FEB 2007

MIDLOTHIAN PUBLIC LIBRARY

W9-AJP-721

MIDLOTHIAN
PUBLIC LIBRARY

THE OFFICIAL PRICE GUIDE TO

GLASSWARE

FOURTH EDITION

Midlothian
Public Library

□ □ □

14701 S. Kenton Ave.
Midlothian, IL 60445

DEMCO

House of Collectibles
New York Toronto London Sydney Auckland

Copyright © 2007 by Mark Pickvet

Important Notice: All the information, including valuations, in this book has been compiled from reliable sources, and efforts have been made to eliminate errors and questionable data. Nevertheless, the possibility of error, in a work of such immense scope, always exists. The publisher will not be responsible for any losses that may occur in the purchase, sale, or other transaction of items because of information contained herein. Readers who think they have discovered errors are invited to write and inform us, so that the errors may be corrected in subsequent editions.

All rights reserved. No part of this book may be reproduced in any form or by any means, electronic or mechanical, including photocopying, recording, or by any information storage and retrieval system, without the written permission of the publisher. Published in the United States by House of Collectibles, an imprint of The Random House Information Group, a division of Random House, Inc., New York, and simultaneously in Canada by Random House of Canada Limited, Toronto.

House of Collectibles and colophon are registered
trademarks of Random House, Inc.

RANDOM HOUSE is a registered trademark of Random House, Inc.

This book is available at special discounts for bulk purchases for sales promotions or premiums. Special editions, including personalized covers, excerpts of existing books, and corporate imprints, can be created in large quantities for special needs. For more information, write to Special Markets/Premium Sales, 1745 Broadway, MD 6-2, New York, NY 10019 or e-mail specialmarkets@randomhouse.com.

Please address inquiries about electronic licensing of any products for use on a network, in software, or on CD-ROM to the Subsidiary Rights Department, Random House Information Group, fax 212-572-6003.

Visit the House of Collectibles Web site: www.houseofcollectibles.com

4th Edition

Printed in the United States of America

10 9 8 7 6 5 4 3 2 1

ISSN: 0743-8699

ISBN: 978-0-375-72182-3

748.2

MIDLOTHIAN PUBLIC LIBRARY
14701 S. KENTON AVE.
MIDLOTHIAN, IL 60445

CONTENTS

MIDLOTHIAN PUBLIC LIBRARY
14701 S. KENTON AVE.
MIDLOTHIAN, IL 60445

ACKNOWLEDGMENTS

Naturally, a project of this magnitude is never completed alone. Many, many people helped along the way, and I sincerely hope that I do not forget anyone: Robin Rainwater, Kate Pickvet, Louis Pickvet Jr., Leota Pickvet, Julie Pickvet, Louis Pickvet III, Fairy Pickvet, Juli Pickvet, Brad Dubay, Andrea Dubay, Tom Smith, Sandra Smith, David Smith, Alan Smith, Douglas Smith, Ella Kitson, Robert Darnold, Sue Darnold, Rachel Moore, Ward Lindsay, Robert Davidson, Rick Patterson, Paul Traviglia, Joe Renner, David Renner, Linda Renner, Dr. Fred Svoboda, Dr. Arthur Harshman, Dr. David Churchman, Dr. Howard Holter, Dr. Mark Luca, Ronald Robinson, Douglas Warner, Ron Brasseur, Tanya Brasseur, Joy McFadden, Jill Ghattas, Gail Grabow, Bonnie Van Sickle, Donna Williams, Jill Smith, Jack Adamson, Gary Crossen, Joan Mogensen, Herbert Smith, David Hill, James Smith, George Nichols, Julie Barnett, Johanna Billings, Lori Whetzel, John and Karen Halsey, Sheryl Laub, Carol O'Laughlin, Nadine Wallenstein, Carol Buntrock, Brad and Vera Decker, Gordon Ferguson, Tammy and Forrest Kimble, John Lander, Carl Mann, Joan Lynn, Kathy Simon, Rota Erickson, Mary Blake, Larry Dearman, Ruth Bagel, Larry Mitchell, Connie DeAngleo, Brian Hill, Joseph Bourque, Don Kime, Virginia Scott, Wilma Thurston, Karen Skinner, Tom McGlauchlin, Adrienne Esco, Eunice Booker, Mary Sharp, Ellen Hem, Larry Branstad, Marie Heath, Kathy Harris, Marie McGee, Judy Maxwell, Barbara Hobbs, Harold Mayes, Pat McNeil, Hallie Nicholl, Sue Kelly, Judy Givens, Norman Madalin, Sandy Redmond, Jo Anne Andrews, Pam Sullivan, Bob Gingerich, Linda Walker, Melissa Boarman, Janet Davis, and Richard Godwin.

Librarians and personnel from the following libraries: Carnegie Institute, Chrysler Museum Library, Corning Museum of Glass Library, Detroit Public Library, Fenton Art Glass Company Library, Flint Public Library, Harvard Widener Library, Historical Society of Pennsylvania, Library of Congress, Milwaukee Public Library, New York Public Library Annex, Toledo-Lucas County Library, Toledo Museum of Art Library, and the libraries of the University of Michigan. Museum and Company Personnel: Christine Mack from the

Allen Memorial Art Museum; C. J. Arnsbarger from the Anchor-Hocking Corporation; Anndora Morginson from the Art Institute of Chicago; David Reese from the Bartlett-Collins Company; Barbara Anderson from the Bergstrom-Mahler Museum; William Blenko Jr., Richard Blenko, and Virginia Womack from the Blenko Glass Company; M. E. Walker from the Block China Corporation; Theresa Cederholm from the Boston Public Library; Bernard C. Boyd, Susan Boyd, and Luke Boyd from the Boyd Art Glass Company; Kimberly Cady from the Cabell County Library in Huntington, West Virginia; Ann Lloyd and Sarah Nichols from the Carnegie Museum of Art; Donna Sawyer, Rosemary Dumais, Gary Baker, and Peter Dubeau from the Chrysler Museum; Jane Shadel Spillman, Jill Thomas-Clark, Gail Bardhan, Rosalind Young, and Virginia Wright from the Corning Museum of Glass; Darlene Antonellis-Lacroix from the Currier Gallery of Art; Frank Thrower and Sophia Dewhurst from Dartington Crystal; William Gates from the East Liverpool Museum of Ceramics; Frank Fenton from the Fenton Art Glass Company; David Dalzell, former president of the Fostoria Glass Company; Cathleen Latendresse from the Henry Ford Museum; Jack Wilkie from the Franklin Mint; Lisa Gibson from the Gibson Glass Company; Jim Hill from the Greentown Glass Museum; Arthur Harshman from the Indiana Glass Company; Reva Ashcraft from the Jefferson County Historical Association of Steubenville, Ohio; Ulrica Hydman-Vallien, Bertil Vallien, Kjell Engman, Gunnel Sahlin, and Goran Warff at Kosta-Boda; Julia Lee Cook from the Libbey Glass Company; Carrie Brankovich from the Lotton Art Glass Company; Erika Hoglund and Mats Jonasson from the Maleras Glassworks; Marie Ann Coil from the Muncie Public Library in Muncie, Indiana; Josef Marcolin and Pamela Nicola of Murano Glass; Cherry Goldner and Katherine McCracken from the National Heisey Glass Museum; Philip F. Hopke from the New England Crystal Company; Mia Karrison from the Nybro Glass Company; Donna Baron of Old Stourbridge Village; Maj Britt from Orrefors; Erica Smith and Frances Haggart from Perthsire Paperweights; Peter Moore from the Pilgrim Glass Corporation; Kirk Nelson from the Sandwich Glass Museum; Lawrence Selman of Seman Paperweights; Paula Belanger of the Showcase Antique Center; Sheila Machlis Alexander from the Smithsonian Institute; Maria Ayckbourna from Swarovski Crystal; Mary O'Reilly and Michelle Power from Tipperary Crystal; Sandra Knudsen from the Toledo Museum of Art; the Havenmeyer collection at the University of Michigan Museum of Art; Viviana Terkuc from Venini Art Glass; Don Ritz from the former Viking Glass Company; William Hosley and Linda Roth from Wadsworth Athenum; Ellen Marts, Beverly Narbut, and Gay Taylor at the Wheaton Village Museum; and Redmond O'Donahough, Ruth Coughlan, Sean Flynn, Tom Gleeson, Pat Brophy, Karen Power, John Stenson, and Pat Boyce from Waterford Crystal.

Finally, a special thanks to the editors, assistant editors, and other personnel who put up with me at Random House/House of Collectibles!

INTRODUCTION

The oldest glass items known to man come from obsidian, a type of glass formed when the heat of a volcano fuses masses of silica or sand together. Obsidian is ordinarily shiny and black, and is at times translucent. Humans were chipping obsidian into arrow heads, knives, razors, spear heads, and a variety of other tools as early as 75,000 b.c. Naturally, the glassy obsidian contained the ultra-sharp edges necessary for superb early toolmaking. Few edges are ever as hazardous as glass, of which most of us have been painfully reminded on occasion. Aside from weapons and tools, obsidian was formed into mirrors, bowls, jewelry, and ceremonial masks.

There are other ways that glass can occur naturally. The terms *tektites* and *fulgurites* are two such examples. Tektites are small, rounded bodies of glass that form as a result of the impact of fiery meteorites upon sand on both the Earth and moon. Tektites have been found in Eastern Europe, Indonesia, Vietnam, Australia, the United States, and other places. Yellowish lumps of tektites are occasionally found in the dunes of the Sahara Desert. Fulgurites are crude, brittle, slender tubes of glass that are formed when lightning strikes a sandy area with the right combination of minerals.

Glass objects were worked as early as 2000 b.c., and the Egyptian and Mesopotamian regions of the modern-day Middle East and North Africa is where glassmaking began.

While working on an encyclopedia project on the subject of glass, I came across some interesting information on the origins of milk glass. Archaeological records, although somewhat sketchy, indicate that an opaque white glass was made in Ancient Egypt around the 16th and 15th centuries b.c. It was originally given its unique nontransparent coloring by the inclusion of ashes from calcined bones. The origin of the bones was anybody's guess. Some say that they likely were from domesticated animals as well as those that were hunted. Early nomads, bands, tribes, and communities tended to be very frugal and used every scrap of material from a slain beast, right down to the bones. Some legends note that the bodies of their fallen enemies were at times burned, thus, yielding ashes that may have been used in such enterprises as glassmaking.

The Chinese were producing milk-glass snuff bottles around the 2nd century b.c., but they generally found glass products inferior to true porcelain and considered them cheap reproductions. Small milk-glass bottles and jars have been unearthed in Persian cities from the 7th century. The jars were used to hold precious spices, perfumes, and medicines or drugs. In his famous work published in 1612, *L'arte Vetraria (The Art of Glass)*, Venetian master glass craftsman Antonio Neri included a formula for making milk-white glass. Actually, the Venetians are credited with inventing the modern formula for milk glass in the 15th century. The semi-opaque opalescent glass could still be colored with compounds of arsenic and calcined bones; however, the Venetians perfected a formula using tin oxide. Modern milk glass today usually contains aluminum or tin, and fluorine as an additive. Milk glass became popular in the 17th and 18th centuries as a substitute for the more expensive decorated Chinese porcelain. An entirely new style of hand-painted, gilded, and elaborately decorated milk-glass products became known as Bristol glass because it originated in Bristol, England, in the 1760s, though some say the style was copied directly from Bohemian makers earlier in the 18th century.

Other European countries jumped on the milk-glass bandwagon and came up with their own names. The Germans call it *Milchglas* or *Porcellein-Glas*, the Italian term is *lattimo*, and the French refer to it as *blanc-de-lait*. The popularity spread to America as well, and in modern times milk glass is often trimmed, hand-painted, or machine enameled, since almost any color goes with white. There are many covered animal-shape dishes in milk glass, such as the commonly seen hens and roosters, as well as a few uncommon ones, such as horses and lions. One thing to be wary of is covers that do not match the bottoms. Milk-glass collectors refer to this as a marriage; nevertheless, unmatched pieces are always worth less than matching pairs (matched covers generally fit the bottoms more precisely, too!). Some of the largest sets of tableware ever produced in America have been in milk glass, such as Westmoreland's Beaded Edge & Panel Grape designs, as well as Fenton's Crest & Hobnail patterns. The Fenton patterns are still in production today.

What we are interested in here is the collectibility of glass and the state of that market. So welcome to the fourth edition of the *Official Price Guide to Glassware*. I have an address to which you can mail correspondence:

Mark Pickvet
5071 Watson Drive
Flint, MI 48506

Because of the volume of mail received, please include an SASE for a response and adequate return postage for any photographs you might send (that is, if you prefer that they be returned). I am away at times but do my best to answer any correspondence I receive. Please include a legible address, so that I can reply to your letters. I also have an e-mail address: *MPickvet@aol.com*

Out of the hundreds of letters I've received from the third edition, the most frequently asked questions concerned glass identification and value. This can be a daunting proposition because I have files containing literally hundreds of unidentified pictures of glass. Without a true mark or signature, there are no easy approaches to identifying newer glassware, especially pieces made recently (that is, in the past two to three decades) by individual studio artisans. A lot of this glass consists of bowls, vases, and unique sculptures. Unfortunately, a lot of it changes hands and ends up in rummage, yard, and garage sales, flea markets, gift shops, and antiques shops and shows, thus, making the crucial point of origin impossible to determine. On the flip side, it really is wonderful that nearly anyone can set up their very own glass operation with some simple tools, a small torch or furnace, and perhaps a grinder for cutting stained glass.

Note that expert appraisers will simply put a price on an unidentified piece in the $10 to $35 range. With no history or identifying mark, appraisers are forced to conclude that the piece is really not that special. This is also true of reproduction glass. Take the famous French glass artisan Galle, for example. A typical Galle art-glass original may sell in the hundreds or even thousands of dollars; nevertheless, the history of the piece must be carefully documented. If it is not, an appraiser will assume it is just one of thousands of recent Romanian reproductions that also contain Galle's signature. (The reproductions are generally much more brightly colored than the originals and are usually worth no more than $100.)

Measurements are important. I use two primary sources to determine them: I actually measure the pieces myself, using rulers, templates, vernier calipers, graduated cylinders, measuring cups, beakers, and so on (in my basement laboratory!), and I use manufacturers' listings directly from their company catalogs, advertisements, and trade journals. Because of mold variations or other slight changes made by manufacturers, you can expect variances of as much as half an inch as well as a few ounces in capacity. Expect even more variance in handmade glass. This is particularly true for older art and other handmade styles of glass.

In general, the bigger the piece of glassware, the higher the price. This is the old punch-bowl-to-salt-dip rule; if both are made in the same style, the punch bowl will cost more. The same holds true for tumblers—bigger tumblers sell for more than little tumblers. Take careful note that this is a general rule only; rarity and desirability play a large part in pricing. For instance, a small Acorn Burrs–patterned carnival glass vase whimsey outsells everything else in the pattern by at least a factor of six. Then again, if you check with America's premier art-glass designer of the 20th century, Dale Chihuly, bigger is always better!

This new edition, along with updated and current pricing, contains about 2,000 more prices than the third, along with about 50 additional new categories throughout the main chapters. It has always been and continues to be our goal to provide the most comprehensive listings in a broad number of categories in the field of collectible glassware. It cannot be emphasized enough that the dollar amounts listed here serve as a general guide only and are not intended to set prices. Please refer to the chapter on market and pricing for more information. The outline in the first printing applies to this updated edition. Pressed-pattern, carnival glass, and Depression glass are listed alphabetically by pattern name. Cut glass is alphabetized by company name because so many manufacturers produced the same patterns and basic cuttings. Modern, Art, and Foreign listings include both manufacturers' and pattern names; patterns are used when there is sufficient variety of pieces to list separately. The Modern section also contains some miscellaneous older listings that do not fit within the other categories (fruit or canning jars, for example).

Once again, if you discover any mistakes, errors, discrepancies, or inconsistencies, or have some new or interesting information that you would like to share, I would be happy to hear from you. I would also like to thank all of you who have taken the time to write on a wide variety of glass-related topics. As always, I wish you the best in your collecting endeavors and hope that you find the piece(s) of your dreams—at reasonable prices!

Mark Pickvet

MARKET REVIEW, PRICING, AND CARE OF GLASSWARE

THE GLASS MARKETPLACE

In recent years, glass collectors have proliferated to an astounding degree. Much of this can be attributed to the rise of reproduction carnival glass in the 1960s, along with the continued popularity of Depression glass. Post-Depression glass is gaining in momentum as more and more patterns from the 1940s to the present are readily found at auctions and antiques shops, and on the Internet. The number of small studio art-glass companies and individual artisans continues to increase worldwide at what seems an exponential rate. Historically speaking, the hub of the glass world in the United States centered around the East, Midwest, and Southeast. Nearly all the original factories were in Massachusetts, Pennsylvania, New York, West Virginia, Ohio, and Indiana. With the exception of Bartlett-Collins in Oklahoma, all glass manufactured in America through the Depression years came from east of the Mississippi River. As a result prices and availability are still somewhat higher for those living in the western half of the country. Beginning in the latter half of the 20th century, a good many new art-glass companies sprang up in the West, especially in California and Washington. Seattle alone has several hundred glass artisans and draws many to the Pilchuk Glass School. There are schools in the East, too, notably around Corning, New York, and in Wheaton Village in New Jersey. Small companies, artists, and even a new museum or two can be found scattered throughout the country, and even across the world.

As the years go by, supply continues to be a problem, which directly influences pricing. Pressed, cut, art, and carnival glass is generally available only through auctions, choice shows, and exclusive dealers. Depression and even some modern glass is slowly following the trends of its predecessors; however, both are still available through general shows and common dealers. Prices on art and carnival glass continue to increase, whereas cut and pressed wares seem to have stabilized over the past couple of decades. Depression glass seems to edge up in value little by little as the years go by.

The best deals on glass are generally found by tracking the trends followed by dealers. Attend numerous auctions, know the value of patterns and styles so you can recognize a good deal when it comes along, answer advertisements in newspapers by private collectors, look in the rummage/garage sale ads for those selling glassware, join a club in your area of interest, and attend large antiques and flea markets. Always use caution when dealing on the Internet (see appendix 2). At nearly every large show you'll find a wide variety of dealers. Those who specialize in glass usually sell it at or near the prices listed in popular price guides. The best deals at shows tend to come from dealers who specialize in other merchandise. If these particular dealers have only a few glass items along with a variety of other merchandise, they may not know its value, or they may simply offer it at a price higher than what they paid to realize a profit, a price that may be substantially less than what the piece is worth.

Online auction houses have had a significant effect on the marketplace. They have certainly added a new factor in pricing dynamics. Since I have been observing these types of auctions over the past decade, my opinion is that they tend to benefit the seller by raising the prices not only of glass, but also of a wide variety of antiques, collectibles, and so forth. Dealers can now reach literally millions of households, whereas they once were limited to one community or region. An example is the dark ruby red Cape Cod pattern tableware made by Wheaton Industries for Avon that was discontinued in 1997. If you enter "Avon Cape Cod" in eBay's search box, you will get hundreds of listings. I can recall in the early 1990s seeing this stuff plastered all over flea markets and rummage sales for as little as a dollar for some of the smaller pieces (for example, saucers, small drinking goblets, candleholders). There were hundreds of thousands of pieces made in this pattern; nevertheless, the demand of those wishing to complete their sets is exceeding supply. When this happens, the prices invariably go up. I am amazed to see what apparently are harder-to-find items in this pattern selling for high prices. For instance, a set of four napkin holders now exceeds $50, two-tier tidbits go as high as $75, flat-based tumblers run about $50 for a set of four, and the larger soup/cereal bowl exceeds $25 for just one! Note again that this is not rare or old glass.

IDENTIFYING GLASS

There is no substitute for a good education. Glass now covers such a wide variety of forms and patterns that it is difficult to study them all. Most collectors focus on a certain category, color, style, manufacturer, or form. This book is divided into seven chapters covering the most popular categories. There is also no substitute for experience in collecting glass. Reading and studying books, visiting museums and art galleries, joining a club (see appendix 1), speaking with dealers and visiting their shops, and attending auctions, if only as a nonbidding participant, can all enhance your knowledge of glassware. Learn to recognize the exact marks and signatures of the various makers, particularly of the items or producers in which you are most interested. The simplest of forgeries is that of a well-known maker applied to what was previously an unmarked object of lesser quality and value. Appendix 5 contains a directory of manufacturers' marks.

Glass that is considered highly collectible dates back to pressed items in the 1820s. Glass products dating from before that are generally found in museums. Pressed glass is identified by embossed or molded patterns. Such things as ribbing, arches, flutes, bull's-eyes, cables, thumbprints, and other geometrical or lacy designs are common on pressed glass. Cut glass designs were often similar to pressed glass, but only higher-grade crystal formulas were used, along with designs that were cut by hand rather than applied by machine. As a result, cut glass is sharper, thicker, and much brighter or glossier compared with pressed glass.

Whereas pressed glass was done by hand-pressing machines, Depression glass was made by automated machines. The techniques are very similar in that glass is pressed into a mold and the main pattern is built into the mold. The main difference is that Depression glass was made in greater quantities and the majority of it was produced in bright, vivid colors. Older pressed items occasionally contained colors, but they were generally duller and easily distinguished from Depression glass.

Art glass contains many unique styles such as color experimentation, opaque and opalescent styles, cameo or relief-cut styles, gaudy objects and colors, ornamental styles, unique shadings, and a general Victorian-age fondness for ostentation. The most popular object for art-glass stylings appears on vases. Vases range from a few inches in height to several feet. Most are found in the 6- to 20-inch range and include such styles as trumpets, jack-in-the-pulpit, lily, tulip, rose bowls, and so on. Other objects include lamps, pitchers, baskets, and paperweights. Art glass was generally made to be displayed rather than for any practical use.

Carnival glass was originally considered a cheap, gaudy version of art glass. Carnival glass was pressed into molds and then sprayed with metallic salts to produce the oily surface coloring. Carnival glass is usually fairly easy to identify, but it can be confused with more modern and reproduction iridescent forms. To make matters more confusing, some Depression glass included light marigold iridescent forms. Carnival glass had a short history and was made only from the turn of the century until the mid-1920s.

Other glass objects that have found their way into the hands of collectors are more specific, which simplifies identification. These might include such collectibles as fruit jars, bottles, character glass, advertising glass, Disney glass, Fire King ovenware, marbles, paperweights, souvenir glass, insulators, thimbles, and so on. The most challenging aspect of glass identification these days is the presence of a good deal of unmarked studio art glass. Without a true mark or signature, there are no easy approaches to identifying newer glassware, especially those pieces made by individual studio artisans in the past few decades. A lot of this glass consists of bowls, vases, and unique sculptures. Unfortunately, a lot of it changes hands and ends up in rummage, yard, and garage sales, flea markets, gift shops, consignment shops, and antiques shops and shows, thus, making the crucial point of origin impossible to determine.

This is also true of reproduction glass. Take the famous French artisan Emile Galle, for example. A typical Galle art-glass original may sell in the hundreds or even thousands of dollars; nevertheless, the history of the piece must be well documented. If it is not, an appraiser will assume it is just one of thousands of recent Romanian reproductions that also contain Galle's signature—the reproductions are usually worth $50 to $100.

PRICING

With the huge variety of glass shows, numerous auctions, and national advertising, prices are becoming more standardized for glass collectibles. The values listed in this book should serve as a general guide only. They are not intended to set prices; rather, they are determined from hundreds of these shows, dealers, auctions, mail-order listings, experts in the field, and private collectors. Neither the author nor the publisher assumes responsibility for any losses that might be incurred as a result of using this guide. The purpose of this book is to provide the most up-to-date and realistic prices for rare as well as common collectible glassware.

Prices listed in this book are based on glass in excellent or mint condition. Glass that is chipped, heavily scratched, cracked, poorly finished, or with other major problems has very little value. Age, condition, demand, availability, and other factors are directly relevant to pricing. Take special note that dealers pay only about one-half to two-thirds of the quoted prices, sometimes less if they think it will be difficult to sell the piece. Liquidity for collectibles in general is a volatile area. The categories themselves involve several different aspects regarding condition and are outlined as follows:

Pressed Glass

Pressed patterns are the oldest styles of glass priced in this guide, at least when it comes to matching pieces. They are, for the most part, 19th-century hand-pressed items that vary a good deal in consistency. Further complicating matters is the general lack of patents, and hence, numerous companies and individuals making the same designs in different molds. The result is objects with wide variations in shape, pattern, type, and general formula. Ribbing may be thicker or thinner; vines may be single or double; gridding or checkering may be narrow or wide; and even clear glass tends to take on a pale purple tinge. Manganese in the basic formula is responsible for amethyst coloring; a little too much, coupled with prolonged exposure to the sun, is responsible for this tinting.

Beware of tinging as well as serious flaws within older pressed glass from the 19th century. Some clear Depression patterns and reproductions are at times confused with older and more valuable pressed designs. Thinner examples can be quite fragile, but for the most part, the formulas used in pressed glass have held together well. Speaking of formulas, most pressed glass was produced in a good grade of lead crystal, sometimes referred to as flint. Nonlead or lime glass (referred to as nonflint) was also used in pressing and is less valuable than true lead crystal. One last item of note is to look out for patterns that are irregular, out of balance, or slightly stretched, or pieces that appear off-center, including the pattern.

Art Glass

There is simply no other category of glass that requires as much attention as art glass. Pieces that run into the thousands and even the hundreds of thousands of dollars deserve the following 10-point plan:

1. Mint Condition—The tiniest chip or crack; any missing portion; any part that is repaired or reground; discoloration; staining; internal bubbles that have burst; variations in cutting, engraving, or enameling; or any problems no matter how minor should at the very least reduce the prices listed in this guide; serious flaws make them virtually worthless. The only exception would be for a few minor scratches on the underside of the base upon which the object rests.

2. The Source or Dealer—Having a knowledgeable and reputable dealer is essential when purchasing. A dealer should stand by the work, which might turn out to be a reproduction or even a fake. A signed certificate of authenticity should pose no difficulty for a dealer, auction house, or similar organization.

3. Appraisal—Get a second opinion if there is the least bit of doubt. Museum personnel, licensed appraisers, or others with knowledge in the field should be called upon.

4. Education—There is no substitute for experience in the art-glass field. Reading and studying books, visiting museums and art galleries, speaking with dealers and visiting their shops, and attending auctions even if only as a nonbidding participant can all enhance your knowledge in this category.

5. Marks and Signatures—Learn to recognize the exact marks and signatures of the various makers, particularly on the items or products in which you are most interested. The simplest of forgeries is that of a well-known maker applied to what was previously an unmarked object of lesser quality and value.

6. Low Prices—Glass objects of rarity and significant value are rarely sold for small fractions of their actual worth. Carder, Steuben, Tiffany, Galle, and others are simply not found at flea markets and rummage sales. The majority of art glass in the past was purchased almost exclusively by the upper echelons of society.

7. High Prices—On the flip side of No. 6, do not get caught up in bidding wars at auctions in the heat of the moment. At times, a collector searching for a matching or highly desirable piece may pay an exorbitant price. Of course, if you who have found the piece of your dreams, it is, after all, your money to spend as you see fit. Visiting a few galleries, signing up on "want lists" with specific dealers, and a bit of traveling may get you the piece you are looking for without excessive bidding.

8. Age—Older glass will usually have some telltale sign of wear. A slight bit of fading that does not detract from the item's overall appearance may be evident. Tiny or random scratches on the base are common for art glass; most are there simply because the object has stood in one place for so long. A piece that appears brand new just might be!

9. Color—No matter how close they come, the color of reproduction glassware always seems to differ slightly or to some larger degree from the originals. Much of it is caused by the original formulas and ingredients used in the glassmaking process. Sand, lead, and other additives are nearly impossible to duplicate through the decades, especially when they are obtained from different sources or regions. The raw materials and sand banks of a hun-

dred years ago no longer exist in some parts of the country. Certain elements such as high-grade uranium are no longer available for glass production. The slightest variation in color, shade, or hue from known examples can act as a clue to the existence of a reproduction.

10. Be Choosy—If the other nine requirements have been satisfied, a question still arises about the individual design. Occasionally, ill-formed, twisted, or unnatural shapes are referred to as "grotesque" and may look quite odd or lack value compared with graceful, free-flowing objects of beauty. Aside from the practical side, a true object of art should capture your imagination and stir an emotion (unless you are buying for investment or reselling).

Cut Glass

Like art glass, cut glass was an exclusive product for the wealthy. Because of the extremely heavy lead content as well as the extensive hand-cutting, hand-engraving, and hand-polishing involved, reproductions of the original cut patterns have not been made using these methods. Because of the thick, heavy cuts, some lead cut glass has a thickness that exceeds half an inch. One of the biggest mistakes people make is assuming that thick glass is strong and durable. Cut glass is fragile because cutting weakens the glass structurally, especially deeper and asymmetrical cutting.

Quality and condition are the two most prevalent factors when inspecting cut glass. Light refraction—a natural crystal gleam—is far superior to a cheaper acid finish, and uniform weight, balance, and thickness, true symmetrical cuts that are sharp and precise, a lack of cloudiness, and a resonating bell-like sound when tapped with a fingernail are all determining factors of quality. Nicks, tiny chips, discoloration, a dull finish, and scratches all reduce the value of fine cut glass. Any major flaws such as heavy scratching or chipping render the object virtually worthless.

Carnival Glass

Originally, carnival glass was produced as a cheap substitute for art glass; however, prices for some carnival glass have easily reached and exceeded the art-glass level. Less expensive common items should be given the same general visual and hand inspection as all glassware. The rare and incredibly valuable items such as red carnival should follow the 10-point procedure outlined under "Art Glass."

Carnival glass is characterized by an iridescent metal flashing, the one area of inspection that differentiates it from most other glassware. The iridization should flow smoothly and consistently over the entire object. Gaps, discolorations, dull areas from excessive wear, or any incomplete flashing reduces the price. The base color in most pieces should be observed only on the underside; if it can be viewed in significant areas or portions on the outside, it may be a sign that the iridization has worn off or was incomplete.

Reproductions pose problems in carnival glass. Some iridized Depression glass and later iridized examples resemble the original carnival designs. Naturally, those that cause the most severe problems are new pieces made in the original molds. Fortunately, some companies marked the new wares to distinguish them from the old, such as Imperial, which marked them "IG."

Depression Glass

In no other category is the chip as much of a factor in condition as in Depression glass. As a rule, most Depression glass was mass-produced cheaply in machines in great quantities for the general public. Through constant everyday use, coupled with the thinner designs that were no longer hand-cut, chipping is a severe problem with Depression glass. Foots, rims, lids, handles, joints, and so on should all be carefully inspected for chips. Run your finger around these places with your eyes closed to discover chips by touch.

Minor flaws such as an occasional tiny air bubble, slight inconsistent coloring from piece to piece, and tiny trails of excess glass do not detract from the value of Depression glass. A typical Depression mold might last for thousands of machine pressings, and it was impossible to match perfectly batch after batch of color. As a result, it is possible to accumulate a matching patterned set of more than 50 pieces that vary slightly in color. Major flaws such as excess scratching, large trails of glass, rough mold lines, chips, missing pattern designs, and so on render Depression glass virtually worthless.

Reproductions pose a few difficulties; however, there appear to be major differences in the new versions. The most prevalent difference is color. New reproduction colors appear washed out, dull, and not as attractive as the originals. Other differences involve dimensions and new colors that were not produced in the original versions.

Modern Glass

There is little to report on glass produced within the last 50 years or so. In short, it should be in nothing less than new condition. Occasionally, enameling on cheaper advertising or character glass may fade or scratch easily, but if those items are abundantly available, less than perfect pieces should be passed over unless they are highly desired and scarce. Even brand new items should be inspected for any damage or flaws that may have occurred in manufacture, transport, or shipping, or simply from being moved around frequently on display shelves.

CARE OF GLASS

There have been horror stories of glass shattering or spontaneously breaking from changes in temperature, sitting in one place for too long, or simple movement. Some of it is grounded in myth; however, glass does require some minimal care. Machine and pressed glasswares are generally sturdy and were designed for utilitarian purposes. Fancier items such as art glass were designed for display purposes only as true objects of art. Glass will break from sudden temperature changes. Much depends on how fragile the piece in question is. A warm piece of glass at room temperature may break if suddenly exposed to cold weather outside. When transported, glass should be carefully wrapped and then remain wrapped for several hours until it adjusts to the destination's temperature. Milk glass has been known to be especially vulnerable to temperature changes.

Never wash glassware until it has adjusted to room temperature. Lukewarm or warm water should be used. Scalding hot water can easily destroy glass. Mild nonabrasive cleaning solutions should be used only on ordinary pressed wares such as Depression glass. Some art forms should not be washed with water at all! Anything beyond a light feather dusting may affect the finish. Avoid using a dishwasher for cleaning most any collectible glass; hot water and detergents can destroy or damage most finishes. I once acted as an appraiser in an insurance claim where an entire dishwasher load of Waterford crystal was basically ruined. Keep the good stuff out of the dishwasher! Stains on crystal have been successfully removed by lightly rubbing a lemon half or vinegar on the glass and then rinsing with lukewarm water. Also note that distilled water is preferred for cleaning rather than hard water or water with a high mineral content. When washing glass in a sink, aside from using nonabrasive cleansers, it is also advisable to cushion the sink with a towel or perhaps a rubber mat. Dropping glass on brittle porcelain or steel is obviously asking for trouble. It is best to simply air-dry glass in the open on a towel; however, a soft lint-free cloth shouldn't cause too many problems. Fine glass can scratch easily, too, so when dusting, a soft, lint-free cloth, perhaps dampened with a very mild ammonia solution, is recommended.

Exposing older lead crystal to direct sunlight for lengthy periods of time can cause the manganese to react and turn the object a light shade of purple. Collectible glass is best stored in sturdy cabinets or on well-secured shelves away from direct sunlight. Occasionally, it should be cleaned and moved. Avoid excess stacking as well as sliding or twirling glass. Also, avoid contact with hard or abrasive materials—protective felt works well for the bottom surface of display areas. Another item of note is to avoid packing fine glass in newspaper or other moisture-absorbing materials for long periods of time. Moisture can cause staining, and mold might form, too. Soft cloth or bubble wrap is more suitable.

There is sometimes a debate with chemists as to whether glass is a liquid or a solid. It appears to be a solid, but some low-quality forms have been known to run over time. Check out an old abandoned home sometime and observe any remaining windows. Occasionally, you will find glass that has thickened and bulged at the bottom. Fortunately, the effect of gravity is a rarity in collectible glass; however, sitting in one spot for decades may cause a gradual run over time. Older glass was not designed for the high pressure and extreme temperatures of both dishwashers and freezers. Likewise, microwave use is not recommended, even though it has been proved that the lead in glass does not react to microwave energy. New glass products are acceptable for microwave use as long as it is recommended by the manufacturer; older items are not. To date, I have never seen a recommendation that glass can safely be placed in a freezer. Glass subjected to below-freezing temperatures is highly vulnerable to cracking and breakage.

Speaking of lead, over time, toxic amounts of lead can leach from lead crystal into its contents; therefore, it is advisable not to store food or liquids in a lead crystal container. This is especially true for such things as oil and vinegar in cruets, which can react more quickly with lead than other liquids and/or foods. A similar reaction with alcoholic beverages occurs in prolonged storage in lead crystal decanters. Warnings have been posted specifically for pregnant women advising them not to drink regularly from lead crystal; furthermore, infants should not be fed from fancy lead crystal baby bottles (even if it was a gift from your mother-in-law!). To err on the side of safety, lead crystal should be used only for special occasions, and then thoroughly emptied, washed, and stored away when not in use.

Metal implements are usually not matched well with glassware because of the damage they may cause. Table sets such as old pressed wares and Depression glass, and even newer items such as Avon's Cape Cod pattern will scratch when used with metal utensils. Over time, the scratches build up. Such items as cake and pie pans that have had cuts made directly on them with metal utensils are particularly vulnerable. They may not destroy the piece; nevertheless, they will certainly damage it and reduce its value. Molten wax can be quite damaging to candlesticks, especially if the wax burns within 3 inches or less of the actual candle cup.

Dripless candles are preferable. If wax does indeed adhere to a candlestick, then denatured alcohol can be gently applied to remove it. I've seen it suggested that hot water be used to melt the wax, but, as mentioned above, beware of extreme temperatures, particularly for fragile items that may break.

History has shown that glass has survived the test of time. Look in the major museums such as the Corning Museum of Glass or the Chrysler Museum and you will find pieces that have survived for centuries. With a little careful attention, your pieces will last as well.

— 1 —
FOREIGN GLASS AND GLASSMAKING

A question that may never be answered fully is what brought on the development or discovery of glass. Some believe it was invented completely by accident. Legend has it that a desert nomad in ancient Egypt lighted a wood fire in a sand pit and that the ashes fused with the sand into a glassy substance. Further experimentation was carried on from there until a workable material was created. No matter how glass was invented, archaeological records and surviving glass objects date the existence of glass to the time of the Egyptians, roughly 3,500 years ago.

The prime ingredients of glass are silica, a form of sand, and ashes from plants and trees. Ash is an alkali that aids the sand in melting at a lower temperature. Stabilizing substances such as carbonate of soda or lime are crushed into fine powders and added to the batch. They not only assist in the fusion process but also protect against excessive moisture. Metals and other ingredients or additives were altered through the centuries, but the basic formula for the most part has remained intact.

The technique of core-forming used by the Egyptians did not change for centuries until the rise of the Roman Empire. The first step in core-forming is the construction of a base or core, ordinarily a mixture of clay and dung. Hot glass was then spun around the core. The core-formed glass was quite dark or opaque and often decorated with brightly colored glass threads that were woven around it.

The average citizens of ancient Egypt usually did not possess such ornaments as the new glassware. It was reserved for the wealthy, such as high priests, nobles, the pharaoh's assistants, and the pharaoh himself. Core-formed objects were usually made into containers for ointments, oils, and perfumes. These artistic items were present on thrones, buried with mummies in their cases, and even placed in the tombs of pharaohs.

Core-forming was the exclusive method of early glassmaking, but advances and new ideas followed as the centuries passed. The Mesopotamians cast glass into moldlike containers. Simple clay molds may have lasted for only one good cast, but molds did have their beginning here. Another innovation of the Mesopotamians was the addition of an extra step in the finishing process. After casting, the surface of the glass was polished by revolving wheels fed with abrasives. These basic techniques of mold-casting and polishing were adopted later by European and American glassmakers.

The second significant step in the history of glassmaking other than its actual discovery was the art of glassblowing. Around 50 B.C., or just over 2,000 years ago, the Romans developed the process of blowing short puffs of air through a hollow metal tube into a gather, or molten blob of glass. Glassmakers would heat up a batch of glass to the melting point, inflate a bubble quickly at the end of the rod, and then work it quickly while it was still warm into many shapes and sizes. Glassblowing was the first significant alternative to the ancient methods of casting and core-forming.

With the advent of blowing, glass was no longer a luxury product created exclusively for the wealthy. The Romans produced a great variety of glass, and fortunately a good deal of it survived or was recreated from archaeological digs. The most popular or common items blown were drinking vessels. Drinking cups were used primarily for drinking fermented beverages. Gladiator beakers and souvenir beakers depicting gruesome gladiator scenes, battles, heroes, chariots, and so forth were designed for drinking wine. Glass was also blown into molds, and bottles were often decorated with the same scenery. Other popular shapes blown from glass included figureheads, gods and goddesses, and particularly grapes or grape clusters to celebrate wine and the vine from which it was derived. The same grape patterns can be found in 19th-century carnival and Depression wares.

The Romans experimented with many styles of decorating that were adapted later. The Greeks borrowed cutting techniques from the Mesopotamians but learned to cut shallow grooves and hollows more precisely, similar to that applied to gemstones. The Romans advanced further with cutting, engraving, and polishing with the use of stone and wooden wheels. A glass object was held against a wheel and fed with an abrasive paste. Shallow, deep, and fancy cuts were made, based for the most part on the cutter's skill.

Enameling developed long before glassware. The painting of cave walls, rocks, clay, pottery, and so forth has been a part of every culture since the dawn of civilization. The Romans enameled their glassware much like we do today, only without the complex machinery. With the Romans, colored glass was pulverized into a powder, mixed with oils like a paint, and then applied to a glass article. The piece was then reheated to permanently fuse the enamel. Romans, for the most part, manipulated cold glass and cold painting.

Until the 5th century, the Romans ruled the Western world and the advances by the West were found somewhere within their vast empire. In the East, China delved into glassmaking in the form of beads, jewelry, and jadelike carved glass figurines about the same time as the Romans. Much of it was exported or traded away, since glass was not highly regarded. The Chinese spent more time and effort creating the finest porcelain in the world for the coming centuries. Later, but not until the 18th and 19th centuries, glass became somewhat popular in China. Cut-glass snuff bottles for inhaling opium and porcelain reproductions of vases were made of opaque glass to resemble porcelain. It was in the Middle East or the Islamic world, however, and then on to Europe that advances were made in the history of glassmaking.

Islamic glass dates as far back as the 8th century. The Romans had experimented with some cameo or relief cutting, but the Islamic cutters took it a step farther. Relief cutting is a difficult, time-consuming, and expensive process. It involves outlining a design on a glass surface and then carefully cutting away part of the background to leave the original design raised in relief. Relief-cut glass was once again reserved for the upper echelon of society. Plants, geometric patterns, fish, quotations from the Koran, and a wide variety of other designs were highlighted by highly skilled artists in relief upon vases, perfume sprinklers, beakers, bottles, and many other articles.

Common items for ordinary people might include bowls, bottles, and drinking glasses primarily for wine consumption. Enameling was done on lamps, which housed oil for fuel and floating wicks. The period of Islamic glass ended very early in the 15th century when, in 1401, the Mongol conqueror Tamerlane destroyed Damascus and captured the glass artisans. He brought them and their skills to Samarkand.

When Europe moved into the Middle Ages, glassmaking nearly became extinct. A few primitive vessels such as bowls and drinking vessels were created but hardly anything of note for decades. The 12th century, coupled with the rise in power of the Catholic Church, was responsible for a new chapter in glassmaking history.

Gothic architecture and the creation of the stained-glass window brought glassmaking to new heights. Stained materials from oils, plants, and vegetable matter were added to glass's basic ingredients. The development of coloring glass with some experimental metals led to colored glass being cast into flat cakes, cut into small pieces, and then formed into mosaics. Brilliantly colored glass was included in some of the finest European architecture. Huge cathedral windows sparkled in shades of all the basic colors, adorning the greatest and most elaborate churches ever built, such as Notre Dame and Westminster Abbey.

In the second millennium, the first glassmakers' guild and the hub of the glassmaking world centered around the city of Venice. By the early 13th century, Venice had become the trade center of the Western world. Venetian glassmakers formed a guild to guard their trade secrets as commercial production of glass flourished once again.

The glass industry in Italy was ordered by proclamation to move all operations to the nearby island of Murano. The reason was because of the potential hazard for great furnace fires, which could easily destroy the entire city if an accident occurred in one of the glass houses. The glass trade was such an integral part of the commerce of Venice that Venetian glassmakers were forbidden by law to leave Murano. The penalty for escape was death, though many did manage to do so.

It was not all that unfortunate for the glass craftsmen living and working on Murano. Their skills and reputation were highly regarded, and their daughters were allowed to marry noblemen. For the most part the city of Venice had a Western world monopoly on the art of glassmaking. Their craftsmen held the secrets of furnace construction, glass formulas—including the ideal proportion of ingredients—and the use of tools and toolmaking. Knowledge was passed down only to their sons or those rarely admitted to the guild. The secrets were well guarded until 1612, when Antonio Neri made them available in his book titled *L'Arte Vetraria,* which translates into *The Art of Glass*. Neri was a master glass craftsman and understood the complete process involved in its production. It is easy to see that Neri enjoyed his trade, for he is famous for saying, "Glass is more gentle, graceful, and noble than any metal and its use is more delightful, polite, and sightly than any other material at this day known to the world."

The biggest effect the Venetians had on the evolution of glassmaking was the development of cristallo in the 16th century. Next to the discovery of glass itself by the Egyptians and the invention of glassblowing by the Romans, the creation of a nearly colorless glass formula was a significant innovation. The glass was adapted to the world's finest mirrors, far superior to those made of bronze, steel, or polished silver. Venetians produced glass beads for jewelry and rosaries that rivaled that of gemstones. Glass jewelry was also used for barter in the African slave trade.

Venetian glass was produced in colors that would resurface in art glass in the 19th century and Depression glass in America in the early 20th century. Emerald green, cobalt blue, amethyst, pink, amber, and later, in the 17th century, a milky white glass all flowed steadily from the factories on Murano. The monopoly and production of fine Venetian glass dominated the world market through most of the 17th century.

Glass was a significant factor in science and technological advances. Clear optical lenses for microscopes, telescopes, improved eyeglasses, test tubes, beakers, flasks, tubing, and a host of other laboratory apparatuses were vital for scientific experimentation. The Venetian cristallo did not interfere with chemicals, and one could easily observe chemical reactions and the results through the clear glass. As with most glass at this point, the finest Venetian styles were created for the wealthy. Anyone of importance in the West graced their tables with glass wine goblets, fancy bowls, and vessels created in Venice. The Venetian glass cutters were the first to use diamond-point engraving. Until the 17th century, India was the sole source of diamonds, and the majority of trade between East and West passed through Venice. With diamonds readily available, the glass artisans of Venice adapted them to their cutting wheels.

The one serious complaint with Venetian glass that surfaced was its inherently frail nature. There was no question that the glass was exquisite and the best made in the world to that point, but it was thin, fragile, and not easily transported. It broke easily in shipment, and the quest for a more durable formula was actually achieved by the English.

Shortly after the time of the Venetians, a few other glass houses sprang up around northern Europe. Europe was still in the midst of the feudal system, and a few glass houses existed near the manors of noblemen. Wood ashes or potash was readily available and aided in melting the sand mixture. Heavy concentrations of iron in the soil produced glass of a pale or murky green color. These so-called "forest glass houses" made windows and drinking vessels of poor quality; however, both were very practical items.

Huge drinking vessels were particularly popular in Germany, where beer was drunk in large quantities. Some held several quarts, and amazingly enough, some drinkers tried to drain them in a single gulp. Some lost their bets whereas others succeeded, but the practice was frowned upon by some such as Martin Luther, who referred to these vessels as "fools' glasses."

In the late 16th and 17th centuries, Germans and Bohemians began cutting and decorating their glass. Their drinking glasses contained patriotic designs, coats of arms, biblical figures and references, mythological figures, and scenes of daily life. They experimented with the formulas of making glass and actually developed a form of crystal that was easier to cut than the thin Venetian cristallo. In Bohemia and Brandenburg specifically, this new glass could be cut on rapidly rotating stone and copper wheels. The Germans were responsible for the perfection of wheel engraving and engraved many of the same designs that were enameled. As the center of the West's trade shifted away from Venice, so did the advances in glassmaking. The English adopted the Venetian style and began their own unique technological advances beyond the experts at Murano.

This early world glassmaking history certainly has relevance for the past two centuries of glassmaking. Sand and ash are still the two primary ingredients for the production of glass. Many of the colors used in art and Depression glass were invented or even perfected long ago. Enameling, wheel-cutting, cameo-engraving, and other decorating techniques can be traced far into the distant past. However, there was still room for significant improvements and experimentation. Both occurred in Europe and America.

England did little in the way of original glassmaking until the 17th century, although English artisans did manage to produce some window glass and a few crude drinking glasses in the 13th century. In 1571, Giacomo Verzelini and nine other Italian glassmakers escaped to London from Murano via Antwerp. Three years later Verzelini received a patent from Queen Elizabeth to create glass in the Venetian style, the secrets of which he was well familiar with. For the next 100 years, England was well on its way to becoming the world leader in the production of practical glassware.

In 1615, English glassmakers were forced to switch from wood to coal as fuel for their furnaces. Wood was outlawed because of a severe shortage; what was available was reserved for shipbuilding. Coal posed special problems, for it was dirtier and the fumes produced could easily ruin molten glass during the blowing process.

The first significant item that England produced for export was the "black bottle" in the mid-17th century. It was actually a very dark green, primarily because of the iron and other elements in the sand used in the glass formulas. It was nearly black, and this actually served to protect the contents from light. The bottle was made of thick glass that was very durable; unlike the fragile thin Venetian glassware, the black bottle rarely broke in shipping.

Throughout the mid-17th and 18th centuries, England was the largest supplier of bottles in the Western world.

A more important goal of English glassmakers was to find a cross between the delicate, clear Venetian glass and the strong, thick black bottle. They preferred the elegance and clarity of cristallo coupled with the durability of the black bottle. The solution arrived in 1676 with George Ravenscroft. Ravenscroft was an English glassmaker who lived and studied for several years in Venice. He forever etched his name in the history of glass development by perfecting a formula for heavy lead glass that is still regarded as an excellent formula today.

The new batch held great advantages and was a significant factor in ending the Venetian dominance. When heated, it remained in a workable condition for a lengthier period of time, which in turn allowed the glass artisan to indulge in fancier and more time-consuming endeavors. It was superior in clarity, weight, strength, and light-capturing ability. The workability of the first true lead crystal was responsible for a host of new stem formations, particularly in goblets. Airtwists, spiral twisted patterns in the internal stem of a goblet, teardrops, knops or knobs, balusters, and others all refracted light as never before. With Ravenscroft's discovery, the English truly succeeded in their goal.

The English further experimented with refraction in their cutting techniques. Before the early 18th century, they borrowed cutting techniques from the Germans and Bohemians. The new style began with covering the surface of a glass object with an orderly geometric pattern of facets. This technique combined with the new crystal formula maximized refraction, which in turn produced a brilliant sparkling effect. This new beautifully patterned cut glass was applied to chandeliers, candlesticks, centerpieces, and drinking glasses. Previously, rooms in typical English homes were dark. Candles were heavily taxed and, therefore, expensive. Glass served to lighten things up and replaced candles until it, too, became too popular and was subject to taxation.

The new lead glass could be formed into thicker articles and was much easier to cut than the Venetian glass. Sturdier everyday items such as firing and dram glasses followed in the late 18th century. Firing glasses obtained their name from the noise of several being slammed upon the table simultaneously, which sounded like a group musket firing. Firing glasses were built with extremely thick bases and withstood the abuse inflicted upon them in taverns. The base might be as much as an inch thick.

Durable glass products from England were exported in large quantities. Some were shipped to the Far East in the 17th century, but many more were shipped in the 18th century. The English East India Company exported significant amounts of glass to India, second only to what they shipped to America.

In 1780 Parliament lifted a 35-year ban on the exportation of Irish glass. Irish glass was tax-free, and many of England's skilled glassworkers moved to Ireland. English and Irish glass was virtually identical in style and impossible to distinguish from each other except for marks. Glassworkers in Ireland turned out huge quantities for American markets across the Atlantic. Glassmaking cities such as Dublin, Belfast, Cork, and probably the most famous city for fine glass, Waterford, survived well into the 19th century. Some have been reorganized, such as Waterford, and continue to operate today.

America's founding fathers and people who had access to glassware on America's East Coast used British- and Irish-made glass well into the 1820s, until the invention of the mechanical pressing machine. Glassware imported by America included water tumblers, decanters, firing glasses, wineglasses and other stemware, rummers, drams, fluted glasses, finger basins, bottles, punch jugs, liqeuers or cordials, saltcellars, mustard dishes, butter, keepers globes, and anything else the English and Irish factories turned out.

Whereas American companies were gearing up in the 19th century, England and Ireland lost a significant share of their largest market; however, they still exported a good deal of glass to America. More glass found its way into domestic life, and more decorations were applied to it. Landscapes, buildings, city views, nature, and portraiture were all engraved, stained, or enameled upon English glassware. Beakers often contained entire maps of famous battles and scenes of daily life.

In 1845, Parliament finally removed the excise tax on English glass. By the 1850s England still had the reputation of producing some of the finest glassware in the world. The World's Fair in London in 1851, dubbed "The Great Exposition of the Works of Industry of All Nations," contained a huge display of glass. The Crystal Palace Exposition featured a giant building containing 400 tons of sheet glass or about 300,000 handblown panes. The displays and products at this exhibit could not but help stimulate the glass industry.

Complete matching table sets of glassware that were later produced in great quantity in America during the Great Depression had their roots in England. Table service items included stemmed drinking glasses in many different shapes and sizes, water beakers, beer tankards, decanters, bowls, sugar bowls and creamers, saltshakers, butter dishes, honey jars, flower vases, candlestick holders, bonbon dishes, carafes and pitchers, and so on.

A variety of other glass items other than tableware were made in England, too. Jugs, water basins, powder boxes, jewelry dishes and boxes, toothbrush holders, soap dishes, and other glass objects were popular. The hand-pressing method invented in America was used in England very soon after its initial development. Though most were made in France, paperweights were popular in England in the mid-19th century. England and other European countries were the first to spark a revival of cameo cut glass, which had not been present for centuries since the Islamic glass cutters. John Northwood was credited for the revival of relief-cutting in cameo colors. A blue or plum color cased in white with classic Greek and Roman themes was raised in relief on vases, flasks, plaques, and many other items.

England began and then followed the art-glass trends in the later 19th century. Thomas Webb, along with his sons, was one of the largest producers of Cameo, Burmese, Peachblow, and a variety of other designs. Several English firms also adopted the cheaper carnival glassmaking techniques from America in the 20th century. With the help of the

7

English, Australian glass houses were built and produced carnival glass, too. The later 19th century was a significant time for the entire European community as others joined in.

The biggest influence the French had in the world of glassmaking was their leadership role in both paperweight making and the art nouveau movement. The 1840s and 1850s are often considered the golden age of paperweights as makers such as Baccarat, St. Louis, Clichy, and others sparked a trend that was revived a century later. Paperweights may well be the most popular specialty in glass collecting today. Later in the 19th century, Eugene Rousseau and Emile Galle were the initial French designer-artists and first displayed their fancy glass at the Paris Exposition Universelle. From the time Admiral Matthew Perry opened trade with Japan to the West, Rousseau was deeply influenced by Asian art. This renewed interest in Eastern art in the form of rugs, porcelain, prints, paintings, and so on was also popular in America throughout the art nouveau period. Rousseau and Galle did not limit themselves to Far Eastern influence but rather combined it with traditional German and Italian Renaissance shapes. Galle, more than Rousseau, was the inspiration for this period. The new art form appeared not only in glass but in architecture, paintings, posters, book illustrations, furniture, wallpaper, fabric, embroidery, jewelry, and numerous other mediums. Unlike many of the manufacturers of cut glass, Galle signed his works, which sparked others to continue this tradition.

Art glass was richly ornamental, with little in the way of rules. It was full of originality, displaying crackle effects, metal particles, asymmetrical designs, long sinuous lines, weaving tendrils, flowing rhythms, and wild color effects. Colors and opaqueness were experimented with, and impractical items made of glass had no constructive use except for display and value as works of art. Whimsies abounded, and such things as insects, animals, fruits, and other recurring themes in nature were all recreated in glass. Rather than typical pretty floral designs, thistle pines, pinecones, and simple plants such as grains of wheat were present on this glass. There were no set limits or traditions to follow.

Galle went on to direct the highly acclaimed Nancy School of Art in Nancy, France. The institute dedicated itself to originality, innovation, and artistic achievement in glass. In the 1880s and 1890s the city of Nancy became the hub of the art-glass movement in Europe. Enameled, gilded, engraved, and bizarre color effects were all part of Galle's designs; however, he is most noted for his superb cameo-relief creations in glass. Nancy attracted many other noted figures such as Jean Daum, second only to Galle in reputation. When Galle died in 1904, the quality of work in his factory suffered, and many believe it was the beginning of the decline of an era.

One other noteworthy French designer and artisan was Rene Lalique. Lalique began his career as a maker of art-glass jewelry in the 1890s. He was commissioned by Coty Parfums to produce fancy decorative perfume bottles for Coty's various fragrances. At this point the true artist was born and Lalique's famous creations branched into glass sculpture. Figures, nudes, vases, and even car-hood ornaments were formed into frosted crystal works of art. He experimented a little with colors but worked primarily with crystal. Many of his creations contain several separate views, such as a bowl formed by three kneeling nude figures.

Other European countries were part of the art nouveau movement. Austrian makers included Johannn Lutz, E. Bakalowits, and Moser and Sons; Val St. Lambert was a famous glass city in Belgium; the islands near Venice continued to produce millefiori designs dating back to the 13th century; and even famous American artists such as Louis Comfort Tiffany and Frederick Carder visited Europe to gain firsthand knowledge and ideas of glassmaking trends.

The remainder of this chapter is devoted to pricing trends in foreign glassware primarily from the past two centuries. Please refer to the previous section on Market Review and Pricing for an explanation of the guides contained within this work.

African Glass
20th Century–Present

Over the past couple of decades, some small African glass novelty companies have sprung up. Local glass artisans in Ngwenya, a small village in Swaziland, produce handmade animals, and Moroccan artisans decorate glass with gold.

Bowl, 9", Frosted & Cut Design of an Elephant Parade, African Wildlife Foundation Commission	$175
Elephant, 3" Tall, Crystal with Green Swirling, Ngwenya	$35
Elephant Sculpture, 5⅞" Tall, Crystal Elephant on Frosted Base	$175
Rhinoceros, 2¾" Long, Crystal with Green Swirling, Ngwenya	$30
Tumbler, 4 oz., Paneled Red, Blue, or Green with Gold Scrolling, Morocco	$12.50
Water Buffalo, 2½" Long, Crystal with Green Swirling, Ngwenya	$30

Alexandrite
Thomas Webb and Sons, England, 1890s–Early 1900s

This English art glass consists of gradual shading from pale yellow or amber to a pinkish rose color, and finally to blue. See additional material under "Webb, Thomas & Sons" near the end of the chapter.

Bowl, Finger, 5", Fluted, Matching Underplate	$800
Bowl, Finger with Matching Underplate, Honeycomb Pattern	$2,300
Creamer, 3" Tall, Pitcher Style, Thumbprint Pattern	$2,300
Goblet, 8½" Tall, Wafer Base, Textured Leaves on Stem	$2,300
Match Holder with Square Top, 3" Square, 2½" Tall, Diamond Quilted Pattern	$835
Pitcher, 5½" Tall, Petal Top, Applied Handle	$2,250
Plate, 5½", Crimped, Thumbprint Pattern	$1,050

Plate, 6", Rippled	$1,050
Punch Cup, 2¾" Tall, Applied Citron Handle	$635
Tazza, 1½" x 4½", Amber Pedestal Feet, Diamond Quilted Pattern	$950
Toothpick Holder, 2½" Tall, Dark or Light Color Shading	$1,000
Toothpick Holder, 3" Tall, Globe-Shape Body, Square Top	$825
Toothpick Holder, 3" Tall, Ruffled	$800
Tumbler, 3" Tall, Honeycomb Pattern	$950
Vase, 3" Tall, Diamond Quilted Pattern	$635
Vase, 4" Tall, Jack-in-the-Pulpit Style, Honeycomb Pattern	$1,175
Vase, 4½" Tall, Honeycomb Pattern	$785
Vase, 6" Tall, Ruffled, Honeycomb Pattern	$885
Wineglass, 4½" Tall, Honeycomb Pattern	$1,375
Wineglass, 4½" Tall, Thumbprint Pattern	$1,475

Argentinian Glass
1920s–Present

The first glass company established in Buenos Aires was the Regolleau Christalerias Company. They began producing practical tableware and produced some carnival glass items early on. A couple of others—Cristalerias Papini and Cristalerias Piccardo—followed soon afterward. The companies were all nationalized in the 1940s, and only Rigolleau and Papini (name changed to Cristalux) are still in operation.

Ashtray, Beetle Shape, Carnival Blue	$500
Ashtray, R. & C. Design, Carnival Marigold or Blue	$140

Australian Carnival Glass
1918–1930s

The most famous Australian factory to produce carnival glass was the Crystal Glass Works Limited in Sydney. The majority of glass was produced in marigold, purple, and amethyst. As you can see from the listings below, native wildlife is a popular theme of Australian carnival glass.

Bowl, 5", Australian Swan Pattern, Marigold (Purple $210)	$185
Bowl, 5", Banded Diamonds Pattern, Marigold or Amethyst	$85
Bowl, 5", Emu Pattern, Marigold or Amethyst	$265

Bowl, 5", Kangaroo Pattern, Marigold or Amethyst	$135
Bowl, 5", Kingfisher Pattern, Marigold or Amethyst	$175
Bowl, 5", Kiwi Pattern, Marigold or Amethyst	$275
Bowl, 5", Kookaburra (Bird) Pattern, Marigold or Purple	$150
Bowl, 5", Magpie Pattern, Marigold (Amethyst $225)	$125
Bowl, 5", Thunderbird Pattern, Marigold or Purple	$200
Bowl, 5½", Australian Swan Pattern, Marigold (Purple $125)	$85
Bowl, 6", Magpie Pattern, Marigold or Amethyst	$325
Bowl, 8" Style Pattern, Marigold or Amethyst	$150
Bowl, 8¾", Pin-Ups Pattern, Marigold or Amethyst	$165
Bowl, 9", Australian Swan Pattern, Marigold (Purple $475)	$250
Bowl, 9", Butterfly Bower Pattern, Marigold or Amethyst	$150
Bowl, 9", Heavy Banded Diamonds Pattern, Marigold or Amethyst	$140
Bowl, 9", Kangaroo Pattern, Marigold (Purple $675)	$525
Bowl, 9", 12-Sided, Kingfisher Pattern, Marigold (Purple $350)	$225
Bowl, 9", Kookaburra (Bird) Pattern, Marigold or Purple	$400
Bowl, 9", Thunderbird Pattern, Marigold or Purple	$350
Bowl, 9½", Australian Swan Pattern, Marigold (Purple $500)	$265
Bowl, 9½" Kangaroo Pattern, Marigold or Amethyst	$700
Bowl, 9½", Kingfisher Pattern, Marigold or Amethyst	$325
Bowl, 9½", Thunderbird Pattern, Marigold or Amethyst	$400
Bowl, 10", Banded Diamonds Pattern, Marigold or Amethyst	$135
Bowl, 10", Emu Pattern, Marigold or Amethyst	$1,350
Bowl, 10", Kiwi Pattern, Marigold (Amethyst $1,250)	$400
Bowl, 10", Kookaburra (Bird) Pattern, Marigold or Purple	$375
Bowl, 10", Magpie Pattern, Marigold (Amethyst $700)	$300
Bowl, Berry, Heavy Banded Diamonds Pattern, Marigold or Purple	$100
Bowl, Berry, Magpie Pattern, Marigold	$75
Bowl, Octagonal, Emu Pattern, Marigold, Purple, or Amber	$115
Bowl, Pin-Up Square on Stem Pattern, Marigold or Purple	$115
Butter Dish, Triands Pattern, Marigold	$85

Cake Plate, 10", Butterflies and Waratah Pattern, Marigold (Amethyst $375)	$500
Cake Plate, Butterfly Bower Pattern, Marigold or Purple	$265
Cake Plate, Flower Flannel Pattern, Marigold	$235
Cake Plate, Ostrich Pattern, Marigold, Amethyst, or Purple	$375
Compote, Butterflies and Bells Pattern, Marigold or Purple	$275
Compote, Butterflies and Waratah Pattern, Marigold (Amethyst $375)	$250
Compote, Butterfly Bower Pattern, Marigold or Purple	$400
Compote, Butterfly Bush Pattern, Marigold or Amethyst	$400
Compote, Flower Flannel Pattern, Marigold or Amethyst	$190
Compote, Hobnail and Cane Pattern, Marigold or Amethyst	$175
Compote, Ostrich Pattern, Marigold, Amethyst, or Purple	$215
Compote, Rose Panels Pattern, Marigold	$175
Compote, S-Band Pattern, Marigold or Amethyst	$115
Compote, Wild Fern Pattern, Marigold (Purple $275)	$185
Creamer, Australian Pattern, Marigold or Amethyst	$110
Creamer, Australian Panels Pattern, Marigold or Amethyst	$95
Creamer, Banded Panels Design, Marigold or Amethyst	$100
Creamer, Blocks and Arches Pattern, Creamer	$55
Epergne, Sungold Pattern, Amethyst (White $850)	$550
Mug, Souvenir, Paneled Flute Design, Inscribed "Greetings From Mt. Gambier," Marigold (White $500)	$175
Pitcher, Water, Banded Diamonds Pattern, Marigold, Amethyst, or Purple	$1550
Pitcher, Water, Blocks and Arches, Marigold or Amethyst	$275
Plate, 5½", Golden Cupid Pattern, Crystal with Gold	$125
Plate, 9", Golden Cupid Pattern, Crystal with Gold	$175
Sugar, Australian Pattern, Marigold or Amethyst	$115
Sugar, Australian Panels Pattern, Marigold or Amethyst	$90
Sugar, Banded Panels Design, Marigold or Amethyst	$80
Sugar, Diamond Band Pattern, Marigold or Amethyst	$80
Tumbler, Banded Diamonds Pattern, Marigold or Amethyst	$575
Tumbler, Blocks and Arches, Marigold, Amethyst, or Purple	$110
Tumbler, Vertical Grape Pattern, Light Marigold	$55

Vase, Shallow Bowl with Flower Holder in Center, 3-Tiered Threaded Design, Ice Green	$100
Vase, Tropicana Pattern, Marigold	$1,850

Austrian Glass
19th Century–Present

Older Austrian glass from several factories can be difficult to distinguish from other European makers because of the country's historical association with Germany, Bohemia, and the Austro-Hungarian Empire. Oftentimes (such as at auctions), Austrian glass products are combined with other miscellaneous European glassware that might include items from France, England, Germany, and other countries.

Bowl, 4¾", Iridescent Purple with Pink and White Threading	$240
Brandy Glass, 5¾" Tall, Crystal	$10
Compote, 3¾" Tall, Lime Green with Black Foot, Enameled Black Lattice Design	$290
Goblet, 8" Tall, Iridescent Light Green	$255
Goblet, 8½" Tall, Crystal, Curved Stem, Kirkland Design	$12.50
Lamp, 13" Tall, Metal Base, 10" Iridescent Amber Shade with Pink Threading	$1,875
Paperweight, Round, 1½" Diameter, Multicolor Center with Edelweiss and Gentian Floral Design	$75
Perfume Bottle, 4¾" Tall, Opaque White with Gold-Plated Stopper and Necklace Chain	$50
Perfume Bottle, 7¼" Tall, Opaque White with Gold-Plated Stopper and Necklace Chain	$60
Royal Pumpkin Coach (Cinderella's), 3" Tall, Drawn by 2 Mice, Mirrored Base Gold Crown, Chain, Wheel Hubs, and Visor	$87.50
Shot Glass, Square Shape, 2½" Tall, 2 oz., Crystal with Etched Floral Pattern Around Glass	$20
Shot Glass, 2¾" Tall, Crystal with Gold Rim and Multicolored Enameled Flags and Coat-of-Arms	$12.50
Vase, 3¼" Tall, Ruffled, Iridescent Blue with Gold Vines and Jeweled Butterflies	$540
Vase, 4⅛" Tall, Iridescent Gold with Amber Spots	$375
Vase, 6½" Tall, Light Orange with Deep Amethyst Rim and Handle	$440
Vase, 7" Tall, Silver Rim, Iridescent Green with Applied Serpent Design	$425
Vase, 8" Tall, Conch Seashell Shape, Iridescent Gold with Green Seashell Foot	$440
Vase, 9¾" Tall, Scalloped, Iridescent Yellow with Orange Design on Base	$565

Austrian Engraved Beaker. *Courtesy of the Corning Museum of Glass.*

Vase, 10¾" Tall, Ruffled, Iridescent Purple with Silver Overlay	$925
Vase, 12" Tall, Iridescent Yellow with Gilding	$590

Baccarat Glass Company
France, 1765–19th Century, 1953–Present

Producing what came to be known as "The Crystal of Kings," the original Baccarat company was founded in 1764 in Baccarat, France. Early on, the company produced practical lead crystal items. In 1846, they began producing art-style paperweights along with tableware, cut glass, and other decorative glass. The company is still in operation today with a factory, museum, and showroom in Baccarat, as well as a second museum and showroom in Paris. Baccarat is known for producing some of the finest crystal, colored glass, and paperweights being made in the world today. Since 1953, they have resumed paperweight production and are also noted for high-quality clear lead crystal products. Beware of imitation sulphide paperweights made in America, especially those of several presidents, such as Kennedy, Lincoln, and Eisenhower.

Angel Christmas Figurine, 6⅝" Tall, 5½" Wide, Crystal	$235
Angel with Trumpet Figure, 6" Tall, Crystal	$185
Bassacuda Letter Opener, 10" Long, Crystal	$275
Bear, 4⅝" Long, 2¾" Tall, Crystal	$210
Bottle, Scent, 4" Tall, White and Gold (Cyclamen)	$600
Bottle, Scent, 4¼" Tall, Rose Tiente Swirl Design	$105
Bottle, Scent, 4½" Tall, Front Label (Mitsonko)	$120
Bottle, Scent, 6¾" Tall, Rose Tiente Swirl Design	$140

Cristalleries de Baccarat. *Reproduced directly from a 1993 Baccarat advertisement.*

Baccarat Loch Ness Monster, 4-Piece. *Photo by Robin Rainwater.*

Baccarat Camel Centerpiece. *Photo by Mark Pickvet.*

Bottle, Scent, 7½" Tall, Rose Tiente Swirl Design	$160
Bowl, 5½", 2" Tall, Amberina Swirl Design	$105
Bowl, Rose, 5", Rose Tiente Swirl Design	$90
Bowl, 15½" Scalloped Rim, Light Amber, Rose Tiente Sunburst Design	$1,050
Box with Cover, Rectangular (3" x 2"), Rose Tiente Swirl Design	$125
Bull, 6½" Long, 3½" Tall, Head Lowered, Crystal	$285
Bunny, 2½" Tall, 2¾" Long, Crystal	$85
Bunny, 3¼" Tall, Crystal	$90
Bunny, 3⅓" Tall, Easter, Blue, Pink, or Crystal	$130

Butterfly Pin, 1¾" Across, Ruby Red with 18 kt. Gold Accents	$365
Candelabra, 24" Tall, Frosted Child on Stem, 2-Holder, with Central Prism	$2,275
Candlestick, 7" Tall, Footed, Swirled Amberina Shading	$105
Candlestick, 7⅛" Tall, Flared Base, Light Amberina, Rose Tiente Swirl Design	$135
Candlestick, 9" Tall, Crystal Bamboo Spiral Pattern	$140
Candlestick, 15¾" Tall, Crystal, Frosted Cherub Base, 8 Prisms	$1,500
Carafe, Tumble-Up, Rose Tiente Swirl Design	$120
Cat, 4½" Tall, 5" Long, Arched Back, Crystal	$235
Cat, 6¾" Tall, Batting in Air, Crystal	$255
Cologne Bottle with Stopper, 5" Tall, Swirled Amberina Shading	$160
Compote, 4" Tall, Amberina	$225
Compote, 8¾" Tall, 7¾" Diameter, Circular Base, Frosted Cherub on Stem	$285
Cordial, Amber with Gold Geese Decoration	$45
Cougar Head, 5½" Tall, 5" Wide, Crystal	$440
Dachshund, 3¼" Tall, 6" Long, Crystal	$225
Decanter with Stopper, 9½" Tall, Amber, Gold Geese Decoration	$225
Decanter with Stopper, 10" Tall, Light Amberina, Rose Tiente Swirl Design	$265
Decanter with Stopper, 10" Tall, Crystal, Etched Wild Turkey Design	$365
Decanter with Stopper, 13" Tall, Etched Floral Design	$275
Decanter with Stopper, 14" Tall, Cut and Etched (for J. G. Monnet & Co.)	$285
Dove Crystal Christmas Ornament, 3¼" Long, 1999	$75
Duck, 1⅝" Tall, 2⅝" Long, Crystal, Amethyst, Amber, or Emerald Green	$110
Eagle, 9⅝" Tall, 7⅛" Wide, Crystal	$735
Elephant, 2⅝" Tall, 2¾" Long, Crystal, Trunk Up	$85
Elephant, 3" Tall, Trunk Down, Crystal	$105
Epergne, Bronze Mounts, Onyx Footed Plinth, Amberina Shading	$400
Epergne, 15" Tall, Marbled Base, Swirled Amberina Shading	$400
Figure Skating Figurine, 11¾" Tall, Crystal	$315
Flower Holder, 12" x 2", Bridge Shape, 5" Tall, Sapphire Blue, Swirl Design	$240
Frog, 1¾" Tall, 1⅞" Long, Amber or Moss Green	$100
Frog, 4½" Tall, Crystal with 22 kt. Gold Crown	$175
Goblet, 5" Tall, Engraved Grape and Vine Design, Signed	$225

Heart Shape, 2¾" Long, Ruby Red	$110
Heart Shape, 3" Long, Amethyst, Blue, or Green	$115
Horse Head, 4½" Tall, 5¾" Long, Crystal	$225
Inkwell with Silverplated Lid, 2¾" Tall, Square, Floral Design	$105
Ladybug, 1¼" Tall, 2¼" Long, Crystal, Amber, Light Green, or Yellow	$95
Lamp, 4" Tall, Rose Tiente Swirl Design, Fairy Figure, Circular Base	$325
Lamp, Peg, 8" Tall, Ruffled Shades, Rose Tiente Swirl Design	$550
Lamp, Hurricane, 22" Tall, Bobeche with 4½" Prisms, Amberina	$675
Loch Ness Monster, 4 Pieces, 3¾" Tall, 9" Long, Crystal (Green $475)	$350
Marlin, 10¼" Long, Crystal (Blue Marlin Swordfish)	$750
Mother with Child Figurine 9¼" Tall, Crystal	$265
Mug, Swirled Amberina Shading, Thumbprint Pattern	$125
Nude Figerine, 4¾" Tall, 5⅛" Wide, Sitting and Reading Poetry, Crystal	$275
Otter, 5¾" Tall, Standing, 4" Long Including Tail, Crystal	$255
Otter, 7" Long, Reclining, 2¼" Tall, Crystal	$265
Paperweight, 2⅝", 10 Twisted Ribbons Radiating from a Millefiori Center	$575
Paperweight, 3", Multicolored Pansy Floral Design	$465
Paperweight, 3⅛", Double Clematis Design	$2,175
Paperweight Set of 12, Franklin Mint Commission, 1976: Green, Amber, or Blue Ground, 6 Side Windows, Sulphides of Abraham Lincoln, Admiral De Grasse, Alexander the Great, Charlemagne, George Washington, Joan of Arc, Julius Caesar, Louis XIV, Napoleon Bonaparte, Peter the Great, Queen Elizabeth, and Simon Bolivar (Great Leaders of History Series, $60 each)	$750
Paperweight, Sulphide, Faceted, Crystal Alexander the Great Design	$350
Paperweight, Sulphide, Faceted, Crystal Julius Caesar Design	$350
Paperweight, Sulphide, Faceted, Crystal Charlemagne Design	$475
Paperweight, Sulphide, Faceted, Crystal Winston Churchill Design	$675
Paperweight, Sulphide, Faceted, Crystal Admiral DeGrasse Design	$400
Paperweight, Sulphide, Faceted, Crystal Dwight D. Eisenhower Design	$500
Paperweight, Sulphide, 2½", Ben Franklin Design (Antique)	$1,575
Paperweight, Sulphide, 2½", Crystal Patrick Henry Design	$295
Paperweight, Sulphide, 2¾", Crystal Andrew Jackson Design	$295
Paperweight, Sulphide, Faceted, Crystal John F. Kennedy Design	$575

Paperweight, Sulphide, Faceted, Red and White Overlaid John F. Kennedy Design	$1,875
Paperweight, Sulphide, Faceted, Crystal Martin Luther King Design	$435
Paperweight, Sulphide, 3" Faceted, Robert E. Lee Design, 1955	$410
Paperweight, Sulphide, 3", Faceted, Crystal Abraham Lincoln Design	$515
Paperweight, Sulphide, 2¾", Crystal James Monroe Design	$335
Paperweight, Sulphide, 4", Faceted, Crystal Mount Rushmore Design	$485
Paperweight, Sulphide, Faceted, Crystal Napoleon Design	$415
Paperweight, Sulphide, Faceted, Crystal Thomas Paine Design	$435
Paperweight, Sulphide, Faceted, Crystal Peter the Great Design	$400
Paperweight, Sulphide, Faceted, Pope John XXIII Design	$175
Paperweight, Sulphide, 2¾", Pope Pius XII Design, Signed "David," 1959	$175
Paperweight, Sulphide, 3¼", Faceted, Outer Canes, Faceted, Queen Elizabeth Design, 1977	$375
Paperweight, Sulphide, 3¼", Queen Victoria Design (Antique)	$575
Paperweight, Sulphide, Faceted, Crystal Harry Truman Design, Gold Base	$525
Paperweight, Sulphide, Faceted, Crystal George Washington Design	$575
Paperweight, Sulphide, Faceted, Crystal Woodrow Wilson Design	$475
Paperweight, Packed Canes Design, Dated 1956	$325
Paperweight, Scattered Canes, Muslin Background, Dated 1846	$1,950
Pig, 2¾" Tall, 2¾" Long	$85
Plate, Rose Tiente Swirl Design	$60
Rabbit, 3¼" Tall, Crystal	$85
Santa Claus Figurine, 4¼" Tall, Crystal, with Present	$150
Scottie Dog, 5" Tall, Begging, Crystal	$200
Shaving-Brush Holder, Rose Tiente Swirl Design	$110
Shot Glass, 2¼" Tall, Flared, Millefiori Paperweight Base	$270
Snowman Christmas Ornament with Angel, 2⅝" Tall, 2½" Wide, Flat Crystal, Etched "Noel 1998"	$65
Snowman Figurine, 4¾" Tall, Crystal	$150
Soap Dish, 4½" Across, 2" Tall, Vaseline	$70
Starfish, 5½" Diameter, Crystal	$205
Tiger, 5½" Tall, Crystal, Sitting	$300

Tumbler, 3¾" Tall, Rose Tiente Swirl and Gold Floral Design	$285
Tumbler, 4" Tall, Rose Tiente Swirl Design	$95
Vase, 3½" Tall, Satinized Crystal with Enameled and Cut Busts of Caesar, Cleopatra, and Mark Antony	$575
Vase, 4¼" Tall, Paneled Green Clover Design	$87.50
Vase, 6⅛" Tall, Colbalt Blue and White Lace Design	$255
Vase, 7" Tall, Cylindrical, Crystal, Cut Ovals	$105
Vase, 7" Tall, Ovoid Design, Hexagonal Top, Crystal	$240
Vase, 8" Tall, French Cameo, Signed	$475
Vase, 8" Tall, French Cameo, Matte Crystal and Enamel Design	$750
Vase, 8" Tall, Coiled Snake Design, Signed	$390
Vase, 9½" Tall, Crystal Architectual Design	$1,500
Vase, 10" Tall, Opalescent, Scenic View with Birds Design	$440
Vase, 12" Tall, Jack-in-the-Pulpit Design, Amethyst	$325
Vase, 16" Tall, Crystal in Bronze Base, Scalloped Rim, Domed Foot, Fluted Panels	$4,275
Wineglass, 9" Tall, 6 oz., Crystal Round Base and Stacked Geometric Stem, Various Transparent Color Bowls	$150

Bohemian Glass
Germany, 17th Century–Present

The original Bohemian glass was characterized by heavy stone engraving overlaid with colored glass. A later design included the cutting of two layers of colored glass. The object was then gilded or enameled. Bohemia is now part of western Czechoslovakia, but once encompassed Austria, Southern Germany, and Czechoslovakia. Individual items can be difficult to date because the glass has been continuously produced for more than 300 years. Noted makers include Carl Goldberg, Count Arnost Harrach, Hartmann & Dietrichs, Carl Hosch, H. G. Curt Schlevogt, and many others.

Basket, 10½" Tall, Milk White with Transparent Amber Handle and Base	$375
Beaker, 5⅜" Tall, Ruby Red, Deer and Trees Decoration	$130
Bowl, 6", Engraved Castle, Deer, and Foliage Designs	$120
Bowl, 8", Cranberry Overlay, Various Enameled Designs	$170
Bowl, 12½", Cut Cobalt Blue to Crystal	$285
Candlestick, 9" Tall, Ruby and Crystal Cut, Bird or Deer Decoration	$82.50
Chalice, 6" Tall, Fluted, Footed, Crystal to Ruby Coloring, Stag Design	$140

Compote, 9", White to Green, Multicolored Floral Design $190

Cruet with Stopper, 6½" Tall, Ruby Flashed with Engraved Floral and Foliage Design $365

Decanter with Stopper, 9" Tall, Opaque Shading of Pink to White, Cut Floral Design $375

Decanter with Stopper, Ruby Red, Building and Floral Design $140

Decanter with Stopper, 12" Tall, Narrow, Etched and Cut Patterns $190

Goblet, 5½" Tall, Ruby Red Scroll Design $140

Goblet, 7" Tall, Ruby Red, Battle Monument Baltimore Decoration $575

Goblet, 7¼" Tall, Multicolored Enameled Floral Cameo Design (Cameo Enameling Only) $175

Jar, 13" Tall, Applied Prunts, Footed, Enameled Design of Man with Drinking Cup, Verse on Reverse Side $325

Lamp Shade, 5" Tall, 9" Diameter, Milk Glass with Multicolored Cameo Design of Bear on Fallen Log $2,375

Mantel Lustre, 12" Tall, Tulip Form Top, Hanging Crystal Prisms, Green with White Overlay, Enameled Floral Design $450

Mantel Lustre, 13" Tall, Tulip Form Top, Hanging Crystal Prisms, Green with White Overlay, Enameled Floral Design $500

Mantel Lustre, 14" Tall, Ruby Red with Gilding and Enameled Floral Design $510

Medallion, Oval (2" x 1½"), Crystal, Nude Figure of Woman with Loincloth and Basket on Head $400

Mug, Beer, 5½" Tall, Cranberry to Clear Etched $85

Plate, 12", Crystal, Engraved Building Design in 4 Views $600

Pokal with Cover, 8" Tall, Ruby Red and Crystal, Floral and Building Scenery $1,450

Pokal, 16" Tall, Ruby Red, Niagara Falls and Building Decoration $2,375

Pokal with Faceted Finial, 24" Tall, Green with Multicolored Shield and Grape Decoration $3,875

Stein, 5" Tall, Ruby Red, Niagara Falls Decoration $375

Stein, 5⅛" Tall, Ruby Red, Floral Paneled Design $375

Stein, 5½" Tall, Ruby Red, Hunting Dog and Forest Decoration $385

Stein, 6¼" Tall, Ruby Red, Castle, Scroll, and Vine Decoration $395

Tumbler, 3¾" Tall, Ruby Red, Windmill Decoration $87.50

Tumbler, 4" Tall, Crystal, Engraved Chalet with Heavy Grass, Lake, and Bridge Scene $225

Tumbler, 7" Tall, Crystal with Multicolored Enameled Monastery Design (Various Styles)
$275

Tumbler, 7" Tall, Crystal with Applied Multicolored Beading, Multicolored Knight and Shield Design
$325

Urn with Cover, 22" Tall, Ruby Red, Stag and Woodland Scene
$685

Vase, 5" Tall, Crystal, Engraved Cameo Face of Woman
$190

Vase, 6" Tall, Circular Pedestal Base, Double Loop Handle, Coralene
$375

Vase, 7½" Tall, Multicolored Swirl Design
$125

Vase, 8¼" Tall, Cased with White, Enameled Floral Design
$140

Vase, 8¼" Tall, Scalloped, Cobalt Blue Overlay
$175

Vase, 9" Tall, Emerald Green with White and Gold Enameled Floral Design
$250

Vase, 9½" Tall, Violet Red Case with Opal White, Gilded Scroll and Trim, Green and Turquoise Beading
$475

Vase, 10" Tall, Cut Windows, Blue, Yellow and Ruby Red Coloring
$275

Vase, 10½" Tall, Cobalt Blue Encased in Crystal
$140

Vase, 11" Tall, Crystal, Many Engraved Miniature Crescent Moons Design
$170

Vase, 14" Tall, Enameled Butterfly Design on White Opal Glass
$1,575

Wineglass, 6" Tall, Crystal, Engraved Pinwheel Design
$55

Wineglass, Knob Stem, Dark Ruby Red, Monkey Design
$80

Bristol Glass
Europe (England, France, Germany, and Italy), 18th–19th Centuries

Bristol Glass is usually characterized by an opaque or semi-opaque base color that is further decorated by use of enamels. It originated in Bristol, England, in the 17th century and spread to other parts of Europe. Some Bristol Glass may have been made in Czechoslovakia/Bohemia and simply sold by English merchants. A little of it was produced in America by the New England Glass Company and a few others.

Basket, 10½" Tall, Ruffled, Pink Opaline, Bird Design
$255

Biscuit Jar with Silver-Plated Cover, 7½" Tall, Tan Birds and Foliage with Silver-Plated Handle and Rim
$285

Bowl, 3¾", 1¾" Tall, 3 Snail Feet, Blue with Yellow Foliage and Floral Design, Gold Bands
$80

Bowl, 7", Lily Shape, Amethyst Color
$75

Bowl, Rose, 4¼" Diameter, 4½" Tall, Footed, Crimped, Turquoise with Gold Floral, Foliage, and Trim
$160

Candlestick, 6½" Tall, Turquoise with Multicolored Floral and Foliage Design	$120
Candlestick, 7" Tall, Opaque Green with Gold Band	$87.50
Chandelier, 4-Light, Crystal Bell and Prism Design	$2,175
Cologne Bottle with Gold Ball Stopper, 4" Tall, Green with Gold Dot and Star Design	$125
Cologne Bottle with Ball Stopper, 5¾" Tall, Turquoise with Gold Band and Enameled Floral Design	$115
Cologne Bottle with Stopper, 10" Tall, Pink with Gold Band and Foliage Design	$175
Cracker Jar with Silver-Plated Cover, Rim, and Handle; 6½" Tall, Opaque Blue with Multicolored Floral and Foliage Design	$265
Ewer, 10" Tall, Clambroth with Blue Edging	$115
Lamp, 10" Tall, Square Shade, Shell-Footed, Enameled Birds and Floral Design	$750
Mug, 5" Tall, Opaque White with Enameled Eagle	$415
Pitcher, Water, 8½" Tall, Applied Crystal Handle, Light Green with Enameled Floral and Birds Design	$125
Salt Dip, Rectangular, White with Multicolored Enameled Floral Design	$55
Sweetmeat Jar, 5" Tall, Silver-Plated Rim, Cream with Multicolored Enameled Floral Design	$175
Urn with Cover, 15" Tall, Enameled Floral Design	$200
Vase, 3¾" Tall, Turquoise with Gold Bands and Multicolored Enameled Florals with White Dots	$90
Vase, 5¼" Tall, Turquoise with Gold Bands and Floral Design	$155
Vase, 6½" Tall, Brown with Gold Floral Design	$100
Vase, 7½" Tall, Opaque Gray with Multicolored Enameled Boy or Girl	$115
Vase, 8½" Tall, Cylindrically Shaped, Blue with Multicolored Enameled Floral, Butterfly, and Building Design	$125
Vase, 9½" Tall, Green with Gilded Leaf Design	$90
Vase, 10" Tall, Handled, Enameled Green Design	$165
Vase, 10" Tall, Enameled Gold and Pink Floral Design	$150
Vase, 11½" Tall, Pink with Multicolored Enameled Angel in Chariot Design	$225
Vase, 11¾" Tall, Opal, Enameled Floral Design	$175
Vase, 13" Tall, Footed, Turquoise with Gold Leaf and Scrolling	$285
Vase, 13½" Tall, Amethyst Tint, Enameled Floral Design	$175
Vase, 14½" Tall, Cone Shape, Blue with White Floral Design	$265

Vase, 14½" Tall, Dark Gray with Red and White Floral Design	$265
Vase, 16½" Tall, Opaque White with Enameled Floral and Butterfly Design	$200
Vase, 18" Tall, Ruffled, Enameled Hydrangeas with Gilding	$325

Caithness Glass, Ltd.
1960–Present

Caithness was founded in 1960 and has factories at Perth, Wick, and Oban in the region of Perthshire, Scotland. In its beginning, Caithness specialized in paperweights, but it soon expanded into novelties as well as some limited crystal tableware. Noted glass artisan Paul Ysart joined Caithness in 1962, and Caithness acquired the Whitefriars name in 1981.

Bottle with Round Crystal Stopper, 3¾" Tall, Blue Ground with Multicolored Floral Paperweight Base	$90
Bowl, 7¼" Diameter, 5" Tall, Clear Round Base, Blue Bottom and Sides, Engraved Dolphins' Design	$100
Paperweight, 1¾" Globe, Green Ground, Green Shamrock and White Floral Design, Top Viewing Window	$75
Paperweight, 1¾" Globe, Colbalt Blue Ground, Multicolored Thistle and Floral Design, Top Viewing Window	$75
Paperweight, 2" Globe, Clear to Ultramarine Ground, Multicolored Dragonfly in Flight over Leaves, Limited Edition of 500	$300
Paperweight, 2" Globe, Various "Flower of the Month" Designs (Multicolored Floral Designs, 1 for Each Month), Price Is for Each	$60
Paperweight, 2" Globe, Blue Ground, White Snowflake and Floral Design, Top Viewing Window	$75
Paperweight, 2½" Globe, Cobalt Blue Ground, Tan and White Teddy Bear Design	$75
Paperweight, 2⅜", Aqua Ground, Purple and White Pansy, Controlled Bubbling, Front Viewing Window	$125
Paperweight, 3", Globe, Blue with Controlled Bubbles, Engraved Dolphins Front Viewing Window	$65
Paperweight, 3" Globe, Blue and Pink Kingfisher Design	$45
Paperweight, 3" Globe, Green with Controlled Bubbles, Engraved Scottish Highlander Cattle, Front Viewing Window	$65
Paperweight, 3" Globe, Sorcerer's Apprentice—Swirled Mass of Green and White Ribbons/Bubbles	$40
Paperweight, 3" Globe, Clear with Controlled Bubbling, Red, White, and Blue Decreasing Spiral Design, Front Viewing Window	$50

Paperweight, 3⅛" Globe, Clear and White Muslin Ground, Blue and Yellow Forget-Me-Nots, Green Leaves, Limited Edition of 50 $375

Paperweight, 3⅛" Globe, Cobalt Blue Ground, Blue Star over Joseph and Mary Figures, Limited Edition of 75 $700

Paperweight, 4" Tall, Pear Shape, Blue Ground, Sculptured Seaweed Shapes, Limited Edition of 500 $100

Paperweight, 4¼" Tall, Blue and Speckled White Ground, Multicolored Spiral Design, Limited Edition of 650 $85

Vase, 8¼" Tall, Light Blue or Green with Various Engraved Designs (Barn Owl, Dolphins, Hummingbird, or Swan) $65

Vase, 9" Tall, Crystal with Seaform Green, Blue, or Yellow Swirling, Various Engraved Designs (Angelfish, Deer, Kingfisher, Otter, Orchids, or Whale) $65

Canadian Glass
Mid-1820s–Present

Canadian Glass is often ignored in the collecting field (except by Canadian collectors); however, a good deal of glass was made in Canada dating as far back as the mid-1820s. The Mallorytown Glass Works in Ontario was the first to produce glass, and others followed the pressed-, art, and cut-glass trends of Europe and America. Much of the glass made in Canada in the 19th century was practical (such as bottles, tumblers, tableware, windows, and fruit or canning jars). Dominion (several pressed patterns such as Rayed Heart and Athenian) and Diamond were two successful companies that followed Mallorytown. Dominion eventually became Jefferson, a major producer of art nouveau lamps. Two others known for pressed glasswares in the late 19th century are the O'Hara Glass Company Ltd. and the Burlington Glass Works. There were also many noted Canadian cut-glass manufacturers, including Gowans, Kent & Company, Ltd., Gundy-Clapperton Company, Lakefield Cut Glass Company, and the most well known, Roden Brothers.

Bowl, 5", Cut Hobstar Design, Gowans, Kent, & Co.	$135
Bowl, 6", Cut Buzzstar Design, Gundy-Clapperton	$155
Bowl, 6", Handled, Canadian Pattern, Burlington Glass Works	$40
Bowl, Chandelier Pattern, O'Hara	$34
Bowl, 7", 4½" Tall, Footed, Canadian Pattern, Burlington Glass Works	$70
Bowl, 8", Footed, Athenian Pattern, Dominion Glass Co.	$85
Bowl, 8", Pressed Maple Leaf Pattern	$60
Bowl, 8", Rayed Heart Pattern, Dominion Glass Co.	$110
Bread Plate, 10", Canadian Pattern, Burlington Glass Works	$50
Butter Dish with Cover, Athenian Pattern, Dominion Glass Co.	$135

Butter Dish with Cover, Canadian Pattern, Burlington Glass Works	$95
Butter Dish with Cover, Chandelier Pattern, O'Hara	$95
Butter Dish with Cover, Rayed Heart Pattern, Dominion Glass Co.	$150
Cake Stand, 9¼", Canadian Pattern, Burlington Glass Works	$95
Cake Stand, Chandelier Pattern, O'Hara	$70
Canning Jar with Zinc Cover, Embossed "Best," 1 qt.	$4
Canning Jar with Glass Lid, Clear with Embossed "Improved Gem," 1 pt.	$7.50
Canning Jar with Glass Lid, Clear with Embossed "Improved Gem," 1 qt.	$8.50
Canning Jar with Glass Lid, Clear with Embossed "Perfect Seal," 1 pt.	$7.50
Canning Jar with Glass Lid, Clear with Embossed "Perfect Seal," 1 qt.	$8.50
Canning Jar, Amber, Embossed "Canadian Queen," 1 qt. (rare)	$415
Celery Dish, Chandelier Pattern, O'Hara	$47.50
Celery Dish, 9" Oblong, Rayed Heart Pattern, Dominion Glass Co.	$110
Celery Vase, Canadian Pattern, Burlington Glass Works	$65
Compote with Cover, 6", Canadian Pattern, Burlington Glass Works	$100
Compote, 6" to 7" Diameter, Canadian Pattern, Burlington Glass Works	$42.50
Compote, 6" or 7", Chandelier Pattern, O'Hara	$47.50
Compote, 7" Diameter, Pressed Maple Leaf Pattern	$62.50
Compote with Cover, 7", Canadian Pattern, Burlington Glass Works	$110
Compote with Cover, 8", Canadian Pattern, Burlington Glass Works	$120
Compote with Cover, 8", Chandelier Pattern, O'Hara	$80
Compote, 9" Diameter, 6½" Tall, Cut Diamond and Hobstar Design, Roden Brothers	$215
Cookie Jar with Silver-Plated Lid and Top Handle, Silver-plated Beaver Finial on Handle, 10½" Tall, Enameled Grape Decoration	$375
Cordial, Canadian Pattern, Burlington Glass Works	$37.50
Creamer, Athenian Pattern, Dominion Glass Co.	$62.50
Creamer, Canadian Pattern, Burlington Glass Works	$65
Creamer, Chandelier Pattern, O'Hara	$37.50
Creamer, 4" Tall, Pitcher Style, 2-Handled, Cut Maple Leaf Pattern	$185
Creamer, Rayed Heart Pattern, Dominion Glass Co.	$90
Goblet, Canadian Pattern, Burlington Glass Works	$47.50
Goblet, Etched, Chandelier Pattern, O'Hara	$37.50

Goblet, 5½" Tall, Pressed Honeycomb Pattern with Faceted Design within Combs (Copper Wheel–Engraved), Diamond Glass Co., 1890s — $160

Goblet, 6" Tall, Pressed Raspberry Pattern, 1890s — $80

Hat, 2¾" Tall, Canadian Pillar Pattern, Lamont Glass Co., 1890s — $67.50

Heart Shape, 1" Thick, 2" Long, Various Iridized Colors, 1990s, Robert Held — $26

Inkwell, Chandelier Pattern, O'Hara — $415

Jam Jar with Cover, Ribbed Lid, Canadian Pattern, Burlington Glass Works — $80

Lamp, 14" Tall, Bronze Base, Cobalt Blue with Enameled Palm Trees Design, Jefferson Glass Co. — $1,575

Lamp, Kerosene, 16" Tall, Emerald Green Base and Globe, #102 Style, Dominion Glass Co., 1880s — $325

Lamp, 18" Tall, Opal with Enameled Water Scene with 2 Sailing Ships, Jefferson Glass Co. — $800

Mug, Canadian Pattern, Burlington Glass Works — $50

Nappy, 4", Athenian Pattern, Dominion Glass Co. — $37.50

Paperweight, 2½" Tall, 10⅛" Circumference, Opal 5-Petal Lily on Multicolor Chips' Background, Cobalt Blue Writing "Souvenir de Wallaceburg, Ont," 1910s — $340

Paperweight, 3⅛" Tall, 10¼" Circumference, Cased 5-Petal Lily on Bubble Stem, Opal Glass Petals with Emerald Green and Multicolored Chips Background, 1890s — $375

Pitcher, Milk, 6½" Tall, Cut Buzzstar Pattern, Roden Brothers — $325

Pitcher, Milk, Canadian Pattern, Burlington Glass Works — $105

Pitcher, Water, Canadian Pattern, Burlington Glass Works — $135

Pitcher, Water, Chandelier Pattern, O'Hara — $57.50

Pitcher, Water, 10⅜" Tall, Footed, Handblown Crystal, Excelsior Glass Co., 1880s — $215

Pitcher, Water, 11½" Tall, Footed, Pressed Maple Leaf Pattern — $265

Pitcher, 11½" Tall, 64 oz., Cut Colonial Pattern — $425

Plate, 6", 2-Handled, Canadian Pattern, Burlington Glass Works — $32.50

Powder Jar with Cover, 3½" Tall, 4" Diameter, Cut Regina Pattern, Roden Brothers — $155

Salt and Pepper Shakers, 3" Tall, Milk Glass, Pressed Butterfly and Tassel Pattern — $115

Salver, 9" Diameter, 5½" Tall, Athenian Pattern, Dominion Glass Co. — $105

Sauce Dish, Flat, Canadian Pattern, Burlington Glass Works — $17.50

Sauce Dish, Footed, Canadian Pattern, Burlington Glass Works — $22.50

Spooner, Canadian Pattern, Burlington Glass Works — $50

Spooner, Chandelier Pattern, O'Hara	$42.50
Spooner, Rayed Heart Pattern, Dominion Glass Co.	$70
Sugar, 3½" Tall, 2-Handled, Cut Maple Leaf Pattern	$135
Sugar with Cover, Athenian Pattern, Dominion Glass Co.	$90
Sugar with Cover, Canadian Pattern, Burlington Glass Works	$95
Sugar with Cover, Chandelier Pattern, O'Hara	$55
Sugar with Cover, Rayed Heart Pattern, Dominion Glass Co.	$140
Sugar Shaker, Chandelier Pattern, O'Hara	$110
Toothpick Holder, 2¼" Tall, Pressed Canadian Beaded Oval and Fan Pattern	$70
Tray, Celery, 11½" x 4" Oval, Cut Aster Pattern, Roden Brothers	$365
Tumbler, 5" Tall, Diamond Crosscut Pattern	$80
Tumbler, 5½" Tall, Cut Buzzstar Pattern	$90
Vase, 8" Tall, Slender Form, Ruffled, 4" Long Fluted Design	$52.50
Vase, 9" Tall, Ruffled, Crystal to Cranberry Shading, Chalet Artistic Glass, Ltd.	$275
Vase, 11" Tall, Footed, Ruffled, Long Flutes with Pressed Floral Band at Top, Jefferson Glass Co.	$100
Wineglass, Canadian Pattern, Burlington Glass Works	$47.50

Chinese Glass
1680–Present

Glassware in China was made to resemble the more desirable porcelain and was first named Peking Glass because that was where most of it was made originally. The Chinese considered glass inferior and merely an imitation of porcelain. However, they experimented with opaque glassware, including cameo designs. The name Peking is also attributed to glassware made in other cities in China (such as Po-shan) whose final finish was applied in Peking factories (originally at the Peking Imperial Glassworks).

Modern Chinese items include reverse painted glass—glass that is painted on the inside with traditional themes, such as mountains, waterfalls, pagodas, and bamboo. The artist must actually paint the mirror image, or reverse of the image, so that it shows correctly in front. Note that it is not a good idea to put live plants or—especially—flowers in water within a reverse-painted object, as natural materials can destroy the finish. Reverse-painted items are recommended for holding silk flowers only.

Bowl, 5¾", White with Green Cranes and Lotus Plants	$105
Bowl, 7", Blue on White Cameo, Floral Design	$265

Peking (Chinese) Reverse Painted Bowl. *Photo by Robin Rainwater.*

Peking Glass Vase. *Photo by Robin Rainwater.*

Bowl, 7", Multicolored Flowers, Leaves, and Butterfly Design on White Cameo	$375
Bowl with Cover, 7½", Red on White Cameo, Bird on Floral Branches Design	$460
Bowl, 8", Green with Engraved Garden (Pagodas and Foliage), Yin and Yang Design	$325
Bowl, 11", Ribbed, Multicolored Floral Cameo Design	$400
Bowl, Rose, 3¾" Tall, 4½" Diameter, Frosted, Reverse Painted with Multicolored Asian Designs	$57.50
Candlestick, 6" Tall, Dragon Foot, Green Cased Center with Oak Leaf Top	$165
Cup, 3½" Tall, Flared, Blue on White Cameo, Dragon and Cloud Design	$310
Jar with Cover, 4¾" Tall, Ruby Red with Engraved Horse and Tree Design on Both Front and Back	$2,525
Snuff Bottle, 2¼" Tall, White with Green Floral Design	$140
Snuff Bottle, 3" Tall, Green on White Cameo, Sailing Sheep with Painted Peony	$400
Tumbler, Bamboo Spike Design, Carnival Marigold Color	$85
Tumbler, Shanghai Pattern, Carnival Marigold Color	$85
Urn with Cover, Teakwood Stand, Blue and Whitle Floral Stand	$290

Vase, 3½" Tall, Pink Floral Design on White Cameo	$1,075
Vase, 6" Tall, Red on White Cameo, Butterflies and Peony Design	$215
Vase, 7" Tall, Frosted, Reverse Painted with Multicolored Oriental Scenery	$85
Vase, 8" Tall, Cameo Yellow Floral Design on White	$290
Vase, 8" Tall, Teal on White Cameo, Dragonfly and Water Lily Design	$325
Vase, 8½" Tall, Bulbous, Red on White Cameo, Floral Design	$325
Vase, 9" Tall, Red on White Cameo, Birds and Pine Tree Design	$350
Vase, 9" Tall, Green on White Cameo, Raven and Pine Tree Design	$350
Vase, 9¼" Tall, Red on White Cameo, Monkey in Pine Tree Design	$350
Vase, 9¼" Tall, Red on White Cameo, Monkey in Pine Tree Design	$350
Vase, 10" Tall, Blue on White Cameo, Bird in Floral Tree Design	$390
Vase, 10" Tall, Yellow on White Cameo, Monkey in Pine Tree Design	$390
Vase, 10" Tall, Gourd Shape, Red on White Cameo, Peony Design	$390
Vase, 10¼" Tall, Hexagonal, Red on White Cameo, Floral Panel Design	$425
Vase, 11½" Tall, White Satin Ground, Cobalt Blue Cameo Butterfly and Floral Design	$1,150
Vase, 12" Tall, Bulbous, White with Dark Red Floral Design	$450
Vase, 12½" Tall, Red on White Cameo, Floral Design	$675

Clichy
France, 1840s–1880s

The French classic period of paperweight manufacturing ran from about 1845 to 1870. The factories in the town of Clichy (a suburb of Paris), like Baccarat and St. Louis, produced many, then closed during the later art nouveau period. A revival in the 1950s of paperweight production occurred in all these famous French glassmaking towns (with the exception of Clichy), and their production has flourished ever since.

Paperweight, 2", White Mill Canes with Pink and Green Floral Design	$850
Paperweight, 2¼", Con Mill, 4 Rows in Blue and White Basket	$1,800
Paperweight, 2¼", 30 Pink and White Swirled Threads	$1,575
Paperweight, 2½", Con Mill, Turquoise with Cane Gar and Florets	$800
Paperweight, 2½", Multicolored Densely Packed Millefiori Design, Signed	$3,850
Paperweight, 2½", Multicolored Densely Packed Millefiori Design, Hexagon Shape, Signed	$4,250

Paperweight, 2⅝", Checkered Barber Pole Design with 18 Canes, Twists, and Filigree Rods	$3,150
Paperweight, 2⅝", Two-Tone Green and White Spiral Design	$425
Paperweight, 2¾", Multicolored Mill Canes with Pink and Green Rose	$950
Paperweight, 2¾", Pattern Mill, Faceted, Canes with Rose and 5 Rings	$950
Paperweight, 3", Con Mill, Star Cane Cluster with 3 Rings and Rose	$1,475
Paperweight, 3", Con Mill, 8-Point Star Cane in Basket	$2,175
Paperweight, 3", Pinwheel, 44 Amethyst Rods, White Tubes and Turquoise Floret	$1,875
Paperweight, 3", Scattered Mill, Pink Rose in Center	$1,000
Paperweight, 3⅛", Large Dark Pink Camomile Design	$785
Paperweight, 3⅛", Crystal with Dark Emerald Green 4-Leaf Clover	$2,675
Paperweight, 3½", Multicolored Florettes Separated by Varied Threaded White Strips	$925
Paperweight, 3¾", Con Mill, Cane Gar, 7-Rose Design (1 in Center)	$925
Paperweight, Sulphide, 2¾", White Cameo of Comte de Chambord on Deep Cobalt Blue Ground	$625
Paperweight, Sulphide, 3⅜", Translucent Ground, Alfred de Musset Design	$650

Czechoslovakian Glass
1918–Present

Czechoslovakia was officially recognized as a separate country in 1918. Before dividing into two countries in January 1993, a good deal of glass was made by several firms. Much of it is simply marked "Czechoslovakia" or "Made in Czechoslovakia," but older items contain a wide variety of manufacturers' marks. It was made in many styles, including colored art (especially orange), carnival colors, and engraved crystal. Since 1993, glass has been marked as above or may be labeled "Czech Republic." The most famous name in Czechoslovakian glass is that of Moser (see separate listings under Moser Glass). Newer Mary Gregory items made in Czechoslovakia have become more collectible and are selling for one-half to two-thirds of the original 19th-century Mary Gregory (see the Mary Gregory section later in this chapter).

Basket, 5½" Tall, Crystal Thorn Handle, Red with Streaking	$185
Basket, 7½" Tall, Orange with Applied Black Trim and Handle	$165
Basket, 8" Tall, Black with Ruffled Yellow Top, Black Handle	$165
Bean Pot with Cover, 2½" Tall, Carnival Marigold	$100
Bell, 5" Tall, Ruby Red with Crystal Ball Finial and Gilded Filigree Design	$45

Czechoslovakian Glass. *Reproduced directly from a 1989 Czechoslovakian advertisement.*

Bell, 6" Tall, Cobalt Blue with 22 kt. Gold Gilding, Matches Decanter Set Below, Czech Republic	$50
Biscuit Jar with Cover, 6½" Tall, 4¾" Diameter, Crystal, Diamond Pattern, Ceska	$90
Bottle, Inca Pattern, Carnival Marigold or Amethyst	$950
Bowl, 5½", Footed, Came Cut Dark Green on Light Orange	$475
Bowl, 7", Crystal with Transparent Multicolored Bubble Design, Czech Republic	$50
Bowl, 7½", Orange Spatter on Bright Yellow, Purple Base	$80
Bowl, 8", Fleur-de-Lys Pattern, Carnival Marigold	$425
Bowl, 8½", 4¾" Tall, Crystal, Striped Pattern, Ceska	$55
Bowl, 10", Oval, Zipper Stitch Pattern, Carnival Marigold	$75
Bowl, 12", Flared, Red	$77.50
Bowl, Rose, Classic Arts Pattern, Carnival Marigold	$550
Bowl, Rose, Fleur-de-Lys Pattern, Carnival Marigold	$550
Box with Cover, 4" Across, Ruby Red with Cut Floral Design	$87.50
Candlestick, 10½" Tall, Orange with Multicolored Base	$55
Candy Dish with Cover, 5", Crystal with Transparent Multicolored Bubble Design, Czech Republic	$50
Chandelier, Faceted Crystal, Brass Mountings, 7-Light, 21" Tall, 20" Across, Czech Republic	$650
Chandelier, Faceted Crystal, Brass Mountings, 14-Light, 26" Tall, 26" Across, Czech Republic	$1,000

Compote, 6¾", Footed, Ruby Red with Gold Gilding, Enameled Cameo Design	$115
Compote, 6¾", Footed, Ruby Red with Gold Gilding	$140
Compote, 10", Footed, Orange and Black	$150
Cordial, Barber Bottle Design, Carnival Marigold	$60
Cordial, Zipper Stitch Pattern, Carnival Marigold	$135
Decanter Set, 10" Tall with Multifaceted Round Stopper, Crystal with Vertical Ribbing, 6 Matching 2" Shot Glasses, Czech Republic	$75
Decanter Set, 11½" Tall, 16 oz., Cobalt Blue with 22 kt. Gold Gilding, Gilded Stopper, 6 Matching 3¾" Cobalt Blue and Gilded Stemmed Glasses, Czech Republic	$225
Decanter with Stopper, Green with Gold Trim	$70
Decanter with Stopper, Cone Shape, Ruby Red Handle, Opalescent Crackle Design	$265
Decanter with Stopper, Zipper Stitch Pattern, Carnival Marigold	$1,275
Fernery with Flower Frog, 4½" Diameter, Amber	$100
Goblet, Ruby Red with Heavy Gold Gilding	$40
Ice Bowl with Insert, 7" Diameter, 5½" Tall, Crystal, Vertical Ribbed Design, Ceska	$115
Lamp, 9" Tall, Crystal Bubble Sphere on Pedestal with Art Deco Dancer	$535
Nude Statue, 2 Nude Women, 8½" Tall, Light Blue and Frosted Opalescent Design	$178
Perfume Bottle with Crystal Figural Stopper, 5½" Tall, Amber	$265
Perfume Bottle with Crystal Figural Stopper, 3" Tall, Ruby Red	$275
Perfume Bottle with Frosted Pink Floral Dome Stopper, 5½" Tall, Crystal with Frosted Nude Applicator Connected to Stopper	$1,565
Perfume Bottle with Stopper, 6½" Tall, Crystal with Blue Art Deco Design	$265
Perfume Bottle with Nude Figural Stopper, 6½" Tall, Amethyst	$475
Perfume Bottle with Stopper, 7" Tall, Crystal, Daffodils Design	$165
Perfume Bottle with Stopper, 7½" Tall, Crystal, Cut Hobstar Design	$90
Perfume Bottle with Frosted Loving Couple Stopper, 11½" Tall, Crystal with Engraved Floral Design	$785
Perfume Bottle with Stopper, Horizontal Ribbed Design, Carnival Marigold	$135
Pin Box, Horizontal Ribbed Design, Carnival Marigold	$85
Pitcher, Water, 10" Tall, Topaz with Green Streaking and Blue Threading	$185
Pitcher, Water, 11½" Tall, Black Handle, Orange with Colorful Jungle Bird Design	$185
Plate, Chop, 12", Fleur-de-Lys Pattern, Carnival Marigold	$750
Powder Jar with Cover, Classic Arts Pattern, Carnival Marigold	$550

Puff Box, Horizontal Ribbed Design, Carnival Marigold	$110
Ring Tree, Horizontal Ribbed Design, Carnival Marigold	$80
Soap Dish, Horizontal Ribbed Design, Carnival Marigold	$67.50
Tray, Barber Bottle Design, Carnival Marigold	$65
Tray, Zipper Stitch Pattern, Carnival Marigold	$265
Tumbler, Horizontal Ribbed Design, Carnival Marigold	$90
Vanity Set, 4-Piece (Small Water Bottle with Stopper, Oval Dish, and Tray), Crystal, Beaded Medallion Pattern	$95
Vase, 4" Tall, Hexagonal, Footed, Multicolored Spatter Design	$65
Vase, 4½" Tall, Cobalt Blue Spatter Design	$65
Vase, 4¾" Tall, Footed, Blue with Black Rim	$70
Vase, 5½" Tall, Ruffled, White with Rose Interior	$87.50
Vase, 6" Tall, Ruffled, Cased Blue with White Interior	$215
Vase, 6½" Tall, Orange with Silver-Deposit Floral Design	$60
Vase, 6½" Tall, 4 Blown Applied Crystal Feet, Orange Curved Figure-6 Design	$95
Vase, 7" Tall, Classic Arts Pattern, Carnival Marigold	$575
Vase, 7" Tall, Frosted with Horses Raised in Relief	$125
Vase, 7" Tall, Horizontal Ribbed Design, Carnival Marigold	$80
Vase, 7" Tall, Ribbed Orange with Cobalt Blue Leaf Trim	$75
Vase, 7" Tall, Inca Pattern, Carnival Marigold or Amethyst	$1,050
Vase, 7½" Tall, Jack-in-the-Pulpit Style, Orange with Black Spots	$95
Vase, 7½" Tall, Crystal Crackle with Embossed Floral Design	$50
Vase, 8" Tall, Fleur-de-Lys Pattern, Carnival Marigold	$750
Vase, 8" Tall, Ruffled, Tangerine Blue Design	$140
Vase, 8" Tall, Ruffled, Yellow with Black Snake Design	$240
Vase, 8½" Tall, Ruffled, Blue with Pink Interior	$140
Vase, 8½" Tall, Black-Lined Rim, Orange with Enameled Black Medallions	$95
Vase, 8½" Tall, Frosted Three Graces Design (Malachite Green, $225)	175
Vase, 9" Tall, Crystal with Multicolored Ribbon Bands, Czech Republic	$55
Vase, 9" Tall, Tricorner Top, Gloss Black over Orange Design	$100
Vase, 9¼" Tall, Cut Crystal Diamond Design with Frosted Classic Lady Design, Czech Republic	$125

Vase, 9½" Tall, Fan Style, Amber with Blue Threading	$140
Vase, 10" Tall, Classic Arts Pattern, Carnival Marigold	$1,050
Vase, 10", Crystal with Transparent Multicolored Bubble Design, Czech Republic	$50
Vase, 11" Tall, Square Shape, Emerald Green with Floral Design in Relief	$290
Vase, 11½" Tall, Pebble and Fan Design, Carnival Blue Iridized Amber	$1,000
Vase, 12" Tall, Ruffled, Green with Black Trim	$230
Vase, 12" Tall, White to Emerald Green Cut Overlay, Scalloped Rim, Floral and Gold Trim	$385
Vase, 13" Tall, Canary Yellow with Black Handles	$165
Vase, 13" Tall, Ruby Red with Heavy Gold Gilding	$165
Vase, 15" Tall, Trumpet, Curled Lip, Amethyst with Mottled Amethyst Globed Base, Czech Republic	$130
Vase, 15½" Tall, 3⅞" Diameter, Tapers in at Top, Crystal with 12 Interlocking Circles	$385
Vase, Fish Shape, Carnival or Iridized Colors	$525
Whiskey Tumbler, 21½" Tall, Green with Gold Trim (Matches Decanter Above)	$17.50

Daum, Nancy Glass
Daum Glass, France, 1875–present

Jean Daum (1825–85) purchased a glass company in 1875 in Nancy, France. Daum, Nancy Daum, Daum Freres, Cristalleries de Nancy, and Daum & Cie are all names associated with glass made by this company. Daum began as a producer of many styles of art nouveau glass, particularly opaque and *pate-de-verre* styles. Next to Galle, Daum was the most important factory producing French art glass, including cameo designs during the art nouveau period. Note that A. Walter was a designer for the firm from 1908 to 1914; many Daum items contain his signature. Walter went on to found his own firm in 1919. Other techniques used by Daum produced intaglio, inlaid, enameled, acid-cut, and copper wheel–engraved items. When Jean died, his sons and grandsons continued glass production. The Daum factory as well as the glass school in Nancy continue to operate today, producing many opaque art sculptural forms as well as some clear and transparent colored forms of crystal.

Ash Tray, 6" Across, Pate de Verre Design (A. Walter)	$835
Basket, 7" Tall, Black, Red, and Yellow Cameo Floral Design	$700
Beaker, 4½" Tall, Footed, Green with Gold Flowers	$190
Bird Figurine, 1¾" Long, Various Pate de Verre Colors with 24 kt. Gold-Plated Bronze Feet	$155
Bowl, 3¾", Translucent Blue, Green, and Yellow, Butterfly Design	$2,675

Daum Figurines. *Photo by Mark Pickvet.*

Daum Sculpture. *Photo by Mark Pickvet.*

Bowl, 6", Yellow, Orange, and Blue Enameled Mulberry and Floral Cameo Design
$1,350

Bowl, 8¼", Footed, Flared, Light Opalescent Orange with Green Streaking, Etched and Burgundy Enameled Blossoms on Green Vines, Gold Trim $1,575

Bowl, 10", Pedestal Base, Cameo $1,675

Bowl, 12", Amber, Etched Triangles in Panels $1,125

Bowl, 13½", Rose Pink Shaded to Yellow, Enameled Sunflower Design with Gold Trim, Signed $5,000

Box with Hinged Cover, 3" Diameter, Leaves and Berries with Grasshopper on Cover, Signed "A. Walter" $5,675

Box, Square with Hinged Domed Cover, 6" Diameter, Cameo River Scene	$4,175
Box with Hinged Cover, 6" Tall, Green and Blue with Pyramid on Cover, Signed "A. Walter"	$3,675
Butterfly Figurine, 3" Tall, 3" Long, Various Pate de Verre Colors	$155
Case, 3" Tall, Gray and Tan with Enameled Floral Design	$1,275
Cat Figurine, 10½" Tall	$775
Cruet with Stopper, 7¼" Tall, Green with Multicolored Cameo Foliage and Berries, Gold and Silver Accents	$2,000
Decanter with Red Stopper, 11" Tall, Crystal with Gray Streaking	$475
Dog Figurine with Ball, 4" Long, Pate de Verre Amber Dog with Pate de Verre Blue Ball	$155
Dragon, 4¾" Long, Pate de Verre Green or Lavender	$225
Ducks' Sculpture 2½" Tall, 2 Pate de Verre Mandarin Yellow Ducks on Nest	$155
Egg, Glass with Glass Base, Gilded Pedestal Foot, 5" Tall, Opalescent, Acid Etched with Cameo-Engraved Ducks	$2,125
Ewer, 8¾" Tall, Pedestal Foot, Pink to Green Shading, Applied Cabochon Insects, Signed	$6,775
Labrador Dog Figurine, 1½" Tall, 3" Long, Resting on Log, Multiple Shades of Amber	$125
Labrador Dog Figurine, 3" Tall, 2¼" Wide, Sitting, Multiple Shades of Amber	$155
Lamp, 7" Tall, Marble Base, Green and Brown Forest Lake Scene	$2,675
Lamp, 7½" Diameter Shade, Amber Base, Red Floral Cameo Design	$11,000
Lamp, 14½" Tall, 9¼" Domed Shade, Etched Vertical Rib and Dot Design on Base and Shade, Signed	$4,550
Lamp, 19¼" Tall, 3-Arm Iron Mounted, Multicolored Winter Landscape Scene	$8,275
Lamp, 30½" Tall, 2-Piece (Lighted Base and Dome), Opaque Blue and Yellow with Multicolored Floral Design	$21,500
Panther Sculture, 6" Tall, 6" Long, Pate de Verre, Amber Panther on Green Branch	$850
Paperweight, 10", Sea Nymph Rising from Surface, Signed "Cheret"	$6,850
Perfume Bottle, 4¾" Tall, 2¾" Wide, Pate de Verre Shaded Purple and Green, Iris Floral Finial	$325
Pitcher, Water, Tortoiseshell Cameo Design, Signed	$560
Powder Box with Sterling Silver Cover, Multicolored Floral Design	$1,160
Rose Bloom, 4" Long, Various Pate de Verre Colors	$200

Salt Dip, 2" Square, 1" Tall, Yellow Floral Cameo Design, Enameled Design	$1,850
Sherbet, 4¼" Tall, Apricot with Gold Mica	$170
Swan Figurine, 2½" Tall, 3½" Long, Pate de Verre, Yellow, Blue, or Pink	$160
Tray, 7" Long, Salamander with Ivy Leaves and Yellow Blossoms, Signed "A. Walter"	$4,850
Tray, 7½" Long, Triangular, Gray with Mallard Duck Faces, Signed "A. Walter"	$3,150
Tumbler, 4¾" Tall, Green Leaves and Purple Violets Design	$1,850
Tumbler, Wooded Winter Snow Scene, Signed	$450
Vase, 4" Tall, Amber, Sailing Ship Design	$1,375
Vase, 4½" Tall, Opalescence with Enameled Floral and Foliage Design, Gold Accents	$1,475
Vase, 4¾" Tall, Pale Green with Large Air Bubbles	$325
Vase, 5" Tall, Pedestal Foot, Cameo Ducks Design	$2,875
Vase, 5" Tall, Violet Pedestal Foot, Yellow and Turquoise	$1,150
Vase, 5¼" Tall, Red Millefiore Design	$1,050
Vase, 5½" Tall, Green to Purple Shading, Sunflower and Daisy Floral Design	$1,350
Vase, 6½" Tall Frosted with Pine Forest and Lake Scene	$550
Vase, 6¾" Tall, 3-Layered Cameo	$675
Vase, 7" Tall, 5" Diameter, Cameo Red and Yellow on Aqua, Floral Design, Signed "A. Walter"	$2,350
Vase, 8" Tall, 8" Diameter, Flared, Vertical Ribs, Gray	$1,250
Vase, 9" Tall, Light Blue to Cobalt Blue Shading, Gold Mica	$2,875
Vase, 10" Tall, Slender, Blue, Orange, and Yellow Cameo Berry Cluster Design	$2,150
Vase, 10½" Tall, Enameled Joan of Arc Design	$2,675
Vase, 11½" Tall, Flared, Frosted Peach with Etched Floral and Insect Design, Gold Trim, Signed	$55,000
Vase, 12" Tall, Ovoid Shape, Yellow with Etched Leaves	$3,500
Vase, 13" Tall, Ovoid Shape, Yellow with Etched Leaves	$2,675
Vase, 13½" Tall, Cone Shape, Footed, Yellow with Enameled Flower Blossoms	$6,875
Vase, 14" Tall, Gold Gilded on Amethyst, Cameo Iris and Dragonfly Design	$2,350
Vase, 15½" Tall, Mottled, Shaded Gray, Enameled Cornflower Design	$5,650
Vase, 15½" Tall, White with Green Holly Berries	$1,350

Vase, 16" Tall, Green and Gold Gilt on Yellow, Cameo	$2,150
Vase, 16" Tall, Multicolored Cameo Iris Floral Design with Gilded Leaves and Dragonfly	$7,675
Vase, 18" Tall, Red and Yellow Spatter with Gold Mica	$2,150
Vase, 18¾" Tall, Folded Rim, Iridescent Smoky Blue, Etched Scrolling and Lozenges, Signed	$3,150
Vase, 20" Tall, Applied Black Berries on Dark Gray Ground	$1,150
Vase, 27" Tall, Amethyst with Yellow Center, Autumn Woodland Cameo Scene	$10,500
Wine Goblet, Engraved and Enameled Lily Design, Signed	$435
Woman Figurine, 7" Tall, Seated with Head in Hands, Yellow, Signed "A. Walter"	$2,350

De Vez Cameo Glass Saint-Hilaire Touvier de Varreaux Co.,
France, Late 19th–Early 20th Century

The De Vez Cameo Glass company was also known as Cristallerie de Pantin, which merged with Legras & Çie around 1920. The firm is best known for cameo art–style glass (all of the items listed below are cameo cut). Some of the items produced by the company are marked "Degue" after one of their most noted craftsman, or "Pantin" for the company's name. The name De Vez was a pseudonym for the firm's art director, De Varreux. Additional French cameo items are listed in the French Cameo glass section below. See Legras & Cie later in the chapter for additional listings.

Bowl, Rose, 3" Tall, Black on Gold and Pink Satin, Lake and Forest Scene, Signed "De Vez"	$1,375
Compote, 4", Brown and Rust on Yellow, Clear Interior, Village Scene with River and Mountains, Signed "De Vez"	$1,475
Lamp, 15" Tall, Dark Red Shade and Base, Egyptian Scene, Signed "Degue"	$3,875
Lamp, 17¼" Tall, 10½" Diameter Shade, White and Yellow on Red, Etched Morning Glories, Signed "Degue"	$3,050
Vase, 4" Tall, Rust on Amber, Lakeside Scene, Signed "De Vez"	$585
Vase, 4" Tall, Heart Shape, Pedestal Foot, Amethyst on Frosted White, Cut Harbor Scene, Signed "De Vez"	$785
Vase, 6" Tall, Crystal with Pink Mottling, Art Deco Cameo-Engraved Design, Signed "Degue"	$700
Vase, 6¾" Tall, Gray on White Overlaid in Orange and Green, Cut Dutch River Scene, Signed "De Vez"	$785

Vase, 6¾" Tall, White and Purple on Burnt Orange, Etched Flowering Sea Anemones, Signed "Degue" $585

Vase, 7" Tall, Blue on Pink, Etched Alsatian River and Village Scene, Signed "De Vez"
$1,175

Vase, 8" Tall, Burgundy on Amber, Winding River and Trees Design, Signed "De Vez"
$1,575

Vase, 10" Tall, Red and Blue on Yellow, Cut Sailboat River, Butterfly, and Mountain Scene; Signed "De Vez" $1,250

Vase, 10½" Tall, Orange and Purple on Grayish Yellow, Cut Houseboat on River and Mountain Scene, Signed "De Vez" $1,375

Vase, 11" Tall, Purple on Multicolored Ground, Floral Design, Signed "Degue" $1,375

Vase, 11" Tall, Shaded Red and Yellow Mums, Signed "De Vez" $900

Vase, 15¾" Tall, Gray and Pink on Yellow, Cut Red and Blue Floral Design, Signed "Degue" $1,050

Vase, 16½" Tall, Tan on Grayish Green, Cut Triangle Design, Signed "Degue" $2,275

Vase, 17" Tall, Flared, Amethyst, Cut Intersecting Arch Design $1,475

Vase, 18½" Tall, Orange and Brown on Blue, Etched Tree Design, Signed "Degue"
$1,475

English Cameo Glass
1850s–1890s

Cameo glass is made in two or more layers; the first (inner) is usually a dark color and the casing (outer) is white. Classic, floral, natural, and other scenes were carved in as many as five layers. The technique was applied by manufacturers in nations such as France. The primary English makers were Thomas Webb & Sons and Stevens & Williams. Note that brothers George and Thomas Woodall worked for Webb.

Bowl, Rose, 3½", White on Rose Mother-of-Pearl, Wild Rose Design, Diamond Quilted Pattern $2,175

Bowl, 4" Tall, 6" Diameter, Ruffled, Pink on White Satin with Apple Blossoms, Signed "Stevens & Williams" $975

Bowl, 5" Diameter, 2" Tall, White on Cranberry, Floral Design, Signed "Webb" $975

Bowl, 6" Tall, White on Blue, Dragon Design (Webb) $2,900

Bowl, 7" Diameter, Aqua on Blue, Seaweed and Shell Design $2,900

Cup, Loving, 7½" Tall, 3 Applied Handles, Light Gold on Dark Gold (Webb) $465

Epergne, 10½" Tall, White on Red, Mirrored Base, Floral Design $4,950

English Cameo. *Photo by Robin Rainwater. Courtesy of the Corning Museum of Glass.*

English Cameo Art Vases. *Photo by Mark Pickvet.*

Mustard Pot with Silver-Plated Cover and Rim, 3¼" Tall, 1⅞" Diameter, Pink on White Cameo, Cut Floral and Foliage Design — $435

Perfume Bottle with Faberge Stopper, 3¼" Tall, White on Blue, Floral Design — $7,750

Perfume Bottle with Cut Stopper, 4" Tall, White on Saffron, Floral Design, Signed "Webb" — $1,900

Plate, 13" Round, White on Amber, Winged Horse and Rider (Stevens & Williams) — $3,750

Platter, 14" Round, 4-Color (White, Red, Light Blue, and Tan Florals) on Green Cameo (Webb) — $8,750

Saucer, 6", White Circular Floral Design on Rust (Stevens & Williams) — $875

Sweetmeat Jar with Silver Cover, 6" Tall, White on Light Blue, Fancy Leaf Design — $2,450

Vase, 5" Tall, White on Blue Mother-of-Pearl, 5" Diameter, Apple Blossom Design, Diamond Quilted Pattern — $2,450

Vase, 5" Tall, White on Blue, Floral Design, Signed "Stevens & Williams" — $1,900

Vase, 5" Tall, White on Red, Honeysuckle Design, Signed "Webb" — $1,900

Vase, 5" Tall, White on Yellow, Violets and Leaves Design — $2,250

Vase, 6" Tall, White on Blue, Floral Design — $2,450

Vase, 6" Tall, White on Citron, Signed "Webb" $2,450

Vase, 6" Tall, White on Amethyst, Beetle and Nasturtiums Design, Signed "Stevens & Williams" $3,950

Vase, 6½" Tall, White on Amber to Rose Shading, Ovoid Geranium Design, Signed "Webb" $1575

Vase, 7" Tall, Blue with White Figure, Signed "Woodall" $8,250

Vase, 7" Tall, Rose on White, Scroll Design, Signed "Webb" $1,900

Vase, 7" Tall, White on Tan, Signed "Stevens & Williams" $1,900

Vase, 7½" Tall, Tan with White Figure, Signed "Woodall & Webb" $9,250

Vase, 8" Tall, White Woman with Harp (Siren) on Brown, Signed "Geo. Woodall" $8,250

Vase, 8" Tall, White on Yellow, Tall Grass Design, Signed "Woodall" $3,950

Vase, 8" Tall, White on Blue, Rose Design, Signed "Stevens & Williams" $2,400

Vase, 8" Tall, White on Red Mother-of-Pearl (Webb) $5,750

Vase, 8¾" Tall, Classic 2-Handled Style, White Child on Black (Joseph Northwood) $8,250

Vase, 9" Tall, White on Blue, Floral Design on Body and Neck $3,750

Vase, 9" Tall, White on Peachblow, Floral Design, Signed "Webb" $5,750

Vase, 9" Tall, White on Red, Signed "Stevens & Williams" $1,900

Vase, 9¾" Tall, White on Reddish Orange, Bird, Dragonfly, and Iris Design, Signed "Webb" $3,750

Vase, 10" Tall, White on Red, Signed Webb $3,750

Vase, 11½" Tall, White on Red, Signed "Webb" $3,950

Vase, 11¾" Tall, Opalescent White on Blue (Webb) $4,250

Vase, 11¾" Tall, Classic 2-Handled Style, White Floral and Stork Design on Dark Blue $4,250

Vase, 12" Tall, Gourd Shape, White on Yellow, Horsemen Design $4,450

Vase, 12" Tall, Banded Neck, White on Peach, Floral Design, Signed "Stevens & Williams" $3,950

Vase, 12" Tall, White on Red, Floral and Plums Design, Signed "Stevens & Williams" $3,950

Vase, 12½" Tall, Mother-of-Pearl (Ivory-Like), Signed "Webb" $4,400

Vase, 13" Tall, Tan with White Figures, Signed "Woodall & Webb" $11,500

Vase, 23½" Tall, White on Red, Foxgloves Design (Webb) $8,850

English Carnival Glass
1910–Early 1930s

Carnival glass first arrived in England from America, and as it caught on, several factories began making it. The three best-known producers were Davisons of Gateshead, Guggenheim Ltd. of London, and the Sowerby Company of Gateshead-on-Tyne. Given the popularity of tea in England, there are many standard serving-type items such as butter dishes, creamers, sugars, bowls, and water sets. As in America, its popularity quickly died, and production was phased out in the late 1920s and early 1930s.

Banana Dish, Cut Arches Pattern, Marigold	$115
Banana Dish, Moonprint Pattern, Marigold (Sowerby)	$185
Basket, Thin Handle, Alternating Diamonds with Floral Design, Marigold (Davisons of Gateshead)	$85
Bean Pot with Cover, Fruit and Berries Design, Marigold or Blue	$575
Boat, Row (Used for Holding Pens/Pencils), Daisy Block Pattern, Marigold or Amethyst (Sowerby) (Aqua Opalescent $850)	$325
Bonbon Dish, Illinois Daisy Pattern, Marigold (Davisons of Gateshead)	$65
Bowl, 4", Intaglio Daisy Pattern, Marigold (Sowerby)	$37.50
Bowl, 4", Modern Pattern, Marigold	$55
Bowl, 4", Pineapple Pattern, Carnival Colors (Sowerby)	$55
Bowl, 4½", Intaglio Daisy Design, Marigold (Sowerby)	$55
Bowl, 4½", Mitred Diamonds and Pleats, Marigold and Blue	$47.50
Bowl, 5", Lattice Heart Pattern, Carnival Colors (Sowerby)	$47.50
Bowl, 5", Prism and Cane Pattern, Carnival Colors (Sowerby)	$80
Bowl, 6", Footed, Thistle and Thorn Pattern, Marigold	$67.50
Bowl, 7", Footed, Diving Dolphins Pattern, Marigold (Sowerby) (Blue, Green, or Amethyst $475)	$325
Bowl, 7", English Hob and Button Pattern, Carnival Colors	$85
Bowl, 7", Pineapple Pattern, Carnival Colors (Sowerby)	$85
Bowl, 7½", Intaglio Daisy Design, Marigold (Sowerby)	$85
Bowl, 7¾", Intaglio Daisy Pattern, Marigold (Sowerby)	$62.50
Bowl, 8", Illinois Daisy Pattern, Marigold (Davisons of Gateshead)	$80
Bowl, 8", Moonprint Pattern, Marigold (Sowerby)	$65
Bowl, 8", Pinwheel Pattern, Carnival Colors	$90
Bowl, 8½", Feathered Arrow Pattern, Marigold (Guggenheim)	$67.50

Bowl, 8½", Mitred Diamonds and Pleats, Marigold and Blue	$57.50
Bowl, 9", Petals and Prisms, Marigold	$80
Bowl, 10", English Hob and Button Pattern, Carnival Colors	$115
Bowl, 10", Grape and Cherry Pattern, Marigold (Sowerby) (Blue $250)	$105
Bowl, 10", Lattice Heart Pattern, Carnival Colors	$80
Bowl, 14", Moonprint Pattern, Marigold (Sowerby)	$115
Bowl, Oval or Round, Finecut Rings Pattern, Marigold (Guggenheim)	$165
Bowl, Flora Pattern, Marigold or Blue (Sowerby)	$165
Bowl, Hobstar and Cut Triangles Design, Marigold (Green or Amethyst $115)	$85
Bowl, Oval or Round, Footed, Lea Pattern, Marigold or Amethyst (Sowerby)	$70
Bowl, Prism and Cane Pattern, Marigold (Sowerby) (Purple $135)	$80
Bowl with Cover, Diamond Pinwheel Pattern, Marigold (Davisons of Gateshead)	$55
Bowl, Fruit, Petals and Prisms, Marigold	$115
Bowl, Rose, Classic Arts Pattern, Marigold (Davisons of Gateshead)	$185
Bowl, Rose, Hobstar and Cut Triangles Design, Marigold (Green or Amethyst $125)	$85
Bowl, Rose, Intaglio Daisy Pattern, Marigold (Sowerby)	$75
Bowl, Rose, Footed, Kokomo Pattern, Marigold, Green or Blue (Sowerby)	$80
Bowl, Rose, Pineapple Pattern, Carnival Colors (Sowerby)	$165
Bowl, Rose, Sea Thistle Pattern, Marigold	$85
Bowl, Rose, Vining Leaf Variant Design, Marigold	$350
Butter Dish, 10" Diameter, Cathedral Pattern (Davisons of Gateshead) (Amethyst or Blue $75)	$55
Butter Dish, Diamond Pinwheel Pattern, Marigold (Davisons of Gateshead)	$115
Butter Dish, Hobstar Reversed Pattern, Marigold, Blue, or Amethyst (Davisons of Gateshead)	$75
Butter Dish, Moonprint Pattern, Marigold (Sowerby)	$165
Butter Dish, Pineapple Pattern, Carnival Colors (Sowerby)	$105
Butter Dish, Split Diamond Pattern, Marigold or Amethyst (Davisons of Gateshead)	$95
Butter Dish, Triands Pattern, Marigold	$80
Butter Dish with Cover, Beaded Swirl Pattern, Marigold (Sowerby)	$135
Butter Dish with Cover, Finecut Rings Pattern (Guggenheim)	$185
Butter Dish with Cover, Rose Garden Pattern, Marigold (Blue, Green, Amethyst, or Purple $375)	$185

Butter Dish with Cover, Shooting Star Pattern, Marigold	$185
Cake Plate, Footed, Diamond Ovals Pattern, Marigold (Sowerby)	$185
Cake Plate, Footed, Thistle and Thorn Pattern, Marigold	$185
Cake Stand, Finecut Rings Pattern, Marigold (Guggenheim)	$185
Candleholder, Victorian Crown or Coronation Pattern, Marigold	$325
Candlestick, Moonprint Pattern, Marigold (Sowerby)	$60
Carafe, Daisy and Cane Pattern, Marigold (Sowerby)	$125
Casserole Dish with Cover, Fruit and Berries Pattern (Blue $425)	$350
Celery Dish, Finecut Rings Pattern, Marigold (Guggenheim)	$135
Celery Vase, Heavy Prisms Pattern, Marigold (Davisons of Gateshead) (Blue or Purple $175)	$135
Celery Vase, Triands Pattern, Marigold	$80
Chalice, 7" Tall, Cathedral Pattern, Marigold (Davisons of Gateshead) (Amethyst or Blue $150)	$115
Cheese Dish, Moonprint Pattern, Marigold (Sowerby)	$165
Coaster, Rayed Star Design, Marigold	$50
Compote, Beaded Swirl Pattern, Marigold or Blue (Sowerby)	$80
Compote, Cathedral Pattern, Marigold (Davisons of Gateshead) (Amethyst or Blue $85)	$60
Compote, Daisy and Cane Pattern, Marigold (Sowerby)	$42.50
Compote, Footed, Diamond Ovals Pattern, Marigold (Sowerby)	$55
Compote, Diamond Pinwheel Pattern, Marigold (Davisons of Gateshead)	$80
Compote, Diamond Prisms Pattern, Marigold	$80
Compote, Hobstar and Cut Triangles Design, Marigold (Green or Amethyst $125)	$90
Compote, Lattice Heart Pattern, Carnival Colors (Sowerby)	$90
Compote, Moonprint Pattern, Marigold (Sowerby)	$60
Compote, Pineapple Pattern, Carnival Colors (Sowerby)	$85
Compote, Stippled Diamond Swag Design; Marigold, Blue, or Green	$90
Compote, 5", War Dance Pattern, Marigold	$115
Cookie Jar, Illinois Daisy Pattern, Marigold (Davisons of Gateshead)	$115
Cordial, Star and Fan Pattern, Marigold	$135
Cordial, Zipper Stitch Pattern, Marigold	$55
Cracker Jar with Metal Cover, Fans Pattern, Marigold (Davisons of Gateshead)	$265

Creamer, Apple Panels Pattern, Marigold (Sowerby) (Blue $85)	$55
Creamer, Beaded Swirl Pattern, Marigold or Blue (Sowerby)	$80
Creamer, Cathedral Pattern, Marigold (Davisons of Gateshead)	$60
Creamer, Diamond Ovals Pattern, Marigold (Sowerby)	$70
Creamer, Diamond Top Pattern, Marigold	$60
Creamer, Diamond Vane Pattern, Marigold	$55
Creamer, English Button Band Pattern, Marigold	$70
Creamer, Finecut Rings Pattern, Marigold (Guggenheim)	$135
Creamer, Footed, Lea Pattern, Marigold or Amethyst (Sowerby)	$65
Creamer, Hobstar Panels, Marigold	$65
Creamer, Moonprint Pattern, Marigold (Sowerby)	$65
Creamer, Petals and Prisms, Marigold	$80
Creamer, Pineapple Pattern, Carnival Colors (Sowerby)	$80
Creamer, Rose Garden Pattern, Marigold (Blue, Green, Amethyst, or Purple $110)	$65
Creamer, Sea Thistle Pattern, Marigold	$70
Creamer, Shooting Star Pattern, Marigold	$70
Creamer, Split Diamond Pattern, Marigold or Amethyst (Davisons of Gateshead)	$65
Creamer, Sunken Daisy Pattern, Marigold (Blue $75)	$55
Creamer, Thistle and Thorn Pattern, Marigold	$80
Creamer, Triands Pattern, Marigold	$65
Creamer, Zipper Design, Marigold	$70
Decanter with Stopper, Daisy and Cane Pattern, Marigold or Blue (Sowerby)	$300
Decanter with Stopper, Star and Fan Pattern, Marigold	$800
Decanter with Stopper, Zipper Stitch Pattern, Marigold	$450
Epergne, Cathedral Pattern, Marigold (Davisons of Gateshead)	$600
Epergne, with Metal Base, English Hob and Button Pattern, Marigold Colors	$250
Epergne, Fountain Pattern, Marigold (Sowerby)	$375
Flower Holder, Cathedral Pattern, Marigold (Davisons of Gateshead)	$115
Frog, Flower, Flower Block Design, Carnival Colors (Sowerby)	$80
Frog, Flower with Base, Hobstar Reversed Pattern, Marigold (Davisons of Gateshead)	$75
Frog, Flower, Zip Zip Pattern, Marigold	$90

Hen Dish with Cover, Marigold (Sowerby)	$200
Hen Dish with Cover, Miniature, Marigold (Sowerby)	$250
Jam Jar, Finecut Rings Pattern, Marigold (Guggenheim)	$165
Jam Jar with Cover, Moonprint Pattern, Marigold (Blue $150) (Sowerby)	$115
Lamp, Fountain Pattern, Marigold (Sowerby)	$375
Nut Dish, Bow and English Hob Design, Marigold	$65
Nut Dish, Thistle and Thorn Pattern, Marigold	$90
Paperweight, Sphinx Design, Amber	$800
Pitcher, Milk, Fans Pattern, Marigold (Davisons of Gateshead)	$175
Pitcher, Milk, Moonprint Pattern, Marigold (Sowerby)	$175
Pitcher, Milk, Rose Garden Pattern, Marigold (Blue, Green, Amethyst, or Purple $850)	$500
Pitcher, Toy (Miniature), Fancy Cut Pattern, Marigold	$275
Pitcher, Water, Banded Grape and Leaf Pattern, Marigold	$550
Pitcher, Water, Beaded Swirl Pattern, Marigold or Blue (Sowerby)	$275
Pitcher, Water, Fans Pattern, Marigold (Davisons of Gateshead)	$275
Plate, Hobstar and Cut Triangles Design, Marigold (Green or Amethyst $145)	$95
Powder Box with Cover, Paneled, Sculptured Lady Handle on Lid, Marigold (Davisons of Gateshead)	$165
Powder Jar, Classic Arts Pattern, Marigold (Davisons of Gateshead)	$185
Punch Bowl, Cathedral Arches Pattern, Marigold	$575
Punch Cup, Cathedral Arches Pattern, Marigold	$60
Sauce Dish, Split Diamond Pattern, Marigold or Amethyst (Davisons of Gateshead)	$47.50
Spittoon, Daisy and Cane Pattern, Blue (Sowerby)	$375
Spooner, Diamond Top Pattern, Marigold	$47.50
Spooner, Hobstar Reversed Pattern, Marigold (Davisons of Gateshead)	$80
Spooner, Rose Garden Pattern, Marigold (Blue, Green, Amethyst, or Purple $95)	$65
Spooner, Triands Pattern, Marigold	$65
Sugar, Apple Panels Pattern, Marigold (Sowerby), (Blue $85)	$55
Sugar, Beaded Swirl Pattern, Marigold or Blue (Sowerby)	$80
Sugar, Diamond Ovals Pattern, Marigold (Sowerby)	$70

Sugar, Diamond Top Pattern, Marigold	$60
Sugar, Diamond Vane Pattern, Marigold	$55
Sugar, English Button Band Pattern, Marigold	$70
Sugar, Footed, Hobstar Panels, Marigold	$65
Sugar, Moonprint Pattern, Marigold (Sowerby)	$70
Sugar, Petals and Prisms, Marigold	$80
Sugar, Pineapple Pattern, Carnival Colors (Sowerby)	$80
Sugar, Rose Garden Pattern, Marigold (Blue, Green, Amethyst, or Purple $90)	$70
Sugar, Sea Thistle Pattern, Marigold	$70
Sugar, Shooting Star Pattern, Marigold	$70
Sugar, Split Diamond Pattern, Marigold or Amethyst (Davisons of Gateshead)	$65
Sugar, Sunken Daisy Pattern, Marigold (Blue $75)	$52.50
Sugar, Thistle and Thorn Pattern, Marigold	$80
Sugar, Triands Pattern, Marigold	$67.50
Sugar Dish with Cover, Finecut Rings Pattern, Marigold (Guggenheim)	$165
Sugar Dish with Cover, Beaded Swirl Pattern (Davisons of Gateshead)	$90
Sugar Dish with Cover, Signet Pattern, Marigold	$105
Sugar Dish with Cover, Zipper Design, Marigold	$110
Swan Dish with Cover, Marigold (Sowerby) (Amethyst, Purple, or Blue $400)	$250
Toothpick Holder, African Shield Pattern, Marigold	$165
Toothpick Holder, Banded Diamond and Fans Pattern, Marigold	$115
Tray, Serving, Star and Fan Pattern, Marigold	$275
Tray, Serving, Zipper Stitch Pattern, Marigold	$185
Tumbler, Banded Grape and Leaf Pattern, Marigold	$165
Tumbler, Beaded Swirl Pattern, Marigold or Blue (Sowerby)	$80
Tumbler, Fans Pattern, Marigold (Davisons of Gateshead)	$110
Tumbler, Toy (Miniature), Fancy Cut Pattern, Marigold	$80
Vase, 5" Tall, Thin Rib and Drape Design, Carnival Colors (Sowerby)	$185
Vase, 6" Tall, Thistle Design, Marigold	$80
Vase, 6½" Tall, Pinwheel Pattern, Carnival Colors	$135
Vase, 7" Tall, Classic Arts Pattern, Marigold (Davisons of Gateshead)	$215

Vase, 8" Tall, Pinwheel Pattern, Carnival Colors	$185
Vase, 10" Tall, Classic Arts Pattern, Marigold (Davisons of Gateshead)	$275
Vase, 13½" Tall, Fine Prisms and Diamonds Pattern, Marigold, Blue, Green, or Purple	$115
Vase, 14" Tall, Thin Rib and Drape Design, Carnival Colors (Sowerby)	$285
Vase, Daisy and Cane Pattern, Marigold or Blue (Sowerby)	$135
Vase, Finecut Rings Pattern, Marigold (Guggenheim)	$135
Vase, Flora Pattern, Marigold or Blue (Sowerby)	$165
Vase, Footed Prisms Pattern, Marigold (Sowerby) (Blue or Green $175)	$110
Vase, Moonprint Pattern, Marigold (Sowerby)	$80
Vase, Pebble and Fan Pattern, Vaseline (Cobalt Blue or Amber $600)	$175
Vase, Rose Garden Pattern, Blue, Green, Amethyst, or Purple	$300
Vase, Seagull Design, Marigold	$975
Vase, Spiralex Pattern, Marigold, Blue, Green, or Amethyst	$115
Vase, Square Diamond Pattern, Blue	$165
Vase, Sunflower and Diamond Pattern, Marigold (Blue $135)	$90
Vase, Tropicana Pattern, Marigold	$1,500
Vase, Vining Leaf Variant Design, Marigold	$375

Finnish Glass
20th Century

Glass has been made in Finland since the late 17th century. The first firms were established by Swedish glassmakers who made practical items such as windows and tableware. Although similar to modern Swedish art styles, a distinct form of Finnish art glass surfaced in the late 1920s with the opening of such firms as Riihimaki, Iittala, and Notsjo. Finland as well as Sweden produced some carnival glass in the 1930s after the fad had pretty much ended in America, England, and Australia.

Decanter with Stopper, Banded Diamonds and Bars Pattern, Carnival Marigold	$750
Decanter with Multicolored Transparent Rooster Stopper, Light Bluish Gray Glass	$375
Lollipop Isle Sculpture, Crystal Base with Multicolored Lollipop Stems (Notsjo)	$575
Pitcher, Water, Grand Thistle Pattern, Carnival Blue or Amethyst Color	$775
Tumbler, 2¼" Tall, Banded Diamonds and Bars Pattern, Carnival Marigold	$550
Tumbler, 4" Tall, Banded Diamonds and Bars Pattern, Carnival Marigold	$550

Tumbler, Grand Thistle Pattern, Carnival Blue or Amethyst Color	$150
Vase, 3½" Tall, Fan Shape, Lead-Free Glass	$15
Vase, 5½" Tall, Heavy Crystal with Controlled Air Bubble Design (Notsjo)	$160
Vase, 7½" Tall, Ruffled, Lead-Free Glass	$25
Vase, 8" Tall, Bishop's Mitre Pattern, Carnival Blue	$225
Vase, Orchid, 13½" Tall, Bullet Design with Oval Center Hole, Heavy Crystal	$265

French Cameo Glass
Various Producers, 1850s–Early 20th Century

Colorful French Cameo Glass is cut in relief as is standard practice in cameo style glass. The technique was applied by other nations, notably England (see English Cameo Glass). The prices listed below are for smaller French companies or individual artisans such as Richard, Verrerie D'Art, and others. Additional listings can be found in this chapter for major French companies and artists under Baccarat, Daum, De Vez, Galle, La Verre, and St. Louis.

Bowl, 6", Red on Brown, Etched Foliage (Richard)	$475
Ewer, 9" Tall, Thistle Design (Roux Chalon)	$675
Lamp, 19" Tall, Green and Pink Floral Design	$1,550
Lamp, 21" Tall, Blue, Amber, and Green on Translucent White, Signed "LeMaitre"	$2,750
Vase, 3" Tall, Amethyst and Crystal, Orchid Design (Verrerie D'Art)	$1,075
Vase, 3½" Tall, Cranberry on Frosted Crystal, Floral and Leaf Design (Fritz Heckert)	$400
Vase, 3¼" Tall, Purple on White, Rose and Thorn Design (Weis)	$775
Vase, 6" Tall, Violet and Crystal Foliage Design (Vessiere)	$750
Vase, 8" Tall, Red to Black, Blue Foot (Richard)	$425
Vase, 9" Tall, Pate de Verre Design (Argy-Rousseau)	$1,850
Vase, 11" Tall, Brown and Red Floral Design	$1,000
Vase, 14" Tall, Green, Enameled Floral Design	$775
Vase, 15" Tall, Footed, Gray, Orange, and Red; Cherry Branch Design (Ledoux)	$1,350
Vase, 17" Tall, Light Orange with Brown and Green Mottling, Grape and Leaf Design	$2,350
Whiskey Tumbler, 2" Tall, Floral Pattern	$375

Galle, Emile
France, 1874–Early 1900s

Galle (1846–1904) was a French glassmaker and pioneer in 19th-century art nouveau–style glass. He established his own glass operation in 1867 at Nancy, France, and is noted for unique styles of art cameo glass, cut cased glass, and floral designs created in several color effects and styles. He was also one of the first to begin signing his works, which sparked a trend followed by other artisans. Galle passed away in 1904: however, the factory he founded continued to produce art glass until 1931. (After his death, items produced contain his signature and an added star.) Beware of recent Romanian reproductions with Galle's signature, especially lamps and vases. In fact, appraisers today assume that glass with the Galle signature is a Romanian reproduction unless the history of the object can be well documented. Romanian reproductions are generally worth about $50 to $100 and tend to be much brighter in color.

Biscuit Jar with Cover, 8" Tall, Footed, Purple on Light Gray Cameo, Flower Blossom Design, Signed $2,375

Bowl, 2½", Crystal on Orange Cameo, Berries and Leaves Design, Signed "Galle" $1,075

Bowl, 4½", Dark Green with Enameled Tropical Flowers, Signed $2,150

Bowl with Cover, 6", Swirled Green with Seascape and Floral Design $2,750

Bowl, Oblong Boat Shape (7" x 5"), Brown Design on Peach to Green Cameo, Tree and Stream Scene, Signed $1,900

Bowl, 8", Ruffled, Amber with Enameled Flowers and Dragonflies, Signed "Emile Galle Fecit" $800

Bowl, 8½", Pedestal Base, Signed $650

Bowl, 10", Rose Pink on Green Cameo, Magnolia Blossoms and Foliage Design, Signed $4,000

Box with Domed Cover, 2½" Tall, Amethyst on Frosted Crystal Cameo, Cut Dragonfly on Cover, Leaf and Berry Design on Base $1,275

Champagne Glass, 5¼" Tall, Etched and Enameled, Signed $385

Chandelier, 9" Diameter, Cameo Orange on Light Blue, Dragonfly and Tulip Design, Signed $7,900

Compote, 4", Enameled Pink Flowers Interior, Carved Leaf Design Exterior $1,175

Compote, 6½", Enameled Pink Pods Interior, Frosted Exterior with Maple Leaves $1,375

Compote, 8", Circular Foot, Lime Green and Amber on Tangerine Cameo, Vine and Foliage Design, Signed $3,300

Cup, Footed, Light Amber, Enameled Thistle Design, Signed $685

Decanter with Handle and Stopper, 8" Tall, Amber with Enameled Pink Thistle Design, Signed $1,900

Decanter with Stopper, 8¼" Tall, Enameled Lady in Dress, Signed "Galle"	$2,150
Decanter with Stopper, 11¼" Tall, Apple Blossom and Dragonfly Design	$1,675
Ewer, 8" Tall, Amber with Gilding and Multicolored Floral Design, Signed	$2,750
Ewer, 11¼" Tall, Olive Green with Floral Design	$3,750
Goblet, 8" Tall, Blue Floral Cameo Design, Signed	$1,350
Inkwell, 5¾", Layered Amber with Foliage Design	$1,875
Lamp, Candle, 7" Tall, Pedestal Stand, Multicolored Cameo Floral Design, Signed	$2,675
Lamp, 12½" Tall, Violet Blue on Yellow and White Cameo Shade, Chrysanthemum Design, Signed on Shade and Base	$17,750
Lamp, 17" Tall, Pink Dome Shade, Trumpet Base, Cameo Grape and Vine Design, Signed	$13,750
Lamp, 19¼" Tall, Pelican Design on Bronze Base, Sprayed Flower Blossoms on Shade, Signed	$11,850
Lamp, 27" Tall, Circular Base, Long Stem, Mushroom Dome Top with Brass Fixtures, Red to White Shaded Woodland Scene	$12,850
Medallion, Napoleon Profile, 3½" Diameter, Signed	$335
Perfume Bottle with Frosted Stopper, 4½" Tall, Cameo Green on Green Fern Design, Signed	$2,700
Perfume Bottle with Stopper, 4¾" Tall, Enameled Scene of Man in Boat on Lake, Signed	$2,375
Pitcher, 3" Tall, Green Serpent Handle, Enameled Red and Brown Floral Design, Signed	$2,175
Pitcher, 3" Tall, Frosted Handle, Enameled Bleeding Hearts Design, Signed	$1,675
Powder Jar with Cover, 6" Tall, Red Carved Flowers on Green Cameo, Signed "Galle"	$2,400
Ring Tree, 11¾" Tall, Crystal Tree with Enameled Insects on Base	$1,275
Saucer, Light Amber, Enameled Thistle Design, Signed	$385
Shot Glass, 2½" Tall, Pink and Green on Frosted Cameo, Maple Seed Design, Signed	$875
Tumbler, 4" Tall, Cameo Cut Crystal, Signed "Galle"	$535
Tumbler, 4½" Tall, Enameled Arabesques, Signed	$310
Vase, 2" Tall, Miniature, Pinecone Decoration, Signed	$275
Vase, 3¾" Tall, Miniature, Blue and Green Floral Design, Signed	$850
Vase, 4½" Tall, Dark Red with Enameled Green and Gold Lizard, Signed "Galle"	$635
Vase, 5" Tall, Cabbage Shape, Signed	$400

Vase, 5" Tall, Scalloped, Pinched Sides, Oriental Algae and Starfish Design, Signed $8,750

Vase, 5½" Tall, Purple Sweet Peas on Frosted Cameo, Signed "Galle" $875

Vase, 6" Tall, Light Brown and Green on Gray Cameo, Fruit and Acorn Branch Design, Signed "Galle" $1,275

Vase, 6½" Tall, Cameo Violet on Frosted to Yellow Shading, Signed $1,650

Vase, 7" Tall, Frosted Burnt Orange and Foliage Design, Signed $565

Vase, 7" Tall, Slender, Brown on Yellow Cameo, Hyacinth Design, Signed $925

Vase, 7½" Tall, Light Mauve to Pink Shading, Applied Stems and Flower Blossoms, Signed $685

Vase, 8" Tall, Light and Dark Mauve, Signed $815

Vase, 8½" Tall, Footed, Flared, Olive Green on Gray Cameo, Chestnut Branch and Foliage Design, Signed $1,675

Vase, 9½" Tall, Pedestal Foot, Cobalt Blue on Yellow Cameo, Wild Floral and Foliage Design, Signed $1,775

Vase, 9½" Tall, Various Applied Ceramic Decorations, Signed $585

Vase, 10" Tall, 3-Color, Olive Green to Blue to Rose Floral Cameo Design, Signed "Galle" $2,650

Vase, 10" Tall, Light Tan with Enameled Floral Design, Signed $2,200

Vase, 10½" Tall, Flared, Amber on Turquoise Cameo, Seascape and Water Lily Design, Signed $3,175

Vase, 11½" Tall, Hexagonal Shape, Brown and Tan Cameo Foliage, Signed $3,950

Vase, 12" Tall, Slender, Green and Brown on Yellow Cameo, Queen Anne's Lace Design, Signed $4,000

Vase, 13½" Tall, Flask Shape, Poppy Blossoms Design, Signed $8,350

Vase, 14" Tall, Leaves, Berries, and Foliage Design Signed $4,850

Vase, 15" Tall, Fruit and Vine Cameo Design, Signed "Galle" $1,075

Vase, 15" Tall, Purple Columbine Blossoms on Frosted Gray Cameo, Signed "Galle" $5,250

Vase, 15½" Tall, Rolled Neck, Tan on Cream Cameo, Etched Floral and Branch Design, Signed $4,350

Vase, 16¾" Tall, Chestnuts and Foliage Design, Signed $5,250

Vase, 17½" Tall, Amber on Crystal Cameo, Multicolored Enameled Chrysanthemum Design, Signed $5,350

Vase, 19" Tall, Inverted Cylinder, Tan on Ice Blue Cameo, Lily Design, Signed $2,450

Vase, 19½" Tall, Falling Maple Leaves Design, Signed	$3,450
Vase, 20" Tall, Circular Base, Dark Amethyst to Yellow Shading, Lilac Floral Design, Signed	$4,250
Vase, 20¼" Tall, Jack-in-the-Pulpit Style, Foliage and Flower Blossoms Design, Signed	$9,350
Vase, 21" Tall, Slender Form, Snails on Base, Cameo Lake Scene with Birds, Trees, and Boats	$11,500
Vase, 24¾" Tall, Butterflies and Iris Blossoms Design, Signed	$9,850
Vase, 25½" Tall, Cushioned Foot, Flared, Tan on Gray Cameo, River and Forest Scene, Signed	$5,600
Vase, 33½" Tall, Dark Tan to Light Orange Cameo, Floral Design, Signed "Galle"	$5,750
Whiskey Tumbler, 2¾" Tall; White, Blue, and Green Cameo on Crystal and Pink Background, 4-Petal Flower Design, Signed	$875

German Glass
20th Century

German glass has been made for centuries, but the listings below include modern examples only. Older items can be found under Bohemian Glass. Not surprisingly, many of the modern examples include thimbles, crystal Hummels, fancy steins, and a variety of other collectibles.

Apple, 3½" Tall, 3" Diameter, Long Stem	$26
Basket, 8½" Tall, 6½" Diameter, Crystal and Frosted Bow Tie Design	$45
Bowl, 5½", 4¼" Tall, Crystal with a Transparent Blue and Yellow Bird Figurine Attached to Rim	$46
Bowl, 9⅝", Crystal and Frosted Bow Tie Design	$45
Bowl, Salad, 10", 5½" Tall, Silver-Plated Base Crystal, Diamond and Oval Pattern	$31
Brandy Snifter, 6½" Tall, Crystal	$5.50
Candy Dish with Cover, 6¾" Tall, 5¾" Diameter, Canopy Shape, Frosted Embossed Carousel Horses, Transparent Gold Ball Finial on Cover	$53.50
Candy Dish with Cover, 8¼" Tall, 6½" Diameter, Crystal and Frosted Bow Tie Design	$50
Cat Paperweight, 2" Tall, 3" Long, Amethyst	$36
Cat Salt and Pepper Shakers, 3½" Tall and 2" Tall, Gorham Crystal	$35
Crane Figurine, 9¾" Tall, Transparent Pink	$45
Egg, 3¼" Tall, 12 oz., Crystal with Frosted Blue Finish, All-Over Floral Design	$37.50

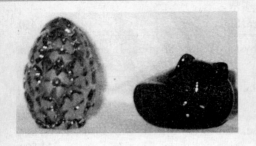

German Dansk Egg and Cat. *Photo by Robin Rainwater.*

German Glass Examples from Zweisel, Germany. *Photo by Mark Pickvet.*

Hummel Figurines, 2" Tall, Frosted Crystal (For Mother, Little Sweeper, March Winds, Sister, Soloist, or Village Boy), Goebel	$72.50
Hummel Figurines, 3" Tall, Frosted Crystal (Apple, Tree Girl, The Botanist, Meditation, Merry Wanderer, The Postman, Visiting an Invalid), Goebel	$80
Hummel Figurines, 3⅝" Tall, Frosted Crystal (Apple Tree Girl, Merry Wanderer, The Postman, Visiting an Invalid), Goebel	$82.50
Mug, Barrel Shape, Crystal with Etched Grape and Leaf Pattern, Green Handle	$11.50
Pear, 4" Tall, 2½" Wide, Long Stem	$25
Photo Frame, 11¼" x 9½" Rectangle, Crystal with Diamond and Shell Border	$45
Pig Figurine, 5" Long, 3" Tall, Pink with Green Clover	$50
Pilsner Glass, 9½" Tall, 14 oz., Crystal	$6.50
Pitcher, Water, Targon Pattern, Carnival Marigold	$2,150
Rabbit Salt and Pepper Shakers, 3¼" Tall and 2" Tall, Gorham Crystal	$35
Romer, 11½" Tall, 6¼" Diameter Pewter Base, Green Tinted Bowl Etched with "Anno Domini 2000," Millennium Limited Edition of 200	$250
Spittoon, Targon Pattern, Carnival Marigold	$4,250
Stein, 6½" Tall, Pewter Lid and Finial on Handle; Ruby Red, Engraved Block Cameos of Various Woodland Wildlife, Barrel Shape, 500-Piece Limited Edition	$290
Stein, 8½" Tall, Pewter Lid and Finial on Handle, Deep Blue with Engraved Fisherman in Water and Ducks, Limited Edition (250)	$315
Stein, 9½" Tall, Pewter Lid and Finial on Handle, Crystal with Engraved Royal Blossom, 7-Diamond Pattern	$140

Stein, 9½" Tall, Pewter Lid and Finial on Handle, Ruby Red with Engraved Stag and Woodlands $250

Stein, 10¾" Tall, Pewter Lid and Finial on Handle, Crystal with Etched Apple Tree and Garden Design $150

Stein, 10½" Tall, Pewter Lid and Finial on Handle; Ruby Red, Cobalt Blue, or Edelweiss Green with Engraved Floral Design, 250-Piece Limited Edition $275

Stein, 10½" Tall, Pewter Lid and Finial on Handle, Cobalt Blue with Engraved Bacchus Design, Limited Edition of 500 $300

Stein, 11" Tall, Etched Crystal Garden of Eden Design, Applied Amber Handle, Pewter Lid and Thumb Grip, Poschinger Glashutte, Limited Edition of 250 $225

Stein, 14" Tall, Crystal Millennium Edition, Crystal with Engraved "Millennium 2000," Poschinger Glashutte $500

Stein, 14¼" Tall, Pewter Lid and Thumb Grip, Cobalt Blue with Engraved American Eagle Design, Crystal Handle, Limited Edition of 100 $400

Thimble, Crystal, Cut Diamond Pattern $23.50

Thimble, Crystal with Cut Diamond Pattern and Gold Base $25

Thimble, Crystal with Engraved Owl Design $25

Thimble, Crystal with Engraved Swan Design $30

Thimble, Crystal with Etched Edelweiss Flower $17.50

Thimble, Crystal, Gold-Plated, Etched Floral Design $25

Thimble, Crystal with Hand-Painted Amish Symbol $25

Thimble, Crystal with Heart and Leaves $25

Thimble, Crystal with Hand-Painted Floral Design $20

Thimble, Crystal with Rainbow-Colored Glass Decorations $20

Thimble, Lavender, Light Blue, Ruby Red, Yellow, or Amethyst with Etched Floral and Grape Design $20

Thimble, Cobalt Blue with 22 kt. Gold Floral Design $30

Thimble, Ruby Flashed Crystal with Etched Hummingbird $25

Thimble, Blown within a Miniature Antique Milk Bottle, 20" Tall, Crystal $12.50

Thimble, Stein Shape with Gold-Plated Lid and Handle, Ruby Red or Emerald Green with Etched Star Design $22.50

Thimble, Stein Shape with Gold-Plated Lid and Handle, Cobalt Blue with Etched Star Design and Enameled Gold Floral Design $22.50

Tumbler, Targon Pattern, Carnival Marigold $525

Tumble-up, 8" Tall, Crystal 17 oz. Carafe and Matching 6 oz. Tumbler, Etched Floral Design $35

Vase, 5¼" Tall, Opaque Teal with Embossed Swallows Around Glass $45

Vase, 6½" Tall, Heart-Shape Top, Grooved Sides, Crystal, Gorham $35

Vase, 8¼" Tall, Crystal and Frosted Bow Tie Design $45

Vase, 8½" Tall, Fan Shape, Crystal, Star and Lovebird Cuts $35

Vase, 10" Tall, Cut Crystal Pineapple Design, Gorham $40

Wineglass, 6 oz., Green Base and Stem, Crystal Bowl with Gold Rim and Gold Leaf and Grape Design $11

Hungarian Glass
20th Century

The most notable products made in modern Hungary are colored cut crystal dinnerware such as goblets, wineglasses, tumblers, bowls, and plates. Typical cut colors include ruby red, cobalt blue, emerald green, and amethyst. The colors are strong and sharp and are at times cased in layers, too. The Horchow Company is one in modern-day Hungary producing this glass, and their products can be found in boutiques, jewelry stores, and by mail through such companies as Bloomingdale's and Fifth Avenue Crystal.

Bear Figurine, 6" Long, Crystal $50

Bell, 7½" Tall, 3½" Wide, Diamond and Fan Cased Cut Crystal in Ruby Red or Cobalt Blue $37.50

Bowl, 9", Cut Palmette Pattern (Diamond Hex Dots with Large Fans), Cobalt Blue or Ruby Red $185

Bowl, 9", Cased Green and Crystal, Crystal Salamanders Cut in Relief, 4⅞" Tall $250

Bowl, 9", Cobalt Blue with Cased Crystal Arch and Diamond Continuous Design $150

Bowl, 9", Ruby Red with Cased Crystal Pinecones, Greens, and Cinnamon Sticks Design $150

Bowl, 9¼", 6 Scallops with 6 Cut Floral and Leaf Designs, Ruby Red in Cased Crystal $160

Bowl, 10", Cobalt Blue with Cut Crystal Gazelles $275

Bowl, 10", 6" Tall, Cobalt Blue with Cased Crystal Roman Numerals I–XII, Millennium Edition $200

Bowl, 10", 7½" Tall, Footed, Ruby Red with Cased Crystal Romanov Design, Artist Magda Nemeth, Limited Millennium Edition of 350 $275

Bowl, Rose, 5½" Diameter, 4½" Tall, Cut Astor Pattern, Emerald Green, Cobalt Blue, Amethyst, or Ruby Red $57.50

Hungarian Glass Bowl. *Reproduced directly from a 1992 Hungarian catalog.*

Bull Figurine, 6" Long, Crystal	$50
Candy Jar with Cover, 7" Tall, 6½" Diameter, Crystal with Etched Carousel Design	$50
Carafe, 1 qt., Amethyst, Emerald Green, Ruby Red, Red, or Cobalt Blue, Cased Crystal Butterfly Design	$150
Centerpiece Stemmed Bowl, 10½" Tall, 10" Diameter, Crystal Stem, Ruby Red Bowl with Cased Chinese Mandarin Player, Copper Wheel–Engraved Imperial Garden Pattern	$325
Centerpiece Stemmed Bowl, 11" Tall, 11" Diameter, Cobalt Blue with Heavy Cased Large Pineapple Fan Design, Artist Magda Nemeth, Limited Edition of 750	$225
Centerpiece Stemmed Bowl, 13½" Tall, 9¼" Diameter Cobalt Blue with Heavy Cased Crystal Fans, Cross-Hatching, and Rainbow Swirls; Crystal Base and Stem	$200
Cordial, 2 oz., Cut Essex Pattern (Diamond and Fan Variation), Emerald Green, Cobalt Blue, Amethyst, or Ruby Red	$27.50
Egg, 4½" Tall, Cobalt Blue with Cased Crystal Pineapple Design	$60
Egg, 4¾" Tall, 3" Diameter, Ruby Red or Emerald Green with Cased Angel Blowing a Trumpet	$60
Goblet, 8½" Tall, Crystal with Green Stem, Frosted Wavy Leaves on Bowl	$15
Goblet, 8½" Tall, Crystal Spiral Stems, Various Colored Bowls with Alternating Panels of Etched Grapes and Starburst Reliefs	$50
Goblet, 9" Tall, Ruby Red with Etched Holly and Berry Design	$50
Goblet 10 oz., Crystal Cut Fluted Stem, Cut Cased Crystal and Cobalt Blue Floral Patterned Bow	$100
Highball Glass, 14 oz., Amethyst, Emerald Green, Ruby Red, or Cobalt Blue, Cased Crystal Butterfly Design	$50

Ice Bucket, 7" Diameter, Engraved Cheetah Design	$200
Jam Jar with Lid and Spoon 5" Tall, 3⅛" Diameter, Cobalt Blue or Ruby Red, Engraved Fruit Design, Crystal Spoon and Crystal Ball Finial on Lid	$35
Old-Fashioned Glass, 14 oz., Amethyst, Emerald Green, Ruby Red, or Cobalt Blue, Cased Crystal Butterfly Design	$50
Perfume Bottle, 4½" Tall, Purple, Green, or Light Blue; Engraved Butterfly and Floral Design, Faceted Stopper	$65
Tumbler, 3½" Tall, 4" Diameter, Cut Fan Pattern, Various Colors	$45
Tumbler, 5½" Tall, Cut Fan Pattern, Various Colors	$40
Tumbler, 7" Tall, Various African Engraved Safari Designs (Matches the Ice Bucket Above)	$65
Tumbler, 8" Tall, Cut Fan Pattern, Various Colors	$45
Urn with Cover, 14" Tall, Cobalt Blue with Crystal Cased Heavy Cross-Hatching, Crystal Ball Finial on Cover	$45
Vase, 3" Tall, 2" Diameter, Amethyst with Cased Crystal Dragonfly Design	$40
Vase, 3" Tall, 2" Diameter, Cobalt Blue with Cased Crystal Honey Bee Design	$40
Vase, 3" Tall, 2" Diameter, Emerald Green with Cased Crystal Butterfly Design	$40
Vase, 3" Tall, 2" Diameter, Ruby Red with Cased Crystal Ladybug Design	$40
Vase, 10" Tall, Ruby Red with Cased Crystal Floral Design	$175
Vase, 11¾" Tall, 3-Layered Amber Tortoiseshell Design	$57.50
Wineglass, 6½" oz., Crystal Cut Fluted Stem, Cut Cased Crystal and Cobalt Blue Floral Patterned Bowl	$100

Indian Glass
1928–Present

Glass was first made in India in the early 16th century. This so-called Mogul Period lasted until 1857 and was characterized by glass that was engraved, gilded, and enameled mostly in Persian styles (sometimes referred to as Mogul or Mughal glass). Most of this glass was made in limited quantities and is not readily found in collections except in museums. The Jain Glass Works was founded in the north-central area of India in 1928 by Shri Chhadamilal Jain. At one time it was the largest glass-producing firm in India. The company was known for making tableware, tumblers, globes, lamp chimneys, and iridized carnival glass, which they called "lustre" glass. Jain closed in 1986; nevertheless, there are several small glass firms as well as studio artisans who operate today in India.

Pitcher, Banded Grape and Leaf Pattern, Carnival Marigold, Jain	$675
Pitcher, Beaded Spears Pattern, Carnival Marigold, Jain (Carnival Amethyst $600)	$500

Tumbler, Australian Daisy Pattern, Carnival Marigold, Jain	$225
Tumbler, Banded Grape and Leaf Pattern, Carnival Marigold, Jain	$115
Tumbler, Beaded Mirrors' Pattern, Carnival Marigold, Jain	$160
Tumbler, Beaded Spears' Pattern, Carnival Marigold, Jain (Carnival Amethyst $225)	$200
Tumbler, Bride's Bouquet Pattern, Carnival Marigold, Jain	$250
Tumbler, Canary Tree Pattern, Carnival Marigold, Jain	$240
Tumbler, Mirror and Crossbar Pattern, Carnival Marigold, Jain	$300
Tumbler, Mirrored Peacocks Pattern, Carnival Marigold, Jain	$325
Vase, 8½" Tall, Goddess Design, Carnival Marigold, Jain	$1,250
Vase, 8¾" Tall, Carnival Marigold Elephant Design, Jain	$550

Irish Glass
18th Century–Present

Glass has been made in Ireland for centuries, and much of it was and still is imported to the United States. The most famous name is Waterford (see separate listings) but the cities of Cork, Dublin, and Tipperary also housed large factories and produced significant quantities of glass in the past. A few of the newest rivals for Waterford's cut crystal are Cavan, Galway, Tipperary, Galway, Kerry Glass, Tower, and Tyrone.

Apple, 3¼" Tall, Crystal with 40 Shades of Green, Kerry Glass	$40
Basket, 6" Tall, 4½" Diameter, Cut Crystal with Gold-Plated Handle, Faux Pearl Finial, Killarney	$45
Bell, 6" Tall, Green Glass with Crystal Handle, Engraved Claddagh Design, Duiske of Ireland	$35
Biscuit Jar with Cover, 8" Tall, Crystal with Diamond Cuts, Galway	$90
Bowl, 4¾", Crystal with Diamond Cuts, Tipperary	$40
Bowl, Rose, 3½", Internal Gold-Plated Votive, Killarney	$40
Bunny Figurine, 3" Tall, Crystal with 40 Shades of Green, Kerry Glass	$30
Bunny Figurine, 4" Tall, Crystal with 40 Shades of Green, Kerry Glass	$35
Candleholder, 6" Long, Aladdin's Lamp Style, Crystal with Diamond and Straight Cuts, Tipperary	$40
Candy Dish, 4⅛" Tall, Footed, Crystal Cut Diamond and Fan Design, Tipperary	$25
Candy Jar with Cover, 9" Tall, Cut Crystal Square Design, Tower	$50
Centerpiece Bowl, Footed, 10", Crystal Cut Interlocking Chain Design, Tipperary	$125

Tipperary Bowl. *Photo by Mark Pickvet.*

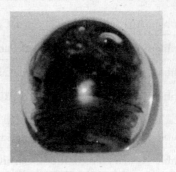

Terry Glass of Ireland. *Photo by Mark Pickvet.*

Tipperary Crystal of Ireland. *Photo by Mark Pickvet.*

Chandelier, 24" Tall, 21" Wide, Crystal with Cut Diamonds, 5-Light, Brass Fittings	$1,775
Clock, Miniature Grandfather, 4½" Tall, Crystal Diamond Cuts, Galway	$70
Clock, Miniature Grandfather, 7¾" Tall, Cut Crystal Killarney	$50
Cornucopia Nut Dish, Footed, Crystal with Diamond and Oval Cuts, Galway	$75
Creamer, 4" Tall, Pitcher Style, 10 oz., Crystal with Cross Cuts, Tipperary	$40
Dolphin Figure, 5" Long, 2½" Tall, Crystal and Sapphire Blue Swirled Design	$35
Football, 3¾" Long, Crystal with Cut Threads, Tipperary	$105
Globe, 4¾" Tall, Crystal with Etched Continents, Diamond Cut Crystal Base, Cavan Crystal	$150

Golf Ball, Regulation Size, Frosted with Cut Crystal Dimples, Tipperary	$50
Lamp, 9" Tall, Cut Crystal Hurricane, Impression for Candle, Tower	$65
Lamp, 9½" Tall, 4½" Diameter, Hurricane, Diamond Cut Crystal, Impression for Candle, Tower	$65
Lamp, 11" Tall, Cut Diamond and Fan Crystal Globe Base, Base is 6¾" Diameter, Galway	$80
Mug, Coffee, 5½" Tall, 8 oz., Low Handle, Crystal with Etched Harp, Shamrocks, and "Irish Coffee"	$21.50
Ornament, Hanging, 3" Long, Green Shamrock within Crystal, Galway	$35
Paperweight, 3½" Tall, Oval-Globe Shape, Ocean Blue Swirled Design, Kerry Glass	$31.50
Paperweight, 4" Tall, Slender Oval Egglike Shape, Crystal with 40 Shades of Green and a Stone from Blarney	$50
Paperweight, 4½" Tall, Oval-Globe Shape, Crystal with 40 Shades of Green Swirls, Kerry Glass	$30
Pig Figurine, 3½" Long, 2" Tall, Crystal with 40 Shades of Green Swirls	$40
Pinecone, 3¾" Tall, Crystal, Rough-Edge Faceted Diamond Cuts	$100
Pitcher, Water, 7¾" Tall, 20 oz., Crystal with Fan Cuts, Tipperary	$77.50
Plate, 8½", Diamond Cuts with Etched Claddagh Coat of Arms, Galway	$85
Potato Figurine, 3" Long, 2" Wide, Crystal, Galway	$35
Ring Tree, 4" Diameter, Cut Crystal Triangle Pattern, Tower	$25
Sherbet, 4¾" Tall, Crystal with Etched Shamrocks	$35
Slipper, Crystal, 3" Tall, 6½" Long, Tipperary	$45
Stein, 7" Tall, Crystal with Pewter Lid, Pewter Shamrocks on Front and Lid	$36
Tumbler, 4¾" Tall, 5 oz., Footed, Crystal with Fan Cuts, Tipperary	$30
Tumbler, 3" Tall, 9 oz., Cashel Pattern, Tipperary	$25
Tumbler, 12 oz., Old-Fashioned Style, Crystal with Etched Shamrocks	$9.50
Vase, 3" Tall, Crystal with Diamond and Oval Cuts, Tipperary	$25
Vase, 5" Tall, Crystal with Diamond and Fan Cuts, Tipperary	$40
Vase, 7" Tall, Castle Shape, Crystal Cut Diamond and Fan, Tipperary	$75
Vase, 8" Tall, Crystal with Cut Diamonds and Leaves, Galway	$70
Vase, 10" Bud, Crystal, Cut Square Pattern, Tower	$50
Vase, 10" Tall, Crystal Cut Millennium Vase, Tipperary	$85
Wine Goblet, 8 oz., Crystal with Etched Harps	$10

Jonasson, Mats; Maleras Glasbruk

1960s–Present

Mats Jonasson is a Swedish designer who was born in 1945. He is a third-generation master glass craftsman and specializes in reverse sculpting of crystal (irregularly shaped ice blocks) for Maelras Glasbruk of Sweden. The blocks are usually carved on the reverse side to provide a mirrored three-dimensional image when viewed from the front. Jonasson has created a huge variety of wildlife as well as a few other designs using this method.

Angelfish Ice Sculpture, 4¼" Tall	$100
Buffalo Ice Sculpture, 6" Long	$130
Camel, Dromedary Ice Sculpture, 4¾" Long	$130
Cardinals Ice Sculpture, 6¼" Long, Pair	$155
Cheetah Ice Sculpture, 6½" Long, Limited Edition	$750
Chipmunks Ice Sculpture, 3¾" Long, Pair	$85
Dolphin Ice Sculpture, 2" Long	$42.50
Dolphins Ice Sculpture, 5¾" Long, Pair	$135
Dragon Ice Sculpture, 4" Long	$100
Eagle Ice Sculpture, 7¾" Long, Bald Eagle	$180
Elephant Ice Sculpture, 6" Long	$60
Elephant Ice Sculpture, 7" Long, Limited Edition	$650
Elephant Ice Sculpture, 8" Long	$130
Foal Ice Sculpture, 4¾" Long	$95
German Shepherd Ice Sculpture, 6¼" Tall	$150
Goats Ice Sculpture, 6" Long, Pair of Mountain Goats	$170
Gorilla Ice Sculpture, 7½" Long	$350
Grizzly Bear Ice Sculpture, 5" Tall	$125
Grizzly Bear Ice Sculpture, 6¾" Long	$250
Heron Ice Sculpture, 6½" Long	$150
Hippopotamuses Ice Sculpture, 4½" Long, Pair	$175
Horse Ice Sculpture. 4¾" Long, Foal	$105
Hummingbird Ice Sculpture, 3" Long	$65
Hummingbird Ice Sculpture, 4¾" Long	$125
Iguana Ice Sculpture, 3½" Long	$100

Kangaroo Ice Sculpture, 4½" Long	$100
Kitten Ice Sculpture, 2" Long	$42.50
Kitten Ice Sculpture, 3¾" Long	$70
Lion Cub Ice Sculpture, 4¾" Long	$95
Lion and Lioness Ice Sculpture, 6¼" Long	$335
Loon Ice Sculpture, 2¾" Long	$80
Loon Ice Sculpture, 5¼" Long	$180
Lynx Ice Sculpture, 6" Long	$140
Marlin Ice Sculpture, 7¾" Long	$300
Moose Ice Sculpture, 4" Long	$100
Orangutan Ice Sculpture, 4¾" Tall, Face Only	$130
Osprey Ice Sculpture, 4¾" Long	$130
Owl Ice Sculpture, 3¾" Long, Owlet	$75
Owls Ice Sculpture, 5½" Long, Three Owls	$115
Owl Ice Sculpture, 6¼" Long, Barn Owl	$135
Owl Ice Sculpture, 7¼" Long, Eagle Owl	$240
Owls Ice Sculpture, 5" Long, 5 Owlets	$100
Paperweight, 3" Round, Crystal, Cat, Dove, Eagle, Koala, Mouse, or Wren	$52.50
Polar Bear Ice Sculpture, 4" Long	$100
Polar Bear Ice Sculpture, 6" Long	$130
Polar Bear Cub Ice Sculpture, 2" Long	$42.50
Rabbit Ice Sculpture, 3¾" Long	$75
Rhinoceros Ice Sculpture, 4¼" Long	$150
Rooster Ice Sculpture, 6" Long	$130
Sandpiper Ice Sculpture, 4" Long	$115
Sea Horse Ice Sculpture, 5¾" Long	$130
Seal Ice Sculpture, 2½" Long, Baby Seal	$52.50
Seal Ice Sculpture, 3¼" Long, Baby Seal	$80
Seals Ice Sculpture, 8" Tall, Pair, Limited Edition to 975	$535
Swan Ice Sculpture, 3½" Long	$85
Swans Ice Sculpture, 4" Long, Swan and Cygnet	$150

Tiger Ice Sculpture, 6¼" Tall	$175
Tiger Ice Sculpture, 7" Tall	$200
Water Buffalo Ice Sculpture, 8" Long, Limited Edition	$725
Whale Ice Sculpture, 6" Long, Blue Whale	$200
Whale Sculpture, 5¾" Tall, 9¼" Long, Blue Whale	$275
Wolf Ice Sculpture, 6" Tall	$115
Wolf Ice Sculpture, 7" Long, Limited Edition	$700

Kosta Boda
1742–Present

The original Kosta Glassworks was established in 1742 in Sweden and is one of the oldest glassmakers still in operation today. The factory originally produced windows, then later added chandeliers and tableware. In 1946, it merged with Afors and the Boda Glassworks to form Kosta Boda. Boda was established in 1864 by two previous employees of Kosta. Kosta Boda is noted for decorative cut glass, tableware, and many traditional Scandinavian art styles of glass. Together in 1970, Kosta, Boda, Johansfors, and Afors became part of the Afors Group, the largest glass-producing firm in Sweden. The group also acquired other small Swedish glass firms, such as Skruff and Sendvik. Orrefors joined in 1990—see additional listings under Orrefors later in the chapter.

Bowl, 5", 3½" Tall, Bulbous, Flared, Cranberry with White Gridding, Kosta	$250
Bowl, 5¼", 3" Tall, Blue Crystal, Kosta	$565
Bowl, 6", Frosted with Green Swirls, Kosta	$375
Bowl, 6¼", 5" Tall, Crystal Cased to Green, Brown Swirls, Etched "Kosta Sweden"	$435
Bowl, 7", Oblong, Canoe or Kayak Shape, Crystal with White Trim, Kosta	$155
Bowl, Rose, 5" Tall, 6¼" Diameter, Crystal Cased to Green, Green and Brown Internal Swirling, Kosta	$355
Decanter with Stopper, 9¼" Tall, 17 oz., Cut Crystal Prince Design, Kosta Boda	$350
Dish, Rectangular with Cover, 10¼" Long, Hand-Painted Nevada Desert Navajo Pattern, Kosta Boda	$200
Egg, 2½" Tall, Cobalt Blue with Black Speckles (Matches Egg Cup), Kosta Boda	$75
Egg Cup, 4⅛" Tall, Frosted White and Blue Amazon Pattern, Kosta Boda	$150
Ice Sculpture, Jagged Outer Edge, Engrave Reindeer Drinking from a Pool of Water (Kosta)	$1,975
Pitcher, 7½" Tall, Crystal with Applied Opaque Green Handle, Enameled Floral Design, Kosta Boda	$100

Pitcher, 7⅞" Tall, Crystal with Applied Handle, Ulrica Pattern Kosta Boda	$100
Platter, 12", Engraved Floral Ulla Pattern, Kosta Boda	$125
Vase, 3" Tall, 3" Diameter, Frosted with Multicolored Applied Stripes, Kosta	$175
Vase, 6¾" Tall, Flattened Oval Shape, Blue and Green Spiral Striping, Kosta	$475
Vase, 8" Tall, Crystal with Hand-Painted Face, Open Minds Pattern, Kosta Boda	$225
Vase, 8½" Tall, Crystal with Etched Female Nude	$535
Vase, 11" Tall, Tilted Square Sails Design, Crystal, Kosta Boda	$200
Vase, 12" Tall, Teardrop Form, Cased Crystal to Red, Kosta	$325
Vase, 13" Tall, Cut Crystal Twist Design, Black-Lined Interior, Kosta	$650
Vase, 14" Tall, Crystal with White Interior, Seaweed Design, Kosta	$675
Vase, 14⅛" Tall, Crystal with Enameled Tulips Design, Kosta Boda	$175

Lalique Glass
René Lalique, France, Late 19th Century–Present

René Lalique (1860–1945) worked in the 1890s as a jeweler making paste glass jewelry. M. F. Coty contracted Lalique to design perfume bottles and Lalique's glass creations propelled him into becoming France's premier designer of the 20th century. Lalique's figural glass is usually made of high-quality lead crystal and may be frosted or enameled; a few rare items were produced in black. The different figures are often formed into useful objects and may be molded or blown in several identical designs. Figures also may be cameo-engraved, heavily etched, and contain smooth, satiny acidized or pearlized finishes. Dating is a big problem with Lalique glass. Older molds have been reused, but some signed marks are helpful. Until his death in 1945, most were marked "R. Lalique." The "R" was dropped a little later. Other pieces may contain "R. Lalique, France" for a signature.

Ashtray, 4½" Long, 8 Girls' Faces Around the Edge	$135
Ashtray, 5½" Long, Fish with Bubbles Design, Signed "R. Lalique"	$265
Ashtray, Mouse in Center, Yellow, Signed "R. Lalique, France"	$435
Beaker, 4" Tall, 6 Panels of Classical Standing Figures	$195
Bell with Finch Finial	$185
Birds, Flying, 12" Tall, Framed, Signed "R. Lalique"	$2,850
Birds, Love, Menu Holder, Framed, Signed "R. Lalique"	$285
Bowl, 8", Opalescent, Mermaids Design	$1,850
Bowl, 8", Berry Foot, Gray, Mistletoe Design, Signed "R. Lalique"	$365
Bowl, 8", Opalescent Blue, Nudes Design in Relief	$835

Lalique Glassware. *Reproduced directly from a 1930 Lalique catalog.*

Lalique Glassware. *Reproduced directly from a 1997 Lalique advertisement.*

Lalique Glassware. *Photo by Robin Rainwater.*

Lalique Glassware. *Photo by Robin Rainwater.*

Bowl, 9½", Opal, Fish and Waves Design, Signed "R. Lalique, France"	$1,050
Bowl, 9½", Footed, Dog and Foliage Design, Signed "R, Lalique, France"	$1,050
Bowl, 9½", Opal, Dahlias Design, Signed "R. Lalique, France"	$985
Bowl, 10", Amber Finish, Black Flower Design, Signed "R. Lalique, France"	$1,175
Bowl, 10", Opal, Peacock Feather Design, Signed "R. Lalique, France"	$1,075
Bowl, 12", Fish and Bubbles Design	$785
Bowl, 13", Frosted Satin, 12 Molded Monkey Faces Around Rim, Madagascar Pattern, Signed "R. Lalique France"	$7,500
Bowl, 14¼", Calypso, Nude Maidens in the Sea	$1,850
Bowl, Ivy, Globe Shape, 14" Diameter, Frosted and Green Maple Leaf Design	$1,075
Bowl, Rose, 5¾", Frosted, Ball-Shape Flower Blooms and Stems	$320
Box, 4" Diameter, Black Rooster and Wheat Design, Signed "Lalique" (without Original Box $4,250)	$6,650
Box with Cover, 5½", Enameled Black with Molded Dahlia Cover, Signed	$1,550
Buffalo Figurine, 4½" Tall, Frosted	$290
Candelabrum, 4-Light, Brown Pheasants Design	$2,450
Candlestick, 6" Tall, Embossed Geometric Designs, Signed	$285
Cat, Crouching, 9" Long, Satin Frosted Finish, Signed	$625
Cat, Persian, Sitting, 3½" Tall, Satin Frosted Finish	$250
Cat, Sitting, 8¼" Tall, Satin Frosted Finish	$265
Chalice, 9½" Tall, Oval Bowl with Foliage Design, Signed	$350
Chandelier, Bowl Form with 4 Chains, 14" Diameter, Framed Design, Signed "R. Lalique"	$3,950
Cherub Figurine with Flute, 3½" Tall, Frosted	$300
Cherub Figurine with Lyre, 3½" Tall, Frosted	$300
Cherub Figurine with Mandolin, 3½" Tall, Frosted	$300
Christmas Ornament, Various Round and Crescent Colored Designs, Annual Issue 1980s–Present, 2"–3"	$100
Clock, Miniature Quartz Set in Frosted Heart, 1¾" Across	$250
Clock, Pendulum, 4½" Square, Opal, Nudes, Signed "R. Lalique"	$2,950
Cockatoo Figurine, 11¾" Tall, Satin Frosted Finish	$2,350
Duck Figurine, Resting, 1¾" Across, Frosted	$135
Duck Figurine, Standing, 2¾" Tall, Frosted	$135

Elephant Figurine, 4½" Long, Satin Frosted Finish	$325
Falcon Mascot, 6" Tall, Framed, Signed "R. Lalique"	$1,250
Fish, Angel, 2" Tall, 2½" Long, Various Frosted Colors, Signed "Lalique France"	$110
Fish, Blow, 1" Tall, 2" Long, Various Frosted Colors, Signed "Lalique France	$110
Fish, 5" Tall, Polished Crystal	$85
Frog, 2¼" Tall, Opaque Frosted Green	$90
Gazelle Bookends, Leaping Gazelles, 4" x 4"	$425
Girl, Nude with Goat, 4" Tall, Signed "Lalique"	$375
Hood Ornament, 3¾" Tall, Ram's Head, Frosted Gray, Signed "R. Lalique France"	$1,750
Hood Ornament, Fish Design, 3⅞" Tall, Frosted, Signed "R. Lalique France"	$4,150
Hood Ornament, 4⅝" Tall, Eagle's Head	$1,850
Hood Ornament, 5" Tall, 5 Rearing Horses Design	$5,250
Hood Ornament, 5½" Long, Kneeling Nude with Flowing Hair	$3,750
Hood Ornament, 5⅞" Tall, Full Perched Falcon, Partially Frosted, Signed "R. Lalique"	$2,000
Hood Ornament, 6½" Long, Frosted Dragonfly Design	$5,750
Hood Ornament, 7½" Long, Light Amethyst Rooster Design	$6,250
Hood Ornament, 7½" Tall, Frosted Nude Design	$7,750
Hood Ornament, 7¾" Long, Greyhound Design	$2,250
Hood Ornament, 8" Long, Frosted Yellow Dragonfly Design	$6,250
Horse Head Bookends, 6½" Tall, 3¾" Wide, Longchamps Crystal Horse Head, Chrome Radiator Cap on a Black Base, Pair	$8,250
Inkwell, 6" Diameter, Spiraled Serpents, Signed "R. Lalique"	$4,150
Jaguar Figurine, 3½" Tall, 4" Long, Frosted Bombay Design	$325
Jaguar Figurine, 3" Tall, 4" Long, Frosted Columbo Design	$325
Jaguar Sculpture, 3½" Tall, 4½" Long, Frosted Madras Design (2 Jaguars Embracing)	$525
Jardiniere, 5¼" Diameter, 2 Antelope-Designed Handles	$2,850
Knife Rest, 4" Long, Frosted Ends, Signed	$100
Lamp, 16½" Tall, Square Base and Stem, Brown to Light Tan Peacock Design, Light Tan Floral Shade, Signed "Lalique"	$7,750

Lizard Figurine, 6½" Tall, Green	$285
Mascot, Kneeling Nudes Bending Backward, 5" Tall, Signed "R. Lalique, France"	$4,650
Nude Woman Figurine, 13½" Tall, Satin Frosted Finish, Signed	$500
Owl Figurine, 2" Tall, Frosted	$150
Owl Figurine, 3" Tall	$135
Panda Figurine, 2¾" Tall, Frosted	$250
Paperweight, Owl 3½", Frosted	$155
Paperweight, Eagle Head, 4½", Amber	$1,400
Pendant, Heart-Shape Frosted Angel Design, 1" Across	$200
Perfume Bottle with Stopper, 3½" Tall, Framed Crystal, Deux Fleurs Brand, Signed "R. Lalique France"	$475
Perfume Bottle with Stopper, 4½" Tall, 4 Paneled Turtles with Heads Back	$6,650
Perfume Bopttle with Stopper, 4¾" Tall, Frosted Clairfontaine Design	$350
Perfume Bottle with Stopper, 6" Tall, Transparent Brown Finish, Coty Amber Antique Brand, Signed "R. Lalique"	$1,400
Perfume Bottle with Stopper, 6" Tall, Footed, Framed Design, Roses Brand, Signed "R. Lalique"	$775
Perfume Bottle with Stopper, 7" Tall, Black Enamel, Forvil Le Parfum Brand, Signed "R. Lalique, France"	$885
Perfume Bottle with Ball Stopper, 8" Tall, Disk Form, Nina Ricci Brand	$285
Perfume Bottle with Kneeling Nude Garlanded Stopper, 10½" Tall, Light Amber Floral Design	$1,200
Plate, 8", Engraved Hunting Dog, Signed "Lalique"	$550
Plate, Collector, Frosted Crystal, *Deux Oiseaux* (Two Birds) Frosted Crystal, 1965	$1,150
Plate, Collector, 8½", Frosted Crystal, *Rose de Songerie* (Dream Rose), 1966	$425
Plate, Collector, Frosted Crystal, *Ballet de Poisson* (Fish Ballet), 1967	$275
Plate, Collector, Frosted Crystal, 1968 Through 1976	$150
Plate, 9", Opalescent Seashell Design	$1,150
Powder Box with Cover, 3⅝" Diameter, Dancing Nudes and Garland Design	$425
Rabbit Figurine, Various Frosted Designs, 2"–2½" Tall/Long	$150
Rooster, 3" Tall, Frosted on Clear Crystal Base	$150
Rooster Mascot, 8" Tall, Framed, Signed "R. Lalique, France"	$750

Seal, 5½" Tall, Frosted on Jagged Clear Crystal Vase	$1,050
Sparrow, 4¼" Long, Satin Frosted Finish	$145
Stallion Bookends, 8¼" Tall, 6⅜" Wide, Satin Frosted, Pair	$1,850
Tray, 15½" Oval, Clear and Frosted Carnation Blossoms Design	$1,150
Vase, 4¾" Tall, 4" Wide, Dampierre Design	$425
Vase, 5" Tall, Footed, Frosted Swirled Body with 2 Applied Doves	$275
Vase, 5" Tall, Bulbous, Fish Design	$925
Vase, 5½" Tall, Male Nudes in Base "Holding Up" Vessel	$3,150
Vase, 6" Tall, Black on Opal Coloring, Band of Rabbits Design, Signed "R. Lalique"	$1,650
Vase, 6¾" Tall, Globe Shape, Swimming Fish with Lengthy Fins and Tails	$425
Vase, 7" Tall, Frosted, Nesting Birds Design	$425
Vase, 7" Tall, Globe Shape, Frosted, Antelope Design, Signed	$425
Vase, 7" Tall, Globe Shape, Blue, Fern Leaf Design, Signed "R. Lalique"	$1,450
Vase, 7" Tall, 10¼" Diameter, 8 Nude Dancing Children, Frosted Satin	$16,250
Vase, 7½" Tall, 6 Nudes Holding Urns Design	$2,750
Vase, 8" Tall, Gray, Ibex and Floral Design, Signed "R. Lalique, France"	$2,000
Vase, 8" Tall, 2 Doves Design, Signed "Lalique"	$450
Vase, 8½" Tall, Blue Opal, Snail Shell Design, Signed "R. Lalique, France"	$2,650
Vase, 9½" Tall, Globe Shape, All-Over Molded Fish Design	$2,150
Vase, 9½" Tall, Opal, 4 Pairs of Lovebirds, Signed "R. Lalique, France"	$3,650
Vase, 9½" Tall, Globe Shape, Dark Gray, Large Fish Design, Signed "R. Lalique"	$21,500
Vase, 9½" Tall, 6 Alternating Panels of Female Nudes	$4,750
Vase, 10" Tall, Ovoid Shape, Framed Archers Design	$4,750
Vase, 10" Tall, Bulbous, Amber, Coiled Serpent Design, Signed "R. Lalique"	$19,500
Vase, 10" Tall, Frosted, Naked Maidens Design Around Vase	$5,650
Vase, 10" Tall, Smoke-Colored Eagles and Feathers Design	$3,850
Vase, 11" Tall, Tapered Neck, Frosted, Mythological Creatures Design	$1,850
Vase, 13½" Tall, Black, Alligator and Pineapple Branch Design, Signed "R. Lalique"	$13,750
Wineglass, 6" Tall, Crystal and Frosted, Dancing Nudes on Stem	$215
Yorkshire Terrier, 2½" Tall, Frosted	$365

Legras & Cie
Late 19th Century–Present

J. F. Legras established a glassmaking firm at St. Denis, France, in the 1880s. The firm was best known for cameo-engraved items until 1920; during this early period, items were marked with either "Legras or "Mont Joye" or "Mont Joye & Cie." In 1920, they merged with the Pantin Glassworks. After the merger, items were marked "Pantin," "Degue," or "De Vez." Those marked with the De Vez or Degue signatures can be found under De Vez Cameo Glass earlier in the chapter.

Basket, 6½" Tall, Amber with Brown and Cream Spatter, Gold Aventurine Cased over Cranberry	$400
Bowl, 7", Frosted Cameo Over Crystal, Enameled Sunset Winter Scene (Legras)	$450
Bowl, 8½" Cameo Crystal and Frosted with Enameled Black and Red Floral Design (Legras)	$750
Compote, 7½" Diameter, 5¼" Tall, Tri-Cornered, Beige and Cream Cameo Leaf Design	$625
Vase, 4¼" Tall, Multicolor Enameled Landscape Cameo Scene (Legras)	$925
Vase, 5" Tall, Green on Light Yellow Cameo, Maple Leaves and Pod Design (Legras)	$450
Vase, 6" Tall, Caramel Base with Cameo-Engraved Opal Landscape Scene	$575
Vase, 7" Tall, Opaque Yellow with Cameo-Engraved Coral and Shell Design	$500
Vase, 8¾" Tall, Gray, White, and Yellow Cameo Design with Enameled Burgundy Floral Design (Legras)	$550
Vase, 11½" Tall, Red and Amythest Floral Cameo Design (Mont Joye)	$650
Vase, 16" Tall, Bulbous Pink on Gray Cameo, Grapevine Design (Legras)	$2,150
Vase, 25½" Tall, Bulbous Base and Stick Neck, Gray and Red Raspberry and Vine Cameo Design, Legras	$850

Leverre Cameo Glass
1908–33

During the early 20th century, French glassmaker Charles Schneider founded a French firm in 1908 that remained in business until 1933. Most products produced were cameo-engraved and exported to the United States. They were primarily marketed through Ovington's of New York City. Products were usually marked "Leverre," "LeVerre Francais," or with the Schneider name.

Bowl, 13½", Bunn Feet, Wine on Rust, Cameo Floral Cluster Design (Le Verre Francais)	$2,375
Chandelier, 13" Tall, Burgundy to Brown on Yellow, Cameo, Trumpet Flower Design on Conical Shade (Le Verre Francais)	$3,350

Lamp, Boudoir Style, 14" Tall, 6½" Diameter Shade, Amethyst to Blue Shaded Cameo-Engraved Geometrical Design (Le Verre Francais)	$1,750
Pitcher, 6" Tall, Shaded Orange and White Cameo (Schneider)	$525
Vase, 5¾" Tall, Shaded Orange and White Cameo (Schneider)	$900
Vase, 9½" Tall, Footed, Urn Shape, Purple on Pink and Orange Cameo, Swag Design (Le Verre Francais)	$1,275
Vase, 11½" Tall, Trumpet Style, Crystal Foot, Amethyst on Green Foliage (Le Verre Francais)	$950
Vase, 15½" Tall, Footed, Mottled Yellow Base with Cameo-Engraved Blue and Orange Seed Pod Design (Le Verre Francais)	$1,050
Vase, 18" Tall, Footed, Multicolored on Yellow and Rust Cameo, Art Deco Floral Design (Le Verre Francais)	$2,150
Vase, 19" Tall, Footed, Brown on Yellow Cameo, Geese Design (Le Verre Francais)	$2,850
Vase, 22" Tall, Cylindrically Shape, Orange on Light Green Cameo, Floral Top (Le Verre Francais)	$3,750

Lismore
Waterford Crystal Ltd., 1951–Present

Lismore is one of the new Waterford's most popular cut patterns. For older as well as other, newer items, see the Waterford listings near the end of this chapter.

Bell, 3" Tall, Ring Handle	$50
Biscuit Jar with Cover, 7" Tall	$150
Bowl, 4", 2¼" Tall	$40
Bowl, 5"	$70
Bowl, 9½"	$140
Bowl, 10"	$200
Brandy Snifter	$50
Cake Plate, 11", 5" Tall, Footed	$175
Cake Server 12" Long, Crystal Lismore Handle	$75
Cake Shop, Village Collection, 2" Tall, 2½" Long	$75
Candlestick, 5" Tall	$65
Carafe, Wine, 22 oz.	$145
Carafe, Water or Wine, 30 oz.	$155

Waterford Crystal. *Reproduced directly from a 1995 advertisement, courtesy of the Waterford Glass Co.*

Champagne Glass	$40
Church, Village Collection, 4" Tall, 4" Long	$85
Claret Glass	$40
Cordial Glass	$30
Cottage, Village Collection, 2" Tall, 3½" Long	$75
Creamer, Pitcher Style, 3" Tall	$50
Decanter, Ship's with Faceted Stopper, 9½" Tall	$290
Decanter, Whiskey, 10" Tall	$275
Decanter, Wine	$225
Honey Jar with Cover, 4⅛" Tall	$85
Hors D'Oeuvres Disk, 9" Across, 3 Sections	$100
Hotel, Village Collection, 3" Tall, 3" Long	$75
Ice Bucket, 7¾" Tall, 7" Diameter	$125
Napkin Ring 1½" x 2"	$20
Perfume Bottle with Brass Top and Atomizer, 4½" Tall	$80
Pitcher, Milk, 24 oz.	$140
Place Card Holder, 1" x 2¼"	$20
Plate, 8"	$45
Post Office, Village Collection, 1½" Tall, 2¼" Long	$75
Salt and Pepper Shakers, 6" Tall, Round Feet, Silver-Plated Tops	$150

Sauce Boat, Small Cup-Pitcher Style, 8 oz.	$60
Schoolhouse, Village Collection, 2½" Tall	$75
Sherbet	$50
Shot Glass, 1.6 oz., 2½" Tall	$32.50
Sugar Bowl, 1¾" Tall	$35
Sugar Shaker with Silver-Plated Top, 8" Tall	$70
Surgery, Village Collection, 2" Tall	$75
Tray, Rectangular, 11" x 7"	$100
Tumbler, 5 oz.	$30
Tumbler, 9 oz., Old-Fashioned Style	$35
Tumbler, 10 oz.	$40
Tumbler, 10 oz.	$40
Tumbler, 10 oz., Iced Tea, Footed	$50
Tumbler, 12 oz., 6½" Tall	$45
Tumbler, 12 oz., Old-Fashioned Style	$40
Vase, Bud, 4" Tall	$45
Vase, 8½" Tall, Round Base	$100
Vase, 9" Tall, Wedge and Olive Cuts	$175
Wineglass, 10 oz.	$60
Wineglass, Red or White	$40
Wineglass, Oversize	$95

Loetz Glass
Austria, 1840s–Early 1900s

The original Loetz Glassworks was founded in 1840 in western Austria (Klostermule) by Johann Lotz (1778–1844). Lotz earned a reputation early on as a maker of high-quality glassware. During the art nouveau period, he produced iridescent glass similar to that of Carder at Steuben and Tiffany. A few other Loetz originals include threaded glass and cameo designs. Identification can be difficult since much of Loetz' work was not signed, and at times cheaper imitation iridescent glass has been attributed to Loetz. Note that the name Lotz was purposefully given the English spelling Loetz in 1900, supposedly to represent the international nature of the firm.

Basket, Bride's, Red with Enameled Design, Silver Holder	$785
Basket, 9" Tall, Lilac and Green Spotted Design with Flower Prunts	$240

Loetz Vase. *Photo by Mark Pickvet. Courtesy of the Corning Museum of Glass.*

Basket, 10" Tall, Amber with Iridescent Blue Threading, Prunt Handle	$900
Basket, 17½" Tall, 9½" Diameter, Iridescent Green with Applied Crystal Handle	$475
Biscuit Jar with Cover, Square Shape, Iridescent Pink	$525
Bowl, 2½", Miniature, Green Papillon with Silver Deposit	$385
Bowl, 5", Opalescent White, Prunt Design	$125
Bowl, 6½", Ruffled, 3 Applied Purple Handles	$135
Bowl, 9", Ruffled, Iridescent Purple	$415
Bowl, 9½", Scalloped, Iridescent Gold Leaf Design	$550
Bowl, 12", Iridescent Gold, Applied Glass Decoration	$625
Bowl, Rose, 4", Iridescent Shades of Red	$115
Bowl, Rose, 4½", Staghorn Base, Green with Purple Threading	$425
Candlestick, 10" Tall, Red and Green Fern Design	$315
Chalice, 5½" Tall, Iridescent Blue-Green, Teardrop Design	$2,750
Cookie Jar with Silver-Plated Cover, Pink Florette Design	$425
Cracker Jar with Silver-Plated Cover, Rim, and Bail Handle; 7½" Tall, Iridescent Green with Threading	$400
Epergne, 4 Green Trumpet-Style Lilies and Small Baskets Design	$650
Ewer, 6" Tall, Iridescent Green with Applied Handles	$575
Ewer, 10½" Tall, Cobalt Blue with Iridescent Silver Spots, Engraved "Loetz Austria"	$5,250
Jar with Cover, 8" Diameter, Cameo Floral Design, Signed "Loetz"	$825

Lamp, Candle, 12" Tall, Gold Spotted Shade and Base, Red and Green Leaves Design
$825

Lamp, Table, 20" Tall, Bronze Serpent Base, Iridescent Threaded Green Globe Shade
$5,350

Perfume Bottle with Stopper, 5½" Tall, Silver Accents, Iridescent Green with White Threading
$525

Pitcher, 5½" Tall, Square Top, Ribbed Handle, Iridescent White Crackle Design $600

Pitcher, Syrup with Silver-Plated Lid, 8" Tall, Iridescent Cobalt Blue $1,100

Toothpick Holder, Silver Overlay Design $235

Vase, 3¾" Tall, 5¾" Diameter, Flared, Ruby Red with Iridescent Blue Mottling $2,500

Vase, 4½" Tall, Iridescent Silver to Blue, Signed "Loetz" $585

Vase, 5" Tall, Iridescent Gold, Signed "Loetz" $365

Vase, 6" Tall, Pinched Sides, Iridescent Blue $625

Vase, 6" Tall, Iridescent Blue to Gold, Lily Pad Design, Signed "Loetz" $625

Vase, 6" Tall, Iridescent Gold, Signed "Loetz" $385

Vase, 6" Tall, Iridescent Green $185

Vase, 6" Tall, Iridescent Purple to Silver, Signed "Loetz" $415

Vase, 6½" Tall, Iridescent Yellow to Gold, Blue and Platinum Wave Design $1,900

Vase, 6½" Tall, Green with Blue Serpent Around Neck $525

Vase, 7" Tall, Iridescent Blue in Silver-Plated Holder $350

Vase, 7" Tall, Bottle Form, Applied Iridescent Grape Design $215

Vase, 7" Tall, 13" Diameter, 3-Lobe Rim, Iridescent Green to Silver to Blue, Swirls and Spots Design
$1,650

Vase, 7" Tall, Iridescent Purple $215

Vase, 8", Pinched Sides, Iridescent Blue Swirl Design $650

Vase, 8" Tall, Ruffled, Opalescent Green Swirl Design $215

Vase, 8" Tall, Pedestal Base, Iridescent Bronze $275

Vase, 9" Tall, Pinched Sides, Iridescent Blue to Gold with Pink Highlights $700

Vase, 9" Tall, Bronze Holder, Ruffled, Iridescent Gold Wavy Design $1,850

Vase, 9¼" Tall, Bronzed Leaf and Floral Design on Green Cameo $1,950

Vase, 9¾" Tall, Pinched, Ribbed, Iridescent Gold $900

Vase, 10" Tall, Iridescent Gold with Silver Overlay $1,275

Vase, 10½" Tall, Swirled Onyx Design $1,050

Vase, 11" Tall, Iridescent Bronze with Purple Threading	$1,300
Vase, 11½" Tall, Jack-in-the-Pulpit Style, Dome Foot, Iridescent Blue and Gold Floral Design	$1,350
Vase, 12" Tall, Ruffled, Blue with Pink Interior	$335
Vase, 12" Tall, Iridescent Gold, Floral Decoration	$650
Vase, 12" Tall, Iridescent Dark Blue to Light Blue	$800
Vase, 12" Tall, Ruffled, Iridescent Crystal with Pink Interior	$315
Vase, 12½" Tall, Iridescent Blue to Green	$700
Vase, 13" Tall, Amber with Gold and Rose Decoration	$365
Vase, 13¼" Tall, Bronzed Leaves on Yellow	$2,350
Vase, 14" Tall, Green on Gray Cameo, Butterfly and Floral Design	$1,950
Vase, 16" Tall, Gray with Iridescent Blue and Silver Trailings, Green Grass, Silver Overlay on Base and Rim, Signed "Loetz Austria"	$22,500
Vase, 19" Tall, Iridescent Blue and Silver Peacock Design	$1,850
Vase, 19¾" Tall, Footed, Flared, Iridescent Pink with Silver Overlay Bands	$4,350

Mary Gregory Glass
Various Companies, 1870s– Present

Mary Gregory glass is characterized by crystal and colored glassware (most commonly pastel pink) decorated with white enameled designs of one or more boys and/or girls playing in Victorian scenes (newer pieces illustrate children standing and not playing). Gregory worked as a decorator for the Boston & Sandwich Glass Company from 1870 to 1880; however, she did not decorate the glassware of her namesake. The original Mary Gregory appears to have been produced in Bohemia in the late 19th century and not with Boston & Sandwich as originally believed. Pieces that exceed $100 in price are generally elaborate European items from the late 19th and early 20th centuries.

In fact, Victorian figures have been made throughout Europe (in Germany, England, France, Italy, Switzerland, and especially Czechoslovakia) as well as later in America by Fenton, Westmoreland, and others. The newer pieces are generally worth about one-third to one-half of the original Mary Gregory items but are gaining somewhat in value and popularity. Originally, white-faced pieces were made in America, whereas tinted faces were produced in Europe; however, there has been some overlap. Few categories exhibit the price ranges found in Mary Gregory glass—from $15 to $20 for low-quality, poorly finished more recent items up to several hundred dollars for older, high-quality items.

Bottle, Wine with Crystal Bubble Stopper, 7⅛" Tall, Cranberry, Boy Design	$225
Bottle, Wine with Amber Faceted Stopper, 9" Tall, Amber, Boy Design	$250

Mary Gregory Art Glass. *Photo by Mark Pickvet.*   **Mary Gregory Art Glass.** *Photo by Robin Rainwater.*

Bottle, Wine, 9½" Tall, Sapphire Blue with Enameled White Girl Design	$225
Bottle, Wine with Crystal Bubble Stopper, 10" Tall, Cranberry, Girl Design	$275
Bowl, 5", Cranberry, Girl Fishing	$100
Box with Hinged Cover, 3¾" x 3¾", Brass Foot, Lime Green, Boy Design	$275
Box with Hinged Cover, 4" x 3⅝", Amber, Girl with Scarf	$375
Box with Hinged Cover, 6" x 3⅝", Blue, Girl Feeding Bird	$525
Candy Dish with Cover, 7½", 3-Footed, Girl and Boy	$275
Cheese Dish with Dome Cover, 9", Cranberry, 2 Girls and Boy	$400
Cookie Jar with Cover, Cranberry, Girl Sitting on Fence	$550
Cruet with Crystal Stopper, 6" Tall, Green or Cobalt Blue, Some Bronzing (Neck and Bands), Boy or Girl Design, Crystal or Colored Handle (Cranberry $100)	$75
Cruet with Crystal Stopper, Blue with Crystal Handle, Boy with Flower	$375
Cruet with Amber Stopper, 9½" Tall, 3-Petal Top, Amber, Boy Design	$325
Decanter with Stopper, 10" Tall, 3-Petal Top, Lime Green, Young Girl	$265
Decanter with Stopper, 13½" Tall, Amber, Boy in Riding Outfit	$375

Goblet, 4¾" Tall, Cranberry with Crystal Pedestal Foot, Girl with Hat	$125
Goblet, 5¾" Cranberry, Boy Feeding Birds	$150
Mug, 3⅞" Tall, Amber, Boy and Girl Design	$165
Mug, 4" Tall, Blue, Boy with Balloons	$165
Pitcher, 5" Tall, Green with Gold Trim, Boy and Floral Design	$225
Pitcher, Water, 9" Tall, Cranberry with Crystal Spout, Boys Design	$500
Pitcher, Water, 9½" Tall, Crimped, Crystal, Girl Chasing Butterfly	$250
Pitcher, Water, 10" Tall, Tankard Style, Blue, Girl Tending Sheep	$350
Plate, 8", Black, Girl in Swing	$75
Tumbler, 2½" Tall, Cranberry, Girl and Boy Design	$150
Tumbler, 3½" Tall, Green, 2 Girls, 1 Boy, and 3 Trees Design	$125
Vase, 4" Tall, Blue, Boy in Garden	$135
Vase, 4½" Tall, Cranberry with Crystal Pedestal Foot, Girl	$165
Vase, 4¾" Tall, Cobalt Blue, Girl Sitting with Flower Basket	$215
Vase, 6½" Tall, Cranberry, Boy or Girl	$265
Vase, 6½" Tall, Sapphire Blue, Boy and Girl	$185
Vase, 7½" Tall, Cobalt Blue, Boy with Hat and Oars	$185
Vase, 7¾" Tall, Pink with White Interior, Girl with Butterfly Net	$185
Vase, 9" Tall, Pedestal Foot, Cranberry, Boy Blowing Bubbles	$365
Vase, 9½" Tall, Cranberry, Girl with Umbrella	$325
Vase, 9¾" Tall, Black Amethyst, Girl with Hat	$265
Vase, 10" Tall, Scalloped, Amber, Boy or Girl	$325
Vase, 10" Tall, Cranberry, Boy or Girl	$250
Vase, 10¾" Tall, Black Amethyst, Boy or Girl	$350
Vase, 11½" Tall, Scalloped, Pedestal Base, Gold Trim	$375
Vase, 11¾" Tall, Blue, Boy Kneeling Offering Heart to Girl	$525
Vase, 12" Tall, 5½" Diameter, Pink, Girl Sitting on Branch	$375
Vase, 15" Tall, Black Amethyst, Boy Chasing Butterfly with Net	$525
Vase, 17" Tall, Cranberry, Boys and Girls Gathering Apples	$625
Vase, 17" Tall, Black Amethyst, Girl with Hat, Umbrella, and Basket	$625

Mexican Glass
1920s–Present

One factory known to produce a little carnival glass was the Cristales de Mexico. The company's products usually contain an "M" within a "C" mark on the underside. The Oklahoma and Ranger patterned water sets appear to be close copies of Imperial Glass Company's original designs. Modern Mexican designs include chili peppers and jalapeno peppers and transparent colored trims such as emerald green or cobalt blue.

Candleholder, Footed, 4½" Tall, Carnival Marigold and Green Coloring, Cross and Bleeding Heart Design	$525
Canister, 12" Tall, Crystal with Red Chili Pepper Stopper	$45
Creamer, Ranger Pattern, Carnival Marigold	$50
Cruet, Crystal, Ruby or Emerald Green Chili Pepper Stopper with Green Stem, No Handle, Carafe Shape	$30
Cruet, Crystal, Ruby or Chili Pepper Stopper with Green Stem, 4½" Tall, 6" Diameter, Crystal Applied Handle, Pitcher Shape	$30
Cruet, Crystal, Ruby Red Chili Pepper Stopper with Green Stem, Crystal Handle, 5" Tall	$20
Cruet, Crystal, Ruby Red Chili Pepper Stopper with Green Stem, Crystal Handle, 7" Tall	$22.50
Decanter with Stopper, Oklahoma Pattern, Carnval Marigold	$875
Decanter with Stopper, Ranger Pattern, Carnival Marigold	$275
Decanter with Dolphin Finial Stopper, 11½" Tall, Crystal	$60
Donkey and Cart, 9¾" Long, 4½" Tall, Milk-Glass Reproduction	$35
Goblet, 8 oz., Clear Stem and Base with Cobalt Blue Bowl, Various Sand-Etched Native American Designs	$20
Goblet, 16 oz., Circular Base, Thick Stem, Cobalt Blue	$10
Pitcher, Water, Crystal with Emerald Green Rim and Lip, Applied Emerald Green Handle	$30
Pitcher, Water, Oklahoma Pattern, Carnival Marigold	$525
Pitcher, Water, Ranger Pattern, Carnival Marigold	$250
Punch Bowl, 11", 9½" Tall, Cut Crystal Sunflower Floral Design	$75
Punch Cup, 6 oz., Cut Crystal with Emerald Green or Cobalt Blue Trim	$7.50
Punch Ladle, Crystal	$7.50
Shot Glass, 2¾" Tall, Crystal with Emerald Green or Cobalt Blue Trim	$10

Stirrer (For Crystal Pitcher Above with Emerald Green Accents), Green Cactus at End
$10

Tumbler, Emerald Green Rim, Green Saguaro Cactus Stem (Matches Pitcher and Stirrer Above)
$20

Tumbler 5½" Tall, 8 oz., Crystal with Cobalt Blue Rim
$6

Tumbler, 7" Tall, 18 oz., Handblown Bent Crystal Design with Emerald Green Rim
$17.50

Tumbler, Water, Oklahoma Pattern, Carnival Marigold
$400

Tumbler, Water, Ranger Pattern, Carnival Marigold
$150

Mideastern Glass
1980s–Present

Though glass was first invented in Egypt thousands of years ago, the ancient glass of the region (such as Islamic) is housed in museums, and rarely are such items offered for sale. Modern examples from the last few decades are suddenly springing up on the collector market. The Israeli pieces listed are made by David Barak in his studio in Herzlia, Israel.

Bowl, 3", Silver Decoration at Top, Cinnamon Red, Dark Green, or Ultramarine, Israel
$57.50

Bowl, 5", Silver Decoration at Top, Cinnamon Red, Dark Green, or Ultramarine, Israel
$110

Creamer, 4½" Tall, Silver Handle and Decoration at Top, Cinnamon Red, Dark Green, or Ultramarine, Israel
$77.50

Menorah, Crystal Ice Sculpture with Mountainous Jerusalem Landscape, Slots for 9 Candles
$110

Perfume Bottle with Gold Stopper, 4½" Tall, Handblown, Amber with Gold Accents, Egypt
$36

Perfume Bottle with Gold Stopper, 5" Tall, Handblown, Ruby Red with Gold Floral Accents, Egypt
$36

Perfume Bottle with Red and Blue Female Figural Stopper, Tall, Handblown, Fluted, Blue and Red Diamond Design, Egypt
$36

Perfume Bottle with Gold Stopper, 5½" Tall, Handblown, Amber with Gold Accents, Egypt
$36

Perfume Bottle with Gold Stopper, 5½" Tall, Handblown, Rose Red with Gold Accents, Egypt
$41

Perfume Bottle with Gold Stopper, 6½" Tall, Handblown, Aquamarine with Gold Accents, Egypt
$41

New From Egypt
No Two
Exactly Alike

Egyptian Glass. *Reproduced directly from a 1996 Egyptian glass advertisement.*

Egyptian Perfume Bottle. *Photo by Robin Rainwater.*

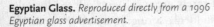

Perfume Bottle with Amethyst and Crystal Stopper, Handblown, Amethyst with Gold Lines and Etched Vining $41

Saltcellar, 2" Tall, Silver Overlay Decoration, Cinnamon Red, Dark Green, or Ultramarine, Israel $57.50

Sugar, 5" Tall, Silver Lid and Decoration at Top, Cinnamon Red, Dark Green, or Ultramarine, Israel $80

Vase, 6" Tall, Silver Stem and Trailings, Cinnamon Red, Dark Green, or Ultramarine, Israel $80

Vase, 6½" Tall, Silver Stem and Trailings, Cinnamon Red, Dark Green, or Ultramarine, Israel $87.50

Vase, 7" Tall, Crystal with Etched Hebrew Characters, 2 Styles (Shalom and Song of Songs), Price Is for Each $82.50

Vase, 8" Tall, Silver Stem and Trailings, Cinnamon Red, Dark Green, or Ultramarine, Israel $105

Vase, 9" Tall, 2-Handled, Opaque Frosted Blue with Seals on the Handles, Tehran, Iran $55

Vase, 9½" Tall, Silver Stem and Trailings, Cinnamon Red, Dark Green, or Ultramarine, Israel $135

Vase, 11" Tall, Linen Bopp Style, Varied Spiraling Concentric Rings, Designer Karim Rashid $150

Vase, 12" Tall, Silver Stem and Trailings, Cinnamon Red, Dark Green, or Ultramarine, Israel $290

Vodka Set, Ice Bucket (5" Tall, 5½" Diameter) and Six 3-oz. Liqueur Stems (5¾" Tall, Slim), Made in Turkey $50

Millefiori Glass
Venice, Italy, 14th Century–Present

Millefiori is an ancient glass technique in which tiny multicolored glass discs are imbedded into the surface of an object to produce a mosaic effect. The term means "thousand flowers," for each little disc is made to resemble flowers. The discs were made by slicing fused glass canes or cylindrical rods. These cross sections were in turn arranged in a desired pattern, refired, and shaped into the desired item. The pieces listed below are Venetian designs from the later 19th century to the present. Very few American pieces were made in this style (Carder's Tessera is one example).

Basket with Red and White Twist Handle, 4¼" Diameter, Solid Millefiori (No Capacity) $775

Bowl, Finger, 2", 2 Applied Crystal Handles, Pink, Green, and White Canes	$75
Bowl, Finger, 3", Blue Ground	$105
Bowl, 4", 1" Deep	$55
Bowl, 4", 2 Applied Crystal Handles, Blue and White Canes	$100
Bowl, 6", Brass Holder	$235
Bowl, 8", Scalloped, Folded Sides, Amethyst and Silver Floral Decorations	$175
Christmas Ornament, 2¾", Bell Shape	$35
Christmas Ornament, 3½" Diameter Ball, Hollow	$40
Christmas Ornament, 5" Tall, Teardrop Shape, Hollow	$40
Clock, 7½" Tall, Quartz, Alternating Multicolored Vertical Panels of Colored Glass, Center Panel of Multicolored Millefiori	$125
Clock, 8½" Tall, Quartz, Scattered Millefiori Multicolored Glass Beads and Marbles	$135
Creamer, 4" Tall, Scattered Design on White Ground	$235
Cruet with Stopper, 5" Tall, Allover Millefiori, Including Handle and Stopper	$450
Cup, 2½" Tall	$90
Decanter with Stopper, 12" Tall, Dark Amethyst with Multicolored Opalescent Floral Design	$1,250

Venetian Millefiori Bowl, late 18th century. *Photo by Robin Rainwater.*

Venetian Millefiori Paperweights. *Photo by Robin Rainwater.*

Egg Shape, 3" Tall, Multicolored Millefiori	$55
Epergne, 16" Tall, Bowl with 3 Ruffled Trumpet-Style Vases	$350
Goblet, 7½" Tall, Crystal Stem and Base, Multicolored Canes	$235
Lamp, 7" Tall, Dome Shade, Millefiori Base	$375
Lamp, 10" Tall, Shade and Base in Lavender Cane Form	$500
Lamp, 11½" Tall, Electric, Millefiori Shade and Base	$625
Lamp, 19" Tall, 9" Diameter Dome Shade, Millefiori Shade and Base	$875
Letter Opener, Glass, 6¾" Long, Multicolor Millefiori Handle, Silver Blade	$80
Magnifying Glass, 5" Long, Multicolor Millefiori Handle, Crystal Lens Enclosed in Silver Circle	$90
Paperweight, 2½" Diameter, Multicolor Millefiori Black Rosone Design	$80
Paperweight, 2½" Diameter, Multicolor Millefiori Fish Design	$80
Paperweight, 3", Allover Crowned Design	$135
Paperweight, 3", Pink Center with 6 Turquoise Canes, Gold Dust Design	$80
Perfume Bottle with Latticino and Gold-Tipped Stopper, 4½" Tall, 4½" Diameter	$75
Perfume Bottle with 24 kt. Gold Leaf Hand Twist Stopper, Blue and White Millefiori Design with Gold Leaf, 4¾" Tall	$75
Pitcher, Water, 7½" Tall, 32 oz., Transparent Blue Ground, Applied Crystal Handle with Gold Leafing, Multicolored Millifiori	$185
Pitcher, Water, 8" Tall, Crystal Circular Base and Applied Crystal Handle with Gold Leafing, Multicolored Millefiori	$215
Powder Jar with Cover, 2½" Tall, 2¾" Diameter, Blue with Multicolored Floral Design	$350

Saucer (Matches Cup)	$60
Sugar with Cover, 4" Tall, Blue	$285
Toothpick Holder, 2¾" Tall, Blue Ground	$105
Tumbler, 4" Tall, Blue and Green Millefiori Design	$185
Tumbler, 4" Tall, 9 oz., Multicolored Millefiori Design (Matches 8" Pitcher Above)	$70
Tumbler 4½" Tall, 12 oz., Multicolored Millefiori Design (Matches 7½" Pitcher Above)	$75
Turtle Figurine, 5" Long, 2" Tall, Multicolored Millefiori Shell, Head, Tail, and Feet with Gold Leaf	$100
Turtle Paperweight, 3" Long, 1½" Wide, Rounded Millefiori Body, Cobalt Blue Feet, Tail, and Head	$35
Vase, 4" Tall, Miniature, Blue Ground	$185
Vase, 4½" Tall, Handkerchief Style, Multicolored Canes	$160
Vase, 6½" Tall, Cobalt Blue with Multicolored Canes	$275
Vase, 7" Tall, Multicolored Millefiori	$285
Vase, 8" Tall, Ruffled, Applied Crystal Handle, Multicolored Canes	$295
Vase, 8" Tall, 2-Handled, Millefiori Design in Curving Rows	$425
Vase, 8" Tall, Blue Ground	$800
Vase, 15" Tall, Asymmetrical Tilted Design, Pierced Hole, Polychrome Patchwork	$4,100
Vase, Dragonfly with Netting Design, Signed	$900
Vase, Ruffled, Violet Ground	$235
Watch, 1" Diameter Face, Quartz, Rimmed with Multicolored Millefiori Design	$75

Moser Glass
Czechoslovakia, 1857–Present

Ludwig Moser (1833–1916) was a famous Austrian glassmaker who opened an art-glass studio in 1857 at Meierhofen, near Karlsbad, Czechoslovakia. Moser is noted for deeply carved and richly enameled wildlife sculptural scenery upon glass, cut colored scenery, classical cameo designs, and a good deal of gilding. In 1900, his four sons, Rudolf, Gustav, Richard, and Leo, joined the firm, and the name was amended to Ludwig Moser & Sohne. Leo (1879–1974) became the firm's director, and in 1922, he and Richard purchased Meyr's Neffe, their largest rival at the time in Bohemian-styled art glass. Moser Glass is still being produced today; also note that the "Moser" or "Moser Karlsbad" signatures refer to glass made by the Moser family. Items marked "Malachite" are characterized by swirled layers of dark green shades, just like the mineral for which it is named.

Basket, 5½" Tall, Malachite, Green Cherub Design $425

Basket, 6" Tall, 6½" Diameter, Malachite, Woman and Cherubs Design, Marked "Moser/Carlsbad" $265

Bell, 5½" Tall, Cut Cranberry and Crystal, Gold Scrolling $115

Bowl, 5", Cut Panels, Signed "Moser-Alexandrite" $285

Bowl, 9", 5" Tall, Green with Engraved Floral Design $475

Box with Hinged Cover, 3" Tall, 4" Diameter, Malachite, Nude Woman on Cover, Marked "Moser/Carlsbad" $215

Box with Hinged Cover, 5", Ball Feet, Cameo Gold Amazon Warriors on Cobalt Blue $575

Box with Hinged Cover, 5¾", Cranberry, Gold Vines $215

Candlestick, 4" Tall, Amethyst, Signed $140

Candlestick, 10½" Tall, Amethyst, Gold Band of Warriors $375

Candlestick, 14" Tall, Cranberry Overlay with Gilded Scrolls $785

Chalice, 6¾" Tall, Amethyst to Crystal, Gold Leaves Design $750

Compote, Blue and Crystal Floral Decoration, Gold Rim $185

Cordial, 2¾" Tall, Cranberry with Gilded Scrolling $75

Cruet with Stopper, 5" Tall $340

Cup and Saucer, Amber with Gilded Scrolling and Multicolored Floral Design $350

Decanter with Stopper, 12½" Tall, Cranberry, Gold Grapes $715

Decanter with Stopper, 16" Tall, Applied Prunts and Glass Jewels $625

Ewer, 6" Tall, Green with Multicolored Enameled Fern Design $650

Ewer, 9" Tall, Cornucopia Shape, Pedestal Base, Aquamarine with Gold Foliage and Flowers $1,250

Ewer, 10¾" Tall, Cranberry, Applied Prunts and Glass Jewels $1,350

Ewer, 11½" Tall, Multicolored Beads, Enameled Floral Design $875

Ewer, 12" Tall, Multicolored Leaves on Amber Base, Blue Handle $975

Perfume Bottle with Cut Stopper, 3" Tall, Amethyst Prism Cut Design $340

Perfume Bottle with Stopper, 4½" Tall, Cobalt Blue with Gold Figures $215

Perfume Bottle with Stopper, 10" Tall, Crystal with Heavy Gold Decoration $600

Pitcher, 4¾" Tall, Bulbous, Flared Foot, Ruby Red with Gold Bands $725

Pitcher, Water, 7" Tall, Crackle Glass with Multicolored Enameled Fish and Seaweed Design $375

Pitcher, Water, 8½" Tall, Footed, Amber with Blue Trim	$500
Pitcher, Water, 8½" Tall Amber with Multicolored Enameled Floral Design	$300
Pitcher, Water, 10" Tall, 4 Gilded Feet, Green with Multicolored (Including Gold) Floral and Scroll Design	$685
Toothpick Holder, 2½" Tall, Malachite with Multicolored Enameled Angels	$275
Toothpick Holder, 3" Tall, Cranberry on Crystal Pedestal Base	$175
Tumbler, 4½" Tall, Cranberry with Gold Floral Design	$140
Urn, 14" Tall, White to Cranberry Cut, Enameled Floral Design with Gold	$885
Vase, 2½" Tall, Cranberry with Gilding, Multicolored Enameled Floral Design	$265
Vase, 3" Tall, Cobalt Blue, Gold Bands, Enameled Asian Woman Design	$215
Vase, 3½" Tall, Miniature, Amethyst	$160
Vase, 4" Tall, 4 Gilded Feet, Cranberry with Multicolored Enameled Design of Bird, Acorn, and Foliage	$750
Vase, 5" Tall, Gold Foliage with Enameled Acorns and Oak Leaves	$285
Vase, 5" Tall, Malachite, Nude Woman and Floral Design, Marked "Moser/Carlsbad"	$195
Vase, 6" Tall, Paneled Pattern, Cranberry with Enameled Blue and Gold Design	$265
Vase, 6½" Tall, Amethyst, Gold Rim, Engraved Tulips Design	$415
Vase, 7" Tall, Amber and Blue, Enameled Floral Design	$800
Vase, 8" Tall, 6" Diameter, 4-Footed, Blue Floral Design with Gold Scrolling	$1,250
Vase, 8¾" Tall, Smoke Crackle, Enameled Orchid Design	$875
Vase, 9" Tall, Cranberry with Gold Medallions and Enameled Beading	$535
Vase, 9" Tall, Urn Style, Cranberry Rose Medallion Design, 2 Gilded Handles	$1,000
Vase, 9½" Tall, Malachite, Nude Woman and Grapes Design, Marked "Moser/Carlsbad"	$300
Vase, 9½" Tall, Ruffled, Pink Flowers with Gilding	$265
Vase, 10", Handled, Overall Enamel Design, Signed	$725
Vase, 10" Tall, Amethyst, Gold Trim, Birds and Lily Pads Design	$575
Vase, 10" Tall, Dark Amber with Enameled Elephant Design	$775
Vase, 10" Tall, 3" Diameter, Cameo Poppy Design	$2,825
Vase, 10" Tall, Bulbous, Cobalt Blue, Signed	$215
Vase, 11" Tall, Cobalt Blue, Gold Rim, Engraved Elephants and Palm Trees	$2,350
Vase, 11½" Tall, Crystal with Intaglio Engraved Purple Flowers	$850

Vase, 12½" Tall, Blue with Multicolored Enameled Flowers, Butterflies, and Bees	$340
Vase, 12½" Tall, Raised Scroll Design with Applied Metal Bees, Signed	$650
Vase, 13" Tall, Cobalt Blue to White Shading, Multicolored Enameled Floral Design, Gold Trim	$775
Vase, 15" Tall, Flared, Crystal to Green with Engraved Floral Design	$950
Vase, 16" Tall, Green with Multicolored Enameled Pink and Blue Floral Design	$1,200
Vase, 20" Tall, Trumpet Form, Gold Feet and Border, Light Purple with Enameled Nude Design	$1,250
Vase, 22" Tall, Handled, Emerald Green with Gold Leaves, Dutchman in Reserve Design	$1,850
Whiskey Tumbler, 3" Tall, Cranberry with Gold Grapes	$140

Nailsea Glass
England, 1788–Present

This glass is named for the small town of Nailsea, England, where glass was first produced by the Nailsea Glass House in 1788. The original factory produced novelty items as a particular style developed. It was characterized by colored or crystal glass decorated with contrasting loops, swirls, or spirals. The style spread to other parts of England and even a little to America.

Bell, 11¾" Tall, White with Dark Pink Loopings	$110
Bottle, Bellows, 8½" Long, Opaque White with Cranberry and Crystal Loopings	$175
Bottle, Bellows, 11" Long, Crystal with Pink and White Loopings	$130
Bowl, Finger, 4", Crystal with Blue and White Streaking	$105
Bowl, Finger, 4½", 4-Fold Rim, Chartreuse with White Loopings	$400
Bowl, 4½" Tall, 2¼" Tall, Citron with White Looping	$155
Candlestick, 10" Tall, Bulb Stem, Cone-Shape Base, Crystal with White Loopings	$195
Cologne Bottle, 5¾" Tall, Milk White with Blue and Cranberry Loopings; Crystal Stopper with Blue, Pink, and White Loopings	$535
Flask, 6½" Tall, Milk White with Dark Blue Loopings	$155
Flask, 7½" Tall, Crystal with Cranberry and White Loopings	$195
Flask, 7¾" Tall, Cobalt Blue with White Loopings	$225
Lamp, 6" Tall, Ruffled Base, Blue with White Loopings	$550
Lamp, 7" Tall, Blue Shade with White Loopings	$675
Mug, 5½" Tall, Crystal with Blue and White Loopings	$365

Nailsea. *Photo by Robin Rainwater.*

Pitcher, Water, 6½" Tall, Footed, Crystal with White Loopings	$1,200
Pitcher, Water, 9½" Tall, Applied Crystal Handle and Feet, Cranberry with White Loopings	$1,500
Powder Horn Novelty, 12" Long, Light and Dark Blue Shading with White Loopings	$235
Rolling Pin, Black with White Loopings	$250
Rolling Pin, Blue with White Loopings	$315
Rolling Pin, 18" Long, Crystal with Pink Loopings	$225
Rolling Pin, 19" Long, Crystal with Pink Loopings	$235
Salt Dip, 3¾" Diameter, Footed, Crystal with White Loopings	$185
Tumbler, 4½" Tall, Milk White with Blue Loopings	$125
Vase, 4½" Tall, Rolled Edge, Blue with White Loopings	$165
Vase, 8" Tall, 5" Diameter, Flared Rim and Base, Crystal with White Loopings	$225
Vase, 8½" Tall, Flared and Ruffled Rim, Crystal Pedestal Foot, Crystal with Red, White, and Blue Loopings	$575
Vase, 9¾" Tall, Footed, Blue with White Loopings	$600
Witch Ball, 4½" Diameter, Crystal with Thin White Loopings	$235

Orrefors Glasbruck
1898–Present

The Orrefors Glasbruck was established in 1898 in Smaland, Sweden. The company started out as a basic tableware manufacturer and began producing more art styles in the

Orrefors of Sweden. *Photo by Mark Pickvet.*

Orrefors of Sweden. *Photo by Mark Pickvet.*

Orrefors of Sweden. *Reproduced directly from a 1982 Orrefors advertisement.*

1910s and 1920s. By 1925, the company had gained fame for its unique crystal engraving, particularly for the spectacular Graal line developed by master glassblower Knut Berquist and designers Simon Gate and Edward Hald. The firm is still in operation today, producing high-quality crystal, cased glass, stemware, and traditional Swedish art-styled items. In 1990, they merged with Kosta-Boda to become part of the Afors Group, but distinct glass is still made under the Orrefors name. See additional listings earlier in this chapter under Kosta Boda.

Bowl, 4½"Crystal, Corona Design	$55
Bowl, 5", Crystal with Etched Mother and Child	$275
Bowl, Crystal with Etched Male Nude Figures	$310
Bowl, 6", 3⅜" Tall, Crystal Faceted Cuts	$85

Bowl, 6", Flared, Pomona Style, Crystal $100

Bowl with Underplate, 7¾", Flared, Crystal with 4 Panels, Engraved Nude Maidens in Each Panel $2,250

Bowl, 8¼", 4" Tall, Crystal, Interlocking Cut Honeycomb Design $100

Clock, 3⅛" Octagon, Crystal, Beveled $110

Decanter with Melon-Ribbed Stopper, 11" Tall $110

Decanter with Stopper, 11¾" Tall, Crystal with Engraved Underwater Fisherman $235

Pitcher, Water, 38 oz., Crystal $115

Plate, Commemorative, Annual Cathedral Series, Crystal, 1970 and Up (1973—$77.50, 1974—$67.50, 1977—$110) $37.50

Plate, Commemorative, Annual Mother's Day Series, Crystal, 1970 and Up (1975—$67.50) $27.50

Platter, 16¼" x 13" Oval, Crystal with Airtrapped Bubbled Concentric Ring Design, Signed "Orrefors Ariel No. 1799E, Edvin Ohrstrom" $295

Urn with Cover, 10½" Tall, Crystal with Engraved Garden of Eden Design $1,375

Vase, 4" Tall, Crystal with Etched Woman Viewing Moon and Stars $415

Vase, 4¾" Tall, Globe Shape, Crystal with Internal Fish and Seaweed Design $650

Vase, 4¾" Tall, Engraved Internal Fish and Green Seaweed Design on Crystal, Engraved "Orrefors Sweden Graal #2960 Edward Hald" $775

Vase, 4⅞" Tall, Globe Shape, Crystal with Green and Black Swimming Fish, Graal Design $1,500

Vase, 5" Tall, Crystal with Engraved Bird in Flight $140

Vase, 5½" Tall, Green with Internal Engraved Sea Diver and Mermaid, Engraved "Orrefors Graal—301B" $585

Vase, 6" Tall, Crystal with Internal Engraved Green Tropical Fish and Plants, Engraved "Orrefors—Sweden—Graal—Nu 454—B—Edward Hald" $585

Vase, 6¾" Tall, Crystal with Internal Engraved Green Jellyfish and Plants, Graal Design $1,550

Vase, 7⅛" Tall, Engraved Male Nude Diver $785

Vase, 7¼" Tall, Crystal with Internal Engraved Fish and Seaweed, Graal Design $650

Vase, 7⅝" Tall, Prism "Thousand Windows" Cut Crystal Pattern $325

Vase, 8¼" Tall, Crystal, Square Base $165

Vase, 8¼" Tall, Engraved Gondolier and Woman on Reverse, Signed, Graal Design $2,850

Vase, 8½" Tall, Thick Crystal Base, Vertically Striped in Lila, Graal Design $1,750

Vase, 8½" Tall, Light Blue, Three Engraved Seagulls	$250
Vase, 8¾" Tall, Crystal with Interior Decoration of Amorphic Figures Playing Games, Inscribed "Orrefors 1938 Graal"	$7,850
Vase, 9" Tall, Flared, Crystal with Engraved Male Nude Diver, Fish, and Waves	$1,175
Vase, 10¼" Tall, Frosted Slim Female Archer, Signed "Orrefors"	$175
Vase, 11" Tall, Footed, Crystal with Engraved Sailboat and Water Design	$2,150
Vase, 12⅜" Tall, Footed, Spherical Center Section, Amber	$375
Vase, 13¾" Tall, Black Footed, Crystal with Engraved 3 Male Nude Divers	$3,950
Wineglass, Crystal, Illusion or Prelude Pattern	$35

Peachblow
Thomas Webb & Sons, England, 1890s–Early 1900s

Peachblow, sometimes spelled as two separate words (Peach Blow), was an art form originally made in America, usually in shades from a rose pink at the top to a white or grayish white at the bottom. The style was briefly popular in England as well, near the end of the art nouveau movement. See the end of the chapter for more on Thomas Webb & Sons.

Biscuit Jar with Cover, 6" Tall, Pine Needles and Butterfly Design with Gold Decoration	$1,100
Bowl, 2½", 3¾" Tall, Gold Butterfly and Pine Needles Design	$365
Bowl, 4", 2½" Tall, Satin Finish with White Lining, Gold Butterfly and Pine Needles Design	$385
Bowl, Rose, 2¾", 3" Tall, 8-Crimped	$300
Cologne Bottle with Stopper, 5" Tall	$700
Cologne Bottle with Silver Stopper, 5" Tall, Gilded Branch Design	$950
Creamer, Rolled Rim, Coralene Seaweed Design	$600
Pitcher, Water, 9" Tall, Tankard Style, Signed	$475
Plate, 8¼", Crimped, Gold Prunus Design	$475
Vase, 3¾" Tall, 2¾" Diameter, Gold Prunus Design	$425
Vase, 4½" Tall, Gold Flowers with Silver Centers Design	$575
Vase, 5" Tall, Footed, Applied Crystal Flowers and Leaves	$600
Vase, 5¾" Tall, 3" Diameter, Gold Floral and Insect Design	$400
Vase, 5¾" Tall, Coralene Seaweed Design	$400
Vase, 6" Tall, Ruffled, Blue Interior, Enameled Floral Design	$425

Vase, 6½" Tall, 3½" Diameter, Gold Prunus and Bee Design	$550
Vase, 7" Tall, 4" Diameter, Gold Prunus Design	$400
Vase, 7" Tall, Gold Floral, Leaves, and Dragonfly Design	$825
Vase, 7¼" Tall, Gold Prunus Design	$425
Vase, 7½" Tall, Gold Bands, Floral, and Butterfly Design	$875
Vase, 7½" Tall, Gold and Purple Floral Design	$375
Vase, 8" Tall, Pinched Sides, Acid Cut	$825
Vase, 8" Tall, Slender, Lined	$750
Vase, 8¼" Tall, Horizontal Ribbing, White Interior	$400
Vase, 8½" Tall, Gold Branches with Blossoms and Leaves Design	$525
Vase, 9⅞" Tall, Bottle Shape, Gold Floral and Leaves Design	$575
Vase, 10" Tall, 6" Diameter, Gold Prunus Design	$825
Vase, 11¾" Tall, 5¾" Diameter, Clear Feet and Floral Design	$875
Vase, 15" Tall, 7" Diameter, Rose Shaded to Pink, Gold Floral and Birds Design	$1,475

Peloton Glass
Bohemia (Western Czechoslovakia), 1880–Early 20th Century

Peloton Glass was first patented by Wilhelm Kralick in 1880 and is characterized by short random lengths and shapes of colored streaks (or threads) on an opaque-colored base. The base is most often opal white. The streaking was added by rolling the threads directly into the base when the article was removed from the oven. Pieces were further decorated by enameling.

Biscuit Jar with Cover, 6" Tall, Multicolored Threading on Opal White	$550
Biscuit Jar with Silver-Plated Cover and Handle, 7" Tall	$725
Biscuit Jar with Silver-Plated Cover and Handle, 7¾" Tall, Pink Ribbed with White Interior and Multicolored Strands	$1,300
Bowl, 6½", 3 Applied Crystal Feet, Opaque White with Brown and Yellow Decorations, Ribbed	$350
Bowl, Rose, 2½", 6-Crimped, Multicolored Threading on Opal White	$240
Bowl, Rose, 2½", 6-Crimped, Crystal Feet, Multicolored Threading on Lavender	$240
Bowl, Rose, 2½", 6-Crimped, Wishbone Feet, Multicolored Strings on Cased Pink	$240
Cruet with Crystal Stopper, 7" Tall, Pastel Filaments on Light Blue Ground	$350
Pitcher, Water, 6½" Tall, Applied Crystal Handle, Multicolored Threaded Design	$250

Pitcher, Water, 7½" Tall, Clear and White Threading, Enameled Leaves and Floral Design	$475
Pitcher, Water, 8" Tall, Crystal Overshot Style	$425
Pitcher, Water, 8" Tall, Blue and Green Shaded Butterfly Design	$1,050
Pitcher, 11" Tall, Amber with Multicolored Threading, Reeded Handle	$625
Plate, 6", Ruffled, Crystal with Multicolored Threaded Design	$175
Plate, 7", Single Colors on a Translucent Ground	$375
Toothpick Holder, 3" Tall, Crystal with White Threading	$150
Toothpick Holder, 3¼" Tall, Crystal with Multicolored Threaded Design	$175
Tumbler, 3¼" Tall, Crystal with Multicolored Threading	$150
Vase, 3" Tall, Miniature, Applied Legs, Violet	$325
Vase, 3⅛" Tall, Crystal with White Threading	$235
Vase, 3¾" Tall, 6-Petal Feet, 4-Corner Top, Multicolored Threaded Design	$340
Vase, 4" Tall, Folded Tricorn Top, Multicolored Threading on Opal White	$425
Vase, 4" Tall, Bulbous, Ribbed, Pastel Strings on Pink Shading	$600
Vase, 4¼" Tall, Tricorner Top, Folded Rim, Melon Ribbed, Clear with White Lining and Multicolored Threading	$350
Vase, 5" Tall, Tricorner Top, Blue and White Threading	$365
Vase, 5¼" Tall, Ruffled, Yellow and White Threading	$375
Vase, 6" Tall, Crimped, Multicolored Threading on Crystal to Lavender Shading	$475
Vase, 6¾" Tall, Yellow with White Interior and Threading	$425
Vase, 7" Tall, Clear with Cranberry Threading	$325
Vase, 7" Tall, 5 Wishbone Feet, Ribbed, Multicolored Threading on Opal White	$525
Vase, 8" Tall, Tiny Multicolored Flaking on Opal White	$550
Vase, 9" Tall, Multicolored Threading on Opal White	$565
Vase, 13" Tall, Multicolored Threading on Opal White	$750

Perthshire Paperweights Ltd.
Crieff, Scotland, 1970–Present

Perthshire has been in business only since 1970, and already many of their limited editions are valued at several hundred dollars along with a few in the thousands. Perthshire is one of many companies that have sparked a great revival in paperweight-making and collecting.

Perthshire Paperweights. *Photo by Mark Pickvet.*

Perthshire Paperweights. *Photo by Mark Pickvet.*

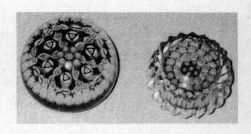

Perthshire Paperweights. *Photo by Mark Pickvet.*

Bowl, 4½", Blue Rim, White Vertical Latticino Bands, Millefiori Base	$125
Inkwell, 7½" Tall, Millefiori Base and Stopper	$450
Paperweight, 2⅜", Cobalt Blue Ground, 3 Interlaced Elliptical (Celestial Design), Garlands that connect into a Millefiori 6-Sided Figure	$110
Paperweight, 2½", Cobalt Blue Ground, Cross Composed of Yellow Stardust Canes Encircled by a Millefiori Garland, Limted Edition of 300	$110
Paperweight, 2½", Cobalt Blue Ground, Star of David Composed in White Stardust Canes Encircled by a Millefiori Garland, Limited Edition of 300	$110
Paperweight, 2½", Clear Base, 6 Side Windows and 1 Top, Multicolored Toucan on Branch, Limited Edition of 250	$300

Paperweight, 2¾", Crystal Ground with 16 Side View Windows and 1 Top, Multicolored Pair of Budgies on a Eucalyptus Branch, Limited Edition of 175 $550

Paperweight, 2¾", 1998 Holiday Issue, Crystal Ground, 5 Side Windows and 1 Top, Multicolored Boy Pulling Sled in Snow—Winter Scene, Limited Edition of 200 $450

Paperweight, 2⅞", Mill Heart on Red Ground $200

Paperweight, 2⅞", Opal Blue Ground, Multicolored Butterfly within a Millefiori Circle $785

Paperweight, 3", Pattern Mill, Central Cane with Ribbon Twist and Other Canes $125

Paperweight, 3", Multicolored Central Cluster of Canes Encircled by 12 Radiating Twists, Dividing Panels of Millefiori, Limited Edition of 200 $325

Paperweight, Panda, 3", Translucent Blue, Limited Edition (300) $875

Paperweight, 3⅛", 86-Petal Dahlia in Canes $675

Paperweight, 4¼", Crystal Ground with 6 Side View Windows and 1 Top, White and Yellow Flower Blooms on Green Stems, Limited Edition of 150 $1,000

Paperweight, 3¼", Thistles within Stardust Canes $400

Paperweight, 3½", Sea Horse and 2 Fish, Pink Seaweed, Crab, and Shell $350

Paperweight, 3¾", Crystal Globe Filled with 100s of Millefiori Pieces, Signed "Peter McDougall," Limited Edition of 30 $2,500

Perfume Bottle with Glass Swirl Threaded Stopper, Millefiori Base $175

Piedouche, 3½" Tall, Clear Round Base; Blue, White, and Clear Vertically Lined Stem; Multicolored Millefiori Mushroom Top, Limited Edition of 125 $1,250

Shot Glass, 2⅞" Tall, 5-Petal Yellow Lampwork Flower on Translucent Blue Ground $90

Tumbler, Millefiori Base $100

Polish Glass
20th Century–Present

Glass was first made in and around Poland beginning as early as the late 14th century. Early products were practical items like windowpanes and tableware. After the Middle Ages, Polish glass was made in the typical Venetian and Bohemian styles of the day. Beginning in the later 20th century, contemporary Polish styles consist primarily of cased and cut/heavily engraved crystal dinnerware such as goblets, wineglasses, tumblers, bowls, jars, and plates. Look for Polish products in fine gift stores, boutiques, jewelry stores, and by mail order through such companies as Tyrol's and Fifth Avenue Crystal.

Basket, 9" Tall, Crimped Base, Shell Edge, Cut Crystal Lily and Fan Design $42.50

Bowl, 6" Tall, 8" Diameter, Crimped Base, Shell Edge, Cut Crystal Lily and Fan Design $37.50

Bowl, 11" Oval, Vertical Line and Hexagon-Cube Cuts, Crystal with Frosted Panels
$52.50

Bowl, 13½", Emerald Green on Swirled Crystal Base $60

Bowl, Rose, 5" Diameter, Cut Crystal Diamond and Fan Pattern $26

Candy Dish with Cover, 6" Diameter, 6" Tall, Cobalt Blue with Crystal Base and Crystal Ball Finial $35

Centerpiece, Stemmed Bowl, 11¾" Diameter, 9½" Tall, Amber $77.50

Champagne Glass, 7¼" Tall, 2½" Wide Bowl, Crystal with Cut Optic Pattern in Lower Bowl $10

Cornucopia, 11" Long, 9" Tall, Crystal with Engraved Starbursts, Facets, and Thumbprints $85

Creamer, 6" Tall, Pitcher Style with Handle and Lip, Circular Base, Crystal Faceted and Frosted Design (Matches Sugar Below) $27.50

Cross, 7¾" Across, Crystal Christian Symbol on Round Base $35

Decanter with Crystal Ball Stopper, 14" Tall, 6½" Wide, Circular Hole in Center $52.50

Jesus Figurine, 12" Tall, Frosted Sacred Heart Design on Crystal Base $40

Lamp, 13" Tall, 6½" Diameter Circular Base, Brass Accents, Brass Shell Electric Switch, Cut Diamonds and Fluted Circular Base, Large Cut Fans on Lamp $125

Lamp, 29" Tall, Cut Diamonds and Fluted Circular Base, Fluted Stem with Hanging Faceted Prisms, 7½" Diameter Globe with Engraved Floral Design, Crystal Chimney
$315

Mary Figurine, 12" Tall, Frosted Blessed Mother Design on Crystal Base $40

Pitcher, Water, 8½" Tall, 28 oz., Torus Doughnut Hole Blown into Body $37.50

Plate, 10½" Square, Cut Matzo Design $50

Plate, 11", Cut Star of David Design $50

Rabbit Figurine, 4" Long, 2¾" Long, Pink $11

Rabbit Figurine, 5½" Tall, 3" Long, Pink $11

Sherbet, 6" Tall, 4" Diameter Bowl, Teardrop Stem $12

Sugar Dish with Cover, 7" Tall, No Handles, Ball Stopper on Cover, Crystal Faceted and Frosted Design (Matches Creamer Below) $27.50

Vase, Bud, 7" Tall, Tapers Wider at Top, Cut Crystal Diamond Design with Engraved Grape Leaves $32.50

Vase, Bud, 8" Tall, Crystal with Cut Spiral Pinwheel Design $35

Vase, 9" Tall, Crimped Base, Shell Edge, Cut Crystal Lily and Fan Design $37.50

Romanian Glass
20th Century–Present

Modern Romanian glass includes companies that make crystal table and barware that is both cut and occasionally decorated with gold accents, as well as those that make more colorful art glass. The most significant concern of collectors today is the many recent reproductions of Galle art glass. Romanian reproductions contain the famous artisan's signature but tend to be made in much brighter colors than the originals of the later 19th-century Art Nouveau Period. In fact, unless the heritage of the piece can be indisputably traced, any colored glass with a Galle signature is considered by experts and appraisers alike to be a Romanian reproduction (usually worth $50–$100).

Goblet, Water, 7" Tall, 12 oz., Crystal Stem, Various Colored Bowls (Pink, Green, Red, or Blue) with Etched Central Floral Design	$30
Ice Bucket, 8½" Tall, Crystal with 2 Tab Handles, Off-Center Slanted Design	$40
Martini Glass, 4" Tall, 2 oz., Crystal, Globe Base with Cone-Shape Insert	$20
Vase, 8" Tall, Opaque Yellow with Brown Accents, Pouring Pitcher Style with 1 Handle	$75
Vase, 10¼" Tall, Opaque Blue with 2 Applied Green Scrolled Tab Handles at Top	$60
Vase, 11½" Tall, Opaque Green with Brown Accents, Urn Style with 2 Handles	$100
Vase, 13" Tall, Opaque Orangish Red with 2 Brown Handles	$115
Vase, 19" Tall, Opaque Orange with 2 Brown Handles, Urn Style	$125
Wineglass, 6½" Tall, Crystal Stem with Cased Cut Cobalt Blue Grape and Geometric Design	$30
Wineglass, 8" Tall, 8 oz., Crystal Stem, Various Colored Bowls (Pink, Green, Red, or Blue) with Etched Central Floral Design	$30

Russian Glass
20th Century–Present

Glassware has been produced in Russia since the early 11th century. The first operations were forest glasshouses, which were found in heavily wooded or forested areas so that a ready supply of ash was on hand. These glasshouses or huts produced drinking vessels as well as some jewelry and beads. Beginning in the 17th century, two known firms near Moscow, Dukhanino and Izmailovskii, produced practical items (Izmailovskii began in 1668 under Tsar Alexis I). In the 18th century, several state-run glass operations produced a good deal of ornamental and art wares for the royal families—that is, glass that was colored, etched, engraved, relief cut, gilded, and so forth. Tsar Peter the Great established the first St. Petersburg glass firm specifically for the royal family. In the early 19th century, a government decree banned the importation of any foreign glass; as a result, many glass-making companies sprang up throughout the countryside, most near major western cities. Aside from practical wares, some art items were also produced during Europe's art nouveau movement in the later 19th and early 20th centuries, again mostly for the royal family. The products of state-run factories that made glassware from 1917 to 1991 are usually referred to as Soviet glass. In the post-Communist era, many collectible glass products are now produced in Russia, though some are commissioned from other European countries: cut and colored glass eggs in the Faberge style, novelties, and fancy cut, colored, and cased tableware. Guscrystal is Russia's oldest crystal producer still in operation, and several modern firms have sprung up in and around St. Petersburg.

Bowl, 17" Diameter, Cased Cut with Crystal and Various Colors (Emerald Green, Sapphire Blue, or Ruby Red), Guscrystal $200

Centerpiece Raised Bowl, 6½" Tall, 8" Diameter, Cased Cut with Crystal and Various Colors (Amber, Cobalt Blue, or Ruby Red), Guscrystal $100

Champagne Glass, 5 oz., Crystal with Etched Alexandra Pattern, Guscrystal $15

Clown Figurine, 12" Tall, Multicolored Millefiori Body, Chubby Faberge Style $140

Clown Figurine, 14" Tall, Blue and White Horizontally Swirled Body, Red and Black Accents, Sailor Style $150

Clown Figurine, 15" Tall, Thin with Blue and White Horizontally Swirled Body, Red and Amber Accents, Shy Style $140

Cordial Glass, 1 oz., Crystal with Etched Alexandra Pattern, Guscrystal $10

Decanter Set, 10" Tall, Crystal Decanter with Stopper, 6 Matching 3" Tall Shot Glasses, 10½" Diameter Serving Tray, Cut Geometric Pattern, Guscrystal $100

Egg, 2½" Tall, Crystal with Various Etched/Engraved Designs (Coronation, Crown, Leaves, Primrose, Rose Trellis, Songbird, Stars, Swan, or Wreath), Faberge $80

Egg, 2¾" Tall, Cobalt Blue with Cut Crystal Lines and Stars, 24 kt. Gold-Plated Stand, Faberge $100

Egg, 2¾" Tall, Emerald Green with Cut Crystal Leaf Cuts, 22 kt. Gold-Plated Stand, Faberge $100

Egg, 2¾" Tall, Emerald Green with Cut Crystal Primrose Design, 24 kt. Gold-Plated Stand, Faberge $100

Egg, 2¾" Tall, Ruby Red with Cut Crystal Hearts and Diamonds, 24 kt. Gold-Plated Stand, Faberge $100

Egg, 2¾" Tall, Ruby Red with Cut Crystal Lines and Circles, 24 kt. Gold-Plated Stand, Faberge $100

Egg, 2¾" Tall, Yellow with Cut Crystal Coronation Floral Design, 24 kt. Gold-Plated Stand, Faberge $100

Egg, 3" Tall, Various Colors (Cobalt Blue, Emerald Green, or Ruby Red), Engraved Romanov Double Eagle Design Encrusted with 18 kt. Gold, Faberge $110

Egg, 7" Tall, Including Gold-Plated Sterling Stand, Cranberry with Copper Wheel–Engraved Cupid Figurine, Faberge, Limited Edition of 995 $600

Goblet, 10 oz., Crystal with Etched Alexandra Pattern, Guscrystal	$15
Paperweight, Tsar Crystal Block Style, 2" Square, Etched with Monogram of Nicholas II	$35
Paperweight, Rectangular, 2¾" Tall, 1½" Wide, Crystal Block Style, Etched Lighthouse Design	$65
Paperweight, Rectangular, 3" Tall, 2" Wide, Crystal Block Style, Etched with Russian Samovar	$80
Paperweight, 3" Square, Crystal Block Style, Etched with Double-Headed Eagle Imperial Design	$90
Pharmaceutical Bottle, 3" or 4" Tall, Molded Design (5" Tall $25)	$20
Samovar, 14" Tall, Green Glass with Hand-Painted Peasant Scene, Brass Accents	$325
Vase, 8¾" Tall, Crystal, Vertical Beveled Design	$30
Vase, 10⅜" Tall, Cut Crystal Pinwheel and Diamond Design, Separate Bottom Section for Votive Candle	$55
Vase, 12" Tall, 7½" Diameter, Cased Cut Crystal and Colors (Cobalt Blue or Ruby Red), Imperial Thistle Pattern	$400
Vase, 18" Tall, 5½" Diameter, Cased Cut with Crystal and Various Colors (Amethyst, Emerald Green, Sapphire Blue, or Ruby Red)	$300

Sabino Art Glass
France, 1920s–1930s, 1960s–1970s

Marius-Ernest Sabino first made a variety of art-glass items (mostly figurines) in the 1920s. When the art nouveau period in France ended in the 1930s, Sabino halted production. He resurfaced in the 1960s with his own handmade molds and a special formula for a gold-satinized, light creamy blue opalescent glass. Sabino died in 1971 and his family continued export of the glass but were unable to duplicate his original formula.

Bird, Nesting, 2" Long	$90
Bird, Perched, 2" Long	$80
Bird, Wings Down, 2" Tall	$90
Birds Figure, 2 Babies Perched on Branch, 3" Tall	$37.50
Birds Figure, 2 Birds, 3½" Tall, 4½" Across	$250
Birds Figure, 3 Birds, 5" Tall	$275
Birds Figure, 3 Birds Perched on Branch, 5" Across	$300
Birds Figure, 5 Birds Perched on Branch, 8" Across	$1,300
Bowl, 5", Fish Design	$90

Bunny Rabbit, 2" Tall	$70
Butterfly, 2¾" Tall, Small, Wings Open	$60
Butterfly, 6" Tall, Large	$75
Cat, 2" Tall, Sleeping	$50
Cat, 2¼" Tall, Sitting	$55
Cherub, 2" Tall	$50
Chick, Baby, 3¾" Tall, Jumping, Wings Up	$75
Chick, Baby, Drinking, Wings Down	$60
Clock, 6¼" Tall, Opalescent Case, Overlapping Arcs Design	$1900
Collie, 2" Tall	$62.50
Dove, Small, Head Up	$45
Dragonfly, 6" Tall, 5¾" Long	$165
Elephant	$50
Figurine, Isadora Duncan	$800
Figurine, Madonna, Robed, 5" Tall	$150
Figurine, Nude, 6¼" Tall, Kneeling Female with 3 Doves	$335
Figurine, Nude with Long Flowing Hair, 6¾" Tall	$350
Figurine, Semi-Nude, Partially Draped, 7¼" Tall	$450
Figurine, Nude, Suzanne the Dancer, 9" Tall	$3,750
Figurine, Venus de Milo, Large	$100
Fish, 2" Long	$50
Fish, 4" Tall, 4" Long	$100
Fox	$40
Gazelle	$115
German Shepherd, 2" Tall	$50
Hand, Either Left or Right	$260
Hen	$45
Knife Rest, Bee or Fish Design	$45
Knife Rest, Blue Glass, Duck Ends	$55
Mockingbird, Large	$125
Mouse, 3" Long	$67.50

Owl, 4½" Tall	$77.50
Pekingese, 1¼" Tall	$45
Perfume Bottle, 6" Tall, Loosely Draped Figures Around Bottle	$200
Perfume Bottle, 6¼" Tall, Frivolities, Opal Women and Swans Design	$100
Pigeon, 6¼" Tall	$150
Poodle, 1¾" Tall	$45
Rabbit, 1⅞" Long	$45
Rooster, 3½" Tall	$50
Rooster, Large, 7" Tall	$450
Scottish Terrier, 1½" Tall, 4" Long	$125
Snail, 1" Tall, 3" Long	$50
Squirrel, 3½" Tall, Oval Base	$55
Stork, 7¼" Tall	$155
Tray, Shell, Small	$50
Tray, Swallow, Small	$45
Turkey Bookends (2 Turkeys—1 Upright and 1 Sitting on Each Bookend), Pair	$535
Turtle	$42.50
Vase, 5½" Tall, Square, Rectangular Block Design	$400
Vase, 10" Tall, Rectangular Form, Female Nude on Each Side	$2000
Vase, Opal, Colombes Design	$550
Vase, Oval and Pearl Design	$285
Woodpecker	$80
Zebra, 5½" Tall, 5½" Long	$175

St. Louis
France, 1840s–Early 1900s, 1950s–Present

St. Louis (pronounced "Sohn Louwhie") is a famous eastern French glassmaking town that was producing glass as far back as the 16th century (1586). In the 1840s, the Compagnie des Verreries et Crustalleries de St-Louis was noted most for making paperweights, but production halted when the popularity of paperweights severely declined in the early 1870s. The firm, in the Alsace-Lorraine in eastern France, was part of Germany from 1871 to 1918 as well as a partner with rival Baccarat. The marks "Arsal," "Arsale," "D'Argental," and "St. Louis-Munzthal" can all be found upon St. Louis glass from that time, especially cameo-engraved items produced during the art nouveau period (D'Argental is actually the

French name for the German "Munzthal"). The St. Louis factory produced art wares during the art nouveau movement. In 1952, paperweight production was revived, and St. Louis continues today as a major producer of sulphide, lampwork, overlaid, and millefiori paperweights.

Atomizer with Silver-Plated Top, 4" Tall, 3" Diameter, Cranberry Cut on Crystal Cameo, Cut Floral and Scroll Design $285

Bear Cub, 5¼" Tall, Frosted with Clear Ball Base $110

Clarinet-Playing Jazz Figurine, 5¾" Tall, Frosted Man on Crystal Base, Black Clarinet $350

Paperweight, 2⅜", Hollow White Canes (Honeycomb Effect) with Green Interior, Millefiori Center $2,675

Paperweight, 2⅜", 10 Red and Green Spiral Twists Alternating with 10 White Spiral Twists, Blue and White Millefiori Center $625

Paperweight, 2½", 15-Petal Blue Clematis, Red and White Ground $2,175

Paperweight, 2½", Dark Pink Camomile with 4 Green Leaves and 1 Bud $485

Paperweight, 2⅝", Cobalt Blue Large Pansy Design $850

Paperweight, 2⅝", 2 Strawberries with 5 Blossoms $1,875

Paperweight, 2¾", Camomile with 52 Blue Petals, Cane Center $550

Paperweight, 2¾", Double Pink Clematis, Double Swirl on White Lattice Ground $425

Paperweight, 2¾", 45-Petal Dahlia, Star Base, Blue and Amber Cane Stamen $3,875

Paperweight, 2¾", 2 Red and 2 White Turnips in Swirled Basket $1,875

Paperweight, 2⅞", Multicolored Butterfly with Millefiori Wings and Circular Border $2,950

Paperweight, 2⅞", 9-Petaled Red Clematis with 3 Green Leaves, Millefiori Center, Blue and White Jasper Ground $2,250

Paperweight, 2⅞", Marbleized Turquoise and White Swirls $585

Paperweight, 3", Double Clematis Design, Double Swirl on a White Lattice Ground $1,800

Paperweight, 3" Globe, Light Yellow Interlocking Hexagons, View Hole in Top, Black and Yellow Internal Honeybees, Limited Edition of 150 $1,500

Paperweight, 3", Shaded Pink Large Dahlia Blossom $5,500

Paperweight, 3", Red and White Flower Bouquet $685

Paperweight, 3⅛", 3 Apples and 3 Pears in White Lattice Bowl $2,250

Paperweight, 3⅛", Millefiori Mushroom, Green Stem, Blue and White Filigree Base $2,450

Paperweight, 3⅛", 5-Petaled Blue, White, and Red Flowers with Millefiori Centers, Green Leaves $950

Paperweight, Sulphide, 2", King Edward VIII Plaque Design $315

Paperweight, Sulphide, 3", Faceted, Marquis de Lafayette Design $315

Paperweight, Sulphide, Faceted, Pope John Paul II Design $195

Perfume Bottle with Stopper, 6½" Tall, Orange and Brown Floral and Bird Design on Amber $1,575

Saxophone-Playing Jazz Figurine, 5⅞" Tall, Frosted Man on Crystal Base, Yellow Saxophone $350

Seal with Ball, 6" Tall, Frosted with Clear Ball Base and Clear Ball on Seal's Nose $135

Trumpet-Playing Jazz Figurine, 5¾" Tall, Frosted Man on Crystal Base, Yellow Trumpet $350

Vase, 6" Tall, Amethyst on Frosted Ground, Floral and Foliage Design (D'Argental) $535

Vase, 6" Tall, Green on Chartreuse, Morning Glory Design (Arsal) $1,575

Vase, 6" Tall, Blue, Enameled Floral Design (St. Louis) $1,000

Vase, 10" Tall, Cranberry Cut Design with Opalescent Iris Decoration $575

Vase, 10" Tall, Slender Bottle Form, Red and Green on Light Green to Red Shading (D'Argental) $1,875

Vase, 10" Tall, Purple on Yellow, Lilies and Iris Design (Arsal) $2,150

Vase, 11½" Tall, Light Pink with Purple and Green Irises (Arsal) $2,400

Vase, 12" Tall, Brown and Red, Ship Design (D'Argental) $900

Vase, 13" Tall, Elongated Feet, Dark Brown on Green and Rust, Trees and Fence Design (D'Argental) $1,950

Vase, 13¾" Tall, 3¼" Square Base, Cobalt Blue Encased in Crystal $195

Vase, 14" Tall, 3" Square Base, Crystal or Burgundy $200

Vase, 17" Tall, Burgundy on Amber Grapevines Design (D'Argental) $2,650

Wineglass, 8½" Tall, Bell Shape, Cranberry to Clear, Double Teardrop Design (D'Argental) $485

Wineglass, Teardrop Stem, Amethyst to Clear, Cut Hobstar and Fern Pattern (D'Argental) $585

Stevens and Williams
England, 1830s–1930s

William Stevens and Samuel Cox Williams produced glass in the village of Stourbridge, England, located in Britain's most famous glass region. Their factory was named the

Brierly Hill Glassworks, but many of their products are signed "Stevens & Williams." They made several art styles of glass (such as Alexandrite, Engraved Crystal, and Silver Decorating), including an inexpensive method of manufacturing cameo glass up into the 1930s. See additional listings under English Cameo Glass.

Basket, 13½", Amber Footed, Thorn Handle, Draped Leaf Design	$775
Bell, 6½" Tall, Pink and White Overlay	$450
Biscuit Jar with Sterling Silver Cover, 7½" Tall, Ruffled Leaves Design with Pink Lining	$475
Bowl, 3¾", 2½" Tall, Ruffled, Pale Orange	$215
Bowl, 4¾", 3⅛" Tall, Flared, Amber Rim, White with Pink Lining, Applied Amber Leaves and Berries	$225
Bowl, 7½", 6" Tall, Crimped, Amber Rim, Floral Design	$400
Bowl, Rose, 2¾", Blue, Thumbprint Pattern	$240
Bowl, Rose, 3½", Crimped, Opaque White	$185
Bowl, Rose, 4¼", Cranberry	$275
Candlestick, 10" Tall, Moss Agate	$185
Compote, 6", Honeycomb Stem, Engraved Poppies and Pods Design	$265
Cruet with Stopper, 8" Tall, 4" Diameter, Applied Blue Handle, Light Blue with White Crackle Design	$215
Decanter with Stopper, 11" Tall, Footed, Amber with Crystal Trim	$525
Ewer, 5¼" Tall, Amber Branch Handle, Cherry Design	$185
Goblet, 7" Tall, Crystal Foot and Stem, Red Cut Overlay Bowl	$265
Goblet, 8½" Tall, Gold Cut Overlay Floral Design on Green Ground	$300
Lamp, Miniature, 5¼" Tall, Ruffled Rim on Base, Stripe Pattern	$775
Perfume Bottle with Stopper, 4½" Tall, Moss Agate	$165
Perfume Bottle with Stopper, 9" Tall, Green and Crystal Swirl Design	$240
Perfume Bottle, 13" Tall, Swirled, Blue with Gold and Enameled Berries	$400
Pitcher, 5" Tall, Opalescent Cranberry, Hobnail Pattern	$225
Pitcher, 6" Tall, Opalescent Yellow, Vertical Stripes, Reeded Shell Handle	$250
Salt Dip, White Threading, Enameled Berry Design	$185
Toothpick Holder, 3¼" Tall, Cased Green and Crystal, 3-Footed	$200
Vase, 4" Tall, Fluted, Milk White with Pink Lining, Fluted Rim, Applied Red Cherries and Crystal Foliage	$215
Vase, 5" Tall, 3" Diameter, Pink with White Leaves and Engraved Grass	$475

Vase, 5¾" Tall, Amber and Gold, Loop and Berry Design	$325
Vase, 5¾" Tall, 4" Diameter, Dark Pink with Opal Interior and Ruffled Amber Leaves	$215
Vase, 6½" Tall, Opaque Cream with Pink Cherries	$225
Vase, 6½" Tall, 3¾" Diameter, 8-Crimped Rim, Pink with Ruffled Leaves Design	$265
Vase, 7" Tall, Satin, Opal with Multicolored Cased Shadings	$325
Vase, 7½" Tall, Ruffled, Amber Feet, Pink with Apple Leaves	$285
Vase, 8¾" Tall, Silveria Design	$325
Vase, 9¼" Tall, 6½" Diameter, Footed, Opaque Yellow with White Lining, Applied Amber Foliage Design	$275
Vase, 11½" Tall, Ruffled, Amber and Cranberry Floral Design	$465
Vase, 12" Tall, 5" Diameter, Clear Opal Rim and Leaves, Coral with White Interior	$500
Vase, 13" Tall, Pear Shape, Multicolored Floral Design	$375
Vase, 15¼" Tall, Jack-in-the-Pulpit Style, Pink and White	$450

Swarovski and Other Crystal Miniatures

Various Companies, 1976–Present

Crystal miniatures are highly collectible and are made throughout Europe, in Austria, Germany, Sweden, France, Ireland, and other countries. The largest producer is Swarovski of Austria, who introduced the first ones in 1976—Swarovski items all contain the company mark (see appendix 5). A few are made in the United States as well. Most are faceted and animals are the most popular medium, although new unique and larger items are appearing constantly. Colors are used primarily for accents, though a few pieces contain more colored surface area of a color than crystal. Black, red, frosted, metal, and recently introduced gold accents by Swarovski can all be found on crystal miniatures.

Airplane, F-14 Tomcat, 1" Tall, 2⅝" Long	$125
Airplane, F/A-18 Hornet, 1" Tall, 1¾" Long	$105
Airplane, Stealth Fighter, 2" Long	$50
Airplane, 2⅛" Long, 2¼" Wingspan	$135
Anchor, Ship's, 1½" Tall, Gold Chain	$55
Angel, 1⅜" Tall	$175
Angel, 3¾" Tall	$225
Angelfish, 1¾" Long, Frosted Fins	$55
Apple, 1¼" Tall, Rainbow Colors	$55

Swarovski Silver Crystal Miniatures. *Photo by Robin Rainwater.*

Swarovski Miniature Crystal Horse. *Photo by Robin Rainwater.*

Automobile, Antique Roadster, 3¼" Long	$275
Baby Carriage, 2⅛" Tall	$175
Balloon, Hot Air, 1½" Tall, Red Basket	$75
Basket of Violets, 1¼" Tall	$70
Beagle, 1¾" Tall, Sitting Position	$55
Beagle, 1¾" Long, Lying Down, Frosted Tail Up	$55
Bear, 1⅛" Tall, Holding Pink Balloon, Black Eyes and Nose	$45
Bear, 1¼" Tall, Grandma or Grandpa with Spectacles	$65
Bear, 1⅜" Tall, Scuba Diving Bear with Treasure Fish and Swimming Fish	$95

Bear, 1½" Tall, with Captain's Hat and Stern Wheel	$60
Bear, 1½" Tall, Red Heart and "I Love You" Disc	$40
Bear, 1⅝" Tall, with Gold Club, Green Cap, Amethyst Ball, and Red Feet	$85
Bear, 1¾" Tall, with Party Hat, Cake, and Horn	$50
Bear, 1¾" Tall, with Baseball Bat	$75
Bear, 1¾" Tall, with Tennis Racket	$75
Bear, 2⅛" Tall, with Golf Club and Ball	$125
Bears, 2⅜" Tall, 2 at Candlelight Dinner on Circular Base, Moonlighted Window in Background	$150
Beaver, 1¾" Tall, 2 Swarovski Varieties	$90
Beaver, 3" Long	$175
Bee, Bumble, ½" Tall, ⅝" Long	$35
Birthday Cake, 2" Tall, Pedestal Base and Single Candle	$250
Blowfish, 2" Long, Frosted Fins	$65
Blowfish, 3" Long, Frosted Fins	$185
Butterfly, 1" Long, Octagonal Base with Pink Flower	$45
Cable Car or Trolley, 1¼" Long	$50
Cable Car or Trolley, 4" Long	$175
Cactus, ¹⁵⁄₁₆" Tall, in Pot and Flowering	$300
Candle, Christmas, 1½" Tall, Holly Berries on Base	$30
Cannon, 2" Tall, 2⅝" Long, 3" Round Mirror Base, 3 Black Cannonballs	$185
Car, 1⅝" Long, Red Taillights	$62.50
Carousel, 2¼" Tall, 1⅛" Diameter, 2 Horses	$110
Carousel, 2½" Tall, 3 Horses	$165
Carousel Horse, 2½" Tall, 1½" Square Base	$65
Carousel Horse with Bear Holding Balloon, 2⅜" Tall	$100
Castle on Green Base, 1" Tall	$40
Castle with Changing Color Base, 2¼" Tall, Rainbow Stairway on Base	$175
Castle with Changing Color Base, 2½" Tall, Rainbow Stairway on Base	$235
Castle, 3" Tall, Slender, Amber Base, 2" Wide	$75
Castle with Changing Color Base, 4³⁄₁₆" Tall, Camelot	$575
Cat, ⅝" Tall, Siamese Kitten, Black Ears and Feet	$35

Cat, ¾" Tall, 1¾" Long, Crouched	$37.50
Cat, 1" Tall, Kitten with Red Ball	$65
Cat, 1⅜" Tall, Siamese Mother, Black Ears and Feet	$50
Cat, 1¾" Tall, Standing, Black Eyes and Nose	$100
Cat Staring at Fish in Fishbowl, 1¾" Tall	$110
Cat, 2" Tall, Black Eyes and Nose, Metal Tail and Whiskers	$600
Cat, 2⅞" Tall, Black Eyes and Nose, Metal Tail and Whiskers	$200
Cat Sitting in Rocking Chair, 3" Tall	$90
Cats in a Basket, 1" Tall, 2½" Long, 2 Sleeping	$62.50
Cats, 1½" Tall, Mother with Kitten	$75
Cats, 1½" Tall, 1" Across, 2 Kittens Together	$45
Cheetah, 4" Tall, 2 Swarovski Varieties	$350
Chess Set, 32 Pieces with 13½" Square Glass Board	$1,350
Chick, 1" Tall, Chubby, Silver Feet and Beak	$40
Chickens, 1" Tall, Circular Base, 2 Chicks and Red Hearts	$55
Christmas Tree, 2" Tall, with Tiny Kitten and Present	$65
Christmas Tree, 3⅜" Tall, with Tiny Kitten and Present	$95
Christmas Tree with Presents, 6" Tall, 6" Diameter, Colorful Accents, Limited Edition (1,000)	$975
Church, Twin Tower Cathedral, 2¼" Tall	$175
Church, 2¾" Tall, ¾" Square Base, Rainbow Colors	$175
Cocker Spaniel, ½" Tall, Puppy	$20
Cocker Spaniel, ¾" Tall	$25
Cottage, Honeymoon, 1¾" Tall, Multicolored Accents	$135
Crab, 1⅛" Tall, 1½" Long, Claws Up	$55
Crab, Hermit, 1½" Long	$55
Dachshund, 1¼" Long, Black Eyes and Nose, Metal Tail	$200
Dachshund, 2¹⁵⁄₁₆" Long, Black Eyes and Nose, Metal Tail, Several Swarovski Varieties	$200
Dice, Pair (Actual Size), Red or Black Dots	$50
Dog, ⅞" Tall, Puppy, Black Eyes and Nose	$32.50
Dog with Dog House, 1" Tall	$67.50

Doll, 1¼" Tall, Gold Accents	$60
Dolphins, 2¼" Tall, 2 (1 with Ball), Rainbow Base	$47.50
Dolphins, 4¾" Long, Pair on Base	$1500
Dragon, Holding Crystal Ball, 5½" Long	$500
Dragonfly, 1⅝" Long, Thin Silver Thread Bones	$67.50
Dragster, 4" Long, Red Exhaust Vents	$105
Duck, ¾" Long, Black Eyes and Yellow Beak	$32.50
Dumbo, Flying Disney Elephant with Frosted Hat, 2¹³⁄₁₆" Long	$750
Dumbo, Flying Disney Elephant, 2½" Tall, 5 Swarovski Varieties	$4,500
Dumbo, Flying Disney Elephant with Hat, 2⅝" Long	$1,500
Elephant, 3¼" Tall, 4½" Long, Frosted Tusks	$325
Elephant, 4⅜" Long, Frosted Tusk	$1,750
Falcon Head, 4" Tall, 2 Swarovski Varieties	$2,000
Fire Engine, 1½" Long	$85
Fish, Puffer, ¾" Tall, 1⅝" Long	$55
Fox, 2¾" Long, Frosted Nose and Tail	$175
Frog, ½" Tall	$20
Gingerbread House on Square Mirrored Base, 2½" Tall, Multicolored	$185
Harp, 4" Tall	$225
Heart Shape, 1⁷⁄₁₆" Long	$85
Hedgehog, 1½" Long, Black Eyes and Nose, Silver Whiskers	$55
Hedgehog, 2⅛" Long, Black Eyes and Nose	$90
Hedgehog, 2¾" Long, Black Eyes and Nose	$155
Hippopotamus, 1¼" Long, Black Eyes, Red Mouth	$40
Hippopotamus, 2¼" Long, Black Eyes	$125
Horse, Rocking, 2" Tall, 2¼" Long	$75
House, Victorian, 3" Tall, Multicolored Accents	$260
Hummingbird, ⅝" Tall, 1" Long	$55
Ice Cream Sundae, 1" Tall, Multicolored Accents	$45
Jack-in-the-Box, 1⅜" Tall, Multicolored Accents	$55
Juke Box, 2" Tall, 1¾" Wide	$115

Kangaroo with Baby in Pouch, 2 1/16" Long, Black Accents	$100
Kiwi Bird, 1 3/4" Long, Black Eyes, Frosted Beak	$100
Kiwi Bird, 2 1/8" Tall, Black Eyes, Frosted Beak	$175
Knight, 3" Tall, with Shield and Sword	$75
Koala Bear, 1 1/8" Tall, Black Eyes and Nose	$55
Koala Bear, 1 3/4" Tall, Black Eyes and Nose	$85
Koala Bears on Mirrored Base, 1 1/2" Tall, 2 Bears Sharing a Heart	$85
Kudu, Frosted Horns, 3 7/8" Long	$625
Ladybug, 1" Long, Black Accents	$40
Lighthouse, 2 1/2" Tall, Gold Circular Base	$65
Lighthouse with Changing Color Base, 2 1/2" Tall, Rainbow Stairway on Base	$135
Lion, 5" Long, Frosted Tail	$650
Lobster, 3" Long, Gold Feelers	$60
Lute, 3 3/8" Long	$175
Meadowlark, 1 3/8" Tall	$47.50
Mickey Mouse, Disney, 2 1/4" Tall	$750
Moose, 7/8" Tall	$35
Moose, 1" Tall, 1 1/2" Long	$55
Motorcycle, 3" Long, 2" Tall	$215
Mouse, 1/2" Long	$150
Mouse, 1 11/16" Tall, Black Eyes and Nose, Metal Tail and Whiskers	$50
Mouse, 1 3/4" Tall, Grandpa or Grandma on Rocking Chairs	$75
Mouse, 2 7/8" Tall, Black Eyes and Nose, Metal Tail and Whiskers, 2 Swarovski Varieties	$1,000
Mouse, 3 3/4" Tall, Black Eyes and Nose, Metal Tail and Whiskers	$1,750
Movie Camera, 2 3/4" Tall, Gold Accents	$60
Octopus, 1 1/2" Wide	$30
Octopus, 2 1/2" Wide	$50
Otter, 1 1/2" Tall, 1 1/4" Long	$57.50
Owl, 1" Tall	$22.50
Owl, 1 15/16" Tall, Frosted Face	$125

Owl, 2⅝" Tall, Frosted Face	$150
Owl, 6½" Tall, Frosted Face	$2,000
Panda Bear, ¾" Tall, Black Ears, Arms, and Legs	$30
Paperweight, 1½" Diameter, Swarovski Logo	$125
Paperweight, 1½" Diameter, Swarovski Austria Tour	$475
Pegasus (Winged Horse), 6" Long	$500
Penguin, 1¼" Tall	$45
Penguin, 1½" Tall	$50
Penguin, 3⅜" Tall	$150
Petrol Train Wagon, 1⅝" Long	$100
Piano, Grand with Stool, 2 9/16" Tall	$275
Pig, ⅞" Tall, Black Eyes and Pink Nose	$32.50
Pig, 2" Long, Several Swarovski Varieties	$55
Pig, 3" Long	$450
Pigs in Race Car, 1¼" Tall, 2½" Long, 2 Pigs	$85
Pineapple, 1¼" Tall, Gold Top	$45
Pineapple, 2¼" Tall, Gold Top	$65
Pineapple, 3" Tall, Gold Top	$115
Polar Bear, 3½" Long, Black Eyes and Nose	$250
Rabbit, ½" Tall, ¾" Long, Lop-Eared	$22.50
Rabbit with Pool Table, Cue Stick, and Balls, 1⅛" Tall	$87.50
Rabbit, 1½" Tall, Skiing	$60
Rabbit in Basket, 2" Tall, Red Bow and Base	$45
Rabbits, 1" Tall, 2" Across, 2 Bunnies Sharing a Heart	$55
Rabbits on Beach Under Palm Tree, 1⅞" Tall	$125
Raccoon, 1" Tall, Black Eyes, Nose, and Tail	$42.50
Radio, Vintage Style, 1" Tall, Gold Accents	$40
Red Wagon (Flyer) with Bunnies, 1½" Long	$85
Rhinoceros, 2⅜" Long, Black Eyes, Frosted Horns	$150
Rhinoceros, 2⅞" Long, Black Eyes, Frosted Horns	$175
Rocking Horse, 2¾" Tall, Black Accents	$150

Rooster, 1⅞" Tall, Red Accents	$75
Rooster, 1¹⁵⁄₁₆" Tall, Frosted Crown	$75
Sail Boat, 1⅛" Tall, 1" Square Base	$35
Santa Maria Ship, 4⅝" Long	$425
Saxophone, 4¼" Tall, Small Metal Stand	$150
Scorpion, 2¾" Long, Tail Up	$77.50
Seal, Baby, ½" Tall, ¾" Long, Silver Whiskers	$17.50
Seal, 3½" Long, Black Accents, Silver Whiskers, Several Swarovski Varieties	$175
Seals, Pair on Base, 4" Long	$650
Sheep, 1¼" Tall, Black Legs and Face	$45
Shell with Faux Pearl, 1" Tall, 1" Long	$42.50
Shell with Faux Pearl, 2" Long	$105
Shell with Faux Pearl, 2½" Long	$175
Ship, Cruise, 2¼" Long, 1" Tall	$115
Sleigh, 4¼" Long	$350
Slot Machine, 1¾" Tall, Gold and Red Accents	$135
Slot Machine, 2¼" Tall, Gold and Red Accents, Black Ball on Handle	$185
Snail, ¾" Tall	$15
Snail, 1" Tall	$17.50
Snail, 1½" Long, Frosted Head, Black Accents	$100
Snowman on Skis, 1⅛" Tall, Red Scarf	$47.50
Space Shuttle on Green Globe Base, 3" Tall	$450
Squirrel, 1½" Tall, Black Eyes, Holding Acorn	$45
Squirrel, 2¾" Tall, Frosted Tail	$175
Starship *Enterprise*, Star Trek, Red and Yellow Accents	$200
Stork, 3" Tall, with Baby in Beak	$75
Sundae Glass with Multicolored Ice Cream Scoops, 2" Tall	$45
Swan, ¾" Tall, 1" Long	$40
Swan, 1½" Tall, 1½" Long, Several Swarovski Signature Varieties	$85
Swan, 6½" Tall	$5,000
Taj Mahal, 4½" Tall, 4" Square, Limited Edition (2000)	$875

Tank, M-1A, 1⅜" Tall, 2¼" Long	$95
Telephone, ¾" Tall, Red or Black Buttons	$47.50
Tender Train Call, 1¼" Long	$75
Train Engine, ¾" Tall, 1¼" Long	$47.50
Train Engine, 1¼" Tall, 2" Long	$115
Train Engine, 2½" Long	$165
Tunnel of Love Sculpture, 2 Doves on Boat in Arch, 2" Tall, 2" Wide	$150
Turkey, 1⅝" Long	$70
Turtle, 1⅛" Long	$17.50
Turtle, 2¼" Long, Black Eyes	$75
Turtle, 3" Long, Black Eyes	$100
Turtle, 9½" Long, Black Eyes	$7,500
Turtledoves, Pair on Base, 3½" Long	$1,250
Tweety Bird Sculpture, 2⅜" Tall (Looney Tunes)	$165
Unicorn, 4⅜" Long	$650
Vase, 2" Tall, 6 Red Roses with Green Stems	$65
Violin with Bow and Stand, 4¼" Long	$175
Whale, 3¼" Long	$250
Whales, Mother and Baby on Base, 4⅛" Long	$625
Wishing Well with Bucket of Flowers, 2" Tall	$67.50
Woodpeckers, 2 on Tree, 4⅛" Tall	$2250
Yosemite Sam on Wooden Base, 3½" Tall (Looney Tunes)	$165

Swedish Glass
20th Century

One of the oldest Swedish glass firms noted for high-quality glass products established in 1742 was the Kosta Company. Much of their contemporary art forms of the early to mid-20th century are highly collectible (see Kosta Boda earlier in this chapter). Most of the other glass firms in Sweden can trace their roots to Kosta. The Eda Glassworks in the Varmland region produced some glass, including carnival items (including all those listed below) in the early 20th century. Other Swedish firms experimented later with crystal art forms and engraving; the Orrefors Glasbruck (established 1898 in Smaland) is noted for engraving, particularly for their spectacular Graal line, and Mats Jonasson is a contemporary designer of crystal animal sculptures. Both are listed separately earlier in this chapter.

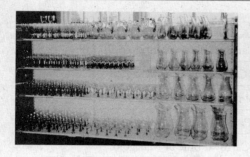

Kosta-Boda of Sweden. *Photo by Mark Pickvet.*

Nybro Glass (Sweden). *Photo by Mark Pickvet.*

Maleras of Sweden. Mats Jonasson Engraved Crystal Ice Sculptures. *Photo by Mark Pickvet.*

Bird Figurine, 3" Tall, Ruby Red, Early 1980s	$25
Bowl, Berry, 5", Grand Thistle Pattern, Marigold Carnival	$30
Bowl, Berry, 5", Grand Thistle Pattern, Green, Purple, or Smoke Carnival	$50
Bowl, 6", Rose Garden Pattern, Carnival Colors	$110
Bowl, 8¼", Rose Garden Pattern, Carnival Colors	$95
Bowl, 9½", Oval, Boat Shape, Crystal, Mottled Upper Rim, Nybro	$50
Bowl, 10", Cathedral or Curved Star Pattern, Carnival Blue or Marigold	$85
Bowl, Rose, Rose Garden Pattern, Carnival Colors	$875
Butter Dish with Cover, Cathedral or Curved Star Pattern, Carnival Blue or Marigold	$275

Butter Dish, Rose Garden Pattern, Carnival Colors	$475
Chalice, Cathedral or Curved Star Pattern, Carnival Blue or Marigold, 7" Tall	$200
Compote, Cathedral or Curved Star Pattern, Carnival Blue or Marigold	$75
Compote, 474 Pattern Variant, Carnival Green	$125
Creamer, Footed, Cathedral or Curved Star Pattern, Carnival Blue or Marigold	$100
Epergne, Cathedral or Curved Star Pattern, Carnival Blue or Marigold	$350
Golfer Ice Sculpture, 6" Tall, Golfer Swinging, Nybro	$100
Pitcher, Water, Cathedral or Curved Star Pattern, Carnival Blue or Marigold	$3,150
Pitcher, Water, Grand Thistle Pattern, Blue Carnival	$2,850
Pitcher, Water, Rose Garden Pattern, Carnival Colors	$875
Plate, 8", Crystal with Copper Wheel–Engraved Head of Greek Goddess Helena, 1940s	$650
Platter, Oval, 14½" x 8¼", Engraved Fishing Boat, Nybro	$125
Sugar, Footed, Cathedral or Curved Star Pattern, Carnival Blue or Marigold	$100
Tumbler, Grand Thistle Pattern, Blue Carnival	$675
Tumbler, Cathedral or Curved Star Pattern, Carnival Blue or Marigold	$475
Vase, 6¾" Tall, Cylindrical, Blue and Amber Gondolier	$2,150
Vase, 9" Tall, Rose Garden Pattern, Carnival Colors	$375
Vase, Crystal with Separate Base, Copper Wheel–Engraved Egyptian Dancer, 1940s	$785
Vase, Cathedral or Curved Star Pattern, Carnival Blue or Marigold, 9½" Tall	$275
Vase, Letter, Rose Garden Pattern, Carnival Colors	$325
Vase, Seagull Design, Carnival Marigold	$1,150

Val St. Lambert
Belgium, 1822–Present

The original Val St. Lambert company was established by Francois Kemlin and Auguste Lelievre in 1822. The firm followed the French in the art nouveau movement in the later 19th century. They produced cameo glass as well as glass styled similar to that of Lalique. Though their quality has always been outstanding, they have never achieved the reputation of their French counterparts; hence, their products sell for less in sales and auctions today. The firm is still in operation today and is Belgium's most noteworthy producer of cased crystal and colored art-glass styles.

Bowl, 6", Blue Rim, Crystal Overlay, Engraved Design, Signed	$185
Bowl, 8", Scalloped, Applied Teardrops	$235

Val St. Lambert Vases. *Photo by Mark Pickvet.*

Val St. Lambert. *Photo by Mark Pickvet.*

Bowl, 12", Cranberry to Crystal Shading	$425
Bowl, 12", Green with Applied Crystal Handle	$275
Bowl, 15¾", Cut Crystal, Various Cased Colors (Cobalt Blue, Emerald Green, or Ruby Red)	$325
Bowl, Rose, 10", Cut Crystal, Cased Cobalt Blue	$250
Box with Cover, 4" Diameter, 3¾" Tall, Opaque Blue with Opalescent Basket-Weave Pattern, Ring Finial	$125
Candlestick, 6¼" Tall, Crystal Elysee Design	$105
Candlestick, 11" Tall, Crystal Elysee Design	$135
Candlestick, 11" Tall, 4-Footed, Bird Design	$90
Cat, Kitten Figurine, 3¾" Long	$65
Cat Figurine, 3¾" Long	$80
Cat Figurine, 6¾" Long	$125
Coaster, 3¼" Diameter, Engraved Signs of the Zodiac, 12 Styles (Price Is for Each)	$20
Compote, 3½", Applied Loop Handles, Flared Foot, Amberina with a Ruby Red Rim	$225
Decanter with Stopper, 15¼" Tall, Cut Crystal, Cased Light Green	$250
Decanter with Stopper, 16⅜" Tall, Cranberry on Frosted Crystal Cameo, Floral and Foliage Design	$1,350
Decanter with Stopper, 16⅞" Tall, Cut Crystal, Cased Ruby Red	$300
Ewer, 14" Tall, Red on Crystal Cameo, Wildflower and Foliage Design	$1,250

Goblet, Water, 7½" Tall, Engraved Crystal with Wide Gilded Band at Top—Grapes and Foliage	$50
Hand Shape, 3⅛" Long, Solid Crystal (Cobalt Blue $80)	$60
Heart Shape, Solid Crystal, 3¼" Across (Emerald Green $85)	$65
Knife Rest, 4½" Long, Amber, 1963	$105
Koala Figurine, 2¼" Tall	$65
Owl Figurine, 2¼" Tall	$65
Perfume Bottle with Stopper, 5" Tall, Embossed Frosted Blue Design	$115
Perfume Bottle with Stopper, 5¼" Tall, Cranberry to Crystal, Signed	$275
Puff Box with Cover, Opalescent Blue	$135
Rabbit Figurine, 2¼" Long, Crystal	$65
Rabbit Figurine, 4" Long, Crystal	$85
Rabbit Figurine, 6½" Long, Crystal	$125
Tumble-Up, Cameo Cranberry, Signed (Includes Tumbler and Matching Underplate)	$900
Tumbler, 5½" Tall, Translucent Pink, Signed	$115
Vase, 5¾" Tall, Multicolored Enamel Coloring on Cameo Olive Green Base	$875
Vase, 6" Tall, Ruby Red on Crystal Cameo, Leaf and Foliage Design	$375
Vase, 6" Tall, Green, Sweet Gum Leaves and Balls Design	$415
Vase, 6" Tall, Multicolored on Opal Gray Cameo, Sailboat Design	$1,450
Vase, 7" Tall, 3 Notches on Collar, Crystal	$185
Vase, 7" Tall, 3" Diameter, Notched Collar, Light Green on Frost Cameo, Floral Design	$850
Vase, 7¾" Tall, Gray with Scrolled Foliage Bands	$400
Vase, 8" Tall, Cameo Cranberry	$675
Vase, 8¼" Tall, Cut Crystal, Cased Ruby Red	$225
Vase, 9" Tall, Ovoid Shape, Amber with Embossed Acanthus Leaves	$285
Vase, 9" Tall, Red Floral Design on Yellow Cameo	$975
Vase, 10" Tall, Double Gourd Shape, Lavender Floral Design	$675
Vase, 10" Tall, Lavender on Frosted Crystal Cameo, Wildflower and Foliage Design, Signed	$1,350
Vase, 10½" Tall, Red Floral and Branch Cameo Design on White	$1,450
Vase, 12" Tall, Cut Crystal, Cased Cobalt Blue	$350

Vase, 12½" Tall, Purple on Frosted Crystal Cameo, Foliage Design	$950
Vase, 15" Tall, Cut Crystal, Cased Emerald Green	$375
Vase, 15¾" Tall, Cut Crystal, Cased Ruby Red	$400
Vase, 16½" Tall, Cameo with Multicolored Enameled Floral Design	$1,050
Vase, 17½" Tall, Silver, Green, and Yellow Cameo Floral Design on Cream Base	$1,750

Vallerysthal Glass
France, 1830s–Present

The original name of this company comes from Val De Vallery, a Frenchman who purchased an existing factory in Lorraine, France. The firm survived the German annexation of the Alsace-Lorraine region in 1870 and then merged with the Portieux Glassworks in 1872. The firm followed the trends of the art nouveau movement, producing art styles including cameo-engraved glass. Beginning in 1899, the company produced many covered animal dishes. Vallerysthal shut down during World War II, but the factory itself survived and remained in operation until 1977. In 1986, a new firm named Cristallerie de Vallerysthal opened and continues in operation today, producing novelty items, tableware, and reproductions from some of the original molds.

Box with Cover, 4" Tall, 3½" Diameter, Light Opaque Blue	$100
Cow Covered Dish, Crystal, Early 1900s	$125
Dog Covered Dish, Dog on Rug, Amber, Early 1900s	$150
Fish Covered Dish, Milk Glass, Early 1900s	$125
Goblet, 6¼" Tall, Light Opaque Blue	$75
Hen Covered Salt Dish, Opalescent White	$75
Plate, 6", Green, Thistle Pattern	$75
Plate, 8", Light Opaque Blue with Enameled Floral Design	$65
Rabbit Covered Dish, Clear and Frosted Design, 1899	$100
Squirrel Covered Dish, Light Opaque Blue, Early 1900s	$115
Swan Covered Dish, Light Opaque Blue, Early 1900s	$115
Tumbler, 4½" Tall, Light Opaque Blue	$50
Turtle Butter Dish with Cover, Snail Finial, Milk Glass	$125
Vase, 6" Tall, Pink on Crystal Cameo-Engraved Leaf Pattern	$1,000
Vase, 7¾" Tall, Green on Red Cameo-Engraved, Red and Green Berry and Branch Design	$425
Vase, 13¾" Tall, Footed, Red on Amber Cameo-engraved, Branch and Berry Design, Gilded Trim	$2,500

Venetian Glass
Venice, Italy, 11th Century–Present

Original Venetian-style glass is usually characterized by millefiori and other colorful designs on very fragile or thin soda- or lime-based glass. For centuries the Venetians dominated the world in glass products, particularly clear glass objects such as mirrors and tableware. The items priced below are mostly from the late 18th century to the present; older items do not surface often (most surviving works are in museums or permanent private collections). Newer items are also thicker than the thin cristallo of old. Venetian glass is still made on the Island of Murano near Venice today, using many of the same designs and techniques employed for centuries. Note some of the neat encased fish/sea/aquarium sculptures and novelty items of late. Beware that modern Venetian items vary widely in quality from poorly finished, unsigned, pale-colored objects, to those in the same style that may be signed, highly polished, and with deep, rich coloring (it pays to visit the many different shops on Murano to compare). See also the Millefiori and Venini sections for additional listings.

Aquarium, Heart-Shape Paperweight, 3½" Across, Crystal with Multicolored Encased Tropical Fish and Plants	$100
Aquarium Sculpture, 4½" Tall, 4½" Wide, Crystal with Multicolored Encased Tropical Fish and Plants	$175
Aquarium Sculpture, 5¼" Tall, 6" Wide, Crystal with Multicolored Encased Tropical Fish and Plants	$200
Aquarium Sculpture, 5⅜" Tall, 5¼" Wide, Crystal Fishbowl Shape with Multicolored Encased Tropical Fish and Plants	$225
Aquarium Sculpture, 5½" Tall, 5" Diameter, Crystal with Multicolored Tropical Fish and Plants Encased in Bowl, Transparent Sapphire Rim	$215
Aquarium Sculpture, 6" Globe Diameter, Transparent Blue with Multicolored Encased Tropical Fish and Plants	$235
Aquarium Sculpture, 7" Tall, 6" Wide, Crystal with Multicolored Encased Tropical Fish and Plants	$225
Basket, 5" Tall, Ruby Red with Crystal Base, Rim and Handle	$155
Bird Figurine, 3½" Tall, Latticino Design, Gold-Flecked Beak	$80
Bird Figurine, 8" Tall, Crystal Pedestal Base, Blue and White Design	$65
Birds, Figural Pair, 10" Tall, Ruby Red to Clear Shading	$185
Bird Figurine, 11½" Tall, Blue and Crystal with Gold Flecking, Crystal Base, 2 Styles	$100
Bird Figurine, 15" Tall, Green with Gold Flecks	$100
Birds in Tree Sculpture, 20 Birds in Large Tree, 20" Tall	$250

Murano Aquarium Sculptures, Venetian Glass.
Photo by Mark Pickvet.

Venetian Glass Candy. *Photo by Robin Rainwater.*

Bottle, Water, 9" Tall, Cranberry, Enameled Decoration	$155
Bowl, 6½", Green and Gold Ribbons with Latticino Bands, Flower Finial	$235
Bowl, 7", Red and White Stripes	$185
Bowl, 9" Oval, 3¾" Tall, Cranberry with Opalescent Ribbing	$200
Bowl, 17½", Scalloped, Light to Dark Blue Shading with Gold Swirls	$275
Candleholder, 6" Tall, Ovoid Design, Seated Female Figure	$925
Candlestick, 5" Tall, Dolphin Stem, Gold Flecks with Berry Prunts	$40
Candlestick, 5¾" Tall, Ruby Red Bowl, Holder and Circular Base, Crystal Stem with Grape Bunch	$105
Candlestick, 10½" Tall, Crystal Angel Shape, Amber Halo	$57.50
Candlestick, 12" Tall, Crystal with Gold Dust	$155
Cat Sculpture, 5½" Tall, Crystal Cat with Blue Tail, 1 Encased Fish, Blue Accents	$125
Cat Sculpture, 6" Tall, Crystal Cat with Blue Tail, 2 Encased Fish, Blue Accents	$135
Cat Sculpture, 8½" Tall, Ultramarine Cat with Encased Fish, Crystal Accents	$140
Clown Figurine, 5" Tall, Multicolore Millefiori Body with Multicolored Accents (Baby)	$80
Clown Figurine, 7⅞" Tall, Red Tomato-Shape Body, Multicolor Accents	$100
Clown Figurine, 8" Tall, Blue, White, and Yellow Vertical Striped Body, Multicolor Accents	$90
Clown Figurine, 9" Tall, Pastel Pink, White, and Green Vertical Striped Body, Multicolor Accents (Mother)	$125

Clown Figurine, 9½" Tall, Green and White Horizontal Striped Body, Multicolor Accents $100

Clown Figurine, 10" Tall, Green and Yellow Squash-Shape Body, Multicolor Accents $100

Clown Figurine, 10" Tall, Pastel Blue, White, and Yellow Vertical Striped Body, Multicolor Accents (Father) $155

Cockatoo Figurine, 12½" Tall, 5" Wide, Crystal with White Latticino, Gold Crests and Perches $125

Cockatoo Figurine, 15½" Tall, 5½" Wide, Green and Crystal with Gold Dust, Black Beak $175

Compote, 6" Tall, Green with White and Gold Decorations $185

Creamer, 4" Tall, Pitcher Style, Red Clover Design $415

Decanter with Stopper, 13" Tall, Silver Speckled Amber with Star Canes $465

Decanter with Stopper, 18" Tall, Ruby Red with Heavy Gold Gilding, Gilded Foot, Handle and Stopper $335

Decanter with Cone-Shape Stopper, 20" Tall, Multicolored Vertical Bands $400

Dresser Tray, 16" x 10" Rectangular, Frosted, Brass Mounts $200

Dolphin Figurine, 8" Long, 4½" Tall, Ultramarine, Child $50

Dolphin Figurine, 12" Long, 7½" Tall, Ultramarine, Mother $110

Dove Figurine, 6" Long, 3½" Tall, Pink and White with Gold Dust, 2 Styles $80

Duck Figurine, 12" Tall, Pink with Gold Decorations $85

Duck Figurine, 15" Tall, Green to Crystal Shading $165

Egg, 3" Tall, Crystal with Blue and White Floral Blossoms on Green Stems $50

Elephant Figurine, 7" Tall, Blue, Yellow, and Orange Design $55

Elephant Figurine, 8" Tall, Ultramarine with Gold Dust $95

Elephant Figurine, 8" Tall, White with Gold Decoration $75

Elephant Figurine, 10" Tall, Turquoise $65

Epergne, 15½" Tall, Bowl with 3 Vases, Ruby Red with Applied Crystal Accents $535

Figurine, Sea Nymph Riding on a Wave, 10" Tall, Crystal with Gold Decorations $385

Fish-in-a-Bag Figurine, 2½" Tall, 1 Orange Goldfish Encased in Crystal Bag $25

Fish-in-a-Bag Figurine, 3" Tall, 3 Orange Goldfish Encased in Crystal Bag, Applied Blue Ribbon $50

Fish-in-a-Bag Figurine, 4" Tall, 1 Orange Goldfish Encased in Crystal Bag, Applied Blue Ribbon $80

Fish-in-a-Bag Figurine, 5½" Tall, Orange Goldfish Encased in Crystal Bag, Applied Blue Ribbon $100

Fish Figurine, Balloon Style, 6" Tall, 10" Long, Blue or Green, Crystal Fins with Gold Leafing $100

Fish Figurine, 9¾" Tall, Ruby Red with Gold-Flecked Fins $145

Fish Figurine, 13" Tall, Blue with Crystal Base $85

Fish Figurine, 15" Long, Sailfish, Yellow and Orange on a White Base $95

Flask with Ruby Red Stopper, 11½" Tall, Crystal with Enameled Red and Green Floral Decoration $65

Frog Figurine, 4" Tall, 4½" Long, Green with Gold Accents $100

Goblet, Water, 9" Tall, Ruby Red Bowl and Base, Crystal Dolphin Stem with Gold Flecks $215

Goblet, Water, 9" Tall, Tall Stem, White and Red Latticino Design $235

Heart Paperweight, 3½" Across, 1" Tall, Multicolored Fish, Coral, and Seaweed Design $85

Horse Figurine, 4" Long, Blue $45

Horse Figurine, 10" Long, Blue $60

Lamp, 8" Tall, Miniature, Millefiori Mushroom-Style Shade and Base $435

Lamp, 20" Tall, 11" Millefiori Mushroom Shade with Matching Base $485

Lamp, 20" Tall, 4-Arm Stand, 11" Swirled Silver, Gold, and Silver Shade $500

Oriental Figurine, 5½" Tall, Kneeling Female, Transparent Blue and Crystal Body, Black Hat $80

Oriental Figurine, 7½" Tall, Standing Male, Transparent Blue and Crystal Body, Black Hat $80

Owl Figurine, 7" Tall, Multicolored with Millefiori Eyes and Iridescent Silver Leaf $125

Paperweight, Car Shape, 1½" Tall, 5½" Long; Amethyst, Blue, Cobalt Blue, Emerald Green, or Yellow $35

Paperweight, Pear Shape, Pale Yellow Glass with Hollow Red Center, Green Stem and Leaf, Air Bubble Pattern $235

Peacock Figurine, 17⅓" Tall, 6½" Wide, Green, Orange, and Crystal with Gold Dust $250

Pelican Sculpture, 9" Tall, Ultramarine and Crystal with Encased Tropical Fish in Beak (Pouch) $175

Pelican Sculpture, 10½" Tall, Transparent Blue, Round Crystal Base and Crystal Accents, Tropical Fish Encased in Crystal Beak (Pouch) $200

Pelican Sculpture, 14½" Tall, Crystal Footed Base, Crystal to Bright Sapphire Blue Body, Orange Goldfish Encased in Crystal Beak (Pelican's Pouch) $300

Penguin Figurine, 5" Tall, Black, White and Crystal $65

Penguin Figurine, 8" Tall, Black, White and Crystal $85

Penguin Figurine, 10" Tall, Black, White and Crystal $100

Penguin Sculpture, 8" Tall, 5½" Wide, Crystal with Encased Goldfish, Black Beak and Feet $150

Penguin Sculpture, 11¼" Tall, 7" Wide, Crystal with Encased Fish, Red, Blue, and Green Accents $225

Perfume Bottle with Ruby Red Stopper, 3¼" Tall, Crystal with Enameled Red and Green Floral Design $55

Pheasant Figurine, 15½" Long, Crystal with Blue Decorations $165

Pitcher, Syrup, 5½" Tall, Crystal with Multicolored Threading $375

Pitcher, Water, 10½" Tall, 42 oz., Crystal with Alternating Colored Strips and Gold, Applied Handle $150

Plate, Boomerang Shape, 10" Long, Yellow with Internal Slices of Murrhine $105

Ram Figurine, 8" Long, Blue $55

Rooster Figurine, 9¾" Tall, Standing Position, Amber with Gold Dust $155

Rooster Figurine, 13½" Tall, Resting Position on Base, Multicolored Design, Limited Edition of 500 $350

Squirrel Figurine, 11" Long, Crystal with Multicolored Decorations $115

Swan Figurine, 4½" Long, Ruby Red with Gold Flecked Wings, Inverted Thumbprint Pattern $110

Swan Figurine Dish, 7½" Long, Ruby Red with Crystal Wings and Accents $60

Tumbler, Water, 4" Tall, Millefiori Purple Shades $115

Turtle Figurine, 5¾" Long, Green Shell, Crystal Head, Tail, and Feet, Gold Dust $80

Unicorn Bust, 10" Tall, Crystal with Gold Dust $150

Vase, 6" Tall, Multicolored Spatter on Ruby Red $62.50

Vase, 7" Tall, Black with Green Looping and Gold Decorations, Signed $750

Vase, 8" Tall, Handled, Red and White Floral Design $260

Vase, 8" Tall, Millefiori Floral and Net Design $750

Vase, 8" Tall, Blue with Red Lines and Millefiori Floral Design $725

Vase, 8" Tall, Handled, Millefiori Vertical Bands $425

Vase, 8½" Tall, Cornucopia Style with Circular Base, Ruby Red with Applied Crystal Flowers	$175
Vase, 9" Tall, 7½" Wide, Multicolored Aquarium with 4 Fish and Kelp, Ultramarine Transparent Ground	$300
Vase, 11" Tall, 5" Diameter, Moth-Blown, Edelweiss Green with Etched Dark Green and White Birch Forest Design	$325
Vase, 12" Tall, Paneled, Crystal with Amber and Brown Lining	$300
Vase, 12" Tall, Scalloped, Inverted Ribbing on Neck, Ruby Red	$215
Vase, 12" Tall, Ruby Red with Applied Crystal Swan Handle	$215
Wineglass, 4" Tall, Clear with Encrusted Gold Band	$135
Wineglass, 6½" Tall, Ruby Red with Heavy Gold Gilding, Gilded Foot	$65
Wineglass, 6" Tall, Sea Serpent–Shape Stem	$57.50

Venini Art Glass
Murano, Italy, 1921–Present

Contemporary art glass is still being made on the famous island of Murano using ancient methods combined with modern technology. Most items listed below are signed "Venini" or "Venini Murano" or even "Murano Made in Italy." Venini (named after Paulo Venini, who first established a glass factory in 1921 and died in 1959) is one of the most recognizable names in the modern Venetian glass world.

Bell, 5" Tall, Alternating Pink and White Filigree Swirls	$80
Bird Figurine, 12" Tall, Transparent Iridescent, Signed "Murano Made in Italy"	$1,650
Bottle with Mushroom-Shape Stopper, 5¼" Tall, Crystal Cased in Ruby Red	$650
Bottle with White Stopper, 13" Tall, White Lower Half, Olive Green Upper Half	$550
Bowl, 4½", Alternating White and Turquoise Filigree Swirls	$375
Bowl, 5½", Squared, Light Blue with Bubbles and Gold Decorations, Signed "Venini Murano Made in Italy"	$525
Bowl, 7¾", 3½" Tall, Moss Green with Bubbles	$135
Bowl, 10", Crystal with Colored (Amethyst, Gold, and White) Spiral Stripes	$185
Bowl, 16½" Oval, Iridescent Green, Stamped "Venini Murano—Made in Italy"	$475
Bowl, 21", Flared, Ruffled Sides, Crystal and Opaque White, Engraved "Venini Italia"	$635
Candlestick, 15½" Tall, Domed Circular Foot, Pale Smoke Color	$375
Candy Dish, 2¼" Tall, 5" Diameter, Light Green and White Ribbon Design	$185

Candy Dish with Cover, 6" Tall, Frosted, Pinecone Pattern	$100
Decanter with Stopper, 8" Tall, Clear Cased Amber with Incised Surface	$1,350
Decanter with Stopper, 14" Tall, Clear Cased Amber with Incised Surface	$1,850
Decanter, Clown Figurine Design, 14" Tall, Multicolored Body with Cobalt Blue Hat and Tie	$375
Hourglass, 7" Tall, Blue and Green, Signed	$675
Musician Figurine with Gown and Headpiece, 9" Tall	$425
Perfume Bottle with Stopper, 6" Tall, Alternating Scarlet and Teal Stripes	$775
Toothpick Holder, 3" Tall, Multicolored Design	$100
Vase, Handkerchief, 3¾" Tall, Pink and White Latticino Design	$335
Vase, 4" Tall, 6" Diameter, Egg Form, 2 Rim Openings, Cameo, 3 Color Layers	$5,650
Vase, Handkerchief, 5¾" Tall, Crystal with Blue and White Latticino Design	$375
Vase, Handkerchief, 6" Tall, White Cased in Crystal	$425
Vase, 7" Tall, Spherical, Green, Signed "Venini—Italia"	$500
Vase, Handkerchief, 8" Tall, White with Yellow Interior	$675
Vase, 8½" Tall, Black Circular Base, Alternating Black and Yellow Laced Stripes	$1,050
Vase, Handkerchief, 9" Tall, Tan Cased to White	$725
Vase, Bottle, 10" Tall, Dark Green with Red and White Band	$1,350
Vase, 10½" Tall, Double-Neck Design, Opaque Blue with Multicolored Peacock Design	$1,050
Vase, 11" Tall, Handkerchief, Flared, Iridescent Pink	$2,150
Vase, 12" Tall, Crystal with Amber and Tan Interior and 2 Holes That Completely Pass Through Body	$1,050
Vase, 14" Tall, Cylindrical, Red and Blue Swirled Stripes Design	$625
Vase, 15½" Tall, Dark Pink Cased Cylindrical Body with Gray and Purple Lining, Signed "Venini Murano Italia"	$2,500
Vase, 17" Tall, Bulbous, Flared Rim, Pale Amethyst	$1,875
Vase, 24" Tall, Classic Form, Crystal Cased to White	$775

Verlys Art Glass
French Holoplane Company and the A. H. Heisey Company of America, 1932–1951

Verlys was established in 1932 as an art-glass branch of the French Holoplane Company in France. The Heisey Glass Company of Newark, Ohio, obtained the rights and formulas for Verlys and produced similar, but somewhat cheaper products from 1935 to 1951. French-made pieces have a molded signature, whereas the American-made pieces have a diamond etched signature in script. The glass itself is usually crystal with satinized frosting and/or etching similar in style to Lalique. Engraving is usually a heavier, deeper cut than etching. A few Verlys pieces can be found in color, too.

Ashtray, 4½" Diameter, Floral Border, Frosted Dove Design	$60
Ashtray, 4½" x 3½" Rectangular, White Opalescent with Engraved Butterfly Design	$125
Bookends, 6" Tall, Frosted Girl and Deer Design, Pair	$225
Bowl, 6", Crystal, Pinecone Design	$75
Bowl, 6", Satin Blue or Amber, Pinecone Design	$125
Bowl, 8½", 3-Footed, Crystal, Etched Thistle Design	$175
Bowl, 11½", Crystal, Etched Birds and Bees Design	$250
Bowl, 11½", Frosted Floral Design	$100
Bowl, 12", Crystal, Etched Tassels Design	$150
Bowl, 13½", Frosted Crystal, Poppy Design	$225
Bowl, 14", Engraved Orchid Design	$250
Bowl, 14", Etched Dragonfly Design	$250
Bowl, 16", Crystal, Pinecone Design	$110
Box with Cover, 6½" Diameter, Etched Butterfly Design	$125
Compote with Cover, 6" Tall, Frosted Crystal, Pinecone Design	$85
Pigeon Figurine, 4½" Tall, Frosted Crystal	$300
Plate, 5", Frosted Fish Design	$85
Plate, 6¼", Crystal, Pinecone Design	$95
Vase, 4½" Tall, 6½" Diameter, Fan Style, Frosted Lovebirds Design	$175
Vase, 5" Tall, Footed, Fiery White Opalescent Design with Molded Butterflies	$225
Vase, 5" Tall, Crystal, Lovebirds Design	$150
Vase, 5" Tall, Crystal with Etched Butterflies	$225
Vase, 8" Tall, Crystal with Etched Thistle Design	$275
Vase, 8" Tall, Frosted Dancers (Spring and Fall)	$185
Vase, 9" Tall, Fiery White Opalescent Design with Etched Thistles	$325
Vase, 9½" Tall, Molded Mandarin Male Figure	$175
Vase, 9¾" Tall, Frosted and Molded Stalks of Leaf Design	$200
Vase, 11" Tall, Frosted Satin Blue, Molded Mermaid Design	$675

Waterford Glass Company
Ireland, 1783–1851, 1951–Present

The new Waterford is not unlike the old in style—that is, the production of fine crystal with cut decorations. Original items were made of a fine grade of crystal as good as any in the world at the time. The new items, including tableware, functional products, and some novelty items, are also made of high-quality lead crystal and are becoming quite collectible, too. The new Waterford has prospered, and by the early 1970s, they had become the largest producer of handmade crystal in the world, a distinction they hold today. Of particular note are the handmade limited-edition masterpiece collection items. Additional Waterford listings can be found under Lismore.

Anchor, 5" Tall, 5" Wide	$90
Angelfish Figurine, 3" Tall	$60
Angelfish Sculpture, 4½" Tall, 2 Angelfish on Base	$90
Baseball, 3" Diameter (Regulation Size)	$100
Baseball, 3" Diameter (Regulation Size), Engraved with New York Yankees Logo	$125
Bear Figurine, Teddy, 3" Tall	$50
Bear Figuirne, 3" Tall, 6" Long	$100
Bell, 3½" Tall, Millennium Edition	$60
Bell, 4¾" Tall, Etched Crest Design	$70
Biscuit Jar with Cover, 6" Tall, Diamond and Slender Leaf Cuts	$175
Block, ABC Baby Style, 2" Dimensions, Beveled Crystal	$65
Bookends, 5¼" Diameter ¼ Circle Wedges, 1⅝" Thick, Diamond and Fan Cuts, Pair	$175
Bootie, Baby, 4" Long	$65
Bowl, Heart Shape, 4½" Across, Wedge Cut	$55
Bowl, Potpourri, 4⅝", 2¼" Tall, Leaf Design	$55
Bowl, 6¼" Oblong, 3½" Wide, 1½" Tall, Vertical Ribbed Sides and Diamond Base	$60
Bowl, 7", 3½" Tall, Leaf and Diamond Design	$85
Bowl, 8", Calais Pattern	$70
Bowl, 8", 3½" Tall, Colleen Pattern	$135
Bowl, 9", 6½" Tall, Round Base, Leaf and Diamond Cuts	$400
Bowl, 10", 7½" Tall, Footed, Diamond and Wedge Cuts	$1,250
Bowl, 11", Cut Apprentice Pattern	$650
Bowl, Oval (11" x 7"), Notched, Diamond and Fan Cuts	$150

Waterford Hedgehog. *Photo by Mark Pickvet.*

Waterford Lamps. *Photo by Mark Pickvet.*

Waterford Vase. *Photo by Mark Pickvet.*

Waterford Crystal. *Photo by Robin Rainwater.*

Waterford Crystal. *Reproduced directly from a 1995 Waterford catalog. Courtesy of the Waterford Glass Co.*

Bowl, Rose, 5½" Tall, 5¼" Diameter, Calais Pattern	$85
Box with Cover and Heart Finial, 4½" Diameter	$45
Box with Hinged Lid, Shell Shape	$100
Brandy Glass, Alana Pattern	$55
Brandy Glass, Colleen Pattern	$60
Brandy Glass, Kylemore Pattern	$60
Brandy Glass, Patrick Pattern	$55
Bride and Groom Figurine, 7" Tall	$150
Brush, Makeup, 6" Long, Crystal Handle	$45
Bull Figurine, 5½" Long, 3¾" Tall	$100
Butter Dish with Cover, ¼ lb. Size, 7¼" Long, 2½" Tall, Open Diamond Cut Design	$165
Butterfly Figure, 3½" Across	$55
Candelabra, 9¼" Tall, 2-Tiered Candleholder, Diamond and Wedge Cuts with Teardrops	$775
Candelabra, 9¾" Tall, Single Holder, Prisms	$400
Candleholder, 3⅝" Tall, Scalloped, Round Base	$50
Candleholder, 2-Piece, Base Bowl and Small Shade, Diamond Cuts	$150
Candlestick, Globe Shape, 2½" Diameter, Diamond Pattern	$45
Candlestick, 4½" Tall, Palladia Pattern	$70
Candlestick, 5½" Tall, Stemmed, Diamond Cuts	$50
Candy Dish, Heart Shape, 7¾" x 7½"	$65
Cat Figure, 3" Tall, Sitting Upright	$50
Cat Figure, Regal Cat, 5" Tall	$100
Centerpiece Stemmed Bowl, 9" Tall, Diamond and Vertical Cuts	$850
Champagne Glass, Alana Pattern	$45
Champagne Glass, Castletown Pattern	$75
Champagne Glass, Colleen Pattern	$55
Champagne Glass, Kylemore Pattern	$55
Champagne Glass, Patrick Pattern	$50
Champagne Glass, Powerscourt Pattern	$65
Chandelier, 22" Tall, 15" Wide, 5 Large Teardrops	$2,275

Chandelier, 23" Tall, 22" Wide, 57 Teardrops	$2,550
Chandelier, 30" Tall, 30" Wide, 9 Large Teardrops	$3,125
Claret Glass, Alana Pattern	$50
Claret Glass, Castletown Pattern	$75
Claret Glass, Colleen Pattern	$55
Claret Glass, Kylemore Pattern	$55
Claret Glass, Patrick Pattern	$50
Claret Glass, Powerscourt Pattern	$65
Clock, 2⅝" Tall, 4" Long, Kensington Pattern	$75
Clock, 2¾" Tall, Crystal Shell Shape	$65
Coaster, 5" Diameter, Diamond Cuts	$55
Conch Shell, 5" Long, 2¼" Tall	$110
Creamer, Pitcher Style, Cut Ovals, Gold Rim	$45
Creamer, Footed, Pitcher Style, Leaf Cuts	$75
Cruet, 4¼" Tall (No Stopper), Diamond Cut	$50
Decanter, Cut with Etched Christmas Tree	$225
Decanter, Claret with Faceted Stopper, 12½" Tall, Old-Fashioned Style, Diamond Cut	$700
Decanter, Ship's with Faceted Stopper, 9½" Tall, Diamond Cuts	$325
Decanter, Whiskey, Kylemore Pattern	$200
Decanter, Whiskey, Patrick Pattern	$175
Decanter, Wine, Alana Pattern	$225
Decanter, Wine, Castletown Pattern	$350
Decanter, Wine, Colleen Pattern	$225
Decanter, Wine, Patrick Pattern	$200
Decanter, Wine, Powerscourt Pattern	$375
Dog Figurine, 2¼" Tall, Westie	$60
Dolphin Figurine on Base, 5¼" Tall, Leaping	$80
Dolphin Sculpture, 7⅜" Tall, 7" Wide, 2 Dolphins on Base	$150
Dove Figure, 1¾" Tall, 5" Long	$75
Dreidel Spinning Shape, 5" Tall, 2½" Square, Prism Faceted Cut	$125

Duck, Mallard, 2½" Tall, 3¾" Long, Wedge-Cut Feathers	$100
Egg, 2" Tall, 2-Piece, Opens to Reveal Pewter Bunny	$90
Egg, 3¼" Tall, 2¼" Wide, Annual Editions Beginning in 1991 (Price Is for Each)	$125
Egg, 3½" Tall, 2¼" Wide, Diamond and Sunburst Pattern	$100
Egg, 5½" Tall, Pedestal Stand, Diamond Cuts	$115
Fish, Leaping Salmon Figure, 8½" Tall	$125
Frame, Photo, Heart Shape, 4½" Tall, 4¼" Wide	$55
Frog Figure, 2⅜" Tall	$75
Gavel, 5½" Long	$75
Ginger Jar with Cover, 8" Tall, Diamond and Rosette Pattern	$175
Globe Sculpture, 6½" Diameter, 14" Tall with Mahogany Base, Diamond Cut Continents	$2,750
Goblet, Alana Pattern	$50
Goblet, Castletown Pattern	$75
Goblet, Cut with Etched Christmas Tree	$50
Goblet, Colleen Pattern	$55
Goblet, Kylemore Pattern	$55
Goblet, Patrick Pattern	$50
Goblet, Powerscourt Pattern	$65
Golf Ball, Regulation Size, 2½" Diameter	$85
Golf-Club Head, 3" Tall	$75
Golf Shoe, 6" Long	$75
Harp, 5" Tall, 2" Wide	$70
Heart-Shape Box, 2¾" x 2¾", 2-Piece	$65
Hedgehog Figurine, 2¼" Long, 1¾" Tall	$60
Horse Figure, Rearing, 3¾" Tall, 2¾" Wide	$55
Horse Figure on Base, 8½" Long	$250
Ice Bucket, 5⅜" Tall, Silver-Plated Handle, Diamond Cut	$165
Lamp, 13" Tall, Diamond Pattern	$500
Lamp, 18" Tall, Diamond Pattern	$800
Lamp, 20" Tall, Brass Base, Crystal Part 8¾" Tall	$250

Leprechaun Figurine with Pot of Gold, 3" Tall, 3½" Wide	$75
Madonna Figure with Child, 7" Tall	$150
Mug, Christening, 3" Tall	$70
Mug, Tankard Style, 4½" Tall, 13 oz., Diamond and Long Slender Leaf Cuts	$85
Mustard Pot with Cover, 3" Tall, Perpendicular Cuts	$45
Napkin Ring, Oval, Open Diamond Cut Design	$40
Owl Figure, 3⅛" Tall	$75
Owl Figurine on Base, 4" Tall	$100
Panda Bear Figurine, 5" Tall	$100
Paperweight, 3", Globe Shape, Star of Hope Design	$100
Paperweight, 3¼" Globe Shape, Various Engraved Floral Designs	$75
Paperweight, 3¼" Tall, Diamond Shape, Diamond Cuts	$75
Paperweight, 3½" Diameter, Diamond and Star Cuts	$75
Paperweight, 3½" Long, 2¾" Wide, Strawberry Shape	$75
Paperweight, 4", Shamrock Design	$125
Paperweight, 4½" Long, 1¼" Tall, Open Diamond Cuts, Turtle Design	$75
Paperweight, 5" Tall, Number "1" Shape, Diamond Cuts	$75
Perfume Atomizer, 4" Tall, Diamond Cuts	$85
Perfume Bottle with Stopper, 6½" Tall, Nocturne Design	$50
Pig Figurine, 2" Tall, 1¾" Wide	$60
Pitcher, Water, 24 oz., Cut Design with Etched Christmas Tree	$150
Pitcher, Water, 32 oz., Long Slender Oval Cuts	$175
Plate, 8", Cut Diamonds and Etched Golfer in Center	$100
Ram, 2" Tall, 3¼" Long	$65
Ring Holder, 2¾" Tall, Heart Base (3" Across)	$45
Sail Boat, 5½" Tall, 4¾" Long, Cut Ovals	$115
Salmon Figurine on Base, 8½" Tall	$185
Salt Cellar, 2⅝" Tall, Stemmed, Boat Shape, Tiny Diamond Cuts	$85
Salt and Pepper Shakers, 6" Tall, Round Feet, Silver-Plated Tops, Diamond and Leaf Cuts	$100
Santa Claus Figure, 5½" Tall	$140

Sea Horse Figure, 3½" Tall	$50
Sea Horse Figure, 6¾" Tall	$200
Sconce, 2-Light, 11¼" Tall, 12½" Wide, Two 4½" Diamond Cut Plates Each with 8 Teardrops	$850
Seal Pup Figurinee on Base, 3½" Long	$85
Sherbet, Alana Pattern	$50
Sherbet, Castletown Pattern	$85
Ship, Sailing, 5¾" Across	$140
Ship, Titanic, 11½" Long, 1⅝" Wide	$140
Stein, 6" Tall, Diamond and Narrow Leaf Cuts	$100
Sugar, Cut Ovals, Gold Rim	$50
Sugar, Footed, Leaf Cuts	$65
Sugar Shaker with Silver-Plated Top, 6½" Tall, Stemmed, Diamond and Leaf Cut	$65
Swan, Cygnet Figurine, 2¾" Long, 2¼" Tall	$50
Teddy Bear Figure, 3" Tall	$55
Thimble, 1½" Tall	$40
Tray, Shell Shape, 5" x 4½", 1" Tall	$55
Tray, Oval (8" x 6"), Central Star, Vertical Flutes	$65
Tumbler, 9 oz., Old-Fashioned Style, Alana Pattern	$45
Tumbler, 9 oz., Castletown Pattern	$70
Tumbler, 9 oz., Colleen Pattern	$45
Tumbler, 9 oz., Old-Fashioned Style, Kylemore Pattern	$50
Tumbler, 9 oz., Patrick Pattern	$40
Tumbler, 9 oz., Powerscourt Pattern	$55
Tumbler, 9 oz., Wide Diamond Pattern	$40
Tumbler, 9 or 10 oz., Cut with Etched Christmas Tree	$40
Tumbler, 12 oz., Colleen Pattern	$55
Tumbler, 12 oz., Old-Fashioned Style, Patrick Pattern	$45
Tumbler, 12 oz., Powerscourt Pattern	$60
Vase, 4" Tall, Diamond and Flute Design	$55
Vase, 7" Tall, Slender, Diamond and Vertical Cuts	$60
Vase, 7" Tall, Cut Floral Pattern, Mother's Day Design	$75

Vase, 7⅝" Tall, Prism "Thousand Windows" Pattern	$275
Vase, 9" Tall, Araglin Pattern	$150
Vase, 9" Tall, Calais Pattern	$60
Vase, 10" Tall, Round Base, Wide Neck, Wedge and Diamond Cuts	$200
Vase, 12" Tall, Engraved Butterfly Design, Limited Edition of 2,500	$650
Vase, 12" Tall, Engraved Dolphin Design, Limited Edition of 2,500	$750
Vase, 12" Tall, Round Base, Flared Top, All-Over Cut Pattern, Masterpiece Collection	$925
Vase, 13½" Tall, Engraved Lilies' Design, Limited Edition of 2,500	$950
Vase, 14" Tall, Cut with Engraved St. Patrick's Design, Limited Edition of 200	$1,500
Vase, 14" Tall, Engraved Yacht Design, Limted Edition of 2,500	$850
Wineglass, Alana Pattern	$40
Wineglass, Castletown Pattern	$75
Wineglass, Colleen Pattern	$50
Wineglass, Oversize, Colleen Pattern	$100
Wineglass, Kylemore Pattern	$50
Wineglass, Patrick Pattern	$45
Wineglass, Powerscourt Pattern	$60

Webb, Thomas & Sons
Stourbridge, England, 1837–1930s

Webb is simply the most famous English name in the art-glass world. They were a major part of the European art nouveau movement and followed American trends as well. They borrowed Peachblow and Burmese designs from America but also produced Alexandrite, Cameo, and a host of other designs. The firm still operates today as Webb's Crystal Glass Company, Ltd., primarily producing crystal stemware. Additional listings for Webb can be found under Alexandrite, English Cameo, and Peachblow.

Biscuit Jar with Cover, 7½" Tall, Pink Satin with Floral Design on Body and Cover	$625
Biscuit Jar with Cover, 8" Tall, Frosted Yellow, Signed	$1,550
Bowl, 3½", Ruffled, Enameled Floral and Butterfly Design, Signed	$425
Bowl, 4", 2½" Tall, Ruby Red Cut to Green, Floral Wreath and Swag Design	$500
Bowl, 4⅞", Crimped, Mother-of-Pearl, Diamond Quilted Pattern	$765
Bowl, 5", Ruffled, Burmese	$225
Bowl, 5¾", Pink with White Lining, Intaglio Flowers and Branches	$900

Bowl, Rose, 6", 5" Tall, Yellow to Cream Satin with White Interior — $425

Bowl, 6¼", Applied Rim, Burmese with Floral Design — $1,750

Centerpiece, 12½" Diameter, 7" Tall, Ruffled, Blue Overlay with Enameled Floral Design — $600

Creamer, 2⅝" Tall, Fluted, Burmese with Green Leaves Design — $785

Epergne, 21" Tall, Center Trumpet Design with 3 Hanging Baskets, Cranberry and Vaseline — $1,400

Ewer, 3¾" Tall, 5¼" Diameter, Ivory Handle, Green to White Satin, Apples and Leaves Design — $625

Flask with Threaded Silver Stopper, 5¾" Tall, Swan's Head Design — $2,650

Perfume Bottle with Sterling Silver Stopper, 3½" Tall, Burmese with Purple Floral Design — $850

Perfume Bottle with Sterling Silver Stopper, 4¾" Tall, Burmese with Gold Branches Design — $975

Perfume Bottle with Stopper, 5½" Tall, Ivory Satin with Gold Bamboo and Multicolored Floral Design — $575

Perfume Bottle with Silver Top, 6" Tall, Red to Yellow to Dark Amber Shading — $375

Perfume Bottle with Stopper, Citron, Vine and Floral Decoration — $900

Pitcher, Water, 6½" Tall, Loop Handles, Ivory, Blooming Bamboo Plant Design — $1,850

Pitcher, Water, 7½" Tall, Red to White Shading — $675

Plate, 6½", Ruffled, Butterscotch, Diamond Quilted Pattern — $115

Salt Dip, Rectangular, Red — $675

Toothpick Holder, 2⅝" Tall, Hexagonal Collared Top, Burmese — $415

Tumbler, 5" Tall, Red to White Shading — $225

Vase, 2½" Tall, Miniature, Blue with Enameled Butterfly and Floral Design — $700

Vase, 3" Tall, Miniature, Red with Carved White Fuchsias — $400

Vase, 3⅜" Tall, Ivory with Gold Butterfly and Floral Design — $275

Vase, 3½" Tall, Vertical Ribs, Burmese — $200

Vase, 3¾" Tall, Hexagonal Top, Burmese with Lavender Floral and Leaves Design — $465

Vase, 4½" Tall, Green with Gold Leaves and Hydrangea Blossoms — $475

Vase, 4¾" Tall, Pink and White Burmese, Oriental Floral, House, and Birds Design — $500

Vase, 5" Tall, 2¾" Diameter, Gold on Coral, Floral and Bees Design — $325

Vase, 5" Tall, Pink Interior, Gold Floral and Butterfly Design — $425

Thomas Webb & Sons, Cameo Vase. *Photo by Robin Rainwater. Courtesy of the Chicago Art Institute.*

Webb Cameo. *Photo by Robin Rainwater. Courtesy of the Corning Museum of Glass.*

Vase, 6" Tall, Ruffled, Satin, Diamond Quilted Pattern	$425
Vase, 6" Tall, Footed, Cut Crystal, Red and White Trumpet Floral Design	$3,150
Vase, 6½" Tall, Red to Pink Shading	$475
Vase, 7" Tall, Light Satin Blue with White Lining, Berries and Foliage Design, Gold Scrolling	$500
Vase, 7" Tall, Urn Shape, 2 Applied Handles, Ribbed, Iridescent Gold	$1,850
Vase, 7¼" Tall, 5" Diameter, Flared, Applied Bronzed Handles, Orange Satin with White Lining, Gold Fern, Daisies, and Butterfly Design	$1,050
Vase, 8¼" Tall, Burmese with Green Leaves and Coral Flower Buds	$865
Vase, 8½" Tall, Ribbed, Fish-Scale and Vine Design, Signed	$3,500
Vase, 8½" Tall, Amber with Enameled Butterflies and Cattails Design	$625
Vase, 9" Tall, Butterfly and Floral Design, Burmese	$2,250
Vase, 9" Tall, 5" Diameter, Bulbous, Flared Rim, Red with White Lining, Gold Fern Design	$775
Vase, 10" Tall, Amethyst Cameo Design, Signed	$1,450
Vase, 10" Tall, Bottle Shape, Burmese with Mums and Leaves Design	$1,350

Vase, 10½" Tall, Gourd Shape, Blue with White Floral Design	$2,850
Vase, 11" Tall, Gourd Shape, Footed, Yellow Satin with Cream Interior	$500
Vase, 12" Tall, Ruffled, Coral Design with Cream Interior	$575
Vase, 14" Tall, Red with Enameled Floral Decorations	$750
Vase, 15" Tall, Flared, Multicolored Floral Design	$775

– 2 –
PRESSED GLASS

The American glass industry experienced a shaky start, but it was not for lack of ambition. Glass was first made in the New World by the Spaniards, who set up a glasshouse in 1535 in Argentina, and another in 1592 at the town of Cordoba del Tucaman in the Territory of the Rio de la Plata, where they remelted broken glass from Europe and formed it into crude, usable objects. Both were short-lived operations.

The first permanent English settlement was established in North America at Jamestown, Virginia, in 1607. In 1608, Captain Christopher Newport brought eight Polish and Dutch glassmakers, who founded a glasshouse in 1609. Some crude tableware items, mostly bottles, were made and were included in the first cargo exported from the New World. The operation lasted only a short while. A second glasshouse was constructed in Jamestown in 1620 by the London Company, and six Italian workers were imported to work there. The principal products were beads and marbles, which were used to trade with the Native Americans. This glasshouse, too, survived only a few short years.

Still, America had an abundance of all the necessary ingredients: excellent sources for ash, plenty of sand, and massive forests for fuel. The Germans, with very limited success, would be the next immigrants to attempt glassmaking in the New World. In 1739 a German immigrant named Caspar Wistar built a factory in New Jersey. He hired skilled German glassworkers and became the first commercially successful glass manufacturer in the United States. Just as it had been in the forest glasshouses of Europe, the immediate need, and practical use, for glass products was for bottles and windows. Wistar also made some crude tableware and a few scientific glass vessels for Benjamin Franklin. It was surprising that any glass was made at all, since England banned the manufacturing of glass in the colonies in order to maintain their monopoly on glass production. The Wistar house, however, did not survive for long.

Pressed Glass Decanters. Left to right: Flute & Pine Tree, Baroque Shell, Diamond Quilted, and Vertically Ribbed Patterns. *Photo Courtesy of the Sandwich Glass Museum.*

Pressed Glass Decanters. Left to right: Flute & Pine Tree, Baroque Shell, Diamond Quilted, and Vertically Ribbed Patterns. *Photo Courtesy of the Sandwich Glass Museum.*

From 1763 to 1774 another German by the name of Henry W. Stiegel operated a glasshouse in Manheim, Pennsylvania. Stiegel acquired some of the former employees of Wistar's business and hired a few additional experienced foreign workers from Germany and England. He went bankrupt in 1774 but did manage to create some window and bottle glass. The American Revolution forced his glasshouse to shut down permanently.

One year after the Revolution another German immigrant opened a glass factory in America. In 1784 John Frederick Amelung produced a fair amount of hand-cut tableware, much of it engraved. Amelung's factory also made Benjamin Franklin a pair of bifocals. They, too, could not operate consistently at a profit and shut down in 1795.

There were many reasons for these failures, even though there was a great demand for glass in the colonies. Foreign competition and pressure from the English government were significant reasons for those failures. Glasshouses or manufacturing plants were well established in England and Ireland, producing large quantities of cheap glass. Early Americans lacked the capital and many of the skills necessary to manufacture glass. Transportation problems resulted in shipping that was too difficult and costly across the Alleghenies. People out West used crude bowls, teacups, and bottles to consume food and spirits.

The Alleghenies were a disadvantage to eastern manufacturers but a boom to those living in eastern Ohio, northern West Virginia, and western Pennsylvania. The mountains served as a barrier to foreign and eastern glass long before the great canals were built. In 1797 the first frontier glasshouse about 60 miles south of Pittsburgh was constructed by Albert Gallatin, an immigrant from Switzerland. Later that year a bottle factory was built in Pittsburgh by James O'Hara and Isaac Craig. This factory was named the Pittsburgh Glass Works, and in 1798 they merged with Gallatin's New Geneva Glass Works. They did manage to produce handblown windows, bottles, and a bit of tableware, but they were unable to operate profitably. They sold out to Edward Ensell soon afterward.

Pittsburgh and the surrounding area was an ideal place to manufacture glassware. Wood for fuel was readily available; later, massive coal deposits were discovered in the region. Large sand or sandstone deposits lie along the numerous riverbeds, and red lead for fine crystal production was available nearby in the Illinois Territory. The commercial markets were wide open in every direction except back East. Areas north to Canada, west to the Pacific, and south to the major trading centers of New Orleans and the Gulf of Mexico were all accessible by easy river transport. Yet despite these strategic advantages, many early attempts ended in failure.

America's early successes in glassmaking can be traced to many individuals, but one figure stands out in particular. Deming Jarves not only founded many companies but obtained knowledgeable foreign workers, the proper ingredients and good formulas, and wrote an important trade volume in 1854 titled *Reminiscences of Glassmaking*. Most important, he was able to obtain enough financial backing to keep the businesses operating long enough to achieve long-standing profit margins.

In the 1790s the Boston Crown Glass Company was chartered to produce window glass and managed to do very little. The only noteworthy contribution worth mentioning is that they were the first to introduce lead crystal in America. Many of the workers left and went on to form the Boston Porcelain and Glass Company in 1814. They built a factory in 1815 and made a few limited lead-glass products before failing in 1817. Deming Jarves, with three associates (Amos Binney, Daniel Hastings, and Edmund Monroe), purchased the holdings of it and incorporated it into a new company in 1818. It was dubbed the New England Glass Company, which settled in East Cambridge, Massachusetts.

From the very beginning they operated profitably and continuously reinvested in new equipment and recruited skilled workers from Europe. Jarves assumed a leading role as first agent and manager. He was a prosperous businessman and held a monopoly on red lead production early on in America. Red lead is a vital ingredient for making fine lead crystal. Jarves left New England Glass in 1826 and went on to form the Boston & Sandwich Glass Company, another successful operation.

What Jarves accomplished in the East, the team of Bakewell, Ensell, and Pears was working on in the West. In 1807 Edward Ensell founded a small glass company in Pittsburgh, but it was purchased by Benjamin Bakewell and associates in 1808. Benjamin sent his son Thomas Bakewell and a trusted clerk named Thomas Pears on numerous trips to Europe to hire experienced glassworkers. Thomas Pears split off in 1818 to start a bottle factory, but it failed and he rejoined the Bakewells. He quit again in 1825 and moved to Indiana but came back once again in 1826. He died soon afterward, but his son John Palmer Pears became manager of the glasshouse and the name changed to Bakewell, Pears & Company.

These early successes were somewhat of a rarity. The first period or what is referred to as the early American period of American glass lasted from 1771 to 1830. Several glass companies were founded east and west of the Alleghenies, but nearly all ended in failure. Cheap European glass and the lack of protective tariffs hurt eastern glassmakers. Out West, skilled workers were difficult to obtain, and the necessary capital was not available to sustain long-term growth and operation. A few economic depressions such as the one after the War of 1812 were also factors in those shutdowns. Except for a few enterprising men such as Jarves, this first period in American glass history was marked with unprofitability and failure.

The middle period in American glass history dates from 1830 to about 1880. The Baldwin Bill in 1830 placed import duties and high tariffs on foreign imports. The new tariffs worked, and the glass industry in the United States was given a much-needed boost. Along with taxes, the American invention of a mechanical pressing machine in the late 1820s led to the mass production of glassware. The invention of this hand press was America's greatest contribution to glassmaking. It was as important as the discovery of lead crystal, glassblowing, and the invention of glass itself. Hand-pressing revolutionized the industry; it was very fast, efficient, and could be done with less-skilled workers.

Pressed glass was made by forcing melted glass into shape under pressure. Early on, a plunger was used to force or press molten glass into iron molds. A mold was made of two or more parts and imparted lines or seams where the mold came apart. With each piece the mold was reassembled and filled again. Some of the marks left by the mold were hand-finished to remove them. Molds might contain patterns within them, were usually hinged, and could be full-size single-piece molds or separate for more complicated objects. Candlesticks, vases, common table items, and especially matched sets of tableware were easily manufactured by hand-pressing.

Pressed items were made in great quantities, especially in the factories Jarves opened. The New England Glass Company, which eventually became Libbey, and the Boston & Sandwich Glass Company were two of the most successful companies producing pressed glass in America. Many followed in the mid-19th century such as Adams & Company; Bakewell, Pears & Company; McKee Brothers; Bryce Brothers; Hobbs, Brocunier & Company; and King & Son.

Individual patterns were rarely patented by any one company. Even when patents were obtained, designs were copied. Ashburton or Hex Optic, Bull's-Eye, Cable, Thumbprints, Hamilton, Comet, Grapes, Pineapples, Ribs, Sunbursts, Pillars, Flutes, and others are at times difficult to distinguish from one another.

William Leighton invented a cheap lead substitute in 1864. Leighton was employed by Hobbs, Brocunier & Company at the time and developed a glass formula that substituted lime for the much more expensive lead. The glass products manufactured with lime still maintained a good degree of clarity. Though the brilliance was not as sharp as lead crystal, the price savings and practicality of it more than made up for the difference in quality. Most companies were forced to switch to lime to remain competitive.

Pressed glass remained somewhat affordable compared with art and cut glass in the late 19th and early 20th centuries, too. Fire polishing developed in England in 1834 was adopted in America. Fire polishing removed mold and tool marks by reheating and gave glass a shinier finish that was a little closer to fine cut crystal.

Simple, clear pressed-glass articles were combined with other design features and decorating techniques. Pressed glass was made in many colors, flashed, cut occasionally like simple fluting, cased, enameled, and might contain applied blown accessories such as handles and feet. All still qualify as pressed-glass items; nevertheless, the quality and dull colors were still far behind the elegance of cut crystal and the beauty of fancy art glass. Then again, the price for obtaining it wasn't necessarily out of reach for the average American.

Other makers in the late 19th and early 20th centuries in America included the conglomerate U.S. Glass; George Duncan & Sons; Central Glass Company; and Indiana Tumbler & Goblet Company. Many others continued the mass production of pressed-glass items. Many of these later pressed patterns were more elaborate, patented, and not as easily copied—a great aid in identification!

Actress
Labelle Glass Company, 1870s–1880s; Adams & Company, 1880s

Actors and actresses are formed on this pattern in frosted portraits with light ridges. The pieces are also framed by stippled shell forms rising off the sides of the glass. Note that Imperial reproduced a few items, including the pickle dish. Colored pieces are reproductions; decrease the prices listed below by 65–75 percent for them.

Bowl, 6", Footed	$50
Bowl, 7", Footed	$55
Bowl, 8"	$95
Bowl, 8", Footed	$65
Bowl, 9½", Footed	$100
Butter Dish with Cover	$125
Cake Stand, 7" Tall, 10" Diameter	$175
Candlestick	$140
Celery Dish, Pinafore Design	$175
Celery Vase	$150
Cheese Dish with Cover, "The Lone Fisherman" Design	$275
Compote, 5"	$55
Compote, 10"	$105
Compote, 12"	$140
Compote with Cover, Low, 6" Diameter	$265
Compote with Cover, 8" Tall, 12" Diameter	$330
Creamer	$85
Dresser Tray	$75
Goblet	$105

Actress Pattern Milk Pitcher. *Drawing by Mark Pickvet.*

Honey Dish with Cover	$140
Jam Jar with Cover	$150
Mug, Pinafore Design	$60
Mustard Jar with Cover	$105
Pickle Dish, Embossed "Love's Request Is Pickles"	$65
Pitcher, Milk (Small), 6½" Tall, Pinafore Design	$325
Pitcher, Water (Large), 9" Tall, Romeo and Juliet Design	$275
Platter, Round, "Miss Nielson" Design	$175
Platter, Oval, 7" x 12", Pinafore Design	$150
Platter, Oval, 9" x 13", "Miss Nielson" Design	$175
Relish Dish, 4½" x 7"	$40
Relish Dish, 5" x 8"	$45
Relish Dish, 5½" x 9"	$50
Salt and Pepper Shakers	$90
Salt Dip	$80
Sauce Bowl, Flat	$35
Sauce Bowl, Footed	$45
Spooner	$75
Sugar Dish with Cover	$115
Tray, Embossed "Give Us This Day"	$125

Pressed Adonis. *Drawing by Mark Pickvet.*

Adonis
Mckee Brothers, 1890s

The Adonis pattern is characterized by horizontal bands and drapes. The bands rise vertically while tapering to a point near the top. For colors, most notably yellow and blue, double the prices listed below. This pattern is also referred to as Washboard or Pleat & Tuck.

Bowl, 5"	$13
Butter Dish with Cover	$55
Cake Plate, 11"	$25
Cake Stand, 10½"	$35
Celery Vase	$30
Compote, 4½"	$22.50
Compote, 8"	$35
Compote with Cover	$50
Creamer	$27.50
Pitcher, Syrup	$85
Pitcher, Water	$45
Plate, 10"	$22.50
Relish Dish	$18
Salt and Pepper Shakers	$40
Sauce Dish, 4", Flat	$12.50

Spooner	$25
Sugar Dish with Cover	$42.50
Tumbler	$20

Alabama
U.S. Glass Company, Early 1890s

Alabama was the first of U.S. Glass's famous state series. It is also known as Beaded Bull's-Eye and Drape, in which the top or upper half of "Alabama" pieces have the bulls' eyes while the bottom or lower half contain a drapery pattern. Green pieces are priced the same as the clear, whereas prices for a few rare ruby flashed items should be doubled.

Bowl, 5"	$21.50
Butter Dish with Cover	$80
Cake Stand	$57.50
Celery Holder, Upright	$50
Compote, Open, 5" Tall	$40
Compote with Cover	$150
Creamer	$45
Honey Dish with Cover	$110
Nappy with Handle	$30
Pitcher, Syrup, with Lid	$90
Pitcher, Milk	$90
Pitcher, Water	$100
Relish Dish, Oblong, 3 Varieties	$30
Spooner	$30
Sugar with Cover	$75
Toothpick Holder	$75
Tumbler	$30

America
American Glass Company and Riverside Glass Works, Early 1890s

This pattern is also referred to as Swirl and Diamond and is often confused with other similar patterns. Double the prices listed below for any colored glass.

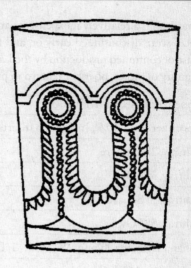

Alabama Pattern Tumbler. *Drawing by Mark Pickvet.*

Bowl, 8½"	$35
Butter Dish with Cover, Pedestal Base	$65
Carafe	$50
Celery Vase	$42.50
Compote, 8" Tall, 8" Diameter	$65
Creamer, Tankard Style, Applied Handle	$42.50
Goblet	$36
Pitcher, Tankard Style, 64 oz., Applied Handle	$70
Relish Dish	$24
Sauce Dish, 4½", Flat	$14
Spooner	$22.50
Sugar with Cover, Individual (Small)	$32.50
Sugar with Cover (Large)	$57.50
Tumbler	$26

American
Fostoria Glass Company, 1915–83

Fostoria's American pattern is sometimes confused with block optic or cubist patterns of the Depression. Some colors were added during the Depression, including amber, green, and yellow (increase prices listed below by 50 percent) as well as blue and some iridized or carnival colors (double the prices listed below).

American is a relatively inexpensive pattern because of its long production; however, some pieces were discontinued early on and have increased in value. Others have fallen off because of continued production by the Lancaster Colony Corporation. For sheer variety and quantity of pieces, no other pattern in pressed glass comes close to this one.

Appetizer Dish, Individual, 3¼"	$40
Appetizer Tray, 10½", Includes 6 Inserts	$325
Ashtray, 2⅞" Square	$12.50
Ashtray, 3⅞" Oval	$16
Ashtray, 5" Square	$50
Ashtray, 5½" Oval	$30
Banana Dish, 9" Oblong, 3½" Wide, 1 Tab Handle	$35
Basket, Reed Handle, 10"	$95
Bell (Rare)	$450
Boat Dish, 8½" Oblong	$20
Boat Dish, 9" Oblong, 2-Part	$25
Boat Dish, 12" Oblong	$27.50
Bonbon Dish, 6", 3-Footed	$30
Bonbon Dish, 7", 3-Footed	$35
Bonbon Dish, 8", 3-Footed	$40
Bottle, Bitters, 5¾" Tall, Includes Tube	$80
Bottle, Catsup, with Stopper	$150
Bottle, Water, 9¼" Tall, 44 oz.	$150
Bowl, 3½"	$21.50
Bowl, 3¾" Oval	$21.50
Bowl, 4¼"	$21.50
Bowl, 4½" Oval	$21.50
Bowl, 4¾" Flared	$21.50
Bowl, 5"	$22.50
Bowl, 5" Flared	$22.50
Bowl, 6"	$27.50
Bowl, 7"	$45
Bowl, 8"	$55

Fostoria Glassware, American Pattern. *Reproduced directly from an early-20th-century Fostoria catalog.*

Bowl, 8", 3-Footed	$75
Bowl, 8", Footed, 2-Handled Trophy Cup	$150
Bowl, 9", Round or Oval	$32.50
Bowl, 9½" Centerpiece	$55
Bowl, 9½" x 6" Oval, 3 Divisions	$45
Bowl, 10" Round or Oval	$40
Bowl, 10" Oval, 2 Divisions	$45
Bowl, 10½", 3-Footed	$45
Bowl, 11", Centerpiece, Round or Tricorner	$65
Bowl, 11½" Round or Oval	$50
Bowl, 11¾" Oval	$50
Bowl, 12"	$75
Bowl, 12¼", Shrimp (Rare)	$450
Bowl, 13"	$85
Bowl, 15", Hat-Shape Centerpiece	$225
Bowl, 16", Centerpiece, Footed	$225
Bowl, Rose	$55
Butter Dish with Cover, ¼ lb. Size	$35
Butter Dish with Cover, 5¾" Dome Diameter, 7¼" Underplate Diameter	$135
Cake Plate, 7½"	$17.50

Cake Salver, 10" Round, 2-Handled	$150
Cake Salver, 10" Square	$200
Cake Salver, 11" Round	$50
Cake Stand, 12", 3-Footed	$75
Candelabra, 2-Light, 4⅛" Tall, 8½" Across	$75
Candelabra, 2-Light, 4⅜" Tall, Footed	$50
Candelabra, 2-Light, 6½" Tall	$135
Candelabra, 2-Light, 6½" Tall, Prisms	$170
Candlestick, 2" Tall	$45
Candlestick, 3" Tall	$17.50
Candlestick, 6" Tall	$35
Candlestick, 6¼" Tall, Round Foot	$100
Candlestick, 7" Tall	$110
Candlestick, 7¼" Tall	$150
Candy Dish with Cover, Hexagonal, Footed	$75
Candy Dish with Cover, Triangular, 3-Part	$100
Celery Dish, 10" Oblong	$25
Celery Vase, 6" Tall, 3½" Diameter	$25
Cheese Dish with Cover, Dome and Underplate	$100
Cigarette Box with Cover, 4¾"	$45
Claret Glass, 4⅝" Tall, 3½ oz.	$25
Claret Glass, 4⅞" Tall, 7 oz.	$55
Coaster, 3½" or 3¼"	$11
Cocktail Glass, 2⅞" Tall, 3 oz., Footed	$17.50
Cocktail Glass, 3½" Tall, 4 or 4½ oz., Footed	$20
Cocktail Glass, 4" Tall, 3½ oz., Footed	$18.50
Cologne Bottle with Stopper, 5¾" Tall, 6 oz.	$75
Cologne Bottle with Stopper, 7½" Tall, 8 oz.	$85
Cologne Bottle with Stopper, 7¼" Tall, 9 oz.	$95
Comport, 4" or 4½", Open	$17.50
Comport, 5" or 5¼", Open, No Stem	$20
Comport, 8½", Open, No Stem	$50

Comport, 9½", Open, No Stem	$75
Compote, 5", Open	$17.50
Compote, 5", Covered	$35
Compote, 6½", Open, 5¼" Tall, Square Shape	$85
Compote, 6½", Covered, 8" Tall	$125
Compote, 6¾", Covered	$40
Compote, 7", Open	$22
Compote, 16" Diameter, 20" Tall	$175
Cookie Jar with Cover, 8⅞" Tall	$350
Cordial, 2⅞" Tall, Footed	$25
Cordial, 3⅛" Tall, Footed	$35
Cracker Jar with Cover, 8¾" Tall, 5¾" Diameter	$300
Cracker Jar with Cover, 10" Tall, 5¾" Diameter	$375
Creamer, Individual, 3 oz. (Tiny)	$11
Creamer, Individual, 5 oz. (Small)	$12.50
Creamer, 4¼" Tall, 9½ oz. (Large)	$15
Cruet with Stopper, 6½" Tall, 5 oz.	$75
Cruet with Stopper, 7" Tall, 7 oz.	$85
Cup, 7 or 8 oz., with or without Feet, Several Styles	$12.50
Cup, Custard, 6 oz., 2 Styles	$11.50
Decanter with Stopper, 9¼" Tall, 24 oz.	$100
Decanter with Sterling Silver Stopper, 10" Tall	$165
Decanter with Stopper, 2 Styles, Metal Holder and Chain, Engraved Tabs (Scotch or Rye)	$190
Fernery, 3-Footed	$12.50
Flower Pot with Cover (Rare), 5½"	$1850
Fruit Dish with Cover and Spoon, 10" (Rare)	$2,250
Glove Box with Cover, Rectangular (9½" x 3½")	$375
Goblet, 4¾" Tall, 4½ oz.	$12.50
Goblet, 4⅜" Tall, 9 oz.	$14
Goblet, 5½" Tall, 9 oz.	$15
Goblet 5¾" Tall, 12 oz.	$17.50

Goblet, 6⅛" Tall, 10 oz.	$20
Goblet, 6¾" Tall, 9 oz.	$17.50
Goblet, Hexagonal, 7" Tall, 10 oz.	$18
Gravy Boat with Underplate	$60
Hairpin Box with Cover, Rectangular (3½" x 1½")	$325
Hair Receiver, 3" x 3"	$425
Handkerchief Box with Cover, Rectangular (5½" x 4½")	$350
Hat, 2½" Tall	$20
Hat, 3" Tall	$30
Hat, 4" Tall	$70
Ice Bucket, 6½" Diameter, with Tongs	$65
Ice Bucket, 7" Tall, 10" Diameter, Metal Handle	$90
Ice Tub, 5½", with Liner	$100
Ice Tub, 6½", with Liner	$115
Jam Jar with Cover	$75
Jelly Dish with Cover, 4½" Diameter, 7" Tall	$100
Jelly Dish with Cover, 5½" Diameter, 2-Handled	$110
Jewel Box with Cover, Square (4½" x 4½")	$250
Jewel Box with Cover, Rectangular (4¼" x 3¼"), 2-Drawer (Rare)	$5,000
Jewel Box with Cover, Rectangular (5¼" x 2¼")	$375
Lamp, Candle, 8½"	$150
Lamp, Hurricane, 12"	$225
Lamp, Perfume	$65
Lemon Dish with Cover, 5¼"	$65
Marmalade Jar with Cover and Notch, Chrome Spoon	$65
Mayonnaise Set, 3-Piece (Dish, Plate, and 1 Spoon)	$45
Mayonnaise Set, 3-Piece (Divided Dish and 2 Spoons)	$55
Molasses, Can, 2 Styles	$450
Mug, 3¼" Tall, 5½ oz.	$45
Mug, Beer, 4½" Tall, 12 oz.	$75
Mustard Jar with Cover and Spoon, 3¾" Tall	$50

Napkin Ring, 2"	$20
Nappy, 4¼" Tall, 1 Handle, Round or Square	$15
Nappy, 4½", 1 Handle	$16
Nappy, 5", 1 Handle	$17.50
Nappy, 5", 2-Handled	$50
Nappy, 5", Tricorner, 1 Looped Handle	$17.50
Nappy, 5¼", 1 Handle	$20
Nappy, 5¼", 2-Handled	$22.50
Nappy, 6", 1 Handle	$18.50
Nappy, 7", 1 Handle	$25
Nappy, 8", 1 Handle	$27.50
Nappy, 8½", 2-Handled	$45
Nut Dish, Oval (3¾" x 2¾")	$12.50
Nut Dish, 4½" Oval	$16
Olive Dish, Oval (6" x 3½")	$16
Pickle Dish, Oval (8" x 4")	$18
Pickle Jar with Cover, 6" Tall	$350
Picture Frame	$17.50
Pin Tray, 5¼" Oval	$225
Pitcher, Syrup with Metal Lid, 5¼" Tall, 6 oz.	$250
Pitcher, Syrup with Metal Lid, 6¾" Tall, 11 oz.	$250
Pitcher, 16 oz.	$40
Pitcher, 32 oz.	$65
Pitcher, 44 oz., 7½" Tall	$80
Pitcher, 48 oz., 6½" Tall, Footed	$80
Pitcher, 48 oz., 8" Tall, Footed	$80
Pitcher, Water, 55 oz., 8" Tall	$110
Pitcher, Water, 58 oz., 7¼" Tall	$115
Pitcher, 69 oz., Jug Style	$140
Pitcher, Water, 71 oz.	$150
Pitcher, Water, ½ Gallon, Ice Lip, with or without Foot	$150

Pitcher, Water, ½ Gallon, No Ice Lip	$325
Plate, 6" or 7"	$12.50
Plate, Crescent, 7½" x 4⅜"	$55
Plate, 8", Sauce Liner, Oval	$30
Plate, 8½"	$15
Plate, 9"	$17.50
Plate, 9½"	$25
Plate, 10", Square Shape, Pedestal Base	$22.50
Plate, 10½"	$22.50
Plate, 11½"	$25
Plate, Torte, 13½", Oval	$55
Plate, Torte, 14"	$75
Plate, Torte, 18"	$150
Plate, Torte, 20"	$225
Plate Torte, 24"	$275
Platter, 10½" Oval	$50
Platter, 12" Oval	$65
Platter, 12" Round	$100
Platter, 12½" Round	$110
Platter, 13" Round	$115
Pomade Box with Cover, 2" Square	$350
Puff Box with Cover, Cube Shape (3" x 3" x 2⅞")	$250
Puff Box with Cover, Rectangular (3⅛" x 2¾")	$250
Punch Bowl, 12", Footed	$200
Punch Bowl with Stand, 14", 10" Tall, 2 Gallon	$400
Punch Bowl with Stand, 18", 12" Tall, 3¾ Gallon	$450
Punch Cup, Several Styles	$12.50
Relish Dish, 8½" Oval, 2-Section	$27.50
Relish Dish, 9" Oval, 4-Part	$45
Relish Dish, 9½" Oval, 3-Section	$40
Relish Dish, 10" Square, 4-Section	$100

Relish Dish, 10½" Oval, 3-Section	$42.50
Relish Dish, 11" Oblong, 2-Section	$45
Relish Dish, 11" Oblong, 3-Section	$47.50
Relish Dish, 11" Square, 4-Section	$225
Ring Holder	$25
Salt Dip	$11
Salt and Pepper Shakers, 2 Styles (3" or 3¼" Tall)	$35
Sandwich Server with Center Handle, 10½"	$45
Sandwich Server with Center Handle, 11½"	$50
Saucer, 6"	$6
Saucer, Ice Cream, 2 Styles	$50
Sherbet, 3⅛" Tall, 6 oz.	$11
Sherbet, 3¼" Tall, 5 oz.	$11
Sherbet, 3½" Tall, 4½ or 5 oz.	$11
Sherbet, 3½" Tall, 4½ oz., with Handle	$12.50
Sherbet, 3½" Tall, 4½ oz., Octagonal Stem	$14
Sherbet, 4⅛" Tall, 5½ oz.	$15
Sherbet, 4¼" Tall, Flared, Hexagonal Stem	$15
Sherbet, 4½" Tall, 4½ oz.	$15
Spoon, Serving	$37.50
Spooner, 3¾" Tall	$35
Straw Holder with Cover, 10" Tall	$300
Sugar, Open, Individual, 2¼" (Tiny)	$15
Sugar, Open, Individual, 6 oz., 2-Handled (Small)	$17.50
Sugar with Cover, 6¼" Tall (Large)	$25
Sugar Shaker with Chrome Top, 4¾" Tall	$55
Tidbit, 7" Tall, 3-Footed	$45
Toothpick Holder, 2¼" Tall	$27.50
Tray, 5" x 2½" Rectangular	$85
Tray, Oval, 6", 2-Handled	$40
Tray, Oval, 6¾" x 3"	$25

Tray, Celery, Oval, 10" x 4½"	$45
Tray, Oval, 10" x 5", 2-Handled	$45
Tray, Square, 10"	$175
Tray, Square, 10¾"	$175
Tray, Rectangular, 10½" x 7½"	$85
Tray, 12" Round	$175
Tray, Serving, Oval, 11½" x 8"	$75
Tray, Ice Cream, Oval, 13½" x 10"	$200
Tray, Fruit, 16" Round, 4" Tall	$125
Tumbler, 2⅞" Tall, 3 oz.	$15
Tumbler, 3⅜" Tall, 6 oz.	$16
Tumbler, 3⅞" or 4" Tall, 8 oz.	$17.50
Tumbler, 4¼" Tall, 8 oz.	$20
Tumbler, 4¾" Tall, 5 oz.	$16
Tumbler, 5" Tall, 9 oz.	$20
Tumbler, 5¼" Tall, 8 oz.	$22.50
Tumbler, 5", 5¼", or 5½" Tall, 12 oz.	$24
Vase, 4½" Tall	$75
Vase, 6" Tall	$35
Vase, 6" Tall, Flared	$25
Vase, Bud, 6" Tall, Footed	$25
Vase, 6" Tall, Urn Shape, Footed	$40
Vase, 6½" Tall, Flared	$25
Vase, 7" Tall, Flared	$75
Vase, 7½" Tall, Urn Shape, Footed	$45
Vase, 8" Tall	$45
Vase, 8" Tall, Flared	$80
Vase, 8" Tall, Cylindrically Shaped, 3½" Diameter	$65
Vase, 8½" Tall, Bud, Flared or Cupped	$35
Vase, 9" Tall, Square-Footed	$65
Vase, 9½" Tall, Flared	$165

Vase, 9½" Tall, Flared, Swung	$225
Vase, 10" Tall, Cylindrically Shaped, 4" Diameter	$100
Vase, 10" Tall, 6" Diameter, Cupped	$225
Vase, 10" Tall, 8" Diameter	$125
Vase, 12" Tall, Cylindrically Shaped, 4½" Diameter	$250
Vase, 14" Tall, Flared, Swung	$275
Vase, 15" Tall, Narrow	$125
Vase, 16" Tall, Flared, Swung	$375
Vase, 20" Tall, Narrow	$375
Vase, 25" Tall, Narrow	$475
Whiskey Tumbler, 2 oz.	$17.50
Wineglass, 4¼" Tall, 2½ oz.	$16.50

Apollo
Adams and Company, 1870s

Prices below are for crystal; increase them 25–35 percent for frosted pieces, and double them for any ruby flashed examples.

An Apollo pattern made by McKee is quite different from Adams's. This pattern is also referred to as Shield Band or Canadian Horseshoe.

Bowl, 4"	$12.50
Bowl, 5"	$15
Bowl, 6"	$17.50
Bowl, 7"	$25
Bowl, 8"	$30
Butter Dish with Cover	$50
Cake Stand, 8"	$50
Cake Stand, 9"	$60
Cake Stand, 10"	$70
Celery with Base, Upright	$40
Cheese Dish with Cover	$105
Compote, Open, 5", High	$40

Compote, Open, 7", Low	$35
Compote with Cover, 8"	$75
Creamer	$45
Cruet with Stopper	$75
Egg Holder	$35
Goblet	$40
Lamp, 10"	$150
Pickle Dish	$25
Pitcher, Syrup with Lid	$135
Pitcher, Water	$80
Plate, 9½", Square	$32.50
Salt Dip	$25
Sauce Dish, Flat	$12.50
Sauce Dish, 5", Footed	$15
Spooner	$35
Sugar Dish with Cover	$55
Sugar Shaker	$35
Tray	$50
Tumbler	$35
Wineglass	$40

Arched Grape
Boston & Sandwich Glass Company, 1870s–1880s

Arched Grape is one of the many typical grape patterns produced throughout the 19th century. As the name implies, this one consists of a simple grape pattern within arches. Note that this pattern was not produced in full lead crystal.

Butter Dish with Cover	$65
Celery Vase	$45
Champagne Glass	$40
Compote with Cover (Low)	$60
Compote with Cover (High)	$75
Cordial Glass	$45
Creamer	$45

Cordial Arched Grape Pattern Glass. *Drawing by Mark Pickvet.*

Goblet	$35
Pitcher, Water	$85
Sauce Dish, 4"	$12.50
Spooner	$35
Sugar Dish	$30
Sugar Dish with Cover	$55
Wine Goblet	$35

Ashburton
Various Companies, 1840s–1880s

Ashburton is a large thumbprint pattern and was made in some quantity by Boston & Sandwich, New England, McKee, and many others. There are a few rare pieces such as the toddy jar, butter dish, and creamer. Ashburton has been steadily increasing in price over the past few years, especially for the larger and rarer pieces.

Double the prices listed below for any colored pieces; a few flashed ruby red, yellow, amber, green, and opalescent pieces have been found.

The creamer along with the sugar, wineglass, and goblet have all been reproduced, which is cause for some concern. Reduce the prices listed below by 60–70 percent for reproductions.

Ale Glass, 5" Tall, Crystal	$100
Bitters Bottle	$75
Bottle, Whiskey, 1 pt.	$65

Bottle, Whiskey, 1 qt.	$85
Bowl, 6½"	$85
Butter Dish with Cover	$200
Candy Dish (No Cover), 7½"	$80
Carafe	$190
Celery Dish	$105
Celery Dish, Scalloped	$120
Champagne Glass	$95
Claret Glass, 5¼" Tall	$60
Cordial, 4½" Tall	$100
Creamer	$235
Decanter with Stopper, 16 oz.	$225
Decanter with Stopper, 32 oz.	$275
Decanter with Stopper, 48 oz.	$325
Egg Holder, Single	$75
Egg Holder, Double	$100
Flip Glass with Handle	$155
Goblet, Barrel-Shape Cup, Flared	$60
Goblet, Straight Sides	$55
Honey Dish	$22.50
Lamp	$175
Mug, 7"	$105
Pitcher, Syrup with Lid, 16 oz., Jug Style	$300
Pitcher, Milk, 32 oz.	$350
Pitcher, Water, 48 oz.	$500
Plate, 6⅝"	$85
Sauce Dish, Small	$15
Sauce Dish, Large	$25
Spooner	$55
Sugar Dish with Cover	$175
Toddy Jar with Cover, Matching Underplate	$400

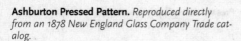

Ashburton Pressed Pattern. *Reproduced directly from an 1878 New England Glass Company Trade catalog.*

Toddy Jar with Cover, Handled, Matching Underplate	$450
Tumbler, Bar, Lemonade, or Water	$85
Tumbler, Water, Footed	$125
Tumbler, Whiskey, with Handle	$150
Water Bottle, Tumble-Up	$115
Wineglass	$55

Atlas
Adams & Company, 1880s; Bryce Brothers, 1889; and U.S. Glass Company, 1890s

Atlas is a fairly plain crystal style that contains circular bulges near the bottom of most pieces. Double the prices for any ruby flashed or engraved examples.

Bowl, 9"	$25
Butter Dish with Cover	$55
Cake Stand, 8" Tall	$45
Cake Stand, 9" Tall	$50
Cake Stand, 10" Tall	$60
Celery Vase	$40
Champagne Glass, 5½" Tall	$35
Compote with Cover, 5"	$60
Compote, 7"	$45

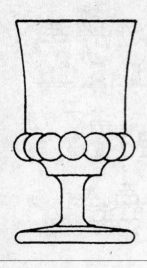

Pressed Atlas Glass. *Drawing by Mark Pickvet.*

Compote with Cover, 8"	$75
Cordial Glass	$40
Creamer, 2 Styles	$35
Goblet	$40
Marmalade Jar with Cover	$55
Molasses Can	$75
Pitcher, Syrup	$75
Pitcher, Water, 2 Styles	$75
Salt and Pepper Shakers	$30
Salt Dip, Individual (Small)	$20
Salt Dip, Master (Large)	$25
Sauce Bowl, Flat	$15
Sauce Bowl, Footed	$20
Spooner	$35
Sugar Dish with Cover	$50
Toothpick Holder	$25
Tray, Water	$85
Tumbler	$35
Whiskey Glass	$25
Wineglass	$35

Balder
U.S. Glass Company, 1890s–Early 1900s

Prices below are for plain crystal items. For emerald green, increase them by 50 percent; for ruby red, double them.

A few pieces of this pattern were trimmed in gold (add 25 percent to the prices listed below for any not listed), but it is difficult to find those where the gold lining or trim is completely intact. Note that gold trim can usually be removed from clear or colored glass with a pencil eraser, but be careful with flashed items; the flashing could easily be scraped or rubbed off, too!

Although Balder is the popular name, it is also known as U.S. Glass Company's Pennsylvania pattern in their state series.

Biscuit Jar with Cover	$85
Bowl, 4"	$25
Bowl, 8"	$30
Bowl, 8", Square	$30
Butter Dish with Cover	$80
Carafe, 1 pt.	$50
Carafe, Water, 1 qt.	$70
Celery Tray	$35
Celery Vase	$50
Champagne Glass	$30
Cheese Dish with Cover	$80
Compote, Ruffled	$55
Creamer, Individual (Small)	$20
Creamer, Large	$30
Cruet with Stopper	$55
Cup	$17.50
Decanter with Stopper	$125
Goblet	$30
Molasses Can	$85
Pitcher, Syrup with Metal Lid	$60
Pitcher, Water	$75

Plate, 8"	$30
Punch Bowl	$200
Punch Cup	$17.50
Saltshaker	$15
Sauce Dish	$12.50
Spooner	$26
Sugar, Handled (Small)	$20
Sugar with Cover (Large)	$50
Tankard	$130
Toothpick Holder	$40
Tumbler, Juice	$16
Tumbler	$35
Whiskey Tumbler	$50
Wineglass	$25

Baltimore Pear
Adams & Company, 1870s–1880s; U.S. Glass Company, 1890s–Early 1900s

Because the pattern consists of two pears, it is also referred to as Double Pear or Twin Pear. A few other names include Fig, Gypsy, or Maryland Pear. Reduce the prices by half for reproduction pink or cobalt blue items.

Bowl, 6"	$35
Bowl, 9"	$40
Butter Dish with Cover	$85
Cake Stand, 9"	$75
Celery Vase	$55
Compote, Up to 5", Open	$35
Compote, 5" Up to 7", Open	$45
Compote, Over 7", Open	$55
Compote with Cover, Up to 5"	$60
Compote with Cover, 5" Up to 7"	$70
Compote with Cover, Over 7"	$80
Creamer	$40

Goblet	$40
Pickle Dish	$27.50
Pitcher, Milk	$85
Pitcher, Water	$105
Plate, 8½"	$35
Plate, 10"	$45
Plate, 12½", Bread	$75
Relish Dish	$35
Sauce Dish	$15
Sauce Dish, Footed	$20
Spooner	$45
Sugar Dish with Cover	$60
Tray, 10½"	$50

Barred Oval
George Duncan & Sons and U.S. Glass Company, 1890s–Early 1900s

The frosted (increase prices by 50 percent) items can be found a little more frequently than the rare ruby red (triple the prices listed below). The pattern is characterized by five horizontal bars that pass through the center of the ovals in each object.

Bottle, Water	$65
Butter Dish with Cover	$115
Celery Dish	$40
Compote, Open	$45
Creamer	$45
Cruet with Faceted Stopper	$100
Goblet	$35
Pitcher, Water	$100
Plate, 5"	$25
Sauce Dish	$17.50
Spooner	$30
Sugar Dish with Cover	$65
Tumbler	$35

Basket Weave
Various Companies, 1880s–1890s

Double the prices listed below for amber, blue, green, yellow, and vaseline. Beware of modern reproductions of pitchers, tumblers, and goblets.

Bowl, Berry	$25
Bowl, Finger	$30
Bowl with Cover	$40
Butter Dish with Cover	$40
Cake Plate	$50
Compote with Cover, 7"	$55
Cordial	$35
Creamer	$30
Cup	$25
Egg Holder, Single	$20
Egg Holder, Double	$30
Goblet	$30
Lamp	$60
Mug	$25
Pickle Dish	$30
Pitcher, Syrup, with Metal Lid	$75
Pitcher, Milk	$110
Pitcher, Water	$75
Plate, 8¾", 2-Handled	$27.50
Platter, 11", 2-Handled	$35
Salt Dip	$15
Salt and Pepper Shakers	$50
Sauce Dish, Round	$20
Saucer	$15
Spooner	$27.50
Sugar Dish with Cover	$40
Tray, Bread, 11"	$20

Tray, 12"	$25
Tumbler, Footed	$20
Wineglass	$30

Beaded Grape Medallion
Boston Silver Glass Company, Late 1860s–1871

The feet of certain objects may be plain or banded. The traditional grape design is in a cameo or medallion form. Color flashed versions were made during the Depression era; the prices below apply to them as well.

Bowl, Oval, Small	$35
Bowl, Oval, Large, 8½"	$45
Butter Dish, Acorn Finial	$75
Castor Bottle	$95
Celery Vase	$50
Champagne Glass	$50
Compote with Cover, Low, Oval	$90
Compote with Cover, High, Oval (10" x 7")	$110
Cordial	$80
Creamer, Applied Handle	$60
Egg Holder	$35
Goblet	$40
Honey Dish	$30
Lamp, Handled	$115
Pickle Dish	$45
Pitcher, Water	$175
Plate, 6"	$45
Salt Dip, Round, Flat	$30
Salt Dip, Oval, Flat	$30
Salt Dip, Footed	$35
Spooner	$35
Sugar Bowl with Cover, Acorn Finial	$90

Beaded Grape Medallion Wine Goblet. *Drawing by Mark Pickvet.*

Bedford
Fostoria Glass Company, 1901–05

The Bedford was one of Fostoria's first lines of glass and was referred to as Line No. 1000 by Fostoria.

Bonbon Dish, 5", 1 Handle	$25
Bonbon Dish, 6", 1 Handle	$30
Bowl, Berry, 7"	$30
Bowl, Berry, 8"	$35
Bowl, 9" Oval	$40
Bowl, 10" Oval	$45
Butter Dish with Cover	$100
Celery Vase	$40
Claret Glass	$40
Compote, 6", Open	$40
Compote with Cover, 6"	$85
Compote, 7", Open	$45
Cracker Jar with Cover	$175
Creamer, Individual (Small)	$30
Creamer (Large)	$45
Cruet with Hollow Stopper	$70

Bedford Glassware Line. *Reproduced directly from an early-20th-century Fostoria catalog.*

Cup, Custard	$30
Goblet	$40
Ice Cream Tray, Rectangular	$55
Pitcher, Jug Shape	$90
Salt Dip, Individual	$22.50
Spooner	$35
Sugar with Cover, Individual (Small)	$55
Sugar (Large)	$65
Sugar Shaker	$65
Toothpick Holder	$55
Tumbler, Water	$35
Whiskey Tumbler	$22.50
Wineglass	$40

Bellflower
Various Companies, 1840s–1880s

Also known as the Ribbed Leaf and Bellflower, this pattern boasts some of the oldest, rarest, and most valuable early pattern glass made in America. It is also characterized by fine vertical ribbing. Some pieces may have a single or double vine within the pattern. A few rare colors such as amber and cobalt also exist, for which the prices below should be doubled. The Boston & Sandwich Glass Company was the original maker of this pattern, but others such as the McKee Brothers produced it, too.

Bowl, 6"	$115
Bowl, 8"	$135
Bowl, Flat with Scalloped Edge	$135
Bowl, Flat, Scalloped and Pointed Edge	$175
Bowl, Oval, 7" x 5"	$65
Bowl, Oval, 9" x 6"	$75
Butter Dish with Cover, Plain Edge	$135
Butter Dish with Cover, Beaded Edge	$160
Butter Dish with Cover, Rayed Edge	$185
Cake Stand	$2,075
Celery Vase	$240
Champagne Glass	$135
Compote, Open, Low, 6¾"	$115
Compote, Open, High, 8"	$135
Compote, Open, High, 8½" Tall, 9¾" Diameter	$150
Compote with Cover, Low, 8"	$165
Compote with Cover, High, 8"	$185
Cordial, Several Styles	$85
Creamer	$175
Cruet with Stopper	$135
Decanter with Stopper, 16 oz.	$325
Decanter with Stopper, 32 oz.	$350
Decanter with Bellflower-Pattern Stopper, 16 or 32 oz.	$600
Egg Holder, Straight Sides	$55
Egg Holder, Flared Sides	$60
Goblet (Several Styles)	$85
Honey Dish, 3¼" x 2½"	$37.50
Lamp, Bracket, All Glass	$425
Lamp, Marble Base	$235
Mug, Applied Handle	$285
Pickle Dish	$75

Bellflower Glass. *Drawing by Mark Pickvet.*

Pitcher, Syrup with Lid, Round	$875
Ptcher, Syrup with Lid, 10-Sided	$1,150
Pitcher, Milk	$750
Pitcher, Water (2 Styles)	$375
Plate, 6"	$125
Salt Dip, Footed	$55
Salt Dip with Cover, Footed	$200
Sauce Dish, Various Styles	$35
Spooner	$60
Sugar, Octagonal	$425
Sugar Dish with Cover	$225
Tumbler, Footed	$250
Tumbler, Water	$150
Whiskey Tumbler	$200
Wineglass, Several Styles	$125

Berry or Barberry
Boston & Sandwich Glass Company, 1860s; Mckee Brothers, 1880s

The berries on this pattern may be round or oval and the number of them varies as well, particularly on the goblets. A few odd-colored pieces continue to pop up; double the prices listed below for pale green, pale blue, amber, or yellow. This pattern is also known as Olive or Pepper Berry.

Bowl, Oval, 6"	$25
Bowl, Oval, 7"	$30
Bowl, 8", Round	$30
Bowl with Cover, 8"	$65
Bowl, Oval, 8" x 5½"	$40
Bowl, 9", Oval	$45
Butter Dish with Cover, 8", 2 Styles	$90
Cake Stand	$150
Celery Dish	$55
Celery Vase	$65
Compote with Cover, Low, 8"	$75
Compote with Cover, High, 8"	$65
Compote with Cover, High, Shell Finial, 8"	$90
Cordial	$60
Creamer	$45
Cup Plate	$20
Egg Holder	$40
Goblet	$35
Honey Dish, 3½"	$25
Pickle Dish	$25
Pitcher, Syrup with Pewter Lid	$185
Pitcher, Water, Applied Handle	$155
Plate, 6"	$25
Salt Dip, Footed	$32.50
Sauce Dish	$30
Sauce Dish, Footed	$35
Spooner, Footed	$37.50
Sugar Dish with Cover	$60
Tumbler, Footed	$30
Wineglass	$35

Bleeding Heart
Boston & Sandwich Glass Company, 1860s–1870s; King and Son & Company, 1870s; and U.S. Glass Company, 1890s

This pattern was originally known as Floral, and the floral design is usually separated by a vertical line above the halfway point of each object. King and Son also produced this pattern in white opaque (milk) glass, for which the prices listed below should be increased by 25 percent.

Bowl, 7¼", Oval	$40
Bowl, 8"	$50
Bowl with Cover, 9¼", Oval	$75
Butter Dish with Cover	$95
Cake Stand, 9" to 9½" Tall	$85
Cake Stand, 10" Tall	$100
Cake Stand, 11" Tall	$115
Compote with Cover, Low-Footed, 7"	$70
Compote with Cover, Low-Footed, 7½"	$75
Compote with Cover, Low-Footed, 8"	$85
Compote with Cover, High-Footed, 8"	$90
Compote with Cover, 8½", Oval	$65
Compote with Cover, High-Footed, 9"	$115
Creamer, Applied Handle	$65
Creamer, Molded Handle	$35
Dish with Cover, 7"	$65
Egg Holder, Straight-Sided	$55
Egg Holder, Barrel Shape	$60
Egg Rack, 3-Egg	$385
Goblet, Knob on Stem (Several Styles)	$45
Honey Dish	$20
Mug	$50
Pickle Dish, Oval, 8¾" x 5"	$40
Pitcher, Milk, Applied Handle	$250
Pitcher, Water, Applied Handle	$185
Plate (Several Styles)	$85

Pressed Glass. Bleeding Heart Pattern. *Drawings by Mark Pickvet.*

Pressed Glass. Block and Fan Pattern. *Drawings by Mark Pickvet.*

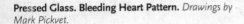

Platter, Oval	$85
Relish Dish, 4 Divisions, Oval, 5½" x 3½"	$125
Salt Dip, Round, Footed, Master (Large)	$65
Salt Dip, Oval, Flat (Small)	$40
Sauce Dish, Round, Flat	$22.50
Sauce Dish, Oval	$27.50
Spooner	$40
Sugar Dish with Cover	$75
Tray, Oval	$55
Tumbler, Footed	$85
Tumbler, Water	$85
Wineglass	$55

Block and Fan
Richards & Hartley Glass Company, 1880s; U.S. Glass Company, 1890s

This design is also known as the Romeo, or Red Block and Fan pattern. It is characterized by horizontal bands of fans that circle the top and bottom of each object. Between the fans are horizontal rows of blocks. There are a few rare ruby flashed pieces (double the prices listed below).

Biscuit Jar with Cover	$75
Bowl, Finger	$57.50

Bowl, 4"	$22.50
Bowl, 8"	$45
Bowl, Orange	$55
Bowl, Rose	$40
Butter Dish with Cover	$75
Cake Stand, 9"	$45
Cake Stand, 10"	$55
Carafe	$60
Celery Tray	$35
Celery Vase	$45
Compote, Open, 8"	$45
Condiment Set, 4-Piece (Salt and Pepper Shakers, Cruet, and Tray)	$110
Cordial	$55
Creamer, Individual (Small)	$25
Creamer, 3 Styles	$40
Cruet without Stopper, Small	$40
Cruet without Stopper, Large	$55
Goblet	$55
Ice Tub	$55
Jam Jar without Cover	$95
Lamp	$175
Pickle Dish	$32.50
Pitcher, Milk	$60
Pitcher, Syrup	$100
Pitcher, Water, Pedestal Base	$85
Plate, 6"	$20
Plate, 10½"	$30
Relish Dish, Rectangular	$35
Salt and Pepper Shakers	$55
Sauce Dish, Square, Flat	$20
Sauce Dish, 4", Circular, Footed	$25

Spooner	$35
Sugar, Open	$45
Sugar Dish with Cover	$60
Sugar Shaker	$50
Tray, Ice Cream	$85
Tumbler	$45
Wineglass	$55

Bow Tie
Thompson Glass Company, 1889–92

This pattern is also referred to as American Bow Tie. The pattern is characterized by fans and center circles that resemble bow ties, hence the name. The only known producer was the Thompson Glass Company, a firm that operated for only a few short years.

Bowl, 8"	$45
Bowl, Orange, 10", Footed	$125
Bowl, Oval, 10¼"	$75
Butter Dish with Cover	$75
Butter Pat	$35
Cake Stand, 9"	$67.50
Compote, Open, 5½" (High)	$65
Compote, Open, 6½" (Low)	$55
Compote, Open, 8" (Low)	$65
Compote, Open, 9¼" (High)	$75
Creamer	$55
Goblet	$65
Honey Dish with Cover	$65
Marmalade Jar	$85
Pitcher, Milk	$100
Pitcher, Water	$100
Punch Bowl	$125
Relish Dish, Rectangular	$35
Salt Dip, Individual (Small)	$25

Salt Dip, Master (Large)	$50
Saltshaker	$50
Sauce Dish, Flat	$20
Spooner	$40
Sugar Dish, Open	$55
Sugar Dish with Cover	$70
Tumbler	$55
Wineglass	$65

Broken Column
Various Companies, 1880s–1890s

This pattern is also referred to as Irish Column, Bamboo Irish Column, Rattan, Ribbed Fingerprint, or Notched Rib. It is characterized by raised columns that project outward from the object. Known producers were the Colombia Glass Company, the Portland Glass Company, and the U.S. Glass Company; there may have been others as well.

Some pieces have ruby notches or flashing (double the prices below); others are trimmed in gold (increase the prices below by about a third); and a few are found in cobalt blue (double the prices below). Beware of reproductions—the goblet and compotes have been reproduced for the Smithsonian Institution and the Metropolitan Museum of Art. Smithsonian reproductions are marked "S.I."

Banana Dish, Flat	$65
Banana Stand	$215
Basket with Handle, 13½" Long, 12" Tall	$150
Biscuit Jar with Cover	$100
Bottle, Water	$100
Bowl, Finger	$35
Bowl, 4"	$25
Bowl, 6", with Cover	$55
Bowl, 7", with Cover	$65
Bowl, 8", with Cover	$75
Bowl, 8½"	$50
Bowl, 9"	$55
Bread Tray	$75

Butter Dish with Cover	$100
Cake Stand, 9"	$90
Cake Stand, 10"	$100
Carafe, Water	$85
Celery Dish	$75
Celery Tray, Oval	$50
Champagne Glass	$110
Claret Glass	$85
Compote, Open, 8"	$85
Compote with Cover, 5¼" Diameter, 10¼" Tall	$100
Compote with Cover, 10"	$125
Creamer	$55
Cruet with Stopper	$100
Cup	$20
Decanter	$100
Goblet	$65
Marmalade Jar	$100
Pickle Castor	$265
Pitcher, Syrup with Lid, Jug Shape	$185
Pitcher, Water	$110
Plate, 4"	$32.50
Plate, 7¾"	$45
Relish Dish	$35
Saltshaker	$55
Sauce Dish, Flat	$15
Spooner	$45
Sugar Dish with Cover	$85
Sugar Shaker	$100
Toothpick Holder	$175
Tumbler	$55
Wineglass	$90

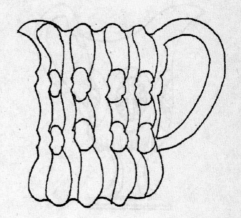

Broken Column Syrup Pitcher. *Drawing by Mark Pickvet.*

Buckle
Various Companies, 1850s–1870s

The original Buckle pattern is attributed to Boston & Sandwich, but others followed (Union Glass Co., Burlington of Canada, and Gillinder & Sons). Those listed "with Band" are identical in pattern except for an extra horizontal band at the top of each piece. The pattern is also sometimes referred to as Oaken Bucket or Early Bucket.

Some pieces were made in a finer grade of crystal (add 25 percent to the prices below); a few light blue pieces also have been found (double the prices below). Water pitchers in this pattern are very rare.

Bowl, 6", Rolled Rim	$65
Bowl, 7", Rolled Rim	$70
Bowl, 8", Rolled Rim	$75
Bowl, 10", Rolled Rim	$80
Bowl, 6", with Band, Flat Rim	$40
Bowl, 7", with Band, Flat Rim	$45
Bowl, 8", with Band, Flat Rim	$50
Butter Dish with Cover	$110
Cake Stand, 9¾"	$45
Champagne Glass	$60
Compote, Open, 6"	$75
Compote, Open, 8½"	$60

Pressed Buckle Glass. *Drawing by Mark Pickvet.*

Compote, Open, with Band	$45
Compote with Cover, with Band	$70
Cordial, with Band	$55
Creamer, Pedestal Foot, Applied Handles	$65
Creamer, with Band	$55
Egg Holder	$40
Egg Holder, with Band	$40
Goblet	$45
Goblet, with Band	$45
Pickle Dish, Oval	$45
Pitcher, Water, Applied Handle	$800
Pitcher, Water, with Band	$575
Salt Dip, Oval, Flat, Pattern in Base Only	$20
Salt Dip, Footed	$25
Salt Dip, Footed, with Band	$20
Spooner, Scalloped	$35
Spooner, with Band	$30
Sugar Dish with Cover	$70
Sugar Dish with Cover, with Band	$60
Tumbler	$50

Tumbler, with Band	$45
Wineglass	$45

Bull's-Eye
Various Companies, 1850s–1870s

The original Bull's-Eye was made by both the New England Glass Company and the Boston & Sandwich Glass Company. A few pieces were produced in green, red, milk white, and other colors, for which prices below should be doubled.

Several variations of the basic Bull's-Eye design were produced by the U.S. Glass Company; the Union Glass Company; Dalzell, Gilmore & Leighton; and others. These include Bull's-Eye with Diamond Point, Bull's-Eye and Daisy, Bull's-Eye and Fan, Bull's-Eye with Fleur-de-Lys, Bull's-Eye and Pillar, Bull's-Eye and Star, and others. The prices are comparable for all basic pattern variants.

Bitters Bottle	$90
Bottle, Water, Tumble-Up	$200
Bowl	$55
Butter Dish with Cover	$175
Carafe	$55
Castor Bottle with Stopper	$75
Celery Vase	$95
Champagne Glass	$125
Cologne Bottle with Stopper	$125
Compote, Open, Low Footed	$70
Compote, Open, High	$90
Cordial	$85
Creamer with Applied Handle	$150
Cruet with Stopper	$150
Decanter with Stopper, 16 oz.	$200
Decanter with Stopper, 32 oz.	$350
Egg Cup with Cover	$225
Egg Holder	$60
Goblet	$80
Goblet, with Knobbed Stem	$95
Jam Jar with Cover	$125

Pressed Bull's-Eye. *Drawing by Mark Pickvet.*   **Pressed Bull's-Eye.** *Photo by Mark Pickvet.*

Jelly Dish	$55
Lamp	$175
Mug, 3½", Applied Handle	$125
Pickle Dish, Oval	$55
Pitcher, Water	$325
Relish Dish, Oval	$37.50
Salt Dip, Footed, Individual (Small)	$50
Salt Dip with Cover, Oblong, Footed, Master (Large)	$135
Spooner	$50
Sugar Dish with Cover	$175
Toothpick Holder	$55
Tumbler, Small, 3½"	$55
Tumbler, Water	$105
Whiskey Tumbler	$75
Wineglass	$60

Button Arches
Duncan & Miller Glass Company, 1890s

The arched button design of this pattern appears on the lower quarter or fifth of most objects. Button Arches was a popular medium for souvenirs, and most pieces can be found with ruby red, ruby flashed, etched, engraved, and frosted band designs.

The prices below are for plain crystal. Increase the prices by 50 percent for ruby or ruby flashed and by 25 percent for any etching, engraving, or frosted bands. There are a few clambroth (a streaky tan-white opalescent hue) or off-white opaque pieces in this pattern as well (double the prices).

Note that some pieces, particularly goblets, wineglasses, and toothpick holders, have been reproduced.

Bowl, 8"	$40
Cake Stand, 9¼"	$60
Compote	$37.50
Creamer	$40
Cruet with Stopper	$90
Cup	$27.50
Goblet	$35
Mug, Small, 3"	$35
Mug, Large, 4"	$40
Pitcher, Syrup	$185
Pitcher, Water	$125
Punch Cup	$25
Salt and Pepper Shakers	$60
Spooner	$30
Sugar Dish with Cover	$60
Toothpick Holder	$40
Tumbler, Water	$35
Wineglass	$35

Cabbage Rose
Central Glass Company, 1880s–1890s

The pattern is usually on the lower half to two-thirds of each object and is separated from the clear unpatterned portion by a horizontal band. Any colored glass in this pattern is a reproduction by the Mosser Glass Company from the early 1960s (reduce prices by two-thirds to three-fourths).

Basket with Handle, 12"	$150
Bitters Bottle, 6½" Tall	$150

Bowl, 6"	$32.50
Bowl with Cover, 7½"	$75
Bowl, Oval, 7½"	$37.50
Bowl, Oval, 9½"	$45
Butter Dish with Cover	$85
Cake Stand, 9¼"	$50
Cake Stand, 11"	$75
Cake Stand, 12½"	$85
Celery Vase	$55
Champagne Glass	$60
Compote, Open, 7½"	$90
Compote, Open, 9½"	$110
Compote with Cover, 6"	$105
Compote with Cover, 7" to 7½"	$115
Compote with Cover, 8" to 8½"	$130
Compote with Cover, 9"	$140
Compote with Cover, 10"	$155
Cordial	$55
Creamer, Applied Handle	$65
Egg Holder	$55
Goblet	$50
Mug	$70
Pickle Dish	$42.50
Pitcher, 32 oz., Milk	$175
Pitcher, 48 oz., Water	$175
Relish Dish, 8½"	$45
Salt Dip, Footed, Beaded Rim	$35
Sauce Dish (Several Varieties)	$20
Spooner	$40
Sugar, Open	$45
Sugar Dish with Cover	$75

Tumbler, Water	$50
Wineglass	$50

Cable
Boston & Sandwich Glass Company, 1850s–1960s

Color pieces are very rare and include opaque blue, opaque green, and some with amber panels; double the prices below for any colored examples. Cable was produced to commemorate the laying of the Trans-Atlantic Cable linking Europe to America. A few pattern variations were introduced later by other manufacturers.

Bowl, 8", Footed	$55
Bowl, 9"	$80
Butter Dish with Cover	$135
Cake Stand, 9"	$115
Celery Vase	$85
Champagne Glass	$275
Compote, 5½" Diameter (High)	$75
Compote, 7" Diameter (Low)	$65
Compote, 9" Diameter (Low)	$65
Compote, 9¾" Tall, 10" Diameter	$125
Compote, 5¾" Tall, 11" Diameter	$125
Cordial	$150
Creamer	$350
Decanter with Stopper, 16 oz.	$300
Decanter with Stopper, 32 oz.	$350
Egg Holder	$75
Egg Holder with Cover	$250
Goblet	$80
Honey Dish	$55
Lamp, All Glass, 8¾" Tall (Glass Base)	$175
Lamp, with Marble Base, 8¾" Tall	$150
Lamp, Miniature	$550
Mug	$135

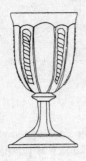

Pressed Cable Glass. *Drawing by Mark Pickvet.*

Pressed Glass. Right to left: Cable, Waffle, Star & Bull's-Eye, and Bar Patterns. *Courtesy of the Sandwich Glass Museum. Photo by Mark Pickvet.*

Pitcher, Syrup	$350
Pitcher, Water	$750
Plate, 6"	$100
Salt Dip, Individual, Flat	$40
Salt Dip, Footed	$50
Salt Dip with Cover	$125
Sauce Dish	$35
Spooner	$50
Sugar Dish with Cover	$135
Tumbler, Footed	$225
Wineglass	$185

California
U.S. Glass Company, 1890s

The California pattern is also known as Beaded Grape. There is a horizontal line of beading at the top, and vertical bands frame the grape design.

Some pieces were trimmed in gold (add 25 percent to the prices below if the gold is completely intact). For the rarer emerald green, double the prices below. Reproductions were made by Westmoreland in colors and milk glass; prices for them are the same as for the crystal.

Bowl, 5¼", Square	$22.50
Bowl, 6¼", Square	$27.55

Bowl, 7¼", Square	$32.50
Bowl, 8", Round	$37.55
Bowl, 8¼", Square	$42.50
Bowl, Oblong	$30
Butter Dish with Cover	$75
Cake Stand, 9"	$75
Celery Tray, Oblong	$37.50
Celery Vase	$45
Compote, Open, 4" Tall	$37.50
Compote, Square, 5"	$60
Compote, Square, 6"	$70
Compote with Cover, 7" Tall	$85
Compote with Cover, 8" Tall	$100
Compote with Cover, 9" Tall	$115
Cordial	$45
Creamer	$50
Cruet with Swirl Stopper	$85
Goblet	$45
Jelly Dish with Cover, 4" Tall	$55
Olive Dish, Tab Handle	$27.50
Pickle Dish	$30
Pitcher, 32 oz., Milk, Round	$85
Pitcher, 32 oz., Milk, Square	$95
Pitcher, 48 oz., Water, Round	$95
Pitcher, 48 oz., Water, Square	$105
Pitcher, 64 oz., Water, Round	$125
Plate, 8½" Square	$35
Platter, 10¼" x 7¼" Oblong	$60
Salt and Pepper Shakers with Metal Tops	$60
Salt Dish, 4½"	$20
Sauce Dish, 3½"	$17.50
Sauce Dish, 4"	$20

Sauce Dish with 2 Handles	$25
Spooner	$40
Sugar Dish with Cover	$65
Sugar Shaker	$60
Tray, Bread	$35
Toothpick Holder	$50
Tumbler, Water	$35
Vase, 6" Tall	$35
Wineglass	$45

Carolina
Bryce Brothers, 1880s–1891; U.S. Glass Company, 1891–Early 1900s

This pattern was originally made by Bryce Brothers as the Inverness pattern. It is also referred to as Mayflower. When Bryce Brothers became part of the U.S. Glass Company conglomerate, the pattern became Carolina in the state series, which it is best known as today.

For any green or ruby flashed items (some made as souvenirs), double the prices below; for the rare amethyst-stained glass in this pattern, triple the prices below. Finally, increase the prices below by 25 percent for any pieces with fully intact gold trim.

Bowl, Berry	$27.50
Butter Dish with Cover	$45
Cake Stand	$45
Compote, 8" (High)	$47.50
Compote, 9½" (High)	$50
Creamer	$30
Goblet	$35
Jelly Dish	$20
Mug	$27.50
Pitcher, Milk	$60
Plate, 7½"	$20
Relish Dish	$20
Saltshaker	$20

Sauce Dish, Flat	$12.50
Sauce Dish, Footed	$15
Spooner	$27.50
Sugar Dish with Cover	$40
Tumbler	$20
Tumbler, Souvenir	$25
Wineglass	$35

Colorado
U.S. Glass Company, 1890s–Early 1900s

The state series of U.S. Glass continues with the Colorado pattern, which is also referred to as Lacy Medallion.

There are several color variations associated with the Colorado. For green, cobalt blue, and ruby red increase the prices below by 50 percent. For clambroth, double the prices below. For the rare amethyst-stained glass in this pattern, triple the prices below. Finally, increase the prices below by 25 percent for engraved pieces. Note that some pieces may also contain enameled decorations (same price), silver frames or feet (increase price by 25 percent), and some gold trim (increase price by 25 percent if the gold is completely intact).

Banana Stand	$45
Bowl, 6"	$32.50
Bowl, 7½", Footed	$40
Bowl, 8½", Footed	$52.50
Bowl, Triangular	$35
Butter Dish with Cover	$75
Cake Stand	$70
Celery Vase	$45
Cheese Dish, Footed	$45
Compote, 5"	$27.50
Compote, 6"	$35
Compote, 9¼"	$65
Creamer, Individual (Small)	$35
Creamer (Large)	$55
Cup	$25

Mug	$30
Nappy, 7¼"	$30
Pitcher, Milk	$175
Pitcher, Water	$175
Plate, 6¾"	$35
Plate, 8"	$40
Salt and Pepper Shakers, 3-Footed	$65
Sauce Dish, Ruffled	$22.50
Sherbet	$35
Spooner	$45
Sugar, Individual, 2 Open Handles (Small)	$35
Sugar with Dish Cover (Large)	$70
Toothpick Holder	$45
Tray, 4", Crimped	$30
Tray, 4", Flared	$30
Tray, 8", Crimped	$40
Tray, 8", Flared	$40
Tumbler	$30
Tumbler, Souvenir	$35
Vase, 12" Tall	$50
Wineglass	$35

Connecticut
U.S. Glass Company, 1898–Early 1900s

This state series of U.S. Glass is not as common as many of the others. Double the prices below for ruby flashed, stained, engraved, or transfer etched.

Biscuit Jar with Cover	$50
Bowl, 4"	$20
Bowl, 5½"	$25
Bowl, 8", Flared	$30
Butter Dish with Cover	$55

Cake Stand, 10"	$50
Celery Tray	$27.50
Celery Vase	$35
Compote, 7"	$35
Compote with Cover	$50
Creamer	$35
Goblet	$40
Lamp with Enameled Decoration	$105
Lemonade Glass with Handle	$27.50
Olive Dish, Reeded Applied Handle	$27.50
Pitcher, Water, Tankard Shape, 3 Styles	$55
Relish Dish	$22.50
Salt and Pepper Shakers	$45
Spooner	$30
Sugar Dish with Cover	$45
Sugar Shaker	$45
Toothpick Holder, 2 Styles (Flared or Transfer Etched)	$60
Tray, 8", Oblong	$35
Tumbler	$30
Wineglass	$40

Cord and Tassel
Central Glass Company, 1870s

Several of these objects (creamer, cruet, lamp, mug, pitcher, and sugar) contain handles that were either applied or pressed. The price is the same for either method.

Bowl, Oval	$45
Butter Dish with Cover	$85
Cake Stand	$65
Celery Vase	$55
Compote with Cover, 8"	$85
Cordial	$45

Pressed Glass. Cord and Tassel Pattern. *Drawing by Mark Pickvet.*

Pressed Glass. Cord Drapery Pattern. *Drawing by Mark Pickvet.*

Creamer	$50
Cruet with Stopper	$85
Egg Holder	$50
Goblet	$45
Lamp, Low Pedestal	$125
Mug	$55
Pitcher, Water	$140
Sauce Dish, Flat	$27.50
Spooner	$37.50
Sugar with Cover	$75
Wineglass	$45

Cord Drapery
Indiana Tumbler and Goblet Company, 1890s–Early 1900s

Colors include amber, canary yellow, cobalt blue, emerald or opaque Nile green, and white (increase prices 60–70 percent for color examples). Chocolate pieces are two to three times more valuable than these colors and are listed under Chocolate in the Art Glass section.

Bowl, Berry	$32.50
Bowl, Oval, Deep	$45
Butter Dish with Cover	$70

Cake Stand	$60
Compote, Open, Fluted	$65
Compote with Cover, 8"	$225
Creamer	$55
Cruet with Dewey Stopper (Amber Only)	$375
Goblet	$50
Jelly Dish with Cover	$65
Pitcher, Syrup with Lid	$125
Pitcher, Water	$125
Plate, 6"	$45
Punch Cup	$24
Relish Dish, 9¼" x 5¼"	$40
Salt and Pepper Shakers	$55
Sauce Dish	$25
Spooner	$35
Sugar	$55
Tumbler	$45
Wineglass	$50

Croesus
Riverside Glass Works, 1890s

Croesus is characterized by curves, shells, and diamonds. Double the prices below for emerald green, and triple them for the rare amethyst color. For intact gold trim, increase the prices below by 25 percent.

Beware of reproductions. Toothpick holders and tumblers have been reproduced in America, and the four-piece table set has been reproduced in Japan.

Bowl, Scalloped Rim	$40
Bowl with Cover, 7"	$65
Butter Dish with Cover	$90
Celery Dish	$40
Compote with Cover, 6" Diameter, 10½" Tall	$100
Creamer, Small (Individual)	$32.50

Creamer, Medium (Berry)	$45
Creamer, Large (Regular Table Size)	$55
Cruet with Stopper	$175
Pitcher, Water	$90
Salt and Pepper Shakers	$65
Sauce Dish	$30
Spooner	$35
Sugar Bowl with Cover	$85
Table Set, 4-Piece	$225
Toothpick Holder	$60
Tray	$55
Tumbler, Water	$50

Crystal Wedding
Adams Glass Company, 1880s; U.S. Glass Company, 1890s

Crystal Wedding was also produced in amber, blue, yellow, and ruby stained (double the prices). For any frosted, engraved, or banded designs, increase the prices below by 25 percent.

Beware of reproductions: those little covered candy jars have been reproduced extensively in both crystal and a wide variety of colors.

Banana Stand	$125
Basket, Fruit	$140
Bowl, 4½"	$20
Bowl, 7", Scalloped Rim	$55
Bowl with Cover, 7", Square	$85
Bowl, 8", Square	$60
Bowl with Cover, 8", Square	$85
Butter Dish with Cover	$85
Cake Plate, Square	$55
Cake Stand, 9", Square Shape	$85
Cake Stand, 10", Square Shape	$90
Celery Dish	$50
Celery Vase	$55

Pressed Crystal Wedding. *Photo by Robin Rainwater.*

Claret Glass	$60
Compote with Cover, Low, 5", Square	$55
Compote with Cover, High, 7" Diameter, 13" Tall	$110
Creamer	$60
Cruet with Square Stopper	$150
Goblet	$60
Lamp, 9"	$315
Nappy with Handle	$35
Pickle Dish, Oblong	$50
Pitcher, Syrup	$175
Pitcher, Milk, Round	$125
Pitcher, Milk, Square Shape	$150
Pitcher, Water, Round	$175
Pitcher, Water, Square Shape	$225
Plate, 10"	$35
Relish Dish	$30
Salt Dish, Individual (Small)	$30
Salt Dish, Master (Large)	$40
Salt and Pepper Shakers	$100
Sauce Dish	$20

Spooner	$40
Sugar Bowl with Cover	$85
Tumbler, Water	$45
Vase, 2 Styles (Footed or Swung)	$75
Wineglass	$60

Cupid and Venus
Richards & Hartley Glass Company, 1870s–1880s

This pattern is sometimes referred to as Guardian Angel, and the mythological figures appear in beaded medallion form. Amber and a few vaseline items have been found. Double the listed prices below for colors.

Bowl, Oval	$75
Butter Dish with Cover	$115
Cake Plate, 11"	$85
Celery Vase, Scalloped Rim	$65
Champagne Glass	$125
Compote, Open	$50
Compote with Cover, Low	$75
Compote with Cover, High	$90
Cordial	$80
Creamer	$55
Goblet	$75
Marmalade Jar with Cover	$175
Mug, 2"	$35
Mug, 2½"	$40
Mug, 3½"	$45
Pickle Castor	$35
Pickle Castor in Frame, Metal Lid	$235
Pitcher, Milk, 7½"	$90
Pitcher, Water	$115
Plate, 10½"	$45
Plate, 10½", Handled	$50

Cupid and Venus Pattern Mug. *Drawing by Mark Pickvet.*

Sauce Dish, Round, Flat	$20
Sauce Dish, 3½", Footed	$22.50
Sauce Dish, 4", Footed	$25
Sauce Dish, 5", Footed	$27.50
Spooner	$40
Sugar with Cover	$90
Wineglass	$100

Daisy & Button

Gillinder & Sons, 1876; Hobbs, Brockunier and Company, 1880s; George Duncan & Sons, 1880s; Richards & Hartley, 1890s; Bryce Brothers, 1890s; U.S. Glass Company, 1890s; Dunkirk Glass Company, Early 1900s

This fairly common and prolific pressed pattern was manufactured by several companies. The original Daisy & Button was created by Gillinder & Sons and was displayed at the great Philadelphia Centennial Exhibition in 1876. The pattern is a geometric design consisting of spoked circles (like daisies) and open or plain circles (the buttons). The design is much like a cut-glass look-alike.

As with the variety of producers, there are several design variations along with some unique and rare dishes. Crossbars, ovals, panels, narcissus floral designs, prisms, ornaments, and others can all be found to enhance the basic pattern.

Colors include amber, yellow, light and dark blue, rose, red, and green; increase prices below by 50 percent. For vaseline, double the prices below. For intact gold trim, increase prices by 25 percent.

Beware of reproductions, especially with small pieces (such as toothpick holders and tumblers). L. G. Wright Company reproduced some pieces, including a 6" long boat-shape (canoe) dish.

Ashtray, 3-Footed	$15
Boat Dish, 8½" Oblong	$27.50
Boat Dish, 12" Oblong	$30
Boat Dish, 14" Oblong	$32.50
Bowl, Finger, Crossbars in Pattern	$27.50
Bowl, 7", Crossbars in Pattern	$30
Bowl, 7", Paneled Pattern	$27.50
Bowl with Cover, 7½", Paneled Pattern	$50
Bowl, 8", Crossbars in Pattern	$32.50
Bowl, 8", Paneled Pattern	$32.50
Bowl, 8", Triangular	$65
Bowl with Cover, 8½", Paneled Pattern	$65
Bowl, 8¾", Hexagonal	$45
Bowl, V-Ornament Design	$35
Butter Dish with Cover, Round	$100
Butter Dish with Cover, Square	$115
Butter Dish with Cover, Flat or Footed, Crossbars in Pattern	$75
Butter Dish with Cover, Narcissus Flower Design	$85
Butter Dish with Cover, Oval Medallion in Pattern	$75
Butter Dish with Cover, Paneled Pattern	$100
Butter Dish with Spartan Helmet-Shape Cover (Rare)	$265
Butter Dish with Cover, V-Ornament Design	$75
Butter Pat	$35
Castor Set, 4 Bottles, Glass Tray	$85
Castor Set, 5 Bottles, Metal Tray	$125
Celery Dish, Oval Medallion in Pattern	$37.50
Celery Dish, Thumbprints in Pattern	$37.50
Celery Dish, V-Ornament Design	$37.50

Celery Vase, Narcissus Flower Design	$40
Compote with Cover, 7", Crossbars in Pattern	$50
Compote with Cover, 8", Crossbars in Pattern	$60
Compote, Narcissus Flower Design	$50
Compote, 8", Paneled Pattern	$50
Compote, 9½", Scalloped Rim	$40
Creamer	$50
Creamer, Crossbars in Pattern	$37.50
Creamer, Narcissus Flower Design	$40
Creamer, Prisms in Pattern	$40
Creamer, Oval Medallion in Pattern	$37.50
Creamer, Paneled Pattern	$50
Creamer, Thumbprints in Pattern	$37.50
Creamer, V-Ornament Design	$37.50
Cruet with Stopper, Crossbars in Pattern	$65
Cruet with Square Stopper, Paneled Pattern	$175
Cup, V-Ornament Design	$27.50
Decanter with Stopper, Narcissus Flower Design	$125
Dish, Fan Shape	$22.50
Dish with Fly-Shape Cover (Rare)	$215
Dish, Oblong, V-Ornament Design	$30
Egg Holder	$25
Goblet, Crossbars in Pattern	$40
Goblet, Narcissus Flower Design	$40
Goblet, Oval Medallion in Pattern	$45
Goblet, Thumbprint Panels	$55
Hat Vase, 2½"	$27.50
Ice Tub	$35
Inkwell	$37.50
Lamp, Crossbars in Pattern	$105
Leaf-Shape Dish, 5"	$17.50

Mug, Crossbars in Pattern	$35
Parfait	$27.50
Pickle Castor in Frame, V-Ornament Design	$100
Pitcher, Milk (1-qt.), Crossbars in Pattern	$80
Pitcher, Syrup, Crossbars in Pattern	$75
Pitcher, Water, Bulbous, Reeded Handle	$85
Pitcher, Water, Tankard Style	$75
Pitcher, Water (2-qt.), Crossbars in Pattern	$80
Pitcher, Water, Narcissus Flower Design	$80
Pitcher, Milk or Water, Oval Medallion in Pattern	$85
Pitcher, Water, Paneled Pattern	$135
Plate, 5"	$35
Plate, 6"	$20
Plate, 7", Square	$22.50
Platter, 13", Round	$37.50
Platter, Oval, 2-Handled	$50
Platter, Oval, Paneled Pattern	$65
Punch Bowl with Stand	$110
Salt and Pepper Shakers, Pewter Tops	$65
Salt and Pepper Shakers, Crossbars in Pattern	$55
Salt and Pepper Shakers, Narcissus Flower Design	$55
Sauce Dish, Narcissus Flower Design	$20
Sauce Dish, Oval Medallion in Pattern	$25
Sauce Dish, 4½", Paneled Pattern	$20
Sauce Dish, 4½", Footed, Paneled Pattern	$25
Sherbet	$27.50
Slipper, 5"	$45
Slipper, 11½"	$50
Spooner, Crossbars in Pattern	$27.50
Spooner, Narcissus Flower Design	$30
Spooner, Oval Medallion in Pattern	$30

Spooner, V-Ornament Design	$30
Sugar Dish with Cover	$75
Sugar Dish with Cover, Crossbars in Pattern	$55
Sugar Dish with Cover, Narcissus Flower Design	$60
Sugar Dish with Cover, Oval Medallion in Pattern	$55
Sugar Dish with Cover, Paneled Pattern	$75
Sugar Dish with Cover, Thumbprints in Pattern	$55
Sugar Dish, V-Ornament Design	$55
Toothpick Holder	$35
Toothpick Holder, V-Ornament Design	$40
Tray, Ice Cream, 14" x 9"	$42.50
Tray, Water, Crossbars in Pattern	$42.50
Tray, Water, Narcissus Flower Design	$50
Tumbler, Water	$50
Tumbler, Water, Crossbars in Pattern	$40
Tumbler, Water, Narcissus Flower Design	$40
Tumbler, Water, Paneled Pattern	$50
Tumbler, Water, V-Ornament Design	$40
Wall Pocket	$100
Wineglass, Crossbars in Pattern	$40
Wineglass, Narcissus Flower Design	$40

Dakota
Ripley and Co., 1880s; U.S. Glass Company, 1890s

Dakota is also known as Baby Thumbprint or Thumbprint Band because of the single band of thumbprints that make up the pattern.

Colors include ruby flashed (increase prices by 50 percent) and the rare cobalt blue (triple the prices below). Some pieces have been etched or engraved with berries, ferns, trees, foliage, and a variety of wildlife (increase prices by 25–35 percent).

Basket with Metal Handle, 10"	$250
Bottle, 5½" Tall	$100

Bowl, 8"	$45
Butter Dish with Cover	$100
Cake Cover, 8"	$225
Cake Stand, 10" to 10½"	$85
Celery Tray	$35
Celery Vase, Flat Base	$50
Compote with Cover, 5"	$65
Compote, Open, 6"	$45
Compote with Cover, 6"	$75
Compote with Cover, 7"	$85
Compote, Open, 8"	$45
Compote with Cover, 8"	$95
Compote, Open, 10"	$75
Compote with Cover, 10"	$110
Creamer, Pedestal Base	$60
Cruet with Stopper	$125
Goblet	$35
Jug, 1 qt.	$100
Pitcher, Milk	$100
Pitcher, Water	$100
Plate, 10"	$80
Salt and Pepper Shakers	$100
Sauce Dish, 4", Flat	$20
Sauce Dish, 5", Footed	$25
Spooner, Pedestal Base	$35
Sugar Dish with Cover	$75
Tray, Condiment	$85
Tray, 12" x 10"	$90
Tray, 13", Ruffled Edge	$100
Tumbler, Water	$50
Wineglass	$35

Delaware

U.S. Glass Company, Bryce Brothers, and King Glass Company, Late 1890s–Early 1900s

Delaware is also called American Beauty, New Century, and Four Petal Flower. As one of the alternate names implies, the pattern is characterized by long thin leaves and four-petaled flowers.

Delaware was made in a variety of colors, including a pale red or rose stain and green (increase prices below by 50 percent), and the rarer opaque green, custard, and milk glass (double the prices). Gold trim was also applied to many of the pieces (increase prices by 25 percent for complete, intact gold trim).

Banana Bowl, Boat Shape	$75
Basket, Bride's, Silver Holder	$105
Bowl, Finger	$30
Bowl, 8", with or without Flutes	$35
Bowl, 9", with or without Flutes	$40
Bottle with Stopper	$100
Butter Dish with Cover	$85
Celery Vase	$85
Creamer	$55
Cruet with Stopper	$100
Cup	$20
Lamp Shade	$100
Pin Tray	$35
Pitcher, Milk (Jug Shape)	$125
Pitcher, Water	$125
Pomade Box	$125
Puff Box	$125
Punch Cup	$22.50
Sauce Dish, 5½", Boat Shape	$20
Spooner	$50
Sugar Dish with Cover	$85
Tankard, 9¼"	$115
Toothpick Holder	$65

Tumbler	$35
Vase, 6" Tall	$30
Vase, 8" Tall	$35
Vase, 9½" Tall	$45

Diamond Horseshoe
Brilliant Glass Works, Late 1880s; Greensburg Glass Company, 1880s–1890s

This Diamond Horseshoe design is sometimes referred to as Aurora. A few were engraved (increase prices below by 25 percent) and ruby flashed (double the prices).

Butter Dish with Cover	$90
Cake Stand	$65
Compote, Open	$40
Compote with Cover	$65
Creamer	$45
Decanter with Stopper	$100
Goblet	$40
Pitcher, Water	$85
Salt and Pepper Shakers	$45
Spooner	$30
Sugar	$45
Wineglass	$40

Diamond Point
Various Companies, 1830s–1880s

The original Diamond Point was produced by the Boston & Sandwich Glass Company as early as the 1830s. Bryce, Richards & Company produced it in the 1850s, and others (New England, for example) followed later.

There are many rare pieces, and some colors were produced (triple the listed prices for color). Also note that the prices below are for full lead crystal (or flint glass) pieces. For cheaper lime formulas, decrease the prices below by about a third.

Ale Glass, 6¼" Tall	$95
Bowl with Cover, 7"	$70
Bowl, 7" Oval	$50

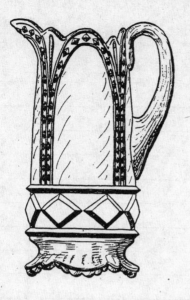

Pressed Glass. Aurora or Diamond Horseshoe Pattern. *Drawing by Mark Pickvet.*

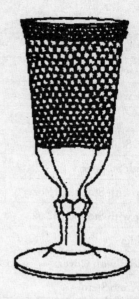

Pressed Glass. Diamond Point Pattern. *Drawing by Mark Pickvet.*

Bowl with Cover, 8"	$75
Bowl, 8" Oval	$55
Bowl, 9" Oval	$60
Bowl, 10" Oval	$70
Butter Dish with Cover	$150
Cake Stand, 14"	$210
Candlestick	$100
Castor Bottle	$35
Celery Vase	$85
Champagne Glass	$100
Claret Glass	$100
Compote, 6", Open	$70
Compote, 7", Open	$75
Compote, 8", Open	$80
Compote, 10½", Open, Flared	$125

Compote, 11", Open, Scalloped	$135
Compote with Cover, 6"	$130
Compote with Cover, 7"	$165
Compote with Cover, 8"	$200
Cordial	$175
Creamer, Scalloped, Footed	$150
Cruet with Stopper	$185
Decanter with Stopper, 16 oz.	$225
Decanter with Stopper, 32 oz.	$275
Egg Holder	$50
Egg Holder with Cover	$85
Goblet, Knob Stem	$65
Honey Dish	$40
Lamp	$235
Lemonade Glass	$65
Mug	$95
Mustard Jar with Cover	$50
Pitcher, Syrup, 16 oz.	$250
Pitcher, Syrup, 16 oz., Footed	$275
Pitcher, Milk, 32 oz.	$275
Pitcher, Milk, 32 oz., Footed	$300
Pitcher, Water, 48 oz.	$325
Pitcher, Water, 48 oz., Footed	$350
Plate, 3 to 3¼"	$35
Plate, 5½"	$40
Plate, 6"	$45
Plate, 7"	$55
Plate, 8"	$60
Plate, Pie, 6" (Deep)	$75
Plate, Pie, 8" (Deep)	$85
Salt Dip with Cover, Footed	$90

Pressed Diamond Point. *Photo by Mark Pickvet.*   **Pressed Diamond Point.** *Photo by Mark Pickvet.*

Sauce Dish	$40
Spooner	$55
Sugar Dish with Cover, Footed	$125
Tumbler, Water	$75
Whiskey Tumbler	$95
Wineglass	$85

Dot
Bryce Brothers, 1870s–1880s

Dot is also known as Beaded Oval and Scroll because of the large beaded vertical ovals that alternately enclose the scroll design.

Bowl, 6¼"	$35
Bowl, 8"	$45
Butter Dish with Cover	$85
Cake Stand	$55

Dot or Beaded Oval & Scroll Water Pitcher. *Drawing by Mark Pickvet.*

Compote, Open	$40
Compote with Cover	$65
Cordial	$45
Creamer	$40
Goblet	$40
Pickle Dish	$35
Pitcher, Water	$85
Salt and Pepper Shakers	$55
Sauce Dish, Flat	$20
Spooner	$35
Sugar, Open	$40
Sugar with Cover	$65
Wineglass	$40

Excelsior
Various Companies, 1850s–1870s

Excelsior was made primarily by the Boston & Sandwich Glass Company, McKee Brothers, and C. Ihmsen and Company. To a lesser extent, others produced it, too. A few pale green items are occasionally found (increase the prices by 50 percent).

The pattern variant referred to below was produced exclusively under McKee Brothers and is sometimes referred to as Tong. The ovals have a wider diameter (nearly circular) but converge at the bottom to what is nearly a point. In short, they are somewhat heart-shaped on the variant.

Ale Glass	$75
Bar Bottle	$95
Bitters Bottle	$110
Bowl, 10"	$135
Bowl with Cover	$165
Butter Dish with Cover	$150
Butter Dish with Cover (McKee Pattern Variant)	$115
Candlestick, 9½" Tall	$150
Celery Vase (McKee Pattern Variant)	$90
Celery Vase, Scalloped (McKee Pattern Variant)	$100
Champagne Glass	$65
Claret	$55
Compote, Open	$100
Compote with Cover	$150
Cordial (McKee Pattern Variant)	$65
Creamer, 2 Styles	$125
Creamer (McKee Pattern Variant)	$125
Decanter, 16 oz., with or without Foot	$100
Decanter, 32 oz.	$110
Egg Holder, Single	$50
Egg Holder, Double	$55
Goblet, Barrel-Shape Bowl, Maltese Cross Design (Boston & Sandwich)	$90
Goblet (McKee Pattern Variant)	$55
Lamp, Hand	$125
Lamp, Whale Oil, Maltese Cross Design (Boston & Sandwich)	$285
Mug, Applied Handle	$75
Pickle Jar with Cover	$60
Pitcher, Syrup with Lid	$400
Pitcher, Milk	$425

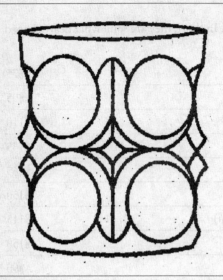

Pressed Excelsior Pattern. *Drawing by Mark Pickvet.*

Pitcher, Water (McKee Only)	$450
Salt Dip, Footed	$35
Spooner, 4¾"	$65
Spooner (McKee Pattern Variant)	$75
Sugar with Cover, 6½"	$175
Sugar with Cover, 8½"	$225
Sugar with Pagoda-Style Cover	$150
Sugar with Cover (McKee Pattern Variant)	$135
Tumbler, Bar	$55
Tumbler, Water, Various Styles	$50
Tumbler, Footed (McKee Pattern Variant)	$55
Whiskey Tumbler, Maltese Cross Design (Boston & Sandwich)	$75
Wineglass	$55

Fan and Flute
U.S. Glass Company, 1890s

This pattern was also referred to as Millard. The fluted panels may be stained with amber (increase the listed prices below by 50 percent) or with ruby red (double them). The panels might also be engraved rather than pressed (increase prices by 25 percent).

Bowl, 7"	$20
Bowl, 8"	$24

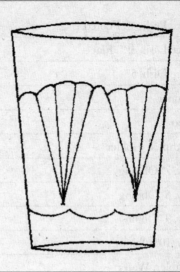

Fan & Flute Tumbler. *Drawing by Mark Pickvet.*

Bowl, 9"	$28
Butter Dish	$50
Cake Stand	$50
Celery Tray	$32.50
Celery Vase	$37.50
Compote, 6", Open	$25
Compote, 7", Open	$30
Compote, 8", Open	$35
Compote, 9", Open	$40
Creamer	$37.50
Cruet with Stopper	$55
Cup	$24
Goblet	$35
Pitcher, Syrup, with Lid	$85
Pitcher, Milk	$85
Plate, 7"	$18
Plate, 9"	$22.50
Plate, 10"	$24
Saltshaker	$28
Sauce Dish, 4", Flat	$12.50

Sauce Dish, 4", Footed	$15
Sauce Dish, 4½", Flat	$14
Sauce Dish, 5"	$17.50
Spooner	$27.50
Sugar	$37.50
Toothpick Holder	$40
Tray, 7" Oblong	$27.50
Tray, 8" Oblong	$32.50
Tray, 9" Oblong	$37.50
Tray, 10" Oblong	$42.50
Tumbler, Water	$32.50
Wineglass	$35

Feather
Mckee Glass Company, 1896–1901; Beatty-Brady Company, Early 1900s; Cambridge Glass Company, Early 1900s

Feather has many names, including the original Doric as well as Finecut and Feather, Cambridge Feather, Feather and Quill, Indiana Feather, Prince's Feather, Swirl, and Indiana Swirl. Like so many pressed designs, this one resembles cut glass with alternating panels of rosette points and beaded flutes.

Colors are very scarce and valuable. For green, amber, or ruby red, triple the prices; for chocolate, quadruple them. Wineglasses made in cranberry or pink stain were reproduced in the 1950s by the Jeannette Glass Company (they purchased McKee); for these, cut the price in half.

Banana Dish, Boat Shape	$80
Bowl, 6" to 6½"	$30
Bowl, 7" to 7½"	$35
Bowl, 8" to 8½"	$40
Bowl, Berry, Square	$40
Bowl, Oval, 8½"	$30
Bowl, Oval, 9" x 7", Footed	$40
Bowl, Oval, 9¼"	$35
Butter Dish with Cover	$75

Cake Plate	$75
Cake Stand, 8" to 8½"	$55
Cake Stand, 9½"	$60
Cake Stand, 11"	$80
Celery Vase	$55
Champagne Glass	$75
Compote, Open, 4"	$25
Compote, Open, 6"	$35
Compote, Open, 7"	$45
Compote, Open, 8"	$50
Compote with Cover, 4¼"	$125
Compote with Cover, 7"	$150
Compote with Cover, 8¼" to 8½"	$175
Cordial	$135
Creamer, Scalloped	$50
Cruet with Stopper	$85
Goblet	$65
Honey Dish	$25
Jam Jar with Cover	$150
Pickle Castor	$155
Pickle Dish	$40
Pitcher, Syrup	$150
Pitcher, Milk	$75
Pitcher, Water	$95
Plate, 7"	$40
Plate, 8"	$45
Plate, 9½"	$55
Plate, 10"	$65
Platter	$65
Relish Dish, 8"	$35
Saltshaker	$40

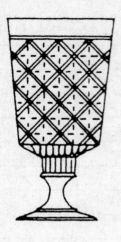

Pressed Feather Glass. *Drawing by Mark Pickvet.*

Sauce Dish, Flat	$20
Sauce Dish, Footed	$25
Spooner, Scalloped	$35
Sugar Dish with Cover	$75
Toothpick Holder	$95
Tumbler, Water	$55
Wineglass	$40
Wineglass, Scalloped Band	$55

Finecut
Bryce Brothers, 1880s; U.S. Glass Company, 1890s

Finecut is a diamond design with four dashes (two vertical, two horizontal) within each diamond. It is also known as Flower in Square. Colors include amber, blue, and vaseline; double the prices for colored items.

Bowl, 8¼"	$17.50
Bread Plate	$32.50
Butter Dish with Cover	$55
Cake Stand	$45
Celery Tray	$32.50
Celery Vase in Silver Holder	$65
Creamer	$42.50

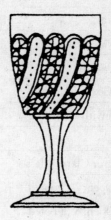

Pressed Fine Cut Glass. *Drawing by Mark Pickvet.*

Goblet	$30
Pitcher, Water	$75
Plate, 7"	$21
Plate, 10"	$27.50
Relish Dish	$17.50
Sauce Dish, 4", Flat	$14
Spooner	$22.50
Sugar Dish with Cover	$47.50
Tray, Water	$35
Tumbler, Water	$25
Wineglass	$30

Fine Rib
New England Glass Company, 1850s–1870s

There were many ribbed designs created by other companies, but there are some distinctions with this New England pattern. The ribbing is very fine and extends from the top to the bottom of each piece. Nearly all the pieces have scalloped bottom panels. Some bowls and compotes also have wavy rims.

Ale Glass	$75
Bitters Bottle	$85
Bottle, Water, Tumble-Up	$95

Bowl, 7" Oval	$50
Bowl, 8" Oval	$55
Bowl, 9" Oval	$60
Bowl, 10" Oval	$65
Bowl with Cover, 7"	$85
Butter Dish with Cover	$150
Celery Vase	$75
Champagne or Claret Glass	$65
Compote, Open, 7", Footed	$75
Compote, Open, 8", Footed	$80
Compote, Open, 9", Footed	$85
Compote, Open, 10", Footed	$90
Compote with Cover, 7", Footed	$125
Compote with Cover, 8", Footed	$150
Creamer	$100
Cruet with Stopper	$125
Cup, Custard	$65
Decanter with Stopper, 16 oz.	$125
Decanter with Stopper, 32 oz.	$150
Egg Holder	$50
Goblet	$55
Honey Dish	$35
Lamp, Handled	$225
Mug	$75
Pitcher, Syrup with Lid, 16 oz.	$350
Pitcher, Milk, 32 oz.	$250
Pitcher, Water, 48 oz.	$275
Plate, 6"	$60
Plate, 7"	$70
Salt Dip, Flat	$45
Salt Dip with Cover, Footed	$125
Sauce Dish	$37.50

 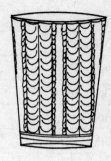

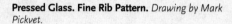

Pressed Glass. Fine Rib Pattern. *Drawing by Mark Pickvet.*

Pressed Glass. Fishscale Pattern. *Drawing by Mark Pickvet.*

Tumbler, Water	$65
Whiskey Taster with Handle	$75
Whiskey Tumbler	$75
Wineglass	$55

Fishscale
Bryce Brothers, 1880s–1890s

Fishscale is also known as Coral. It contains vertical bands of half circles from the top to the bottom of each object that resemble the scales of fish.

Ashtray, Daisy & Button Slipper Design (Slipper Is Amber, Blue, Crystal, or Topaz), Attached to Rectangular Tray (Tray Contains the Fishscale Pattern)	$55
Bowl, 6"	$35
Bowl, 7"	$40
Bowl, 8"	$45
Bowl with Cover, 7" Square, Round Base	$65
Bowl with Cover, 8" Square, Round Base	$75
Butter Dish with Cover	$85
Cake Stand, 8¾" to 9"	$50
Cake Stand, 10"	$55
Cake Stand, 11"	$60
Celery Vase	$57.50

Compote, Open, 7"	$40
Compote, Open, 8"	$45
Compote, Open, 9"	$50
Compote, Open, 10"	$55
Compote with Cover, 6"	$70
Compote with Cover, 7"	$80
Compote with Cover, 8"	$90
Creamer	$45
Goblet	$45
Lamp, Handled	$125
Mug	$75
Pickle Dish	$35
Pitcher, 32 oz.	$75
Pitcher, 64 oz.	$100
Pitcher, 1 gal.	$150
Plate, 7"	$30
Plate, 8"	$35
Plate, 8", Square	$40
Plate, 9", Square, Round Corners	$45
Salt and Pepper Shakers	$75
Sauce Dish, 4", Flat	$18
Sauce Dish, 4", Flared, Footed	$22.50
Spooner	$27.50
Sugar with Cover	$65
Tray, Oblong, Scalloped Edge (for Shakers)	$50
Tray, Water, Round	$65
Tumbler	$40

Fleur-de-Lys
Adams and Company, 1880s–1890s

Fleur-de-Lys is also referred to as Fleur-de-Lys and Drape, or Fleur-de-Lys and Tassel. For green and opal colors, increase the prices by 50 percent.

The basic design is in relief and includes upright fleur-de-lys with upside-down tassels (or drapes).

Bottle, Water	$65
Butter Dish with Cover	$85
Cake Stand	$60
Celery Vase	$45
Claret Glass	$50
Compote, Open	$50
Compote with Cover	$80
Cordial	$60
Creamer	$50
Goblet	$45
Lamp	$175
Mustard Jar with Ribbed Cover	$95
Pitcher, Syrup with Lid	$115
Pitcher, Milk	$90
Pitcher, Water	$105
Sauce Dish, 4", Flat	$24
Sauce Dish, 4½", Flat	$27.50
Spooner	$27.50
Sugar with Cover	$85
Tumbler	$40
Wineglass	$45

Florida
U.S. Glass Company, 1890s

This state series pattern of U.S. Glass contains alternating clear curved panels with curved herringbone designs; hence the substitute names Herringbone, Paneled Herringbone, and Emerald Green Herringbone. For amber, green, or any other colors, double the prices.

Berry Set	$85
Bowl, 7¾"	$20
Butter Dish with Cover	$57.50

Cake Stand, Small	$40
Cake Stand, Large	$65
Celery Vase	$37.50
Compote, Square, 6½"	$27.50
Creamer	$37.50
Cruet with Stopper	$50
Goblet, 5¾" Tall	$35
Mustard Set, 3-Piece (Jar, Cover, Underplate)	$50
Nappy, Handled	$25
Pitcher, Syrup	$75
Pitcher, Water	$65
Plate, 7½"	$16
Plate, 9½"	$21
Relish Dish, Square, 6"	$20
Relish Dish, Square, 8½"	$25
Saltshaker	$35
Sauce Dish	$12.50
Spooner	$27.50
Sugar Dish with Cover	$47.50
Tumbler	$26
Wineglass	$35

Flute
Various Companies, 1850s–Early 1900s

The original Flute patterns were usually six or eight large rounded flutes that encompassed the majority of the object. Most pieces contain a plain band across the top. Many companies had their own individual names such as Bessimer Flute, Brooklyn Flute, New England Flute, Reed Stem Flute, Sandwich Flute, Sexton Flute, and so on.

Some Flute pieces were made in colors such as blue, green, and others (double the prices).

Ale Glass	$40
Berry Set, Children's, 7-Piece	$60
Bitters Bottle	$55
Bowl, Scalloped	$40

Candlestick	$32.50
Champagne Glass	$32.50
Compote, 8" Diameter	$45
Creamer	$37.50
Cup, Custard	$40
Decanter, 32 oz.	$85
Egg Holder, Single	$25
Egg Holder, Double	$35
Goblet	$35
Honey Dish	$25
Lamp, Whale Oil	$140
Mug, Applied Handle	$50
Mug, Toy, 2 oz. with Handle	$30
Pitcher, Water	$120
Salt Dip, Footed	$25
Sauce Dish, Flat	$20
Spooner	$26
Sugar Dish with Cover	$47.50
Tumbler, 4 oz.	$26
Tumbler, 6 oz.	$30
Tumbler, 8 oz.	$35
Tumbler, Bar, 12 oz.	$40
Whiskey Tumbler, 2 oz.	$15
Wineglass	$30

Georgia
Richards and Hartley, 1890s; U.S. Glass Company, Early 1900s

This state series of U.S. Glass is also known as Peacock Feather because of its vertical paneling of feathers capped off by large round ovals. This pattern is very rare in blue—triple the prices. A few have been found with gold trim or gold decorations; increase prices by 25 percent for intact gold.

Bonbon Dish, Footed	$35
Bowl, 8"	$37.50

Butter Dish with Cover	$55
Cake Stand, Miniature (Children's)	$40
Cake Stand, 9"	$50
Cake Stand, 10"	$55
Cake Stand, 11"	$60
Castor Set, 2 Bottles	$67.50
Celery Tray, 11¾"	$42.50
Compote, 5"	$25
Compote, 6"	$30
Compote, 7"	$35
Compote, 8"	$40
Compote with Cover, 5"	$42.50
Compote with Cover, 6"	$47.50
Compote with Cover, 7"	$52.50
Compote with Cover, 8"	$57.50
Condiment Set (Cruet with Stopper, Salt and Pepper Shakers, Undertray)	$125
Creamer, Miniature (Children's), 2" Tall	$40
Creamer	$42.50
Cruet with Stopper	$65
Decanter with Stopper	$85
Dish, Oval	$37.50
Lamp with Pedestal Base	$100
Lamp, Oil, 7" Tall	$100
Mug	$32.50
Nappy with Handle	$32.50
Pitcher, Syrup, Metal Lid	$75
Pitcher, Water	$85
Plate, 5¼"	$20
Relish Dish	$20
Salt and Pepper Shakers	$50
Sauce Dish	$15

Spooner	$40
Sugar Dish with Cover	$55
Sugar Shaker	$50
Tumbler	$40

Hamilton
Boston & Sandwich Glass Company, 1860s–1880s

The leaf pattern variant is sometimes referred to as Hamilton with Leaf. The horizontal diamond band in the middle of each piece in the original Hamilton is replaced by leaves in the pattern variant.

The Hamilton with Leaf pattern was also produced by others in the 1890s. Occasionally the leaves can be found frosted (add 25 percent to the prices).

Butter Dish with Cover	$125
Butter Dish with Cover (Leaf Pattern Variant)	$150
Castor Bottle with Stopper	$85
Celery Vase	$65
Celery Vase (Leaf Pattern Variant)	$75
Compote, Open, Low Foot	$45
Compote, Open, High Foot	$50
Compote, Open, (Leaf Pattern Variant)	$55
Compote with Cover, 6"	$85
Compote, 7", Scalloped Rim	$50
Cordial (Leaf Pattern Variant)	$55
Creamer	$50
Creamer, Molded Handle (Leaf Pattern Variant)	$65
Decanter with Stopper	$215
Egg Holder	$45
Egg Holder (Leaf Pattern Variant)	$65
Goblet	$45
Honey Dish	$30
Lamp, 7" Tall, 2 Styles (Leaf Pattern Variant)	$190
Pitcher, Syrup with Metal Lid	$275

Pressed Hamilton Pattern. *Drawing by Mark Pickvet.*

Pitcher, Water	$250
Pitcher, Water (Leaf Pattern Variant)	$265
Plate, 6"	$100
Salt Dip, Footed (Leaf Pattern Variant)	$40
Sauce Dish, 4"	$20
Sauce Dish, 5"	$24
Spooner	$37.50
Spooner (Leaf Pattern Variant)	$47.50
Sugar, Open	$50
Sugar Dish with Cover (Leaf Pattern Variant)	$100
Tumbler, Bar (Leaf Pattern Variant)	$100
Tumbler, Water	$90
Whiskey Tumbler	$125
Wineglass	$90
Wineglass (Leaf Pattern Variant)	$100

Heart With Thumbprint
Various Companies, 1880s–1900s

There are several rare and valuable pieces in this pattern, especially those in color. For transparent green, double the prices; for the rare custard, blue custard, opaque green, or ruby stained, triple them. Increase the prices by 25 percent for any items with completely intact gold trim.

This pattern has many names and is called Bull's-Eye in Heart, Columbia, Columbian, and Heart and Thumbprint. The Tarentum Glass Company was the primary manufacturer, but others followed.

Banana Dish, 10" Long	$125
Barber Bottle	$125
Bowl, Finger	$50
Bowl, 7", Square	$40
Bowl, 9"	$50
Bowl, 9½", Square	$50
Bowl, 10", Scalloped	$55
Bowl Rose, Small	$40
Bowl Rose, Large	$70
Butter Dish with Cover	$150
Cake Stand, 9"	$175
Carafe	$125
Card Tray	$27.50
Celery Vase	$75
Compote, 7½", Ruffled Rim	$225
Compote, 8½"	$175
Cordial, 3" Tall	$165
Creamer, Individual (Small)	$40
Creamer	$70
Cruet with Stopper	$100
Goblet	$75
Hair Receiver with Cover	$75
Ice Bucket	$75
Lamp, Small	$125
Lamp, Oil, 8" Tall	$150
Mustard Dish with Silver-Plated Cover	$150
Nappy, 6¼", Triangular	$37.50
Pitcher, Water	$235
Plate, 6"	$35

Pressed Heart with Thumbprint. *Drawing by Mark Pickvet.*

Plate, 10"	$55
Powder Jar with Cover	$80
Punch Cup	$27.50
Salt and Pepper Shakers	$110
Salt Dip	$35
Sauce Dish, Crimped, 5"	$35
Spooner	$55
Sugar Bowl, Individual, Handled	$40
Sugar Bowl with Cover	$125
Toothpick Holder	$150
Tray, 8¼" x 4¼"	$40
Tumbler, Water	$60
Vase, 6" Tall	$45
Vase, 10" Tall	$75
Wineglass	$65

Honeycomb
Various Companies, 1850s–1890s

Honeycomb has been referred to as Cincinnati, Vernon, Hex Optic, and others. Bakewell, Pears & Company; Lyons Glass Company; McKee Brothers; and others all made this pattern. Honeycomb variations were made later, during the Depression.

Note that the prices below are for full lead crystal (sometimes referred to as flint); cut them in half for lime glass (noncrystal or nonflint). Colors include amber, cobalt blue, green, opal, and topaz (double the prices).

Ale Glass	$60
Barber or Bitters Bottle	$75
Bowl, Finger	$55
Bowl, 6" to 6½"	$40
Bowl, 7" to 7½"	$45
Bowl, 8" to 8½"	$50
Bowl, 9" to 9½"	$55
Bowl, 10" to 10½"	$60
Bowl, Oval	$50
Bowl with Cover, 6"	$75
Bowl with Cover, 7"	$85
Bowl with Cover, 7¼", Acorn Finial	$115
Bowl with Cover, 8"	$95
Butter Dish with Cover	$85
Cake Stand	$65
Castor Bottle with Stopper	$75
Celery Vase	$70
Champagne Glass	$60
Claret Glass	$50
Compote, Open, 6"	$40
Compote, Open, 6½" to 7"	$50
Compote, Open, 6½" to 7", Low Foot	$45
Compote, Open, 7½" to 8", Scalloped	$55
Compote, Open, 8", Low Foot	$60
Compote, Open, 9"	$65
Compote, Open, 10"	$70
Compote with Cover, 6½" to 7"	$75
Compote with Cover, 7", Low Foot	$70
Compote with Cover, 8"	$90

Pressed Honeycomb Pattern. *Drawing by Mark Pickvet.*

Compote with Cover, 8", Low Foot	$85
Compote with Cover, 9¼"	$105
Cordial, 3½" Tall	$60
Creamer, 5½" Tall, Applied Handle	$50
Cup, Custard	$45
Decanter with Stopper, 16 oz.	$100
Decanter with Stopper, 32 oz.	$115
Egg Holder	$40
Goblet, Barrel-Shape Bowl	$50
Honey Dish with Cover	$27.50
Jelly Glass, Pedestal Base	$80
Jug, 8 oz.	$55
Jug, 16 oz.	$65
Jug, 32 oz.	$75
Jug, 48 oz.	$85
Lamp, All Glass	$110
Lamp, Marble Base	$125
Lemonade Glass	$50
Mug, 8 oz.	$50
Pitcher, Water, Applied Handle	$185

Plate, 6"	$40
Plate, 7"	$50
Pomade Jar with Cover	$65
Relish Dish	$40
Salt and Pepper Shakers	$65
Salt Dip, Footed	$32.50
Salt Dip with Cover, Footed	$65
Sauce Dish	$25
Spooner	$75
Sugar Dish with Cover	$75
Sugar Dish with Frosted Rosebud Finial	$90
Tumbler, 5½ oz.	$50
Tumbler, 8 oz.	$60
Tumbler, 8 oz., Footed	$70
Vase, 7½" Tall	$55
Vase, 10½" Tall	$85
Whiskey Glass with Handle	$150
Wineglass	$45

Horn of Plenty
Various Companies, 1830s–1870s

Horn of Plenty and Comet are virtually identical; however, Comet is attributed solely to the Boston & Sandwich Glass Company. Horn of Plenty was also made by Boston & Sandwich as well as Bryce Brothers, McKee Brothers, and possibly others.

This is an old, rare, and valuable pattern. A few pieces were made in amber, canary yellow, cobalt blue, and an opalescent white (double the prices). Note that the lamp is completely glass. The water tumbler and goblet have been reproduced in amber and crystal.

Bottle, Bar, with Stopper	$150
Bowl, 8½"	$235
Bowl, Oval (8" x 5½")	$235
Butter Dish with Cover, 6" Diameter	$225
Butter Dish with Cover, George Washington's Head Finial	$800

Butter Dish with Cover (Comet Pattern, Boston & Sandwich)	$225
Cake Stand, 9½" (Frosted—Same Price)	$125
Celery Vase	$185
Champagne Glass	$185
Compote, 8" Tall, Open	$150
Compote, 12" Tall, Open	$175
Compote, Open (Comet Pattern, Boston & Sandwich)	$175
Compote with Cover, 6"	$185
Compote with Cover, 13"	$215
Cordial	$175
Creamer, 5½" Tall	$200
Creamer, 7" Tall	$225
Creamer (Comet Pattern, Boston & Sandwich)	$225
Decanter with Stopper, 16 oz.	$185
Decanter with Stopper, 32 oz.	$215
Decanter with Stopper, 64 oz.	$260
Egg Holder	$80
Goblet (Comet Pattern, Boston & Sandwich)	$165
Honey Dish, 3¼"	$40
Lamp, All Glass, 15"	$300
Lamp, Marble Base	$275
Mug, Applied Handle	$175
Mug (Comet Pattern, Boston & Sandwich)	$175
Pickle Dish	$125
Pitcher, Milk	$800
Pitcher, Water	$700
Pitcher, Water (Comet Pattern, Boston & Sandwich)	$800
Plate, 6"	$110
Salt Dip, Oval	$65
Sauce Dish, 4½"	$35
Sauce Dish, 5" to 5¼"	$40
Sauce Dish, 6"	$45

McKee Brothers. *Reproduced directly from a late-19th-century McKee Brothers catalog.*

Horn of Plenty. *Photo by Robin Rainwater.*

Spooner	$65
Spooner (Comet Pattern, Boston & Sandwich)	$110
Sugar with Pagoda Cover	$265
Sugar Dish with Cover (Comet Pattern, Boston & Sandwich)	$200
Tumbler, Water (Comet Pattern, Boston & Sandwich)	$175
Whiskey Tumbler	$140
Whiskey Tumbler (Comet Pattern, Boston & Sandwich)	$275
Wineglass	$185

Illinois
U.S. Glass Company, 1890s

This state series of U.S. Glass is also known as Clarissa or Star of the East because of the large eight-point star in the pattern. For any ruby flashed, ruby stained, or green items, double the prices.

Basket, 11½", Applied Handle	$125
Bowl, Finger	$35
Bowl, 5"	$30
Bowl, 6", Square	$35
Bowl, 8"	$40
Bowl, 9", Square	$45
Butter Dish with Cover	$75

Candlestick	$55
Celery Tray, 11"	$50
Cheese Dish with Cover	$85
Compote, 5"	$45
Compote, 9"	$65
Creamer, Individual (Small)	$35
Creamer (Large)	$45
Cruet with Stopper	$75
Decanter with Stopper	$105
Marmalade Jar	$155
Olive Dish	$26
Pitcher, Syrup, Pewter Lid	$125
Pitcher, Milk, Silver-Plated Rim	$200
Pitcher, Milk, Square Shape	$85
Pitcher, Water, Square Shape	$90
Plate, 7", Square	$32.50
Relish Dish, 7½" x 4"	$18
Relish Dish, 8½" x 3"	$24
Salt Dip, Individual (Small)	$20
Salt Dip, Master (Large)	$30
Salt and Pepper Shakers	$50
Sauce Dish	$18
Spooner	$42.50
Straw Holder with Cover	$315
Sugar Dish, Individual (Small)	$35
Sugar Dish with Cover (Large)	$75
Sugar Shaker	$75
Tankard with Silver-Plated Rim	$100
Toothpick Holder	$40
Toothpick Holder with Advertising	$55
Tray, 12" x 8"	$60
Tumbler	$40

Pressed Glass, Illinois. *Drawing by Mark Pickvet.*

Vase, 6", Square Shape	$45
Vase, 9½" Tall	$70

Iowa
U.S. Glass Company, Early 1900s

Iowa is more accurately described as Paneled Zipper. For colors (ruby or red stained, amber, green, yellow, or blue), double the prices. For crystal pieces with any gold trim or gold decoration, increase the prices by 25 percent. For colored pieces with any gilding, increase the prices by 150 percent.

Bowl, Berry	$30
Bread Plate	$90
Butter Dish with Cover	$65
Cake Stand	$45
Carafe	$45
Compote with Cover, 8"	$50
Creamer	$37.50
Cruet with Stopper	$50
Cup	$25
Decanter with Stopper, 2 Styles	$65
Goblet	$35
Lamp	$150

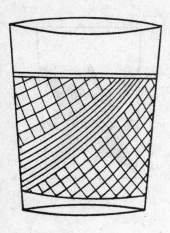

Pressed Glass, Iowa. *Drawing by Mark Pickvet.*

Olive Dish	$25
Pitcher, Water	$65
Punch Cup	$20
Saltshaker	$27.50
Sauce Dish, 4½"	$17.50
Spooner	$37.50
Sugar Dish with Cover	$47.50
Toothpick Holder	$35
Toothpick Holder, Footed	$55
Tumbler, Water	$35
Vase, 8" Tall	$35
Whiskey Jug with Stopper	$75
Wineglass	$35

Jacob's Ladder
Bryce Brothers, 1870s–1880s; U.S. Glass Company, 1890s

The original name for Jacob's Ladder was Maltese because of the cross design on many pieces. A few rare colored pieces (amber, blue, green, and yellow) were also made; double the listed prices for those.

Bowl, 6"	$30
Bowl, 7", Oval	$35

Bowl, 8", Oval	$40
Bowl, 8¾" to 9"	$45
Bowl, 9", in Silver-Plated Holder, Footed	$150
Bowl, 9¾" to 10", Oval	$50
Bowl, 10¼" to 11", Oval	$50
Butter Dish with Cover, Maltese Cross Finial	$90
Cake Stand, 8"	$55
Cake Stand, 9"	$60
Cake Stand, 11"	$65
Cake Stand, 12"	$70
Castor Bottle with Stopper	$40
Celery Dish	$40
Celery Vase, 9" Tall	$50
Compote, Open, 7½"	$45
Compote, Open, Scalloped Edge, 8½"	$45
Compote, Open, Scalloped Edge, 9¾"	$55
Compote, Open, 10"	$50
Compote, Open, with Silver-Plated Holder	$125
Compote, Dolphin	$325
Compote with Cover, 6"	$90
Compote with Cover, 7½"	$115
Compote with Cover, 9½"	$150
Cordial	$65
Creamer, Footed	$45
Cruet with Maltese Cross Stopper, Footed	$110
Goblet	$75
Honey Dish, 3½"	$17.50
Marmalade Dish, Maltese Cross Finial	$100
Mug	$100
Perfume Bottle with Maltese Cross Stopper	$100
Pickle Dish	$45
Pitcher, Syrup with Metal Lid	$125

Pressed Glass, Jacob's Ladder Pattern. *Drawing by Mark Pickvet.*

Pitcher, Syrup with Metal Lid, Knight's Head Finial	$155
Pitcher, Water, Applied Handle	$210
Plate, 6" to 6¼"	$30
Relish Dish, 9½" x 5½"	$25
Salt Dip, Master, Round, Flat	$40
Salt Dip, Master, Footed	$50
Sauce Dish, 3½", Flat, Footed	$15
Sauce Dish, 4", Flat, Footed	$18
Sauce Dish, 4½", Footed	$20
Sauce Dish, 5", Flat, Footed	$22.50
Spooner, 6"	$40
Sugar Dish with Cover, Maltese Cross Finial	$100
Tray, Oval	$45
Tumbler, 8 oz.	$100
Wineglass	$45

Kansas

Co-Operative Glass Company, 1890s; U.S. Glass Company, 1901–1906; Jenkins Glass Company, 1915–25

Kansas is also known as Jewel with Dewdrop, which more accurately describes the pattern. Prices should be doubled for ruby stained items. The smaller mugs have been reproduced in crystal, vaseline, amber, and blue (worth about $15 each).

Banana Stand	$100
Bowl, 7", Oval	$45
Bowl, 8"	$50
Bread Plate	$55
Butter Dish with Cover	$75
Cake Plate	$55
Cake Stand, 7½" (Medium)	$60
Cake Stand, 10" (Large)	$90
Celery Vase	$85
Compote, with Cover, 5"	$65
Compote, 6"	$40
Compote with Cover, 6"	$70
Compote, 8"	$55
Compote with Cover, 8"	$90
Creamer	$50
Goblet	$65
Mug	$60
Mug, Tall	$40
Pitcher, Syrup with Lid	$140
Pitcher, Milk	$100
Pitcher, Water	$120
Relish Dish, 8½", Oval	$30
Salt and Pepper Shakers	$100
Sauce Dish, 4"	$20
Spooner	$35
Sugar Dish with Cover	$75
Sugar Shaker	$55
Toothpick Holder	$75
Tumbler, Water	$50
Whiskey Tumbler	$50
Wineglass	$60

Kentucky

U.S. Glass Company, 1890s–Early 1900s

Kentucky is a basic diamond column pattern that is separated by flowing vertical divisions. Prices should be doubled for ruby stained or cobalt blue items. As one would surmise, this is another in the U.S. Glass Company's state series.

Bowl, 8"	$30
Butter Dish with Cover	$65
Cake Stand, 9½"	$50
Creamer	$35
Cruet with Stopper	$55
Cup	$17.50
Goblet	$40
Nappy with Handle	$20
Olive Dish with Handle	$35
Pitcher, Water	$75
Plate, 7", Square	$22.50
Punch Cup	$17.50
Salt and Pepper Shakers	$40
Sauce Dish, Square Shape, Footed	$15
Spooner	$40
Sugar Dish with Cover	$45
Sugar Shaker	$35
Toothpick Holder	$50
Tumbler, Water	$30
Wineglass	$35

Lattice

King, Son & Company, 1880s

Lattice is also known as Diamond Bar and is characterized by occasional vertical diamond bands that resemble latticework. There are usually horizontal diamond bands at the top and bottom of each object as well.

Bowl, 8", Oval	$37.50
Butter Dish with Cover	$75

Lattice Pattern Pitcher. *Drawing by Mark Pickvet.*

Cake Stand, 8"	$55
Celery Vase	$45
Compote with Cover, 8"	$75
Cordial	$55
Creamer	$40
Goblet	$40
Lamp	$135
Marmalade Jar	$165
Pickle Dish	$35
Pitcher, Syrup with Lid	$100
Pitcher, Water	$125
Plate, 6¼"	$27.50
Plate, 7¼"	$32.50
Plate, 10"	$45
Platter, Oval (11½" x 7½"), Embossed "Waste Not, Want Not"	$65
Salt and Pepper Shakers	$65
Sauce Dish, Flat	$16
Sauce Dish, Footed	$18
Spooner	$27.50

Sugar with Cover	$60
Tray	$75
Wineglass	$40

Loop and Dart
Boston & Sandwich Glass Company, 1860s–1870s; Richards & Hartley, 1880s

This pattern consists of a series of overlapping loops and darts downward. It is a stippled pattern as well. Note that the prices are for full lead crystal or flint glass; for the cheaper nonlead or nonflint glass, reduce them by 25–35 percent.

Bowl, 9", Oval	$50
Butter Dish with Cover	$65
Cake Stand, 10"	$60
Celery Vase	$45
Compote, with Cover, 8", Low	$85
Compote with Cover, 8", High	$100
Creamer	$50
Cruet with Stopper	$125
Egg Holder	$35
Goblet	$40
Lamp, Oil	$125
Pitcher, Water	$100
Plate, 6"	$45
Relish Dish	$30
Salt Dip, Footed	$55
Sauce Dish	$15
Spooner	$37.50
Sugar Dish with Cover	$75
Tumbler, Footed	$40
Tumbler, Water	$35
Wineglass	$40

Louisiana
Bryce Brothers, 1870s–Early 1880s; U.S. Glass Company, Late 1890s–Early 1900s

Another in the U.S. Glass Company's state series, Louisiana is also known as Sharp Oval and Diamond for the interlocking ovals that contain the diamond design and end in a sharp point. It is also known as the Granby pattern. For any gold trim or frosted accents, increase the price by 25 percent.

Bowl, 9"	$30
Butter Dish with Cover	$85
Cake Stand	$75
Celery Vase	$40
Compote with Cover, 8"	$85
Creamer	$40
Goblet	$40
Jelly Dish, 5"	$45
Match Holder	$45
Mug	$35
Nappy with Cover, 4"	$45
Pitcher, Water	$75
Relish Dish	$22.50
Spooner	$40
Sugar Dish with Cover	$55
Sugar Shaker	$35
Tumbler, Water	$35
Wineglass	$40

Madora
Bryce, Higbee & Company, 1880s–1890s; Higbee Glass Company, Early 1900s

Madora is sometimes referred to as Arrowhead or Arrowhead in Oval because of the large arrowhead design in the center of the pattern. A few pieces were embossed with a bee (the Higbee Glass Company trademark) and are a little more valuable than those without it (increase prices by 25 percent).

Basket, 7" Long	$75
Bowl, Rose, with Foot and Stem	$45
Cake Stand	$60
Celery Dish with Handles	$45
Creamer	$40
Plate, 7", Square	$30
Punch Cup	$24
Salt Dip, Individual	$22.50
Salt and Pepper Shakers	$55
Sherbet	$35
Sugar Dish with Cover	$60
Wine Goblet	$35

CHILDREN'S MINIATURES:

Butter Dish with Cover	$45
Creamer	$30
Spooner	$25
Sugar with Cover	$45
Complete Set of 6 Pieces	$150

Maine
U.S. Glass Company, Late 1890s–Early 1900s

Maine, a pattern in the U.S. Glass Company's state series, is also known as Paneled Stippled Flower or Stippled Primrose because of its frame and stippled floral design. Pieces contain vertical ribbing as well. For any colored trim or stains, increase the prices by 25–35 percent; for any emerald green, double them.

Bowl, 8"	$35
Bread Plate, 10" x 7¼", Oval	$45
Butter Dish with Cover	$65
Cake Stand	$50
Compote, 7"	$35
Compote, 8"	$45
Compote, 9"	$50

Creamer	$35
Cruet with Stopper	$85
Jelly Dish with Cover	$60
Mug	$45
Pitcher, Milk	$75
Pitcher, Syrup	$85
Pitcher, Water	$75
Relish Dish	$22.50
Salt and Pepper Shakers	$65
Sauce Dish	$18
Sugar Dish with Cover	$55
Sugar Shaker	$35
Toothpick Holder	$125
Tumbler, Water	$35
Wineglass	$50

Maryland
Bryce Brothers, 1880s; U.S. Glass Company, 1890s–Early 1900s

To accurately describe this pattern, Maryland is often referred to as Inverted Loop and Fan or Loop and Diamond. For ruby flashed or ruby stained pieces, double the prices; for any with gold trim or gold decoration, increase the prices by 25–35 percent.

Banana Dish	$35
Bowl, Berry	$20
Bread Plate	$27.50
Butter Dish with Cover	$75
Cake Stand, 8"	$45
Celery Tray	$25
Celery Vase	$35
Compote, Open	$32.50
Compote with Cover	$65
Creamer	$35
Goblet	$35

Pressed Glass, Maryland. *Drawing by Mark Pickvet.*

Olive Dish with Handle	$25
Pitcher, Milk	$55
Pitcher, Water	$65
Plate, 7"	$30
Relish Dish, Oval	$25
Saltshaker	$35
Sauce Dish	$17.50
Spooner	$35
Sugar Dish with Cover	$55
Toothpick Holder	$125
Tumbler	$35
Wineglass	$45

Massachusetts
U.S. Glass Company, 1898–1900s

Colors in this pattern are somewhat rare and include emerald green, ruby stained, and cobalt blue (double the prices). Note that the butter dish with cover has been reproduced in crystal, pink, light green, and iridized marigold ($30–$35). Because of its style, this pattern is also referred to as Arched Diamond Points or Star and Diamonds.

Banana Stand	$150
Bar Bottle with Metal Whiskey Tumbler Cover	$100

Basket, 4½", Applied Handle	$65
Bonbon Dish, 5", Handled	$30
Bottle, Water	$115
Bowl, 6", Square	$22.50
Bowl, 9", Square	$27.50
Butter Dish with Cover	$85
Celery Tray	$37.50
Champagne Glass	$40
Cologne Bottle, 7½" Tall	$75
Compote	$42.50
Cordial	$65
Creamer	$40
Cruet with Stopper, 3½" Tall (Small)	$100
Goblet	$55
Gravy Boat	$50
Jug, Shaped Much Like a Teapot (Rum Jug)	$135
Lamp	$115
Mug	$27.50
Mustard Jar with Cover	$50
Olive Dish with Handle	$20
Pitcher, Syrup	$75
Pitcher, Water	$125
Plate, 8"	$37.50
Punch Cup	$21.50
Relish Dish, 8½"	$35
Salt and Pepper Shakers	$60
Sauce Dish, 4", Square	$20
Sherry Glass	$52.50
Shot Glass	$37.50
Spooner, Handled	$27.50
Sugar Dish with Cover, Handled	$65

Toothpick Holder	$75
Tumbler	$37.50
Vase, 6½" Tall	$40
Vase, 7" Tall	$45
Vase, 9" Tall	$55
Vase, 10" Tall	$60
Whiskey Tumbler	$37.50
Wineglass	$55

Michigan
U.S. Glass Company, Late 1890s–Early 1900s

Another in U.S. Glass's state series, Michigan is also known as Loop and Pillar, which more adequately describes the basic pattern. The series also includes some miniature or toy pieces originally designed for children.

For ruby stained, blue stained, or yellow stained pieces, double the prices. For any additional decorations, such as gold trim, etching, or enameling, increase the prices by 25 percent.

Bowl, Finger	$21
Bowl, 7½"	$35
Bowl, 8½" to 9"	$42.50
Bowl, 10" to 10½"	$50
Bowl, Fruit	$85
Butter Dish with Cover, Miniature (Toy)	$75
Butter Dish with Cover	$85
Celery Vase	$50
Compote, 4½"	$55
Compote, 9¼"	$75
Creamer, Miniature (Toy)	$75
Creamer, Individual (Small)	$35
Creamer	$45
Cruet with Stopper	$85
Cup	$20
Goblet	$55

Honey Dish	$17.50
Mug, Lemonade	$32.50
Nappy with Handle	$42.50
Olive Dish, 2-Handled	$21
Pickle Dish	$21
Pitcher, Syrup, Metal Lid	$100
Pitcher, Water, Miniature (Toy), Tankard Style	$65
Pitcher, Water, 8" Tall	$75
Pitcher, Water, Tankard Style, 12" Tall	$100
Plate, 5½"	$21
Punch Bowl, 8"	$65
Punch Cup	$17.50
Relish Dish	$27.50
Salt and Pepper Shakers	$60
Sauce Dish, Handled	$21
Sherbet, 2-Handled	$22.50
Spooner, Miniature (Toy)	$55
Spooner	$55
Sugar Bowl with Cover, Miniature (Toy)	$75
Sugar Dish, Individual (Small)	$35
Sugar Bowl with Cover	$65
Sugar Shaker	$35
Toothpick Holder	$100
Tumbler, Water	$45
Vase, Bud	$45
Vase, Footed	$55
Wineglass	$50

Minnesota
U.S. Glass Company, Late 1898–Early 1900s

Minnesota, another pattern in U.S. Glass's state series, is characterized by alternating stars in diamonds with circles in half ovals. For ruby stained or green, double the prices; for any additional decorations, such as gold trim, etching, or enameling, increase the prices by 25 percent.

Banana Stand	$75
Basket	$75
Biscuit Jar with Cover	$75
Bonbon Dish, 5"	$21
Bowl, 5", Flared	$27.50
Bowl, 9½", Oval	$35
Bowl, 10", Oval	$40
Bowl, Rose	$55
Butter Dish with Cover	$65
Carafe	$45
Celery Tray, 10"	$35
Celery Tray, 13"	$45
Compote, 6", Round	$45
Compote, 6", Square	$50
Compote, 7", Round	$50
Compote, 7", Square	$55
Compote, 8", Round	$55
Compote, 8", Square	$60
Compote, 9", Square	$65
Compote, 10", Flared	$75
Creamer, Individual (Small)	$25
Creamer	$37.50
Cruet with Stopper	$55
Cup	$24
Goblet	$45
Hair Receiver	$37.50
Humidor with Metal Jeweled Cover	$215
Match Safe	$35

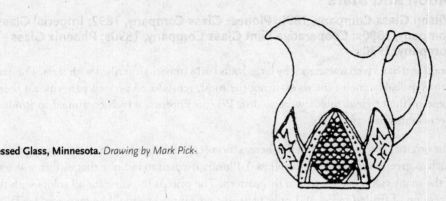

Pressed Glass, Minnesota. *Drawing by Mark Pickvet.*

Mug	$35
Olive Dish	$21
Pitcher, Syrup	$75
Pitcher, Water, Tankard Style	$105
Plate, 5"	$30
Plate, 7⅜"	$30
Pomade Jar with Cover	$47.50
Relish Dish	$26
Saltshaker	$35
Sauce Dish, Boat Shape	$25
Spooner	$35
Sugar Bowl with Cover	$47.50
Toothpick Holder, 3-Handled	$45
Toothpick Holder, 3-Handled, with Advertising	$85
Tray, 8" Long	$25
Tumbler, Juice	$27.50
Tumbler, Water	$32.50
Wineglass	$45

Moon and Stars

Wilson Glass Company, 1890; Pioneer Glass Company, 1892; Imperial Glass Company, 1890s; Cooperative Flint Glass Company, 1890s; Phoenix Glass Company, 1930s

Moon and Stars is characterized by large round orbs (moons) inscribed with stars. This pattern is probably one of the most, if not the most, reproduced pressed patterns out there. Some of the original molds were sold in 1937 to Phoenix, which continued to produce pieces in this pattern.

The original was made in crystal, whereas most reproductions boast a wide variety of color (such as greens, reds, blues, and yellows). Plurals are used to indicate that differing shades of the many colors are evident in this pattern. The price is the same for all colors with the exception of frosted pieces and milk glass, for which prices should be increased by 25–35 percent.

Ashtray, 8"	$25
Bowl, 6"	$30
Bowl, 12½"	$45
Butter Dish with Cover	$85
Cake Stand	$75
Celery Dish	$22.50
Compote	$25
Compote with Cover, 7"	$35
Compote with Cover, 8"	$40
Compote with Cover, 10"	$50
Creamer	$60
Goblet	$45
Lamp Shade, 4"	$25
Lamp, Table	$115
Pitcher, Water	$150
Salt and Pepper Shakers	$45
Sugar Bowl with Cover	$80
Toothpick Holder	$25
Tumbler, Water	$55
Tumbler, Water, Footed	$60
Wineglass	$45

Pressed Glass, Moon & Star. *Photo by Robin Rain-water.*

Nevada
U.S. Glass Company, Early 1900s

Another in U.S. Glass's state series, Nevada is a fairly simple pattern consisting of a horizontal band of loops at the bottom as well as at the top; in between is clear, unpatterned crystal. Increase the prices by 25 percent for any additional decorations, such as frosted pieces and gold trim, etching, or enameling.

Biscuit Jar with Cover	$75
Bowl, Finger	$30
Bowl with Cover, 6"	$45
Bowl, 7"	$30
Bowl with Cover, 8"	$55
Butter Dish with Cover	$80
Cake Stand, 10"	$45
Celery Vase	$30
Compote, 6"	$30
Compote with Cover, 6"	$47.50
Compote, 7"	$37.50
Compote, with Cover, 7"	$55
Compote, 8"	$42.50
Compote, with Cover, 8"	$65
Creamer	$37.50

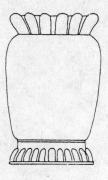

Pressed Glass, Nevada. *Drawing by Mark Pickvet.*

Cruet with Stopper	$50
Cup	$20
Pickle Dish, Oval	$20
Pitcher, Syrup, Tin Lid	$60
Pitcher, Milk, Tankard Style	$60
Pitcher, Water	$65
Pitcher, Water, Jug Style	$65
Pitcher, Water, Tankard Style	$65
Salt Dip, Individual (Small)	$20
Salt Dip, Master (Large)	$25
Saltshaker	$25
Sauce Dish, 4", Round	$16
Spooner	$42.50
Sugar Dish with Cover	$47.50
Toothpick Holder	$45
Tumbler, Water	$25

New England Pineapple
Boston & Sandwich Glass Company, 1860s

The pineapples of this pattern are pressed into large oval shapes that encompass the majority of each object. Many pieces are quite scarce and valuable in this pattern.

Pressed Glass, New England Pineapple. *Drawing by Mark Pickvet.*

Bowl, Fruit	$175
Butter Dish with Cover	$225
Castor Bottle	$110
Celery Vase	$225
Champagne Glass	$175
Compote, Open	$80
Compote with Cover, 6"	$225
Cordial	$150
Creamer, 6½"	$200
Cruet with Stopper	$150
Decanter with Stopper, 16 oz.	$275
Decanter with Stopper, 32 oz.	$325
Egg Holder	$80
Goblet, 2 Styles	$80
Honey Dish	$40
Mug	$150
Pitcher, Water	$365
Plate, 6"	$150
Salt Dip, Footed	$85
Sauce Dish	$40

Spooner	$80
Sugar Dish	$125
Sugar Dish with Cover	$225
Tumbler, Water	$125
Tumbler, Water, Footed	$150
Whiskey Tumbler, 2 oz.	$110
Wineglass	$80

New Hampshire
U.S. Glass Company, Early 1900s

Another in U.S. Glass's state series, New Hampshire is also known as Bent Buckle, which more accurately describes the basic pattern of interlocking buckles. It has also been called Modiste. For ruby stained or rose stained pieces, double the prices. For any additional decorations, such as gold trim, etching, or enameling, increase the prices by 25 percent.

Biscuit Jar with Cover	$75
Bowl, 5½", Flared	$17.50
Bowl, 8½"	$22.50
Bowl, 8½", Flared	$24
Bowl, 8½", Square Shape	$27.50
Butter Dish with Cover	$60
Cake Stand, 8¼"	$40
Carafe	$75
Celery Vase	$45
Compote, Open	$45
Compote with Cover, 5"	$55
Compote with Cover, 6"	$65
Compote with Cover, 7"	$75
Creamer, Individual (Small)	$25
Creamer	$40
Cruet with Stopper	$65
Goblet	$45

Mug	$27.50
Pitcher, Syrup, Metal Lid	$100
Pitcher, Water, Bulbous, Applied Handle	$100
Pitcher, Water, Molded Handle	$85
Relish Dish	$25
Salt and Pepper Shakers	$75
Sauce Dish	$17.50
Sugar Dish, Individual (Small)	$25
Sugar Bowl with Cover	$55
Toothpick Holder	$35
Vase	$45
Wineglass	$35

New Jersey
U.S. Glass Company, 1900–08

Another of U.S. Glass's state series, New Jersey is also known as Loops and Drops, which more accurately describes the pattern. Prices should be doubled for the rare emerald green and ruby stained examples. Increase the prices by 25 percent for intact gold trim.

Bottle, Water	$65
Bowl, 8", Flared	$32.50
Bowl, 9"	$37.50
Bowl, 10", Oval	$42.50
Bowl, Fruit, 12½"	$65
Bread Plate	$37.50
Butter Dish with Cover	$90
Butter Dish with Cover, Footed	$150
Cake Stand, 8"	$75
Carafe, Water	$70
Celery Tray, Rectangular	$32.50
Compote with Cover, 5"	$55
Compote, 6¾"	$40

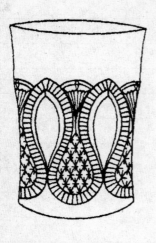

Pressed Glass, New Jersey. *Drawing by Mark Pickvet.*

Compote, 8"	$65
Compote with Cover, 8"	$80
Compote, 10½"	$70
Creamer	$42.50
Cruet with Stopper	$65
Goblet	$50
Molasses Can	$110
Olive Dish	$21
Pickle Dish, Rectangular	$21
Pitcher, Syrup with Lid	$115
Pitcher, Milk, Applied Handle	$85
Pitcher, Water, Applied Handle, 2 Styles	$100
Plate, 8"	$37.50
Salt and Pepper Shakers, Small	$45
Salt and Pepper Shakers, Hotel	$60
Sauce Dish	$16
Spooner	$35
Sugar Dish with Cover	$75
Sweetmeat Jar, 8"	$85
Toothpick Holder	$65

Tumbler, Water	$37.50
Wineglass	$50

Oregon
U.S. Glass Company, Early 1900s

Oregon is also known as Beaded Loop or Skilton, and is characterized by oval beading and diamonds that resemble cut glass. The beading intersects, as do the horizontal bands of ovals at the top. Prices should be doubled for the rare emerald green. Flashed pieces were made during the Depression years and sell for about the same price as basic crystal. Note that some partial flashing is present on some pieces (flashed feet on the footed tumbler, for instance).

Bowl, 3½"	$15
Bowl with Cover, 6"	$55
Bowl with Cover, 7"	$65
Bowl with Cover, 8"	$75
Butter Dish (2 Styles)	$75
Cake Stand, 6" (Small)	$45
Cake Stand, 7¾" (Medium)	$55
Cake Stand, 9½" (Large)	$65
Carafe, Water	$45
Celery Vase	$40
Compote, 5½"	$55
Compote, 6"	$40
Compote with Cover, 7"	$70
Compote, 8"	$50
Cordial	$40
Creamer	$40
Creamer, Footed	$45
Cruet with Stopper	$65
Goblet	$40
Honey Dish	$25
Jelly Dish	$50

Mug	$45
Pickle Dish, Boat Shape	$45
Pitcher, Syrup with Lid	$100
Pitcher, Milk	$85
Pitcher, Water, 64 oz.	$100
Relish Dish, 7½" Oval	$25
Salt Dip	$25
Salt and Pepper Shakers	$50
Sauce Dish, 3½"	$15
Sauce Dish, 4"	$20
Spooner	$27.50
Spooner, Footed	$32.50
Sugar, Open	$40
Sugar, Footed	$45
Sugar Dish with Cover	$65
Sugar Shaker	$45
Toothpick Holder	$80
Tray, 7½", Oval	$35
Tray, 9½", Oval	$50
Tray, 10½", Oval	$55
Tray, Bread	$50
Tumbler, Water	$40
Tumbler, Footed	$45
Vase	$55
Wineglass	$50
Wineglass, Pedestal Base	$65

Panelled Dewdrop
Campbell, Jones & Company, 1870s–1880s

This pattern is sometimes referred to as Striped Dewdrop and is characterized by vertical strips or panels of dewdrops. Some pieces may or may not have rows of dewdrops on the base.

Panelled Dewdrop Champagne Glass. *Drawing by Mark Pickvet.*

Butter Dish with Cover	$85
Celery Vase	$45
Champagne Glass	$40
Cheese Dish with Cover	$100
Compote, Open, 8", Footed	$65
Cordial	$40
Creamer, Applied Handle	$45
Goblet, Plain Base	$40
Goblet, Dewdrops on Base	$45
Honey Dish with Cover, 11"	$150
Marmalade Jar	$75
Mug, Applied Handle	$40
Pickle Dish	$60
Pitcher, Water	$85
Plate, 7"	$35
Plate, 11"	$65
Platter, Oval	$45
Platter, Oblong, Handles	$60
Relish	$21
Sauce Dish, Flat	$16

Sauce Dish, Footed	$18
Spooner	$25
Sugar with Cover	$65
Tumbler, Water	$35
Wineglass	$40

Panelled Grape
D. C. Jenkins Glass Company, Early 1900s

This pattern is also known as Heavy Panelled Grape. Note that the listed prices are for clear glass only. This pattern was heavily reproduced in milk glass, carnival glass, and other colors (reduce prices by 65–70 percent).

Ale Glass	$75
Bowl, Oval	$45
Bowl with Cover	$75
Butter Dish with Cover	$85
Celery Vase	$55
Compote, Open	$55
Compote with Cover	$85
Cordial	$60
Creamer, 4½" Tall	$55
Cup	$45
Goblet	$75
Pitcher, Syrup	$185
Pitcher, Milk	$165
Pitcher, Water	$185
Sauce Dish, 4¼", Round	$30
Sauce Dish, Oval	$35
Sauce Dish, Footed	$37.50
Spooner	$37.50
Sugar Dish, Open	$40
Sugar with Cover	$65

Pressed Glass. Panelled Grape Pattern. *Drawings by Mark Pickvet.*

Pressed Glass. Panelled Thistle Pattern. *Drawings by Mark Pickvet.*

Toothpick Holder	$65
Tumbler, Water	$65
Wineglass	$75

Panelled Thistle
Various Companies, 1910s–Early 1920s

The Higbee Glass Company was the original maker of this pattern, and they referred to it as Delta. The Jefferson Glass Company of Toronto, Canada, and the Dominion Glass Company also produced items in this pattern. Some pieces have Higbee's bee mark (increase prices by 25 percent). A few reproductions have been made, including colored salt dips, clear salt dips that are taller than 1 inch, and a slim flared toothpick holder. Reduce prices by 50–75 percent for them.

Basket, Various Styles	$115
Bowl, 6½"	$40
Bowl, 7"	$45
Bowl, 8½"	$55

Bowl, 9"	$60
Bowl, Footed	$55
Butter Dish, Flanged, with Cover	$85
Cake Stand, 9¾" Diameter	$60
Celery Vase, Handled	$55
Celery Dish	$40
Compote, 5", Open	$40
Compote, 8", Open	$50
Cordial	$42.50
Creamer, Knob Feet	$47.50
Cruet (without Stopper)	$55
Cup, Custard	$35
Goblet, Straight	$37.50
Goblet, Flared	$42.50
Honey Dish with Cover, Square, Footed	$95
Pickle Dish, 8¼"	$30
Pitcher, Milk, 32 oz.	$90
Pitcher, Water, 64 oz.	$105
Plate, 6"	$35
Plate, 7¼"	$40
Plate, 8¼"	$45
Plate, 9½"	$50
Plate, 10¼"	$55
Salt Dip, Individual, 1" Tall, Footed	$24
Salt and Pepper Shakers	$65
Sauce Dish, Several Styles	$24
Spooner, 2-Handled	$40
Sugar Bowl with Cover, 2-Handled	$75
Toothpick Holder	$65
Tray, Celery	$45
Tumbler, Water	$37.50

Wineglass, Flared	$42.50
Wineglass, Straight	$37.50

Pennsylvania
U.S. Glass Company, 1890s

This is another of the state series produced by U.S. Glass. Colors include green, ruby or ruby stained, and blue (double the prices). Increase the prices by 25 percent for any fully intact gold trim.

Biscuit Jar with Cover	$90
Bowl, 4"	$26
Bowl, 8"	$32.50
Bowl, 8", Square	$35
Butter Dish with Cover	$90
Carafe	$75
Celery Tray	$37.50
Celery Vase	$55
Champagne Glass	$35
Cheese Dish with Cover	$100
Compote	$55
Creamer	$40
Cruet with Stopper	$60
Cup	$24
Decanter with Stopper	$125
Goblet	$35
Molasses Can	$100
Pitcher, Syrup	$75
Pitcher, Water	$85
Pitcher, Water, Tankard Style	$125
Punch Bowl	$215
Punch Cup	$20
Saltshaker	$20

Sauce Dish	$16
Shot Glass	$50
Spooner	$32.50
Sugar Dish with Cover	$65
Toothpick Holder	$50
Tumbler, Juice	$22.50
Tumbler, Water	$32.50
Whiskey Tumbler	$50
Wineglass	$35

Pineapple and Fan
Adams & Company, 1880s; U.S. Glass Company, 1890s

This pattern is also referred to as Cube with Fan because of the cube or pineapple-like design on the lower half of each piece. The fan design is on the top portion and the cubes are flat beveled squares. A few objects have been found in color; for green increase the prices below by 50 percent; for ruby stained, double them.

Bowl, 8"	$40
Bowl, 9"	$45
Butter Dish with Cover	$85
Cake Stand	$60
Celery Vase	$50
Creamer	$40
Custard Cup	$27.50
Goblet	$42.50
Mug	$35
Piccalilli Jar with Cover	$85
Pitcher, 16 oz.	$55
Pitcher, 32 oz.	$65
Pitcher, 64 oz., Tankard Style	$85
Pitcher, 96 oz., Tankard Style	$115
Salt Dip, Individual	$18
Sauce Dish, 4"	$16

Sauce Dish, 4½"	$17.50
Spooner	$37.50
Sugar with Cover	$60
Tumbler, Water	$35
Wineglass	$40

Pointed Thumbprint
Bakewell, Pears & Co., 1860s; Bryce Bros., 1890s

The thumbprints on this pattern are pointed on the ends and as a consequence, resemble almonds. The pattern was also referred to as Fingerprint and Almond Thumbprint. Bryce Brothers produced a cheaper lime glass in the early 1890s in the same pattern; the prices are for lead glass (reduce by two-thirds for nonlead). A few have been found in milk glass (same price as listed for crystal).

Bowl, 4½", Footed	$60
Butter Dish with Cover, Cable Edge	$125
Celery Vase	$65
Champagne Glass	$65
Compote, 10½"	$75
Compote with Cover, 4¾", 2 Styles	$85
Compote with Cover, 7"	$95
Compote with Cover, 10"	$125
Compote with Cover, 4¾"	$60
Compote with Cover, 7" Tall	$70
Compote with Cover, 10" Tall	$90
Cordial Glass	$50
Creamer	$65
Cruet with Stopper	$75
Decanter	$100
Egg Holder	$50
Goblet	$55
Pitcher, Water	$150
Punch Bowl	$175

Salt Dip, Flat	$30
Salt Dip, Footed	$32.50
Salt Dip with Cover, Footed	$50
Spooner	$30
Sugar with Cover	$85
Sweetmeat Jar with Cover	$95
Tumbler	$65
Wineglass	$50

Primrose
Canton Glass Company, 1880s

The flower and leaf design of this pattern includes vertical panels and horizontal ribbing. Several items were made in a variety of colors aside from the usual crystal. For amber, green, and yellow, increase the prices by 50 percent. For amethyst (slag), cobalt blue, vaseline, and black, double them.

Bowl, Berry	$27.50
Bowl, Waste	$37.50
Butter Dish with Cover	$80
Cake Stand	$60
Celery Vase	$45
Compote with Cover, 6"	$50
Compote with Cover, 7½"	$60
Compote with Cover, 8"	$70
Compote with Cover, 9"	$85
Cordial	$45
Creamer	$40
Egg Holder	$37.50
Goblet, Knob Stem	$40
Goblet, Plain Stem	$35
Marmalade Jar	$65
Pickle Dish	$32.50
Pitcher, 7½" Tall	$65

Pressed Primrose Pattern. *Drawing by Mark Pickvet.*

Plate, 4½"	$24
Plate, 6"	$26
Plate, 7"	$28
Plate, 8¾", Cake, Handled	$40
Platter, Oval (12½" x 8"), Flower Handles	$55
Sauce Dish, Flat	$18
Sauce Dish, 4", Footed	$21
Sauce Dish, 5½", Footed	$23.50
Spooner	$30
Sugar with Cover	$60
Tray, Water	$55
Wineglass	$35

Ribbed Grape
Boston & Sandwich Glass Company, 1850s–1860s

This pattern is characterized by grape clusters, leaves, vines, and vertical ribbing. Colors include an aqua or bluish green and opaque white, for which the prices should be doubled.

Bowl, Berry	$75
Butter Dish with Cover	$125
Celery Vase	$85
Compote, 8", Open, Footed	$85

Ribbed Grape Pattern. *Photo by Robin Rainwater.*

Ribbed Grape Pattern. *Drawing by Mark Pickvet.*

Compote with Cover, 6"	$175
Cordial	$125
Creamer	$150
Goblet, 2 Styles	$80
Pitcher, Water	$225
Plate, 6"	$55
Plate, 7½"	$65
Sauce Dish, Flat	$40
Spooner	$55
Sugar with Cover	$125
Tumbler, Water	$85
Whiskey Tumbler	$100
Wineglass	$55

Ribbed Palm
Mckee Brothers, 1860s–1870s

The palm leaves in this pattern are quite large and usually begin at the bottom and nearly reach the top. The remaining portion consists of vertical ribbing. There are quite a few rare pieces such as the creamer and pitcher.

A few odd colors such as green and ruby stained have been found; double the prices for those.

Ribbed Palm Pattern. *Drawing by Mark Pickvet.*

Bowl, 6", Flat Rim	$45
Bowl, 6", Oblong, Scalloped	$55
Bowl, 7", Oblong, Scalloped	$60
Bowl, 8", Oblong, Scalloped	$65
Bowl, 9", Oblong, Scalloped	$70
Butter Dish with Cover	$135
Celery Vase	$80
Champagne Glass	$100
Compote, 7", Open, Scalloped	$80
Compote, 8", Open, Scalloped	$100
Compote, 10", Open, Scalloped	$150
Compote with Cover, 6"	$150
Cordial	$100
Creamer, Applied Handle	$200
Egg Holder	$50
Goblet	$75
Lamp, 3 Styles	$160
Pickle Dish	$57.50
Pitcher, 9" Tall, Applied Handle	$260
Plate, 6"	$50

Salt Dip, Pedestal Base	$45
Sauce Dish, 4"	$30
Spooner	$45
Sugar with Cover	$125
Tumbler, 8 oz.	$100
Whiskey Tumbler	$100
Wineglass	$75

Roman Rosette
Bryce, Walker & Company, 1870s; U.S. Glass Company, 1890s

The rosettes in this pattern are quite large and circle around each object. The pattern is a typical all-over Sandwich design in that many similar patterns of it have been reproduced and referred to as Old Sandwich glass.

A few odd colors such as applied amber and ruby decorations have been found in the original pattern; double the prices for those.

Bowl, 5"	$22.50
Bowl, 6"	$27.50
Bowl, 7"	$32.50
Bowl, 8" to 8½"	$37.50
Bowl with Cover, 9"	$80
Bread Plate	$40
Butter Dish with Cover	$75
Cake Stand, 9"	$55
Cake Stand, 10"	$65
Castor Bottle with Stopper	$75
Castor Stand (Holds 3 Castor Bottles)	$35
Celery Vase	$45
Compote with Cover, 4½" to 5"	$60
Compote with Cover, 6"	$75
Compote with Cover, 7"	$85
Compote with Cover, 8"	$95
Cordial	$60

Pressed Roman Rosette. *Drawing by Mark Pickvet.*

Creamer, 16 oz.	$45
Goblet	$50
Mug	$45
Mustard Jar	$60
Pickle Dish	$40
Pitcher, Syrup with Metal Lid	$100
Pitcher, Milk, 32 oz.	$125
Pitcher, Water	$150
Plate, 7¼" to 7½"	$70
Platter, Oval (11" x 9")	$45
Relish Dish, 9"	$35
Salt and Pepper Shakers	$50
Sauce Dish, Flat, 4"	$18
Sauce Dish, Flat, 4½"	$23.50
Sauce Dish, Footed	$26
Spooner	$35
Sugar Dish with Cover	$60
Tray for Shakers (Small)	$16
Tumbler, Water	$75
Wineglass	$60

Sawtooth

Boston & Sandwich Glass Company, 1860s; New England Glass Company, 1860s

The sawteeth are a little sharp for a pressed pattern but are still easily distinguished from cut glass. The teeth usually begin at the bottom of each object and proceed about three-quarters of the way up. This pattern is often confused with Diamond Point; however, the teeth or diamonds in Sawtooth are larger and more pronounced than the smaller ones associated with Diamond Point.

Original pieces usually have sawtooth rims, knobbed stems, and applied handles. Reduce the prices by 25 percent if any of these are lacking. For any colored pieces, double the prices.

Bowl, 5"	$24
Bowl, Berry, 8"	$45
Bowl, Berry, 9"	$50
Bowl, Berry, 10"	$55
Bowl with Cover, 7"	$70
Butter Dish, Miniature (Children's)	$85
Butter Dish with Cover	$100
Cake Stand, 9"	$110
Cake Stand, 10"	$125
Celery Vase, Pointed Edge	$60
Celery Vase, Rolled Edge	$75
Champagne Glass	$75
Compote, 6", Open	$40
Compote, 7", Open	$50
Compote, 8", Open	$60
Compote, 10", Open	$75
Compote with Cover, 6"	$70
Compote with Cover, 7"	$75
Compote with Cover, 8"	$85
Compote with Cover, 9"	$95
Compote with Cover, 10", Knob on Stem	$175
Compote with Cover, 11", Knob on Stem	$200

Pressed Sawtooth Pattern. *Drawing by Mark Pickvet.*

Compote with Cover, 12", Knob on Stem	$225
Cordial	$50
Creamer, Miniature (Children's)	$75
Creamer	$60
Cruet with Stopper	$125
Decanter with Stopper, 32 oz.	$125
Egg Holder	$45
Goblet, Knob on Stem	$55
Honey Dish	$30
Jar with Cover, Acorn Finial	$100
Lamp	$135
Pitcher, Water, 64 oz.	$175
Salt Dip	$26
Salt Dip with Cover, Footed	$45
Sauce Dish, 4"	$25
Sauce Dish, 5"	$27.50
Spooner	$45
Spooner, Octagonal	$55
Spooner, Miniature (Children's)	$55

Sugar Dish with Cover	$65
Sugar Dish, Miniature (Children's)	$75
Tray, 10", Oval	$45
Tray, 11", Oval	$50
Tray, 12", Oval	$60
Tray, 14", Oval	$75
Tumbler, Juice, 3½" Tall	$30
Tumbler, Water	$40
Tumbler, Water, Footed	$55
Wineglass, Knob on Stem	$50

Star-In-Bull's-Eye
U.S. Glass Company, Early 1900s

The eyes of this Bull's-Eye pattern are large, and the circles overlap at the edges. The star pattern is within the bull's-eyes, as the pattern name suggests. A few other pieces besides the water tumbler may be found trimmed in gold; add 25 percent to the prices if the gold is completely intact. For ruby stained pieces, double the prices.

Bowl, Berry	$37.50
Butter Dish with Cover	$70
Cake Stand	$60
Celery Vase	$45
Compote, 6", Open, Flared	$40
Compote with Cover	$65
Creamer	$45
Cruet with Stopper, 4" Tall	$70
Goblet	$45
Pickle Dish, Diamond Shape	$40
Pitcher, Syrup, Metal Lid	$135
Pitcher, Water	$110
Relish Dish	$35
Salt Dip	$26

Pressed Glass. Star-in-Bull's Eye Pattern. *Drawing by Mark Pickvet.*

Pressed Glass. Sunburst Pattern. *Drawing by Mark Pickvet.*

Pressed Glass. Teardrop and Thumbprint Pattern.
Drawing by Mark Pickvet.

Sauce Dish	$21
Spooner	$32.50
Sugar with Cover	$60
Toothpick Holder, Single	$50
Toothpick Holder, Double	$60
Tumbler, Water, Gold Band	$40
Whiskey Tumbler, 2 oz.	$50
Wineglass	$45

Sunburst

D. C. Jenkins Glass Company, Early 1900s

The original Sunburst pattern by Jenkins was also referred to as Squared Sunburst. It is a fairly common pattern, with the exception of the rare Sunburst-patterned toothpick holder.

Bowl, Oblong (Deep)	$37.50
Butter Dish	$37.50
Cake Plate	$42.50
Celery Vase	$37.50
Compote with Cover	$57.50
Cordial	$37.50
Creamer, Individual (Small)	$22.50
Creamer, 4½" Tall (Large)	$27.50
Cup	$20
Egg Holder	$27.50
Goblet	$32.50
Marmalade Jar	$55
Pickle Dish, Single	$30
Pickle Dish, 8", 2 Divisions	$42.50
Pickle Dish, 10", 2 Divisions	$52.50
Pitcher, Milk	$55
Pitcher, Water	$65
Plate, 6"	$30
Plate, 7"	$35
Plate, 11"	$45
Saltshaker	$30
Sauce Dish, 1 Handle	$21
Spooner	$17.50
Sugar, Open Individual (Small)	$17.50
Sugar with Cover (Large)	$42.50

| Toothpick Holder | $75 |
| Tumbler, Water | $27.50 |

Teardrop
Ripley & Company, 1870s–1880s; U.S. Glass Company, 1890s

The basic Teardrop is sometimes referred to as Teardrop and Thumbprint because of the band of thumbprints that usually rests above the teardrops. There are many variations of teardrop and thumbprint patterns.

Some pieces may be engraved or enameled (increase prices by 25 percent). Other colors include ruby flashed and cobalt blue (double the prices).

Bowl, 7"	$35
Bowl, Oval	$37.50
Biscuit Jar with Cover	$125
Butter Dish with Cover	$75
Cake Stand	$60
Celery Dish	$40
Compote, Open	$50
Creamer	$45
Cruet with Stopper	$125
Goblet	$40
Pitcher, Syrup with Metal Lid	$115
Pitcher, Water	$115
Plate, 10"	$45
Relish Dish	$32.50
Saltshaker	$40
Sauce Dish, 4", Flat	$18
Sauce Dish, Footed	$22.50
Spooner	$32.50
Sugar, Open	$45
Sugar with Cover	$65

Tumbler, Water	$40
Wineglass	$40

Teardrops and Diamond Block
Adams & Company, 1870s–1880s; U.S. Glass Company, 1890s

This pattern is characterized by large teardrops at the bottom of each object. The remaining portion of each object is in a block diamond design. It is also referred to as Jacob's Tears, Job's Tears, and Art. Some pieces have been found with ruby flashing, which are a bit more valuable (increase the prices by 50 percent). Milk glass in this pattern is reproduction—reduce the prices by 50–60 percent.

Banana Dish, Oblong, Flat	$105
Banana Stand	$105
Basket, 10" Tall	$90
Bowl, 6", Footed	$40
Bowl, 7"	$45
Bowl, 8"	$60
Butter Dish with Cover	$75
Cake Stand, 9"	$65
Cake Stand, 10"	$75
Celery Vase	$50
Compote, 8", Open	$55
Compote, 9", Open	$65
Compote, 10", Open	$75
Compote with Cover, 7", Footed	$115
Cracker Jar with Cover	$155
Creamer, 2 Styles	$60
Cruet with Stopper	$135
Goblet	$65
Jug, Vinegar, 48 oz.	$115
Mug	$65
Pitcher, Milk	$125
Pitcher, Water, 64 oz.	$125

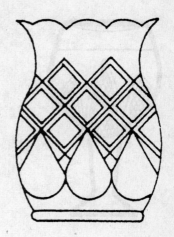

Teardrop & Diamond Back Pattern. *Drawing by Mark Pickvet.*

Pitcher, Water, 80 oz.	$150
Plate, 10"	$50
Relish Dish	$35
Sauce Dish, 4", 2 Styles	$25
Spooner	$35
Sugar Dish with Cover	$75
Tumbler	$55
Wineglass	$65

Teasel

Bryce Brothers, 1870s; New Martinsville Glass Company, Early 1900s

The original design was made by Bryce Brothers and was modeled after the teasel plant that is used to comb wool. The later New Martinsville version was originally called Long Leaf Teasel, and a few extra pieces (butter dish and cruet) were produced that were not part of the Bryce Brothers' production line.

Bowl, 8", Pedestal Base	$42.50
Bowl, Oval (9" x 5")	$45
Butter Dish with Cover (New Martinsville)	$67.50
Cake Stand	$55
Celery Dish	$40
Compote, Open	$40

Teasel Pattern Wineglass. *Drawing by Mark Pickvet.*

Cracker Jar with Cover	$85
Creamer	$45
Cruet with Stopper (New Martinsville)	$65
Goblet, Several Styles	$40
Honey Dish with Cover, Oblong	$85
Pitcher, Water	$85
Plate, 7"	$30
Plate, 9"	$35
Sauce Dish, Round, Flat	$18
Spooner	$32.50
Sugar Dish with Cover	$60
Toothpick Holder	$65
Tumbler, Water	$40
Whiskey Tumbler	$50

Tennessee
King, Son & Company, 1890s; U.S. Glass Company, Late 1890s–Early 1900s

Another in U.S. Glass's state series, Tennessee is more accurately described by its alternative names of Jewel and Crescent or Jeweled Rosette.

For ruby stained or green, double the prices; for any additional decorations, such as gold trim, etching, or enameling, increase them by 25 percent.

Bowl with Cover, 7"	$50
Bowl, 8"	$40
Bread Plate	$47.50
Butter Dish with Cover	$75
Cake Stand, 8"	$40
Cake Stand, 9½"	$45
Cake Stand, 10½"	$50
Celery Vase	$40
Compote with Cover, 5"	$50
Compote, 6", Open	$35
Compote, 7", Open	$40
Compote with Cover, 7"	$60
Compote, 8", Open	$45
Compote, 10", Open	$70
Creamer	$37.50
Cruet with Stopper	$75
Goblet	$50
Mug	$45
Pitcher, Syrup with Metal Lid	$105
Pitcher, Milk	$75
Pitcher, Water	$85
Relish Dish	$30
Saltshaker	$35
Spooner	$40
Sugar Dish with Cover	$57.50
Toothpick Holder	$85
Tumbler, Water	$40
Wineglass	$65

Texas

U.S. Glass Company, Late 1890s–Early 1900s

One of the rarest of U.S. Glass's state patterns, Texas is also referred to as Loop with Stippled Panels. For ruby or red stained items, double the prices. For crystal pieces with gilded tops, increase the prices by 25 percent; for colored pieces with gilded tops, increase the prices by 150 percent.

Bowl, Berry, 7"	$40
Bowl with Cover, 6"	$65
Bowl with Cover, 7"	$75
Bowl with Cover, 8"	$85
Bowl, 9", Scalloped	$45
Butter Dish with Cover	$150
Cake Stand, 9½"	$75
Celery Dish	$65
Celery Vase	$75
Compote, 5½" Diameter, Open	$55
Compote, 6", Scalloped Rim	$75
Creamer, Individual (Small)	$40
Creamer (Large)	$65
Cruet with Stopper, Inverted Pattern	$225
Goblet	$100
Horseradish Dish with Cover and Opening for Spoon	$75
Pickle Dish, 8½"	$40
Pitcher, Syrup with Metal Lid	$350
Pitcher, 48 oz., Inverted Pattern	$275
Pitcher, Pattern Variant	$425
Plate, 8¾" to 9"	$65
Preserve Dish, Oval	$55
Saltshaker	$75
Salt and Pepper Shakers, Small	$125
Salt and Pepper Shakers, Large	$150
Sauce Dish	$18.50
Sauce Dish, Footed	$27.50
Spooner	$60
Sugar, Open	$40

Sugar with Cover, Individual (Small)	$125
Sugar with Cover, Individual (Large)	$150
Toothpick Holder	$50
Tray, 11¼" x 6½"	$75
Tumbler, Water, Inverted Pattern	$55
Tumbler, Water, Pattern Variant	$55
Vase, 6½" Tall (Straight or Cupped)	$35
Vase, 8" Tall (Straight or Cupped)	$45
Vase, 9" Tall (Straight or Cupped)	$55
Vase, 10" Tall (Straight or Cupped)	$65
Wineglass	$90

Thousand Eye
Various Companies, 1870s–Early 1900s

The original Thousand Eye pattern was first made by Adams & Company around 1875. Many Adams pieces in this pattern contain a three-knob stem finial. In the 1880s, Richards & Hartley produced pieces in this pattern with plain stems and scalloped bottoms. Others followed with their own variations; nevertheless, the basic pattern contains rows upon rows of circles from which the Thousand Eye name is derived. For colors such as amber, blue, green, vaseline, yellow, and any opalescence, double the prices.

Bowl, Serving, Carriage Shape	$55
Bowl, Waste	$65
Bread Plate, 10"	$50
Butter Dish with Cover	$65
Cake Stand, 10"	$35
Cake Stand, 11"	$45
Celery Dish, Hat Style	$45
Celery Vase, 7"	$55
Cologne Bottle with Faceted Stopper	$55
Compote, 5", Open	$32.50
Compote, 6", Open	$35
Compote, 7", Open	$40

Compote, 8", Open	$45
Compote, 8" Open, Square	$55
Compote with Cover, 8", Square	$75
Compote, 9", Open	$55
Compote, 10", Open	$60
Cordial	$40
Creamer, Small, 4"	$35
Creamer, Large, 6"	$45
Cruet with Faceted Stopper, 6"	$50
Egg Holder	$60
Goblet	$45
Hat Shape or Vase	$50
Honey Dish with Cover, 7¼" x 6"	$100
Inkwell, 2" Square, Patterned Lid Only	$45
Jelly Dish	$25
Lamp, Kerosene, 12"	$125
Lamp, Kerosene, 15"	$150
Lamp Shade, Inverted Beehive Shape, Christmas Light	$40
Mug, Miniature or Toy, 2½"	$25
Mug, 3½"	$30
Nappy with Handle, 5"	$40
Nappy with Handle, 6"	$45
Nappy with Handle, 8"	$55
Pickle Dish	$30
Pitcher, Syrup, Pewter Lid	$80
Pitcher, Milk, 7"	$100
Pitcher, Water, 36 oz.	$100
Pitcher, Water, 64 oz.	$125
Pitcher, Water, 128 oz.	$175
Plate, 6", Mold-Embossed Clock and ABCs Around Rim	$55
Plate, 6", Square	$35

Plate, 8", Square	$37.50
Plate, 10", Square	$50
Platter, 11", Oval	$50
Platter, 11" x 8", Oblong	$50
Salt and Pepper Shakers	$55
Salt and Pepper Shakers, with Bands	$75
Salt Dip, Individual (Small)	$65
Salt Dip, Master, Carriage Shape	$70
Salt Dip, Master, 4"	$17.50
Salt Dip, Master, 4", Footed	$20
Sauce Dish	$35
Spooner	$45
String Holder, Beehive Shape	$45
Sugar Dish with Cover	$65
Toothpick Holder	$40
Tray, 12½" Diameter	$50
Tray, 14", Oval	$65
Tumbler, Water	$75
Wineglass	$35

Thumbprint
Bakewell, Pears & Company, 1860s

The original Thumbprint pattern was first named Argus by Bakewell and Pears. It has also been referred to as Early Thumbprint. Solid but transparent colors in this pattern are extremely scarce (triple the prices).

For the more recently reproduced ruby flashed King's Crown pattern by the U.S. Glass Company conglomerate, including Tiffin, cut the prices below in half. For those produced (by Fostoria) for the Henry Ford Museum in Dearborn, Michigan, in crystal, red, green, or cobalt blue, reduce the prices by 50–70 percent.

Ale Glass, 7½" Tall	$150
Ashtray	$45
Bowl, 4" to 6"	$55

Bowl with Cover	$225
Butter Dish, 2 Styles	$165
Cake Plate	$135
Castor Bottle	$160
Celery Vase, 2 Styles	$140
Champagne Glass	$95
Claret Glass	$155
Compote, Open, 6"	$80
Compote, Open, 8"	$90
Compote, Open, 9"	$100
Compote with Cover, 6", Hexagonal	$135
Compote with Cover, 7", Hexagonal	$165
Compote with Cover, 8", Hexagonal	$190
Compote with Cover, 10", Hexagonal	$225
Cordial	$90
Creamer, Applied Handle	$125
Decanter with Stopper, 32 oz.	$185
Egg Holder	$60
Goblet, Barrel Shape	$65
Goblet, Ring Stem	$80
Honey Dish	$35
Lamp, 10" Tall	$115
Mug, Applied Handle, 8 oz.	$110
Pickle Dish	$55
Pitcher, Water	$500
Punch Bowl with Stand, 12" Diameter, 23½" Tall	$1650
Salt Dip, Individual (Small)	$27.50
Salt Dip, Master (Large)	$37.50
Sauce Dish, 4", Flat	$32.50
Sauce Dish, 4½", Flat	$37.50
Spooner	$55

Pressed Thumbprint Pattern. *Drawing by Mark Pickvet.*

Sugar with Cover	$165
Tumbler, Bar	$90
Tumbler, Footed	$65
Vase, 9½" Tall	$85
Whiskey Tumbler, 2 oz.	$85
Wineglass	$70

Tulip with Sawtooth
Bryce, Richards and Company, 1850s

The original pattern name was simply Tulip, but "Sawtooth" was added because that design was patterned at the bottom of the tulips. The original pieces were made primarily in crystal, but some cheaper lime substitutes have been found; reduce the prices by 50 percent for noncrystal.

Bowl, Berry	$65
Butter Dish with Cover	$150
Celery Vase	$85
Champagne Glass	$125
Compote, 8", Open	$55
Compote with Cover (Low)	$75
Compote with Cover, Small	$85
Compote with Cover, Large	$100

Cordial	$75
Creamer	$125
Decanter with Stopper, 8 oz.	$150
Decanter with Stopper, 16 oz.	$200
Decanter with Patterned Stopper, 32 oz., Handled	$275
Egg Holder with Cover	$225
Goblet, 7" Tall, Knob Stem	$75
Honey Dish	$50
Pitcher, Water	$300
Plate, 6"	$75
Pomade Jar	$100
Salt Dip, Master	$40
Salt Dip, Petal Rim, Pedestal Base	$55
Spooner	$45
Sugar Dish, Open	$75
Tumbler, Bar	$75
Tumbler, Water	$70
Tumbler, Water, Footed	$75
Whiskey Tumbler	$75
Wineglass	$75

Vermont
U.S. Glass Company, 1899–1903

Another of U.S. Glass's state patterns, Vermont is also known as Honeycomb with Flower Rim and Inverted Thumbprint with Daisy Band.

There are quite a few color variations. For gold trim or gilding, increase the prices by 25 percent; for amber, blue, green, slag, and milk glass, increase the prices by 50 percent; for cobalt blue and decorated custard, double the prices. The reproduced toothpick holder in chocolate or opalescent, by Mosser and Degenhart, should be listed at $65.

The candlestick that was produced in custard only was originally referred to as Jeweled Vermont.

Basket (Several Varieties)	$50
Bowl, Berry	$35

Bowl, Waste	$45
Butter Dish with Cover	$75
Candlestick (Custard Only)	$80
Card Tray	$30
Celery Tray	$37.50
Celery Vase	$47.50
Compote, Open	$45
Compote with Cover	$65
Creamer, 4¼"	$37.50
Goblet	$47.50
Pickle Dish	$26
Pitcher, Water	$100
Relish Dish	$32.50
Saltshaker	$30
Sauce Dish	$25
Spooner	$32.50
Sugar	$37.50
Sugar Dish with Cover	$50
Toothpick Holder	$45
Tumbler, Water	$40
Vase	$35

Virginia or Banded Portland
Portland Glass Company, 1890s; U.S. Glass Company, 1901

This pattern in the U.S. Glass state series is also called Banded Portland and Maiden Blush. Flashed-on colors of blue, green, ruby red, pink, and yellow have also been discovered, for which the prices below should be doubled.

Bottle, Water	$80
Bowl, 4"	$15
Bowl, 6"	$30
Bowl with Cover, 6"	$50
Bowl, 7½"	$35

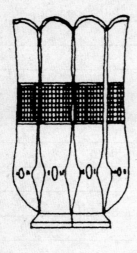

Pressed Glass, Virginia. *Drawing by Mark Pickvet.*

Bowl, 8"	$40
Bowl with Cover, 8"	$100
Butter Dish with Cover	$75
Cake Stand	$65
Candlestick	$45
Carafe	$90
Celery Dish	$40
Celery Vase	$45
Cologne Bottle	$65
Compote, 6"	$45
Compote with Cover, 6"	$85
Compote with Cover, 7"	$100
Compote with Cover, 8"	$115
Creamer, Individual, Oval (Small)	$30
Creamer, Large, 6 oz.	$45
Cruet with Stopper	$75
Cup	$25
Decanter	$65
Dish, Sardine, Oblong	$60
Dresser Tray	$60

Goblet	$45
Jelly Dish with Cover	$125
Lamp, 2 Styles	$65
Nappy, Square	$20
Olive Dish	$25
Pin Tray	$22.50
Pitcher, Syrup with Lid	$75
Pitcher, Water, Tankard Style	$100
Pomade Jar with Cover	$45
Punch Bowl	$135
Punch Cup	$25
Relish Dish, 6½"	$30
Relish Dish, 8¼"	$35
Ring Holder	$85
Salt and Pepper Shakers	$75
Sauce Dish, 2 Styles, Round or Flat	$15
Spooner	$35
Sugar Dish, Individual (Small)	$30
Sugar Dish with Cover	$65
Sugar Shaker	$55
Toothpick Holder	$45
Tumbler	$35
Vase, 6" Tall	$35
Vase, 9" Tall	$45
Wineglass	$45

Waffle
Boston & Sandwich Glass Company, 1850s–1860s; Bryce, Walker & Company, 1850s–1860s

There is some confusion about which company produced this pattern first, because records are sketchy. A few colors, including opaque white, have been found (double the prices). The simple square Waffle design has been reproduced in a variety of forms.

Bowl, 8"	$55
Butter Dish with Cover	$150
Cake Stand	$70
Celery Vase, 9" Tall	$100
Champagne Glass	$125
Claret Glass	$135
Compote, 6", Open	$75
Compote, 8", Open	$85
Compote with Cover, 7"	$125
Compote with Cover, 9"	$150
Cordial	$75
Creamer, 6¾" Tall	$150
Cruet with Stopper	$125
Decanter with Stopper, 16 oz.	$150
Decanter with Stopper, 32 oz.	$200
Egg Holder	$55
Goblet, Knob Stem	$75
Lamp, Complete Glass	$225
Lamp, Applied Handle, Marble Base	$200
Pitcher, Water, 9½" Tall	$500
Plate, 6"	$90
Relish Dish, Oval (6" x 4"), Scalloped	$65
Salt Dip, Footed	$55
Salt Dip with Cover	$125
Sauce Dish, 4"	$35
Spooner	$75
Sugar Dish with Cover	$200
Toy Mug, Applied Handle	$150
Tumbler, Water	$85
Whiskey Tumbler	$85
Wineglass	$75

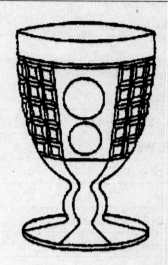

Waffle & Thumbprint Pattern. *Drawing by Mark Pickvet.*

Waffle and Thumbprint
Various Companies, 1850s–1870s

Here is one variation of the Waffle where the rectangles are interspersed with thumbprints. For noncrystal pieces, reduce the prices by 50 percent.

The Boston & Sandwich Glass Company; the New England Glass Company; and Curling, Robertson & Company were the primary producers of this pattern. The pattern is also known as Bull's-Eye and Waffle, Palace, or Triple Bull's-Eye.

Bottle, Footed	$150
Bowl, Rectangular (7" x 5")	$45
Bowl, Rectangular (8" x 6")	$55
Butter Dish with Cover	$150
Celery Vase	$120
Champagne Glass	$105
Claret Glass	$135
Compote with Cover, 6"	$150
Compote with Cover, 7"	$170
Compote with Cover, 8"	$190
Cordial	$110
Creamer	$150
Decanter with Stopper, 16 oz.	$185
Decanter with Stopper, 32 oz. (Pointed Paneled Stopper)	$225

Egg Holder	$65
Goblet	$85
Goblet, Knob Stem	$90
Lamp, 9½"	$150
Lamp, 11", Whale Oil	$200
Pitcher, Water	$550
Salt Dip	$55
Spooner	$65
Sugar Dish with Cover	$200
Sweetmeat Jar with Cover, 6"	$200
Tumbler, Water	$100
Tumbler, Water, Footed	$110
Whiskey Tumbler	$100
Wineglass	$85

Wildflower
Adams & Company, 1870s; U.S. Glass Company, 1890s

This pattern is characterized by six-petaled flowers with leaves, stems, and berries that form a continuous design around each object. There is also vertical flute-like ribbing at the bottom and vertical trapezoidal bands at the top.

Colors include amber, cobalt blue, green, and yellow (double the prices). The goblet, flat sauce dish, water tumbler, wineglass, and 10-inch diameter plate have all been reproduced in this pattern (reduce prices by 75 percent).

Bowl, 7½"	$45
Bowl, Waste	$65
Butter Dish with Cover	$75
Butter Dish with Cover, Footed	$85
Cake Plate with Metal Handle	$100
Cake Stand, Small, 8½"	$50
Cake Stand, Large	$60
Celery Dish	$40
Compote, Open (High)	$45

Wildflower Pattern. *Drawing by Mark Pickvet.*

Compote, Open, 8" (Low)	$37.50
Compote with Cover, 6"	$65
Compote with Cover, 8"	$75
Cordial	$60
Creamer	$40
Goblet	$40
Pickle Dish, 5¾", Square	$30
Pickle Dish, 6¼", Square	$35
Pickle Dish, 7¾", Square	$40
Pickle Dish with Cover, 7¾", Square	$75
Pitcher, Syrup with Metal Lid	$125
Pitcher, Water	$100
Plate, 9¾", Square	$40
Plate, 10"	$75
Platter, 10", Oblong	$75
Salt and Pepper Shakers	$65
Sauce Dish, Round, Flat	$18
Sauce Dish, Square, Flat	$22.50
Sauce Dish, 3½", Round, Footed	$30
Sauce Dish, 4", Round, Footed	$35

Wisconsin Pattern. *Drawing by Mark Pickvet.*

Spooner	$35
Sugar with Cover	$55
Tray, Round	$40
Tray, Oval (13" x 11")	$50
Tumbler, Water	$40
Wineglass	$40

Wisconsin
U.S. Glass Company, 1898–Early 1900s

The last of U.S. Glass's state patterns, Wisconsin is also known as Beaded Dewdrop. It is characterized by vertical tears or drops that section off oval beaded designs. Toothpick holders have been reproduced in color; for those, reduce the price by 75 percent.

Banana Stand	$85
Bowl with Cover, 6", Oval	$55
Bowl, 7"	$47.50
Bowl, 8"	$52.50
Butter Dish with Cover	$85
Cake Stand, 8½"	$65
Cake Stand, 9½"	$75
Candy Dish	$40
Celery Dish	$50

Celery Vase	$70
Compote, Open, 5"	$40
Compote, Open, 6"	$45
Compote, Open, 8"	$60
Compote, Open, 10"	$80
Compote with Cover, 5" Tall	$65
Compote with Cover, 6" Tall	$75
Compote with Cover, 7" Tall	$85
Compote with Cover, 8" Tall	$95
Condiment Set, 5-Piece (Shakers, Mustard Dish, Horseradish Dish, and Tray)	$175
Creamer, Individual (Small)	$45
Creamer (Large)	$65
Cruet with Stopper	$90
Cup	$35
Goblet	$75
Jelly Dish, Handled	$40
Lamp	$135
Marmalade Jar with Cover	$135
Mug	$40
Pickle Dish	$40
Pitcher, Syrup with Lid	$125
Pitcher, 32 oz., Milk	$85
Pitcher, 48 oz., Water	$95
Plate, 6¾"	$30
Punch Cup	$35
Relish Dish	$32.50
Salt and Pepper Shakers, Short	$55
Salt and Pepper Shakers, Tall	$65
Sauce Dish, 4", Flat	$18.50
Saucer	$20
Spooner	$37.50

Sugar, Individual (Small)	$45
Sugar Dish with Cover	$85
Sugar Shaker	$100
Sweetmeat Dish with Cover, 5", Footed	$55
Toothpick Holder, 3-Footed Base	$65
Tray, 6", Oval, Handled, with Cover	$60
Tumbler	$55
Wineglass	$75

Zipper
Richards & Hartley, Late 1880s–1890s

The original pattern name was Cobb; however, Zipper more accurately describes the long vertical rows of horizontal dashes. Note that this pattern was made in lime-based glass only (nonlead or nonflint).

Bowl, 7"	$25
Bowl, 9½" x 6" Oblong	$30
Butter Dish with Cover	$55
Celery Vase	$35
Cheese Dish with Cover	$65
Compote, Open	$30
Compote with Cover, 8"	$50
Creamer, 2 Styles (High or Low Footed)	$40
Cruet with Stopper	$55
Goblet	$30
Marmalade Jar with Cover	$55
Pickle Dish	$30
Pitcher, Milk, 32 oz.	$60
Pitcher, Water, 64 oz.	$65
Relish Dish, 10"	$25
Salt Dip	$12.50
Saltshaker	$22.50
Sauce Dish	$12.50

Sauce Dish, Footed	$15
Spooner	$35
Sugar Dish, Open	$30
Sugar Dish with Cover	$55
Tumbler, Water	$30

– 3 –
CUT GLASS

The Brilliant period of American glassmaking lasted from 1880 to 1915. It was characterized by deep cutting, exceptional brilliance or sparkle, heavy lead crystal formulas, and
elaborate and ornate designs. Cut glass was made by steel or iron wheels revolving in a
trough while a stream of water mixed with abrasives dripped down upon the wheel from
above. This initial process was known as roughing and was responsible for the first cutting.
Heavier wheels were used to make deeper and sharper cuts. The glass then proceeded to a
hard stone wheel, where the rough cut was smoothed out. At this point a polisher would
polish it on a softer wooden wheel, and then a buffer would further smooth it on a buffing
wheel. Buffing was eventually replaced with acid polishing in the 1890s, but true craftsmen
argued that acid polishing was inferior because it wasn't permanent and gradually wore
away. Acid polishing also left a somewhat dull finish, obstructing the brilliance of the piece
to a small degree.

The aim of a cutter was to remove imperfections and impart facets to capture a good deal
of light, creating a prismatic effect. American inventions improved on cutting. Flat-edged
wheels made square-ended cuts and convex-edged wheels made hollowed cuts. Americans
added mitre-edged wheels, which made curved or V-shape cuts. Mitre-edged wheels were
invented in the late 1870s and freed cutters from depending on straight line cuts. Wheels
were made not only of stone and steel but also of copper and carborundum.

Electricity, when available, was used to power the wheels as well as to provide the craftsmen with better lighting by which to see; of course, it may have added more hours to their
workday, too! Additional steps were added to the cutting process as finer wheels and
milder abrasives made cutting more precise.

Copper wheel cutting or engraving was the end in the evolutionary process for the finest
cut glass. As many as 150 wheels of various diameters, from the very large down to the size

of a pin, were used. A copper wheel engraver held the final pattern in his mind without outlining it on the glass. Glass objects were pressed to the revolving wheel, which instantly cut through or roughened the surface. It was then rubbed repeatedly with oils with one's fingers as it was placed on and off the wheel.

Before electricity, lathes were operated by foot-powered treadles and were somewhat limited in size. An electrically operated lathe made heavier wheels possible, including large diamond-point cutting wheels. It might take weeks, months, and even years to finish a single piece on copper wheels.

Elaborate carving such as cameo engraving was also completed on copper wheels. Stone wheels were primarily used for depth, whereas copper was best for fine detailed work. Copper wheel engravers were compensated at a higher rate than cutters and were some of the most highly skilled artisans in the glassmaking business.

Along with blowers, copper wheel engravers commanded salaries as high as $6 a day in the 1880s, common cutters about $3.50 to $4 a day, and ordinary general workmen about $14 to $20 a week based on a six-day workweek. The higher wages provided incentive to foreign workers to immigrate to America. In Europe, English and Irish glassmakers earned $7 to $9 per week; Germans and Austrians earned much less, at $3 a week. American wages were typically three to four times greater than those of their European counterparts. One disadvantage was that European glassmakers produced cheaper glass products in terms of price. Even after a 45 percent tariff was placed on imported glass in 1888, European glassware was still highly competitive. America's own advantages included an abundance of cheap fuel (a problem in Europe) and advanced mechanization.

To make fine cut glass, a high-quality handblown blank was necessary. Many decorating companies purchased blanks of high-quality lead glass from major glass companies for their cutters to work. Traditionally, blowers had to be very skilled artisans. It took years of training, hard work, and the ability to perform effectively under pressure—especially in poor working conditions—to become a successful blower. A blower typically had to work near a blinding furnace with roasting heat, eye-watering smoke, and hands that were constantly scorched and dirtied with coal dust. It was surprising indeed that such exquisite objects could be blown from these stoke-hole-like conditions. Under such pressures, the glassblower had to exercise the utmost skill, control, patience, steady nerve, and judgment, all mixed further with creativity and occasional bouts of spontaneity. In short, glassblowing has always been an art rather than a craft.

There were many other positions one could fill in the glassmaking trade. A gatherer was one who gathered a blob of molten glass at the end of a blowpipe, pontil, or gathering iron for the blower. Cutters ordinarily apprenticed for three years at a small salary, usually after completing eight grades of formal education. The best cutters might work up to becoming copper wheel engravers after years of practice.

At the turn of the 20th century, women held some jobs in the glass business, though glassmaking was primarily a man's field of work. Women dusted glass in showrooms and sales rooms, distributed glass to cutters, updated catalogs, made drawings of blanks, waxed the glass before an acid dip, and washed or dried glass before packaging it. A rare enameler or cutter might have been female.

The production of glass itself was not an easy, inexpensive, or safe practice. The basic ingredients of sand, potash, lead for the best crystal, and a few other additions were mixed in a huge clay pot and heated to extreme temperatures. A batch was termed "metal" by chemists, and the best metal batch always contained the highest lead content. Cut glass was usually made with a company's best metal formula. Molten glass had to be gathered by a worker to press into a mold or simply for the blower to work. Several tools were available, including a pontil, which was used to remove expanded glass objects from the blowing iron; however, it did leave a mark. It was later replaced with a special rod called a gadget. A gadget had a spring clip on the end of it to grip the foot of a glass piece and hold it while another worker trimmed the rim and applied whatever finishing touches were needed.

Ovens were important, especially those with a special opening called a "glory hole." A glory hole was a small-size opening in the side of the oven where objects could be reheated and reworked without destroying the original shape. A lehr was an annealing oven that toughened glass through gradual cooling. A muffle kiln was a low-temperature oven used for firing on or permanently fusing enamels.

A variety of technical jargon and tools were associated with the glassmaking process. Moil was waste glass left on the blowpipe or pontil. Pucellas were like tongs and were used to grip or grasp glass objects. Arrissing was the process of removing sharp edges from glass. Cracking-off involved removing a piece of glass from the pontil by cooling, gently tapping, and then dropping it into a soft sand tray. Fire polishing was the art of reheating objects at the glory hole to remove tool marks.

Glass did not always turn out perfectly and "sickness" resulted. Sick glass was usually not tempered or annealed properly and showed random cracks, flaking, and possible disintegration. Seeds were tiny air bubbles in glass indicating an underheated furnace or impurities caused by flecks of dirt.

A variety of other techniques were present in American glassmaking, including a good deal of originality. Cutting was done primarily in geometrical patterns. Pictorial, cameo, and intaglio (heavily engraved) designs were all cut regularly. Acid etching was the process of covering glass with an acid-resistant layer, scratching on a design, and then permanently etching the design with acids. Acid polishing gave cut glass a polished surface by dipping the entire object into a mild solution of sulfuric or hydrofluoric acid. Hand-painting and firing on enamels were two additional finishing techniques.

Sandblasting was a distinctly American process whereby a design was coated with a protective layer and the exposed surfaces were sandblasted with a pressurized gun. Trimming with enamels such as silver, gold, and platinum were in use in the early 1900s, before World War I. Staining, gilding, monogram imprinting, rubber stamping, and silk screening were other cheaper methods of decorating glass developed in the early 20th century. In 1913 a gang-cut wheel was invented in America to make several parallel incisions at once. It made rapid and inexpensive cutting possible, such as cross-hatching and blunt-edged flower petals. For the most part cut glass was simply that—undecorated crystal except for the elaborate cutting.

The decline of superb cut crystal reached its lowest point as World War I neared. The exclusive market it catered to turned around as the wealthy preferred more art deco or art nouveau styles and new, fancy European imports. Cheaper glass formulas, labor troubles, increased imports, more and more machine-made glass, and lead needed for the war effort were all factors leading to the end of the Brilliant period in American glass history.

Some of the biggest names in the cut-glass world were Libbey, T. J. Hawkes, C. Dorflinger, Mt. Washington/Pairpoint, John Hoare, T. B. Clark, H. P. Sinclaire, and Tuthill. Hundreds of cut-glass patterns were made, and though many were patented, they were still copied or similar variations of them were produced by others. There were also many common designs or combinations of them shared by all, including rosettes, hobstars, fans, strawberry diamonds, geometric cuts, flutes, buzzstars, cross-hatching, blocks, hobnails, and so on. Fortunately, more distinct marks and signatures were applied to cut glass products than any other category of glass. (See the appendix on "Manufacturers' Marks.")

Alford, C. G. & Co.
1872–1918

Alford was a jeweler and repaired watches in New York City. There is some debate about whether the company cut any glass or simply applied their mark to what was completed by others and then sold the glass in their store. Research supports that they only sold cut glass.

Bonbon Dish, Hobstar Bottom, Signed "Alford"	$200
Celery Dish, 12" Oval, 4 Hobstars in Each Corner, Signed "Alford"	$300
Cruet with Faceted Ball Stopper, Brunswick Pattern	$275
Decanter with Faceted Stopper, 9½" Tall, 32 oz., No Handle, Hobstar and Fan Design, Viola Pattern	$800
Nappy, 6", Trieste Pattern	$225
Plate, 7¼", Large Center Hobstar Surrounded by 8 Smaller Hobstars, Signed "Alford"	$150
Punch Bowl, 12", 5½" Tall, Triest Pattern	$1,050
Vase, 14" Tall, Brunswick Pattern, Signed "Alford"	$400

Almy & Thomas
1903–1918

Although they were not a large maker of cut glass, the team of Charles H. Almy and G. Edwin Thomas cut high-quality blanks provided by the Corning Glass Works.

Bowl, 8", Notched Rim, Alternating Star and Hobstar Design	$225
Decanter with Faceted Stopper, 7" Tall, Notched Handle, Fan and Star Pattern	$725
Decanter with Faceted Stopper, 8¾" Tall, Brunswick Pattern	$850
Whiskey Tumbler, 3" Tall, Fan and Star Pattern	$150

American Cut Glass Company
1897–1915

This company was established in 1897 in Chicago by William Anderson. Anderson was a designer and craftsman for Libbey from 1887 to 1906 and cut glass on the side for American. The company moved to Lansing, Michigan, in 1900 and continued to produce a limited amount of cut glass until World War I.

Bowl, 8", Notched edge, Star Pattern	$250
Tray, 10" x 5" Rectangular, Large Center Hobstar Surrounded by 8 Smaller Hobstars	$475
Tray, 12" Diameter, Lansing Pattern	$475
Tray, 14" Diameter, Lansing Pattern	$550
Tray, 17½" x 10" Rectangular, Ice Cream, Mary Pattern	$2,750

Averbeck Cut Glass Company
1892–1923

Averbeck first operated as a jewelry store. In 1892 they began selling cut glass by mail order. They employed glass cutters in a small factory in Honesdale, Pennsylvania, and purchased glass wholesale from small, relatively unknown cutting shops, applying their trademark to the finished pieces.

Bonbon Dish, Diamond Pattern	$85
Bowl, 5", American Beauty or Ruby Pattern	$150
Bowl, 6" Nappy, Acme, American Beauty Boston, Frisco, Occident, Paris, Puck, Saratoga, Ruby, Spruce, or Webster Pattern	$175
Bowl, 7", Acme, American Beauty Boston, Frisco, Occident, Paris, Puck, Saratoga, Ruby, Spruce, or Webster Pattern	$200
Bowl, 8", Azalea Pattern	$250
Bowl, 8", Acme, American Beauty Boston, Frisco, Occident, Paris, Puck, Saratoga, Ruby, Spruce, or Webster Pattern	$225
Bowl, 9", Acme, American Beauty Boston, Frisco, Occident, Paris, Puck, Saratoga, Ruby, Spruce, or Webster Pattern	$250
Bowl, Banana, 10" Oval, Genoa Pattern	$500

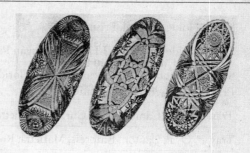

Celery Trays. *Reproduced directly from an early-20th-century Averbeck catalog.*

Bowl, 10", Acme, American Beauty Boston, Frisco, Occident, Paris, Puck, Saratoga, Ruby, Spruce, or Webster Pattern	$275
Bowl, 11½", Roosevelt Pattern	$325
Carafe, 1 qt., Georgia or Napoleon Pattern	$185
Compote, Georgia or Napoleon Pattern	$400
Creamer, American Beauty, Florida, Georgia, Lady Curzon, Liberty, Melba, Priscilla, Ruby, or Vienna Pattern	$85
Cruet with Stopper, 7½" Tall, Florida Pattern	$160
Decanter with Stopper, 9¼" Tall, Acme Pattern	$850
Decanter with Stopper, 10" Tall, Electric Pattern	$1,150
Decanter with Stopper, 12" Tall, Alabama Pattern	$1,275
Goblet, Alabama, Florida, Priscilla, or Radium Pattern	$75
Jug with Stopper, 6" Tall, Liberty Pattern	$350
Jug with Stopper, 8" Tall, Genoa Pattern	$375
Pickle Dish, 8" Oval, Canton, Empress, Marietta, Saratoga, Royal, or Ruby Pattern	$225
Pitcher, 10½" Tall, 2 qt., Florida, Georgia, or Naples Pattern	$350
Plate, 6", Spruce Pattern	$150
Plate, 7", Boston, Lowell, Saratoga, or Vienna Pattern	$175
Punch Bowl with Base, 10", Occident or Vienna Pattern	$1,050
Punch Bowl with Base, 12", Occident or Vienna Pattern	$1,450
Punch Bowl with Base, 14", Occident or Vienna Pattern	$1,750

Spoon Holder, 4" Tall, Prism	$150
Spoon Holder, 5½" Tall, 2-Handled, Logan Pattern	$175
Sugar, 2-Handled, American Beauty, Florida, Georgia, Lady Curzon, Liberty, Melba, Priscilla, Ruby, or Vienna Pattern	$85
Tray, 7" Oval, Canton, Lady Curzon, Marietta, Priscilla, Ruby, or Saratoga Pattern	$350
Tray, 8" Oval, Canton, Empress, Marietta, Royal, Ruby, or Saratoga Pattern	$325
Tray, 12" Oblong, Diamond, Frisco or Liberty Pattern	$450
Tray, 14" Oblong, Frisco, Ruby, or Vienna Pattern	$450
Tray, 14" Oblong, Ruffled Edge, Acme Pattern	$475
Tray, 14½" Oval, Cape Town Pattern	$525
Tumbler, Maude Adams Pattern	$55
Vase, 8" Tall, Liberty or Radium Pattern	$175
Vase, 10" Tall, Liberty or Radium Pattern	$225
Vase, 12" Tall, Liberty or Radium Pattern	$250
Vase, 14" Tall, Liberty or Radium Pattern	$300
Vase, 14" Tall, Saratoga Pattern	$750
Vase, 15" Tall, Nice Pattern	$750
Vase, 17" Tall, Naples Pattern	$1,000
Vase, 18" Tall, Nice Pattern	$1,250

Bergen, J. D., Company
1880–1922

James D. Bergen operated a cut-glass business under a variety of names, and, like so many others in the 19th and early 20th centuries, he recruited relatives to work in his cutting shop. Names included the Bergen Cut Glass Company, Bergen-Phillips Cut Glass Company, Bergen and Son, Bergen Glass Works, and the Bergen Glass Company.

Basket, Small, Straight Cuts	$115
Basket, Large, Straight Cuts	$150
Bell, 6" Tall, Premier Pattern	$225
Bell, 7" Tall, Premier Pattern	$275
Bonbon Dish, 6", Bedford, Emblem, Evelyn, or Pilgrim Pattern	$125
Bonbon Dish, 7", Bedford, Emblem, Evelyn, or Pilgrim Pattern	$150
Bonbon Dish, Heart Shape, Emblem Pattern	$375

Bergen, Bottle and Tobacco Jar. *Reproduced directly from an early-20th-century J. D. Bergen catalog.*

Bergen Bowls. *Reproduced directly from an early-20th-century J. D. Bergen catalog.*

Bergen Bowls. *Reproduced directly from an early-20th-century J. D. Bergen catalog.*

Bottle, Wine with Straight Cut Stopper, 12¾" Tall, Tasso Pattern	$600
Bowl, 6" Oval, Ripple Pattern	$175
Bowl, 7", Ambrose, Bermuda, Chester, Elsa, Florence, Golf, Hampton, Hilda, Kenwood, Ivanhoe, Renwick, or Roosevelt Pattern	$150
Bowl, 7" Oval, Caprice Pattern	$200
Bowl, 7" Oblong, Keystone Pattern	$225
Bowl, 8", Ambrose, Bermuda, Chester, Elsa, Florence, Golf, Hampton, Hilda, Kenwood, Ivanhoe, Renwick, or Roosevelt Pattern	$200
Bowl, 8", 6 Circles, Notched Edge, Azalea Design	$300
Bowl, 8", Goldenrod Pattern	$225

Bowl, 9", Ambrose, Bermuda, Chester, Elsa, Florence, Golf, Hampton, Hilda, Kenwood, Ivanhoe, Renwick, or Roosevelt Pattern $275

Bowl, 10", Ambrose, Bermuda, Chester, Elsa, Florence, Golf, Hampton, Hilda, Kenwood, Ivanhoe, Renwick, or Roosevelt Pattern $325

Bowl, Rose, 3¼" Tall, 4" Diameter, 3-Footed, Buzz Saw and Fan $150

Butter Dish with Domed Cover, 6" Tall, 8" Diameter Underplate, Bedford Pattern $550

Candelabra, 3-Light $375

Candlestick, 7" Tall, Victoria Pattern $175

Candlestick, 10" Tall, Victoria Pattern $225

Carafe, 1 to 1½ pts., Ansonia, Gilmore, Goldenrod, Golf, Marie, Meteor, Newport, or Waverly Pattern $225

Carafe, 1 qt., Ansonia, Gilmore, Goldenrod, Golf, Golf, Marie, Meteor, Newport, or Waverly Pattern $300

Celery Dish, 2-Handled, Logan Pattern $525

Cheese Dish with Domed Cover, 9" Tall, Glenwood Pattern $800

Compote, 5", Magnet Pattern $150

Compote, 6", Beacon, Enterprise, Magnet, or Waltham Pattern $175

Compote, 7", Beacon, Enterprise, Magnet, or Waltham Pattern $200

Compote, 8", Beacon, Enterprise, Magnet, or Waltham Pattern $225

Compote, 9", Beacon, Enterprise, Magnet, or Waltham Pattern $275

Compote, 10", Beacon, Enterprise, Magnet, or Waltham Pattern $325

Compote with Cover, Arcadia Pattern $2,250

Creamer, Avon, Bedford, Detroit, Emblem, Glenwood, Gilbert, Golf, Grace, Magnet, Oregon, or Superior Pattern $85

Cruet with Stopper, Avon, Bedford, Detroit, Emblem, Glenwood, Gilbert, Golf, Grace, Magnet, Oregon, Superior, or Waverly Pattern $160

Cup, Bedford, Bermuda, Corsair, Edna, Electric, Frisco, Golf, Kenwood, Magnet, Marlow, Monticelle, Premier, Progress, Wabash, or Webster Pattern $75

Decanter with Stopper, 8" Tall, Bedford, Electric, Glenwood, Premier, or Savoy Pattern $550

Glove Box with Hinged Cover, Harvard Pattern with Engraved Floral Design $2,250

Goblet, Bedford, Electric, Glenwood, Premier, or Savoy Patterns $55

Goblet, Star Base, Three 16-Point Hobstars, Strawberry Diamond and Fan Vesicas, Signed $125

Hairpin Box with Cover, 3 Applied Feet, Chair Bottom Design, Harvard Pattern, Signed "Bergen" $1,500

Humidor with Cover, 8"Glenwood Pattern, Signed "Bergen" $875

Knife Rest, 2½" $25

Knife Rest, 3¼" $30

Knife Rest, 5" $35

Lamp, 14½" Tall, Premier Pattern, Top and Bottom Globes $2,250

Lamp, 22" Tall, Kenwood Pattern, Top and Bottom Globes $2,500

Mustard Jar with Cover, 4" Tall, 2½" Diameter, Notched Prism Pattern, Faceted Lid Finial, Lid Is Notched for Matching Crystal Spoon $325

Pitcher, 1 pt., Allyn, Delta, Electric, Goldenrod, Persian, Premier, Princeton, or Vienna Pattern $225

Pitcher, 1½ pt., Allyn, Delta, Electric, Goldenrod, Persian, Premier, Princeton, or Vienna Pattern $275

Pitcher, 1 qt., Allyn, Delta, Electric, Goldenrod, Persian, Premier, Princeton, or Vienna Pattern $325

Plate, 6", Ambrose, Bermuda, Chester, Elsa, Florence, Golf, Hampton, Hilda, Kenwood, Ivanhoe, Renwick, Roosevelt, Sunflower, Vienna, or White Rose Pattern $125

Plate, 7", Ambrose, Bermuda, Chester, Elsa, Florence, Golf, Hampton, Hilda, Kenwood, Ivanhoe, Renwick, Roosevelt, Sunflower, Vienna, or White Rose Pattern. $150

Plate, 8", Ambrose, Bermuda, Chester, Elsa, Florence, Golf, Hampton, Hilda, Kenwood, Ivanhoe, Renwick, Roosevelt, Sunflower, Vienna, or White Rose Pattern $175

Plate, 9", Ambrose, Bermuda, Chester, Elsa, Florence, Golf, Hampton, Hilda, Kenwood, Ivanhoe, Renwick, Roosevelt, Sunflower, Vienna, or White Rose Pattern $200

Plate, 10", Ambrose, Bermuda, Chester, Elsa, Florence, Golf, Hampton, Hilda, Kenwood, Ivanhoe, Renwick, Roosevelt, Sunflower, Vienna, or White Rose Pattern $225

Pomade Jar with Cover, Prism Pattern $175

Powder Jar with Cover, Swirled Comet Pattern, Signed "Bergen" $500

Punch Bowl with Stand, 12", Marlow Pattern $1,500

Punch Bowl with Stand, 14", Glenwood Pattern $2,750

Punch Bowl with Stand, Wabash Pattern $2,550

Saucer, 5", Bedford, Bermuda, Corsair, Frisco, Golf, Kenwood, Magnet, Progress, or Webster Pattern $75

Saucer, 6", Bedford, Bermuda, Corsair, Edna, Electric, Frisco, Golf, Kenwood, Magnet, Progress, Premier, Wabash, or Webster Pattern $100

Sugar, 2-Handled, Avon, Bedford, Detroit, Emblem, Glenwood, Gilbert, Golf, Grace, Magnet, Oregon, or Superior Pattern	$85
Tray, 6" Oblong, Slanted, Key West Pattern	$150
Tray, 6½" Oblong, Straight Sides, Magnet Pattern	$175
Tray, 7" Oval, Laurel Pattern	$200
Tray, 7½" Oblong, Short Handle, Emblem Pattern	$250
Tray, 9" Oblong, Circular Center, 5" Wide, Dariel Pattern	$475
Tray, Oval, 9" x 5", Hawthorne Pattern	$300
Tray, Rectangular (11½" x 7"), Hobstars and Diamonds	$425
Tumbler, Allyn, Delta, Electric, Goldenrod, Persian, Premier, Princeton, or Vienna Pattern	$55
Vase, 6" Tall, Notched Prism	$225
Vase, 21" Tall, 9" Diameter, 2-Part, Sunbeam Pattern	$600

Blackmer Cut Glass Company
1894–1916

Arthur L. Blackmer was a businessman and salesman for his company and employed others to make the glass. Like so many others, the business did not survive World War I.

Bowl, 7", Starling Pattern	$175
Bowl, 7", Troy Pattern	$150
Bowl, 9", Columbia Pattern	$250
Compote, 9" Diameter, 6½" Tall, Celtic or Medina Pattern	$200
Creamer, Eudora or Ruby Pattern	$125
Cruet with Faceted Stopper, 6" Tall, Oregon Pattern	$325
Decanter with Cut Stopper, Concord Pattern	$525
Ice Tub, Angled Cradle Shape, Columbia Pattern	$850
Nappy, 6", Regal Pattern	$225
Nappy, 6", Notched Edge, Troy Pattern	$150
Plate, 7", Newport or Zephyr Pattern	$175
Plate, 8", Doris Pattern	$200
Platter, 12" Round, Crescendo Pattern	$600
Relish Dish, 7" Across, Tab Handle, Sultana Pattern	$225

Sugar Dish, Eudora or Ruby Pattern	$125
Tray, 10" Round, Emerson Pattern	$250
Tray, 12" Oval, Plymouth Pattern	$375
Tumbler, 8" Tall, Constellation Pattern	$175
Vase, 11" Tall, 12" Diameter, Sultana Pattern	$550
Vase, 12" Tall, 4" Diameter, Prudence Pattern	$375

Clark, T. B. and Company
1884–1930

Thomas Byron Clark operated the second-largest cut-glass operation in all of Pennsylvania (Dorflinger was the largest). Clark actually used Dorflinger's blanks early on, and the quality of Clark's products rank with the best.

Bonbon Dish, Adonis, Arbutus, Dorrance, Jewel, Manhattan, St George, Venus, or Winola Pattern	$125
Bonbon Dish with Handle, Irving, Jefferson, or St. George Pattern	$150
Bowl, 6", Footed, Manhattan Pattern	$225
Bowl, Rose, 7", Manhattan Pattern	$250
Bowl, 8", Prima Donna Pattern, Signed "Clark"	$400
Bowl, 8" Square, Corinthian Pattern	$300
Bowl, 8", Adonis, Arbutus, Desdemona, Magnolia, Manhattan, Priscilla, Venus, or Winola Pattern	$275
Bowl, 9", Adonis, Arbutus, Desdemona, Magnolia, Manhattan, Priscilla, Venus, or Winola Pattern	$300
Bowl, 9¼", Scalloped Sawtooth Edge, Hanover Pattern	$325
Bowl, 10", Adonis, Arbutus, Desdemona, Magnolia Manhattan, Priscilla, Venus, or Winola Pattern	$325
Bowl, 12", Notched Edge, Strawberry Diamond Pattern, Signed "Clark"	$375
Bowl, Oval (11½" x 9"), Quatrefoil Rosette Pattern, Signed "Clark"	$500
Carafe, 1 qt., Jewel, Manhattan, Priscilla, or Winola Pattern	$225
Cheese Dish with Dome Cover, Manhattan Pattern	$825
Claret Jug with Sterling Silver Stopper, Arbutus Pattern, Signed "Clark"	$1,350
Cologne Bottle with Stopper, 6 oz., Globe Shape, Jewel or Venus Pattern	$500
Compote, 5" Diameter, 5½" Tall, Hobstars, Signed "Clark"	$325

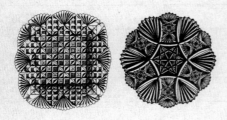

Strawberry Diamond & Star (left) and Seashell Pattern (right). *Reproduced directly from a T. B. Clark 1886 and 1882 patent.*

Compote, 8" Tall, Harvard Pattern Variant	$450
Compote, 10" Diameter, Arbutus Pattern	$400
Creamer, 3½" Tall, Cut Thistle Design	$150
Creamer, 4" Tall, Strawberry Diamond and Star Pattern	$350
Cruet Bottle with Stopper, Huron or Manhattan Pattern	$175
Decanter with Stopper, 32 oz., No Handle, Winola Pattern	$500
Decanter with Stopper, 32 oz., with Handle, Winola Pattern	$525
Decanter with Stopper, 32 oz., with Handle, Strawberry Diamond and Fan Pattern	$450
Goblet, Winola Pattern	$100
Jug, Whiskey, Ball-Faceted Stopper, 7½" Tall, Applied Handle, Hobstar, Diamond, and Fan	$375
Mug, Jewel or Winola Pattern	$150
Nappy, 5", Jewel, Manhattan, or Winola Pattern	$125
Nappy, 6", Jewel, Manhattan, or Winola Pattern	$150
Nappy, 7", Arbutus, Desdemona, Jewel, Manhattan, or Winola Pattern	$175
Nappy, 8", Arbutus, Desdemona, or Manhattan Pattern	$200
Nappy, 9", Arbutus, Desdemona, or Manhattan Pattern	$225
Nappy, 10", Arbutus, Desdemona, or Manhattan Pattern	$250
Pitcher, Milk, 32 oz., Venus Pattern	$400
Pitcher, Water, 48 oz., Venus Pattern	$450

Pitcher, Water, Triple Square Pattern, Signed "Clark"	$550
Plate, 6", Harvard Pattern Variant	$100
Plate, 7", Prima Donna Pattern, Signed "Clark"	$175
Plate, 7", Venus Pattern	$150
Plate, 12", Pinwheel Pattern, Signed "Clark"	$475
Platter, 12" Round, Waldorf Pattern	$475
Punch Bowl, 12", Desdemona Pattern	$1,200
Punch Bowl, 14", Arbutus Pattern	$875
Punch Bowl with Stand, 14" Diameter, Desdemona Pattern	$2,150
Relish, 9" Diameter, 4-Part, 2-Handled, 4 Hobstars	$275
Sugar Dish, 3½" Tall, Cut Thistle Design	$150
Sugar with Cover, 4½" Tall, Strawberry Diamond and Star Pattern	$450
Sugar Shaker with Sterling Silver Top, Henry VIII Pattern	$275
Tray, Celery, 11", Adonis, Desdemona, Dorrance, Manhattan, Nordica, or Winola Pattern	$350
Tray, Celery, Pinwheel Design, Signed "Clark"	$250
Tray, 11½" x 8" Rectangular, Jewel Pattern	$650
Tray, Celery, 11⅞" Oval, Pinwheels and Hobstars Design	$350
Tray, 12" Oval, Baker's Gothic Pattern	$375
Tray, Bread, 12½", Hobstars and Fans with Engraved Leaves	$400
Tray, 13", Adonis, Manhattan, Venus, or Winola Pattern	$450
Tumbler, 8 oz., Arbutus, Jewel, or Winola Pattern	$55
Tumbler, 8 oz., Coral Pattern	$150
Tumbler, 8 oz., Strawberry Diamond and Fan Design	$125
Vase, 4" Tall, Notched Rim, Wide Style, Henry VIII Pattern	$225
Vase, 8" Tall, Circular Base, Jewel Pattern	$200
Vase, 9" Tall, Orient Pattern	$225
Vase, 10" Tall, Circular Vase, Jewel Pattern	$250
Vase, 10¼" Tall, 8½" Wide, Mistletoe Pattern	$1,250
Vase, 12" Tall, Circular Base, Jewel Pattern	$275
Vase, 15" Tall, Circular Base, Adonis or Palmetto Pattern	$375

Vase, 18" Tall, Circular Base, Adonis or Palmetto Pattern	$575
Whiskey Tumbler, Strawberry Diamond and Fan Design	$85
Wineglass, Winola Pattern	$85

Dithridge and Company
1881–1901

Dithridge was a large supplier of lead blanks and did a little cutting of their own as well.

Pitcher, 10" Tall, Corset Shape, Scalloped, Sunburst and Geometric Design	$425
Tray, Oval, 6⅞" Long, Angled Cut Squares Alternating with Diamond Cross-Cut Squares	$200
Wineglass, 4¾" Tall, Strawberry Diamond and Fan Pattern	$175

Dorflinger, Christian and Sons
1852–1921

Fine cut glass by Christian Dorflinger and his sons graced the table of many a president. Dorflinger spared no expense in finding excellent workmen, obtaining the best lead and other ingredients, and above all, demanding high-quality workmanship. Dorflinger was one of the largest producers of cut crystal glassware until World War I.

Bowl, Finger, with Underplate, Picket Fence Pattern	$115
Bowl, 6½" Square, Strawberry Diamond Pattern	$175
Bowl, 8", Notched Edge, Amore Pattern	$200
Bowl, 8", Gladys Pattern	$225
Bowl, 9", Alternating Small and Large Diamond-Checkered Pattern ("#28" Pattern)	$250
Bowl, 9", Large Leaf (6 Leaves) Design, Paola Pattern	$175
Bowl, 9" Diameter, 7" Tall, Prince of Wales Design, Plumes Pattern with Hobstar Foot	$525
Bowl, 9¼" Diameter, Cranberry Cut to Clear; Floral, Leaf, Fan, and Scrolled Design	$500
Bowl, 10" Oval, Strawberry Pattern	$325
Bowl, Rose, Brilliant Pattern	$250
Bowl, Rose, 5½" Tall, 7" Diameter, Sawtooth Edge, Hob Diamond Pattern	$275
Carafe, 7¼" Tall, 5½" Diameter, Hob Diamond Pattern	$325
Carafe, 8¼" Tall, Split Pattern	$325
Cheese Dish with Dome Cover, 7", Russian Pattern	$850

Florentine Pattern. *Reproduced directly from an 1888 Dorflinger patent.*

Cologne Bottle with Stopper, 7½", Princess Pattern	$500
Cookie Jar with Cover, 6¼" Tall, Hobstar Base, Sterling Silver Cover Marked "Gorham," Sussex Pattern	$575
Creamer, Notched Prism Handles, Colonial Pattern	$150
Creamer, Russian Pattern	$150
Cruet, Fan and Star Design, Pattern #80	$250
Cruet with Stopper, 8" Tall, Globe Shape, Gladys Pattern	$375
Cruet with Stopper, 1¼" Tall, Marlboro Pattern	$400
Decanter with Silver Stopper, 12" Tall, Parisian Pattern	$850
Decanter, Renaissance Pattern	$350
Fernery, Picket Fence Pattern	$90
Goblet, 5½" Tall, Mitred Stem, Parisian Pattern	$275
Ice Bucket with Underplate, Handle Tabs, Marlboro Pattern	$2,150
Lamp, Banquet Oil, 4-Part, Matching Cut Chimney, Paper Label	$750
Lamp, Gone with the Wind, 20" Tall, 12" Base Diameter, Hobstar and Diamond Design	$1,450
Parfait, 6" Tall, Kalana Lily Pattern	$150
Perfume with Stopper, Hobstar Base, Marlboro Pattern	$250
Pitcher, Cream, 4½" Tall, Parisian Pattern	$275
Pitcher, Cream, 6" Tall, Parisian Pattern	$275
Pitcher, Cereal, 5" Tall, Diamond and Fern Cuts (Dorflinger's "#80" Pattern)	$300

Pitcher, Water, 7¼" Tall, Globe Shape, Applied Handle, Strawberry Diamond and Fan Pattern	$350
Pitcher, Water, 7½" Tall, Colonial Pattern	$350
Pitcher, Water, 8" Tall, Colonial Pattern	$350
Pitcher, Water, 8½" Tall, Globe Shape, Scalloped, Sunburst Base, Paneled Neck, Strawberry Diamond and Fan Pattern	$450
Plate, 5", Hobstar and Lace Design	$85
Plate, 6¼", Picket Fence Pattern	$95
Plate, 7", Parisian Pattern	$125
Plate, 7", Russian Pattern	$200
Plate, 7½", Scalloped and Serrated Rim, American Pattern	$100
Plate, 8" Gladys Pattern	$175
Plate, 8½", Parisian Pattern	$2,000
Punch Bowl with Stand, 14⅛" Diameter, 11½" Tall, 24-Point Hobstar on Center and Base, 12 8-Point Hobstars, Marlboro Pattern	$2,500
Punch Bowl Ladle, Cranberry to Clear, Montrose Pattern	$3,500
Salad Set, 3-Piece, 10" Handled Square Bowl, Parisian Pattern, Sterling Silver Fork and Spoon	$2,250
Salt Dip, Paperweight Style, Parisian Pattern	$125
Sugar Dish, Notched Prism Handles, Colonial Pattern	$150
Sugar Dish, No Handles, Russian Pattern	$150
Tray, 11" Oval, Middlesex Pattern	$300
Tray, 12½" Oval, Ice Cream, Pinwheels	$575
Tumbler, Juice, 3¾" Tall, Old Colony Pattern	$175
Tumbler, Juice, 3⅞" Tall, Parisian Pattern	$200
Vase, 6" Tall, Kalana Pansy Pattern	$150
Vase, 7½" Tall, Kalana Geranium Pattern	$175
Vase, 10" Tall, Hobstars with 5 Large Bull's-Eyes	$300
Vase, 10" Tall, Kalana Wild Rose Pattern with Amethyst Flowers Design	$325
Vase, 10" Tall, 7" Diameter, Russian Pattern	$375
Vase, 12" Tall, Flared Top and Bottom, Kalana Pansy Design	$350
Vase, 12" Tall, Circular Base, Diamond and Horizontal Step Cutting	$400

Vase, 14" Tall, Cosmos Pattern	$400
Vase, 14" Tall, Circular Base, Notched Top Edge, Parisian Pattern	$450
Vase, 15" Tall, Inverness Pattern	$350
Whiskey Tumbler, Old Colony Pattern	$100
Wineglass, Knobbed Stem, Colonial Pattern	$125

Eggington, O. F. Company
1896–1920

Oliver F. Eggington was once manager of T. G. Hawkes's cutting department and went on to establish the Eggington Rich Cut Glass Company with Walter F. Eggington. Eggington purchased its blanks from the Corning Glass Works and patented a few patterns such as the Magnolia and Trellis.

Bowl, Finger, 5", Bull's-Eye and Hobstar Pattern, Signed "Eggington"	$90
Bowl, 5¾", Notched Edge, Cluster Pattern	$150
Bowl, 7", Cambria Pattern	$150
Bowl, 7", Checkerboard Pattern	$1,000
Bowl, 7¼", Trellis Pattern	$225
Bowl, 7½", Lotus Pattern	$250
Bowl, 8", Chain of Hobstars, Triple Bands	$250
Bowl, 8", Cluster Pattern	$275
Bowl, 9", Marquise or Roman Pattern	$225
Bowl, 10", Arabian Pattern, 5" Tall	$2000
Bowl, 10", Calve Pattern, Signed	$250
Butter Dish with Cover, 5" Dome Cover, 7" Plate, Lotus Pattern, Signed	$625
Celery Dish, 11¾" x 4¾" Oval, Arabian Pattern	$400
Creamer, 4" Tall, Trellis Pattern Variation, Signed	$250
Cruet with Faceted Stopper, 12½" Tall, Trellis Pattern	$2750
Decanter with Matching Stopper, Creswick Pattern	$3250
Ice Bucket, 8" Tall, Tab Handles, Creswick Pattern	$475
Jam Jar with Cover, 6" Tall, 4" Diameter, Fluted and Notched Rim, Rayed Base, Chain of Hobstars Design	$525
Nappy, 6", Notched Edge, Lotus Pattern	$100

Magnolia Pattern. *Reproduced directly from a 1903 Eggington patent.*

Nappy, 7", Notched Edge, 1 Handle, Lotus Pattern	$150
Pitcher, Water, 10" Tall, Thistle Pattern, Signed "Eggington"	$275
Plate, 7", Lotus or Tokio Pattern, Signed	$125
Plate, 7", Prism Pattern	$150
Plate, 8", Magnolia Pattern, Signed "Eggington"	$175
Platter, 12" Diameter, Trellis Pattern, Signed "Eggington"	$475
Platter, 14" Diameter, Cluster Pattern, Signed	$550
Punch Bowl with Stand, 14" Diameter, 13" Tall, Arabian Pattern, Signed	$1,600
Punch Cup, Stemmed, Arabian Pattern	$125
Relish, 8" Oval, Arabian Pattern	$225
Spooner, 8", Star and Hobnail Design	$100
Spooner, Oval, 8" x 4", Flat, Lotus Pattern	$100
Sugar, 4" Tall, Rose-Bowl Shape, Trellis Pattern Variation, Signed	$250
Tray, 10" x 8" Rectangular, Trellis Pattern	$750
Tray, Celery, 12" Oval, Lotus Pattern	$250
Tray, Ice Cream, 12" Oval, Calve Pattern	$250
Tumbler, Thistle Pattern, Signed "Eggington"	$125
Vase, 12" Tall, Victoria Pattern	$550
Vase, 14" Tall, Urn Shape, 4 Hobstars with Comet Swirls Design	$2,500

Elite Cut Glass Company
1918–24

Elite was best known for their Expanding Star pattern in cut glass, which consists of strawberry diamonds and fans, as well as stars and hobstars that expand outward.

Bowl, 9", Expanding Star Pattern	$275
Ice Tub, 9", 2-Handled, Expanding Star Pattern	$375
Punch Bowl, 14", Expanding Star Pattern	$550
Spooner, 7" x 5" Rectangular, Expanding Star Pattern	$115

Empire Cut Glass Company
1895–1924

Empire was founded by Harold Hollis in New York City. In 1902 he sold it to his employees, who operated it as a cooperative until 1904. It was then sold to Henry C. Fry, who continued producing cut glass under the Empire name into the 1920s.

Bonbon Dish, Applied Curled-Up Handle, Atlantic Pattern	$225
Bowl, 6", Notched Edge, Saxonia Pattern	$175
Bowl, 8", Albemarle, Dupont, Isabella, Manhattan, Nelson, or Typhoon Pattern	$250
Bowl, 8", Shallow, Japan Pattern	$225
Bowl, 8", Kremlin Pattern	$275
Bowl, 9", Berkshire or Iorio Special Pattern	$300
Carafe, Water, 7¾", Peerless Pattern	$200
Celery Dish, 11½" Oval, Princeton Pattern	$300
Compote, 4⅜" Tall, 7" Diameter, Atlantic Pattern	$300
Decanter with Faceted Ball Stopper, Diamond and Fan Design	$400
Nappy, 6", Notched Edge, Orinoco or Prince Pattern	$125
Plate, 8", Notched Edge, Plymouth Pattern	$175
Relish Dish, 8", 2 Applied Handles, 4 Divisions, Madame Pattern	$225
Tray, 12" Oblong, Notched Edge, Atlantic Pattern	$375
Tray, 13" Long, Celery, Plaza Pattern	$300
Tray, 14" Oblong, Notched Edge, Elsie Pattern	$425
Vase, 9" Tall, Waldorf Pattern	$300
Vase, 12" Tall, Circular Base, Viola Pattern	$650

Empire Pattern. *Reproduced directly from a 1912 Jewel Cut Glass patent.*

Enterprise Cut Glass Company
1905–17

Enterprise actually obtained a good deal of their blanks for cutting from Belgium; others they purchased from the Union Glass Works. As with so many others, the advent of World War I cut off vital supplies, and they went out of business in 1917.

Bowl, 7½", Buzz Star Pattern	$150
Bowl, 7½", Notched Edge, Star Pattern	$175
Decanter with Stopper, 13" Tall, Large Hobstar on Globe-Shape Base, Vertically Cut Neck	$625
Pitcher, 7" Tall, Tankard Style, Daisy Pattern	$350
Pitcher, Milk, 8" Tall, Sunburst Pattern	$375
Pitcher, Water, 13½" Tall, Imperial Pattern	$525
Plate, 8¼", Notched Edge, Daisy Pattern	$150
Punch Bowl with Stand, 11" Diameter, 10" Tall, Majestic Pattern	$3,150
Punch Bowl with Stand, 14" Diameter, 16½" Tall, 8½" Deep, Royal Pattern	$4,250
Tray, Celery, 12½" Oval, Notched Edge, Rose Pattern	$500
Tray, Ice Cream, 14" x 7½" Oval, Buzz Star Pattern	$600
Tumbler, Sunburst Pattern	$75
Vase, 13" Tall, Circular Diamond Cut Base, Large Hobstar Design	$1,350

Fry, H. C. and Company
1901–34

Henry C. Fry worked for a variety of glass firms before finally establishing his own business in 1901. Fry was diversified in his product line, which not only included cut glass, but also pressed, etched, his famous ovenware, and blown blanks.

Bonbon Dish, 5" Square, King George Pattern	$150
Bowl, 4", Wheat Pattern	$125
Bowl, 6", 4 Ovals with Crosscuts and Chains of Stars	$175
Bowl, 6", Wheat Pattern	$175
Bowl, 7¾", Chicago Pattern, Signed "Fry"	$500
Bowl, 8", Cleo Pattern, Signed "Fry"	$225
Bowl, 8", Nelson, Pineapple, or Wheat Pattern	$200
Bowl, 8", 2 Circular Handles, Trojan Pattern	$275
Bowl, 9", Rayed Base, Chain Hobstars and Fans, Signed "Fry"	$300
Bowl, 10", Frederick, Keystone, or Wheat Pattern	$250
Decanter with Faceted Stopper, 10" Tall, Genoa Pattern	$625
Lamp, 20" Tall, Notched Prism Pattern with Hobstars	$1,550
Mayonnaise Bowl, 5" Diameter, Circular Pedestal Base, Swirled Wheat Pattern	$200
Nappy, 1 Handle, Carnation Pattern	$125
Plate, 7", Brighton Pattern	$200
Plate, 8", Wheat Pattern	$150
Platter, 8¾" Diameter, Raised Notch Edge (1⅜" Tall), Asteroid Floral Pattern Variant, Signed "Fry"	$325
Platter, 12" Round, Frederick Pattern, Signed "Fry"	$700
Platter, 12" Oblong, Atlantic Pattern	$475
Powder Box with Hinged Cover, 5½" Diameter, 3½" Tall, Silver-Hinged Frame around Box and Cover, Carnation Pattern	$525
Sandwich Server with Center Handle, 10" Diameter, Asteroid Pattern	$450
Serving Dish, 9¾", Tricorner, Flaring Notched Prism Pattern	$725
Sherbet, 4" Tall, Chicago Pattern	$100
Tray, Bread, 12" Oval, Elba Pattern	$450

Tray, Bread, 12" Oval, Typhoon Pattern	$475
Tray, 14" Oblong, Notched Edge, Elsie Pattern	$400
Tray, 14" Oval, Sciota Pattern	$500
Tray, 14" Rectangular, Leman or Nelson Pattern	$575
Tumbler, Highball, 5½" Tall, Pinwheel Center, Hobstar on Base	$125
Tumbler, 6" Tall, Georgia Pattern	$150
Umbrella Stand, 24" Tall, Star, Diamond, and Bull's-Eye Design	$5,000
Vase, 9" Tall, Trumpet Style, Vardin Pattern	$175
Wineglass, Supreme Pattern, Signed "Fry"	$75

Hawkes, T. G. Company
1880–1903

One of the big names in the cut-glass world, Thomas Gibbon Hawkes was an Irish immigrant with a long family history of glass artistry. He was a direct descendant of the Hawkes family of Dudley, England, and the Penrose family of Waterford, Ireland. Hawkes came to America in 1863 and fell in with some famous cut-glass makers, including John Hoare, Henry Sinclaire, and Oliver Eggington. Hawkes purchased blanks from the Corning Glass Works through 1904. He then teamed up with various relatives and Frederick Carder to form the Steuben Glass Works.

Hawkes's painstaking details and such famous patents as the Russian, Louis XIV, Brazilian, Nautilus, and many others established him as one of the elite of America's cut-glass manufacturers.

Basket, 9" Tall, 8" Diameter, 3 Thumbprints on Applied Handle, Hobstar Base, Hobstar and Fans	$1,275
Basket, 12" Tall, 8½" Diameter, Barrel Shape, Notched Handle, Cut Horizontal Rows with Vertical Divisions	$825
Basket, 10" Diameter, Russian Pattern	$600
Bonbon Dish, 5", Strawberry Diamond and Fan Pattern	$110
Bonbon Dish, 5" Round, Russian Pattern	$135
Bowl, 4", Finger, Millicent Pattern	$135
Bowl, 4½", Harvard Pattern	$140
Bowl, 6", Festoon Pattern	$150
Bowl, 7", Gladys Pattern	$175
Bowl, 7", 2" Tall, Kohinoor and Hobstar Pattern, Signed "Hawkes"	$350
Bowl, 7" Oblong, Panel Pattern	$300

T. G. Hawkes Cut Glass Hobnail Platter. *Photo by Mark Pickvet.*

T. G. Hawkes Cut Glass. *Photo courtesy of Corning Museum of Glass.*

Bowl, 7", Straight Sides, Venetian Pattern	$275
Bowl, Rose, 7½", 8" Tall, Queens' Pattern, Signed "Hawkes" on Bottom and Liner	$750
Bowl, 8", 3½" Tall, Kohinoor Pattern, Signed	$625
Bowl, 8", Nautilus Pattern	$525
Bowl, 8", Crimped, Russian Pattern	$350
Bowl, 8", Footed, Russian Pattern	$375
Bowl, 8" Square, Notched Edge, Festoon Pattern	$250
Bowl, 8¾", Brazilian Pattern	$300
Bowl, Fruit, 9", Millicent Pattern	$325
Bowl, 9", Hobstars and Bull's-Eye Clusters (Queens' Pattern Variant)	$550
Bowl, 9", Russian Pattern	$400
Bowl, Centerpiece, 9" Diameter Base, 4" Diameter Bowl, Scalloped, 24-Point Hobstar Bottom, Hobstar Pattern, Signed "Hawkes"	$625
Bowl, 9¼", Scalloped, Engraved Dahlias and Swirls	$500
Bowl, 10", Comet Pattern, Signed "Hawkes"	$450
Bowl, 10", Devonshire Pattern	$450
Bowl, 10", Harvard Pattern	$350
Bowl, 10", Footed, Russian Pattern	$450
Bowl, 12", Chrysanthemum or Russian Pattern, Signed "Hawkes"	$825
Butter Dish with Cover, 5" Cover Diameter, Jersey Pattern	$750
Candelabra, 17" Tall, 3-Light, Brazilian Pattern	$3,350

Candleholder, 3½" Tall, Hollow Bulb Stem, Intaglio Floral Design	$110
Candlestick, 12" Tall, Swirled Pillar Stem, Russian Patterned Square Foot	$375
Candlestick, Rayed Base, Faceted Ball, Paneled Stem	$300
Carafe, Water, Devonshire Pattern	$800
Celery Dish, Boat Shape, Harvard Pattern	$600
Cheese Dish with Cover, Aberdeen Pattern	$500
Cocktail Shaker with Cover, 9", Diamond Cut Design	$335
Cologne with Stopper, Bell Shape, Gravic Design, Signed "Hawkes"	$485
Compote, 7" Diameter, 7" Tall, Open, Venetian Pattern	$250
Compote, 13" Diameter, 10" Tall, Panel Pattern, Signed "Hawkes"	$675
Compote, Large, Hobstar and Thumbprints Enclosed in Diamonds	$575
Cordial, Square Base, Cut Diamond Design, 1 oz.	$85
Cruet with Stopper, 6" Tall, Venetian Pattern	$550
Cruet with Stopper, 9" Tall, Dundee Pattern	$1250
Decanter with Stopper, 12" Tall, Brunswick Pattern	$750
Decanter with Silver-Hinged Stopper, Chrysanthemum Pattern	$700
Decanter with Stopper, 12" Tall, Grecian Pattern	$750
Globe, Rose, 6½" Tall, Circular Pedestal Base, Brunswick Pattern	$185
Goblet, 5¾" Tall, Gravic Floral Design, Signed "Hawkes"	$135
Goblet, 6¾" Tall, Intaglio 3-Fruit Design	$175
Humidor, Tobacco, 8" Tall, Large Cut Oval Ball on Cover, Brunswick Pattern	$785
Humidor, Tobacco, 8½" Tall, Large Cut Oval Ball on Cover, Marlboro Pattern	$885
Ice Bowl, 7" Round, 5" Tall, 2 Tab Handles, Iceland Pattern	$515
Ice Cream Tray, Oval (15½" x 10½"), Chrysanthemum Pattern	$815
Ice Tub, 5" Tall, 6" Across, Rayed Base, Strawberry Diamond and Fan Pattern	$385
Knife Rest, 5" Long, Faceted	$85
Napkin Ring, 1¾" Diameter, Hobstar Design	$95
Nappy, 6", Handled, Engraved Flowers between Hobstars	$110
Nappy, 6", Handled, Jupiter Pattern	$150
Nappy, 8", Russian Pattern, Signed "Hawkes"	$275
Olive Dish, 9" Acorn Shape, Strawberry Diamond Pattern	$425

Pitcher, Syrup with Sterling Silver Lid, 4½" Tall, St. Regis Pattern	$515
Pitcher, Syrup with Sterling Silver Lid, 7" Tall, Brunswick Pattern, Signed	$1,550
Pitcher, Milk, 6½" Tall, 7½" Wide, Intaglio and Chrysanthemum Pattern, Signed "Hawkes"	$2,050
Pitcher, Water, 10" Tall, Panel Pattern, Signed "Hawkes"	$1,050
Pitcher, Water, 11" Tall, Pedestal Base, Queens' Pattern, Signed "Hawkes"	$1,575
Pitcher, Water, 11½" Tall, Chrysanthemum Pattern	$1,275
Pitcher, Water, 12" Tall, Intaglio Cut and Chrysanthemum Pattern, Signed "Hawkes"	$1,775
Pitcher, Cocktail, 16" Tall, Silver-Plated Stirrer, Cut Band Design	$350
Plate, 7", Astor, Cambridge, Grecian, or Venetian Pattern	$225
Plate, 7", Chrysanthemum Pattern	$250
Plate, 7½", Queens Pattern	$375
Plate, 7½", Napoleon Pattern	$275
Plate, 8", Engraved Chantilly Lace Deisgn, Signed "Hawkes"	$250
Plate, 8", Notched Edge, Russian Pattern	$300
Plate, 8½", Venetian Pattern	$300
Plate, 9", Venetian Pattern, Signed "Hawkes"	$325
Plate, 10", Constellation or Holland Pattern	$275
Plate, 11", Cardinal Pattern, Signed "Hawkes"	$375
Plate, 12", Constellation or Panel Pattern	$350
Plate, 12", Venetian Pattern, Signed "Hawkes"	$425
Plate, 13", Kensington Pattern	$1250
Plate, 13½", Scalloped, 8-Point Hobstar, Stamped "Hawkes"	$1275
Platter, 11½" Round, Panel Pattern, Signed "Hawkes"	$775
Platter, 12½" Oval, Albany Pattern	$700
Platter, 13" Round, Venetian Pattern	$750
Platter, 14" Round, Constellation Pattern	$450
Platter, 14" Round, North Star Pattern	$900
Platter, 15½" Round, Kings' Pattern	$925
Platter, 16" Round, Constellation Pattern	$550

Powder Box with Hinged Cover, Chrysanthemum Pattern, Signed	$585
Punch Bowl with Stand, 12" Diameter, 12" Tall, Queens' Pattern, Signed "Hawkes"	$3,150
Salt and Pepper Shakers, Alberta Pattern	$285
Tray, Dresser, 10" Oval, Sheraton Pattern	$300
Tray, 11" Oval, Devonshire, Naples, or Wild Rose Pattern	$475
Tray, 11½" Square, Chrysanthemum Pattern	$2250
Tray, Ice Cream, 14" (Nearly Rectangular), Ruffled Edge, Mars Pattern	$425
Tray, Ice Cream, 14" Oval, Russian Pattern	$735
Tray, Oblong, 15" x 8", Nautilus Pattern, Signed "Hawkes"	$1550
Vase, 4½" Tall, 3 Engraved Medallions, Gracia Pattern, Signed "Hawkes"	$275
Vase, 9" Tall, Diamond and Hobstar Pattern	$375
Vase, 10" Tall, Trumpet Style, Fish-Scale Design Along Sides, Diamond and Hobstar Design at Top	$400
Vase, 11" Tall, Globe Holder, Globe Knob Stem, Circular Base, Russian Pattern	$450
Vase, 11½" Tall, Sterling Silver Foot, Knob Stem, Millicent Pattern	$375
Vase, 12" Tall, Brunswick Pattern	$425
Vase, 12" Tall, Globe Top, Circular Base, Franklin Pattern	$450
Vase, 12" Tall, Engraved Ferns and Roses with Bands of Hobstars	$475
Vase, 13" Tall, Globe Holder, Globe Knob Stem, Circular Base, Russian Pattern	$550
Vase, 14" Tall, Flared, Notched Rim, Circular Base, Brighton Pattern	$785
Vase, 14" Tall, 6" Diameter, Lattice and Rosette Pattern, Signed "Hawkes"	$815
Vase, 18" Tall, Pedestal Base, Queens' Pattern, Signed "Hawkes"	$925
Whiskey Tumbler, 2¾" Tall, Monarch Pattern, Signed "Hawkes"	$125
Wineglass, 5½" Tall, Double Knob, Circular Foot, Engraved Iris Design	$100
Wineglass, 6½" Tall, Square Base, Cane or Queens' Pattern	$125

Hoare, J. and Company
1868–1921

John Hoare was one of the early leaders of America's Brilliant period in glassmaking. He and his father, James, were both born in the famous glassmaking town of Cork, Ireland. The Hoare family was also associated with Thomas Webb & Sons and other firms in England. John Hoare also paid the boat fare for Thomas G. Hawkes, who was employed briefly with the Hoares.

Hoare's quality also elevated the company's cut-glass products to some of the best ever produced. This is evidenced by the numerous awards they received at various expositions, such as the gold medal award at the Columbian Exposition in Chicago in 1893. The firm remained in business until James Hoare II died in 1921.

Basket, Small, 2¾" Diameter, 5" Tall, Applied Thumbprint Handle, Crosby Pattern	$185
Basket, 18" Tall, Flared Top; Diamond, Fan, and Hobstar Cuts	$900
Bell, 6" Tall, Monarch Pattern	$135
Bonbon Dish, 5" Round, Croesus Pattern	$135
Bowl, 7", Rolled Side, Creswick Pattern	$275
Bowl, 7¾", Trellis Pattern, Signed "Hoare"	$725
Bowl, Rose, 7" Diameter, 6" Tall, Wedding Ring Pattern	$675
Bowl, 8", Croesus Pattern	$225
Bowl, 8" Square, Pebble Pattern	$375
Bowl, 8", Strawberry Diamond and Fan Pattern, Signed "Hoare"	$235
Bowl, 8¼" Diameter, 2½" Tall, Scalloped, Serrated Rim, 8 Oval Mitres with 6 Rows of Hobstars between the Ovals, Marked "J. Hoare & Co./1853/Corning"	$625
Bowl, 9", Footed, Corning Pattern	$300
Bowl, 9" Square, Croesus Pattern	$350
Bowl, 10" Square, Corning Pattern	$400
Bowl, 11" Square, Marquise Pattern	$475
Bowl, Centerpiece, 11½" Diameter, 5½" Tall, Scalloped and Swirled Leaves with Alternating Strawberry and Diamond Pattern	$1550
Bowl, 14", Shallow, Diamond and Bar Design, #5336 Pattern	$725
Butter Pat, Hobstar and Crossed Oval Pattern, Signed "Hoare"	$85
Candlestick, 8" Tall, Cross-Hatched Diamond Design	$350
Candlestick, 10" Tall, Colonial Pattern	$175
Carafe, Queen's Pattern, Signed "J. Hoare and Company"	$550
Celery Dish, 11¼" Long, Harvard Pattern, Signed "Hoare"	$225
Centerpiece, Canoe Shape, 12½" Long, 4" Tall, Scalloped, Quarter Diamond Pattern	$1,250
Champagne Glass, Sunburst Base, Circular Foot, Fluted and Notched Hourglass Stem, Hobstars Between Mitre Cuts	$125
Creamer, Swirled Hobstar and Fan Design	$150
Cruet with Stopper, 6" Tall, Strawberry Diamond and Fan Pattern, Signed "Hoare"	$450

Decanter with Stopper, 8" Tall, 16 oz., Hindoo Pattern	$425
Decanter with Stopper, 8½" Tall, Prism Pattern	$325
Decanter with Sterling Silver Stopper, 9" Tall, Wheat and Thistle Design	$975
Decanter with Stopper, 13½" Tall, Wedding Ring Pattern	$850
Ewer, 12" Tall, Pedestal Base, Rookwood Pattern	$4,250
Ewer, 14½" Tall, Pedestal Base, Rookwood Pattern	$5,000
Handkerchief Box with Hinged Cover, Nassau Pattern, Silver Overlay by Birks	$1,275
Ice Cream Tray, 13" Long, Scalloped Hobstar and Strawberry Diamond Border, Oval Hobstar and Fans on Center, Marked "J. Hoare and Company"	$875
Jug, Whiskey with Stopper, 10" Tall, 7" Diameter, 1 gal., Monarch Pattern, Signed	$2,750
Nappy, 1 Handle, 7", Elfin Pattern	$150
Pitcher, Water, 9¼" Tall, Applied Handle, Notched Rim, Hindoo Pattern	$500
Pitcher, Water, 9¼" Tall, Flared Bottom, Sunburst Base, Scalloped, Large Hobstars, Signed "J. Hoare & Co./1853/Corning"	$525
Pitcher, Water, 12" Tall, Eleanor Pattern	$2,500
Pitcher, Water, 12" Tall, Wheat Pattern	$675
Plate, 6", Acme Pattern	$150
Plate, 7", Square, Corning Pattern	$200
Plate, 7", Hexagonal, Nassau Pattern	$200
Plate, 8", Square, Corning Pattern	$225
Platter, 12", Circular, Carolyn Pattern	$500
Platter, 14", Circular, Creswick Pattern	$575
Platter, 14", Circular, Hindoo Pattern	$600
Punch Bowl with Stand, 12" Diameter, 13" Tall, Limoge Pattern	$3,750
Punch Bowl, 12", 6" Tall, Wheat Pattern	$3,150
Punch Bowl, 12½", Newport Pattern	$2,850
Punch Bowl with Base, Oval (20" x 13"), 10" Tall, Croesus Pattern	$4,250
Punch Cup, Handled, Croesus Pattern	$125
Relish Dish, 6" Long, 3-Lobed, Hobstar and Facets Design	$125
Relish Dish, 7" Long, Brighton Pattern	$150
Sachet Jar with Cover, 4" Tall, Hindoo Pattern	$500

Sugar Dish, Swirled Hobstar and Fan Design	$150
Tobacco Jar with Cover, 6½" Tall, 4½" Diameter, Strawberry Diamond and Fan Design	$725
Tobacco Jar with Cover, 7⅛" Tall, Hobstars, Swags, and Facets	$775
Tobacco Jar with Cover, 8" Tall, 5" Diameter, Carolyn Pattern	$1,350
Tray, Celery, Oval (9½" x 4"), Strawberry Diamond and Fan Pattern	$275
Tray, Celery, Oval (10½" x 5"), Large Hobnail Design	$375
Tray, Celery, Oval (11" x 5"), Eclipse Pattern	$425
Tray, Celery, Oval (12" x 4½"), Victoria Pattern	$475
Tray, Ice Cream, 13½" Oval, Wheat Pattern	$925
Tray, Ice Cream, 17" Oval, Meteor Pattern	$1,500
Tray, Ice Cream, 17½", Hobstar Design	$1,500
Tumbler, 3¾", Croesus Pattern	$175
Vase, 12" Tall, 2-Handled, Monarch Pattern	$1,500
Vase, 12" Tall, Trumpet Shape, Prism with Button Squares, 5" Diameter	$375
Vase, 14" Tall, 6½" Diameter, Comet Pattern, Signed	$1,750
Whiskey Tumbler, 2¾" Tall, Monarch Pattern	$125
Wineglass, Monarch Pattern	$115

Hope Glass Works
1872–1923

This small manufacturer of cut glass had trouble operating profitably and went through several changes in ownership, though the company name itself was not altered. They made glass globes, knobs, and shades along with some tableware. In 1899, it was acquired by the DeGoey family, who remained in business until 1951; however, heavy cut-glass production ended in the early 1920s.

Bowl, 7", Shallow, Notched Edge, Large Star Cut Surrounded by 6 Small Hobstars	$150
Creamer, 4½" Tall, Handle and Spout (Pitcher Style), Notched Rim, Applied Notched Handle, Vertically Cut with Mitred Diamond Band at Top	$225
Cruet with Stopper, 5" Tall, Hobstar and Diamond Pattern	$525
Plate, 7", Cut Star in Center Surrounded By Engraved Carnations	$550
Sugar, 4¼" Tall, 2 Notched Handles, Notched Rim, Vertically Cut with Mitred Diamond Band at Top	$200

Hunt Glass Company
1895–1973

Thomas Hunt along with his son, Harold, came to the United States in 1880 from England. The elder Hunt first worked for T. J. Hawkes before establishing his own operation in 1895. Hunt's cut glass was made into the 1930s; after that, the firm switched exclusively to machine-made glass products.

Banana Boat, 11" Oblong, Royal Pattern	$550
Bonbon Dish, 3¾" Square, Royal Pattern	$110
Bowl, 7¾", Royal Pattern	$375
Bowl, 8", Limoges Pattern	$275
Bowl, 8", Royal Pattern	$425
Bowl, 9", Cut Bar and Circle Design	$225
Bowl, Rose, 7½", Royal Pattern	$500
Compote, 3-Part (Bowl, Base, and Stem), 10", 15" Tall, Royal Pattern	$3,850
Creamer, Royal Pattern	$175
Punch Bowl with Stand, 12", Royal Pattern	$1,850
Sandwich Server, Engraved Fruit, Signed	$375
Sugar Dish, Royal Pattern	$175
Tray, 7¾" Oval, Royal Pattern	$225
Tray, Ice Cream, 10½", Hobstar and Fan Design	$275
Tray, Bread, 11½", Royal Pattern	$325
Tray, Ice Cream, 14½", Stafford Pattern	$500
Tumbler, Juice, Royal Pattern	$85

Ideal Cut Glass Company
1902–34

Charles Rose established Ideal at Corning, New York, in 1902. The firm was moved to Canastota, New York, in 1904, then sold to W. B. Hitchcock in 1908. Hitchcock moved it to Syracuse in 1909, and Ideal continued in operation until 1934. All in all, they made very few products, but they did patent a six-petaled flower and a sailing ship pattern in cut/engraved glass.

Lamp, 18" Tall, Hobstar and Fluted Design	$1,550
Pitcher, 14½" Tall, Corset Shape, Serrated Lip, Cut Vertical Rows Alternating with Hobstars	$850

Plate, 8", Engraved Sailing Ship (*Constitution*)	$1,500
Tumbler, Diamond-Poinsettia Pattern	$275
Vase, 12" Tall, Notched Edge, Diamond-Poinsettia Pattern	$1,250

Irving Cut Glass Company
1910–33

Irving was formed by six glass cutters who had previously worked for others (George Reichenbacher, Eugene Coleman, William Hawken, William Seitz, George Roedine, and John Gogard). The firm survived World War I but closed during the Depression.

Bonbon Dish, Butterfly Shape, 6", Elk Pattern	$150
Bowl, 8", Pinwheel Pattern	$200
Butter Dish with Cover, 6" Diameter Dome, 8" Diameter Underplate, Rose Combination Pattern	$750
Butter Dish with Cover, 8" Diameter, 5½" Tall, Zella Pattern	$750
Creamer, Pitcher Style, Applied Handle, Notched Rim, Large Hobstar Design	$275
Goblet, 4½" Tall, White Rose Pattern	$150
Lamp, 22" Tall, Dome Shade, Zella Pattern	$2,750
Nappy, 11" Diameter, 6" Tall, 2-Sectioned, Center Top Handle, Hobstar and Diamond Cut Design	$525
Pitcher, Water, Signora Pattern	$400
Plate, 7", White Rose Pattern	$150
Plate, 10", Victrola Pattern	$450
Pitcher, Water, 9" Tall, Applied Handle, Carnation Pattern	$575
Relish Tray, 9" x 4" Oval, 2 Divisions, Iowa Pattern	$500
Sugar, 2 Applied Handles, Notched Rim, Large Hobstar Design	$275
Tray, Boat Shaped, 9" Oblong, Iowa Pattern	$625
Tumbler, 4" Tall, Signora Pattern	$75

Jewel Cut Glass Company
1906–28

The firm began as the C. H. Taylor Glass Company in 1906 but changed the name to Jewel the following year. The company patented a few patterns, and as the market for fine cut glass declined, they stopped cutting glass and began selling greeting cards in 1928.

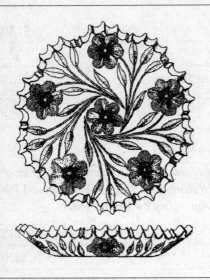

Primrose Pattern. *Reproduced directly from a 1912 Jewel Cut Glass patent.*

Bonbon Dish, 6", 2 Tab Handles, Engraved Floral Design	$275
Bowl, 8", Shallow, Notched Edge, Engraved Primrose Pattern	$350
Bowl, 11", Rolled Rim, Bishop's Hat Design, Aberdeen Pattern	$450
Creamer, 3½" Tall, Aberdeen Pattern	$300
Handkerchief Box with Cover, 7" Square Shape, Aberdeen Pattern	$1,375
Plate, 7", Regency Pattern	$125
Plate, 8", Fluted and Hobnail Design	$150
Plate, 8", Empire Pattern	$200
Platter, 16" Circular, Aberdeen Pattern	$1,250
Punch Bowl with Stand, 14" Diameter, 14" Tall, Aberdeen Pattern	$3,050
Sugar, Open, 3½" Tall, Aberdeen Pattern	$300
Tray, Oval (15¼" x 9½"), Aberdeen Pattern	$500

Keystone Cut Glass Company
1902–18

Keystone was a small company that purchased their blanks from both the Corning Glass Works and Dorflinger. As lead crystal blanks were harder and harder to come by, the business closed just after the end of World War I.

Bowl, 9", 4½" Tall, Notched Edge, Rose Pattern	$325
Butter Dish with Cover, 6" Tall, Rose Pattern	$900
Creamer, 2-Handled, Double Spout, Signed "Keystone Cut Glass Company"	$525

Creamer, 2 Applied Handles, Double Spout, Romeo Pattern	$475
Goblet, 6" Tall, Pluto Pattern	$150
Lamp, 22" Tall, Branning's Fan Scallop Pattern	$2,900
Pitcher, Water, 10¼" Tall, Applied Handle, Pluto Pattern	$475
Sugar, 2-Handled, Signed "Keystone Cut Glass Company"	$525
Sugar, 2 Applied Handles, Notched Edge, Romeo Pattern	$475

Laurel Cut Glass Company
1903–20

Laurel was another of those small companies with a limited distribution network. They produced some cut-glass products and briefly joined with Quaker City directly after World War I. The two separated by 1920 and Laurel ended cut-glass production.

Bowl, 6", Amaranth Pattern	$150
Bowl, 8", Cypress, Everett or Triumph Pattern	$225
Compote, 8" Tall, 8" Diameter, Notched Edge, Hobstar Design	$225
Creamer, Single Handle and Spout, Eunice Pattern	$200
Plate, 8", Central Hobstar Surrounded by 6 Smaller Hobstars	$175
Sugar, 2-Handled, Eunice Pattern	$200
Tray, 8" Oblong, Ruffled Edge, Audrey Pattern	$275
Tumbler, Whiskey, Crescent Pattern	$125

Libbey Glass Company
1888–1936

You will find more listings for Libbey than any other cut-glass manufacturer, and for good reason: Libbey was simply the largest producer of cut glass in the world. Their products rivaled the best anywhere, and they won numerous awards at various expositions. Some of Libbey's famous one-of-a-kind cut-glass creations are housed in the Toledo Museum of Art in Ohio (the company was instrumental in establishing the museum). Libbey ceased heavy cut-glass production in the mid-1930s but continued on as a large producer of machine-made glass products.

Basket, Oval (12¼" x 7¼"), 17" Tall, Intaglio and Brilliant Pattern, Signed "Libbey"	$1,050
Bell, 4½" Tall, Faceted Handle, Puritana Pattern	$575
Bell, 5⅜" Tall, Faceted Handle, Hobstar, Diamond and Fan Design	$365

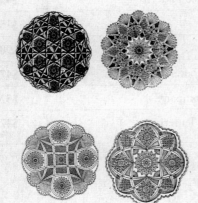

Stratford Pattern (top left), Princess Pattern (top right), Mathilda Pattern (bottom left), and Corinthian Pattern (bottom right). *Reproduced directly from an 1896 Libbey patent.*

Bottle, Water, Imperial Pattern, Signed "Libbey"	$325
Bottle, Whiskey, 14" Tall, Cut Stopper, Intaglio Rye	$375
Bowl, 4½", Flared, Ruffled, Foliage Design, Signed "Libbey"	$200
Bowl, Finger, 5", Etched Floral Design	$165
Bowl, Finger, 5", Intaglio Grape and Leaf Design	$200
Bowl, 7", Colonna Pattern, Signed "Libbey"	$250
Bowl, 8", Star and Feather Pattern	$225
Bowl, 8", 2 Tab Handles, Sunset Pattern	$375
Bowl, 8", Corinthian Pattern	$275
Bowl, 8", Delphos Pattern, Signed "Libbey"	$325
Bowl, 8", Gloria or Isabella Pattern	$275
Bowl, 8½", Hobstars with Fans and Diamond Panels, Signed "Libbey"	$275
Bowl, 9", Columbia Pattern	$300
Bowl, 9", Colonna or Greek Key Pattern	$300
Bowl, 9", Empress Pattern	$325
Bowl, 9", Glenda Pattern, Signed "Libbey"	$325
Bowl, 9", Harvard or Senora Pattern	$425
Bowl, 9", Finely Detailed Snowflake Pattern, Signed "Libbey"	$1,150
Bowl, 10", 5" Tall, Intaglio and Leaves Pattern, Signed "Libbey"	$475
Bowl, 10", Aztec or Florence Pattern	$350

Bowl, 10", Fluted, Kimberly Pattern	$425
Bowl, 10", Tricorner, Marcella Pattern, Signed "Libbey"	$750
Bowl, 10", 16-Point Hobstar on Base, Sultana Pattern, Signed "Libbey"	$450
Bowl, 10⅛", Stratford Pattern	$625
Bowl, 11½" x 4½" Oval, Russian Ambassador Pattern	$975
Bowl, 11½" x 8" Oval, 4½" Tall, Star and Feather Pattern, Signed "Libbey"	$675
Bowl, 12", Geometric Pattern, Signed "Libbey"	$750
Bowl, Fruit with Base, 13", Hobstar and Trellis Cutting	$2,000
Bowl, 13½", Russian Ambassador Pattern	$1,250
Bowl, 14", Shallow, Libbey Pattern, Signed "Libbey"	$750
Bowl, Fruit, Hat Shape, Thistle Pattern, Signed "Libbey"	$600
Bowl, Fan and Hobstars, Eulalia Pattern	$525
Bowl, Rose, 5½" Tall, Senora Pattern	$750
Bowl, Rose, 6½" Tall, 4½" Top Opening, Ribbed, Signed "Libbey" in Circle	$175
Box, Powder, 6"Diameter, Hinged Lid, Florence Pattern	$675
Butter Dish with Domed Cover, Matching Underplate, Columbia Pattern	$875
Butter Dish with Domed Cover, Matching Underplate, Hobstar and Strawberry Diamond Design, Gloria Pattern	$875
Butter Dish with Domed Cover, Rajah Pattern	$875
Cake Plate, 12", Aztec Pattern, Signed "Libbey"	$550
Candlestick, 6" Tall, Fluted, Teardrop Stem, Signed "Libbey"	$200
Carafe, Elsmere Pattern, Signed "Libbey" on Flute	$325
Carafe, Fan, Hobstar and Mitre Cut, Signed "Libbey"	$275
Carafe, New Brilliant Pattern	$300
Celery Dish, 11" Long, Harvard Pattern	$225
Chalice, 11" Tall, Colonna Pattern	$1,000
Champagne Glass, Embassy Pattern, Signed "Libbey"	$115
Champagne Glass, Fern and Flower Design, Signed "Libbey"	$115
Champagne Glass, Imperial Pattern, Signed "Libbey"	$115
Cheese Dish with Dome Cover, Matching Underplate, Columbia Pattern, Signed "Libbey"	$975
Cologne Bottle with Stopper, 6" Tall, 6" Diameter, Globe Shape, Columbia Pattern	$650

Cologne Bottle with Stopper, 8" Tall, Globe Shaped, Columbia Pattern	$675
Compote, 6", 6" Tall, Hobstar, Fan, and Pinwheels, Step-Cut Stem, Signed	$300
Compote, 8½" Diameter, Ozella Pattern	$550
Compote, 10½" Diameter, Knobbed Stem with Teardrop, Geometric Design, Signed "Libbey"	$850
Cordial, 24-Ray Base, Fluted, Faceted Knob, Harvard Pattern, Signed "Libbey"	$125
Cordial, Embassy Pattern, Signed "Libbey"	$125
Cordial, Princess Pattern, Signed "Libbey"	$125
Cordial, 3½" Tall, Sultana Pattern, Signed "Libbey"	$125
Creamer, Hobstars and Strawberry Diamond, Signed "Libbey"	$175
Creamer, Raised Lip, Eulalia Pattern	$175
Creamer, Star and Feather Design	$175
Decanter, Side Handle, Corinthian Pattern	$500
Decanter with Faceted Stopper, 13" Tall, 4½" Diameter, Ellsmere Pattern	$1,550
Decanter with Stopper, 18" Tall, Pedestal Base, Herringbone Pattern, Signed "Libbey"	$3,500
Decanter with Stopper, 19⅛" Tall, Cut Circular Foot, Applied Cut Handle, Tapering Shape, Small Pouring Lip, Sunburst Pattern Variant, Signed "Libbey"	$5,250
Goblet, Columbia Pattern	$150
Goblet, Water, Princess Pattern, Signed "Libbey"	$115
Ice Cream Dish, 17½" Long, Senora Pattern	$1,350
Ice Cream Tray, 12" Diameter, Somerset Pattern	$300
Ice Cream Tray, 14" x 7½", Kimberly Pattern	$400
Ice Cream Tray, 16" x 9¾", 4-Sectioned Cut Flowers, Flashed, Ivernia Pattern, Signed "Libbey"	$1,350
Ice Cream Tray, 18" Diameter, Princess Pattern	$800
Jug, 7" Tall, with Handle, Stopper on Side Spout, Sultana Pattern, Signed "Libbey"	$2,750
Nappy, 5", Melrose or Venetian Pattern, Signed "Libbey"	$115
Nappy, 6", Princess Pattern, Signed "Libbey"	$125
Nappy, 7", Heart-Shape, Heart Pattern, Signed "Libbey"	$200
Nappy; Hobstars, Strawberry Diamond and Fan Design, Signed "Libbey"	$150

Pitcher, Milk, Harvard Pattern	$425
Pitcher, Milk, 7¾" Tall, Corinthian Pattern	$425
Pitcher, Water, 8" Tall, Tankard Style, New Brilliant Pattern	$400
Pitcher, Water, 8" Tall, Tankard Style, Rayed Base, Sunburst with Bands of Hobstars	$400
Pitcher, Water, 8½" Tall, Corinthian Pattern	$475
Pitcher, Water, 9" Tall, Columbia Pattern, Signed "Libbey"	$575
Pitcher, Water, 9" Tall, Kingston Pattern	$500
Pitcher, Water, 11" Tall, Imperial Pattern, Signed "Libbey"	$650
Pitcher, Champagne, 11½" Tall, Iola Pattern	$675
Pitcher, Water, 12" Tall, Aztec Pattern, Signed "Libbey"	$775
Pitcher, Water, 13" Tall, Kingston Pattern	$700
Pitcher, Water, Scotch Thistle Pattern	$475
Plate, 6", Columbia Pattern	$150
Plate, 6¾", Ellsmere Pattern, Signed "Libbey" with Sabre	$175
Plate, 6¾", Ice Cream, Prism Pattern, Signed "Libbey"	$200
Plate, 7", Aztec Pattern, Signed "Libbey"	$200
Plate, 7", Colonna or Kimberly Pattern	$200
Plate, 7", Prism Pattern, Signed "Libbey"	$175
Plate, 7", Spillane Pattern, Signed "Libbey"	$175
Plate, 10", Columbia or Corinthian Pattern	$275
Plate, 10", Kingston Pattern, Signed Libbey	$300
Plate, 10", Princess Pattern	$350
Plate, 11½", 6-Paneled, Thistle Design, Signed "Libbey"	$400
Plate, 11¾", Sultana Pattern, Signed "Libbey"	$425
Platter, 12", Circular, Neola Pattern	$775
Platter, 12", Circular, Ozella Pattern	$625
Platter, 16", Circular, Diana Pattern, Signed	$1,850
Punch Bowl with Stand, Spillane Pattern, Signed "Libbey"	$4,250
Punch Bowl with Stand, 14", Colonna Pattern	$2,750
Punch Cup, Colonna Pattern	$135

Punch Ladle, Faceted, Colonna Pattern	$285
Relish, 6" Diameter, 2½" Tall, Signed "Libbey"	$250
Salt Dip, Pedestal Base, Signed "Libbey"	$150
Salt and Pepper Shakers with Silver Tops, Intaglio Cut Floral Design	$350
Saucer, 5", Hobstars with Asymmetrical Center Star	$125
Sherry Glass, Moonbeam Pattern, Signed "Libbey"	$85
Spooner, 6" Tall, Sultana Pattern	$175
Sugar, Hobstars and Strawberry Diamond, Signed "Libbey"	$175
Sugar, Flared Rim on 2 Sides, Eulalia Pattern	$150
Sugar, 2-Handled, Star and Feather Design	$175
Tankard, Vase, 11¼" Tall, Hobnail and Cross Cutting, Signed "Libbey"	$650
Tankard, 11½" Tall, Hobnail and Cross Cutting, Signed "Libbey"	$850
Tray, Pickle, 8" Oval, Regis Pattern	$215
Tray, 10" Oval, Senora Pattern, Signed "Libbey"	$525
Tray, 10½" Oblong, Puritan Pattern, Signed "Libbey"	$650
Tray, 11¼" x 4½", Wisteria and Lovebird Pattern	$1,500
Tray, 12" Diameter, Senora Pattern, Signed "Libbey"	$725
Tray, 12" Diameter, Scalloped, 6-Paneled, Diamond Point with Star	$1,375
Tray, Celery, 12" x 4⅜", Eight 12-Pointed Hobstars, Fan Center, Diamond and Fan Cuts, Gem Pattern	$250
Tray, 14" Oval, Ice Cream, 2 Tab Handles, Prism Pattern, Signed "Libbey"	$825
Tray, 15¾" Oblong, 9½" Wide, Fishtail Shape, Prism Pattern, Signed "Libbey"	$1,050
Tray, 17½" Oval, Wedgemere Pattern, Signed "Libbey"	$2,150
Tray, Heart Shape, Florence Star Pattern	$575
Tumbler, Juice, Corinthian Pattern	$115
Tumbler, Harvard or New Brilliant Pattern	$100
Tumbler, Scotch Thistle Pattern	$115
Tumbler, Strawberry Diamond Design, Signed "Libbey"	$115
Vase, 5½" Tall, Sawtooth Rim, Bull's-Eyes and Fern Design	$200
Vase, 10" Tall, Fine Ribbed Cuts	$225
Vase, 12" Tall, Corset Shape, Signed "Libbey"	$675

Vase, 12" Tall, Radiant Pattern	$500
Vase, 16" Tall, Rose Cutting, Signed "Libbey"	$425
Vase, 16" Tall, Star and Feather Pattern, Signed "Libbey"	$1,400
Vase, 18" Tall, 2 Notched Handles, Hobstars and Hobnails Design	$2,850
Vase, 18" Tall, Wedgemere Pattern	$2,650
Vase, 20" Tall, 7½" Diameter, Pedestal Base, Kensington Pattern Variation, Signed "Libbey"	$2,500
Wineglass, 5¾" Tall, Circular Foot, Double Knob, Signed "Locke Art"	$150
Wineglass, 7¼" Tall, Cornucopia Pattern	$115
Wineglass, Embassy Pattern, Signed "Libbey"	$115
Wineglass, Cut Stem Only, Signed "Libbey"	$175

Luzerne Cut Glass Company
1910s–Late 1929

Luzerne, like countless others, was a small, obscure company with few surviving products. They were established sometime before World War I and were out of business by 1929.

Tray, 14" Oblong, Notched Edge, 2 Tab Handles, Myron Pattern	$365
Tray, 14½" Oval, Notched Edge, Electra Pattern	$415

Maple City Glass Company
1910–1920s

Maple City purchased a factory formerly run by John S. O'Connor in Hawley, Pennsylvania. O'Connor stayed on briefly with the newly formed company. What few cut-glass products they made were marked with an etched maple leaf. The firm sold out to T. B. Clark in the early 1920s.

Banana Boat, 10" Long, Strawberry Diamond and Hobstars, Marked with Maple Leaf	$365
Bowl, 7", Crossed Oval Design	$175
Bowl, 8", Fenmore Pattern	$200
Bowl, 9", Notched Edge, Emerald Pattern	$225
Celery Dish, Boat Shape, Marked Inside with Maple Leaf	$1,050
Ice Cream Tray, 14½" x 8", Cane, Fan, Hobstar, and Strawberry Design, Marked with Maple Leaf	$750

Mustard Dish with Cover and Matching Underplate, 3½" Tall, Panel and Notched Prism Design, Signed	$350
Pitcher, Milk, 7½" Tall, Pinwheels and Cross-Hatching, Signed	$425
Punch Bowl, 12¼" Diameter, 11½" Tall, Temple Pattern	$3,775
Spooner, 5½" Tall, Large Hobstar and Cross-Hatched Design	$275
Tobacco Jar with Cover, 6" Tall, 5" Diameter, Hemispherical Cut Finial, Hobstar and Fan Design	$1,350
Tray, 12" Oval, Notched Edge, Manchester Pattern	$300
Tray, 14" Oval, Notched Edge, Gloria Pattern	$350
Vase, 7½" Tall, Pansy Pattern	$375

Meriden Cut Glass Company
1895–1923

Meriden, Connecticut, was a small, relatively unknown glassmaking town that featured several small companies. The Meriden Cut Glass Company was one such business that produced blanks for cutting as well as some cut products of their own. They were noted most for the Alhambra pattern, which is also known or more familiar as Greek Key.

Bottle, Worcester with Stopper, 8" Tall, Alhambra Pattern	$725
Cake Salver, 10" Diameter, Stemmed, Alhambra Pattern	$525
Cheese Dish with Domed Cover, Plymouth Pattern	$500
Cruet with Stopper, 8" Tall, Albany Pattern	$650
Cruet with Stopper, 9½" Tall, Alhambra Pattern	$775
Decanter with Stopper, 12½" Tall, Alhambra Pattern	$1,275
Decanter with Stopper, Plymouth Pattern	$750
Decanter with Stopper, 6" Tall, Wheeler Pattern	$600
Fern Dish with Metal Liner, 8½" Diameter, Alhambra Pattern	$1,050
Humidor with Cover, 9½" Tall, 6" Diameter, Alhambra Pattern	$2,750
Ice Tub with Silver Rim and Handle, 9", Alhambra Pattern	$2,500
Nappy with Center Handle, Florence Pattern	$200
Pitcher, Water, 9" Tall, Large, Heavy Sterling Silver Top, Including Pouring Lip, Alhambra Pattern	$1,250
Pitcher, Water, 12½" Tall, Tankard Style, Sterling Silver Top, Alhambra Pattern	$1,750
Plate, 7", Alhambra Pattern	$150

Plate, 7" Square, Notched Edge, Hobstars and Circles Inscribed in Squares	$225
Plate, 10", Alhambra Pattern	$300
Relish Dish, Old Irish Pattern	$300
Tray, 12½", Hobstar Design	$1,000
Tray, 13" Oval, Alhambra Pattern	$1,250
Tumbler, 4½" Tall, Thalia Pattern	$375
Vase, 16" Tall, Alhambra Pattern	$4,000

Monroe, C. F. Company
1880–1916

C. F. Monroe was better known as an art-glass company; however, they employed glass cutters as well.

Bowl, 7", Rockmere Pattern	$225
Bowl, 8", Notched Edge, Monroe Pattern	$200
Bowl, 9½", Footed, Central Hobstar with Chain of Smaller Hobstars, Silver Rim	$575
Carafe, 9½" Tall, Nevada Pattern	$250
Fernery, 80" Tall, Silver Rim, Allover Hobstar and Fan Pattern	$575
Hairpin Box with Lid, 4" Diameter, Brass Rim at Top of Box and Bottom of Lid, Fluted Base, Hobstar and Fan Design on Lid	$550
Pitcher, Syrup with Silver-Plated Lid and Handle, Hobstar and Fan Pattern	$775
Powder Box with Cover, 5½" Diameter, Silver Rim at Top of Box and Bottom of Cover, Hobstar, Fan, and Strawberry Diamond Design on Base and Cover	$750
Powder Box with Cover, 6" Diameter, Silver Rim at Top of Box and Bottom of Cover, Fluted Base, Large Center Hobstar on Cover	$700
Powder Box with Cover, 6" Diameter, Brass Rim at Top of Box and Bottom of Cover; Central Hobstar with Star and Fan Design on Base and Cover	$750
Powder Box with Cover, 7½" Diameter, Silver Rim at Top of Box and Bottom of Cover, Fluted Base, Central Hobstar with Several Small Hobstars on Cover, Jewel Pattern	$775
Powder Box with Cover, 8" Diameter, Silver Rim at Top of Box and Bottom of Cover, Fluted Base, Central Hobstar with Several Small Hobstars on Cover	$800
Vase, 14" Tall, Ariel Pattern	$775
Watch Box with Cover, 3" Diameter, Brass Rim at Top of Box and Bottom of Cover, Fluted Base, Pinwheel Design on Cover	$500

Monroe Pattern. *Reproduced directly from a 1902 C. F. Monroe patent.*

Mt. Washington Glass Works

1837–94

Mt. Washington is best known for its famous art-glass products, but they were also a significant producer of cut glass. They patented many designs, including several floral patterns such as the Rose, Rose variations, Daisy, and others. Mt. Washington eventually became part of the Pairpoint Manufacturing Company in 1894, which continued with several of Mt. Washington's cut lines. (See additional listings under "Pairpoint.")

Bonbon Dish, 5", Finger-Hold Handle, Priscilla Pattern	$175
Bowl, 6", Bedford Pattern	$150
Bowl, 8", Magnolia Pattern	$225
Bowl, 8", Russian Pattern	$275
Bowl, 8¾", Picket Fence with 24-Point Star Base, Acid Finish	$275
Bowl, 10" Princess Pattern	$375
Butter Tub with Cover, 2-Handled (Cover Has Indentation for Handles), 5" Diameter, 8" Diameter Matching Underplate, Diamond and Star Pattern	$2,775
Champagne Glass, 5" Tall, Diamond and Star Pattern with Hobstar Base	$150
Cheese Dish with 9¼" Matching Underplate, Nevada Pattern	$775
Cracker Jar with Cover, Strawberry Diamond and Fan Pattern	$825
Creamer, Bedford, Corinthian, Regent, Strawberry Diamond and Fan, or West Pattern	$200
Decanter with Stopper, Right-Angle Handle, Bedford Pattern	$675
Decanter with Stopper, No Handle, Corinthian Pattern	$700

Decanter with Stopper, Westminster Pattern $725

Jam Jar with Hinged Cover, Handled, Strawberry Diamond and Hobstar Pattern, Marked "M.W." on Cover $475

Mug, 8 oz., Regent, Westminster, or Wheeler Pattern $150

Mustard Jar with Cover, 1 Handle, Strawberry Diamond and Fan or Westminster Pattern $335

Pitcher, Water, Corinthian Pattern $300

Pitcher, Water, Regent, Strawberry Diamond and Fan, or Westminster Pattern $375

Pitcher, Water, 8" Tall, Radiant Pattern $400

Pitcher, Water, 11½" Tall, Wheeler Pattern $450

Plate, 5½", Hortensia Pattern $125

Plate, 6", Corinthian, Priscilla, Strawberry Diamond and Fan, or Westminster Pattern $150

Plate, 7", Bedford, Corinthian, Priscilla, Regent, or Westminster Pattern $175

Plate, 7", Square, Madora Pattern $250

Plate, 8", Bedford, Butterfly and Daisy, Corinthian, or Westminster Pattern $200

Platter, 14½" Circular, Silver Rim, Daisy Pattern $1,650

Platter, 15" Oval, Large Diamond with Octagon Cuts $600

Punch Bowl with Base, 14" Diameter, Regent Pattern $3,750

Punch Ladle, Regent Pattern $550

Relish Dish, 3 Divisions, Strawberry Diamond and Fan Pattern $225

Salt and Pepper Shakers, Ribbed, Pillar Pattern, Metal Holder with Handle $375

Spoon Holder, 6" Oblong, Strawberry Diamond and Fan Pattern $115

Spoon Holder, 7" Oblong, Strawberry Diamond and Fan Pattern $135

Sugar, Bedford, Corinthian, Regent, Strawberry Diamond and Fan (without Cover), or Westminster Pattern $200

Sugar with Cover, Strawberry Diamond and Fan Pattern $250

Sugar Shaker, Egg Shape, Metal Top, Corinthian, Strawberry Diamond and Fan, or Wheeler Pattern $550

Tray, Dresser, Tulip Pattern $250

Tray, 9" Square, Corinthian Pattern $475

Tray, 12" x 5½" Rectangular, Block Diamond or Strawberry Diamond and Fan Pattern $300

Tray, 14" Oblong, Strawberry Diamond and Fan Pattern	$325
Tray, 14½" x 7¾" Rectangular, Diamond with Fans on Edges	$750
Tray, Irregular, 1 Large Semicircle for Pitcher, 2 Smaller Semicircles For Tumblers, Strawberry Diamond and Fan Pattern	$425
Tumbler, 3¾" Tall, Block Diamond Design	$85
Whiskey Tumbler, 2½" Tall, Westminster Pattern	$125
Wineglass, 6⅛" Tall, Fluted Stem, Angular Ribbon Pattern with Star Base	$150

Ohio Cut Glass Company
1904–12

This firm was established at Bowling Green, Ohio, in 1904. Ohio worked primarily as a cutting shop for Pitkin & Brooks; nevertheless, products were advertised and labeled with the Ohio Cut Glass Company name. The company was managed by Thomas Singleton and produced cut glass until 1912. The factory burned to the ground in 1912 and was not rebuilt.

Bowl, 8", Large Central Buzz Star and Fan Design, Sawtooth Rim	$175
Bowl, 8", Large Central 16-Point Star and Fan Design, Sawtooth Rim	$175
Celery Dish, 8" Oval, Hobstar and Diamond Design	$200
Creamer, 3", Diamond and Fan Design	$85
Creamer, 3", Pinwheel and Fan Design	$85
Cruet with Ball-Faceted Stopper, 5½ oz., Strawberry Diamond and Fan Design	$150
Nappy, 5", No Handles, Hobstar and Fan Design	$100
Nappy, 5", 1 Handle, Crosshatch, Diamond, and Star Design	$125
Sugar Dish, 3", Diamond and Fan Design, 2-Handled	$85
Sugar Dish, 3", Pinwheel and Fan Design, 2-Handled	$85

Pairpoint Glass Corporation
1894–1938

As noted under Mt. Washington, Pairpoint purchased them in 1894 and continued production of cut glass. They also patented several lines, including the Tulip, Anemone, and others.

Bonbon Dish, 5", 2 Tab Handles, Salem Pattern	$175
Bottle, Whiskey with Stopper, 10" Tall, 1 qt., Old English Pattern	$1,750
Bowl, 8", Notched Edge, Montrose or Wisteria Pattern	$350

Priscilla Pattern. *Reproduced directly from an 1894 Pairpoint patent.*

Bull's-Eye Pattern. *Reproduced directly from an 1898 Pairpoint patent.*

Bowl, 9", Notched Edge, Montrose Pattern	$375
Bowl, 11", Myrtle Pattern	$525
Bowl, 12", Berwick Pattern	$675
Bowl, 12", Notched Edge, Wisteria Pattern	$675
Bowl, 14", Notched Edge, Wisteria Pattern	$875
Cheese Dish with Cover, Strawberry Diamond Pattern	$1,275
Cologne Bottle with Stopper, 2 oz., Arbutus Pattern	$250
Comport, 6½" Tall, Diamond-Hob Design	$200
Comport, 8" Tall, Diamond-Hob Design	$250
Compote, 10" Tall, Teardrop Stem, Hobstar Base, Avila Pattern	$375
Compote, 10" Tall, Hobstar and Fan Design, Uncatena Pattern	$375
Creamer, Domed Base, Colias Pattern	$125
Cruet with Flower Cut Stopper, Ramona Pattern	$325
Flower Holder, 13½" Diameter, Butterfly and Daisy Pattern	$525
Handkerchief Box with Cover, 7" Square, 3⅛" Tall, Silver-Plated Rim and Under Rim on Lid, Engraved Floral Design	$700
Mug, 4" Tall, Tyrone Pattern	$275
Nappy, 5", "+" Shape, Block Diamond Design	$115
Nappy, 5½" Heart Shape, Fairfax Pattern	$200
Nappy, 7¾", Essex Pattern	$150

Nappy, 8", Bombay or Montank Pattern	$175
Plate, 8", Clarina or Vintage Pattern	$115
Spoon Holder, 7¾" Oval, Canton Pattern	$125
Spoon Holder, 2 Handles, Malden Pattern	$150
Sugar, Domed Base, Colias Pattern	$125
Sugar Tray, Domino, Rectangular with Tab Handles	$225
Tray, 8¼" x 4" Rectangular, Wakefield Pattern	$225
Tray, 9" Oval, Essex Pattern	$250
Tray, 9¼" Oval, Kingston Pattern	$275
Tray, 10", Triangular, Russian Pattern	$400
Tray, 10" Oval, Russian Pattern (Persian Variation)	$325
Tray, 14" Oblong, Ruffled Edge, Silver Leaf Pattern	$500
Vase, 6" Tall, Fan Scroll Pattern	$200
Vase, 8" Tall, Fan Scroll Pattern	$225
Vase, 10" Tall, Savoy Pattern	$400
Vase, 12" Tall, Fan Scroll Pattern	$350
Whiskey Tumbler, 2½" Tall, Butterfly and Daisy Pattern	$100

Pitkin & Brooks
1872–1920

Edward Pitkin and Jonathan Brooks Jr. formed a wholesale glass and china business in 1872. They later opened various cutting shops and employed cutters to produce products with their P & B mark. They sold the glass in their wholesale business and patented several lines, such as Korea, Wild Daisy, Heart and Hobstar, and others. Overall, the company was one of the larger producers of cut-glass products.

Basket, 6", Eldorado Pattern	$350
Basket, 8", Eldorado Pattern	$450
Basket, 8", Footed, Zesta Pattern	$500
Bonbon Dish, 3½", Square, Mars Pattern	$85
Bonbon Dish, Heart Shape, 5½", Earl Pattern	$150
Bonbon Dish, 6"; Beverly, Eric, Erminie, Oriole, or Prince Pattern	$110
Bonbon Dish, 6¾", Rajah Pattern	$115
Bonbon Dish, 7½", Myrtle Pattern	$115

Pitkin & Brooks Carnation Water Set. *Reproduced directly from an early-20th-century Pitkin & Brooks catalog.*

Pitkin & Brooks Crete P&B Grade, Footed. *Reproduced directly from an early-20th-century Pitkin & Brooks catalog.*

Bonbon Dish with Cover, 10", Delmar Pattern	$325
Bowl, 6½", Venice Pattern	$125
Bowl, 7", Clarion or Marietta Pattern	$150
Bowl, 8", Athole, Border, Carnegie, Cleo, Corsair, Duchess, Elsie, Empress, Lyre, Marietta, Mars, Meadville, Mikado, Myrtle, Nellore, Oriole, Plymouth, Rajah, or Winona Pattern	$200
Bowl, 8", Shallow, Belmont or Venice Pattern	$175
Bowl, 8", 3½" Tall, Notched Edge, Hobstar and Diamond Pattern	$175
Bowl, 9", Corsair, Empress, Heart, Marietta, Mars, Meadville, Rajah, Venice, or Winona Pattern	$275
Bowl, 9½", Mars Pattern	$300
Bowl, 10", Marietta, Oriole, Pinto, or Rajah Pattern	$300
Candlestick, 8", Oro Pattern	$200
Candlestick, 14" Tall, Heart Pattern	$375
Carafe, 1 qt., Belmont, Carolyn, Heart, Mars, Meadville, Myrtle, Rajah, Sunburst, Venice, or Winfield Pattern	$175
Celery Dish, 12", Plaza Pattern	$350
Compote, 5" Diameter, 9" Tall, Heart Pattern	$200
Compote, 5", Cress, Myrtle, Villa, or Zeller Pattern	$135
Compote, 5", 2-Handled; Crete or Memphis Pattern	$150
Compote, 6", Atlas, Cress, or Radium Pattern	$155
Compote, 6", 2-Handled, Crete or Memphis Pattern	$185

Compote, 7", 2-Handled; Crete or Memphis Pattern	$225
Compote, 7", McKinley or Myrtle Pattern	$200
Compote, 7" Tall, Border Pattern	$425
Compote, 7½", Heart or Savannah Pattern	$215
Compote, 8", Glee, Mars, or Rajah Pattern	$235
Compote, 10", Rajah Pattern	$250
Compote, 10", 2-Handled, Border Pattern	$250
Compote, 12", Rajah Pattern	$300
Compote, 14", Rajah Pattern	$350
Compote, 11¾" Tall, 10½" Diameter, 2-Part, Floral Design, Plymouth Pattern, Signed	$775
Creamer, Belmont, Border, Byrns, Carolyn, Duchess, Garland, Halle, Heart, Mars, Meadville, Myrtle, Oriole, Plymouth, Prism, Rajah, Sunburst, Triumph, or Venice Pattern	$135
Cup, Belmont, Border, Byrns, Carolyn, Duchess, Garland, Halle, Heart, Mars, Meadville, Myrtle, Oriole, Plymouth, Prism, Rajah, Sunburst, Triumph, or Venice Pattern	$75
Cruet with Stopper, Garland or Sunray Pattern	$150
Decanter with Stopper, 1 qt., Garland Pattern	$275
Fernery, 7¾" Diameter, Paneled Floral and Diamond Design, Signed	$215
Glove Box with Cover, 11" Long, Delmar Pattern	$350
Goblet, Belmont, Heart, Sunrise, or Venice Pattern	$75
Hair Receiver with Cover, 5", Aurora Borealis, Esther, Hiawatha, or Larose Pattern	$185
Humidor with Cover, 8½", Zesta Pattern	$375
Jewelry Box with Cover, 6" Oval, Merrimac Pattern	$275
Jewelry Box with Cover, 7" Oval, Delmar or Sparkle Pattern	$325
Knife Rest, 3½", Barbell Shape	$35
Knife Rest, 4½", Barbell Shape	$40
Knife Rest, 5½", Barbell Shape	$45
Knife Rest, 6", Barbell Shape	$50
Lamp, 17" Tall, 32 Prisms, Engraved Chrysanthemum Design	$1,850
Lamp, 22" Tall, 32 Prisms, Engraved Poppy Design	$2,150
Lamp, 23" Tall, 12" Diameter Shade, Plymouth Pattern, Signed	$2,250
Nappy, 5", Tab Handle, Mars, Meadville, Mikado, or Venice Pattern	$85

Nappy, 6", Tab Handle, Heart Pattern	$225
Nappy, 6", Tab Handle, Mars, Meadville, Mikado, or Venice Pattern	$100
Nappy, 6", Seymour Pattern	$150
Nappy, 7", Corsair, Meadville, Mikado, or Myrtle Pattern	$200
Nappy, 7½", 2 Tab handles, Phena Star Pattern	$225
Nappy, 8", Corsair, Meadville, or Myrtle Pattern	$250
Nappy, 9", Corsair or Meadville Pattern	$275
Pickle Dish, 7", Meadville or Nellore Pattern	$215
Pitcher, 1½ qt., Kelz Pattern	$275
Pitcher, 2 qt., Orleans Pattern	$375
Pitcher, 12" Tall, Heart Pattern	$1,050
Plate, 7", Rosette and Buzz Star Pattern	$150
Plate, 7", Hexagonal, Star Pattern	$225
Plate, 7", Mars or Wild Daisy Pattern	$150
Plate, 9", Roland Pattern	$175
Plate, 12", Roland Pattern	$225
Plate, 14", Roland Pattern	$275
Pomade Box with Cover, 2¾", Electra Pattern	$250
Puff Box with Cover, 5", Aster or Esther Pattern	$275
Puff Box with Cover, 6", Heart Pattern	$300
Punch Bowl with Base, 10", Crete, Keystone, or Rajah Pattern	$1,000
Punch Bowl with Base, 12", Beverly, Carolyn, Crete, Derby, Garland, Heart, Keystone, Korea, Plymouth, Sunburst, or Sunray Pattern	$1,450
Punch Bowl with Base, 14", Belmont, Beverly, Carolyn, Derby, Heart, Keystone, or Plymouth Pattern	$1,750
Punch Cup; Beverly, Carolyn, Crete, Derby, Garland, Heart, Keystone, Korea, Plymouth, Rajah, Sunburst, or Sunray Pattern	$85
Relish Tray, 7", Osborn Pattern	$250
Salt Dip, 1½", Vertical Star Cuts	$25
Salt and Pepper Shakers, Various Cut Designs	$65
Saucer, 5", Beaver, Corsair, Kenwood, Meadville, Mikado, or Myrtle Pattern	$150
Saucer, 6", Beaver, Corsair, Kenwood, Meadville, Mikado, or Myrtle Pattern	$175

Sherbet, Merlin Pattern	$75
Spoon Boat, 11⅝" x 4⅝" Canoe Shape, Hobstar Design	$525
Spoon Tray, 7½" Oblong, Cortez Pattern	$250
Sugar, Belmont, Border, Byrns, Carolyn, Duchess, Garland, Halle, Heart, Mars, Meadville, Myrtle, Oriole, Plymouth, Prism, Rajah, Sunburst, Triumph, or Venice Pattern	$135
Tray, 10", Hobstar Center, Myrtle Pattern	$300
Tray, 10" Oval, Nellore Pattern	$300
Tray, 10¾" Oval, Nellore Pattern	$325
Tray, 11" Oblong, 5 Large Hobstars, Cortez Pattern	$350
Tray, 11" Oval, Meadville or Myrtle Pattern	$300
Tray, 11½" Oblong, Halle Pattern	$350
Tray, 11¾" Oval, Rajah Pattern	$375
Tray, 12" Oval, Athole, Bowa, or Princess Pattern	$375
Tray, 12" Oval, Notched Edge, Bowa Pattern	$375
Tray, 13½" Across, Oak Leaf Shape, Notched Prisms and Vesicas	$775
Tumbler, Various Cut Patterns	$75
Vase, 8" Tall, Hiawatha or Rosabella Pattern	$225
Vase, 10" Tall, Rosabella Pattern	$325
Vase, 10" Tall, Star and Fan Design	$450
Vase, 12" Tall, Rosabella Pattern	$425
Vase, 13" Tall, Star and Fan Design	$700
Vase, 16" Tall, Star and Fan Design	$950

Quaker City Cut Glass Company
1902–27

Quaker City was also known as the Cut Glass Corporation of America. Few examples of their products have been found that are easily identified. They used paper labels with a bust of William Penn, but the gummed labels easily fell off or were removed. The most impressive and extremely valuable pieces are the tall vases that were typically made in three separate pieces that screw together.

Bonbon Dish, 5½" Oval, Notched Edge, Mystic Pattern	$150
Bowl, 4" Tall, Footed, Ruffled Edge, Berlyn Pattern	$300
Bowl, 4½" Tall, Footed, Notched Edge, Whirlwind Pattern	$225

Bowl, 9", Notched Edge, Columbia or Marlborough Pattern	$225
Compote, Angora Pattern	$575
Cup, 4" Tall, Eden Pattern	$300
Plate, 11", Du Barry Pattern	$325
Punch Bowl with Stand, 11", Diameter, 10" Tall, Elgin Pattern	$1,500
Punch Bowl with Stand, 14" Diameter, 15" Tall, Majestic Pattern	$5,000
Punch Cup (Matches Bowl), Majestic Pattern	$250
Vase, 20" Tall, 3-Part, Empress Pattern	$5,500
Vase, 24" Tall, 3-Part, Empress Pattern	$6,000
Vase, 36" Tall, 3-Part, Riverton Pattern	$7,500

Sinclaire, H. P. Company
1904–29

The Sinclaires were associated with several famous glassmakers. Henry P. Sinclaire Sr. was the secretary of the Corning Glass Works from 1893 until he died in 1902. Henry P. Sinclaire Jr. was the secretary of T. J. Hawkes from roughly the same time (1893–1903) and went on to establish his own business. He purchased blanks from the Corning Glass Works and patented several cut patterns before being forced to close during the Depression.

Bonbon Dish, 7" Rectangular, Strawberry Diamond or Assyrian Pattern	$175
Bowl, Fruit, 8" Diameter, 5" Tall	$350
Bowl, 9", 2¾" Tall, Hobstar and Mitred Cuts, Signed "Sinclaire"	$275
Bowl, 9" Top Diameter, 4" Tall, Assyrian Pattern	$425
Bowl, 9½", Adam Pattern	$350
Butter Dish, 6" Rectangular, Open, Strawberry Diamond Pattern	$185
Champagne Glass, Ivy Pattern, Signed "Sinclaire"	$115
Children's Miniature Cereal Set, 2-Piece, Pitcher and Bowl, Queen Louise Pattern, Signed "Sinclaire"	$500
Clock, Mantel, 8" Tall, Copper Wheel–Engraved, Signed "Sinclaire"	$600
Cologne Bottle with Stopper, 6" Tall, Floral Design, Signed "Sinclaire"	$285
Cordial, Star Base, Greek Key Pattern, Signed "Sinclaire"	$125
Creamer, Queen Louise Pattern, Signed "Sinclaire"	$175
Creamer, 6" Tall, Vintage Pattern, Signed "Sinclaire"	$250
Cup, Loving, 9¼" Tall, 8½" Diameter, 2-Handled, Signed "Sinclaire"	$1,550

Decanter with Stopper, 5" Tall, Bengal Pattern, Signed "Sinclaire"	$400
Decanter with Stopper, Queen's Pattern, Signed "Sinclaire"	$625
Epergne, 2-Part, 14" Tall, 10½" Diameter, Engraved Floral and Foliage Design, Signed "Sinclaire"	$1,500
Flower Pot, Intaglio Border, Geometric Design, Signed "Sinclaire"	$350
Ice Cream Tray, Rectangular (14" x 9"), Assyrian Pattern, Signed "Sinclaire"	$1,250
Lamp, 17" Tall, Flower Basket Pattern	$1,450
Nappy, 3¼" Triangular Shape, Cumberland Pattern	$150
Olive Dish, 7¼" x 4", 16 12-Point Hobstars in a Chain, Etched Floral and Foliage Design	$175
Pitcher, 7" Tall, Westminster Pattern, Signed "Sinclaire"	$350
Pitcher, 8½" Tall, Barrel Shape, Scalloped, Strawberry and Diamonds above Vertical Panels	$475
Pitcher, 9" Tall, Pedestal Base, Signed "Sinclaire"	$2,500
Pitcher, Water, 11" Tall, Adam Pattern	$475
Plate, 5", 32-Point Star on Base, Diamond Cross Cut, Signed "Sinclaire"	$125
Plate, 7", Assyrian Pattern, Signed "Sinclaire"	$275
Plate, 10", Adam Pattern	$375
Plate, 12", Stars and Garlands, Signed "Sinclaire"	$450
Platter, 13¼", Circular, Assyrian Pattern, Signed "Sinclaire"	$725
Platter, 15", Circular, Hiawatha Pattern, Signed "Sinclaire"	$785
Punch Bowl with Stand, 18" Diameter, 11½" Tall, Constellation Pattern	$2,750
Sugar with Cover, Queen Louise Pattern, Signed "Sinclaire"	$250
Sugar, Open, Vintage Pattern, Signed "Sinclaire"	$250
Teapot with Lid, 8" Tall, Intaglio and Damascus Pattern, Signed "Sinclaire"	$3,400
Tray, 7" x 4¾", Hobs in Chain Design, Engraved Border, Signed "Sinclaire"	$175
Tray, 10" x 7" Oval, Crosscut, Fans and Hobstars	$300
Tray, 10½" x 8" Rectangular, Assyrian Pattern	$525
Tray, 12" x 5", Assyrian Pattern	$375
Tray, 12" x 5", Flared Ends, Scalloped Sides, Geometric Cutting with Hobstars, Signed "Sinclaire"	$350
Tray, 12" x 5" Rectangular, Adam Pattern, Signed "Sinclaire"	$425

Tray, 14" Oval, 2 Tab Handles, Diamond and Threading with Engraved Floral Design in Center	$800
Tray, 15" Circular, Cornwall Pattern	$850
Vase, 6½" Tall, Flower Center, Bengal Pattern	$900
Vase, 11" Tall, Flower Center, Flute and Panel Border	$425
Vase, 12" Tall, 5" Diameter, Assyrian Pattern, Signed "Sinclaire"	$525
Vase, 14" Tall, 5" Diameter, Assyrian Pattern, Signed "Sinclaire"	$825
Vase, 15½" Tall, Queen Louise Pattern, Signed "Sinclaire"	$500
Vase, 16" Tall, Stratford Pattern, Signed "Sinclaire"	$600
Wineglass, Ivy Pattern, Signed "Sinclaire"	$125

Standard Cut Glass Company
1902–27

Standard was founded in New York City by Harry Broden in 1893. The company produced some limited cut and engraved glass until World War I.

Bowl, 8", Bruce, Lazarre, Pinto, Prismatic Stars, or Tartan Pattern	$175
Bowl, 9", Bruce, Lazarre, Pinto, Prismatic Stars, or Tartan Pattern	$200
Bowl, 10", Bruce, Lazarre, Pinto, Prismatic Stars, or Tartan Pattern	$225
Celery Tray, 8½" Oval, Strawberry Diamond and Fan Design	$300
Creamer, Large Diamond Design, Applied Handle, Notched Rim	$175
Cruet with Stopper, 5¾" Tall, Fan and Diamond Design	$250
Vase, 7" Tall, Trumpet Style, Diamond and Fan Design	$185
Vase, 8" Tall, Trumpet Style, Diamond and Fan Design	$200
Vase, 9" Tall, Trumpet Style, Diamond and Fan Design	$215
Vase, 10" Tall, Trumpet Style, Diamond and Fan Design	$250

Sterling Cut Glass Company
1904–50

The firm was established in 1904 as the Sterling Glass Company by Joseph Phillips. It was joined in 1913 by Joseph Landenwitsch. The company was briefly known as Joseph Phillips & Company. Apparently, what little cut glass they produced was in the early teens, for in 1919, Phillips became a salesman for the Rookwood Pottery Company and Landenswitsch became president of Phillips Glass Company, another offshoot.

Later the company reorganized as the Sterling Cut Glass Company. Pieces made by Sterling are scarce and quite valuable. Aside from fine cutting, many Sterling pieces contain elegant engraving as well.

Compote, 12" Diameter, 12" Tall, Arcadia Pattern	$850
Plate, 10", Fruits and Butterfly Design, Eden Pattern	$1,750
Plate, 10", Engraved Floral Border, Regal Pattern	$1,250
Tray, 11" Oval, Arcada Pattern	$550
Tray, 13½" x 6" Oval, Intaglio Cut Daisy Design	$500

Straus, L. & Sons
1888–1917

A Bavarian immigrant, Lazarus Straus came to America (Georgia) in 1852 along with his wife, Sara, and two sons, Isidor and Nathan. The family moved to New York City and opened an import business selling china and glassware. Lazarus, along with his sons, began cutting their own glass products around 1888 and usually marked every piece with "Straus Cut Glass" with a faceted gem within a circle. The firm ceased cut-glass production in the later World War I era.

Bowl, 6" Bijoux Pattern	$125
Bowl, 7", Rex Pattern	$150
Bowl, 8", Notched Ovals Edge, Daisies and Diamonds Pattern	$175
Bowl, 8", Norma Pattern	$200
Bowl, 9", Hobstar Design with Hobnail and Miter Cuts, Sawtooth Rim	$225
Bowl, 9", Notched Edge, Americus Pattern	$200
Bowl, 9", Tassel Pattern	$225
Bowl, 10", Warren Pattern	$275
Bowl, 11½" Oval, Imperial Pattern	$325
Bowl, 12" Square, Venetian Pattern	$375
Bowl, Rose, 5½", Electra Pattern	$450
Carafe, Water, Drape Pattern, Signed "Straus"	$325
Celery Dish, Encore Pattern, Signed "Straus"	$250
Cheese Dish with Dome Cover, 9" Diameter Underplate, 6" Diameter Dome, Corinthian Pattern	$775
Compote, 12" Tall, Corinthian Pattern	$750

Inverted Kite Pattern (left-top and bottom) and Imperial Pattern (right). *Reproduced directly from 1892 and 1893 patents.*

Creamer, 3" Tall, Notched Handle, Prism and Bull's-Eye Design	$175
Creamer, 5" Tall, 4½" Diameter, Ulysses Pattern	$450
Decanter with Cut Stopper, 11" Tall, Americus Pattern	$525
Ice Tub, 6" Diameter, 5½" Tall, Corinthian Pattern	$400
Pitcher, Water, 12" Tall, Drape Pattern	$1,250
Plate, 7", Antoinette, Drape, Inverted Kite, or Rex Pattern	$125
Plate, 8", Notched Edge, Lily of the Valley or Pansy Pattern	$150
Plate, 8", Venetian Pattern	$175
Plate, 10", Maltese Urn Pattern	$375
Platter, 12" Round, Maltese Urn Pattern	$625
Punch Bowl, 12½" Diameter, Corinthian Pattern	$1,500
Sugar, 3" Tall, Notched Handles, Prism and Bull's-Eye Design	$175
Sugar Dish with Cover, 5½" Tall, 5" Diameter, Ulysses Pattern	$550
Tray, Celery, 11" Oblong, 2 Hobstars and Crosscuts	$325
Tray, Celery, Acorn Shape, Rosettes and Crosscuts	$450

Tray, Ice Cream, 18" x 10" Rectangular, Drape Pattern	$2,000
Wineglass, Encore Pattern	$125

Taylor Brothers Company, Incorporated
1902–15

The Taylor brothers, Albert and Lafayette, first formed Taylor Brothers and Williams along with John H. Williams in 1902. Williams moved on soon afterward and was dropped from the title. The company managed to stay afloat for only a short period of time and filed bankruptcy in 1911. They hung on a little longer until World War I forced them out permanently. One of the most interesting designs of the company was that of cut casserole dishes; not many produced this particular object in cut glass.

Bowl, 9" Diameter, 4½" Tall, Ferns, Hobstars, and Stars	$325
Bowl, 9", Pentagonal, Palm Pattern	$525
Casserole Dish with Cover, 8½", 7" Tall, Palm Pattern, Signed	$2,150
Casserole Dish with Hobstar Cover, 9", 2 Handles, Palm Pattern, Signed	$2,350
Casserole Dish with Cover, 2 Handles, Pedestal Base, Hobstar and Diamond Pattern, Signed	$2,650
Compote, 13½" Tall, 10" Diameter, Fine Diamond and Fan Pattern	$1,350
Nappy, 5", 1 Handle Tab, Large Fluted Star in Center, Small Hobstars and Crosscuts	$225
Nappy, 6", 1 Tab Handle, Large Star Surrounded by 6 Smaller Stars	$200
Platter, 12" Round, Ruffled Edge, Palm Pattern, Signed	$425
Tray, Ice Cream, 10" Oval, Scalloped, Hobstar Rings within a Crystal Band	$650
Tray, 10½" Oval, Ruffled Edge, Arcadia Pattern	$525
Tray, 11½" x 6½" Oval, Hobstars, Stars and Diamonds	$450
Tray, 14½" x 9" Oval, 32-Point Hobstar Base, Strawberry Diamond and Chain of Hobstars Design	$1,750
Toothpick Holder, 2¼" Tall, Geometric Pattern	$150

Thatcher Brothers
1891–1907

George Thatcher, who previously worked at the Boston & Sandwich Glass Company, the Mt. Washington Glass Company, and in the cutting department of Smith Brothers; joined his brother Richard to form Thatcher Brothers. They produced some cut glass before going out of business during the panic of 1907.

Bowl, 8¼", Notched Edge, Rosette and Foliage Design	$175
Vase, 10½" Tall, Cylindrical, Diamond and Fan Design (Alternating Large Diamonds and Tiny Diamond Sections)	$450
Vase, 13" Tall, Circular Base, Stemmed, Vertically Ribbed Bulbous Midsection, Rosette and Foliage Design	$600

Tuthill Cut Glass Company
1900–23

Charles Guernsey Tuthill formed the C. G. Tuthill & Company in 1900. His brother James and sister-in-law Susan joined with him in 1902 and the name was amended to the Tuthill Cut Glass Company. The quality of their products was outstanding and much of it was attributed to Susan, who served as somewhat of an inspector, constantly measuring depth, observing details, and not allowing glass to leave the factory that was in less-than-perfect condition. As a result, Tuthill won numerous awards and their products rivaled those of the best cut-glass producers in the country. They patented many patterns, including several floral and fruit designs: Tomato, Tiger Lily, Grape, Cosmos, Orchid, Grapefruit, and others.

Basket, Oval, 9" Long, 5" Tall, Poppy Pattern	$950
Basket, Rectangular, Intaglio and Brilliant Pattern	$1,175
Basket, 21" Tall, Vintage Pattern	$2,875
Bottle, Whiskey with Stopper, 12" Tall, Cornell Pattern	$775
Bowl, 6", Hobstar and Fan Design	$250
Bowl, 7", Phlox Pattern	$275
Bowl, 7", Wild Rose Pattern	$425
Bowl, 8", Rose Pattern	$400
Bowl, 8", Hobstar and Fan Design	$450
Bowl, 8", 2½" Tall, Rolled Rim, Bishop's Hat Design, Vintage Pattern	$1,350
Bowl, 9½", Rex Pattern	$350
Cake Plate, 12", 2" Tall, 24-Point Hobstars and Fans, Signed "Tuthill"	$675
Candlestick, 12" Tall, Rosemere Pattern, Signed "Tuthill"	$625
Candy Box with Cover, 6" Round, 3" Tall, Vintage Pattern	$1,850
Charger, 12½", Intaglio Strawberry Leaf and Vine Design	$500
Cologne Bottle with Sterling Silver Stopper, Wild Rose Pattern, Signed "Tuthill"	$650
Compote, 8¼" Top Diameter, 3½" Tall, Rosemere Pattern	$325
Compote, 6½" Diameter, 14½" Tall, Intaglio Vintage Pattern	$225
Creamer, 4" Tall, Large Hobstar Design	$200

Cruet with Stopper, 8" Tall, Poppy Pattern, Signed "Tuthill"	$485
Cruet with Stopper, 10" Tall, Pedestal Base, Vintage Pattern, Signed "Tuthill"	$550
Decanter with Stopper, 11" Tall, 6" Diameter, Intaglio and Brilliant Pattern, Signed "Tuthill"	$1,000
Decanter with Stopper, 12" Tall, Handled, Primrose Pattern	$625
Lamp, 22" Tall, 12" Diameter Shade, Rex Pattern, Signed "Tuthill"	$5,750
Mayonnaise Set, 2-Piece, 6" Hexagonal Bowl with Matching 6" Hexagonal Underplate, Phlox Pattern, Signed "Tuthill"	$750
Mayonnaise Set, 2-Piece, 5" Bowl with 6" Matching Underplate, Stars and Arcs Pattern, Signed "Tuthill"	$575
Mug, Dawson Pattern	$175
Pitcher, 9" Tall, Rose Pattern, Signed "Tuthill"	$1,050
Plate, 5⅞" x 4½", Oval, Rosemere Pattern, Signed "Tuthill"	$275
Plate, 7", Rex Pattern, Signed "Tuthill"	$525
Plate, 9", Quilted Diamond Pattern	$350
Plate, 9" x 7" Oval, Vintage Pattern	$675
Plate, 10", Rosemere Pattern	$700
Plate, 10", Silver Rose Pattern	$750
Plate, 10", Three Fruits or Wild Rose Pattern	$475
Platter, 12", Circular, Vintage Pattern, Signed "Tuthill"	$700
Platter, 13", Circular, Wild Rose Pattern, Signed "Tuthill"	$775
Platter, 14¼", Circular, Wild Rose Pattern, Signed "Tuthill"	$875
Punch Bowl, 13" Diameter, 16" Tall, Scalloped, Footed, Engraved Grape Clusters and Leaves, Alternating Cross Cuts and Hobstars, Signed "Tuthill"	$6,500
Punch Cup, 3½" Tall, Flared, Circular Foot, Stemmed, Vintage Pattern	$175
Sugar, 3¾" Tall, 2-Handled, Large Hobstar Design	$200
Toothpick Holder, 4" Tall, Stemmed, Wild Rose Pattern, Signed "Tuthill"	$225
Tray, 7½" x 5½" Rectangular, Dresser, Vintage Pattern	$450
Tray, 8½" Oval, Scalloped, Intaglio Floral Design	$300
Tray, Celery, 12" Long, Pinwheel Design, Signed "Tuthill"	$475
Tray, 12", Circular, Engraved Blackberry Design	$500
Vase, 10" Tall, Cylindrically Shaped (4" Diameter from Top to Bottom), Rex Pattern, Signed "Tuthill"	$3,250

Vase, 11" Tall, Urn Shape, 2 Handles, Vintage Pattern	$925
Vase, 16½" Tall, Slender Form, Vintage Pattern	$675

Unger Brothers
1901–18

Another small company with limited production, the two Unger brothers produced some silver housewares and cut glass before closing for good just after World War I.

Bowl, 8", Shallow, Notched Edge, Fontenoy Pattern	$185
Bowl, 8", Pinwheel Design with Hobstar Center	$165
Nappy, 6", Applied Handle, Florodora Pattern	$185
Perfume Bottle with Sterling Silver Screw Top, 4" Tall, Russian Pattern	$925
Pitcher, Water, 10" Tall, Notched Handle, Ruffled Ridge, Hobart Pattern	$575
Pitcher, Water, 11" Tall, Tankard Style, Notched Handle, Ruffled Ridge, Hobart Pattern	$600
Plate, 7", 6 Hobstars in a Circular Pattern	$125
Plate, 12", Notched Edge, La Voy Pattern	$425
Tankard, 11" Tall, Hobart Pattern	$325
Tray, 14" Rectangular, Duchess Pattern	$400

Westmoreland Specialty Company
1889–1937

Westmoreland was established by two brothers, George Robinson West and Charles Howard West, in 1889 in Grapeville, Pennsylvania. The company was reorganized as the Westmoreland Glass Company in 1924 and lasted until 1985, but ceased cut-glass production after it was purchased by the Brainard family in 1937.

Westmoreland was not known as a huge cut-glass producer; nonetheless, some have argued that they produced more cut glass in the 1920s and 1930s than any other glass manufacturer in America. Of course, the 1920s and 1930s was a time of colored Depression glass and the Brilliant period of American cut glass had ended back in the midteens.

Westmoreland cut-glass products tend to contain more engraving rather than cutting. A few pieces are occasionally found marked with Westmoreland's "Keystone W" trademark.

Candlestick, 7" Tall, Engraved Floral Design	$62.50
Candlestick, 8" Tall, Bead and Reel Design	$75

Cigarette Bow with Cover, 6" x 3½" Rectangular, Engraved Floral and Irish Setter Design	$250
Pitcher, Water, 2 qt., Colonial Pattern (Sunburst and Grecian Cut)	$150
Relish Dish, 8¼" Diameter, 4 Divisions, 2 Tab Applied Handles, Engraved Butterfly and Floral Design	$125
Salt Dip, Hexagon Shape, Cut Stars on Each Side	$50
Salt Dip, Round, Hobstar Design	$40
Sandwich Tray with Center Handle, 6" Diameter, Crosshatched Diamond Design with Engraved Grape Clusters	$50
Tray, 10" Octagon, Engraved Floral Design	$50
Tumbler, Colonial Pattern (Sunburst and Grecian Cut)	$50
Vase, 7" Tall, Hexagonal Base, Grecian and Sunburst Design	$75
Vase, 9" Tall, Hexagonal Base, Grecian Cut with Engraved Thistle Design	$100
Vase, 12" Tall, Hexagonal Base, Grecian and Sunburst Design	$100
Wineglass, 5" Tall, 4 oz., Etched Trellis Floral Design	$50

– 4 –
AMERICAN ART GLASS

In the midst of America's Brilliant period, a new form of glass arose. This new "art nouveau" or "art glass" period began in the 1880s and lasted well into the early 20th century. Artists, designers, and other creative people who had not previously worked in glass turned their talents into some of the most unique and spectacular glass objects ever composed. Some have a legitimate argument that the Brilliant period, coupled with the introduction of art glass, began in America with the Philadelphia Centennial Exhibition in 1876. As with the expositions taking place in Europe, these events allowed glassmakers to display some of their finest pieces to date. The Philadelphia event featured a massive cut chandelier and a glass fountain that was 17 feet in height. The fountain was an ornamental design with cut crystal prisms lighted by 120 gas jets and surmounted by a glass figure of Liberty.

The art nouveau movement had its beginnings in France with Rousseau and Galle (see the "Foreign Glass" section in chapter 1); however, America produced its own share of world-class designers. Two of the most famous American art glass sculptors were Louis Comfort Tiffany and Frederick Carder. Tiffany was an American painter who visited Paris in 1889 and observed Galle's work in person at the Exposition Universelle. He was also the son of the jewelry magnate who had founded Tiffany & Co., the famous jewelry store. Louis Comfort Tiffany began his work in glass by producing stained-glass windows without using stains or paints. The color, detail, and illusion were created within the glass itself by plating one layer of glass over another. He broadened his work to include lamps and was one of the first to experiment with iridescent glass. He named his iridescent products Favrile or Tiffany Favrile. The word was derived from the English *febrile*, which means "belonging to a craftsmen or his craft." Iridescence is produced by firing on combinations of metallic salts that in turn create a wide variety of coloring effects. Luminous colors and metallic luster produced a silky smooth or delicate patina on Tiffany's glass. According to Tiffany, his main inspiration was the decayed objects from Roman glass discovered in archaeological excavations.

With great success at presenting his works at the World's Exposition in Chicago in 1893, orders poured in, and he further expanded his work to other art forms. Tableware, vases, flowers, unique shapes, and many other table items were blown from Tiffany's skilled hands. His designs were never decorated or painted; they were made by combinations of different colored glass during the blowing operation. His goods were displayed at various places throughout Europe, including the 1900 Paris Exposition, which in turn inspired young European artists to copy his style.

Frederick Carder was an apprentice of the famous English glass artisan John Northwood. Carder emigrated from Stourbridge, England, and founded the Steuben Glass Works in Corning, New York. He created several varieties of lustrous lead glass such as Aurene, one such ornamental iridescent form. He sold Steuben to the Corning Glass Works in 1918 but continued to produce some of the finest crystal forms in the world through 1936 for Corning. Carder's glass was also exhibited at numerous national and international expositions, galleries, and museums.

Many others followed in the footsteps of Tiffany and Carder. So much experimentation took place that more distinctive styles were invented in America than in all of Europe combined. Many American firms copied or attempted to reproduce popular designs of others, and, at times, the experimentation led to new creations. In 1883 Joseph Locke, an Englishman employed by the New England Glass Company, was the first to obtain a patent for Amberina. In 1885 another English immigrant named Frederick Shirley patented Burmese for the Mt. Washington Glass Works. Burmese products were sent to Queen Victoria of England as gifts, who was so impressed with the style that she ordered more. Mt. Washington shared the formula with Thomas Webb & Sons of England, who also produced Burmese products. In 1886 Shirley also patented Pearl Satin Glass for Mt. Washington. In 1887 Locke patented Agata Glass for New England.

More patents followed for a huge variety of art styles, including Amethyst, Aurora, Cintra, Cluthra, Cranberry, Crown Milano, Custard, Intarsia, Lava, Mercury, Peach Blow, Slag, Rubina, Satin, and Spatter, among others. See the individually priced categories as well as the glossary for descriptions of these particular designs. Many classic styles have been revived since the 1970s by several small art-glass studios throughout America. A few are listed in chapter 7 in the section on "Modern and Miscellaneous Collectible Glassware."

Amberina
New England, Libbey, Mt. Washington, Tiffany, and Others, 1880s–1920

Amberina is a single-layered style of glass created by the New England Glass Company in 1883. It is characterized by an amber color at the bottom of an object that gradually shades into red at the top. The shading could very well change with each new object and the colors could be reversed. The red might be a brilliant ruby red or a deep violet or purple sometimes referred to as fuchsia, and a little genuine gold dust was at times mixed with the transparent amber. The New England Glass Company placed a high-quality vibrantly colored thick Amberina plating on some of their wares. These particular items are very rare and valuable.

Libbey continued the production of Amberina after acquiring the New England Glass Company. Libbey sold patent rights for Amberina to others such as Tiffany. Several varieties of Amberina have been reproduced by many companies and individuals. Reproductions exist, too, as well as less valuable flashed-on and enameled examples. Flashed-on and enameled items usually include metal oxides that produce an iridescent finish or enamel that flecks or eventually peels. The original Amberina has no such iridescence and was rarely enameled.

Bar Bottle with Faceted Stopper, 8" Tall, Swirled Rib Pattern	$400
Basket, 7½" Tall, Signed "Libbey"	$2,000
Bonbon Dish, 7" Oval, Shallow, Daisy and Button Pattern (Hobbs Brocunier)	$550
Bottle, Perfume with Stopper, Signed "Libbey"	$950
Bowl, 2¾", 4½" Tall, Plated Amberina	$3,750
Bowl, 3", Fluted, Plated Amberina	$3,750
Bowl, 3", Scalloped, Fine Coloring, Plated Amberina	$5,500
Bowl, 5¼", Plated Amberina, Ruffled Top (New England Glass Co.)	$2,250
Bowl, Finger, 5⅜", 2½" Tall (New England Glass Co.)	$250
Bowl, 5⅜", 2¾" Tall, with Scalloped Rim	$300
Bowl, Rectangular, 5½" x 2½" (Libbey)	$325
Bowl, Rose, 6", Hobnail	$425
Bowl, Melon, 7" Tall, Ribbed, 4-Footed	$550
Bowl, 7½", Scalloped, Diamond Quilted Pattern	$225
Bowl, 7½", 3½" Tall, Plated Amberina, Scalloped Rim, White Lining, Paper Label "Aurora/NEGW" (New England Glass Co.)	$3,000
Bowl, 8", Scalloped, Plated Amberina	$5,750
Bowl, 9" Square, Daisy and Button Pattern	$300
Bowl, 10" Oval, Daisy and Button Pattern (Hobbs Brocunier)	$375
Bowl, Footed, Lustrous Rose, Old Iron Cross Mark (Imperial)	$250
Butter Dish, 4¾", Ribbed, Silver-Plated Base with Unicorn in Center, Plated Amberina	$2,750
Butter Dish with Cover, Diamond Block Pattern	$325
Butter Pat, 2¾" Square, Daisy and Button Pattern	$275
Carafe, 6¾" Tall, Ruffled Tricorner Top (New England Glass Co.)	$350
Carafe, 7½" Tall, Reverse Amberina, Inverted Thumbprint Pattern	$350
Carafe, 8" Tall, Hobnail	$375

Castor Set, 2 Cruets with Stoppers, Salt and Pepper Shakers with Pewter Tops, and Silver-Plated Tray (New England Glass Co.) $1,750

Celery Vase, 6½" Tall, Light Color, Diamond Quilted Pattern $450

Celery Vase, Plated Amberina $3,000

Champagne Glass, 6" Tall with Hollow Stem (New England Glass Co.) $385

Cheese Dish with Cover, 9½" Diameter, 7" Tall, Optic Pattern $550

Cheese Dish with Cover, 9½" Diameter, 8" Tall, Large Circles in Cover and Round Knob, Flared Rim (New England Glass Co.) $700

Cologne Bottle with Faceted Cut Stopper, 5" Tall, Inverted Thumbprint Pattern (New England Glass Co.) $325

Compote, 4¼" Diameter, 7" Tall, Crimped Rim, Diamond Quilted Pattern (New England Glass Co.) $700

Compote, 5" Diameter, Signed "Libbey" $750

Compote, 6½", 8" Tall, Signed "Libbey" $825

Compote, 8¾" Diameter, Inverted Thumbprint Pattern (New England Glass Co.) $450

Cordial (Gunderson-Pairpoint) $75

Creamer, 2½" Tall, Plated Amberina (New England Glass Co.) $3,750

Creamer, 2⅝" Tall, Amber Handle, Scalloped, Inverted Thumbprint Pattern (New England Glass Co.) $450

Creamer, 4¾" Tall, Ribbed, Ribbed Feet, Hollow Knobby Stem, Signed "Libbey" $1,350

Creamer, 5" Tall, Pitcher Style, Ribbed, Plated Amberina $5,500

Cruet, 6½" Tall with Faceted Stopper, Amber Handle, Plated Amberina $3,000

Cruet with Stopper, 7¾" Tall, Inverted Thumbprint Pattern (New England Glass Co.) $450

Cup, Punch, Diamond Quilted Pattern (New England Glass Co.) $350

Cup, Punch, Plated Amberina (New England Glass Co.) $2,000

Decanter with Stopper, 9" Tall, 4" Diameter, Applied Amber Handle $400

Decanter with Faceted Cut Stopper, 10½" Tall, Inverted Thumbprint Pattern $475

Decanter with Faceted Amber Stopper, 12" Tall, Diamond Quilted Pattern (New England Glass Co.) $550

Dish, Canoe Shape, 8" Long, Daisy and Button Pressed Design $1,150

Goblet, Rose Amber (Mt. Washington Glass Co.) $275

Hat, 6" Wide $140

Ice Bucket with Tab Handles, 7¼" Diameter, 5½" Tall, Floral and Foliage Decorations
$350

Lamp Shade, 14", Plated Amberina (New England Glass Co.) $5,050

Lemonade Glass, Plated Amberina $1,750

Marmalade Dish with Metal Cover, 5¼" Tall, Thumbprint Pattern (Mt. Washington Glass Works) $300

Mug, Barrel Shape, 2½" Tall with Thumbprint Pattern $265

Mug, 7½" Tall, Reverse Color, Inverted Thumbprint Pattern $465

Mug, Amber Handle, Ribbed, Plated Amberina $2,550

Parfait, Plated Amberina (New England Glass Co.) $1,550

Pitcher, Syrup with Pewter Top, Inverted Thumbprint Pattern (New England Glass Co.)
$550

Pitcher, Syrup with Top, 6" Tall, Plated Amberina (New England Glass Co.) $7,500

Pitcher, Milk, 5" Tall, Melon Ribbed, Applied Amber Handle, Herringbone Pattern $275

Pitcher, 6¾" Tall, Tankard Style, Diamond Quilted Pattern (New England Glass Co.)
$825

Pitcher, 7" Tall, Square Top, Inverted Thumbprint Pattern (New England Glass Co.)
$350

Pitcher, 7" Tall, Cornered Spout, Plated Amberina (New England Glass Co.) $7,500

Pitcher, 7½" Tall, Ribbed, Inverted Thumbprint Pattern, Reverse Amberina Color, Signed "Libbey" $750

Pitcher, Water, 8" Tall, Reverse Color Design $500

Pitcher, 9½" Tall, Ruffled, Amber Handle, Inverted Thumbprint Pattern $375

Pitcher, 10" Tall, Amber Handle, Inverted Thumbprint Pattern, Signed "Libbey" $475

Pitcher, 12", Engraved Otus and Ephialtes Holding Mars Captive, Title Panel, Signed "J. Locke" $1,250

Plate, 7" (New England Glass Co.) $135

Punch Cup, 2½" Tall, Diamond Quilted Pattern (New England Glass Co.) $200

Punch Cup, 2¾" Tall, Ribbed, Amber Handle, Plated Amberina $2,250

Salt Dip, 4½" Long, Daisy and Button Pattern $150

Saltshaker, Pewter Top, Reverse Amberina Color Pattern $250

Salt and Pepper Shakers, Inverted Thumbprint Pattern (Mt. Washington Glass Co.) $500

Salt and Pepper Shakers, Diamond Quilted Pattern $325

Salt and Pepper Shakers, Plated Amberina	$5,550
Sauce Dish, 5½" Square, Daisy and Button Pattern (Hobbs Brocunier)	$300
Spittoon, Hourglass Shape with Ruffled Edge	$600
Spooner, Round with Scalloped Top and Square Mouth, Venetian Diamond Pattern (New England Glass Co.)	$600
Spooner, 5" Tall, Plated Amberina	$2,350
Sugar, 4½" Tall, Ribbed, Ribbed Feet, Hollow Knobby Stem, Signed "Libbey"	$1,500
Sugar, 2½" Tall, Plated Amberina (New England Glass Co.)	$3,750
Sugar Shaker, 4" Tall, Butterfly on Lid, Inverted Thumbprint Pattern	$525
Swan, 5" Tall (Pairpoint-Bryden)	$85
Toothpick Holder, Reversed Color Pattern	$250
Toothpick Holder, 2" Tall, Ribbed, Plated Amberina	$3,050
Toothpick Holder, 2½" Tall, 3-Footed, Daisy and Button Pattern (Hobbs Brocunier)	$300
Toothpick Holder, 2½" Tall, Round with Square Rim, Diamond Quilted Pattern (New England Glass Co.)	$200
Tumbler, Inverted Thumbprint Pattern	$140
Tumbler, Inverted Thumbprint Pattern, Signed "Libbey"	$165
Tumbler, Ribbed, 5" Tall, Plated Amberina	$2,250
Tumbler, Swirled	$175
Tumbler, Swirled, 3¾" Tall, Gold Amber (New England Glass Co.)	$175
Tumbler, Diamond Pattern, Fuchsia Shading at the Top (New England Glass Co.)	$250
Tumbler, 3¾" Tall, Plated Amberina (New England Glass Co.)	$2,250
Vase, 4" Tall, Cylindrically Shaped (New England Glass Co.)	$185
Vase, 4⅛" Tall, Plated Amberina (New England Glass Co.)	$3,050
Vase, 4⅝" Tall, Pressed Stork Pattern, Scalloped Top (New England Glass Co.)	$650
Vase, Lily, 6" Tall (Mt. Washington Glass Works)	$425
Vase, Lily, 6¼" Tall, Plated Amberina (New England Glass Co.)	$2,550
Vase, Swirled, Satinized, Reverse Amberina Color Pattern, Enameled Gold Flowers	$1,750
Vase, 7" Tall with Tricorner Top (New England Glass Co.)	$525
Vase, 7" Tall, Cylindrically Shaped, Ruffled, Inverted Thumbprint Pattern	$200
Vase, 7" Tall, Jack-in-the-Pulpit Style, Fuchsia to Amber Shading	$550
Vase, Lily, 7¼" Tall, Plated Amberina	$3,150

Vase, Lily, 7½" Tall, Signed "Libbey"	$625
Vase, 7¾" Tall, Applied Swirled Circular Domed Foot, Drinking Horn Shaped with Coiled Tail (Libbey)	$1,450
Vase, 8" Tall, Lily Shaped, Plated Amberina	$2,850
Vase, 8⅛" Tall, Applied Crystal Spiral Stem	$275
Vase, 8¾" Tall, Cylindrically Shaped, Swirled	$225
Vase, 9½" Tall, 2-Handled, Signed "Libbey"	$775
Vase, 10" Tall, Jack-in-the-Pulpit Style, Signed "Libbey"	$850
Vase, 10½" Tall, Swirled, Amber Rigaree, Footed	$275
Vase, 10½" Tall, Lily Shaped, Metal Stand, Plated Amberina	$4,550
Vase, 11" Tall, Signed "Libbey"	$1,250
Vase, 12" Tall, Three Applied Feet, Swirl Rib Pattern	$350
Vase, 13" Tall, Ruffled Rim, Circular Base, Inverted Thumbprint Pattern	$400
Vase, 14" Tall, 6" Diameter, Fluted Rim	$550
Vase, 23½" Tall, Ribbed, Knob Stem (New England Glass Co.)	$1,850
Whiskey Bottle with Stopper, 9½" Tall, Rippled Pattern	$300
Whiskey Glass, 2⅝" Tall, Diamond Quilted Pattern (New England Glass Co.)	$185

Aurene Steuben Glass Works
1904–33

Aurene was produced in five basic colors: blue, brown, gold, green, and red. The pieces remain Steuben's most desirable and popular colored glass designs; however, they are quite scarce today. Aurene is characterized by an iridescent sheen applied by spraying on various metallic salts and other chemical mixtures. Base colors were ordinarily clear, amber, or topaz. Matte finishes were applied by spraying on tin or iron chloride solutions. Alabaster and calcite were necessary for the green and red colors, respectively.

Atomizer, 5", Ribbed, Iridescent Gold	$325
Basket, 5" Tall, Ruffled, Gold with Light Green Highlights	$1,500
Basket, 8" Diameter, 8" Tall, Iridescent Gold with Applied Handle	$650
Basket, 8" Diameter, 9½" Tall, Iridescent Gold with Applied Handle	$850
Basket, 12½" Tall, Crimped Rim, Gold with Applied Berry Prunts	$1,400
Bonbon Dish, 4½", 1¼" Tall, Scalloped, Blue	$585
Bowl, Finger, 3", Red, Signed "F. Carder"	$5,250
Bowl, 6", Blue	$375

Aurene Art Glass. *Courtesy of the Corning Museum of Glass.*

Bowl, 6" Oval, Gold	$500
Bowl, 9", 3½" Tall, Footed, Gold	$575
Bowl, 10", Blue	$650
Bowl, Oval (4" x 2"), Calcite and Gold	$185
Bowl, 14" Centerpiece, Gold	$1,000
Candlestick, 4¾" Tall, 10" Wide, Gold	$625
Candlestick, 8" Tall, Gold, Marked "Aurene 686"	$675
Candlestick, 10" Tall, Air Twist Stem, Blue	$850
Candlestick, 12" Tall, Tulip Shape, Gold	$775
Cologne Bottle with Stopper, 5½" Tall, Bell Shaped, Iridescent Gold, Marked "Aurene 1818"	$825
Cologne Bottle with Stopper, 6½" Tall, Ribbed, Iridescent Gold	$925
Compote, 4", 5¾" Tall, Iridescent Gold	$850
Compote, 6", Blue	$1,250
Compote, 8", Gold	$1,150
Cordial, 3½" Tall, Twisted Stem, Gold	$275
Cordial, 7" Tall, Blue	$575
Darner, Stocking, Blue	$775
Darner, Stocking, Gold	$625
Decanter with Stopper, 10¾" Tall Dimpled Body, Circular Foot, Gold, Marked "Aurene 2759"	$675

Goblet, 6¼" Tall, Twisted Stem, Gold	$375
Goblet, 8" Tall, Venetian Style, Gold	$550
Jardiniere, 6½" Tall, 3 Applied Handles, Gold	$1,500
Lamp, 12" Tall, Gold, Gilded Heart and Foliage	$4,250
Perfume Bottle with Stopper, 5⅞" Tall, Blue	$875
Perfume Bottle with Stopper, 8" Tall, Blue, Signed	$925
Plate, 8½", Gold	$350
Punch Bowl, 12", 5½" Tall, Footed, Blue	$1,150
Salt Dip, 2" Tall, Pedestal Foot, Gold, Signed	$275
Salt Dip, 8 Ribs, Blue	$425
Shade, 4½" Tall, Iridescent Green with Calcite Interior, Platinum Foliage Design	$1,500
Shade, 4½" Tall, Tulip Shape, Gold	$350
Shade, 6½" x 6", Green with Calcite Interior, Platinum Foliage Design	$1,550
Shade, Iridescent Brown with Calcite Lining, Blue Drape Design	$625
Shade, Iridescent Light Brown with Gold Leaves and Threading, Gold Lining	$375
Sherbet with Matching Underplate, Gold	$425
Tray, Oblong Stretched Border, Footed, Blue, Signed "Carder"	$875
Tumbler, 6" Tall, Iridescent Gold, Signed	$275
Vase, 2" Tall, Ovoid Form, Flared Rim, Iridescent Amber with Green Scrolling	$1,000
Vase with Holder, 4" Tall, Gold	$575
Vase, 5" Tall, Blue, Signed	$675
Vase, 5½" Tall, Iridescent Gold with Green and White Floral Design	$2,150
Vase, 6" Tall, Jack-in-the-Pulpit Style, Gold	$1,650
Vase, 6" Tall, Stick Style, Iridescent Blue	$725
Vase, 6" Tall, Iridescent Gold	$625
Vase, 6¼" Tall, Stump Shape, 3-Pronged, Gold, Signed	$725
Vase, 6½" Tall, 3-Stemmed, Blue	$1,000
Vase, 6¾" Tall, Iridescent Gold with Calcite Interior	$625
Vase, 7" Tall, Gold with Green Foliage and White Flowers	$3,500
Vase, 8¼" Tall, Gold, Inscribed "Steuben"	$1,500
Vase, 8½" Tall, Blue	$475
Vase, 9" Tall, 9" Top Diameter, Ruffled, Iridescent Gold	$1,250

Vase, 9" Tall, 3-Handled, Gold	$850
Vase, 9½" Tall, Cylindrical, Blue	$550
Vase, 10" Tall, Blue Button Design, Signed "F. Carder"	$1,650
Vase, 10" Tall, Blue, Paneled Design	$1,450
Vase, 10½" Tall, Green with Gold Interior, Rim, and Heart and Vine Decoration	$3,750
Vase, 11" Tall, Fan Shape, Iridescent Gold	$1,450
Vase, 12½" Tall, Blue with White Floral Design	$1,550
Vase, 12¾" Tall, Cylindrical, Footed, Flared Neck, Iridescent Gold	$1,550
Vase, 18" Tall, Cylindrical, Narrow, Gold	$1,250
Wineglass, 6" Tall, Air Twist Stem, Gold	$600

Boston & Sandwich Glass Company
1825–1880s

One of America's early successful firms, Boston & Sandwich was noted most for "sandwich" or pressed glass, from which its name is derived. They manufactured large amounts of this new hand-pressed glass but occasionally created objects of art in the form of lacy glass in the French style, paperweights, opal wares, engraved glass, and so on.

Basket Bride's, 9" Diameter, Overshot, Twisted Handle, Crystal	$300
Bottle with Screw-On Cap, 2½" Tall, Marbleized Cobalt and White	$175
Bottle, 8" Tall, Triple Cased with Cut Windows	$215
Bowl, 9", Lacy Design, Peacock Eye coloring	$175
Bowl with Matching Underplate, 3" Tall, Ruffled, Ruffled, Canary Yellow	$175
Butter Dish with Cover, 5" Tall, Bluerina (Blue to Amber Shading) with Enameled Floral Design	$700
Candlestick, 1⅞" Tall, Miniature, Crystal	$50
Candlestick, 6¾" Tall, Hexagonal Base, Clambroth, Dolphin Design	$475
Candlestick, 7" Tall, Circular Base, Petal Socket, Canary Yellow	$285
Candlestick, 7" Tall, Circular Diamond Point Base, Petal Socket, Canary Yellow	$355
Candlestick, 7" Tall, Clambroth, Petal and Loop Design	$235
Candlestick, 7" Tall, Hexagonal, Amber	$450
Candlestick, 7¼" Tall, Hexagonal Base, Green Socket, Clambroth Foot and Stem	$675
Candlestick, 7½" Tall, Hexagonal, Amber	$475
Candlestick, 7½" Tall, Hexagonal Base, Amethyst	$525

Boston & Sandwich Vase, Ruby Overlay. *Photo by Robin Rainwater. Courtesy of the Sandwich Glass Museum.*

Candlestick, 9" Tall, Cobalt Petal Socket, Clambroth Column	$325
Candlestick, 9¼" Tall, Hexagonal Base, Light Blue	$450
Candlestick, 9¾" Tall, Cobalt Socket, Clambroth Base and Stem, Acanthus Leaf Design	$450
Candlestick, 10¼" Tall, Single Step Base, Clambroth, Dolphin Design	$550
Candlestick, 10¼" Tall, Single Step Base, Green, Emerald Dolphin Design	$850
Candlestick, 10¼" Tall, Single Step Base, Blue Socket, Gilded, Clambroth, Dolphin Design	$800
Candlestick, 10¾" Tall, Double Step Base, Clambroth, Dolphin Design	$500
Candlestick, 11½" Tall, Crucifix Design, Canary Yellow	$450
Candlestick, 11½" Tall, Crucifix Design, Green	$750
Candlestick, 12" Tall, Hexagonal, Dark Blue	$500
Candlestick, Clambroth with Translucent Blue Acanthus Leaves	$750
Cheese Dish with Cover, 8", Crystal Overshot	$365
Claret Glass, 4½" Tall, Craquelle Finish with Ruby Threading	$100
Claret Glass, 5" Tall, Canary Yellow with Threading	$185
Cologne Bottle with Stopper, 6" Tall, Paneled Design, Amethyst	$650
Cologne Bottle with Ball Stopper, 8" Tall, Square Shape, Crystal Overshot	$250
Epergne, 12" Tall, Ruffled Bowl with Ruby Threading, Cut Circular Tray	$325
Ewer, 11" Tall, Clambroth with Applied Emerald Green Handle, Sterling Silver Fittings	$250

Fishbowl, 16½" Tall, Ruffled Crystal Base with Dolphin's Tail, Crystal Bowl with Etched Fish and Plants $850

Ice Cream Dish, 4¼" Diameter, 4¼" Tall, Circular Pedestal Base, White Casing with Ruby Threads $225

Ice Cream Tray, 13" Long, Crystal Overshot $200

Jam Jar, 3½" Tall, Opaque Blue, Bear Design $525

Jam Jar, 3¾" Tall, Clambroth, Bear Design $550

Jug, 6¾" Tall, Barrel Shape, Etched Bees and Floral Design, Crystal with Ruby Threading $225

Lamp, Kerosene, Jade Green with White Overlay $6,250

Paperweight, 2⅜" Diameter, Latticino with Pears, Cherries and Green Leaves $675

Paperweight, 2½" Diameter, Blue Poinsettia, Green Stem, Jeweled Leaves on White Latticino $1,000

Paperweight, 2½" Diameter, White Latticino Basket with Multicolored Flowers and Green Leaves $1,100

Paperweight, 2⅝" Diameter, White Latticino with Flowers, Green Leaves, Blue and White Canes $750

Paperweight, 2⅝" Diameter, Latticino with Pink Poinsettia and Green Leaves $375

Paperweight, 2¾" Diameter, 12-Ribbed Blue Dahlia Petals, Latticino Basket, Yellow Cane, Emerald Green Stem $475

Paperweight, 2¾" Diameter, 6-Petaled Flower and Leaves $825

Paperweight, 2⅞" Diameter, Candy Cane Design $265

Paperweight, 3" Diameter, Jasper with Jenny Lind Sulphide Bust $300

Paperweight, 3" Diameter, Sulphide Bird Design, Red, White, and Blue $350

Paperweight, 3½" Diameter, Sulphide Design of Queen Victoria and Prince Consort, Clear Glass $250

Pipe, 15" Long, Crystal with White Loopings $425

Pitcher, 6½" Tall, Amber Overshot, Green Reeded Handle $325

Pitcher, 8½" Tall, Tortoise-Shell Design, Amber Handle $475

Pitcher, 10" Tall, Fluted Top, Opalescent Amber $375

Pitcher, 10½" Tall, Blue Overshot, Amber Lip and Handle $525

Pitcher, 11" Tall, Pink Overshot with Crystal Handle $625

Pitcher, 12" Tall, Pear Shape, Fluted Rim, Crystal Crackle Design $385

Punch Bowl with Cover, 11" Tall, Overshot, Globe Shape, Fruit Stem Finial $625

Salt Dip, Boat Shape, 3½" Long, Blue Paddle Wheeler, Marked "Lafayet" on Wheels, Signed "B. & S. Glass Co." $725

Salt Dip, Rectangular (2⅞" x 1⅞"), Oval Knobs on Base, Scrolled, Stippled, Transparent Green, French Lacy Design $250

Salt Dip, Rectangular (2⅞" x 1⅞"), 4-Footed, Gothic Arches on Feet, Opalescent Blue
$250

Salt Dip, 3⅛" Diameter, Blue with Pressed Floral Design $325

Saltshaker, 2¾" Tall, Barrel Shape, Threaded Rim with Pewter Top, Dark Blue, Sunburst on Base, Marked "Patented December 25, 1877" $200

Tankard, 7¼" Tall, Engraved Cattails and Lilies, Amber with Threading $425

Tankard, 7½" Tall, Engraved Cattails, Water Lilies, and Crane; Crystal with Ruby Threading
$375

Tankard, 9" Tall, Dark Amber Overshot $750

Tankard, 11" Tall, Crystal Overshot, Reeded Handle $200

Tieback Knob, Cobalt to Clear Coloring over Mercury $125

Tieback Knob, Cranberry to Clear Coloring over Mercury $125

Tumbler, 3¼" Tall, Engraved Cattails and Lilies, Crystal with Ruby Threading $155

Tumbler, 3¾" Tall, Engraved Foliage, Crystal with Ruby Threading $165

Tumbler, 5½" Tall, Canary Yellow with Threading $215

Tumbler, 5½" Tall, Crystal with Blue Threading $225

Tumbler, 6" Tall, Engraved Floral Design on Top, Cranberry Threading on Bottom $225

Vase, 4" Tall, Enameled Floral Design $165

Vase, 6½" Tall, Bluerina (Blue to Amber Shading), Floral Design $375

Vase, 8½" Tall, Celery, Scalloped, Hourglass $150

Vase, 9¼" Tall, Flared, 3 Scrolled Gilded Feet, Opaque White with Red Enameled Leaves
$385

Vase, 9½" Tall, Tulip Style, Footed, Amethyst $1,250

Vase, 10" Tall, Cranberry Cut to Clear Roundels $475

Burmese
Mt. Washington Works and Pairpoint Manufacturing Company, 1880s–1950s

Burmese is characterized by a gradual shading of bright or canary yellow at the base to a salmon pink at the top. It is also thin and rather brittle. The colors were created by the addition of expensive elements, namely gold and uranium. The most common decorations applied were gold enamels (real gold mixed with acid) and popular cut patterns. Mt. Washington actually obtained an exclusive patent for producing Burmese in 1885. Production of it continued when Pairpoint purchased Mt. Washington (including some reissues made in the 1950s). Reproductions are difficult if not impossible to make because of the federal government's restrictions on the use of uranium. Mt. Washington also gave the English firm of Thomas Webb & Sons permission to produce this style.

Basket, Thorn Handle, 1950s (Gunderson)	$375
Bell, 6¾" Tall, Flared Base, Applied Amber Handle	$550
Bell, 11¾" Tall, Emerald Green Handle	$2650
Biscuit Jar, Barrel Shape, Silver-Plated Top, Oak Leaves and Acorn Design, Paper Label	$1,550
Bowl, 4", Fluted Edge	$350
Bowl, 4¾", Ice Cream, Ruffled	$375
Bowl, 6½", Footed, Applied Burmese Decoration	$1,500
Bowl, 7", Curled Feet (Gunderson)	$450
Bowl, 12", Scalloped	$1,050
Bowl, Rose, Gold Handles, Ivy Decor, Dickens' Verse	$3,150
Bowl, Rose, 2½", Hexagonal Top	$300
Butter Dish with Domed Cover, 9", Applied Crystal Handle, Satinized	$875
Castor Set, 5-Piece, Salt and Pepper Shakers with Silver-Plated Tops, 2 Globe-Shape Cruets with Pointed Stoppers, Footed Silver-Plated Stand	$3,500
Celery Vase, 10" Tall, Footed, Fluted Rim	$500
Cologne Bottle with Stopper, 5" Tall	$1,250
Cracker Jar with Cover, 6½" Tall, Acidized Finish, Applied Handles	$1,550
Creamer, 4" Tall, 3½" Diameter, Footed	$1,250
Creamer, 5½" Tall, Pitcher Style, Hobnail Pattern	$2,250
Cruet with Stopper, 7" Tall, Acid or Gloss Finish	$1,250
Cup, Satin Shading	$275
Epergne, 2 Circular Bowls, 4" Tall, Ruffled, Enameled Flowers, 4-Footed Silver-Plated Stand	$4,150

Burmese Art Glass. *Photo by Mark Pickvet.*

Ewer, 9" Tall, Squat Dome, Enameled Decoration	$2,150
Hat, 1⅛" Tall, 3" Brim, Upside Down, Gloss Finish	$700
Hat, 3½" x 2¾", Upside Down (Bryden)	$175
Hat, 3" Tall, 4" Brim, Upside Down, Diamond Quilted Pattern (Gunderson)	$375
Lamp, 3¾" Tall, Crimped Top and Plate, Fairy (Gunderson)	$650
Mustard Pot, Silver Cover, Acidized, Ribbed	$385
Perfume Bottle with Cut Stopper	$475
Pig, Miniature, ⅞" Long (Gunderson)	$185
Pitcher, 4¾" Tall, Square Lip, Yellow Reeded Handle, Enameled Mums	$875
Pitcher, 5" Tall, Inverted Thumbprint Pattern, Egyptian with Bow in Chariot Design	$1,450
Pitcher, Syrup with Silver Lid, 6" Tall, Enameled Decoration	$2,250
Pitcher, 6¾" Tall, Acidized, Ivy Design, Dickens Verse	$4,500
Pitcher, 9" Tall, Acidized, Gold Outlined Foliage Design	$2,750
Pitcher, 9" Tall, Tankard Style, Acidized, Gloss Finish	$1,250
Plate, 6"	$225
Plate, 9", Satinized (Gunderson)	$550
Salt and Pepper Shakers, Barrel Shape, Pewter Tops	$475
Saucer, Satin Shading	$200
Shade, 5¼" x 3¾", Satin Finish	$325
Sugar Shaker, 4" Tall, Globe Shape, Leaves and Berries Design	$875

Sweetmeat Jar with Cover, Silver-Plated Rim, Top Handle, Enameled Floral and Foliage Design	$475
Toothpick Holder, Circular Base, Square Top, Enameled Floral Design	$675
Toothpick Holder, Bowl Shape, Hexagonal Top, Satin Finish	$375
Toothpick Holder, Diamond Quilted Pattern	$475
Tumbler, 3⅞" Tall, Satin Finish	$250
Tumbler, 4" Tall, Dull or Shiny Finish (Gunderson)	$250
Tumbler, Thomas Hood Versed	$1,850
Vase, 2½" Tall, Bulbous, Diamond Quilted Pattern	$175
Vase, 3" Tall, Bulbous, 3-Petal Folded Rim	$285
Vase, 3¼" Tall, Ruffled	$275
Vase, 4" Tall, Ruffled, Fluted Base	$375
Vase, 4" Tall, Ruffled, Acidized, Enameled Foliage Design, 4-Footed Silver-Plated Holder	$850
Vase, 5" Tall, Ruffled, Footed	$375
Vase, 5" Tall, Enameled Yellow Handles, Pink and Yellow Enameled Floral Design	$2,350
Vase, 5½" Tall, Flared Rim, Acidized	$575
Vase, 6" Tall, Lily Shape, Paper Label	$1,000
Vase, 6¾" Tall, Jack-in-the-Pulpit Design, Enameled	$775
Vase, 7" Tall, Lily Shape, Paper Label	$850
Vase, 7" Tall, Acidized, Hobnail Pattern (Gunderson)	$400
Vase, 8" Tall, Lily Shape, Paper Label	$250
Vase, 9" Tall, Crimped, Jack-in-the-Pulpit Design	$875
Vase, 10" Tall, Lily Shape, Paper Label	$975
Vase, 10¾" Tall, Enameled Daisy and Butterfly Design, Versed (Poetry)	$3,250
Vase, 11¾" Tall, Enameled Daisy and Butterfly Design	$3,000
Vase, 11¾" Tall, Acidized, Enameled Scroll and Floral Design	$2,750
Vase, 11¾" Tall, Enameled Daisy and Butterfly Design, Montgomery Verse	$3,250
Vase, 12" Tall, Gloss Finish, Jack-in-the-Pulpit Design	$1,750
Vase, 12" Tall, Enameled Daisy and Butterfly Design, Montgomery Verse	$3,550
Vase, 12" Tall, Ibis and Pyramid Design	$5,500
Vase, 12" Tall, Crimped, Folded Rim, Floral Stem, Jack-in-the-Pulpit Design	$1,650

Vase, 12" Tall, Lily Shape, Paper Label	$1,250
Vase, 13½" Tall, Ruffled Foot and Top	$1,500
Vase, 14" Tall, Lily Shape, Paper Label	$1,250
Vase, 14½" Tall, Crimped Rim, Jack-in-the-Pulpit Design	$1,450
Vase, 15" Tall, 2-Handled, Enameled Yellow to Pink	$6,500
Vase, 17½" Tall, Egyptian Man with Staff Design	$5,850
Vase, 24" Tall, Lily Shape, Paper Label	$1,850
Vase, 26" Tall, Slender, Yellow to Pale Pink Coloring	$1,750
Whiskey Taster, 2¾" Tall, Diamond Quilted Pattern	$325

Central Glass Company
1866–1939

The Central Glass Company was established in 1866 in Wheeling, West Virginia. They were noted for many pressed patterns, etched crystal tableware, various art styles, and especially coin glass (separate listings follow). They were also one of the first to develop popular colors of the Depression era. Central closed permanently in 1939.

Bowl, 7½", Crystal, Etched Oak Leaf Band Pattern	$50
Bowl, 11½", Rolled Edge, Balda Lavender Pattern	$55
Butter Dish with Cover, Crystal, 2-Handled, Log Cabin Pattern	$385
Cake Stand, 12", Crystal, Etched Rose Pattern	$100
Candlestick, 9" Tall, Chinese Red with Gold Band, Crystal Top	$37.50
Candlestick, 9" Tall, Crystal, Frosted/Etched Cherub on Stem	$150
Candlestick, 15" Tall, Cobalt Blue with White Opal Highlights	$165
Celery Vase, 8" Tall, Crystal, Etched Rose Pattern	$85
Compote with Cover, 7" Tall, Stemmed, Crystal, Log Cabin Pattern	$385
Compote with Cover, 9", Crystal, Etched Rose Pattern	$150
Compote, 11", Amethyst with White Opal Highlights	$200
Compote, 13", Cobalt Blue with White Opal Highlights, Matches Candlestick	$215
Creamer, Crystal, Log Cabin Pattern	$150
Hair Receiver with Cover, Chippendale Pattern	$25
Lamp, 8¼" Tall, Oil, Crystal, Etched Oak Leaf Band Pattern	$110
Pickle Dish, Oblong, Owl Shaped, Crystal	$85
Pitcher, 8½" Tall, Crystal, Log Cabin Pattern	$325

Plate, 11½", Chinese Red Color with Wide Gold Band	$55
Salt Dish, Master, 4" Long, Rectangular, Tab Handles Crystal, Log Cabin Pattern	$85
Sandwich Server with Center Handle, Chinese Red Color with Wide Gold Band	$55
Sugar Dish with Cover, Crystal, Log Cabin Pattern	$225

Chocolate Indiana Tumbler and Goblet Company,
1900–03; Fenton Glass Company, 1907–10

Chocolate refers to the color of this earthy opaque glass. Variances are from a light tan to caramel to a deep chocolate brown. The dark chocolate color is most desirable and may sell for a 10–20 percent premium above lighter colors. Lighter Chocolate articles are sometimes incorrectly referred to as Caramel Slag Glass. Aside from a few novelty items such as glass animals, Chocolate-colored was produced in numerous patterns such as Austrian, Cactus, Dewey, Geneva, Melrose, Shuttle, and many others, including several floral and leaf designs. Jacob Rosenthal created the formula for the Indiana Tumbler & Goblet Company at Greentown, Indiana, and shared it with a few other select factories, including Fenton.

Berry, 4", Waterlily and Cattails (Fenton)	$140
Berry Set, 8" Diameter Fruit Bowl with 6 Sauce Dishes, Leaf Pattern	$600
Bowl, Fruit, 8" Diameter	$185
Bowl, Fruit, 9¼" Diameter, Cactus Pattern	$140
Bowl, 9½", Footed, Panther Pattern (Fenton)	$160
Bowl, Oval, 8¼" x 5¼", Geneva Pattern	$125
Butter Dish with Cover, Cactus Pattern	$325
Butter Dish with Cover, Pedestal, Cactus Pattern	$525
Butter Dish with Cover, 4" Diameter, Dewey Pattern	$250
Butter Dish with Cover, 5" Diameter, Dewey Pattern	$275
Butter Dish with Cover, Waterlily and Cattails (Fenton)	$200
Compote, 4½" Diameter, 3½" Tall, Geneva Pattern	$250
Compote, 5¼" Diameter, 5" Tall, Cactus Pattern	$225
Compote, 6" Diameter, Melrose Pattern with Scalloped Rim	$375
Compote, 7¼" Diameter, 5" Tall, Cactus Pattern	$235
Compote, 8¼" Diameter, Cactus Pattern	$340
Creamer, Cactus Pattern	$150
Creamer, Cord Drapery Pattern	$150
Creamer, Leaf Pattern	$125

Fenton Chocolate Art Glass. *Photo by Robin Rainwater. Courtesy of the Fenton Art Glass Museum.*

Creamer, Shuttle Pattern	$125
Creamer, Stirgil Pattern, Large (6" Tall)	$135
Creamer, Waterlily and Cattails (Fenton)	$135
Cruet with Stopper, Cactus Pattern	$325
Cruet with Stopper, Leaf Pattern	$300
Dolphin Dish with Cover, 9" Long, 4" Tall	$525
Fernery, 3-Footed, Fenton Vintage Pattern	$325
Hat Pin Box, Orange Tree Pattern	$425
Jelly Dish with Cover, Cord Drapery Pattern	$250
Lamp, Kerosene, Wild Rose Pattern	$375
Mug, Cactus Pattern	$125
Mug, Herringbone Pattern	$125
Mug, Shuttle Pattern	$150
Nappy, Triangular, Handled, Leaf Pattern	$125
Nappy, Handled, Masonic Pattern	$175
Pitcher, Syrup with Lid, Cactus Pattern	$200
Pitcher, Syrup with Lid, Cord Drapery Pattern	$425
Pitcher, Water, Cord Drapery Pattern	$400
Pitcher, Water, Deer Pattern	$575
Pitcher, Water, Feather Pattern	$950

Pitcher, Water, Heron Pattern	$450
Pitcher, Water, Indiana Feather Pattern	$975
Pitcher, Water, Ruffled Eve Pattern	$675
Pitcher, Water, Squirrel Pattern	$575
Pitcher, Water, Waterlily and Cattails (Fenton)	$575
Pitcher, Water, Wild Rose Pattern	$625
Relish, Oval (8" x 5"), Leaf Pattern	$125
Salt and Pepper Shakers, Leaf Pattern	$325
Sauce Dish, Cactus Pattern	$100
Sauce Dish, Dolphin Pattern	$375
Sauce Dish, Geneva Pattern	$100
Sauce Dish, Leaf Pattern	$100
Sauce Dish, Tassel Pattern	$200
Sauce Dish, Wild Rose Pattern	$150
Spooner, Austrian Pattern	$300
Spooner, Cactus Pattern	$175
Spooner, Cord Drapery Pattern	$165
Spooner, Dewey Pattern	$165
Spooner, Leaf Pattern	$165
Spooner, 2-Handled, Waterlily and Cattails (Fenton)	$165
Spooner, Wild Rose Pattern	$250
Stein, 8½" Tall, Pub Scene	$375
Sugar, Cord Drapery Pattern	$150
Sugar with Cover, Cactus Pattern	$250
Sugar with Cover, Chrysanthemum Pattern	$550
Sugar with Cover, Leaf Pattern	$185
Sugar with Cover, Waterlily and Cattails (Fenton)	$200
Sweetmeat Dish with Cover, Cactus Pattern	$625
Toothpick Holder, Cactus Pattern	$160
Toothpick Holder, Geneva Pattern	$225
Toothpick Holder, Picture Frame Design	$1,150

Tray, 11" Long, Leaf Pattern	$200
Tray, Oval (10¾" x 5½"), Leaf Pattern	$165
Tray, Serpentine, Dewey Pattern	$100
Tumbler, Biscuit Pattern	$250
Tumbler, Cactus Pattern	$125
Tumbler, Cord Drapery Pattern	$425
Tumbler, Leaf Pattern	$115
Tumbler, Sawtooth Pattern	$135
Tumbler, Shuttle Pattern	$150
Tumbler, Waterlily and Cattails (Fenton)	$150
Tumbler, Wild Rose Pattern	$200
Vase, 5¾" Tall, Fleur-De-Lis Pattern	$350
Vase, Scalloped Flange Pattern	$125

Coin Glass Central Glass Company
1890s

The first coin glass produced in America was made in 1892, the centennial year of the United States Mint. Silver dollars, half dollars, quarters, 20-cent pieces, dimes, and half dimes were reproduced in glass relief and then placed on each article. The coins in relief were usually frosted on clear crystal glass, but clear, amber, red, and gold examples were also made. The patterns were not identical to the actual minted coins; however, five short months after production, they were outlawed by the U.S. government as being a form of counterfeiting. Other medallions were allowed, such as Christopher Columbus ("Columbia coin glass") and other foreign explorers ("foreign coin glass"), as well as coats-of-arms. Fostoria also created a good deal of coin glass in the later 20th century, including some commissioned by Avon.

Bowl, 6", Scalloped Top, Frosted Coins	$450
Bowl, 6", Oval, Frosted Coins	$400
Bowl, 7", Scalloped Top, Frosted Coins	$475
Bowl, 7", Oval, Frosted Coins	$425
Bowl, 8", Scalloped Top, Frosted Coins	$500
Bowl, 8", Oval, Frosted Coins	$450
Bowl, 9", Scalloped Top, Frosted Coins	$525
Bowl, 9", Oval, Frosted Coins	$475

Bread Tray, Frosted Half Dollars and Silver Dollars	$550
Butter Dish with Cover, Half Dollars and Silver Dollars	$850
Cake Stand, 10" Diameter, Frosted Silver Dollars	$625
Cake Stand, 10" Diameter, Clear Silver Dollars	$425
Champagne Glass, Frosted Dimes	$550
Claret Glass, Frosted Half Dimes	$525
Compote, 5½" Diameter, 5½" Tall, Frosted Dimes and Quarters	$400
Compote with Cover, 6" Diameter, 9½" Tall, Silver Dollar	$625
Compote, 6½" Diameter, 8" Tall, Frosted Dimes and Quarters	$400
Compote, 7" Diameter, 5¾" Tall, Frosted Dimes and Quarters	$675
Compote, 8" Diameter, 11¼" Tall, Frosted Coins	$875
Compote with Cover, 8" Diameter, 11½" Tall, Frosted Coins	$900
Compote with Cover, 8" Diameter, High Pedestal, 1892 Quarters and Half Dollars	$625
Compote with Cover, 9" Diameter, Frosted Coins	$1,000
Compote with Cover, 6⅞" Tall, Frosted Coins	$800
Creamer, Frosted Coins in Base, 1 Handle	$525
Cruet with Stopper, 5½" Tall, Frosted Coins	$875
Epergne, Frosted Silver Dollars	$2,050
Goblet, 6½" Tall, Frosted Dimes	$475
Goblet, 7" Tall, Frosted Half Dollars	$575
Lamp, 4¾" Tall, Frosted 20-Cent Pieces	$600
Lamp, Kerosene, Handled, 5¼" Tall, Clear Quarters in Base	$625
Lamp, Kerosene, Pedestal Base, Frosted Quarters	$825
Lamp, Kerosene, Pedestal Base, Amber Stained Silver Dollars	$950
Lamp, Milk Glass, 8" Tall, Columbian Coin	$575
Mug, Frosted Coins	$625
Pickle Dish, Oval, 7½" x 3¾", Clear Coins	$350
Pitcher, Milk, Frosted Half Dollars	$775
Pitcher, Water, Frosted Coins	$850
Pitcher, Water, Gilded Columbian Coins in Base	$625
Preserve Tray, Single Crystal Silver Dollar in Center	$425

Relish, Frosted Coins	$375
Saltshaker with Pewter Top	$250
Sauce Dish, 4" Diameter, Frosted Quarters	$300
Spooner, Frosted Quarters	$550
Sugar with Cover, Frosted Coins	$700
Toothpick Holder, Clear or Frosted Coins	$350
Tray, Water, 10" Diameter, Frosted Dollars	$675
Tumbler, Frosted 1878 Dollar in Base	$335
Tumbler, Frosted 1879 Dollar in Base	$325
Tumbler, Frosted 1882 Dollar in Base	$325
Tumbler, Frosted Coins around Base	$250
Vase, Clear Dimes	$275
Vase, Frosted Quarters	$475
Vase, Clear Quarters	$400
Wineglass, Frosted Half Dimes	$775

Consolidated Lamp and Glass Company
1894–Early 1900s

Consolidated is best known for lamps and glass blown under the Florette and Guttate pattern names. Several color styles are apparent on much of their wares, including blue, green, pink, white, and yellow, many in opaque art styles, some trimmed in gold, and others in either satin or gloss finishes. A few articles were even made in apricot, Pigeon Blood (brown highlighting over ruby red, similar to that of a pigeon's darker or reddish-brown blood), and gilded forms. Nearly everything the company produced was functional tableware or for lighting.

Boat-Shape Dish, 13" Long, Frosted Lovebirds Design	$375
Bowl, 8", Opaque Blue, Dancing Sea Nymph Design	$400
Bowl, 10", Yellow, Orchid Design	$175
Butter Dish with Cover, White with Gold Trim	$175
Butter Dish with Cover, Pink, Florette Pattern	$285
Cake Plate, 12", Green, Bird and Iris Floral Design	$160
Candlestick, 6¾" Tall, Hummingbird Design	$185
Candlestick, 10½" Tall, Yellow, Iris Design	$90

Cigarette Box with Cover, Purple Lilac Design	$165
Cookie Jar, Pink with Silver-Plate	$375
Creamer, Pink Satin, Florette Pattern	$175
Cruet with Stopper, White	$300
Lamp, Miniature, Enameled Floral Design	$450
Lamp, Miniature, Various Leaf and Scrolling	$475
Lamp 8½" Tall, Pink, Guttate Pattern	$475
Lamp, 9" Tall, Pink and White, Florette Pattern	$500
Lamp, 10½" Tall, Enameled Daisies	$525
Lamp, 11" Tall, Milk Glass with Blue Floral Design	$550
Lamp, 11" Tall, Avocado Green with Yellow Scrolling	$550
Lamp, 12" Tall, Gone with the Wind, Regal Iris Pattern, Carnival Marigold	$3,650
Lamp, Oil, 12" Tall, Florette Pattern	$550
Lamp, 14" Tall, Apricot with Gilded Edging, Enameled Blue Floral Design	$775
Lamp, 15" Tall, Pink with White Floral Design, Gilded Edging	$825
Mustard Dish, Pink, Florette Pattern	$175
Pitcher, Syrup with Silver-Plated Rim, Blue	$350
Pitcher, Water, White, Guttate Pattern	$150
Pitcher, Water, White with Gold Trim, Guttate Pattern	$175
Pitcher, Water, Yellow Casing, Guttate Pattern	$475
Pitcher, Water, 7¼" Tall, Pink, Florette Pattern	$385
Plate, 8¼", Pink, Dancing Sea Nymph Design	$150
Salt and Pepper Shakers with Tops, Pink Casing, Guttate Pattern	$175
Salt and Pepper Shakers with Tops, Pink, Florette Pattern	$275
Spooner, Pink, Florette Pattern	$200
Sugar Dish, Pink, Florette Pattern	$175
Sugar Shaker with Top, Pink Casing, Guttate Pattern	$275
Sugar Shaker with Top, Pink, Florette Pattern	$235
Toothpick Holder, Yellow, Florette Pattern	$150
Toothpick Holder, Cranberry, Guttate Pattern	$200
Tumbler, Pink Casing, Guttate Pattern	$85

Tumbler, 6" Tall, Pink, Dancing Sea Nymph Design	$175
Vase, 7½" Tall, Florentine, Milk White	$125
Vase, 8" Tall, Pinecone Design, Opal Blue	$150
Vase, 8¼" Tall, Frosted Grasshoppers on Green Background	$150
Vase, 12" Tall, Green, Florette Pattern	$250
Vase, 18" Tall, Gold on Milk Glass, Blackberry Design	$300

Coralene
Mt. Washington Glass Works, 1880s–1890s

Coralene is sometimes referred to as mother-of-pearl for its pearly or coral-like sheen. Small glass beads of clear, colored, or opalescent glass are applied to an object, then fired on. There were several pattern styles, but most include coral, seaweed, and floral designs. Beware of reproductions or remakes where the beading is not fired on; it chips and flakes very easily.

Bowl, Rose, 3" Tall, 4½" Diameter, Crimped, Amber Foot, Pink with Yellow Seaweed Design	$450
Bowl, 5½", Blue, Herringbone Pattern with Pink Coral	$650
Cracker Jar with Silver-Plated Rim, Cover, and Handle; Beaded Fruit, Foliage, and Coral	$775
Cruet with Stopper, Pink Satin with Yellow Coral	$500
Decanter with Stopper, 10" Tall, Yellow Seaweed Decoration	$575
Mug, 2" Tall, Orange Seaweed with Turquoise Handle	$175
Perfume Bottle with Sterling Silver Stopper, 4¼" Tall, Mother-of-Pearl with Multicolored Coral	$525
Pitcher, 6¼" Tall, Yellow with White Lining, Multicolored Coral	$375
Pitcher, 7½" Tall, Orange and Green Coral, Orange Handle	$425
Pitcher, 8" Tall, Blue and Yellow Coral Design	$675
Pitcher, Water, 9½" Tall, Blue and Yellow Seaweed, White Handle, Blue Inner Casing	$925
Toothpick Holder, Yellow Seaweed with White Shading	$425
Tumbler, 4" Tall, Yellow Seaweed with Pink Shading	$300
Tumble-Up, Carafe with Lid, White Coral on Light Pink Cranberry	$450
Vase, 4" Tall, Blue with White Lining, Yellow Beading and Coral	$425

Coralene Vase. *Reproduced directly from an 1880s Mt. Washington advertisement.*

Vase, 5" Tall, White with Pink Coral Design	$125
Vase, 5" Tall, Yellow and Green Coral on a Dark Brown Background	$335
Vase, 5¾" Tall, Blue with Beaded Yellow Seaweed, White Inside	$600
Vase, 6" Tall, Ruffled, Blue Coral Design with White Floral Beading	$275
Vase, 6" Tall, Mother-of-Pearl, Floral and Sprayed Beading Design	$575
Vase, 7" Tall, Footed, Tan Satin Design	$775
Vase, 7½" Tall, Blue with Yellow Coral and Seaweed	$350
Vase, 8½" Tall, Flared Rim, Yellow Seaweed	$500
Vase, 9" Tall, Urn Shape, Vertical Rainbow Colors	$900
Vase, 9" Tall, Orange on White Coloring	$1,100
Vase, 10¼" Tall, Reeded and Scrolled Feet, Gold Rim, Green Leaves and Pink and Blue Floral Beading on a Cranberry Background	$575
Vase, 12" Tall, Blue with Yellow Beading and Coral	$1,450

Cranberry
Various Producers, 1820s–Present

Cranberry is sometimes referred to as a light ruby or rose red colored glass. It is a transparent glass the color of dark pink or light red cranberries. It was created by adding tiny amounts of gold oxide as the primary coloring agent. Larger amounts of gold produce a darker, true ruby red. Cranberry glass is one of the oldest forms of art glass in America and was made by many companies. Beware of cheaper flashed, coated, and stained articles in an identical or similar color. They chip and scratch more easily if the color is not consistent throughout the entire glass, inside and out. Cranberry is still being made today by a variety of individuals and modern art-glass companies.

Basket, 6" Tall, Vertical Ribbing, Scalloped, Clear Handle, Circular Foot	$250
Basket, 8" Tall, Ruffled, Crystal Handle	$275
Basket, 9" Tall, Applied Amber Feet and Handle, Gold Flecking	$175
Bell, 5" Tall, Dark Coloring	$150
Bell, 7" Tall, Gold Tracing	$550
Bell, 7½" Tall, Swirled with Crystal Handle	$400
Bell, 12" Tall, Clear Handle, Green Clapper	$375
Bottle, Perfume with Stopper, 3¼" Tall	$175
Bottle, Perfume with Cut Stopper, 8¼" Tall, Brass Ormolu at Base	$275
Bottle, Square, 8½" Tall, Vertical Ribbing	$185
Bowl, Finger, 3¼" Diameter, Ruffled	$150
Bowl, 4" Diameter with Hinged Cover	$225
Bowl, 7½" Diameter, Enameled Flowers	$265
Bowl, Flower, Ruffled, 3" Tall	$135
Bowl, Rose, Ruffled, Threaded Body, 3½" Diameter	$150
Box with Hinged Lid, 3" Tall, 3½" Square, Ribbed, Gold Decoration	$300
Butter Dish with Cover, Hobnail Pattern	$150
Candlestick, 9½" Tall, Swirled Design	$100
Castor Set, Pickle Dish in Silver-Plated Frame with Lid and Tongs (Several Designs)	$450
Chalice with Cover, 16" Tall, Gilded with Enameled Figure of Girl	$365
Cheese Dish, Cranberry Dome with Crystal Ball Handle and Crystal Underplate (Hobbs Brocunier)	$275
Cologne Bottle with Stopper, 6" Tall, Silver Overlay	$435
Cordial, 4" Tall, Gold Paneled, Clear Stem and Base	$135
Cracker Jar with Silver-Plated Cover, Rim, and Handle, 7¼" Tall, Square Shape, Gold Floral and Leaf Design	$475
Creamer, 4¼" Tall, Ruffled, Clear Handle, Shell Feet	$165
Creamer and Sugar Set in Silver-Plated Holder (Several Varieties)	$385
Cruet with Silver-Plated Stopper, 5½" Tall	$175

Cruet with Stopper, 6" Tall, Clear Handle	$300
Cruet with Cut Crystal Stopper, 6½" Tall, Clear Handle	$335
Cruet with Cut Crystal Stopper, 13" Tall, 4" Diameter, Gold Rose Decoration	$275
Cup, Loving, 3½" Tall, 3-Handled, Silver Overlay	$775
Cup, Punch, Clear Handle, Enameled Flowers	$75
Decanter without Stopper, 6" Tall	$225
Decanter with Crystal Cut Stopper, 10" Tall	$350
Decanter with Clear Stopper, 10½" Tall, Clear Handle, Enameled Floral Design	$375
Decanter with Clear Stopper, 11" Tall, Clear Handle, Inverted Thumbprint Pattern	$375
Decanter with Crystal Cut Stopper, 13" Tall, Applied Crystal Handle, Gold Rose and Foliage Design	$400
Epergne, 12" Tall, Single Trumpet Style	$300
Epergne, 12" Tall, Double Trumpet Style	$450
Epergne, 13½" Tall, 3 Trumpets, Crystal Base, Enameled Floral Design	$500
Epergne, 19" Tall, 5-Piece, Ruffled Bowl, Center Lily, 3 Jack-in-the-Pulpit Vases	$1,250
Ewer, 8½" Diameter, Applied Crystal Handle, Floral Decoration	$350
Hat, 2½" Tall	$200
Hat, 3" Tall, Silverplated Rim	$275
Lamp, Kerosene, 8½" Tall, Brass Base with Cranberry Shade	$500
Lamp, Kerosene, Swirled Shade, Brass Frame for Hanging	$525
Lamp, Oil, 18" Tall, Thumbprint Patterned Globe, Enameled Design	$725
Mug, 4" Tall, Clear Handle, Inverted Thumbprint Pattern	$135
Nappy, 6½", Cut Strawberry and Diamond (C. Dorflinger and Sons)	$675
Pitcher, Syrup, 6¾" Tall, Silver-Plated Handle and Spout	$475
Pitcher, 7½" Tall, Ruffled, Clear Handle, Enameled Floral Design	$350
Pitcher, Square Top, Bull's-Eye Pattern	$450
Pitcher, Water, 8" Tall, Inverted Thumbprint Pattern	$250
Pitcher, 8½" Tall, Tankard, Inverted Thumbprint Pattern	$550
Pitcher, 9" Tall, Swirl Pattern with Enameled Flowers	$350
Plate, 6" Diameter	$75
Plate, 8" Diameter	$85
Salt Dip, Footed, Enameled Floral Decoration	$225

Salt & Pepper Shakers, Metal Tops, Enameled Floral Design	$250
Sugar Bowl with Cover, Guttate Pattern (Consolidated)	$250
Sugar Bowl with Cover, Shell Feet	$200
Sugar Shaker with Silver Top, 6½" Tall, Drape Pattern	$165
Toothpick Holder, Barrel Shaped, Inverted Thumbprint Pattern	$200
Tumbler, 3½" Tall, Clear Pedestal Foot, Enameled Floral Design with Gold Decoration	$110
Tumbler, 4¾" Tall, Small Thumbprint Pattern	$115
Urn with Cover, 8¾" Tall, 5½" Diameter, Applied Floral Handle, Applied Crystal Floral Design	$1,000
Vase, 4¼" Tall, 4¼" Diameter, Ovoid with Flared Neck	$125
Vase, 5¼" Tall, 5¼" Diameter, Footed, Silver Leaves and Gold Floral and Butterfly Design	$475
Vase, 6¾" Tall, Flared, Clear Pedestal Base	$150
Vase, 7½" Tall, Enameled Gold and White Flowers	$175
Vase, 7½" Tall, Ruffled, Clear Circular Foot	$225
Vase, 8" Tall, Ruffled	$225
Vase, 8½" Tall, Enameled Gold and White Flowers	$235
Vase, 9½" Tall, Circular Base, Applied Crystal Floral and Foliage Design	$245
Vase, 10" Tall, Slender Form, Enameled Floral Design	$250
Vase, 12" Tall, Bubble Connector (Pairpoint)	$300
Vase, 12" Tall Cylindrical, 3-Footed	$250
Vase, 14" Tall, Pedestal Foot, Enameled White Scrolling	$300

Crown Milano
Mt. Washington Glass Works, 1890s

Crown Milano is another of Mt. Washington's patented art-glass patterns. It is character-ized by heavy gold enameling upon an opal or earth-toned background. Some contain jewel work or settings for glass beads. The name was derived from the signature, which is typically a crown within a wreath. For the most part, Crown Milano is identical in design to that of the older but less popular Albertine, glass originally created by Albert Steffin.

Basket, Bride's, 9" Tall, Folded Rim, White with Enameled Floral Design	$650
Basket, Bride's, 14¼" Tall, Ruffled, Yellow with Enameled Floral Design, Footed Silver-Plated Stand, Signed	$1,250

Crown Milano Basket. *Photo by Robin Rainwater.*

Biscuit Jar with Cover, 6" Tall, Thistle and Gold Enameled Design, Signed on Bottom and Cover	$1,950
Biscuit Jar with Cover, 8¼" Tall, White, Enameled Desert Scene, Cover Contains Silver Decoration, Pairpoint Stamp	$1,500
Biscuit Jar with Cover, 9" Tall, Floral and Foliage Design, Signed	$1,250
Bowl, 6", Crimped, Gold Rim, Pansy Design	$375
Bowl, 8", Fan Shape, Shallow, White Pansy Design	$475
Bowl, 9½", 3-Cornered, Yellow-Green Pansy Design	$575
Bowl, Rose, 4", Yellow with Gold Lines and Enameled Floral Design	$375
Cracker Jar with Silver-Plated Cover, Rim, and Handle, 5¾" Tall, 5¼" Diameter, Multicolored Floral Design with Gold Scrolling	$925
Cracker Jar with Cover, 7¼" Tall, Gold and Green Foliage Design, Signed	$950
Creamer, 3¼" Tall, Ribbed, White with Gold Decoration, Signed	$650
Ewer, Shepherd, Flock and Church Enameled Design	$4,250
Ewer, 10" Tall, Twisted Handle, Paneled Design	$2,250
Jar with Cover, 5¼" Tall, White Opal with Gold Beading	$950
Jardiniere, 6" Tall, 8" Diameter, Pink with Multicolored Cyrsanthemum Design, Gold Rim	$625
Jardiniere, 7" Tall, 9¼" Diameter, Pansy Design, Gold Rim	$825
Lamp, 1¾" Tall, Asian Man and Camel Design on Shade, Elephants on Base Globe, Metal Base	$5,850

Pitcher, Syrup, Silver-Plated Lid, 7½" Tall, White to Orange Shading, Blue Daisy and Green Foliage Design with Gold Butterfly	$850
Pitcher, Water, 12" Tall, White Floral Design, Signed	$1,750
Pitcher, Water, 13½" Tall, Bulbous, Rural Scene, Gold Decoration	$1,950
Powder Jar with Cover, 3" Tall, Ribbed, Enameled Floral Design, Signed	$850
Salt Dip, Pink Floral Design	$175
Spooner, Diamond Quilted Pattern, Chrysanthemum Design with Gold Trim	$750
Sugar with Cover, 6" Tall, Ribbed, Handled, White with Gold Decoration	$750
Sugar Shaker, 3" Tall, Ribbed, Orange to Yellow Shading, Foliage Design	$625
Sweetmeat Jar with Cover, 5" Tall, Embossed, Gold Wash Design, Signed	$1,000
Tumbler, Gloss Finish, 3¾" Tall, Enameled Floral and Wreath Design	$1,250
Urn with Crown-Shaped Cover, 16½" Tall, Foliage Decoration	$5,250
Vase, 3" Tall, Enameled Leaf Design	$750
Vase, 4" Tall, Iris and Foliage Design, Signed	$925
Vase, 5½" Tall, Scroll and Floral Design, Signed	$1,850
Vase, 6" Tall, Ribbed, Cream Ground with White Peony Blossoms	$1,500
Vase, 7" Tall, Swirled, Bulbous, Cactus and Foliage Design	$3,650
Vase, 8½" Tall, Swirled, Wild Fowl Design, Signed	$3,250
Vase, 9" Tall, Globular, Scrolls on Neck, Gold and Tan Fern Design	$1,350
Vase, 9½" Tall, 2-Handled, Opaque White with Multicolored Floral Design	$1,750
Vase, 10½" Tall, Duck Design	$4,250
Vase, 11" Tall, Baluster Shape, Gloss Finish, Gilded Handles, "The Courting Couple" Design, Scrolled Ribbons, Signed	$3,250
Vase, 11" Tall, Bulbous, Chrysanthemum Design, Signed	$1,600
Vase, 12¼" Tall, Flared Base, Rolled Rim, Gold Design and Beading on a Tan Ground	$1,650
Vase, 13" Tall, Angel Design	$3,250
Vase, 13" Tall, White to Green Shading, Gold Enamel	$1,350
Vase, 14" Tall, Handled, Floral Design	$1,750
Vase, 14" Tall, Handled, Acorn Design with Gold Trim, Signed	$1,950
Vase, 15" Tall, Gold Dragon Design, Signed	$2,750
Vase, 17" Tall, Duck Design, Signed "Frank Guba"	$6,250

Custard
Various Producers, 1890s–1915

Custard refers to the milky white to deep yellow opaque coloring like that of custard pudding. It is sometimes referred to as buttermilk because the color also resembles yellow buttermilk. Uranium salts are often added to produce a vibrant yellow opalescence that is very mildly radioactive (safe for one to handle!) and reacts to black light. Custard-style glass originated with the English and Bohemian makers in the 1870s and 1880s. American makers soon followed with their own formulas. As with most art glass, a variety of decorations and colors were applied to the base custard-colored glass. These include flashing or enameling of blue, brown, green, pink, red, and even gold gilding or painting. Flower enameling is the most common, but the basic glass itself was produced in numerous patterns by a host of companies.

Banana Boat, 4-Footed, 11" Oval, Geneva Pattern, Northwood	$165
Bowl, 7½", Ruffled, Grape and Cable Pattern, Northwood	$100
Bowl, 8", Banded Ring Pattern	$225
Bowl, 8½", Maple Leaf Pattern	$325
Bowl, 10½", Argonaut Shell Pattern	$300
Bowl, 11", Ruffled, Footed, Grape Pattern	$600
Bowl, 11½", Fan and Feather Pattern	$500
Bowl, 12", 3-Footed, Maple Leaf Pattern	$650
Butter Dish with Cover, Gold Decoration, Argonaut Shell Pattern	$475
Butter Dish with Cover, Beaded Circle, Cherry and Scale, Diamond, Grape, or Maple Leaf Pattern	$400
Butter Dish with Domed Cover, Gold Louis XV Pattern, Northwood	$375
Cologne Bottle with Stopper, 5½" Tall, Grape Pattern, Northwood	$850
Cologne Bottle with Stopper, 6¼" Tall, Scrolled Design	$425
Compote, Footed, Gold Louis XV Pattern, Northwood	$185
Cracker Jar with Cover, 2-Handled, Grape and Cable Pattern, Northwood	$775
Creamer, Argonaut Shell, Banded Ring, Beaded Circle, Chrysanthemum, Fan, Maple Leaf, Scrolled, or Victoria Pattern	$185
Creamer, Gold Louis XV Pattern, Northwood	$235
Cruet with Stopper, 5½" Tall, Banded Ring, Chrysanthemum, Grape, or Scrolled Pattern	$500
Cruet with Stopper, 6" Tall, Beaded Circle Pattern	$1,250
Cruet with Stopper, 6¼" Tall, Intaglio Design	$550

Cruet with Stopper, Gold Louis XV Pattern, Northwood	$525
Dresser Tray, Grape and Thumbprint Pattern, Northwood	$425
Goblet, Beaded Swag Pattern, Heisey	$100
Humidor with Cover, 7½" Tall, Grape Design	$350
Humidor with Cover, 8" Tall, Grape Design	$875
Jelly Dish, Everglade or Maple Leaf Pattern	$500
Jelly Dish, Inverted Fan and Feather Pattern	$550
Mug, Souvenir (Several Varieties)	$100
Napkin Ring, Souvenir (Several Varieties), Diamond Pattern	$175
Nappy, 6½", Ruffled	$115
Pickle Dish, 7½" Long, Beaded Swag Pattern	$425
Pitcher, Syrup with Lid, Geneva Pattern, Northwood	$375
Pitcher, Syrup with Lid, Scroll Pattern	$550
Pitcher, Water, 8" to 10" Tall, Argonaut Shell, Beaded Circle, Chrysanthemum, Diamond, Grape, Maple Leaf, Drape, or Scrolled Pattern	$550
Pitcher, Water, Gold Louis XV Pattern, Northwood	$425
Plate, 7½", Prayer Rug Design, Imperial	$125
Punch Bowl, Footed, Fan and Feather Pattern	$4,250
Punch Bowl with Stand, Grape and Cable Pattern, Northwood	$1,500
Punch Cup, Grape and Cable Pattern, Northwood	$100
Salt and Pepper Shakers, with Tops, Geneva Pattern	$225
Salt and Pepper Shakers, with Pewter Tops, Fan and Feather Pattern, Pink and Gold Trim	$725
Sauce Dish, Various Styles and Patterns	$100
Spooner, Argonaut Shell, Banded Ring, Beaded Circle, Everglade, Fan and Feather, Geneva, Grape, Maple Leaf, or Scrolled Pattern	$200
Sugar with Cover, Argonaut Shell, Banded Ring, Beaded Circle, Chrysanthemum, Maple Leaf, Scrolled, or Victoria Pattern	$275
Sugar with Cover, Gold King Louis XV Pattern, Northwood	$300
Toothpick Holder, 2¾" Tall, Chrysanthemum or Fan and Feather Pattern	$600
Toothpick Holder, Rose Decoration (Jefferson)	$375
Toothpick Holder, Wild Bouquet Pattern	$800

Toothpick Holder, 3" Tall, Ribbed Drape Pattern	$250
Toothpick Holder, Souvenir, Various Styles	$100
Tumbler, Banded Ring, Beaded Circle, Chrysanthemum, Everglade, Intaglio, Maple Leaf, Prayer Rug, Scrolled, or Victoria Pattern Tumbler	$175
Tumbler, Gold Louis XV Pattern, Northwood	$150
Vase, 6" Tall, Georgia Gem Pattern	$400
Vase, 7" Tall, Butterfly and Berry Design	$150
Vase, 7½" Tall, Banded Ring or Scrolled Pattern	$450
Vase, 10" Tall, Grape and Gothic Arch Pattern, Northwood	$350
Vase, Hat Shape, Ruffled, Grape and Arch Pattern	$125
Vase, Souvenir (Several Varieties)	$125
Whiskey Tumbler, Souvenir, Several Varieties	$100
Wineglass, Diamond Pattern	$115
Wineglass, Souvenir, Heisey	$100

Cut Velvet
Various Producers, 1880s–Early 1900s

Cut Velvet is characterized by two separate layers fused together that are blown into a mold. The result is a design that is raised on relief along with a satiny velvet texture. Although this style was made in a variety of colors and patterns, it is most often found in the Diamond Quilted pattern.

Bottle, 7¼" Tall, Pink with White Lining, Diamond Quilted Pattern	$275
Bottle, 8¼" Tall, Blue with White Lining, Diamond Quilted Pattern	$285
Bowl, Finger, 3½" Diameter, Pink with White Lining	$250
Bowl, Flower, 4" Diameter, Blue with White Lining	$250
Bowl, Flower, 4¼" Tall, Pink and White or Blue and White Shading, Diamond Quilted Pattern	$285
Bowl, 7" Ribbed, Tan	$335
Bowl, Rose, 3½", Crimped (4 or 6), Blue or Pink, Diamond Quilted Pattern	$250
Bowl, 3¾", 4" Tall, Blue, Diamond Quilted Pattern	$275
Creamer, 3½" Tall, Diamond Quilted Pattern	$425
Creamer, 5¼" Tall, Tan with White Lining, Ribbed	$250
Ewer, 11" Tall, Pink and White Shading, Diamond Quilted Pattern	$450

Ewer, 12" Tall, Pink and White Shading, Diamond Quilted Pattern	$475
Perfume Bottle with Stopper, 7½" Tall, Blue, Diamond Quilted Pattern	$275
Pitcher, 4½" Tall, Pink with White Lining, Amber Handle, Honeycomb Pattern	$575
Pitcher, Water, Yellow, Diamond Quilted Pattern	$750
Pitcher, 7½" Tall, Blue, Diamond Quilted Pattern	$450
Punch Cup, Pink with White Lining, Diamond Quilted Pattern	$155
Tumbler, 3½" Tall, Pink, Diamond Quilted Pattern	$350
Tumbler, 5" Tall, Pink or Blue, Diamond Quilted Pattern	$150
Vase, 5" Tall, 3" Diameter, Blue with White Lining, Diamond Quilted Pattern	$150
Vase, 5¼" Tall, Blue with White Lining	$150
Vase, 6" Tall, Ribbed, Butterscotch Color	$350
Vase, 6" Tall, 3¼" Diameter, Blue with White Lining, Diamond Quilted Pattern	$200
Vase, 6¼" Tall, Green with White Lining, Diamond Quilted Pattern	$225
Vase, 6½" Tall, Pleated Top, Dark Blue, Diamond Quilted Pattern	$550
Vase, 7" Tall, Ruffled, Footed, Pink to White Shading, Diamond Quilted Pattern	$275
Vase, 8" Tall, Blue with Vertical Ribbing	$285
Vase, 8" Tall, Blue Satin, Diamond Quilted Pattern	$475
Vase, 8¾" Tall, Blue, Diamond Quilted Pattern	$525
Vase, 9" Tall, Ruffled, Blue, Diamond Quilted Pattern	$550
Vase, 9¼", Flared, Ruffled, Diamond Quilted Pattern	$275
Vase, 10" Tall, Tricorner Rim, Pink with White Lining, Vertically Ribbed Design	$250
Vase, 11" Tall, Pink, Herringbone Pattern	$375
Vase, 11" Tall, Amethyst, Diamond Quilted Pattern	$575
Vase, 12" Tall, Jack-in-the-Pulpit Style, Iridescent Yellow and White with Red Lining	$400
Vase, 14" Tall, Butterscotch Color with White Lining, Diamond Quilted Pattern	$675

De Vilbiss
1900–1930s

The De Vilbiss Company purchased blank vases from other companies such as Cambridge, Fenton, Steuben, and so on. They decorated them by adding such things as bulbs, collars, decorations, and gilding. Many were signed, stamped, or labeled with the "De Vilbiss" or the "De Vilbiss—Made in U.S.A." trademark. They were most famous for perfume spray bottles, referred to as atomizers.

Bottle, Perfume, 5" Tall, Footed, Gold Trim	$240
Bottle, Perfume, 7" Tall, Gold Crackle with Black Trim	$185
Bottle, Perfume, Metallic Black with Chrome Neck	$135
Dresser Set, 7-Piece, Gold Trim with Enameled Flowers, Signed "De Vilbiss"	$1,150
Hairpin Box, Hinged Lid, Iridescent with Gilding	$225
Lamp, Perfume, 7" Tall, Glass Insert with Nude Figure	$350
Lamp, Perfume, 12" Tall, Glass Insert with Nude Figure	$525
Perfume Atomizer, 4¾" Tall, Gold Crackle Design with Beaded Flower at Top	$175
Perfume Atomizer, 6" Tall, Crystal Base, Orange Stain	$150
Perfume Atomizer, 6¼" Tall, Tasseled Bulb, Black	$135
Perfume Atomizer, 6½" Tall, Cranberry, Signed "De Vilbiss"	$150
Perfume Atomizer, 7¼" Tall, Crystal, Gold Draped Woman on Stem	$375
Perfume Atomizer, 7¾" Tall, Iridescent Orange, Signed "De Vilbiss"	$425
Perfume Atomizer, 9¼" Tall, Black and Gold	$235
Perfume Atomizer, Blue with Black Enameling	$135
Perfume Atomizer, Green with Cut Leaves, Signed "De Vilbiss"	$235
Perfume Atomizer, Gilded with Black Enameling	$175
Perfume Atomizer, Iridescent Amber, Signed "De Vilbiss"	$350
Perfume Atomizer, Gilded, Tapered Top, Amber Jewel Set in Cap	$425
Pin Tray, Black with Gold Trim	$75
Pin Tray, Rectangular (5½" x 3¼"), Black and Gold Decoration, Orange Stain	$75
Tray, Iridescent with Gilding	$100

Durand Art Glass Company
1897–1931

Victor Durand Jr. and his father, Victor Durand Sr., were from the famous glass town of Baccarat, France. Both Durands worked for Whitall-Tatum before establishing the Vineland Flint Manufacturing Company in 1897. Victor Durand Jr. established a firm in his own name in 1924 and continued producing art glass until his death in an automobile accident in 1931. Durand was one of the few companies (like Steuben and Tiffany) to make fancy blown art glass during the Depression years. They produced a variety of objects in various colors and patterns but are noted most for vases. Most of their products either contain a silver and black label "Durand" or an engraved silver signature in script. The script may also contain a wide V shape beneath it.

Bowl, 4½", Iridescent Blue with White Heart and Foliage Design	$500
Bowl, Flower, 6", Ruffled, Iridescent Gold, Signed "Durand"	$525
Bowl, Flower, 7½" Diameter, Iridescent Blue, Signed "Durand"	$1,100
Bowl, 10" Diameter, Orange and Gold	$750
Bowl, Blue and Silver, King Tut Pattern, Signed "Durand"	$850
Bowl with Cover, Red and White, Moorish Crackle Pattern	$375
Box with Cover, 3¼" x 2¾", Green and Gold, King Tut Pattern, Signed "Durand"	$1,450
Candlestick, 9" Tall, Amber with Blue Feathering	$185
Candlestick, 10" Tall, Green, King Tut Pattern	$800
Compote, 5½", Amethyst	$425
Compote, 7" Diameter, Gold and Iridescent, Numbered and Signed "Durand"	$600
Cup, Iridescent Gold, Signed "Durand"	$350
Decanter with Stopper, 12" Tall, Blue to Clear Shading, Signed "Durand"	$650
Jar with Cover, 7" Tall, Iridescent Red with Silver Threading	$4,250
Jar with Cover, 11" Tall, Green with White Iridescence, Signed "Durand 1994-8"	$1,750
Jar with Cover, 11" Tall, Calcite with Gold Feathers, Signed "Durand"	$1,850
Jar with Cover, 11" Tall, Vertical Ribs, Green Triple Overlay, Signed "Durand"	$3,500
Lamp, Electric, 7½" Tall	$1,100
Lamp, 24" Tall, Pulled Leaf Design with Threaded Overlay	$1,050
Light with Iron Holder, 9¾" Tall, Green, King Tut Pattern	$850
Perfume with Stopper, 6" Tall, Gold	$950
Plate, 8", Blue with Feathering	$425
Plate, 8", Red with White Feathers	$450
Plate, 8", Red and White, Engraved "Bridgeton Rose"	$475
Saucer, Iridescent Gold, Signed "Durand"	$250
Shade, 5½" Tall, Blue, White, and Gold Design (2 Styles)	$225
Sherbet, Green with White Feathering, Signed "Durand"	$425
Sherbet with Matching Underplate, 2-Piece Set, King Tut Pattern	$550

Tazza, 7¾" x 6¼", Iridescent Gold, Signed "Durand"	$1,250
Tumbler, Amber, Signed "Durand"	$175
Vase, 4" Tall, Iridescent Amber, Signed "Durand"	$250
Vase, 4" Tall, Iridescent Blue Feathering	$400
Vase, 4½" Tall, Iridescent Gold, Signed "Durand"	$425
Vase, 5½" Tall, Green and Gold on Opal, Egyptian Crackle Pattern	$1,050
Vase, 6" Tall, Green with Iridescent Gold and Platinum	$1,250
Vase, 6" Tall, Inverted Rim, Transparent Yellow, Raindrop Pattern, Signed "Durand 1968-6"	$1,000
Vase, 6¼" Tall, Flared, Iridescent Blue with Silver Threading, Signed "Durand 1710-6"	$1,250
Vase, 6¼" Tall, Gold Luster, Heart and Vine Design	$775
Vase, 6¼" Tall, Iridescent Orange with White Interior, Swirled Green King Tut Pattern, Signed "Durand"	$775
Vase, 6½" Tall, Blue and Black Cameo, Signed "Durand"	$2,500
Vase, 7" Tall, Iridescent Amber with Iridescent Bluish Green Scrolling King Tut Pattern, Signed "Durand"	$875
Vase, 7" Tall, Iridescent Blue	$625
Vase, 7" Tall, Oiled Luster with Opal, Signed "Durand"	$625
Vase, 7" Tall, Intaglio Cut, Signed "Durand"	$2,250
Vase, 7¼" Tall, Iridescent Gold, Signed "Durand"	$550
Vase, 7½" Tall, Iridescent Blue with White Hearts and Vines	$1,750
Vase, 8" Tall, Iridescent Green with Silver, King Tut Pattern, Signed "Durand"	$2,000
Vase, 8" Tall, Intaglio Cut with Iridescent Gold, Signed "Durand 20161-8"	$1,300
Vase, 8" Tall, Urn Shaped, Green and Gold, King Tut Pattern	$1,550
Vase, 8" Tall, Handled, Iridescent Yellow and Gold with Blue Edge, Engraved "Durand 1974-15"	$1,500
Vase, 8¼" Tall, Flared, Cased Amber to Gold with Iridescent Amber Lining, Green Scrolling, King Tut Pattern, Signed "Durand"	$1,250
Vase, 9", Green and Gold, King Tut Pattern	$1,150
Vase, 9" Tall, Green with White Interior and Silver Swirls, King Tut Pattern, Signed "Durand"	$1,250
Vase, 9¼" Tall, Blue and Ivory with Gold Interior	$1,250

Vase, 9¼" Tall, Urn Shape, White Exterior with Blue Color and Gold Threading, Yellow Interior, Signed "Durand"	$950
Vase, 9¾" Tall, White with Red Collar and Foot	$1,500
Vase, 9¾" Tall, Cut Vertically, Red and Clear Overlay	$1,175
Vase, 10" Tall, Iridescent Cobalt Blue, Signed "Durand"	$1,600
Vase, 10" Tall, Intaglio Cut, Crystal with Red Casing, Signed "Durand"	$1,250
Vase, 10" Tall, Iridescent Gold with Silver, King Tut Pattern, Signed "Durand 1910"	$1,050
Vase, 10" Tall, White, Orange, and Gray with Heart-Shape Leaves	$850
Vase, 10½" Tall, Frosted Glass with Blue and White Overlay, Signed "Durand"	$1,250
Vase, 10¾" Tall, Intaglio Cut with 4 Layers, Signed "Durand 1911-70"	$1,350
Vase, 10¾" Tall, Iridescent Gold, Jack-in-the-Pulpit Style	$850
Vase, 11½" Tall, Blue Exterior with Silver Interior, Signed "Durand"	$1,350
Vase, 12" Tall, Iridescent Amber with Opalescent Heart and Foliage, Signed "Durand"	$775
Vase, 12" Tall, Iridescent Blue with Gold Crackle, Signed "Durand"	$950
Vase, 12½" Tall, Red with Silver Exterior, Gold Interior, King Tut Pattern, Signed "Durand"	$1,650
Vase, 12½" Tall, Green with Pink Highlights, King Tut Pattern, Signed "Durand"	$1,650
Vase, 13" Tall, Green with White Feathers	$600
Vase, 15" Tall, Amber with Gold Iridescence	$1,250
Vase, 15½" Tall, Ivory on Gold, King Tut Pattern, Signed "Durand 1974-15"	$1,450
Vase, 16" Tall, Bulbous, Iridescent Blue, Signed "Durand"	$1,350
Vase, 16¼" Tall, Bulbous, Iridescent Blue to Purple Shading, Signed "Durand 1716-16"	$1,550
Wineglass, Yellow with Feathering	$300

Favrile
Louis Comfort Tiffany, 1892–1920s

Developed and patented in 1892, Favrile is characterized by multicolored iridescent base colors decorated with applied or embedded designs. Favrile was one of the leading designs in the art nouveau period, and others sought to copy or create similar color effects. Refer to "Tiffany" and "Tiffany Lamps" near the end of the chapter for additional listings.

Collection of Favrile Art Glass Vases. *Courtesy of the Corning Museum of Glass.*

Bonbon Dish, 5" Diameter, 3" Tall, Bluish Green Opalescent, Internal Herringbone Design, Stamped "L.C.T. Favrile 1700"	$750
Bowl, 4", Iridescent Gold with Purple and Green Highlights	$750
Bowl, 5¼", Iridescent Gold, Ribbed Design	$850
Bowl, 6¼", Iridescent Opal Blue	$950
Bowl, 8", 3¾" Tall, Footed, Iridescent Gold, Signed "L.C. Tiffany Favrile 1848"	$1,050
Bowl, 10", 3½" Tall, Iridescent Gold, Ribbed, Stamped "L.C. Tiffany Favrile 1925"	$775
Candlestick, 20" Tall, Gold with Bronze Base, Lily Pad Design, Stamped "27466"	$1,150
Candy Jar with Cover, 9¾" Tall, Circular Foot, Iridescent Blue, Marked "X236 L.C. Tiffany—Favrile"	$2,500
Chandelier, 50" Tall Alamander Leaded Glass, 6 Chains, 6 Gold Favrile Shades Marked "L.C.T.," Multicolored Floral Design	$36,500
Compote, 5" Tall, Blue, Signed "L.C.T. Favrile"	$1,550
Compote, 5¼" Tall, Ruffled, Gold, Signed "L.C. Tiffany—Favrile"	$850
Floriform, 11¼" Tall, Gold Ribbing, Signed "L.C. Tiffany Favrile—455H"	$1,350
Flower Bowl with Frog, 10¾" Diameter, Blue Floral Design, Bowl Signed "Louis C. Tiffany—Furnaces Inc. Favrile," Frog Signed "L.C. Tiffany—Favrile"	$2,650
Frog, Flower, 3¾" Tall, Double, Signed "L.C. Tiffany Favrile—5678K"	$700
Jar, Ginger with Cover, 8½" Tall, Yellow with Green Glaze, Signed "L.C. Tiffany—Favrile"	$2,650
Jug with Handle, 4" Tall, Blue, Signed "L.C. Tiffany—Favrile"	$1,150
Lamp, 17¾" Tall, Venetian Style, Gilded Shade in Bronze Mount, Iridescent Gold, Signed "L.C.T."	$4,000

Lamp, 28" Tall, 22" Diameter, Cabochon Jewels; Iridescent Amber, Blue, and Green; Dragonfly Border $46,500

Perfume with Stopper, 4¼" Tall, Iridescent Blue with Blue Highlights, Signed "L.C. Tiffany Favrile—923OG" $950

Plate, 8¼", Cobalt Blue and Iridescent Gold, Egyptian Chain Design, Stamped "L.C. Tiffany Favrile X77" $1,750

Plate, 10½", Iridescent Green, Signed "L.C. Tiffany" $1,150

Sherbet, 3½" Tall, Gold, Intaglio Engraved Grapes, Signed "1225 L.C.T. Favrile" $875

Tazza, 10" Diameter, 5½" Tall, Domed Foot, Iridescent Blue with Purple Highlights $2,400

Vase, 2½" Tall, Urn Shape, Red Exterior, Yellow Interior, Signed "1611K L. C. Tiffany Favrile" $2,000

Vase, 3½" Tall, Iridescent Gold, Green Leaf Deisgn, Signed "L.C. Tiffany #5212" $750

Vase, 4" Tall, Flared, Iridescent Gold, Signed "1027-883 GM—L.C. Tiffany Favrile" $650

Vase, 5" Tall, Ovoid Form, Yellow with Cobalt, Signed $18,500

Vase, 5½" Tall, Flared, Iridescent Gold, Dimpled Surface, Signed $1,250

Vase, 6" Tall, Crystal with Multicolored Morning Glories, Signed "L.C. Tiffany—Favrile" $3,250

Vase, 6¼" Tall, Inverted Rim, Multicolored Cameo Floral Design, Signed "L.C. Tiffany—Favrile" $5,000

Vase, 7" Tall, Opal Blue with Gold Foliage, Signed $850

Vase, 7¼" Tall, Flask Shape, Lava, "L.C. Tiffany - Favrile" $21,500

Vase, 8" Tall, Iridescent Blue and Swirled Design, Signed $1,500

Vase, 8" Tall, Flared, Iridescent Ruby Red with Black Foot and Rim, Engraved "1636 K L.C. Tiffany Favrile" $7,500

Vase, 9" Tall, Urn Shape, Iridescent Gold, Cameo Foliage, Signed "Louis C. Tiffany Favrile 6368N" $3,000

Vase, 9¼" Tall, Floriform, Gold with Green Lily Pads, Signed "L.C. Tiffany—Favrile" $1,500

Vase, 10" Tall, Iridescent Gold, Intaglio Floral Design, Signed "1153—3643K L.C. Tiffany Favrile" $2,750

Vase, 11¼" Tall, Jack-in-the-Pulpit Style, Blue, Signed "L.C. Tiffany—Favrile" $3,650

Vase, 12" Tall, Floriform, Blue with Trailing Green, Lily Pads, Signed "L.C. Tiffany—Favrile" $3,750

Vase, 13" Tall, Double Gourd Form, Internal Cross-Thread Diamond Design in Blue, Green, and Orange; Aquamarine Body and Iridescent Gold, Signed "L.C. Tiffany Favrile 1540P" $3,650

Vase, 15" Tall, Opal White, Iridescent Wavy Green and Gold Design	$2,250
Vase, 15½" Tall, Green with Amber Lily Pads and Millefiori Flowers, Signed "L.C. Tiffany—Favrile"	$4,750
Vase, 16½" Tall, Jack-in-the-Pulpit, Iridescent Gold, Foot Inscribed "7841B L.C. Tiffany Favrile"	$5,250
Vase, 18½" Tall, Opal with Gold Feathering	$6,500
Vase, 19¼" Tall, Urn Shape, Gold Foot, Iridescent Blue on Gold with Blue and Amber Bands, Signed "5622G L.C. Tiffany—Favrile"	$6,500
Vase, 19½" Tall, Jack-in-the-Pulpit Style, Blue, Signed "L.C. Tiffany—Favrile"	$37,500
Vase, 23¼" Tall, Cylindrical, Opaque Olive Green with Iridescent Gold Trailings, Stamped "L.C. Tiffany—Favrile 2900G Exhibition Piece"	$38,500
Wineglass, 8" Tall, Circular Foot, Opalescent Pink Bowl, Green Stem, Signed "L.C.T. Favrile"	$525

Fostoria Glass Company
1887–1920s

Iris is Fostoria's most recognizable form of art glass and was produced before 1920. It is often confused with Steuben's Aurene and Tiffany's Favrile. Iris is identified by paper labels and usually has a base color of opal glass. The interiors are highlighted in gold and the exteriors in a wide variety of iridescent colors. Like Fenton, many of Fostoria's patterns appear in later chapters. The company remained in operation until 1986.

Bowl, Opal with Gold, Iris Pattern	$275
Compote with Cover, Opal ith Gold, Iris Pattern	$300
Epergne, 14½" Oblong Bowl, 9" Tall, Single Flower, Opalescent Pink, Heirloom Cutting	$175
Figurine, Chinese Lotus, 12¼" Tall, Silver Mist Figurine	$300
Figurine, St. Francis, 13½" Tall, Silver Mist Figurine	$400
Lamp, 15" Tall, Opal with Green and Gold, Footed	$1,500
Lamp, 15¼" Tall, Domical Shade, Baluster Base, Opal with Green Feathers, Amber Edge	$1,500
Owl Bookends, Black Glass, Pair	$500
Shade, 7", Opal with Green, Iris Pattern	$250
Shade, Opal with Gold Over Green, Iris Pattern	$250
Shade, Gilded with Green and Gold, Iris Pattern	$250
Shade, Ruffled, White with Gold, Gold Lining, Iris Pattern	$275

Shade, 4-Sided, Opal with Green and Gold, Iris Pattern	$275
Shade, Green, Platinum King Tut Pattern	$575
Shade, Opalescent with Green and Gold Outlining, Iris Pattern	$250
Vase, 4½" Tall, Footed, Opal with Gold, Iris Pattern	$250
Vase, 8" Tall, Flared, Royal Blue Color	$200
Vase, 8½" Tall, Opal with Green, Iris Pattern	$275
Vase, 24" Tall, Swung Style, Opalescent Pink, Heirloom Cutting	$150

Fry, H. C. Glass Company
1902–34

Fry glass is usually found in fine cut and ovenware examples; however, as with many others, the H. C. Glass Company experimented with color effects. Their most noteworthy artistic products were opal or opaline Foval and Pearl Art styles. Both are characterized by a white opalescence with color accents. Some of their products were also decorated with silver and colored threading.

Basket, 7½" Tall, 7½" Diameter, Opal with Blue Handle	$500
Bowl, 10", White Opal with Blue Trim	$350
Bowl, 11", Centerpiece, White Opal, Cobalt Blue Feet	$250
Bowl, 12", Centerpiece, Green Base, Opalescent	$425
Bread Pan, Fry Ovenware, Opalescent	$75
Butter Dish with Cover, Pearl Oven Ware	$115
Candlestick, 10", White Opal with Blue Threading	$165
Candlestick, 12" Tall, White Opal with Jade Green Threading and Rim	$650
Candlestick, 12" Tall, White Opal with Blue Handle	$185
Casserole Dish, Miniature (Children's), 4" Diameter, Fry Ovenware	$90
Casserole Dish with Cover, 1½ qt., Oval, Blue Finial, Fry Ovenware, Dated 1925–6	$85
Coffeepot with Cover, White Opal with Blue Handle and Finial	$625
Compote, 7", Opalescent White with Blue Threading	$400
Creamer, Opal with Blue Handle	$250
Cruet, Opal with Cobalt Blue Handle and Cobalt Blue Stopper	$500
Cup, White Opal with Cobalt Blue Handle	$110
Cup, Opal with Jade Green	$95
Cup with Underplate, Handled, Opaque Blue	$115

Custard Cup, Fry Ovenware, Dated 1919	$35
Decanter with Stopper, 9" Tall, Footed, Foval with Applied Blue Handle	$225
Measuring Cup, ½ Cup, 3-Spout, Fry Ovenware	$115
Nappy, Handled, Opaline	$100
Pie Plate, Fry Ovenware	$45
Pitcher, Water, 8" Tall, Blue and White Opal with Amethyst Handle	$475
Pitcher with Cover, Clear Craquelle with Jade Green Handle	$215
Plate, 7½", Jade with Silver Floral Decoration	$175
Plate, Grill, 10½", Pearl Oven Ware	$50
Platter, 17", Fry Oven Ware	$85
Reamer, Juice, Opaline	$85
Saucer, White Opal	$45
Saucer, Opal with Jade Green	$60
Sherbet, Opal with Blue Stem and Foot	$135
Sugar, Opal with Blue Handles	$125
Teapot with Cover, Opaline with Green Spout and Handle	$325
Toothpick Holder, 2¼" Tall, Opal with Blue Handles	$100
Vase, 8", White Opal with Lavender Top, Signed "Fry"	$300
Vase, 9½", White Opal with Blue Top, Signed "Fry"	$225
Vase, 11" Tall, Opaline with Blue Spiral Twist and Blue Rim	$325
Vase, Clear Craquelle with Applied Amethyst Rosettes	$105
Vase, Opal with Blue Pedestal Vase	$450

Gillinder & Sons
1867–92

The Gillinders built a small glasshouse and presented many of their products during the 1876 Centennial Exposition in Philadelphia. Some are even marked "Centennial 1876" or "Gillinder and Sons, Centennial Exhibition." They also gave away small novelty items as souvenirs such as glass hats and slippers. Many of their products are frosted, cut, and pressed into many shapes. "Lion" below refers to a head finial, whereas the frosted lion appears on the object as a frosted design. The cameo vases are particularly rare and valuable. For lion pieces that are not frosted, reduce the prices by 25 percent.

Bowl with Cover, Oval (6½" x 4¼"), Frosted Lion	$125
Bowl with Cover, Oval (6⅞" x 3⅞"), Frosted Lion	$175

Bowl with Cover, Oval (7½" x 4¾"), Frosted Lion	$200
Bowl with Cover, Oval (8" x 5"), Frosted Lion	$175
Bowl with Cover, Oval (9" x 5½"), Frosted Lion	$225
Bread Plate, 12", Frosted Lion	$125
Bust, Abraham Lincoln, 6" Tall, Opaque White	$675
Bust, William Shakespeare, 5" Tall, Frosted Bust	$475
Bust, George Washington, 5" Tall	$425
Butter Dish with Cover, Lion Head Finial	$200
Cake Stand, Frosted Lion Design	$125
Celery Vase, Etched Lion Design	$150
Celery Vase, Frosted Lion	$125
Champagne Glass, Frosted Lion	$200
Cheese Dish with Cover, Lion Head Finial	$450
Children's Miniature Set, 5-Piece Lion (Creamer and Sugar, Covered Compote, Stemmed Glass, Stemmed Covered Compote)	$575
Compote, 7¾" to 8" Diameter, Frosted Lion	$165
Compote, 7" Oval, Lion Finial	$175
Compote, 8" Oval, Frosted Lion	$185
Compote, 9" Oval, Frosted Lion	$200
Compote with Cover, 6¾" Oval, 7" Tall, Lion	$200
Compote with Cover, 7" Diameter, 11" Tall, Lion	$225
Compote with Cover, 7¾" Oval, Lion	$225
Compote with Cover, 8" Diameter, 13" Tall, Lion	$250
Cordial, Frosted Lion	$200
Creamer, Frosted Lion	$125
Duck Dish (Duck Cover), Amber	$100
Egg Cup, 3½" Tall, Frosted Lion	$150
Figurine, Buddha, 5¾" Tall, Orange, Signed "Gillinder"	$175
Figurine, Buddha, 6" Tall, Amber	$100
Goblet, 6¼" Tall, Frosted Lion	$125
Jar, Marmalade, with Cover, Lion Finial	$175
Paperweight, Challinor, 3" Diameter, Faceted, Concentric Colored Rings	$425

Paperweight, Frosted Lion	$200
Paperweight, Intaglio Portrait of Abraham Lincoln	$175
Paperweight, Ruth the Gleaner	$200
Pitcher, Syrup with Metal Lid, Frosted Lion	$400
Pitcher, Milk, 6½" Tall, Frosted Lion	$475
Pitcher, Water, 8¼" Tall, Frosted Lion	$375
Pitcher, Water, Hexagonal, Alternating Draped Women in Gothic Arches	$575
Plate, 10", Blaine Design, Signed "Jacobus"	$325
Plate, 10", Warrior, Signed "Jacobus"	$250
Plate, 10½", Handled, Frosted Lion	$125
Platter, Oval (10½" x 9"), Lion Handles	$150
Platter, 12¼" Oval, Frosted Lion Center	$150
Relish Dish, 8½" Long, Frosted Lion Handles	$100
Salt Dip, Rectangular, 3½" Long, Frosted Lion	$450
Sauce Dish, 5" Diameter, Footed, Frosted Lion	$75
Slipper, Lady's Glass, Marked "Gillinder & Sons Centennial Exhibition"	$90
Spooner, Frosted Lion	$100
Sugar Dish with Cover, 3½" Tall, Frosted Lion	$150
Toothpick Holder, 2½" Tall, Baby Chick	$175
Vase, 6½" Tall, Frosted Lion	$150
Vase, Frosted, Pressed "Gillinder Centennial"	$90
Vase, Cameo, 6¾" Tall, White Leaves on Blue Background	$2,350
Vase, Cameo, Ruffled, Footed, Floral Design on a Ruby Red Background	$3,150
Vase, Cameo, 7¾" Tall, Floral Design on Yellow Background, Flared	$2,450
Vase, Cameo, 8½" Tall, Floral Design on Blue Background, Flared	$2,850
Wineglass, 5¾" Tall, Frosted Lion	$250

Handel and Company
1885–1936

Some of the most exquisite lamps ever made in America were fabricated by Handel and signed by numerous individual artists working in the company. Chipped glass effects, hand-decorated interiors, bent inserts, metal or leaded shades, fired-on metallic stains, gilding, cameo-engraving, and etchings can all be found on these famous lamps. Even the bases were quite elaborate; copper, brass, bronze, and white plated metals were used and decorated as well. Handel also produced some tableware, opal glass, and a few nonglass products (wood, metal, porcelain, and pottery items).

Bowl, 8", Enameled Trees Design, Signed	$250
Cake Plate, 10", 2 Handles, Pink Floral Design with Gold Edge	$175
Candlestick, 8½" Tall, Footed, Frosted with Enameled Landscape and Windmills	$1,000
Candlestick, 9" Tall, Amber with Etched Floral Design	$375
Cigar Holder with Hinged Lid, 6" x 3¼", Bear Design	$375
Humidor with Pewter Cover, 5" Tall, Opal, Owl and Branch Design, Signed and Numbered	$575
Humidor with Cover, Shriner's Fez and Printed "Cigars" on Cover, Brown and Green, Gold and White Trim, Man Riding Camel Design	$1000
Humidor with Pewter Cover, Opal with Brown and Green, Horse and Dog Design, Signed "Braun"	$625
Humidor with Silver-Plated Cover, Green Ground, Indian Design, Signed	$575
Lamp, 6¾" Tall, Double Green and Yellow Mica Shades	$1,550
Lamp, 7" Tall, Crystal Flecked Design, Bronze Base, Signed	$1,250
Lamp, 7¼" Tall, Cone Shade, Blue and White Globe, Metal Base	$675
Lamp, 8½" Tall, Glass Base, Blue Floral Design	$1,450
Lamp, 9" Tall, Multicolored Floral Design on Red Background	$6,850
Lamp, 9" Tall, Multicolored Parrots and Tropical Foliage Design	$4,850
Lamp, 9¼" Tall, 3-Footed, Shaded Amber to Blue	$1,275
Lamp, 9½" Tall, Brass Base, Amber and Brown Swirled Shade	$1,300
Lamp, 10" Tall, Green and Yellow Floral Design on a White Background, Brass Base, Signed	$2,350
Lamp, 10½" Tall, Green and Red Floral Design on a Yellow Background, Signed	$1,650
Lamp, 11" Tall, Red and White Floral Design on a Brown Background, Signed	$4,650
Lamp, 11¼" Tall, Green and White Lily Design, Signed "Handel"	$6,850
Lamp, 12" Tall, Multicolored Lake and Trees on Yellow Background, Signed	$6,900
Lamp, 12" Tall, Windmill Design, Dark Bronze Base	$2,350
Lamp, 12" Tall, Light Ice Blue Mica Shade with Birds and Foliage, Brass Base	$10,750
Lamp, 14" Tall, Bronze Base, Orange Wavy Pattern with Yellow Domed Shade	$1,250

Lamp, 15" Tall, Reverse Painted Shade, Multicolored Landscape Design with Tan Trees and Orange Water on a Green Background	$3,150
Lamp, Wall Globe, 16" Diameter, Black with Pink Roses and Blue and Yellow Parrots, Signed	$11,500
Lamp, Wall Globe, 18" Diameter, Cobalt Blue Bird on Floral Background	$750
Lamp, 19" Tall, Amber and Green, Tan Shade, Metal Base	$2,250
Lamp, 22½" Tall, Green Domed Shade, Multicolored Storm at Sea Design	$3,650
Lamp, 22½" Tall, Red Domed Shade, Pine Needle Design	$3,250
Lamp, 26" Tall, Bronze Base, Multicolored Rainforest Scene	$11,000
Lamp, 28" Tall, Leaded Blue Domed Shade, Bronze Base, Egyptian (Sphinx) Design	$11,750
Lamp, 29" Tall, Leaded Blue Domed Shade, Metal Base, Tree and Foliage Design	$13,500
Pitcher, 9½", Pink Roses and White Carnations	$425
Vase, 5½" Tall, 4" Diameter, White Floral Design on Green Background	$525
Vase, 7½" Tall, Green Trees and Foliage on Yellow Background	$775
Vase, 10" Tall, Green and Brown Forest Design, Signed	$2,450
Vase, 12" Tall, Multicolored Floral and Scrolled Design, Signed	$1,000

Heisey, A. H. Glass Company
1896–1957

A. H. Heisey himself began producing glass as early as the 1860s; however, it wasn't until the official A. H. Heisey Glass Co. was established at Newark, Ohio, in 1896 that a good deal of glass came from the factory. Heisey was noted early on for producing some cut patterns and finely etched glass, along with some limited art styles. The company followed glass trends by later producing some carnival, Depression, and post-Depression crystal patterns before closing permanently in 1957.

Boat Dish, 11" Long, Winged Scroll Pattern	$175
Bowl, 8", Green with Gold Trim, Fancy Loop Pattern	$50
Bowl, 11", Cornucopia Shaped, Cobalt Blue, Warwick Pattern	$525
Bowl, 11½", Bluish Green, Ridgeleigh Pattern	$300
Bowl, 12", Centerpiece, Amber with Etched Floral Design, Waverly Pattern, Sea Horse Foot	$275
Bowl, Rose, 4", Emerald Green, Pineapple and Fan Pattern	$125
Butter Dish with Domed Cover, Winged Scroll Pattern	$275

Candlestick, 6" Tall, Yellow with Chintz Etching	$100
Candy Box with Cover, Crystal with Etched Rose, Bow Knot Finial, Waverly Pattern	$250
Cocktail Glass, Crystal with Burgundy Bands and Gold Trim	$50
Cocktail Shaker, 7¾" Tall, Engraved Forest Scene	$175
Cordial, Alexandrite, Carcassone Pattern	$175
Cruet with Stopper, Winged Scroll Pattern	$300
Cup, Yellow, Empress Pattern	$40
Cup, Custard, Winged Scroll Pattern	$100
Decanter with Stopper, Alexandrite, Carcassone Pattern	$675
Goblet, 6½" Tall, Cobalt Blue	$150
Humidor with Cover, 8¼" Tall, Winged Scroll Pattern	$325
Ice Bucket, Dolphin Feet, Sterling Overlay	$150
Lamp, Hurricane, Lariat Pattern	$75
Lemon Dish with Cover in Farberware Metal Holder, 6½" Long (Oval), Dolphin Finial, Empress Pattern	$100
Match Holder, Winged Scroll Pattern	$275
Mug, Beer, 12 oz., Yellow, Old Sandwich Pattern	$175
Mug, Beer, 18 oz., Cobalt Blue, Old Sandwich Pattern	$375
Mustard Jar with Cover, 4¼" Tall, Green, Twist Design	$125
Nut Dish, Alexandrite, Empress Pattern	$200
Pitcher, Syrup with Silver-Plated Lid, Winged Scroll Pattern	$625
Pitcher, Water, 9" Tall, Winged Scroll Pattern	$475
Pitcher, 9½" Tall, 48 oz., Dolphin Foot, Sahara Yellow Color	$225
Pitcher, Water, Tankard Style, 3 qt., Crystal, Engraved Greek Key Pattern	$325
Plate, 5", Pink, Yeoman Pattern	$15
Plate, 6", Yellow, Old Sandwich Pattern	$20
Plate, 7", Square, Alexandrite	$75
Punch Bowl, 15" Diameter, Cobalt Blue, Victorian Pattern	$250
Punch Cup, Cobalt Blue, Victorian Pattern	$15
Sauce Dish, 4½" Diameter, Winged Scroll Pattern	$75
Saucer, Yellow, Empress Pattern	$15

Spooner, Winged Scroll Pattern	$175
Toothpick Holder, Custard, Various Souvenir Styles	$100
Toothpick Holder, Emerald Green, Gold Trim	$125
Tumbler, Footed, 12 oz., Cobalt Blue, Carcassone Pattern	$100
Vase, 9" Tall, Tulip Shape, Footed, Cobalt Blue	$550

Hobbs, Brockunier and Company
1863–91

The most popular art form created by this company was Frances Ware. It is characterized by an amber color, fluted rims, a hobnail pattern, and an allover camphor staining. The purpose of the stain is to invoke a somewhat dull or flat finish.

Bonbon Dish with Cover, 6", Amber Finial Frances Ware	$200
Bowl, 3½", Finger, Amber Rim, Frances Ware, Hobnail Pattern	$55
Bowl, 4", Frances Ware, Hobnail Pattern	$65
Bowl, 7½", Frances Ware, Hobnail Pattern	$85
Bowl, 8" Square, Frances Ware	$150
Bowl, 9", Frances Ware	$135
Bowl, 14¼" x 4¾" Boat Shape, Daisy and Button Pattern	$500
Butter Dish with Cover, Amber Rim, Frosted, Hobnail Pattern	$200
Butter Dish with Cover, Frosted, Frances Ware	$200
Carafe, Water, Frosted with Amber Flashing, Block Design	$200
Celery Vase, Square Shaped, Daisy and Button Pattern, Vaseline	$125
Cheese Dish with Cover, Blue Ball Handle and Crystal Underplate, Circle Pattern, Bluerina Color	$1,000
Creamer, Amber Rim, Hobnail Pattern	$85
Creamer, Amber Rim, Frosted, Hobnail Pattern	$135
Creamer, Amber Rim, Frosted, Frances Ware, Hobnail Pattern	$125
Cruet with Stopper, Amber Rim, Frosted Hobnail, Frances Ware	$750
Cruet with Stopper, Opalescent Vaseline, Hobnail Pattern	$550
Custard Cup, Applied Handle, Footed, Hexagon Patter	$60
Pitcher, Syrup with Pewter Lid, Frosted, Frances Ware, Hobnail Pattern	$300
Pitcher, Milk, 5" Tall, Amber Rim, Hobnail Pattern	$275

Pitcher, Milk, 5½" Tall, Frosted, Frances Ware	$300
Pitcher, Water, 8" Tall, Globe Shape, Amber Neck and Rim, Hobnail Pattern	$350
Pitcher, Water, 8½" Tall, Square Top, Frances Ware, Amber Rim, Frosted Hobnail Pattern	$350
Pitcher, Water, 9" Tall, Cranberry Crackle Design with Applied Crystal Handle	$350
Pitcher, Water, Hexagon Block Pattern, Ruby Stained with Engraved Leaf Design Applied Crystal Handle	$350
Plate, 5¾" Square, Frosted, Frances Ware, Hobnail Pattern	$55
Saltshaker, Amber Rim, Frances Ware, Hobnail Pattern	$175
Sauce Dish, Frances Ware, Hobnail Pattern	$65
Spooner, Amber Rim, Frosted, Hobnail Pattern	$95
Sugar with Cover, Amber Rim, Hobnail Pattern	$125
Sugar with Cover, Amber Rim, Frosted, Hobnail Pattern	$175
Toothpick Holder, Daisy and Button Pattern	$275
Toothpick Holder, 2" Tall, Frances Ware	$125
Tray, 12" x 7", Frances Ware	$150
Tray, 14" x 9½", Frosted, Frances Ware	$325
Tumbler, Amber Ribbon, Hobnail Pattern	$500
Tumbler, 4" Tall, Frosted, Frances Ware	$85
Vase, 7" Tall, Fluted Rim, Opalescent Pink with White Hobnails	$375

Holly Amber
Indiana Tumbler and Goblet Company, 1903

Holly Amber is a rare pressed art design featuring holly leaves on colored glass that shades from a light creamy opalescent to a darker brown-amber. The color is sometimes referred to as Golden Agate. It was made only from January 1, 1903, to June 13, 1903.

Bowl, Berry, 7½" Oval, 4½" Tall	$700
Bowl, Berry, 8½", 3½" Tall	$1,050
Bowl, 10" Rectangular	$1,100
Butter Dish with Cover, 7¼", Domed with Tapered Top	$1,750
Cake Salver, 9½" Diameter	$2,250
Compote with Cover, 4½"	$1,750
Compote, 4¾", Open	$550

Compote with Cover, 6½" Diameter	$2,000
Compote with Cover, 8½" Diameter	$2,150
Compote with Cover, 12½" Diameter	$2,250
Creamer, 3" Tall	$1,250
Cruet with Stopper, 6¼" to 6½" Tall	$2,550
Cup, Handled, 5" Tall	$850
Dolphin Dish with Cover, 7"	$1,750
Match Holder	$525
Mug, Handled, 4" Tall, Amber White Handle	$725
Mug, Handled, 4½" Tall, Amber White Handle	$825
Nappy, 1 Handle	$475
Parfait, 6" Tall	$750
Pickle Dish, 6½" x 4", 2-Handled	$625
Pitcher, Syrup with Tin or Silver-Plated Lid, 5¾" Tall	$2,150
Pitcher, Water, 8¾" Tall	$2,750
Plate, 7½", Square	$950
Plate, 9¼"	$3,500
Relish Dish, 7½" Oblong	$950
Salt and Pepper Shakers	$1,750
Sauce Dish	$450
Spooner, 4" Tall, 2⅝" Base Diameter, 3½" Top Diameter	$550
Sugar Dish with Cover	$1,850
Toothpick Holder, 2½" Tall	$750
Toothpick Holder, 5" Tall, Pedestal Base	$1,500
Tumbler, 4" Tall, Holly Branch Panels, Transparent Amber Rim	$650
Tumbler, Water, Wreath in Base	$650
Vase, 6" Tall, Footed	$925

Honesdale Decorating Company
1901–32

Honesdale operated as a branch of C. Dorflinger and Sons. It served primarily as a decorating firm for glass vases and other articles by enameling, engraving, etching, gilding, and using silver and gold trims. Fired-on iridescent colors were used as well. The company was sold to a Viennese glassmaker named Carl Prosch, who had also worked for Dorflinger. The business was permanently closed in 1932.

Bowl, 8", Cameo Design with Green Scrolls	$375
Goblet, 7" Tall, Gold Design and Border (Heisey Blank)	$100
Plate, 8½", Amethyst with Gold Rim	$150
Tumbler, 4½" Tall, Crystal with Enameled Rooster	$50
Tumbler, 6¼" Tall, Crystal with Gold Trim	$75
Vase, 5" Tall, Light Iridescent with Blue Cameo Scrolls	$375
Vase, 6½" Tall, Multicolored Floral Design on a Blue Base	$450
Vase, 7" Tall, Flared, Yellow Cameo Mums Outlined in Blue	$475
Vase, 8½" Tall, Green, Purple, and Red Floral Design Outlined in Gold, Gold Beaded Rim, Signed	$625
Vase, 9" Tall, Green Acid Cut Back Design, Crystal Base with Gold Trim, Signed	$650
Vase, 9" Tall, Green Cameo Scrolls with Gold	$675
Vase, 10" Tall, Green and Gold Cameo, Signed	$650
Vase, 10" Tall, Yellow Cameo Outlined in Crystal	$550
Vase, 10¾" Tall, Blue Cameo with Gold, Gilded Rim	$750
Vase, 11" Tall, Amethyst Cameo on Crystal, Gilded, Signed	$625
Vase, 11" Tall, Red Cameo with Hunting Scene	$1,350
Vase, 11½" Tall, Blue Cameo on Crystal Base, Gilded, Signed	$850
Vase, 12" Tall, Iridescent with Gilding	$575
Vase, 12" Tall, Red Cameo on Frosted Crystal, Gold Outline, Flared	$875
Vase, 12" Tall, Green Cameo with Gold Outline, Geese and Cattails Design	$850
Vase, 12½" Tall, Blue Cameo on Frosted Crystal, Gilded Outline, Etched Floral and Scroll Designs, Signed "Honesdale"	$1,000
Vase, 13½" Tall, Blue and Yellow Floral Design on a Crystal Base, Gilded Outline	$625
Vase, 14" Tall, Crystal with Gilding, Signed "Honesdale"	$575
Vase, 14" Tall, Emerald Green Background with Gilding, Floral Design	$325
Vase, 14" Tall, Orange and Crystal Cameo, Gilding, Chrysanthemum and Foliage Design	$1,500
Vase, 14½" Tall, Gilded, Etched, Versailles Pattern	$350
Vase, 17½" Tall, Crystal with Gold Tracing, Basket-Weave Design	$1,350

Imperial Glass Company
1901–1920s

Imperial was a major manufacturer of both carnival and Depression glass but did experiment early with iridescent art forms such as vases. Imperial Jewels was a pressed and blown colored glass introduced in 1916.

Bowl, 6½", Opaque Green, Jewels	$100
Bowl, 8½", Opaque Blue and Purple, Jewels	$275
Bowl, 9", Ribbed, Amber, Signed	$250
Bowl, 10", Light Blue with Pressed Pillar Flutes	$50
Bowl, Rose, Amethyst, Jewels, Signed	$185
Candlestick, 7¾" Tall, Black Amethyst, Jewels	$250
Candlestick, 10" Tall, Crystal with Ruby Red Holder and Base	$135
Candy Dish with Cover, Pink, Jewels	$65
Compote, 7½", Iridescent Teal, Jewels	$85
Pitcher, Water, 8½" Tall, Cobalt Blue, Hobnail Pattern	$450
Pitcher, Water, 10" Tall, Opaque Yellow with White Loops, Applied Crystal Handle	$275
Plate, 8", Iridescent Green, Jewels	$65
Plate, 9", Opal White, Jewels	$85
Sweetmeat Jar with Cover, Blue, Jewels	$185
Vase, 6" Tall, Iridescent Blue with White Foliage	$315
Vase, 6" Tall, Amethyst, Jewels	$225
Vase, 6" Tall, Ruffled, Ruby Red	$250
Vase, 6½" Tall, Green Loops on Blue Oval	$300
Vase, 7" Tall, Iridescent White, Gold Loops	$400
Vase, 7¾" Tall, Flared, Footed, Iridescent Green Ground, Silver Designs	$575
Vase, 8" Tall, Frosted Ground, Iridescent Blue Designs	$250
Vase, 8½" Tall, Blue, Imperial Jewels	$425
Vase, 9" Tall, Blue Loops on Opal	$425
Vase, 9" Tall, White Foliage on Green Background, Orange Neck	$275
Vase, 9½" Tall, 3-Handled, Green Floral Design with Orange Interior	$475
Vase, 10" Tall, Opaque White, Blue Loops	$375
Vase, 10" Tall, Green Scrolling, Orange Interior	$275

Vase, 10½" Tall, Orange with Gold Swirls	$375
Vase, 11¼" Tall, Green Leafing on White, Orange Interior	$575

Kew Blas
Union Glass Company, 1893–1924

W. S. Blake, the superintendent at Union Glass, created the name Kew Blas by rearranging the letters of his name. It was made in a variety of colors such as brown, cream, green, tan, white, and several shades of these basic colors. Kew Blas is fairly scarce and is often confused with other art glass produced in the same colors by other companies. It is also sometimes found etched or signed on the underside.

Bowl, 5", Flared, Ribbed, Iridescent Gold	$275
Bowl, 6", Light Blue Opal, 3-Footed, Flared, White Interior, Signed	$525
Bowl, 6½", Iridescent Gold and Green, Zipper Pattern, Signed	$825
Bowl, 14", Red, Feather Design, Signed	$1,500
Bowl, Rose, 4½", Tan with Iridescent Green and Gold Zipper Pattern	$1,000
Candlestick, 8" Tall, Iridescent Gold with Swirled Stem, Signed	$400
Candlestick, 9" Tall, Calcite and Gold with Green Feather Design, Signed	$425
Compote, 5" Tall, 4" Diameter, 3-Footed, Iridescent Gold	$425
Compote, 6" Tall, 4½" Diameter, Iridescent Gold Design	$500
Compote, 7" Tall, Ribbed, Stem Twist, Iridescent Gold with Pink Highlights	$550
Creamer, 3¼", Iridescent Gold, Signed	$625
Cup; Iridescent Green, Gold, and Ivory, Applied Handle, Feather Design, Signed	$900
Decanter with Enameled Stopper, 15" Tall, Ribbed, Gold	$1,250
Goblet, 6" Tall, Knob Stem, Iridescent Gold	$400
Pitcher, 4½" Tall, Gold with Green Feather Design, Gold Interior, Swirled Handle	$900
Salt Dip, Iridescent Gold	$250
Saucer, Iridescent Green, Gold, and Ivory, Feather Design, Signed	$325
Tumbler, 3½" Tall, 4-Sided, Iridescent Gold	$625
Tumbler, 4" Tall, Gold with Feather Design	$575
Vase, 4¼" Tall, 5¼" Diameter, Emerald Green with Iridescent Purple Lining, Hexagon Pattern	$800
Vase, 5½" Tall, Iridescent Gold on White	$650
Vase, 5¾" Tall, Flared, Ruffled, Iridescent Amber, Fish-Scale Pattern	$650

Kew Blas Bowl. *Photo by Robin Rainwater.*

Vase, 6" Tall, Calcite, Wavy Gold Design, Gold Interior	$725
Vase, 6½" Tall, Green and Gold Feathers on an Iridescent Gold Background, Signed	$1,075
Vase, 7" Tall, Gold and Green with Diagonal Stripes, Signed	$650
Vase, 8½" Tall, Iridescent Gold	$550
Vase, 9" Tall, Calcite, Gold and Green Feather Design, Signed	$1,050
Vase, 10" Tall, Iridescent Gold with Green Foliage	$550
Vase, 12" Tall, Iridescent Gold, Cattail Design	$1,400
Wineglass, 4¾" Tall, Twisted Stem, Iridescent Gold, Signed	$265

Kimble Glass Company
1930s

Cluthra-designed art glass was Kimble's only popular product. It is characterized by brilliant gloss-finished colors with cloud formations and multiple air bubbles of varying sizes. It is often confused with Steuben's Cluthra, which usually has a higher concentration of bubbles. Some pieces are signed in silver with the Kimble name or a *K* with a date and number code. Also, a few can be found with the Durand-Kimble signature, indicating a brief partnership between the two companies.

Bowl, Globe Shape, Blue with Streaked Orange and Brown, Cluthra Design, Signed, Numbered	$350
Vase, 4¼" Tall, Light Blue and Orange, Cluthra Design, Signed	$350
Vase, 5" Tall, Green to White Shading, Cluthra Design	$475
Vase, 5" Tall, Blue, Cluthra Design, Signed	$475

Vase, 6" Tall, White, Cluthra Design, Signed	$275
Vase, 6½" Tall, Green, Orange, White, and Yellow, Cluthra Design, Signed	$1,350
Vase, 6½" Tall, Flared, Triple-Hued, Cluthra Design	$850
Vase, 7¾" Tall, White, Signed	$325
Vase, 8" Tall, Green with White Enameling, Signed	$350
Vase, 8½" Tall, Footed, Orange and White, Cluthra Design	$375
Vase, 10" Tall, Crystal with Green to White Shading, Enameled Floral Design, Signed	$325
Vase, 10" Tall, Blue, Cluthra Design	$450
Vase, 11½" Tall, Blue and White, Cluthra Design, Signed	$450
Vase, 12" Tall, White with Enameled Design, Signed "Durand-Kimball"	$550
Vase, 12" Tall, Jade Green and White, Cluthra Design, Signed, Numbered	$550
Vase, 18" Tall, Blue and Yellow, Cluthra Design, Signed	$775

Libbey Art Glass
1878–1930s

Although Libbey is better known for brilliant cut crystal, they did continue some of the traditions of the New England Glass Company, which William L. Libbey purchased. Amberina was their most popular form of art glass, but a few other items such as souvenir items (from the 1893 World's Fair), Maize (corn-cob designs), ornamental glassware, and experimental shading. (See additional entries under "Amberina" and "Peach Blow.")

Bowl, 2½", Cream-Colored Satin, Signed	$975
Bowl, 7", Flared, Pink with Trapped Bubbles, Swirl Pattern, Signed	$375
Bowl, 8¾", Opaque White with Green Leaves, Maize Pattern	$275
Box, 4¼", Cream Satin Finish, Enameled Daisies, Marked "World's Fair 1893," Signed "Libbey Cut"	$525
Candlestick, 6" Tall, Crystal Stem and Foot, Red Feather Top, Signed	$1,075
Candlestick, 6" Tall, Crystal Foot and Stem, Opalescent Cup with Pink Interior, Signed "Libbey"	$1,150
Candlestick, 8" Tall, Air Twist Stem	$275
Celery Vase, 6½" Tall, Clear Iridescent, Maize Pattern, Amber Kernels and Blue Leaves	$400
Champagne Glass, Squirrel Stem, Signed "Libbey"	$250
Cocktail Glass, Crow Stem, Signed "Libbey"	$125

Cocktail Glass, Opalescent Kangaroo Stem, Signed "Libbey" — $225

Compote, 3⅜" Tall, 5¾" Diameter, Circular Foot, Gold Knob, Blue to Iridescent Gold Shading — $600

Cruet with Stopper, Clear Iridescent, Maize Pattern — $275

Cup, Marked "World's Fair 1893" — $125

Cup, Vaseline, Marked "World's Fair 1893" — $175

Goblet, 6¼" Tall, Raised Blown Opalescent Drops Over Bowl, Low Circular Foot, Morning Mist Pattern — $215

Goblet, 9⅛" Tall, Circular Foot, 4 Globe-Shape Bubbles in Stem; Ruby Flashed Bowl with Engraved Scroll, Foliage, and Ribbons, "Campanille" Pattern — $800

Goblet, 9¼" Tall, Cut Circular Foot, Rub Knob on Stem, Cased Pink and White Victorian Cameo Cut Design, 4 Lady Cameos Separated by Columns — $5,850

Goblet, 10¾" Tall, Engraved Circular Foot, Spiral Engraved Stem with Ruby Threading, Engraved Fruit Baskets and Scrolls on Bowl — $800

Paperweight, Lady's Head, Marked "World's Fair 1893" — $275

Paperweight, Frosted, Lady's Head Design, Marked "Columbian Exposition 1893" — $475

Pitcher, Syrup with Pewter Lid, 6" Tall, Iridescent Gold Corn Cob, Blue Husks, Maize Pattern — $675

Plate, 7¾", Ship (Santa Maria), Sepia-Hued — $675

Salt and Pepper Shakers, Blue, Egg Design, Marked "1893 Exposition" — $450

Salt and Pepper Shakers, Brass Tops, Maize Pattern — $350

Saucer, Leaf Shape, Marked "World's Fair 1893" — $85

Saucer, Vaseline, Marked "World's Fair 1893" — $105

Sugar Shaker, 5½" Tall, Brass Top, Opaque Cream with Blue Husks — $250

Sugar Shaker, 5½" Tall, Brass Top, Opaque Cream with Green Husks — $375

Sugar Shaker, 5½" Tall, Brass Top, Opaque Cream with Yellow Husks — $300

Tazza, 6" Tall, Opalescent Bowl and Foot, Crystal Stem, Blue-Swirled Threading — $1,150

Toothpick Holder, Pink Shading to White, Blue and Green Floral Pattern, Gold Inscribed "Little Lob" — $175

Toothpick Holder, Yellow with Green Leaves Outlined in Gold, Maize Pattern — $575

Tumbler, 3" Tall, Crystal Foot, Dark Green Prunts, Signed "Libbey" — $215

Tumbler, Iridescent Gold Ear with Blue Leaves, Maize Pattern — $325

Vase, 4½" Tall, Mushroom Shape, Signed "Libbey" — $1,175

Vase, 6½" Tall, Domed Circular Foot, Engraved Sitting Gazelle, Modern American Series	$300
Vase, 8" Tall, Opaque White with Green Husks, "Maize" Pattern	$275
Vase, 8" Tall, Crystal Pedestal Base, White Opal with Pink Feathering, Signed	$625
Vase, 9" Tall, Flared, Vertically Ribbed, White Opal with Blue Feathering, Signed	$300
Vase, 10" Tall, Opalescent Rabbit Base	$325
Vase, 10⅞" Tall, Flared, 3 Bubble Round Strawberry-Shape Feet, Crystal, Modern American Series	$325
Vase, 11¼" Tall, Circular Foot, Amber Stem, Signed "Libbey"	$875
Vase, 12½" Tall, Circular Foot, Ribbed, Signed "Libbey"	$1,225
Vase, 13½" Tall, Footed, Emerald Green with Engraved Floral Design, Signed "Libbey"	$1,000
Wineglass, 5" Tall, Opalescent Monkey Stem, Crystal Bowl, Signed "Libbey"	$175
Wineglass, 6" Tall, Kangaroo Stem, Crystal, Signed "Libbey"	$250
Wineglass, Opalescent Polar Bear Stem, Crystal Bowl, Signed "Libbey"	$185

Locke Art Glass
1891–1920s

After leaving the New England/Libbey Glass Companies in 1891, Joseph Locke founded his own cutting and decorating shop. Blanks were purchased from Dorflinger, and, as a result, some of Locke's art glass is similar to Dorflinger's Kalana designs. Locke's knowledge and original designs were instrumental in New England/ Libbey's production of Amberina, Pomona, Peach Blow, and so on. He continued producing these styles with his own company.

Brandy Glass, 3¼" Tall, Etched Floral Design, Paper Sticker	$165
Champagne Glass, 6" Tall, Poppy Pattern	$155
Goblet, 6¼" Tall, Etched Vines, Signed	$165
Goblet, 6¾" Tall, Etched Floral Design, Signed	$165
Parfait, Footed, Etched Kalana Poppy, Signed	$200
Pitcher, 8" Tall, Etched Vintage Pattern, Signed	$625
Pitcher, 8" Tall, Etched Rose Pattern, Signed	$375
Pitcher, 8½" Tall, Tankard Style, Ornate Handle, Grape and Line Design	$1,150
Pitcher, 13½" Tall, Tankard Style, Etched Vintage Pattern, Signed	$1,550

Plate, 7", Etched Poinsettias, Signed	$300
Punch Cup, Poppy Pattern, Signed "Locke Art"	$115
Salt Dip, Rectangular (2¼" x 1¼"), Pedestal Foot, Vintage Pattern	$110
Sherbet, Etched with Various Fruit, Signed	$300
Sherbet, 3½" Tall, Etched Grapes and Vines	$125
Sherbet, 3¾" Tall, Etched Vines, Signed	$250
Tray, Rectangular, 15¾" x 8", Etched Floral Design	$475
Tumbler, 5¼" Tall, Ribbed, Etched Vintage Pattern	$165
Tumbler, 5¾" Tall, Etched Grape and Vine Design, Signed	$135
Vase, 5" Tall, Ruffled, Etched Floral Design, Signed	$875
Vase, 5" Tall, Flared, Poppies and Flower Buds	$650
Vase, 6" Tall, Engraved Poppies	$300
Vase, 6¼" Tall, Flared, Etched Roses, Signed	$750
Vase, 10½" Tall, Crimped Folded Rim, Ribbed, Etched Fern Design	$225
Vase, 10¾" Tall, Gold Tinted Roses and Leaves, Signed "Locke Art—Mount Oliver, Pennsylvania"	$1,350
Whiskey Tumbler, 2⅝" Tall, Engraved Wheat Pattern	$185
Wineglass, Ribbed, Poppy Design	$135

Mercury Glass
Various Companies, 1850s–1900s

Original glass in this style actually contains the element mercury from which it derives its name; however, a solution of silver nitrate also served as a substitute. Mercury was mixed with tin and lead into a solution that was used to coat the interiors of hollow glass objects. The excess liquid was poured out and the open pontil area was sealed with a plug. Many of the plugs were lost or removed, which causes the glass to oxidize and discolor. The exteriors were further decorated by enameling, engraving, staining, and etching. A few contain gold or silver gilting on the inner side. The glass is also sometimes referred to as "silvered" and is confused with genuine silver articles.

Bottle, 7½" Tall, 4½" Diameter, Flashed Amber with Etched Grapes and Leaves	$275
Bowl, Flower, 2" Tall, Ribbed	$100
Bowl, 6", Enameled White Floral Design	$75
Bowl, 9½" Diameter, 3-Footed	$150
Bowl, Rose, 10" Diameter, Gold Foliage	$225

Candlestick, Miniature (Children's)	$75
Candlestick, 6" Tall, Dome Base, Gold	$115
Candlestick, 6¼" Tall, Gold Shading	$105
Candlestick, 10½" Tall, Flared Rim, Domed Foot	$135
Candlestick, 11" Tall, Enameled Floral Design	$100
Candlestick, 12" Tall, White Enameled Flower Design	$185
Carafe with Stopper, 12" Tall	$100
Centerpiece, 10", Round Base with Spherical Top	$115
Compote, 6¼" Tall, White Enameled Floral Design	$105
Compote, 8¼" Tall, Gold to Amber Shading	$175
Crystal Ball, Witch's, Bronze Stand, 18" Tall	$250
Curtain Tieback, 3½" Diameter, Etched Vine and Grape Pattern with Pewter Shank	$35
Curtain Tieback, 3½" Diameter, Etched Fruit and Vine Pattern with Pewter Shank, Marked "New England Glass Co., patented January 15, 1855"	$85
Curtain Tie-Back, 4½" Diameter, Starflower Design with Pewter Shank	$90
Doorknob	$45
Drawer Pulls or Knobs, 1¼" Diameter	$45
Dresser Jar with Cover, 8" Tall, Knob Finial	$125
Flower Holders, Auto	$55
Goblet, 5⅛" Tall, White Enameled Floral Design with Amber Interior	$55
Lamp, 10" Tall, Vintage Design with Pewter Connections	$350
Match Holder	$85
Mug, 3" Tall, Child's, Applied Crystal Handle	$55
Perfume, 2¾" Tall, Amber Dauber, Striped Design	$85
Pitcher, 9" Tall, Water, Engraved Floral Design, Clear Handle	$375
Pitcher, 11½", Water, Applied Clear Handle	$175
Rolling Pin	$175
Salt Dip, 1½" Tall, 3" Diameter	$75
Salt Dip, 3" Tall, Pedestal Base, Amber Interior, Etched Floral Design, Signed "N.E.G."	$275
Sugar, 6¼" Tall, 4¼" Diameter Domed Cover with Knob, Footed Floral Design	$75
Toothpick Holder, 3½" Tall, Pedestal Base	$65

Toothpick Holder, 5" Tall, Pedestal Base, Etched Fern Design	$75
Urn, 3" Tall, Pedestal Base, Gold Lining	$150
Urn, 12½" Tall, Pedestal Base	$250
Vase, 5½" Tall, Enameled Foliage Design	$55
Vase, 7" Tall, Enameled Blue Deer and Foliage Design	$75
Vase, 7½" Tall, Silver with White Enameled Birds	$85
Vase, 9½" Tall, White and Purple Floral and Butterfly Design with Red Berries	$100
Vase, 10" Tall, Silver Paneled Design with Multicolored Enameled Floral Sprays	$225
Vase, 12½" Tall, Pedestal Foot, Flared Neck, Floral Design Around Center	$150
Vase, 14¼" Tall, Bulbous, Blue and White Floral Design	$275
Wig Stand, 10" to 10½" Tall	$150
Wineglass, Etched with Enameling	$75

Monroe, C. F. Company; Kelva, Nakara, and Wave Crest
1880–1916

C. F. Monroe was a small art decorating company in Meriden, Connecticut. They primarily applied opal enamels in both satin and brightly colored finishes to blanks provided to them by Pairpoint as well as French factories. The company produced only three products, and none is easily distinguished from the others except by name. Most are either signed or stamped "KELVA," "NAKARA," or "WAVE CREST."

Ashtray, 4½", Opal Scrolls and Pink Apple Blossoms	$350
Bonbon Dish with Silver Handle, Yellow to White Shading, Blue Floral and Foliage Design, Signed "WAVE CREST"	$650
Bonbon Tray, Swirled with Beading, Signed "NAKARA"	$475
Box, Glove, Rectangular 8½" x 4½", Hinged Cover, Signed "WAVE CREST"	$875
Box, Hexagonal, 4" Across, Hinged Cover, Signed "NAKARA"	$475
Box, Hexagonal, 4" Tall, Hinged Cover, Signed "NAKARA"	$475
Box, Octagonal, Hinged Cover, Signed "KELVA"	$775
Box, Jewelry, 7", Signed "WAVE CREST"	$325
Box, Ring, 3½", Gray and Blue Floral Design, Signed "KELVA"	$475
Box, Ring, 3½", Signed "WAVE CREST"	$275
Box, Round, 6" Diameter, Hinged Cover, Signed "NAKARA"	$625
Box, Hexagonal, 8" Across, Hinged Cover, Pink and White, Signed "KELVA"	$500

C. F. Monroe Art Glass. *Photo by Mark Pickvet.*

Box, Round, 8¼" Diameter, Hinged Cover, Woman's Picture on Cover, Signed "NAKARA"	$1,150
Box, Trinket, Signed "NAKARA"	$300
Box, 8½" Wide, Picture of 2 Women in Garden, Signed "NAKARA"	$975
Box, Hinged Lid, Gold Decoration and Opal Flowers, Signed "WAVE CREST"	$925
Candlestick, 7¼" Tall, Signed "KELVA"	$175
Cigarette Holder, Hexagonal	$525
Cracker Jar with Silver-Plated Cover, 6" Tall, Silver-Plated Handle, Enameled Scroll Design, Wave Crest	$425
Creamer, Swirl Pattern with Silver-Plated Mounts	$185
Cruet with Brass Handle and Stopper, Angel Design, Wave Crest	$475
Ewer, 14" Tall	$250
Ewer, 14½" Tall, Enameled Fishing Scene	$275
Ewer, 15½" Tall, Ribbed	$300
Fernery, 7" Wide, Gold and White Design, Wave Crest (Unsigned)	$425
Fernery, 11" Tall, 8" Wide, Scalloped, Beading, Wild Rose and Foliage Design, Signed "WAVE CREST"	$1,050
Hairpin Dish, 5½" Length, Green with Pink and White Floral Design, Signed "NAKARA"	$300
Hairpin Dish, 3¼" Diameter, Signed "WAVE CREST"	$175
Hair Receiver with Cover, 4" Tall, Small Floral Decoration, Signed "KELVA"	$375

Hair Receiver, Diamond Shape with Cover, White Beading and Blue Enamel, Signed "NAKARA" $550

Humidor with Hinged Cover, 5" Tall, Green and Blue Forget-Me-Not Design, White Beading, Marked "Tobacco" in Purple Lettering, Signed "Wave Crest" $550

Humidor with Hinged Cover, 6" Tall, Blue, Gold "CIGARS" Lettering, Signed "KELVA" $850

Humidor with Cover, 6" Tall, Tan with Floral Design, Signed "KELVA" $800

Humidor with Cover, 6" Tall, Brass Rim on Top of Base and Bottom of Cover, Floral Design, Embossed "Cigars," Signed "Wave Crest" $925

Ice Bucket, 11" Tall, 6" Diameter, Silver Cover and Handle, Wild Rose Design, Wave Crest $825

Ice Bucket, 13¼" Tall, Light Blue, Wild Rose Design, Signed "WAVE CREST" $1,050

Jar, Biscuit with Silver-Plated Cover and Handle, 8" Tall, Lilac Design, Wave Crest $575

Jar, Biscuit with Silver-Plated Cover, 10" Tall, Swirl Pattern $600

Jar, Blown-Out with Cover, 3" Tall, Wave Crest (Unsigned) $400

Jar, Tobacco with Metal Cover, 6¾" Tall, Lettered "Tobacco," Signed "NAKARA" $950

Jar, Toothpowder with Embossed Brass Cover, Signed "WAVE CREST" $575

Jardiniere, 7" Tall, Straight Sides, Ring Feet, Enameled Floral Design with Gold Trim, Wave Crest $575

Jardiniere, 12" Tall, White, Gold Decoration, Nakara $675

Lamp Base, Blown-Out, 17" Tall, Frosted Crystal Shade, Wave Crest (Unsigned) $875

Lamp, Table, Signed "WAVE CREST" $550

Letter Holder, Footed Base, Wave Crest (Unsigned) $425

Perfume Bottle with Brass Stopper and Double Handles, 3½" Tall, Pink and Purple Floral Design, Wave Crest $325

Pitcher, Syrup with Silver-Plated Lid, 4" Tall, Raised Paneled Floral Design, Wave Crest $825

Pitcher, Syrup, Swirled with Silver-Plated Top and Handle, Enameled Pink Roses $675

Planter, 7½" Tall, Beaded Brass Rim, Signed "WAVE CREST" $550

Plate, 7", Pale Blue with Enameled Pind Lilies, Signed "WAVE CREST" $650

Platter, Rectangular (11" x 8"), Scrolled Edge, Enameled Roses, Wave Crest $600

Salt and Pepper Shakers with Pewter Tops, 3" Tall, Moss Green, Enameled Floral Design, Kelva $450

Salt and Pepper Shakers with Pewter Tops, Signed "WAVE CREST" $500

Salt Dip, Brass Rim, 2 Brass Handles, Floral Design, Wave Crest $150

Sugar, Swirl Pattern with Silver-Plated Mounts	$200
Sugar Shaker with Silver-Plated Top, 4" Tall, Floral Design, Wave Crest	$225
Toothpowder Jar with Brass Cover, 3½" Tall, White and Pink Floral Design	$400
Vase, 4" Tall, Blue and White with Paneled Pink Flowers, White Beaded Rim, Wave Crest	$425
Vase, 5" Tall with Bronze-Footed Holder	$250
Vase, 6" Tall, Bronze-Footed Holder, White with Enameled Pink and Blue Floral Design, Wave Crest	$275
Vase, 8" Tall, Bulbous, Footed Ormolu Base, Blue to Yellow Shading, White Beading and Floral Design, Signed "NAKARA"	$450
Vase, 10" Tall, White with Enameled Pink and Orange Chrysanthemums, Beaded White Rim, Wave Crest	$650
Vase, 11¼" Tall, Blue with Burmese Shading, Enameled Orchids, Nakara	$1,150
Vase, 12" Tall, 9" Wide, Handled, Footed, Signed "WAVE CREST"	$800
Vase, 13" Tall, Hexagonal, Marbled Background with White Rim, Signed "KELVA"	$750
Vase, 14" Tall, Green Background with Silver-Plated Feet, Signed "KELVA"	$875
Vase, 17½" Tall, 4-Footed Brass Base, 2 Brass Handles Connected with Brass Rim, Cartouche Hand-Painted Maiden Outlined in Gold and Mauve, Wave Crest	$1,850
Whisk Broom Holder, 8½", Signed "WAVE CREST"	$875

Mother-of-Pearl
Various Companies, 1880s–Early 1900s

Mother-of-Pearl is characterized by two or more layers of glass in a satin, pearl-like finish, and internal indentations that purposefully trap air bubbles. The two major producers of this pearlized glass were the Mt. Washington Glass Works and the Phoenix Glass Works. Other firms such as Steuben, Tiffany, Libbey, and a few others also created glass in this manner. A host of decorating techniques and coloring effects were applied to Mother-of-Pearl. Decorations include applied beading, cameo engraving, enameling, and gold leafing.

Colors are much like those of pearls—shaded light blues, light pinks, light purples, light yellows, and sparkling off-whites. These techniques were also applied to numerous popular cut patterns of the 19th century, including Diamond Quilted, Herringbone, Raindrops, Ribbed, Thumbprints, and so on.

Basket, 5½" Tall, Ruffled, Pink with Frosted Handle, Herringbone Pattern	$325
Basket, 12" Tall, Thorn Handle, Moire Pattern with Enameled Decoration	$825
Bottle, Cologne, 4½" Tall, Apricot with Silver Stopper, Drape Design	$275

Bowl, Rose or Flower, 4" Tall, 3½" Diameter $850

Bowl, Bride's, 10" Diameter, Scalloped, Ribbed, Amber with Gold Floral Design, Diamond Quilted Pattern $1,250

Bowl, 11", 4" Tall, Ruffled, Frosted Feet, Blue, Ribbon Pattern $575

Bowl, Bride's, 11" Diameter, Ruffled, Blue and White with Gold Highlights, Herringbone Pattern $575

Box with Hinged Cover, 4½" Tall, Brass Handle, Blue with White Lining, Gold Leaves and Scrolls $375

Cookie Jar with Cover, Green with Silver-Plated Cover, Handle, and Rim; Enameled Chrysanthemums $285

Creamer, Frosted Handle, Apricot, Raindrop Pattern $225

Creamer, 4½" Tall, Blue Frosted Handle and White Lining, Teardrop Pattern $400

Creamer, 5" Tall, Blue with Frosted Handle, Diamond Quilted Pattern $400

Cruet, with Stopper, 6" Tall, Pink with White Interior, Diamond Quilted Pattern $250

Cruet with Stopper, 6½" Tall, Blue with Frosted Handle $800

Ewer, 10½" Tall, 2 Frosted Handles, Pink with White Interior $1,550

Ewer, 12" Tall, Shaded Rose, Swirl Pattern $1,350

Lamp, 9¾" Tall, 3-Footed, Brass Base, Raindrop Patterned Shade $1,150

Lamp, 12¼" Tall, Brass Base, Pink and White Floral Design, Signed $1,450

Lamp, 20½" Tall, Brown, Brass Foots and Mounts, Swirl Pattern $1,550

Mug, 3½" Tall, Frosted Handle, Pink to White Floral Design, Diamond Quilted Pattern $350

Perfume Bottle with Stopper, 5" Tall, Blue, Diamond Quilted Pattern $425

Pitcher, Cream, 5½" Tall, Ruffled, Frosted Handle, Herringbone Pattern $475

Pitcher, Syrup with Lid, Red, Beaded Drape Pattern $625

Pitcher, Water, 9¼" Tall, Oval Top, Frosted Handle, Enameled Blue Foliage Design $575

Salt and Pepper Shakers with Pewter Tops, 3½" Tall, Pink to White Shading, Raindrop Pattern $450

Sugar with Dome Cover, Apricot, Raindrop Pattern $275

Sugar Shaker, 5" Tall, Cranberry Floral and Stork Design, Inverted Thumbprint Pattern $825

Tumbler, 3¾" Tall, Apricot, Herringbone Pattern $225

Tumbler, 4" Tall, Enameled Daisies and Leaves, Diamond Quilted Pattern $325

Vase, 3" Tall, Miniature, Salmon, Diamond Quilted Pattern $265

Vase, 4¾" Tall, Blue, Enameled Floral Design, Diamond Quilted Pattern	$275
Vase, 5" Tall, Ruffled, Pink, Diamond Quilted Pattern	$335
Vase, 5½" Tall, Folded-In Square Top, Blue, Hobnail Pattern	$750
Vase, 5¾" Tall, Rose Design, Acorn Pattern	$675
Vase, 6" Tall, Yellow to White Shading, Hobnail Pattern	$1,050
Vase, 6½" Tall, White Ground with Gold Design, Ribbon Pattern	$1,550
Vase, 6¾" Tall, Ruffled, Rose, Herringbone Pattern	$325
Vase, 7¼" Tall, Dark Pink, Drape Pattern	$325
Vase, 7¼" Tall, Ruffled, Light Caramel, Ribbed, Raindrop Pattern	$375
Vase, 8" Tall, White, Enameled Peacock Tail (Eye) Design	$675
Vase, 9" Tall, Triple-Ring Neck, Peach, Diamond Quilted Pattern	$375
Vase, 9" Tall, Ruffled, Yellow with White Lining, Enameled Floral Design, Silver-Plated Holder, Ribbon Handles	$425
Vase, 10" Tall, Ruffled, Green with White Lining, Diamond Quilted Pattern	$725
Vase, 11" Tall, Shaded Apricot, Raindrop Pattern	$650
Vase, 11½" Tall, Ruffled, Blue, Loop and Teardrop Pattern	$675
Vase, 13" Tall, Ruffled, Blue, Herringbone Pattern	$525
Vase, 16" Tall, Ribbed, Chartreuse Lining, Zipper Pattern	$725

Mt. Washington Glass Works
1837–94

With such influences as Deming Jarves, William L. Libbey, A. H. Seabury and others, Mt. Washington became a major producer of art-glass tableware and vases in the later part of the 19th century. A huge variety of styles and designs including Amberina, Burmese, Crown Milano, Mother-of-Pearl, Peach Blow, and countless others were all part of Mt. Washington's output. Several additional listings can be found under these design names. Note that Royal Flemish refers to a Mt. Washington patented design that resembles stained-glass windows (individual pieces of glass separated by lead line borders).

Basket, Bride's, 6" Tall, 5½" Diameter, Cameo, Blue and White Floral Design, Silver-Plated Holder	$1,050
Basket, Bride's, 12" Tall, Cameo, Flared, 4-Footed, Pink and White Design, Silver-Plated Holder	$1,550
Bowl, 7½", Cameo, Red and White, Floral Design with Winged Griffins	$1,150
Bowl, 8½", Cameo, Blue and White Floral Design	$750

Mt. Washington Burmese Lamp. *Photo by Robin Rainwater.*

Bowl, 9½" Cameo, Pink and White Floral Design	$1,250
Bowl, Rose, Cameo, White and Yellow Daisies	$475
Bowl, Rose, 6", 5¼" Tall, Pink and Blue Enameled Floral Design	$425
Candlestick, 7¼" Tall, Silver Holder, Enameled Pink Floral Design	$375
Compote, 5½" Diameter, 11" Tall, Reverse Painted Vintage Design, Ambero Style	$775
Cookie Jar with Cover, 6" Tall, Pink, Royal Flemish Design	$2,350
Cracker Jar, 6" Tall, Crystal with Enameled Brownies, Signed "Napoli"	$1,550
Cookie Jar with Cover, 6¼" Tall, Gold Thistle Design	$1,250
Cracker Jar, 6½" Tall, Pastel Floral Pattern, Albertine	$1,150
Cracker Jar with Cover, 6½" Tall, Royal Flemish Leaf Design	$1,150
Cruet with Stopper, 5¾" Tall, Rose Amber, Inverted Thumbprint Pattern	$725
Dresser Tray, 8" x 8" Square, Satinized Green Foliage and Purple Irises	$275
Ewer, 11⅜" Tall, Twisted Handle and Neck, Royal Flemish Design	$625
Ewer, 15½" Tall, Rope Handle, Overlaid Royal Flemish Design	$2,450
Ewer with Cover, 16" Tall, Rope Handle, Royal Flemish, Coat-of-Arms Decoration	$6,250
Hat Pin Holder, Mushroom Shape, Lusterless, Satin Finish, Fern and Flower Design	$375
Lamp, 19¾" Tall, Kerosene, Milk Shade, Pink and Yellow Floral Design, Globular Glass Base, Footed (Shells and Ram's Head)	$2,250
Lamp, 42" Tall, Electric, Crystal Shade, Blue Aqua, Gold Lions and Shields, Red Accents, Royal Flemish Design	$8,750

Mustard Jar with Hinged Cover, Leaf Design on Pink and White Background, Silver-Plated Rim and Cover $425

Paperweight, 4⅛" Diameter, Blue and White Shaded Rose, Green Stem, Serrated Green Leaves $35,000

Pitcher, Syrup with Lid, Multicolored Floral Design Outlined in Gold $2,450

Pitcher, Syrup with Metal Lid, Barrel Shape, Ribbed, Metal Handle, Floral Design $650

Pitcher, Syrup with Lid, Multicolored Floral Design Outlined in Gold $2,450

Pitcher, Syrup with Metal Lid, Barrel Shape, Ribbed, Metal Handle, Floral Design $650

Pitcher, Water, 9" Tall, Tan and Brown with Red Scrolls, Royal Flemish Design $3,250

Pitcher, Water, 10" Tall, Crystal, Crab Decoration $925

Plate, 10", Lusterless, Enameled Pansies $115

Plate, 12", Lusterless, Enameled Portrait of Woman $175

Punch Bowl with Base, 16" Diameter, 13½" Tall, Palmer Cox Brownie Scene, Gold Trim, Royal Flemish Design $27,500

Salt Dip, 4-Footed, Ribbed, Pink and Yellow Pansies with Gold Highlights $275

Saltshaker, Egg Shaped, White with Enameled Foliage, Metal Chick's Head Top $600

Saltshaker, Rose Amber, Inverted Thumbprint Pattern $250

Salt and Pepper Shakers, 2½" Tall, Egg Shape, Pewter Tops, Opaque White with Various Enameled Floral Designs $600

Sugar Shaker, Cream White with Pink and Blue Enameled Floral Design $500

Sugar Shaker, Ribbed, Purple Violet Design $375

Toothpick Holder, 2⅛" Tall, Lusterless, White with Enameled Leaves $425

Vase, 3¾" Tall, Lava with White Outlines, Multicolored Mica Chips $2,450

Vase, 4½" Tall, Lava, Applied Handles, Acidized $2,550

Vase, 4¾" Tall, Satin Finish, Enameled Forget-Me-Not Design $825

Vase, 5¼" Tall, Rolled Rim, Venetian Diamond, Enameled Floral Design $775

Vase, 5¾" Tall, Multicolored Dark Lava Design $2,000

Vase, 6" Tall, Opaque White, Pink Ground, Gilded Rings, Enameled Bird on Branch $250

Vase, 6½" Tall, Lava, Multicolored Imbedded Glass Flecks $4,850

Vase, 7¼" Tall, Gold Tracing and Edging, Floral Design $2,650

Vase, 7½" Tall, 2-Handled, Royal Flemish, Tan and Brown Medallion Design $2,750

Vase, 8" Tall, Brown Shading, Gold Outlining, Royal Flemish Design with Winged Gargoyle $4,350

Vase, 8¼" Tall, Pear Shape, Floral Design, Inscribed "Progressive/Fuchre /November 16, 1886"	$2,450
Vase, 9" Tall, 7½" Diameter, Yellow Opal, Chrysanthemum Design	$800
Vase, 9" Tall, Globe Base, Gold Trim, Frog and Reeds Design, Signed "Napoli"	$1,250
Vase, 10" Tall, Enameled Floral Design, Signed "Napoli"	$875
Vase, 10½" Tall, Enameled Dragonflies and Floral Design	$1,000
Vase, 10½" Tall, Tan and Red Panels, Gold Beading at Top and Base, Red Top, Royal Flemish Design, Gold Serpent and Falcon on Front and Back	$5,750
Vase, 11" Tall, Gourd Shape, Brown to Gold Satin, Seaweed Design	$675
Vase, 13" Tall, Royal Flemish, Camel and Rider Paneled Design	$5,850
Vase, 15" Tall, Royal Flemish, Duck Decorations	$3,650
Vase, 16" Tall, Boy on Front and Foliage on Back, Signed "Verona"	$1,550

Nash, A. Douglas Corporation
Early 1900s–1931

The Nashes, including Arthur J. and his two sons, A. Douglas and Leslie, all worked for various glass companies in England and America, including Tiffany. Under the A. Douglas Nash Corporation, art glass was produced for the most part in the style of Tiffany (Leslie Nash once managed the Tiffany Glass Furnace at Corona, New York). Chintz glass is the most recognizable form of Nash's designs and is characterized by a spoked, rayed, or striped pattern emanating from the center of an object. A multitude of colors on iridescent backgrounds is also characteristic of Nash's products. Some pieces were decorated in gold or platinum luster or trims as well.

Bowl with Underplate, Iridescent Gold and Platinum, Signed, Numbered	$575
Bowl, 4", Red with Silver Stripes, Chintz Design	$750
Bowl, 4½", Blue with Silver and Red Stripes, Chintz Design	$550
Bowl, 10¼", Ruffled, Iridescent Green, Signed	$825
Bowl, Centerpiece, 15½", Amber, Blue, and Green Opalescent Chintz Design	$875
Box with Hinged Cover, 5" Diameter, Blue, Chintz Design, Signed	$450
Candlestick, 4" Tall, Ball Stem, Red and Gray, Chintz Design	$450
Candlestick, 5" Tall, Red with Silver Highlights, Chintz Design	$550
Chalice, 4½" Tall, Fluted; Gold, Pink, and Platinum; Signed, Numbered	$875
Cologne Bottle with Stopper, 5" Tall, Alternating Stripes of Green and Blue, Chintz Design	$725
Compote, 7¼" Diameter, 4½" Tall, Green, Chintz Design, Signed	$425

Compote, 8" Diameter, 5" Tall, Green with Red and Gray Spiraled Rim, Chintz Design	$525
Cordial, 4" Tall, Blue and Green, Chintz Design	$150
Cordial, 4¼" Tall, Red with Silver, Chintz Design	$165
Goblet, 5" Tall, Pedestal Foot, Blue and Silver, Chintz Design, Signed	$215
Goblet, Twisted Stem, Wafer Foot, Pink Threaded Bowl, Signed "Libbey-Nash"	$225
Nut Dish, 1¼" x 4", Ruffled, Iridescent Gold	$350
Perfume Bottle with Stopper, 8" Tall, Blown-Out Bottom, Iridescent Gold	$875
Plate, 6½", Chartreuse and Orchid Spirals from Center, Chintz Design	$250
Plate, 8", Green and Blue, Chintz Design	$250
Salt Dip, 4" Diameter, Iridescent Bronze, Blue and Violet Highlights, Signed	$325
Vase, 4¼" Tall, Flared, Iridescent Amber, Signed "Nash-544"	$675
Vase, 4¾" Tall, Pedestal Base, Iridescent Blue and Gold, Signed "Nash-644"	$475
Vase, 5½" Tall, Iridescent Gold on White	$525
Vase, 5¾" Tall, Red Ground with Silver Stripes, Chintz Design, Signed	$975
Vase, 6¾" Tall, Square Curved Rim, Iridescent Gold, Signed "Nash-539"	$650
Vase, 7" Tall, 4" Across, Square Shaped, Flared, Iridescent Gold, Signed	$675
Vase, 8½" Tall, Blue with Iridescent Silver Scrolling, Chintz Design	$700
Vase, 9" Tall, Red and Gray, Chintz Design	$600
Vase, 9" Tall, Ribbed, Opaque Red with White Polka Dots, Signed "Nash GD154"	$1,250
Vase, 10" Tall, Trumpet Shape, Green and Blue, Chintz Design, Signed	$725
Wineglass, 6" Tall, Green and Lavender, Chintz Design, Signed	$225

New England Glass Company
Early 1818–78

Another Deming Jarves–founded company, New England Glass was blessed with many gifted designers—Joseph Locke, Henry Whitney, and Louis Vaupel, to name just a few. The company's output was huge and spanned across all lines of glass from early pressed practical wares to fancy art glass. New England's art examples included Agata, Amberina, Pomona, and a host of others. Libbey purchased the company in 1878 and continued to produce many of the same styles.

Bowl, Finger, 4½", Scalloped, Agata Style	$1,350
Bowl, 7", Opaque Blue	$950

Bowl, 8", Opaque Green	$1,450
Bowl, 8½", Ruffled, Amber Rim, Pomona Style	$425
Creamer, Agata Style	$1,450
Cruet with Stopper, 5½" Tall, Opaque Green	$2,000
Cruet with White Stopper, 5½" Tall, Globe Shape, Ruffled, Pink Handle, Agata Style	$3,250
Paperweight, 2⅝" Diameter, Latticino Ground, 3 Red and White Flower Buds, Green Leaf Tips	$4,250
Paperweight, 2¾" Diameter, Pink Poinsettia with White Center and Green Stem and Leaves, White Latticino Basket	$1,050
Paperweight, Apple with Cut Slice, 3" Diameter, Crystal Base (Francois Pierre)	$4,250
Pitcher, 4¼" Tall, Square Top, White Reeded Handle, Agata Style	$1,850
Pitcher, 6¼" Tall, Square Top, Pomona Style, Cornflower Design	$675
Pitcher, 8¼" Tall, Amber Top, Pomona Style, Cornflower Design	$550
Pitcher, 10" Tall, Pear Shape, Crystal with Vertical Cleats Below the Waist	$425
Plate, 6½", Fluted Rim, Agata Style	$950
Punch Bowl, 9¼", Amber Trim, Pomona Style	$1,650
Punch Cup, Amber Trim, Pomona Style	$135
Salt Dip, 3" Long, 2⅛" Tall, 4-Footed, Floral Design, Signed	$325
Saltshaker, 3¾" Tall, Agata Style	$550
Spooner, 4½" Tall, Opaque Green with Gold Band	$1,250
Sugar, 3" Tall, 2 Handles, Gold Band of Berries and Leaves, Pomona Style	$550
Sugar, 4" Tall, Flared, Square Neck, 2 Handles, Gold Decoration, Agata Style	$1,950
Sugar Shaker, 4" Tall, Ribbed, Fig Form, Lime Opal with Pink Floral Design	$925
Toothpick Holder, Square Top, Agata Style	$675
Toothpick Holder, Gold-Stained Collar, Pomona Style	$450
Tray, 12½" x 7½", Ruffled, Gold Rim, Stained Cornflower Design, Pomona Style	$1,050
Tumbler, 3¾" Tall, Agata Style	$950
Tumbler, 3¾" Tall, Opaque Green with Gold Band (Several Styles)	$1,250
Tumbler, 3¾" Tall, Amber Top, Pomona Style, Cornflower Design	$265
Tumbler, 4" Tall, Agata Style	$975
Vase, 4½" Tall, 4 Pitched Sides, Ruffled, Crimped, Agata Style	$2,550

Vase, 5¾" Tall, Agata Style	$2,450
Vase, 6" Tall, Circular Foot, Agata Style	$2,750
Vase, 7" Tall, Trumpet-Shaped, Footed, Amethyst Molded Ovals Design	$250

Onyx Glass
Various Companies, 1889–Early 1900s

The first patent for onyx-styled glass was obtained by George Leighton in 1889 while working for the Dalzell, Gilmore, and Leighton Company. They referred to their design as Findlay Onyx. They did experience difficulties in perfecting a durable formula, for their onyx products were brittle and cracked easily. Onyx glass is characterized by parallel layers of colors, at times thin enough to be translucent. Lustrous forms of platinum or silver, opal forms, concentric rings on the base, and varying degrees of relief because of the layering technique are all aspects of onyx glass.

Bowl, 4", Red and White Floral Design	$575
Bowl, 7½", Cream and Beige	$375
Bowl, 8", White with Silver Flowers, Findlay	$1,350
Butter Dish with Cover, 6" Diameter, 4½" Tall, Platinum Design on Cream Background	$2,250
Celery Vase, 6½" Tall, White with Silver Flowers, Findlay	$575
Creamer, Raised White Opalescent Design on Red Background	$1,500
Muffineer, 5", White	$575
Mustard Jar with Silver-Plated Cover, 3⅜" Tall, Red Leaves on an Opalescent White Background, Findlay	$1,500
Paperweight, Pig, Findlay	$300
Pitcher, Syrup with Silver-Plated Lid, 7" Tall, Ivory with Gold Decoration	$750
Pitcher, Syrup, with Silver-Plated Lid, 7½" Tall, Metal Handle, Silver Design on Ivory Background	$750
Pitcher, 7½" Tall, Cream Color, Findlay	$1,050
Pitcher, Water, 8" Tall, Silver Color, Findlay	$1,425
Saltshaker with Metal Cover, 2¾" Tall, Silver Flowers on Brown Background	$575
Saltshaker with Metal Cover, 2¾" Tall, Raised Silver Flowers on Cream Background	$450
Spooner, Opalescent White Flowers on Red Background	$1,150
Spooner, Silver Design on Cream Background	$675
Sugar with Cover, Raised White Opalescent Design on Red Background	$1,250

Sugar with Cover, 6" Tall, Platinum Flowers on Cream Background	$750
Sugar Shaker, 5" Tall, Light Brown	$700
Sugar Shaker with Metal Cover, 5¾" Tall, Silver Flowers on Cream Background	$650
Toothpick Holder, 2½" Tall, Cinnamon Swirled Design, Findlay	$475
Toothpick Holder, 2¾" Tall, Raised Silver Design on Ivory Background	$400
Tumbler, 3¼" Tall, Barrel Shape, Silver Design on Cream Background	$525
Tumbler, 3½" Tall, White with Silver Floral Design	$575
Tumbler, 4" Tall, Dark Red and White Floral Design	$1,250
Vase, 5" Tall, Cream with Silver Floral Design	$875
Vase, 6½" Tall, Raised Silver Flowers on Cream Background, Findlay	$925

Pairpoint Manufacturing Company, Inc.
1894–1958

Pairpoint merged with and eventually resumed all glass manufacturing operations from Mt. Washington by 1894. Pairpoint produced a wide variety of items, from functional tableware and lamps to fancy art-glass and cut designs. Robert Gunderson and Robert Bryden were also active with the firm in the mid-20th century.

Bowl, 6½", 2½" Tall, Amber with Cobalt Blue Feet	$325
Bowl, 8", Green with Crystal Swan Handles (Small), (Gunderson-Pairpoint)	$200
Bowl, 8", Footed, Green with Crystal Swan Handles, (Large), (Gunderson-Pairpoint)	$475
Bowl with Cover, 8", 6½" Tall, 2 Handles, Fish with Chrysanthemum Design, Signed "Pairpoint Limoges 2502/50"	$1,150
Bowl, Bride's, 9", Cut Rim, Medallion Design, Footed Silver-Plated Frame	$425
Bowl, Bride's, 9½", Daisy and Bluebell Design, Silver-Plated Holder, Signed "Pairpoint"	$975
Bowl, 12", Footed Base, Ruby and Blue Twist Design	$375
Bowl, 14", Footed Base, Ruby and Blue Twist Design	$425
Bowl, 16", Footed Base, Ruby and Blue Twist Design	$475
Bowl, Centerpiece, Turned-Down Rim, Amber with Silver Overlay	$400
Box with Hinged Cover, Oval, Cream with Gold Foliage, Signed "Pairpoint"	$725
Box with Hinged Cover, Oval, Scalloped, Cream with Gold Foliage, Signed "Pairpoint"	$750
Candlestick, 4½" Tall, Mushroom Top, Green with Crystal Bubble in Stem	$125

Candlestick, 5" Tall, Ruby and Blue Twist Design	$275
Candlestick, 10" Tall, Engraved Floral Holder, Air-Twist Stem, Veneti Design	$300
Candlestick, 10½" Tall, Prism Cut, Ball Connector, Emerald Green	$250
Candlestick, 16" Tall, Emerald Green	$425
Candy Dish with Cover, Engraved Dewdrop Design, Canaria Pattern, Crystal Bubble Finial	$275
Compote, 4" Tall, 6" Diameter, Aurora Pattern	$175
Compote, 4¼" Tall, 6" Diameter, Ruby with Crystal Bubble in Stem	$165
Compote, 4⅝" Tall, 8" Diameter, Ruby and Blue Twist Design	$235
Compote, 5" Tall, Ruby with Crystal Bubble in Stem	$265
Compote, 6½" Tall, 12" Diameter, Paperweight Base, Amber with Crystal Bubble in Stem	$225
Compote, 6½" Tall, 10½" Diameter, Green with Crystal Bubble in Stem	$225
Compote, 7¼" Tall, 6¼" Diameter, Amber with Crystal Bubble in Stem	$225
Compote, 7½" Tall, Black with Silver Overlay	$425
Compote, 8" Tall, 8" Diameter, Floral Design, Green with Crystal Ball Stem, Silver Overlay, Marked "Rockwell"	$325
Compote, Upturned Foot, Colias Pattern, Light Green with Crystal Ball Connector	$325
Compote with Cover, Green with Crystal Bubble Connector	$225
Cracker Jar with Cover, 7¼" Tall, Melon with Gold Tracings, Signed "Pairpoint" (Cover Signed "M.W.")	$725
Cracker Jar with Silver-Plated Rim, Cover, and Handle; 5¾" Tall, Milk White with Blue Scenery	$675
Decanter with Stopper, 10" Tall, Green Threaded Design	$850
Goblet, Engraved Grape Design, Canaria Pattern	$175
Hat, 3¼" Tall, Opaque Pink to Blue Coloring	$100
Humidor with Silver-Plated Cover and Rim, 5½" Tall, Blue Landscape Scene with Ships and Windmills	$1,150
Lamp, Boudoir, 5" Diameter Shade, Rose Bouquet Design, Tree Trunk Base, Signed "Pairpoint"	$3,250
Lamp, Table, 8" Diameter Shade, Brass Base, Dogwood Border, Signed "Pairpoint"	$3,250
Lamp, 9¼" Tall, Miniature, Kerosene, Blue and White Windmill Design, Signed "Delft"	$575

Lamp, 13¾" Tall, 4-Sectioned Shade, Metal Base (Tree), Enameled Apples and Apple Blossoms $5,850

Lamp, 15¾" Tall, Frosted Domed Shade, Enameled Desert Scene (Sunset) $3,350

Lamp, 21" Tall, Metal Base, Multicolored Leaf Design, Grape Pattern, Shade Stamped "The Pairpoint Corp." $4,500

Lamp, 21" Tall, 14" Diameter Shade, Brass Base, Floral and Butterfly Design, Papillon Pattern $6,000

Lamp, 23" Tall, 16" Diameter Shade, Brass Base, Hunting Scene with Man and Deer $2,250

Lamp, 24¼" Tall, Red Domed Shade, Green and Black Flower Blossoms in Relief $2,250

Lamp, 26" Tall, Tropical Foliage and Birds on Shade $6,250

Lamp, Floor, 48" Tall, Metal Base, Signed Shade "Garden of Allah" (on Reverse) $7,500

Paperweight, Crystal Cut Base, Yellow Rose Design (Bryden-Pairpoint) $250

Paperweight, 7" Tall, Crystal Fish with Bubbles Design $90

Pitcher, Miniature, 3" Tall, Violet with White Design, Paper Label "Pairpoint-Bryden" $135

Pitcher, Water, 12" Tall, Footed, Green with Applied Crystal Handle, Bubbled Stem $225

Plate, 8", Enameled Floral, Spanish Galleon, or Whale Decoration $115

Plate, 12", Enameled Floral, Spanish Galleon, or Whale Decoration $185

Powder Jar with Hinged Cover, 6" Diameter, Crystal, Viscaria Pattern $325

Swan, 12" Tall, Crystal Head and Neck, Ruby Red Body $725

Tumbler, 8" Tall, Enameled Floral, Spanish Galleon, or Whale Decoration $185

Urn with Cover, 6" Tall, Osiris Design (Amethyst, Blue, Green, or Yellow) $350

Urn with Cover, 6½" Tall, Osiris Design (Amethyst, Blue, Green, or Yellow) $350

Vase, 5" Tall, Ruffled, Cobalt with Crystal Bubble in Stem $265

Vase, 6" Tall, Hand-Painted Multicolred Sailing Scene $325

Vase, 8" Tall, Enameled Floral, Spanish Galleon, or Whale Decoration $400

Vase, 8" Tall, Rolled Rim, Ruby with Crystal Bubble in Stem $250

Vase, 8" Tall, Osiris Design, Various Styles and Colors (Amethyst, Blue, Green, or Yellow) $250

Vase, 9" Tall, Osiris Design, Various Styles and Colors (Amethyst, Blue, Green, or Yellow) $300

Vase, 9" Tall, Ruby Cornucopia Design with Crystal Bubble in Stem $300

Vase, 9" Tall, Village Scene, Signed "Ambero" $1,250

Vase, 9¾" Tall, Cut Green to Crystal Design, Colias Pattern	$375
Vase, 10" Tall, Osiris Design, Various Styles and Colors (Amethyst, Blue, Green, or Yellow) $350	
Vase, 10" Tall, Ruby with Crystal Bubble in Stem	$375
Vase, 12" Tall, Flared, Ruby with Crystal Ball Connector	$425
Vase, 13" Tall, 6½" Diameter, Trumpet Style, Footed, Cobalt Blue with Crystal Bubbled Handle	$400
Vase, 14½" Tall, Cameo Vintage Design, Signed	$1450
Vase, 15" Tall, Amethyst with Cover	$450
Wineglass, Black Foot and Stem, Red Bowl, with or without Silver Overlay	$135

Peach Blow
Various Companies, 1880s–1950s

Peach Blow is similar to Burmese except that the uranium oxide was replaced with cobalt or copper oxide in the general formula. The shading of Peach Blow varies from a light grayish-blue color at the base to a rose pink or peach color at the top. Cobalt generally produces a slightly darker shade at the base than copper. Also like Burmese, Peach Blow is found in numerous finishes, patterns, and enamels, tends to be thin and fragile, and is rather desirable and valuable. Unlike Burmese, Peach Blow was produced by several companies such as Mt. Washington/Pairpoint/Gunderson; Hobbs, Brocunier; New Martinsville; New England/ Libbey; and even foreign makers, including Thomas Webb & Sons of England.

Biscuit Jar with Cover, 7¼" Tall, Enameled Design (Mt. Washington)	$875
Bottle, Banjo, 6¼" Tall (Gunderson)	$275
Bottle, Water, 7" Tall, Pyramid Shape (Wheeling)	$1,450
Bowl, Finger, 2½", Crimped, Acid Finish (New England)	$850
Bowl, 3½", Applied Leaf Design (Gunderson)	$175
Bowl, 4", Pinched Edge (Mt. Washington)	$2,750
Bowl, 4", Scalloped, Diamond Quilted Pattern (Mt. Washington)	$2,450
Bowl, 4½" Diameter, 2½" Tall, White Interior (Hobbs Brocunier)	$375
Bowl, 4½" Diameter, 3" Tall, Ruffled, 3-Footed (Mt. Washington)	$1,750
Bowl, 5" Diameter, Scalloped (New Martinsville)	$100
Bowl, 5½" Diameter, 2½" Tall, 10 Pleated Sides, Wild Rose Pattern (New England)	$475
Bowl, 8" Diameter, Ruffled (New Martinsville)	$185
Bowl, 10", Ruffled, Ribbed, Yellow Interior, Gilded (Mt. Washington)	$675

Peachblow Art Glass. *Photo by Mark Pickvet.*

Bowl, Bride's, 10¾" Diameter, Fluted (New Martinsville)	$285
Bowl, Ruffled Sharp Vibrant Color (Boston & Sandwich)	$475
Bowl, Rose, 4", Floral Decoration (New England)	$550
Bowl, Rose, 5", Floral Decoration (New England)	$650
Bowl, Rose, Gold Design, Marked "World's Fair 1893," Libbey	$600
Butter Dish with Cover (Gunderson)	$425
Celery Dish, 4¾" Tall, Square Top, Scalloped (New England)	$725
Creamer, Handled (Mt. Washington)	$3,350
Creamer, Cased White Interior (Wheeling)	$675
Cruet with Cut Stopper, Tricorner Spout, Crystal Handle (Wheeling)	$1,950
Cruet with Stopper, 7" Tall, Acid Finish (Wheeling)	$1,450
Cruet with Stopper, 8" Tall, Ribbed Shell Handle (Gunderson)	$1,250
Cup, Satin Finish (Gunderson)	$185
Darner, Stocking (New England)	$185
Decanter with Amber Stopper, 9" Tall, Amber Handle, Acid Finish (Wheeling)	$1,850
Ewer, 6" Tall, (Gunderson)	$265
Ewer, 8" Tall, Rigaree Decoration (Wheeling)	$1,750
Hat, 2⅞", Diamond Quilted Pattern (Gunderson)	$165
Lamp, Hall, Brass Frame	$1,850
Lamp, 21" Tall, Gone with the Wind Style, Crystal Chimney (Hobbs Brocunier)	$13,500

Muffineer, 5½" (Hobbs Brocunier)	$725
Mug (Gunderson)	$150
Pear, 4½" Tall, Blown, Curved Stem (New England)	$475
Perfume Bottle with Stopper, Enameled Apple Blossoms (Mt. Washington)	$2,850
Pitcher, Acidized, Yellow Handle (Mt. Washington)	$3,400
Pitcher, 5" Tall, Square Top, Amber Handle (Wheeling)	$1,400
Pitcher, Syrup with Pewter Lid, 7" Tall (Wheeling)	$1,750
Pitcher, Water, 7", Amber Handle (Hobbs Brocunier)	$2,000
Pitcher, Water, 7" Tall, Square Handle (Mt. Washington)	$4,000
Pitcher, Water, 8½" Tall, Acid Finish (Wheeling)	$1,650
Pitcher, Water, 10" Tall, Amber Ring Handle (Wheeling)	$1,850
Plate, 8" (Gunderson)	$400
Powder Jar with Silver-Plated Lid, 4" Tall, Floral and Leaf Design	$375
Punch Cup, 2" Tall, Dull Acid Finish (New England)	$475
Punch Cup, Gloss Finish (New England)	$475
Punch Cup, Amber Handle, Opaque White Handle (Wheeling)	$550
Saltshaker with Silver-Plated Top, 2½" Tall, (Wheeling)	$500
Saltshaker, 3" Tall	$550
Saucer, Satin Finish (Gunderson)	$135
Spooner, 5" Tall, Ruffled (New England)	$335
Sugar, 2½" Tall, Handled, Label (Mt. Washington)	$2,650
Sugar, Enameled "World's Fair 1893" (Libbey)	$675
Sugar Shaker with Silver-Plated Top, 5" Tall, Dull Acid Finish (Wheeling)	$625
Sugar Shaker, 5½" Tall (New England)	$1,150
Sugar Shaker, 5½" Tall, Ringed Neck (Wheeling)	$725
Toothpick Holder, 2¼" Tall, Tricorner Top, Satin Finish (New England)	$700
Toothpick Holder, 2⅜" Tall, Square Rim, Silver-Plated Holder, 5" Tall (New England)	$850
Toothpick Holder, 2½" Tall, Square Rim, Silver-Plated Holder, 5½" Tall (New England)	$875
Toothpick Holder, 2¾" Tall, Enameled Floral Design (Mt. Washington)	$3,850
Tumbler, 3¾" Tall (Gunderson)	$325

Tumbler, 3¾" Tall (New England)	$775
Tumbler, 4" Tall, Acid Finish, Daisy Decoration (Mt. Washington)	$2,450
Tumbler, Dark Gloss Cobalt Finish (Hobbs Brocunier)	$475
Vase, 2¼" Tall, Miniature, Acid Finish, Gold Decoration (Wheeling)	$825
Vase, 3" Tall, Applied Prunts (Mt. Washington)	$325
Vase, 4¼" Tall, Crimped (Gunderson)	$250
Vase, 4¼" Tall, Crimped (New England)	$400
Vase, 4½" Tall, Ruffled, Fold-Over Rim, 5 Frosted Feet (Boston & Sandwich)	$375
Vase, 4½" Tall, Scalloped, Flared, Ribbed (Mt. Washington)	$2,850
Vase, 5" Tall, Ruffled (Gunderson)	$550
Vase, 5½" Tall, Bulbous (New England)	$550
Vase, 6¼" Tall, Trumpet Shape (Mt. Washington)	$1,850
Vase, 6½" Tall, Lily (New England)	$725
Vase, 7" Tall, Bulbous Body with Stick Neck (New England)	$775
Vase, 8" Tall, Bulbous (Mt. Washington)	$1,500
Vase, 8" Tall, Gourd Shape (Wheeling)	$975
Vase, 9" Tall, Barrel Shape, Ruffled, Enameled Birds and Leaves and Insects (Boston & Sandwich)	$500
Vase, 9¼" Tall, Trefoil Shape (Gunderson)	$450
Vase, 10¼" Tall, Oval, Narrow Neck, Amber Holder with 5 Griffins Design (Hobbs Brocunier)	$1,950
Vase, 10½" Tall, Ruffled, Footed (Mt. Washington)	$4,650
Vase, 10½" Tall, Crimped, Jack-in-the-Pulpit Design (Mt. Washington)	$7,850
Vase, 10½" Tall, Spangled, 2 Applied Crystal Reeded Handles (Hobbs Brocunier)	$3,650
Vase, 11" Tall, Bulbous, Dull Finish	$1,350
Vase, 12" Tall, Trumpet Shape, Rose to White Shading (New England)	$1,650
Vase, 13" Tall (Wheeling)	$1,250
Vase, 15½" Tall, Lily (New England)	$1,750
Vase, 18" Tall, Trumpet Shape (New England)	$2,250
Vase, 3 Turned-Down Sides, Ruffled (Mt. Washington)	$4,850
Whiskey Tumbler, 2" Tall, Acid Finish (New England)	$425
Wineglass, 5" Tall (Gunderson)	$200

Phoenix Glass Company
1880–1950s

Much of Phoenix's art glass is similar to that of Lalique. Figures have a smooth, satiny, acidized finish and are sometimes colored. Cameo engraving, pearlized finishes, and heavy etching are also part of Phoenix's designs. Glass made by Phoenix is also similar to certain styles produced by Consolidated, though the colors of Phoenix are limited and more common. Phoenix ended art-glass production in the 1950s. The firm eventually became a division of Anchor-Hocking in 1970.

Ashtray, 5½" Long, Pearl Floral Design on Coral Background	$115
Banana Dish, Pearl Opalescent	$225
Basket, 4½" Tall, Opaque Pink Cameo with Molded Dogwood	$85
Bowl, 8", Ruffled, Divided, Gilded Floral Pattern on Satin Background, Opaque Pink	$500
Bowl, 10", Flower, Floral Design on Pink Background	$235
Bowl, Powder, Blue Hummingbird Design	$150
Bowl, Berry with Cover, Pearl Opalescent	$215
Bowl, 11", Yellow, Tiger Lily Design	$165
Candleholder, Strawberry Shape, 4¼" Tall, Tan	$115
Candleholder, Water Lily Shape, 4¼" Tall, Green on Crystal	$135
Candlestick, 6¾" Tall, Green, Bird of Paradise Design	$165
Candy Box, 6½" Diameter, Crystal with White Violets on a Light Blue Background	$235
Candy Dish with Cover, 6¾", Periwinkle Blue Cameo	$215
Canoe Dish, 8" Long, Opaque White with Green Lemons and Foliage Design	$125
Centerpiece Bowl, 14", Footed, Diving Nudes, Crystal	$275
Compote, Fish Design, Amber	$135
Compote, 6", Pedestal Base, Amethyst Pastel, Dolphin Design	$265
Compote with Cover, Pearl Opalescent	$265
Creamer, Pearl Opalescent	$155
Lamp, 6½" Tall, Frosted White, Pinecone Design	$135
Lamp, 10½", Foxglove Pattern, Yellow, Green, and White	$165
Lamp, 14" Tall, Foxglove Pattern, Aqua, Orange, and White, Marble Base	$265
Plate, 6¼", Yellow, Green, and White Chrysanthemums	$90
Plate, 12", Bird of Paradise Design, Various Color Styles	$90

Pitcher, Water, Pearl Opalescent	$675
Sugar, Pearl Opalescent	$165
Sugar with Cover, Lacy Dewdrop Pattern, Blue Design	$135
Tumbler, Pearl Opalescent	$275
Vase, 5" Tall, Pearl Floral Design on Light Blue Background	$115
Vase, 5½" Tall, Brown and White, Hummingbird Design	$85
Vase, 6½" Tall, Rectangular, Frosted, Pair of Lovebirds Design	$135
Vase, 7" Tall, Fern Design, Blue	$145
Vase, 8" Tall, Frosted, Katydid Pattern	$135
Vase, 8" Tall, Praying Mantis Pattern, Pink	$155
Vase, 8" Tall, Freesia, Flared, Crystal Satin, Sea Green Background	$155
Vase, 8¼" Tall, Fan Shaped, Bronze-Colored Grasshopper	$265
Vase, 8¾" Tall, Milk Glass on Tan Background, Primrose Design	$235
Vase, 9¼" Tall, Fish Design, Blue	$265
Vase, 9¼" Tall, Milk Glass, Wild Geese Design on Blue Background	$235
Vase, 9¼" Tall, Opalescent Satin, Wild Geese Design	$235
Vase, 9½" Tall, Two-Tone Apricot	$215
Vase, 9½" Tall, 12" Diameter, Frosted, Flying Geese Design	$235
Vase, 10" Tall, Frosted Madonna Pattern, Dark Blue	$400
Vase, 11" Tall, Cream Ground, Dancing Nudes	$575
Vase, 11" Tall, Brown and Green Dogwood Design	$315
Vase, 11" Tall, Bulbous, Red Ground with Iridescent Flowers	$285
Vase, 11½" Tall, Pearlized Light Blue, Philodendron Design	$225
Vase, 12" Tall, White, Dancing Females in Relief	$285
Vase, 12¼" Tall, Pink Peonies with Turquoise Leaves Design	$265
Vase, 14½" Tall, Nudes, Blue and White	$725
Vase, 17" Tall, Blue Ground, Thistle Design	$650

Pigeon Blood
Various Companies, Late 1880s–Early 1900s

Pigeon Blood is characterized by a somewhat transparent deep scarlet red (or blood red). Pieces produced in Pigeon Blood tend to have a glossy or shiny finish. Note that the red coloring characteristic of this style was applied to many cut glass patterns, too.

Bowl, 4½", 2⅜" Tall, Inverted Thumbprint Pattern	$175
Bowl, 6" Diameter, Gold Floral Design	$115
Bowl, 8½" Tall, 3-Footed, Crystal Feet and Handles	$210
Bowl, Rose, 5", Floral Design with Gold Highlights	$100
Butter Dish with Cover, Enameled White Floral Design	$575
Carafe with Silver-Plated Neck, Beaded Drape Pattern	$225
Cookie Jar with Cover; Silver-Plated Cover, Handle, and Rim; Florette Pattern (Consolidated)	$325
Creamer, 3½" Tall, Enameled Floral Design	$275
Cruet with Stopper, 5¾" Tall, Enameled Scrolls	$250
Decanter with Stopper, 9½" Tall	$250
Lamp, 10½" Tall	$850
Pitcher, Syrup with Lid, 4¾" Tall	$450
Pitcher, 7" Tall, Clear Handle	$325
Pitcher, 7¼" Tall, Gilded, Ribbed Handle, Ruffled Top (Consolidated)	$375
Pitcher, Milk, 7¼" Tall	$250
Pitcher, Tankard Style, 10" Tall, Diamond Quilted Pattern	$285
Pitcher, Water, 11" Tall	$525
Salt and Pepper Shakers (Consolidated)	$225
Salt and Pepper Shakers, Several Styles	$225
Sugar Shaker, Several Styles	$425
Sugar Dish, 3½" Tall, Enameled Floral Design	$275
Spooner, Several Styles	$110
Toothpick Holder, Ribbed	$95
Toothpick Holder, Loop Pattern	$175
Tumbler, Enameled Design, Several Styles	$90
Vase, 6" Tall, 2-Handled	$325
Vase, 7¼" Tall, Enameled Floral Design	$225
Vase, 8¼" Tall, Enameled Floral Design	$250
Vase, 10½" Tall, Enameled Floral Design	$275
Wineglass, 6" Tall	$65

Pink Slag
Indiana Tumbler and Goblet Company, 1880s–Early 1990s

Pink Slag is an opaque pressed glass with swirled or marbleized shading from white to pink. It was made primarily in tableware. The rarest and most valuable pattern was Indiana's Inverted Fan and Feather. Pink Slag is also referred to as Agate or Marble. Offshoots of this marbleized design were produced by others in various colors; however, the style is not that common. Swirling is not an easy effect to achieve, because colors tend to blend into one rather than remaining separate or partially mixing to achieve slag.

Bowl, 6½", Inverted Fan and Feather Pattern	$1,125
Bowl, 9", Footed, Inverted Fan and Feather Pattern	$900
Bowl, 10"	$825
Butter Dish with Cover, 6" Diameter, Inverted Fan and Feather Pattern	$1,550
Compote, 5", Inverted Fan and Feather Pattern	$775
Creamer, 3½" Tall, Handled, Inverted Fan and Feather Pattern	$875
Creamer, 4½" Tall, Pitcher Style, Inverted Fan and Feather Pattern	$950
Creamer, 4¾" Tall, 4-Footed, Beaded Handle, Inverted Fan and Feather Pattern	$1,000
Cruet with Stopper, 6" Tall, Inverted Fan and Feather Pattern	$2,250
Cruet with Stopper, 6½" Tall	$1,500
Lamp, 8¼" Tall	$1,250
Pitcher, 8" Tall, Inverted Fan and Feather Pattern	$2,750
Punch Cup, 2½" Tall, Inverted Fan and Feather Pattern	$525
Saltshaker with Metal Top, Inverted Fan and Feather Pattern	$425
Sauce Dish, 2½" Tall, Ball-Shape Feet, Inverted Fan and Feather Pattern	$475
Spooner, Inverted Fan and Feather Pattern	$475
Sugar with Cover, 4" Tall, Inverted Fan and Feather Pattern	$1,100
Sugar with Cover, 5½" Tall, Inverted Fan and Feather Pattern	$1,250
Toothpick Holder, Inverted Fan and Feather Pattern	$875
Tumbler, 3½" Tall	$525
Tumbler, 4" Tall, Inverted Fan and Feather Pattern	$650
Tumbler, Grape and Vine Design	$250

Pomona
New England Glass Company, 1885–Early 1900s

Pomona is an art style of glass patented by Joseph Locke in 1885. It was produced by applying or dipping an object into acid to produce a mottled, frosted appearance. Pieces were then further decorated by staining and etching, usually floral patterns (especially the cornflower).

Bowl, Finger, 3", Matching 4½" Underplate, Ruffled Rim, Blue Cornflower Design	$85
Bowl, 4½", 3" Tall, Amber Stained	$300
Bowl, 8", Scalloped Amber Rim, Inverted Thumbprint Pattern	$125
Bowl, 10", Blue Cornflower Design	$375
Bowl, 10", 4¼" Tall, Crimped Sides, Blue Pansy and Butterfly Design	$400
Butter Dish with Cover and 8" Underplate, 4½" Tall, Reeded Handle, Stained Gold Foliage Design	$1,350
Celery Vase, 6¼" Tall, Ruffled Rim, Crystal Base, Blue Cornflower Design	$475
Champagne Glass, 5" Tall, Amber Stained	$275
Creamer with Amber Handles, Inverted Thumbprint Pattern	$325
Cruet with Stopper, 5½" Tall, Applied Clear Handle, Blueberry Design with Gold Leaves	$425
Cruet with Stopper, 7¼" Tall, Crimped Foot, Applied Handle, Blue Cornflower Design	$750
Goblet, 6" Tall, Amber Stained	$300
Marmalade Jar with Cover, 6" Tall, Amber Trim, Ribbed Swirl Design	$175
Nappy, 5¼", Applied Handle, Blue Cornflower Design	$200
Pitcher, 6¾" Tall, Tankard Style, Applied Crystal Handle, Gold Stained, Diamond Quilted Pattern	$550
Pitcher, 12¼" Tall, Tankard Style, Gold Grass and Blue Butterfly Design	$850
Punch Bowl, 14", Blue Cornflower Design	$2,250
Punch Cup, Blue Cornflower Design	$175
Sauce Dish, 4", Amber Rim, Inverted Thumbprint Pattern	$55
Sugar Dish with Applied Amber Handles, Inverted Thumbprint Pattern	$325
Toothpick Holder, 3¼" Tall, Tricorner Top	$250

Toothpick Holder, 3¼" Tall, Blue Cornflower Design	$200
Tumbler, 3" to 4" Tall, Blue Cornflower Design	$175
Vase, 3" Tall, Fan Shape, 6" Across, Ruffled Rim, Blue Cornflower Design	$275
Vase, 5¾" Tall, 4½" Diameter, Crimped, Ruffled Foot, Blue Cornflower Design	$575
Vase, 6" Tall, Ruffled, Blueberry Design	$425
Vase, 9" Tall, Tricorner Top, Diamond Quilted Pattern	$225

Purple Slag
Challinor, Taylor and Company; and Others, 1870s–20th Century

Purple Slag is a style of glass characterized by colorful violet or purple swirling, or marbleized designs. Purple Slag was a popular art form of the Challinor, Taylor and Company of Tarentum, Pennsylvania, which produced it in the 1870s and 1880s. Other American and English firms produced it as well. In the later 20th century, Imperial and Kemple were two known American producers. Like Pink Slag and other slag glass in general, swirled or marbleized shaded glass is not an easy effect to achieve.

Boot Glass, Rectangular, 3" Tall, 2" Long	$75
Bowl with Cover, 6", Beaded Rim Design	$100
Bowl, 8", Heart and Vine Design	$65
Bowl, 8½", Shallow, Rimmed Like Pie Pan	$125
Bread Tray, Tam O' Shanter Design	$325
Butter Dish with Cover, Paneled Grape Design	$100
Cake Stand with Pedestal Base, 10½"	$100
Celery Vase, 9¼" Tall, Pedestal Foot	$125
Compote, 4½"	$85
Creamer, Various Styles	$100
Demitasse Cup and Saucer, 2" Tall	$65
Lion Covered Animal Dish	$175
Mug, Various Molded Animal Styles	$100
Owl Figurine, 4½" Tall, Imperial	$100
Pitcher, 7½" Tall, Molded Basket-Weave Design with Fans	$300
Plate, 10"	$65
Plate, 10½", Lattice Edge	$75
Platter, 13" Diameter, Lattice Edge	$125

Rabbit Covered Animal Dish	$300
Salt Dip, Master	$85
Sugar Dish, 1 or 2 Handled, Various Styles	$100
Thimble, Whimsey, 2" Tall, Shaped Like Giant Thimble	$100
Toothpick Holder, Acanthus and Scrolled Design	$150
Tumbler, 4½" Tall, Ribbed	$60
Vase, 4" Tall, Argonaut Shell Pattern	$55
Vase, 5" Tall, Fan Style	$65
Vase, 6" Tall, Jack-in-the-Pulpit Style	$75

Quezal Art Glass and Decorating Company
1901–25

Because Quezal was founded by two men who had worked for Tiffany (Martin Bach and Thomas Johnson), Quezal's products are very similar in nature to Tiffany's. Brilliant iridescent forms of blue, gold, white, green, and so on were much like Tiffany's Favrile. The name Quezal was patented in 1902, and the name was often engraved in silver block letters on the underside; pieces not signed are confused with both Tiffany and Steuben.

Bowl, 5½", Flared, Iridescent Gold	$300
Bowl, 6", Ruffled, Iridescent Gold	$350
Bowl, 7", Fluted, Iridescent Gold	$550
Bowl, Center with Base, 13", Flared, Ribbed, Iridescent Gold with Blue to Violet Shading, Signed	$1,250
Candlestick, 7¾" Tall, Iridescent Blue, Signed	$325
Compote, 6", Pedestal Base, Iridescent Gold, Signed	$475
Compote, 7", Thin Stem, Iridescent Gold, Signed	$500
Cup, Scroll Handle, Iridescent Gold, Signed	$450
Decanter with Stopper, 11½" Tall, Flared, Iridescent Green and Gold Feather Design, Signed	$4,250
Lamp, 6" Tall, Bronze Feet, Iridescent Gold, Signed	$1,450
Lamp, Double, Claw Feet, Pearlized Base, Calcite with Gold Interior	$950
Lamp, 28" Tall, Onyx and Metal Base and Stand, Ribbed Opal Shade with Gold Leaf and Green Bands, 5" Shade That Is Signed Twice	$1,250
Perfume Bottle with Stopper, 8" Tall, 4-Sided Cone Shape, Iridescent Gold	$425
Plate, 6", Scalloped, Iridescent Gold	$275

Plate, 8", Scalloped, Iridescent Gold	$325
Salt Dip, 1¾", Scalloped, Ribbed, Iridescent Gold	$200
Salt Dip, 2¾", Gold, Signed "Quezal"	$325
Saucer, 7", Stretched, Iridescent Gold	$350
Sconce, Double Branched, Gilded, 5" Shades	$650
Shade, 4½" Diameter, Yellow with Gold Lining	$350
Shade, 4¾" Diameter, Ribbed, Iridescent Gold with Colored Highlights	$200
Shade, 6" Tall, Iridescent Gold with Blue and Violet Highlights	$275
Shade, 6¾" Tall, Iridescent Green with Gold Lining, King Tut Pattern	$1,250
Shade, 7" Tall, Flared, Ribbed Sides, Yellow, Signed "Quezal"	$375
Shade, 7" Tall, Opal with Gold Lining	$1,175
Shade, 7¾" Tall, Bullet Shape, Opal with Green Feathers and Gold Edging	$775
Shade, 8⅜" Tall, Opal with Yellow Feathers	$900
Shade, 13½", Green Pulled Feathers with Gold Lining, Signed "Quezal"	$1,050
Spittoon, 3½" Tall, Bulbous, Latticed Green and White with Gold Feathers, Marked "Quezal S 813"	$725
Toothpick Holder, 2¼" Tall, Melon Ribbed, Iridescent Blue to Violet Shading with Green and Gold Foliage	$275
Vase, 4" Tall, Ivory with Gold and Green Feather Design	$1,275
Vase, 4½" Tall, Ruffled and Stretched Rim, Signed	$525
Vase, 5" Tall, Iridescent Dark Blue, Gold Leaves	$1,450
Vase, 6" Tall, Iridescent Reddish Gold, Lightning Design	$1,550
Vase, 7" Tall, Footed, Fluted and Crackled Rim, Amber with White Leaves and Green Edge, Marked "Quezal 167"	$1,350
Vase, 7" Tall, Iridescent Blue, Signed "Quezal"	$575
Vase, ¾" Tall, Gold Rim, Green with Silver Feathers, Signed "Quezal 12"	$1,350
Vase, 8" Tall, Footed, Flared, Iridescent Blue, Signed	$725
Vase, 8½" Tall, Jack-in-the-Pulpit Style, Overhanging Rim, Footed, Iridescent Gold with Yellow Leaves, Inscribed "Quezal"	$1,350
Vase, 8¾" Tall, Jack-in-the-Pulpit Style, Iridescent Gold and Scrolling	$1,250
Vase, 8¾" Tall, Ruffled, Iridescent Green with Gold Lining and Gold Feathers, Signed	$1,550

Vase, 9" Tall, Footed, Opaque Cream Color with Green and Gold Foliage, Signed "Quezal N.Y."	$2,500
Vase, 10" Tall, Iridescent Gold with Silver Overlay	$1,150
Vase, 11" Tall, Iridescent Blue with Silver Scrolling	$1,250
Vase, 11" Tall, Trumpet, Ribbed, White with Gold Lattice and Gold Interior, Marked "Quezal 6"	$1,100
Vase, 12" Tall, 9" Diameter, Banded Floral and Feather Design, Gold Interior, Marked "Quezal #437"	$6,750
Vase, 13½" Tall, Jack-in-the-Pulpit Style, Amber	$4,650
Vase, 15" Tall, Jack-in-the-Pulpit Style, White with Gold and Green Feather Design	$5,650
Vase, 16" Tall, Jack-in-the-Pulpit Style, Footed, Ruffled and Flared Rim, Green and Gold Feather Design with Iridescent Gold Lining, Signed	$5,750
Whiskey Tumbler, 2¾" Tall, Iridescent Gold, Signed	$250
Wineglass, 6" Tall, Iridescent Gold, Signed	$500

Reading Artistic Glass Works
1884–86

Although the company went bankrupt after two short years, Reading Artistic Glass Works did manage to produce some fine art glass. Amberina, opalescent, decorated cut patterns, and so on were all made in that short time period. The opalescent colors are particularly noteworthy and exist in beautiful blues, greens, pinks, purples, whites, yellows, and others.

Bowl, 6", Ruffled, Opalescent Blue	$225
Carafe, 10½" Tall, Red with Crystal Spout	$350
Carafe, 1½" Tall, Pink with Crystal Spout	$375
Ewer, 13" Tall, Red with Clear Spout	$375
Pitcher, Water, 10½" Tall, Pink, Thumbprint Pattern	$500
Pitcher, Water, 11" Tall, Pink and White Frosted Coin Dot Design	$525
Vase, 7¾" Tall, Overshot, Blue Opal	$475
Vase, 9½" Tall, Pink with Dark Red Opalescent Neck	$825
Vase, 13½" Tall, Opalescent Yellow, Swirled Design	$550
Vase, 14" Tall, Black with Applied Black Neck Ring	$575
Vase, 14½" Tall, Footed, Opaque Yellow, 2 Applied Clear Crystal Handles	$550

Rubena or Rubina Crystal
Various Companies, 1880s–1890s

Rubena is characterized by a gradual shading from crystal at the bottom to ruby red at the top. Some pieces have shading that is not gradual but contains a distinct line of color separation. Pieces are also at times accented with clear crystal (such as on the handles, lids, stoppers, and feet). Many cut patterns were decorated with Rubena shading. George Duncan and Sons is credited with the original introduction of this design, and others soon followed.

Basket, 6" Tall, 4" Diameter	$165
Bowl, 4½", Daisy and Scroll Pattern	$100
Bowl, 5½", Inverted Thumbprint Pattern	$135
Bowl, 6½", Frosted	$135
Bowl, 8", Royal Ivy Pattern	$165
Bowl, 9", Frosted, Royal Ivy Pattern	$185
Bowl, Oval, 9½", Overshot	$235
Bowl, Rose, 5½", 4¾" Tall, Gold Floral Design	$185
Butter Dish with Cover, 7" Tall, Gilded, Signed "Northwood"	$325
Butter Dish with Cover, Frosted, Royal Ivy Pattern	$375
Butter Dish with Cover, Royal Oak Pattern	$425
Candlestick, 9" Tall, Cranberry to Clear Coloring	$135
Carafe, Water, 8" Tall, Cranberry to Clear Coloring	$250
Castor Set, Pickle Dish with Silver-Plated Holder and Tongs (Northwood)	$425
Castor Set, Pickle Dish, Silver-Plated Frame and Cover, Frosted Insert	$425
Cheese Dish with Cover, 6½" Tall, 10" Diameter	$375
Compote, 8½" Tall, Footed, Honeycomb Pattern	$275
Condiment Set, 4-Piece, 2 Square Bottles, Rectangular Salt Dip, Silver-Plated Holder	$375
Cookie Jar with Cover, 9½" Tall, Ribbed	$425
Cracker Jar with Sterling Silver Cover, 7" Tall, 6" Diameter, Cut Fan and Strawberry Pattern	$1,250
Creamer, Frosted, Royal Ivy Pattern	$325
Creamer, Royal Oak Pattern	$200
Creamer, Frosted, Royal Oak Pattern	$425
Cruet with Stopper, 5¼" Tall, Frosted, Royal Ivy Pattern	$550

Cruet with Stopper, 5½" Tall, Royal Oak Pattern	$625
Cruet with Cut Crystal Stopper, 6" Tall, Overshot	$500
Cruet with Stopper, 10" Tall	$175
Decanter with Stopper, 8" Tall, Signed "Northwood"	$400
Decanter with Stopper, 9" Tall, Applied Crystal Handle	$225
Ice Bucket, Silver Handle, Enameled	$200
Jam Jar with Cover, Swirl Pattern	$250
Jelly Dish, Triangular, Crimped, Silver-Plated Holder	$300
Mug, 3¾" Tall, Octagonal, Gold and Silver Trim	$115
Mustard Jar with Silver-Plated Color, Enameled Floral Design, Thumbprint Pattern	$235
Perfume Bottle with Faceted Stopper, 5¾" Tall	$215
Perfume Bottle with Silver-Plated Stopper, 6¼" Tall, Diamond Quilted and Drape Pattern	$185
Perfume Bottle with Crystal Faceted Stopper, 6½" Tall, Cut-Paneled Design	$195
Pitcher, Syrup with Metal Lid, 4¾" Tall	$500
Pitcher, Syrup with Metal Lid, 5¼" Tall, Inverted Thumbprint Pattern	$335
Pitcher, Syrup with Metal Lid, 5¼" Tall, Royal Ivy Pattern	$450
Pitcher, Water, 8½" Tall, Royal Ivy Pattern	$700
Pitcher, Water, 8½" Tall, Royal Oak Pattern	$550
Punch Cup, 4¼" Tall	$75
Salt Dip, 2" Tall, Hexagonal, Silver-Plated Stand	$200
Saltshaker, Threaded (Northwood)	$165
Salt and Pepper Shakers, Frosted, Royal Ivy Pattern	$185
Salt and Pepper Shakers, Frosted, Royal Oak Pattern	$275
Sauce Dish, Several Styles	$75
Spooner, Frosted, Royal Ivy Pattern	$150
Spooner, Frosted, Royal Oak Pattern	$175
Sugar, Frosted, Royal Ivy Pattern	$225
Sugar with Cover, Royal Oak Pattern	$265
Sugar with Cover, Frosted, Royal Oak Pattern	$450
Sugar Shaker, Frosted, 5¼" Tall, Royal Ivy Pattern	$350

Sugar Shaker, Frosted, 5¼" Tall, Royal Oak Pattern	$325
Toothpick Holder, Several Styles	$185
Tumbler, Enameled Floral Design, 5½" Tall, Diamond Quilted Pattern	$115
Tumbler, Enameled Design, 6" Tall, Inverted Thumbprint Pattern	$125
Tumbler, 6" Tall, Royal Ivy Pattern	$150
Tumbler, Frosted, 6" Tall, Royal Oak Pattern	$150
Vase, 6" Tall, Ribbed Interior, Frosted with Etched Floral and Leaf Design, Mt. Washington	$325
Vase, 8" Tall, Pedestal Foot, Ribbed, Flared	$175
Vase, 8" Tall, Enameled Floral Decoration	$225
Vase, 8¾" Tall, Trumpet Shape, Ruffled, Gold Floral Decoration	$275
Vase, 10" Tall, Footed, Applied Crystal Decoration	$225
Vase, 10" Tall, Ruffled, Enameled Floral Design with Gold Trim	$225
Vase, 13" Tall, Trumpet Shape, Crystal Pedestal Foot, Crystal Applied Threading	$275

Rubena Verde or Rubina Verde
Various Companies, 1880s–1890s

Rubena Verde is similar to many of the other shaded designs in Amberina, Peach Blow, and Rubena Crystal. The colors in Rubena Verde vary from an aqua green or greenish yellow at the base to a ruby red at the top. Hobbs, Brocunier, and Company is usually noted as the original maker; however, others followed soon afterward.

Basket, Bride's, 8" Diameter, Silver-Plated Holder	$375
Basket, Bride's, 8" Diameter, Hobnail Pattern	$675
Bowl, 4", Threaded Design	$150
Bowl, 4¼", Ruffled, Hobnail Pattern	$135
Bowl, 7", Scalloped, Enameled Gold Decorations	$235
Bowl, 8", 3-Footed, Circle Pattern (Hobbs Brocunier)	$275
Bowl, 9½", Ruffled, Inverted Thumbprint Pattern	$225
Bowl, Rose, 5", Crimped, Hobnail Pattern	$165
Butter Dish with Cover, Daisy and Button Pattern	$275
Celery Vase, 12" Tall, 6" Diameter, Cherry Blossoms and Butterflies Design	$325
Cheese Dish with Yellow Ball Stopper and Yellow Matching Underplate, Circle Pattern (Hobbs Brocunier)	$375

Creamer, 5" Tall, Reeded Handle, Inverted Thumbprint Pattern	$485
Cruet with Stopper, 4" Tall, Rounded Design, Inverted Thumbprint Pattern	$625
Cruet with Stopper, 6½" Tall, Frosted, Hobnail Pattern (Hobbs Brocunier)	$625
Cruet with Stopper, 6¾" Tall, Triple-Lipped Top, Inverted Thumbprint Pattern	$625
Cruet with Stopper, 7" Tall, Vaseline Handle, Inverted Thumbprint Pattern (Hobbs Brocunier)	$625
Cup with Yellow Handle, Circle Pattern (Hobbs Brocunier)	$115
Epergne, 22" Tall, Trumpet in Center of Bowl, Hanging Baskets	$575
Perfume Bottle with Stopper, No Handle, 5½" Tall, Inverted Thumbprint Pattern (Hobbs Brocunier)	$525
Pitcher, Syrup with Silver-Plated Lid, 5" Tall, Inverted Thumbprint Pattern	$250
Pitcher, Syrup with Lid, Hobnail Pattern	$275
Pitcher, Water, 7½" Tall, Enameled Floral Design	$550
Pitcher, Water, 8" Tall, Square Top, Greenish Yellow Handle, Hobnail Pattern	$485
Pitcher, Water, 8" Tall, Clear Handle, Tri-Cornered Lip, Enameled Daisy Design	$525
Pitcher, Water, 9" Tall, Inverted Thumbprint Pattern	$600
Salt and Pepper Shakers, 4½" Tall, Pewter Tops, Enameled Floral Design	$350
Sweetmeat Dish, 5¾" Tall, Octagonal, Notched Edge, Greenish Yellow Trim, Silver-Plated Holder	$215
Toothpick Holder, 4" Tall, Opalescent Hobnail Pattern	$175
Tumbler, 4" Tall, Diamond Quilted Pattern	$185
Tumbler, 4" Tall, Hobnail Pattern	$350
Vase, 6" Tall, Ruffled	$185
Vase, 6½" Tall, Scalloped, Reverse Color Pattern	$215
Vase, 6¾" Tall, Crimped, Footed	$165
Vase, 7" Tall, Scalloped, Enameled Floral Design	$250
Vase, 8" Tall, Jack-in-the-Pulpit Style, Applied Greenish Yellow Feet	$275
Vase, 8¼" Tall, Applied Crystal Feet and Crystal Foliage	$175
Vase, 9¼" Tall, Pedestal Feet, Drape Pattern	$235
Vase, 11" Tall, Ruffled, Green Rim, Drape Pattern	$450
Wineglass, 4¼" Tall, Inverted Thumbprint Pattern	$185
Witchball with Chain, Hobnail Pattern (Hobbs Brocunier)	$150

Satin Glass
Various Companies, 1880s–Early 1900s

Satin glass is characterized by opaque milk, opal, or colored glass with a distinctive white lining. The satin texture or finish was created by a thin coating or washing with hydrofluoric acid.

Basket, 4¾" x 3" Oval,¾" Tall, Pinched Rim, Applied Frosted Crystal Handle, White with Pink Lining, Herringbone Pattern	$375
Bell, 6" Tall, Blue	$65
Biscuit Jar with Silver-Plated Cover and Handle, 7" Tall, Pink Florette Pattern	$400
Biscuit Jar with Silver-Plated Cover and Handle, 9" Tall, White Floral Pattern	$325
Bowl, Finger, 4½", Diamond Quilted Pattern	$75
Bowl, 6½", 3-Lobed Rim, Olive Green with White Interior, Gold Floral Design	$265
Bowl, 8", Ruffled, Rainbow Colors	$365
Bowl, 9¼", 3⅜" Tall, 3 Applied Frosted Feet, Ruffled, White with Pink Interior, Diamond Quilted Pattern	$475
Bowl, Rose, 3½", 3¼" Tall, 8-Crimped, Blue Overlay with Embossed Floral Design	$185
Cookie Jar with Silver-Plated Cover, 8" Tall, 5" Diameter, Shell and Seaweed Overlay Design	$475
Creamer, Blue, Marked "World's Fair—1893" (New England)	$425
Cruet with Stopper, 7" Tall, Multicolored	$550
Epergne, 18" Tall, Enameled Bird and Floral Design	$450
Ewer, 8½" Tall, Swirled White with Multicolored Enameled Stripes	$525
Ewer, 9¾" Tall, Blue with Frosted Handle, Enameled Flower Design	$300
Ewer, 12¾" Tall, Pedestal Foot, Frosted Handle, Enameled Floral Design	$425
Ewer, 15" Tall, Applied Crystal Rope Handle, Pink with White Lining	$1,150
Lamp, Miniature, 5" Tall, Ruffled Base and Shade, Swirled Pink Design	$525
Lamp, Miniature, 8½" Tall, Globe Shade, Square Base, Red with Crystal Chimney, Drape Pattern	$500
Lamp, 8½" Tall, Gone with the Wind Style, Brass Foot, Red with 2 Winged Griffins on Each Globe	$875
Pitcher, Milk, 6½" Tall, Blue, Diamond Quilted Pattern	$825
Pitcher, Water, 7½" Tall, Square Top, Reeded Handle, White Liner	$375
Spittoon, White Casing on Light Blue Background	$200
Sugar, Blue, Marked "World's Fair—1893" (New England)	$385

Sugar Shaker, 4" Tall, Blue with Embossed Leaf Design	$350
Toothpick Holder, ¼" Tall, Blue and White Enameled Design	$155
Vase, 3½" Tall, Bulbous with Fan-Shape Top, Pink with White Interior, Ribbon Pattern	$275
Vase, 6" Tall, Conical, Ribbed, Ruffled, Blue	$165
Vase, 6½" Tall, Footed, Ribbed, Pink Overlay with Enameled Floral Design	$135
Vase, 7" Tall, Gourd Shape, Light Blue to Turquoise Coloring	$325
Vase, 7½" Tall, Acid Cut Back Squares, Pink Overlay with Enameled Floral Design	$325
Vase, 8" Tall, Gourd Shape, Blue	$200
Vase, 8" Tall, Ribbed, White with Green Lining	$225
Vase, 9" Tall, Blue Overlay with Gold Scrolls and Enameled Floral Design	$225
Vase, 10½" Tall, Peach Overlay with Enameled Floral Design	$240
Vase, 11" Tall, Ribbed, Blue Overlay with Enameled Floral and Jewel Design	$250
Vase, 18" Tall, Blue, Iris Decoration	$425
Vase, Ruffled, Pink and White Swirls, White Lining (Mt. Washington)	$550

Sinclaire, H. P. Company
1904–29

Sinclaire was primarily a producer of cut, engraved, or etched glassware. They obtained their blanks early on from some of the best lead crystal makers (such as Corning, Dorflinger, and Baccarat), but after 1920 they produced their own blanks. In the 1920s Sinclaire created many art objects in various colors similar to those of Steuben.

Bowl, 10", Pedestal Foot, Black with White Edge, Signed	$375
Bowl, 11", Ruffled, Blue with Etched Floral Design	$225
Bowl, 11½", Pink with Etched Floral Design	$235
Candlestick, 7½" Tall, Blue with Etched Scrolls	$90
Candlestick, 8" Tall, Dark Amber Etched Design, Signed	$100
Candlestick, 9½" Tall, Yellow with Etched Floral Design	$125
Candlestick, 10" Tall, Crystal, Engraved Vintage Design, Signed	$150
Candlestick, 10¼" Tall, Swirl Ribbed, Light Green, Signed	$100
Cologne Bottle with Stopper, 5¼" Tall, Etched Floral Design, Signed	$350
Compote, Dark Amber, Etched Design, Signed	$225
Compote, Rolled Rim, Pedestal Foot, Light Green	$175

Decanter with Stopper, 8" Tall, Crystal, Etched Floral and Foliage Design	$225
Perfume Bottle with Stopper, 6" Tall, Electric Blue	$300
Pitcher, Green with Amber Handle, Etched Vintage Pattern	$375
Plate, 8½", Amber, Leaf Design	$65
Tumbler, Green with Amber Base, Etched Vintage Pattern	$100
Urn, 8" Tall, Celeste Blue	$175
Vase, 5" Tall, Iridized Blue, Signed	$200
Vase, 5½" Tall, 4" Diameter, Interior Ribbing, Amethyst	$95
Vase, 6" Tall, Amethyst to Crystal Coloring, Lily Pattern	$325
Vase, 7½" Tall, Celeste Blue	$165
Vase, 12" Tall, Crystal, Etched Flower and Foliage Design	$235
Vase, 12", Olive Green with Etched Floral Design	$275
Vase, 13½" Tall, Crystal, Etched Tulip Design	$575
Wineglass, Green to Crystal Coloring, Duchess Pattern	$90

Smith Brothers
1874–99

The Smith Brothers (Harry and Alfred) were originally part of a decorating department at Mt. Washington. They formed their own decorating company but still used many blanks provided by their previous employer. Smith Brothers was noted for many cut, engraved, and enameled floral patterns. They also decorated glass in the majority of the popular art designs of the day such as Burmese, Peach Blow, gilding, silver or silver plating, and numerous other color and color effects.

Bowl, 4", Purple Rim, Floral Design	$265
Bowl, 5½", Beaded Edge, Blue and Purple Floral Design	$500
Bowl, 6", Melon Ribbed, Iridescent Gold, Beaded White Rim	$500
Bowl, 7½", Blue and White Floral Design, Gold Rim	$525
Bowl, 8", Green and White Floral Design Gilding	$700
Box with Cover, Square, 3¼" x 3¼", Pink and White Floral Design	$425
Cookie Jar with Cover, 7¼" Tall, Pink and White Floral Design	$1,000
Cookie Jar with Cover, 8½" Tall, Multicolored Floral Design on Cream Background, Signed	$1,550
Cracker Jar, Cube Shape, Silver-Plated Cover and Handle, Enameled Crab Design	$950

Cracker Jar with Cover, 7" Tall, Silver-Plated Top, Ridge and Handle, Various Enameled Floral and Foliage Designs	$875
Creamer, Cream with Enameled Gold Flowers	$350
Creamer, Cream with Enameled Lady's or Soldier's Head, Silver-Plated Handle and Rim	$375
Humidor with Cover, 6" Tall, 5" Diameter, Pansy Design on Body and Cover	$450
Humidor with Silver-Plated Humidor Cover, 6½" Tall, Cream, Pansy Design, Signed	$850
Humidor with Silver-Plated Humidor Cover, 7" Tall, Cream, Floral Design, Signed	$875
Lamp Shade, Various Enameled Floral and Foliage Designs	$165
Mustard Jar with Silver-Plated Hinged Cover, Silver-Plated Handle, Various Enameled Floral Designs	$325
Mustard Dish, Handled, Pansy Design, Signed	$275
Pitcher, Syrup with Silver-Plated Rim, Handle, and Cover, 4¾" Tall, Melon Ribbed, Pastel Floral Design	$775
Pitcher, Water, 8½" Tall, White with Gold Floral Decoration	$275
Plate, 6⅜", Ship Design (**Santa Maria**)	$675
Plate, 7", Ship Design	$675
Plate, 7¾", Ship Design (**Santa Maria**)	$700
Salt Bowl, Various Enameled Floral Designs	$100
Saltshaker, Various Enameled Floral Designs	$150
Saltshaker, Egg Shape, Various Enameled Floral Designs	$175
Sugar with Silver-Plated Cover, Cream with Gold Enameled Flowers, Silver-Plated Handle	$385
Sugar with Silver-Plated Cover, Cream with Gold Enameled Lady's or Soldier's Head, Silver-Plated Handle	$385
Sugar Shaker, 3" Tall, Ribbed, Silver-Plated Top, White with Purple Columbines	$775
Sweetmeat Dish, Raised Gold, Enameled Pansies, Rampant Lion Mark	$600
Toothpick Holder, 2¼" Tall, Vertical Ribbed (Columns), White with Enameled Flowers	$200
Toothpick Holder, 2½" Tall, Vertically Ribbed, Blue with Enameled Rose Design	$250
Tumbler, Blue with Enameled Stork Design	$75
Vase, 2½" Tall, Ribbed, Daisy Design, Signed	$425

Vase, 2½" Tall, Ribbed, Gold Lettering "Season's Greetings," Signed	$425
Vase, 3¾" Tall, Beaded Rim, Melon Ribbed, Multicolored Enameled Floral Design	$215
Vase, 4½" Tall, Pinched Sides, Carnation Design	$575
Vase, 5" Tall, Cream with Enameled Flowers, Signed	$375
Vase, 5¼" Tall, Triangular Shape, Pale Yellow with White Floral Design	$400
Vase, 6¼" Tall, Bulbous, Embossed Rope Rim, Gold Trim, Multicolored Enameled Floral and Foliage Design	$300
Vase, 7¾" Tall, Cream with Birds and Floral Design, Signed	$635
Vase, 8½" Tall, Flask Style, Enameled Ship (*Santa Maria*), Signed	$1,650
Vase, 8½" Tall, Floral Mum Design, Signed	$800
Vase, 9" Tall, Cylindrical, Enameled Bird Design, Signed	$375
Vase, 10" Tall, Banded Glass at Top and Bottom, Pink, Enameled Bird and Reed Design	$325
Vase, 12½" Tall, Crystal with Purple and White Irises, Green Foliage, and Gold Trim	$625

Spatter Glass
Various Companies, 1880s–Early 1900s

Spatter refers to spotted or multicolored glass that has a white inner casing and crystal outer casing. At times, leftover colored glass was combined and blown into a mold to create a splotching or spattering effect. Many objects of a whimsical nature were produced in this fashion.

Basket, 5¼" Tall, 4¾" Diameter, Crimped and Ruffled Rim, Applied Crystal Handle, Blue, Pink, and White Spatter, White Lining	$185
Basket, 6" Tall, Multicolored, Earth-Tone Spatter, White Lining	$150
Basket, 8¼" Tall, Green Spatter, White Lining	$300
Basket, Bride's, 10" Tall, Crimped, Rainbow Spatter	$235
Bowl, 5", Rainbow Spatter, White Lining	$150
Bowl, 6½", Blue Spatter, White Interior	$165
Bowl, 8", Pink Spatter	$185
Bowl, 10", Pleated Top, Blue Spatter	$185
Bowl, Centerpiece, 13½", Swirled, Footed, Two Applied Amber Handles, Yellow with White Spatter	$200
Bowl, Rose, 4½" Tall, Blue Spatter	$85

Candlestick, 8" Tall, Rainbow Spatter on Blue Background $95

Candlestick, 8½" Tall, Pink Spatter on White Background $115

Candy Jar with Cover, 6¼" Tall, 3½" Diameter, Yellow and Blue Spatter, Enameled Floral Design $175

Cruet with Stopper, 7½" Tall, Blue and Yellow Spatter $285

Cruet with Stopper, 8" Tall, Crystal Handle, Blue and White Spatter (Mt. Washington) $315

Decanter with Crystal Heart-Shape Stopper, 8¾" Tall, Applied Crystal Handle, Blue and White Spatter $225

Decanter with Crystal Faceted Stopper, 10" Tall, Pinched Sides, Red and White Spatter $275

Ewer, 11" Tall, 3¾" Diameter, Footed, Tricorner Rim, Applied Crystal Handle, Pink with Yellow Lining, Yellow and White Spatter, Floral and Butterfly Design $250

Pitcher, Milk, 5½" Tall, Cranberry and Frosted Coloring with Rainbow Swirled Spatter $315

Pitcher, Water, 8" Tall, Rainbow Spatter on Blue Background $255

Pitcher, Water, 8¼" Tall, Blue and White Spatter $275

Rolling Pin, 15" Long, 2" Diameter, White with Maroon and Cobalt Blue Spatter $275

Salt Dip, 1¾" Tall, Crystal Footed, Blue and White Spatter $125

Sugar Shaker, Cased Cobalt Blue, Orange and White Spatter $200

Toothpick Holder, 2½" Tall, Rainbow Spatter on Red Background $150

Tumbler, 5¾" Tall, Green and White Spatter $90

Vase, 5¼" Tall, Blue and White Spatter $140

Vase, 6" Tall, Yellow Casing with Gold Spatter $150

Vase, 6" Tall, Speckled Pink and White Spatter $150

Vase, 7" Tall, Crimped, Opalescent Blue with White Spatter, White Lining $150

Vase, 7¼" Tall, Petal-Shape Crystal Feet, White Lining, Yellow and White Spatter $200

Vase, 8" Tall, White Lining, Rainbow Spatter $150

Vase, 8¾" Tall, Flared, Pink, White, and Yellow Spatter $175

Vase, 9" Tall, Crystal Thorn Handles, Rainbow Spatter $200

Vase, 10½" Tall, Pink, White, and Red Spatter $225

Vase, 11" Tall, Ruffled, Blue Spatter $250

Vase, 12" Tall, 3-Petal Top, Yellow and White with Enameled Floral Design $275

Steuben Glass Works
1903–33

In Steuben's precrystal era, few names command as much attention in the art-glass world as Frederick Carder and Thomas J. Hawkes, who formed the original company. Hawkes was a maker of superb-quality crystal, and Carder, like Tiffany, studied the art movement in Europe as well as various art styles from around the world. Carder soon became a world-class designer, and the majority of Steuben's art-colored glass creations are attributed to him or, at the very least, to his direction. The majority of the objects created were signed "Steuben" or with Carder's signature. For further examples, refer to "Aurene" earlier in the chapter.

Ashtray, Topaz with Blue Leaf Handle, Signed	$200
Bowl, 4", Blue to Alabaster Shading, Acid Cut Back	$2,150
Bowl, 4¾" Diameter, 11" Tall, Air-Trapped Mica Flecks, Silverina Design	$1,150
Bowl, 6" Tall, Pedestal Base, Bubbled Crystal	$350
Bowl, 8" Tall, Acid Cut Back, Plum Jade	$3,150
Bowl, 6½" Diameter, 12" Tall, Cranberry to Clear Shading	$500
Bowl, 6½" Diameter, 12" Tall, Folded Rim, Ivory	$425
Bowl, 11", Pomona Green	$200
Bowl, Centerpiece, 12" Diameter, Ribbed, Pedestal Foot, Celeste Blue, Signed "Steuben"	$475
Bowl, Centerpiece, 13" Diameter, Selenium Red, Signed "Steuben"	$675
Bowl, Centerpiece, Acid Cut Back, Jade, Etched York Pattern	$3,250
Bowl, Centerpiece, 16", Footed, Bristol Yellow, Signed	$1,000
Bowl, Centerpiece, Topaz with Floral Design, Signed	$600
Bowl, Footed, Green Pomona Foot, Oriental Poppy Design, Signed "Steuben"	$1,350
Bowl, 4-Lobed, Wavy Rim, Vertical Ribbed, Green to Clear Shading, Stamped "Steuben"	$450
Candelabra, 14½" Tall, Silverina Design	$650
Candelabra, Lamp Style, Double, Rib Swirled Flame Center, Flemish Blue Design	$525
Candlestick, 6" Tall, Acid Cut Back, Jade Green on Alabaster Background, Rose Pattern	$300
Candlestick, 10" Tall, Amber, Double Twist Stem	$275
Candlestick, 12" Tall, Ribbed, Dome Foot, Double Ball Stem, Amber	$250
Candlestick, 14" Tall, Swan Stem, Venetian Style, Green	$225
Candlestick, Alabaster Foot, Rosaline Designed Cup, Signed	$225

Steuben Art Glass. *Photo by Mark Pickvet.*

Candlestick, Airtraps, Amethyst, Silverina Design, Signed	$300
Candy Dish with Cover, 6" Tall, Pedestal Base, Blue and Topaz	$275
Chalice, 12" Tall, Griffin Handles, Snake Stem, Cobalt with Gold Foil and White Streaks	$375
Champagne Glass, 5¾" Tall, Crystal Twist Stem, Black Rim, Cerise Design	$275
Champagne Glass, 6¼" Tall, Oriental Poppy Design, Signed	$550
Compote, Iridescent with Stripes, Rose Cintra Design, Venetian Style, Applied Prunts, Green Rim	$300
Compote with Cover, 12" Tall, Venetian Style, Topaz, Paperweight Pear Finial, Signed "F. Carder—Steuben"	$425
Cordial, 4¾" Tall, Knobbed Baluster Stem, Selenium Red	$250
Cup and Saucer Set, Rosaline Design	$225
Decanter with Stopper, 9" Tall, Swirl Ribbed, Bristol Yellow	$750
Goblet, 6" Tall, Pomona Green, Signed	$125
Goblet, 6" Tall, Verre de Soie Design	$125
Goblet, 7" Tall, Green, Threaded Design, Signed	$175
Goblet, 7⅛" Tall, Cintra Design Stem and Border, Opalescent, Signed	$450
Goblet, 9" Tall, Twisted Amethyst Stem, Crystal Bowl	$200
Lamp, Marble Base with 2 Bronze Nudes (Kneeling), Moss Agate Design	$4,150
Lamp Base, 14" Tall, Acid Cut Back, Plum Jade, Oriental Design	$1,850
Lamp, 17" Tall, Calcite with Gold and Green Feathers	$2,850

Mug, 6" Tall, Footed, Crystal with Green Handle and Decoration, Matsu-no-ke Design $400

Nude, Figural, Black Jade with Knees in Crystal Circle $1,750

Nut Dish, 5" x 3", Pedestal Base, Black with Jade Threading $225

Parfait, 6½" Tall, Stemmed, Rosaline and Alabaster Design $240

Pear, 5¼" Tall, Blown, Jet Black, Marked "F. Carder-Steuben" $600

Perfume Bottle with Green Stopper, 4" Tall, Bulbous, Verre de Soie Design $525

Perfume Bottle with Stopper, 12" Tall, Celeste Blue $600

Perfume Bottle with Stopper, Bristol Yellow with Black Threading, Signed $300

Pitcher, 8½" Tall, Ribbed, Pomona Green with Applied Amber Handle $300

Pitcher, 9" Tall, Tankard Style, Bristol Yellow and Black with Jade-Threaded Rim, Diamond Quilted Pattern $375

Plaque, 8" x 6½", Thomas Edison $1,150

Plaque, 5½" Square, Mottled Green and White with Flesh-Toned Bare-Breasted Woman, Pate-de-Verre Design, Signed "F. Carder 1915" $2,000

Plate, 8", Intaglio Border, Crystal to Amethyst Coloring $175

Plate, 8", Crystal with Black Threading $100

Plate, 8¼", Copper Wheel–Engraved Rim, Marina Blue Design $175

Plate, 8½", Crystal with Amethyst Rim, Signed $200

Plate, 8½", Jade Green $150

Plate, 8½", Opalescent with Blue and Red Cintra Edge $200

Powder Jar with Cover, Rosa Design, Signed $200

Salt Dip, Verre de Soie Design $150

Shade, Bell Shaped, Verre de Soie Design $150

Shade, Calcite with Acid Etched Gold Design $225

Shade, Opal, Yellow Feathering Outlined in Green, Gold Lining $250

Sherbet with Matching Underplate, Calcite with Blue Lining $400

Sherbet with Matching Underplate, Jade Green Design $175

Sugar Shaker, 8" Tall, Verre de Soie Design $525

Tumbler, 5" Tall, Amber with Flemish Blue Rim $125

Tumbler, 5" Tall, Rainbow Iridescence, Verre de Soie Design $125

Urn, 13" Tall, Banjo Shape, Footed, Venetian Style, Topaz $250

Vase, 4¾" Tall, Rosaline Design	$775
Vase, 5" Tall, Flared, Ribbed, Ivrene Design	$250
Vase, 5" Tall, Selenium Red Design	$300
Vase, 5" Tall, Yellow to White Cluthra Design	$800
Vase, 6" Tall, Acid Cut Back, Black Jade on Alabaster, Pussy Willow Design, Signed	$2,500
Vase, 6" Tall, Pedestal Foot, Ruffled, Ribbed, Iridescent, Ivrene Design	$450
Vase, 6" Tall, Trumpet Shape, Footed, Ivrene Design, Signed	$525
Vase, 6" Tall, Trumpet Shape, Alabaster Pedestal Foot, Rosaline Design, Signed	$325
Vase, 6½" Tall, Jack-in-the-Pulpit, Iridescent Ivrene Design, Signed	$775
Vase, 6½" Tall, Footed, Opaque White Swirls, Oriental Jade Design	$350
Vase, 7" Tall, Thorned, 3-Pronged, Emerald Green Design	$425
Vase, 7½" Tall, Crystal, Acid Finish, Diatreta Geometric Design	$18,500
Vase, 8" Tall, Acid Cut Back, Alabaster to Jade Shading	$950
Vase, 8" Tall, Acid Cut Back, Alabaster, Jade Green Rim	$1,050
Vase, 8" Tall, White Cluthra Design, Signed	$1,750
Vase, 8¼" Tall, Trumpet Shape, Domed Pedestal Foot, Ribbed, Celeste Blue Design	$300
Vase, 8¾" Tall, Footed, Celeste Blue	$325
Vase, 9¼" Tall, Pedestal Foot, Engraved Floral Rosaline Design	$900
Vase, 9¼" Tall, Alabaster Foot, Engraved Floral Rosaline Design	$1,250
Vase, 9½" Tall, Ribbed, Jade Green	$350
Vase, 10" Tall, Ribbed, Pedestal Foot, Bristol Yellow	$350
Vase, 10" Tall, Flat Oval Shape, Large Bubbles, Dark Red to White Shading, Cluthra Design	$1,350
Vase, 10¼" Tall, Inverted Lip, Ribbed, Ivory Design, Signed	$375
Vase, 10½" Tall, Flared, Swirled, Bubbled Cluthra Cream Design	$1,000
Vase, 10¾" Tall, Footed, Amber with Variegated Greens and Blues, Signed	$1,350
Vase, 11½" Tall, Green to Yellow Jade Shading, Acid Cut Back	$1,850
Vase, 12" Tall, Floriform, Ivory with Black Trim	$1,400
Vase, 12" Tall, Domed Foot, Flared, Selenium Red, Signed	$1,850
Vase, 13" Tall, Trumpet Shape, Fluted, Green Florentia Design, Signed	$2,500

Vase, 13¼" Tall, Cameo Green Cintra Overlaid with Alabaster, Acid Etched Chrysanthemum Design $7,250

Vase, 13½" Tall, Tyrian Design, Signed $13,500

Vase, 14" Tall, Blue Jade, Alabaster and Black Swirls, Acid Cut Back, Signed "F. Carder" $6,000

Vase, 16" Tall, Folded Rim, Optic Ribs, Marina Blue Design $575

Vase, 19½" Tall, Footed, Flared, Jade Green, Oriental Pagoda and Landscape Design, Signed $1,850

Vase, Fish Attached to Pedestal, Red, Signed Steuben $300

Wineglass, Green Swirled, Signed $200

Wineglass, 4¾" Tall, Ribbed, Inverted Baluster Stem, Topaz $175

Wineglass, 7¼" Tall, Twisted Stem, Jade and Alabaster, Signed $200

Wineglass, 8½" Tall, 2 Knobs, Circular Foot, Oval Bowl with Molded Bubbles and Threading, Transparent Green, Marked "Steuben" $150

Tiffany, Louis Comfort
1880s–1920s

The outright leader of the art nouveau period in America, Louis Comfort Tiffany, along with members of the Nash family, sparked the entire art-glass movement in the United States. Color effects, experimentation, iridescent forms, expensive metallic designs (bronze, gold, silver, platinum, and others), and a host of original art styles from around the world are all characteristic of Tiffany's work. See also "Favrile" and "Tiffany Lamps" for additional entries.

Bonbon Dish, 4" Diameter, Iridescent Yellow Orange with Opalescent Foot and Stem, Signed $425

Bowl, Finger, Matching Underplate, Ruffled, Ribbed, Iridescent Gold, Signed $175

Bowl, 5", Ruffled, Blue $775

Bowl, 7", Ruffled, Iridescent Gold, Intaglio Cut $1,050

Bowl, 10", Iridescent Gold with Green Ivy, 2 Flower Frogs $925

Bowl, 12", Footed, Opal and Yellow, Signed $1,150

Bowl, 12", Centerpiece, Opalescent Pastel Blue $1,350

Candelabrum, 2-Light, 12" Bronze with Green Glass Inserts $1,650

Candlestick, 8" Tall, Iridescent Gold, Signed $350

Chalice, 11" Tall, Iridescent Gold with Green Leaves $1,650

Cologne Bottle with Double-Lobed Stopper, 10" Tall, Signed $1,350

Tiffany Favrile Jack-in-the-Pulpit Vase. *Photo by Mark Pickvet.*

Compote, 12" Diameter, Stemmed, Blue, Signed	$1,550
Cordial, 11½" Tall, Iridescent Gold, Signed	$350
Decanter with Stopper, 8¾" Tall, Gold, Merovingian Pattern	$1,750
Decanter with Stopper, 9" Tall, Brown Agate Design with Vertical White Lines, Signed	$1,650
Inkwell, Square (4" x 4"), Hinged Lid, Insert, Bronze with Green Slag, Pine Needle Design, Signed	$550
Inkwell, Square, Embossed Brass Frame, Paneled, Marked "Tiffany Studios, N.Y. 844"	$675
Parfait, 5" Tall, Footed, Pastel Lavender and Opalescent, Signed	$500
Plate, 6", Pastel Blue, Signed "LCT"	$385
Plate, 8¼", Cobalt Blue, Opalescent Flared Rim, Green and Gold Egyptian Chain Pattern, Signed	$1,750
Plate, 11", Light Bluish Green, Opalescent Starburst Design	$425
Punch Bowl with Stand, 15½" Diameter, Iridescent Gold	$2,750
Punch Goblet, 3½" Tall, Hollow Stem, Gold, Signed	$300
Salt Dip, Ruffled, Iridescent Blue and Gold, Signed "Tiffany"	$265
Shade, Iridescent Orange with Opal Lining, King Tut Pattern	$475
Shade, 5" Tall, Opal, Green King Tut Pattern	$950
Shade, 6¼" Tall, Banded at Base and Rim, Acid Etched Leaves and Berries	$400
Shade, 10" Diameter, Domical, Gray, Green, and Iridescent Amber	$1,650
Sherbet, 4¼" Diameter, Yellow Orange with Opalescent Edge	$425

Sherbet, 5" Tall, Blue, Signed "L.C.T. T511"	$1,100
Shot Glass, Iridescent Gold with Applied Lily Pads, Signed	$525
Stamp Box, 3 Glass Inserts, Signed "Tiffany Studios"	$255
Stamp Box, Rectangular (4" x 2¼"), Bronze with Green Slag, 3 Compartments, Pine Needle Design	$325
Toothpick Holder, Iridescent Gold, Inverted Dimple Design, Signed "L.C.T.—#R8844"	$450
Tumbler, 4" Tall, Pinched Sides, Iridescent Gold, Signed	$425
Vase, 2" Tall, Miniature, Swirled Green with Berry Clusters	$1,350
Vase, 3½" Tall, Miniature, Footed, Iridescent Gold, Opalescent Amber and White Zipper Design, Signed "LCT 8604"	$1,250
Vase, 4" Tall, Paperweight Style, Cameo Floral and Intaglio Design, Signed	$6,850
Vase, 4¼" Tall, Urn Shape, Iridescent Gold with Opalescent White Flowers and Green Leaves, Marked "L.C.T. US099"	$5,350
Vase, 4¼" Tall, Paperweight Style, Crystal with Cream, Mauve, and Olive Morning Glories, Signed "L.C.T. Y6889"	$2,150
Vase, 4½" Tall, Lava with Cobalt Overlay, Gold Trailings, Signed	$27,500
Vase, 4½" Tall, Tall Collar, Iridescent Red, Signed	$3,850
Vase, 5" Tall, Tan and Brown Agate Design, Signed	$1,050
Vase, 5¼" Tall, Cylindrical, Cream Neck, Silver Band Beneath Neck, Translucent Green Glass Edge, Marked "L.C.T. Q4511"	$1,050
Vase, 5¼" Tall, Ribbed, Dimpled, Iridescent Blue	$1,050
Vase, 5½" Tall, Ribbed, Dimpled, Iridescent Blue	$1,250
Vase, 5½" Tall, Millefiori, Iridescent Gold with White Flowers and Green Leaves	$2,450
Vase, Bud, 6" Tall, Iridescent Gold, Signed, Numbered	$850
Vase, 6" Tall, Crystal Base, Pastel Yellow, Signed	$725
Vase, 6½" Tall, Iridescent Red and Black Paneled Design, Signed	$4,650
Vase, 6½" Tall, Iridescent Lava, Banded or Beaded Decoration, Signed	$7,150
Vase, 7" Tall, Paperweight Style, Peacock Feather Design, Signed	$5,850
Vase, 7¼" Tall, Flask Shape, Lava, Inscribed	$5,150
Vase, 7½" Tall, Iridescent Shades of Green, Millefiori and Gold Leaves Design, Signed	$2,650
Vase, 8" Tall, Paperweight Style, Squared Body, Iridescent Gold with Opaque Green and Milk Floral and Foliage Design, Signed "L.C.T. 42232"	$4,250

Vase, Bud, 8¼" Tall, Iridescent Gold, Green Triangle Design, Signed	$800
Vase, 8½" Tall, Iridescent Brown with Double Threading, Signed	$1,350
Vase, 9" Tall, Ribbed, Pedestal Ribbed Foot, Iridescent Gold Foliage	$1,550
Vase, 9½" Tall, Iridescent Brown, Cypriote Design	$3,650
Vase, 10" Tall, Laminated Tan and Brown Agate Striped Design, Signed	$3,850
Vase, 10" Tall, Interior Ribbed, Iridescent Yellow, Signed "L.C. Tiffany"	$1,150
Vase, 11" Tall, Iridescent Red with Gold Overlay, Signed	$1,450
Vase, 12" Tall, Paperweight Style, Gladiolus Design, Signed	$5,850
Vase, 13" Tall, Pedestal Base, Ribbed, Iridescent Gold with Blue Highlights, Signed	$2,150
Vase, 13¼" Tall, Jack-in-the-Pulpit Style, Gold, Signed "L.C.T. W8426"	$2,350
Vase, 14½" Tall, Trumpet Shape, Pedestal Base with Ball, Iridescent Gold Foliage	$3,150
Vase, 15" Tall, Bronze Base, Green Striations, Iridescent Gold Foliage	$3,250
Vase, 16" Tall, Floriform, Iridescent Gold, Signed "L.C.T. 9708A"	$3,350
Vase, 16½" Tall, Paperweight Style, Bronze Base, Blue Floral Design	$8,750
Vase, 17¼" Tall, Curved Gooseneck Style, Amber with Gold Feathers, Signed "L.C.T. M4386"	$3,850
Vase, 18" Tall, Flower Form, Bronze Base, Floriform, Pink Cameo Decoration	$3,850
Vase, 19" Tall, Stick Shape, Bronze Support, Iridescent Blue, Signed	$1,350
Vase, 19" Tall, Jack-in-the-Pulpit Style, Iridescent Gold, Floriform, Signed	$1,550
Vase, 22½" Tall, Flared, Cobalt Blue with Iridescent Gold and Multicolored Peacock Feathered Design, Signed "L.C. Tiffany F2888"	$17,500
Vase, 27" Tall, Iridescent Amber Green with Iridescent Brown Feather Design, Signed	$16,500
Water Goblet, 7" Tall, Iridescent Gold, Vintage Pattern, Signed	$725
Wineglass, 4" Tall, Gold Foot and Bowl with Amber Stem, Signed	$375
Wineglass, 8½" Tall, Gold with Crystal Stem, Signed "L.C.T."	$1,350

1870s–1920s

If one had to attribute one major object or design to Louis Comfort Tiffany, it would be a toss-up between Favrile and lamps. World-renowned Tiffany lamps have been command-ing auction prices in six figures for many of the larger works for quite some time. Permis-sible reproductions pose some problems, but fraudulent copies (posing as originals) should be carefully looked out for. Also, some museums such as the Smithsonian, the Metropoli-tan Museum in New York, and the Museum of Fine Arts in Boston, just to name a few, have commissioned many small reproduction stained-glass Tiffany lamps. Most sell for a

Tiffany Lamps. *Photo by Mark Pickvet. Courtesy of the Chicago Art Institute.*

Tiffany Lamps. *Photo by Robin Rainwater.*

Tiffany Lamp. *Reproduced directly from a Shot Glass Club of America auction catalog.*

few hundred dollars. A vast majority of the original lamps are signed "L.C.T.," "Louis C. Tiffany," "Tiffany Studios," or other titles containing the name Tiffany. Beware of any fraudulent signatures, and, as with any art glass that sells for several thousand dollars or more, be sure to obtain a certificate of authenticity before purchasing any Tiffany product.

Candelabrum, 15", 6-Branched, Green Glass Cabochons, Snuffer in Central Handle, Circular Mark $5,250

Ceiling Fixture, 17", Iridescent Gold Shades, Inscribed "L.C.T." $4,500

Chandelier, 22" Diameter, Multicolored Hanging Head Dragonfly Design, Impressed "Tiffany Studios New York" $37,500

Chandelier, 24" Diameter, Pink and Blue Iris Blossom Design, Impressed "Tiffany Studios New York" $35,000

Chandelier, 25" Diameter, Multicolored Rose Bush Design, Impressed "Tiffany Studios New York" $35,000

Chandelier, Wisteria, 25" Diameter, Multicolored, Impressed "Tiffany Studios New York" $38,500

Chandelier, 27" Diameter, Multicolored Fish Design, Impressed "Tiffany Studios New York" $34,500

Chandelier, 30" Diameter, Multicolored Grape Trellis Design, Impressed "Tiffany Studios New York" $48,500

Chandelier, 48" Diameter, Amber Blocked Design, Bronze Chain and Accents, Impressed "Tiffany Studios New York" $35,000

Lamp, Candle, 5" Tall, Turtle-Back Tile Design, Impressed "Tiffany Studios New York" $6,750

Lamp, Desk, 10" Tall, White Floriform Shade, Green Leaf and Foliage Design, Lacy Base, Signed "Tiffany Studios New York 403" $4,250

Lamp, Bronze Desk, 11¼" Tall, Turtle-Back Tile Design, Top Hook-Loop for Hanging, Impressed "Tiffany Studios New York" $11,500

Lamp, Candle, 11½" Tall, Shades of Blue Butterfly Design $3,500

Lamp, Candle, 12" Tall, Gold Candlestick, Amber, Green Acorn Design, Signed $8,500

Lamp, Candle, 13" Tall, Gold Shade, Ruffled, Gold Candlestick, Opal Insert, Green Feather Design, Signed $2,750

Lamp, Candle, 13" Tall, Turtle-Back Tile Design, Impressed "Tiffany Studios" $8,500

Lamp, Desk, 13" Tall, Iridescent Green and Gold Shade $4,250

Lamp, Table, 13" Tall, Globular Shade, Iridescent Blue Portrait Style $2,750

Lamp, 13½" Tall, Bronze Base and Stem with Iridescent Green Shade, Pine Needle Design $2,850

Lamp, 14" Tall, Iridescent Gold, Daffodil Design $7,750

Lamp, Bronze Desk, 14½", Adjustable Oval Shade, Circular Cast Foot, Green Glass Cabochons, Green Floral Design, Impressed "408 Tiffany Studios New York" $3,250

Lamp, 15" Tall, Bronze Base and Stem, 9" Globe Shade with Carved Butterflies and Dragonflies $5,500

Lamp, Electric Candle, 15" Tall, Gold Shade, Opal and Green Riser, Signed on Base and
Shade $2,500

Lamp, Gone with the Wind, 15", Signed Shade, Signed Bronze Base, Off-White Satin
Background, Orange Feathers, Signed "Tiffany Studios" $5,000

Lamp, 16", Leaded Acorn, Green and White Shade, Signed $4,500

Lamp, 16", Red, Amber, and Green Shaded Canterbury Bells, Signed $13,500

Lamp, 16¾", Pony White Wisteria with Pink and Green Florals $26,500

Lamp, 16½", Leaded Amethyst and Green Shade, White and Yellow Roses and Butterflies
                                                                                               $87,500

Lamp, 17" Tall, Leaded Dogwood Shade, Pink and Rose Blossoms, Green Foliage, Octagonal Bronze Base with Ivy, Impressed "Tiffany Studios New York" $22,500

Lamp, 18", Deep Violet 16" Dragonfly Shade, Glass Base Enclosing Fuel Canister, 5 Dragonflies and Floral Design in Relief on Base, Impressed "Tiffany Studios New York"
                                                                                               $97,500

Lamp, 20", Blue and Green Dragonfly Designed 14" Shade, Impressed "Tiffany Studios
New York" $65,000

Lamp, Table, 20¼", Feathered Green and White Shade, Lily Pad Vase, Marked "Tiffany
Studios New York 381" $10,500

Lamp, Bronze Table, 20½", 16" Multicolored Bamboo-Designed Shade, Impressed
"Tiffany Studios New York" $38,500

Lamp, Bronze Table, 21¼", Leaded Shade, 4 Raised Feet, Orange Acorns, Green Panels,
Marked "Tiffany Studios New York" $3,750

Lamp, Bronze Table, 21½", Seven Lily-Shape Gold Globes, Base Marked "Tiffany Studios
New York" $12,500

Lamp, Table, 22", Leaded Yellow Daffodil Shade, Urn-Shape Base, Blue to Green Shading, Green Base, Signed "Grueby" on Base $18,500

Lamp, Table, 22", Spiderweb, Apple Blossom Design, Signed $16,500

Lamp, Bronze Table, 22", Multicolored 16" Fish Design Shade $27,500

Lamp, Bronze Table, 23¼", Leaded Shade, 5 Ball Feet, Multicolored Dragonflies, Stamped
"Tiffany Studios New York" $13,250

Lamp, Bronze Table, 25" Tall, Leaded 19" Shade, Mottled Green Tile Effect, Stamped
"Tiffany Studios New York" $14,500

Lamp, Bronze Table, 26", Leaded Hemispherical Shade "558," Bronze Base, "366," Multi-colored Floral and Leaf Design, Impressed "Tiffany Studios" $15,500

Lamp, Bronze Table, 26½", Leaded Domical Shade, 4-Footed Bronze Base, Pink and Blue Flowers, Yellow Centers, Impressed "Tiffany Studios New York 1475-13" $31,500

Lamp, Bronze Table, 27½", Leaded Domical Shade, Bronze Treeform Base, Blue Flowers with Bright Green and Yellow Leaves, Signed "Tiffany Studios New York" $70,000

Lamp, Bronze Desk, 29½", Twin Green Hemispherical Shades, Bronze Base, Gravity Feed Fuel Canister $4,250

Lamp, 31½", 10" Diameter Globe Shade, Multicolored Autumn Leaf Design $48,500

Lamp, Bronze Floor, 56" Tall, 8-Footed, Iridescent Gold Shade, Green and Brown Foliage, Impressed "Tiffany Studios 425" $12,500

Lamp, Bronze Floor, 63", Leaded Glass Turtle-Back Tile Design 20" Shade, Impressed "Tiffany Studios New York" $18,500

Lamp, Bronze Floor, 64½", Leaded Domical Shade, 4-Footed Base, Impressed "Tiffany Studios New York 387" $13,500

Lamp, Bronze Floor, 68", Red and Yellow Salamander 27" Shade, Impressed "Tiffany Studios New York" $48,500

Lamp, Bronze Floor, 79", Gold Patina Base, 24" Shade with Molted Yellow Flower Clusters and Green Leaves on Blue Ground, Impressed "Tiffany Studios New York" $85,000

Vasa Murrhina
Various Companies, 1884–1890s

The name Vasa Murrhina originated from the Vasa Murrhina Art Glass Company in 1884. The company ornamented its glass by rolling it with flakes or flecks of mica. Colored glass particles or tiny metallic sprinkles produced much the same effect. The company went out of business because of flaws in their basic formulas. These flaws were responsible for causing more than two-thirds of their final glass products to crack. Many other companies adopted this decorating technique and produced some glassware in this fashion.

Basket, 6" Tall, Crystal Twisted Handle, Pink with Silver Mica $325

Basket, 7" Tall, Red to Pink Coloring $375

Bottle with Screw-On Metal Silver-Plated Cap, 5" Cap, Pink with Gold Mica and Butterfly Design $425

Bowl, Finger, 4", Cranberry with Silver Mica $225

Bowl, 4¾", Ruffled, Pink and Red with Gold Mica $325

Bowl, Rose, 5", Blue with Yellow and Silver Mica $175

Creamer, Ribbed, Cobalt with Gold Mica $185

Vasa Murrhina Art Glass. *Photo by Mark Pickvet.*

Creamer, 4½" Tall, Crystal Handle, Pink and Red with White Lining and Silver Mica	$175
Cruet with Crystal Stopper, 6" Tall, Crystal Handle, Pink with Silver Mica	$325
Cruet with Stopper, 6¼" Tall, Blue with Silver Mica	$300
Ewer, 9½" Tall, Ruffled, Pink, Blue, and Yellow with White Lining and Silver Mica	$275
Mug, 4½" Tall, White with Gold Mica	$175
Perfume Bottle with Silver Threaded Stopper, 5" Tall, Butterfly Design, Silver Mica	$425
Pitcher, 7¾" Tall, Blue with Silver Mica	$300
Pitcher, Syrup with Metal Lid, 5¾" Tall, Blue with Gold Mica	$350
Pitcher, Water, 8½" Tall, Bulbous, Brown and Red with Gold Mica	$475
Sugar, Ribbed, Cobalt Blue with Gold Mica	$185
Toothpick Holder, 2" Tall, Yellow with Red and Silver Mica	$175
Tumbler, Various Designs with Gold or Silver Mica	$300
Vase, 6" Tall, Bulbous, White with Amber and Gold Mica	$200
Vase, 6¼" Tall, Fluted, Footed, White with Gold Mica	$200
Vase, 6¾" Tall, Applied Crystal Handle, Blue with Gold Mica	$175
Vase, 7¼" Tall, Slender, Cranberry with Gold Mica	$250
Vase, 8" Tall, Trumpet Shape, Dark Red with White and Silver Mica	$275
Vase, 8½" Tall, Yellow Design on White Background, Silver Mica, White Lining	$275
Vase, 9¼" Tall, Blue with White and Lighter Blue Splotches, Gold Mica	$300

Vase, 10" Tall, Fluted Top, Multicolored Mica Flecks	$300
Vase, 12¼" Tall, Pink with Silver Mica	$350

Vaseline Glass
Various Companies, 1870s–Mid-20th Century

Vaseline glass was once made with a small amount of uranium, which imparts a light greenish-yellow color (a greasy appearance like vaseline). Low-grade uranium compounds, the nonradioactive variety, are still occasionally used in glassmaking; nevertheless, the formulas have changed significantly since the World War eras of the early and mid-20th century. High-quality Vaseline glass usually glows vibrantly under black light; in contrast, cheaply made products do not and are usually not finished as well either. Note that the English usually refer to Vaseline glass as Lemonescent. Some pressed glass, novelties, souvenir glass, and art wares were made in this style. Vaseline was also occasionally made in an opalescent form (vaseline-colored glassware with a white opalescent edge or background) that is usually found in iridized carnival glass as well as some art glass.

Basket, 6¾" Tall, Ruffled, Opalescent, Hobnail Pattern	$125
Basket, 8¾" Tall, Bonnet Shape	$150
Bowl, 7" x 4½" Oval, Barred Forget-Me-Not Pattern	$50
Bowl, 9", Daisy and Button Pattern	$125
Bowl, Rose, 4¾", Ruffled, Opalescent Hobnail Pattern	$85
Bread Plate, Souvenir, General Grant, Inscribed "Patriot & Soldier"	$125
Butter Dish with Domed Cover, Opalescent Hobnail Pattern	$150
Candlestick, 9½" Tall	$175
Candlestick, 12" Tall, Petal and Loops Pressed Design	$1,500
Canoe Dish, 13½" Long, Daisy and Button Pattern	$125
Celery Vase, 7½" Tall, Ribbed, Scalloped Top, Footed, Opalescent	$175
Compote, 5", Opalescent	$75
Cordial Glass 3¾" Tall, Hexagonal	$200
Cruet, Dewey Campaign, Greentown Glass	$200
Fish Bowl, 13½" x 7"	$400
Mug, Deer and Pine Design	$150
Perfume Bottle with Maltese Cross Stopper, 4" Tall, Octagonal Body	$150
Pitcher, 7" Tall, Applied Clear Ribbed Handle, Opalescent, Hobnail Pattern	$175
Plate, 8", Octagonal	$25

Salt Dip, Various Pressed Styles	$15
Toothpick Holder, Various Pressed Styles	$17.50
Toothpick Holder, Various Pressed Souvenir Styles	$27.50
Tumbler, Dewey Campaign, Greentown Glass	$100
Tumbler, 5½" Tall, Daisy & Button Pattern	$75
Vase, 6" Tall, Light Cranberry Ruffled Rim, Swirled Feather Pattern	$150
Vase, 8" Tall, Jack-in-the-Pulpit Style, Opalescent Stripes	$150
Vase, 8½" Tall, Bud, Opalescent, Hobnail Pattern	$100
Vase, 10" Tall, Waffle and Thumbprint Pattern	$425

– 5 –
CARNIVAL GLASS

The problem with art glass was the same as that with fine, brilliantly cut crystal: it was too expensive for the average citizen and catered to an exclusive, limited market. An inexpensive pressed substitute did arrive for Tiffany, Steuben, and the English Victorian glass, and that was carnival glass. Nearly all the carnival glass made in the United States was produced from about 1905 to the late 1920s. In the beginning the new pressed glass was not called carnival but borrowed its name from Tiffany's Favrile and Steuben's Aurene. It soon added other exotic names, such as New Venetian Art, Parisian Art, Aurora, and Art Iridescent.

The techniques of making this glass were also borrowed from the art nouveau movement. Color is natural in glass based on various oxides that are present in sand. Ordinarily, iron and common metals produce light green to brown glass. The addition of various metallic oxides, variations in heat and length of time in the furnace, and minor formula changes all produced astounding effects on color. Carnival glass contains a base color, which is the color of the glass before any iridescence is fired on it. The base color is usually present on the bottom underside of an iridized glass object.

There were two major groups of colored carnival glass. The bright carnival colors consisted of red, blue, green, purple, amethyst, amber, and marigold. The pastel colors were a bit more rare and were made up of clear, white, ice green, ice blue, clambroth, lavender, aqua opalescent, peach opalescent, and smoke. Red was the rarest and one of the most expensive to make, because fair amounts of gold oxides were required to produce it. Naturally, red is the most valuable color today and commands very high prices. The pastel colors are also not as common and are quite valuable, too.

Marigold was the most popular carnival color and is the one usually envisioned when one thinks of carnival glass. Marigold was made up of an orange-brown-colored flashing that was applied to clear glass and then sprayed with iridescence. Pastels usually had clear bases with a very light coating of iridescence. Lavender naturally had a purple tint; aqua a bluish-green tint; peach a yellow-orange tint; smoke a light gray; and clambroth a pearly white or light yellow sheen. Other opaque and opalescent shadings were made, too. Of all the colors, marigold remains the most abundant and the most inexpensive to acquire.

The glass itself was first manufactured into simple bowls and vases. As its popularity increased, water sets, table sets, punch bowls, berry and ice cream sets, dresser sets with matching cologne bottles, other bottles (wines, whiskey, soda), powder jars, trays, hat pin holders, lamps, paperweights, mugs, beads, advertising items, and souvenir pieces all followed. Unlike fancy art glass, carnival glass was sold in china shops and general stores and through mail order, and was used to make containers for food products such as pickles and mustard. Carnival-glass pieces were the first to be used as prizes for promotional items for tea companies, candy companies, and furniture stores (like Depression glass would be soon afterward).

Carnival glass was exported to England and other parts of Europe. It even reached as far as Australia. Several foreign countries began producing it, too, including England, Australia, Sweden, and others; however, the fad was a short-lived one. By the late teens, the demand lessened; by the early 1920s, the fad had pretty much ended. The new modern decor trends of the 1920s had no place for this odd, oily-looking glassware. Manufacturers were left with huge inventories, and this remaining stock was sold to fairs, bazaars, and carnivals (hence the name carnival glass) at below-wholesale prices to rid themselves of it. Those who were stuck with it packed it away until the 1950s.

Five companies produced the majority of carnival glass in America: the Fenton Art Glass Company of Williamstown, West Virginia; the Imperial Glass Company of Bellaire, Ohio; the Millersburg Glass Company of Millersburg, Ohio; the Northwood Glass Company of Wheeling, West Virginia; and the Dugan Glass Company of Indiana, Pennsylvania. Noted individuals were Frank and John Fenton, who founded Fenton. John went on with another brother named Robert to establish Millersburg. Jacob Rosenthal was also employed by the Fentons and developed many carnival-glass formulas. Edward Muhleman founded Imperial, and Harry Northwood (son of English glass artisan John Northwood) established Northwood. Harry Northwood's managers Thomas E. Dugan (Harry Northwood's cousin) and W. G. Minnemeyer went on to form the Dugan Glass Company.

Fenton and Imperial both made iridescent products in the modern era. Nearly all of Fenton's recent works are easily distinguished from the older versions, and Fenton continues in operation today. Imperial began reproducing carnival glass in the early 1960s using some of the original molds; however, the new glass is marked "IG" on the base or bottom. Imperial survived several rough moments in the past and finally shut down for good in 1982. A few other companies that produced limited amounts of carnival glass were Cambridge, Jenkins, Heisey, Indiana, Federal, Fostoria, McKee-Jeannette, Westmoreland, and U.S. Glass.

Carnival Glass by Pattern
ACANTHUS
Imperial Glass Company

This pattern is characterized by a large acanthus leaf and was also listed by Imperial as their #465 pattern. The prices listed are for the standard colors of blue, green, amethyst, or purple. For marigold, reduce them by 50 percent; for rare opalescent varieties such as aqua or clambroth, double them.

Bowl, 8"	$100
Bowl, 8½"	$125
Bowl, 9"	$150
Bowl, 9½"	$175
Plate, 10"	$325

Acorn Burrs
Northwood Glass Company

This pattern is characterized by raised acorns and oak leaves around each object. The prices listed are for the standard colors of blue, green, amethyst, or purple. For marigold, reduce them by 50 percent; for the rare opalescent varieties including white, blue, green, and aqua, triple them.

Bowl, Berry, 5"	$55
Bowl, Berry, 10"	$175
Butter Dish with Cover	$275
Creamer	$250
Pitcher, Water	$850
Punch Bowl with Base	$2,000
Punch Cup	$90
Spooner	$250
Sugar Dish with Cover	$250
Tumbler	$100
Vase, Whimsey	$3,500

Carnival Glass. Acorn Burrs Pattern. *Drawing by Mark Pickvet.*

Carnival Glass. Aztec Pattern. *Photo by Robin Rainwater.*

Adam's Rib
Dugan Glass Company

This is a fairly simple vertically ribbed pattern. The prices listed are for marigold; for the pastel ice colors of green or blue, double them.

Candlestick	$65
Candy Dish with Cover	$125
Pitcher, Water	$175
Tumbler	$50
Vase, Fan Shape	$65

Apple Tree
Fenton Art Glass Company

This pattern is characterized by branches with leaves and apples in low relief. Prices are for marigold; double them for any colors such as blue or pastels.

Pitcher, Water	$500
Tumbler	$50
Vase	$7,500

Aztec Pattern Glass. *Drawing by Mark Pickvet.*

Aztec
McKee Brothers

This is the same Whirling Star or Aztec pattern pressed by McKee in clear glass. Carnival colors were added later to a few of the surviving original molds. McKee was a very small producer of carnival glass. The prices below are for both marigold and clambroth.

Bowl, Rose	$425
Creamer	$275
Pitcher, Water	$1,500
Sugar	$275
Tumbler	$750

Banded Drape
Fenton Art Glass Company

As the name implies, this pattern contains parallel lines that drape or are curved around the object. Unlike most carnival glass, the pieces in this pattern tend to be enameled with leaves and lilies. The prices listed are for the standard colors of blue and green with enameling (reduce them by 25 percent for no enameling). For marigold, reduce them by 50 percent; for any rare opalescent varieties such as white, double them.

Pitcher, Water	$500
Tumbler	$75

Beaded Shell
Dugan Glass Company

The scallop shell of this pattern is large, and usually three or four of the shells together circle each table item. The beading circles out in a radius from the bottom of each shell. The rims of many pieces are simply the top of the shell, and the bases are ridged shells pointing downward. The prices listed are for the standard colors of blue, green, amethyst, or purple. For marigold, reduce them by 25 percent; for any rare opalescent varieties, triple them.

Bowl, Berry, 5", Footed	$50
Bowl, Berry, 6½", Footed	$75
Bowl, Berry, 9", Footed	$100
Butter Dish with Cover	$150
Creamer with Cover	$125
Mug	$200
Mug, Whimsey (Irregular)	$500
Pitcher, Water	$675
Spooner	$100
Sugar with Cover	$125
Tumbler	$85

Bells and Beads
Dugan Glass Company

This pattern is characterized by swirled bell-shape flowers with beaded stems. The prices listed are for the standard colors of blue, green, amethyst, or purple. For marigold, reduce them by a third; for any opalescent varieties such as peach, double them.

Bowl, 6¾"	$100
Bowl, 7½"	$125
Compote	$85
Gravy Boat, Handled	$85
Hat	$65
Nappy	$100
Plate, 6¾"	$125
Plate, 8"	$175

Big Basketweave
Dugan Glass Company

This pattern is characterized by a large vertical basket-weave pattern as opposed to smaller weaves produced by other companies. Dugan referred to it as Wicker Weave rather than the name adopted by collectors. This pattern has a wide variety of vases, including shorter, squat varieties as well as longer, slender ones. The prices listed are for the standard colors of blue, green, amethyst, or purple. For marigold, reduce them by 50 percent; for any opalescent varieties, double them.

Basket, Small	$75
Basket, Large	$150
Vase, 4"	$175
Vase, 5½"	$200
Vase, 6¼"	$225
Vase, 7"	$250
Vase, 8¾"	$175
Vase, 10½"	$200
Vase, 12"	$225
Vase, 14"	$250

Birds and Cherries
Fenton Art Glass Company

This pattern is characterized by five birds perched upon cherry branches; the entire design is in relief. Plates and bowls are quite scarce. The prices listed are for the standard colors of blue, green, amethyst, or purple. For marigold, reduce them by 50 percent; for any rare pastel varieties, increase them by 50 percent.

Bonbon Dish	$85
Bowl, 5"	$450
Bowl, 9"	$750
Compote	$90
Plate, 10"	$2,000

Blackberry
Fenton Art Glass Company

This pattern is characterized by blackberries in the interior with a basket-weave design on the exterior. The prices listed are for the standard colors of blue, green, amethyst, or purple, as well as any pastel or opalescent varieties, with the exception of the rare and elusive red, for which prices should be tripled. For marigold, reduce the prices by one-third.

Hat Vase	$150
Plate	$1,750
Spittoon	$4,000
Vase	$1,250

Blackberry Wreath
Millersburg Glass Company

This pattern is characterized by blackberry branches curved together to form a wreath; within the wreath is fruit and foliage. The prices listed are for the standard colors of blue, green, amethyst, or purple. For marigold, reduce them by one-third.

Bowl, Up to 6"	$150
Bowl, 6" Up to 7"	$175
Bowl, 7" Up to 8"	$200
Bowl, 8" Up to 9"	$250
Bowl, 9" to 10"	$300
Compote	$175
Plate, 6"	$3,000
Plate, 8"	$4,500
Plate, 10"	$6,000
Spittoon (Whimsey)	$5,000

Brocaded Patterns
Fostoria Glass Company

Fostoria produced a number of brocaded pastel floral patterns, primarily in ice green and ice blue, though other colors such as pink, white, and vaseline were also produced (same price as below). Fostoria's brocaded patterns were made using the technique of acid cut back. A gold edge was then applied to finish most items. Floral/foliage patterns consist of acorns, daffodils, daisies, palms, poppies, roses, and so on.

Bonbon Dish	$100
Bowl, 8"	$85
Bowl, 9"	$115
Bowl, Center, Footed	$250
Bowl, Rose	$225
Cake Plate	$175
Cake Tray with Center Handle	$175
Compote	$150
Goblet	$200
Ice Bucket	$325
Nappy	$100
Perfume Box with Cover	$275
Tray, Bread	$250
Tray, Dresser	$200
Vase	$275

Butterfly and Berry
Fenton Art Glass Company

This pattern is characterized by alternating panels of monarch butterflies and triangular-shape berries, along with a notched rim. The prices listed are for the standard colors of blue, green, amethyst, or purple; as well as any pastel or opalescent varieties, with the exception of the rare red (multiply by a factor of 10!). For marigold, reduce the prices by 50 percent. As usual with most original carnival glass, particularly with Fenton, red pieces are quite rare and extremely valuable.

Bowl, Berry, 5"	$125
Bowl, Berry, 10", Footed	$175
Bowl, Fernery	$750
Butter Dish with Cover	$275
Creamer with Cover	$150
Cuspidor	$3,000
Hat Pin Holder	$2,000

Fenton Carnival Butterfly & Berry Pattern. Blue & Marigold. *Photo by Mark Pickvet. Courtesy of the Fenton Art Glass Museum.*

Nut Dish	$750
Pitcher, Water	$650
Plate, Footed, Blue	$1,750
Spittoon, 2 Styles	$3,000
Spooner	$150
Sugar Dish with Cover	$250
Tumbler	$100
Vase, 10" Tall	$150

Cane
Imperial Glass Company

This pattern is characterized by vertical panels along with a starred base. The prices are the same for both marigold and clambroth varieties; for any other colors, double the prices.

Bowl, 7½"	$35
Bowl, 8½"	$40
Bowl, 9"	$45
Bowl, 10"	$50
Compote	$65
Goblet	$75
Pickle Dish	$40

Captive Rose
Fenton Art Glass Company

This pattern is characterized by roses surrounded by diamonds, circles, and scales. The prices listed are for the standard colors of blue, green, amethyst, or purple. For marigold, reduce them by one-third; for any pastel or opalescent varieties, double them.

Bonbon Dish	$100
Bowl, 8½"	$100
Bowl, 10"	$125
Compote	$100
Plate, 7"	$650
Plate, 9"	$750

Cattails and Water Lilies
Fenton Art Glass Company; Northwood Glass Company

Along with the cattails and water lilies, there is some molding at the bottom of this design (soil and grass). The prices listed are for the standard colors of blue, green, amethyst, or purple. For marigold, reduce them by one-third; for any of Fenton's rare red in this pattern, multiply by a factor of 10.

Bonbon Dish	$150
Bowl, Berry, 9"	$125
Bowl, Oblong, Banana, 4-Footed	$200
Creamer	$150
Jelly Dish (Resembles Toothpick Holder)	$150
Pitcher, Water	$350
Spooner	$150
Sugar Dish with Cover	$175
Tumbler	$100

Checkerboard
Westmoreland Glass Company

Checkerboard is a diagonal cross-cut pattern and all pieces, with the possible exception of punch cups, are quite rare. Note that this pattern has been reproduced. Reproductions con-

Checkerboard Tumbler. *Drawing by Mark Pickvet.*

tain Westmoreland's newer mark (beginning in 1949) which consists of an intertwined *W* and *G*. Reproductions are worth only a small fraction of the value of the originals (about 5–10 percent). The prices here are for purple; for marigold, reduce them by one-third, for any pastels such as clambroth, double them.

Cruet with Stopper	$450
Goblet	$450
Pitcher, Water	$4,000
Punch Bowl	$5,000
Punch Cup	$150
Tumbler	$750
Vase	$2,500
Wineglass	$375

Cherry
Millersburg Glass Company; Dugan Glass Company

The five Dugan bowls, Dugan plate, and Dugan cruet are a separate pattern from the remaining Millersburg pieces. Dugan's Cherry is characterized by cherry branches with the fruit in medallion form within the interior of the bowls. Millersburg's Cherry pattern consists of exterior panels of cherry foliage raised in relief. The prices listed are for the standard colors of blue, green, amethyst, or purple. For marigold, reduce them by 50 percent. Some of Dugan's pieces in this pattern can be found in peach opalescent (double the prices). A few of the Millersburg pieces were made in a Hobnail pattern (double the prices).

Banana Bowl (Dugan)	$300
Banana Dish	$4,000
Bowl, 4"	$100
Bowl, 5", Ruffled (Dugan)	$65
Bowl, 5½"	$110
Bowl, 6", Ruffled Footed (Dugan)	$75
Bowl, 7"	$200
Bowl, 8" Ruffled (Dugan)	$125
Bowl, 8½", Ruffled, Footed (Dugan)	$350
Bowl, 9"	$250
Bowl, 10", Ice Cream	$325
Butter Dish with Cover	$425
Compote	$1,750
Creamer	$300
Cruet with Stopper (Dugan)	$400
Pitcher, Milk	$1,500
Pitcher, Water	$1,750
Plate, 6" (Dugan)	$500
Plate, 6" (Millersburg)	$2,500
Plate, 7½"	$3,250
Plate, 10"	$3,500
Powder Jar with Cover	$2,500
Spooner	$275
Sugar Dish with Cover	$325
Tumbler, 2 Styles	$250

Cherry And Cable
Northwood Glass Company

Cherry and Cable contains a line or cable that runs around each item; four leaves run through the cable and branch down into two groupings of three cherries. Also, around the bottom are circular thumbprints (eight total). This pattern has been reproduced in miniature. The primary color was marigold as priced below; double the prices for blue carnival pieces made in this pattern.

Carnival Glass. Cherry and Cable Pattern. *Drawing by Mark Pickvet.*

Carnival Glass. Circle Scroll Pattern. *Drawing by Mark Pickvet.*

Bowl, Berry, 5"	$85
Bowl, Berry, 9"	$135
Butter Dish with Cover	$500
Creamer	$250
Pitcher, Water	$1,750
Sugar with Cover	$275
Spooner	$225
Tumbler	$450

Cherry Circles
Fenton Art Glass Company

Fenton's Cherry Circles includes groups of three cherries in a wide band around the center of each object surrounded by foliage wreaths. The prices listed are for the standard colors of blue, green, amethyst, or purple. For marigold, reduce the prices by one-third; for any opalescent or pastel varieties, double them; and for the rare red, increase them by a factor of 10.

Bonbon Dish	$200
Bowl, 8"	$85
Compote	$125
Plate, 9"	$350
Plate, 10", Chop	$500

Cherry Wreath
Dugan Glass Company

The cherries in this wreath design are either the color of the basic flashing or are flashed in red. The prices listed below are for blue, green, amethyst, or purple. For marigold, reduce them by one-third; for those flashed in red, increase the prices by 50 percent; and finally, for any pastels, double the prices.

Butter Dish with Cover	$250
Creamer	$150
Cuspidor	$2,000
Lamp, Cherub	$500
Pitcher, Water	$500
Sugar	$150
Spooner	$125
Tumbler	$100

Chesterfield
Imperial Glass Company

This is a fairly simple pattern with long vertical panels or flutes. The prices are the same for both marigold and white. For the pastel colors of blue, smoke, clambroth, white, or teal, increase the prices by 50 percent. For any rare red varieties, quadruple them.

Bowl, Rose	$50
Candlestick	$40
Candy Jar with Cover	$100
Compote, 6½"	$45
Compote, 11½"	$80
Goblet, 5½" Tall	$50
Mug, Lemonade	$75
Pitcher, Water	$175
Punch Bowl with Base	$600
Puch Cup	$50
Salt Dip	$100
Sherbet, 2 Varieties	$35

Toothpick Holder	$300
Tumbler	$40

Circle Scroll
Dugan Glass Company

The scroll design of this pattern is inscribed in circles that band around each object. Above and below the circles are vertical panels with circular ends. The prices listed are for the standard colors of amethyst or purple. Note that the amethyst is sometimes found in a very dark shade such as black amethyst (same price). For marigold, reduce the prices by one-third.

Bowl, 5"	$55
Bowl, 10"	$85
Butter Dish with Cover	$450
Creamer	$250
Hat Shape	$125
Pitcher, Water	$2,500
Spooner	$225
Sugar Dish with Cover	$450
Tumbler	$550
Vase	$300

Coin Dot
Fenton Art Glass Company; Westmoreland Glass Company

The original Coin Dot was produced by Fenton and is characterized by various sizes of pressed coins around each item. Westmoreland produced a slight variant as noted by the pieces listed below. The primary pricing is for blue, green, amethyst, or purple. For marigold, reduce them by one-third; for opalescent varieties (peach or aqua), triple them; and finally for any rare red, multiple the prices by a factor of 10.

Basket (Westmoreland Pattern Variant)	$175
Bowl, 6"	$60
Bowl, 9"	$65
Bowl, 10"	$75

Bowl, Rose	$175
Bowl, Rose (Westmoreland Pattern Variant)	$175
Bowl (Westmoreland Pattern Variant)	$100
Compote (Westmoreland Pattern Variant)	$125
Pitcher, Water	$550
Tumbler	$275

Colonial
Imperial Glass Company

This is a typical Colonial pattern featuring wide arched panels around each object. Most pieces have been found in marigold, for which the prices have been recorded below. For any green, double them; for any red, multiply them by 5.

Candlestick	$150
Creamer	$60
Goblet	$60
Mug	$75
Pitcher, Water	$1,000
Sugar	$60
Tumbler	$100
Vase	$80

Columbia
Imperial Glass Company

This is a fairly simple pattern with vertical panels or flutes that encompass about half of each object. This was also knows as Imperial's #246 pattern and was produced in non-iridized versions. The prices below are for green, amethyst, purple, or any pastel colors (such as smoke or clambroth). For marigold, reduce them by 50 percent.

Bowl, Rose	$400
Cake Plate	$200
Compote, 2 Styles (Bases Differ)	$225
Vase	$150

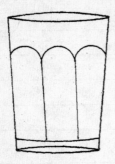

Colonial Tumbler. *Drawing by Mark Pickvet.*

Cosmos and Cane
U.S. Glass Company

This pattern is characterized by ferns and flowers that are placed from the bottom to just below the rim; between the foliage is a diamond trellis design. This pattern was produced mostly in white, for which the prices are listed below. For marigold or a similar honey amber color, reduce them by 50 percent. A few pieces exist in amethyst, for which the prices should be doubled.

Basket, White	$750
Bowl, Berry, 5"	$150
Bowl, Berry, 8"	$175
Bowl, Berry, 10"	$200
Bowl, Rose, 2 Styles	$1,500
Butter Dish with Cover	$325
Compote, 2 Styles	$400
Creamer	$225
Pitcher, Water	$1,500
Plate, Chop	$1,500
Sherbet	$175
Spittoon	$3,500
Spooner	$200
Sugar Dish with Cover	$250

Tray	$350
Tumbler	$200
Tumbler with Advertising	$300

Country Kitchen
Millersburg Glass Company

Country Kitchen includes flowers, triangular ridges, and wavy bands around each object. Cuspidors and spittoons are very rare and valuable. Basic prices are for green, amethyst, or purple; for marigold, reduce them by one-third. For any pastels such as vaseline, double the prices.

Bowl, Berry, 5"	$150
Bowl, Berry, 8"	$225
Bowl, Berry, 9"	$325
Bowl, Berry, 10"	$425
Butter Dish with Cover	$800
Creamer	$550
Cuspidor	$5,000
Spittoon	$5,000
Spooner	$500
Sugar	$550
Vase, Whimsey	$750

Crab Claw
Imperial Glass Company

Crab Claw is an interlocking pattern that resembles cut glass. Within the design can be found curved files, hobstars, diamonds, and half flowers. Basic prices are for green, amethyst, purple, or smoke; for marigold, reduce them by one-third. For any pastels such as vaseline, double the prices.

Bowl, 5"	$50
Bowl, 10"	$75
Bowl, Fruit, Footed	$150
Cruet with Stopper	$2,000

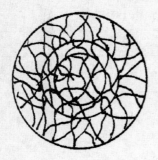

Crackle Plate. *Drawing by Mark Pickvet.*

Pitcher, Water	$750
Tumbler	$150

Crackle
Various Companies

If any carnival glass can be called "common," then Crackle is a prime candidate. It is true to the name *carnival* in that large amounts were given away as prizes at fairs, exhibitions, and so on. Imperial was probably the largest maker of Crackle carnival. Basic prices are for marigold; for any other colors, including pastels or opalescent varieties, double them.

Bowl, Berry, 5"	$17.50
Bowl, Berry, 6"	$22.50
Bowl, Berry, 8"	$27.50
Bowl, Berry, 9"	$32.50
Bowl, Berry, 10"	$37.50
Candlestick, 3½" Tall	$27.50
Candlestick, 7" Tall	$32.50
Candy Jar with Cover	$40
Creamer	$37.50
Pitcher, Water, Dome Base	$100
Planter, Window	$150
Plate, 6"	$25

Plate, 7"	$30
Plate, 8"	$35
Punch Bowl with Base	$100
Punch Cup	$17.50
Saltshaker	$40
Sherbet	$25
Spittoon	$75
Sugar	$37.50
Tumbler	$25
Vase, Auto	$35
Vase, Wall	$50

Dahlia
Dugan Glass Company

The large dahlias in this pattern are in relief and are spaced a little farther apart than typical pressed patterns. With the exception of the epergne, the pattern was made exclusively by Dugan. The prices listed below are for amethyst or purple. For marigold, reduce them by 50 percent; for any pastels (mostly white), double the prices.

Bowl, 5", Footed	$55
Bowl, 10", Footed	$150
Butter Dish	$175
Creamer	$125
Epergne (Fenton)	$350
Pitcher, Water	$1,050
Spooner	$100
Sugar	$125
Tumbler	$200

Diamond Lace
Imperial Glass Company

This pattern is characterized by long diagonal frames with central starbursts, beading, and stippling. The prices listed below are for green or amethyst. For marigold, reduce them by one-third; for any pastel or opalescent varieties, double them.

Bowl, Berry, 5½"	$50
Bowl, Berry, 8"	$90
Bowl, Berry, 9"	$100
Bowl, Fruit, 10½"	$125
Bowl, Rose, Whimsey	$3,500
Pitcher, Water	$400
Tumbler	$100

Diamond Point Columns
Imperial Glass Company; Northwood Glass Company; and Fenton Art Glass Company

This pattern is characterized by alternating rows of panels with checkered diamonds. Most production was in marigold, which is priced below. A few odd-colored pieces have been found (such as purple, green, blue, white, and vaseline); double the prices for any color other than marigold.

Banana Dish	$100
Basket (Northwood)	$1,500
Bowl, 4½"	$25
Butter Dish	$50
Compote	$50
Creamer	$40
Pitcher, Milk	$60
Plate, 7"	$60
Powder Jar with Cover	$60
Spooner	$35
Sugar	$40
Vase	$50

Diamonds
Millersburg Glass Company

As the name implies, this is an allover pressed diamond design. The diamonds are a bit larger than those regularly associated with pressed glass. The prices are for green, amethyst, or purple; for marigold, reduce them by one-third. For any aqua opalescent pieces, double the prices.

Carnival Glass. Dahlia Pattern. *Drawing by Mark Pickvet.*

Carnival Glass. Double Dolphin Pattern. *Drawing by Mark Pickvet.*

Pitcher, Water, with Spout	$425
Pitcher, Water, without Spout	$625
Punch Bowl with Base	$3,500
Spittoon	$10,000
Tumbler	$100

Double Dolphin
Fenton Art Glass Company

Each object usually contains a pair of scaled dolphins with flipped tails in raised relief. The colors were made in a variety of light iridescent pastels, including ice blue, ice green, pink, topaz, tangerine, amethyst, and white. Double the prices for any red.

Bowl, 8"	$90
Bowl, 9", Footed	$125
Bowl, 10"	$100
Bowl, 11", Footed	$135
Cake Plate with Center Handle	$100
Candlestick	$50
Candy Dish with Cover	$125
Compote	$90
Vase, Fan Style	$100

Dragon and Lotus
Fenton Art Glass Company

Dragon and Lotus is an easily recognized pattern; as the name implies, each piece has alternating dragons and lotus blossoms in ovals around each object. The prices listed are for the standard colors of blue, green, amethyst, and purple. For marigold, reduce the prices by one-third; for any opalescent or pastel varieties, double them; and for the rare red, increase them by a factor of 10.

Bowl, 9"	$200
Bowl, 9", Footed	$225
Nut Dish or Bowl	$400
Plate, 9½"	$2,000

Elks
Fenton Art Glass Company, Millersburg Glass Company, Dugan Glass Company

This pattern is characterized by an elk head with a clock upon the antlers (pointing to 12). Around the elk's head is floral and foliage designs. Dugan made only a nappy and Millersburg produced a bowl and paperweight in this pattern; the remaining advertising/souvenir pieces are from Fenton. The prices listed are for the standard colors of blue, green, amethyst, or purple. Marigold pieces in this pattern are actually rare and sell at the same price.

Bell, 1911 Atlantic City, Blue	$2,250
Bell, 1914 Parkersburg, Blue	$2,750
Bell, 1917 Portland, Blue	$20,000
Bowl, 8" (Millersburg)	$2,250
Bowl, Atlantic City, Blue	$1,500
Bowl, Detroit	$1,200
Nappy (Dugan)	$7,500
Paperweight (Millersburg)	$2,750
Plate, Atlantic City	$2,000
Plate, 1914 Parkersburg	$2,000

Estate
Westmoreland Glass Company

The design of Estate resembles that of a maze of lines decorated around the objects. Carnival pieces in this line are relatively small. The basic prices are for marigold, but a few odd

Millersburg Carnival Elks Pattern. *Photo by Robin Rainwater. Courtesy of the Fenton Art Glass Museum.*

Estate Mug. *Drawing by Mark Pickvet.*

colors have been found. For regular aqua, ice blue, ice green, or peach opalescent, double them; for aqua opalescent or smoke, triple them.

Creamer	$65
Mug	$100
Perfume Bottle with Stopper	$350
Sugar	$65
Vase, 3" Tall, Stippled	$75
Vase, 6" Tall, Bud	$65

Fashion
Imperial Glass Company

This pattern consists of diamonds, jewels, sunbursts, and beading over the entire surface of each object. The prices listed are for the colors blue, green, amethyst, purple, or smoke. For marigold, reduce them by 50 percent; for any opalescent or pastel varieties, double them; and for any rare red, multiply them by a factor of 10.

Basket, Bride's	$300
Bowl, 9"	$100
Bowl, Fruit, with Base	$150
Bowl, Rose	$625
Butter Dish	$225
Compote	$500

Fashion Pitcher. *Reproduced directly from a 1910s Imperial Glass catalog.*

Creamer	$150
Pitcher, Water	$750
Punch Bowl with Base	$1,500
Punch Cup	$40
Sugar	$150
Tumbler	$125

Fentonia
Fenton Art Glass Company

Fentonia consists of scales and stitches within beaded frames. The pattern is set diagonally on each object and nearly covers the entire surface (except a little at the top). The pattern variant is known as Fentonia Fruit and includes fruit within the diamonds of the pattern. The variant is rarer and more valuable than the original. The prices listed are for the standard colors of blue, green, amethyst, or purple. For marigold, reduce the prices by one-third.

Bowl, 5", Footed	$60
Bowl, 6", Footed (Fentonia Fruit)	$125
Bowl, 7½", Footed	$85
Bowl, Berry, 9"	$80
Bowl, 9½", Footed	$90
Bowl, 10", Footed (Fentonia Fruit)	$200

Bowl, Fruit, 10"	$110
Butter Dish with Cover	$250
Creamer, 2 Styles	$100
Pitcher, Water	$700
Pitcher, Water (Fentonia Fruit)	$825
Spooner	$100
Sugar Dish with Cover, 2 Styles	$150
Tumbler	$125
Tumbler (Fentonia Fruit)	$500
Vase (Fentonia Fruit)	$275

Fern
Northwood Glass Company, Fenton Art Glass Company

Fern, as the name suggests, is simply a series of ferns that alternate with branches emanating from the center. It is an interior pattern, but some ferns and foliage are also found upon the exterior. The three Fenton bowls were made in blue; all other listed pieces are priced for blue, green, purple, or amethyst; for marigold, reduce them by 50 percent. For any odd pastels such as ice green or ice blue, double the prices; for any rare red, multiply them by a factor of 10.

Bowl, 7" (Northwood)	$100
Bowl, 7" (Fenton), Blue	$850
Bowl, 8" (Fenton), Blue	$950
Bowl, 8¼"	$125
Bowl, 9" (Fenton), Blue	$1,000
Compote (Northwood)	$125
Hat (Fenton)	$85

Field Thistle
U.S. Glass Company

This pattern consists of swirled foliage with daisies as well as a central medallion with a clear glass daisy. The pattern covers the entire exterior of each object and was produced mostly in marigold as priced below. For any pastels such as ice green or ice blue, double the prices.

Bowl, 6"	$60
Bowl, 10"	$75
Butter Dish with Cover	$150
Compote, Large	$175
Creamer	$125
Plate, 6"	$275
Plate, 9"	$375
Pitcher, Water	$250
Spooner	$100
Sugar	$125
Tumbler	$60
Vase	$625

File
Imperial Glass Company

File is characterized by a series of rounded panels with ridges or files. A central band divides two rows of these file designs into pyramidlike shapes. Aside from Imperial, it was also made in England. The prices listed are for the colors of amethyst and purple. For marigold, reduce them by one-third. A few odd pieces exist in pastel colors; increase the prices for those by 50 percent.

Bowl, 5"	$45
Bowl, 7"	$55
Bowl, 9"	$60
Bowl, 10"	$65
Butter Dish with Cover	$300
Compote	$55
Creamer	$150
Pitcher, Water	$550
Spooner	$125
Sugar Dish with Cover	$175
Tumbler, Juice (Small)	$350
Tumbler, Juice (Large)	$200
Vase	$150

Fine Rib

Northwood Glass Company, Fenton Art Glass Company, Dugan Glass Company

This is a simple pattern of vertical ribbing that varies little from one maker to another. The prices listed are for the standard colors of blue, green, amethyst, or purple. For marigold, reduce them by 50 percent; for any pastel colors, double them. For opalescent varieties, namely peach or aqua opalescent, triple them. Finally, for any rare Fenton red pieces, multiply the prices by a factor of 10.

Banana Dish	$200
Bowl, 5"	$45
Bowl, 9"	$75
Bowl, 10"	$80
Compote	$200
Lamp Shade	$125
Plate, 8"	$85
Plate, 9"	$100
Vase, 7"	$80
Vase, 8"	$100
Vase, 12"	$125
Vase, 14"	$150

Floral and Optic

Imperial Glass Company

This pattern consists of wide panels edged by a bordering band of grapes and leaves. Basic prices are for marigold. For odd colors such as smoke, iridized milk glass (similar to marigold but flashed over milk glass instead of clear glass), or aqua opalescent, triple the prices. For any rare red, multiply them by a factor of 10.

Bowl, 8"	$30
Bowl, 8", Footed	$35
Bowl, 9"	$35
Bowl, 9, Footed	$40
Bowl, 10"	$40
Bowl, 10", Footed	$45
Bowl, Rose, Footed	$85
Cake Plate	$75

Flute
Imperial Glass Company, Millersburg Glass Company, Northwood Glass Company

There are quite a few Flute designs but most are very similar in design and price. Imperial's has wide paneled flutes, thick glass, and circular bases. Some Millersburg products have 16 thin flutes, whereas others were made with much wider flutes, and Northwood's wide flutes are more arched or ridged when compared with the others. The prices are for the standard colors of blue, green, amethyst, or purple. For marigold, reduce them by one-third; for any pastel colors or opalescent varieties, double them.

Bowl, 4"	$65
Bowl, 5"	$70
Bowl, 5½'	$90
Bowl, 10"	$250
Bowl, 10" (Northwood Only)	$75
Bowl, Custard, 11" (Imperial Only)	$350
Butter Dish	$200
Butter Dish with Cover	$250
Celery Dish	$425
Compote, 6", Clover-Shape Base	$650
Creamer	$125
Cruet (Imperial)	$175
Cup	$45
Pitcher, Water	$625
Punch Bowl	$500
Punch Bowl with Base	$700
Punch Cup	$55
Ringtree (Northwood Only)	$250
Salt Dip, Footed (Northwood Only)	$40
Sauce Dish, 5" Diameter	$45
Sherbet (Northwood Only)	$55
Spooner	$100
Sugar	$125

Sugar Dish with Cover	$175
Toothpick Holder	$200
Toothpick Holder, Handled	$350
Tumbler, Several Styles	$200
Vase, 6"	$425
Vase, 16"	$500
Vase, 19"	$550
Whiskey Tumbler	$50

Four Flowers
Dugan Glass Company, Riihimaki of Finland, Eda Glassworks of Sweden

As the name implies, this pattern consists of four flower blossoms in a squared design with four large leaves. The primary design was also produced by Riihimaki of Finland, where a similar variant was made by Eda of Sweden; the variant has a three-petaled floral design within the four leaves. The prices listed below are for the standard colors of blue, green, amethyst, or purple. For marigold, reduce them by 50 percent; for any pastel colors (smoke, vaseline, teal, or amber), double them. Finally, for any peach opalescent varieties, triple the prices.

Banana Bowl	$400
Bowl, 5"	$45
Bowl, 6"	$50
Bowl, 7"	$55
Bowl, 8"	$55
Bowl, 8½", Footed	$125
Bowl, 9"	$100
Bowl, 10"	$125
Bowl, 11"	$150
Bowl, Rose	$1,000
Plate, 6½"	$325
Plate, 9"	$500
Plate, 10"	$550
Plate, 10½"	$575

Four Seventy-Four
Imperial Glass Company

The pattern called "Four Seventy-Four" consists of a large central four-petaled flower on a large stalk with thin leaves. These flowers are framed by interlocking broken arches of sunbursts. The ridges are usually notched also. The prices listed are for the colors green, amethyst, or purple. For marigold, reduce them by one-third; for any pastel colors (such as teal, lavender, pink, olive, and lime green), double them. For any aqua opalescent varieties, triple them. Finally, for any rare red, multiply the prices by a factor of 10.

Bowl, 8"	$90
Bowl, 9"	$100
Butter Dish with Cover	$250
Compote	$200
Cordial	$225
Creamer	$125
Goblet	$100
Pitcher, Milk	$425
Pitcher, Water, 2 Styles	$600
Punch Bowl with Base	$1,250
Punch Cup	$45
Sherbet	$100
Sugar	$125
Tumbler	$100
Vase, 7" Tall	$400
Vase, 8" Tall	$425
Vase, 10" Tall	$1,150
Vase, 14" Tall	$1,250
Wineglass	$150

Frosted Block
Imperial Glass Company

This pattern is characterized by stippled glass in panels separated by beading. Some pieces may be marked "Made in USA." Dealers in carnival glass have indicated that they add a surcharge of a quarter or a third to pieces that are marked in this manner on the underside.

This pattern was made primarily in marigold as priced below. Double the prices for clam-broth, white, smoke, or any other unusual colors.

Bowl, 5"	$25
Bowl, 6½"	$30
Bowl, 7", Square	$55
Bowl, 7½"	$35
Bowl, 8"	$40
Bowl, 8", Square	$60
Bowl, 9"	$45
Bowl, Rose	$85
Butter Dish with Cover	$75
Compote	$50
Creamer	$40
Nut Dish	$40
Pickle Dish, Oval, Handled	$85
Pitcher, Milk	$125
Plate, 6½"	$45
Plate, 7½"	$50
Plate, 9" to 9½"	$55
Spooner	$40
Sugar	$40
Tray, Celery	$45
Vase, 6" Tall, Pedestal Feet	$45

Fruits and Flowers
Northwood Glass Company

Fruit and Flowers contains slight variations of apples, pears, and cherries, all with leaves, vines, and foliage. The prices listed below are for the standard colors of blue, green, amethyst, or purple. For marigold, reduce them by one-third; for any pastels, double the prices; and for any opalescent varieties, quadruple them.

Banana Dish, 7"	$375
Bonbon Dish	$100

Fruit & Flowers Pattern. *Photo by Robin Rainwater.*

Bowl, Berry, 5"	$75
Bowl, Berry, 7"	$85
Bowl, Berry, 8"	$200
Bowl, Berry, 9"	$150
Bowl, 10", Footed	$175
Nappy, Tab Handle, Shallow, 7"	$250
Plate, 7"	$225
Plate, 8"	$250
Plate, 9½"	$275

Garden Path
Dugan Glass Company

This is an allover pattern design that consists of circular scrolling around a central six-petaled star. Garden Path actually comes in two pattern styles: one has a smooth or slightly ruffled edge, and the other has a notched edge (the basic pattern is the same). The prices listed below are for amethyst, purple, white, or peach opalescent. For marigold, reduce them by 50 percent.

Bow, 5"	$115
Bowl, 7"	$125
Bowl, 8"	$350
Bowl, 9"	$375

Bowl, 9½"	$400
Bowl, 10"	$500
Bowl, Rose	$400
Compote	$400
Plate, 6"	$600
Plate, Chop (Divided)	$6,000

Golden Honeycomb
Imperial Glass Company

This pattern contains a large central medallion of a sunburst at the base, and the exterior surface contains rows of thumbprints inscribed within squares or honeycombs. It is also known as Hex Optic. The prices listed below are for marigold; double them for any other colors.

Bonbon Dish, 5" Diameter	$50
Bowl, 5"	$35
Bowl, 7"	$50
Compote	$50
Creamer	$50
Lamp, Oil	$175
Lamp Shade	$100
Plate, 7"	$55
Pitcher, Water	$150
Sugar	$50
Tumbler	$40

Grape
Imperial Glass Company

Imperial's Grape is a fairly common pattern except for the larger items (cuspidors, pitchers, and punch bowls). Other Grape designs such as Fenton's and Northwood's are usually referred to as Grape and Cable (see separate listings). Grape comes in a wide variety of colors. The prices listed below are for the standard colors of blue, green, amethyst, or purple. For marigold, reduce them by one-third; for any pastels (aqua, amber, clambroth, smoke, olive green, ice green, ice blue, white, vaseline, and so on), double the prices. For any opalescent varieties, quadruple them; and for any rare red specimens, multiply the prices by 10.

Basket	$1,250
Bottle, Water	$200
Bowl, Berry, 5"	$40
Bowl, Berry, 6"	$50
Bowl, Berry, 8"	$70
Bowl, Berry, 8¾"	$75
Bowl, Berry, 9"	$85
Bowl, Berry, 10"	$90
Bowl, Fruit, 11"	$100
Bowl, Fruit, 12"	$125
Bowl, Rose	$500
Compote	$85
Cup	$100
Cuspidor	$2,750
Decanter with Stopper, Wine	$275
Goblet	$75
Lamp Shade	$125
Nappy	$50
Pitcher, Milk	$375
Pitcher, Water	$375
Plate, 6"	$100
Plate, 6½"	$125
Plate, 7"	$175
Plate, 8½", Ruffled	$200
Plate, 9"	$125
Plate, 12"	$325
Punch Bowl with Base	$400
Punch Cup	$50
Saucer	$45
Spittoon	$2,750
Tray, Center Handle	$125

Tumbler	$50
Wineglass	$65

Grape and Cable
Northwood Glass Company, Fenton Art Glass Company

Fenton produced many fewer pieces than Northwood (only those noted in parentheses below). The Fenton pattern contains grape bunches alternating with large-veined leaves, which are both attached to a vine. The cable is a diagonal series of ridges curving up and down directly below the rim. Northwood's design consists of large bunches of grapes raised in relief from the center, and they, too, alternate with the leaves. The cable is formed at the base with teardrops. A few variations include accents such as bands, rows of thumbprints or basket weave, and so forth (same prices). The prices below are for the standard colors of blue, green, amethyst, or purple. For marigold, reduce them by one-third; for any pastels, double the prices; and for any rare red (Fenton only) or opalescent varieties, multiply the prices by 10.

Banana Boat, 12", Footed	$350
Basket, Bride's (Fenton)	$2,500
Bonbon Dish	$100
Bowl, 4", Ice Cream	$50
Bowl, Berry, 5"	$45
Bowl, 5½"	$50
Bowl, 5½", Scalloped	$55
Bowl, 7", Footed (Fenton)	$125
Bowl, 7", Footed	$70
Bowl, 7", Scalloped	$65
Bowl, 8", (Fenton)	$75
Bowl, 8", Scalloped	$75
Bowl, 8¼", Footed (Fenton)	$135
Bowl, Berry, 9", Scalloped	$110
Bowl, 9", Footed	$110
Bowl, Berry, 10"	$150
Bowl, 11", Ice Cream	$325
Bowl, 11½", Scalloped	$175
Bowl, Orange, Footed (Fenton or Northwood)	$250

Grape & Cable Pattern. *Photo by Robin Rainwater.*

Fenton Carnival. Left to right: Grape & Cable, Fenton Flowers, Grape & Cable Patterns. *Reproduced directly from a 1920 Butler Brothers catalog.*

Bowl, Orange, Footed, with Advertising (Fenton)	$2,750
Butter Dish	$300
Candlestick	$250
Centerpiece, Footed	$1,000
Cologne Bottle with Stopper	$700
Compote	$750
Compote with Cover	$1,000
Cookie Jar with Cover	$1,500
Creamer	$150
Cup	$375
Cuspidor	$6,500
Decanter with Stopper	$750
Dresser Tray	$300
Fernery	$1,750
Hat	$150
Hat Pin Holder	$375
Lamp, Candle	$800
Lamp Shade	$225
Nappy	$100

Pin Tray	$275
Pitcher, Tankard	$2,750
Pitcher, Water	$750
Plate, 6"	$300
Plate, 7½"	$325
Plate, 9", Footed (Fenton)	$200
Plate, 9½"	$500
Plate, Footed	$300
Plate with Advertising	$625
Powder Jar with Cover	$250
Punch Bowl with Base, 12" (Rare in Aqua Opalescent; $125,000 for the Set with 12 Matching Cups)	$750
Punch Bowl with Base, 16"	$800
Punch Bowl with Base, 24"	$3,500
Punch Cup, 2 Styles	$50
Saucer	$150
Sherbet	$60
Shot Glass or Whiskey Tumbler	$300
Spittoon	$6,500
Spittoon (Fenton)	$2,500
Spooner	$150
Sugar	$150
Sugar with Cover	$225
Sweetmeat Dish	$500
Sweetmeat Compote with Cover	$2,000
Tobacco Jar with Cover	$1,250
Tumbler, 6 oz.	$125
Tumbler, 12 oz.	$150
Tumbler, 16 oz.	$175
Vase	$5,000

Grape & Gothic Arches Tumbler. *Drawing by Mark Pickvet.*

Grape and Gothic Arches
Northwood Glass Company

This typical grape pattern includes leaves and large grape bunches connected by a vine around each piece. In the background are pointed arches that resemble a picket fence. The prices below are for the standard colors of blue, green, amethyst, or purple. For marigold, reduce them by one-third; for any pastels, mostly a pearl color similar to clambroth, double the prices.

Bowl, 5"	$50
Bowl, Berry, 10"	$125
Butter Dish with Cover	$175
Creamer	$100
Pitcher, Water	$500
Spooner	$90
Sugar Dish with Cover	$125
Tumbler	$75

Greek Key
Northwood Glass Company

Greek Key is a common pattern found in other mediums and consists of a maze of interlocking *e* designs. At the top of each item are semicircles with tiny flower circles surrounded by seven petals; in the middle is the maze design, and at the bottom are stretched diamonds with circles at the top. The prices listed below are for the standard colors of blue, green, amethyst, or purple; for marigold, reduce them by one-third. For any pastels such as ice blue or ice green, or aqua opalescent, quadruple the prices.

Bowl, 7"	$200
Bowl, 8½"	$225
Bowl, 8½", Dome Footed	$225
Hat Pin (Pattern Variant)	$125
Pitcher, Water	$1,250
Plate, 9"	$1,250
Plate, 11"	$1,500
Tumbler	$350

HEAVY GRAPE
Imperial Glass Company,
Dugan Glass Company

Aside from a couple of Dugan bowls, the pieces priced below are all Imperial's. Imperial's Heavy Grape has exterior flutes with the grape bunch and leaves inside. Dugan's is also an interior pattern with a grape-leaf center surrounded by a circular pattern of alternating leaves and grape bunches. Heavy Grape comes in a variety of colors. The prices listed below are for the standard colors of blue, green, amethyst, or purple. For marigold, reduce them by one-third; for any pastels (aqua, amber, clambroth, smoke, olive green, ice green, ice blue, white, vaseline, and so on), double the prices; for any opalescent varieties, quadruple them; and for any rare red specimens, multiply the prices by 10.

Bowl, 5" (Dugan)	$200
Bowl, Berry, 5"	$35
Bowl, Berry, 6"	$40
Bowl, Berry, 7"	$50
Bowl, Berry, 8"	$55
Bowl, Berry, 8¾"	$75
Bowl, Berry, 9"	$200
Bowl, 10" (Dugan)	$800
Bowl, Berry, 10"	$225
Bowl, Fruit, 11", with Base	$350
Bowl, Fruit, 12", with Base	$400
Compote	$55

Nappy	$55
Plate, 6"	$450
Plate, 8"	$225
Plate, 11"	$400
Punch Bowl with Base	$750
Punch Cup	$75

Heisey Carnival Glass
A. H. Heisey Company

Although not a huge producer of carnival glass, Heisey did make some iridized glass during this time period. Basic prices are for marigold; for any other colors, including pastel or opalescent varieties, double them.

Bottle, Water (Line #357)	$300
Breakfast Set	$350
Candy Jar with Cover, 11" Tall, Stemmed, Floral Spray Design	$375
Compote, Cartwheel Style	$275
Compote, Colonial Pattern	$125
Creamer	$225
Dresser Tray, Colonial Pattern	$150
Frog Dish with Cover	$875
Hair Receiver, Colonial Pattern	$150
Perfume Bottle, Colonial Pattern	$125
Puff Box, Colonial Pattern	$150
Punch Cup (Flute Design)	$50
Spittoon	$175
Sugar	$225
Sugar Dish with Cover	$275
Toothpick Holder	$250
Tray	$200
Tumbler (Line #357)	$90
Tumbler, Colonial Pattern	$80
Turtle Dish with Cover	$400
Vase, Colonial Pattern	$100

Higbee Carnival Glass
Higbee Glass Company

Like Heisey above, Higbee was not a huge producer of carnival glass. Because the company was established in 1907 near the beginning of the carnival fad, it is easy to see that they would have produced some iridized glassware of the period. Note that much of Higbee's glass contains a raised honeybee trademark; dealers usually charge 25–35 percent more when the mark is present. The prices below are for standard marigold without the mark; double them for any other colors.

Bowl, Diamond Fountain Pattern	$125
Bowl, 7", Floral Oval Pattern	$65
Bowl, 8", Floral Oval Pattern	$70
Creamer, Floral Oval Pattern	$75
Creamer, Hawaiian Lei Pattern	$85
Cruet with Stopper, Diamond Fountain Pattern	$1,000
Goblet, Floral Oval Pattern	$90
Mug, Arched Fleur-de-Lys Pattern	$275
Mug, Nell Pattern	$100
Mug, Ribbed Ellipse Design	$125
Pitcher, Water, Heavy Heart Pattern	$850
Pitcher, Water, Paneled Thistle Design	$750
Plate, Diamond Fountain Pattern	$300
Plate, 7", Floral Oval Pattern	$125
Sugar, Floral Oval Pattern	$75
Sugar, Hawaiian Lei Pattern	$85
Tumbler, Heavy Heart Pattern	$165
Tumbler, Paneled Thistle Design	$125

Hobnail
Millersburg Glass Company

In general, hobnail patterns are common, especially with Westmoreland; however, in carnival glass, they are quite rare. The knobs of the Millersburg pieces are glossy and refract well. Note that there are fewer rows of hobs on the pattern variant. The prices listed below are for the standard colors of blue, green, amethyst, or purple; for marigold, reduce them by one-third.

Bowl (Marigold Has Cherries in Pattern)	$1,250
Bowl, Rose	$550
Bowl, Rose (Pattern Variant)	$1,250
Butter Dish	$750
Creamer	$425
Hat Vase	$2,250
Jardiniere (Pattern Variant)	$1,250
Pitcher, 6" Tall, Miniature	$500
Pitcher, Water	$3,750
Spittoon	$1,250
Spooner	$400
Sugar Dish with Cover	$625
Tumbler, 2½" Tall, Miniature	$125
Tumbler	$1,250
Vase	$400
Vase (Pattern Variant)	$1,000

Hobstar
Imperial Glass Company

This Hobstar design is the same pattern as those typically found on cut glass. The molding does contain some fine faceting and is often confused with cut glass. The pattern variant contains hobstars surrounded by beaded broken arches. The prices listed below are for the colors green, amethyst, purple, or smoke; for marigold or clambroth, reduce them by 50 percent.

Basket, Bride's, Marigold	$150
Bowl, 5"	$55
Bowl, 6", Ruffled	$60
Bowl, 8", Ruffled	$65
Bowl, 9" (Pattern Variant)	$80
Bowl, 10"	$100
Bowl, 12", Ruffled	$85
Bowl, Fruit, with Base	$200
Bowl, Fruit, with Base (Pattern Variant)	$250

Hobnail Carnival. *Photo by Mark Pickvet. Courtesy of the Fenton Art Glass Museum.*

Butter Dish with Cover	$225
Cookie Jar with Cover	$175
Creamer	$100
Pickle Castor	$1,500
Punch Bowl with Base	$1,250
Punch Cup	$90
Spooner	$90
Sugar Dish with Cover	$150
Vase, Flared	$250

Hobstar and Feather
Millersburg Glass Company

The feathers surround the finely sharp molded hobstar within this pattern. Rims are usually scalloped, and the bottom contains a horizontal band. The prices listed below are for the standard colors of blue, green, amethyst, or purple; for marigold, reduce them by one-third. For any unusual colors, including pastels, double the prices.

Bowl, 5"	$550
Bowl, 5", Diamond Shape	$600
Bowl, 5", Heart Shape	$550
Bowl, 10", Square	$2,500
Bowl, Rose	$4,000

Butter Dish with Cover	$2,100
Card Tray	$400
Compote, 6"	$2,250
Compote, 10"	$7,500
Creamer	$900
Punch Bowl with Base	$4,500
Punch Cup	$100
Sherbet	$900
Spooner	$850
Sugar Dish with Cover	$1,250
Tumbler	$1,250
Vase	$5,000

Hobstar Band
Imperial Glass Company

Small hobstars are contained within pointed ovals at the top of each object in this pattern. The lower part contains vertical beading. Most pieces were made in marigold; for any other colors, triple the prices. A few rare amethyst and green pieces have been discovered.

Bowl, 8"	$150
Bowl, 10"	$200
Butter Dish	$125
Celery Dish	$125
Compote	$125
Pitcher	$325
Tumbler	$75

Holly
Fenton Art Glass Company

Holly is characterized by holly leaves and vines emanating from the center. The foliage also creates a raised circular pattern in relief. This pattern comes in a variety of color styles. The prices listed below are for the standard colors of blue, green, amethyst, or purple. For marigold, reduce them by one-third; for any pastels or unusual color varieties, double the prices; and for any rare peach opalescent or red, multiply the prices by 10.

Bowl, 7¼"	$165
Bowl, 8"	$125
Bowl, 10"	$150
Bowl, Rose	$600
Compote, 5" (Small)	$175
Goblet	$100
Hat Vase	$100
Plate, 9"	$900

Holly Sprig
Millersburg Glass Company

This pattern is often referred to as Whirl because of the whirling shape of the design. Within the design are holly leaves and berries in a circular style. The prices listed below are for the standard colors of blue, green, amethyst, or purple. For marigold or clambroth, reduce them by one-third; for any rare vaseline examples, double the prices.

Bonbon Dish, 2 Styles	$100
Bonbon Dish, with Advertising	$200
Bowl, 5½", Ruffled	$300
Bowl, 6", Ruffled	$325
Bowl, 7"	$350
Bowl, 7" Square	$350
Bowl, 7", Tricorner	$350
Bowl, 8", Ruffled	$400
Bowl, 8" Square	$375
Bowl, 8", Tricorner	$375
Bowl, 9"	$200
Bowl, 9", Ruffled	$225
Bowl, 9", Tricorner	$400
Bowl, 10"	$225
Bowl, 10"	$250
Bowl, 10", Tricorner	$425
Bowl, Rose	$650

Compote	$650
Nappy, Tricorner	$125
Sauce Dish	$350
Tray, Handled	$475

Inverted Feather
Cambridge Glass Company

Cambridge was not a major producer of iridized or carnival glass; however, they did manufacture a few inverted patterns. Inverted Feather covers each piece entirely, with scrolls, hobstars, ridged frames, florals, and draped beading. Basic colors are green and amethyst; for marigold, reduce the prices by one-third.

Butter Dish with Cover	$575
Compote	$175
Cracker Jar with Cover	$750
Creamer	$450
Cup	$125
Parfait Dish	$250
Pitcher, Milk	$2,000
Pitcher, Water	$7,000
Punch Bowl with Base	$4,750
Punch Cup	$125
Spooner	$400
Sugar	$450
Tumbler	$750
Wineglass	$500

Inverted Strawberry
Cambridge Glass Company

The second of Cambridge's inverted patterns, this one is characterized by diamond-molded strawberries with branches and leaves around each item. Basic colors are blue, green, purple, and amethyst; for marigold, reduce the prices by one-third.

Bowl, Berry, 5"	$75
Bowl, 7½", Square	$500

Bowl, Berry, 9"	$350
Bowl, 10½"	$375
Butter Dish with Cover	$1,250
Candlestick	$275
Celery Dish	$1,000
Compote (Small)	$600
Compote (Large)	$525
Creamer	$375
Cruet with Stopper	$2,000
Cuspidor	$1,400
Honey Dish	$250
Pitcher, Milk	$4,000
Pitcher, Water	$2,500
Powder Jar	$350
Spittoon	$1,400
Spooner	$325
Sugar	$375
Sugar, Stemmed	$1,250
Tumbler	$275

Inverted Thistle
Cambridge Glass Company

This pattern is similar to Inverted Strawberry except that the strawberries are replaced with thistle. The thistle branches and leaves are also formed into scrolls. Basic colors are green, blue, purple, and amethyst; for marigold, reduce the prices by one-third. Double the prices for any opalescent varieties.

Bowl, 5"	$200
Bowl, 9"	$375
Box with Cover	$450
Butter Dish with Cover	$700
Creamer	$475
Pitcher, Milk	$3,250

Carnival Glass. Inverted Thistle Pattern. *Drawing by Mark Pickvet.*

Carnival Glass. Luster and Clear Pattern. *Drawing by Mark Pickvet.*

Pitcher, Water	$4,000
Plate, Chop	$2,750
Spittoon	$4,250
Spooner	$450
Sugar	$475
Tumbler	$450

Kittens

Fenton Art Glass Company

This is a cute pattern consisting of kittens scrambling over each other to drink from a long oval bowl. Standard colors are blue, purple, and amethyst; for marigold, reduce the prices by 50 percent. A few pieces have been found in pastel colors such as aqua, smoke, vaseline, and a light lavender; increase the price by 50 percent for any pastels.

Bowl, 4"	$400
Bowl, Flared Rim, Straight Sides	$500
Bowl, 6"	$400
Cup	$400
Plate, 4½"	$450
Saucer	$300
Spittoon	$7,500

Spooner	$300
Vase, 3" to 3¼" Tall	$450

Lattice and Daisy
Dugan Glass Company

This pattern contains daisy blossoms and leaves in the center of each object. On the borders are two thick rows of interlocking diamonds or latticework. The prices listed below are for blue, green, amethyst, and purple. For marigold, reduce them by 50 percent; for any pastel white, increase them 50 percent.

Bowl, 5"	$75
Bowl, 9"	$225
Pitcher, Water	$1,500
Tumbler	$125

Leaf Tiers
Fenton Art Glass Company

Leaf Tiers contains rows of overlapping leaves around each object. All pieces in this pattern are footed. Pricing is for blue, green, or amethyst. For marigold, reduce the prices by one-third.

Banana Dish, Footed	$350
Bowl, Berry, 5", Footed	$75
Bowl, Berry, 10", Footed	$100
Butter Dish, Footed	$325
Creamer, Footed	$150
Pitcher, Water, Footed	$750
Spooner, Footed	$125
Sugar Dish, Footed	$150
Tumbler, Footed	$250

Little Flowers
Fenton Art Glass Company

Little Flowers contains two bands of flowers around a central floral circle. The inner row consists of tiny flowers, whereas those in the outer row are larger and are connected by stems from the center. The prices listed below are for the standard colors of blue, green, amethyst, or purple. For marigold, reduce them by one-third; for any pastels or unusual color varieties, double the prices; and for any rare Amberina or red, multiply the prices by 10.

Bowl, 5½" Round	$85
Bowl, 5½" Square	$225
Bowl, 6"	$100
Bowl, 6", Tricorner	$200
Bowl, 9½"	$175
Bowl, 10"	$250
Plate, 7"	$325
Plate, 10"	$2,750

Little Stars
Millersburg Glass Company

This pattern consists of a large central seven-petaled flower surrounded by six-pointed stars. The prices listed below are for green or amethyst. For marigold or clambroth, reduce them by one-third. Blue is rare in this pattern; quadruple the prices.

Bowl, 4"	$800
Bowl, 7"	$450
Bowl 9"	$600
Bowl, 10½"	$900
Plate, 7½"	$1,500

Lotus and Grape
Fenton Art Glass Company

Lotus and Grape consists of alternating grape bunches and lotus leaves around a floral central circle. The pattern variant has a laced or notched edge. The prices listed below are for the standard colors of blue, green, amethyst, or purple. For marigold, reduce them by one-third; for any pastels or unusual color varieties (such as aqua and vaseline), double the prices; and for any rare red, multiply the prices by a factor of 10.

Absentee Bowl	$2,000
Bonbon Dish	$150
Bonbon Dish, Footed, Pattern Variant	$150
Bowl, 6", Footed, Pattern Variant	$90

Bowl, 7"	$125
Bowl, 8½"	$150
Bowl, Rose, Footed, Pattern Variant	$500
Plate, 9½"	$2,500

Lustre and Clear
Imperial Glass Company

This is a somewhat transparent marigold color with pillars that end at the rim. There are also matching flutes. For any colored pieces other than marigold (such as amber, green, blue, and clambroth), double the prices below; for any rare red, multiply them by 10.

Bowl, 5"	$35
Bowl, 10"	$45
Bowl, Rose	$100
Butter Dish	$100
Compote	$55
Creamer	$45
Nappy	$55
Pitcher, Water	$250
Salt and Pepper Shakers	$100
Sugar	$45
Tray, Celery, 8"	$55
Tumbler	$65
Vase, 8", Footed	$125
Vase, Wall	$55

Lustre and Flute
Northwood Glass Company

This pattern is characterized by vertical flutes or columns topped off by a band of lattice-work. The prices listed below are for green, amethyst, or purple. For marigold, reduce them by one-third.

Bonbon Dish, 2-Handled	$65
Bowl, 5½"	$45
Bowl, 8"	$75

Compote	$60
Creamer	$65
Hat	$40
Nappy	$75
Punch Bowl with Base	$550
Punch Cup	$35
Sherbet	$50
Sugar	$65

Lustre Rose
Imperial Glass Company

This early Imperial pattern consists of a band of roses within thorns and other foliage. The colors priced below include amber, green, purple, amethyst, pastel blue, or smoke. For marigold or clambroth, reduce them by one-third; for any rare red, multiply them by a factor of 10.

Bowl, Berry, 5"	$50
Bowl, 6", Ruffled	$60
Bowl, 7"	$65
Bowl, 8"	$75
Bowl, 9"	$85
Bowl, Berry, 9", Footed	$250
Bowl, 10"	$100
Bowl, 11", Footed	$150
Bowl, 12", Footed	$175
Bowl, Rose	$175
Butter Dish	$125
Cake Plate	$325
Creamer	$85
Fernery, Footed	$200
Pitcher, Milk	$175
Pitcher, Water	$300
Plate, 6"	$250
Plate, 9"	$275

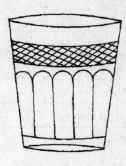

Lustre Flute Tumbler. *Drawing by Mark Pickvet.*

Spooner	$75
Sugar Dish with Cover	$115
Tumbler	$85

Maple Leaf
Dugan Glass Company

The maple leaves in this pattern are intertwined within ridging that gives a raised appearance. Above the design is a horizontal line of semicircles around each piece. Basic colors are blue, amethyst, or purple; for marigold, reduce them by one-third.

Bowl, 4½", Ice Cream, Stemmed (Small)	$55
Bowl, 9", Ice Cream, Stemmed (Large)	$115
Butter Dish with Cover	$175
Creamer	$75
Pitcher, Water	$350
Spooner	$70
Sugar Dish with Cover	$100
Tumbler	$60

Melon Rib
Imperial Glass Company

Melon Rib is a fairly simple pattern that consists of wide horizontal ribbing. Prices are for marigold, which is the only known color produced in this pattern.

Bowl, 10"	$40
Candy Jar with Cover	$75
Decanter with Stopper	$125
Pitcher, Water	$100
Puff Box with Cover	$55
Salt and Pepper Shakers	$55
Tumbler	$35

Memphis
Northwood Glass Company

Memphis is a cutlike geometric pattern with starred ovals and diamonds. Basic prices are for green or amethyst; reduce them by one-third for marigold. There are a few rare colors, including pastel white (double the prices), blue or lime green (triple the prices), and ice blue or ice green (multiply the prices by 5). Pieces also exist in plain crystal without any carnival flashing, for which the prices should be reduced by two-thirds.

Bowl, 5"	$65
Bowl, 10"	$350
Bowl, 12"	$400
Bowl, Fruit, with Base	$650
Creamer	$100
Punch Bowl with Base	$750
Punch Cup	$75
Sugar	$100

Octagon
Imperial Glass Company

Octagon, as the name implies, consists of eight panels with very large molded lines. The panels contain a variety of stars, diamonds, beads, arches, and other geometrical designs. The colors priced below are aqua, green, purple, amethyst, pastel blue, white, and smoke. For marigold or clambroth, reduce them by one-third.

Bowl, 4½"	$50
Bowl, 8½"	$80
Bowl, 10"	$175
Bowl, 12"	$225

Bowl, Rose, Marigold	$750
Butter Dish with Cover	$450
Compote, 5", Small	$300
Compote, Large	$350
Cordial	$350
Creamer	$350
Cup	$100
Decanter with Stopper	$550
Goblet	$125
Nappy, Handled	$300
Pitcher, Milk	$300
Pitcher, Water, 8", Small	$650
Pitcher, Water, Large	$750
Salt and Pepper Shakers	$575
Sherbet	$125
Spooner	$300
Sugar Dish with Cover	$325
Toothpick Holder	$500
Tumbler, 2 Styles	$100
Vase, 8" Tall	$225
Wineglass	$125

Omera
Imperial Glass Company

Omera is also known as "Smooth Panels," which describes this fairly simple wide-paneled pattern. Imperial also made this design in clear glass as well as noniridized Depression colors later. The colors priced below are for marigold and clambroth. Double them for any other carnival glass colors except red, for which they should be multiplied by 10.

Bowl, 6"	$30
Bowl, 8"	$40
Bowl, 10"	$50
Bowl, Rose	$80

Celery Dish with Handle	$50
Nappy	$40
Plate, 8"	$60

Optic and Buttons
Imperial Glass Company

Vertical panels with a band of beads at the top make up this simple pattern by Imperial. The prices below are for marigold or clambroth; double them for any others, such as smoke or lavender.

Bowl, 5"	$35
Bowl, 6"	$40
Bowl, 8"	$45
Bowl, 10"	$50
Bowl, 12" 2-Handled	$60
Bowl, Rose	$110
Compote	$55
Cup	$200
Goblet	$75
Nut Cup, 2-Handled	$200
Pitcher, Water	$225
Plate, 6"	$55
Plate, 7"	$65
Plate, 9½"	$80
Plate, 10½"	$90
Salt Dish, Open, 2-Handled	$175
Saucer	$125
Tumbler, 2 Styles	$75
Wineglass	$75

Orange Tree
Fenton Art Glass Company

This pattern is characterized by a thick tree trunk with three branches; the branches contain orange blossoms with stippled centers. Fenton made a lot of this pattern, and in a wide

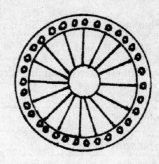

Optic and Buttons Plate. *Drawing by Mark Pickvet.*

variety of colors. The prices below apply to aqua, amber, blue, green, lavender, vaseline, purple, amethyst, ice green, and ice blue. For marigold, teal, or clambroth, reduce the prices by 50 percent. Double the prices for white (pastel or milk); triple them for Amberina, and multiply them by a factor of 10 for red or opalescent varieties (peach, aqua, or even marigold opalescent).

Bowl, Berry, 5½", Footed	$55
Bowl, 8"	$125
Bowl, Berry, 9", Footed	$135
Bowl, 10"	$145
Bowl, 11", Footed	$150
Bowl, Orange, 12", Footed	$175
Bowl, Rose	$125
Butter Dish with Cover	$650
Centerpiece, 12", Footed	$2,000
Compote	$75
Creamer, 2 Styles	$75
Cruet	$3,000
Cup, Loving	$600
Goblet	$225
Hat Pin Holder	$500
Mug	$175

Mug, Shaving	$200
Pitcher, Water, Footed	$700
Pitcher, Water, Pattern Contains Scrolls	$1,000
Plate, 8"	$1,500
Plate, 9½"	$1,600
Pwder Jar with Cover	$250
Punch Bowl with Base	$550
Punch Cup	$40
Sherbet	$100
Spooner	$70
Sugar	$75
Sugar with Cover	$100
Tumbler, Footed	$80
Tumbler, Pattern Contains Scrolls	$100
Vase	$2,500
Wineglass	$100

Palm Beach
U.S. Glass Company

Although U.S. Glass was not a huge maker of iridized glass, they did produce a few odd pieces and patterns during the carnival-glass era. Molds that contain large grapes and leaves were once used by U.S. Glass to make pressed glass in this same design. The prices below are for honey amber, lime green, and marigold. Double them for any other colors, such as amethyst and pastel white.

Banana Dish	$125
Bowl, 5"	$90
Bowl, 6"	$110
Bowl, 9"	$65
Bowl, Rose	$300
Butter Dish	$150
Creamer	$100
Pitcher, Water	$375

Plate, 9"	$250
Spooner	$85
Sugar Dish with Cover	$125
Tumbler	$150
Vase	$400

Pansy
Imperial Glass Company

The pansies in this pattern are cluttered with arches and other foliage on a stippled background. The prices below are for green, purple, or amethyst. For marigold, reduce the prices by 50 percent. Double the prices for unusual colors such as blue, smoke, lavender, and aqua opalescent.

Bowl, 8¼"	$175
Bowl, 9½", Ruffled	$200
Creamer	$60
Dresser Tray, Oval	$100
Nappy	$75
Pickle Dish, Oval	$65
Plate, Ruffled	$225
Relish Dish	$175
Sugar	$60

Peach
Northwood Glass Company

In this pattern, two peaches are bunched together with branches and vines framed with horizontal beading. The design is set in low relief and also contains two outer horizontal bands (one near the top and one at the bottom). The pattern was made mostly in white, which is priced below. Marigold and blue pieces are rare—double the prices for them.

Bowl, Berry, 5"	$65
Bowl, Berry, 9"	$175
Butter Dish with Cover	$325
Creamer	$175

Peach Tumbler. *Drawing by Mark Pickvet.*

Pitcher, Water	$1,000
Spooner	$150
Sugar Dish with Cover	$250
Tumbler	$200

Peacock
Millersburg Glass Company

The feathers of the peacock in this pattern are set in relief, and the peacock itself is framed by a wreath of foliage. In the background are Greek columns and ferns at the bird's feet. The prices below apply to green, purple, amethyst, and clambroth pieces. For marigold, reduce them by one-third; for any rare blue or vaseline, triple the prices.

Banana Dish	$3,750
Bowl, 5"	$350
Bowl, 6"	$350
Bowl, 7½"	$500
Bowl, 9"	$600
Bowl, 10", Ice Cream	$1,750
Bowl, Rose	$5,000
Plate, 6"	$1,500
Plate, Chop	$2,250
Spittoon	$8,000

Peacock and Urn

Fenton Art Glass Company, Millersburg Glass Company, Northwood Glass Company

The patterns from the three companies that produced Peacock and Urn are all similar. The ridgework on the urn is more rigid in Millersburg than in Fenton's; Millersburg's also contains a stylized bee within the bird's beak. The circle of leaves within the foliage wreath is less detailed and contains more plain, glossy space on the Northwood design. One of the Millersburg variants includes wreaths that are sprays of foliage rather than a complete all-encompassing design. Some of the scrolling has no beading as in the original pattern. The colors priced below are blue, green, purple, amethyst, vaseline, white, ice green, ice blue, and smoke. For marigold or clambroth, reduce them by one-third. For any rare red or opalescent varieties, such as aqua, peach, or moonstone, multiply the prices by 10.

Bowl, 5"	$225
Bowl, 6" Ice Cream	$250
Bowl, 8½"	$350
Bowl, 9"	$375
Bowl, 9½"	$425
Bowl, 10"	$650
Compote	$1,500
Goblet	$250
Plate, 6"	$600
Plate, 6" Stippled	$750
Plate, 9", Footed	$500
Plate, 10½"	$4,500
Plate, 11"	$1,750
Plate, Chop, 12"	$2,000
Spittoon	$4,000

Peacock at the Fountain

Northwood Glass Company, Dugan Glass Company

There are only two Dugan pieces, a pitcher and tumbler, as noted below. The remaining pieces are from Northwood. The peacock in this pattern is quite large, standing upright on a block pedestal that contains a daisy growing from between the bricks. The fountain contains lined ridges where the water sprays from it. Prices below are for blue, green, purple, amethyst, or white. For marigold, reduce them by one-third; for ice blue or ice green, double them; and for any rare aqua opalescent, multiply them by 10.

Peacock and Urn Pattern. *Photo by Robin Rainwater.*

Bowl, Berry, 5"	$100
Bowl, Berry, 9"	$250
Bowl, Orange, Footed	$750
Butter Dish with Cover	$400
Compote	$800
Creamer	$175
Pitcher, Water	$750
Pitcher, Water (Dugan)	$650
Punch Bowl with Base	$1,250
Punch Cup	$60
Spittoon	$17,500
Spooner	$150
Sugar with Cover	$300
Tumbler	$75
Tumbler (Dugan)	$100

Peacock Tail
Fenton Art Glass Company

The pattern is characterized by a center circle of feathers with concentric circles that emanate out from each feather. The colors priced below are blue, green, purple, amethyst, or

Peacock at the Fountain Pattern. *Photo by Robin Rainwater.*

white. For marigold, reduce them by one-third; for any rare red, multiply them by a factor of 10.

Bonbon Dish with Handle	$85
Bowl, 4"	$55
Bowl, 5"	$60
Bowl, 7"	$70
Bowl, 8"	$125
Bowl, 10"	$150
Compote	$60
Hat Vase	$60
Plate, 6"	$275
Plate, 9"	$325

Persian Garden
Dugan Glass Company

Persian Garden is a geometric pattern with a center medallion. Rows of arches with flowers and checkerboards flow outward from the medallion, ending in a band of fountains with teardrops near the rim of each piece. The prices below are for blue, green, purple, amethyst, white, lavender, or peach opalescent. For marigold, reduce them by one-third.

Bowl, Berry, 5"	$75
Bowl, Ice Cream, 6"	$150

Bowl, Berry, 10"	$350
Bowl, Ice Cream, 11"	$550
Bowl, Fruit with Base	$650
Plate, 6"	$500
Plate, Chop, 13"	$5,000

Persian Medallion
Fenton Art Glass Company

This pattern is characterized by varying shapes of floral medallions with bands of petaled circles, with teardrops inscribed within the circles. Some bowls have a grape and cable patterned exterior (same price). The prices below are for blue, green, purple, amethyst, or white. For marigold, reduce them by one-third; for amber, vaseline, ice green, or ice blue, double them; and for any rare red, multiply them by 10.

Bonbon Dish	$150
Bowl, 5"	$65
Bowl, 8¾"	$175
Bowl, 10", Collar Base	$325
Bowl, Orange	$475
Bowl, Rose	$325
Compote, Small	$275
Compote, Large	$350
Hair Receiver	$115
Plate, 6"	$325
Plate, 7"	$300
Plate, 9" to 9½"	$650
Plate, Chop	$1,000
Punch Bowl with Base	$675
Punch Cup	$50
Spittoon,	$8,500

Poppy Show
Imperial Glass Company, Northwood Glass Company

The Poppy Show patterns are similar between the two companies. Both contain poppies, leaves, stems, and vines. Northwood produced only the bowls and plate as noted below; the

Carnival Glass, Persian Medallion Pattern. *Photo by Mark Pickvet, Courtesy of the Fenton Art Glass Museum.*

Carnival Glass, Persian Medallion Pattern. *Photo by Mark Pickvet, Courtesy of the Fenton Art Glass Museum.*

remaining pieces are Imperial's. Note that Imperial reproduced this product in the 1960s. Reproductions are marked "IG" on the underside and sell for about 10 percent of the originals priced below (original blue, green, purple, amethyst, amber, white, ice green, ice blue, smoke, or lime green). For marigold or clambroth, reduce the prices below by one-third; for any rare aqua opalescent, multiply them by a factor of 10.

Bowl, 7" (Northwood)	$100
Bowl, 8½" (Northwood)	$1,250
Bowl, 9" to 9½" (Northwood)	$2,250
Lamp, Table	$3,500
Lamp, Hurricane	$3,250
Plate, 9" (Northwood)	$2,500
Vase, 12" Tall	$1,250

Prism & Daisy Band
Imperial Glass Company

This is a simple, finely vertically ribbed pattern with a banded row of daisies at the top. The basic color is marigold, which is priced below. Double the prices for any other colors.

Bowl, 5"	$100
Bowl, 8"	$950
Compote	$2,750
Creamer	$2,750

Sugar	$2,500
Vase	$2,750

Ranger
Imperial Glass Company, Inwald of Sweden, Christales de Mexico, Chrystal Glass of Australia

Ranger is a fairly simple arched block pattern that was produced mostly in marigold. Imperial was known to make a clambroth piece or two (same price).

Bowl, 4½"	$45
Bowl, 6"	$60
Bowl, 9"	$85
Bowl, 10"	$100
Butter Dish with Cover	$200
Cracker Jar with Cover	$125
Creamer	$60
Decanter with Stopper	$250
Nappy	$75
Perfume Bottle with Stopper, 5¼"	$175
Pitcher, Milk	$175
Pitcher, Water	$625
Sherbet	$75
Shot Glass	$500
Sugar Dish with Cover	$100
Toothpick Holder	$150
Tumbler	$150
Vase, 8" Tall, Pedestal Feet	$125
Vase, 10" Tall	$100

Raspberry
Northwood Glass Company

The raspberries of this pattern are shaped by beaded circles in low relief. Below the raspberries is a wide basket-weave panel. The colors priced below are blue, green, purple, amethyst, amber, or horehound (Northwood's name for a dark amber color like root beer).

Reduce them by one-third for marigold; double the prices for teal, lavender, or white; and quadruple them for lime green, ice green, or ice blue.

Bowl, Berry, 5"	$55
Bowl, Berry, 9"	$85
Bowl, Serving, Footed	$90
Compote	$75
Pitcher, Milk	$400
Pitcher, Water	$475
Sauce Boat, Footed	$200
Tumbler	$75

Robin
Imperial Glass Company

This pattern shows a robin perched on a branch with leaves. Original colors include marigold and smoke, which are priced below. Reproductions later in the 20th century by Imperial were in white, blue, pink, and red. All reproductions have Imperial's "IG" mark on the underside and are worth about one-third to one-half of the originals.

Mug	$75
Pitcher, Water	$200
Tumbler	$45

Sailboats
Fenton Art Glass Company

As you might expect from the name, the basic design includes sailboats within curved frames. Each frame includes a single sailboat on the water with clouds in the background. The primary frames are separated by smaller frames that include a four-petaled star that resembles the blades of a windmill. The prices below are for amber, aqua, blue, green, lime green, purple, and amethyst. Reduce them by 50 percent for marigold or lavender; double them for Amberina or vaseline; and for any rare red, multiply them by a factor of 10.

Bowl, 6"	$100
Compote	$150
Goblet	$350
Plate, 6"	$700
Wineglass	$125

Scale Band
Fenton Art Glass Company

This pattern consists of alternating panels of scales and fluted (at the top band) vertical ribs. The prices below apply to blue, green, and white pieces. Reduce them by 50 percent for marigold; double them for vaseline; multiply them by a factor of 10 for any rare red or opalescent varieties (aqua or peach opalescent).

Bowl, 6"	$100
Bowl, 8½"	$150
Bowl, 10"	$200
Plate, 6½"	$250
Plate, 7"	$350
Pitcher, Water	$500
Tumbler	$125

Seaweed
Millersburg Glass Company

This design consists of beads in bubble form, spiraling scrolls that twirl outward from the center, and a wavy background. The prices below are for green, purple, and amethyst pieces; reduce them by 50 percent for marigold or clambroth. Blue is rare; quadruple the prices for any blue pieces.

Bowl, 5"	$600
Bowl, 6" to 6½"	$750
Bowl, 9"	$625
Bowl, 10"	$850
Bowl, 10½", Ice Cream	$1,500
Bowl, 10½", Ruffled	$525
Lamp	$500
Plate, 10"	$2,500

Singing Birds
Northwood Glass Company

As the pattern name implies, the birds sitting on the branches have their beaks open as if they are singing. The prices below are for blue, green, purple, amethyst, lavender, or horehound (Northwood's name for a dark amber color like root beer). Reduce them by one-third for marigold; double them for olive green, white, smoke, ice green, or ice blue; and for any rare aqua opalescent, multiply them by a factor of 10.

Bowl, Berry, 5"	$45
Bowl, Berry, 10"	$90
Butter Dish with Cover	$375
Creamer	$150
Mug	$175
Mug, Stippled	$300
Mug, Pouring (with Spout)	$1,000
Pitcher, Water	$650
Sherbet	$650
Spooner	$125
Sugar	$175
Tumbler	$100

Ski Star
Dugan Glass Company

Dugan's Ski Star pattern is much like a kaleidoscope, featuring stars within circles and stars surrounding the circles. The star in the pattern is often compared to the eight points of a compass. The prices below are for blue, green, amethyst, or purple. Reduce them by 50 percent for marigold; double them for peach opalescent.

Banana Dish	$225
Basket, Handled	$275
Bowl, 5"	$90
Bowl, 8"	$225
Bowl, 10"	$250
Bowl, Rose	$400
Plate, 6"	$175
Plate, 7½"	$200
Plate, 10"	$250

Smooth Rays
Dugan Glass Company, Imperial Glass Company, Northwood Glass Company, Westmoreland Glass Company

Smooth Rays consists of pillared or vertical panels along with a circular rayed base (Imperial pieces have more of a star base); nevertheless, the basic pattern between all companies is nearly identical. The prices below are for blue, green, amethyst, or purple. Reduce them by 50 percent for marigold, clambroth, or smoke; double them for amber, teal, milk glass (white or light blue made by Westmoreland exclusively), opalescent varieties (aqua, blue, or peach), or for Northwood's Alaska (marigold flashed over green glass).

Bonbon Dish	$60
Bowl, 6"	$60
Bowl, 8"	$90
Bowl, 9"	$50
Bowl, 10"	$60
Bowl, Rose	$175
Champagne Glass	$85
Compote, 5"	$50
Compote, 7½"	$60
Cup, Custard	$35
Goblet	$60
Pitcher, Water	$150
Plate, 7"	$100
Plate, 8"	$75
Plate, 9"	$100
Plate, 12"	$100
Tumbler	$45
Wineglass	$60

Springtime
Northwood Glass Company

Springtime contains chained daisies within panels set in relief. Along the top and bottom of each piece are borders that resemble basket-weave designs. The prices below are for blue and green; reduce them by one-third for marigold.

Bowl, Berry, 5"	$75
Bowl, Berry, 9"	$225
Butter Dish with Cover	$475
Creamer	$400
Pitcher, Water	$1,250
Spooner	$375
Sugar	$425
Tumbler	$125

S-Repeat
Dugan Glass Company

This pattern consists of large stylized S shapes that repeat around each object. The prices below are for amethyst or purple. Marigold is actually rare in this pattern; double the prices for any marigold pieces.

Creamer	$100
Pitcher, Water	$1,000
Punch Bowl with Base	$5,000
Punch Cup	$100
Sugar	$250
Toothpick Holder	$125
Tumbler	$150

Stag and Holly
Fenton Art Glass Company

As the name implies, this pattern consists of alternating deer (stags) and branched holly leaves. There is also a large holly berry in the center. The prices below are for blue, green, amethyst, purple, and aqua. Reduce them by 50 percent for marigold; double them for amber; and multiply them by 10 for any rare red.

Bowl, 9"	$350
Bowl, 10"	$375
Bowl, 13"	$450
Bowl, Rose	$1,500

Plate, 9"	$1,750
Plate, 13"	$3,000

Star and File
Imperial Glass Company

This is a simple geometric pattern consisting of a wide chain of hobstars separated by filed spears. Most pieces exist in marigold or clambroth as priced below; however, a few rare colors pop up now and then, and the prices listed here should be tripled for them.

Bonbon Dish	$45
Bowl, 7", Round or Square	$40
Bowl, 7", 2-Handled	$45
Bowl, 8", Round or Square	$45
Bowl, 8", 2-Handled	$50
Bowl, 9½"	$55
Bowl, Rose	$85
Celery Vase, 2-Handled	$60
Champagne Glass	$50
Compote	$50
Cordial, 1 oz.	$75
Creamer	$40
Cup, Custard	$35
Decanter with Stopper	$150
Goblet	$50
Nut Dish	$50
Pickle Dish	$50
Pitcher, Water	$325
Plate, 6" to 6½"	$70
Relish Dish, Oval, 2-Handled	$60
Sherbet	$50
Spooner	$35
Sugar	$40
Tumbler	$100

Vase, Handled	$60
Wineglass	$70

Star Medallion
Imperial Glass Company

A wide band encompasses about three-quarters of each piece; in the center of it are sharp-edged patterned stars. Surrounding the stars are hobstars extending out from small diamond patterning. The colors priced below include marigold, smoke, or clambroth; double them for any other color varieties.

Bonbon Dish	$45
Bowl, 6"	$30
Bowl, 6", Square	$40
Bowl, 7"	$35
Bowl, 7", Square	$45
Bowl, 9", Square	$60
Butter Dish with Cover	$125
Celery Vase, Handled	$100
Compote	$55
Creamer	$70
Cup, Custard	$30
Goblet	$60
Pickle Dish	$50
Pitcher, Milk	$100
Pitcher, Water	$150
Plate, 5"	$55
Plate, 6"	$60
Plate, 7½"	$65
Plate, 10"	$80
Punch Bowl	$250
Punch Cup	$40
Sherbet	$40
Spooner	$65

Stippled Rays Pattern. Northwood Amethyst. *Photo by Mark Pickvet. Courtesy of the Fenton Art Glass Museum.*

Sugar	$70
Tray, Celery	$75
Tumbler, 2 Varieties	$40
Vase, 6" Tall	$50

Stippled Rays
Fenton Art Glass Company, Imperial Glass Company, Northwood Glass Company

The Fenton version contains the most variety of pieces, all except the footed creamer and sugar. This interior pattern is characterized by alternating stippled spears with clear portions that emanate from the center into a large star. The Imperial pattern is in low relief with scalloped edges. The only two pieces known to have been made by Imperial are the footed creamer and sugar. Northwood produced a compote along with the 8-inch and 10-inch bowls. The prices below are for amber, blue, green, amethyst, purple, and smoke. Reduce them 50 percent for marigold; double them for amberina, lime green, ice green, ice blue, black amethyst, vaseline, or pastel white; and multiply them by 10 for any rare red.

Bonbon Dish	$55
Bowl, 5"	$60
Bowl, 8"	$70
Bowl, 9"	$75
Bowl, 10"	$85

Bowl, 11"	$100
Compote	$60
Creamer	$80
Creamer, Footed	$85
Plate, 7"	$150
Sugar	$90
Sugar, Footed	$85

Stork and Rushes
Dugan Glass Company

The stork is a common bird found in many carnival examples. Imperial also made several items such as vases and ABC plates with a stork pattern motif. The prices below are for blue, amethyst, purple, or aqua. Reduce them by one-third for marigold and multiply them by 10 for any rare aqua opalescent.

Basket with Handle	$200
Bowl, Berry, 4½"	$50
Bowl, Berry, 10"	$75
Butter Dish with Cover	$225
Creamer	$100
Hat Vase	$75
Mug	$150
Pitcher, Water	$300
Punch Bowl with Base	$350
Punch Cup	$40
Spooner	$90
Sugar Dish	$150
Tumbler	$75

Strawberry
Dugan Glass Company, Fenton Art Glass Company, Millersburg Glass Company, Northwood Glass Company

Millersburg pieces contain strawberries and large or wide strawberry leaves in a circular design. The leaves are much thinner on Northwood's pattern. To date, all that has been found by Fenton and Dugan are the bonbon dish and epergne, respectively. The prices below are for blue, green, amethyst, or purple pieces. Reduce them by 50 percent for marigold; double them for vaseline, lime opalescent, lavender, ice blue, or ice green; triple them for peach opalescent or Northwood's horehound (color of root beer or horehound candy); and multiply them by 10 for any rare red or aqua opalescent pieces.

Banana Boat	$1,500
Bonbon Dish	$75
Bowl, 5"	$125
Bowl, 6½"	$150
Bowl, 8"	$325
Bowl, 8½"	$375
Bowl, 9½", Tricorner	$700
Bowl, 10"	$425
Compote	$500
Epergne (Dugan)	$1,250
Gravy Boat	$1,500
Hat Pin	$1,650
Plate, 7"	$300
Plate, 9"	$350
Plate, 9", Stippled	$1,750

Ten Mums
Fenton Art Glass Company

The basic design contains 10 floral mounds or mums that surround a common mum within a centralized circle. Between the outer mums and the center circle are leaves that also wind in a circular pattern. The prices below are for blue, green, amethyst, or purple. Reduce them by 50 percent for marigold; double them for pastel white; and triple them for any peach opalescent.

Bowl, 8"	$325
Bowl, 9", Footed	$750
Bowl, 11"	$350
Pitcher, Water	$1,000
Plate, 10"	$1,250
Tumbler	$125

Tree Bark Tumbler. *Drawing by Mark Pickvet.*

Tree Bark

Imperial Glass Company, Jeannette Glass Company

Tree Bark is a very simple, rough pattern. The exterior contains haphazard vertical ridges that resemble the bark of trees. The pattern variant was produced by Jeannette and contains straighter barklike designs than the original. The prices are for marigold; for any other colors, double them.

Bowl, 7½"	$25
Bowl, Console	$40
Candlestick, 4½"	$25
Candlestick, 7"	$35
Candleholder with Marble Stand, Pattern Variant	$100
Candy Jar with Cover	$50
Pickle Jar, 7½"	$60
Pitcher, Water	$85
Pitcher, Water, Pattern Variant	$75
Pitcher, Water, with Lid	$100
Planter, Pattern Variant	$75
Plate, 7"	$45
Plate, 8"	$60
Sauce Dish, 4"	$20
Tumbler, 2 Styles	$35

Tumbler, Pattern Variant	$30
Vase, Cone or Ovoid Shape	$50

Twins
Imperial Glass Company

This pattern contains a sunburst in the center surrounded by a wreath of teardrop rosettes. The remaining portion consists of rounded arches and ridges in relief. It is much like an allover pattern resembling that of cut glass. The prices below are for blue, green, amethyst, purple, or smoke. Reduce them 50 percent for marigold or clambroth.

Basket, Bride's	$200
Bowl, Berry, 5"	$35
Bowl, 7", Footed	$60
Bowl, 8"	$60
Bowl, Berry, 9"	$60
Bowl, 10", Footed	$70
Bowl, Fruit with Base	$200
Plate, 9½"	$750
Plate, 13"	$850
Punch Bowl with Base	$750
Punch Cup	$75
Vase, 7"	$125
Vase, 8"	$150

Two Flowers
Fenton Art Glass Company

There are more than two flowers in this basic pattern, contrary to the pattern name. The name comes from the pair of flowers that encircle a common floral pattern within the center of each object. The prices below apply to blue, amethyst, purple, green, aqua, smoke, or vaseline pieces. Reduce them by one-third for marigold; double them for any pastel white; and multiply them by 10 for any rare red.

Bowl, 5", Footed	$75
Bowl, 8", Footed	$85
Bowl, 8½"	$250
Bowl, 10", Footed	$300

Bowl, Rose	$200
Plate, 9", Footed	$750
Platter, 13", Round	$4,500

Vintage
Fenton Art Glass Company, Millersburg Glass Company, U.S. Glass Company, Dugan Glass Company

Vintage is another common grape and leaf pattern that is somewhat sparse and in low relief on each piece. Unlike the Fenton pieces, the Millersburg pieces contain hobnails. The wineglass is the only U.S. Glass piece listed. The prices below are for blue, green, amethyst, purple, or aqua. Reduce them by one-third for marigold; double them for vaseline, pastel blue, or lime green; triple them for Amberina; and multiply them by a factor of 10 for any rare red or aqua opalescent.

Bonbon Dish	$65
Bowl, Berry, 4½"	$45
Bowl, 5" (Millersburg)	$1,500
Bowl, 6", Tricorner	$75
Bowl, 6½"	$50
Bowl, Berry, 8"	$55
Bowl, 8", Flat	$55
Bowl, 9" (Millersburg)	$1,000
Bowl, 10", Flat	$90
Bowl, Orange, Footed	$125
Bowl, Rose	$150
Compote	$50
Cup	$40
Epergne, 2 Styles	$175
Fernery, 2 Styles	$125
Mug, Pattern Variant with Band (Dugan)	$250
Nut Dish, 6-Footed	$85
Pitcher, Pattern Variant with Band (Dugan)	$500
Plate, 7"	$400
Plate, 7¾"	$450

Plate, 9"	$500
Plate, 11", Ruffled	$300
Perfume Bottle with Stopper (Dugan)	$650
Powder Jar with Cover (Dugan)	$300
Punch Bowl with Base	$500
Punch Cup	$40
Sandwich Server	$75
Spittoon	$7,500
Tray, Card	$100
Tray, Dresser, 7" x 11" (Dugan)	$150
Tumbler, Pattern Variant with Band (Dugan)	$750
Vase	$1,750
Wineglass (U.S. Glass)	$60

Waffle Block
Imperial Glass Company

Waffle Block is a simple allover square pattern resembling waffles, as the name implies. The prices below are for marigold or clambroth; double them for any other colors such as purple or teal. (Teal in carnival glass is much like an ice-green color, but a bit darker.)

Basket, 10"	$65
Bowl, 7"	$40
Bowl, 8", Square	$50
Bowl, 9"	$45
Bowl, Fruit, with Base, 11½"	$75
Bowl, Rose	$85
Butter Dish with Cover	$125
Creamer	$70
Nappy	$50
Parfait	$40
Pitcher, Water	$150
Plate, 6"	$35
Plate, 10"	$90

Vintage Pattern. Fenton Marigold. *Photo by Mark Pickvet. Courtesy of the Fenton Art Glass Museum.*

Plate, 12"	$100
Punch Bowl with Base	$250
Punch Cup	$25
Salt and Pepper Shakers	$85
Sherbet	$40
Spittoon	$100
Sugar	$70
Tumbler, 2 Styles	$300
Vase, 8" Tall	$40
Vase, 10" Tall	$50
Vase, 11" Tall	$60

Water Lily and Cattails
Fenton Art Glass Company, Northwood Glass Company

As the name implies, the pattern contains alternating water lily blossoms with cattails. Fenton made the most pieces, whereas Northwood produced only beverage sets (pitchers and matching tumblers). The prices below are for the basic colors of blue, green, purple, or amethyst; reduce them by 50 percent for marigold.

Bonbon Dish	$100
Bowl, Berry, 4½"	$60
Bowl, 6", Tricorner	$75

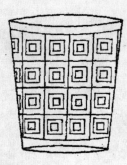

Waffle Block Tumbler. *Drawing by Mark Pickvet.*

Bowl, 8"	$200
Bowl, 10½"	$600
Butter Dish with Cover	$400
Creamer	$175
Pitcher	$1,000
Spittoon	$5,500
Spooner	$150
Sugar Dish with Cover	$225
Toothpick Holder	$200
Tumbler	$200
Vase	$225

Whirling Star
Imperial Glass Company

Whirling Star consists of rayed stars and hobstars within heavy lined framing. Pieces were made mostly in marigold as priced below; double the prices for any other colors.

Bowl, 9"	$45
Bowl, 11"	$55
Compote	$60
Pitcher, Water	$400

Punch Bowl with Base	$200
Punch Cup	$20
Tumbler	$85

Wide Panel
Imperial Glass Company, Fenton Art Glass Company, Northwood Glass Company, Westmoreland Glass Company, U.S. Glass Company

The panels extend about three-quarters of the way up the glass and end in three horizontal bands at the top for the most common items in this pattern. With so many companies producing this simple design, there are a number of variations, including varying degrees of width in the panels, pieces with only one or no top bands, and so on. The only U.S. Glass and Westmoreland pieces are noted below. The prices here are for blue, green, amethyst, purple, or white pieces. Reduce them by one-third for marigold or clambroth; double them for ice blue, ice green, teal, pink, or smoke; triple them for amber or vaseline; quadruple them for any peach opalescent; and multiply them by a factor of 10 for any rare red or aqua opalescent.

Bowl, 6", Square	$75
Bowl, 7"	$50
Bowl, 7½" (Westmoreland)	$35
Bowl, 8"	$125
Bowl, 8¼" (Westmoreland)	$40
Bowl, 9"	$150
Bowl, 9" (Millersburg)	$125
Bowl, 10"	$60
Bowl, 11"	$90
Bowl, 12"	$100
Bowl, 13"	$125
Bowl, Rose	$250
Cake Plate, 12"	$250
Cake Plate, 15"	$300
Candy Dish with Cover	$75
Compote	$50
Compote, Miniature	$45
Console Set, 3-Piece (Bowl and 2 Candlesticks)	$125

Epergne, 5-Piece	$2,000
Goblet (Small)	$75
Goblet (Large)	$100
Lemonade Glass, Handled	$50
Pitcher, Water	$500
Plate, 6"	$35
Plate, 8"	$75
Plate, 10"	$100
Plate, 11"	$125
Platter, 12"	$150
Platter, 14", Round	$175
Punch Bowl	$500
Punch Cup	$50
Salt Dip (U.S. Glass Company)	$55
Spittoon	$750
Vase, 7"	$45
Vase, 8"	$50
Vase, 9"	$55
Vase, 12"	$100
Vase, 15"	$225
Vase, 21"	$350

Windmill
Imperial Glass Company

The windmill in this pattern is raised in the center and is surrounded by trees within a ridged oval. Outside of the oval frame is floral designs and paneled sides. The colors priced below include amber, amethyst, purple, green, smoke, teal, lavender, olive green, or clam-broth. Reduce them by 50 percent for marigold; double them for pastel blue or vaseline.

Bowl, Berry, 4"	$30
Bowl, Berry, 5"	$35
Bowl, Berry, 8"	$50
Bowl, Berry, 9"	$60

Bowl, 9", Footed	$65
Bowl, Fruit, 10½"	$50
Pickle Dish, Oval	$100
Pitcher, Milk	$175
Pitcher, Water	$225
Tray, Dresser, Oval	$100
Tumbler	$55

Wishbone
Northwood Glass Company, Imperial Glass Company

Wishbone contains a central small circular medallion surrounded by curving tweezerlike spears shaped like wishbones. Overlapping these wishbone designs are winged mothlike critters; beyond them is a continuous line of scrolling. The only Imperial piece listed is the flower arranger. The prices below are for green, amethyst, smoke, or lavender. Reduce them by one-third for marigold or clambroth; double them for aqua, white, or horehound; quadruple them for any blue, ice green, ice blue, or lime green; and multiply them by 10 for any rare aqua opalescent.

Bowl, 8"	$225
Bowl, 9", Footed	$200
Bowl, 10"	$250
Epergne	$1,000
Flower Arranger (Imperial)	$100
Pitcher, Water	$1,250
Plate, 9", Footed	$750
Plate, 10"	$3,000
Plate, Chop, 11"	$4,000
Tumbler	$150

Wreathed Cherry
Dugan Glass Company

The cherries in this pattern are of a slightly darker color and are raised in relief. Surrounding the cherries is a wreath of draped scalloped ridges that form a continuous band. Each wreath frames a bunch of three cherries. The prices below apply to blue, green, amethyst (including black or a very dark amethyst), purple, or white pieces; reduce them by one-third for marigold or clambroth.

Carnival Windmill Tumbler. *Photo by Robin Rainwater.*

Bowl, Berry, 5", Oval	$55
Bowl, Berry, 10½", Oval	$175
Bowl, Berry, 12"	$200
Butter Dish with Cover	$250
Creamer	$100
Pitcher, Water	$500
Spooner	$90
Sugar	$125
Toothpick Holder	$200
Tumbler	$75

Wreath of Roses
Fenton Art Glass Company, Dugan Glass Company

Wreaths of vines and foliage surround this simple rose design. The prices here are for blue, green, amethyst, purple, or lavender. Reduce them by one-third for marigold; double them for amber, aqua, or white; and quadruple them for any rare peach opalescent.

Bonbon Dish	$100
Bonbon Dish, Stemmed	$90
Bowl, Rose (Dugan)	$90
Compote	$60
Compote (Dugan Pattern Variant)	$75

Nut Dish (Dugan)	$100
Punch Bowl with Base	$750
Punch Cup	$40
Spittoon (Dugan)	$750

Zig Zag
Fenton Art Glass Company, Millersburg Glass Company, Northwood Glass Company

Fenton's Zig Zag is mostly a wavy or irregular enameled band with additional enameled floral designs. Northwood and Millersburg pieces contain many molded wavy lines around a central circle. The prices below are for blue, green, amethyst, purple, white, or ice green pieces; reduce them by one-third for marigold or clambroth.

Bowl, 9½" (Millersburg)	$450
Bowl, 9½", Ruffled (Millersburg)	$500
Bowl, 10", Tricorner (Millersburg)	$750
Card Tray (Millersburg)	$1,250
Pitcher, Enameled Floral Design (Fenton)	$500
Pitcher (Northwood)	$5,500
Tumbler, Enameled Floral Design (Fenton)	$75
Tumbler (Northwood)	$750

– 6 –
DEPRESSION GLASS

It had been nearly 40 years since the United States had experienced a serious economic downswing. Many, including a new generation, had either forgotten or had not lived through the hard times of the 1890s. A major shock was on its way, for looming over the horizon was the nation's greatest and worst recession—the Great Depression of the late 1920s and 1930s. Several factors were responsible for this decline. The Agricultural Marketing Act of 1929 and the Hawley-Smoot Tariff enacted in 1930 increased rates on both farm and manufacturing goods. President Herbert Hoover signed the bill despite widespread opposition by most leading economists. The tariff alone raised the cost of living, encouraged inefficient production, and hampered exports. Foreign retaliation against expensive exports followed.

Through September 1929 the stock market continued an upward trend, but the increase was caused by speculation and manipulation of existing securities. Banks gambled heavily on this speculation, businesses overstocked inventories, consumer spending was suddenly reduced by a factor of four, commodity prices rapidly declined, and interest rates soared. Despite these poor economic indicators, the stock market boomed, but it all came to a grinding halt on October 23, 1929. Security prices unexpectedly fell drastically from panic selling. The following day nearly 13 million shares were dumped on the market, a new record. Five short days later the record was broken again as the volume reached 16 million shares. The dumping of so many shares caused the market to crash and spawned the Great Depression. Thousands of banks closed, robbing nearly $3 billion from depositors; more than 100,000 businesses went bankrupt; the Gross National Product was nearly cut in half; and millions of Americans were out of work. Even agricultural output suffered from poor weather conditions and low prices. As a result massive foreclosures followed.

Despite the nation's severe problems, more glass was manufactured during these years than at any other time period in American history—an amazing feat, considering the state of the nation's economy. A great battle ensued in the glass industry between glasshouses that produced handmade pieces, and machineware. Hand-cut crystal was far superior in quality, but it was very expensive and lost out to mass-produced machine-made glass on price alone. The new manufactured glass was flawed and cheaply made, but the price was several times lower than handmade glass. Flaws included noticeable air bubbles, slight inconsistent coloring, and tiny trails of excess glass, among others. These minor flaws do not detract from the functional value, but chips and cracks render glass virtually worthless. The glass companies that folded during the Depression were those that did not convert to automation. Competing with "Two for a Nickel" tumblers and complete sets of tableware that sold for as little as $2 was impossible, especially considering the depressed state of the nation.

Machine-made glassware first appeared on the market in significant quantities after the end of World War I. It sold well, but intense competition and price cutting followed. The profit margin on such products was very low, and a higher sales volume was required to sustain such profits—not an easy objective to achieve during an upcoming depression. Cheap handmade imported glass also nearly tripled in quantity in the 1920s providing even more competition for American glass manufacturers.

Despite these difficulties, the Depression era was a banner time for glass production in the United States. More patterns, shapes, and colors were produced in this period than in any other period in American glass history. Depression glass includes nearly all glass made in America from the 1920s and 1930s. It was marketed to middle- and working-class Americans because it could be sold at very low prices. The affordable glass could be purchased by the piece or in complete sets. It was available from general or department stores and factory outlets, through mail order, and wherever house furnishings and kitchenware were sold. Table sets usually included soup and serving bowls, tumblers, plates, and saucers. Added to this could be creamers and sugars, punch sets, vases, candy and cracker jars, water pitchers, butter dishes, dessert dishes, serving platters, salt and pepper shakers, measuring cups, and nearly everything imaginable for the table. Some sets number more than 100 distinct pieces in the same pattern!

The gaudy art and oily-looking carnival glass colors went out of style quickly and were replaced by the simple singular nonopaque colors of the new Depression glass. Color was added to many of America's gadgets in the Roaring '20s, including such things as automobiles and appliances. Colored glass pieces were used as cheap prizes at fairs and exhibitions; complete sets were given away as promotional items with furniture and appliance purchases; and smaller pieces served as bonuses in oatmeal cans, cereal boxes, and household supply containers. With the coming of Depression glass, glass was so inexpensive that it was no longer a luxury for the well-to-do only. Middle- and working-class Americans purchased it in large quantities. Colored glass had been in existence for centuries, but the Depression was when it reached its peak in popularity. It was also when nearly every company producing glass in America perfected color and further experimented with new combinations. Pink was by far the most common, which is evidenced by the slightly lower value of pink Depression glass. In terms of quantity, green was a close second to pink, followed by amber. Other colors, though somewhat rarer, can also be found in glass of this period. To produce color, metallic as well as nonmetallic elements are necessary. Metals produce the most vibrant and distinct colors, whereas nonmetallic agents such as phosphorous, selenium, sulphur, and tellurium serve to heighten or intensify specific colors.

Manganese produces an amethyst color and is the oldest known metal, dating back to Egyptian times around 1400 B.C. Copper imparts a light blue color and was also used by the ancient Egyptians. Cobalt is responsible for the richest, deepest, and most powerful blue coloring. Cobalt blue has been a staple throughout history. Examples of this beautiful blue glass were found in King Tut's tomb, and it was used in stained-glass windows of 12th-century Europe, and extensively as a pottery glaze for both the Tang and Ming dynasties of China.

Lead produces the most outstanding clear crystal. Generally, the higher the concentration of lead, the better clarity and quality of the crystal. Silver also produces crystal, though not as fine or as cheaply as lead. Chromium is responsible for a dark green color that can be heightened by other elements. Iron can be mixed with chromium for a darker green or with sulphur and carbon to produce amber-colored glass. Manufacturers usually avoid sand containing high concentrations of iron because it tends to make glass a murky green or dull brown. Gold, one of the more expensive coloring agents, imparts a brilliant ruby red color. Andread Cassius in 1685 is usually credited with this discovery. Luxurious ruby red glass generally has a higher value than most other colors because of the addition of gold. Toward the end of the Depression and beyond, selenium served as gold's replacement to produce a dark ruby red color. Rarer colors exist, too, such as a prominent bright yellow produced from uranium and smoky gray-colored glass from nickel.

Aside from coloring, decorating techniques flourished during the Depression years. Some hand-etching and copper wheel–engraving survived, but technological advances made it possible for machines to do it more quickly and efficiently. The quality did suffer to some extent, but the labor savings alone more than made up for it. Crackle glass was made by dipping hot glass fresh from a machine mold into cold water to induce numerous cracks over the entire surface. It was then necessary to reheat the cracked glass and reform it within the mold. Frosted glass gained some in popularity and consisted of a complete light acid etching over the entire exterior surface of the object. The result was a murky, light gray coloring. Machines applied enameling in exactly the right position, which was much quicker than application by hand. Enameled glass was then refired to fuse the paintlike substance permanently. Silk screens were also used to apply patterns, monograms, crests, and so forth. Even decals were fired on some cheaper glassware. Aside from these numerous innovations, the most permanent trademark decorating technique applied to Depression glass consisted of simple patented patterns pressed into molds by machine.

The popularity of Depression glass faltered in the late 1930s as Americans tired of the colored glass. A return to crystal as well as new technological advances in ceramics and plastics ended the era of one of the most notable and prolific periods in American glass history. Depression glass was packed away for years until collectors of the 1960s began reassembling sets. A major resurgence in Depression glass popularity ever since has produced a multitude of collectors; skyrocketing prices; numerous clubs, books, and newsletters; and simply the most popular form of glass collecting in America.

Adam

Jeannette Glass Company, 1932–34

A few odd pieces of this pattern were made in yellow and opaque blue (or delphite); triple the prices below for them. With most patterns, green is slightly more valuable than pink, but Adam is an exception. A good deal of green is available along with the pink. The pattern contains a large central flower with vertical ribbing. There are a few rare pieces, including two versions of the original butter dish. Be careful that the Adam Sierra butter dish bottom or top is not mixed up with the plain Adam or plain Sierra pattern (see the Sierra listings). Note that the butter dish has been reproduced but that the color of the new is shaded more lightly than that of the original. Also note that the candy-jar lid and sugarbowl lid are identical, a common and practical occurrence in Jeannette's glassware.

Ashtray, 4½"	$35
Bowl, 4¾"	$25
Bowl, 5¾"	$55
Bowl, 7¾"	$35
Bowl, 9", with Cover	$95
Bowl, 10" Oval	$45
Butter Dish with Cover (Green Is Rare—$500)	$100
Butter Dish with Cover (Sierra Pattern—Pink Only)	$1,550
Cake Plate, 10", Footed	$35
Candlestick, 4" Tall	$60
Candy Jar with Cover	$125
Coaster, 3¼"	$27.50
Creamer	$30
Cup	$30
Lamp	$350
Pitcher, Milk, 1 qt., with or without Round Base	$55
Plate, 6"	$12.50
Plate, 7¾", Square	$20
Plate, 7¾", Round	$80
Plate, 9", Square	$35
Plate, 9" Grill, 3 Divisions	$32.50
Platter, 11¾"	$37.50
Relish Dish	$30

Salt and Pepper Shakers	$120
Saucer, 6", Square	$10
Saucer, 6", Round	$75
Sherbet	$40
Sugar with Cover	$45
Tumbler, 4½"	$40
Tumbler, 5½"	$75
Tumbler, 7½"	$90
Vase, 7½" (Pink Is Rare—$425)	$100

American Pioneer
Liberty Works, 1931–34

Color and size variances are often found in nearly all, if not all, Depression patterns. Differing shades of green are common in the American Pioneer pattern. Piece sizes often vary because of mold or manufacturing changes. American Pioneer is a round hobnail pattern. Primary colors are pink, green, and crystal. For crystal, reduce the prices by 25 percent. A few pieces have also been discovered in amber; double the prices for those.

Bowl, 5", 2-Handled	$25
Bowl with Cover, 8¾"	$155
Bowl, 9", 2-Handled	$35
Bowl with Cover, 9¼"	$155
Bowl, 10¾"	$75
Candlestick, 6½"	$65
Candy Jar with Cover, 2 Varieties (Narrow and Wide)	$140
Cheese and Cracker Set, 2-Piece, Plate with Indentation and Matching Compote	$80
Coaster, 3½"	$40
Cocktail Glass, 3⅞" Tall	$50
Creamer, 2 Styles	$30
Cup	$17.50
Dresser Set, 2 Cologne Bottles with Stoppers, Powder Jar, and Matching Tray	$450
Goblet, 6" Tall	$60
Ice Bucket or Pail	$80
Lamp with Metal Pole	$85

Lamp, Globe Shape	$150
Lamp, 8½" Tall	$135
Mayonnaise Dish	$90
Pilsner Glass, 5¾" Tall, 11 oz.	$160
Pitcher with Cover, 5" Tall	$225
Pitcher with Cover, 7" Tall	$275
Plate, 6"	$17.50
Plate, 6", 2-Handled	$20
Plate, 8"	$17.50
Plate, 11½", 2-Handled	$40
Saucer	$7.50
Sherbet, 3½" Tall	$25
Sherbet, 4¾" Tall	$45
Sugar, 2-Handled, 2 Styles	$30
Tumbler, 5 oz.	$45
Tumbler, 8 oz., 4" Tall	$55
Tumbler, 12 oz., 5" Tall	$65
Vase, 7" Tall, Several Styles	$135
Vase, 9" Tall	$275
Whiskey Tumbler, 2¼" Tall, 2 oz.	$80
Wineglass, 4" Tall	$55

American Sweetheart
Macbeth-Evans Glass Company, 1930–36

The pattern contains a slightly irregular edge caused by sets of three vertical ribs. The ribbing is only on the edges for the flatter pieces. American Sweetheart comes in a wide variety of opaque or nearly opaque colors. A light nearly transparent milk white, a deep cobalt blue, ruby red, beige, and some trimmed pieces in gold can all be found. Blue and red are beautiful but rare (double the listed prices below). For gold trim and opaque versions, increase the prices by 25 percent.

Bowl, 3¾" or 4½"	$100
Bowl, 6"	$22.50
Bowl, 9" or 9½"	$80

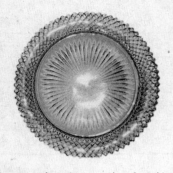

American Sweetheart Pattern. *Photo by Robin Rain-water.*

Bowl, 10", Oval	$80
Bowl, 11", Oval	$85
Bowl, 18" Console	$500
Creamer	$17.50
Cup	$20
Lamp Shade	$525
Pitcher, 2 qt., 7½" Tall	$1,000
Pitcher, 2½ qt., 8" Tall	$800
Plate, 6" or 6½"	$7.50
Plate, 8"	$15
Plate, 9"	$17.50
Plate, 9¾" or 10¼"	$40
Plate, 11", Chop	$25
Plate, 12"	$27.50
Platter, 13", Oval	$75
Platter, 15½" Round	$250
Salt and Pepper Shakers	$600
Saucer	$5
Sherbet, 2 Styles	$27.50
Sugar Dish	$17.50

Sugar Dish with Cover (Rare)	$500
Tidbit, 2-Tier	$125
Tidbit, 3-Tier	$325
Tumbler, 5 oz., 3½" Tall	$110
Tumbler, 9 oz., 4¼" Tall	$100
Tumbler, 10 oz., 4¾" Tall	$135

Aunt Polly
U.S. Glass Company, Late 1920s

Aunt Polly–patterned glass is difficult to find in perfect condition. Minor flaws are evident in much Depression glass, but the seams and mold lines are rather heavy and uneven with this pattern. The pattern is diamond on the bottom half and paneled on the top half (plates are just the opposite). The blue is light in color and the most popular shade, but there are also varying shades of green and a few iridescent pieces. Reduce the price by 50 percent for colors other than blue.

Bowl, 4¾", 2 Styles	$25
Bowl, 5½", 1 Handle Tab	$30
Bowl, 7¼" Oval, 2-Handled	$50
Bowl, 8"	$55
Bowl, 8½" Oval	$140
Butter Dish with Cover	$300
Candy Jar with Cover, 2-Handled ($100 if Not Blue)	$525
Compote, 5¼", Footed, 2-Handled	$75
Creamer	$65
Pitcher, 1½ qt., 8" Tall	$240
Plate, 6"	$17.50
Plate, 8"	$25
Salt and Pepper Shakers	$275
Sherbet	$17.50
Sugar Dish with Cover ($35 without Cover)	$225
Tumbler, 3½" Tall, 8 oz.	$40
Tumbler, 6½" Tall, Footed	$100
Vase, 6½" Tall	$60

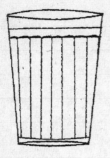

Aurora Pattern Tumbler. *Drawing by Mark Pickvet.*

Avocado Pattern Tumbler. *Drawing by Mark Pickvet.*

Aurora
Hazel Atlas Glass Company, Late 1930s

The prices are primarily for cobalt blue, which is the most desirable color. Pieces were also made in pink and green (same price) as well as crystal (cut price in half).

Bowl, 4½"	$65
Bowl, 5½"	$25
Cup	$18
Pitcher, Milk, 4½" Tall	$37.50
Plate, 6½"	$15
Saucer	$7.50
Tumbler, 4¾" Tall	$35

Avocado (No. 601)
Indiana Glass Company, 1923–33

The primary colors in this pattern are pink and green, with a bit of crystal (reduce the prices by 50 percent for crystal). Reproductions abound in this pattern, as is typical with the Indiana Glass Company. Avocado was remade in the 1970s under the Tiara product line in pink, frosted pink, yellow, blue, red, amber, amethyst, and dark green. Reduce prices by 50 percent for all reproduction items except pitchers and tumblers, for which these prices should be reduced by 90 percent.

Bowl, 5¼", 2-Handled	$35
Bowl, 7", 1 Handle	$40

Bowl, 7½"	$60
Bowl, 8" Oval, 2-Handled	$40
Bowl, 9½"	$175
Cake Plate, 10¼", 2-Handled	$65
Creamer	$40
Cup, 2 Styles	$40
Pitcher, 2 qt.	$1,150
Plate, 6½"	$20
Plate, 8¼"	$25
Relish, 6", Footed	$35
Saucer	$27.50
Sherbet	$65
Sugar	$40
Tumbler	$275

Beaded Block
Imperial Glass Company, 1927–1930s

Beaded Block comes in a variety of colors. The primary colors are green, pink, and amber. For crystal, reduce the prices by one-third. Other colors are a medium blue, vaseline, iridescent, red, opalescent, and milk white; double the prices for them. This pattern contains squares separated by vertical and horizontal beaded rows. Imperial reproduced a few of these, but all of Imperial's reproductions are marked "IG" on the bottom. Note that there are many bowls in Beaded Block.

Bowl, 4½" to 5½", with or without Handles	$20
Bowl, 6" to 6¼", with or without Handles	$25
Bowl, 6¾", Flared	$27.50
Bowl, 7" to 7½", Plain, Fluted, or Flared Edges	$30
Bowl, 8¼"	$35
Celery Dish	$35
Compote	$30
Creamer	$27.50
Marmalade Dish, Stemmed, 2 Styles	$27.50
Pickle Dish, 2-Handled	$30

Pitcher, 1 pt., 5¼" Tall	$125
Plate, 7¾" Square	$22.50
Plate, 8¾"	$27.50
Sugar	$30
Vase, 6", Footed	$30

Block or Block Optic
Hocking Glass Company, 1929–33

The pattern consists of ridged horizontal ribbing intersecting with vertical ribbing to create the block effect. The basic colors are green, pink, and yellow. A few frosted and crystal pieces exist but are not highly desired (reduce the prices below by 50 percent). Pieces have also been found in amber (same price), and the covered butter dish comes in a few rare colors such as cobalt blue ($575) and opalescent green ($275).

Bowl, 4¼"	$12.50
Bowl, 4½"	$35
Bowl, 5¼"	$27.50
Bowl, 7" to 7¼"	$175
Bowl, 8½"	$40
Bowl, 11¾", Console	$80
Butter Dish with Cover	$75
Candlestick	$60
Candy Jar with Cover, 2 Styles	$85
Cocktail Glass, 4¼" Tall	$45
Compote	$100
Creamer, Several Styles	$17.50
Cup, Several Styles	$10
Goblet, 5¾" Tall, 9 oz.	$40
Goblet, 7¼" Tall, 9 oz.	$50
Ice Bucket	$75
Ice Tub	$90
Mug	$40
Pitcher, Water, Several Styles, 1½ qt.	$125
Pitcher, Water, 2½ qt.	$150

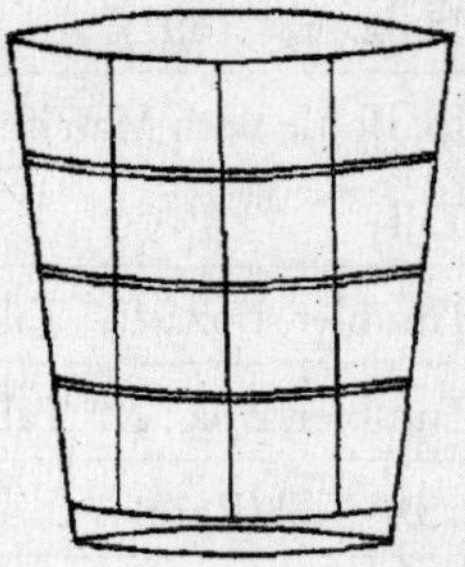

Block Pattern Whiskey Tumbler. *Drawing by Mark Pickvet.*

Plate, 6"	$6
Plate, 8"	$10
Plate, 9"	$40
Plate, 9" Grill (divided)	$70
Plate, 10¼"	$30
Platter, 12¾"	$35
Reamer	$32.50
Salt and Pepper Shakers	$95
Sandwich Server with Handle	$85
Saucer, 2 Styles	$12.50
Sherbet, 3¼" Tall	$12.50
Sherbet, 4¾" Tall	$20
Sugar, Several Styles	$17.50
Tumbler, 3 oz., 2⅝" Tall	$30
Tumbler, 3 oz., 3¼" Tall, Footed	$35
Tumbler, 5 oz., 3½" Tall	$32.50
Tumbler, 9 to 9½ oz., with or without Feet	$22.50
Tumbler, 10–11 oz., 5" Tall	$27.50
Tumbler, 10–11 oz., 6" Tall, Footed	$40
Tumbler, 12 oz., 4⅞" Tall	$35

Tumbler, 15 oz., 5¼" Tall	$50
Tumble-Up, Bottle with Matching Tumbler	$80
Vase, 5¾" Tall	$375
Whiskey Tumbler, 1 oz., 1⅝" Tall	$50
Whiskey Tumbler, 2 oz., 2¼" Tall	$40
Wineglass, 3½" Tall (Rare)	$500
Wineglass, 4½" Tall	$50

Bow Knot
Unknown Manufacturer, Depression Years

The only color of Bow Knot is green, and the center consists of a hexagonal flower surrounded by scrolling bowlike designs.

Bowl, 4½"	$22.50
Bowl, 5½"	$37.50
Cup	$12.50
Plate, 7"	$17.50
Sherbet	$25
Tumbler, 5" Tall, 10 oz., with or without Foot	$30

Cameo or Ballerina or Dancing Girl
Hocking Glass Company, 1930–34

Cameo is a very beautiful, highly collectible, and easily recognizable pattern with the cameo dancing girl design. Pink, green, and yellow are the primary colors. Pink is rarer, as evidenced by the numerous exceptions below. A few pieces were made in crystal with a platinum rim (reduce the prices below by 25 percent); a few others appear in frosted green (reduce the prices below by 50 percent). Reproductions exist with the salt and pepper shakers in pink, green, and cobalt blue (1970s), but the colors are weaker and easily distinguished from the originals. Miniature sets that contain about 40 pieces have been reproduced in pink, green, and yellow and are easily distinguished because of their tiny size and pale colors (see the following chapter for prices).

Bowl, 4¼"	$12.50
Bowl, 4¾"	$165
Bowl, 5½" (Rare in Pink—$175)	$40
Bowl, 7¼"	$65

Cameo Pattern. *Photo by Robin Rainwater.*

Bowl, 8¼" (Rare in Pink—$200)	$55
Bowl, 9" (Rare in Pink—$165)	$85
Bowl, 10" Oval	$50
Bowl, 11", 3-Footed	$110
Butter Dish with Cover (Rare in Yellow—$1,750)	$275
Cake Plate, 10", 3-Footed	$30
Cake Plate, 10½"	$175
Candlestick	$65
Candy Jar with Cover, 4" Tall (Rare in Pink—$550)	$125
Candy Jar with Cover, 6½" Tall	$225
Cocktail Shaker, Crystal with Metal Lid	$1,000
Compote (Rare in Pink—$225)	$50
Cookie Jar with Cover	$65
Creamer, 2 Styles	$35
Cup, 2 Styles (Rare in Pink—$100)	$20
Decanter with Stopper, 10" Tall	$250
Domino Tray	$175
Goblet, 6" Tall (Rare in Pink—$225)	$75
Ice Bucket, 2 Tab Handles (Rare in Pink—$775)	$275
Jam Jar with Cover, 2" Tall	$225

Pitcher, Milk, 1 pt., 5¾" Tall (Rare in Yellow—$2,500)	$275
Pitcher, 1 qt., 6" Tall	$80
Pitcher, Water, 2 qt., 8½" Tall (Rare in Pink or Yellow—$1,750)	$85
Plate, 6" or 7" (Rare in Pink—$100)	$7.50
Plate, 8" (Rare in Pink—$50)	$15
Plate, 8½" Square (Rare in Yellow—$275)	$60
Plate, 9½" or 10" (Rare in Pink—$75)	$25
Plate, 10½", with or without Handles	$20
Plate, 10½" Grill, No Handles (Rare in Pink—$75)	$17.50
Plate, 10½", Grill, 2-Handled (Rare in Pink—$75)	$75
Platter, 12", 2 Tab Handles	$40
Relish, 7½", Footed, 3 Divisions	$45
Salt and Pepper Shakers (Rare in Pink—$1,000)	$100
Sandwich Server with Center Handle (Rare—Green Only)	$7,000
Saucer with Ring	$225
Saucer, 6" (Rare in Pink—$100)	$6
Sherbet, 3" to 3⅛" Tall (Rare in Pink—$85)	$20
Sherbet, 5" Tall (Rare in Pink—$125)	$50
Sugar, 2 Styles (Rare in Pink—$150)	$35
Tumbler, 5 oz., 3¾" Tall (Rare in Pink—$100)	$40
Tumbler, 9 oz., with or without Feet, 4" to 5" Tall (Rare in Pink—$125)	$35
Tumbler, 10 oz., with or without Feet, 4¾" to 5" Tall	$40
Tumbler, 11 oz., 5" Tall (Rare in Pink—$100)	$45
Tumbler, 11 oz., Footed, 5¾" Tall (Rare in Pink—$150)	$75
Tumbler, 15 oz., 5¼" Tall (Rare in Pink—$150)	$100
Tumbler, 15 oz., Footed, 6⅜" Tall	$525
Vase, 5¾" Tall	$275
Vase, 8" Tall	$50
Water Bottle	$45
Wineglass, 3½" Tall	$1,000
Wineglass, 4" Tall (Rare in Pink—$275)	$100

Cherry Blossom
Jeannette Glass Company, 1930–39

Cherry Blossom's primary colors are pink and green. A few pieces were made in a light opaque blue sometimes referred to as delphite blue (same prices). A few others were made in yellow, amber, red, and opaque green; quadruple the prices. A few reproductions have been made in Cherry Blossom, including water sets (pitchers and tumblers), bowls, cups and saucers, butter dishes, salt and pepper shakers, the two-handled tray, and the cake plate (reduce the prices 50 to 75 percent for repros). The colors differ in the reproductions and include brighter versions of pink and green, along with yellow, cobalt blue, ruby red, iridized colors, and transparent blue.

Bowl, 4¾"	$25
Bowl, 5¾"	$55
Bowl, 7¾"	$95
Bowl, 8½"	$60
Bowl, 9" Oval	$55
Bowl, 9", 2-Handled	$75
Bowl, 10½", 3-Footed	$110
Butter Dish with Cover	$125
Cake Plate, 10¼", 3-Footed	$45
Coaster	$17.50
Creamer	$25
Cup	$25
Mug	$300
Pitcher, Milk, 1 qt., 6¾" Tall	$80
Pitcher, 1½ qt., 8" Tall, with or without Feet	$75
Plate, 6"	$12.50
Plate, 7"	$27.50
Plate, 9"	$30
Plate, 9", Grill, 3 Divisions	$35
Plate, 10", Grill	$150
Platter, 9" Oval	$1,150
Platter, 11" Oval	$60
Platter, 13" Oval	$80

Cherry Blossom Pattern. *Photo by Robin Rainwater.*

Platter, 13" Oval, 3 Divisions	$85
Salt and Pepper Shakers	$1,350
Saucer	$7.50
Sherbet	$25
Sugar with Cover	$45
Tray, 10½"	$37.50
Tumbler, 4 oz., 3½" Tall	$30
Tumbler, 4 oz., 3¾" Tall	$27.50
Tumbler, 8–9 oz., 4½" Tall	$45
Tumbler, 12 oz., 5" Tall	$85

CHILDREN'S MINIATURE SET, PRODUCED IN PINK AND DELPHITE BLUE:

Creamer	$55
Sugar	$55
Plate, 6"	$15
Cup	$45
Saucer	$10
14-Piece Set	$375

Cherryberry
U.S. Glass Company, Early 1930s

Iridized pieces are often confused with earlier carnival glass because of the similar marigold color. Cherryberry is very similar to Strawberry except for the difference in the berries. The basic colors are pink and green; however, most pieces can be found in crystal and a light iridized marigold color (reduce the prices by 25 percent for crystal or marigold).

Bowl, 4"	$12.50
Bowl, 6¼"	$125
Bowl, 6½"	$30
Bowl, 7½"	$35
Butter Dish with Cover	$215
Compote	$35
Creamer, Small	$27.50
Creamer, Large, 4½" Tall	$50
Olive Dish, 5", 1 Tab Handle	$25
Pickle Dish, 8¼" Oval	$25
Pitcher	$215
Plate, 6"	$12.50
Plate, 7½"	$25
Sherbet	$12.50
Sugar, Small (Open)	$25
Sugar, Large with Cover	$115
Tumbler, 3½" Tall	$45

Chevron
Hazel Atlas Glass Company, 1937–39

The prices below are for cobalt blue. Pink is rare (double the prices below); for plain crystal, reduce them by 35 percent. Five molded arrowheads make up the basic pattern. I have received more letters about this design than any other, simply because the publisher placed the blue pitcher on the cover of both the first and second editions of this book. Chevron was used as a Kellogg's cereal promotion in the late 1930s. Pitchers were once in-store promotions; customers received a free pitcher when they purchased two boxes of cereal.

Creamer, 3" Tall, 4¾" Long	$22.50
Pitcher, 4⅛" Tall, 5⅞" Long	$27.50
Sugar Dish, 3" Tall, 5½" Long	$32.50

Circle
Hocking Glass Company, 1930s

Many pieces have a star on the bottom, and all contain horizontal ribbing. Pink and green are the two primary colors. For any crystal pieces, reduce the prices below by 25–35 percent. Many goblets have green stems with crystal bowls (same price). As with a good deal of Depression glass, color variations from one batch to the next often vary, and many pieces of Circle have a yellowish-green tone.

Bowl, 4½"	$12.50
Bowl, 5" to 5½"	$15
Bowl, 8"	$22.50
Bowl, 9½"	$25
Creamer	$15
Cup, 2 Styles	$7.50
Decanter	$65
Goblet, 2 Styles	$15
Pitcher, 2 qt.	$75
Pitcher, 2½ qt.	$50
Plate, 6"	$5
Plate, 8¼"	$8
Plate, 9½"	$15
Platter, 10"	$20
Reamer (Fits the 2½ qt. Pitcher)	$20
Saucer	$4
Sherbet, 3⅛" Tall	$7.50
Sherbet, 4¾" Tall	$8.50
Sugar	$15
Tumbler, 4 oz., 3½" Tall	$10
Tumbler, 8 oz., 4" Tall	$12.50
Tumbler, 10 oz., 5" Tall	$20
Tumbler. 15 oz.	$30
Wineglass	$15

Cloverleaf Pattern Flat Tumbler. *Drawing by Mark Pickvet.*

Cloverleaf
Hazel Atlas Glass Company, 1930–36

The clover leaves are placed between two circular bands near the tops or outer rims of each piece. The primary colors are pink, green, and yellow. The pattern was also produced in black (double the prices) and crystal (reduce them by 25–35 percent).

Ashtray, 4"	$37.50
Ashtray, 5¾"	$50
Bowl, 4"	$40
Bowl, 5"	$55
Bowl, 7"	$65
Bowl, 8"	$85
Candy Dish with Cover	$100
Creamer	$25
Cup	$14
Plate, 6"	$10
Plate, 8"	$15
Plate, 10¼" Grill, 3 Divisions	$32.50
Salt and Pepper Shakers (Rare in Yellow—$150)	$50
Saucer	$5
Sherbet	$15
Sugar, 2-Handled	$25

Depression Glass. Colonial Block Pattern. *Drawing by Mark Pickvet.*

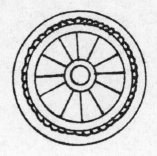

Depression Glass. Colonial Rope Pattern. *Drawing by Mark Pickvet.*

Tumbler, 9 oz., 4" Tall	$65
Tumbler, 10 oz., 3¾" Tall	$45
Tumbler, 10 oz., 5¾" Tall, Footed	$40

Colonial Block
Hazel Atlas Glass Company, Early 1930s

The block pattern is similar to Block Optic, but the Colonial Block pieces contain a star in the bottom or center. The prices here are for green and pink. For crystal, frosted, and re-production milk glass, reduce the prices by 50 percent. For any black or cobalt blue, double the prices. Most pieces in this pattern are marked with the Hazel-Atlas *H* and *A* overlapping symbol. This symbol is sometimes confused with both Atlas-Mason (overlapping *A* and *M*) and Anchor-Hocking because of the *A* and *H* beginning letters. Refer to the appendix on manufacturers' marks.

Bowl, 4"	$10
Bowl, 7"	$25
Butter Dish with Cover	$75
Butter Tub with Cover	$60
Candy Jar with Cover	$50
Creamer	$15
Goblet	$16
Pitcher	$55
Powder Jar with Cover	$22.50

Sherbet	$12.50
Sugar Dish with Cover, 2-Handled	$27.50
Tumbler, 5¼" Tall, Footed	$60

Colonial Fluted or Rope
Federal Glass Company, 1928–33

The pattern contains vertical ribbing with a roping on the outer or top edge. The basic color is green. Reduce the prices below by 25–35 percent for crystal. Some pieces are marked with the Federal trademark (*F* inscribed in a shield on the underside).

Bowl, 4"	$15
Bowl, 6"	$17.50
Bowl, 6½"	$40
Bowl, 7½"	$27.50
Creamer	$12.50
Cup	$10
Plate, 6"	$5
Plate, 8"	$8
Saucer	$3
Sherbet	$10
Sugar with Cover, 2-Handled	$30

Colonial Knife and Fork
Hocking Glass Company, 1934–38

This pattern consists of wide arched flutes with extra vertical ribbing between the flutes. The basic colors are pink, green, and crystal. For crystal, reduce the prices below by 50 percent. Some pieces were produced in milk white as well as with a gold trim (same price as listed below). There are also a few rare, darker royal ruby items in this pattern, for which these prices should be quadrupled.

Bowl, 3¾"	$60
Bowl, 4½", Berry	$35
Bowl, 4½", Soup	$85
Bowl, 5½"	$90
Bowl, 7"	$75

Depression Tumblers. Left: Mayfair Open Rose Pattern. Right: Colonial Knife & Fork Pattern. *Photo by Robin Rainwater.*

Bowl, 9"	$45
Bowl, 10" Oval	$50
Butter Dish with Cover (Rare in Pink—$750)	$75
Celery Dish	$175
Cheese Dish with Cover	$275
Claret Glass, 5¼" Tall	$30
Cocktail Glass, 4" Tall, 3 oz.	$35
Cordial Glass, 3¾" Tall, 1 oz.	$35
Creamer (Rare in Pink—$75)	$30
Cup	$16
Goblet, 5¾" Tall, 8½ oz.	$40
Mug, 4½" Tall (Rare in Green—$1,000)	$600
Pitcher, 7" or 8" Tall, with or without Ice Lip	$100
Plate, 6"	$10
Plate, 8½"	$12.50
Plate, 10"	$70
Plate, 10" Grill, 3 Divisions	$30
Platter, 12" Oval	$40
Salt and Pepper Shakers	$175

Saucer	$10
Sherbet, 2 Styles	$30
Sugar with Cover, 2-Handled (Rare in Pink—$100)	$50
Tumbler, 3 oz., 3¼" Tall, Footed	$30
Tumbler, 5 oz., 3" Tall	$30
Tumbler, 5 oz., 4" Tall, Footed	$45
Tumbler, 9 oz., 4" Tall	$27.50
Tumbler, 10 oz., 5¼" Tall, Footed	$55
Tumbler, 11 oz., 5⅛" Tall	$45
Tumbler, 12 oz.	$60
Tumbler, 15 oz.	$80
Whiskey Tumbler, 2½" Tall, 1½ oz.	$20
Wineglass, 4½" Tall, 2½ oz.	$35

Coronation or Banded Rib or Saxon
Hocking Glass Company, 1936–40

The wide vertical ribbing in this pattern ends about halfway up, merging into very thin banded rims spaced closely together. The prices are for pink and green. Saucers were made in crystal ($1), and several pieces were also made in Hocking's dark red named royal ruby, for which prices should be doubled.

Bowl, 4¼"	$65
Bowl, 4¼", 2 Tab Handles	$10
Bowl, 6½", 2 Tab Handles	$10
Bowl, 8"	$200
Bowl, 8", 2 Tab Handles	$17.50
Cup	$7.50
Pitcher, 2 qt., 7¾" Tall	$600
Plate, 6"	$4
Plate, 8½" (Rare in Green—$50)	$7.50
Saucer	$4
Sherbet (Rare in Green—$85)	$10
Tumbler, 5" Tall, 10 oz., Footed (Rare in Green—$200)	$40

Crackle Candy Jar. *Photo by Robin Rainwater.*

Crackle Glass
Various Companies, 1920s–1930s

Crackle glass was made by plunging hot objects into lukewarm or cold water to induce cracks; the object was then refired or replaced in a mold. Many companies produced it, but not in huge quantities. The colors are usually amber, green, and pink; for crystal, reduce them by 50 percent.

Candlestick, "By Cracky" Pattern (L. E. Smith)	$17.50
Candy Jar with Cover, "By Cracky" Pattern (L. E. Smith)	$50
Frog, "By Cracky" Pattern (L. E. Smith)	$35
Pitcher, Iced Tea with Cover, "Craquel" Pattern (U.S. Glass)	$150
Pitcher, Iced Tea with Cover, Jack Frost Design (Federal)	$125
Pitcher, Lemonade, Jack Frost Design (Federal)	$100
Pitcher, Water, Jack Frost Design, Depression Colors (Federal)	$100
Plate, 7", "By Cracky" Pattern (L. E. Smith)	$12.50
Plate, 8" Octagonal, "By Cracky" Pattern (L. E. Smith)	$27.50
Sherbet, "By Cracky" Pattern (L. E. Smith)	$12.50
Tumbler, Iced Tea, Footed, "Craquel" Pattern (U.S. Glass)	$12.50
Tumbler, Iced Tea, Jack Frost Design (Federal)	$15
Tumbler, Lemonade, Jack Frost Design (Federal)	$17.50
Tumbler, Water, Jack Frost Design (Federal)	$15

Crow's Foot

Paden City Glass Company, 1930s

Crow's Foot is a very simple pattern consisting of vertical rows of teardrops (usually four sets that are far apart and somewhat squared off) that end in a fan. There are more or fewer teardrops, depending on the size of the piece. Collectors are generally attracted to the colors in this pattern, which include the desirable ruby red, cobalt blue, and black (double the prices for these particular colors). The prices below are for the basic colors of amber, amethyst, yellow, and white. For crystal, reduce the prices by one-third.

Bowl, 4⅞" Square	$17.50
Bowl, 6"	$25
Bowl, 6½"	$27.50
Bowl, 8½" Square, 2-Handled	$32.50
Bowl, 8¾" Square	$35
Bowl, 10", Footed	$40
Bowl, 10" Square, 2-Handled	$42.50
Bowl, 11" Oval	$25
Bowl, 11" Square	$40
Bowl, 11" Square, Rolled Edge	$45
Bowl, 11½"	$45
Bowl, 11½", 3-Footed	$50
Cake Plate, Square, Low Foot	$50
Candleholder	$35
Candlestick, 5¾" Tall	$20
Candelstick, Square, Mushroom Shape	$25
Candy Dish, 6⅛", 3¼" Tall, 3-Footed	$100
Candy Dish with Cover, 6½", 3-Part (2 Styles)	$40
Cheese Stand, 5"	$17.50
Compote, 6¼", 3¼" Tall	$20
Compote, 7", 6⅝" Tall	$35
Compote, 7⅜", 4¾" Tall	$40
Creamer, with or without Feet	$10
Cup, with or without Feet	$7.50

Gravy Boat, 2 Spouts	$55
Gravy Boat with Pedestal Base	$75
Mayonnaise Dish, 3-Footed	$30
Plate, 5¾"	$2.50
Plate, 8"	$7.50
Plate, 8½" Square	$7.50
Plate, 9¼"	$20
Plate, 9½", 2-Handled	$40
Plate, 10⅜", 2-Handled	$30
Plate, 10⅜" Square, 2-Handled	$27.50
Plate, 10½"	$55
Plate, 11"	$27.50
Platter, 12"	$27.50
Relish Dish, 3 Divisions	$55
Sandwich Server with Center Handle	$40
Sandwich Server with Center Handle, Square	$30
Saucer, 6"	$2.50
Saucer, 6" Square	$2.50
Sugar Dish, with or without Feet	$10
Tumbler, 4¼" Tall	$45
Vase, 4⅝" Tall	$45
Vase, 10¼" Tall, Cupped	$65
Vase, 10¼" Tall, Flared	$50
Vase, 11¼" Tall, Flared	$90

Cube or Cubist
Jeannette Glass Company, 1929–33

Cube is often mixed up with many similar pressed crystal patterns such as Fostoria's American pattern. The basic colors are pink and green, but quite a few others exist. For crystal, amber, or milk white, reduce the prices by 50 percent. For yellow, blue, or ultramarine, double them.

Bowl, 4½", 2 Styles	$12.50
Bowl, 6½"	$17.50

Jeanette Cube-Patterned Pitcher and Tumblers. *Reproduced directly from a 1930 Jeanette Advertisement.*

Cube or Cubist Pattern. *Photo by Robin Rainwater.*

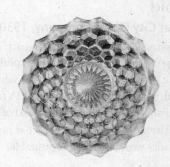

Cube or Cubist Pattern. *Photo by Robin Rainwater.*

Bowl, 7¼"	$20
Butter Dish with Cover	$85
Candy Jar with Cover	$40
Coaster	$10
Creamer, 2½"	$5
Creamer, 3½"	$12.50
Cup	$11
Pitcher	$265
Plate, 6"	$5

Plate, 8"	$12.50
Powder Jar with Cover, 3-Footed	$40
Salt and Pepper Shakers	$45
Saucer	$4
Sherbet	$12.50
Sugar, 2½"	$5
Sugar with Cover, 3"	$25
Tray, for the Large Creamer and Sugar, 7½", Made in Crystal Only	$7.50
Tumbler, 4" Tall, 9 oz.	$80

Cupid
Paden City Glass Company, 1930s

Two winged Cupid figures face each other between a cameolike bell in this pattern. The primary colors priced below are pink, green, and blue; but pieces have been found in amber, blue, black, and yellow, for which the prices should be increased by 50 percent. For crystal, reduce them by 50 percent. A few pieces with silver overlay that are marked "Made in Germany" on the base have also been discovered in this pattern (same price). Paden City Depression products are somewhat rare, difficult to find, and desirable. These three characteristics make them quite valuable.

Bowl, 8½", Oval, Footed	$300
Bowl, 9¼" Footed	$325
Bowl with Center Handle, 9¼"	$300
Bowl, 10¼" to 10½"	$250
Bowl, 11"	$250
Cake Plate, 11¾"	$250
Cake Stand, Footed	$250
Candlestick	$150
Candy Jar with Cover, with or without Feet	$450
Casserole Dish with Cover	$550
Compote	$225
Compote with Cover, 3-Part	$325
Creamer, 4½" to 5", with or without Feet	$200
Cup	$100
Ice Bucket or Tub	$350

Cupid Pattern. *Reproduced directly from a 1929 U.S. patent.*

Lamp with Silver Trimming	$525
Mayonnaise Dish, 3-Piece (6" Dish, 8" Plate, and Spoon)	$250
Plate, 10½"	$175
Samovar	$1,100
Saucer	$35
Sugar, 2-Handled, 4¼" to 5", with or without Feet	$200
Tray with Center Handle, 10¾"	$250
Tray, 11", Oval, Footed	$275
Tumble-Up, Water Bottle with Tumbler	$550
Vase, 8¼"	$700
Vase, 10"	$350
Vase, Fan Shape	$500

Della Robbia
Westmoreland Glass Company, Late 1920s–Early 1930s

Della Robbia is most often found in crystal with applied colors, which is priced below. This is a molded fruit pattern, usually with red apples, yellow pears, and purple grapes, though the tinting varies from light to dark. The basic pattern was also made in pink, milk glass, and opaque blue; increase prices by 25–35 percent for those particular colors.

Basket, 9"	$225
Basket, 12"	$325

Bowl, 5"	$40
Bowl, 12", Footed	$150
Bowl, 13", Rolled Edge	$150
Bowl, 14" Oval	$275
Bowl, 15", Bell Shape	$275
Cake Salver, 14"	$175
Candelabra, 4" Tall, 2-Light	$150
Candlestick, 4" Tall	$40
Candy Dish	$100
Candy Jar with Cover, Scalloped	$125
Champagne Glass, 6 oz.	$30
Cocktail Glass, 3¼ oz.	$30
Compote, 6½", 3⅝" Tall, Footed	$35
Compote, 8", Bell Shape	$125
Compote, 12", Bell Shape, Footed	$150
Compote, 13"	$150
Creamer, Footed	$25
Cup	$22.50
Goblet, 6" Tall, 8 oz.	$35
Heart Dish, 8", 1 Handle	$175
Nappy, 4½", 1 Handle	$35
Nappy, 6", 1 Handle, Bell Shape	$40
Nappy, 6½", 1 Handle	$40
Nappy, 7½", 1 Handle	$50
Nappy, 8", 1 Handle, Bell Shape	$75
Nappy, 9", 1 Handle	$100
Pitcher, 1 qt.	$275
Plate, 6", Liner	$15
Plate, 6⅛"	$12.50
Plate, 7¼"	$25
Plate, 9"	$40

Plate, 10½"	$100
Platter, 14"	$175
Platter, 18"	$225
Punch Bowl, 14"	$350
Punch Cup	$20
Salt and Pepper Shakers	$65
Saucer	$12.50
Sherbet, 5 oz., 4¾", High Footed	$30
Sherbet, 5 oz., Low Footed	$27.50
Sugar Dish, Footed	$25
Torte Plate, 14"	$125
Tumbler, 5 oz.	$30
Tumbler, 8 oz.	$32.50
Tumbler, 8 oz., Footed	$35
Tumbler, 11 oz., Footed	$40
Tumbler, 12 oz., 5¼" Tall	$45
Tumbler, 12 oz., Bell Shape	$45
Tumbler, 12 oz., Bell Shape, Footed	$45
Wineglass, 3 oz.	$35

Diamond Quilted or Flat Diamond
Imperial Glass Company, Late 1920s–Early 1930s

Be careful not to confuse this pattern with a similar diamond pattern by Hazel Atlas. The quilting on Hazel Atlas pieces ends in a straight line at the top of each piece. Those of Imperial's end unevenly in points at the top. The prices listed below are for pink and green. For the rarer colors such as light blue, black, red, and amber, double the prices below; for crystal, reduce them by 50 percent.

Bowl, 4¾"	$12.50
Bowl, 5"	$10
Bowl, 5½", 1 Tab Handle	$10
Bowl, 7"	$12.50
Bowl, 10½"	$25

Cake Salver, 10"	$75
Candlestick	$17.50
Candy Jar with Cover, Footed	$85
Champagne Glass, 6" Tall, 9 oz.	$15
Compote, 7¼", 6" Tall	$55
Compote with Cover, 11½"	$115
Cordial, 1 oz.	$15
Creamer	$15
Cup	$12.50
Ice Bucket	$65
Mayonnaise Set with Ladle, Plate, and Compote	$60
Pitcher, 2 qt.	$65
Plate, 6"	$6
Plate, 7"	$8
Plate, 8"	$10
Platter, 14"	$18
Punch Bowl with Stand	$525
Sandwich Server with Center Handle	$40
Saucer	$5
Sherbet	$12.50
Sugar, 2-Handled	$15
Tumbler, 6 oz., Footed	$10
Tumbler, 9 oz.	$12.50
Tumbler, 9 oz., Footed	$15
Tumbler, 12 oz.	$12.50
Tumbler, 12 oz., Footed	$17.50
Vase, Fan Shape, Double Dolphin Handles	$75
Whiskey, 1½ oz.	$10
Wineglass, 2 or 3 oz.	$15

Diana
Federal Glass Company, 1937–41

Diana is sometimes confused with spirals, swirls, and twisted patterns; however, the centers of Diana pieces are swirled where the others are plain. The shading also seems to be a little duller on the Diana pieces. Basic colors are pink and amber. For crystal, crystal trimmed in colors, or frosted pieces, reduce the prices by 50 percent.

Ashtray, 3½"	$5
Bowl, 5"	$15
Bowl, 5½"	$25
Bowl 9"	$25
Bowl, 11"	$45
Bowl, 12"	$40
Candy Jar with Cover	$55
Coaster	$12.50
Creamer	$15
Cup	$17.50
Cup, 2 oz. Demitasse	$45
Junior Set, 6 Cups, 7 Saucers with a Round Metal Rack (Rack Contains Grooves for Saucers and Hooks for Hanging Cups)	$325
Plate, 6"	$6
Plate, 9½"	$20
Plate, 11¾"	$35
Platter, 12" Oval	$35
Salt and Pepper Shakers	$110
Saucer	$6
Saucer, Demitasse (4½")	$12.50
Sherbet	$15
Sugar, 2-Handled	$15
Tumbler, 9 oz., 4⅛" Tall	$45

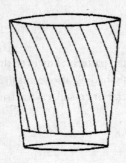

Diana Pattern Tumbler. *Drawing by Mark Pickvet.*

Dogwood or Apple Blossom or Wild Rose
Macbeth-Evans Glass Company, 1928–32

The primary pieces are in pink and green. For yellow double the prices; for Cremax, Monax, and crystal pieces, reduce the prices below by 50 percent. Beware of undecorated glass made by MacBeth-Evans in the same shape as Dogwood patterned glass; it has been passed off as this pattern but is worth 50–60 percent less.

Bowl, 5½"	$40
Bowl, 8½"	$85
Bowl, 10¼" (Rare in Pink—$575)	$350
Cake Plate, 11" Footed	$1,250
Cake Plate, 13" Footed	$175
Coaster	$600
Creamer, 2 Styles (Rare in Green—$50)	$25
Cup, 2 Styles (Rare in Green—$50)	$25
Pitcher, 8" Tall, 80 oz.	$525
Plate, 6"	$12.50
Plate, 8"	$12.50
Plate, 9¼"	$50
Plate, 10½" Grill, 3 Divisions	$35
Platter, 12" Salver	$40
Platter, 12", Oval	$750

Dogwood Plate Pattern. *Reproduced directly from a 1928 Dogwood patent.*

Saucer	$10
Sherbet, Footed (Rare in Green—$125)	$50
Sugar, 2-Handled, 2 Styles (Rare in Green—$50)	$25
Tidbit Set, 2-Tiered (8" and 12" Plates with Metal Handle)	$200
Tumbler, 5 oz., 3½" Tall	$300
Tumbler, 10 oz., 4" Tall (Rare in Green—$110)	$55
Tumbler, 11 oz., 4¾" Tall (Rare in Green—$110)	$55
Tumbler, 12 oz., 5" Tall (Rare in Green—$150)	$80

Doric
Jeannette Glass Company, 1935–38

Doric's primary colors are pink and green. For the rare opaque delphite blue, yellow, or ultramarine, quadruple the prices below. A reproduction iridescent three-part candy dish was produced in the 1970s in the Doric pattern with the original molds and is priced at only about $10. The candy and sugar lids are not interchangeable as in most Jeannette patterns, because the candy lid is a little wider and much taller than the sugar. Note that the complete relish set in Doric consists of the 8" x 8" bottom tray, two 4" x 4" top trays, and one 4" x 8" top tray.

Bowl, 4½"	$12.50
Bowl, 5"	$475
Bowl, 5½"	$100
Bowl, 8¼"	$40

Bowl, 9", 2-Handled	$30
Bowl, 9", Oval	$50
Butter Dish with Cover	$100
Cake Plate, 10", 3-Footed	$35
Candy Dish with Cover	$50
Candy Dish, 3-Part	$15
Candy Dish, 3-Part in Metal Holder	$50
Coaster	$22.50
Creamer	$20
Cup	$15
Pitcher, 1 qt., 5½" Tall (Very Rare in Delphite Blue—$1,350)	$75
Pitcher, 1½ qt., 7½" Tall	$1,000
Plate, 6"	$7.50
Plate, 7"	$30
Plate, 9"	$25
Plate, 9" Grill, 3 Divisions	$35
Platter, 12", Oval	$45
Relish, 4", Square	$17.50
Relish, 4" x 8", Rectangular	$25
Salt and Pepper Shakers	$50
Saucer	$6
Sherbet	$20
Sugar with Cover, 2-Handled	$55
Tray, 8" Square	$35
Tray, 10", 2-Handled	$27.50
Tumbler, 4" Tall, 10 oz., Footed	$90
Tumbler, 4½" Tall, 9 oz., Footed	$100
Tumbler, 5" Tall, 12 oz., Footed	$100

Doric Pattern Creamer. *Drawing by Mark Pickvet.*

Doric and Pansy
Jeannette Glass Company, 1937–38

This pattern is a derivative of the plain Doric in that it has flowers (pansies) inserted where the original Doric has blank or clear glass. Colors are pink, green, and ultramarine. For crystal, reduce the prices by 50 percent. Color variations do exist in the ultramarine from a bluish tint to almost green (same price).

Bowl, 4½"	$25
Bowl, 8"	$90
Bowl, 9", 2-Handled	$40
Butter Dish with Cover	$500
Cup	$17.50
Creamer	$115
Plate, 6"	$12.50
Plate, 7"	$45
Plate, 9"	$45
Salt and Pepper Shakers	$450
Saucer	$6
Sugar, 2-Handled	$125
Tray, 10", 2-Handled	$37.50
Tumbler, 4½" Tall, 9 oz.	$150
Tumbler, 4¼" Tall, 10 oz.	$625

601

"PRETTY POLLY PARTY DISHES" (CHILDREN'S SET):

Cup	$45
Saucer	$10
Plate	$11
Creamer	$50
Sugar	$50
14-Piece Tea Set	$350

Early American Sandwich
Duncan and Miller Glass Company, 1925–1930s

The primary colors of Early American Sandwich are pink, green, and amber. For crystal, reduce the prices below by 50 percent. Duncan and Miller was the first to recreate the old Sandwich designs in the new automatic machine-pressed process of the Depression era. Ruby red and a yellow-green color were added in the 1940s (increase the prices by 25 percent). Indiana later acquired a few of the molds and reproduced some items, but the colors are different. Indiana also developed their own Sandwich pattern that does not contain as many spirals as the original Duncan and Miller products. The prices actually tend to stay down because of the amount and different varieties of Sandwich out there.

Ashtray, 2¾", Square	$8
Basket, 6" Tall	$85
Basket, 10" Tall	$85
Basket, 10" Tall, Ruffled	$95
Bonbon Dish with Handle	$25
Bonbon with Cover, 7½" Tall	$80
Bowl, 4"	$8
Bowl, 4" (Fits 6½" Plate)	$10
Bowl, 5"	$12.50
Bowl, 5", Footed	$15
Bowl, 6", 3 Styles	$16
Bowl, 6", Footed	$18
Bowl, 10", 3 Divisions	$27.50
Bowl, 11", 2" Tall, Serrated	$37.50
Bowl, 11½", Shallow, 1½" Tall	$250
Bowl, 11½", Crimped	$27.50

Bowl, 12", Oblong, 3¾" Tall	$35
Bowl, 12", Flared	$40
Butter Dish with Cover	$250
Candelabrum, 1-Light	$50
Candelabrum, 3-Light, 10"	$85
Candelabrum, 3-Light, 16"	$100
Candlestick, 4"	$15
Candlestick, 2-Branch, 5"	$25
Candlestick, 3-Branch, 5"	$30
Candy Jar with Cover, 5" Tall	$75
Candy Jar with Cover, 8½" Tall	$100
Cheese and Cracker Set, 2-Piece (13" Plate, 5½" Cheese Stand)	$90
Cigarette Box with Cover	$50
Cigarette Holder, 3", Footed	$35
Compote, 5½", Inner Liner	$30
Compote, 6" (2 Styles)	$35
Compote, 7½", Flared	$50
Creamer, 3" Tall	$22.50
Creamer, 4" Tall	$27.50
Cruet with Stopper 5¾" Tall, 3 oz.	$55
Cup, 6 oz.	$10
Deviled Egg Platter, 12" (Holds 1 Dozen Eggs)	$225
Fruit Cup, 2½", 6 oz.	$15
Jelly Dish, 3" Diameter	$12.50
Ladle	$25
Lamp, Hurricane, 15"	$225
Mayonnaise, 2¾" Tall, 5" Diameter	$12.50
Parfait, 5¼", 4 oz.	$17.50
Pickle Dish, Oval (7" x 3¾")	$20
Pitcher, Syrup, 1 pt.	$125
Pitcher, 1 qt.	$150

Plate, 5"	$6
Plate, 6"	$7.50
Plate, 6½", Indentation for 4" Finger Bowl	$8.50
Plate, 7"	$10
Plate, 8"	$12.50
Plate, 9½"	$17.50
Plate, 12"	$20
Plate, 12" Grill, 3 Divisions	$22.50
Plate, 13"	$25
Relish, Oval (7" x 3¾"), 3 Divisions	$20
Relish, Oval (10" x 4½"), 3 Divisions	$25
Relish, Rectangular (10½" x 6¾"), 3 Divisions	$30
Salt and Pepper Shakers with Glass Tops	$75
Salver, Cake, 12"	$40
Salver, Cake, 13"	$45
Saucer	$6
Sherbet, 4¼", 5 oz.	$15
Stemware, 2¾", 5 oz., Low Foot	$15
Stemware, 4¼" or 4½", 3 oz.	$15
Stemware, 5¼", 5 oz.	$17.50
Stemware, 6", 9 oz.	$20
Sugar, 2¾" Tall, Low Footed, 2-Handled	$22.50
Sugar, 3¼" Tall, Low Footed, 2-Handled	$27.50
Sugar Shaker, 13 oz.	$27.50
Sundae, 3½", 5 oz., Flared	$25
Tray, 6" Round, 1 Handle	$15
Tray, 8" Oval, 2 Handles	$20
Tray, 10" Oval	$25
Tray, Rectangular (10½" x 6¾")	$25
Tumbler, 3¼" Tall, 5 oz., Footed	$17.50
Tumbler, 4¾" Tall, 9 oz., Footed	$20

Tumbler, 5¼" or 5½" Tall	$25
Urn with Cover, 12"	$175
Vase, 3" Tall, Footed	$20
Vase, 4½" Tall	$25
Vase, 5" Tall, Footed	$30
Vase, 10" Tall, Footed	$65

English Hobnail
Westmoreland Glass Company, 1920s–1985

In the earliest of Westmoreland's advertisements, English Hobnail was referred to as a Sandwich Reproduction. It is also Westmoreland's #555 pattern and was produced by the company in crystal until the company closed in the 1980s. The colors covered in the pricing are pink, green, amber, and a light copper blue. For cobalt blue, black, or ruby red, double the prices below; for crystal, reduce them by 50 percent.

Ashtray (Many Styles)	$27.50
Basket, 5", Handled	$50
Bonbon Dish, 1 Handle	$30
Bottle, Toilet, 5 oz.	$30
Bowl, 3"	$20
Bowl, 4"	$55
Bowl, 4½" to 5", Several Styles	$20
Bowl, 6" to 6½", Several Styles	$22.50
Bowl, 7"	$25
Bowl, 8", Several Styles	$35
Bowl, 8", Footed, 2-Handled	$85
Bowl, 9", Oval	$40
Bowl, 10"	$45
Bowl, 11"	$50
Bowl, 12"	$50
Bowl, 12", Oval	$55
Butter Dish with Cover, 6½" Diameter	$65
Candelabra, 2-Light	$55

Candlestick, 3½" Tall	$27.50
Candlestick, 8½" to 9" Tall	$45
Candy Dish, 3-Footed	$65
Candy Jar with Cover, Small	$70
Candy Jar with Cover, Large, 15" Tall	$250
Celery Dish, 9" Tall	$27.50
Celery Dish, 12" Tall	$37.50
Chandelier, 17" Shade, Prisms (Crystal Only—$450)	
Cheese Dome with Cover, 6"	$80
Cheese Dome with Cover, 8¾"	$90
Cigarette Box with Cover	$35
Cigarette Jar with Cover	$55
Claret Glass, 5 oz.	$25
Coaster, 3"	$12.50
Cocktail Glass, 3 oz.	$25
Cologne Bottle with Stopper	$55
Compote, 5" to 5½", Footed, Several Styles	$30
Compote, 6" to 7", Footed, Several Styles	$40
Compote, 8", Footed	$65
Cordial, 1 oz.	$35
Creamer, Hexagonal	$27.50
Creamer, Square Footed	$50
Cruet with Stopper, 2 oz.	$50
Cruet with Stopper, 6 oz.	$80
Cup	$22.50
Cup, Demitasse	$60
Decanter with Stopper	$185
Egg Cup	$90
Goblet, 5 oz.	$25
Goblet, 6¼ oz.	$30
Goblet, 8 oz.	$35

Ice Tub, 4"	$55
Ice Tub, 5½"	$75
Jam Jar with Cover	$80
Lamp, 6¼" Tall	$75
Lamp, 9¼" Tall	$150
Marmalade Dish with Cover	$65
Mayonnaise Dish, 6"	$25
Nut Dish, Footed	$22.50
Pitcher, 1½ pt.	$175
Pitcher, 1 qt.	$225
Pitcher, 2 qt., 2 Styles	$325
Plate, 5½"	$12.50
Plate, 6" to 6½", Several Styles	$14
Plate, 6¾" to 7¾", Several Styles	$15
Plate, 8" to 9", Several Styles	$17.50
Plate, 10" to 11", Several Styles	$50
Plate, 11½" to 12½", Several Styles	$55
Platter, 14"	$65
Puff Box with Cover	$55
Punch Bowl (Crystal Only—$250)	
Punch Bowl Stand (Crystal Only—$75)	
Punch Cup (Crystal Only—$10)	
Punch Ladle (Crystal Only—$15)	
Relish Dish, 8", 3 Divisions	$40
Salt and Pepper Shakers	$175
Salt and Pepper Shakers, Footed	$100
Salt Dip, 2", Footed	$75
Saucer	$5
Saucer, Demitasse	$17.50
Sherbet, Several Styles	$20
Sugar, 2-Handled, Hexagonal	$27.50

Sugar, Square Footed	$50
Tidbit, 2-Tier	$55
Tumbler, 5 oz.	$22.50
Tumbler, 8 oz.	$27.50
Tumbler, 10 oz.	$32.50
Tumbler, 12 oz.	$35
Urn with Cover, 15" Tall	$425
Vase, 7½" Tall	$100
Vase with Cover, 7½" Tall	$150
Vase, 8" Tall	$150
Vase, 8½" Tall	$125
Vase, 10" Tall	$125
Whiskey, 1½ oz.	$25
Wineglass, 2 oz.	$35

(Philbe) Fire-King Dinnerware
Hocking Glass Company, 1937–38

The primary colors of this pattern are pink and green. For the more desirable light copper blue, increase the prices by 25–35 percent; for crystal, reduce them by 50 percent. Hocking introduced the original Fire-King dinnerware near the end of the Depression-glass era. Many pieces are trimmed in platinum (same price). Near the end of the Depression, Anchor and Hocking merged, producing an incredible amount of Fire-King products that can be found in a variety of shapes and styles (see the next chapter).

Bowl, 5½"	$55
Bowl, 7¼"	$85
Bowl, 10" Oval	$105
Candy Jar with Cover	$775
Cookie Jar with Cover	$1,100
Creamer	$150
Cup	$125
Goblet	$210
Pitcher, 1 qt., 6" Tall	$750
Pitcher, 2 qt., 8½" Tall	$1,100

Philbe Fire-King Plate. *Reproduced directly from a 1937 U.S. patent.*

Plate, 6"	$75
Plate, 8"	$45
Plate, 10" or 10½"	$85
Plate, 10½" Grill, 3 Divisions	$85
Platter, 11½"	$75
Platter, 12", 2 Tab Handled	$150
Saucer, 6"	$75
Sherbet	$500
Sugar, 2-Handled	$150
Tumbler, 4 oz., Footed, 3½" Tall	$175
Tumbler, 9 oz., 4" Tall	$125
Tumbler, 10 oz., Footed, 5¼" Tall	$90
Tumbler, 15 oz., Footed, 6½" Tall	$100

Floral and Diamond Band
U.S. Glass Company, 1920s

This pattern contains a large six-petaled flower with diamond bands near the top or outer rim. The diamond banding is not complete, because it is cut off by smaller six-petaled flowers. The mold lines also tend to be a little rough. The prices below are for pink and many varying shades of green ranging from light green to bluish or aqua greens. Some green is nearly opaque and appears frosted or satinized. For the rarer marigold or black pieces, double the prices; for crystal, reduce them by 50 percent.

Bowl, 4½"	$15
Bowl, 5¾", 2-Handled	$17.50
Bowl, 8"	$22.50
Butter Dish with Cover	$160
Compote	$25
Creamer, Small	$15
Creamer, 4¾" (Large)	$22.50
Pitcher, 8" Tall	$150
Plate, 8"	$55
Sherbet	$11
Sugar, Small	$15
Sugar with Cover, 5¼" (Large), 2-Handled	$100
Tumbler, 4" Tall	$35
Tumbler, 5" Tall	$55

Floral Poinsettia
Jeannette Glass Company, 1931–35

Floral Poinsettia is an allover pattern of large poinsettia blossoms combined with vertical ribbing. The prices below are for amber, pink, and green pieces; however, there are other variations. For opaque blue (delphite), opaque green (jadeite), yellow, or red, triple the prices; for crystal, reduce them by 50 percent. Note that the salt and pepper shakers have been reproduced in pink, dark green, and cobalt blue (reduce the prices by 75–80 percent). Also, as referenced below, there are quite a few rare and valuable pieces in this pattern.

Bowl, 4"	$25
Bowl, 5½" (Rare)	$800
Bowl, 7½"	$35
Bowl with Cover, 8"	$75
Bowl, 9" Oval	$35
Bowl, Rose (Rare)	$575
Butter Dish with Cover	$125
Candlestick	$50
Candy Jar with Cover	$55
Canister, 5¼" Tall (Coffee, Tea, Cereal, or Sugar)	$25

Coaster	$17.50
Compote, 9" (Rare)	$1,000
Creamer	$25
Cup	$17.50
Dresser Set (Rare)	$1,500
Frog, Flower (Rare)	$750
Ice Tub, 3½" Oval, 2 Tab Handles (Rare)	$1,000
Lamp	$300
Pitcher, Milk, 1½ pt., 5½" Tall (Rare)	$600
Pitcher, 1 qt., 8" Tall	$50
Pitcher, 1½ qt., 10¼" Tall	$285
Plate, 6"	$10
Plate, 8"	$17.50
Plate, 9"	$25
Plate, 9" Grill, 3 Divisions (Rare)	$325
Platter, 10¾" Oval	$35
Platter, 11" or 12", Oval	$100
Refrigerator Dish with Cover, 5" Square	$85
Relish Dish, Oval, 2-Part, 2 Tab Handles	$30
Salt and Pepper Shakers, 2 Styles	$75
Saucer	$15
Sherbet	$25
Sugar with Cover, 2-Handled	$35
Tray, 6" Square, 2-Handled	$25
Tray, 9¼", Oval (for Dresser Set)	$225
Tumbler, 3 oz., Footed, 3½" Tall (Rare)	$200
Tumbler, 5 oz., Footed, 4" Tall	$27.50
Tumbler, 7 oz., Footed, 4¾" Tall	$27.50
Tumbler, 9 oz., 4½" Tall (Rare)	$225
Tumbler, 9 oz., Footed, 5¼" Tall	$65
Vase, 3-Footed	$525
Vase, 7" Tall, Octagonal (Rare)	$500

Florentine No. 1 or Old Florentine or Poppy No. 1
Hazel Atlas Glass Company, 1932–35

Florentine No. 1 is not that difficult to distinguish from Florentine No. 2 on the following page. The main difference is that the majority of pieces in No. 1 are hexagonal, whereas all those in No. 2 are round. The prices below are for pink, green, and yellow. For cobalt blue, double them; for crystal, reduce them by 50 percent. Note that in both Florentine designs, the butter and oval bowl covers are interchangeable. Also, the salt and pepper shakers have been reproduced in pink and cobalt blue; reduce the prices by 75–80 percent for reproductions.

Ashtray, 5½"	$35
Bowl, 5"	$17.50
Bowl, 5", Ruffled	$25
Bowl, 6"	$35
Bowl, 8½"	$40
Bowl with Cover, 9½", Oval	$85
Butter Dish with Cover	$190
Coaster, 3¾"	$27.50
Compote (Rare in Green—$50)	$25
Creamer	$22.50
Creamer, Ruffled	$50
Cup	$15
Pitcher, 1 qt., 6½" Tall	$55
Pitcher, 1½ qt., with or without Ice Lip, 7½" Tall (Rare in Yellow—$225)	$150
Plate, 6"	$10
Plate, 8½"	$15
Plate, 10"	$27.50
Plate, 10" Grill, 3 Divisions	$22.50
Platter, 11½" Oval	$30
Salt and Pepper Shakers	$70
Saucer	$6
Sherbet	$16
Sugar Dish, Ruffled (No Cover)	$50
Sugar with Cover	$50

Tumbler, 4 oz., 3¼" Tall	$20
Tumbler, 5 oz., 3¾" Tall	$27.50
Tumbler, 9 oz., 4" Tall	$27.50
Tumbler, 10 oz., 4¾" Tall	$30
Tumbler, 12 oz., 5¼" Tall	$35

Florentine No. 2 or Poppy No. 2
Hazel Atlas Glass Company, Mid- to Late 1930s

As with Florentine No. 1, the prices are for pink, green, and yellow. For unusual colors such as amber, cobalt blue, light blue, and fired-on versions, double the prices below; for crystal reduce them by 50 percent.

Ashtray, 3¾"	$32.50
Ashtray, 5½"	$42.50
Bowl, 4½"	$22.50
Bowl, 4¾"	$25
Bowl, 5½"	$40
Bowl, 6"	$45
Bowl, 7½"	$100
Bowl, 8"	$40
Bowl, 9"	$35
Bowl with Cover, 9", Oval	$85
Butter Dish with Cover	$175
Candlestick	$35
Candy Dish with Cover	$175
Coaster, 3¼"	$22.50
Compote	$35
Creamer	$15
Cup	$12.50
Custard Cup	$90
Gravy Boat	$85
Parfait, 6" Tall	$45
Pickle Dish, 10", Oval	$40

Pitcher, Milk, 24 oz., 6¼" Tall	$200
Pitcher, Milk, 28 oz., 7½" Tall	$50
Pitcher, Water, 1½ qt., 7½" Tall	$225
Pitcher, Water, 2½ qt., 8¼" Tall (Rare in Yellow—$500)	$275
Plate, 6"	$7.50
Plate, 6¼", with Indentation	$32.50
Plate, 8½"	$12.50
Plate, 10"	$20
Plate, 10¼" with Indentation for 4¾" Bowl	$45
Plate, 10¼" Grill, 3 Divisions	$22.50
Platter, 11" Oval	$22.50
Platter, 11½", Matches Gravy Boat	$50
Relish Dish, 10", 3 Divisions	$35
Salt and Pepper Shakers	$65
Saucer	$6
Sherbet	$15
Sugar with Cover, 2-Handled	$45
Tray, Condiment	$85
Tumbler, 5 oz., 3⅜" Tall	$16
Tumbler, 5 oz., Footed, 3¼" or 4" Tall (2 Styles)	$20
Tumbler, 6 oz., 3½" Tall	$22.50
Tumbler, 9 oz., 4" Tall	$22.50
Tumbler, 9 oz., Footed, 4½" Tall	$40
Tumbler, 12 oz., 5" Tall (2 Styles)	$45

Flower Garden with Butterflies or Butterflies and Roses
U.S. Glass Company, Late 1920s

This is a very dense allover pattern of leaves, butterflies, and five-petaled flowers. The colors included in the pricing are pink, green, aqua, and amber. For light blue or yellow, increase the prices by 50 percent; for crystal decrease them by 50 percent; and for any black, quadruple them. The black pieces are rare and particularly valuable, as is most black Depression glass. Note that some of the pieces have gold banding or rings near the top or around the edging; however, the prices do not vary for these features.

Ashtray	$200
Bonbon Dish with Cover	$85
Bowl with Cover, 7¼"	$150
Bowl, 8½"	$60
Bowl, 9"	$65
Bowl, 11"	$75
Bowl, 12"	$80
Candlestick, 4"	$35
Candlestick, 8"	$75
Candy Jar with Cover, 6"	$175
Candy Jar with Cover, 7½"	$175
Cheese and Cracker Dish, Footed	$110
Cigarette Box with Cover	$60
Cologne Bottle with Stopper	$250
Compote, Various Styles, 5¾" Tall and Under	$45
Compote, Various Styles, More Than 5¾" Tall	$85
Creamer	$85
Cup	$75
Heart-Shape Jar with Cover	$1,500
Mayonnaise Set, Dish, Plate, and Ladle	$100
Plate, 7"	$25
Plate, 8", 2 Styles	$25
Plate, 10" with or without Indentation	$50
Powder Dish	$85
Powder Jar with Cover, 2 Styles	$150
Sandwich Server with Center Handle	$80
Saucer	$30
Sugar, 2-Handled	$85
Tray, 10", Oval	$65
Tray, 11¾", Rectangular	$75
Tumbler, Various Styles	$225

Fortune Plate. *Drawing by Mark Pickvet.*

Vase, 6¼" Tall	$125
Vase, 8" Tall	$125
Vase, 9" Tall	$150
Vase, 10" to 10½" Tall	$175

Fortune
Hocking Glass Company, 1937–38

The only colored glass in this pattern is pink. For crystal, reduce the price by 25–35 percent. The pattern contains angled vertical flutes for somewhat of an optic effect. This angling also produces a notched edge except for the drinking vessels, which are cut off by a horizontal line and, therefore, have a smooth outer edge.

Bowl, 4"	$10
Bowl, 4½"	$12.50
Bowl, 4½", with 2 Tab Handles	$15
Bowl, 5¼"	$17.50
Bowl, 7¾"	$25
Candy Dish with Cover	$32.50
Cup	$12.50
Plate, 6"	$6
Plate, 8"	$27.50
Saucer	$5

| Tumbler, 3¼" Tall, 5 oz. | $12.50 |
| Tumbler, 4" Tall, 9 oz. | $15 |

Fruits
Hazel Atlas Glass Company, 1931–33

The primary colors in this pattern are pink and green. For crystal reduce them by 50 percent; for any odd iridized pieces, use the same prices as for pink and green. A pair of fruits appears together with leaves at the top or outer edge of this vertically paneled pattern.

Bowl, 5"	$35
Bowl, 8"	$55
Cup	$12.50
Pitcher	$110
Plate, 7"	$90
Plate, 8"	$15
Saucer	$7.50
Sherbet	$15
Tumbler, 3½" Tall	$65
Tumbler, 4" Tall	$30
Tumbler, 5" Tall, 12 oz.	$175

Georgian Lovebirds
Federal Glass Company, 1931–36

This is a pretty pattern with lovebirds sitting side by side on most pieces except tumblers, hot plates, and some plates. Also, on some pieces, the design is in the center only, whereas others include it on the edges too. The main color made in this pattern was green. Quadruple the prices for any rare amber examples; reduce them by 50 percent for crystal.

Bowl, 4½"	$12.50
Bowl, 5¾"	$27.50
Bowl, 6½"	$75
Bowl, 7½"	$70
Bowl, 9" Oval	$70
Butter Dish with Cover	$110
Coaster	$17.50

Georgian Lovebirds. *Photo by Robin Rainwater.*

Creamer, 3"	$15
Creamer, 4"	$20
Cup	$12.50
Hot Plate, 5"	$60
Pitcher	$575
Plate, 6"	$10
Plate, 8"	$15
Plate, 9¼"	$32.50
Platter, 11½", 2 Tab Handles	$75
Saucer	$5
Sherbet	$16
Sugar with Cover, 2-Handled, 3"	$75
Sugar with Cover, 2-Handled, 4"	$200
Tumbler, 4" Tall, 9 oz.	$75
Tumbler, 5¼" Tall, 12 oz.	$150

Heritage
Federal Glass Company, Late 1930s–1970s

The prices below are for pink and green pieces. For light blue, increase them by 50 percent; for crystal, decrease them by 50 percent. This pattern was reproduced in the 1960s and 1970s in green, amber, and crystal. Most are marked "MC" (for McCrory's), and the patterns are weaker for the new pieces. The new green is also darker than the original, and some of the crystal was trimmed in gold. Heritage is similar to Sandwich patterns in that it includes an allover pressed pattern. As with most Depression glass, reproductions sell for only about 20–25 percent of the originals' prices.

Bowl, 5"	$65
Bowl, 8½"	$165
Bowl, 10½"	$30
Creamer	$35
Cup	$10
Plate, 8"	$12.50
Plate, 9¼"	$15
Plate, 12"	$20
Saucer	$6
Sugar, 2-Handled	$35

Hex Optic or Honeycomb
Jeannette Glass Company, 1928–32

This is a rather simple pressed hexagonal pattern. The primary Depression colors are pink and green. Iridescent or light marigold pieces were reproduced in the 1950s, for which the prices below should be reduced 25–35 percent.

Bowl, 4¼"	$10
Bowl, 7¼"	$15
Bowl, 7½"	$12.50
Bowl, 8¼"	$22.50
Bowl, 9"	$27.50
Bowl, 10"	$32.50
Butter Dish with Cover	$100
Creamer, 2 Styles	$8
Cup, 2 Styles	$6
Ice Bucket with Metal Handle	$25
Pitcher, Milk; 1 qt., 5" Tall	$35
Pitcher, Water, 1½ qt., 9" Tall	$55
Pitcher, Water, 2 qt., 8" Tall	$275

Plate, 6"	$5
Plate, 8"	$7.50
Platter, 11"	$18
Reamer (Fits Ice Bucket)	$60
Refrigerator Dish with Cover, 4" Square	$17.50
Salt and Pepper Shakers	$35
Saucer	$4
Sugar, 2-Handled, 2 Styles	$8
Sugar Shaker	$250
Sherbet	$7.50
Tumbler, 7 oz., Footed, 4¾" Tall	$10
Tumbler, 9 oz., 3¾" Tall	$8
Tumbler, 9 oz., Footed, 5¾" Tall	$12.50
Tumbler, 12 oz., 5" Tall	$10
Tumbler, 16 oz., Footed, 7" Tall	$15
Whiskey, 2" Tall, 1 oz.	$10

Hobnail
Hocking Glass Company, 1934–36

Hobnail is a common pattern among many companies; that is one reason for the relatively low prices. A few of the original Hobnail molds were used to make Moonstone, a hobnail derivative of Anchor-Hocking's in the 1940s. This is primarily a crystal pattern, which is priced below. Some of the crystal pieces are trimmed in red, and a few pieces come in pink (cups and saucers, plates, and the sherbet dish); increase the prices below by 25–35 percent for trimmed or pink pieces.

Bowl, 5½"	$6
Bowl, 7"	$7.50
Cup	$6
Creamer, Footed	$6
Decanter with Stopper, 32 oz.	$35
Goblet, 10 oz.	$10
Goblet, 13 oz.	$12.50
Pitcher, 18 oz.	$25

Pitcher, 2 qt.	$30
Plate, 6"	$2.50
Plate, 8½"	$5
Saucer	$2.50
Sherbet	$5
Sugar, Footed	$6
Tumbler, 3 oz., Footed	$7.50
Tumbler, 5 oz., Footed	$7.50
Tumbler, 5 oz.	$6
Tumbler, 9 oz.	$7.50
Tumbler, 10 oz.	$8
Tumbler, 15 oz.	$15
Whiskey, 1½ oz.	$7.50

Horseshoe or No. 612
Indiana Glass Company, 1930–33

This is a pattern that Indiana did not patent a name for except the designation *No. 612*. Horseshoe is simply a nickname that stuck because of the large ovals on the pattern that curl in like horseshoes at the end. Horseshoe pieces also vary in thickness (same price). Basic colors are green and yellow. Most pink pieces are rare; quadruple the prices for them. For crystal, reduce these prices by 50 percent.

Bowl, 4½"	$35
Bowl, 6½"	$40
Bowl, 7½"	$30
Bowl, 8½"	$45
Bowl, 9½"	$55
Bowl, 10½", Oval	$40
Butter Dish with Cover	$1,050
Candy Dish with Cover, Metal Holder (Same Price in Pink)	$225
Creamer	$22.50
Cup	$17.50
Pitcher, 2 qt.	$350
Plate, 6"	$12.50

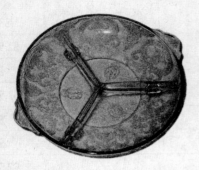

Horseshoe Pattern. *Photo by Robin Rainwater.*

Plate, 8½"	$15
Plate, 9½"	$17.50
Plate, 10½"	$25
Plate, 10½" Grill, 3 Divisions	$150
Platter, 10¾" Oval	$40
Platter, 11½"	$40
Relish, 3-Part, Footed	$37.50
Saucer	$7.50
Sherbet	$20
Sugar, 2-Handled	$22.50
Tumbler, 4¼" Tall	$185
Tumbler, 4¾" Tall	$200
Tumbler, 5½" Tall, Footed	$40
Tumbler, 6¼" Tall, Footed	$200

Iris or Iris and Herringbone
Jeannette Glass Company, 1928–32, 1950s–1970s

This pattern consists of floral irises along with vertical ribbing. Except as noted, the prices are for plain and decorated crystal, as well as the reproduction marigold, blue, and amethyst (1950s–1970s). For the rarer green and pink, quadruple the prices below.

Iris Pattern. *Photo by Robin Rainwater.*

Bowl, 4½" (Rare in Crystal—$50)	$10
Bowl, 5"	$150
Bowl, 5", Ruffled, Sauce Dish	$15
Bowl, 7½" (Rare in Crystal—$175)	$75
Bowl, 8" (Rare in Crystal—$100)	$35
Bowl, 9½"	$25
Bowl, 11"	$75
Bowl, 11½"	$35
Butter Dish with Cover	$75
Candlestick	$27.50
Candy Jar with Cover	$200
Claret Glass, 4½" Tall, 3 oz.	$25
Coaster	$125
Cocktail Glass, 4 oz., 4½" Tall	$35
Creamer	$17.50
Cup	$17.50
Cup, Demitasse (Rare in Iridescent—$175)	$40
Goblet, 4 oz., 5½" Tall (Rare in Iridescent—$250)	$35
Goblet, 8 oz., 5½" Tall (Rare in Iridescent—$250)	$35
Lamp Shade, 11½"	$125

Nut Set (Metal Base and Holder for Nut Crackers and Picks)	$150
Pitcher, 9½" Tall, Footed	$55
Plate, 5½"	$17.50
Plate, 8"	$125
Plate, 9"	$75
Platter, 11¾"	$55
Saucer	$17.50
Saucer, Demitasse	$175
Sherbet, 2½" Tall	$30
Sherbet, 4" Tall (Rare in Iridescent—$250)	$35
Sugar with Cover, 2-Handled	$30
Tumbler, 4" Tall	$175
Tumbler, 6" Tall, Footed	$25
Tumbler, 6½" Tall, Footed	$40
Vase, 9"	$35
Wineglass, 4" to 4½" Tall	$35

Jubilee
Lancaster Glass Company, Early 1930s

Be very careful of other, less valuable Lancaster patterns. True Jubilee has an open-centered flower in the pattern with 12-petal flowers surrounding it. Other patterns have 16 petals or 12 petals with a smaller petal between each large one. The only two colors are pink and yellow, and most pieces in this pattern are rare.

Bowl, 8", 3-Footed	$275
Bowl, 9", 2-Handled	$150
Bowl, 11", 3-Footed	$275
Bowl, 11½"	$200
Bowl, 11½", 3-Footed	$250
Bowl, 13", 3-Footed	$275
Cake Plate, 11", 2-Handled	$80
Candlestick	$110
Candy Jar with Cover, 3-Footed	$375
Champagne Glass, 7 oz., 5½" Tall	$110

Jubilee Plate. *Drawing by Mark Pickvet.*

Cheese and Cracker Set	$300
Cocktail Glass, 4¾" Tall, 4 oz.	$85
Cordial, 1 oz., 4" Tall	$275
Creamer	$50
Cup	$40
Goblet, Water, 11 oz., 7½" Tall	$185
Mayonnaise Set (Plate, Bowl, and Ladle)	$325
Plate, 7"	$27.50
Plate, 8¾"	$30
Platter, 13½"	$100
Platter, 14", 3-Footed	$250
Saucer, 2 Styles	$15
Sherbet	$80
Sugar, 2-Handled	$80
Tray, 11", with Center Handle	$250
Tumbler, 5" Tall, Footed, 6 oz.	$110
Tumbler, 6" Tall, 10 oz.	$125
Tumbler, 6" Tall, 12 oz.	$175
Vase, 12" Tall	$400
Wineglass, 3 oz., 5" Tall	$175

Kitchenware
Various Companies, 1920s–1930s

The basic colors are pink, green, amber, yellow, and light blue. For opaque versions and crystal, reduce the prices by 50 percent. For cobalt blue, ruby red, amethyst, or ultramarine, double them; and for any black, quadruple them. Some of the largest makers of kitchen products during the Depression era were Hocking/Anchor-Hocking (many canister sets, Vitrock, Fire King, and nearly every type of piece made); Jeannette (Jennyware products—most made in ultramarine as well as other colors); Hazel Atlas (famous for the Crisscross pattern); McKee (many opaque and milk-white patterns, some with colored dots, red or black ships, and other motifs); and a host of others.

Kitchenware can be difficult to identify at times because of the many plain and unmarked styles. These products were also made in every color, including the opaque styles of delphite blue, jadeite green, custard yellow or beige, milk whites, fired-on colors, and others. Many were decorated by embossing and enameling as well as the widespread use of fired-on decals or transfers.

A few additional notes: Cookie jars are generally larger than patterned cracker jars; canisters come in a huge variety of shapes and markings—flour, sugar, coffee, tea, cereal, spices, salt, oatmeal, cocoa, etc.; glass silverware, primarily knives, serving spoons, and ladles are getting more difficult to find; cups may have as many as three spouts; range bowls or sets are often marked "drips" or "drippings" and have matching canisters; the only known cobalt-blue water cooler was made by L. E. Smith; reamers are probably the most prolific—increase prices by 50 percent if there is a matching collecting bowl or cup; and finally, mechanical items such as extractors, grinders, and so on should include a glass collecting device.

Bottle, Water (Usually with Metal Screw-On Lid)	$45
Bowl, Mixing, Up to 7"	$17.50
Bowl, Mixing, 7⅛" Up to 9"	$22.50
Bowl, Mixing, More Than 9"	$27.50
Butter Dish with Cover, ¼ lb. Stick Size	$35
Butter Dish with Cover, 1 lb. Block Size	$50
Cake Preserver with Cover	$100
Cake Tub	$50
Canister, Covered, Up to 16 oz.	$40
Canister, Covered, 17–28 oz.	$45
Canister, Covered, 29–48 oz.	$50
Canister, Covered, More Than 48 oz.	$75
Cocktail Shaker, Covered	$30

Depression Kitchenware. *Photo by Robin Rainwater.*

Cookie Jar with Cover	$40
Cruet with Stopper	$60
Dispenser, Liquid (Usually Glass with Metal Spigot)	$175
Dispenser, Liquid 2-Part (Usually with Glass Top and Bottom, May Have Metal Handles, Spigot, and Base)	$350
Egg Beater Jar	$40
Egg Cup	$17.50
Funnel	$65
Ice Bucket or Pail, Up to 24 oz.	$35
Ice Bucket or Pail, More Than 24 oz.	$45
Iron (Very Rare)	$1,150
Juice Dispenser	$150
Knife	$45
Ladle, Small	$20
Ladle, Large	$40
Marmalade Jar with Cover and Matching Spoon	$90
Measuring Cup, ¼ Cup	$17.50
Measuring Cup, ⅓ Cup	$20
Measuring Cup, ½ Cup	$22.50
Measuring Cup, 1 Cup	$25
Measuring Cup, 2 Cup	$35

Measuring Cup, More Than 2 Cups	$50
Mechanical Attachments	$55
Mustard Dish with Matching Cover and Matching Spoon	$90
Pie Dish	$55
Pitcher, Syrup, Up to 16 oz.	$65
Pitcher, 17–28 oz.	$75
Pitcher, 29–48 oz.	$85
Pitcher, More Than 48 oz. (Add $25 to Pitchers with Lids)	$100
Punch Ladle	$40
Range Bowl, Uncovered	$22.50
Range Bowl, Covered	$37.50
Reamer, Lemon, Small, Under 3" Tall	$12.50
Reamer, Lemon, Small, More Than 3" Tall	$17.50
Reamer, Orange, Large, Under 3" Tall	$17.50
Reamer, Orange, Large, More Than 3" Tall	$20
Refrigerator Bowl with Cover, Round, Up to 8" Diameter	$22.50
Refrigerator Bowl with Cover, Round, More Than 8" Diameter	$35
Refrigerator Bowl with Cover, Square or Rectangular, Up to 32 Square Inches	$35
Refrigerator Dish with Cover, Square or Rectangular, More Than 32 Square Inches	$40
Rolling Pin (Cobalt Blue—$425)	$225
Salt and Pepper Shakers	$65
Salt Box	$90
Scoop	$60
Soap Dish	$27.50
Straw Dispenser (Usually with Metal Cover)	$175
Sugar Shaker	$37.50
Teapot (Very Rare in Colors)	$850
Tray, Oval or Rectangular	$30
Tumblers, Up to 8 oz.	$17.50
Tumblers, More Than 8 oz.	$22.50
Water Cooler with Spout	$200

Lace Edge or Open Lace
Hocking Glass Company, 1935–38

Lace patterns are notorious for chipping and cracking because of the delicate edging. Be sure to scrutinize pieces very carefully before purchasing. Chipped, cracked, or damaged glass has little value except for historical purposes. Several companies produced Lace-styled glassware, but Hocking's pink is a bit duller than others. The primary color is transparent pink. For satinized or frosted pink, and crystal, reduce the prices below by 50 percent.

Aquarium, 1 gal., Crystal Only	$45
Bowl, 6½"	$30
Bowl, 7¾"	$65
Bowl, 8¼"	$55
Bowl, 9½"	$50
Bowl, 10½", 3-Footed	$275
Butter Dish with Cover	$100
Candlestick	$175
Candy Jar with Cover	$75
Compote with Cover, 7"	$75
Compote, 9", No Cover (Rare)	$925
Cookie Jar with Cover	$100
Creamer	$35
Cup	$30
Flower Bowl with Crystal Frog	$55
Plate, 7¼"	$30
Plate, 8¼"	$30
Plate, 8¾"	$32.50
Plate, 10½"	$40
Plate, 10½" Grill, 3 Divisions	$35
Plate, 10½" Relish, 3-Part (Parallel Divisions)	$35
Platter, 12¾" or 13", with or without Divisions	$75
Relish Bowl, 7½", 3-Part	$75
Saucer	$12.50
Sherbet	$125
Sugar, 2-Handled	$35

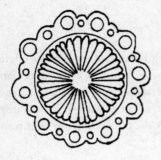

Lace Edge Plate. *Drawing by Mark Pickvet.*

Tumbler, 3½"	$150
Tumbler, 4½" Tall	$30
Tumbler, 5" Tall	$100
Vase, 7" Tall (rare)	$650

Laced Edge or Katy Blue
Imperial Glass Company, Early 1930s

The prices below are for light blue and green with opalescent edging on all pieces. Imperial referred to the opalescent coloring as Sea Foam. As with Hocking's Lace Edge, beware of damaged edges.

Basket, No Handle	$250
Bowl, 4½"	$37.50
Bowl, 5"	$42.50
Bowl, 5½" to 6"	$45
Bowl, 7"	$95
Bowl, 9"	$110
Bowl, 11", Oval	$175
Bowl, 11", Oval, Divided	$135
Candlestick	$95
Cup	$40
Creamer	$50

Mayonnaise, 3-Piece (Bowl, Plate, and Ladle)	$150
Plate, 6½"	$22.50
Plate, 8"	$40
Plate, 10"	$100
Plate, 12"	$100
Platter, 13"	$200
Saucer	$17.50
Sugar, 2-Handled	$50
Tidbit, 2-Tiered, Includes 8" and 10" Plates	$125
Tumbler, Various Styles	$75
Vase	$110

Laurel
McKee Glass Company, 1930s

The colors are pale opaque versions and consist of the company names Jade Green, White Opal, French Ivory, and Poudre Blue. Blue is the most valuable and sells for about double the prices listed below. The ivory has an aged yellow look to it like genuine older ivory. The patterns tend to be weak on some small pieces such as the salt and pepper shakers. The ivory children's pieces are available with red, green, or orange trim—increase the prices below by 25–35 percent for them. Some pieces of the children's set were also embossed with a Scottish terrier motif, which is by far the most valuable and desirable; triple the prices for ivory pieces with the dog, and quadruple them for the rare green.

Bowl, 5"	$15
Bowl, 6"	$16
Bowl, 6" with 3 Legs	$17.50
Bowl, 8"	$42.50
Bowl, 9"	$35
Bowl, 9¾", Oval	$40
Bowl, 10½" with 3 Legs	$45
Bowl, 11"	$50
Candlestick, 4"	$25
Champagne Glass, 5"	$55
Cheese Dish with Cover	$75
Creamer, Short	$15

Creamer, Tall	$20
Cup	$12.50
Plate, 6"	$10
Plate, 7½"	$12.50
Plate, 9⅛"	$17.50
Plate, 9⅛", Grill	$20
Platter, 10¾", Oval	$35
Salt and Pepper Shakers	$65
Saucer	$5
Sherbet	$17.50
Sugar, Short	$15
Sugar, Tall	$20
Tumbler, 4½" Tall, 9 oz.	$55
Tumbler, 5" Tall, 12 oz.	$65

CHILDREN'S TEA SET:

Creamer	$30
Cup	$25
Plate	$12.50
Saucer	$10
Sugar	$30
Complete 14-Piece Set	$225

Lincoln Inn
Fenton Art Glass Company, Late 1928–39

This is a fairly simple pattern characterized by vertical ribbing that does not quite make it to the top of each piece. It also contains more colors than most others. Basic prices are for pink or rose, green, light blue, amethyst, amber, and opaque shades of green (such as jade green). For cobalt blue, ruby red, and black, double the prices below; for crystal, reduce them by 50 percent. Fenton was not a huge producer of Depression glass, and, like many others, they fought to survive and had many unprofitable years in the 1930s. They did indeed pull through and continue to operate today in Williamstown, West Virginia.

Ashtray	$15
Bonbon, Square or Oval, 2-Handled	$15

Bowl, 4"	$12.50
Bowl, 5"	$12.50
Bowl, 6", 2 Styles	$15
Bowl, 9"	$25
Bowl, 9¼", Footed	$35
Bowl, 10½", Footed	$40
Candy Dish, Oval, Footed	$25
Compote	$20
Creamer	$17.50
Cup	$12.50
Goblet	$25
Nut Dish, Footed	$16
Olive Dish, Handled	$16
Pitcher, 1½ qt., 7¼" Tall	$750
Plate, 6"	$6
Plate, 8"	$12.50
Plate, 9¼"	$14
Platter, 12"	$22.50
Salt and Pepper Shakers	$200
Sandwich Server with Center Handle	$125
Saucer	$5
Sherbet, 2 Styles	$15
Sugar, 2-Handled	$17.50
Tumbler, 4 oz.	$12.50
Tumbler, 5 oz., Footed	$14
Tumbler, 9 oz.	$25
Tumbler, 9 oz., Footed	$17.50
Tumbler, 12 oz., Footed	$25
Vase, 9¾" Tall, Footed	$100
Vase, 12" Tall, Footed	$125
Wineglass	$25

Lorain Basket
Indiana Glass Company, 1929–32

This pattern is also referred to as Indiana's No. 615 and consists of heavy scrolling around the edges and corners with a large center design. The primary colors are green and yellow. For crystal, reduce the prices by 50 percent. Edges tend to be a bit rough because of poor molding, especially the inner rims of bowls. Note that sherbets were reproduced in milk white and an opaque green in the 1950s and 1960s (reduce prices 50–60 percent).

Bowl, 6"	$65
Bowl, 7¼"	$65
Bowl, 8"	$140
Bowl, 9¾", Oval	$65
Creamer	$30
Cup	$17.50
Plate, 5½"	$15
Plate, 7¾"	$17.50
Plate, 8½"	$30
Plate, 10¼"	$65
Platter, 11½"	$50
Relish, 4-Part, 8" Square, 2-Handled	$35
Saucer	$7.50
Sherbet	$35
Sugar, 2-Handled	$30
Tray, 2-Handled	$35
Tumbler, 4¾" Tall, 9 oz., Footed	$35

Madrid
Federal Glass Company, 1932–39

Madrid is characterized by a large center diamond shape surrounded by scrolling. Scrolling occurs on the edges as well. The basic colors are pink, green, and amber. Light blue is rarer; double the prices for those pieces. For crystal, reduce them by 50 percent. Federal referred to the blue color as Madonna Blue. Reproductions are a problem with Madrid. In 1976 Federal reproduced it under the name Recollection for America's Bicentennial. It was issued in amber only and dated "1976." When Federal went out of business, the Indiana Glass Company purchased the molds and removed the 1976 date from them. Indiana has also produced many pieces in a lighter pink and brighter blue; reduce prices 75 percent for reproductions.

Ashtray, 6" Square	$225
Bowl, 4¾"	$22.50
Bowl, 5"	$10
Bowl, 7"	$20
Bowl, 8"	$22.50
Bowl, 9½"	$30
Bowl, 10", Oval	$25
Bowl, 11"	$22.50
Butter Dish with Cover	$100
Cake Plate, 11¼"	$25
Candlestick	$15
Coaster	$60
Cookie Jar with Cover	$55
Creamer	$15
Cup	$10
Gravy Boat with Platter (rare)	$2,000
Jell-O Mold	$17.50
Lazy Susan (Wood with Glass Coasters—Rare)	$1,000
Marmalade	$27.50
Pitcher, Milk, 1 qt., 5½" Tall	$50
Pitcher, 2 qt., 8" Tall (Rare in Green—$175)	$65
Pitcher, 2½ qt., with or without Ice Lip, 8½" Tall (Rare in Green—$250)	$90
Plate, 6"	$6
Plate, 7½"	$12.50
Plate, 9"	$12.50
Plate, 10½"	$55
Plate, 10½" Grill, 3 Divisions	$20
Platter, 11¼"	$20
Platter, 11½", Oval	$25

Relish Dish, 10¼"	$20
Salt and Pepper Shakers, 3½" Tall	$65
Salt and Pepper Shakers, 3½" Tall, Footed	$150
Saucer	$5
Sherbet, 2 Styles	$12.50
Sugar with Cover	$65
Tumbler, 4" Tall, 5 oz.	$20
Tumbler, 4" Tall, 5 oz., Footed	$30
Tumbler, 4¼" Tall, 9 oz.	$25
Tumbler, 5½" Tall, 10 oz.	$35
Tumbler, 5½" Tall, 12 oz.	$35

Manhattan or Horizontal Ribbed
Anchor-Hocking Glass Company, 1938–43

The basic Depression color is pink. Unless otherwise noted, for crystal, reduce the prices by 50 percent; for ruby red, double them. The pattern is a rather simple vertically ribbed design. Anchor-Hocking produced a similar pattern in 1987 named Park Avenue, but the pieces have different dimensions.

Ashtray, 4", Round	$25
Ashtray, 4½", Square	$35
Bowl, 4½"	$20
Bowl, 4½", Handled	$22.50
Bowl, 5¼"	$150
Bowl, 5½", Handled	$25
Bowl, 7½"	$25
Bowl, 8", Tab Handles	$32.50
Bowl, 9"	$55
Bowl, 9½", 1 Handle	$50
Candlestick	$25
Candy Dish, 3-Footed	$20
Candy Dish with Cover, 3-Footed	$80
Coaster	$35

Compote	$45
Creamer	$17.50
Cup (Crystal—$25, Rare in Pink)	$275
Pitcher, Milk, 1½ pt.	$80
Pitcher, 2½ qt.	$85
Plate, 6" (Crystal—$10, Rare in Pink)	$85
Plate, 8½" (Crystal—$25, Rare in Pink)	$200
Plate, 10¼" (Crystal—$27.50, Rare in Pink)	$225
Platter, 14", 3 Divisions (Crystal—$27.50, Rare in Pink)	$250
Relish Tray with 5 Glass Inserts and Center Bowl	$125
Salt and Pepper Shakers	$55
Saucer (Crystal—$10, Rare in Pink)	$85
Sherbet	$22.50
Sugar, 2-Handled	$17.50
Tumbler, Various Styles	$25
Vase, 8" Tall	$55
Wineglass	$15

Mayfair
Federal Glass Company, 1934

Prices are for green and amber; for crystal, reduce them by 50 percent. The green pieces actually differ in pattern somewhat from the amber and crystal. Hocking obtained a patent on the name Mayfair before Federal did; as a result, Federal redesigned the molds twice to produce the Rosemary pattern (listed later in this chapter). The green are part Mayfair and part Rosemary, because they were a result of Federal's design before the final conversion. Most consider the green Mayfair. The pieces caught between the switch have arching in the bottom but no waffling or grid design between the top arches as in the original Mayfair. The glass under the arches of Rosemary are plain.

Bowl, 5", Shallow	$14
Bowl, 5", Deep	$25
Bowl, 6"	$27.50
Bowl, 10" Oval	$37.50
Creamer	$20
Cup	$12.50

Plate, 6¾"	$12.50
Plate, 9½"	$17.60
Plate, 9½" Grill, 3 Divisions	$17.50
Platter, 12" Oval	$40
Saucer	$6
Sugar	$20
Tumbler, 4½" Tall, 9 oz.	$40

Mayfair Open Rose
Hocking Glass Company, 1931–37

This pattern is easily recognized and consists of a large stemmed rose with vertical ribbing. Pink and ice blue are the colors priced below. Green and yellow are much rarer; double the prices; for crystal, reduce them by 50 percent. Some pieces have been satinized or frosted along with some enameling (reduce the prices below by 25–35 percent for them). There are many extremely rare and valuable pieces in this pattern. Since the 1970s, there have been many reproductions of this pattern. The colors as well as some dimensions are different with the new pieces. Salt and pepper shakers, cookie jars, small pitchers, and whiskey tumblers have all been reproduced; reduce prices by 75–80 percent for most reproductions.

Bowl, 5"	$65
Bowl, 5½"	$45
Bowl, 7"	$55
Bowl, 9", 3-Footed (Extremely Rare)	$6,000
Bowl, 9½", Oval	$75
Bowl with Cover, 10"	$150
Bowl, 11¾" or 12"	$85
Butter Dish with Cover (Common in Pink—$75)	$400
Cake Plate, 10" Footed	$80
Cake Plate, 12", 2-Handled	$90
Candy Dish with Cover (Common in Pink—$75)	$350
Celery Dish, 9" or 10", with or without Divisions	$75
Claret Glass, 5¼" Tall	$1,000
Cocktail Glass, 4" Tall	$150
Cookie Jar with Cover (Common in Pink—$75)	$325
Cordial, 3¾" Tall, 1 oz. (Extremely Rare)	$1,250

Mayfair Open Rose Pattern. *Photo by Robin Rainwater.*

Creamer (Common in Pink—$40)	$100
Cup (Common in Pink—$25)	$100
Decanter with Stopper, 1 qt.	$250
Goblet, 4⅛" Tall, 2½ oz.	$1,000
Goblet, 5¾" Tall, 9 oz.	$125
Goblet, 7¼" Tall, 9 oz.	$275
Pitcher, Milk, 1 qt., 6" Tall (Common in Pink—$75)	$200
Pitcher, 8" Tall, 2 qt. (Common in Pink—$75)	$225
Pitcher, 8½" Tall, 2½ qt. (Common in Pink—$125)	$250
Plate, 5¾"	$25
Plate, 6½", with or without Indentation	$25
Plate, 8½"	$45
Plate, 9½"	$75
Plate, 9½" Grill, 3 Divisions	$65
Plate, 11½" Grill, 2-Handled	$75
Platter, 12" Oval, 2-Handled, with or without Divisions	$125
Relish, 8½", No Divisions	$300
Relish, 8½", 4 Divisions	$75
Salt and Pepper Shakers (Common in Pink—$75)	$350
Salt and Pepper Shakers, Footed (Extremely Rare)	$8,500

Sandwich Server with Center Handle	$85
Saucer	$40
Sherbet, 2¼" Tall	$200
Sherbet, 3" Tall	$25
Sherbet, 4¾" Tall	$100
Sugar Dish (Common in Pink—$35)	$100
Sugar Dish with Cover (Cover Is Extremely Rare)	$1,600
Tumbler, 3¼" Tall, 3 oz., Footed	$100
Tumbler, 3½" Tall, 5 oz. (Common in Pink—$50)	$150
Tumbler, 4¼" Tall, 9 oz. (Common in Pink—$40)	$125
Tumbler, 4¾" Tall, 11 oz.	$200
Tumbler, 5¼" Tall, 14 oz. (Common in Pink—$75)	$300
Tumbler, 5¼" Tall, 10 oz., Footed (Common in Pink—$55)	$175
Tumbler, 6½" Tall, 15 oz., Footed (Common in Pink—$65)	$325
Vase	$150
Whiskey Tumbler, 2¼" Tall, 1½ oz.	$75
Wineglass, 4½" Tall, 3 oz.	$125

Miss America or Diamond
Hocking Glass Company, 1933–38

Miss America is a pressed diamond pattern with rays in the center of equal length. The basic colors are pink and green. For ruby red or light blue, quadruple the prices; for crystal or flashed-on crystal, reduce them by 50 percent. Reproductions do cause problems with this pattern. Butter dishes, shakers, tumblers, and pitchers were all remade; however, as with most reproductions, the colors vary significantly from the original Depression colors (usually the new colors are lighter and the pattern is not as heavy).

Bowl, 4½"	$17.50
Bowl, 6½"	$27.50
Bowl, 8"	$100
Bowl, 8¾"	$85
Bowl, 10" Oval	$50
Bowl, 11"	$250
Butter Dish with Cover	$650

Cake Plate, 12", Footed	$75
Candy Jar with Cover	$200
Celery Dish, 10½" Long	$50
Coaster	$40
Cocktail Glass, 4¾" Tall, 5 oz.	$100
Compote	$35
Creamer	$27.50
Cup	$25
Goblet, Water, 5½" Tall, 10 oz.	$60
Pitcher with or without Ice Lip, 2 qt.	$185
Plate, 5¾"	$12.50
Plate, 6¾"	$15
Plate, 8½"	$27.50
Plate, 10¼"	$40
Plate, 10¼" Grill, 3 Divisions	$35
Platter, 12¼" Oval	$50
Relish Dish, 8¾", 4 Divisions	$32.50
Relish Dish, 11¾", 4 Divisions (Crystal—$25, Rare in Other Colors)	$6,000
Salt and Pepper Shakers	$75
Saucer	$8.50
Sherbet	$20
Sugar	$27.50
Tumbler, 4" Tall, 5 oz.	$60
Tumbler, 4½" Tall, 10 oz.	$60
Tumbler, 5¾" Tall, 14 oz.	$100
Wineglass, 3¾" Tall, 3 oz.	$125

Moderntone

Hazel Atlas Glass Company, 1934–42 (Glass Colors), 1940s–1950s (Platonite Colors)

The basic colors of this pattern are cobalt blue and amethyst, although there are a few pink and green examples out there (same price). Note that the cobalt is slightly lighter than ordinary cobalt blue, but still fairly valuable. The amethyst is a dark, almost burgundy color.

Platonite colors are fired on like porcelain and include varying shades of turquoise, orange, yellow, pink, gray, red, green, burgundy, and gold. There are also a few opaque white pieces with red or blue trims as well as white pieces with an Asian river scene. Those with the scenery are priced the same as those below; reduce the prices by 50 percent for regular platonite colors or for plain crystal. The children's sets come in basically the same Platonite colors as the full-scale pieces; however, the nonpastel colors are more desirable.

Ashtray, 7¾" with Match Holder in Center	$185
Bowl, 4¾"	$30
Bowl, 5" Berry with Rim	$32.50
Bowl, 5" Berry without Rim	$40
Bowl, 5" Cereal, Deep	$65
Bowl, 5" Soup, Ruffled	$65
Bowl, 6½"	$85
Bowl, 7½"	$165
Bowl, 8" with Rim	$125
Bowl, 8" without Rim	$150
Bowl, 8¾"	$60
Butter Dish with Metal Cover	$125
Cheese Dish, 7" with Metal Cover	$550
Creamer	$16
Cup	$14
Cup without Handle (Custard)	$27.50
Plate, 5⅞"	$10
Plate, 6¾"	$15
Plate, 7¾"	$16
Plate, 9"	$22.50
Plate, 10½"	$65
Platter, 11" Oval	$65
Platter, 12", Oval	$90
Salt and Pepper Shakers	$55
Saucer	$7.50
Sherbet	$17.50
Sugar Dish with Metal Cover	$55

Tumbler, 5 oz.	$75
Tumbler, 9 oz.	$50
Tumbler, 12 oz.	$150
Whiskey Tumbler, 1½ oz.	$55

CHILDREN'S "LITTLE HOSTESS PARTY SET"

Creamer, 1¾"	
Dark	$22.50
Pastel	$15
Cup, ¾"	
Dark	$20
Pastel	$12.50
Plate, 5¼"	
Dark	$17.50
Pastel	$10
Saucer, 3⅞"	
Dark	$15
Pastel	$10
Sugar, 1¾"	
Dark	$22.50
Pastel	$15
Teapot with Cover, 3½" (rare)	
Dark	$100
14-Piece Set	
Dark	$375
Pastel	$150

Moondrops
New Martinsville Glass Company, 1932–40

As the name suggests, this pattern contains a row of orblike ovals, usually along the bottom of each piece (along the bowls for stemware). Moondrops comes in a variety of colors; prices below are for amber, pink, ice or light blue, amethyst, smoke or gray, and various shades of green (light, forest, and even opaque jadite). For the more desirable ruby red or cobalt blue, double the prices; for plain crystal, reduce them by 50 percent.

Ashtray	$20
Bowl, 4¼"	$40
Bowl, 5¼"	$17.50
Bowl, 5⅜", 3-Footed, Tab Handle	$50
Bowl, 6¼"	$60
Bowl, 8⅜", Footed	$30
Bowl, 9½", Ruffled, 3-Footed	$40
Bowl, 9¾" Oval	$50
Bowl, 9¾" Oval, 2-Handled	$45
Bowl, 12", 3-Footed	$50
Bowl, 13"	$50
Butter Dish with Metal Cover	$300
Candelabra, 5¼" Tall, 3-Light	$60
Candlestick, 2" Tall, Ruffled	$15
Candlestick, 4½" Tall	$16
Candlestick, 5" Tall, Ruffled	$17.50
Candlestick, 5" Tall, Winged Decorations at Top	$35
Candlestick, 8½" Tall, Metal Stem	$20
Candy Dish, 8", Ruffled	$25
Casserole Dish with Cover, 9¾"	$125
Celery Dish, 11"	$30
Cocktail Shaker with Metal Top	$35
Cocktail Shaker with Metal Top and Handle	$40
Compote, 4"	$25
Compote, 11½"	$65
Cordial Glass, 2⅞" Tall, ¾ oz.	$35
Creamer, 2¾" (small)	$12.50
Creamer, 3¾"	$12.50
Cup	$11.50
Decanter, 7¾" Tall	$45
Decanter, 8½" Tall	$50

Decanter, 10¼" Tall (rare)	$450
Decanter, 11¼" Tall	$60
Goblet, 4¾" Tall, 5 oz.	$20
Goblet, 5¾" Tall, 8 oz.	$25
Goblet, 6¼" Tall, 9 oz., Metal Stem	$25
Gravy Boat	$125
Mayonnaise Dish, 5¼"	$50
Mug, 4⅞" Tall, 9 oz.	$30
Mug, 5⅛" Tall, 12 oz.	$20
Perfume Bottle	$225
Pickle Dish, 7½"	$25
Pitcher, 7" Tall, 1½ Pint	$100
Pitcher, 8" Tall, 1½ Pint	$125
Pitcher, 8⅛" Tall, 1 Quart	$125
Pitcher, 8⅛" Tall, 1½ Quart	$150
Plate, 5⅞"	$10
Plate, 6"	$12.50
Plate, 6⅛"	$7.50
Plate, 7⅛"	$14
Plate, 8½"	$15
Plate, 9½"	$25
Platter, 12", Oval	$30
Platter, 14"	$25
Platter, 14", 2-Handled	$27.50
Powder Jar, 3-Footed	$175
Relish Dish, 8½", 3-Footed, 3 Divisions	$25
Saucer	$7.50
Sherbet, 2⅝" Tall	$12.50
Sherbet, 4½" Tall	$17.50
Sugar Dish, 2¾" (small)	$12.50
Sugar Dish, 3½"	$12.50

Toy Mug, 2¾" Tall, 2 oz., with Handle	$12.50
Tumbler, 3¼" Tall, 3 oz., Footed	$12.50
Tumbler, 3⅝" Tall, 5 oz.	$12.50
Tumbler, 4⅜" Tall, 7 oz.	$12.50
Tumbler, 4⅜" Tall, 8 oz.	$12.50
Tumbler, 4⅞" Tall, 9 oz.	$17.50
Tumbler, 5⅛" Tall, 12 oz.	$17.50
Tray, 7½" (Fits Small Creamer and Sugar)	$25
Vase, 7½" Tall, Ruffled	$65
Vase, 8½" Tall, Bud	$200
Vase, 9¼" Tall	$200
Whiskey Tumbler, 2¾" Tall, 4 oz.	$12.50
Wineglass, 4" Tall, 4 oz.	$17.50
Wineglass, 4¾" Tall, 4 oz.	$35
Wineglass, 5⅛" Tall, 3 oz., Metal Stem	$15
Wineglass, 5½" Tall, 4 oz., Metal Stem	$16

Mt. Pleasant Double Shield

L. E. Smith Company, 1920s–1934

The pattern is plain and simple with elegant banding, arcs, and rounded triangles around the edges. The basic colors are pink and green. For cobalt blue, milk white, and dark amethyst (almost black), double the prices; for crystal, reduce them by 50 percent. Many pieces were trimmed in platinum, and if the band is completely intact, the piece is worth a bit more (add 10–15 percent). In case the band is scattered or only partial, the remaining part can be erased lightly with a pencil eraser. Some of the black amethyst pieces contain enameled roosters or baskets of fruit, and the milk pieces contain black bands; quadruple the prices for those.

Bonbon, 7" with Handle	$20
Bowl, 4"	$22.50
Bowl, 5", Footed	$16
Bowl, 6", Square, 2-Handled	$16
Bowl, 7", 3-Footed	$20
Bowl, 8", 2-Handled, Square or Scalloped	$25
Bowl, 9", Footed	$25

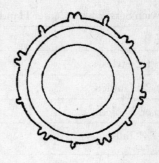

Mt. Pleasant Plate. *Drawing by Mark Pickvet.*

Bowl, 9¼" Square, Footed	$25
Bowl, 10"	$30
Bowl, 10", 2-Handled	$30
Cake Plate, 10½", Footed	$35
Candlestick, Single	$15
Candlestick, Double	$20
Creamer	$25
Cup	$12.50
Leaf-Shape Dish, 8" Long	$15
Leaf-Shape Dish, 11¾" Long	$20
Mayonnaise Dish, Footed	$22.50
Mint Dish, 6", Center Handle	$22.50
Plate, 7", 2-Handled	$15
Plate, 8", Square or Scalloped	$16
Plate, 8", 2-Handled	$17.50
Plate, 8¼", Indentation for Matching Cup	$17.50
Plate, 9", Grill, 3 Divisions	$17.50
Plate, 10½", 2-Handled	$25
Platter, 12", 2-Handled	$30
Salt and Pepper Shakers, 2 Styles	$40

Sandwich Server with Center Handle	$25
Saucer	$4
Sherbet, 2 Styles	$14
Sugar, 2-Handled	$25
Tumbler, Footed	$17.50
Vase, 7¼" Tall	$25

New Century
Hazel Atlas Glass Company, 1930–35

This pattern is sometimes referred to as Lydia Ray, which was a temporary name used by Hazel Atlas but not patented. It is characterized by vertical ribbing cut off near the top with three horizontal bands. Round pieces usually have rays that are equidistant from the center. The basic colors are pink and green. Double the prices for cobalt blue or amethyst; reduce them by 50 percent for crystal.

Bowl, 4½"	$25
Bowl, 4¾"	$27.50
Bowl, 8"	$30
Bowl with Cover, 9"	$85
Butter Dish with Cover	$75
Coaster	$35
Cocktail Glass, 3½ oz.	$35
Cordial, 1 oz.	$55
Creamer	$10
Cup	$15
Decanter with Stopper	$80
Pitcher, 7¾" Tall, 2 qt., with or without Ice Lip	$50
Pitcher, 8" Tall, 2½ qt., with or without Ice Lip	$65
Plate, 6"	$7.50
Plate, 7"	$12.50
Plate, 8½"	$15
Plate, 10"	$22.50
Plate, 10" Grill, 3 Divisions	$17.50
Platter, 11" Oval	$27.50

Salt and Pepper Shakers	$50
Saucer	$5
Sherbet	$12.50
Sugar with Cover	$35
Tumbler, 3½" Tall, 5 oz.	$17.50
Tumbler, 3½" Tall, 8 oz.	$27.50
Tumbler, 4" Tall, 5 oz., Footed	$22.50
Tumbler, 4¼" Tall, 9 oz.	$25
Tumbler, 5" Tall, 9 oz., Footed	$27.50
Tumbler, 5" Tall, 10 oz.	$25
Tumbler, 5¼" Tall, 12 oz.	$35
Whiskey, 2½" Tall, 1½ oz.	$25
Wineglass, 3 oz.	$35

Newport Hairpin
Hazel Atlas Glass Company, Late 1930s

This pattern was made near the end of the Depression and is characterized by intersecting vertical waves. The prices below are for pink, cobalt blue, and dark amethyst. Platonite colors were made in the 1940s–1950s and can be found in the next chapter.

Bowl, 4¼"	$25
Bowl, 4¾"	$25
Bowl, 5¼"	$45
Bowl, 8¼"	$50
Creamer	$20
Cup	$17.50
Plate, 6"	$10
Plate, 8½"	$20
Plate, 8¾"	$35
Platter, 11½"	$50
Platter, 11¾" Oval	$55
Salt and Pepper Shakers	$55
Saucer	$7.50

Sherbet	$20
Sugar, 2-Handled	$20
Tumbler, 4½" Tall, 9 oz.	$50

Nora Bird
Paden City Glass Company, 1929–1930s

The bird on each piece is etched in two poses; one in flight and the other ready for take-off. The pattern is similar to Paden City's Peacock and Wild Rose. The primary Depression colors are pink and green. There are a few crystal pieces in this pheasantlike etched pattern (reduce the prices by 35 percent). For any rare amber examples, double the prices.

Candlestick	$90
Candy Dish with Cover, 6½", 3 Divisions	$225
Candy Jar with Cover, 5¼" Tall, Footed	$225
Creamer, 2 Styles	$65
Cup	$75
Ice Tub, 6"	$225
Mayonnaise Dish with Inner Liner	$125
Plate, 8"	$35
Saucer	$22.50
Sugar, 2-Handled, 2 Styles	$65
Tumbler, 2¼" Tall	$60
Tumbler, 3" Tall	$65
Tumbler, 4" Tall	$75
Tumbler, 4¾" Tall, Footed	$85
Tumbler, 5¼" Tall	$85

Normandie Bouquet and Lattice
Federal Glass Company, 1933–40

The prices below are for pink and amber with a few exceptions for pink. For the light iridescent marigold color, reduce them by 25–35 percent. Depression iridescent as a general rule is much cheaper than true carnival glass and does not cause too many problems for experienced collectors. The color in carnival versions is usually solid all the way through and the pieces much thicker than Depression. Iridescent Depression is also usually a sprayed-on coating over crystal, which produces a very lighter marigold color.

Normandie Bouquet. *Reproduced directly from a 1933 U.S. patent.*

Bowl, 5"	$12.50
Bowl, 6½"	$37.50
Bowl, 8½"	$35
Bowl, 10", Oval	$45
Creamer	$17.50
Cup	$12.50
Pitcher, Water, 2½ qt. (Rare in Pink—$200)	$100
Plate, 6"	$7.50
Plate, 7¾"	$15
Plate, 9¼"	$17.50
Plate, 11" (Rare in Pink—$125)	$50
Plate, 11", Grill, 3 Divisions	$25
Platter, 11¾"	$35
Salt and Pepper Shakers	$85
Saucer	$5
Sherbet	$12.50
Sugar with Cover (Rare in Pink—$250)	$125
Tumbler, 4" Tall, 5 oz. (Rare in Pink—$100)	$40
Tumbler, 4¼" Tall, 9 oz. (Rare in Pink—$75)	$25
Tumbler, 5" Tall, 12 oz. (Rare in Pink—$125)	$50

Old Cafe
Hocking Glass Company, 1936–40

The primary color is pink. For crystal, reduce the prices below by 50 percent. The royal ruby red color was produced for one year only, 1940; double the prices for any red.

Bowl, 3¾"	$10
Bowl, 4½", Tab Handle	$12.50
Bowl, 5"	$15
Bowl, 5½"	$20
Bowl, 6½", Tab Handles	$27.50
Bowl, 9", 2 Tab Handles	$17.50
Candy Dish	$15
Candy Jar with Cover	$25
Cup	$12.50
Lamp	$75
Olive Dish	$12.50
Pitcher, Milk, 1 qt., 6" Tall	$100
Pitcher, 2½ qt.	$150
Plate, 6"	$4
Plate, 10"	$65
Saucer	$4
Sherbet	$15
Tumbler, 3" Tall	$17.50
Tumbler, 4" Tall	$25
Vase, 7¼" Tall	$50

Old English Threading
Indiana Glass Company, Late 1920s–Early 1930s

The pattern contains many concentric ribs spaced very closely together. The basic Depression colors are pink, green, and amber. For crystal or a dark forest green, reduce these prices by 50 percent.

Bowl, 4"	$22.50
Bowl, 9", Footed	$37.50

Bowl, 9½"	$42.50
Candlestick	$22.50
Candy Dish with Cover	$65
Candy Jar with Cover	$75
Compote, 6½" Diameter, 3½" Tall, 2-Handled	$27.50
Compote, 2-Handled	$27.50
Creamer	$22.50
Egg Cup	$20
Fruit Stand, 11", Footed	$55
Goblet	$40
Pitcher with Cover	$150
Plate	$25
Sandwich Server with Center Handle	$65
Sherbet, 2 Styles	$25
Sugar with Cover, 2-Handled	$65
Tumbler, 4½" Tall, Footed	$30
Tumbler, 5½" Tall, Footed	$40
Vase, 5½" Tall	$60
Vase, 8" Tall, Footed	$60
Vase, 12" Tall, Footed	$75

Orchid
Paden City Glass Company, 1930s

As the name indicates, this pattern is characterized by etched orchids. Leaves and stems are also included in the design. Many of the pieces are square in shape or contain square bases. The prices below are for pink, green, yellow, and amber. For the more desirable cobalt blue and ruby red, double the prices; for the rare black, triple them. Reduce the prices by 50 percent for any plain crystal.

Bowl, 5"	$30
Bowl, 8½", 2-Handled	$85
Bowl, 8¾" Square	$85
Bowl, 10", Footed	$115

Bowl, 11" Square	$115
Cake Stand, 2" Tall	$100
Candlestick	$65
Candy Dish with Cover, 3 Divisions, 2 Styles	$115
Compote, 6¼", 3¼" Tall	$40
Compote, 7", 6½" Tall	$75
Creamer	$60
Ice Bucket	$125
Mayonnaise Set (Bowl, Plate, and Ladle)	$100
Plate, 8½"	$55
Sandwich Server with Center Handle	$85
Sugar, 2-Handled	$60
Vase, 8" Tall	$115
Vase, 10" Tall	$150

Ovide
Hazel Atlas Glass Company, 1930–35

The prices below are for green, yellow, platonite, and black. The opaque Platonite pieces are white with fired-on color trims. Some of the Platonite pieces contain decorations such as flying geese, windmills, a bar and ball design, and so on (triple the prices for decorated glass). This pattern has also been referred to as New Century though it is patented as Ovide.

Bowl, 4¾"	$10
Bowl, 5½"	$15
Bowl, 8"	$27.50
Candy Dish with Cover	$45
Cocktail, Footed	$6
Creamer	$10
Cup	$8
Plate, 6"	$5
Plate, 8"	$7.50
Plate, 9"	$10
Platter, 11"	$12.50

Ovide Plate. *Drawing by Mark Pickvet.*

Salt and Pepper Shakers	$30
Saucer	$4
Sherbet	$10
Sugar	$10
Tumbler	$15

Oyster and Pearl
Anchor-Hocking Glass Corporation, 1938–40

The pattern consists of a starlike outcropping from a circular center. On the arms or legs of each star are three progressively smaller circles. The pieces priced below include crystal, pink, and fired-on opaque versions of pink, green, and white. For ruby red, double the prices. Oyster and Pearl was made at the tail end of the Depression after the merger of the two companies. It represents a transition period from the colored glass of the Depression to the more ceramic and porcelainlike solid colors of the post-Depression era.

Bowl, 5½", 1 Handle	$15
Bowl, 6½", 2-Handled	$20
Bowl, 10½"	$30
Candleholder	$20
Heart-Shape Bowl, 1 Handle	$17.50
Platter, 13½"	$27.50
Relish Dish, 2 Divisions, 10½" Long	$20

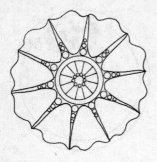

Oyster and Pearl Plate. *Drawing by Mark Pickvet.*

Panelled Aster

U.S. Glass Company, Early 1930s

As the name indicates, this pattern contains asters separated into vertical sections. Watch for rough mold seams with this pattern. Primo is the official U.S. Glass name for this pattern; however, Panelled Aster is the more common name. The prices below are for pink, green, yellow, and light amber.

Bowl, 4½"	$25
Bowl, 5½"	$30
Bowl, 8"	$40
Bowl, 9"	$45
Bowl, 11", 3-Footed	$50
Cake Plate, 10", 3-Footed	$40
Coaster	$12
Creamer	$17.50
Cup	$15
Pitcher	$325
Plate, 6"	$12.50
Plate, 7½"	$15
Plate, 10"	$27.50
Plate, 10", Grill, 3 Divisions	$20
Saucer	$4

Panelled Aster. *Reproduced directly from a 1932 U.S. patent.*

Sherbet	$17.50
Sugar, 2-Handled	$17.50
Tray, 2-Handled	$40
Tumbler, Various Styles	$35

Parrot
Federal Glass Company, 1931–32

Parrot is an easily recognized pattern and consists of two parrots sitting together on one branch and a lone parrot on the other branch. The branches contain palmlike leaves. The basic colors are green and amber. For light blue, double the prices; for crystal, reduce them by 50 percent.

Bowl, 5"	$30
Bowl, 7"	$55
Bowl, 8"	$110
Bowl, 10", Oval	$80
Butter Dish with Cover (Rare in Amber—$1,500)	$500
Creamer	$75
Cup	$50
Hot Plate, 2 Styles (rare)	$1,050
Marmalade Dish, 7"	$50
Pitcher, 2½ qt., 8½" Tall	$3,000

Parrot Plate. *Drawing by Mark Pickvet.*

Plate, 5¾"	$40
Plate, 7½"	$45
Plate, 9"	$55
Plate, 10½", Grill, Round or Square, 3 Divisions	$50
Platter, 11¼" Oblong	$80
Salt and Pepper Shakers	$325
Saucer	$20
Sherbet	$35
Sugar with Cover, 2-Handled (Rare in Amber—$600)	$225
Tumbler, 4¼" Tall, 10 oz.	$175
Tumbler, 5½" Tall, 10 oz., Footed	$175
Tumbler, 5½" Tall, 12 oz.	$200
Tumbler, 5¾" Tall, Footed	$175

Patrician or Spoke
Federal Glass Company, 1933–37

The Depression colors for this pattern are pink, green, and amber. For crystal, reduce the prices below by 25–35 percent. The inner circle of each piece resembles a wheel with spokes, hence the nickname. The pattern also develops into a star, contains zigzag designs near the outer edges or tops of each pieces, and has an additional edging made of semicircles.

Bowl, 4¾"	$25
Bowl, 5"	$16
Bowl, 6"	$35
Bowl, 8½"	$45
Bowl, 10", Oval	$45
Butter Dish with Cover (Rare in Pink—$250)	$125
Cookie Jar with Cover	$625
Creamer	$17.50
Cup	$15
Marmalade Dish	$45
Pitcher, 8" Tall, 2 Styles	$175
Plate, 6"	$12.50
Plate, 7½"	$17.50
Plate, 9"	$20
Plate, 10½"	$50
Plate, 10½", Grill, 3 Divisions	$25
Platter, 11½" Oval	$40
Salt and Pepper Shakers	$90
Saucer	$12.50
Sherbet	$17.50
Sugar with Cover, 2-Handled	$100
Tumbler, 4" Tall, 5 oz.	$37.50
Tumbler, 4¼" Tall, 9 oz.	$37.50
Tumbler, 5¼" Tall, 8 oz., Footed	$70
Tumbler, 5½" Tall, 14 oz.	$55

Patrick
Lancaster Glass Company, 1930s

Patrick was made in two colors, pink and yellow. The pattern consists of etched floral and scrolled designs.

Bowl, 5¾"	$125
Bowl, 9", 2-Handled	$200

Bowl, 11"	$175
Candlestick	$100
Candy Dish, 3-Footed	$200
Cheese and Cracker Set	$185
Cocktail Glass, 4" Tall	$100
Creamer	$85
Cup	$75
Goblet, 4¾" Tall, 6 oz.	$100
Goblet, 6" Tall, 10 oz.	$125
Mayonnaise Set (Bowl, Plate, and Ladle)	$225
Plate, 7"	$25
Plate, 7½"	$30
Plate, 8"	$50
Sandwich Server with Center Handle	$175
Saucer	$25
Sherbet	$80
Sugar, 2-Handled	$85
Tray, 11", 2-Handled	$85
Tumbler, Several Styles	$100
Wineglass	$100

Peacock and Wild Rose
Paden City Glass Company, 1930s

Once again there are a variety of colors in this Paden City pattern. Those priced below are pink, green or blue-green, amber, light blue, and yellow. For ruby red and cobalt blue, double them; for black, triple them; and for crystal, reduce them by 50 percent. Black is about the only color in all of Depression glass that outprices ruby red and cobalt blue. This holds true in this pattern. The green is a very pale bluish green or much like a light ultramarine. The pattern is similar to Peacock Reverse, but the peacock faces forward.

Bowl, 5"	$110
Bowl, 8½" Oval, Footed	$225
Bowl, 8¾", Footed	$200
Bowl, 9½", Footed	$225

Bowl, 9½", Center Handle	$185
Bowl, 10½"	$210
Bowl, 10½", Footed	$225
Bowl, 10½", Center Handle	$150
Bowl, 11"	$200
Bowl, 14"	$250
Cake Plate, Footed	$175
Candlestick	$110
Candy Dish with Cover	$225
Cheese and Cracker Set	$225
Compote	$150
Ice Bucket or Tub	$250
Pitcher, Milk, 1 qt., 5" Tall	$375
Pitcher, Water, 2 qt.	$550
Plate, 7½"	$100
Relish, 3 Divisions	$125
Tumbler, Several Styles	$125
Vase, 10" Tall, 2 Styles	$275
Vase, 12" Tall	$325

Peacock Reverse
Paden City Glass Company, 1930s

The peacock in the pattern is referred to as Reverse because its head is turned to face its tail section, whereas the body remains straight. The prices listed are for pink, green, yellow, and amber. For ruby red and cobalt blue, double them; for black, triple them; for crystal, reduce them by 50 percent. This pattern was supposedly made in pink, green, yellow, amber, blue, red, black, and crystal. Advertisements and catalogs list all of the above colors, including crystal, but not all have been rediscovered at this point. As is common with Paden City's glassware, there are only a limited number of pieces and what is for sale is difficult to locate.

Bowl, 5", Square	$50
Bowl, 8¾" Square	$125
Bowl, 8¾" Square, 2-Handled	$125
Bowl, 11¾"	$150

Candlestick	$85
Candy Dish, Square	$200
Compote, 3¼" Tall	$85
Compote, 4¼" Tall	$105
Creamer	$110
Cup	$100
Plate, 6"	$35
Plate, 7½"	$75
Plate, 8½"	$75
Plate, 10½", 2-Handled	$110
Sandwich Server with Center Handle	$100
Saucer	$30
Sherbet	$80
Sugar, 2-Handled	$110
Tumbler, 4" Tall, 10 oz.	$100
Vase, Several Styles	$250

Petalware
Macbeth-Evans Glass Company, 1930–40

The colors priced below include traditional Depression pink, Monax (an opaque white named by MacBeth-Evans), and Cremax (an opaque beige also named by MacBeth-Evans). For a few odd cobalt blue pieces, triple the prices; for crystal, reduce them by 50 percent; and for fired-on decorations on the Monax or Cremax examples, double the prices. The fired-on decorations include mostly floral and fruit patterns on the Monax bases. Florette is one name given to the red flower pattern, whereas fruits consist of apples, blueberries, cherries, grapes, oranges, pears, plums, and strawberries. Some pieces are trimmed in red, which are somewhat rare and valuable, mostly in the floral patterns (quadruple the prices below). Some of the white or Cremax items contain gold banding, which is also priced slightly higher if the gold is completely intact—add 10–15 percent.

Bowl, 4½"	$17.50
Bowl, 5¾"	$15
Bowl, 7"	$75
Bowl, 9"	$27.50
Creamer, Footed	$10

Cup	$15
Lamp Shade, Several Styles	$16
Mustard Dish with Metal Cover	$25
Pitcher, 80 oz.	$75
Plate, 6"	$4
Plate, 8"	$7.50
Plate, 9"	$15
Plate, 11"	$17.50
Plate, 12"	$20
Platter, 13", Oval	$25
Saucer	$3
Saucer, Soup Liner	$20
Sherbet, 4", Footed	$35
Sherbet, 4½", Footed	$12.50
Sugar	$15
Tidbit Servers (Lazy Susan), Several Styles	$20
Tumblers, Several Styles	$20

Pineapple and Floral or No. 618
Indiana Glass Company, 1932–37

The prices below are for amber, green, and a somewhat dull fired-on opaque orangish red. As with so many of Indiana's patterns, Pineapple and Floral was reproduced in an avocado color in the 1960s and more recently in the 1980s in several colors such as pink, cobalt blue, and crystal; reduce the prices by 50 percent. The mold seams are a little thick and jagged with this pattern, so be careful that they are not too rough. Minor flaws ordinarily do not pose problems in Depression glass, but major ones do.

Ashtray, 4½"	$24
Bowl, 4¾"	$25
Bowl, 6"	$30
Bowl, 7"	$15
Bowl, 10", Oval	$30
Comport	$10
Creamer	$12.50

Cream Soup	$25
Cup	$12.50
Plate, 6"	$7.50
Plate, 8⅜"	$10
Plate, 9⅜" (Rare in Green—$40)	$20
Plate, 11½"	$25
Plate, 11½", with Indentation	$50
Platter, 11", with 2 Closed Handles	$25
Platter, Relish, 11½", Divided	$40
Saucer	$6
Sherbet, Footed	$25
Sugar	$12.50
Tumbler, 4¼", 8 oz.	$35
Tumbler, 5", 12 oz.	$90
Vase, Cone Shape	$125

Pretzel
Indiana Glass Company, 1930s

The pricing below is for crystal or embossed crystal pieces; for ultramarine, double the prices. As with many of Indiana's numbered patterns, Pretzel is the adopted name because of its wavy overlapping pretzel-like design. It was patented simply as No. 622. As with so much of Indiana's glass, Pretzel did not escape reproductions. The celery tray was reissued in the 1970s in amber, avocado green, and blue; reduce the price for those pieces by 75 percent.

Bowl, 4½"	$10
Bowl, 7½"	$15
Bowl, 9½"	$22.50
Celery Tray, 10¼"	$20
Creamer	$10
Cup	$7.50
Leaf-Shape Dish, 7"	$10
Pickle Dish, 2-Handled	$10
Pitcher, 1 qt.	$450

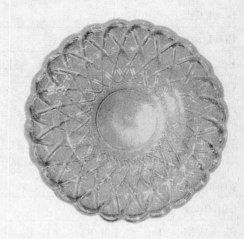

Pretzel Pattern Plate. *Photo by Robin Rainwater.*

Plate, 6"	$7.50
Plate, 6", 1 Handle	$8
Plate, 7¼", Square	$10
Plate, 8½"	$12.50
Plate, 9½"	$15
Platter, 11½"	$20
Saucer	$2.50
Sugar, 2-Handled	$10
Tumbler, 3½" Tall, 5 oz.	$50
Tumbler, 4½" Tall, 9 oz.	$45
Tumbler, 5½" Tall, 12 oz.	$75

Princess
Hocking Glass Company, 1931–35

Princess is a pretty, popular pattern characterized by a somewhat paneled curtain design. Note that many pieces are octagonal in shape. The basic prices are for pink, green, and light amber. For bright yellow (named Topaz by Hocking) and light blue, double the prices.

Ashtray	$90
Bowl, 4½"	$35
Bowl, 5"	$45
Bowl, 9"	$50

Bowl, 9½"	$60
Bowl, 10", Oval	$40
Butter Dish with Cover (Rare in Topaz—$1,000)	$125
Cake Plate, 10"	$40
Candy Dish with Cover	$85
Coaster	$65
Cookie Jar with Cover (Rare in Blue—$1,000)	$85
Creamer	$22.50
Cup (Rare in Blue—$150)	$15
Pitcher, Milk, 1 qt., 6" Tall (Rare in Topaz—$750)	$75
Pitcher, Milk, 24 oz., 7⅜" Tall, Footed (Rare)	$600
Pitcher, 2 qt., 8" Tall	$100
Plate, 5½"	$12.50
Plate, 8"	$17.50
Plate, 9½"	$35
Plate, 9½" Grill, 3 Divisions (Rare in Blue—$350)	$20
Plate, 10½" Grill, 3 Divisions, 2-Handled	$20
Platter, 12", 2 Tab Handles	$35
Relish Dish, No Divisions	$225
Relish Dish, Divided	$35
Salt and Pepper Shakers	$75
Sandwich Server with Center Handle (Rare in Topaz—$200)	$35
Sugar Shaker	$50
Saucer (Rare in Blue—$75)	$12.50
Sherbet	$35
Sugar with Cover	$50
Tumbler, 3" Tall, 5 oz.	$40
Tumbler, 4" Tall, 9 oz.	$35
Tumbler, 4¾" Tall, 9 oz., Footed	$75
Tumbler, 5¼" Tall, 10 oz., Footed	$40
Tumbler, 5¼" Tall, 13 oz.	$50

Princess Pattern. *Photo by Robin Rainwater.*

Tumbler, 6½" Tall, 13 oz., Footed	$125
Vase, 8" Tall	$55

Pyramid or No. 610
Indiana Glass Company, 1926–32

Pyramid pieces priced below are in pink, green, and yellow. For crystal or milk glass, reduce the prices by 50 percent. Like a few of Indiana's numbered patterns, the name Pyramid was unpatented but nicknamed by dealers and collectors because of the pattern's shape. Under the Tiara name, Pyramid pieces were reproduced in blue and black in the 1970s (same price as crystal).

Bowl, 5"	$30
Bowl, 6"	$35
Bowl, 8½"	$45
Bowl, 9½", Oval	$50
Creamer	$45
Ice Tub	$125
Ice Tub with Cover	$850
Pickle Dish, 9½"	$45
Pitcher, Milk, 1 qt.	$400
Pitcher, Water, 2 qt.	$500
Relish Tray, 4 Divisions, 2-Handled	$65

Sugar	$45
Tray, for Creamer and Sugar	$40
Tumbler, 8 oz., Footed, 2 Styles	$60
Tumbler, 11 oz., Footed	$85

Queen Mary
Hocking Glass Company, 1936; Anchor-Hocking, 1937–Early 1950s

This pattern is sometimes referred to as Vertical Ribbed because of the up-and-down (vertical) ribbing. The original Depression color was pink, which was first produced in the late 1930s and then carried over into the next decade when Hocking merged with Anchor to form Anchor-Hocking in 1937. Reduce the prices by 50 percent for crystal. For royal ruby and forest green, which were produced in the 1950s, use the same prices listed below.

Ashtray, 2 Styles	$7.50
Bowl, 4"	$6
Bowl, 4", 1 Handle	$7.50
Bowl, 4½"	$8
Bowl, 5"	$15
Bowl, 5½", 2-Handled	$20
Bowl, 6"	$30
Bowl, 7"	$17.50
Bowl, 8¾"	$25
Butter Dish with Cover	$165
Candy Dish with Cover	$50
Candlestick, Double	$22.50
Cigarette Jar, Oval	$10
Coaster, Round	$7.50
Coaster, Square	$8.50
Compote	$30
Creamer, Footed	$60
Creamer, Oval	$17.50
Cup, 2 Styles	$12.50
Mayonnaise Dish	$40
Pickle Dish, 10" Long	$27.50

Pitcher	$250
Plate, 6"	$7.50
Plate, 6½"	$8.50
Plate, 8¾"	$35
Plate, 9¾"	$75
Platter, 12"	$30
Platter, 14"	$35
Relish Dish, 12", 3 Divisions	$25
Relish Dish, 14", 4 Divisions	$30
Salt and Pepper Shakers	$100
Saucer	$7.50
Sherbet	$12.50
Sugar, Footed	$60
Sugar, Oval	$17.50
Tumbler, 3½", 5 oz.	$15
Tumbler, 4" Tall, 9 oz.	$20
Tumbler, 5" Tall, 10 oz., Footed	$80
Vase, 6½" Tall	$25

Radiance
New Martinsville Glass Company, 1936–39

The prices below are for light blue and a light transparent ruby red. For any rare cobalt blue, pink, or green, double the prices; for amber, reduce them by 35 percent; and for crystal, reduce them by 65 percent. Many pieces are decorated with several different designs in gold and platinum. If the design is full and completely intact, add 10–15 percent to the prices below.

Bonbon Dish, 6"	$35
Bonbon Dish, 6", Footed	$40
Bonbon Dish with Cover, 6"	$125
Bowl, 5" with 2 Handles	$25
Bowl, 10", Crimped	$55
Bowl, 10", Flared	$50
Bowl, 12", Crimped	$60

Radiance Cordial. *Drawing by Mark Pickvet.*

Bowl, 12", Flared	$55
Butter Dish	$500
Candlestick, 6", Ruffled	$100
Candlestick, 8"	$75
Candlestick, Double	$85
Celery Dish, 10"	$40
Cheese and Cracker Set	$125
Compote, 5"	$37.50
Compote, 6"	$40
Condiment Set, 4-Piece Set (Includes Tray)	$325
Cordial, 1 oz.	$50
Creamer	$35
Cruet	$100
Cup	$22.50
Decanter with Stopper and Handle	$225
Lamp, 12"	$125
Mayonnaise, 3-Piece Set	$125
Pickle Dish, 7"	$35
Pitcher, 2 qt.	$325
Plate, 8"	$20

Punch Bowl, 9"	$225
Punch Bowl Liner, 14" Plate	$125
Punch Cup	$20
Punch Ladle (Common in Crystal—$25)	$175
Relish Dish, 7", 2-Part	$40
Relish Dish, 8", 3-Part	$50
Salt and Pepper Shakers	$110
Saucer	$12.50
Sugar	$35
Tray, Oval	$50
Tumbler, 9 oz.	$35
Vase, 10", 2 Styles	$125
Vase, 12", 2 Styles	$175

Raindrops or Optic Design
Federal Glass Company, 1929–33

Raindrops is a rather simple pattern with small pressed circles. The prices below are for green; for crystal, reduce them by 50 percent. As with most Federal products, the underside of the pieces contain the company mark (*F* in a shield).

Bowl, 4½"	$8.50
Bowl, 6"	$12.50
Bowl, 7½"	$55
Creamer	$12.50
Cup	$8
Plate, 6"	$5
Plate, 8"	$8.50
Salt and Pepper Shakers	$350
Saucer	$3
Sherbet	$10
Sugar with Cover	$55
Tumbler, 3" Tall, 4 oz.	$7.50
Tumbler, 4" Tall, 5 oz.	$8.50

Raindrops or Optic Pattern. *Photo by Robin Rainwater.*

Tumbler, 4" Tall, 9 oz.	$11
Tumbler, 5" Tall, 10 oz.	$12.50
Tumbler, 5½" Tall, 14 oz.	$15
Whiskey Tumbler, 1¾" Tall, 1 oz.	$10
Whiskey Tumbler, 2¼" Tall, 2 oz.	$10

Ribbon
Hocking Glass Company, Late 1920s–Early 1930s

The basic colors of this pattern are pink and green. For black, double the prices; for crystal, reduce them by 50 percent. This is another simple Depression pattern of vertical panels that nearly reach the top of each item.

Bowl, 4"	$35
Bowl, 5"	$45
Bowl, 7"	$50
Bowl, 8"	$45
Candy Jar with Cover	$55
Creamer	$20
Cup	$8
Plate, 6¼"	$5
Plate, 8"	$8.50

Ribbon Pattern. *Photo by Robin Rainwater.*

Salt and Pepper Shakers	$50
Saucer	$4
Sherbet	$7.50
Sugar, 2-Handled	$20
Tumbler, 5½" or 6" Tall, 10 oz.	$37.50

Rings or Banded Rings
Hocking Glass Company, 1927–33

Depression colors include green and pink along with colored rings applied to crystal. Hocking produced many, many banded ring combinations. These bands came in an incredible number of colors, including black, blue, green, orange, pink, red, and yellow, and differing shades of these colors. Hocking even trimmed or ringed them in metals, including gold, silver, and platinum (same prices). For plain crystal, reduce the prices by 50 percent. The biggest problem with these fired-on enameled rings is that they are difficult to find completely intact. Nicks, scratches, incomplete bands, fading, wear, and other problems plague this type of banding. Damaged banded glass pieces are not worth nearly as much as those where the band is completely intact. The prices below reflect complete, undamaged banding.

Bowl, 5"	$8.50
Bowl, 5¼", 2 Divisions	$45
Bowl, 7"	$17.50
Bowl, 8"	$15

Cocktail Glass, 3¾" Tall, 3 oz.	$22.50
Cocktail Shaker with Metal Top	$35
Creamer	$8.50
Cup	$7.50
Decanter with Stopper	$55
Goblet, Water, 7¼" Tall, 9 oz.	$20
Ice Bucket or Tub	$45
Pitcher, 2 qt., 8" Tall	$40
Pitcher, 2½ qt., 8½" Tall	$50
Plate, 6¼"	$5
Plate, 6½" with Off-Center Ring for Sherbet	$8.50
Plate, 8"	$7.50
Platter, 11¾"	$17.50
Salt and Pepper Shakers	$55
Sandwich Server with Center Handle	$35
Saucer	$4
Sherbet, Fits 6½" Plate	$22.50
Sherbet, 4¾" Tall, Footed	$12.50
Sugar	$8.50
Tumbler, 3" Tall, 4 oz.	$11.50
Tumbler, 3½" Tall, 5 oz.	$12.50
Tumbler, 3½" Tall, Footed	$12.50
Tumbler, 4" Tall, 8 oz.	$20
Tumbler, 4¼" Tall, 9 oz.	$13.50
Tumbler, 4¾" Tall, 10 oz.	$17.50
Tumbler, 5" Tall, 12 oz.	$17.50
Tumbler, 5½" Tall, Footed	$15
Tumbler, 6½" Tall, Footed	$20
Vase, 8" Tall	$45
Whiskey, 2" Tall, 1½ oz.	$15
Wineglass, 4½" Tall, 3½ oz.	$25

Rock Crystal or Early American Rock Crystal
McKee Glass Company, 1920s–1930s

Rock Crystal is a prolific pattern in Depression glass and comes in a wide variety of colors, including varying shades of amber, amethyst, aquamarine, light blue, frosted or decorated crystal, green, milk, pink, vaseline, yellow, frosted colors, and marbleized or slag designs. The prices vary only for ruby red and cobalt blue (double them), and plain crystal (reduce them by 50 percent). The pattern contains a good deal of scrolling and vining around five-petaled flowers.

Bonbon Dish	$40
Bowl, 4"	$27.50
Bowl, 4½"	$27.50
Bowl, 5"	$30
Bowl, 7", 2 Styles	$45
Bowl, 8"	$45
Bowl, 8½", Center Handle	$125
Bowl, 9"	$60
Bowl, 10½"	$65
Bowl, 11½", 2 Divisions	$65
Bowl, 12½", Footed	$150
Bowl, 12½", 5 Divisions	$125
Bowl, 13"	$75
Bowl, 14", 6 Divisions	$110
Butter Dish with Cover	$750
Cake Stand, 11", Footed	$60
Candelabra, Double-Light	$125
Candelabra, Triple-Light	$150
Candlestick, 5½" Tall	$45
Candlestick, 8" Tall	$85
Candy Jar with Cover, 2 Styles	$110
Celery Dish, 12" Long	$55
Champagne Glass, 6 oz.	$30
Claret Glass, 2 oz.	$40

Cocktail Glass, 3½ oz.	$35
Compote, 7"	$40
Compote with Cover, Footed	$60
Cordial, 1 oz.	$55
Cordial, 2 oz.	$40
Creamer, 2 Styles	$40
Cruet with Stopper	$225
Cup	$35
Egg Plate	$75
Goblet, 8 oz.	$35
Goblet, 11 oz.	$40
Ice Dish, Various Styles	$85
Lamp, Electric	$500
Marmalade Dish	$35
Parfait, 3½ oz.	$45
Parfait, 6 oz.	$35
Pitcher, Syrup with Lid	$350
Pitcher, Milk, 1 qt.	$325
Pitcher, Water, 2 qt., 7½" Tall	$425
Pitcher with Cover, 3 qt., 9" Tall	$550
Pitcher, Tankard Style	$750
Plate, 6"	$12.50
Plate, 7½"	$15
Plate, 8½"	$17.50
Plate, 9"	$27.50
Plate, 10½", 2 Styles	$40
Platter, 11½"	$35
Punch Bowl with Stand	$2,000
Punch Cup	$40
Salt and Pepper Shakers, 2 Styles	$150
Salt Dip	$85

Sandwich Server with Center Handle	$55
Saucer	$12.50
Sherbet	$35
Spooner	$100
Sugar with Cover, 2-Handled	$85
Tray, Oval, 7½"	$150
Tumbler, 5 oz., 2 Styles	$30
Tumbler, 9 oz.	$35
Tumbler, 12 oz.	$45
Vase, Cornucopia Style	$125
Vase, 11" Tall	$135
Whiskey Tumbler, 2½ oz.	$35
Wineglass, 3 oz.	$40
Wineglass, 7–7½ oz.	$35

Romanesque
L. E. Smith Glass Company, Early 1930s

Romanesque is a fancy lacy pattern that is an almost allover pattern (usually there is a clear band between the outer fringe lacing and the main pattern in the center of each object). Most plates in this design are octagonal, too. The prices below are for amber, green, and yellow. Double them for any rare black; reduce them by 50 percent for plain crystal.

Bowl, 10", 4¼" Tall, Footed	$60
Bowl, 10½"	$50
Cake Plate, 11½", 2¾" Tall	$45
Candlestick, 2½" Tall	$17.50
Plate, 5½" Octagonal	$7.50
Plate, 7" Octagonal	$10
Plate, 8" Round	$12.50
Plate, 8" Octagonal	$14
Plate, 10" Octagonal	$27.50
Tray	$20
Sherbet, Round Top	$10

Sherbet, Scalloped Top	$12.50
Vase, 7½" Tall	$55

Rose Cameo
Belmont Tumbler Company, 1931

The only color made in Rose Cameo was green. The Belmont Tumbler Company is the only company to file a patent on this pattern, which they did in 1931. Do not confuse it with Hocking's Ballerina. In Rose Cameo, a rose is encircled within the cameo. In Hocking's, a dancing girl or ballerina is encircled.

Bowl, 4½"	$15
Bowl, 5"	$25
Bowl, 6"	$30
Plate, 7"	$17.50
Sherbet	$17.50
Tumbler, 5" Tall, Footed, Rim Design Varies	$30

Rosemary or Dutch Rose
Federal Glass Company, 1935–36

The prices shown here are for green and amber versions of this pattern. Pink is much rarer; increase the prices by 50 percent. Rosemary is a derivative of Federal's Mayfair pattern and includes rose blossoms in the center and within the arches.

Bowl, 5", Berry (Shallow)	$12.50
Bowl, 5", Soup (Deep)	$25
Bowl, 6"	$40
Bowl, 10", Oval	$40
Creamer	$17.50
Cup	$12.50
Plate, 6¾"	$12.50
Plate, 9½"	$17.50
Plate, 9½", Grill, 3 Divisions	$18.50
Platter, 12", Oval	$27.50
Saucer	$7.50

Rosemary Tumbler. *Drawing by Mark Pickvet.*

Sugar, 2-Handled	$17.50
Tumbler, 4¼" Tall, 9 oz.	$40

Roulette
Hocking Glass Company, 1935–39

The primary Depression colors of this pattern are pink and green; for crystal, reduce them by 50 percent. Roulette is sometimes nicknamed Many Windows because of the two horizontal rows of miniature rectangles.

Bowl, 8"	$25
Bowl, 9"	$30
Cup	$10
Pitcher, 1 qt., 8" Tall	$50
Plate, 6"	$7.50
Plate, 8½"	$10
Platter, 12"	$20
Saucer	$5
Sherbet	$8.50
Tumbler, 3¼" Tall, 5 oz.	$30
Tumbler, 3¼" Tall, 7½ oz.	$55
Tumbler, 4¼" Tall, 9 oz.	$35

Tumbler, 5" Tall, 12 oz.	$40
Tumbler, 5½" Tall, 10 oz., Footed	$40
Whiskey Tumbler, 2½" Tall, 1½ oz.	$22.50

Round Robin
Unknown Manufacturer, 1920s–1930s

Round Robin colors are green and iridescent or light marigold. For crystal, reduce them by 50 percent. This is another simple vertically ribbed pattern but with no sure patents. The domino tray is a unique piece to this pattern; it consists of a center ring for a creamer and the remaining surrounding area for sugar cubes.

Bowl, 4"	$12.50
Creamer	$10
Cup	$12.50
Domino Tray	$125
Plate, 6"	$5
Plate, 8"	$7.50
Platter, 12"	$17.50
Saucer	$4
Sherbet	$12.50
Sugar, 2-Handled	$12.50
Tumbler	$30

Roxana
Hazel Atlas Glass Company, 1932–33

Roxana's basic color is yellow, which Hazel Atlas referred to as golden topaz. A few milk-white pieces have been found as well (same price). The basic pattern consists of a stylized floral diamond surrounded by four stalklike leaves. Roxana was a premium, given away in packages of Star Brand Oats.

Bowl, 4½"	$20
Bowl, 5"	$20
Bowl, 6"	$25
Plate, 5½"	$15
Plate, 6"	$15

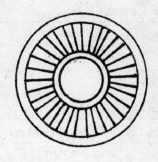

Round Robin Plate. *Drawing by Mark Pickvet.*

Sherbet	$15
Tumbler, 9 oz., 4¼" Tall	$27.50

Royal Lace
Hazel Atlas Glass Company, 1934–Early 1940s

The prices below are for pink and green pieces of Royal Lace. For amethyst and cobalt blue, double them; for crystal, reduce them by 50 percent. Production of this paneled lace pattern by Hazel Atlas continued into the 1940s, but the majority of the colored glass was made in the 1930s. The interesting story of Royal Lace is that General Mills had commissioned Hazel Atlas to manufacture Shirley Temple pieces (cobalt blue glass with pictures of Shirley Temple applied as decals). When General Mills discontinued the order, Hazel Atlas was left with several tanks of molten blue glass. The Royal Lace molds were nearby, which they promptly filled with the blue glass.

Bowl, 4¾"	$40
Bowl, 5"	$45
Bowl, 10"	$45
Bowl, 10", 3-Footed, Straight Edge	$65
Bowl, 10", 3-Footed, Ruffled or Rolled Edge	$125
Bowl, 11" Oval	$45
Butter Dish with Cover	$250
Candlestick, Straight Edge	$50
Candlestick, Ruffled or Rolled Edge	$75

Cookie Jar with Cover	$100
Creamer	$35
Cup	$27.50
Nut Bowl	$450
Pitcher, 1½ qt.	$125
Pitcher, 2 qt., with or without Ice Lip, 8" Tall	$150
Pitcher, 3 qt., 8" to 8½" Tall, with or without Ice Lip	$200
Plate, 6"	$12.50
Plate, 8½"	$17.50
Plate, 9" Grill, 3 Divisions	$35
Plate, 10"	$40
Plate, 10" Grill, 3 Divisions	$40
Platter, 13" Oval	$45
Salt and Pepper Shakers	$115
Saucer	$12
Sherbet	$27.50
Sugar with Cover, 2-Handled	$90
Tumbler, 3½" Tall, 5 oz.	$40
Tumbler, 4¼" Tall, 9 oz.	$40
Tumbler, 5" Tall, 10 oz.	$85
Tumbler, 5½" Tall, 12 oz.	$85

S or Stippled Rose Band
Macbeth-Evans Glass Company, 1930–33

The trimmed colors in this pattern are the most popular and consist of crystal with banding in amber, blue, green, pink, and platinum. The color amber exists in lighter shades that are almost yellow. A few odd pieces in pink, green, and Monax have also been found in this pattern. All are priced the same except for plain crystal (reduce them 25–35 percent) and the exceptions noted below.

Bowl, 5½"	$10
Bowl, 8½"	$20
Cake Plate, 11¾"	$60
Cake Plate, 13"	$85

Creamer	$10
Cup	$7.50
Pitcher, 80 oz., 2 Styles (Rare in Pink or Green—$600)	$150
Plate, 6"	$5
Plate, 8¼"	$7.50
Plate, 9¼"	$11
Plate, Grill	$11
Saucer	$3.50
Sherbet, Footed	$10
Sugar	$10
Tumbler, 3½", 5 oz.	$10
Tumbler, 4", 9 oz. (Rare in Pink or Green—$60)	$12.50
Tumbler, 4¾", 10 oz.	$12.50
Tumbler, 5", 12 oz.	$17.50

Sandwich
Indiana Glass Company, 1920s–1930s

Indiana's Sandwich causes more problems than any other pattern. All the original colors were made during the Depression era; however, all have since been reproduced in one form or another. The problem that arises is that the majority of the original molds were put back into service to make virtually identical pieces. The original pink is much darker than the reproduction pink. The original green is a yellowish green, and the new is a paler shade of green. The original also glows under a dark or black light (a common test for older Depression glass because of the ores used in the ingredients); the new does not glow. The prices below are for the original pink and green. For amber or crystal, reduce them by 50 percent; for any rare red, double them. Other colors of Indiana's Sandwich were produced after the Depression and appear in the next chapter. These include teal blue, smokey blue, milk white, and some odd red. A few red original pieces were made in the 1930s but are nearly impossible to tell from the reproductions; still, any red is usually the most valuable color in this pattern, newer or old.

Ashtray Set, 4-Piece Card Suits	$20
Basket, 10" Tall	$80
Bowl, 4¼"	$10
Bowl, 6"	$10
Bowl, 6", Hexagonal	$12.50

Sandwich Pattern. *Photo by Robin Rainwater.*

Bowl, 8½"	$25
Bowl, 9"	$45
Bowl, 11½"	$55
Butter Dish with Cover	$50
Candlestick, 3½"	$25
Candlestick, 7"	$35
Celery, 10½"	$35
Creamer	$25
Creamer and Sugar Set on Diamond-Shape Tray	$50
Cruet with Stopper	$150
Cup	$7.50
Decanter with Stopper	$125
Goblet, 9 oz.	$30
Mayonnaise	$40
Pitcher, 68 oz.	$55
Plate, 6"	$7.50
Plate, 7"	$10
Plate, 8", Oval with Indentation for the Sherbet	$17.50
Plate, 8⅜"	$10
Plate, 10½"	$25

Plate, 13"	$30
Puff Box	$35
Punch Bowl, 13"	$300
Punch Cup	$25
Salt and Pepper Shakers	$40
Sandwich Server with Center Handle	$45
Saucer	$6
Sherbet, 3¼"	$12.50
Sugar with Cover	$50
Tumbler, 3 oz. Footed	$25
Tumbler, 8 oz. Footed	$30
Tumbler, 12 oz. Footed	$35
Wine, 3" Tall, 4 oz.	$30

Sharon Cabbage Rose
Federal Glass Company, 1935–39

The prices below are for the Depression colors pink, green, and amber; for crystal, reduce them by 50 percent. Note that there are a few rare colored items priced separately below. This pattern gets its name from the roses that resemble cabbage heads. There are several reproductions to be aware of in this pattern. Butter dishes were produced in 1976 in pink, dark pink, green, dark or forest green, light or cobalt blue, red, and amber. The regular pink and green are the only sources of confusion because they resemble the originals. Creamer and sugar sets as well as salt and pepper shakers in very light pink were reissued in the late 1970s and 1980s; however, the color is much fainter than the originals. Candy jars were also reproduced in both pink and green. Beware of dealers, especially those who run online auctions; they tend to list reproductions in Depression glass categories.

Bowl, 5", Berry (Shallow)	$17.50
Bowl, 5", Soup (Deep)	$55
Bowl, 6"	$32.50
Bowl, 7¾"	$65
Bowl, 8½"	$40
Bowl, 9½"	$45
Bowl, 10½"	$50
Butter Dish with Cover	$100

Sharon Cabbage Rose Pattern. *Photo by Robin Rainwater.*

Cake Plate, 11½", Footed	$60
Candy Jar with Cover (Rare in Green—$200)	$75
Cheese Dish with Cover (Rare in Pink or Green—$1,250)	$225
Creamer	$27.50
Cup	$22.50
Marmalade Dish (Rare in Pink—$275)	$60
Pitcher, 2½ qt., with or without Ice Lip (Rare in Green—$525)	$225
Plate, 6"	$11
Plate, 7½"	$27.50
Plate, 9½"	$30
Platter, 12½" Oval	$40
Salt and Pepper Shakers	$75
Saucer	$15
Sherbet	$25
Sugar with Cover, 2-Handled	$60
Tumbler, 4" Tall, 9 oz.	$55
Tumbler, 5¼" Tall, 12 oz. (Rare in Green—$125)	$65
Tumbler, 6½" Tall, 15 oz. (Rare in Amber—$150)	$75
Vase	$175

Sierra Pinwheel Pattern. *Photo by Robin Rainwater.*

Sierra Pinwheel Pattern Creamer, Ribbon Pattern Double-Handle Sugar, Depression Tray with Center Handle. *Photo by Robin Rainwater.*

Sierra Pinwheel
Jeannette Glass Company, 1931–33

The primary colors in this pattern are pink and green, but a few pieces were made in ultramarine (same price). The pattern consists of vertical ribbing that extends out to an irregular edge that is prone to chipping, so examine pieces carefully. Jeannette made a butter dish and cover with a combination of the Adam (see beginning of chapter) and Sierra patterns. This dish along with the cover happens to be worth about $1,550!

Bowl, 5½"	$22.50
Bowl, 8½"	$45
Bowl, 9¼", Oval (Rare in Green—$150)	$75
Butter Dish with Cover	$85
Creamer	$27.50
Cup	$17.50
Pitcher, Milk, 1 qt.	$150
Plate, 9"	$30
Platter, 11", Oval	$65
Salt and Pepper Shakers	$60
Saucer	$12.50
Sugar with Cover, 2-Handled	$52.50
Tray, 10¼", 2-Handled	$26
Tumbler, 4½" Tall, Footed	$85

Spiral
Hocking Glass Company, 1928–30

The two Depression colors made in this pattern are pink and green. For crystal, reduce the prices below by 50 percent. This pattern is sometimes confused with Swirl and Twisted Optic. Swirl is easy because the arc or curves are a bit straighter or not as sharply angled. Like Twisted Optic, Swirl curves go counterclockwise; Spiral curves move clockwise. The important thing to remember is to look at the piece from the correct angle!

Bowl 4¾"	$7.50
Bowl, 7"	$12.50
Bowl, 8"	$15
Bowl, 9"	$20
Creamer	$10
Creamer, Footed	$12.50
Cup	$7.50
Ice Tub	$35
Marmalade with Cover	$40
Parfait, 5¾", Footed	$60
Pitcher, 2 qt., 7½" Tall	$45
Plate, 6"	$3.50
Plate, 8"	$5.50
Platter, 12"	$35
Salt and Pepper Shakers	$50
Sandwich Server with Center Handle	$40
Saucer	$3.50
Sherbet	$7.50
Sugar, 2-Handled	$10
Sugar, 2-Handled, Footed	$12.50
Tumbler, 3" Tall, 5 oz.	$7.50
Tumbler, 5" Tall, 9 oz.	$10
Tumbler, 6" Tall, 10 oz.	$22.50

Spiral Pattern. *Photo by Robin Rainwater.*

Starlight
Hazel Atlas Glass Company, 1938–40

Starlight is a series of overlapping groups of four diagonal bands that form somewhat of a star shape. Some pieces contain a diamond pointlike central circle (mostly the plates). The prices below are for pink. Reduce the prices by 50 percent for any milk white or crystal; double them for any rare cobalt blue.

Bowl 5½", Closed Tab Handles	$15
Bowl, 8½", Closed Tab Handles	$25
Bowl, 11½"	$60
Bowl, 12"	$75
Creamer	$20
Cup	$12.50
Plate, 6"	$7.50
Plate, 8½"	$12.50
Plate, 9"	$17.50
Platter, 13"	$25
Relish Dish	$30
Salt and Pepper Shakers	$50
Saucer	$4
Sherbet	$30
Sugar	$20

Strawberry
U.S. Glass Company, Early 1930s

The basic Strawberry colors are pink and green; however, most pieces can be found in crystal and a light iridized marigold color (reduce the prices below by 25–35 percent for crystal or marigold). This is the sister pattern of Cherryberry, also produced by U.S. Glass. The dimensions of the pieces are identical but the fruits on the pattern are obviously different.

Bowl, 4"	$15
Bowl, 6¼"	$125
Bowl, 6½"	$30
Bowl, 7½"	$35
Butter Dish with Cover	$200
Compote	$27.50
Creamer, Small	$27.50
Creamer, Large, 4½" Tall	$45
Olive Dish, 5", 1 Tab Handle	$25
Pickle Dish, 8¼"	$25
Pitcher, 7¾" Tall	$200
Plate, 6"	$15
Plate, 7½"	$22.50
Sherbet	$12.50
Sugar, Small (open)	$27.50
Sugar, Large with Cover	$125
Tumbler, 3½" Tall	$45

Sunburst
Jeanette Glass Company, Late 1930s

Sunburst is a crystal pattern only and contains a large central star or sunburst design. Some refer to it as Herringbone because of the herringbone design along the rims of each piece. Do note that the inner rims chip easily and bear careful inspection.

Bowl, 4¾"	$10
Bowl, 8½"	$20
Bowl, 10¾"	$30
Candlestick, 2-Light	$35
Creamer	$12.50

Cup	$11.50
Plate, 5½"	$10
Plate, 9¼"	$25
Platter, 11¾"	$30
Relish Dish, 2 Divisions	$17.50
Saucer	$6
Sherbet	$17.50
Sugar Dish	$12.50
Tray, Oval	$15
Tumbler, 4" Tall, 9 oz.	$30

Sunflower
Jeanette Glass Company, 1930s

The basic colors are pink and green. For unusual colors such as ultramarine, delphite blue, and other opaque colors, triple the prices. The pattern consists of sunflower blossoms connected by long stalks or vines along with one large sunflower blossom in the center. The cake plate was once given away free in flour bags and remains one of the most commonly found Depression-glass items.

Ashtray, 5"	$15
Cake Plate, 10" with 3 Legs	$17.50
Creamer	$25
Cup	$20
Plate, 8"	$40
Plate, 9"	$25
Saucer	$12.50
Sugar, 2-Handled	$25
Tumbler, 4¾" Tall, Footed	$40
Trivet, 7" with 3 Legs	$350

Swirl or Petal Swirl
Jeannette Glass Company, 1937–38

Swirl pieces come with two different edge designs—some are plain and others are ruffled. The values are the same for both. The prices below are for pink, ultramarine, amber, light blue, and an opaque or delphite blue. Swirl is fairly easy to keep separate from the Spiral and Twisted Optic patterns because the curves or arcs are not nearly as wide as the others.

Bowl, 5¼"	$17.50
Bowl, 9"	$37.50
Bowl, 10", 2 Tab Handles, Footed	$40
Bowl, 10½", Footed	$35
Butter Dish with Cover	$275
Candleholder, Single Branch	$50
Candleholder, Double Branch	$35
Candy Dish with 3 Legs	$25
Candy Dish with Cover	$175
Coaster	$17.50
Creamer	$20
Cup	$17.50
Pitcher, 1½ qt., Footed (Rare—Ultramarine Only)	$2,000
Plate, 6½"	$10
Plate, 7¼"	$15
Plate, 8"	$16
Plate, 9¼"	$22.50
Plate, 10½"	$35
Platter, 12" Oval	$45
Platter, 12½"	$40
Salt and Pepper Shakers	$75
Saucer	$7.50
Sherbet	$25
Sugar, 2-Handled	$20
Tray, 10½", 2-Handled	$35
Tumbler, 4" Tall, 9 oz.	$35
Tumbler, 4⅝" Tall, 9 oz., Footed	$35
Tumbler, 5" Tall, 9 oz., Footed	$35
Tumbler, 5¼" Tall, 13 oz. (Rare in Ultramarine—$135)	$65

Vase, 6½" Tall	$30
Vase, 8½" Tall	$35

Tea Room
Indiana Glass Company, 1926–31

Colors for Tea Room are pink, green, and amber; for crystal, reduce the prices by 50 percent. Many fountain items were made specifically for ice cream stores, such as banana boats or splits, parfait glasses, footed tumblers, and more; for tearooms as the name of this pattern suggests, look for creamers and sugars, mustards, and marmalades; and even items for restaurants too.

Banana Dish, 7½" Long	$125
Banana Dish, 7½" Long, Footed	$100
Bowl, 4"	$65
Bowl, 5"	$75
Bowl, 8¼"	$75
Bowl, 8¾"	$95
Bowl, 9½" Oval	$85
Candlestick	$40
Creamer, Several Styles	$30
Cup	$65
Goblet	$85
Ice Bucket	$70
Lamp, 9", Electric	$150
Marmalade with Notched Cover	$225
Mustard Jar with Cover	$175
Parfait	$100
Pitcher, 2 qt. (Rare in Amber—$550)	$175
Plate, 6½"	$37.50
Plate, 8¼"	$40
Plate, 10½", 2-Handled	$55
Relish Dish, 3 Divisions	$30
Salt and Pepper Shakers	$75

Sandwich Server with Center Handle	$225
Saucer	$37.50
Sherbet, Several Styles	$40
Sugar, 2-Handled, Several Styles	$30
Sugar with Cover, Several Styles	$225
Sundae Dish, Ruffled	$100
Tray for Rectangular Creamer and Sugar	$55
Tumbler, 6 oz., Footed	$40
Tumbler, 8 oz.	$125
Tumbler, 8 oz., Footed	$40
Tumbler, 11 oz., Footed	$55
Tumbler, 12 oz., Footed	$80
Vase, 6½" Tall	$125
Vase, 9½" Tall	$125
Vase, 9½" Tall, Ruffled	$150
Vase, 11" Tall	$175
Vase, 11" Tall, Ruffled	$300

Thistle
Macbeth-Evans, 1929–30

Primary Thistle colors are pink and green; for crystal, reduce the prices below by 50 percent. Only seven pieces are listed here, with a couple that are rare. The Mosser Glass Company of Cambridge, Ohio, has produced pieces with thicker lines in this pattern, including butter dishes, pitchers, tumblers, and others beginning in the 1980s.

Bowl, 5½"	$35
Bowl, 10¼" (Rare in Pink—$425)	$275
Cake Plate, 13"	$200
Cup	$30
Plate, 8"	$25
Plate, 10¼"	$30
Saucer	$12.50

Thumbprint or Pear Optic
Federal Glass Company, 1929–30

Pear Optic is Federal's official name for this pattern, but it is more commonly referred to as Thumbprint. It is green and contains a common elongated pressed thumbprint design. Note that the design is oval in shape and a little bigger than Raindrops, a similar Federal pattern. Also note that the pieces are marked with Federal's *F* within a shield.

Bowl, 4¾"	$7.50
Bowl, 5"	$10
Bowl, 7"	$12.50
Bowl, 8"	$15
Creamer	$17.50
Cup	$10
Plate, 6"	$6
Plate, 8"	$8
Plate, 9¼"	$12
Salt and Pepper Shakers	$100
Saucer	$4
Sherbet	$10
Sugar	$17.50
Tumbler, 4" Tall, 5 oz.	$10
Tumbler, 5" Tall, 10 oz.	$12.50
Tumbler, 5½" Tall, 12 oz.	$15
Whiskey Tumbler, 2¼" Tall, 1¼ oz.	$12.50

Tulip
Dell Glass Company, Late 1930s–Early 1940s

The Depression colors in the pricing for Tulip are green, amethyst, and a light coppery blue; for crystal, reduce them by 25–35 percent. The basic pattern is somewhat of an allover clear or stippled design that aids in separating the tuliplike blossom designs most often found around the edge or rim. The prices are the same whether the stippling is present or not.

Bowl, 13¼"	$125
Candleholder, 3¾"	$40

Candleholder, 5¼"	$60
Candy Jar with Cover, 7½" Tall	$150
Creamer	$25
Cup	$22.50
Decanter with Stopper	$175
Ice Tub	$100
Plate, 6"	$12.50
Plate, 7¼"	$17.50
Plate, 9"	$40
Saucer	$10
Sherbet, 3¾"	$25
Sugar	$25
Tumbler, 2¾" Tall	$30
Whiskey Tumbler	$30

Twisted Optic
Imperial Glass Company, 1927–30

The Depression colors in the pricing of this pattern are pink, green, and amber. For yellow (canary or a yellow with somewhat of a green tint) or light copper blue, double the prices. Twisted Optic is commonly confused with Hocking's Spiral pattern and less so with some Swirl patterns. The curving spirals of Twisted Optic go counterclockwise, whereas Spiral curves move in a clockwise direction. Spiral was made only in pink and green, whereas Twisted Optic includes light blue, amber, and yellow pieces.

Basket, 10" Tall	$65
Bowl, 4¾"	$15
Bowl, 5"	$10
Bowl, 7"	$12.50
Bowl, 8"	$17.50
Bowl, 9"	$20
Bowl, 10½"	$25
Bowl, 11½"	$27.50
Candlestick, 3" Tall	$15
Candlestick, 8" Tall	$20

Candy Jar with Cover, with or without Feet (Several Styles)	$45
Cologne Bottle with Stopper	$55
Creamer	$10
Cup	$6
Marmalade Dish with Cover	$40
Mayonnaise	$25
Pitcher, 2 qt.	$50
Plate, 6"	$5
Plate, 7"	$6
Plate, 8"	$7.50
Plate, 9", Oval with Indentation	$10
Plate, 10"	$12.50
Powder Jar with Cover	$50
Sandwich Server with Center Handle	$30
Saucer	$4
Sherbet	$8
Sugar, 2-Handled	$10
Tray, 2-Handled	$20
Tumbler, 4½" Tall, 9 oz.	$8
Tumbler, 5¼" Tall, 12 oz.	$10
Vase, 7¼" Tall, 2-Handled	$35
Vase, 8" Tall, 2-Handled	$40
Vase, 8" Tall, Fan Style, 2-Handled	$45

U.S. Swirl
United States Glass Company, Late 1920s

Basic U.S. Swirl colors are pink and green; for crystal, reduce the prices below by 50 percent. A few iridized pieces have been found (same price). Most of the U.S. Swirl pieces have a star in the bottom, which helps in differentiating the pattern from the many other swirls, spirals, and twisted patterns out there.

Bowl, 4½"	$7.50
Bowl, 5½", 1 Handle	$12.50
Bowl, 8"	$20

Bowl, 8¼", Oval	$45
Bowl, 8½", Oval	$60
Bowl, 10", Octagonal, Footed	$100
Butter Dish with Cover	$135
Candy Jar with Cover, 2-Handled	$40
Compote	$30
Creamer	$20
Pitcher, 1½ qt., 8" Tall	$85
Plate, 6"	$4
Plate, 8"	$8
Salt and Pepper Shakers	$65
Sherbet	$8
Sugar with Cover, 2-Handled	$50
Tumbler, 3½" Tall, 8 oz.	$15
Tumbler, 4¾" Tall, 12 oz.	$20
Vase	$27.50

Vernon or No. 616
Indiana Glass Company, 1930–32

This is the last of Indiana's numbered patterns in this chapter. Basic colors are yellow and green; for crystal, reduce the prices here by 50 percent. The yellow is a little more abundant than the green, but neither color is that common. Some of the crystal pieces were trimmed in platinum. With the platinum completely intact, the crystal pieces are worth a few dollars more than the 50 percent reduction to the prices listed below. Once again, sparse or incomplete banding can easily be removed with a pencil eraser; nevertheless, be advised against using any abrasives that will damage the glass.

Creamer, Footed	$32.50
Cup	$22.50
Plate, 8"	$12.50
Plate, 11½"	$35
Saucer	$7.50
Sugar, Footed	$32.50
Tumbler, 5", Footed	$45

Victory
Diamond Glass-Ware Company, 1929–32

The Victory pattern is one of simplicity, consisting of vertical panels (much like a spoke design on the flat rounded pieces). Gravy boats with platters are not commonly found in Depression sets, and the one here is also quite rare. The prices below are for amber, pink, and green; for cobalt blue, double them; for black, triple them. The cobalt blue and the opaque black glass are highly desirable and collectible. Some of the black pieces are trimmed in gold and decorated with flower patterns or other designs. The value is the same as the usual black, which is still about triple what is listed below.

Bonbon Dish	$15
Bowl, 6½"	$17.50
Bowl, 8½"	$25
Bowl, 9", Oval	$37.50
Bowl, 11"	$35
Bowl, 12"	$40
Bowl, 12½"	$40
Candlestick	$25
Cheese and Cracker Set (Indented Plate with Compote)	$55
Compote, 6¾", 6" Tall	$20
Creamer	$20
Cup	$12.50
Goblet, 5" Tall	$30
Gravy Boat with Matching Platter	$250
Mayonnaise Set (Dish, Underplate, and Ladle)	$75
Pitcher, 2 qt.	$250
Plate, 6"	$7.50
Plate, 7"	$10
Plate, 8"	$12.50
Plate, 9"	$22.50
Platter, 12"	$35
Sandwich Server with Center Handle	$40
Saucer	$6
Sherbet	$16

Sugar, 2-Handled	$20
Tumbler, Various Styles	$45

Vitrock Flower Rim
Hocking Glass Company, 1934–37

This is an opaque milk-white glass. The prices listed below are for fired-on colors, which include blue, green, red, and yellow. For plain white, reduce them by 25–35 percent. For the blue decorated Lake Como scenery on white, quadruple the prices.

Bowl, 4"	$7.50
Bowl, 5½"	$20
Bowl, 6"	$7.50
Bowl 7½"	$8.50
Bowl, 9½"	$17.50
Bowl, 9¾"	$20
Creamer, Oval	$8.50
Cup	$5.50
Plate, 7¼"	$4
Plate, 8¾"	$7.50
Plate, 9"	$35
Plate, 10"	$12.50
Platter, 11" to 11½"	$37.50
Saucer	$3.50
Sugar, Oval	$8.50

Waterford or Waffle
Hocking Glass Company, 1938–44

The basic color for this pattern is pink; for crystal, reduce the prices listed here by 50 percent. Pieces can also be found in milk, white, yellow, and reproduction forest green; reduce the prices for those by 25 percent. This pattern is similar to Hocking's Miss America in more ways than one. First it has a similar diamond shape, only the diamonds are much larger on Waterford. Some pieces have the exact same mold design, too, although the patterns differ. Note that Waffle is a nickname only that aids in describing the pattern. This pattern was also made at the tail end of the Depression era (directly after the Miss America pattern).

Ashtray, 4"	$15
Ashtray, 4", with Advertising	$25
Bowl, 5"	$22.50
Bowl, 5½"	$45
Bowl, 8¼"	$35
Butter Dish with Cover (Common in Crystal—$35)	$275
Coaster	$12.50
Creamer	$17.50
Cup	$17.50
Goblet, Various Styles	$37.50
Lamp, Miniature, 4"	$60
Pitcher, Milk, 1 qt. (Common in Crystal—$27.50)	$150
Pitcher, Water, 2½ qt. (Common in Crystal—$40)	$175
Plate, 6"	$10
Plate, 7"	$15
Plate, 9½"	$30
Plate, 10¼", 2-Handled	$25
Platter, 13¾"	$40
Relish, 5 Divisions, 13¾"	$45
Salt and Pepper Shakers (Common in Crystal—$10)	$125
Saucer	$7.50
Sherbet, 2 Styles	$22.50
Sugar with Cover	$50
Tumbler, 3½" Tall, 5 oz.	$100
Tumbler, 5" Tall, 10 oz., Footed	$35
Wineglass	$37.50

Windsor or Windsor Diamond
Jeannette Glass Company, 1936–1940s

The pressed diamond pattern is an allover one; that is, it covers most pieces from top to bottom. The basic colors are pink and green. For odd-colored pieces, including light blue, delphite blue, and yellow, double the prices below. For the rare red Amberina, quadruple them. As with most Depression glass, colored glass production ended with this pattern by 1940; however, pieces were still made in crystal (reduce the prices by 50 percent).

Ashtray	$50
Boat Dish, 11¾" Oval	$50
Bowl, 4¾"	$15
Bowl, 5"	$32.50
Bowl, 5½"	$30
Bowl, 7", 3-Footed	$35
Bowl, 8"	$60
Bowl, 8", 2-Handled	$40
Bowl, 8½"	$35
Bowl, 9", 2-Handled	$45
Bowl, 9½" Oval	$40
Bowl, 10½"	$45
Bowl, 10½", Pointed Edge	$150
Bowl, 12½"	$125
Butter Dish with Cover	$100
Cake Plate, 10¾", Footed	$35
Candlestick, 3" Tall	$45
Candy Jar with Cover	$75
Coaster	$22.50
Compote	$22.50
Creamer, 2 Styles	$20
Cup	$15
Pitcher, 1 pt., 4½" Tall (Common in Crystal—$30)	$150
Pitcher, 1½ qt., 6¾" Tall (Common in Crystal—$25)	$85
Plate, 6"	$10

Windsor Diamond Goblet. *Drawing by Mark Pickvet.*

Plate, 7"	$27.50
Plate, 9"	$30
Plate, 10", 2-Handled	$32.50
Plate, 10¼", 2-Handled	$25
Platter, 11½", Oval	$30
Platter, 13½"	$55
Powder Jar	$75
Relish, 3 Divisions (Common in Crystal—$17.50)	$250
Salt and Pepper Shakers	$60
Saucer	$7.50
Sherbet	$25
Sugar with Cover, 2 Styles	$40
Tray, 4" Square	$55
Tray, 4" Square, 2-Handled	$25
Tray, 9" Oval	$75
Tray, 9" Oval, 2-Handled	$25
Tray, 9¾" Oval (Common in Crystal—$17.50)	$100
Tray, 9¾" Oval, 2-Handled	$40
Tumbler, 3¼" Tall, 5 oz.	$35

Tumbler, 4" Tall, 9 oz.	$35
Tumbler, 4" Tall, Footed	$35
Tumbler, 4½" Tall, 11 oz.	$35
Tumbler, 5" Tall, 11 oz., Footed	$40
Tumbler, 5" Tall, 12 oz.	$55
Tumbler, 7¼" Tall, Footed	$65

– 7 –
MODERN AND MISCELLANEOUS
AMERICAN GLASS

At the turn of the 20th century, America was on a wave of growth fueled by invention, technology, industrialization, and the rise of powerful corporations. The glass industry was no exception. After the Depression, smaller companies were overtaken by larger, machine-production-oriented corporations. Colored glass production of the Depression era was drastically reduced for two primary reasons. One is that many of the elemental metals necessary for coloring were needed for World War II weapons manufacture. The other is that the Depression colors simply went out of style. Many glass manufacturers qualified as industry essentials and produced glass for the war effort. These included radar, X-ray, and electronic tubes as well as heat-treated tumblers manufactured specifically for extra strength.

After the war, big corporations such as Libbey (a division of Owens-Corning) and Anchor-Hocking emerged as industrial giants boasting high-speed machinery and huge-volume capacity. Handmade, hand-cut, hand-etched, and nearly all other operations done by hand that had squeaked through the Depression folded by the late 1950s. Such names as Pairpoint, Heisey, Cambridge, and many more shut down permanently. A few others, such as Fostoria, Imperial, and Westmoreland, survived into the 1980s, but many more were purchased and swallowed by larger firms; some continued operation as divisions of them (Hazel-Ware under Continental Can, for instance). Finally, there were a rare few such as Fenton and Steuben that survived the economic downswings and hard times of the marketplace. They have operated continuously since the early 20th century and continue to etch their mark in glassmaking history.

Despite the difficulties of many companies, a huge variety of collectible glassware has been produced in America since the Depression era. Colors were not totally eradicated, especially with Jeannette, which made several Depression look-alike patterns such as Anniversary. Darker colors such as forest green and royal ruby (Anchor-Hocking), and Moroccan amethyst (Hazel-Ware) were made into large table sets. Animal figures and covered animal dishes have been popular since the 19th century, and modern examples have been made by numerous companies (Heisey, New Martinsville, Fenton, Steuben, Viking, Degenhart, and Boyd, among others). Decorated enameled wares include not only animals but a host of other character figures. Swanky Swigs (a product of Kraft Cheese Spreads in which small tumblers filled with cheese spread were cleaned out, delabeled, and then used as drinking vessels), tumblers, pitchers, and a medley of other items with machine-applied enameling or transfers have flourished over the past 50 years.

As the Depression colors were phased out, a good deal of crystal, milk-glass, and porcelain-like items were produced afterward. Heisey, Cambridge, and Fostoria all made high-quality crystal table sets in the 1940s and 1950s. Fenton's Hobnail and Crest patterns along with Westmoreland's Paneled Grape were the largest sets ever produced in milk glass. Chinex, Fire-King, and a variety of others produced both oven- and tableware that resemble porcelain in a wide assortment of colors. Modern collectible glass includes many reproduction forms such as Imperial's New Carnival, other iridescent forms, carnival-like punch bowl and water sets, popular Depression patterns, Jeannette's miniature Cameo Ballerina, and others that at times can be confusing when compared with the originals. One company that has been controversial for making reproductions is the Indiana Glass Company. In the past few decades the company has reproduced a variety of items in the Sandwich pattern that originally date back to the early Depression years.

Naturally, the people most upset with reproductions are those who have invested or collected the originals, but part of it is caused by selfishness; after all, a company has a legal right to do what it wishes with its own patented lines and machinery. Reproductions give new collectors a chance at acquiring beautiful and appealing patterns. Hundreds of years from now, it will probably matter little whether a particular pattern was produced in the 1930s or 1970s. On the side of the collector, no one really wishes to see their collection devalued or harmed because of remakes. Some companies have responded and made their new pieces with slightly different dimensions in new molds or even with different colors. Exact reproductions with original molds can be confusing to buyers and sellers alike, especially if new pieces are advertised or sold unknowingly as antiques. It is still up in the air whether or not reproductions help or hamper the collector market. Some companies have had mixed results remaking certain styles and patterns of old.

A resurgence in glass and glass collecting has occurred in America in the past few decades. A host of new art-glass companies has surfaced, coupled with a few older ones, and this has resulted in a good deal of high-quality new glassware becoming available in the marketplace. Fenton continues to pour out fancy colored baskets; Steuben, the finest crystal; Pilgrim, a return to cameo-engraving; and such items as spun-glass Christmas ornaments are now available. New marble, novelty, and paperweight makers abound, too. There are also companies who that not involved directly in the manufacturing or production of glass but continue to commission glass lines and new products from various makers. Avon, for example, once commissioned Fostoria to make its own coin-glass items, French producers for their etched crystal Hummingbird dishes, and Wheaton for their ruby red Cape Cod tableware. Others such as Disney, Lenox, and the Franklin Mint have commissioned glassware from various artisans around the world.

The modern art studio glass movement began with Harvey Littleton, a professor of ceramics at the time with the University of Wisconsin. Littleton held a workshop at the Toledo Museum of Art in March 1962 and proved that art glass could be blown by independent artists in small studios. Soon afterward, dozens of independent artists took up the trade, and now hundreds of them have set up studios across the country.

None has been more successful than Dale Chihuly. Chihuly became the first American ever to be granted an apprenticeship with the Venini Glass Factory on the island of Murano near Venice. His creations reside at New York's Metropolitan Museum of Art, the Smithsonian, and in nearly 100 other museums worldwide. He is one of three American artists ever to have a solo show at the Louvre in Paris. Chihuly is noted most for monstrous, multicolored opalescent objects, including huge spheres, massive bowls, flamboyant sea forms, and so on. Individual pieces may command prices exceeding $75,000, and a multipiece work may go as high as $500,000. Some paperweight makers like Paul Stankard are nearing six figures for their works too.

Along with modern glassware, the remaining portion of this chapter also contains some miscellaneous older collectible glass items that do not fit well into the other categories. Some of these items are fruit or canning jars, marbles, insulators, Coca-Cola–embossed glass items, souvenirs, animal figurines, World's Fair glassware, and so on.

Akro Agate
Akro Agate Company, 1914–51

Akro Agate began as a marble manufacturer and quickly became America's leading maker of marbles. They expanded into novelties, children's miniature dishes, and other generally small items. The company made glass in solid, opaque, and transparent colors, but their most famous designs were the swirled or spiraled marblelike colors such as red onyx, blue onyx, and so on. The most common trademark used was a crow in flight clutching marbles within its claws.

Ashtray, Scallop Shell Shape, Marbleized Colors	$18.50
Ashtray, 2⅞" Square, Marbleized Colors	$10
Ashtray, 4", Round, 1931 Firemen's Convention, Solid Opaque Colors	$115
Ashtray, 4", Round, Hotel Edison or Hotel Lincoln, Solid Opaque Colors	$85
Ashtray, 4⅛" Across, Leaf Shape, Marbleized Colors	$17.50
Ashtray, 4½" Hexagonal, Marbleized Colors	$27.50
Ashtray, 5" Square, Marbleized Colors (Black $160)	$80
Ashtray, 5¼" Oval, Heinz 57 Varieties	$75
Basket, 4" Tall, 2-Handled, Marbleized Colors	$37.50
Basket, 5" Tall, 1-Handled, Marbleized Colors	$250
Bell, 5¼" Tall, Solid or Transparent Colors	$40

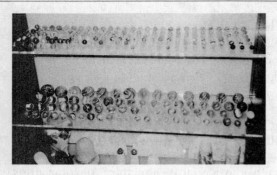

Akro Agate Marbles. *Photo by Robin Rainwater.*

Bell, 5¼" Tall, Marbleized Colors	$60
Bowl, 5¼", 3-Footed, Solid Colors	$17.50
Bowl, 5¼", 3-Footed, Marbleized Colors	$30
Bowl, 7¼", 2 Tab Handles, Solid Colors	$25
Bowl, 7¼", 2 Tab Handles, Marbleized Colors	$35
Bowl, 8", Stemmed, Solid Colors	$150
Bowl, 8", Stemmed, Marbleized Colors	$250
Candlestick, 1¾" Tall, Solid Colors	$100
Candlestick, 1¾" Tall, Marbleized Colors	$150
Candlestick, 4¼" Tall, Solid Colors	$150
Candlestick, 4¼" Tall, Marbleized Colors	$200
Children's Play Set, 8-Piece Concentric Ring Style (Teapot and Cover, Sugar and Creamer, 4 Saucers), Solid Colors (Transparent Cobalt Blue $215)	$185
Children's Play Set, 8-Piece Concentric Ring Style (Teapot and Cover, Sugar and Creamer, 4 Saucers), Marbleized Colors	$285
Children's Play Set, 16-Piece Concentric Ring Style (Teapot and Cover, Creamer and Sugar, 4 Cups, 4 Saucers, 4 Plates), Solid Colors (Transparent Cobalt Blue $500)	$275
Children's Play Set, 16-Piece Concentric Ring Style (Teapot and Cover, Creamer and Sugar, 4 Cups, 4 Saucers, 4 Plates), Marbleized Colors	$385
Children's Play Set, 21-Piece Concentric Ring Style (Teapot and Cover, Creamer and Covered Sugar, 4 Cups, 4 Saucers, 4 Cereal Bowls, 4 Plates), Solid Colors (Transparent Cobalt Blue $575)	$415

Children's Play Set, 21-Piece Concentric Ring Style (Teapot and Cover, Creamer and Covered Sugar, 4 Cups, 4 Saucers, 4 Cereal Bowls, 4 Plates), Marbleized Colors $550

Children's Play Set, 21-Piece Octagonal Style, Dark Green, Blue, or White (4 Plates, 4 Cups, 4 Saucers, Pitcher, 4 Tumblers, Teapot with Cover, Creamer, Sugar) $185

Children's Play Set, 21-Piece Octagonal Style, Lemonade or Ox Blood (4 Plates, 4 Cups, 4 Saucers, Pitcher, 4 Tumblers, Teapot with Cover, Creamer, Sugar) $575

Children's Play Set, 8-Piece Stacked Disc Style (Pitcher with Cover, 2 Cups, 2 Saucers, 2 Plates), Solid Green or White $65

Children's Play Set, 8-Piece Stacked Disc Style (Teapot with Cover, 2 Cups, 2 Saucers, 2 Plates), Solid Colors Other Than Green or White $85

Children's Play Set, 21-Piece Stacked Disc Style (Teapot with Cover, Creamer and Sugar, 4 Cups, 4 Saucers, 4 Plates, Pitcher, 4 Tumblers), Solid Green or White $135

Children's Play Set, 21-Piece Stacked Disc Style (Teapot with Cover, Creamer and Sugar, 4 Cups, 4 Saucers, 4 Plates, Pitcher, 4 Tumblers), Solid Colors Other Than Green or White $185

Children's Play Set, 8-Piece Stacked Disc and Interior Panel Design (Teapot with Cover, 2 Cups, 2 Saucers, 2 Plates), Solid Opaque Colors $160

Children's Play Set, 8-Piece Stacked Disc and Interior Panel Design (Teapot with Cover, 2 Cups, 2 Saucers, 2 Plates), Transparent Cobalt Blue $235

Children's Play Set, 21-Piece Stacked Disc and Interior Panel Design (Teapot with Cover, Creamer and Sugar, 4 Cups, 4 Saucers, 4 Plates, Pitcher, 4 Tumblers), Solid Opaque Colors $425

Children's Play Set, 21-Piece Stacked Disc and Interior Panel Design (Teapot with Cover, Creamer and Sugar, 4 Cups, 4 Saucers, 4 Plates, Pitcher, 4 Tumblers), Transparent Cobalt Blue or Transparent Green $525

Cup and Saucer, Demitasse, 2⅛" Tall, 4¼" Diameter, Solid Colors (Solid Orange or Black $135, Transparent Colors $215) $25

Cup and Saucer, Demitasse, 2⅛" Tall, 4¼" Diameter, Marbleized Colors $35

Flower Pot, 3" Tall, Smooth or Scalloped Top, Solid Colors $22.50

Flower Pot, 3" Tall, Smooth or Scalloped Top, Marbleized Colors $32.50

Jardiniere, 5" Tall, Scalloped or Rectangular Top, with or without Tab Handles, Solid Colors $35

Jardiniere, 5" Tall, Scalloped or Rectangular Top, with or without Tab Handles, Marbleized Colors $55

Marble, Glass, 1 Marble in 1⅛" Square Single Box $825

Marbles, Glass, 5-Piece Set with Original Box $27.50

Marbles, Glass, 10-Piece Set with Original Box $42.50

Marbles, Glass, 25-Piece Set with Original Box	$80
Marbles, Glass, 35-Piece Set with Original Box, Large Opaque Slags	$775
Marbles, Glass, 50–Piece Set with Original Box	$650
Marbles, Glass, 100-Piece Set with Original Box	$325
Marbles, Glass, 100-Piece Set with Original Box, Striped Onyx Marbles	$775
Marbles, Glass, Solitary Checker Set, 25-Piece	$80
Marbles, Glass, Chinese Checker Set, 36-Piece	$80
Marbles, Glass, 10-Piece Set with Popeye Pouch	$875
Marbles, Glass, 70-Piece Set in Tin with Pouch	$575
Puff Box, Apple Style (Includes Cover), Solid Colors (Crystal Only, $80)	$265
Puff Box with Colonial Lady Cover, Solid Colors	$75
Puff Box with Colonial Lady Cover, Transparent Colors	$1,000
Puff Box with Scottish Terrier Cover, Solid Colors	$85
Puff Box with Scottish Terrier Cover, Transparent Colors	$275
Smoker's Set, 4 Small Ashtrays and Cigarette Holder (Holder Resembles a Tumbler), Marbleized Colors	$85
Urn, 3¼" Tall, Square Foot, Marbleized Colors	$27.50
Vase, 3¼" Tall, Cornucopia, Marbleized Colors	$27.50
Vase, 6¼" Tall, Scalloped or Smooth Top, with or without Tab Handles, Solid Colors	$37.50
Vase, 6¼" Tall, Scalloped or Smooth Top, with or without Tab Handles, Marbleized Colors	$55
Vase, 8¾" Tall, Scalloped or Smooth Top, with or without Tab Handles, Solid Colors	$40
Vase, 8¾" Tall, Scalloped or Smooth Top, with or without Tab Handles, Marbleized Colors	$60

Anniversary
Jeannette Glass Company, 1947–49, 1960s–1970s

Pink and crystal Anniversary patterned glass is easily confused with Depression glass and the newer iridized pieces are confused with carnival glass; however, both were produced years later than the older periods. The prices below are for crystal Anniversary; for pink, double the prices. Iridized pieces sell for slightly more than the crystal prices—increase the prices by 25–35 percent. A few pieces were also trimmed in gold, for which prices should be increased by 25 percent.

Bowl, 4¾", Berry	$4
Bowl, 7½"	$10.50
Bowl, 9"	$13.50
Butter Dish with Cover	$32.50
Cake Plate, 12½"	$12.50
Cake Plate with Metal Cover	$25
Candlestick	$7.50
Candy Jar and Cover	$27.50
Compote, 3-Footed	$7.50
Creamer	$6
Cup	$5
Pickle Dish, 9"	$8
Plate, 6¼"	$2.50
Plate, 9"	$7.50
Platter, 12½"	$8
Relish Dish, 8"	$7.50
Relish Dish on Metal Base, 4 Divisions	$14
Saucer	$2
Sherbet	$6
Sugar with Cover	$12.50
Vase, 6½" Tall	$17.50
Wineglass, 2½ oz.	$12

Avon Glass Collectibles
1920s–Present

Though not a maker of glass products, Avon has commissioned hundreds of products as far back as 1886 (their first glass items appeared in the 1920s). Popular modern sets that are or were issued a piece at a time (two or three annually) include the abundant ruby red Cape Cod pattern made by Wheaton Glass Company and discontinued in 1997; the discontinued Hummingbird crystal pattern made in Austria, France, and some other European countries and discontinued in 1994; and even some coin glass and other glass products once produced by Fostoria.

Basket, Candle, Crystal with Gold Handle, Diamond Pattern, Fostoria	$17.50
Bell, 4¾" Tall, Crystal with Red Heart Handle	$17.50

Avon-Commissioned Fostoria Coin Glass. *Photo by Robin Rainwater.*

Bell, 5" Tall, Crystal Heart Handle and Heart Pattern, Fostoria	$17.50
Bell, 5¾" Tall, Etched Frosted Hummingbird Pattern	$25
Bell, 6½" Tall, Red, Cape Cod Pattern	$20
Bowl, Finger, Small (Held Bath Cubes), Red, Cape Cod Pattern	$15
Bowl, 5¼", Etched Frosted Hummingbird Pattern	$16
Bowl, 7½", Rim Soup, Red, Cape Cod Pattern	$30
Bowl, 8¾", Vegetable Soup, Red, Cape Cod Pattern	$35
Bowl, 8¾", Centennial Edition, Red, Cape Cod Pattern	$50
Butter Dish with Cover, 7" Long, ¼ lb. Size, Red, Cape Cod Pattern	$27.50
Cake Plate, 10¾" Diameter, Pedestal Foot, Red, Cape Cod Pattern	$65
Cake Plate, 12" Diameter, Footed, Etched Frosted Hummingbird Pattern	$40
Candleholder, 2⅝" Tall, Etched Frosted Hummingbird Pattern	$16
Candleholder, Hurricane, Red with Clear Chimney, Cape Cod Pattern	$40
Candleholder, 3¾" Diameter, Red, Cape Cod Pattern	$12.50
Candlestick, 3" Tall, Crystal with Holly Decoration	$12.50
Candlestick, 7" Tall, Crystal Heart Pattern, Fostoria	$17.50
Candlestick, 8¾" Tall, Red, Cape Cod Pattern	$17.50
Candlestick Cologne Bottle with Stopper, 5 oz., Red, Cape Cod Pattern	$12.50
Candlette, Turtle Figure (Shell Holds Candle), 4½" Long, Crystal Diamond Pattern	$12.50

Candy Dish, 3½" Tall, 6" Diameter, Red, Cape Cod Pattern — $25

Candy Dish with Cover, 6" Tall, Etched Frosted Hummingbird Pattern — $40

Canning Jar Replica, Blue Glass with Glass Lid and Wire Bail, Pressed Sunburst (Aztec) Pattern — $8.50

Champagne Glass, 5¼" Tall, 8 oz., Red, Cape Cod Pattern — $20

Champagne Glass, 9" Tall, Etched Frosted Hummingbird Pattern — $18.50

Chess Set, 3 oz. Amber Bottles, 6-Piece Set (King, Queen, Rook, Bishop, Knight, and Pawn) — $110

Chess Set, 16 Dark Amber and 16 Light Amber 3 oz. Bottles with Silver-Plated Chess Piece Tops (Complete 32-Piece Set) — $450

Christmas Ornament, 3¼" Across, Hexagon, Red with Plaid Cloth Bow, Cape Cod Pattern — $12.50

Christmas Ornament, 3½" Tall, Etched Frosted Hummingbird Pattern — $12.50

Claret Glass, 5¼" Tall, 5 oz., Red, Cape Cod Pattern — $17.50

Cold Cream Box with Silver Color, Rose Brand, Milk White, Early 1930s — $55

Compote, 4" Tall, Crystal with Holly Decoration — $15

Condiment Tray, Small, Red, Cape Cod Pattern — $15

Creamer, 3½" Tall, Red, Cape Cod Pattern — $17.50

Cruet with Stopper, 5 oz., Red, Cape Cod Pattern — $17.50

Cup, 3½" Tall, Red, Cape Cod Pattern — $15

Cup, 3½" Tall, Red, Cape Cod Pattern, 15th Anniversary — $20

Cup, Loving, No Handle, 6⅞" Tall, Crystal Heart Pattern, Fostoria — $20

Decanter, Miniature with Stopper, 5 oz. Bath Oil, Milk White, Hobnail Design, 1972 — $10

Decanter, Wine, with Stopper, 10½" Tall, 16 oz. (Held Bubble Bath), Red, Cape Cod Pattern — $27.50

Goblet, 8⅛" Tall, Blue with Frosted George Washington Medallion, Fostoria Coin Glass — $20

Goblet, 8⅛" Tall, Blue with Frosted Martha Washington Medallion, Fostoria Coin Glass — $20

Goblet, 8¼" Tall, Etched Frosted Hummingbird Pattern — $18.50

Goblet, Water, with Candle, 9 oz., Red, Cape Cod Pattern — $17.50

Harvester, Amber, 1973 — $8

Heart Box with Cover, 4" Across, Red, Cape Cod Pattern — $20

Mug, 5" Tall, Footed, Red, Cape Cod Pattern — $15

Napkin Ring, 1½" Long, Red, Cape Cod pattern — $15

Picture Frame, Dad's Pride and Joy, Fostoria Crystal, 1982 — $10

Pie Plate, 10¾", Red, Cape Cod Pattern — $35

Pitcher, Miniature Grecian, 5 oz. Bath Oil, Milk White, 1972 — $7.50

Pitcher, Sauce, 5½" Tall, Blue with Frosted Mount Vernon Medallion, Fostoria Coin Glass — $25

Pitcher, Milk, 8" Tall, Etched Frosted Hummingbird Pattern — $35

Pitcher, Water, 8¼" Tall, Red, Cape Cod Pattern — $65

Plate, 7½", Etched Frosted Hummingbird Pattern — $16

Plate, Dessert, 7½", Red, Cape Cod Pattern — $15

Plate, Dinner, 11", Red, Cape Cod Pattern — $30

Platter, Round, 11", Crystal with Holly and Berry Design — $17.50

Platter, Round, 12½", Etched Frosted Hummingbird Pattern — $45

Platter, 13" Oval, Red, Cape Cod Pattern — $50

Powder Box, 3 oz. "Nearness Body," Satin with Blue Speckled Lid, 1956 — $17.50

Powder Sachet, 1½ oz. Cranberry with Silver Cover, 1969 — $12.50

Salt and Pepper Shakers, Red, Cape Cod Pattern — $20

Salt and Pepper Shakers with Stainless Steel Tops, 3" Tall, Etched Frosted Hummingbird Pattern — $27.50

Saltcellar, 4 Feet, Crystal with Matching Silver Spoon, Fostoria — $12.50

Sauce Boat, 8" Long, 1 Handle, Pouring Lip, Red, Cape Cod Pattern — $40

Saucer, 5¾", Red, Cape Cod Pattern — $10

Sugar, 3½" Tall, Red, Cape Cod Pattern — $17.50

Tidbit Tray, 2-Tiered, 9¾" Tall with 7" and 10" Plates, Red, Cape Cod Pattern — $65

Tumbler, 3¾" Tall, Footed, Red, Cape Cod Pattern — $15

Tumbler, 5½" Tall, Red, Cape Cod Pattern — $20

Vase, Grape Bud, 6 oz. Bath Oil, Amethyst, 1973 — $7.50

Vase, 5" Tall, Crystal, Heart Shape, Fostoria — $12.50

Vase, 7½" Tall, Thick, Etched Frosted Hummingbird Pattern — $45

Vase, 8" Tall, Red, Cape Cod Pattern — $30

Vase, Bud, 9½" Tall, Etched Frosted Hummingbird Pattern — $30

Wineglass with Candle, 4½" Tall, Red, Cape Cod Pattern	$15
Wineglass, 6¼" Tall, Etched Frosted Hummingbird Pattern	$18.50

Beaded Edge
Westmoreland Glass Company, Late 1930s–1950s

The original name of this pattern is Westmoreland's Pattern #22 Milk Glass. Beaded Edge is a nickname given to it by collectors. The coral-red color was named by Westmoreland and is simply milk glass with a fired-on red edge. Decorated patterns include eight different fruits as well as eight different flowers for a total of 16 decorated patterns. Westmoreland also made a few pieces in a similar pattern referred to as #108. The prices are for opaque white or milk glass; double them for any coral-red or decorated pieces.

Bowl, 5"	$8
Bowl, 6" Oval	$10
Creamer	$13.50
Creamer with Cover	$21.50
Cup	$7.50
Plate, 6"	$7.50
Plate, 7" or 8½"	$10
Plate, 10½"	$21
Plate, 15", Cake	$37.50
Platter, 12", Oval with 2 Handle Tabs	$40
Relish Dish, 3-Part	$40
Salt and Pepper Shakers	$35
Saucer	$3.50
Sherbet	$10
Sugar	$13.50
Sugar with Cover	$21.50
Tumbler	$12.50

Bicentennial/Patriotic Glass
Various Companies, 20th Century

Many glass companies such as Fenton and Indiana produced souvenir items for America's Bicentennial. Stars and Stripes was a patriotic pattern much like souvenir glass created by

Anchor-Hocking during World War II. Stars and Stripes was adapted from the old Hocking Glass Company Queen Mary molds.

Bell, Patriot Cameo Embossed Design, 1974–76, Chocolate, Patriot Red, or Independence Blue Carnival Colors (Fenton)	$60
Compote with Cover, Bald Eagle Finial, Jefferson Memorial Design, 1974–76, Chocolate Color, Limited Edition of 3,600 (Fenton)	$275
Compote with Cover, Bald Eagle Finial, Jefferson Memorial Design, 1974–76, Independence Blue Carnival Color, Limited Edition of 7,600 (Fenton)	$225
Compote with Cover, Bald Eagle Finial, Jefferson Memorial Design, 1974–76, Patriot Red Color, Limited Edition of 3,600 (Fenton)	$275
Fruit Jar, Ball Ideal, Clear with Various Bicentennial Scenes on Reverse, 1 pt.	$4
Fruit Jar, Ball Ideal, Clear with Various Bicentennial Scenes on Reverse, 1 qt.	$5
Paperweight, Bald Eagle Design with Circle Base; Chocolate, Patriot Red, or Independence Blue Carnival Colors, 1974–76 (Fenton)	$60
Planter, Patriot Cameo Embossed Design, 1974–76, Valley Forge Milk White or Independence Blue Carnival Colors (Fenton)	$60
Plate, Bald Eagle Design, Chocolate or Patriot Red Colors, 1974–76 (Fenton)	$85
Plate, 8", Stars and Stripes Pattern, Crystal, 1942 (Anchor-Hocking)	$20
Plate, Iridized or Marigold Carnival, Various Scenes, Indiana Glass, 1976	$10
Platter, 15", Milk Glass with Multicolored Enameled American Eagle	$55
Sherbet, Stars and Stripes Pattern, Crystal, 1942 (Anchor-Hocking)	$25
Stein, No Lid, Valley Forge Design, Chocolate or Patriot Red Colors, 1974–76 (Fenton)	$85
Swanky Swig Tumbler, Bicentennial Issue (1975–76) in Green, Red, and Yellow, Small, 3¾" Tall	$8.50
Tumbler, 5", 10 oz., Stars and Stripes Pattern, Crystal, 1942 (Anchor-Hocking)	$45

Blenko Glass Company
1922–Present

This company was founded by English immigrant William J. Blenko in 1922. He began as a hand-producer of stained-glass windows, but the company later switched to more contemporary art forms. Characteristic of the company are bright vibrant colors and some art styles such as crackling, bubbling, and unique shapes.

Apple, 2½" Tall, Ruby Red with Applied Crystal Stem	$20
Ashtray, 6½" Diameter, Blue, Bubble Effect	$12.50

Benko Glass. *Photo by Robin Rainwater.*

Ashtray, 7" Diameter, Green, Hinged Clamshell Design	$12.50
Ball, Hollow, 5" Diameter, Ruby Red	$35
Basket, 8¾" Tall, Cobalt Blue	$25
Bowl, Rose, 5½" Tall, Cobalt Blue	$15
Bowl, Rose, 7¾" Tall, Pale Emerald Green	$17.50
Candlestick, Green with Crystal Twist Stem	$40
Champagne Bucket, 11¾" Tall, Top Handle, Opaline Yellow	$25
Compote, 7½" Tall, 9¾" Diameter, Opaline Yellow or Cobalt Blue	$25
Decanter, Ship's, 10" Tall, Green with Crystal Stopper	$37.50
Decanter with Stopper, 13" Tall, Ruby Red	$85
Fish, 10" Tall, Globe Shape, Fin Feet, Large Mouth Opening, Crystal	$37.50
Fish, 16" Long, Fin Feet, Large Mouth Opening, Opaline Yellow	$45
Fish, 22" Long, Fin Feet, Large Mouth Opening, Cobalt Blue	$60
Goblet, Flattened Knob on Stem, Cobalt Blue	$30
Hat Vase, 7½" Tall, 16" Diameter, Crystal with Yellow Band	$40
Highball Glass, Crystal with Green Foot	$20
Penguin, 9½" Tall, Sapphire Blue Cased in Crystal	$37.50
Penguin, 14" Tall, Sapphire Blue Cased in Crystal	$47.50
Pitcher, Milk, 5½" Tall, 32 oz., Green Crackle Design	$22.50
Pitcher, Water, Deep Blue, Bubble Effect	$35

Pitcher, Water, 14" Tall, Ruby Red	$75
Plate, 9", Ruby Red	$17.50
Plate, 12", Crimped, Blue	$25
Platter, 13½" Circular, Circles, Xs, and Squares	$17.50
Punch Bowl, 11" Tall, Aquamarine on Crystal Stand	$185
Punch Cup, Crystal with Ruby Red Handle	$12.50
Sherbet, 6" Tall, Ruby with Crystal Twist Stem	$30
Tumbler, 7" Tall, Ruby Red Crackle Glass	$10
Tumbler, Iced Tea, Footed, Dark Amethyst	$17.50
Vase, 7½" Tall, Flared, Amber	$17.50
Vase, 7½" Tall, 7" Diameter, Opaline Yellow	$30
Vase, 11" Tall, Ruffled, Crystal with Circular Blue Lines	$35
Vase, 11½" Tall, Flared, Footed, Amber with Optic Ribbing	$60
Vase, 14½" Tall, Cylindrical, Pale Emerald Green	$25
Vase, 22" Tall, 11½" Diameter Top, Crystal	$45
Vase, 24" Tall, Tapered Neck at Top, Cobalt Blue	$50

Boyd Art Glass
1978–Present

Boyd began in 1978 by purchasing a factory formerly run by Degenhart. The firm changes trademarks every five years; nevertheless, most resemble a *B* within a diamond (it is usually the lines around the diamond that are changed). The pieces are all miniatures, and colors come in satins, slags, iridescent, and swirls, among others. After a certain production run, the colors are generally retired periodically for each piece. For the most part, common colors run about $8 to $10 per animal or figurine (a little more for additional enameling).

Airplane, Black Carnival	$21.50
Angel, Cobalt Blue	$25
Basket, 4½" Tall, Olde Lyme (Forest Green)	$14
Bear, Fuzzy, Cambridge Blue	$11.50
Bear, Patrick Balloon, Carmel	$11.50
Bear, Patrick Balloon, Enchantment	$28
Bear, Patrick Balloon, Spinnaker Blue	$12.50
Bell, Owl Head Finial, Translucent, White Opal	$14

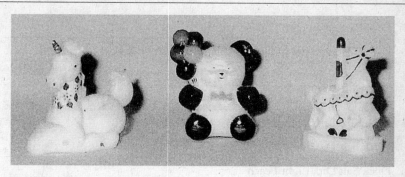

Boyd Glass. *Photo by Robin Rainwater.*

Bunny, Brian, Oxford Gray	$13.50
Bunny, Brian, Ruby Red	$22.50
Bunny, Brian, Vaseline	$13.50
Bunny Salt Dip, Blue	$25
Bunny Salt Dip, Peridot	$30
Bunny Salt Dip, Sunburst	$17.50
Butterfly, Katie, Light Windsor Blue	$11.50
Candy Dish with Cover, Persimmon	$14
Car, Tucker Model, Buckeye	$14
Car Slipper, Platinum Carnival	$20
Cat, Kitten, Miss Cotton, Light Windsor Blue	$10.50
Chick, Bermuda, 1"	$17.50
Chick, Enchantment, 1"	$9.50
Chick, John's Surprise, 1"	$28.50
Chick, Royalty, 1"	$85
Clown, Freddie Hobo, Cobalt Blue Carnival	$12.50
Deer, Bingo, Heliotrope (Very Dark Brown)	$12.50
Dog, Bull Dog's Head, Golden Delight (Amber)	$10
Dog, Parlour Pup #1, Mulberry Mist (Light Lilac)	$10
Dog, Parlour Pup #2, Milk-White Opal	$10

Dog, Parlour Pup #3, Carmel	$10
Dog, Parlour Pup #4, Bermuda Slag (Reddish Brown)	$10
Dog, Pooch, Wintergreen Slage	$40
Doll, Elizabeth, Black Satin	$12.50
Doll, Elizabeth, Lime Carnival	$37.50
Duck Salt Dip, Dove Blue	$12.50
Duck Salt Dip, Light Peach	$10
Duck, Debbie, Shasta White (Light Tan)	$10
Duckling, Shasta White (Light Tan)	$8
Elephant, Zack, Autumn or Ebony	$60
Elephant, Zack, Cobalt Blue or Flame	$50
Elephant, Zack, Furr Green or Peacock Blue	$28
Frog, Jeremy, Green Bouquet	$15
Hen, 3", Carmine	$70
Hen, 3", Pink Champagne	$35
Hen, 5", Ruby Gold	$65
Hen Covered Dish, 5" Long, Shasta White (Light Tan)	$16
Honey Jar with Cover, Lemonade (Vaseline)	$18.50
Horse, Carousel, Candy, Black, or Blue Slag	$15
Horse, Joey, Chocolate	$45
Horse, Joey, December Swirl or Heatherbloom or Rubina	$75
Horse, Joey, Zack Boyd Slag	$15
Jewel Box, Cornsilk	$13.50
Jewel Box, Sam Jones Slag	$45
Kitten with Pillow, Apricot	$25
Kitten with Pillow, Royalty	$27.50
Lamb Covered Dish, 5" Long, Golden Delight (Amber)	$14.50
Lamb Salt Dip, Lime Carnival	$12.50
Mouse, Willie, Lime Carnival	$12.50
Owl, Mulberry Mist (Light Lilac)	$12.50
Penguin, Artie, Black Carnival	$15
Pig, Suee, Shasta White (Light Tan)	$10

Robin Covered Dish, 5" Long, Golden Delight (Amber)	$13.50
Skate Boot, Heather	$15
Slipper Cat, Orange Calico	$13.50
Squirrel, Sammie, Shasta White (Light Tan)	$10
Squirrel, Sammie, Teal	$15
Swan, 3" Long, Azure Blue	$10
Tomahawk, Milk White	$16.50
Toothpick Holder, Forget-Me-Not, Carmine	$42.50
Toothpick Holder, Forget-Me-Not, Teal Swirl	$13.50
Toothpick Holder, Heart, Mint Green	$27.50
Train, 6-Piece, Teal	$75
Train, 6-Piece, Yellow Engine, Baby Blue Coal Car, Dark Cobalt Blue Boxcar, Candyland Coal Hopper, Bamboo Tank Car, and Ruby Red Caboose	$60
Tucker Car, Cobalt Blue	$12.50
Tugboat, Teddy, Peridot Green	$11
Turkey Covered Dish, 5" Long, Shasta White (Light Tan)	$13.50
Turtle, Alexandrite	$10
Unicorn, Lucky, Mulberry Carnival	$11
Vase, Candy Swirl	$16
Vase, Dark Tangerine Slag	$20
Vase, 6" Tall, Beaded, Lilac	$17.50
Woodchuck, Touch of Pink	$9

Bubble or Bull's-Eye or Provincial
Anchor-Hocking Glass Company, 1940–65

The prices below are for the basic colors of forest green, royal ruby, jadeite, and pink. Light, ice blue pieces are scarce—increase the prices by 25–35 percent; for crystal, reduce them by 50 percent.

Bowl, 4"	$18.50
Bowl, 4½"	$11
Bowl, 5"	$12.50
Bowl, 5½"	$14
Bowl, 7¾"	$16

Bowl, 8½"	$20
Bowl, 9" (Rare—Blue Only—$425)	
Candlestick	$25
Cocktail Glass, 3½–5 oz., Various Styles	$12.50
Creamer	$17.50
Cup (Rare in Pink—$125)	$7.50
Goblet, 9–10 oz.	$15
Goblet, More Than 10 oz.	$17.50
Lamp, Several Styles (Crystal Only—$60)	
Pitcher, Water, 1 qt.	$80
Plate, 6¾" (Rare in Green—$20)	$4
Plate, 9½"	$20
Plate, 9½" Grill (Divided)	$25
Platter, 12" Oval	$18
Saucer (Rare in Pink—$50)	$3
Sherbet, 6 oz.	$11
Sugar	$17.50
Tidbit, 2-Tier	$75
Tumbler, 5 or 6 oz.	$8.50
Tumbler, 3¼" Tall, 8 oz.	$12.50
Tumbler, 3¾" Tall, 9 oz.	$12.50
Tumbler, 4½" Tall, 12 oz.	$15
Tumbler, 5⅞" Tall, 16 oz.	$17.50
Tumbler, 5⅞" Tall, 16 oz., Footed	$20
Wineglass	$12.50

Cambridge Animals
1920s–1958

Cambridge was a large producer of crystal dinnerware, especially stemware. The quality of their crystal was quite good, and they survived the Depression by making many color products as well. The firm actually began in 1901. After some good, profitable years in the immediate post–World War II era, Cambridge eventually had trouble competing with cheaper products that assailed the market. The wildlife recreations here are just some of

Cambridge's collectible glassware. Imperial purchased many of the company's molds when Cambridge closed in 1958. Also note that some of the Cambridge animal molds were acquired by the Summit Art Glass Company in the 1980s—some have been reproduced.

Blue Jay Flower Holder, 5½" Tall, Crystal	$125
Blue Jay Flower Holder, 5½" Tall, Green	$375
Blue Jay Flower Holder, 5½" Tall, Moonlight Blue	$225
Buffalo Hunt Console, Mystic Blue	$375
Dog (Bridge Hound), 1½", Variety of Colors	$45
Eagle Bookend	$140
Eagle Flower Frog, 5½" Tall, Crystal	$300
Eagle Flower Frog, 5½" Tall, Pink	$400
Heron, 9", Flower Frog (Small)	$150
Heron, 12", Flower Frog (Large)	$160
Heron and Cattails Cocktail Shaker, 10" Tall, Cobalt Blue with Sterling Silver Cover	$110
Lion Bookend	$160
Pigeon, Pouter, Bookend	$110
Scottish Terrier, Frosted	$110
Scottish Terrier Bookend	$135
Sea Gull Flower Frog	$80
Swan Candlestick, 4½" Tall, Milk White	$240
Swan, 3½" Long, Amber	$100
Swan, 3½" Long, Carmen	$160
Swan, 3½" Long, Crown Tuscan	$70
Swan, 3½" Long, Crystal	$35
Swan, 3½" Long, Ebony	$100
Swan, 3½" Long, Emerald Green	$75
Swan, 3½" Long, Forest Green	$200
Swan, 3½" Long, Milk White	$135
Swan, 3½" Long, Milk White with Gold Trim	$160
Swan, 3½" Long, Peach	$75
Swan, 3½" Long, Pink	$75
Swan, 3½" Long, Royal Blue	$130

Swan, 3½" Long, Smoke or Transparent Gray	$415
Swan, 3½" Long, Yellow (Mandarin Gold)	$75
Swan, 4½" Long, Milk White	$155
Swan, 4½" Long, Ebony, Signed	$135
Swan, 6½" Long, Crystal	$80
Swan, 6½" Long, Carmen or Red	$340
Swan, 6½" Long, Ebony	$175
Swan, 6½" Long, Emerald or Forest Green	$110
Swan, 6½" Long, Milk White	$225
Swan, 6½" Long, Yellow (Mandarin Gold)	$175
Swan, 7" Long, Crystal, Signed	$40
Swan, 8½" Long, Amber	$515
Swan, 8½" Long, Blue (Rare)	$1,250
Swan, 8½" Long, Carmen or Red	$365
Swan, 8½" Long, Crown Tuscan, Variety of Colors	$185
Swan, 8½" Long, Crown Tuscan, Opalescent White with Enameled Floral Design	$785
Swan, 8½" Long, Crystal	$90
Swan, 8½" Long, Ebony	$185
Swan, 8½" Long, Emerald or Forest Green	$175
Swan, 8½" Long, Milk White	$315
Swan, 10½" Long, Ebony	$300
Swan, 10½" Long, Pink	$400
Swan, 12½" Long, Amber	$115
Swan, 12½" Long, Ebony	$365
Swan, 13", Ruby Red with Amber Shading	$200
Turkey Dish with Cover, Blue	$560
Turkey Dish with Cover, Green	$515
Turkey Dish with Cover, Pink	$465
Turtle-Shaped Flower Frog, 5½" Long, Crystal	$185
Turtle-Shaped Flower Frog, 5½" Long, Opaque Pink	$360

Cameo Miniatures
Mosser Glass, Inc., 1980s–Present

The original Cameo was made in full scale during the Depression era. Those pieces listed here are miniature reproductions made in yellow, pink, and green; the prices are the same for all colors. The pattern is a little weaker on the small versions, but they are still very pretty, especially when an entire set is acquired. Thanks to their tiny size, there is no problem whatsoever distinguishing them from the originals. Remember that this version of Cameo is also referred to as Ballerina or Dancing Girl since that is what is pictured in medallion form.

Bowl, Cereal, 2¹¹⁄₁₆"	$5.50
Bowl, Salad, 4³⁄₁₆", 1" Tall	$8.50
Bowl, Soup, 4½"	$6.50
Bowl, Fruit, 5½", 3-Footed, 1½" Tall	$12.50
Bowl, Serving, 5" Oval (including 2 Tab Handles) ⅞" Tall	$11
Butter Dish with Cover, 2¼" Tall, 3½" Underplate Diameter, 2⅝" Dome Diameter	$12.50
Cake Plate, 5" Diameter, 3 Feet, ⅝" Tall	$12.50
Candlestick, 2" Tall	$7.50
Cracker Jar with Cover, 3¾" Tall	$17.50
Creamer, 1¹¹⁄₁₆" Tall	$7.50
Creamer, 2¼" Tall	$7.50
Cup, 1⅛" Tall	$3.50
Goblet, 3" Tall	$6.50
Ice Cream Bucket, 1½" Tall, 2⅝" Diameter, 2 Tab Handles	$11
Jam Jar with Cover, 2½" Tall, 3" Bottom Diameter	$12.50
Mayonnaise Dish, 1⅝" Tall, Stemmed, 2¾" Top Diameter	$8.50
Mayonnaise Jar with Cover, 2½" Tall, 3" Bottom Diameter	$12.50
Parfait, 2⅝" Tall, Round Foot	$5.50
Pitcher, Milk, 3" Tall, Slim	$8.50
Pitcher, Water, 3" Tall, Wide	$12.50
Plate, Dessert, 3¹⁄₁₆"	$3.50
Plate, Octagonal, 4³⁄₁₆" Across	$5.50
Plate, 4¾"	$6.50
Plate, Grill, 5¼"	$6.50

Cameo Miniatures. *Photo by Robin Rainwater.*

Relish Dish, 3¹¹⁄₁₆" Diameter, 2 Tab Handles, ⅞" Tall	$8.50
Saucer, 3"	$3.50
Sherbet, 1⅝" Tall	$4.50
Sugar Dish, 2-Handled, 1⁵⁄₁₆" Tall	$6.50
Sugar, 2-Handled	$7.50
Tray, 5⅞" Oval (Including 2 Tab Handles)	$11
Tumbler, Water, 1¹³⁄₁₆" Tall	$3.50
Vase, 4⅛" Tall	$15

Candlewick
Imperial Glass Company, 1936–82

This is a huge set that was made continuously from the 1930s until Imperial closed for good in 1982. Candlewick is unmarked except for paper labels that are naturally removed; however, it is easily identified by beaded crystal stems, handles, and rims. The name of the pattern comes from pioneer women because the basic design resembles tufted needlework. The majority of Candlewick was made in crystal; however, some limited color pieces were made as well. For ruby red, cobalt blue, and black, double the prices below. For other colors such as light blue, yellow, milk glass, and so on, increase them by 35–50 percent.

Ashtray, 2¾"	$10
Ashtray, 3¼" Square	$45
Ashtray, 4" Round	$12.50
Ashtray, 4¼" x 3" Rectangular	$6

Ashtray, 4½" Heart Design	$15
Ashtray, 4½" Oblong	$12.50
Ashtray, 4½" Square	$47.50
Ashtray, 5" Round	$12.50
Ashtray, 5½" or 6½", Heart Design	$25
Ashtray, 5¾" Square	$55
Ashtray, 6", Matchbook Holder in Center	$175
Ashtray, 6½", Eagle Design	$65
Banana Boat, 10" Oblong	$1,500
Basket, 5" Tall, Beaded Handle	$275
Basket, 6½" Tall	$50
Basket, 11" Tall, Beaded Handle	$300
Bell, 4" Tall	$75
Bell, 5" Tall	$85
Bowl, Bouillon, 2-Handled	$55
Bowl, 3" Finger, with or without Foot	$40
Bowl, 4½" Nappy, 3-Footed	$85
Bowl, 4¾", 2-Handled	$20
Bowl, 5" Fruit (Shallow)	$20
Bowl, 5" Soup (Deep)	$50
Bowl, 5" Across, Heart Shape, 1 Handle	$25
Bowl, 5" Square	$100
Bowl, 5½"	$40
Bowl, 5½" Across, Heart Shape	$27.50
Bowl, 6" (Deep)	$27.50
Bowl, 6" Fruit (Shallow)	$20
Bowl, 6" Across, Heart Shape, 1 Handle	$30
Bowl, 6" Square	$125
Bowl, 6", 3-Footed	$65
Bowl, 6½", Rolled Edge	$30
Bowl, 7"	$25

Bowl, 7", 2 Handles	$25
Bowl, 7" Square	$150
Bowl, 8"	$40
Bowl, 8½"	$40
Bowl, 8½", Divided, 2 Handles	$75
Bowl, 8½", 3-Footed	$140
Bowl, 9"	$50
Bowl, 9", Footed, Crimped Edge	$150
Bowl, 9" Across, Heart Shape	$140
Bowl, 9" Across, Heart Shape, 1 Handle	$180
Bowl, 10"	$55
Bowl, 10", Flared, Fluted, Footed	$225
Bowl, 10", 2 Handles	$150
Bowl, 10", 3-Footed	$175
Bowl, 10½"	$55
Bowl, 11", Flared	$80
Bowl, 11" Oval	$250
Bowl, 12"	$60
Bowl, 12", 2-Handled	$175
Bowl, 13"	$65
Bowl, 14"	$95
Bowl, 14" Oval, Flared	$250
Bowl, Rose, 7½", Footed	$160
Brandy Glass	$35
Bunny on Nest Dish, Blue Satin	$75
Butter Dish with Cover, 5½" Round	$40
Butter Dish with Cover, ¼ lb. Size	$35
Cake Stand, 10", Low Foot	$65
Cake Stand, 11", High Foot	$80
Calendar Desk, 1947 Edition	$250
Candleholder, 3½" Tall	$25

Candleholder, 4½" Tall, 3-Footed	$85
Candleholder, 5" Tall, Heart Design	$75
Candleholder, 6" Tall, Urn Shape	$125
Candleholder, 2-Light, 4" Tall	$55
Candy Box with Cover, 5½" Diameter	$175
Candy Box with Cover, 6½" Diameter	$250
Candy Box with Cover, 7" Diameter	$175
Candy Box with Cover, 7" Diameter, 3 Divisions	$225
Celery Dish, 11" Oval	$75
Champagne Glass, 6 oz., Various Styles	$40
Cigarette Box with Cover	$42.50
Claret Glass, 5 oz., Various Styles.	$50
Clock, 4", Circular	$335
Coaster, 4"	$17.50
Cocktail Glass, 4 oz., Various Styles.	$25
Compote, 4½", Plain Stem	$40
Compote, 5", 2-Beaded Stem	$85
Compote, 5½", Plain Stem	$25
Compote, 5½", 4-Beaded Stem	$35
Compote, 8", Beaded Stem	$110
Compote, 9", Beaded Stem	$135
Compote, Large Oval, Footed	$1250
Cordial, 1–1½ oz., Various Styles	$40
Creamer, Individual (Small)	$12.50
Creamer, Footed	$15
Creamer, Domed Feet	$150
Cruet with Stopper, 4 oz., Various Styles	$65
Cruet with Stopper, 6 oz., Various Styles	$75
Cruet with Stopper, Etched "Oil" or "Vinegar"	$85
Cup, Various Styles	$12.50
Decanter with Stopper, 11½" Tall, 26 oz.	$3,505

Egg Cup	$52.50
Egg Plate, 12", Center Handle	$175
Fork, Large Serving	$27.50
Goblet, Footed, 9 oz.	$22.50
Goblet, Footed, 10 oz.	$25
Goblet, Footed, 11 oz.	$27.50
Goblet, Footed, 12 oz.	$30
Gravy Boat with Underplate	$225
Hurricane Lamp, 2-Piece, Candle Base	$200
Hurricane Lamp, 3-Piece	$250
Ice Tub, 5½" x 8", 2 Handles	$200
Ice Tub, 7", 2 Handles	$250
Jars, Nesting, 3 Together	$425
Jelly Dish with Cover, 5½"	$85
Knife, Butter	$350
Ladle, Mayonnaise or Marmalade	$15
Marmalade Set, 3-Piece (Jar, Lid, and Ladle)	$75
Mayonnaise Set, 4-Piece (Plate, Divided Bowl, 2 Ladles)	$85
Mirror, Standing, 4½" Diameter	$150
Mustard Jar with Cover and Spoon	$65
Nut Cup	$15
Perfume Bottle with Stopper	$55
Pickle Dish, 7½" Oval	$27.50
Pitcher, Low Foot, Small, 14–16 oz.	$265
Pitcher, 20 oz.	$260
Pitcher, 40 oz.	$75
Pitcher, 64 oz.	$85
Pitcher, 80 oz.	$265
Plate, 4½"	$8
Plate, 5½", 2 Handles	$12.50
Plate, 6"	$9

Plate, 6", Off-Center Indentation	$17.50
Plate, 6¾", Crimped, 2-Handled	$27.50
Plate, 7"	$10
Plate, 7½", 2 Handles	$17.50
Plate, 7½" Triangular	$110
Plate, 8"	$11
Plate, 8" with Indentation	$15
Plate, 8" Oval	$25
Plate, 8¼" Crescent	$60
Plate, 8½"	$15
Plate, 8½", 2-Handled	$20
Plate, 9"	$15
Plate, 9" Oval	$20
Plate, 9" Oval, Indentation	$35
Plate, 10", 2 Tab Handles, Various Styles	$30
Plate, 10½"	$45
Plate, 12", 2 Handles, Various Styles	$35
Plate, 12½" Oval	$85
Plate, 12½" Torte, Cupped Edge	$65
Plate, 14", Birthday Cake Design—Holes for 72 Candles	$575
Platter, 13" Oval	$125
Platter, 13½", Cupped Edge	$70
Platter, 14" Round	$125
Platter, 14", Torte, 2-Handled	$65
Platter, 16" Oval	$250
Platter, 17"	$110
Punch Bowl with Matching Underplate	$300
Punch Cup	$17.50
Punch Ladle	$37.50
Relish Dish, 6 to 6½", 2 Divisions	$27.50
Relish Dish, 8½", 4 Divisions	$37.50

Relish Dish, 10½", 3 Divisions, 3-Footed	$115
Relish Dish, 13½", 5 Divisions	$100
Relish Dish, 6 Divisions	$85
Salt and Pepper Shakers, Chrome Tops, Beaded Foot	$25
Salt Dip, 2" or 2¼"	$12
Sandwich Server with Heart Center Handle, 8½"	$45
Sandwich Server, 11¾", Center Handle (Ruby Red $800)	$55
Saucer	$7.50
Sherbet, 5 oz.	$25
Sherbet, 6 oz.	$27.50
Spoon, Large Serving	$27.50
Sugar, Individual (Small)	$12.50
Sugar Dish, Footed	$30
Tidbit, 3-Piece, 2-Tier	$200
Tray, 4½" (for Salt and Pepper Shakers)	$20
Tray, 5½", 2 Upturned Handles	$26
Tray, 5½", Center Handle	$30
Tray, 6½"	$22.50
Tray, 8½", 2 Handles	$32.50
Tray, 9" Oval, Beaded Foot	$35
Tray, 9¼" x 5¼" Rectangular	$55
Tray, 14", 2 Handles	$60
Tumbler, 3 to 4 oz., Various Styles	$22.50
Tumbler, 4½ to 5 oz., Various Styles	$24
Tumbler, 6 oz., Various Styles	$25
Tumbler, 7 oz., Various Styles	$27.50
Tumbler, 9 oz., Footed	$30
Tumbler, 10 oz.	$32.50
Tumbler, 12 oz.	$45
Tumbler, 14 oz.	$30
Tumbler, 16 oz.	$80
Vase, Bud, 4" Tall	$60

Vase, Bud, 5¾" Tall	$65
Vase, 6" Tall	$35
Vase, 6" Tall, Flared Rim	$125
Vase, Bud, 7" Tall	$225
Vase, 8" Tall, Crimped	$75
Vase, 8" Tall, Fan Style, Beaded Handles	$45
Vase, 8½" Tall, Beaded Foot	$100
Vase, 8½" Tall, Flared, Beaded Foot	$225
Vase, 10" Tall, Footed	$200
Wineglass, 3½–5½ oz., Various Styles	$27.50

Canning Jars
1830s–Present

Although canning or fruit jars have been made in the millions for well over a century now, there exist many off-brands and rare colors from the 19th and early 20th centuries that are quite valuable today. Nearly all jars have mold-embossed writing and/or designs. Where a color is not designated below, the jar is clear glass. Also, assume that the top is threaded for a zinc or brass screw-on cap unless "Glass Cover" or "Glass Lid" is indicated.

AD & H Chambers Union Fruit Jar, Blue, Wax Sealer, 1 qt.	$175
A. G. Smalley & Co., Boston & New York, ½ pt.	$18
Acme, Ground Lip Glass, Emerald Green, 1 qt.	$325
Acme LG Co., 1893, ½ gal.	$325
Agee or Agee Victory, Light Green or Amber, 1 qt.	$50
Amazon Swift Seal, Blue, 1 qt.	$12.50
Amazon Swift Seal, Blue, 2 qt.	$17.50
American Eagle & Flag Design, Light Green, 1 qt.	$175
Anchor-Hocking, Embossed Anchor Logo, 1 qt.	$2
Atlas, E-Z Seal, Amber, Glass Cover, 1 qt.	$60
Atlas, E-Z Seal, Apple Green, 1 qt.	$30
Atlas, E-Z Seal, Aqua, Glass Cover, 1 pt.	$37.50
Atlas Good Luck, Clear, Clover Design, 1 qt.	$4
Atlas Strong Shoulder Mason, Aqua, 1 pt.	$6
Atlas Strong Shoulder Mason, Glass Cover, Light Blue or Olive Green, 1 qt.	$27.50

Canning Jars. *Photo by Robin Rainwater.*

Automatic Sealer, Aqua, 1 qt.	$225
Ball Eclipse, Clear, 1 pt.	$6
Ball Ideal, Blue, ½ pt.	$37.50
Ball Ideal, Clear with Various Bicentennial Scenes on Reverse, 1 pt.	$3.50
Ball Ideal, Clear with Various Bicentennial Scenes on Reverse, 1 qt.	$5
Ball Mason, Olive Green, 1 pt.	$40
Ball Perfect Mason, Amber, 2 qt.	$85
Ball Perfect Mason, Blue, Zinc Cover, 1 qt.	$15
Ball Perfect Mason, Dark Olive Green, 1 pt.	$75
Ball Perfect Mason, Emerald Green, 2 qt.	$125
Ball Sanitary Sure Seal, Blue, 1 qt.	$9
Banner, Widemouth, ½ pt.	$50
Banner, Widemouth, Blue, ½ pt.	$85
Banner, Blue, 1 qt.	$12.50
Beaver, Embossed Name and Animal, 1 qt.	$30
Beaver, Embossed Name and Animal, Aqua or Blue, 1 qt.	$90
Beaver, Embossed Name and Animal, Olive Green or Amber, ½ gal.	$850
Best, Amber, Glass Lid, 1 qt.	$200
Boyds, Light Green or Aqua, 1 qt.	$5
Brockway Sur-Grip Mason, Clear, 1 qt.	$5

Buckeye, Aqua, 2 qt.	$175
Burlington, 1 qt.	$62.50
C. F. Spencer's Patent, Rochester, N.Y., Aqua, 1 qt.	$155
Calcutt's, Glass Lid, 2 qt.	$40
Canton Domestic, 1 pt.	$175
Canton Domestic, 1 qt.	$100
Canton, Cobalt Blue, 1870–90, 2 qt.	$5,000
Carter's Butter and Fruit Preserving, Glass Lid, 1897	$165
Champion, Aqua, Pat. Aug. 31, 1869, 1 qt.	$200
Clark's Peerless, Cornflower Blue or Emerald Green, 1 pt.	$75
Clarke, Aqua, Glass Lid, 2 qt.	$75
Coronet with Embossed Crown, 1 qt.	$165
Dandy, Glass Lid, Aqua, 1 qt.	$15
Dolittle, Clear or Aqua, 1 pt.	$50
Double Safety, Clear, ½ pt.	$10
Double Safety, Clear, 2 qt.	$5
Drey Square Mason, Clear, 1 qt.	$10
Eagle, Aqua, 1 qt.	$165
Eclipse, Light Green, 1 qt. (Rare in Amber $1,500)	$150
Electric, Embossed World Globe, Aqua, 1 qt.	$165
Empire, Wing Nut Screw Glass Lid, Aqua, 1 qt. (without Original Lid $275)	$1,150
Erie Lightning, Amethyst, 1 qt.	$100
Eureka, Glass Lid, Aqua, ½ pt.	$35
Everlasting, Aqua, 1 pt.	$50
Everlasting, Aqua, 1 qt.	$40
Excelsior, Aqua, 1 qt.	$75
Fearman's Mincemeat, Amber, 1 qt.	$100
Flaccus Brothers, Embossed Steer, 1 pt.	$125
Flaccus Brothers, Milk Glass, Stag's Head, 1 pt.	$500
Forrest City, Amber, 1 qt.	$125
Forster, Clear, 1 qt.	$20

Franklin Dexter, Aqua, 2 qt.	$75
Gem, Aqua, 1 qt.	$10
Gem, Aqua, 2 qt.	$15
Globe, Wire Closure, Amber, 1 pt. (Rare in Black Amethyst $3,250)	$75
Globe, Wire Closure, Amber, 1 qt.	$100
Globe, Wire Closure, Aqua, 1 qt.	$30
Globe, Wire Closure, Aqua, 2 qt.	$50
Green Mountain CA Co., Aqua, 1 pt.	$15
Haines Patent March 1st 1870, Aqua, 1 qt.	$185
Hamilton Glass Works, Aqua, 1 qt.	$275
Hazel Atlas E-Z Seal, Aqua, 1 pt.	$12.50
Hazel Preserve Jar, Clear, ½ pt.	$50
Helmen's Railroad Mills, Amber, 1 pt.	$75
Hero, Aqua, Glass Cover, 1 pt.	$50
Ideal Imperial, Aqua, 1 pt.	$75
Ideal Imperial, Aqua, 1 qt.	$30
Improved Jam, 2 qt.	$150
Independent, Light Amethyst, 1 qt.	$65
J. M. Clark & Co., Round Shoulder, Green, 1 qt.	$125
Kerr Self-Sealing, Mason, Clear, ½ pt.	$2.50
King, Clear, Banner and Crow Design, 1 pt.	$17.50
L & W, Aqua, 1 qt.	$75
Lafayette, Embossed Portrait, Aqua, 1 pt.	$225
Lafayette, Embossed Portrait, Aqua, ½ gal.	$175
Lightning, Glass Cover, Amber, or Blue, 2 qt.	$85
Lightning, Aqua, 2 qt.	$55
Lightning, Glass Cover, Aqua, 2 qt.	$85
Magic Fruit Jar, Amber, Star Design, 1 qt.	$1,150
Mason, 1858 Trademark, Aqua, 2 qt.	$160
Mason, 3 gal.	$650
Mason, Pat. Nov. 30th, 1858, 1 pt.	$12.50
Mason, Pat. Nov. 30th, 1858, Dark Aqua	$37.50

Mason, Pat. Nov. 30th, 1858, Reverse Cross, Amber, 2 qt.	$150
McDonald's New Perfect Seal, Blue, 1 pt.	$10
Millville Atmospheric, Glass Lid, Aqua, 1 qt.	$50
National, Patented June 27, 1876, 1 pt.	$12.50
Owl, Milk Glass, 1 pt.	$150
Pet, Aqua 1 qt.	$50
Premium, Glass Lid, 1 pt.	$25
Queen, Glass Lid, 1 pt.	$15
Queen Wide Mouth, Square Shape, Glass Lid, 1 pt.	$17.50
Quick Seal, Blue, 1 qt.	$3.50
Royal, Clear, 1 qt.	$7.50
Royal, 1876, Glass Cover, Light Amethyst, 1 qt.	$250
Safety with Glass Cover, Aqua, 2 qt.	$45
Schram Automatic Sealer, Flag, 1 pt.	$15
Sealfast, Glass Cover, 1 qt.	$125
Smalley, Glass Cover, 1 pt. or 1 qt.	$10
Star Glass Co., Aqua, 1 qt. (Cobalt Blue $525)	$55
Swayzee's Improved Mason, Dark Olive, 2 qt.	$75
TM Lightning Reg US Patent Office, Aqua, 1 qt.	$4
Union, Beaver Falls Glass Co., Aqua 2 qt.	$40
Victory, Aqua, 1 qt.	$55
Whitney Mason, Pat'd 1858, Aqua, 1 pt.	$15
Wilcox, Aqua 1 qt.	$100
Woodbury Improved, Aqua, 1 qt.	$65
Worcester, Aqua, 1 qt.	$175
Yeoman's, Waxed Cork Closure, Aqua, 1 qt.	$55

Capri
Hazel Ware, Division of Continental Can, 1960s
The color is listed by Hazel Ware as capri, azure blue, or simply blue. It is a light coppery blue and is a sister pattern of Moroccan Amethyst; that is, many of the pieces are identical in shape in both patterns (only the color differs).

Ashtray, 3¼" Triangular	$7.50
Ashtray, 3¼" Round	$7.50
Ashtray, 3½", Square	$17.50
Ashtray, 6⅞" Triangular	$15
Bowl, 4¾" Octagonal	$8.50
Bowl, 4¾" Swirled	$7.50
Bowl, 5⅜" Round	$10
Bowl, 5¾", Square	$12.50
Bowl, 6", Various Styles	$15
Bowl, 7¾" Oval	$17.50
Bowl, 7¾" Rectangular	$17.50
Bowl, 8¾" Swirled	$20
Bowl, 9" to 9½"	$25
Bowl, 10¾"	$30
Candy Jar with Cover, Footed	$37.50
Chip and Dip Set, 2 Bowls (4¾" and 8¾") with Metal Rack	$37.50
Creamer	$12.50
Cup	$6.50
Cup, Octagonal	$7.50
Goblet, Water, 5½" Tall	$11
Plate, 5¾" Octagonal	$6.50
Plate, 7⅛", Various Styles	$8.50
Plate, 7¼" Octagonal	$9
Plate, 8" Square, with or without Indentation for Cup	$11
Plate, 9" Square, with or without Indentation for Cup	$12.50
Plate, 9½", with Indentation for Cup	$12.50
Plate, 9¾" Octagonal	$12.50
Plate, 9⅞"	$12.50
Plate, 10", with or without Indentation for Cup	$12.50
Saucer, 5½" Square	$2.50
Saucer, 6"	$2.50
Saucer, 6" Octagonal	$3

Sherbet, 4½"	$10
Sugar with Cover	$22.50
Tidbit Set, 3-Tier, Includes 2 Plates (7⅛" and 9⅞") and Round Saucer	$26
Tumbler, 2¾", 4 oz.	$7.50
Tumbler, 3", 4 oz.	$7.50
Tumbler, 3", 5 oz., Pentagon Bottom	$8.50
Tumbler, 3¼", 8 oz.	$9
Tumbler, 4¼", 9 oz., 2 Styles	$10
Tumbler, 5", 12 oz., 2 Styles	$11.50
Tumbler, 6", 10 oz.	$12
Vase, 8½"	$40
Wineglass, 5½"	$11

Century
Fostoria Glass Company, 1950–82

Century is also known or referred to as Fostoria's #2630 Line. Note that the preserve dish is very similar to the candy dish except that it is an inch shorter in height. This is a fairly simple crystal pattern—clear pieces with a ruffled edging. Some are trimmed in silver (same price). A few have been discovered in color—increase the prices for those by 25–35 percent.

Ashtray, 2¾"	$11
Basket with Wicker Handle, 10¼"	$75
Bowl, 4½" with Handle	$14
Bowl, 5"	$15
Bowl, 6"	$25
Bowl, 6¼", Footed	$17.50
Bowl, 7⅛", Triangular, 3-Footed	$18.50
Bowl, 7¼", 3-Footed	$20
Bowl, 8", Flared	$26
Bowl, 8½"	$27.50
Bowl, 9"	$31.50
Bowl, 9½" Oval	$35
Bowl, 9½", with Handles	$36

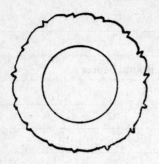

Century Pattern Plate by Fostoria. *Drawing by Mark Pickvet.*

Bowl, 10" Oval, with Handles	$37.50
Bowl, 10½"	$35
Bowl, 10¾", Flared, Footed	$42.50
Bowl, 11", Rolled Edge, Footed	$45
Bowl, 11¼"	$40
Bowl, 12", Flared	$45
Butter Dish with Cover, Rectangular (¼ lb.)	$42.50
Cake Plate, 10", with Handles	$25
Candlestick, 4½"	$20
Candlestick, 7", Double	$35
Candlestick, 7¾", Triple	$45
Candy Jar with Cover, 7"	$42.50
Comport, 2¾"	$17.50
Comport, 4⅜"	$22.50
Cracker Plate, 10¾"	$35
Creamer, 4¼"	$11
Creamer, Individual (Small)	$10
Cruet Bottle with Stopper, 5 oz.	$50
Cup, 6 oz., Footed	$15
Ice Bucket with Metal Handle	$75

Mayonnaise, 3-Piece Set	$35
Mayonnaise, 4-Piece Set (Includes 2 Ladles)	$40
Mustard with Spoon and Cover	$30
Pickle Dish, 8¾" Across	$17.50
Pitcher, 6⅛", 16 oz.	$65
Pitcher, 7⅛", 48 oz.	$115
Plate, 6½"	$7.50
Plate, 7½"	$10
Plate, 7½" Crescent	$40
Plate, 8" with Indentation for Cup	$30
Plate, 8½"	$15
Plate, 9½"	$30
Plate, 10½"	$35
Plate, 14" Cake or Torte	$35
Platter, 12"	$52.50
Preserve with Cover, 6"	$40
Relish, 7⅜", 2-Part	$17.50
Relish, 11⅛", 3-Part	$27.50
Salt and Pepper Shakers, 2⅜" or 3⅛" (2 Styles)	$25
Salt and Pepper Shakers, Individual (Small, 2⅜")	$17.50
Salver, 12¼", Footed	$60
Saucer	$4
Stemware, 3½ oz., 4⅛" Tall	$22.50
Stemware, 3½ oz., 4½" Tall	$27.50
Stemware, 4½ oz., 3¾" Tall	$25
Stemware, 5½ oz., 4½" Tall (Sherbet)	$15
Stemware, 10 oz., 5¾" Tall	$25
Sugar, 4", Footed	$11
Sugar, Individual (Small)	$10
Tidbit, 8⅛", 3-Footed	$20
Tidbit, 10¼", 2-Tier with Metal Handle	$27.50

Tray, 4¼" for Individual Salt and Pepper Shakers	$16
Tray, 7⅛" for Individual Creamer and Sugar Set	$17.50
Tray, 9⅛" with Handles	$27.50
Tray, 9½" with Handles	$32.50
Tray, 11" with Center Handle	$35
Tumbler, 4¾" Tall, 5 oz.	$25
Tumbler, 5⅞" Tall, 12 oz.	$30
Vase, 6"	$20
Vase or Urn, 7½" Tall, with Handles	$75
Vase, 8½" Tall, Oval	$75

Character Glass
Various Producers, 1930s–Present

The term *character glass* is a broad one and refers to pieces that have cartoon and comic book characters, movie stars, and others etched, enameled, or transferred to them, or pieces that might contain fired-on decals. In 1937 Libbey won a contract with Walt Disney to produce tumblers with Snow White and the Seven Dwarfs. The movie was a smash hit, and eight separate tumblers with a picture of each little character enameled upon the surface were filled with cottage cheese and shipped to thousands of dairies across the country. The immense popularity of the "character" tumbler had its beginning here. Other food items included cheese spreads (see listings under "Swanky Swigs"), jams and jellies, and others. Since the 1970s, fast-food restaurants, often with the backing of the soft-drink industry, have promoted decorated tumblers far more than any other medium. See the section on Disney Glass Collectibles as well for additional listings. Note that prices are for a single glass (not the set!).

Actors Series Tumblers (Abbott & Costello, Charlie Chaplin, Laurel & Hardy, Little Rascals, Mae West, or W. C. Fields), Arby's, 1979	$8
Actors Series Tumblers (Jack Albertson, Monty Hall, Teddy Kollack, Jan Murray, Mary Tyler Moore, or Don Rickles), Coca-Cola, 1970s	$15
B. C. Comic Tumblers (Anteater, B. C., Broad, Grog, Thor, or Wiley), Arby's, 1981	$9
Bald Eagle Tumbler, Endangered Species, Burger Chef	$9
Batman Tumblers, 1976 Moon Super Series, 12 Styles	$35
Bullwinkle Tumblers, Ward Collector Series (More Than 20 Styles), Pepsi, 1960s–1970s	$20
California Raisins Tumbler, 12 oz., 1989	$5
Care Bears Mug, Days of the Week, American Greetings	$7.50

Welch's Jelly Character Tumblers. *Photo by Robin Rainwater.*

Care Bears Tumblers (Cheer Bear, Friends Bear, Funshine Bear, Good Luck Bear, Grumpy Bear, or Tenderheart Bear), Pizza Hut, 1983 $15

Alvin and the Chipmunks Tumblers (Alvin, Chipettes, Simon, or Theodore), Hardee's, 1985 $7.50

Clara Peller Tumbler, Where's the Beef? Wendy's $7.50

Dr. Seuss Jelly Tumblers, Several Styles, Welch's, 1997 $2

Endangered Species Series Jelly Tumblers, 12 Styles in All (Panda, Cheetah, Elephant, etc.), Welch's, 1990s $2

Flintstones Kids' Tumblers (Barney, Betty, Fred, or Wilma), Pizza Hut, 1986 $5

Garfield Mugs, 4 Styles, McDonald's, 1987 $4.50

Garfield Tumblers, 4 Styles, McDonald's, 1987 $4.50

Ghostbusters Tumblers, Sunoco, 6 Styles $7.50

Great Muppet Caper Tumblers, 4 Styles, McDonald's, 1981 $4

Hanna Barbera Collector Series Tumblers (Dynomutt, The Flintstones, Huckleberry Hound & Yogi Bear, Josie and the Pussycats, Mumbly, or Scooby Do), Pepsi, 1977 $17.50

Happy Days Tumblers (Fonzie, Richie, Joanie, Ralph, Potsie, or Cunninghams), Pizza Hut/Dr. Pepper $15

Holly Hobbie Tumbler on Parade, Coca-Cola $20

Kelloggs Cartoon Tumblers, 7 Styles (Dig Um, Tony the Tiger, Tony Jr., Toucan Sam, or Snap! Crackle! Pop!), 1977 $12.50

King Kong Tumbler, Burger Chef/Coca-Cola, 1976 $10

Masters of the Universe Tumblers, 6 Styles, 1980s $12.50

McDonaldland Action Series Tumblers, 12 Styles, 1977	$10
Mother's Pizza Tumblers, Coca-Cola, 6 Styles	$10
Muppets Tumblers, The Great Muppet Caper, 4 Styles, 1981	$6
Muppets Jelly Tumblers, Several Styles, Welch's, 1998	$2
Noid Tumblers, 5 Styles, Domino's Pizza, 1988	$4.50
Pac Man Series Tumblers, 11 Styles, Bally, 1980	$7.50
Peanuts Tumblers, 8 Styles, Dolly Madison, 1980s	$10
Peanuts Tumblers, 6 Styles, McDonald's, 1983	$8
Pokemon Jelly Tumblers, Several Styles, Welch's, 1998 and Up	$2
Popeye Tumblers, 8 Styles, Original 1936 Series	$75
Popeye Kollect-a-Set Tumblers, 6 Styles, Burger King/Coca-Cola, 1975	$10
Shirley Temple Bowl, Cobalt Blue with White Figure	$50
Shirley Temple Creamer, Cobalt Blue with White Figure, 1930s	$45
Shirley Temple Mug, Cobalt Blue with White Figure, 1930s	$50
Shirley Temple Pitcher, 9 oz., Cobalt Blue with White Figure, 1930s	$75
Shirley Temple Plate, Cobalt Blue with White Figure, 1930s (Rare)	$350
Shirley Temple Sugar, Cobalt Blue with White Figure, 1930s	$55
Sloth & Goonies Tumbler, Godfather's Pizza, 1985	$6.50
Smurfs' Tumblers, 14 Styles, Hardee's, 1982–1983	$8.50
Star Trek The Motion Picture Tumblers, 3 Styles, Coca-Cola, 1980	$37.50
Star Trek Tumblers, 4 Styles, Dr. Pepper, 1978	$75
Star Trek Tumblers, Cartoon Series Characters (4 Styles), Dr. Pepper, 1976	$65
Star Trek III: The Search for Spock Tumblers (4 Styles), Taco Bell, 1984	$15
Star Wars Return of the Jedi Tumblers (4 Styles), Burger King/Coca-Cola, 1983	$20
Star Wars The Empire Strikes Back Tumblers (4 Styles), Burger King/Coca-Cola, 1980	$20
Star Wars Tumblers (4 Styles), Burger King/Coca-Cola, 1977	$30
Superheroes Cartoon Series Tumblers (More Than 30 Styles), Pepsi, 1976–1979	$20
Superman The Movie Tumblers (6 Styles), Pepsi, 1978	$10
Tom & Jerry Jelly Tumblers, Several Styles, Welch's, 1992	$2.50
Tom & Jerry Tumblers, Several Styles, Pepsi, 1975	$15

Under Dog Series Tumblers (Under Dog, Sweet Polly, or Simon Bar Sinister), Pepsi, 1970s
$25

Universal Studios Monster Tumblers (Creature from the Black Lagoon, Dracula, Frankenstein, Mummy, Mutant, or Wolfman), 1980 $20

Urchins Tumblers (6 Styles), Coca-Cola, 1976 $8.50

Walter Lantz Cartoon Collector Series Tumblers (16 Styles—Andy Panda, Chilly Willy, Woody Woodpecker, etc.), Pepsi, 1977 $21

Warner Brothers Collector Series Tumblers (More Than 30 Styles—Bugs Bunny, Porky Pig, Speedy Gonzales, Elmer Fudd, Daffy Duck, Coyote, Roadrunner, etc.), Pepsi, 1973
$15

Warner Brothers Interaction Series Tumblers (More Than 25 Styles—All Major Characters), Pepsi, 1976 (Special Run Characters $20) $15

Warner Brothers Looney Tunes Collector Series Tumblers (13 Styles), Pepsi, 1979 and 1980
$12.50

Warner Brothers Tumblers (16 Styles), Welch's, 1974 and 1976 $12.50

Wizard of Oz Tumblers (18 Styles), Swift's Peanut Butter, 1950 $22.50

Wizard of Oz Land of Oz Tumblers (5 Styles), Kentucky Fried Chicken, 1984 $20

Ziggy Tumblers (4 Styles), 7-Up, 1977 $6

Ziggy Tumblers (4 Styles), Hardee's or Pizza Inn, 1979 $7.50

Chihuly, Dale
1964–Present

Dale Chihuly has gained a reputation as America's greatest glass artist of the later half of the 20th century and of the new millennium. Chihuly works out of a 25,000-square-foot glass studio in Seattle called the "Boat House"—a house in the shape of a boat. Since losing an eye in a 1976 auto accident, he has been unable to blow his own pieces, but he directs a team of artists and is responsible for most of the designs that come out of his studio. His creations reside at more than 100 museums worldwide. He is one of three American artists ever to have a solo show at the Louvre in Paris. Chihuly is noted most for monstrous, multicolored opalescent objects, including huge spheres, massive bowls, flamboyant sea forms, and so on. Individual pieces may command prices exceeding $75,000, and a multipiece work may go as high as $500,000 (a massive seashell, for instance, filled with dozens of smaller shells).

Basket Set, 1 Large 14" Undertray with 6 Smaller Baskets (4" to 10") Enclosed Within, and 1 Hollow Ball, Opalescent Swirled Orange Design with Black Trim $45,000

Basket Set, 1 Large 18" Oblong Basket with 6 Smaller Baskets (4" to 8") Enclosed Within, Opalescent Swirled Cranberry Design $65,000

Bowl, 18" Across, 12½" Tall Tapering Down to 8½", Ruffled Shell Design, Opalescent Red Shaded to Amber $10,000

Seaform, 1 Massive Shell 20" x 12" Oblong with 14 Smaller Seashells (2" to 6" Long Each), Bright Opalescent Cadmium Yellow with Red Lip Wraps, Swirled Rib Design $225,000

Seashell, 16" Across, 7½" Tall, Opalescent Honeysuckle Blue, Fish-Scale Ribs, Yellow Lip Wraps $12,500

Sphere, Hollow, 24" Diameter, Opalescent Peach with Brown Splotches $15,000

Stalk, 36" Tall, Lime Opal with Opalescent Orange Coils and Swirled Cobalt Blue and Opalescent Amethyst Floral Designs $55,000

Vase, 10½" Tall, 8" Across, Ruffled, Violet Macchia Lined Design with Red Lip Wrap $10,000

Chintz
Fostoria Glass Company, 1940s–1970s

This crystal allover floral pattern is another typical of the post-Depression period. Where it differs from many patterns is that many pieces are quite rare and desirable, and, therefore, very valuable. Chintz was also known as Fostoria's #338 Line.

Bell	$150
Bonbon Dish, 7½", Footed	$37.50
Bowl, 4½"	$75
Bowl, 4½" with 3 Corners	$35
Bowl, 5"	$35
Bowl, 5" with Handle	$35
Bowl, 7½"	$40
Bowl, 8½" with Handles	$80
Bowl, 9¼", Footed	$325
Bowl, 9½"	$85
Bowl, 9½" Oval	$225
Bowl, 10" with Handles	$75
Bowl, 10½" with Handles	$85
Bowl, 11½" Flared	$75
Bowl, #6023 Line (Large), Centerpiece, Footed	$75
Candlestick, 3½" Tall, Double	$37.50
Candlestick, 4" Tall	$25

Candlestick, 5" Tall	$40
Candlestick, 6" Tall, Triple	$60
Candlestick, Double, #6023 Line (Large)	$55
Candy Dish with Cover, 3-Part	$155
Celery Dish, 11" Oval	$55
Champagne Glass, 5½" Tall, 6 oz.	$26
Claret Glass, 5½" Tall, 4½" oz.	$45
Cocktail Glass, 3½" Tall, 4 oz.	$31
Cocktail Glass, 5" Tall, 4 oz.	$30
Cordial, 4" Tall, 1 oz.	$52.50
Compote, 3¼"	$37.50
Compote, 4¾"	$40
Compote, 5½"	$45
Creamer, Individual, 3⅛" Tall, 4 oz. (Small)	$25
Creamer, 3¾", Footed (Large)	$30
Cruet with Stopper, 5½" Tall, 3½ oz.	$125
Cup, Footed	$25
Goblet, 6¼" Tall, 9 oz.	$35
Goblet, 7½" Tall, 9 oz.	$40
Ice Bucket with Metal Handle	$150
Jelly Dish with Cover, 7½"	$100
Mayonnaise Set, 3-Piece, 3½" Holder with Matching Underplate and Ladle	$75
Pickle Dish, 8" Oval	$40
Pitcher, 9¾" Tall, 1½ qt., Footed	$425
Plate, 6"	$16
Plate, 7½"	$21
Plate, 8½"	$30
Plate, 9½"	$60
Plate, 10½" Cake, with Handles	$60
Plate, 11"	$55
Plate, 14" with Upturned Edge	$65
Plate, 16" Cake	$150

Platter, 12" Oval	$115
Platter, 17½", with Upturned Edge	$200
Relish, 6", Square, 2-Part	$45
Relish, 10", Oval, 3-Part	$55
Relish, 5-Part	$65
Salad Dressing Bottle with Stopper, 6½" Tall, 7 oz.	$400
Salt and Pepper Shakers, 2¾" Tall	$110
Sauce Boat, Oval	$85
Sauce Boat, Oval, Divided	$85
Sauce Boat Liner, 8" Oblong	$35
Saucer	$10
Sherbet, 4½" Tall	$25
Sugar, Individual, 2⅞" Tall, 2 Handles (Small)	$25
Sugar, 3½", Footed, 2 Handles (Large)	$30
Syrup, Sani-Cut (with Metal Tab on Pouring Spout)	$450
Tidbit, 8¼" with Upturned Edge, 3-Footed	$45
Tray, 6½" for Individual Creamer and Sugar Set, 2 Tab Handles	$35
Tray, 11" with Center Handle	$55
Tumbler, 5 oz., 4¾" Tall, Footed	$30
Tumbler, 9 oz.	$32.50
Tumbler, 13 oz., 6" Tall, Footed	$35
Vase, 5" (2 Styles)	$100
Vase, 6", Footed	$125
Vase, 7½", Footed	$210
Wineglass	$25

Christmas Candy
Indiana Glass Company, 1940s–1950s

Christmas Candy is sometimes referred to as the No. 624 pattern in Indiana's advertisements. The terrace-green color, which is very desirable, was also referred to as Seafoam by Indiana; others simply refer to it as teal. Crystal Christmas Candy is not all that desirable; reduce the prices shown here by 75 percent for plain crystal.

Bowl, 5¾"	$25
Bowl, 7⅜"	$52.50
Bowl, 9½"	$600
Creamer	$37.50
Cup	$37.50
Mayonnaise or Gravy Bowl with Glass Ladle	$250
Plate, 6"	$15
Plate, 8¼"	$30
Plate, 9½"	$52.50
Plate, 11¼"	$70
Saucer	$12.50
Sugar	$37.50
Tidbit, 2-Tier	$150

Coca-Cola Glass Collectibles
Various Companies, 1886–Present

Coca-Cola was first produced in Atlanta in 1886 and since then has become a major American icon. Just having the patented Coca-Cola or Coke trademarks will often double or triple the price of ordinary collectible items. Naturally, the most popular medium for Coca-Cola glass items are bottles. Over the past five or six decades, well over 1,000 commemorative Coca-Cola bottles have been issued. They have themes such as music legends, presidents, sports stars and coaches, commemorative events such as centennials, and so forth. A few, like the Ty Cobb 1983 Georgia Peach bottle and the Jimmy Carter 1976 bottle, already sell in excess of $100. Nineteenth-century and early-20th-century colored bottles are rare and valuable, too, and also sell for more than $100. An important note is that newer bottles should be full and sealed; if not, their value is reduced by as much as 50 percent.

Ashtray, 4" x 2", Elongated Octagon Shape, 2 Tab Handles, Yellow Glass, Embossed Coca-Cola, Akro Agate, 1930s	$1,000
Ashtray, 4" x 2", Elongated Octagon Shape, No Handles, Pink Glass, Embossed Coca-Cola, Akro Agate, 1930s	$1,000
Ashtray, Crystal with Red Enameled Coca-Cola	$27.50
Bottle, Jimmy Carter, 39th President	$140
Bottle, Green, Christmas, 1923	$30
Bottle, Clemson, 1981 National Football Champions	$10

Coca-Cola Bottle. *Photo by Robin Rainwater.*

Bottle, Cleveland, Ohio, Amber	$60
Bottle, Ty Cobb, the Georgia Peach, 1983	$325
Bottle, Crimson Tide, Bear Bryant, 9½" Tall	$17.50
Bottle, Johnny Lee Steakhouse, 1986	$52.50
Bottle, Macon, Georgia, 1918	$35
Bottle, North Carolina Tarheels National Basketball Champions, 1982	$12.50
Bottle, 75th Anniversary, Amber, 1961	$22.50
Bottle, Wal-Mart 25th Anniversary, 1962–87	$22.50
Bottle, 20" Tall, Light Green Glass with White Coca-Cola, Plastic Bottle Cap (Decoration)	$62.50
Cracker Jar with Metal Lid, 3 qt., Clear with Molded Coca-Cola Script and Bottle, 1990s	$15
Hutchinson Bottle Replica with Glass Stopper, 7" Tall, Light Green Tint, Embossed "Property of Coca Cola Bottling Co."	$20
Hutchinson Bottle Replica with Glass Stopper, 20" Tall, Light Green Tint, Embossed "Property of Coca Cola Bottling Co."	$75
Lamp, 19" Tall, Brass Base and Stem, 37½" Diameter Stained Glass (Burgundy, Cream, and Green Marbles), Coca Cola in White, Electric	$225
Paperweight, 2¼" Diameter, Ruby Red Glass Bottle Cap Design, "Cool Cap" Heirloom Edition, Limited of 1,000, Year 2000, Caithness of Scotland	$100
Paperweight, 3" Diameter, Globe Shape, Multicolored Inner Swirls, "Always Coca-Cola" Icon, Heirloom Edition, Limited Edition of 1,000, Year 2000, Caithness of Scotland	$250

Paperweight, 4" Tall, 3" Diameter, Bell-Shape Soda Glass Design, "Fountain Memories" Heirloom Edition, Limited Edition of 750, Year 2000, Caithness of Scotland, Crystal with Brown Glass Interior $200

Paperweight, 4" Tall, Oval Egg Shape, 3-D Coca-Cola and Bottle Design, Red and Clear "American Dream" Heirloom Edition, Limited Edition of 350, Year 2000 $250

Pitcher, Syrup, Metal Lid, Clear with White Coca-Cola $215

Pitcher, Water, Green, Dallas Cowboys Football $55

Pitcher, Water, 70 oz., Replica Mold-Embossed Contour Design "Coca Cola," Georgia Green Glass, Year 2000 $15

Plate, 13", Clear with Embossed Coca-Cola $65

Shot Glass, 2¼" Tall, 1½ oz., Enameled Green 1969 Christmas $13.50

Shot Glass, 2¼" Tall, 1½ oz., Enameled Red and Green Designs, Annual Issue from 1977 to 1988 (Price Is for Each Glass) $15

Straw Dispenser, 11" Tall, Chrome Base and Top, Enameled Coca-Cola Design $30

Sugar Shaker with Enameled Red Metal Twist-Off Lid, 6" Tall, Enameled Coca-Cola $15

Swag Light, 17" Diameter, Electric, Multicolored Stained Glass, "Drink Coca Cola" $275

Syrup Bottle, 11" Tall, Clear Glass, Molded "Drink Coca Cola", 1920s $800

Tumbler, Various Disney Characters, Several Styles $13.50

Tumbler, Wide Variety of Styles, Enameled White Writing Only $5

Tumbler, Wide Variety of Styles, Enameled Multicolored Designs, Less Than 12 oz. $7.50

Tumbler, Wide Variety of Styles, Enameled Multicolored Designs, 12 oz. to 16 oz.   8.50

Tumbler, Wide Variety of Styles, Enameled Multicolored Designs, More Than 16 oz. $10

Coin Glass
Fostoria Glass Company, 1958–82

Fostoria's Coin Glass is a very popular pattern, and prices continue to rise while availability, especially in emerald green and blue, is quite scarce. There are four basic frosted coin designs, which consist of a liberty bell, a colonial soldier cameo, a torch, and an eagle. Prices below are for crystal, amber, olive green, and a darker ruby or royal red. Double the prices for light blue and triple them for emerald green. Emerald green had only two years of production in the 1960s, so make sure that if you're bidding on an online auction sight, you are well aware of the difference between olive and emerald green. A few odd crystal pieces have gold decorated coins. As long as the gilding is completely intact, the value for them is the same as for emerald green and three times that of regular crystal. Note that the original Fostoria glass has frosted coins; however, Dalzell-Viking (a division of the Lancaster Colony Corporation, which purchased Fostoria) continued to reproduce many of the items without frosted coins until Viking closed in 1997. It is simply cheaper to exclude the frosting. Reproductions without frosted coins generally sell for about half the price of the original Fostoria frosted versions. Also note that there are other Coin patterns out there; Avon, for example, has issued a few in the past (commissioned Fostoria pieces).

Ashtray, 4"	$25
Ashtray, 5"	$27.50
Ashtray, 7½" with Center Coin	$35
Ashtray, 7½" Round	$45
Ashtray, 10"	$45
Ashtray with Cover, 3"	$27.50
Bowl, 8"	$70
Bowl, 8½" Footed	$100
Bowl, 8½", Footed with Cover	$175
Bowl, 9" Oval	$95
Bowl, Wedding with Cover	$125
Candleholder, 4½"	$45
Candlestick, 8"	$60
Candy Box with Cover	$70
Candy Jar with Cover, 6¼"	$70
Cigarette Box with Cover	$70
Cigarette Holder with Cover	$70
Cigarette Urn, 3⅜", Footed	$35
Condiment Set, 4-Piece (Cruet, 2 Shakers, and Tray)	$275
Condiment Tray	$75
Creamer	$27.50
Cruet, 7 oz. with Stopper	$110
Decanter, 16 oz. with Stopper	$275
Goblet, 10½"	$75
Jelly Dish	$37.50
Lamp Chimney, Coach	$75
Lamp Chimney, Handled	$75
Lamp, Oil, 9¾", Handled	$200

Fostoria Coin Glass. *Photo by Robin Rainwater.*

Lamp, Electric, 10⅛", Handled	$225
Lamp, Oil, 13½"	$275
Lamp, Electric, 13½"	$275
Lamp, Oil, 16⅝"	$325
Lamp, Electric, 16⅝"	$325
Nappy, 4½"	$35
Nappy, 5⅜", with Handle	$40
Pitcher, 32 oz., 6¼" Tall	$125
Plate, 8"	$35
Punch Bowl, 14"	$625
Punch Bowl Base	$175
Punch Cup	$50
Salt and Pepper Shakers with Chrome Tops	$110
Salver, Footed	$150
Sherbet, 5¼", 9 oz.	$55
Sugar with Cover	$55
Tumbler, 3⅝", 9 oz.	$50
Tumbler, 4¼", 9 oz.	$60
Tumbler, 5⅛", 12 oz.	$70
Tumbler, 5⅜", 10 oz.	$45

Tumbler, 5³⁄₁₆", 14 oz.	$75
Urn with Cover, 12¾" Tall, Footed	$125
Vase, 8"	$50
Vase, 10" Footed	$75
Wineglass, 4" Tall, 5 oz.	$65

Columbia
Federal Glass Company, 1938–42

Columbia is borderline Depression glass since it was first made in the very late 1930s; nevertheless, the majority of it came out in the early 1940s. A few pieces were made in pink; however, it is a bit paler and lighter than the average Depression pink but still commands prices four or five times that of the crystal priced below. The butter dishes (bottoms and tops) are also available in a variety of flashed designs as well as decals. Complete flashed butter dishes are priced at about $30 except for the ruby red flashed version, which is worth a few dollars more at $35.

Bowl, 5", Crystal	$20
Bowl, 8", Crystal	$25
Bowl, 8½", Crystal	$26
Bowl, 10½", Crystal	$27.50
Butter Dish with Cover, Crystal	$27.50
Cup, Crystal	$10
Plate, 6", Crystal	$5
Plate, 9½", Crystal	$12.50
Plate, 11", Chop, Crystal	$17.50
Saucer, Crystal	$5
Snack Plate, Crystal	$42.50
Tumbler, Small, 4 oz., Crystal	$32.50
Tumbler, Large, 9 oz., Crystal	$37.50

Correia Art Glass
1973–Present

Another recent company, in operation since 1973, Correia has already achieved an excellent reputation. As proof of their achievements, works by Correia can be found in the permanent collections of the Corning Museum of Glass, the Chrysler Museum of Art, the Metropolitan Museum of Art, and the Smithsonian, just to name a few. Everything produced by Correia is completely handmade without using any molds (freehand blowing).

Apple, Opaque Black or Transparent Red	$150
Bowl, Wide Rim, Iridescent Ruby with Gold Swirls	$400
Bowl, Rose, Iridescent Aqua with Gold Swirls	$250
Egg, Luster White Opalescent with Gold Swirls and Red Hearts	$200
Globe Paperweight, 2¼", Luster Gold with Violet Miniature Hearts	$175
Globe Paperweight, 2¼", Dark Opaque Green with Transparent Blue Ring, Saturn Design	$175
Globe Paperweight, 2¼", World Globe, Iridescent Blue with Gold Continents	$175
Globe Paperweight, 2½", Violet with Gold Waves and Crescent Moon	$175
Globe Paperweight, 3", Black or Light Iridescent Gold with Snake in Relief	$175
Globe Paperweight, 3", Opalescent White with Black and White Zebras	$175
Globe Paperweight, 3⅛", Opalescent White with Gold Hearts	$175
Globe Paperweight, 4" Tall, 4¼" Diameter, Curious Cat Design, Black Cat at Top of Fishbowl, Multicolored Fish and Seaweed Encased in Crystal	$350
Lamp, 17½" Tall, Glass Base and 12¼" Shade, Various Iridescent Bright Colors (Base and Shade)	$450
Lamp, Iridescent Blue, Gold Lustre, Etched Design	$950
Perfume Bottle with Crystal Stopper, 3" Tall, Crystal and Aqua Swirls	$175
Perfume Bottle with Black Stopper, 3" Tall, Black and Aqua Striped Design	$275
Perfume Bottle with Crystal Stopper, 4½" Tall, Emerald Green and Aqua Swirls	$300
Perfume Bottle with Crystal Stopper, 7" Tall, Cobalt Blue and Aqua	$300
Vase, 6½" Tall, Iridescent Ruby Red with Gold Swirls	$275
Vase, Jack-in-the-Pulpit Style, Black with Silver Swirls	$375
Vase, Black with Silver Swirls	$225
Vase, Cylinder Form, Black with Silver and Red Swirls	$300

Cremax
Macbeth-Evans Division of Corning Glass Works, Late 1930s–Early 1940s

The Cremax color varies from a lightly tinted milky color to a shinier white porcelain color. For blue-colored pieces as well as those that are decorated, double the prices shown here. Several fired-on and flashed color trims are present on the rims and outer layers, especially on the plates. For the most part, fired-on decals consist of floral designs.

Bowl, 5¾"	$4.50
Bowl, 7¾"	$10
Bowl, 9"	$12
Creamer	$6
Cup	$5
Cup, Demitasse	$18
Plate, 6¼"	$2.75
Plate, 9¾"	$6
Plate, 11½"	$7.50
Saucer	$2.75
Saucer, Demitasse	$6
Sugar, Open	$6

Crest

Fenton Art Glass Company, Early 1940s–Present

For the most part, most of Fenton's Crest pieces are milk glass except for the edging and in some pieces the handles or stoppers. Aqua Crest includes a greenish-blue or aqua trim, and Blue Crest contains a darker blue trim; Emerald Crest has an emerald-green trim; Silver Crest features a crystal trim; Peach Crest also contains a clear glass trim along with an exterior of milk glass and a pink interior; Snow Crest is forest green, rose or ruby red, or amber glass with a milk-white trim; Rose Crest has a pink trim and Silver Rose is opaque pink glass with a clear glass trim; Ruby Crest features a ruby red trim; Ivory Crest is custard glass with a clear glass trim; Gold Crest contains an amber trim; Silver Jamestown consists of a milk-glass exterior, transparent light blue interior, and crystal trim; Silver Turquoise is light blue opaque glass with a crystal trim; Black Crest contains a black trim; and Flame Crest has an orangish-red trim.

From a research standpoint, Fenton's Crest is certainly cause for headaches! Aqua Crest was the original, beginning in 1940. Silver Crest followed in 1943 and remains the most popular; it is still in production today. Emerald Crest was made only from 1949 to 1955. Peach Crest was quite popular and had a lengthy run from 1940 to 1969. Snow Crest was made only from 1950 to 1954. Rose Crest was made from 1944 to 1947. Ivory Crest was made in two short years, 1940 to 1941. Gold Crest had a brief run from 1943 to 1945 and was reissued in 1963 and 1964. Silver Rose was produced in 1956 and 1957. Silver Turquoise was made only from 1956 to 1958. Silver Jamestown was made in 1957 to 1959. Flame Crest and Blue Crest were produced only in 1963. Ruby Crest was made in 1979. Black Crest was made in 1970.

There were more than 100 designated "lines" used for the Crest patterns, but some are older than others. In dating pieces, the formula for the base milk color was changed in 1958;

the originals have a very light opalescence to them when held up to a light. The "Fenton" signature also appears on all products made after 1973. Some pieces contain melon ribbing, too (same price). Note that Fenton did combine similarly colored trims on many of their products such as their cranberry, hobnail, swirled, and other designs; however, they were not referred to as Crest and are not included in the following.

Basic prices listed below are for the most common, Silver Crest. Beginning in the late 1960s, some Silver Crest items contain hand-painted floral designs, increase the prices by 25 percent for these as well as for Aqua Crest. For all other colors, double the prices.

Ashtray	$25
Basket, 2½" to 4½"	$40
Basket, 5" to 5½", Several Styles	$45
Basket, 6½"	$50
Basket, 7"	$55
Basket, 10"	$60
Basket, 12"	$75
Basket, 13"	$85
Bonbon, 5½"	$15
Bonbon, 8"	$20
Bowl, 5"	$25
Bowl, 5", Handled	$40
Bowl, 5½"	$37.50
Bowl, 6½", Crimped	$40
Bowl, 7", Round or Oval	$42.50
Bowl, 8½"	$42.50
Bowl, 8½", Flared	$45
Bowl, 9½"	$50
Bowl, 10", 2 Styles	$55
Bowl, 11"	$57.50
Bowl, 11½", Double Crimped	$67.50
Bowl, 13"	$75
Bowl, 14"	$85
Bowl, Banana, Low Footed	$55
Bowl, Banana, High Footed	$65

Fenton Aqua Crest. *Photo by Robin Rainwater.*

Bowl, Dessert, Low or Shallow Shallow	$37.50
Bowl, Deep Dessert	$40
Bowl, Finger	$25
Bowl, Rose	$37.50
Bowl, Tall, Footed	$62.50
Bowl, Square, Tall, Footed	$100
Cake Plate, Low, Footed	$65
Cake Plate, 13" Tall, Footed	$75
Candleholder, 6" with Crest on the Bottom	$40
Candleholder, Globe Holder	$27.50
Candleholder, Cornucopia Shape	$62.50
Candleholder with Flat Saucer-Shape Base	$27.50
Candleholder, Low, Ruffled	$17.50
Candleholder, High, Ruffled	$35
Candy Box	$75
Candy Box, Tall Stem, Footed	$125
Candy Jar with Cover	$150
Chip and Dip Set, 2-Piece (Low Bowl with Mayonnaise Bowl in the Center)	$75
Comport, Footed, Low	$20
Comport, Footed, High	$22.50

Comport, 6", Flared, Footed	$27.50
Comport, Footed, Crimped	$30
Creamer, Reeded with 1 Handle	$25
Creamer, Reeded with 2 Handles	$30
Creamer, Ruffled	$55
Creamer, Straight Sides	$35
Creamer, Threaded Handled	$20
Cruet with Stopper, 9" Tall	$95
Cup, Reeded or Threaded Handle	$30
Dessert Cup or Dish	$27.50
Epergne Set, 2-Piece, Vase in Bowl	$75
Epergne Set, 3-Piece, 2 Vases in Bowl	$150
Epergne Set, 4-Piece, 3 Vases in Bowl	$175
Epergne Set, 5-Piece, 4 Vases in Bowl	$200
Epergne Set, 6-Piece	$225
Flower Pot with Attached Saucer	$67.50
Lamp, Hurricane	$200
Mayonnaise Bowl	$20
Mayonnaise Ladle (Plain Crystal $10)	$17.50
Mayonnaise Liner	$25
Mayonnaise Set, 3-Piece	$60
Mustard with Cover and Spoon	$65
Nut Dish, Footed, 2 Styles	$17.50
Pitcher, Small	$47.50
Pitcher, Large, 70 oz.	$250
Plate, 5½", 2 Styles	$8
Plate, 6"	$10.50
Plate, 6½"	$15
Plate, 8½"	$30
Plate, 10"	$37.50
Plate, 10½"	$40

Plate, 11½"	$42.50
Plate, 12", 2 Styles	$45
Plate, 12½"	$47.50
Plate, 16", Cake or Torte	$65
Punch Bowl	$400
Punch Bowl Base	$105
Punch Cup	$17.50
Punch Ladle (Plain Crystal Only—$27.50)	
Relish, Divided	$35
Relish, Heart Shape with Handle	$35
Relish Set, 2 Heart-Shape Dishes on Metal Stand	$70
Salt and Pepper Shakers	$125
Saucer	$7.50
Sherbet, Footed	$12.50
Sugar, with Reeded Handles	$25
Sugar, with Ruffled Top	$55
Tidbit, 2-Tier Plates	$75
Tidbit, 2-Tier (Plate and Ruffled Bowl)	$57.50
Tidbit, 3-Tier Plates	$67.50
Tidbit, 3-Tier (2 Plates and Ruffled Bowl)	$90
Top Hat, 5" Vase	$85
Top Hat, 7" Vase	$95
Toothpick Holder	$45
Tray, Sandwich	$35
Tumbler, Footed	$60
Vase, Cornucopia Shape	$65
Vase, 4½" to 5", Several Styles	$16
Vase, 6"	$20
Vase, 6", Crimped	$20
Vase, 6¼", Crimped	$20
Vase, 6¼", Fan Shape	$25

Vase, 6½"	$25
Vase, 7" to 7½"	$32.50
Vase, 8"	$35
Vase, 8", Crimped	$32.50
Vase, 8", Globe Holder	$55
Vase, 8", Wheat	$45
Vase, 8½", Crimped	$55
Vase, 9", 2 Styles	$60
Vase, 10"	$125
Vase, 12"	$125

Daisy
Indiana Glass Company, 1933–1980s

Daisy is sometimes referred to as Indiana's Number 620 pattern run. The listed prices are for the original amber produced in the 1940s. Before that, the pattern was produced in crystal (reduce the prices by 50 percent), and a fired-on red (double the prices). A darker forest green was also added in the 1960s (reduce the prices by 50 percent).

Bowl, 4½", 2 Styles	$9
Bowl, 6"	$27.50
Bowl, 7½"	$17.50
Bowl, 9⅜"	$30
Bowl, 10" Oval	$22.50
Creamer, Footed	$10
Cup	$7.50
Plate, 6"	$3.50
Plate, 7½"	$8
Plate, 8½"	$8.50
Plate, 9⅜"	$10.50
Plate, 10⅜", Grill, 3 Divisions	$12
Plate, 10⅜", Grill, 3 Divisions, with Indentation for 4½" Bowl	$25
Plate, 11½" Cake	$16
Platter, 10¾"	$17.50

Relish Dish, 3 Divisions	$30
Saucer	$2.50
Sherbet	$10
Sugar, 2-Handled	$11
Tumbler, 9 oz. Footed	$20
Tumbler, 12 oz. Footed	$35

Degenhart Crystal Art Glass Factory
1947–78

The company was established in Cambridge, Ohio, in 1947 by John and Elizabeth Degenhart. They were noted for paperweights and miniature colored art novelty items. The company closed in 1978 after Elizabeth's death (John had passed away in 1964). Beginning in 1972, most products can be found with a mold mark that consists of a *D* or a *D* within a heart. (The only exception is the owl, which was marked beginning in 1967.) Some of the company molds were retired; however, Zack Boyd, an employee of Degenhart, purchased many of them and founded the Boyd Art Glass Company in 1978.

Bell, Bicentennial, 1974, Crystal	$10
Bell, Bicentennial, 1974, Canary, Crown Tuscan, Amethyst, Peach, Seafoam, Rose Marie Pink, or Lime Ice	$15
Bell, Bicentennial, 1974, Custard	$26
Bird Salt Dip, 1½", Introduced 1966, Various Colors	$17.50
Bird Salt Dip, 1½", Ebony	$30
Boot, Peachblow, Daisy and Button Pattern, 1950s	$30
Boot, Texas, Green or Peach, 1970s	$20
Chick Covered Dish, 2", Powder Blue or White	$30
Chick Covered Dish, 2", Lemon Custard	$65
Coaster, Sapphire Blue	$8.50
Hat, Miniature, Daisy and Button Pattern, Milk Blue or Vaseline	$17.50
Hat, Miniature, Daisy and Button Pattern, Crown Tuscan or Custard	$25
Hen Dish with Cover, 3", Sapphire Blue, Mint Green, Dark Green, or Amberina	$30
Hen Dish with Cover, 3", Caramel Custard or Pigeon Blood	$55
Hen Dish with Cover, 5", Crystal	$30
Hen Dish with Cover, 5", Sapphire Blue, Bittersweet, or Crown Tuscan	$75
Hen Dish with Cover, 5", Caramel Custard or Pigeon Blood	$100

Lamb Dish with Cover, Canary Yellow or Sapphire Blue	$45
Lamb Dish with Cover, Cobalt Blue or Emerald Green	$55
Owl Figurine, Most Colors (Produced in More Than 200 Colors)	$35
Owl Figurine, Frosty Jade, Lavender Blue, Willow Blue, Fog Opaque, Ivrene, Limeade, or Pigeon Blood	$55
Owl Figurine, Heliotrope or White/Yellow Opalescent	$100
Paperweight, Marbleized Design	$165
Paperweight, Morning Glories Design	$100
Paperweight, Red Floral Design	$85
Paperweight, Star Flower Design	$85
Pooch Figurine, Most Colors (Produced in More Than 100 Colors), Introduced 1976	$20
Pooch Figurine, Heatherbloom, Bittersweet, Buttercup Slag, Fantastic, or Green Caramel Slag	$40
Priscilla Doll Figurine, Most Colors (Produced in 40 Colors), Introduced 1976	$100
Priscilla Doll Figurine, Blue and White or Jade	$125
Robin Dish with Cover, 5", Fawn, Taffeta, or Crown Tuscan	$75
Robin Dish with Cover, 5", Bloody Mary	$100
Tomahawk, Custard Maverick, Introduced 1947	$75
Toothpick Holder, More Than 100 Color Patterns/Designs	$20–$25
Turkey Dish with Cover, Amber or Amethyst	$50
Turkey Dish with Cover, Custard, Gray Slag, Crown Tuscan, Amberina, or Bittersweet	$85
Turkey Dish with Cover, Tomato	$110

Dewdrop
Jeannette Glass Company, 1953–56

Dewdrop is a typical 1950s crystal pattern—nothing too fancy or difficult to obtain. The pattern contains alternating panels of clear glass and tiny horizontal rows of miniature hobs. It was made in crystal only.

Bowl, 4¾"	$6
Bowl, 8½"	$12.50
Bowl, 10⅜"	$20
Butter Dish with Cover	$35
Candy Dish with Cover, 7"	$30

Dewdrop Pattern Plate. *Drawing by Mark Pickvet.*

Creamer	$10
Cup	$5
Leaf-Shape Dish with Handle	$11.50
Pitcher, 1 qt.	$55
Pitcher, 2 qt.	$45
Plate, Indentation for Cup	$5
Plate, 11½"	$20
Punch Bowl, 1½ gal.	$37.50
Punch Bowl Base	$12.50
Sugar with Cover	$15
Tray, Lazy Susan, 13"	$17.50
Tumbler, 9 oz.	$22.50
Tumbler, 15 oz.	$20

Disney Glass Collectibles
1930s–Present

Disney objects range from decorated tumblers to limited edition hand-sculptured crystal items. All have one common characteristic in that they feature Disney characters in some form or another. Those released in limited editions are usually sold out very quickly.

Alice in Wonderland Tumbler, 1950, 8 Styles	$30
Bell, 4½" Tall, Crystal with Gold-Plated Mickey Mouse Ringer	$20

Bookends, 7" Tall, Etched Designs of Snow White and the Evil Queen by Robert Guenther, Limited Edition of 750, 1990s $125

Bowl, 9½" Tall, 8¾" Diameter, 4-Footed, Etched Designs of the 7 Dwarfs by Robert Guenther, Limited Edition of 750, 1990s $200

Centerpiece, 15" Square, 5" Tall, Footed, Etched Designs of Female Villains by Robert Guenther, Limited Edition of 300, 1990s $425

Champagne Bucket, 9½" Tall, 8¾" Diameter, 2 Applied Handles, Etched Design of Cinderella and the Prince $175

Cinderella Tumbler, 1950, 8 Styles $25

Cinderella's Coach, 5¾" Tall, 5" Long, 7⅞" Wide, Crystal Ball Shape with Gold Frame and Finial $100

Cinderella's Slipper on Pillow Base, 2⅜" Tall, 3" Long, 3" Wide, Limited Edition (4,000), Made in Germany $150

Coca-Cola Tumblers with Disney Characters, Several Styles $15

Dalmatians, 101, Tumbler, Wonderful World of Disney $15

Donald Duck Tumbler, 1942, Several Styles $30

Dopey Crystal Figurine, 4½" Tall, Limited Edition (1800) $135

Dopey Paperweight by Robert Guenther, 4", Square, 1990s, Limited Edition of 1,200 $50

Dumbo Crystal Figurine, 4½" Tall, Limited Edition (1,000), Val St. Lambert in Belgium $200

Dumbo Tumbler, 1941, Two-Color, 5 Styles $50

Eeyore Crystal Figurine, 4¼" Tall, Limited Edition (2,000), Made in Germany $175

Evil Queen Paperweight by Robert Guenther, 4", Square, 1990s, Limited Edition of 1,200 (from Snow White) $50

Ferdinand the Bull Tumbler, 4¾" Tall, All Star Parade, 1939 $50

Goofy Frosted Crystal Figurine, 7" Tall, Cristallerie Antonia Imperatore, 1960s $77.50

Goofy Frosted Crystal Figurine, 2⅞" Tall, Goebel $35

Grumpy Paperweight by Robert Guenther, 4", Square, 1990s, Limited Edition of 1,200 $50

Jiminy Cricket Crystal Figurine, 4½" Tall, Limited Edition (1800) $135

Jiminy Cricket Crystal Sculpture, 14" Tall on Wood Lit Base, Engraved Glass Figure, Limited Edition (1,000), Made by Arnold Ruiz $450

Jungle Book Pepsi Tumblers, Several Styles $45

Lady & the Tramp Tumbler, 1955, 8 Styles $35

Little Mermaid Crystal Figurine, 4⅝" Tall, Limited Edition (1,800) $175

Disney *Fantasia* Mickey Mouse. *Photo by Robin Rainwater.*

Maleficent Paperweight by Robert Guenther, 4" Square, 1990s, Limited Edition of 1,200	$50
McDonald's Disneyland Tumbler, 4 Styles	$8
Mickey Mouse Crystal Figurine, 4½" Tall, Limited Edition (1,800)	$150
Mickey Mouse Frosted Crystal Figurine, 2⅞" Tall, Goebel	$35
Mickey Mouse Sorcerer's Apprentice Crystal Figurine, 4½" Tall, Limited Edition (1,800)	$150
Mickey Mouse Through the Years Mug, 1940 Fantasia, Milk White, Pepsi	$20
Mickey Mouse Tumbler, Limited Edition, 1971	$15
Mickey Mouse Club Tumbler, Several Styles	$12.50
Minnie Mouse Frosted Crystal Figurine, 2⅞" Tall, Goebel	$35
Minnie Mouse Mug, Limited Edition, 1971	$15
Pinocchio Tumbler, 4⅝" Tall, 1940s	$25
Plate with Black Marble Stand, 14" Diameter, 5" Height, Etched Snow White and Dopey by Robert Guenther, Limited Edition of 300, 1990s	$425
Pluto Frosted Crystal Figurine, 2⅞" Tall, Goebel	$35
The Rescuers Pepsi Tumblers, 1977, 8 Styles	$12.50
Robin the Boy Wonder Tumbler, 5" Tall	$20
Simba the Lion, Crystal Figurine, 5¼" Tall, Limited Edition (2,000), Made in Germany	$275
Sleeping Beauty Crystal Castle, 4⅝" Tall, Limited Edition (1,800)	$250

Sleeping Beauty Crystal Castle, 5¼" Tall, 4¾" Wide, Made in Germany	$200
Sleeping Beauty Tumbler, 1958, Several Styles	$25
Snow White & the Seven Dwarfs Tumblers, 8 Styles, Originally Held Cottage Cheese, Libbey, Late 1930s, Complete Set	$175
Sorcerer's Apprentice Sculpture, 6¼" Tall, Crystal Wave with Miniature Pewter Mickey Mouse Finial, Franklin Mint	$175
Sorcerer's Apprentice Crystal Hat Sculpture, 3" Tall, 3½" Wide, Includes Hat on Open Book, Limited Edition (2,000), Made in Germany	$100
Snow White Crystal Figurine, 5¼" Tall, Limited Edition (4,000), Made in Germany	$175
Snow White Paperweight by Robert Guenther, 4" Square, 1990s, Limited Edition of 1,200	$50
Tigger Cut Crystal Miniature, 3" Tall, Limited Edition (2,500), Made in Austria	$175
Tinker Bell Crystal Figurine, 4½" Tall, Limited Edition (1,800)	$150
Tumbler, 25th Anniversary (1997), McDonald's Issue, 4 Styles with Disney Characters, 5" Tall, 3¼" Diameter	$3
Ursula Paperweight by Robert Guenther, 4" Square, 1990s, Limited Edition of 1,200	$50
Vase, 8¾" Tall, Crystal, Mickey Mouse Icon Shape	$35
Vase, 22" Tall, 10½" Wide, Etched/Frosted Design of Cruella De Vil by Robert Guenther, Limited Edition of 700, 1990s	$400
Winnie the Pooh Crystal Figurine, 4½" Tall, Limited Edition (1,800)	$200
Winnie the Pooh Cut Crystal Miniature, 1⁵⁄₁₆" Tall, Limited Edition (2,500), Made in Austria	$150
Winnie the Pooh Tumbler, 1950s–1960s, Several Styles	$15

Duncan & Miller Animals
1920s–1955

Like so many others, Duncan and Miller created their own crystal animal figurines from the Depression onward until they closed permanently. Most of their creations are water birds such as swans, ducks, and others in various colors or color accents. A few were made into practical items such as ashtrays, bowls, and cigarette boxes.

Bird of Paradise	$550
Donkey and Pheasant	$450
Donkey with Cart and Peon	$550
Duck, Ashtray, 4"	$22.50
Duck, Ashtray, 8"	$32.50

Duck, Mallard, Cigarette Box with Cover, 4½" x 3½" (Ruby Red $175)	$70
Goose, 6" Tall	$300
Grouse, Ruffled	$2,000
Heron, 7" Tall	$125
Swan, Ashtray, 4", Blue Neck on Crystal Swan	$60
Swan, 3" Tall, Crystal	$40
Swan, 5" Tall, Crystal	$45
Swan, 5½" Tall, Ruby Red with Crystal Neck	$115
Swan, 6" Tall, Ruby Red	$85
Swan, 6½" Tall, Opal Pink	$120
Swan, 7" Tall, Chartreuse	$85
Swan, 7" Tall, Crystal	$75
Swan, 7" Tall, Red with Crystal Neck	$85
Swan, 8" Tall, Crystal with Red Neck	$95
Swan, 8" Tall, Red with Crystal Neck	$105
Swan, 8" Tall, Ruby Red	$100
Swan, 8" Tall, Ruby Red with Floral Design	$105
Swan, 10" Tall, Crystal	$75
Swan, 10" Tall, Blue Opalescent, 12½" Wingspan	$325
Swan, 10" Tall, Green Opalescent, 12½" Wingspan	$290
Swan, 10½" Tall, Milk White with Red Neck	$575
Swan, 10½" Tall, Opal Blue, 12½" Wingspan	$475
Swan, 10½" Tall, Ruby Red with Crystal Neck, 14" Wingspan	$275
Swan, 12" Tall, Milk White with Green or Ruby Red	$390
Swan, 13½" Tall, Ruby Red with Crystal Neck	$265
Swordfish, Crystal	$275
Swordfish, Blue Opalescent	$610

Early American Prescut
Anchor-Hocking Glass Corporation, 1941–99

This is a very common pattern consisting of pressed glass stars and pineapple-like tops with some variants. Those with the Oatmeal designation were once included as premiums in boxes of Crystal Wedding Oats and lack the star design. Those with Pineapple designations were the originals and contain block and pineapple fan designs (stars replaced the blocks in 1960). Beginning collectors often mistake this glass for older pressed designs and even cut glass because of the vintage-like design motif. Crystal is the prevalent design, and is priced below. Occasionally, pieces can be found in color, or with color accents. For any amber, aqua, black, blue, green, milk white, red, or those with hand-painted designs, double the prices.

Ashtray, 4"	$6
Ashtray, 5"	$12
Ashtray, 7¾"	$17.50
Bowl, 4¼"	$20
Bowl, 4¼", Oatmeal	$3
Bowl, 4¼", Scalloped Rim	$7.50
Bowl, 5¼", Scalloped Rim	$8
Bowl, 5⅜"	$5
Bowl, 6¾", 3-Footed	$7.50
Bowl, 7¼"	$8
Bowl, 7¼", Scalloped Rim	$22.50
Bowl, 8¾"	$10
Bowl, 9", Console	$16
Bowl, 9" Oval	$10
Bowl, 9⅜", Gondola Dish	$6
Bowl, 10¾"	$12.50
Bowl, 11¾", Paneled	$175
Box, 4¾", Pineapple	$12.50
Butter Dish with Cover, ¼ lb. Rectangular	$10
Butter Dish with Domed Cover, Pineapple	$17.50
Butter Set, Bottom with Metal Handle and Knife	$17.50
Cake Plate, 13½", Footed	$27.50
Candlestick, 7", Double-Lite	$32.50
Candy Dish with Cover, 5¼"	$12.50
Candy Dish with Cover, 5½" Tall, 7¼" Long	$15
Chip and Dip Set, 10¾" Bowl, 5¼" Brass Holder	$27.50
Coaster	$3

Cocktail Shaker, 9" Tall	$350
Creamer	$5
Cruet with Stopper, 7¾" Tall	$7.50
Cup, 6 oz.	$3.50
Cup, Oatmeal	$3
Jam Jar with Cover, Pineapple	$15
Lazy Susan, 9-Piece Set (Brass Stand, Tray, Center Bowl, 6 Glass Inserts)	$60
Oil Lamp	$300
Pitcher, 12 oz., Milk, Pineapple	$10
Pitcher, Syrup, 12 oz.	$25
Pitcher, Syrup, Pineapple	$15
Pitcher, 18 oz.	$17.50
Pitcher, Square, 40 oz.	$55
Pitcher, 60 oz.	$25
Planter, 6" x 4½"	$20
Plate, 6¾", Indentation (No Ring)	$50
Plate, 6¾", with Cup Ring	$45
Plate, 10"	$12.50
Plate, 11"	$14
Plate, 11", 4-Part with Swirl Dividers	$100
Platter, 11¾", Egg	$45
Platter, 13½"	$17.50
Punch Bowl	$17.50
Punch Cup	$3.50
Punch Ladle	$5
Punch Stand	$12.50
Relish Dish, 8½" Oval, 3-Part	$6.50
Relish Dish, 10", Tab Handle, 2-Part	$8.50
Relish Dish, 13½", 5-Part	$40
Salt and Pepper Shakers, Metal Tops (Plastic Tops $8)	$10
Salt and Pepper Shakers, 2¼" Tall, Individual	$75

Saucer, 4⅜", Oatmeal	$2
Sherbet, 5 oz., Oatmeal	$2
Sherbet, 3½" Tall, 6 oz.	$100
Soap Dish, 5¼" x 3¾", Oatmeal	$16
Sugar Dish with Cover	$6
Sugar Dish with Cover, No Handles, Pineapple	$10
Sugar Dish with Cover, 2-Handled, Pineapple	$12.50
Tray for Creamer and Sugar	$4
Tray, 12" x 6½"	$15
Tumbler, 4 oz., Oatmeal	$2
Tumbler, 5 oz., 4" Tall	$6
Tumbler, 7 oz., Oatmeal	$2.50
Tumbler, 9 oz., Oatmeal	$3
Tumbler, 10 oz., Pineapple	$5
Tumbler, 10 oz., 4½" Tall	$7.50
Tumbler, 15 oz., 6" Tall	$20
Vase, 5" Tall, Footed	$300
Vase, 8½" Tall	$10
Vase, 10" Tall	$15

Fenton Art Glass
1930s–Present

The listings here begin in the 1930s because Fenton primarily manufactured carnival glass before this time period. See additional Fenton listings for carnival glass in chapter 5, under "Chocolate" in chapter 4, under "Lincoln Inn" in chapter 6, and under "Bicentennial," "Crest," "Hobnail," and "Ruby Red Glass" in this chapter. Fenton has a long distinguished career in the glassmaking industry and has survived the upheavals and downswings in the glass market since they have been in business (1905). The firm is best known for colored glass such as vases and baskets made in a huge variety of styles—opalescent, satin, iridescent, fancy patterned, and so on.

Amphora, 14" Tall on Brass Stand, Mulberry Glass with Hand-Painted Mystical Bird, 1999, Limited Edition of 1,250	$350
Basket, 4½" Diameter, Crystal Handle, Opalescent Cranberry, Hobnail Pattern	$110

Fenton Baskets. *Photo by Robin Rainwater.*

Basket, 4½" Diameter, Milk with Rose Trim and Handle	$85
Basket, 5", Black with Crystal Handle, Enameled Floral Design	$55
Basket, 5" Diameter, Opaque Cobalt Blue with Wicker Handle	$175
Basket, 5" Diameter, 3-Footed, Iridescent Amethyst, Pressed Daisy and Star Pattern	$50
Basket, 5" Diameter, Peking Blue (Light Blue and Milk Colored)	$105
Basket, 5" Diameter, Opaque Rose Pastel with Transparent Pink Handle	$95
Basket, 7" Diameter, Opalescent Cranberry with Clear Handle, Coin Dot Pattern	$165
Basket, 7" Diameter, Milk Base, Pink Interior, Black Trim and Handle	$210
Basket, 7½" Diameter, Crystal Handle, Blue Opalescent, Hobnail Pattern	$115
Basket, 10" Diameter, Cranberry Opalescent, Hobnail Pattern	$115
Basket, 10½" Diameter, Mulberry Blue with Clear Handle	$375
Bowl, 6", Cupped, Black Fenton Ebony	$85
Bowl, 13½" Diameter, 2-Handled (17" Long), Jade Green	$175
Candleholder, 4½" Tall, Cornucopia Style, Crystal with Silvertone	$55
Candlestick, 3½" Tall, Double Dolphin Design, Jade Green	$55
Candlestick, 8" Tall, Milk Glass with Ebony Base	$125
Candy Jar with Cover, Double Dolphin Handles, Ebony	$250
Candy Jar with Cover, 10½" Tall, Orange "Flame"	$175
Compote, 5½" Diameter, Plum Opal, Hobnail Pattern	$85
Compote, 7" Tall, 10" Diameter, Black, Mikado Pattern	$375

Cookie Jar with Cover and Wicker Handle, 7" Tall, Ebony, Big Cookies or Circle Pattern	$275
Cruet with Crystal Stopper and Handle, 6" Tall, Lime Opalescent, Hobnail Pattern	$135
Egg, 3¾" Tall, Various Colors and Hand-Painted Designs, More Than 100 Styles	$40–$60
Epergne, 4" Tall, 3 Vases, Petite Blue Opal	$175
Pitcher, Water, Crimped, Hobnail Pattern, Lime Opalescent Color	$210
Plate, Annual Christmas Commemorative, Blue Satin or Carnival, 1970–78 (Price Is for Each)	$25
Plate, Annual Christmas Commemorative, Blue Satin or Carnival, 1979–Up (Price Is for Each)	$17.50
Plate, Annual Mother's Day Commemorative, Blue Satin or Carnival, 1970–Up (Price Is for Each)	$17.50
Sandwich Server with Center Dolphin Handle, 10" Diameter, Emerald Green	$165
Tray, Dresser, 10¾" Across, Fan Shape, Amethyst or Amber, Diamond Optic Pattern	$85
Vase, 6½" Tall, Crimped, Periwinkle Blue	$90
Vase, 7½" Tall, Large Thumbprints, Opalescent Cranberry, Satin Finish	$150
Vase, 7⅝" Tall, Cobalt Blue Base with Multicolored Design and Black Threading, Paper Label "Fenton Art Glass"	$610
Vase, 9" Tall, Blue, Dancing Ladies Pattern	$275
Vase, 9" Tall, Cobalt Blue Base with Multicolored Design and Black Threading	$500
Vase, 9" Tall, Green, Dancing Ladies Pattern	$335
Vase with Cover, 12" Tall, Blue, Dancing Ladies Pattern	$650
Vase, 12" Tall, Cobalt Blue with Engraved Floral Design	$150
Vase, Ivory, Hanging Hearts Design	$275
Vase, Footed, Hearts and Vines Design, Karnak Red	$600

Fire-King Dinnerware and Oven Glass
Anchor-Hocking Glass Corporation, 1940s–1960s

Anchor-Hocking's Fire-King line was made in several patterns. The first and rarest Fire-King Philbe pattern is listed in chapter 6 because it was made during the Depression era. All Fire-King is heat resistant for use in the oven, an advance over nearly all Depression glass. Note that it was not designed for microwave use since widespread household use of microwave ovens didn't begin until the 1970s. In some instances, microwaves have been known to cause cracks in older Fire-King products because of sudden temperature changes. Those made in the later 1970s and afterward are generally safe for microwave use.

Prices listed are for jadeite (light opaque green), azurite (light opaque blue), forest green, royal ruby, gray laurel, peach luster, transparent sapphire blue, turquoise, pink, iridized versions, and milk-white or ivory with colored trims or fired-on decal decorations (for example, floral patterns such as Fleurette, Honeysuckle, Primrose; foliage patterns such as Meadow Green and Wheat; and others such as Gamebirds and Blue Mosaic). Reduce the prices by 50 percent for ivory or milk glass that lacks the colored trim or decorations.

Ashtray, 3½"	$7.50
Ashtray, 4⅝"	$10
Ashtray, 5¾"	$12.50
Bowl, Batter with Spout	$60
Baker, 6 oz., Individual	$7.50
Baker, 1 pt. Round or Square	$7.50
Baker, 1 qt.	$10
Baker, 1½ qt.	$15
Baker, 2 qt.	$20
Bowl, 4" Up to 5"	$8
Bowl, 5" Up to 6"	$10
Bowl, 6" Up to 7"	$12.50
Bowl, 7" Up to 8"	$15
Bowl, 8" to 10"	$20
Bowl, Over 10"	$22.50
Bowl, 4⅜", Pie Plate (Small)	$15
Bowl, 5⅜", Deep Dish Pie Plate	$17.50
Bowl, 16 oz. Measuring	$25
Bowl, Tear, 1 pt.	$12.50
Bowl, Round, 1 qt.	$15
Bowl, Tear, 1 qt.	$16
Bowl, Round, 2 qt.	$17.50
Bowl, Tear, 2 qt.	$18.50
Bowl, Round, 3 qt.	$20
Bowl, Tear, 3 qt.	$22.50
Bowl, Round, 4 qt.	$25
Cake Pan, 8" Round or Square	$12.50

Cake Pan, 8¾", Deep	$25
Cake Pan, 9"	$27.50
Casserole, 10 oz. Individual	$15
Casserole, 1 pt. with Cover (Knob Handle)	$20
Casserole, 1 qt. with Cover (Knob Handle)	$22
Casserole, 1 qt. with Cover (Pie Plate Cover)	$24
Casserole, 1½ qt. with Cover (Knob Handle)	$26
Casserole, 1½ qt. with Cover (Pie Plate Cover)	$28
Casserole, 2 qt. with Cover (Knob Handle)	$30
Casserole, 2 qt. with Cover (Pie Plate Cover)	$32.50
Casserole, 3 qt. with Cover (Knob Handle)	$32.50
Coffee Mug 7 oz. (2 Styles)	$35
Creamer	$10
Cup	$7.50
Cup, Demitasse	$20
Cup, 8 oz. Measuring with 1 Spout	$28
Cup, 8 oz. Dry Measure, No Spout	$125
Cup, 8 oz. Measuring with 3 Spouts	$35
Custard Cup, 5 oz.	$5
Custard Cup, 6 oz. (2 Styles)	$5.50
Egg Plate, 9¾"	$18
Loaf Pan, 9" to 10", Deep	$28
Nipple Cover	$125
Nurser, 4 oz.	$26
Nurser, 8 oz.	$30
Pan, Baking, 5" x 9" with Cover	$30
Pan, Loaf, 5" x 9"	$28
Pan, Baking, 6½" x 10½"	$30
Pan, Baking, 8 x 12½"	$32.50
Percolator Top, 2⅛"	$6
Pie Plate, 8⅜"	$10
Pie Plate, 9"	$12.50

Pie Plate, 9⅝"	$14
Pie Plate, 10⅜", Juice Saver	$125
Pitcher, Up to 1 qt.	$75
Pitcher, 33–48 oz.	$100
Pitcher, 49–64 oz.	$125
Pitcher, More Than 64 oz.	$150
Plate, Up to 6"	$5
Plate, 6" Up to 7"	$6
Plate, 7" Up to 8"	$8
Plate, 8" Up to 9"	$10
Plate, 9" Up to 10"	$12.50
Plate, 10" Up to 12"	$15
Plate/Platter, More Than 12", Round or Oval	$20
Plate, Grill, 9⅝", 3 Divisions	$14
Plate, Grill, 9⅝", 5 Divisions	$15
Refrigerator Jar with Cover, 4½" x 5"	$22.50
Refrigerator Jar with Cover, 5⅛" x 9⅛"	$45
Relish Dish, 11", 3 Divisions	$12.50
Roaster, 8¾"	$55
Roaster, 10⅜"	$80
Saucer, Demitasse	$20
Saucer	$6
Sugar	$10
Sugar Dish with Cover	$20
Table Server with Handles (Hot Plate)	$28
Tray, Rectangular, 11" x 6"	$16
Tumbler, Up to 5 oz.	$6
Tumbler, 5 oz. Up to 7 oz.	$7.50
Tumbler, 7 oz. Up to 9 oz.	$10
Tumbler, 9 oz. Up to 12 oz.	$12.50
Tumbler, More Than 12 oz.	$15
Utility Bowl, 6⅞"	$20

Utility Bowl, 8⅜"	$22.50
Utility Bowl, 10⅛"	$25
Utility Pan, 8⅛" x 12½"	$45
Utility Pan, 10½"	$27.50

Floragold Louisa
Jeannette Glass Company, 1950s

This pattern is often confused with the true Louisa design of the carnival-glass era; however, Floragold pieces contain much lighter iridizing. A few crystal pieces exist that were not iridized (reduce the prices below by about one-third). A few candy dishes were later reproduced in the 1960s and 1970s in light blue, reddish yellow, pink, and the light iridized marigold color (same price). Note that the original salt and pepper shaker tops were plastic (brown or white) but broke easily; metal tops are a common replacement and do not lower the value of the shakers. The shakers were also produced in a milky opaque pink (half the price of the regular shakers).

Ashtray, 4"	$6
Bowl, 4½", Square	$6.50
Bowl, 5½" Round	$42.50
Bowl, 5½" Ruffled	$25
Bowl, 8½", Square	$20
Bowl, 9½" Deep	$47.50
Bowl, 9½" Ruffled	$27.50
Bowl, 12" Ruffled	$15
Butter Dish with Cover, Round (5½" Square Base—Rare)	$900
Butter Dish with Cover, Round (6¼" Square Base)	$47.50
Butter Dish with Cover, Oblong (for¼ lb. stick)	$35
Candlestick, Double	$35
Candy Dish, 1 Handle	$15
Candy Dish, 5¼" Long, 4-Footed	$10
Candy Jar with Cover, 6¾"	$62.50
Coaster, 4"	$6.50
Compote, 5¼" (Rare)	$1,000
Creamer	$11
Cup	$7.50

Pitcher, 1 qt.	$75
Pitcher, 2 qt.	$47.50
Plate, 5¼"	$15
Plate, 8½"	$42.50
Platter, 11¼"	$27.50
Salt and Pepper Shakers with Plastic Tops, Iridescent	$57.50
Saucer, 5¼" (No Cup Ring)	$15
Sherbet, Footed	$17.50
Sugar with Cover, 2-Handled	$22.50
Tidbit Tray with a White Wooden Post	$42.50
Tray, 13½" Oval	$30
Tray, 13½" Oval, Indentation for Covered Candy	$85
Tumbler, Footed, 10 oz.	$25
Tumbler, Footed, 11 oz.	$27.50
Tumbler, Footed, 15 oz.	$95
Vase	$425

Forest Green
Anchor-Hocking Glass Corporation, 1950–67

The original Forest Green by Anchor-Hocking spawned a new color era for glass. The dark green color was copied by others and sold well for the Christmas season along with the Royal Ruby pattern. Depression glass collectors have an easy time distinguishing this color from the lighter Depression green colors; overall it makes dating quite easy. Anchor-Hocking was the only one who actually named a pattern Forest Green; unfortunately, few companies in the modern world produce a true emerald green in glassware.

Ashtray, Several Styles	$10
Bowl, 4¾" or 5¼"	$9
Bowl, 6"	$12.50
Bowl, 7½"	$15
Bowl, 8½" Oval	$25
Bowl with Pouring Spout	$35
Cocktail Glass, 3½ oz.	$11
Cocktail Glass, 4½ oz.	$13.50

Anchor-Hocking Forest Green. *Photo by Robin Rainwater.*

Creamer	$12.50
Cup, Square	$6.50
Goblet, Various Styles, 8 to 11 oz.	$15
Goblet, Various Styles, More Than 11 oz.	$17.50
Mixing Bowl Set, 3 Pieces	$35
Pitcher, 1½ pt.	$27.50
Pitcher, 1 qt.	$32.50
Pitcher, 3 qt.	$45
Plate, 6½" or 6¾"	$8.50
Plate, 8½"	$10
Plate, 10"	$17.50
Platter, Rectangular	$25
Punch Bowl	$35
Punch Bowl Stand	$27.50
Punch Cup, Round	$3.50
Saucer	$2.25
Sherbet	$8.50
Sugar	$12.50
Tumbler, 3" to 5" Tall	$5.50
Tumbler, More Than 5⅛" to 7" Tall	$8.50

Tumbler, Over 7" Tall	$12.50
Vase, 4" Tall	$6
Vase, 6½" Tall	$7.50
Vase, 9" Tall	$12.50
Wineglass, Various Styles, 4 to 5½ oz.	$14

Gibson Glass
1983–Present

Gibson opened a small shop and factory in Milton, West Virginia, in 1983. They offer a fine lineup of paperweights, marbles, Christmas ornaments and figurines, vases, baskets, animals, and other novelty items.

Angel Figure, 6½" Tall, Light Blue Cased in Crystal	$50
Basket, 4½" Tall, Cobalt Blue, Various Molded Pattern Designs	$15
Basket, 4½" Tall, Carnival Cobalt Blue, Various Molded Pattern Designs	$20
Basket, 5" Tall, Crystal with Light Iridescence, Pressed Diamond Pattern	$20
Basket, 8½" Tall, Crimped, Cased Light Blue and Crystal	$60
Bird, 1¾" Tall, 1¾" Long, Cobalt Blue	$8
Bird, 1¾" Tall, 1¾" Long, Light Blue with Crystal Overlay	$12.50
Candy, Glass, Multicolored with Crystal Wrapper, Various Designs	$6
Compote, 8" Diameter, Crimped, Iridescent Pink with Crystal Base and Stem	$50
Cruet with Stopper, 7¾" Tall, Cobalt Blue with Iridescent Spatter	$32.50
Dolphin, 5" Long, Cobalt Blue	$15
Duck, 3¼" Tall, 4" Long, Cobalt Blue	$15
Duck, 3¼" Tall, 4" Long, Crystal	$12
Egg, Cranberry or Light Blue Spatter	$12.50
Marble, 1¼", Multicolored Swirls	$17.50
Marble, 1½", Multicolored Swirls	$20
Marble, 1¾", Multicolored Swirls	$25
Marble, 2", Sulphide, Multicolored Swirls	$27.50
Paperweight, 2" Spherical, Sulphide, Tan and Gray Seal Encased in Crystal	$26
Paperweight, Sulphide, Pastel Pink and Yellow Rabbit in Egg, Limited Edition	$90

Gibson Glass. *Photo by Robin Rainwater.*

Gibson Paperweights. *Photo by Robin Rainwater.*

Penguin, 3" Tall, Cobalt Blue	$10
Vase, 7" Tall, Crimped, Cranberry with Crystal Base	$50
Whale, 4" Long, Cobalt Blue	$15

Harp
Jeannette Glass Company, 1954–57

As the name implies, Harp contains pressed harp designs along with scrolling. It also contains an allover dot design in the mold reminiscent of old Sandwich-patterned glass. Many of the crystal pieces were trimmed in gold or even platinum (increase the prices by 25 percent if completely intact). Transparent colored versions of Harp include a light pink and ice blue, as well as opaque pink and white (double the prices for any colors). It is mostly the cake stand that is indeed found in colors, and these items may or may not be beaded at the foot, whereas others have ruffled or smooth rims (same prices).

Ashtray	$6
Coaster	$6
Cup	$35
Cake Stand, 9", Several Styles	$27.50
Plate, 7"	$17.50
Saucer	$14
Tray with 2 Handles, Rectangular	$37.50
Vase, 7½"	$27.50

Heisey Animals
A. H. Heisey and Company, 1920s–1957

Originally, the famous Heisey animals were relatively inexpensive and were purchased for children and adults alike. They were rather durable and well constructed, but beware of some that might be damaged or scratched from excessive play. Today, Heisey animals are very valuable and difficult to find. Most were made in crystal—exceptions for colors are listed below.

Airedale, 5¾" Tall, Crystal	$550
Airedale, 6" Tall, Crystal	$600
Bull, 4" Tall, Crystal	$1,250
Chick, 1" Tall, Head Up, Crystal	$100
Chick, 1" Tall, Head Down, Crystal	$100
Clydesdale, 7¼" Tall, Crystal	$550
Clydesdale, 8" Tall, Crystal	$650
Dog, Scotty, 3½" Tall, Crystal	$185
Dog, Sealyham Terrier	$150
Dog Head Bookends, 5" Tall, Scott, Pair, Crystal	$300
Dog Head Bookends, 6¼" Tall, Pair, Crystal	$600
Donkey, 6½" Tall, Crystal	$250
Duck, 2¼" Tall, Floating, Crystal	$150
Duck, 2⅝" Tall, Floating, Crystal	$175
Duck, Mallard, 4½" Tall, Wings Half Up, Crystal	$550
Duck, Mallard, 5" Tall, Wings Half Up, Crystal	$250
Duck, Mallard, 6¾" Tall, Wings Up, Crystal	$275
Duck, Wood, 4½" Tall, Crystal	$550
Duck, Wood, 5½" Tall, Crystal	$750
Elephant, 4" Tall, Trunk Down, Crystal	$300
Elephant, 4½" Tall, Trunk Up, Amber	$375
Elephant, 4½" Tall, Trunk Up, Crystal	$325
Elephant, 5⅞" Tall, Crystal	$375
Fish, Angel, Bookends, 6" Tall, Pair, Crystal	$260
Fishbowl, 9" Tall, Crystal	$925
Fish, Candlestick, 5" Tall, Crystal	$250

Fish, Centerpiece, 12" Tall, Tropical Fish with Coral, Crystal	$1,500
Fish, Match Holder, 3" Tall, Crystal	$175
Gazelle, 11" Tall, Crystal	$1,500
Giraffe, 11" Tall, Head Turned to Side, Crystal	$250
Giraffe, 11" Tall, Head Turned to Rear, Crystal	$250
Goose, 2¾" Tall, Wings Down, Crystal	$250
Goose, 4½" Tall, Wings Half Up, Crystal	$185
Goose, 5¾" Tall, Wings Down, Crystal	$275
Goose, 6½" Tall, Wings Half Up, Crystal	$185
Goose, 6½" Tall, Wings Up, Crystal	$185
Hen, 4¼" Tall, Crystal	$450
Hen, 5½" Tall, Crystal	$525
Horse, Pony, 3¾" Tall, Rearing, Crystal	$165
Horse, Plug, 4" Tall, Crystal	$165
Horse, Pony, 4⅛" Tall, Kicking, Crystal	$185
Horse, Plug, 4¼" Tall, Sparky, Cobalt Blue	$1,300
Horse, Pony, 5" Tall, Standing, Crystal	$235
Horse, 7⅜" Tall, Show, Crystal	$600
Horse, 8¼" Tall, Filly, Head Forward, Crystal	$750
Horse, 8¼" Tall, Filly, Head Backward, Crystal	$750
Horse, 8⅞" Tall, Flying Mare, Crystal	$1,500
Horse, 8⅞" Tall, Flying Mare, Sahara Yellow Color	$2,500
Horse Head Bookends, 6⅞" Tall, Pair, Crystal	$250
Horse, Rearing, Bookends, 7⅞" Tall, Pair, Crystal	$350
Pheasant, Asiatic, 10½" Tall	$650
Pheasant, Ringneck, 4¾" Tall, Crystal	$225
Pig, ⅞" Tall, Standing, Piglet, Crystal	$135
Pig, 1" Tall, Sitting, Piglet, Crystal	$165
Pig, 3⅛" Tall, Sow, Crystal	$550
Pigeon, Pouter, 6½" Tall, Crystal	$775
Rabbit, 2⅜" Tall, Head Up, Crystal	$225
Rabbit, 2⅜" Tall, Head Down, Crystal	$225

Rabbit, Paperweight, 2¾" Tall, Crystal	$235
Rabbit, 4⅝" Tall, Crystal	$550
Rabbit Head Bookends, 6¼" Tall, Pair, Crystal	$1,500
Ram's Head Decanter Stopper, Crystal	$450
Rooster, 5⅝" Tall, Crystal	$400
Rooster, 8" Tall, Fighting, Crystal	$550
Rooster Cocktail Glass, 4¼" Tall, Crystal	$60
Rooster Cocktail Shaker, 14" Tall	$175
Rooster Head Decanter Stopper	$110
Rooster Vase, 6½" Tall, Crystal	$175
Sparrow, 2¼" Tall, Crystal	$165
Swan, 2⅛" Tall, Cygnet, Crystal	$135
Swan, 7" Tall, Crystal	$1,000
Tiger Paperweight, 2⅜" Tall	$1,250

Hobnail
Fenton Art Glass Company, 1930s–Present

Fenton's milk glass Hobnail is the largest pattern in terms of the sheer variety of pieces the company ever made. It remains fairly inexpensive and is in great abundance in antique stores throughout the country. There are many other inferior hobnail milk glass products out there, and aside from paper labels that are easily removed, Fenton's pieces are generally not marked. One way to tell the quality of milk glass is the color—the good stuff is like whole milk and vibrantly white; cheaper versions look watered down, like skim milk!

Apothecary Jar with Cover, 11" Tall	$175
Ashtray, 3½", Circular	$7.50
Ashtray, 4", Ball Shape	$35
Ashtray, 4", Octagon Shape	$12.50
Ashtray, 4½" x 3¼", Rectangular	$10.50
Ashtray, 5", Circular	$11
Ashtray, 5", Square	$17.50
Ashtray, 5¼", Octagon Shape	$15
Ashtray, 6½", Circular	$15
Ashtray, 6½", Octagon Shape	$17.50

Fenton Hobnail Milk Glass. *Photo by Robin Rainwater.*

Banana Dish, 12" Long, 5" Wide	$45
Banana Dish, 12" Long, 7" Wide	$50
Basket, Up to 4⅞"	$22.50
Basket, 5" Up to 7"	$27.50
Basket, 7" Up to 9"	$30
Basket, 9" Up to 11"	$37.50
Basket, More Than 11"	$45
Bell, 5" to 7"	$22.50
Bonbon Dish, Up to 6", No Handles	$15
Bonbon Dish, Up to 6", Handled	$17.50
Bonbon Dish, More Than 6", No Handles	$17.50
Bonbon Dish, More Than 6", Handled	$20
Boot, 4"	$16
Bottle with Stopper, 5⅜" Tall	$50
Bowl, 4" Up to 5"	$17.50
Bowl, 5" Up to 6"	$20
Bowl, 6" Up to 7"	$21.50
Bowl, 7" Up to 8"	$22.50
Bowl, 8" to 10"	$30
Bowl, More Than 10"	$40

Butter Dome with Cover, 4¼"	$160
Butter Dish with Cover, ¼ lb. Size, Rectangular	$22.50
Butter Dish with Cover, ¼ lb. Size, Oval	$35
Cake Plate, 13"	$55
Candleholder, 2" Up to 4"	$17.50
Candleholder, 4" Up to 6"	$20
Candleholder, 6" Up to 8"	$22.50
Candleholder, More Than 8"	$25
Candy Dish with Cover, Up to 6"	$37.50
Candy Dish with Cover, More Than 6"	$47.50
Candy Dish without Cover, Up to 6"	$25
Candy Dish without Cover, More Than 6"	$30
Candy Jar with Cover, Up to 7"	$45
Candy Jar with Cover, More Than 7"	$55
Celery Dish, 12"	$100
Cookie Jar with Cover, 11"	$125
Creamer, Up to 3½"	$15
Creamer, More Than 3½"	$17.50
Cruet with Stopper, Up to 7" Tall	$40
Cruet with Stopper, Over 7" Tall	$55
Cup	$8
Cup, Demitasse	$35
Decanter with Stopper, 12"	$250
Egg Cup, 4"	$55
Epergne, 1 Vase	$45
Epergne, 2 Vases	$65
Epergne, 3 Vases	$65
Epergne, 5 Vases	$200
Fairy Light, 4½"	$25
Fairy Light, 8½"	$60
Goblet, Various Styles	$16

Hat Vase	$20
Honey Jar with Cover, 7¼"	$75
Jam Jar with Lid and Spoon, 5"	$40
Jam Set, 4¾" Jar with Lid, Label, and Saucer	$55
Jardiniere, Up to 5" Tall	$16
Jardiniere, More Than 5" Tall	$35
Jelly Dish, 5½" x 4½"	$30
Jelly Set, Two 4¾" Jars with Lids, Ladle and Tray	$65
Lamp, Up to 8½" Tall	$85
Lamp, More Than 8½" Up to 12" Tall	$150
Lamp, More Than 12" Up to 18" Tall	$200
Lamp, More Than 18" Tall	$250
Mayonnaise Set: Bowl, Saucer, and Ladle	$35
Mustard Jar with Notched Cover and Spoon, 3½"	$35
Napkin Ring, 2"	$35
Nut Dish, Various Styles	$17.50
Pickle Dish, 8" Oval	$16
Pitcher, Syrup, Up to 1 pt.	$40
Pitcher, More Than 16 oz. Up to 32 oz.	$50
Pitcher, 33–48 oz.	$65
Pitcher, 49–64 oz.	$85
Pitcher, More Than 64 oz.	$125
Planter, Up to 8"	$25
Planter, More Than 8"	$35
Plate, Up to 6"	$8.50
Plate, 6" Up to 7"	$12.50
Plate, 7" Up to 8"	$15
Plate, 8" Up to 9"	$17.50
Plate, 9" Up to 10"	$20
Plate, 10" Up to 12"	$25
Plate/Platter, More Than 12", Round or Oval	$35

Powder Box with Cover, 4½"	$55
Punch Bowl, Up to 11", Round	$275
Punch Bowl, Over 11", Round	$375
Punch Bowl, 11¼", Octagon	$500
Punch Bowl Base	$100
Punch Cup	$20
Punch Ladle (Crystal $25)	$55
Relish Dish, Up to 8", with or without Divisions	$20
Relish Dish, Over 8" Up to 12", with or without Divisions	$27.50
Relish Dish, More Than 12", with or without Divisions	$35
Salt and Pepper Shakers, Up to 4"	$25
Salt and Pepper Shakers, More Than 4"	$40
Salt Dip, Shell Shape	$50
Saucer	$6
Saucer, Demitasse	$20
Sherbet, 4"	$16
Spooner, 7¼" Long	$100
Stein, 6¾" Tall, 14 oz.	$125
Sugar, Up to 3½"	$15
Sugar, More Than 3½"	$17.50
Sugar with Cover, Up to 3½"	$20
Sugar with Cover, More Than 3½"	$22.50
Sugar Shaker, 4¾"	$125
Tidbit, 2-Tier	$55
Toothpick Holder	$35
Tray, Up to 8" Length	$35
Tray, Over 8" Up to 12" Length	$45
Tray, More Than 12" Length	$75
Tumbler, Up to 5 oz.	$12.50
Tumbler, 5 oz. Up to 7 oz.	$15
Tumbler, 7 oz. Up to 9 oz.	$17.50
Tumbler, 9 oz. Up to 12 oz.	$20

Tumbler, 12 oz. Up to 15 oz.	$22.50
Tumbler, More Than 15 oz.	$27.50
Urn with Cover, 11"	$200
Vase, Up to 6"	$17.50
Vase, 6" Up to 7"	$22.50
Vase, 7" Up to 8"	$27.50
Vase, 8" Up to 9"	$32.50
Vase, 9" Up to 10"	$37.50
Vase, 10" Up to 12"	$42.50
Vase, 12" Up to 18"	$50
Vase, More Than 18"	$60
Wineglass, Various Styles	$16

Holiday or Buttons and Bows
Jeannette Glass Company, 1947–49

This is an all-over geometric pattern nicknamed Buttons and Bows. A few unusual colors include a light iridescent that is nearly yellow, some opaque or what Jeannette called shell pink, and crystal. The prices are for pink with noted exceptions. There are also many variations in the standard pattern. For instance, there are three different cup and saucer sets; two with rayed centers but slightly different dimensions, and one with a plain center. There are two styles of 10-ounce tumblers: one with a flat bottom and one with a very low foot. Sherbets vary, as one has the rayed center star and the other one doesn't. The sherbet plates have slight differences, too.

Bowl, 5⅛"	$15
Bowl, 7¾"	$57.50
Bowl, 8½"	$32.50
Bowl, 9½" Oval	$30
Bowl, 10¾"	$140
Butter Dish with Cover	$45
Cake Plate, 10½", 3 Legs	$125
Candlestick, 3"	$55
Creamer, Footed	$10
Cup (3 Styles)	$10
Pitcher, 4¾", 16 oz. (Crystal $20, Iridescent $25)	$75

Pitcher, 6¾", 52 oz.	$50
Plate, 6", 2 Styles (for Sherbets)	$7.50
Plate, 9"	$17.50
Plate, 13¾"	$115
Platter, 11⅜" Oval (Iridescent $15)	$22.50
Sandwich Tray, 10½" (Iridescent $15)	$20
Saucer (3 Styles)	$4.50
Sherbet (2 Styles)	$7.50
Sugar with Cover	$25
Tumbler, 4", 10 oz., 2 Styles	$25
Tumbler, 4", 5 oz., Footed (Crystal $12.50, Iridescent $15)	$45
Tumbler, 6", Footed	$150

Homespun or Fine Rib
Jeannette Glass Company, 1939–49

This Fine Rib pattern is not unlike the pressed glass of old with a fairly simple vertical ribbing on each piece. The complete children's tea sets are particularly valuable. Prices are for pink; reduce them by 25 percent for plain crystal.

Bowl, 4½"	$15
Bowl, 5"	$32.50
Bowl, 8¼"	$32.50
Butter Dish with Cover	$75
Coaster	$10
Creamer	$15
Cup	$13.50
Plate, 6"	$8
Plate, 9¼"	$25
Platter, 13", 2-Handled	$25
Saucer	$5.50
Sherbert	$22.50
Sugar	$15
Tumbler, 5 oz.	$10

Jeanette Homespun or Fine Rio Pattern. *Reproduced directly from a 1948 advertisement.*

Tumbler, 6 oz. to 7½ oz.	$22.50
Tumbler, 8 oz. to 11½ oz	$24
Tumbler, 12 oz. to 14½ oz.	$37.50
Tumbler, More Than 14½ oz., Footed	$40

CHILDREN'S TEA SET:

Cup	$36
Plate	$12.50
Saucer	$15
Teapot with Cover	$150
Complete Set of 12 Pieces (Crystal Only), Crystal	$185
Complete Set of 14 Pieces (Pink Only), Pink	$400

Imperial's Animals
1920s–1982

Imperial made their first animal figurines when the carnival-glass era ended. Imperial acquired the molds of several other companies after they had gone out of business (Central in 1940, Heisey in 1958, and Cambridge in 1960), all makers of animal figurines. Imperial was considerate enough to mark all of their new products, including reproductions, with the "IG" mark.

Airedale, Caramel Slag	$140
Airedale, Ultra Blue	$110

Chick, Head Down or Up, Milk White	$16
Clydesdale, Amber or Salmon, 5¼" Tall	$385
Clydesdale, Verde Green, 5¼" Tall	$210
Colt, Aqua or Amber (Blue $40)	$80
Cygnet, Black, 4" Tall	$75
Cygnet, Light Blue, 4" Tall	$32.50
Donkey, Caramel Slag or Ultra Blue, 6" Tall	$80
Donkey, Green Carnival, 6" Tall	$135
Elephant, Caramel Slag, 1" Tall	$70
Elephant, Green Carnival, 1" Tall	$115
Elephant, Pink Satin or Light Blue, 4" Tall	$185
Filly, Head Forward, Satin	$90
Filly, Head Backward, Verde Green	$185
Fish Candleholder, Sunshine Yellow	$60
Fish Match Holder, Sunshine Yellow Satin	$32.50
Gazelle, Ultra Blue, 11"	$135
Giraffe, Etched Crystal, 10¼" Tall	$210
Hen, Sunshine Yellow, 4½" Tall	$105
Hen Covered Dish, on Nest, 4½", Beaded Brown	$40
Horse Head Bookends, Pink	$560
Mallard Duck, Wings Down, Caramel Slag or Amber	$215
Mallard Duck, Wings Down, Light Blue Satin	$37.50
Mallard Duck, Wings Half Up, Caramel Slag	$47.50
Mallard Duck, Wings Half Up, Light Blue Satin	$37.50
Mallard Duck, Wings Up, Caramel Slag	$50
Mallard Duck, Wings Up, Light Blue Satin	$37.50
Owl, Milk White	$62.50
Pheasant, Asiatic, Amber	$375
Piglet, Sitting, 1" Tall	$60
Piglet, Standing, Amber	$45
Piglet, Standing, Ruby Red	$115

Piglet, Standing, Ultra Blue	$60
Rabbit, 4⅜" Tall, Ultra Blue	$185
Rabbit, Paperweight, Milk White	$50
Rooster, Amber	$485
Rooster, Fighting, Pink	$240
Sow, Amber, 3⅛" Tall	$465
Swan, Caramel Slag or Iridescent Green	$45
Swan, Milk White	$40
Swan, 8", Purple Slag	$100
Swan Nut Dish, Footed	$47.50
Terrier, 5¾", Caramel Slag	$115
Tiger, Paperweight, Black	$95
Tiger, Paperweight, Jade Green	$120
Wood Duck, Caramel Slag, Ultra Blue Satin, Amber, or Sunshine Yellow Satin	$62.50
Wood Duckling, Floating or Standing, Sunshine Yellow or Sunshine Yellow Satin	$28
Woodchuck, 4½" Tall, Amber	$60

Indiana Custard or Flower and Leaf Band
Indiana Glass, 1930s–1950s

This pattern comes in white or ivory. The ivory is sometimes referred to as French Ivory or Custard and was the original pattern motif. The white was reproduced later (same price). Some Indiana Custard pieces have decals or are patterned with flowers (large or small) as well as winter scenery (increase the prices below by 50 percent).

Bowl, 4⅞"	$10
Bowl, 5¼"	$16
Bowl, 6½"	$27.50
Bowl, 7½"	$37.50
Bowl, 9"	$40
Bowl, 9½" Oval	$37.50
Butter Dish with Cover	$65
Creamer	$17.50
Cup	$37.50

Indiana Custard. *Reproduced directly from a 1933 U.S. patent.*

Plate, 5¾"	$7.50
Plate, 7½"	$17.50
Plate, 8⅞"	$20
Plate, 9¾"	$32.50
Platter, 11½" Oval	$45
Saucer	$7.50
Sherbet	$85
Sugar with Cover	$40

Insulators
Various Producers, 1840s–Present

Insulators date back to the time of telegraph poles in the 1840s. Those most desirable are the threadless styles of old and the odd-colored glass such as cobalt blue, emerald green, or yellow. The most common were clear or aqua-green glass models attached to telephone poles (from Hemingray, Lynchburg, and others). Insulators are generally made of both glass and porcelain. Inspect them carefully, because they were designed for outdoor use. As usual, prices reflect those that are in excellent condition. Those that are cracked, chipped, permanently stained or faded, and so on, are generally worth very little.

AA, Blue-Green	$150
Agee, Purple	$155
American Telephone, Dark Green and Amber	$425
American Telephone & Telegraph, Aqua	$3

Hemingray Insulator. *Photo by Robin Rainwater.*

Armstrong, No. 3, Made in U.S.A., Clear Glass	$3
Armstrong DP-1, Clear Glass	$3
Armstrong DP-1, Green	$6
Armstrong, Dark Amber	$32.50
Brookfield, No. 9, Aqua	$10
Brookfield, Crown-12, Aqua	$5
Brookfield, New York, Emerald Green	$55
Brookfield, 1907 Patent, Aqua	$65
California, Aqua	$15
California, Purple or Yellow	$285
California, Smokey Gray	$55
Chicago, Blue	$85
Columbia, Light Blue	$400
Crown Arc, Aqua	$125
Diamond, Gray	$325
Diamond, Green-Tinted	$7.50
Diamond, Amethyst	$285
Dominion, No. 42, Green-Tinted	$10
Dominion, Blue	$750
H. G. & Co., Aqua	$15

H. G. & Co., Blue	$450
H. G. & Co., Green-Tinted	$20
Hemingray, No. 1, Aqua	$15
Hemingray, No. 3, Aqua	$30
Hemingray, No. 9, Green Milk Glass	$37.50
Hemingray, No. 19, Cobalt Blue	$85
Hemingray, No. 19, Light Blue	$27.50
Hemingray, No. 21, Aqua	$3
Hemingray, No. 38, Aqua	$7.50
Hemingray, No. 40, Aqua with Amber Swirls	$11
Hemingray, No. 42, Aqua	$3
Hemingray, No. 42, Emerald Green	$155
Hemingray, No. 45, Clear Glass	$3
Hemingray, No. 56, Light Green	$25
Hemingray, No. 60, Aqua	$5
Hemingray, No. 79, Aqua	$25
Hemingray, No. D-990, Aqua	$5
Human Services Pioneers, Light Purple or Milk Glass	$20
Kimble, 820, Clear Glass	$7.50
LGT Co., Aqua	$50
Lynchburg, No. 32, Green	$25
Lynchburg, No. 43, Aqua	$10
Lynchburg, No. 44, Aqua	$5
Lynchburg, No. 44, Clear Glass	$5
Lynchburg, No. 44, Blue-Tinted	$7.50
Lynchburg, No. 44, Olive Green	$27.50
McLaughlin, No. 14, Green	$5
McLaughlin, No. 14, Olive Green	$17.50
McLaughlin, No. 19, Emerald Green	$30
McLaughlin, No. 42, Green	$25
N. E. G. M., Aqua	$50

N. E. G. M., Blue	$85
N. E. G. M., Emerald Green	$185
Peacock, Cobalt Blue Mickey Mouse	$1,050
Pyrex, Clear Glass	$3
Pyrex, Sombrero, Carnival	$22.50
Star, Green	$5
W. Brookfield, Aqua with Amber Swirls	$27.50
W. Brookfield, Green	$17.50
W. Brookfield, Purple	$335
Westinghouse, No. 6, Aqua	$275
Westinghouse, No. 6, Light Emerald Green	$335
Whitall Tatum Co., No. 1, Aqua	$3
Whitall Tatum Co., No. 1, Pink	$7.50
Whitall Tatum Co., No. 1, Purple	$17.50

Jamestown
Fostoria Glass Company, 1958–85

The prices below are for crystal. The brown and amber are not all that desirable; reduce the prices by 25–35 percent. Fostoria usually made a fairly good grade of crystal, and the crystal Jamestown pieces are most in demand, followed closely by the other colors—amethyst, green, light blue, smoke, pink, and ruby red (increase prices below by 25–35 percent for these colors). Several lines were used for Fostoria's Jamestown pattern, and many pieces below are similar but differ slightly in dimensions. Stemware had a much longer production run, and, as a consequence, is more easily found than some of the tableware items.

Bowl, 4½"	$20
Bowl, 10"	$42.50
Bowl, 10" with 2 Handles	$47.50
Butter Dish with Cover, ¼ lb. Rectangular	$52.50
Cake Plate, 9½" with 2 Handles	$40
Celery, 9¼"	$35
Creamer, 3½"	$20
Goblet, Various Styles, 4" to 6" Tall	$18
Marmalade Dish with Cover	$65

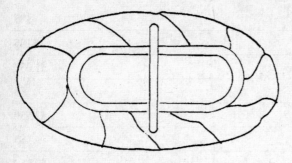

Jamestown Relish Dish. *Drawing by Mark Pickvet.*

Pickle, 8½"	$45
Pitcher, 1½ qt.	$110
Plate, 8"	$18
Plate, 14" Cake	$47.50
Relish, 9", 2-Part	$36
Salad Set, 4-Piece (10" Bowl, 14" Plate, Wooden Fork and Spoon)	$105
Salt and Pepper Shakers with Chrome Tops	$50
Salver, 10" Diameter, 7" Tall	$130
Sauce Dish with Cover	$37.50
Sherbet	$17.50
Sugar, 3½"	$20
Tray, 9½", 2-Handled	$47.50
Tumbler, Less Than 5" Tall	$25
Tumbler, More Than 5" Tall	$30
Wineglass, Various Styles	$18

Lenox, Incorporated
1960s–Present

Lenox began as a porcelain company in 1906. In the later 20th century, the firm expanded into glassware, creating a variety of collectible figurines, stemware, and novelty items. Lenox acquired Bryce Brothers in 1965 and Imperial in 1972. Lenox continued producing glass under the IGC Liquidating Corporation name as a division until selling it in 1982. Lenox continues today as a porcelain and glass producer, but note that some objects sold and marked with the company name are produced in both Europe and Asia.

Angel Figurine, 8½" Tall, Crystal with Frosted Star	$100
Apple, 4¾" Tall, Crystal	$75
Bell, 4¾" Tall, Crystal with Frosted Cherub Finial, Small Brass Chain, and Crystal Ringer	$50
Bird Sculpture, 4" Tall, Crystal Chickadee on Crystal Stump/Floral Base	$50
Bird Sculpture, 4½" Tall, Frosted Chickadee on Crystal Birdbath	$50
Bowl, 9" Diameter, Clear and Frosted Glass Checker Design, Hand-Painted Flowers and Insects in the Alternating Clear Squares	$50
Bowl, 10" Diameter, 8¼" Tall, Crystal with Etched Angelfish, Small Fish, and Sea Plants, Designed by Peter O'Rourke, Limited Edition of 50	$800
Car Sculpture, 1933 Frosted Dusenberg, Commissioned by the Auburn-Cord-Dusenberg Museum	$100
Cat Figurine, 3½" Long, Resting Position	$40
Cat Figurine, 3½" Tall, Female with Bow, Crystal	$40
Cat Figurine, 4" Tall, Partially Standing,Crystal, 2 Different Styles	$50
Cat Figurine, 6" Tall, Crystal with Hand-Painted Floral Design	$85
Cat Figurine, 8½" Long, Crystal, "Morning Stretch" Position	$90
Cat Sculpture, 6⅜" Tall, 2 Cats Fused Together, 1 Clear Crystal and 1 Frosted Crystal	$110
Christmas Ornament, 3" Diameter, Frosted Cherubs, 1997	$25
Cross Sculpture, 7¾" Tall, Faceted Crystal Cross	$40
Dolphin Candlesticks, Pair, 9⅜" Tall, Frosted Dolphin Design on Crystal Wave Base	$160
Dolphin Sculpture, 5⅜" Tall, 10⅛" Long, 3 Crystal Dolphins Leaping from Frosted Wave Base	$160
Eagle Sculpture, 8" Tall on Base, Crystal	$100
Eagle Sculpture, 10¾" Tall on Base, Crystal	$125
Egg, 3¾" Tall, Iridescent Pink with Etched Water Design, Made in England	$40
Elephant Figurine, 3½" Tall, 3½" Long, Crystal	$50
Elephant Sculpture, 5½" Tall, 1 Crystal and 1 Frosted Elephant on Frosted Savannah Grass Base	$200
Elephant Sculpture, 7" Tall, Crystal Elephant on Frosted Savannah Grass Base	$140

Highball, Various Cut and/or Faceted Crystal Designs, Patterns Include Charleston, Firelight, Holiday, Starfire, Windswept, etc. $25

Horse Sculpture, 8" Long, Crystal Galloping Horse on Base with Frosted Accents $140

Lighthouse Sculpture, 8" Long, Crystal with Base, Frosted Accents $100

Lion Sculpture, 7¾" Tall, Crystal Lion on Crystal Base, Frosted Accents $175

Nativity Set, 4-Piece (Joseph–8" Tall, Mary, Crib, and Baby Jesus), Crystal, Dansk $100

Pear, 4½" Tall, Crystal $75

Salt and Pepper Shakers, 2¾" Tall, Crystal Elephants $25

Salt and Pepper Shakers, 2¾" Tall, Crystal Rabbits $25

Salt and Pepper Shakers, 3" Tall, Crystal Cats $25

Salt and Pepper Shakers, 3" Tall, Crystal Dolphins $25

Salt and Pepper Shakers, 3¾" Tall, Crystal Angels $25

Salt and Pepper Shakers, 4⅛" Tall, Crystal Lighthouses $30

Stemware, Various Cut and/or Faceted Crystal Designs, Patterns Include Aria, Charleston, Clarity, Courtyeard, Debut, Encore, Erica, Firelight, Kelly, Madison, McKinley, Monroe, Rhythm, Unity, Windswept, etc. $30

Stemware, Various Cut and/or Faceted Crystal Designs with Gold or Platinum Trim and/or Bands; Patterns Include Citation Gold, Clarity Gold, Classic Shell Gold, Debute Gold or Platinum, Encore Gold or Platinum, Endure Gold, Erica Gold, Eternal Gold, Firelight Gold or Platinum, Golden Sand Dune, Gramercy Gold, Grandview Gold, Hancock Platinum, Landmark Platinum, Phoenix Gold or Platinum, Rhythm Gold or Platinum, Solitaire Platinum, Vintage Jewel Platinum, etc. $40

Swan Sculpture, 2 Swans on Pool, 4¼" Long, Crystal $40

Tumbler, Various Cut and/or Faceted Crystal Deisgns, Patterns Include Charleston, Firelight, Holiday, Starfire, Windswept, etc. $25

Vase, 7¼" Tall, Hand-Painted Bees, Floral, and Leaves Design, Gold Rim and Ring around Base $75

Vase, 8" Tall, Crystal with Frosted Dolphins and Aqua Blue Swirled Wave Design $100

Vase, 8¼" Tall, Crystal with Hand-Painted Butterflies and Flowers $50

Vase, 8¼" Tall, Clear and Frosted Checker Design, Hand-Painted Flowers and Insects in the Alternating Clear Squares $50

Vase, 9¼" Tall, Heavy Crystal with Etched Butterflies $100

Vase, 9¾" Tall, Crystal with Frosted Dolphin $125

Vase, 9¾" Tall, Crystal with Hand-Painted Butterflies, Limited Edition of 500 $300

Vase, 13½" Tall, Crystal Millenium Design with Hand-Painted Flowers, Limited Edition of 2,000 $300

Wolf Sculpture, 7½" Tall, Upright Howling Wolf with Frosted Tail on Crystal Base $80

Lundberg Studios
1973–Present

The original Lundberg Studios was established by brothers James and Steven Lundberg in California in 1973. The two quickly established a reputation for high-quality modern iridescent studio art sculptures and paperweights. Steven moved on to form Steven Lundberg Art Glass, and noted designer Daniel Salazar joined on at Lundberg Studios.

Lamp, 6" Tall Including Metal Base, 5" Diameter Iridescent Blue Planet Saturn with Rings $135

Paperweight, 2⅝" Diameter, White Lace Ground with Multicolored Peony Blossoms and Foliage, Daniel Salazar $350

Paperweight, 2¾" Diameter, White Lace Ground with Pink Rose Blossom and Multicolored Foliage, Daniel Salazar $400

Paperweight, 3" Diameter, Aqua Blue and Turquoise Ground, Multicolored Globe Shape of Planet Earth $175

Paperweight, 3" Diameter, Pink and White Wisteria Clusters, Green Foliage, Blue Ground $250

Paperweight, 3" Diameter, Violet Opaline with Enameled Moon, Stars, and Waves $110

Paperweight, 3¼" Diameter, Iridescent Aqua Ground, Multicolored Kissing Fish, Kelp, and Undersea Design, 24 kt. Gold Flaking, Steven Lundberg $450

Paperweight, 3⅝" Diameter, Ivory Yellow Ground with Lampworked White Crane and Green Bamboo, Daniel Salazar $500

Paperweight, 3⅞" Diameter, White Lace Ground with Pink Rose Blossom and Multicolored Foliage, Daniel Salazar $900

Vase, 4⅝" Tall, Iridescent Gold, Pulled Feather and Split Fern Design $175

Vase, 5½" Tall, 3¾" Diameter, Torch-Worked Crystal by Steven Lundberg, Multicolored Design of a Dragonfly and Cattail Weeds $500

Vase, 6½" Tall, Crystal with Torch-Worked Pink and Purple 4-Petal Flowers with Green Leaves $550

Vase, 7¼" Tall, Iridescent Silver, Blue, Gold, and Purple Shading, Royal Zebra Design, Signed "Lundberg Studios 2000" $150

Vase, 8½" Tall, Iridescent Gold, Pulled Feather and Split Fern Design $200

Vase, 8½" Tall, 5¾" Diameter, Iridescent Gold Tsunami Design $225

Vase, 10¼" Tall, Jack-in-the-Pulpit Style, Iridescent Silver, Blue, Gold, and Purple Shading $200

Milk Glass
Various Companies, Late 19th Century–Present

Milk glass is an opaque or semi-opaque opalescent glass colored originally by a compound of arsenic or calcined bones or tin. The result is a white color resembling milk. Modern milk glass usually contains aluminum and fluorine as additives to produce the desired effect. Milk glass is often trimmed, hand-painted, or machine-enameled with color since most anything goes with white! Common covered dishes such as roosters and hens are priced in the $20 to $25 range, whereas uncommon items such as horses and lions sell for much more.

Apple-Shape Dish, 9½" Across, 2 Divisions, Imperial, 1950s	$35
Basket, 8¾" Long, Laced Edge, Imperial, 1950s	$42.50
Battleship Shape (*The Newark*), 6¼" Long	$100
Battleship Shape (*Maine* from Spanish-American War), 7½" Long	$125
Boar's-Head Covered Dish, 1888 (Rare)	$2,150
Bowl, Fruit, 10⅝", Laced Edge, Monroe Pattern, Fostoria, 1960s	$40
Cake Stand, 10⅜" Square, 6¾" Tall, Hole in Center, Indiana, 1960s	$17.50
Camel Covered Dish, Westmoreland, 1950s	$80
Candleholder, Double, 5¼" Tall, Circular Base, Imperial, 1930s	$45
Candlestick, 4" Tall, Dolphin Stem, Westmoreland	$20
Candlestick, 7½" Tall, Vineleaf Design, Imperial, 1950s	$26
Candy Jar with Cover, 6½" Diameter, Enameled Floral Design	$37.50
Cat Covered Dish, Various Styles	$50
Chick Covered Dish, Double Head, Late 19th Century	$1,275
Chicken Covered Dish, Various Styles	$28
Compote, 7" Diameter, 4⅛" Tall, Circular Base with Bird Stem	$57.50
Compote, Octagon Base, Grape Design, Anchor-Hocking, 1960s	$17.50
Covered Wagon Shape (Conestoga), 6" to 6½" Long	$225
Creamer, 4¾", Chrysanthemum Sprig Design, Northwood	$200
Dog Covered Dish, Various Styles	$50
Dog, Pekingese Covered Dish, Late 19th Century	$775

Donkey and Cart, 9⅜" Long, 4⅛" Tall	$40
Dove Covered Candle Dish, Avon, 1970	$17.50
Duck Covered Dish, Various Styles	$27.50
Eagle Covered Dish (American Eagle Style)	$85
Easter Egg Shape, 2-Piece (Includes Cover), Gold Trim and Enameled Floral Design, 6" Long	$42.50
Egg Shape, 2-Piece (Includes Cover), 2¾" Long	$12.50
Gas Globe, Sinclair or Texaco	$450
Hat Shape, 3¾" Tall, Gold Ruffled Rim, Enameled Floral Design, Fenton	$32.50
Hen Covered Dish, Various Styles	$26
Horse Covered Dish, Various Styles	$60
Iron Covered Dish, 7" Long	$85
Lamb Covered Dish, Various Styles	$26
Lamp, Owl Shape, 7½" Tall	$1,050
Lamp Shade, 7¼" Globe Shape, Embossed Foliage Design	$165
Liberty Bell, 3½" Tall, Metal Clapper	$27.50
Mug, Anchor-Hocking or Hazel Atlas Advertising, 1940s	$10
Perfume Bottle with Stopper, 7" Tall, Pansy Design Outlined in Gold Trim	$55
Pitcher, Milk, 7" Tall, Cambridge, 1940s	$90
Powder Jar with Cover, 5½" Diameter, 4½" Tall, Enameled 3 Kittens Design with Gold Trim, Westmoreland	$70
Punch Bowl, Pineapple Pattern, Westmoreland	$175
Punch Cup, Pineapple Pattern, Westmoreland	$22.50
Rabbit Covered Dish, Various Styles	$26
Rooster Covered Dish, Various Styles	$26
Rooster Covered Dish, 4½" Long, 3¾" Tall, Hazel Atlas Mark	$40
Salt and Pepper Shakers, 3" Tall, Embossed Diamond Quilted Design	$26
Salt and Pepper Shakers, 6" Tall, John and Mary Bull, Aluminum Tops, Imperial, 1950s (Marked "IG")	$52.50
Sugar with Cover, 4¾", Chrysanthemum Sprig Design, Northwood	$260
Swan Covered Dish, Various Styles	$26
Vase, 3¾" Tall, Double Horse Head Design	$17.50
Vase, 6" Tall, Cornucopia Style, Westmoreland, 1930s	$50

GLASSWARE

Vase, 9" Tall, Embossed Loganberry Design, Imperial, 1950s	$32.50
Vase, 9" Tall, Embossed Grape Design, L. E. Smith, 1970s	$27.50
Vase, 9¾" Tall, 11½" Wide, Embossed Geese Design, Consolidated	$160

Moonstone
Anchor-Hocking Glass Corporation, 1941–46

The large round "Moonstones" on the glass articles resemble the hobs on hobnail patterns. The color is a white opalescent that serves as an edging on most pieces. The base is crystal and the opalescent coating does not render the glass opaque. There are a few off-light-green and pink opalescent pieces, for which the prices below should be doubled. Fenton has made a few pieces that are similar to Moonstone, including salt and pepper shakers and cologne bottles; however, the hobs on Fenton's pieces are more pointed than the round ones on Moonstone.

Bowl, 5½"	$18.50
Bowl, 5½", Crimped	$12.50
Bowl, 6½", 2-Handled	$15
Bowl, 7¾"	$16
Bowl, 9½", Crimped	$27.50
Candleholder	$11
Candy Jar with Cover	$37.50
Cigarette Jar with Cover	$26
Cloverleaf-Shape Dish, 3 Divisions	$17.50
Creamer	$11
Cup	$9.50
Goblet, 5½" Tall, 10 oz.	$21.50
Heart-Shape Dish, 1 Handle	$17.50
Plate, 6¼"	$7.50
Plate, 8"	$17.50
Plate, 8½"	$18
Plate, 10"	$25
Platter, 11"	$30
Puff Box with Cover, 4¾", Round	$28
Relish Dish	$13.50

Saucer	$8.50
Sherbet	$10
Sugar, 2-Handled	$11
Vase, 5" Tall	$16

Moroccan Amethyst
Hazel Ware, Division of Continental Can, 1960s

Amethyst is a dark purple color. There are several bowls in unique geometric styles in this collection. Moroccan Amethyst is also a sister pattern of other Hazel designs such as Capri. The pieces are the same shape and dimension; they differ only by color.

Ashtray, 3¼" Triangular	$6.50
Ashtray, 3¼" Round	$6.50
Ashtray, 6⅞" Triangular	$11
Ashtray, 8", Square	$16
Bowl, 4¾" Octagonal	$9
Bowl, 5¾", Square	$12.50
Bowl, 6" Round	$13.50
Bowl, 7¾" Oval	$18
Bowl, 7¾" Rectangular	$16
Bowl, 7¾" Rectangular with Metal Handle	$20
Bowl, 10¾"	$35
Candy Jar with Cover (Short)	$40
Candy Jar with Cover (Tall)	$45
Chip and Dip Set, 3-Piece (5¾" and 10¾" Bowls in Metal Holder)	$47.50
Cocktail Shaker with Cover	$32.50
Cocktail Shaker with Stirrer, 6¼", 16 oz. with Lip	$37.50
Cup	$6.50
Goblet, 4⅜", 5½ oz.	$12.50
Goblet, 5½", 9 oz.	$14
Ice Bucket, 6"	$45
Plate, 5¾"	$6
Plate, 7¼"	$8.50

Plate, 8" Square	$12.50
Plate, 9¾"	$11
Plate, 10", Fan Shape with Indentation for Cup	$11
Plate, 12"	$17.50
Sandwich Server with Metal Handle, 12"	$21
Saucer	$2.50
Sherbet, 4¼", 7½ oz.	$10
Tumbler, 2½", 4 oz.	$10
Tumbler, 3¼", 8 oz.	$16
Tumbler, 4¼", 9 oz.	$12.50
Tumbler, 4¼", 11 oz. with Crinkled Base	$15
Tumbler, 4⅝", 11 oz.	$15
Tumbler, 6½", 16 oz.	$17.50
Vase, 8½", Ruffled	$42.50
Wineglass, 4", 4½ oz.	$12.50

Navarre
Fostoria Glass Company, Late 1930s–1985

Navarre is Fostoria's Plate Etching #327 and is another of Fostoria's numerous etched crystal patterns; most if not all are similarly valued. Nearly all the stemware and one tumbler are available in a light pink or light blue with the same etching. Increase the prices below by 25 percent for pink or blue items; for any rare green, double them.

Bell	$80
Bonbon Dish, 7⅜" Diameter, 3-Footed	$55
Bowl, 4" or 4½", 1 Handle	$16
Bowl, 4⅝", Tricorner	$27.50
Bowl, 5", with or without Handle	$27.50
Bowl, 6", Square	$30
Bowl, 6¼", 3-Footed	$26
Bowl, 7½" Oval, 2 Tab Handles	$40
Bowl, 10" Oval	$85
Bowl, 10½", with or without Handles or Feet	$85

Bowl, 12"	$75
Bowl, 12½" Oval	$90
Brandy Glass, 15 oz., 5½" Tall	$110
Candlestick, 4" Tall	$27.50
Candlestick, 4½" or 5" Tall, Double	$47.50
Candlestick, 5½" Tall	$35
Candlestick, 6" Tall, Triple	$72.50
Candlestick, 6¾" Tall, Double	$65
Candlestick, 6¾" Tall, Triple	$77.50
Candy Dish with Cover	$140
Celery, 9"	$45
Celery, 11"	$55
Champagne Glass, 5 oz., 8" Tall	$110
Champagne Glass, 6 oz., 5⅝" Tall	$35
Cheese Dish, 3¼" Tall, 5¼" Diameter, Stemmed	$42.50
Claret Glass, 4½ oz., 6" Tall	$65
Claret Glass, 6½ oz., 6½" Tall	$70
Cocktail Glass, 4 oz., 3⅝" Tall	$35
Cocktail Glass, 3½ oz., 6" Tall	$37.50
Compote, Various Styles	$42.50
Cordial, ¾ oz., 3⅞" Tall	$55
Cracker Dish, 11", Flat	$45
Creamer, Individual, 3⅛" Tall, 4 oz.	$22.50
Creamer, 4¼" Tall, 6¾ oz.	$27.50
Cruet with Stopper, 6½" Tall	$450
Cup	$23
Goblet, Magnum, 16 oz., 7¼" Tall	$175
Goblet, Water, 10 oz., 7⅝" Tall	$42.50
Ice Bucket, 4½" Tall	$130
Ice Bucket, 6" Tall	$165
Mayonnaise Set, 3-Piece (2 Styles)	$90

Pickle, 6½"	$35
Pickle, 8" or 8½"	$35
Pitcher, Syrup, 5½"	$450
Pitcher, 1 qt.	$300
Pitcher, 1½ qt.	$400
Plate, 6"	$13.50
Plate, 7½"	$17.50
Plate, 8½"	$25
Plate, 9½"	$55
Plate, 10" Cake, 2 Handles	$55
Plate, 10½", Oval	$65
Plate, 11", Cracker	$45
Plate, 14" Cake	$80
Plate, 16" Cake	$110
Relish, 6", Square, 2 Divisions	$40
Relish, 10" Oval, 3 Divisions	$55
Relish, 10", 4 Divisions	$80
Relish, 13¼", 5 Divisions	$100
Salt and Pepper Shakers, 3¼"	$85
Salt and Pepper Shakers, 3½", Footed	$125
Sauce Dish, 6½" x 5¼" Oval	$125
Sauce Dish, 6½", Divided	$55
Sauce Dish Liner, 8", Oval	$35
Saucer	$10
Sherbet, 6 oz., 4⅜" Tall	$27.50
Sherry Glass, 6 oz., 6¼" Tall	$80
Sugar, Individual, 2⅞" Tall	$22.50
Sugar, 3⅝" Tall, 2-Handled	$27.50
Tidbit, 8¼", 3-Footed	$37.50
Tray, 6½" (for Individual Creamer and Sugar Set)	$37.50
Tumbler, 5 oz., 4⅝", Footed	$27.50

Tumbler, 10 oz., 5⅜", Footed	$32.50
Tumbler, 12 oz., 4⅞"	$100
Tumbler, 13 oz., 3⅝"	$100
Vase, Less Than 10" Tall, Various Styles	$100
Vase, 10", Footed	$250
Wineglass, 3¼ oz., 5½" Tall	$45

New Martinsville Animals
1920s–1950s

New Martinsville's line of animals was continued by Viking, which purchased the company in 1944. They used the New Martinsville molds but marked their products as "Rainbow Art" or with the "Viking" name. In 1991 Viking was purchased by Kenneth Dalzell (former president of Fostoria) and some of the old molds were still used; however, Viking closed in 1997 (see the "Viking" entry near the end of this chapter). Most were made in crystal, with a few noted color exceptions listed below.

Bear, Baby, 3" Tall, 4½" Long, Crystal or Light Yellow	$80
Bear, Mama, 4" Tall, 6" Long	$310
Bear, Papa, 4¾" Tall, 6½" Long	$375
Bear, Black, with Wheelbarrow (2-Piece Set)	$290
Bear, Polar	$75
Chick, 1" Tall	$80
Dog Bookends, German Shepherd, Pair	$185
Dog Bookends, Russian Wolfhound, 7¼" Tall, Pair	$210
Dove Bookends, 6" Tall, Frosted, Pair	$90
Duck, Fighting, Head Up or Down (Viking)	$42.50
Eagle	$80
Elephant Bookends, 5½" Tall, Pair	$210
Gazelle Bookends, 8½" Tall, Pair	$145
Hen, 5" Tall	$80
Horse, 12" Tall, Pony, Oval Base	$120
Pelican, 8" Tall, Lavender Tint	$80
Pig, 3¾" Tall, Sow	$300
Piglet, 1¼" Tall	$125

Police Dog on Rectangular Base, 5" Tall, 5" Long	$115
Porpoise	$540
Rabbit, 1" Tall, 3 Styles (Ears Back, Up or Down)	$85
Rabbit, 3" Tall	$110
Rooster, 8" Tall	$115
Seal Candlestick, 4¾" Tall, Baby Seal	$80
Seal Light, 7¼" Tall, with Bulb	$90
Seal with Ball Bookends, Pair	$165
Squirrel Bookends, 5¼" Tall, On Base, Pair	$160
Starfish Bookends, 7¾" Tall, Pair	$185
Swan Bonbon Dish, 6", Cobalt Blue	$65
Swan Bowl, 10½", Amber or Crystal	$55
Tiger Bookends, 6¾" Tall, on Base, Pair	$350

Newport Hairpin

Hazel Atlas Glass Company, 1940–Early 1950s

Fired-on Platonite colors include pink, turquoise, red, and combinations of colors and white. See the previous chapter on Depression Glass for older transparent colors of Newport Hairpin. For solid white colors (a typical milk glass as well as a nearly translucent white), reduce the prices by 25–35 percent.

Bowl, 4¾", Berry	$6.50
Bowl, 4¾", Soup	$10.50
Bowl, 8¼"	$17.50
Creamer	$9.50
Cup	$7.50
Plate, 6"	$2.25
Plate, 8½"	$6.50
Plate, 11½"	$18.50
Plate, 11¾" Oval	$21
Salt and Pepper Shakers	$27.50
Saucer	$1.50
Sherbet	$7.50

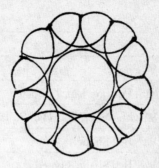

Newport Hairpin Plate. *Drawing by Mark Pickvet.*

Sugar	$9.50
Tumbler	$25

Paneled Grape
Westmoreland Glass Company, 1950–1970s

The white of this pattern is an opaque milk white. Some pieces (mostly plates) are also available at the same prices with colored birds, flowers, and fruits. There are also a few opaque green pieces, and prices for them are the same as well. Paneled Grape is also known as Westmoreland's Pattern #1881 and was hugely successful. In the modern or even post-modern era of glassware, there are few patterns that can boast so many pieces (excluding different color combinations).

Appetizer Set, 3-Piece (Relish Dish, Round Fruit Cocktail, and Small Ladle)	$77.50
Banana Boat, 12", Footed	$175
Basket, 5½"	$62.50
Basket, 6½", Oval	$50
Basket, 8", 2 Styles	$125
Bonbon Dish with Metal Handle, 8"	$57.50
Bottle, Water, 5 oz.	$85
Bowl, 4"	$26
Bowl, 5"	$77.50
Bowl, 6½" Oval	$50
Bowl, 8"	$55

Bowl, 8½"	$60
Bowl, 9"	$85
Bowl, 9", Footed	$85
Bowl with Pouring Lip, 9", Footed	$125
Bowl, 9" with Cover, Round or Square	$100
Bowl, 9½", Bell Shape	$75
Bowl, 9½", Bell Shape, Footed	$125
Bowl, 10", Oval	$85
Bowl, 10½", Round or Oval	$95
Bowl, 11", Round or Oval	$135
Bowl, 11½", Round or Oval	$110
Bowl, 12"	$135
Bowl, 12½", Oval or Bell Shape	$155
Bowl, 14", Shallow	$175
Bowl, Rose	$40
Butter Dish with Cover, Rectangular (¼ lb.)	$45
Cake Salver, 10½"	$75
Cake Salver, 11", Footed	$85
Canape Set, 3-Piece (3½" Fruit Cocktail with Ladle and 12½" Tray)	$175
Candelabra, Triple	$300
Candleholder, 4" Tall, Octagonal	$17.50
Candleholder, 5" Tall	$25
Candleholder, 8" Tall, Double	$40
Candy Box with Cover, 6½"	$60
Candy Jar with Cover, with or without Feet	$45
Canister with Cover, 7"	$160
Canister with Cover, 9½"	$210
Canister with cover, 11"	$275
Celery, 6" Tall	$45
Cheese Dish with Cover	$100
Claret Glass, 3 oz.	$35

Compote, 4½", Crimped	$35
Compote, 6" 2 Styles, Footed	$37.50
Compote with Cover, 7", Footed	$55
Compote, 9", Footed	$90
Condiment Set, 5-Piece (2 Oil Bottles, Salt and Pepper Shakers, and 9" Oval Tray)	$150
Cordial, 2 oz.	$27.50
Creamer, Individual (Tiny)	$17.50
Creamer, 2 Styles	$25
Cruet with Stopper, 2 oz.	$35
Cruet with Stopper, 6 oz.	$45
Cup	$15
Decanter with Stopper	$175
Dresser Set, 4-Piece (2 Water Bottles, Puff Box, and 13½" Oval Tray)	$275
Egg Plate, 12"	$100
Egg Tray, 10" with Metal Center Handle	$75
Epergne Set, 2-Piece (9" Lipped Bowl and 8½" Vase)	$140
Epergne Set, 2-Piece (11½" Bowl and 8½" Vase)	$175
Epergne Set, 2-Piece (12" Lipped Bowl and 8½" Vase)	$225
Epergne Set, 2-Piece (14" Flared Bowl and 8½" Vase)	$275
Epergne Set, 3-Piece (12" Lipped Bowl, 5" Bowl Base, and 8½" Vase)	$360
Epergne Set, 3-Piece (14" Flared Bowl, 5" Bowl Base, and 8½" Vase)	$400
Flowerpot	$65
Fruit Cocktail, 3½", Round or Bell Shape with 6" Plate	$35
Fruit Cocktail, 4½", Round or Bell Shape with 6" Plate	$37.50
Goblet, Water, 8 oz.	$25
Ivy Ball	$52.50
Jardiniere, 5" Tall, 2 Styles	$35
Jardiniere, 6½" Tall, 2 Styles	$42.50
Jelly Dish with Cover, 4½" Tall	$35
Ladle, Small	$15
Lighter	$35

Marmalade Dish with Ladle	$75
Mayonnaise, 4", Footed	$30
Mayonnaise Set, 3-Piece (Round Fruit Cocktail, 6" Plate, and Ladle)	$65
Napkin Ring	$22.50
Nappy, 4½"	$17.50
Nappy, 5", Bell Shape	$26
Nappy, 5", Handled	$35
Nappy, 7"	$35
Nappy, 8½"	$60
Nappy, 9"	$75
Nappy, 10", Bell Shape	$80
Parfait, 6"	$30
Pickle, Oval	$30
Pitcher, 1 pt.	$57.50
Pitcher, 1 qt.	$65
Planter, Freestanding, Various Styles	$55
Planter, Wall, 6"	$100
Planter, Wall, 8"	$150
Plate, 6"	$25
Plate, 7"	$35
Plate, 8½"	$45
Plate, 10½"	$60
Platter, 14½"	$135
Platter, 18"	$225
Puff Box with Cover	$55
Punch Bowl, 13"	$350
Punch Bowl Base	$200
Punch Cup	$15
Punch Ladle	$75
Relish, 9", 3-Part	$50
Salt and Pepper Shakers, 4¼", Small, Footed	$45

Salt and Pepper Shakers, 4½", Large	$57.50
Sauce Boat and Tray	$75
Saucer	$15
Sherbet, 3¾"	$18.50
Sherbet, 4¾"	$21
Soap Dish	$110
Sugar, Individual (Tiny)	$17.50
Sugar, 2 Styles	$25
Sugar with Cover	$35
Tidbit, 2-Tier (8½" and 10½" Plates)	$100
Tidbit Tray with Metal Handle on 8½" Plate	$55
Tidbit Tray with Metal Handle on 10½" Plate	$65
Toothpick Holder	$35
Tray, 9" Oval	$65
Tray, 10" Oval	$95
Tray, 13½" Oval	$110
Tumbler, 5 oz.	$30
Tumbler, 6 oz.	$32.50
Tumbler, 8 oz.	$32.50
Tumbler, 12 oz.	$35
Vase, 4" Tall	$35
Vase, 4½" Tall	$40
Vase, 6" Tall	$35
Vase, 6½" Tall	$40
Vase, 8½" Tall	$35
Vase, 9" Tall, 2 Styles	$42.50
Vase, 9½" Tall	$45
Vase, 10" Tall	$35
Vase, 11" Tall	$45
Vase, 11½" Tall, 2 Styles	$55
Vase, 12" Tall, Handblown	$185

Vase, 14" Tall	$40
Vase, 15" Tall	$45
Vase, 16" Tall	$50
Vase, 18" Tall	$55
Water Bottle, 5 oz.	$75
Wineglass, 5 oz.	$37.50

Pilgrim Glass Company
1949–Present

Pilgrim was established by Alfred E. Knobler in Ceredo, West Virginia, in 1949. Pilgrim is well known in the contemporary art-glass field. Their most impressive designs are superbly crafted cameo products. Along with cameo-engraving, they have revived older styles, including Cranberry, Crackle, Iridescent, and others.

Bottle, 21" Tall, Red with Crystal Stopper, Gurgle Design	$65
Canister with Cover, Amber Color, Crackle Design	$55
Cruet with Crystal Stopper, 7" Tall, Cranberry with Applied Crystal Handle	$50
Decanter with Crystal Ball Stopper, 13" Tall, Blue Glass	$65
Egg, 2½" Tall, Cranberry and Crystal Rose on White Cameo	$225
Egg, 3" Tall, Various Transparent Colors (Green, Amethyst, Blue, etc.) with Cameo Cut Floral and Wildlife Designs)	$40
Egg, 3" Tall, White on Red Cameo, Snowman and Evergreens Design	$250
Lamp, 10" Tall, Brass Base, White on Blue Cameo, Evergreens, and Covered Bridge Scene	$1,275
Lamp, 24" Tall, All Glass (Base, Stem, and Shade), Cranberry with Cameo Floral Design	$1,000
Owl Paperweight, Crystal	$21.50
Paperweight, 4½", Crystal with Blue Flower and Vine Swirls	$55
Perfume Bottle with Stopper, 6" Tall, Cranberry	$95
Pitcher, Miniature, 3½" Tall, Green Crackle	$17.50
Pitcher, Miniature, 4½" Tall, Amethyst, Diamond and Swirl Design, Applied Crystal Handle	$22.50
Pitcher, Miniature, 5" Tall, Transparent Milk Glass, Thumbprint Pattern	$27.50
Pitcher, Milk, 6" Tall, Opaque Tangerine with Frosted Handle	$25

Pilgrim Vases. *Photo by Robin Rainwater.*

Pilgrim Glass Examples. *Photo by Robin Rainwater.*

Pitcher, Water, 7½" Tall, Ruby Red Crackle Design	$45
Plate, 12", Crystal, Christmas Issue, Della Robia Design	$30
Powder Jar with White Cover, 1½" Tall, White "Summer Meadow" on Pink Cameo, Foliage and Clover Design	$350
Vase, 5" Tall, Fluted Top, Crystal Base, White with Cranberry Streaking	$25
Vase, 7" Tall, Black Bears (with White Eyes and Red Mouths) on Green Cameo, Appalachia Folk Art Design	$1,150
Vase, 7" Tall, Light Blue and White Daisies on Green Cameo	$575
Vase, 8" Tall, Bud, Crystal Globe Base, Ruby Red	$35
Vase, 8" Tall, Classic Ming Style, Plum Cast with Milk White Interior	$50
Vase, 9" Tall, 4-Color Cameo, Brown and Tan Koala Bears on Dark Gray Ground	$950
Vase, 10" Tall, Bud, Cranberry	$90
Vase, 11" Tall, 5-Color Cameo; Dark Brown, Tan, and Black Night Hawk Landing Design, White Stars, Shaded Light Gray Ground	$1,375
Vase, 12" Tall, Jack-in-the-Pulpit Style, Cranberry	$125

Vase, 12" Tall, Jack-in-the-Pulpit Style, Iridescent Green with Yellow and Orange Stripes	$115
Vase, 12" Tall, Light Blue on Aqua Cameo, Ladies in the Aviary Design	$425
Vase, 12" Tall, Red and White Rhododendron and Blue Leaves on White Cameo	$950
Vase, 13" Tall, Dark and Light Blue on Tan Cameo, Parrots Design	$450

Planter's Peanuts

1906–Present

The Planters Nut and Chocolate Company was founded in 1906 in Wilkes-Barre, Pennsylvania. The trademark Mr. Peanut figurine was adopted in 1916. In 1961, the company was sold to Standard Brands, Inc., which merged with Nabisco in 1981. There are many barrel-shape jars out there with the peanut finial covers. Early jars were commissioned by Tiffin in the 1930s. Mr. Peanut jars can be difficult to date because many are being reproduced. Be careful, because the older emerald green Depression-style jars sell for about 10 times the price of more recent dark forest green jars.

Aquarium or Fishbowl, Embossed Clear Glass Rectangular Planter's Logo, 1930s–1940s	$175
Jar with Peanut Finial Cover, Barrel Shape, Cobalt Blue, Reproduction	$85
Jar with Peanut Finial Cover, Barrel Shape, Clear Glass with Enameled Mr. Peanut, 1960s–1980s	$37.50
Jar with Peanut Finial Cover, Barrel Shape, Emerald Green, 1930s	$400
Jar with Peanut Finial Cover, Barrel Shape, Dark or Forest Green, 1980s–1990s	$37.50
Jar with Peanut Finial Cover, Octagonal, Emerald Green, 1930s	$400
Jar with Peanut Finial Cover, Square Shaped, Embossed Clear Glass Planter's Design, 1930s	$175
Jar with Knobbed Cover, Round, Embossed Clear Glass Planter's Logo, 1930s–1940s	$125
Jar with Knobbed Cover, Round, Enameled Red and White Planter's Logo, 1960s	$65
Jar with Knobbed Cover, Round, Dark or Forest Green, Planter's Logo, 1980s–1990s	$37.50
Jar with Knobbed Cover, Round, Mr. Peanut 75th Anniversary	$57.50
Marble, Mr. Peanut, 1960	$22.50
Mug, Yellow Glass, Mr. Peanut	$65
Paperweight, Mr. Peanut, Tennis Player, 1938	$85
Pilsener Glass, Mr. Peanut 75th Anniversary	$35
Pitcher, Water, 60 oz., Enameled Black and Yellow Mr. Peanut Design, 1990s	$27.50

Tumbler, Enameled Black and Tan Mr. Peanut	$25
Tumbler, Yellow Glass, Mr. Peanut	$47.50
Tumbler, 16 oz., Enameled Black and Yellow Mr. Peanut Design, 1990s	$5

Pyrex
Corning Glass Works, 1915–Present

The items below are all original crystal Corning Pyrex products. Prices are about the same for decorated milk glass items in the form of enamel transfer produced later. Note that none of the measuring items carry metric system measurements (introduced in the late 1960s). In the late 19th century, Corning produced specialty glass products such as light-bulbs for Edison's new lamps, pharmaceutical and laboratory glass, railroad signal lenses, and so on. Research continued to find a glass that could withstand extreme temperature changes, because flamed railroad lanterns had a habit of shattering when exposed to rain or snow. In 1912, Dr. Otto Schott perfected a boro-silicate glass formula that withstood cold and hot temperature extremes. Initially, the formula worked well for lanterns as well as for battery jars; soon afterward, it was adapted to ovenware and kitchenware, in 1915.

Baking Dish, 9½ oz., Square	$5
Baking Dish, 13" x 9" Rectangular, 2 Tab Handles	$10
Bowl, Mixing, 1½ pt., 2 Tab Handles	$4.25
Bowl, Mixing, 1 qt., 2 Tab handles	$4.75
Bowl, Mixing, 1½ qt., 2 Tab Handles	$5.75
Bowl, Mixing, 2 qt., 2 Tab Handles	$7.50
Bowl, Mixing, 3 qt., 2 Tab Handles	$9.50
Bread Pan, 8½" Rectangular, 2 Tab Handles	$8.50
Cake Dish, 8½", Square	$8.50
Cake Dish, 8½", Square, 2 Tab Handles	$9
Cake Dish, 9", Square	$9
Cake Dish, 9", Square, 2 Tab Handles	$10
Casserole, 1 pt., with Cover, Oval, Knob Handle	$8.50
Casserole, 1 pt., with Cover, Round, Knob Handle	$9
Casserole, 1 qt., with Cover, Oval, Knob Handle	$9.50
Casserole, 1 qt., with Cover, Round, Knob Handle	$12.50
Casserole, 1½ qt., with Cover, Oval, Knob Handle	$13
Casserole, 1½ qt., with Cover, Round, Knob Handle	$13.50

Casserole, 1½ qt., with Cover, Square, Knob Handle	$16
Casserole, 1½ qt., with Cover, Square, Knob Center Handle and 2 Tab Side Handles	$17.50
Casserole, 2 qt., with Cover, Round Knob Handle	$17.50
Casserole, 3 qt., with Pie Plate Cover, Round	$20
Custard Cup, 3 Horizontal Bands	$3.25
Measuring Cup, 1 cup	$4.25
Measuring Cup, 1 pt.	$5.50
Measuring Cup, 1 qt.	$8.50
Mushroom Dish with Dome Cover, 2-Tab Handles on Dish	$85
Pie Plate, 5"	$2.75
Pie Plate, 6"	$3.25
Pie Plate, 7"	$3.75
Pie Plate, 8"	$4.50
Pie Plate, 8½", 2 Tab Handles	$8
Pie Plate, 9"	$5.50
Pie Plate, 10"	$6.50
Pie Plate, 11"	$8.50
Platter, 13⅔" Oval	$21
Platter, 15¾" Oval	$27.50
Refrigerator Dish with Cover, 1½ cup	$5.50
Refrigerator Dish with Cover, 1 pt.	$8
Refrigerator Dish with Cover, 1½ pt.	$11
Refrigerator Dish with Cover, 1 qt.	$13.50
Refrigerator Dish with Cover, 1½ qt.	$16
Roaster with Glass Bowl Cover, 3 qt., 10¼" Diameter, 2 Tab Handles on Top and Bottom	$70
Teapot with Cover, 4-Cup, Short, Squat Style	$67.50
Teapot with Cover, 4-Cup, Tall Style	$105
Teapot with Cover, 6-Cup, Short, Squat Style	$85
Teapot with Cover, 6-Cup, Tall Style	$120

Teapot with Cover, 6-Cup, Engraved Floral Design, Short, Squat Style	$135
Teapot with Cover, 6-Cup, Engraved Floral Design, Tall Style	$175

Royal Ruby
Anchor-Hocking Glass Company, 1938–1970s

Royal Ruby is the older sister pattern of Forest Green. Royal Ruby was first made in the late 1930s but is usually considered as later than the Depression era. The pattern is named for the color, which is a little darker than ruby red. Note that many pieces from Depression patterns were made in this color. These include Coronation, Old Cafe, Oyster and Pearl, Queen Mary, Sandwich, and so on. Anchor-Hocking has a patent on the Royal Ruby name. Both Royal Ruby and Forest Green were made in great quantities, and pieces are usually not too difficult to find. Assembling a complete set in both colors is definitely a challenge! Some pieces contain a combination of crystal and ruby red, at the same prices. Refer to the "Ruby Red" section below for ruby glass made by other companies.

Ashtray, 4½" or 5", Leaf Shape	$7.50
Beer Bottle, 7 oz.	$27.50
Beer Bottle, 12 oz.	$75
Beer Bottle, 16 oz.	$85
Beer Bottle, 32 oz.	$75
Bonbon Dish, 6½"	$12.50
Bonbon Dish, 9"	$16
Bowl, 3¾"	$8.50
Bowl, 4" Ivy (Similar to a Rose Bowl but Narrower)	$12.50
Bowl, 4¼"	$8
Bowl, 4½", 1 Handle	$9
Bowl, 4¾", Round or Square	$10
Bowl, 5", Round or Square	$12.50
Bowl, 5¼"	$15
Bowl, 5½"	$16
Bowl, 5½", 1 Handle	$17.50
Bowl, 6½"	$26
Bowl, 6½", 1 Handle	$18.50
Bowl, 7½", Round or Square	$17.50

Bowl, 8", 2-Handled	$25
Bowl, 8", Oval	$37.50
Bowl, 8½"	$25
Bowl, 9", 2 Tab Handles	$27.50
Bowl, 10"	$42.50
Bowl, 10½"	$50
Bowl, 11½"	$40
Box, 4¼", Crystal with Ruby Red Cover	$16
Candleholder, 3½" Tall	$32.50
Candleholder, 4½" Tall	$42.50
Candy Jar with Cover	$27.50
Celery Dish, 9" Long	$26
Cigarette Box or Card Holder	$75
Cocktail Glass, 3½ or 4½ oz.	$12.50
Cordial	$12.50
Creamer, Several Styles	$12.50
Cup, Round	$7.50
Cup, Square	$9
Goblet, 9 or 9½ oz.	$15
Heart-Shape Dish, 5¼" Long, 1 Handle	$22.50
Ice Bucket	$42.50
Lamp	$42.50
Lamp, Old Café Pattern	$175
Lazy Susan, Crystal Tray with 5 Ruby Red Inserts and Crystal Center Bowl	$105
Leaf-Shaped Dish, 6½" Across	$16
Marmalade Dish, Crystal with Ruby Red Cover, 5⅛"	$13.50
Mint Dish, 8"	$17.50
Mustard Jar, Crystal with Notched Ruby Red Cover and Ruby Red Spoon	$30
Pickle Dish, 6" Long	$17.50
Pitcher, 22 oz., Tilted	$45
Pitcher, 1 qt., Straight or Tilted	$50

Pitcher, 1½ qt., Hobnail Pattern	$75
Pitcher, 2 qt., Bubble or Provincial Pattern	$90
Pitcher, 3 qt.	$100
Plate, 6½"	$6
Plate, 7"	$7.50
Plate, 7¾", Round or Square	$8.50
Plate, 8½", Round or Square	$11
Plate, 9", Round or Square	$12.50
Plate, 9¼", Round or Square	$13
Plate, 9⅜", Bubble or Provincial Pattern	$16
Platter, 13½" to 13¾"	$50
Platter, 14"	$55
Puff Box with Cover, 4⅝", Crystal with Ruby Red Cover	$16
Punch Bowl	$75
Punch Bowl Base	$50
Punch Cup	$6
Relish Tray, Crystal with 5 Ruby Red Inserts and Crystal Center Bowl with Cover	$125
Saucer, Round or Square	$3
Sherbet, Several Styles	$11
Sugar Dish, Several Styles	$12.50
Sugar with Cover, Footed	$26
Tidbit Tray, Center Handle	$30
Tray, Rectangular, 6" x 4½"	$17.50
Tumbler, 3" Tall, Crystal Foot	$15
Tumbler, 3½" Tall	$12.50
Tumbler, 4" Tall	$17.50
Tumbler, 4" Tall, Crystal Foot	$17.50
Tumbler, 4½" Tall, Hobnail Pattern	$17.50
Tumbler, 5" Tall	$20
Tumbler, 6" Tall, Crystal Foot	$20
Tumbler, 6" Tall, Bubble or Provincial Pattern	$22

Tumbler, 8½" Tall, Crystal Foot	$25
Vase, 4" Tall	$12.50
Vase, 6⅜" Tall, Banded Ring Design	$11
Vase, 6½" Tall	$15
Vase, 7¼" Tall	$22.50
Vase, 9"	$20
Water Bottle, 2 Styles (Rare)	$275
Wineglass, Various Styles	$16

Ruby Red Glass
Various Companies, 1890s–Present

Ruby red glass is so named for the deep, rich red color made originally by the addition of gold. In modern times from around the late Depression era and beyond, the element selenium also produces ruby red and has replaced gold as the primary coloring agent. Ruby red glass was made throughout the 20th century by Cambridge, Duncan & Miller, Fenton, Fostoria, Imperial, New Martinsville, Viking, Wright, and others. Those that have survived still make it today. For additional ruby red examples refer to other patterns in this chapter as well as in the previous chapter. These include Royal Ruby, Crest, Coin Glass, Jamestown, references in many Depression patterns, and companies with separate listings such as Blenko, Viking, and Westmoreland.

Ashtray, Ruby Red, 3-Footed, 1930s (Fenton)	$27.50
Banana Boat, 11½" Long, 1930s (New Martinsville)	$50
Basket, 10½" Diameter, Wicker Handle, Embossed Circles, 1933 (Fenton)	$200
Bonbon Dish, 7" Diameter, Basketweave Pattern, 1930 (Fenton)	$80
Bowl, 6", Shallow, 1921 (Fenton)	$80
Bowl, 8", Cupped with Base, 1929 (Fenton)	$90
Bowl, 10", Cupped, 3 Dolphin Feet, 1930 (Fenton)	$150
Bowl, Orange, 10", Crimped, 1921 (Fenton)	$415
Bowl, 11", Crimped, 3-Footed, Pineapple Pattern, 1937 (Fenton)	$190
Bowl, Rose, Reeded Design, 1930s (Imperial)	$40
Candelabrum, 3-Light, 1930s (Imperial)	$175
Candelabrum, 3-Light, 5¼" Tall, 1930s (New Martinsville)	$85
Candleholder, 1-Light, 5¼" Tall, 1930s (New Martinsville)	$60
Candlestick, 3½" Tall, Double Dolphin Design, 1930 (Fenton)	$85

Candlestick, 5" Tall, Horizontally Ribbed, 1930s (Cambridge)	$65
Candlestick, 8½" Tall, Cut Ovals, 1922 (Fenton)	$300
Candy Jar with Cover, 6", Marbleized or Slag Color, 1970s (Imperial, "IG" on Bottom)	$75
Candy Jar with Cover, 7" Across, Clover Leaf Design, 1930s (Paden City)	$150
Chalice with Cover, 9½" Tall, Hapsburg Crown Design, 1960s (Fostoria)	$125
Compote, 10" Diameter, Double Dolphin Handles, 1933 (Fenton)	$200
Creamer, Colony Pattern, 1980s (Fostoria)	$45
Creamer, 4" Tall, Clear Base, 1930 (Fenton)	$50
Cup, 3¼" Diameter, Georgian Pattern, 1930s (Fenton)	$35
Decanter, 21 oz., Georgian Pattern, 1930s (Fenton)	$175
Decanter with Crystal Ball Stopper, Radiance Design, 1940s (New Martinsville)	$175
Epergne, 3-Piece (Stand, Bowl, and Single Vase), 1930s (Paden City)	$350
Fish, Angel, 7¼" Tall, 1960s (Fostoria)	$125
Goblet, 7" Tall, Diamond Optic Pattern, 1928 (Fenton)	$77.50
Jug, Ball Shape, 80 oz., Applied Crystal Handle, 1930s (Cambridge)	$225
Lamp, Electric, 9½" Tall, Diamond Optic Pattern, 1931 (Fenton)	$175
Nappy, 7¾", Laced Edge, Diamond Design, 1930s (Imperial)	$45
Nappy, 8" Diameter, 3-Footed, Crimped, 1934 (Fenton)	$85
Pickle Dish, 7" Long, Diamond Design, 1930s (New Martinsville)	$45
Piggy Bank, 7" Long, 4" Tall, Ruby Red, Mouth Blown, James Joyce	$75
Pitcher, 80 oz., Reeded Design, 1930s (Imperial)	$175
Plate, 7", Cape Cod Pattern (Imperial)	$32.50
Plate, 8", Square, Mount Vernon Design (Imperial)	$37.50
Plate, 10", Sheffield Pattern, 1936 (Fenton)	$87.50
Plate, Torte, 14", Radiance Design, 1930s (New Martinsville)	$87.50
Platter, 12", 2-Handled, 1980s (New Martinsville)	$65
Punch Bowl, Footed, 13" Diameter, 1930s (Cambridge)	$375
Punch Bowl with Underliner Plate, Globe Shaped, Radiance Design, 1930s (New Martinsville)	$575
Punch Cup (Matches Bowl Above), 1930s (Cambridge)	$50
Punch Cup (Matches Bowl Above), Radiance Design, 1930s (New Martinsville)	$45

Punch Ladle (Matches Bowl Above), Radiance Design, 1930s (New Martinsville)	$125
Relish Dish, 8" Diameter, 2-Handled, 1931–56 (Cambridge)	$45
Relish Dish, 8½" Diameter, 3 Divisions, 3-Footed, 1930s (New Martinsville)	$40
Rooster Figurine, 9½" Tall (Viking)	$75
Salt and Pepper Shakers with Chrome Tops, 4½" Tall, Georgian Pattern, 1930s (Fenton)	$140
Sandwich Server with Center Handle, 10½", Threaded Design, 1930s (Paden City)	$150
Sherbet, Footed with Clear Base, 1930 (Fenton)	$55
Sugar, Colony Pattern, 1980s (Fostoria)	$30
Sugar, 3½" Tall, Clear Base, 1930 (Fenton)	$50
Tray, 8½" Long, Leaf Shape, Leaf Vein Design, 1936 (Fenton)	$125
Tray, 12" Rectangular, 2-Handled, 1932 (Fenton)	$125
Tumbler, 4¼" Tall, Large Round Flutes, 1933 (Fenton)	$40
Tumbler, 6" Tall, Plymouth Pattern, 1930s (Fenton)	$45
Tumbler, 12 oz., Reeded Design, 1930s (Imperial)	$30
Vase, 6½" Tall, Jack-in-the-Pulpit Style, 1933 (Fenton)	$100
Vase, Wall, 6½" Tall, 1926 (Tiffin)	$115
Vase, 6¾" Tall, Sheffield Pattern, 1936 (Fenton)	$60
Vase, 8½" Tall, Fan Style, Diamond Optic Pattern, 1928 (Fenton)	$75
Vase, 9" Tall, Embossed Dancers, 1933 (Fenton)	$325
Vase, 12" Tall, Engraved Floral Design, 1931 (Fenton)	$225
Vase, 14" Tall, Cornucopia Shape, 1940s (Duncan & Miller)	$225

Saint Clair Glass Works
1941–Present

St. Clair was founded in Elwood, Indiana, by John St. Clair and his five sons (John Jr., Paul, Ed, Joe, and Bob); all had previously worked for MacBeth-Evans. The firm began as a maker of paperweights and novelty items and added some pressed tableware, lamps, and art styles such as custard glass later. The firm continues today under Joe Rice (nephew of Bob).

Apple, 4" Tall, Crystal with Red Swirling, Applied Green Stem and Leaf at Top, Stamped "Joe St.Clair"	$50
Ashtray, 6", 3 Rests, Various Paperweight Base Color Designs	$75

Ashtray, 6", One Rest and Applied Handle, Orange Floral and Green Foliage Paperweight Base $75

Bell, 6" Tall, Opaque Caramel Slag, Molded Diamond and Foliage Design $40

Bell, 7", Carnival Blue, Bicentennial Style, No Clapper, Stamped "Joe St.Clair" $40

Bird Figurine, 3½" Long, Crystal with Caramel and White Swirling $20

Candleholder, 2½" Tall, 4" Across, Blue Floral Paperweight Style, Applied Crystal Handle $20

Lamp, 25½" Tall, Paperweight Floral Base with Blue, White, Pink, and Maroon Flowers and Foliage, Brass Finial, Electric $150

Paperweight, 3", Sulphide of Abraham Lincoln on a Blue Ground, Stamped "St.Clair 1971" $65

Paperweight, 3", Sulphide of a Donkey Marked with "McGovern 1972"; Red, White and Blue Colors $65

Paperweight, 3", Caramel Slag Floral Design, Stamped "Maude and Bob St.Clair 1979" $50

Paperweight, 3", Clobalt Blue Crimped and Swirled Design, Stamped "Joe St.Clair" $50

Paperweight, 3¼", 5-Petal White Umbrella Flower Over a Multicolored Bed of Shallow Lilies, Signed "Ed St.Clair" $200

Paperweight, 3½", 5 Multicolored Flowers, Stamped "Joe St.Clair" $45

Paperweight, 3¾", Large Red Rose with Green Leaves, Stamped "Joe St.Clair" $55

Papereight, 4", 5 Cobalt Blue Lilies with White Lattice, Stamped "Joe St.Clair" $60

Plate, 8", Iridescent Purple 3D Kewpie Doll Plate, 1 Large Doll in Center Surrounded by 12 Baby Kewpie Dolls, Stamped "Joe St.Clair" $125

Robin Covered Dish, Various Carnival Colors $100

Salt Dish, 3¼" Diameter, Cobalt Blue Carnival with Hobnail Outer Edge, J. F. Kennedy Design $25

Teapot, 4" Tall, 5" Across, Multicolored Swirl and Bubble Design, Stamped "Joe St.Clair" $15

Toothpick Holder, 2⅜" Tall, Various Carnival Colors, Reproduction Cherry Pattern, Stamped "St.Clair" $40

Toothpick Holder, 2½" Tall, Aqua Blue Carnival, 3 Applied Swan Handles, Stamped "Joe St.Clair" $25

Toothpick Holder, 2¾" Tall, Carnival Red, Molded Indian Head Design, Stamped "Original Carnival Society S.C.G.C. 1964–1969" $45

Tumbler, 4" Tall, Reproduction Carnival Grape and Cable Pattern, Stamped "J.St.C" on Inside $25

Turtle Figurine, 5" Across (Nose to Tail), Brown and Tan Swirled Design, Stamped "Joe St.Clair" $35

Vase, 8½" Tall, White and Orange Paperweight Floral Designed Base, Stamped "Joe St.Clair" $75

Sandwich
Anchor-Hocking Glass Company, 1939–1970s

Basic prices are for crystal pieces in this pattern. There are several odd colored pieces—darker royal ruby, forest green, amber (which Anchor-Hocking refers to as Desert Gold), pink, and milk white. Green is the rarest (triple the prices below). Milk white is not that desirable (reduce the prices by 25 percent). For all other colors, double the prices. The pink and royal ruby are the oldest colors and were made for only two short years (1939–40); the rest were made in the 1950s and 1960s. A cookie jar was reproduced in the 1970s in crystal but is an inch taller and noticeably wider by a few inches than the original (priced at $15). This pattern is sometimes confused with Indiana's Sandwich pattern, but there are more leaves surrounding each symmetrical flower pattern in Hocking's Sandwich (four leaves off the main stem as opposed to Indiana's two). One other prolific Sandwich pattern was Duncan Miller's; there are more spiral curves with Duncan Miller's than either Hocking's or Indiana's.

Bowl, 4⅜"	$6.50
Bowl, 4⅞"	$7.50
Bowl, 5", Ruffled	$16
Bowl, 5¼"	$8.50
Bowl, 6½"	$9.50
Bowl, 6¾"	$20
Bowl, 7" to 7¼"	$11.50
Bowl, 8" to 8¼"	$12.50
Bowl, 9"	$27.50
Butter Dish with Cover	$55
Cookie Jar with Cover	$50
Creamer	$10
Cup	$5
Custard Cup	$7.50
Custard Cup, 5 oz., Ruffled	$17.50
Custard Cup Liner	$20

Pitcher, Milk, 1 pt., 6" Tall	$100
Pitcher, 2 qt.	$225
Plate, 7"	$12.50
Plate, 8"	$6
Plate, 9"	$20
Plate, 9" with Indentation for Punch Cup	$7.50
Plate, 12"	$17.50
Punch Bowl, 9¾"	$35
Punch Bowl Stand	$40
Punch Cup	$5
Saucer	$2.50
Sherbet	$10.50
Sugar with Cover	$30
Tumbler, 3 oz.	$17.50
Tumbler, 5 oz.	$15
Tumbler, 9 oz., Footed	$35

Sandwich
Indiana Glass Company, 1920s–Present

Most all pieces listed and priced here were made in a reproduction light green. Indiana's original Sandwich pattern was first made in the 1920s and is listed in chapter 6 under "Depression Glass." The orangish-red color is most desirable and dates as far back as 1933; however, most pieces were made later as reproductions—double the prices for this color. The teal blue color was made in the 1950s to the 1970s, particularly for Tiara home products. Other colors were added for Tiara (amber, crystal, light green, milk white, red, and smokey blue). Teal blue is an aquamarine color and smokey blue is a darker midnight blue but much duller than a cobalt blue. For all Tiara colors other than plain crystal, increase the prices by about 25 percent; for crystal, reduce them by about 25 percent.

Ashtrays, Set of 4 (Card Suits)	$10
Basket, 10"	$50
Basket, 10½", with Handles	$20
Bowl, 4"	$6
Bowl, 4¼"	$6.50

Bowl, 5¼"	$10
Bowl, 6"	$7.50
Bowl, 6", Hexagonal	$12.50
Bowl, 6½"	$8.50
Bowl, 7" to 8¼"	$12.50
Bowl, 8½"	$15
Bowl, 9"	$25
Bowl, 10", Crimped	$17.50
Bowl, 11½"	$27.50
Butter Dish with Cover	$35
Candlestick, 3½"	$15
Candlestick, 7"	$17.50
Candlestick, 8½"	$17.50
Canister, Various Styles	$30
Celery Dish, 10½"	$20
Clock, 12" Diameter	$30
Cookie Jar with Cover	$75
Creamer	$17.50
Creamer and Sugar with Diamond-Shaped Tray	$30
Cruet, 6½" Tall, with Stopper	$150
Cup, 9 oz.	$7.50
Cup for Indented Plate	$5
Decanter with Stopper	$50
Goblet, 8 oz.	$15
Goblet, 9 oz.	$18
Lamp, Wine Decanter Base, Brass Fixtures	$100
Mayonnaise, Footed	$18
Pitcher, 68 oz., with or without Fluted Rim	$80
Plate, 6"	$5
Plate, 7"	$6
Plate, 8"	$7.50

Plate, 8", Oval with Indentation for Sherbet	$12.50
Plate, 8⅜"	$10
Plate, 8½" Oval	$12.50
Plate, 9"	$17.50
Plate, 10½"	$12.50
Plate, 12"	$17.50
Plate, 13"	$25
Puff Box	$25
Punch Bowl	$80
Punch Cup	$10
Salt and Pepper Shakers	$25
Sandwich Server with Center Handle	$35
Saucer, 6"	$5
Sherbet	$8
Sugar	$17.50
Sugar Cover	$17.50
Tidbit, 2-Tier	$25
Tray, 10" (for Wine Decanter and Goblets)	$17.50
Tumbler, 3 oz. Footed	$12.50
Tumbler, 8 oz. Footed	$15
Tumbler, 12 oz. Footed	$17.50
Wine, 3", 4 oz.	$12.50
Wine Set, 8-Piece (Special Edition True Ruby Red $750)	$100

Seneca Glass Company
1891–Present

Seneca was originally established by a group of German immigrants in Fostoria, Ohio, in 1891. They moved operations to Morgantown, West Virginia, in 1896 and produced both blown and cut crystal. They expanded into colored glass during the Depression and later added novelty, Christmas, and rock crystal glassware.

Bowl, 8⅞", Shallow Soup, Crystal, Cut Floral and Leaf Design	$15
Bowl, 14", Cut Crystal, Ribbed, Elegance Pattern	$30

Champagne Glass, 6" Tall, 8 oz., Various Cut/Etched Styles	$10
Cocktail Glass, 6" Tall, 4 oz., Various Cut/Etched Styles	$10
Creamer, 1 Handle, Cut Crystal, Ribbed, Elegance Pattern	$20
Goblet, Stemmed, 5¾" Tall, Cut Crystal, Ribbed, Elegance Pattern	$10
Goblet, Various Cut Crystal Stemmed Designs, Up to 8" Height	$10
Goblet, Various Cut Crystal Stemmed Designs, More Than 8" in Height	$12.50
Platter, 12" Oval, 2 Tab Handles, Cut Crystal, Ribbed, Elegance Pattern	$30
Sugar, 2-Handled, Cut Crystal, Ribbed, Elegance Pattern	$20
Tumbler, 4" Tall, Various Colored Glass Styles	$6

Shell Pink Milk Glass
Jeannette Glass Company, Late 1950s

The color is a very light opaque pink nearly the color of milk glass. There are several pattern variations, but all were produced under the Shell Pink pattern name. There are eagles, pheasants, feathers, fruits, geometric designs, thumbprints, and even insects. The pieces referred to as Napco are marked "Napco, Cleveland" on the bottom and were made specifically for Napco Ceramics of Cleveland, Ohio (same price).

Ashtray, Butterfly Shape	$30
Base with Ball Bearings (for Lazy Susan)	$175
Bowl, 6½", with Cover	$30
Bowl, 8", Footed	$42.50
Bowl, 8", with Cover	$47.50
Bowl, 9", Footed	$32.50
Bowl, 10", Footed	$37.50
Bowl, 10½", Footed	$50
Bowl, 11", 4-Footed	$52.50
Bowl, 17½"	$60
Cake Stand, 10"	$50
Candleholder, Double	$26.50
Candleholder, 3-Footed	$50
Candy Dish, 5½", 4-Footed	$37.50
Candy Dish with Cover, 6½" Tall, Square	$50
Candy Jar with Cover, 5½", 4-Footed	$55

Celery, 12½", 3-Part	$55
Cigarette Box	$250
Compote, 6"	$30
Cookie Jar with Cover, 6½" Tall	$115
Creamer	$25
Goblet, 8 oz.	$25
Honey Jar with Notched Cover for Spoon, Beehive Shape	$55
Napco, Berry Bowl, Footed	$25
Napco, Bowl with Sawtooth Top	$30
Napco, Compote, Square	$25
Napco, Cross-Hatched Design Pot	$25
National Candy Dish	$20
Pitcher, 1½ pt.	$55
Powder Jar with Cover, 4¾"	$55
Punch Base, 3½" Tall	$50
Punch Bowl, 7½ qt.	$100
Punch Cup, 5 oz.	$15
Punch Ladle (Pink Plastic)	$17.50
Relish, 12", 4-Part, Octagonal	$55
Sherbet, 5 oz.	$15
Sugar with Cover	$45
Tray, 10" x 7¾", Oval with Indentation for Cup (Punch Cup Fits the Indentation)	$25
Tray, 12½" x 9¾", Oval with 2 Handles	$67.50
Tray, 13½", Lazy Susan, 5-Part	$75
Tray, 15¾", 5-Part with 2 Handles	$85
Tray, 16½", 6-Part	$90
Tray Set (Lazy Susan with Base)	$250
Tumbler, Various Styles	$20
Vase, 5" Tall, Cornucopia Shape	$35
Vase, 7" Tall	$45
Vase, 9" Tall	$150
Wineglass	$25

Shot Glasses
Various Companies, 1830s–Present

Shot glasses are small articles of glass that generally hold an ounce or two of liquid and are 3 inches in height or less. Shot glasses have been around since the 1830s as whiskey tasters or samplers, and cover nearly every category of glass. The most desirable by collectors are the pre–Prohibition-era whiskey sample or advertising glasses. Most contain etched white writing of a distiller, company, proprietor, or other alcohol-related advertising. These glasses sell for around $35 to $75, but recently some rare examples have auctioned off well in excess of $100 (a few common ones are available for $10–$15). Shot glass collectors are usually quantity collectors, often boasting of hundreds and even a thousand or two glasses. See the Souvenir Glass section below for a few additional ruby red examples.

Barrel Shape	$6–$8
Black Porcelain Replica	$3–$4
Carnival Colors—Plain or Fluted	$65–$85
Carnival Colors with Patterns	$150–$200
Culver 22 kt. Gold	$6–$8
Depression Colors	$8–$12
Depression Colors—Patterns or Etching	$15–$25
Depression Tall—General Designs	$12.50–$15
Depression Tall Tourist	$5–$7.50
Frosted with Gold Designs	$6–$8
General Advertising	$4–$5
General Etched Designs	$5–$7.50
General Frosted Designs	$3–$4
General Porcelain	$4–$6
General Tourist	$3–$4
General with an Enameled Design	$3–$4
General with Gold Designs	$6–$8
Glasses with Inside Eyes	$5–$7.50
Mary Gregory/Anchor-Hocking Ships	$135–$185
19th-Century Cut Patterns	$75–$125
Nude Shot Glasses	$25–$35
Plain Shot Glasses with or without Flutes	$.50–$.75
Pop or Soda Advertising (i.e., Coke or Pepsi)	$12.50–$15

Shot Glasses. *Photo by Robin Rainwater.*

Porcelain Tourist	$3.50–$5.50
Rounded European Designs with Gold Rims	$4–$5
Ruby Flashed Glasses	$35–$45
Square Glasses with Etching	$7.50–$10
Square Glasses with Pewter	$12.50–$15
Square Glasses with 2-Tone Bronze/Pewter	$15–$17.50
Square Shot Glasses—General	$5–$7.50
Standard Glasses with Pewter	$8–$12
Taiwan Tourist	$2–$3
Tiffany/Galle/Fancy Art	$500–$750
Turquoise and Gold Tourist	$6–$8
Whiskey or Beer Advertising—Modern (1940s and up)	$5–$7.50
Whiskey Sample Glasses	$40–$85

L. E. Smith Glass Company
1907–Present

Lewis E. Smith, along with Thomas Wible, established a glass-decorating firm in Jeannette, Pennsylvania, in 1907. Operations were moved to Mt. Pleasant (also in Pennsylvania) shortly afterward, and a second plant was purchased in Greensburg, Pennsylvania, in 1920. In the meantime, Smith left in 1911; however, the company name was never changed. The firm produced a variety of unique items, including food containers, toy glass candy containers, percolator tops, barbershop mugs, egg separators, auto headlamp glass, premium items given away at movie theaters, and novelty items. The firm was acquired by Owens-Illinois in 1975; however, the L. E. Smith name was reacquired and the firm continues producing glassware today.

Basket, 7½" Tall, 7" Wide, Fluted Edge, Light Blue, Hobnail Pattern	$20
Basket, 10½" Tall, 7½" Wide, Pressed Crystal Diamond Design	$30
Basket, 13½" Tall, Red, Bird of Paradise Design, Scalloped Rim	$50
Bear Figurine, 4" Tall, 6½" Long	$200
Bear Figurine, 4½" Tall, Almond Slag	$50
Bird Figurine, 5" Tall, Head Up or Down (2 Styles), Almond Slag	$40
Bookends, Pair, Rearing Horse, 8" Tall, Various Color Styles (Almond Slag, Amber, Cobalt Blue, etc.; Crystal $50)	$65
Bookends, Pair, Rooster, 9" Tall, Ruby Red, 1960, Various Color Styles (Almond Slag, Amber, Cobalt Blue, etc.)	$75
Bowl, 7½", 3½" Tall, Aqua Blue, Fluted Sides, Pressed Grape Pattern in Base	$20
Bowl, 8½", Reproduction Green Carnival, Sawtooth Rim, Star Pattern Design	$20
Bowl, 10", 3-Footed, Oval, Cobalt Blue, Wigwam Pattern	$125
Camel Figurine, 6" Long, 4½" Tall, Colored Design on Square Base, Shriners Label on Base, Various Colors (Amber, Cobalt Blue, etc.; Crystal $45)	$65
Candleholder, 4½" Across, 1½" Tall, 3-Footed, Black Glass, Flared Rim	$10
Casserole Dish with Cover, 9½" Oval, Crystal, Melba Pattern	$25
Cock Fighting Figurine, 9" Tall, Cobalt Blue	$60
Decanter with 6 Matching Whiskey Tumblers, Tumblers Are 2¼" Tall, Decanter Has Stopper, Various Colors (Blue, Amber, and Green), Moon and Stars Pattern	$110
Duck Covered Dish, 7", Black, 1992	$60
Egg Plate, 10¾", Ruby Red, 1990	$65
Elephant Figurine, 1¾" Long, Crystal	$15
Heart-Shaped Dish, 6" Long, Almond Slag	$30
Hen Covered Dish, 6", Almond Slag	$55
Lamp, Hurricane, 12" Tall, Black with Clear Chimney	$40
Plate, 6", Amethyst, Melba Pattern	$10
Plate, 8", Black, George Washington	$100
Plate, 8" Octagonal, Pink, Melba Pattern	$12.50
Plate, 8½", Square, Crystal with Painted V-Ribbon; Red, White and Black Ribbon Design	$15

Plate, 9", Purple Carnival, Abraham Lincoln	$50
Plate, 9", Trellis Design, Yellow Amber	$17.50
Platter, 10", Small Pedestal Foot, Iridescent Blue, Pressed Multiple Star Design	$27.50
Slipper, 2½" Tall, Daisy and Button Pattern, Various Colors (Almond Slag, Amber, Purple Carnival, etc.)	$10
Swan Dish, 8½" Long, 5½" Tall, Black with Gold-Painted Beak	$27.50
Urn-Style Vase, 7" Tall, 2-Handled, Cobalt Blue, Dancing Girl Design	$50
Vase, 7" Tall, Blue, Moon and Stars Pattern	$25

Souvenir Glass
Various Producers, Late 19th Century–Present

Some of the earliest souvenirs were made in 1876 for the nation's centennial celebration; the most popular were glass liberty bells. In the 1880s into the Depression years, ruby flashed or ruby stained over crystal were quite popular and showed up most often in small tumblers and toothpick holders. Today, souvenirs abound with fired-on decals or machine-applied enamels; these include tumblers, mugs, shot glasses, and a variety of other items.

Ashtray, 5" x 3", Black Glass, 1962 World's Fair, Seattle	$27.50
Beer Glass with Handle, 8-Paneled, "M.Gordon, World's Fair, 1893"	$50
Bell, Frosted Handle with Etched "Chicago, Columbian World's Fair 1893"	$80
Butter Dish, Ruby Stained, Button Arches Pattern, Atlantic City 1919	$87.50
Creamer, Miniature, Arched Flutes, Ruby Stained, 1908	$38
Creamer, 4" Tall, Custard with Gold Trim, Chicago Masonic Temple	$75
Liberty Bell Replica, Crystal with Gold Accents, Louisianna Purchase, St. Louis, 1904	$60
Liberty Bell Covered Dish, Globe Finial, Crystal with Embossed "1776" and Various Phrases	$140
Lincoln Glass Bust, Frosted, Gillinder	$350
Mug, Custard with Gold Trim, Hardwick, VT	$45
Mug, Custard, New Rockford, ND	$45
Mug, 1¾" Tall, Ruby Flashed, Pan American Exposition	$35
Mug, Arched Flutes, Ruby Stained, Boston, MA	$40
Mug, Small Corona, Ruby Stained, St. Joseph, MO	$40
Napoleon Glass Bust, Frosted and Clear, Gillinder	$325

Liberty Bell Dish. *Reproduced directly from an 1876 Gillinder & Sons catalog.*

Souvenir Glass. *Photo by Robin Rainwater.*

Paperweight, 2½", Ruby Flashed, Etched Bird and Rose, 1904 St. Louis Fair	$95
Paperweight, 3¼", Crystal, Seashells, 1904 St. Louis Fair	$37.50
Paperweight, 4", Crystal, 1893 Columbian Exposition Agricultural Building	$115
Paperweight, 4", Crystal, 1901 Pan American Exposition, Temple of Music	$95
Plate, 9½" Square, Amber, Ulysses S. Grant, Embossed "Patriot and Soldier"	$75
Plate, 10", Hobnail Border, Cleveland Reform	$48
Plate, 10", Carnival Red, U.S. Capitol Building, Imperial, 1969	$47.50
Plate, 11", Lake Placid Winter Olympics, Roni the Raccoon Mascot	$155
Toothpick Holder, 2⅛" Tall, Ruby Stained Co-Op's Royal, Charleston, 1903	$45
Shakespeare Glass Bust, Frosted, Gillinder	$160
Shot Glass, 2⅜" Tall, Ruby Stained with Etched "Souvenir Bellevue, Mich."	$35
Shot Glass, 2⅜" Tall, Ruby Stained with Etched "Souvenir Chicago, Ill."	$35
Shot Glass, 2⅜" Tall, Ruby Stained with Etched "State Fair 1908"	$35
Toothpick Holder, 4" Tall, Ruby Stained with Etched "Souvenir of Grand Rapids, Mich."	$37.50
Tumbler, 3½" Tall, Lacy Medallion Pattern, Atlantic City 1901	$67.50
Tumbler, 3½" Tall, Etched Crystal, 1893 Columbian Exposition, Mines and Mining Building	$50
Tumbler, 3½" Tall, Custard, Rangley Lakes Maine (Heisey)	$75
Tumbler, 3¾" Tall, Admiral George Dewey Commemorative	$47.50

Tumbler, 5" Tall, Crystal, 1904 St. Louis Fair, Embossed Cascade Gardens	$38.50
Tumbler, 6" Tall, Enameled Eastern Airlines, Various Designs, 1950s	$8
Washington Glass Bust, Frosted Center, Gillinder	$325

Sportsman Series or Sailboat and Windmills or Ships and Windmills

Hazel Atlas Glass Company, Late 1930s

Enameled white designs on this cobalt blue glass include not only sailboats and windmills, but other sports as well. Fishing, golfing, horseback riding, and skiing are also part of this series. Make sure that the design is fully intact. Damaged, worn, or missing designs are worth only a fraction of completely intact decorations. Some pale yellow decorations caused by factory discolorations exist in this pattern, but as long as the complete decoration is there, the value is the same as listed below. There are a lot of tumblers in this design; however, as the price indicates, the 2-ounce whiskey tumbler is rare.

Cocktail Mixer with Stirrer (Metal Lid)	$32.50
Cocktail Shaker (Metal Lid)	$42.50
Cup	$14
Ice Bowl	$42.50
Pitcher, 2½ qt.	$75
Pitcher, 2½ qt., with Ice Lip	$80
Plate, 5⅞"	$32.50
Plate, 8"	$32.50
Plate, 9"	$37.50
Saucer	$22.50
Tumbler, 4 oz.	$35
Tumbler, 5 oz.	$16
Tumbler, 6 oz.	$16
Tumbler, 8 oz.	$20
Tumbler, 9 oz.	$20
Tumbler, 10½ oz.	$22.50
Tumbler, 12 oz.	$27.50
Whiskey Tumbler, 2¼" Tall, 2 oz.	$200

Square
Cambridge Glass Company, 1950s

This was one of Cambridge's last patterns before going out of business. When the Imperial Glass Company acquired many of Cambridge's molds, they reproduced several Square pieces in color such as red and black. Colored pieces sell for about one and a half times the crystal priced below.

Ashtray, 3½"	$11
Ashtray, 6½"	$13.50
Bonbon, 7"	$20
Bonbon, 8"	$27.50
Bowl, 4½"	$15
Bowl, 6½"	$20
Bowl, 9"	$30
Bowl, 10", Round or Oval	$37.50
Bowl, 11"	$42.50
Bowl, 12", Round or Oval	$45
Buffet Set, 4-Piece (Plate, Divided Bowl, and 2 Ladles)	$65
Candleholder, 1¾" Tall	$15
Candleholder, 2¾" Tall	$17.50
Candleholder, 3¾" Tall	$18.50
Candleholder, Cupped	$18.50
Candy Box with Cover	$45
Celery, 11"	$30
Cocktail Glass, 2 Styles	$22.50
Compote, 6"	$27.50
Cordial Glass, 1½ oz., 2 Styles	$27.50
Creamer, Individual (Small)	$12.50
Creamer	$15
Cruet with Stopper, 4½ oz.	$30
Cup	$13.50
Cup, Tea (Small)	$11.50
Decanter, 1 qt.	$110

Goblet, 5 oz.	$15
Goblet, 12 oz.	$17.50
Goblet, Water, 14 oz.	$20
Ice Tub, 7½"	$45
Icer, Cocktail with Liner	$42.50
Juice Glass, 4½ oz., Footed	$15
Lamp, Hurricane, 2-Piece	$75
Mayonnaise Set, 3-Piece (Bowl, Plate, and Ladle)	$50
Plate, 6"	$12.50
Plate, 7"	$15
Plate, 9½"	$30
Plate, 9½", Tidbit	$30
Plate, 11½"	$35
Platter, 13½"	$40
Relish, 6½", 2-Part	$25
Relish, 8", 3-Part	$35
Relish, 10", 3-Part	$45
Rose Bowl, 7½"	$40
Rose Bowl, 9½"	$50
Salt and Pepper Shakers	$35
Saucer	$10
Saucer (Small—for Tea Cup)	$8.50
Sherbet, 2 Styles	$16
Sugar, Individual (Small)	$12.50
Sugar	$15
Tray, 8", Oval (for Individual Creamer and Sugar)	$22.50
Tumbler, 5 oz.	$17.50
Tumbler, 14 oz.	$20
Vase, 5" Tall	$30
Vase, 5½" Tall	$35
Vase, 6"	$30

Vase, 7½" Tall, Footed	$35
Vase, 8" Tall, Footed	$30
Vase, 9½" Tall, Footed	$35
Vase, 11" Tall, Footed	$50
Wineglass, Various Styles	$25

Steuben Crystal
1933–Present

From 1933 on, Steuben concentrated almost exclusively on production of the highest grade of crystal. A few deviations such as silver or gold accents have been added, but no complete colored pieces have been produced since. Some pieces are one-of-a-kind in that they were presented as awards, presentations to heads of state, gifts to museums, and so on (they are not priced here). Steuben's grade of crystal rivals any made in the world today; copper wheel–engraving, prism effects, outstanding designs, and the industry's most gifted artists are all evident in Steuben's glass products. All modern crystal items contain the "Steuben" signature, usually in fine diamond point script.

Apple, 4" Tall, Paperweight	$375
Apple Christmas Ornament, 3"	$100
Ashtray with Single Rest, 5" Across	$100
Balloon Sculpture, 10¼" Tall, 5⅛" Wide, Triangular, 6 Engraved Hot Air Balloons	$13,750
Bear, 2½" Tall, Hand Cooler	$175
Bear, Teddy, 2½" Tall, Hand Cooler	$175
Bear, 7¼" Long	$1,000
Beaver, 3½" Tall	$500
Beaver, 4½" Long	$525
Beaver, 5½" Long	$525
Beaver, 6¼" Tall	$1,100
Beaver, 9" Long	$1,100
Bird, Shore, 8¼" Long, Sleek Slender Design	$500
Bird, Water, 10" Tall, 9¾" Long, in Flight	$1,200
Birdsong Domed Sculpture on Marble Base, 9" Tall, Etched Birds	$14,500
Bookend, 3½" Cube, Air Bubbles	$775
Bowl, 6", Blocks of Cut Lines, 1936	$225

Steuben Crystal. *Photo by Robin Rainwater.*

Steuben Crystal. *Photo by Mark Pickvet. Courtesy of the Chicago Art Institute.*

Bowl, 7", Spiral Base	$400
Bowl, 7¼" Oval, Folded	$225
Bowl, 7¾", Floret, 4 Feet	$475
Bowl, 8¼", Bubbled Spherical Center/Base	$475
Bowl, 8¼", Twist Base	$450
Bowl, 8¾", Orbit Bowl, Bubbled Globe Handle	$650
Bowl, 9" Oval, Folded	$325
Bowl, 9", Ribbed	$325
Bowl, 9¾", Draped Design	$575
Bowl, 9¾", Trillium Design	$650
Bowl, 10", Mardi Gras Style with Circle Impressions	$1,750
Bowl, 10", Sunflower Center/Base	$475
Bowl, 11½", Archaic Etruscan Design	$1,725
Bowl, 11¾", Magnolia	$500
Bowl, 13½", Twist Base	$925
Bowl, 15¼", Low, Footed	$1,350
Bowl, 15½", Sunflower Center/Base	$1,025
Bowl, 16", 3⅞" Tall, Sterling Frame	$17,600
Bowl, 16¼", Engraved Dragonfly Design	$15,500
Bull, 2½" Tall, Hand Cooler	$175

Bull, 9" Long	$1,000
Candelabra, 13" Wide, Bubbled Crescent Base, Silver Strip with 2 Candleholders	$2,750
Candlestick, 4" Tall, Teardrop Design	$150
Candlestick, 4½" Tall, Teardrop in Stem	$550
Candlestick, 4¾" Tall, Scroll Design	$275
Candlestick, 6" Tall, Ruffled, Athena Design	$250
Candlestick, 6" Tall, Twist Stems	$650
Candlestick, 7" to 7½" Tall, Tapered Crystal Block, Fjord Design, 3 Styles	$1,000
Candlestick, 8¾" Tall, Teardrop Design	$675
Candlestick, 9" Tall, Starlight Bubble Design	$700
Candlestick, 9½" Tall, Starlight Bubble Design	$705
Candlestick, 9¾" Tall, Starlight Bubble Design	$710
Candlestick, 10¼" Tall, Baluster	$750
Candlestick, 10½" Tall, Starlight Bubble Design	$720
Candlestick, 10¾" Tall, Starlight Bubble Design	$725
Candy Dish with Cover, 5" Tall, 2¼" Diameter, Ram's Head Finial on Cover	$675
Carousel, 7½" Tall, 4½" Diameter, Engraved Horses with Sterling Pennant	$4,350
Castle Sculpture, 6⅛" Tall, 10⅝" Wide, Black Leather Base	$2,700
Cat, 2½" Wide, Hand Cooler	$175
Cat, Roman, 5¼" Long, Crouched Sitting Position	$475
Cat, 8¾" Tall, Sitting Upright	$825
Cat, 11" Long (Stretched Out)	$825
Cathedral, 15¾" Tall, Prismatic Form, Engraved Cathedral with Apostles	$15,750
Christmas Tree, 6¼" Tall, Cone Shape, Air Bubbles	$625
Circle, 9¾" Diameter, Stardust Bubble Design	$2,750
Circle Sculpture, 6½" Tall, Cut Hemispheres, Black Leather Base	$6,875
Columbus Circular Sculpture on Walnut Base, Crystal Circle with 3 Ships, 4⅝" Diameter	$425
Compote, 10" Diameter, "Cloud Bowl" Design	$700
Crystal Ball, 4½" Diameter, Black Slate Base	$1,400
Cube, Engraved "LOVE & HOPE," 2"	$350

Daisy Sculpture, 7¼" Tall, Engraved Pair of Daisies	$7,500
Decanter with Mushroom Stopper, 9½" Tall, 24 oz., Stardust Bubbled Base	$1,375
Decanter with Circular Stopper, 10" Tall, 32 oz., Ship's Flask Design	$1,450
Decanter with Eagle Finial on Ball Stopper, 10½" Tall, 32 oz.	$1,150
Deer, Engraved Buck Prism Sculpture, 7¼" Tall, Walnut Base	$8,225
Dog, Puppy, 2¾" Wide	$200
Dog, 3¼" Tall, Hand Cooler	$200
Dog, 5" Tall, Ears Down, Head and Flowing Neck	$500
Dog, 6¾" Tall, Stately, Best Friend Design	$1,000
Domes, Flower, 5½" Diameter, Various Engraved State Flowers	$750
Dove Sculptured Dish, 7¼" Long	$500
Dragon, 2" Long, Hand Cooler	$175
Dragon, 7½" Long	$800
Eagle, 2¾" Long, Hand Cooler	$175
Eagle, 3⅛" Tall, 4¼" Wide, Standing with Wings Open	$375
Eagle, 4¾" Tall, 5½" Long, Wings Closed	$775
Eagle, 6¼" Tall, 12" Wingspan, Crystal Ball Base	$725
Eagle, 9½" Tall, in Flight Design	$3,500
Eagle Bowl, 9½" Tall, 4 Copper Wheel–Engraved Eagles, Feathers Form the Top Rim	$27,500
Eagle's Crag, 10¾" Tall, Crystal Ice Sculpture with Miniature Sterling Eagle at Top, Limited Edition	$14,300
Earth Globe on Walnut and Slate Base, Copper Wheel–Engraved Continents	$6,050
Elephant, 3¼" Long, Hand Cooler	$200
Elephant, 5" Tall, Baby	$625
Elephant, 5½" Tall, Trunk Above Head	$650
Elephant, 7½" Tall, Trunk Above Head	$900
Equestrians' Crystal Sculpture, 2¼" Tall, 3" Wide	$425
Excalibur, 4½" Wide Crystal Rock with 8" Sterling Sword (18 kt. Gold Handle)	$3,425
Fawn, Woodland, 4¾" Wide, Semicircle	$325
Fig, 3¼" Tall, Paperweight	$225

Fish, Trigger, Pair Together, 10" Tall	$1,500
Fisherman, Arctic, 6½" Tall, Crystal Ice Sculpture with Engraved Fish and Sterling Fisherman	$4,250
Flag, American Star Spangled Banner on Walnut Base, 6" Long, Engraved Stars and Stripes	$1,750
Fossil Sculpture, 14¼" Tall, 14" Wide	$6,500
Fox, 3¼" Tall, Cub	$200
Fox, 4¼" Tall	$350
Frog, 2½" Long, Hand Cooler	$175
Galaxy, 3½" Sphere, Stardust Galaxy Bubble Design	$850
Gander, 5¼" Tall (Matches Goose)	$400
Gazelle Bookends, 6¾" Tall, Pair	$750
Gazelle Bowl, 6½" Diameter, 6¾" Tall, Copper Wheel–Engraved Gazelles	$25,250
Gmelin Shell, 2¾" Wide, Spiral Design	$225
Golf Green Sculpture with 18 kt. Gold Flag, 7¾" Tall	$5,000
Golf Prism Sculpture, 3½" Tall, 3" Wide	$475
Goose, 4" Tall (Matches Gander)	$400
Heart Paperweight, 1½" Tall, 2⅝" Long, Small Heart within a Large Heart	$200
Heart Paperweight, 2⅞" Wide, Heart Formed by 2 Turtledoves	$350
Heart Pillar, 3½" Tall	$450
Heart Pillar, 4" Tall	$450
Heart Sculpture, 3¼" Tall	$400
Hippopotamus, 3½" Long, Hand Cooler	$200
Hippopotamus, 6¼" Long	$850
Horse, 9" Long, Full Gallop	$1,000
Horse, 11¾" Long	$1,150
Horse Head, 5" Tall	$350
House, 3½" Trapezoidal, 3 Engraveable Lines	$525
Hunter, 6¼" Tall, Ice Sculpture, Frosted Arch, Sterling Hunter in Boat	$4,575
Ice Bear (Sterling Silver) on Crystal Iceberg, 6" Wide, Miniature Bear at Top	$4,175
Jar with Cover, 15" Tall, Engraved Design from Each State in the Union (50 in All)	$3,250
Jungle Sculpture, 12" Long, Wildlife and Foliage	$7,000

Kangaroo, 10¼" Tall $1,500

Lady Bug, 2½" Long, Hand Cooler $200

Leopard in Tree Sculpture, 7½" Tall, 8" Wide, Engraved Leopard Sitting in Tree $13,750

Lion, 9½" Wide, Walnut Base $2,650

Menorah, 9½" Wide, Semicircle with 9 Silver-Plated Candle Cups $3,925

Menorah, 9¼" Wide, Sculptured Block with 9 Silver-Plated Candle Cups on a Marble Base $1,400

Moby Dick Sculpture, 8" Tall, 11¼" Long Frosted Whale Curved Over Boat with Harpooner & Rowers $25,750

Monkey, 2¾" Tall, Hand Cooler $175

Moravian Star, 2½" Tall, 2½" Wide, Engraved Stars, Cube Effect $425

Moth to Flame Bowl Sculpture, 10" Tall, 8¾" Diameter, Air Trap, Engraved Moths $21,500

Mouse, Woodland, 2⅝" Wide, Semicircle $175

Mouse, 3½" Long $350

New York Sculpture, 17" Tall, 3¾" Wide, Engraved Skyscrapers (Woolworth, Chrysler, World Trade Center, and Empire State Buildings) $31,500

Nut Bowl, 6" Wide, Lip on Side $275

Olive Dish, 5½" Diameter, Single Spiral Handle $375

Owl, 2½" Tall, Hand Cooler $175

Owl on Base, 5⅛" Tall $825

Paperweight, 2¾" Tall, Pyramidal, Old Glory Flag $375

Paperweight, 3" Tall, 3" Wide, Triangular Prism Effect ("Cubique") $625

Paperweight, 3¼" Tall, 3" Diameter, Pyramidal with Inner Teardrop $1,425

Peach, 3" Tall, Paperweight $300

Peacock, 10" Tall, 14½" Wide, Semicircle Tail $1,650

Pear, 5¾" Tall, 18 kt. Gold Partridge in a Pear Tree inside Pear $4,225

Pear Christmas Ornament, 3¾" Tall $100

Pelican, 3" Long, Hand Cooler $200

Penguin, 2¾" Tall $200

Penguin, 3½" Tall $225

Peony Jar, 6¼" Tall, 6½" Wide, Copper Wheel–Engraved Peony Design $3,850

Pig, 3⅛" Long, Hand Cooler $175

Pisces Zodiac Sculpture, 2¾" Tall, 2 Fish	$200
Plate, 10", Copper Wheel–Engraved Aquarius Star Design, Aluminum Stand	$3,850
Plate, 10", Various Engraved American Birds (12 Audubon Plates in All)	$750
Plates, 10", Various Engraved Seashell Designs (12 Plates in All)	$750
Plates, 10", Various Engraved Signs of the Zodiac (12 Plates in All)	$750
Plate with Center Handle, 13¼", Droplet Style	$625
Polar Bear, 4" Long	$500
Polar Bear, 5¾" Long	$700
Polar Bear, 5" Tall, 7½" Long	$750
Polo Players Sculpture, 2¼" Tall, 3" Wide	$425
Porpoise, 6⅛" Long (Bottlenosed Dolphin)	$450
Porpoise, 9¼" Long (Bottlenosed Dolphin)	$650
Porpoise, 12⅛" Long (Bottlenosed Dolphin)	$1,200
Prism Sculpture, 7" Tall, 6¼" Wide, Quartz Design	$3,575
Pronghorn, 7" Tall, 14" Wide, Semicircle with 5 Copper Wheel Engraved Pronghorn	$24,500
Quail, 5½" Tall	$475
Rabbit, 2¾" Long, Hand Cooler	$175
Ram, 2½" Long, Hand Cooler	$200
Rhinoceros, 9¾" Long	$1,350
Rose Bouquet Sculpture, 8½" Tall, Engraved Pair of Roses	$5,750
Sailboat, 6½" Wide	$575
Sailboat, 12¾" Tall, Cut Sails with Engraved Lines	$5,200
Sailing Ship Sculpture, 7" Tall, Engraved Ship, Sterling Silver Captain with Telescope	$13,500
Salmon Bowl, 7½" Tall, 10¼" Wide, 7 Copper Wheel–Engraved Salmon, 7 Flies, Bubbles	$19,500
Saturn with Bubbled Ring, 5½" Diameter	$525
Scallop Shell, 3½" Wide	$225
Sea Lion, 5¾" Tall	$825
Seal Sculpture, 8¾" Tall, 2 Engraved Seals Pursuing 3 Tiny Fish	$3,500
Seashell, 3½" Wide, Irregular Spiral Design	$350
Skiers' Prism Sculpture, 3½" Tall, 3" Wide	$475

Snail, 3¼" Tall	$250
Snow Crystal, 2¾" Triangular, Engraved Snowflake	$300
Snow Pine, 4¼" Wide, 5 Straight Sides, Engraved Evergreen Tree	$500
Squirrel, 2¾" Tall, Hand Cooler	$200
Star Paperweight, 4¼" Wide, Pentagram	$875
Star Prism Sculpture, 5" Tall, Slate Base	$1,475
Star of David, 2½" Tall, 2½" Wide, Engraved Stars of David, Cube Effect	$325
Star Stream, 5¼" Tall, Pentagram Swirl Sculpture	$625
Starfish, 4¾" Wide	$225
Stork, 14" Tall, Slender Legs, Circular Base	$625
Stork with Baby, 3" Long	$225
Swan, 6½" Long, Straight Neck	$575
Swan, 7½" Long, Curved Neck	$575
Swan Bowl, 9" Diameter, 8" Tall, Bowl Formed by 3 Copper Wheel–Engraved Swans	$38,500
Swan Sculpture, 7¼" Wide, Engraved Pair of Swans	$7,500
Swordfish Rising from Crystal Sculpture, 7½" Tall	$12,000
Tennis Prism Sculpture, 3½" Tall, 3" Wide, 3 Engraved Tennis Players	$475
Terebra Shell, 4⅝" Long, Spiraled	$225
Trout, 7½" Tall, Engraved Trout and Bubbles with 18 kt. Gold Fly, Limited Edition of 75	$11,500
Trout, 8" Tall with 18 kt. Gold Fly	$2,375
Tumbler, Old-Fashioned, 3½" Tall, 9 oz.	$225
Tumbler, 4⅛" Tall, Stardust Bubbled Base	$350
Tumbler, Highball, 4½" Tall	$275
Turtle, 2½" Long, Hand Cooler	$175
Urn, 6½" Tall, Copper Wheel–Engraved Grecian People	$38,500
Urn, 9½" Tall, 2 Scroll Handles	$1,025
Vase, 5¼" Tall, Classic "Juliet" Style	$225
Vase, 6¼" Tall, Pirouette	$275
Vase, 6½" Tall, Bubbled, Globe Shape	$400
Vase, 6½" Tall, Cinched Waist	$350

Vase, 6½" Tall, Spiral Base	$400
Vase, 6¾" Tall, 3½" Wide, Engraved Angel with Trumpet	$625
Vase, 7" Tall, Handkerchief	$250
Vase, 7⅛" Tall, Circular Base, Engraved Gazelle	$2,750
Vase, 7¾" Tall, Ancient Lyre Design	$450
Vase, 7¾" Tall, Concentric Momentum Design	$1,275
Vase, 8" Tall, Engraved by Waugh, 1935	$1,250
Vase, 8" Tall, Seawave Design	$600
Vase, 8" Tall, Twist Bud Design	$325
Vase, 8" Tall, 8½" Diameter, Sterling Frame	$12,100
Vase, 8⅛", Twist Stem Design	$650
Vase, 8¼" Tall, 8½" Diameter, 24 Cut Facets	$11,550
Vase, 8½" Tall, Classic "Palace" Design	$550
Vase, 9½" Tall, Handkerchief	$675
Vase, 9½" Tall, Mondo, Slender Cylindrical Design	$900
Vase, Archaic Etruscan Design, 9¾" Wide	$1,875
Vase, 10" Tall, Swirled Design	$650
Vase, 11" Tall, Globe Shape, Bubbled	$800
Vase, 11½" Tall, Rose, Clasps on Stem	$775
Vase, 12¼" Tall, Seawave Design	$825
Vase, 12½" Tall, Calypso	$850
Vase, 12½" Tall, Silhouette	$375
Vase, 13" Tall, Calypso	$1,000
Vase, 15½" Tall, Mardi Gras Style with Circle Impressions	$1,600
Vase, 16½" Tall, 6½" Diameter, Sterling Frame	$14,300
Vase, 17½" Tall, Sculptural	$1,000
Vase, Archiac Etruscan Design, 13" Wide	$2,625
Walrus with Sterling Silver Tusks, 7" Long	$3,250
Whale, Nantucket, Limited Edition	$5,500
Whale Sculpture, Ocean's Majesty, 6½" Long, Engraved Mother and Baby Humpback	$10,000
Wreath, Christmas, 3½" Diameter, Engraved Snowflakes and Evergreen Bows	$250

Wren, 3" Wide, Sitting	$200
Zodiac Sphere Sculpture, Engraved Constellations	$13,500

Swanky Swigs
Decorated Jars from Kraft Cheese Spreads, 1933–1970s

Swanky Swigs were originally small jars that could be adapted to juice glasses by soaking off the Kraft Cheese Spread label. Cheese spreads included American Spread, Limburger Spread, Old English, Olive-Pimento, Pimento, Pimento-American, Pineapple, Relish, and Zestful Roka. Even the old original lids to these jars are selling for a dollar or two. Note that the original production runs were from 1933 to 1940 and 1947 to 1958. They were discontinued from 1941 to 1946 and then reissued in the 1970s.

Animal Patterns, Small, Less Than 4"	$12.50
Animal Patterns, Large, More Than 4", Color Combinations Include Black Duck and Horse, Blue Bear and Pig, Brown Squirrel and Deer, Green Cat and Rabbit, Orange Dog and Rooster, and Red Bird and Elephant.	$15
Antique Patterns, Small, Less Than 4"	$15
Antique Patterns, Large, More Than 4", Color Combinations Include Black Coffeepot and Trivet, Blue Kettle and Lamp, Brown Clock and Coal Scuttle, Green Coffee Grinder and Plate, Orange Churn and Cradle, and Red Spinning Wheel and Bellows.	$17.50
Band Patterns, Small, Less Than 4" (1–4 Bands)	$6.50
Band Patterns, Large, More Than 4" (1–4 Bands), Color Combinations Include Black, Blue, Red, Black and Red, Blue and Red, Blue and White, and Red and Green.	$9
Bicentennial Issue (1975–1976), in Green, Red, and Yellow; small, 3¾"	$10
Centennial Celebration Issues (Various States): Small, Less Than 4", Enameled Colors	$12.50
Centennial Celebration Issues (Various States): Large, More Than 4", Enameled Colors	$15
Centennial Celebration Issues (Various States): Cobalt Blue Glasses, 4¾" with Enameled Colors	$42.50
Flower Patterns, Small, Less Than 4"	$15
Flower Patterns, Large, More Than 4", All Enameled Colors for Cornflowers, Daisies, Forget-Me-Nots, Posies, Starbursts, Tulips, and Miscellaneous Flower Designs.	$20
Multiple or Miscellaneous Designs, Small, Less Than 4"	$12.50
Multiple or Miscellaneous Designs, Large, More Than 4", Enameled Designs Include Blocks, Dots, Bursts, etc. in Several Colors.	$15
People Patterns, Small, Less Than 4"	$12.50

Swanky Swig Sailboat Tumbler. *Drawing by Mark Pickvet.*

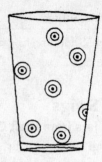

Swanky Swig Circles & Dots Tumbler. *Drawing by Mark Pickvet.*

People Patterns, Large, More Than 4", All Enameled Colors Include Elderly Woman, Woman in Plaid Dress, Man in Pinstripe Suit, and Others	$15
Sailboat Patterns, Small, Less Than 4"	$20
Sailboat Patterns, Large, More Than 4", All Enameled Colors Include Blue, Green, Red, and Yellow (May or May Not Have Enameled Designs)	$25
Solid Opaque Colors, Small, Less Than 4"	$17.50
Solid Opaque Colors, Large, More Than 4", Opaque Colors Include Blue, Green, Red, and Yellow (May or May Not Have Enameled Designs)	$22.50

Thimbles
Various Companies, 1940s–Present

Thimbles come in a variety of styles and materials. Those featured here are made of glass only by American companies. All are of standard size except for those with a decorative finial on top. There are a few other thimbles in chapter 1, most notably from Germany.

Thimble, 1" Tall, Ruffled Edge, Shank Rim Near Bottom (to Hold Rings), Crystal with Gold Trim	$10
Thimble, 1" Tall, Crystal Diamond Pattern with Ruby Red Insert in Top	$27.50
Thimble, 1" Tall, Ruffled, Crystal with Enameled Blue and White Cornflower	$7.50
Thimble, 1" Tall, Crystal with Enameled Red and Yellow Roses with Green Leaves	$7.50
Thimble, 1" Tall, Ruffled, Crystal with Enamel Yellow Roses	$7.50
Thimble, 1" Tall, Scalloped, Etched White Floral Design	$9.50
Thimble, 1" Tall, Cobalt Blue with Multicolored Miniature Paperweight in Top	$42.50

Thimble, 1" Tall, Ruby Red with Multicolored Miniature Paperweight in Top	$42.50
Thimble, 1¼" Tall, Spun Crystal with Multicolored Glass Gem Finial (Several Styles)	$10
Thimble, 1½" Tall, Teapot Shape with Handle, Spout, and Ball Top, Crystal with Blue Applied Porcelain Rose	$12.50
Thimble, 1½" Tall, Spun Crystal with Multicolored Parrot Finial	$12.50
Thimble, 1½" Tall, Spun Crystal with Green and Blue Turtle Finial	$12.50
Thimble, 1¾" Tall, Crystal, Birdbath with 2 Birds Finial	$15
Thimble, 1¾" Tall, Spun Crystal with Multicolored Clown Finial	$10
Thimble, 1¾" Tall, Spun Crystal with Lavender Dragon Finial	$12.50
Thimble, 1¾" Tall, Spun Crystal with Multicolored Mushroom Finial	$10
Thimble, 2" Tall, Bell Shape, Crystal, Octagonal Shape	$12.50
Thimble, 2" Tall, Spun Crystal with Amethyst Elephant Finial	$10
Thimble, 2⅛" Tall, Spun Crystal with Light Blue Dolphin Finial	$10
Thimble, 2⅛" Tall, Spun Crystal with Green Hummingbird Finial	$10
Thimble, 2⅛" Tall, Spun Crystal with Yellow Saxophone Finial	$10
Thimble, 2¼" Tall, Spun Crystal with Light Blue and Clear Sailing Ship Finial	$12.50
Thimble, 2½" Tall, Spun Crystal, Hummingbird and Blossom Finial, Gold Trim and Accents	$35

Tiffin Glass
1916–80

A. J. Beatty & Sons (est. 1852) built a glass factory in Steubenville, Ohio, in 1879. They moved to Tiffin, Ohio, in 1889, and produced some pressed and barware. In 1892, the firm was one of the numerous companies to join the U.S. Glass Co. conglomerate. In 1916 the Tiffin Glass Company operated as a distinct subsidiary and began using a paper label to mark their products. Tiffin is noted for a good deal of tableware produced in crystal (especially stemware), colored Depression styles, and a line of black glassware called Black Satin in the 1920s. Employees of Tiffin purchased the plant in 1963, but sold out to Continental Can in 1966. Interpace acquired it in 1969; however, the glass plant closed permanently in 1980.

Apple Paperweight, Controlled Bubble Design	$125
Ashtray, 6" Diameter, Crystal, Molded Advertisement of Carnegie National Bank	$46
Basket, 7", Satin Finish, Green	$65
Basket, 8", Black Satin	$70
Bowl, 4½", 3-Footed, Swedish Optic Design	$50

Bowl, 9¼", Blue Satin	$25
Bowl, 9¾", Crystal, Cherokee Rose Pattern	$87.50
Cake Plate, 9½" Yellow, 1 Handle, Jack Frost Design	$75
Cake Plate, 10½", Crystal, Flanders Pattern	$77.50
Candelabra, 2-Light, Cerise Design	$80
Candlestick, 8½" Tall, Satin Amberina	$57.50
Candy Jar with Cover, 10" Tall, Satin Green	$77.50
Center Piece, 6", Crystal with Ruby Red Flashing	$175
Champagne Glass, 6" Tall, Crystal, Cherokee Rose Pattern	$30
Champagne Glass, 6¼" Tall, Pink	$42.50
Cocktail Glass, Crystal, Persian Pheasant Pattern	$27.50
Cocktail Glass, 4¼" Tall, Fuchsia	$27.50
Compote, 7½", Flared, Disc Foot, Black Satin	$77.50
Compote, 8½", 5½" Tall, Crystal, Canterbury Pattern	$165
Cordial, Green, Killarney Pattern	$27.50
Cup and Saucer, Pink, Sylvan Pattern	$45
Goblet, 7" Tall, Palais Versailles Pattern	$100
Goblet, 7" Tall, Yellow, Panel Optic Design	$25
Goblet, 8" Tall, Crystal, Cerise Pattern	$30
Goblet, 8" Tall, Topaz, Etched La Fleure Pattern	$45
Hat Vase, 4" Tall, Black Satin	$250
Jar, Advertising, 21" Tall, Crystal, Molded "Heinz"	$135
Perfume Bottle with Stopper, 6" Tall, Black Satin with Enameled Floral Design	$105
Pitcher, 4¾" Tall, 32 oz., Threaded Optic Design, Cornflower Blue with Crystal Handle	$85
Plate, 6", Ruffled, Crystal, Flanders Pattern	$10
Plate, 6", Pink, Flanders Pattern	$20
Plate, 8", Pink, Flanders Pattern	$40
Plate, 10½", Crystal, Byzantine Pattern	$60
Plate, Torte, 14" Crystal, Etched Byzantine Pattern	$67.50
Pumpkin Paperweight, Controlled Bubble Design	$125
Relish Dish, 6¾" Oblong, 3 Divisions, Crystal, Rose Pattern	$50

Relish Dish, 12½" Oblong, 3 Divisions, Crystal, Cherokee Rose Pattern	$87.50
Sherbet, 5⅜" Tall, Crystal, Fuchsia Pattern	$27.50
Tumbler, 5 oz., Juice, Crystal, Rose Pattern	$30
Tumbler, 15 oz., Ice Tea, Crystal, Fuchsia Pattern	$35
Vase, 6" Tall, Crystal, Acid Cut Back Carnation Design	$52.50
Vase, 8" Tall, Crystal, Cherokee Rose Pattern	$52.50
Vase, 8" Tall, Black Satin with Gold Decorations	$140
Vase, 8¼" Long, Cornucopia Style, Copen Blue Design	$150
Vase, 8½" Tall, Pink, Poppy Pattern	$60
Vase, 9" Tall, 2 Handles, Crystal, Fuchsia Pattern	$90
Vase, 10" Tall, Black Satin	$65
Vase, 10½" Tall, Crystal, Cherokee Rose Pattern	$65

Viking Glass Company
1940s–1997

Viking is noted for its ruby red novelties and figurines. Viking purchased New Martinsville in 1944 and continued using some of New Martinsville's original molds; however, the firm marked new issues as "Rainbow Art" or with the Viking name. In 1991 Viking was purchased by Kenneth Dalzell (former president of Fostoria) to become Dalzell-Viking. The company closed its doors permanently in 1997.

Apple Shape, 3¾" Tall, Ruby Red with Green Stem	$21.50
Apple Shape, 5" Tall, Ruby Red with Green Stem	$32.50
Ashtray, Alligator Figural, 11" Long, Orange	$55
Bell, 3½" to 3¾" Tall, Leaf Design, Ruby Red	$22.50
Bell, Liberty Bell Shape, 3¾" Tall, Ruby Red	$27.50
Bell, 4¾" Tall, Mount Vernon Pattern, Ruby Red	$22.50
Bell, 6" Tall, Georgian Pattern, Ruby Red	$26
Bird, 2¾" Long, Cobalt Blue	$11
Bird, 9½" Tall, Cobalt Blue	$35
Bird, 9¾" Tall, Dark Amber	$35
Bonbon Dish, 7", Ruby Red	$22.50
Bowl, 7¾" Diameter, Crystal with Enameled Floral Transfer	$5.50
Bowl, 10" Diameter, Crystal with Enameled Floral Transfer	$8

Dalzell-Viking Owl. *Photo by Robin Rainwater.*

Bowl, 10" Diameter, Light Opaque Swirled Amethyst, Irregular Edge	$21.50
Candlestick, 7" Tall, Black Satin, Spiral Design	$30
Candy Dish, 10" Long, Including 2 Finger Hole Applied Handles, 7" Diameter, Pressed Hobstar and Buzzstar Design on Underside, Notched Edge, Cobalt Blue	$22.50
Candy Jar with 3-Faced Frosted Finial on Frosted Cover, 7" Tall, Crystal, Similar to the Reproduction of the Museum of Fine Arts, Boston (listed at end of chapter)	$27.50
Canoe Dish, Light Blue, Daisy and Button Pattern, Reproduction, 11½" Long	$45
Compote, 5½" Diameter, 2½" Tall, Purple with Candlewick Edging	$12.50
Cube-Shape Box, 3" Dimensions, Clear Glass with Various Molded Designs	$7.50
Dog Figurine, 8" Tall, Lop-Eared, Amber or Blue	$35
Duck, Baby, 5" Tall, Ruby Red or Vaseline	$30
Duck, Mother, 9" Tall, Ruby Red or Dark Teal	$47.50
Egrette Figurine, 12" Tall, Orange	$52.50
Fish Figurine on Base, 9¾", Amber	$65
Lamp, Oil, 9" Tall, Ruby Red	$80
Mushroom Shape, 2" Tall, Ruby Red	$17.50
Owl, 2⅜" Tall, Winking, Clear Glass Miniature	$7.50
Owl, 2⅜" Tall, Winking, Black Glass Miniature	$12.50
Owl Glimmer, 7" Tall, Ruby Red	$35
Paperweight, 3½" Diameter, Circular, 1" Thick, Clear Glass with Large Etched Letters of the Alphabet, 26 Different—Price Is for Each	$5.50

Paperweights, 3½" Diameter, Circular, 1" Thick, Clear Glass with Large Etched Letters of the Alphabet, Set of 26	$150
Paperweight, Lion, 5½", Frosted Design	$40
Paperweight, Tiger, 5¾", Frosted Design	$40
Pear Shape, 8½" Tall, Ruby Red with Green Stem	$52.50
Plate, 8½" Diameter, Light Opaque Swirled Amethyst, Candlewick Edging	$12.50
Rabbit Figurine, 2½" Tall, Black	$22.50
Rabbit Figurine, 6½" Tall, Green	$30
Salt and Pepper Shakers, Diamond and Thumbprint Pattern, Ruby Red	$40
Snowman Glimmer, 9" Tall, Ruby Red	$35
Stove Glimmer, Potbellied Stove Shape, Ruby Red	$35
Strawberry Paperweight, Ruby Red with Green Stem	$22.50
Swan Candleholder, 6¼", Ruby Red with Crystal Neck	$55
Swan Dish, 6¼", Ruby Red with Crystal Neck	$55
Swan Dish, 6½" Long, Ruby Red	$27.50
Vase, 16" Tall, Ruby Red with Crystal Lip	$25

Westmoreland Glass
1889–1985

The operation began as the Westmoreland Specialty Company in 1889 in Grapeville, Pennsylvania. In the beginning as well as in the early 20th century, the company processed such foods as vinegar, mustard, and baking powder to fill the glass containers they made. In 1924 the name was officially changed to the Westmoreland Glass Company so that the business world would associate it with glassmaking. From the company's inception, Westmoreland produced a variety of items adapting readily to America's changing fads. Production included cut, some carnival, and Depression glass, a few art styles, and modern examples included below. See separate listings for Westmoreland products under "Beaded Edge" and "Panel Grape" in this chapter. Also refer to cut examples in chapter 3, "English Hobnail" in chapter 6, and a few carnival examples in chapter 5. Note that Mary Gregory–designed glass originated in Europe in the late 19th century (see chapter 1) and contains Victorian scenes of children. Laced-edge pieces in Westmoreland's Mary Gregory plates are fragile and crack easily along the edges, so take extra precautions when purchasing. Note that you may see the mark or signature of "L Plues," who happened to be a designer for most of Westmoreland's line of Mary Gregory Glass.

Westmoreland Opalescent Green Cherry Candy Jar.
Photo by Robin Rainwater.

Basket, 5" Tall, Mary Gregory (Victorian Scene of Girl), Ruby Red with Enameled White Designs $45

Basket, 14", Maple Leaf Design, Ruby Red $125

Bell, 6½" Tall, Ruby Red with Enameled White Floral Design $35

Bird in Flight Figurine, 5" Wide, Amber Marigold $30

Bowl, 10½", Maple Leaf Design $47.50

Bowl, 8½", Octagon Shape, Crimped, Pink $47.50

Bowl, 13", Octagon Shape, Crystal with Enameled Floral Design $55

Bowl, Rose, 5¾", Laced Edge, Ruby Red $40

Butter Dish with Cover, 8½" Long, ¼ lb. Style, Pressed Cube Design, Ruby Red $60

Cake Stand, 10" Diameter, 4" Tall, Reproduction Cherry and Cable Pattern, Opalescent Green $77.50

Candlestick, 4" Tall, Dolphin Stem, Cobalt Blue $55

Candlestick, 4½" Tall, Laced Edge, Ruby Red $25

Candlestick, 9" Tall, Dolphin Stem, Pink or Green $67.50

Candy Dish with Cover, 3-Footed, Shell Design and Shell Finial, Ruby Red $65

Candy Jar with Cover, Octagon Shape, Pink $60

Candy Jar with Silver Cover, 7½" Tall, Colonial Fluted Design, Light Amethyst with Silver Cover, Enameled Floral Design $115

Candy Jar with Cover, 8" Tall, Fluted, Reproduction Cherry and Cable Pattern, 2-Handled, Opalescent Green $77.50

Cat Dish with Cover, 5½" Long, Light Blue and Milk Opaque Glass	$130
Cheese and Cracker Set (Bowl with Underplate), 10" Diameter, Black with White Enameled Floral Design	$90
Chest with Lid, 4¼" Rectangular, Mary Gregory (Victorian Scene of Girl and Boy), Ruby Red with Enameled White Designs	$65
Cracker Jar with Cover, 8½" Tall, Reproduction Cherry Pattern, Opalescent Green (Ruby Red $150)	$77.50
Creamer, Pouring Spout, Notched Top (Fits Tray Below), Light Blue, Green, or Pink	$25
Creamer, Crystal with Etched Fruit Design	$35
Creamer, Octagon Shape, Black with Enameled Bleeding Heart Floral Design	$35
Creamer, Strutting Peacock Pattern, Ruby Red	$55
Cruet with Stopper, 2 oz., Colonial Pattern, Blue	$70
Cruet with Stopper, 5¼" Tall, Diamond Quilted Design, Ruby Red	$70
Dog Dish with Cover, 5½" Long, Light Blue and Milk Opaque Glass	$130
Dog Dish with Cover, 5½" Long, Milk and Custard Opaque Glass	$155
Flower Bowl Stand, 4" or 5" Diameter, 3-Footed, Yellow with Continuous Etched Leaf Design (Black Glass, No Etching $55)	$45
Goblet, 8 oz., Crystal with Etched Fruit Design	$30
Hat Shape (Straw Hat), Custard with Enameled Red and White Band, 4½" Diameter	$80
Jewel Box with Lid, 4½" Square, Footed, Mary Gregory (Victorian Scene of Boy), Ruby Red with Enameled White Designs	$55
Jewel Box with Lid, 4½" Square, Footed, Mary Gregory (Victorian Scene of Boy), Ruby Red with Enameled White Designs	$55
Lamb Dish with Cover, 5½" Long, Opaque Cobalt Blue Blue and Milk Glass	$185
Lamp, 10" Tall, Lotus Line, Blue or Green	$90
Leaf-Shape Dish, 9" Long, Green with Veining	$26
Pitcher, Milk, 1 pt., Pressed Cube Design, Ruby Red	$65
Plate, 3", Butterfly and Heart Design, Ruby Red	$20
Plate, Heart Shape, 7¼" Across, Mary Gregory (Victorian Scene of Girl), Laced Edge, Ruby Red with Enameled White Designs	$75
Plate, 8½", Mary Gregory (Various Victorian Scenes), Laced Edge, Ruby Red with Enameled White Designs	$75
Plate, 9" Crystal with Etched Fruit Design	$35
Platter, 14", Crystal with Etched Fruit Design	$50

Revolver, Toy, 5" Long, Crystal with Black Stock	$150
Robin Figurine, 5⅛" Tall, Crystal	$26
Rooster Dish with Cover, 5½" Long, Opaque Cobalt Blue and Milk Glass	$275
Sandwich Server with Center Handle, Milk Glass with Crystal Handle and Enameled Floral and Bird Design	$65
Slipper, 5" Long, Ruby Red with Enameled White Shoelace	$32.50
Sugar, 2 Angled Handles, Notched Top (Fits Tray Below), Light Blue, Green, or Pink	$25
Sugar, 2-Handled, Crystal with Etched Fruit Design	$35
Sugar, 2-Handled, Octagon Shape, Black with Enameled Bleeding Heart Floral Design	$32.50
Sugar with Cover, Strutting Peacock Pattern, Ruby Red	$60
Tray with Center Handle (For Creamer and Sugar), 8", Light Blue, Green, or Pink	$30
Tumbler, 1½" Tall, 1 oz., Embossed "Just A Thimbleful," Originally Issued in Crystal, Reissued in Emerald Green and Cobalt Blue (Same Price)	$8.50
Vase, 8½" Tall, Diamond, Circle and Fan Pressed Design, Circular Footed, Ruby Red	$35
Vase, 8¾" Tall, Pressed Buzz Star Design, Ruby Red	$40
Vase, 9½" Tall, Fan Shape, Green with Etched Floral Design	$52.50

L. G. Wright Glass Company
Late 1950s–1999

L. G. Wright was originally a glass salesman for New Martinsville. Beginning as early as the late 1930s, Wright began purchasing glass molds from defunct glass companies. Amazingly, he acquired well over 1,000! In the late 1950s, Wright subcontracted with other companies such as Fenton, Imperial, and Viking to press glass into his molds. Note that he did place his own trademark in most of the molds. Wright passed away in 1969; however, the business was carried on by his wife. The company closed for good in 1999, and all molds were auctioned off to other firms. Most of Wright's products consist of pressed tableware, lamps, vases, rose bowls, covered animal dishes, animal figurines, and other novelty items. In a way, all products with the company name can be considered reproductions of older glass, especially the pressed Daisy and Button pattern.

Ashtray, 5½", Ruby Red, Daisy and Button Pattern	$15
Basket, 7½" Tall, Ruby Red, Daisy and Button Pattern	$27.50
Bell, 6½" Tall, Ruby Red, Daisy and Button Pattern	$30
Bowl, 5", Amber, Daisy and Button Pattern	$15

Cake Plate, 10¼", Light Blue, Daisy and Button Pattern	$15
Canoe Dish, 4¼" Long, Various Colors, Daisy and Button Pattern	$22.50
Canoe Dish, 6½" Long, Various Colors, Daisy and Button Pattern	$30
Cat Covered Dish, 5", Various Slag, Carnival, and Color Designs	$65
Cow Covered Dish, 5", Various Slag, Carnival, and Color Designs	$65
Duck Covered Dish, 11", Various Colors	$75
Goblet, 5" Tall, Light Blue, Daisy and Button Pattern	$12.50
Hen Covered Dish, 5", Various Slag, Carnival, and Color Designs (Rare Ruby Slag $150)	$65
Hen Covered Dish, 8", Various Slag, Carnival, and Color Designs (Rare Ruby Slag $300)	$75
Horse Covered Dish, 5", Various Slag, Carnival, and Color Designs (Rare Ruby Slag $150)	$70
Lamb Covered Dish, 5", Various Slag, Carnival, and Color Designs (Rare Ruby Slag $150)	$70
Lamp, Oil, 12" Tall, Ruby Red, Daisy and Button Pattern	$85
Owl Covered Dish, 5", Various Slag, Carnival, and Color Designs (Rare Ruby Slag $150)	$65
Rooster Covered Dish, 5", Various Slag, Carnival, and Color Designs (Rare Ruby Slag $150)	$65
Slipper, 5" Long, Various Carnival Colors	$15
Swan Covered Dish, 5", Various Slag, Carnival, and Color Designs (Rare Ruby Slag $150)	$65
Swan Salt Dip, 3¼" Long, Cherry Pattern	$30
Tray, 7½" x 4½", 3-Part, Light Blue, Daisy and Button Pattern	$27.50
Turkey Covered Dish, 5", Various Slag, Carnival, and Color Designs (Rare Ruby Slag $150)	$75
Turkey Covered Dish, 8", Various Slag, Carnival, and Color Designs (Rare Ruby Slag $300)	$100
Vase, 7¼" Tall, Corn Cob Design with Applied Handles, Light Blue	$25
Wall Pocket, 6½" Long, Canoe Style, Light Blue, Daisy and Button Pattern	$20

RESOURCES

Periodicals and Clubs

Air Capital Carnival Glass Club
Don Kime
1202 W. 4th Street
Haysville, KS 67060

Akro Agate Collector's Club
Roger Hardy
10 Bailey Street
Clarksville, WV 26301

The Akro Agate Gem
Joseph Bourque
P.O. Box 758
Salem, NH 03079

Aladdin Knights
3935 Kelley Road
Kevil, KY 42053

American Carnival Glass Association
P.O. Box 235
Littlestown, PA 17340

American Cut Glass Association
P.O. Box 482
Ramona, CA 92065

Ancient City Glass Collector's Club
St. Augustine, FL 32084
Emilie Pridgen (904) 794-5955

Antique and Collectible News
P.O. Box 529
Anna, IL 62906

Antique and Collectors Reproduction News
Mark Chervenka
P.O. Box 12130
Des Moines, IA 50312-9403

Antiques and Collecting
1006 S. Michigan Ave.
Chicago, IL 60605

Antique Gazette
6949 Charlotte Parkway, #106
Nashville, TN 37209

The Antique Press
12403 N. Florida Ave.
Tampa, FL 33612

Antique Review
P.O. Box 538
Worthington, OH 43085-9928

The Antique Trader Weekly
P.O. Box 1050 CB
Dubuque, IA 52004-1050

Antique Week
27 N. Jefferson
P.O. Box 90
Knightstown, IN 46148

Arizona Depression Glass Club
2242 E. Campbell
Phoenix, AZ 85034

Art Glass Saltshaker Collectors Society
2832 Rapidan Trail
Maitland, FL 32751

Arts and Crafts Quarterly
P.O. Box 3592, Station E
Trenton, NJ 08629

Avon Times
P.O. Box 9868, Dept. P
Kansas City, MO 64134

Blenko Collectors Society
P.O. Box 1096
Kermit, WV 25674

Boyd Art Glass Collectors Guild
P.O. Box 52
Hatboro, PA 19040

Boyd's Crystal Art Glass
Jody & Darrell's Glass Collectibles
P.O. Box 180833
Arlington, TX 76096-0833

Cambridge Collectors, Inc.
P.O. Box 416
Cambridge, OH 42735

Canadian Carnival Glass Association
Gladys Lawson
532 Chiddington Ave.
London, Ontario, Canada N6C 2W3

Canadian Depression Glass Association
Email: cdga@home.com
Candlewick Club
c/o Virginia R. Scott
275 Milledge Terrace
Athens, GA 30606

Candlewick Club of Florida
120 Red Sky Court
Lake Mary, FL 32746

Candy Container Collectors of America
P.O. Box 352
Chelmsford, MA 10824-0352

Collectible Carnival Glass Association
c/o Wilma Thurston
2360 N. Old S.R. 9
Columbus, IN 47203

Collector Glass News
P.O. Box 308
Slippery Rock, PA 16057

Collectors of Findlay Glass Association
P.O. Box 256
Findlay, OH 45839-0256

Czechoslovakian Collectors
Guild International
P.O. Box 901395
Kansas City, MO 64190

Depression Glass Daze
P.O. Box 57
Otisville, MI 48463

Duncan & Miller Glass Club
P.O. Box 965
Washington, PA 15301

Early American Pattern Glass Society
P.O. Box 340023
Columbus, OH 43234

Fenton Art Glass Collectors of America, Inc.
P.O. Box 384
Williamstown, WV 26187

Fostoria Glass Collectors
21901 Lassen Street, #112
Chatsworth, CA 91311

The Fostoria Glass Society of America, Inc.
P.O. Box 826
Moundsville, WV 26041

Fostoria OH Glass Association
109 N. Main St.
Fostoria, OH 44830

Friends of Degenhart
P.O. Box 186
Cambridge, OH 43725

Fruit Jar Newsletter
364 Gregory Ave.
West Orange, NJ 07052-3743

H. C. Fry Glass Society
P.O. Box 41
Beaver, PA 15009

Gateway Carnival Glass Club
Karen E. Skinner
108 Riverwoods Cove
East Alton, IL 62024

The Glass Art Society
c/o Tom McGlauchlin
Toledo Museum of Art
Toledo, OH 43609

Glass Collectors Club of Toledo
2727 Middlesex Drive
Toledo, OH 43606

Glass Collector's Digest
P.O. Box 553
Marietta, OH 45750-9979

Glass Knife Collector's Club
c/o Adrienne Escoe
4448 Ironwood Ave.
Seal Beach, CA 90740

"*The Glass Post*"
P.O. Box 205
Oakdale, IA 52319-0205

Glass Research Society of New Jersey
Wheaton Village
Milville, NJ 08332

Great Lakes Carnival Glass
c/o Maxine Burkhardt
12875 Chippewa Drive
Grand Ledge, MI 48837

Heart of America Carnival Glass Association
Lucille Britt
3048 Tamarek Drive
Manhattan, KS 66502

Heisey Collectors of America, Inc.
169 W. Church St.
Newark, OH 43055

Heisey Publications
P.O. Box 102
Plymouth, OH 44865

Hoosier Carnival Glass Club
Eunice Booker
944 W. Pine St.
Griffith, IN 46391

International Carnival Glass Association
Lee Markley
R.R. #1, P.O. Box 14
Mentone, IN 46539

Keystone Carnival Glass Club
Mary Sharp
719 W. Brubaker Valley Road
Lititz, PA 17543

Kitchen Antiques & Collectibles News Newsletter
Kana and Darlene DeMore, Editors
4645 Laurel Ridge Drive
Harrisburg, PA 17110

Knife Rests of Yesterday and Today
Beverly Ales
4046 Graham St.
Pleasanton, CA 94566-5619

Kovel's Newsletter
P.O. Box 22200
Beachwood, OH 44122

R. Lalique
11028 Raleigh Court
Rockford, IL 61111

Lincoln-Land Carnival Glass Club
Ellen Hem
N. 951 Hwy. 27
Conrath, WI 54731

Maine Antique Digest
P.O. Box 1429
Waldoboro, ME 04572

Marble Collector's Society of America
P.O. Box 222
Trumbull, CT 06611

Michiana Association of Candlewick Collectors
17370 Battles Road
South Bend, IN 44614

Morgantown Collectors of America
420 1st Ave. N.W.
Plainview, MN 55964

Mount Washington Art Glass Society
P.O. Box 24094
Fort Worth, TX 76124

National Association of Avon Collectors
6100 Walnut, Dept. P
Kansas City, MO 64113

National Depression Glass Association
P.O. Box 69843
Odessa, TX 79769

The National Duncan Glass Society
P.O. Box 965
Washington, PA 15301

The National Early American Glass Club
P.O. Box 8489
Silver Spring, MD 20907

The National Fenton Glass Society
P.O. Box 4008
Marietta, OH 45750

The National Greentown Glass Association
1807 W. Madison St.
Kokomo, IN 46901

The National Imperial Glass Collectors Society
P.O. Box 534
Bellaire, OH 43906

The National Insulator Association
3557 Nicklaus Dr.
Titusville, FL 32780

"*Opaque News*"
The National Milk Glass Collectors Society
Helen Storey
46 Almond Drive
Hershey, PA 17033

The National Reamer Association
c/o Larry Branstad
R.R. 3 Box 67
Frederic, WI 54837

The National Westmoreland
Glass Collectors Club
P.O. Box 372
Export, PA 15632

New England Antiques Journal
4 Church St.
Ware, MA 01082

New England Carnival Glass Association
Ms. Marie M. Heath
H.C.R. 31, Box 15
St. Johnsbury, VT 05819

Northern California Carnival Glass Club
June McCarter
1205 Clifton Drive
Modesto, CA 95355

Ohio Candlewick Collectors' Club
613 S. Patterson St.
Gibsonburg, OH 43431

Old Morgantown Glass Collectors' Guild
420 First Ave. N.W.
Plainview, MN 55964

Pacific Northwest Carnival Club
Pat Dolezal
3515 N.E. Hancock
Portland, OR 97212

Pairpoint Cup Plate Glass Club Collectors of America, Inc.
P.O. Box 52 D
East Weymouth, MA 02189

Paperweight Collectors
P.O. Box 1059
Easthampton, MA 49125

Perfume and Scent Bottle Collectors
2022 E. Charleston Blvd.
Las Vegas, NV 89104

Perfume Bottle Association
P.O. Box 529
Vienna, VA 22183

Phoenix & Consolidated Collectors Association
P.O. Box 81974
Chicago, IL 60681

Rose Bowl Collectors
5214 Route 309
Center Valley, PA 18034

San Diego Carnival Glass Club
Kathy Harris
5860 Torca St.
San Diego, CA 92124

San Joaquin Carnival Glass Club
Marie McGee
3906 E. Acacia Ave.
Fresno, CA 93726

The Shot Glass Club of America
5071 Watson Drive
Flint, MI 48506

Southern California Carnival Glass Collectors
Judy Maxwell
31091 Bedford Drive
Redlands, CA 92373

The Stretch Glass Society
P.O. Box 770643
Lakewood, OH 44107

Tampa Bay Carnival Glass Club
Barbara Hobbs
5501 101st Ave.
N. Pinellas Park, FL 34666

Texas Carnival Glass Club
Kim Smith
902 S. Blackwell St.
Tyler, TX 75023

Thimble Collectors International
6411 Montego Road
Louisville, KY 40228

Three Rivers Depression Era Glass Society
Rte. 88 and Broughton Road
Bethel Park, PA 15102

Tiffin Glass Collectors Club
P.O. Box 554
Tiffin, OH 44883

Tobacco Jar Newsletter
Charlotte Tarses
3011 Falstaff Road, #307
Baltimore, MD 21209

Toothpick Holder Collector's Club
Joyce Ender
P.O. Box 246
Sawyer, MI 49125

Westmoreland Glass Collector's Newsletter
P.O. Box 143
North Liberty, IA 52317

Westmoreland Glass Society
Steven Jensen
4809 420 St. S.E.
Iowa City, IA 52240

Whimsey Glass Club
4544 Cairo Drive
Whitehall, PA 18052

World's Fair Collectors Society, Inc.
Michael Pender
P.O. Box 20806
Sarasota, FL 34238

Internet/Web Sites

One of the most significant changes in the antique and collectibles world is the use of the Internet and World Wide Web. If you simply type in "Glass," "Glass Collecting," "Antiques," or similar key words into any of the popular search engines, you can easily access hundreds of thousands of sites. All of the major online services provide some sort of search functions for key words such as "Glass" or "Antiques," none

867

more so than Google. Most, if not all museums, companies, artisans, and the like have Web sites (a few are listed at the end of this section).

The most significant area concerning glassware, especially when it comes to pricing, are the online auction sites. There are smaller ones like JustGlass.com, but none anywhere near as large as eBay. On any given day, there will be thousands or perhaps even hundreds of thousands of pieces of glass up for auction. To date, I have personally purchased about 200 items, mostly glassware on eBay, and have rarely been disappointed. One seller did not honor my high bid, but he was new, and quickly stopped selling after receiving some negative feedback. Another seller failed to mention a prominent bubble present in the handle of a Mary Gregory glass bell that I had purchased. Most sellers have return policies, and the buyer is usually expected to pay postage, shipping, and insurance. (As a side note, it is a good idea to inquire about these charges if the seller does not list them before bidding.) Here are a few tips for online auctions:

TRUST

How do you trust a dealer or person selling something? In most cases, both sellers and buyers are encouraged to leave feedback about each other. Check the feedback ratings of those with whom you are dealing before you place a bid in an auction. Those with too many negatives do not survive long. Also, the federal government has finally gotten involved with online transactions and is prosecuting for fraud those who accept your payment and then fail to deliver the goods. Notify the auction service right away if you suspect fraud; eBay for instance, has its own investigative force that works closely with public authorities. There is some recourse through services

such as Paypal, too, along with your credit card company.

COMMUNICATION

Do not hesitate to write the seller an e-mail message with any questions you might have. It is to the advantage of the seller to further describe and explain what he or she is listing. Simply do not bid on something if you have any doubts or if the seller does not get back to you. Note also that a seller may have other similar items for sale that you might wish to inquire about. Be careful about accepting responses such as "It's old glass; you can't expect it to be perfect." If you are spending several thousands, it had better be! Know what type of glass might have some minor flaws (such as older pressed styles, including Depression glass) as opposed to those that don't (cut- and fancy art-glass styles, for instance).

TIMING

Keep an eye on the auction's closing date and time. Little can be done for the snipers who wait until the last minute or even second to place a bid. Most everyone with any online auction experience has been outbid at the last minute. Still, some prefer to bid as they are browsing no matter when the auction ends, whereas others like to wait for the closing day before bidding. I prefer to put one good solid maximum bid up front while I am browsing. What is nice about eBay is that they increase your bid only at an increment over the past highest bid. For example, say you bid $50 for a piece of glass that has an opening bid of $20 and an increment of $1. Your bid will now be $21. If someone bids $30, your bid will automatically jump to $31. It will automatically increase up to the limit that you originally put in (in this case, $50).

BIDDING

As a bidder, be 100 percent sure that when you bid, you will honor that bid. In an informal poll of sellers, this is their most frustrating and aggravating concern. About all a seller can do is notify the auction service and leave negative feedback for you. eBay usually will no longer allow you to bid after three such reported cases of not honoring your bid. Sellers can take legal action since a bid is considered to be a binding agreement; nevertheless, few will do so, particularly if the bid was for a relatively small amount.

AUCTION FEVER

Keep in mind that auctions can be addictive. In the heat of bidding, some will occasionally pay a premium over what a piece is approximately worth. This is fine if it is truly a piece you desire or something you've been searching for for a long time. The seller will appreciate it, too! Nonetheless, for more common items, you may wish to check auctions periodically, because the same piece might be listed by someone else in the next day, week, month, or even year, and consequently, may sell for much less. Patience is always a virtue when it comes to auctions. A little experience will allow you to know in most cases what is common and what is not.

SELLER HONESTY

People appreciate honesty in sellers. A full description that includes every little flaw, whether it is a bubble, trailing, unfinished pontil mark, nick, chip, scratch, wear, and so forth, should be noted in detail by the seller. Pictures are vital for selling; if you are going to sell, a digital camera is a necessity, though there are photography services that can be used (but most are quite expensive). A seller's reputation can be made or broken very quickly, especially if deceit is involved. Always check the seller's feedback rating before bidding, and read the comments made by others. It doesn't hurt to check the seller's location, too, as those in foreign lands may not be able to ship to you, not at least without substantial shipping fees. Check those shipping fees as noted above; if none are listed, don't hesitate to ask before bidding.

RESERVE PRICING

This is still an area that I really do not understand insofar as why a seller will put up a secret reserve price that will not be revealed unless a potential buyer bids at least that amount. My personal feeling is that the seller should just list the minimum price he or she will accept to open the bidding. If it's too high, then no one will bid. It is frustrating to bid on something only to receive a message saying that although you are the high bidder, the reserve price has not been met yet. The only advantage I can see for the seller is for him or her to get a feeling of what the piece might sell for on the open market. Sellers take note! In an informal poll of buyers, I found that aside from lack of clear descriptions and listed shipping charges, reserves are one of the biggest pet peeves out there. Some simply don't bother bidding when they see that a secret reserve price has been set.

Here are just a few Web sites related to glassware:

American & Foreign Glass
Jcwiese.com

Angela Bowery's Online Glass Museum
Glass.co.nz/index.htm

Antiques/Depression Glass
sun.com/index.htm

Art and Cut Glass
AACantiques.com

Art Gallery
Cncglassworks.com

Art Glass by Chris Heilman
Hotglassheilman.com

Art Glass Items
Shandgallery.com

Art Glass Items
SpectrumGlass.com

Auctions
*Collectit.net; ebay.com; justglass.com;
sothebys-1.com; usaweb.com/online.html*

Australian Glass
Anu.edu.aa/ita/csa/glass

Books on Glass
*Amazon.com; antiquepublications.com;
books-on-glass.netnz.com; glassbooks.com;
lwbooks.com; schifferbooks.com;
whitehouse-books.com*

British Glass Information
Britglass.co.uk/

Broadfield House Glass Museum
Aboutbritain.com

Buy/Sell/Trade Glass
Cooksmill.com

Caithness of Scotland
Caithnessglass.co.uk

Cameo Glass
Cameoglass.com

Carnival Glass
*Zeus/kspress.com/woodsland/carnivalglass;
accarnivalglass.com; carnivalglass.net;
seekauction.com; texascarnivalglass.com*

Character Glass
Glassnews.com

Colored Glass for Artisans
Chicagoartglass.com

Corning Museum of Glass
Cmog.org

Cut Glass
Classicplaza.com; cutglass.org; handcut.com

Czechoslovakian Glass for Sale
Eledis.com

Depression Glass
*DGshopper.com; antiquenet.com; arsh.com;
dgplace.com; glasskey.com; glassshow.com*

Dorflinger Cut Glass
Dorflinger.org

Duncan & Miller Glass Museum
Duncan-glass.com

Encyclopedia
glass.co.nz/encyclopedia

English Glass
Antique-Glassco.uk

Fenton Glass
fentonglass.com; giftsglass.com

Fostoria Glass Society
Fostoriaglass.org; fostoriacollectors.org

French/Swarovski Crystal
JPcrystal.com

Glass Factories
Glassfactorydirectory.com

Glass Forum
The-forum.com/glass

Glass Line Newsletter
Hotglass.com

Glass Making Techniques
Spectrumglass.com

Glass Sculptures by Leading Artists
Holstengalleries.com; richardsonstudios.com

Glass Search
Opendir.metacrawler.com

Insulators
Insulators.com

Kitchen Glass & Antiques
*Antique-Glass.com; ediesglass.com;
firstclassglass.com*

Kokomo Glass
kog.com

Lalique
R-Lalique.com; rene-lalique.com

Libbey Glass
Toledomuseum.org

Loetz Glass
Gallery.uunet.be/loetzweb

Glass Museum On-Line
glass.co.nz

Northwood Carnival Reproductions
Northwoodglass.com

Paperweights
Selman.com; paperweight.com

Pattern Glass
Whatnotcollectables.com

Pertshire Paperweights
Crieff.co.uk; perthsire.com

Phoenix & Consolidated Glass Club
Collectoronline.com

Replacement Pattern Pieces
replacements.com

Sandwich Glass Museum
Sandwichglassmuseum.org

Stained Glass
*Asgla.com; stainedglassmuseum.org;
stainedglassretailers.com*

Steuben Glass
Steuben.com

Swarovski Crystal
*Always-forever.com; crystalclassics.com;
pure-elegance.com; swarovskicrystal.net;
thecollectiblesstore.com*

Tacoma, WA Museum of Glass
museumofglass.com

Tiffany
*Glass2u.com; tiffanyartglass.com;
tiffanyglass.com; tiffanystainedglass.com*

Toledo Museum of Art
Toledomuseum.org

Venetian Glass
findarticles.com

Waterford Glass
*irishmailorder.com; shamrockshop.com;
waterfordtourism.org; Waterford-usa.com*

West Virginia Glass Companies
State.WV.us/tourism/glassfac/glassco.htm

Westmoreland Glass
Jcwiese.com; frognet.net

Wheaton Village Glass Museum
Wheatonvillage.org
I can also be reached at:
MPickvet@aol.com

Museums

Allen Art Museum
Oberlin College
Oberlin, OH 44074

Art Institute of Chicago
Michigan Ave. and Adams St.
Chicago, IL 60603

The Bennington Museum
W. Main St.
Bennington, VT 05201

Bergstrom Art Center and Museum
165 N. Park Ave.
Neenah, WI 54956

The Cambridge Glass Museum
506 S. 9th St.
Cambridge, OH 43725

Carnegie Institute—Museum of Art
4400 Forbes Ave.
Pittsburgh, PA 15213

Chrysler Museum at Norfolk
Olney Road and Mowbray Arch
Norfolk, VA 23510

Corning Museum of Glass
One Museum Way
Corning, NY 14830

Currier Gallery of Art
192 Orange St.
Manchester, NH 03104

Degenhart Paperweight and Glass Museum, Inc.
P.O. Box 186
Cambridge, OH 43725

Dorflinger Glass Museum
P.O. Box 260
Hawley, PA 18428

Everhart Museum
1901 Mulberry St.
Scranton, PA 18510

Fenton Art Glass Co.
700-T Elizabeth St.
Williamstown, WV 26187

Greentown Glass Museum, Inc
624 W. Main St.
Greentown, IN 46936

Henry Ford Museum
P.O. Box 1970
20900 Oakwood Blvd.
Dearborn, MI 48121

Indianapolis Art Museum
1200 W. 38th St.
Indianapolis, IN

Jones Museum
Douglas Mt. off Hwy. 107
Sebago, ME 04029

Lightner Museum
75 King St.
St. Augustine, FL 32084

Metropolitan Museum of Art
1000 5th Ave.
New York, NY 10028

Milan Historical Museum
10 Edison Dr.
Milan, OH 44846

Minneapolis Institute of Arts
2400 Third Ave. S.
Minneapolis, MN 55404

Museum of Beverage Containers and Advertising
1055 Ridgecrest Dr.
Goodlettsville, TN 37072

Museum of Glass
1801 Dock St.
Tacoma, WA 98402

Museum of Modern Art
11 West 53rd St.
New York, NY 10019

National Bottle Museum
76 Milton Ave.
Ballston Spa, NY 12020

National Duncan Glass Museum
525 Jefferson Ave.
Washington, PA 15301

National Heisey Glass Museum
1609 W. Church St.
Newark, OH 43055

Newark Museum
49 Washington St.
Newark, NJ 07101

New Beford Glass Museum
50 N. Second St.
New Bedford, MA 02740

New Bedford Whaling Museum
18 Johnny Cake Hill
New Bedford, MA 02740

Oglebay Institute—Mansion Museum
Oglebay Park
Wheeling, WV 26003

Old Sturbridge Village
1 Old Sturbridge Village Road
Sturbridge, MA 01566

Philadelphia Museum of Art
P.O. Box 7646
Philadelphia, PA 19101

Portland Art Museum
Seven Congress Square
Portland, ME 04101

Redlands Glass Museum
1157 Orange St.
Redlands, CA 92373

Rockwell Museum
111 Cedar St.
Corning, NY 14830

St. Louis Glass Museum
1 Fine Arts Drive
St. Louis, MO 63110

Sandwich Glass Museum
P.O. Box 103
Sandwich, MA 02563

L.H. Selman Paperweight Gallery
123 Locust St.
Santa Cruz, CA 95060

Seneca County Museum
28 Clay St.
Tiffin, OH 44883

Smithsonian Museum of History
Smithsonian Institution
Washington, DC 29560

Stark Museum of Art
712 Green Ave.
Orange, TX 77630

Texas A & M University
Forsyth Center Galleries
University Memorial Student Center
P.O. Box J-1
College Station, TX 77844

Toledo Museum of Art
P.O. Box 1013
Toledo, OH 43697

Van Andel Museum
272 Pearl St. NW
Grand Rapids, MI 49504

Wadsworth Athenum
600 Main St.
Hartford, CT 06103

Westmoreland Glass Museum
1815 Trimble Ave.
Port Vue, PA 15133

West Virginia Museum of Glass
Main & 2nd Streets
P.O. Box 26452
Weston, WV 26452

Wheaton Village
1501 Glasstown Rd.
Milville, NJ 08332

Sedgewick Co. Historical Museum
204 S. Main St.
Wichita, KS 67202

Winterthur Museum
Route 52
Winterthur, DE 19735

GLOSSARY

ABRASION
The technique of grinding shallow decorations in a glass object by using a wheel. The decorated areas are usually left unpolished.

ACANTHUS
A common gilded decoration applied to glassware in the form of an acanthus leaf. The decoration may be applied in a series of scrolled leaves as well. Acanthus is a spiked plant native to southern Europe.

ACID CUT BACK
The process of dipping an object into acid for a controlled amount of time to achieve a desired cutting depth.

ACID ETCHING
The process of covering glass with an acid-resistant protective layer, scratching on a design, and then applying hydrofluoric acid to etch the pattern into the glass.

ACID POLISHING
The technique of giving cut glass a polished surface by dipping it into a hydrofluoric acid bath.

ACID STAMPING
The process of etching a trademark or signature in glass with acid after it has been annealed. Acid stamps are similar to rubber stamps.

ADAMS AND CO.
Founded by John Adams in Pittsburgh, Pennsylvania, in 1856; Adams was a major producer of pressed pattern glass. The firm became part of U.S. Glass in 1891.

ADVERTISING GLASS
A glass vessel displaying information about a manufacturer, company, proprietor, brand, person, establishment, event, and so on.

AETNA GLASS AND MANUFACTURING CO.
A short-lived pressed-glass manufacturer established in Bellaire, Ohio, in 1880. The firm closed in 1891.

AGATA GLASS
Art glass characterized by mottled purple or brown finishes as a result of alcohol added on top of the color. Agata glass was produced by the New England Glass Company in the late 19th century.

AIR TWIST
An 18th-century English decorating technique in which air bubbles were purposefully injected in the base of an object and then pulled down and twisted into a stem.

AKRO AGATE GLASS CO.
Akro Agate was founded in 1911 in Akron, Ohio. They were most famous for manufacturing opaque marble but added other opaque glass novelty items after they moved operations to West Virginia. The company closed permanently in 1951.

ALABASTER GLASS
A translucent ornamental glass first developed by Frederick Carder at Steuben. Alabaster resembles the white color of the mineral after which it is named and is produced by spraying stannous chloride on a piece before it is reheated.

ALASKAN
A name given to a carnival-glass color produced by the Northwood Glass Company. Alaskan consists of glass with a green base color that is iridized with the common carnival marigold color.

ALBANY GLASS CO.
Albany Glass was first founded in the 1780s in Albany, New York, and lasted until about 1820. They made windows, bottles, and a few other items.

ALBERTINE GLASS
Albertine was produced by the Mt. Washington Glass Company in the late 19th century. It is characterized by opaque glass, ornate decoration, and was applied primarily to show items such as vases. It is sometimes referred to as Crown Milano.

ALE GLASS
An early 17th-century English glass with a capacity of 3–5 ounces, short-stemmed, and used for drinking ale or beer.

ALEXANDRITE GLASS
Art glass produced by Thomas Webb in England in the late 19th century. It is characterized by various shadings of blue, pink or red, and yellow achieved through several stages of refiring.

C. G. ALFORD & CO.
Founded in 1872 in New York City, Alford operated as a watch and jewelry store as well as a cut-glass operation. They closed in 1918.

ALKALI
A soluble salt mixture consisting primarily of potassium carbonate and sodium carbonate. The alkali is an essential ingredient in glass that helps reduce the melting point of silica.

ALMY & THOMAS
Founded in 1903 by Charles H. Almy and G. Edwin Thomas. They purchased the Knickerbocker Cut Glass Company and continued cutting glass until 1918. The Corning Glass Works supplied them with blanks.

ALUMINOSILICATE GLASS
A type of heat-resistant glass developed by Corning for their Flameware brand of Pyrex kitchenware. This formula is more heat resistant than the original borosilicate formula.

AMBER
A yellowish-brown colored glass produced by the addition of iron, carbon, and sulphur. The color resembles fossilized tree sap of the same name.

AMBERETTE
Pressed glassware that was frosted or stained with dark yellow or yellowish brown colors to resemble art glass.

AMBERINA
Art glass produced in America in the late 19th century. It is characterized by transparent glass that is lightly shaded with light amber at the base and gradually shaded darker to ruby red at the top. Joseph Locke received a patent for Amberina in 1883 (see also Plated Amberina).

AMELUNG GLASS
High-quality glass made in America in the late 18th century by German immigrant John Frederick Amelung.

AMERICAN CUT GLASS CO.
Established in 1897 in Chicago by William Anderson (a designer and craftsman for Libbey), the company moved to Lansing, Michigan, in 1900 and continued to produce cut glass until World War I.

AMERICAN FLINT GLASS WORKS
Established at Wheeling, Virginia, in the

1840s (before West Virginia became a state), they produced pressed, mold-blown, and handblown glass in crystal (using flint and lead) and colored glass.

AMERICAN GLASS CO.
Established in 1899 in Indiana, Pennsylvania; the firm purchased the Dugan/Northwood factory and made some pressed wares. They, in turn, sold out to the Diamond Glass Company in 1913.

AMETHYST
A light purple-colored glass produced by the addition of manganese. Some amethyst glass is made so dark that it is referred to as Black Amethyst.

ANCHOR CAP AND CLOSURE CORP.
An American manufacturer established in Long Island City, New York, in the early 1900s; they were a major manufacturer of containers and merged with Hocking in 1937 to form the Anchor-Hocking Glass Corporation.

ANCHOR-HOCKING GLASS CORP.
A huge American glass manufacturer of containers, tableware, and other items established in 1937 when the Anchor Cap and Closure Corporation merged with the Hocking Glass Company.

ANIMAL DISHES
Covered glass dishes or glass objects made in the shapes of various animals, such as roosters, horses, cats, dogs, and elephants. Animal dishes were very popular from about 1890 to 1910, a little during the Depression era, and from the 1970s on.

ANNEALING
A process that toughens glass and eliminates stress by heating and gradually cooling in an annealing oven or lehr.

ANNEALING CRACK
A crack or fissure that develops in glass from improper cooling or annealing.

ANTIMONY
The key metallic agent in producing yellow-colored glass.

AOP
An abbreviation for All-Over Pattern. Allover patterns generally cover the entire glass object but may be limited to the outside only.

APPLIED OR APPLICATION
Attaching molten glass rods to blanks to form handles, foots, pedestals, and so on.

APPLIQUÉD
A decorating technique featuring hand-applied three-dimensional trim. The trim is applied in a molten state while the object itself is still hot, thus becoming a permanent part of the object. The trim is often worked into fruit or flowering vines.

APRICOT
A deep yellow- or dark amber-colored glass.

AQUA OR AQUAMARINE
A light greenish-blue color in glass like the color of seawater.

AQUA OPALESCENT
Aqua- or aquamarine-colored glass with an opalescent edge.

AQUA REGIA
A mixture of two strong acids that serve to dissolve gold dust in the making of red or ruby red glassware. In more recent times, selenium has replaced gold in producing the color red.

ARISSING
The process of removing sharp edges from glass.

ARMORIAL GLASS

A general term used to describe glassware produced throughout Europe in the 17th through 19th centuries. It consists of functional glass objects such as beakers, plates, goblets, and flasks decorated with coats-of-arms that were usually engraved or enameled.

ART OR ART NOUVEAU GLASS

Expensive handblown glass with unusual effects of color, shape, and design. Art glass is primarily ornamental and was most popular from the 1880s to 1920.

ART STUDIO GLASS MOVEMENT

A movement that began in March 1962 with Harvey Littleton, a professor of ceramics with the University of Wisconsin. Littleton held a workshop at the Toledo Museum of Art and proved that art glass could be blown by independent artists in small studios. Out of his new design program at Wisconsin, Littleton's most famous student was Dale Chihuly (see also Chihuly).

ASHTRAY

A shallow bowl-like glass receptacle used for cigarette butts and tobacco ashes.

ATOMIZER

See Cologne Bottle or Perfume Bottle.

ATTERBURY AND COMPANY

A short-lived pressed-glass company that operated in Pittsburgh, Pennsylvania, in the 1850s.

AURENE

Iridescent ornamental art glass created by Frederick Carder at the Steuben Glass Works around 1904.

AVENTURINE

An ancient Egyptian technique of applying small flakes of metal such as gold and copper in colored glass. This technique was popular during the art nouveau period.

AVERBECK CUT GLASS CO.

Established in New York City in 1892; Averbeck ran a jewelry store and a mail-order business featuring cut-glass products. They ceased operation in 1923.

BACCARAT

The original company was founded in 1764 in Baccarat, France, as the Saint-Anne Glassworks. In 1816 Aime-Gabriel d'Artiques purchased the factory and the name was changed to Verrerie de Vonuche Baccarat. Early on, the company produced practical lead-crystal items. In the 1840s, they began producing art-style paperweights along with tableware, cut glass, and other decorative glass. The company is still in operation and is known for making some of the finest crystal in the world today.

BACKSTAMP

An identification mark that is printed or molded on a piece of glass. The mark may include such information as a company name, logo, and item number.

BAKEWELL, PEARS & CO.

An American company established in Pittsburgh, Pennsylvania, in 1807 as the Bakewell, Payn, and Page Co.; they began producing glass furniture knobs and handles and then added tableware and barware. The business closed in 1882.

BALL STOPPER

A spherical glass object that rests at the top of glass bottles, jugs, decanters, etc. Its diameter is larger than the mouth of the vessel.

BALUSTER

A type of English drinking glass or goblet

created in the late 17th century. The stem is in the shape of a short vertical support with a circular section (baluster shape).

BANANA BOAT OR DISH

A long flat or shallow dish, with sides that are possibly curved upward, with or without a separate base, and used for serving bananas or banana splits.

BAR TUMBLER

A glass tumbler with or without flutes produced in the United States in various shapes and sizes beginning in the mid-19th century primarily for hotels and saloons.

BARBER BOTTLE

A colored glass container with a narrow neck and mouth used to hold liquids used by barbers, such as shaving solutions and colognes. Barber bottles may or may not have handles but usually do contain stoppers. They were popular in the late 18th and 19th centuries.

BARBINI GLASSWORKS

Established by Alfredo Barbini in Murano, Italy, in 1950, the company operates today creating Venetian novelties and knick-knacks. Barbini is noted for developing a new technique dubbed *masello*. This involves sculpting a solid block of molten glass without molding or blowing.

BARTLETT-COLLINS CO.

An American company established in Sapulpa, Oklahoma, in 1914; they are noted for tableware, lamps, and glass decorated with Western themes.

BASE

The bottom part of a glass object.

BASE COLOR

The color of glass before any coating is applied, usually the color of carnival glass before it is iridized.

BASKET

A glass receptacle with a semicircular handle used for foods, decoration, or for displaying flowers.

BATCH

The mixture of raw materials fused together before heating.

BAY STATE GLASS COMPANY

Founded in East Cambridge, Massachusetts, in 1851; the company produced some limited cut-glass tableware. Under the direction of Amory Houghton, operations were moved to Somerville, Massachusetts, and renamed the Union Glass Company (see also Union Glass Co.).

BEADING

The process by which chips or small relief beads are fused to a glass object in the form of a continuous row.

BEATTY, ALEXANDER J. & SONS

Established in Steubenville, Ohio, in 1879, the company moved to Tiffin, Ohio, in 1888. As a maker of pressed glass, the company became part of the U.S. Glass Company conglomerate on January 1, 1892. In 1916 the company began operating as a distinct subsidiary known as the Tiffin Glass Company (see also Tiffin).

BEATTY-BRADY GLASS CO.

A pressed-glass manufacturer established in Steubenville, Ohio, in 1850. The company moved to Dunkirk, Indiana, in 1898 and then became part of the National Glass Company in 1899.

BEAUMONT GLASS COMPANY

Established in Martins Ferry, Ohio, in 1895 as a maker of pressed glass, the company was sold to the Hocking Glass Company in 1905.

BEAVER FALLS COOPERATIVE GLASS CO.

A pressed-glass manufacturer established in Beaver Falls, Pennsylvania, in 1879. The firm became the Beaver Falls Glass Company in 1887.

BEER BOTTLE

A glass container with a narrow neck and mouth designed to hold beer. Amber has been the most popular color for beer bottles from the 19th century to the present. Beer bottles usually do not have handles.

BELL OR DINNER BELL

A hollow device with ringer and single top handle used for summoning or signaling when rung (such as to announce dinnertime).

BELLAIRE GOBLET CO.

A pressed-glass manufacturer established in Bellaire, Ohio, in 1879. The firm moved to Findlay, Ohio, in 1888, and then joined the U.S. Glass Company in 1891 as Factory M.

BELMONT TUMBLER CO.

An American company established in 1866 in Bellaire, Ohio; they produced tumblers and some Depression items. The factory burned in 1952 and was never rebuilt.

BERGEN, J. D. CO.

Founded in Meriden, Connecticut, by James D. Bergen and Thomas Niland; Bergen bought out Niland in 1885 and continued operating as a cut-glass operation until 1922.

BERRY BOWL

A concave glass vessel used for serving fruits and other foods. Note that a berry set is a large bowl with one or more matching smaller bowls.

BEST METAL

The highest-quality batch of glass made by a company using the purest ingredients and highest lead content.

BEVEL

Slanted or angle cuts usually beginning at the bottom or sides of a glass object (sometimes referred to as flutes at the bottom).

BISCUIT JAR

A tall, widemouthed canister-shape glass receptacle with cover used for holding biscuits, crackers, or cookies (the predecessor of the cookie jar!).

BITTERS BOTTLE

Small bottles used for containing bitters or tonics made in the United States in the mid- and later 19th century.

BLACK AMETHYST

An extremely dense, nearly opaque shade of purple made by the addition of manganese. Black amethyst glass is so dark that it cannot be seen through when held to light.

BLACK BOTTLE

A dark opaque green English invention in the mid-17th century used for transporting and storing various beverages such as water, beer, wine, and rum.

BLACK GLASS

Dark opaque ebony glass created by the combination of oxide of manganese, cobalt, and oxide of iron added to a batch of glass.

BLACKMER CUT GLASS CO.

Established by Arthur L. Blackmer in New Bedford, Massachusetts, in 1894 and incorporated as A. L. Blackmer in 1902, the company produced cut-glass products until 1916.

BLANK
An uncut piece of glass, ordinarily a bowl or vase, that has been specifically made of heavy, high-quality lead glassware.

BLENKO GLASS CO.
Originally founded by English immigrant William J. Blenko in 1922 in Milton, West Virginia; the company started as a maker of stained-glass windows and later switched to contemporary art forms.

BLOBBING
The process by which chips of colored glass are embedded in the thickness of blown glass to form an irregular scattering of contrasting colors.

BLOWING
The process of blowing air through a metal tube or blowpipe to shape the molten glass blob attached to its end.

BLOWN THREE-MOLD
Glass that is blown into a predesigned mold that is made up of two, three, or even more hinged parts. The three-part mold is the most common and leaves two sets of mold lines. This style of glass originated around 1820 in America and was made throughout the 19th century.

BLOWPIPE
A hollow metal tube used to gather molten glass from the pot; air is then blown through it to shape glass.

BLUE GLASS
In light blue glass, copper is the metallic coloring agent added to a batch of glass. For a deep, dark blue color, refer to Cobalt Blue.

BLUERINA
Art glass made in America in the late 19th century that is very similar to Amberina, but the colors gradually meld from blue at the base to Amberina at the top.

BODA GLASSWORKS
Founded in 1864 in southern Sweden by two workers who had previously worked with the Kosta Glassworks (Scheutz and Widlund). Boda merged with Kosta in 1946 to form Kosta-Boda.

BOHEMIAN GLASS
German-made glass in the 17th century characterized by ornate decoration, heavy cutting, and bright colors.

BONBON OR BONBON DISH
A small, usually flat or shallow circular dish, with or without handles (center handle possible), used for serving small finger foods such as nuts, bonbons, or tiny fruits.

BOOT GLASS
A small glass vessel shaped like a boot with a capacity of about 3 ounces.

BOOZE BOTTLE
A flask made in America in the 1860s in the form of a two-story house by the Whitney Glass Works for Edmund G. Booze.

BOROSILICATE GLASS
The original or first heat-resistant formula for glassware that contains boric oxide. It was developed by the Corning Glass Works for railroad lantern lenses and for battery cases. It was adapted to Pyrex kitchenware in 1915.

BOSTON & SANDWICH GLASS CO.
An American company established in Boston by Deming Jarves in 1825. They produced much pressed and cut glassware before closing in 1888. Boston & Sandwich is considered the first successful American glassmaking firm and is the manufacturer from which the term *Sandwich glass* originates.

BOSTON SILVER GLASS CO.
Established in 1857 by A. Young in Cambridge, Massachusetts; the company pro-

duced some pressed glassware and silver-plating before closing in 1871.

BOTTLE
A glass container with a narrow neck and mouth; may or may not have a handle. Bottles come in all shapes and sizes and can be made of other materials.

BOWL
A concave glass vessel, hemispherical in shape, used for holding liquids and other foods, such as soups, salads, cereal, berries, and vegetables. Bowls commonly come in many other shapes and sizes. The bowl of a wine or stemmed beverage glass is the portion that holds the liquid.

BOX
A glass receptacle that usually contains a cover. The cover may or may not be hinged and the overall shape may be round, oval, or rectangular. Glass boxes are usually very small and were popular during the Victorian era to hold small jewelry and powders.

BOYD ART GLASS CO.
Established in Cambridge, Ohio, in 1978; Boyd is noted for highly collectible miniature art figurines created in a variety of colors and styles.

BRANDY GLASS
A short rounded glass with a foot and tiny stem; shorter but wider compared with a rounded wineglass.

BREAD AND BUTTER PLATE
A round, flat object that is usually 6 inches in diameter.

BRIDE'S BASKET
A fancy bowl held within a silver or silver-plated frame. These were popular wedding gifts during the Brilliant period after they debuted at the World's Columbian Exposition in Chicago in 1893.

BRILLIANT GLASS WORKS
Established by Joseph Beatty Sr. in Brilliant, Ohio, in 1880; the firm produced some pressed glassware before merging with the Novelty Glass Works in 1889.

BRILLIANT PERIOD
The era of American handmade glassware from 1880 to 1915 characterized by fine cutting, engraving, polishing, and fancy patterns.

BRISTOL GLASS
Crystal, colored, and milk glass items produced in several factories in Bristol, England, in the 17th and 18th centuries.

BRISTOL-TYPE GLASS
Nineteenth-century American and English-made Victorian opaque glassware characterized by hand-enameling.

BRYCE BROTHERS
A pressed-glass manufacturer formed after the break-up of Bryce, Walker, and Co. in 1882. The firm moved to Hammondsville, Pennsylvania, in 1889. They specialized in handblown stemware and barware and then joined the U.S. Glass Co. in 1891 as Factory B. The company was moved to Mt. Pleasant, Pennsylvania, in 1896 and continued producing glassware into the 1950s.

BRYCE, HIGBEE AND CO.
A pressed-glass manufacturer established in Pittsburgh, Pennsylvania, in 1879. The firm moved to Bridgeville, Pennsylvania, and became the Higbee Glass Company in 1900.

BRYCE, MCKEE, AND CO.
A short-lived pressed-glass manufacturer established in Pittsburgh, Pennsylvania, in 1850. The firm became Bryce, Walker, and Company in 1854.

BRYCE, WALKER, AND CO.
A pressed-glass manufacturer established

in Pittsburgh, Pennsylvania, in 1854. The firm became Bryce Brothers in 1882.

BUBBLE
An air- or gas-filled cavity within glass. Intentional bubbles are often created for decorative effects, whereas unintentional ones result from improper fusing of the ingredients. Tiny bubbles are also known as seeds.

BUCKEYE GLASS CO.
A pressed-glass manufacturer established in Wheeling, West Virginia, in 1849. The firm moved to Bowling Green, Ohio, in 1888 and closed in 1903.

BULLICANTE
A technique originated in Venice that places air bubbles in a regular pattern within glass (popular in modern paperweights).

BULL'S-EYE
A popular decorating technique in pressed glass whereby raised adjacent circles (bull's eyes) were applied around an object. Bull's-eyes were usually combined with other patterns such as diamond points, thumbprints, panels, and others.

BUMPER
Another term for a firing glass (see Firing Glass).

BURMESE GLASS
Glass objects characterized by various light opaque shadings in pastel colors of pink, yellow, and white produced with the addition of uranium. It was first created by the Mt. Washington Glass Company in the late 19th century and then produced by others.

BUTTER DISH
A glass dish that is ordinarily flat or footed, with or without glass dome or rectangular cover, and used for serving butter, margarine, or other spreads.

BUTTER PAT
A miniature glass plate (round, square, or rectangular) used for serving an individual pat or portion of butter.

BUTTER PLATE
A small glass plate used for serving individual portions of butter, margarine, or other spreads.

BUTTER TUB
A glass vessel shaped as a small bucket or pail (usually smaller than an ice bucket), with or without a semicircular handle, and used for serving butter balls.

CABLE
A pattern in glass that resembles the twisted strands of rope or a cable.

CADDY
A small glass container with a cover used for holding tea or tea bags.

CAKE PLATE
A large flat or footed glass plate, usually round in shape, and used for holding cakes.

CALCITE GLASS
A brightly colored cream-white-colored glass that resembles the mineral calcite (calcite is not used in its manufacture). Calcite glass was first produced by Frederick Carder at the Steuben Glass Works in the early 20th century.

CAMBRIDGE GLASS CO.
Established in Cambridge, Ohio, in 1901; the Cambridge Glass Company was a major producer of colored glassware and cut crystal until 1958, when the factory closed.

CAMEO-ENGRAVING
An engraving process in which the background is carved away to leave the design in relief (see Relief Cutting). Cameo

glass may be produced in more than two layers.

CAMPBELL, JONES, AND CO.
Established in 1865 in Pittsburgh, Pennsylvania, by James Campbell and Jenkins Jones; they operated until 1895 and made mostly pressed glasswares.

CAMPHOR GLASS
A nearly opaque white pressed glass produced in America in the 19th century (see also Frosted Glass).

CANARY YELLOW
A bright yellow-colored glass similar to amber-colored glass (also made with various amounts of iron, carbon, and sulphur).

CANDELABRA OR CANDELABRUM
A branched candlestick with several sockets for holding candles.

CANDLEHOLDER
A small glass tumblerlike vessel designed to hold candles of 2" in diameter or smaller.

CANDLESTICK
A raised glass object with one socket for holding a single candle.

CANDLETTE
A small bowl-like glass object with one socket for holding a single candle.

CANDLEWICK
A style of glass decoration characterized by crystal drop beading around the edges, feet, handles, stems, stoppers/finials, and other trim areas of objects. Imperial was best known for a huge line of tableware in this design that was produced from 1936 to 1982.

CANDY DISH
An open shallow bowl-like glass receptacle used for serving candy; may or may not be footed.

CANDY JAR
A tall, widemouthed glass receptacle with cover used for serving candy; may or may not be footed.

CANE
A cylindrical piece or stick of glass used either for stems of drinking glasses, or, when cut up into small slices, for producing millefiori paperweights.

CANNING JAR
A glass vessel, usually rounded and somewhat cylindrically shaped (though other shapes such as squares exist), used for preserving fruits, vegetables, and meats. Canning jars usually come in standard measurement sizes such as half pints, pints, quarts (the most common), 2 quarts, and gallons. During the later half of the 19th century, it is estimated that hundreds of manufacturers designed nearly 5,000 styles of jars. Originals had glass lids that were held in place by a wax seal or wire bail. Later models supported screw-on bands and lids made of zinc, and then brass or tin. Canning jars are also commonly referred to as fruit or mason jars.

CANTON GLASS CO.
Established in Canton, Ohio, in 1883; the company produced pressed and novelty items before becoming part of the National Glass Company in 1899.

CAPE COD GLASS WORKS
Established in 1858 by Deming Jarves in Boston, the firm produced pressed wares and art designs such as gold ruby, Peach Blow, and Sandwich Alabaster until Jarves's death in 1869.

CARAFE
A large glass bottle with stopper used for serving beverages (usually water or wine). Some carafes contained tumblers that rested upside down as stoppers (see Tumble-Up).

CARAMEL SLAG
See Chocolate Glass.

CARD TRAY
A flat glass object, usually rectangular in shape, with possibly a center handle and two separate sections, and used for holding standard-size playing cards.

CARDER, FREDERICK
A famous glassmaker, designer, and producer. Carder founded the Steuben Glass Company in 1903 and was responsible for most of the factory's production into the early 1930s.

CARNIVAL GLASS
Pressed glassware with a fired-on iridescent finish made in the United States from 1905 to 1925. Reproductions were later produced, beginning in the 1960s.

CARPET
A set of glass canes arranged in a condensed fashion, used in making millefiori paperweights.

CARVING
The removal of glass from the surface of an object, usually by means of handheld tools.

CASED GLASS
Nineteenth-century glass that was blown in multiple layers of separate colors. The glass was then decorated by cutting away all or part of these layers.

CASSEROLE DISH
A deep round, oblong, or square dish; with or without cover; with or without handles or tabs; and used to bake as well as serve food.

CAST GLASS
Glass made in simple molds and then surface-ground with polishing wheels fed by abrasives.

CASTOR SET
A set of glass serving objects held on glass or metal trays. These objects might include small pitchers, cruets, small jars, salt and pepper shakers, and other small dishes.

CELERY DISH
A long flat or shallow narrow glass dish, usually oval in design, and used for serving celery. A few odd celery dishes have been produced in tall cylindrical shapes (see also Celery Vases).

CELERY VASE
A tall glass receptacle resembling a vase used for serving upright stalks of celery. Most were made in the 18th and 19th centuries in pressed cylindrical form and may or may not be stemmed and footed.

CENTERPIECE
A large circular or oval fancy glass bowl used as an adornment in the center of a table. Some contain underplates.

CENTRAL GLASS COMPANY
Established in 1866 in Wheeling, West Virginia; Central was noted for pressed patterns and art coin glass, and as one of the first to develop popular colors of the Depression era. Central closed permanently in 1939.

CENTRAL GLASS WORKS
The firm was established as a cooperative in 1863 by workmen from J. H. Hobbs, Brockunier and Company in Wheeling, West Virginia. The cooperative failed and was reorganized three years later as the Central Glass Company.

CHAIN
Glass threads that are formed or applied to objects in interconnected links or rings.

CHALICE
A fancy drinking vessel with a large

rounded bowl of various sizes and shapes (may or may not be stemmed).

CHALK GLASS
A colorless glass containing powdered chalk. It was developed in Bohemia in the late 17th century for making thick vessels. The vessels were then engraved or enameled.

CHALLINOR & TAYLOR LTD.
Founded in 1866 by David Challinor and Taylor in Pittsburgh, Pennsylvania, the company moved to Tarentum in 1884 and produced pressed glass, lamps, and novelties before becoming part of the U.S. Glass Co. in 1891 as Factory C.

CHAMPAGNE GLASS
A tall glass with foot and stem with a large round but shallow bowl.

CHANDELIER
An ornate branched glass lighting fixture suspended from a ceiling.

CHARTREUSE
Yellowish-green-colored opaque glass.

CHEATERS
Small whiskey tumblers with extremely thick glass bottoms and walls that were made to look as if they held more capacity than they really did.

CHECKERED DIAMOND
A cut design pattern with several small diamonds inscribed within one large one.

CHEESE AND CRACKER DISH
A serving dish with two levels (two-tiered), one for holding cheese or a cheese ball (usually the upper part), and the other for crackers.

CHEESE DISH
A glass dish that is ordinarily flat or footed with a separate glass cover (usually dome shape) that is used for serving cheese. Note that cheese dishes are a little larger than butter dishes.

CHERRY JAR
A small widemouthed glass receptacle with cover used for holding cherries. Most are wider at the bottom and taper off somewhat near the top.

CHIGGER BITE
A small chip or nick in a piece of glass.

CHIHULY, DALE
America's greatest glass artisan of the second half of the 20th century. Chihuly began producing art-glass objects in 1964. He studied at the University of Washington, the University of Wisconsin, the Rhode Island School of Design, and the Venini Glass Factory on the island of Murano in Venice. He later opened his own studio in Seattle and is best known for monstrous, multicolored opalescent objects, including huge spheres, massive bowls, flamboyant sea forms, and so on.

CHIMNEY
A cylindrically shaped glass tube that is open at both ends, used to shield the flame of an oil lamp as well as to trap soot and increase the draft.

CHINTZ
A style of glass patented by A. Douglas Nash and developed by him when he worked for Tiffany. It was characterized by colored ribbed, striped, or swirled glass marvered into opaque, opalescent, and transparent glass. The process was expensive and difficult because the separate colors often ran together.

CHOCOLATE GLASS
A variegated opaque glass that shades from dark brown to light tan. It was first developed by Jacob Rosenthal, who

worked at the Indiana Tumbler and Goblet Company. It is sometimes referred to as caramel slag.

CHOP PLATE
A large flat glass object, usually round or oval in shape, used for serving food. A chop plate serves the same function as a platter, tray, or salver.

CHUNKED
Glass that has been heavily damaged, usually cracked, seriously chipped, or considerably worn.

CIGAR JAR
A large, widemouthed glass canister with cover used for holding and storing cigars and/or tobacco.

CIGARETTE BOX
A small covered glass receptacle designed to hold a single standard pack of cigarettes.

CIGARETTE HOLDER
A flat glass dish or ashtray containing notches that are used for holding cigarettes (may or may not have a cover).

CIGARETTE JAR OR URN
A small, widemouthed glass canister with cover used for holding and storing cigarettes.

CINTRA
A style of art glass developed by Frederick Carder of Steuben. It was produced when a glass object was coated with finely sifted, powdered, colored glass, and then coated with a thin layer of crystal to embed the fused particles. Most objects were made in vertical strips of two separate alternating colors and may or may not contain controlled bubbling.

CISTERN
A large circular basin or oval receptacle used to hold a quantity of water. Glass cis-

terns were first made in Venice as early as the 16th century.

CLAMBROTH OR CLAM BROTH
Grayish-colored, semitransparent glass. In carnival glass, clambroth is an iridized pastel color often compared to ginger ale.

CLAMP
A tool used in place of a pontil to hold a blown glass vessel at its closed end while the open end is being shaped (usually avoids leaving a pontil mark).

CLARET GLASS
A tall glass with foot and stem with a large round, deep bowl specifically designed for serving claret wine.

CLARK, T. B. & CO.
Established in Honesdale, Pennsylvania, in 1884 by Thomas Byron Clark; they cut blanks provided by Dorflinger and became one of the most successful cut-glass companies until they closed in 1930.

CLICHY
A famous French glassmaking town that was noted most for paperweight production beginning in the 1840s. The factories closed in the 1880s as the popularity of paperweights declined.

CLOSED HANDLES
See Tab Handles.

CLUSTER
A collection or gathering of similar canes used in making millefiori paperweights.

CLUTHRA
An art-glass form developed by Steuben in 1920. It is characterized by a cloudy opaque design permeated by varying-size bubbles. Offshoots of the basic design were produced by others such as Kimble.

COASTER
A very shallow or flat container used to

place other glass objects upon (such as tumblers) to protect the surface beneath it, such as tabletops and counters.

COBALT BLUE
Metallic coloring agent producing the most powerful deep dark blue color within glass.

COCKTAIL GLASS
A tall glass with foot, stem, and an angled or straight-edged bowl.

COCKTAIL SHAKER
A tall, tumblerlike glass vessel with cover used for mixing alcoholic drinks.

COIN GLASS
Originally in the 18th and 19th centuries, a tumbler or tankard with a real coin visibly placed in the foot or stem. Later 20th-century versions contain glass coin replicas inscribed within the glass.

COLOGNE BOTTLE
A small glass receptacle with narrow neck and stopper used for holding colognes or perfumes.

COLUMBIA GLASS CO.
A short-lived pressed-glass manufacturer established in Findlay, Ohio, in 1886. The firm became part of the U.S. Glass Company in 1891 as Factory J.

COMBING
A decorating technique where bands of molten or soft-colored glass are dragged along the surface of an object at right angles to form a repetitive pattern.

COMMEMORATIVE GLASSWARE
Glass objects that are decorated, usually with mold-embossed, engraved, or enameled designs, and commemorate a significant event, famous person, or cause. The Romans were noted first for commemorating gladiator events and great battles.

COMPORT OR COMPOTE
A glass serving bowl that may contain a base, stem, or foot/feet used for serving candy, fruits, or nuts. Comports are most commonly referred to as raised candy dishes.

CONCENTRIC RINGS
A decorative technique usually molded or applied with enamels; smaller circles are enclosed by ever-increasing larger circles.

CONDIMENT SET
See Castor Set.

CONSOLE BOWL
A large concave glass vessel, hemispherical in shape, and used as a centerpiece or for serving large items. Console bowls are sometimes accompanied by a pair of matching candlesticks.

CONSOLE SET
A set of tableware that usually consists of three pieces: a pair of candlesticks and a center or console bowl.

CONSOLIDATED LAMP & GLASS CO.
Established in 1894 in Coraopolis, Pennsylvania; the company was noted most for art-glass lamps and its Martele line of art glass. The company closed in 1967.

COOKIE JAR
A tall, widemouthed, canister-shape, glass receptacle (larger than a candy jar) with cover, without feet or stems, and used for holding cookies.

CO-OPERATIVE FLINT GLASS COMPANY
An American pressed-glass manufacturer established in Beaver Falls, Pennsylvania, in 1879. The company ceased operations in 1934.

COPPER
A metallic coloring agent used in glass to produce a light blue or turquoise blue color.

COPPER WHEEL–ENGRAVING
Process of hand-engraving by holding a glass to a revolving copper wheel, which instantly cuts through the surface. Some of the best glass ever produced was done by highly skilled copper wheel engravers who kept the cutting patterns in their minds while altering the cutting with rubbing oil continuously, for hours on end.

CORAL
Various shadings of yellow to red layers applied to glass objects with opaque-colored bases.

CORALENE GLASS
Art glass that was first made in 19th-century Europe and then in America. It is characterized by enamel and colored or opaque glass drops applied to raised branches that resemble coral.

CORDIAL GLASS
A miniature wineglass with a foot, a stem, and a tiny bowl.

CORE-FORMING
Process of glassmaking by spinning glass around a core.

CORK GLASS CO.
The general name for glassware produced by three separate factories in Cork, Ireland, beginning in the late 18th century (c. 1783) and ending in 1841. Objects produced included cut tableware and other practical items.

CORNING GLASS WORKS
An American glass factory established in Corning, New York, in 1868 as the Corning Flint Glass Works. The name was changed permanently in 1875, and the company's most notable purchase was that of Steuben in the 1930s. The company continues to operate today as Corning, Inc. (final name change in 1989).

CORNUCOPIA
A receptacle in the shape of a horned vase. Most have scalloped rims and were used as vases, as wall pockets, or simply as ornaments.

CORREIA ART GLASS
Founded in 1973 by Steven V. Correia in Santa Monica, California; the company's contemporary art products can already be found in major art museums featuring glass, such as the Smithsonian Institution, the Corning Museum of Glass, and the Metropolitan Museum of Art.

COSMOS
Pressed milk glass made in America in the early 1900s.

COVER
An unattached top for closing the mouth of a jar, vase, dish, pot, bowl, or other open vessel. Covers may be flat, domed, contain finials, handled, and so on. Note that they are distinguished from lids, which ordinarily contain hinges.

CRACKER JAR
A tall, widemouthed, canister-shape glass receptacle with cover used for holding crackers. Originally they were referred to as biscuit jars.

CRACKING OFF
The process of removing an object from the pontil. Cooled by scoring, the pipe is then gently tapped and the object falls into a sand tray or V-shape holder held by an assistant.

CRACKLE GLASS
A style of glassware that has a rough irreg-

ular surface resembling cracked ice (sometimes referred to as ice glass). It is made by the technique of crackling.

CRACKLING

A decorating technique applied to glassware by plunging a hot object into cold water to induce cracks and then reforming the piece within a mold.

CRANBERRY GLASS

First developed in England in the 19th century, cranberry glass is characterized by a light red tint (the color of cranberries) produced by the addition of gold dust that is dissolved in two acids (aqua regia). Originally it was a cheaper substitute for ruby red, but now the name is applied to any glass made of the cranberry color.

CREAM SOUP BOWL

A concave glass vessel, hemispherical in shape, usually with two handles, and used for serving soup or other foods.

CREAMER

A small glass cuplike vessel, ordinarily with handle, and used for serving cream (with coffee and tea, usually paired with a sugar dish).

CREMAX

An opaque lightly beige-colored glass first produced and named by the MacBeth-Evans Glass Company.

CREST

A name given to several Fenton Glass products that contain a base color (most often milk glass) and a colored or crystal trim.

CRIMPING

A method of decorating the rims of objects common in such items as bowls and vases. A hand tool is used to manipulate molten glass to form a ribbonlike design.

CRISTALLO

A nearly colorless, highly esteemed soda glass invented by Venetian glassmakers in the 16th century.

CRIZZLING

A deteriorated condition that results from alkaline elements in the glass that react to moisture. The consequence is the formation of droplets or tears of alkaline moisture on the surface. Crizzling is also known as weeping, sweating, or sick glass (also spelled *crisseling*).

CROSS-HATCHING

A glass-cutting technique whereby parallel lines are cut vertically, horizontally, and sometimes diagonally to intersect in a crisscross pattern.

CROWN MILANO

See Albertine.

CRUCIBLE

A pot used for melting glass. Crucibles originated in ancient times and were originally constructed of fired pottery materials.

CRUET

A small glass bottle or decanter with top used to hold a condiment such as oil, vinegar, or salad dressing for use at the table.

CRYSTAL

Colorless glass containing a high lead content.

CRYSTAL GLASS CO.

A pressed-glass manufacturer established in Pittsburgh, Pennsylvania, in 1879. The firm moved in 1882 to Bridgeport, Ohio, where it burned to the ground in 1884. Operations were moved to Bowling Green, Ohio, in 1888. The firm joined the National Glass Company in 1899, was reorganized in 1906, and closed permanently in 1908.

CRYSTAL GLASS WORKS
An Australian company founded in Sydney in the early 1900s; they were noted for carnival and other glass production.

CULLETS
Chards or scraps of glass that are remelted and added to a new batch of glass to aid in the fusion process.

CUMBERLAND GLASS CO.
A short-lived pressed-glass manufacturer established in Cumberland, Maryland, in 1888. The firm became part of the National Glass Company in 1899.

CUP
An open, somewhat bowl-shape or cylindrical vessel, usually with handle, and used for drinking liquids such as coffee, tea, punch, and so on.

CUP PLATE
A flat or shallow concave glass vessel, usually round in shape (occasionally square or oval), and used as an underdish or plate for handleless cups and saucers. Primarily in the 19th century, handleless cups included deep saucers; in turn, the saucers were used to hold hot liquids, which were sipped from them. This necessitated the need for another plate to rest under the cup; hence, the cup plate.

CURLING, R. B. & SONS
An early American pressed-glass manufacturer established in Pittsburgh, Pennsylvania, in 1827. The firm produced some limited pressed wares before becoming Dithridge and Sons in 1860.

CURTAIN TIE-BACK
A small glass ornament affixed to a wall bracket for tying back and holding a curtain in place.

CUSPIDOR
A fancy glass vessel or receptacle used for containing saliva (see Spittoon).

CUSTARD CUP
A smaller than ordinary cup, with or without handle, and used for serving desserts in small portions such as pudding, custard, and Jell-O.

CUSTARD GLASS
A yellowish-colored or yellow cream-colored opaque glass (the color of custard) first developed in the early 1900s. The custard color was originally produced by the addition of uranium salts.

CUT GLASS
Heavy flint glass cut with geometric patterns into the glass with grinding wheels and abrasives. The design is then further smoothed and polished. Cutting originated in Germany and was introduced in the United States in the late 18th century.

CUT VELVET
Colored art glass consisting of two fused, mold-blown layers that leaves the outer surface design raised in relief.

CZECHOSLOVAKIAN GLASS
Glassware produced in the former Bohemian region beginning in 1918, when Czechoslovakia was officially recognized as a separate country. Before it divided in 1992, a good deal of glass was made by several firms in a variety of styles, including colored art (especially orange), carnival colors, and engraved crystal. Glass is still being made, but it is often marked "Czech Republic."

DAISY IN HEXAGON
A cut design pattern featuring a flower inscribed within a hexagon.

DALZELL, GILMORE AND LEIGHTON GLASS CO.
A pressed-glass manufacturer established in Brilliant, Ohio, in 1883. The firm moved to Wellsburg, West Virginia, in 1884 and then to Findlay, Ohio, in 1888.

The company became part of the National Glass Company in 1899.

DARNER
A glass needle with large eye for use in darning. Glass darners are sometimes whimsical creations.

DAUM
A French glass company purchased by Jean Daum in 1875 in the town of Nancy, France. Daum, Nancy Daum, Daum Freres, and Cristalleries de Nancy are all names associated with glass produced by this company. The company began as a producer of many styles of art nouveau glass and continues to operate today.

DE VILBISS CO.
A decorating firm established around 1900 in Toledo, Ohio; the firm primarily decorated perfume bottles and atomizers in many art-glass styles until the late 1930s.

DECAL
A picture, design, or label from specially prepared paper that is transferred to glass, usually by heating.

DECANTER
An ornamental or fancy glass bottle with cover or stopper, with or without handles, and used for serving wine or other alcoholic beverages.

DEGENHART CRYSTAL ART GLASS FACTORY
Established in Cambridge, Ohio, in 1947 by John and Elizabeth Degenhart, the company was noted for paperweights and miniature colored art novelty items. The firm closed in 1978 after Elizabeth's death (John passed away in 1964). Beginning in 1972, most products can be found with a mold mark that consists of a *D* or a *D* within a heart. Some of the company molds were retired; however, Zack Boyd, an employee of Degenhart, purchased

many of them and founded the Boyd Art Glass Company in 1978.

DELPHITE
A lightly colored pale blue opaque glass; it is sometimes referred to as blue milk glass.

DEMITASSE
Matching cups and saucers that are much smaller (half size or less) than their ordinary counterparts. Note that demitasse cups and saucers are still slightly larger than those found in children's miniature tea sets.

DENNIS GLASSWORKS
An English glass operation founded near Stourbridge, England, by the Webb family in 1855. The company early on produced art glass and continues to operate today as part of Dema Glass, Ltd.

DEPRESSION GLASS
Mass-produced, inexpensive, and primarily machine-made glass dinner sets and giftware in several transparent colors produced in America between 1920 and 1940.

DEVITRIFICATION
A deteriorated condition of glass in which crystals have formed within the glass because of technical faults in the manufacturing process.

DIAMOND-DAISY
A cut-glass design pattern featuring daisies inscribed within diamonds or squares.

DIAMOND GLASS CO., LTD.
A Canadian company that operated in Montreal from 1890 to 1902. They were known for many pressed-glass designs, tableware, and lamps.

DIAMOND GLASS-WARE CO.
An American company first established in Indiana, Pennsylvania, in 1891. They were noted for high-quality handmade colored

glassware and closed in 1931 when their factory burned.

DIAMOND POINT
A cut-glass design pattern featuring faceted diamonds that intersect at a common point.

DIAMOND POINT ENGRAVING
Hand-cutting or machine-cutting of glass with a diamond point tool. Note that heat treating hardened metal to a sharp point has since replaced the more expensive diamonds for machine cutting.

DIATRETA GLASS
Art glass made by applying tiny pieces of ornamental glass in patterns to other larger glass objects. This process was first developed by Frederick Carder in the early 1900s.

DINNER PLATE
A flat glass object, usually round in shape, about 8–11 inches in diameter, used for serving supper or dinner.

DIP MOLD
A one-piece mold with an open top used for embossing or imprinting decorations and lettering.

DISPENSERS
A large glass container or bottle with a spigot originally used for obtaining cold water from the refrigerator.

DITHRIDGE & COMPANY
Founded by Edward Dithridge Sr. in Pittsburgh, Pennsylvania, in 1860, Dithridge purchased the Fort Pitt Glass Works, for which he worked in the 1850s. He died in 1873 and his son Edward Dithridge Jr. continued operations until reorganizing and moving to a new location (Martins Ferry, Ohio) in 1881.

DITHRIDGE FLINT GLASS CO.
Founded by Edward D. Dithridge Jr. in 1881 in Martins Ferry, Ohio, the business moved to New Brighton, Pennsylvania, in 1887 (name changed to Dithridge & Sons) and continued to produce cut and engraved glass as well as blanks for others. Dithridge ceased operations in 1891.

DOME COVER
A type of top or cover that is circular and domed in shape, and fits on a collar or ridge of a vessel. They are ordinarily found on many butter and cheese dishes. Some are double-domed with a small domed finial resting on a larger one.

DOMINION GLASS CO.
A Canadian company that operated from 1886 to 1898 (separate from the modern company of the same name) in Montreal. They were noted for pressed wares and lamps.

DOMINO TRAY
A serving dish with a built-in container for cream and surrounding area specifically designed for holding sugar cubes.

DORFLINGER GLASS WORKS
The original factory was established in White Mills, Pennsylvania, in the 1840s by the German immigrant Christian Dorflinger. Dorflinger was noted for making high-quality cut-glass tableware and was a major supplier of lead crystal blanks. The company remained in operation as C. Dorflinger and Sons until 1921.

DOUBLE CRUET
Two glass bottles (cruets) that are fused together into one larger-capacity bottle used for serving condiments.

DOYLE AND CO.
A pressed glass manufacturer established in Pittsburgh, Pennsylvania, in 1866. The

firm became part of the U.S. Glass Company in 1981 as Factory P.

DRAM GLASS

Small English or Irish glasses made of metal used for drinking a single measure of strong liquor (most were made between 1750 and 1850 and imported to the United States).

DRESSER SET

A set of glass bath or bedroom objects held on a matching tray. These objects might include perfume or cologne bottles; jars; and tiny boxes for gloves, hair or hat pins, jewelry; and so on.

DUGAN GLASS CO.

Established in Indiana, Pennsylvania, in 1892 by Harry White, Thomas E. Dugan, and W. G. Minnemyer; they produced a good deal of carnival glass. The firm became the Diamond Glass Co. in 1913 and operated until a fire destroyed it in 1931.

DUNBAR GLASS CO.

Founded in Dunbar, West Virginia, in 1918, the company began as a manufacturer of crystal lamp chimneys. The company also produced some blown and machine-pressed tableware before closing in 1953.

DUNCAN, GEORGE & SONS

George Duncan and Daniel Ripley established the pressed glass firm of Ripley & Co. in 1866 in Pittsburgh, Pennsylvania. The two split in 1874 and went on to form their own companies. George Duncan & Sons was founded in Pittsburgh in 1874 and produced pressed-glass items before becoming part of the U.S. Glass Company in 1891 as Factory D. The firm became part of Duncan Miller in 1903.

DUNCAN MILLER GLASS CO.

Established in 1892 by James and George Duncan Jr. along with John Ernest Miller in Washington, Pennsylvania; the firm produced pressed wares and novelty items through the Depression era. The firm closed in 1955.

DURAND ART GLASS CO.

Established in Vineland, New Jersey, by French immigrant Victor Durand Sr. in 1924; the company produced several art-glass styles until Durand's death in 1931.

EAGLE GLASS AND MANUFACTURING CO.

A short-lived pressed-glass manufacturer established in Wellsburgh, West Virginia, in the 1880s. The firm closed after operating a few short years.

EBONY GLASS

Another name for black-colored or very dark black opaque glass.

EDA GLASSWORKS

A Swedish glass company established in 1833. The firm closed in 1953.

EDINBURGH CRYSTAL GLASS CO.

Established in the late 19th century in Edinburgh, Scotland; the company produced hand-cut crystal wares and exported some of these products to America.

EGG CUP OR HOLDER

A small cuplike vessel without handle with room enough to hold a single egg. Occasionally, double egg holders have been made that have room for two eggs.

EGG PLATE

A flat, thick plate with oval indentations for serving boiled or deviled eggs.

EGGINGTON, O. F. CO.

Established in Corning New York, in 1899 by Oliver Eggington; the company purchased blanks from the Corning Glass

Works and operated as a cut-glass operation until they closed in 1920.

ELECTRIC
An effect attributed to some carnival glass. The iridescence applied is so bright that it resembles neon or electric light.

EMBOSSING
Mold-blown or pressed glassware where the design is applied directly to the object from the mold. Embossed patterns are usually somewhat in relief.

EMERALD GREEN
A deep, powerful green color usually made with chromium and iron (the color of the gemstone emerald).

EMPIRE CUT GLASS CO.
Established in New York City in 1896 by Harry Hollis; Hollis sold the company to his employees, who operated it briefly as a cooperative. They in turn sold it in 1904 to H. C. Fry, who moved operations to Flemington, New Jersey (Flemington Cut Glass Co.).

ENAMELING
A liquid medium similar to paint applied to glassware and then permanently fused on the object by heating.

ENCASED OVERLAY
A single or double overlay design further encased in clear glass.

ENGRAVING
The decoration of glass applied by holding the piece against the edge of revolving wheels made of stone, copper, or other materials.

ENTERPRISE CUT GLASS CO.
Founded by George E. Gaylord in Elmira Heights, New York; the company produced cut glass products until it ceased operation in 1917.

EPERGNE
A large table centerpiece that includes a sizable bowl surrounded by several matching smaller dishes.

ERICKSON GLASSWORKS
Established in Bremen, Ohio, by Swedish immigrants Carl and Steven Erickson in 1943, the brothers produced mold-blown glass products distinguished by heavy casing, controlled bubbles, and a heavy ball for a base. The company ceased operations in 1961.

ETCHING
See Acid Etching.

EWER
A round glass jug-like object, with or without feet, that usually contains a long handle and spout. It is sometimes described as a vase that pours.

EXCELSIOR GLASS WORKS
A pressed-glass manufacturer established in Wheeling, West Virginia, in 1849. The company was part of the Buckeye Glass Company and was moved to Martins Ferry, Ohio, in 1879. The factory burned to the ground in 1894 and was not rebuilt.

FACETED GLASS
Glass objects that are decorated by grinding several small flat surfaces at different angles. Faceting or beveling is commonly found on the stems of drinking glasses as well as on modern crystal miniatures.

FAIRY LAMP
A style of lamp originating in England in the 1840s. They are small candle-burning night lamps that were used in halls, nurseries, children's rooms, in dim corridors of homes, and even as food warmers since most contain a vent hole in the top. Some are two-piece (candle cup and shade), and

others contain three pieces (candle cup, shade, and saucer).

FAN VASE

A style of vase having a narrow bowl with parallel sides made to resemble a triangular fan.

FAVRILE

An American art nouveau style of glass created by Louis Comfort Tiffany in the late 19th century. The original pieces are often referred to as Tiffany Favrile and are characterized by a lustrous iridescent finish in a variety of colors (blue-green and/or gold were the most prevalent).

FEDERAL GLASS CO.

An American company established in Colombia, Ohio, in 1900. They began as a cut-glass operation, switched to automation during the Depression era, and continue to operate today as a subsidiary of the Federal Paper Board Company.

FENTON ART GLASS CO.

Established in Martins Ferry, Ohio, in 1905, the company quickly moved to Williamstown, West Virginia, in 1906. Fenton was a major producer of carnival, opalescent, and other pressed and molded glassware. Fenton still operates today in Williamstown, producing hand-decorated glassware, including lamps and novelty items.

FERN BOWL OR FERNERY

A glass container with a liner, with or without feet, and designed for holding ferns or other plants.

FERN GLASS

Glass objects decorated with etched or engraved ferns or similar leaf patterns.

FIGURINE

A small individual etched or molded statue (or figure).

FILIGRANA

A general term for blown glass made with white or sometimes colored canes.

FILIGREE

A technique developed in Venice that uses glass threads or fine canes twisted around a clear cane to produce finely threaded patterns (see Latticino).

FINDLAY FLINT GLASS CO.

A short-lived pressed-glass manufacturer established in Findlay, Ohio, in 1889. The firm closed within two years.

FINDLAY GLASS

Art glass characterized by varying shades of brown colors.

FINGER BOWL

A small concave glass vessel, usually circular and shallow in shape, and used for rinsing fingers at the table.

FINIAL

A crowning ornament or decorative knob found most often in stemware and at the top of glass covers.

FIRE POLISHING

Reheating a finished piece of glass at the "glory hole" to remove tool marks (more commonly replaced with acid polishing).

FIRED-ON

Finishing colors that are baked on or fused by heating the outer surface of glass objects.

FIRED-ON IRIDESCENCE

A finish applied to glass by adding metallic salts, after which the glass is refired.

FIRE-KING

Kitchenware, dinnerware, and ovenware first produced by the Hocking Glass Company in 1937. A good deal was produced from the 1940s on when Hocking merged with Anchor. Fire-King comes in clear and opaque varieties that are often decorated. Like Pyrex, it was specifically designed with borosilicates, allowing a good degree of heat resistance for oven use.

FIRING GLASS

A small glass vessel with thick base, waisted (tapered in at the middle) sides, and possibly a stem or base that could withstand considerable abuse. The resulting noise of several being slammed at once was comparable to that of a musket firing (hence the name). Some were made of metal, and most were produced in the 18th and early 19th centuries in both Europe and America.

FLAMEWORKING

The technique of shaping objects when they are hot (heated by a gas-fueled torch) from rods or tubes of glass.

FLASHED-ON IRIDESCENCE

A finish applied to glass by dipping hot glass into a solution of metallic salts.

FLASHING

A very thin coating of a different color from that of the base color (thinner than a casting or an overlay).

FLASK

A glass container with narrow neck and mouth, with stopper or cover, and used for carrying alcoholic beverages.

FLINT GLASS

The American term for fine glassware made in the 19th century. A name for lead glass, though original experimenters used powdered flints as substitutes for lead oxides.

FLIP GLASS

An American term for a style of tumbler that is usually around 6–8 inches in height and expands slightly at the rim. Some

sport domed covers with finials. Most were made in the late 18th and 19th centuries.

FLORET OR FLORETTE

A slice from a large cane of several colored rods arranged (usually concentrically) to form a floral pattern.

FLORIFORM

A tall glass vase with narrow stem and top that is in the shape of a flower bloom.

FLOWER BOWL

A large shallow, concave, hemispherical container used for holding or floating flowers with relatively short stems.

FLUTING

Vertically cut decoration in long narrow or parallel sections such as bevels (usually wheel-cut but sometimes molded).

FLUX

A substance such as soda, wood ash, potash, and lead oxide added to the basic ingredients to stabilize and lower the melting point of a batch of glass.

FOLDED FOOT

The turned-over edge of the foot of a wineglass or similar glass object to give added strength to the vessel.

FOOT

The part of a glass other than the base on which it rests.

FOOTMAKER

An assistant to a glassmaker who forms the foot of the glass in the glassblowing process.

FOREST GREEN

A dark green color not as deep or rich as emerald green, first made in the late 1930s and early 1940s by the Hazel Atlas Glass Company, which patented the name. The term has been applied to glassware made by other companies in the same color.

FOSTORIA GLASS CO.
An American glass company founded in Fostoria, Ohio, in 1887; they produced cut crystal items early on, and several Depression tableware patterns, and continued in operation until 1986.

FOUNDING
The making of glass by melting and fusing the ingredients together in a furnace.

FRACTIONAL SHOT
A small glass tumbler with a capacity of less than 1 ounce.

FRANCES WARE
Mold-blown tableware consisting of amber color, fluted rims, and hobnail patterns; it was produced by Hobbs, Brocunier & Co. in the 1880s.

FRANKLIN FLINT GLASS CO.
A pressed-glass manufacturer established in Philadelphia in 1861. It was later purchased by Gillinder & Sons, who operated it until they joined the U.S. Glass Company in 1891.

FREE-BLOWN GLASS
Glassware made through an ancient technique of handblowing by highly skilled craftsmen without the use of molds.

FROG
A small but thick and heavy glass object, usually round or domed, and containing perforations, holes, or spikes for holding flowers in place within a vase.

FROSTED GLASS
A light opalescence or cloudy coloring of a batch of glass using tin, zinc, or an allover acid etching as in Depression glass. A frosted coating can also be applied on the surface of clear or crystal glass by spraying on white acid (a solution of ammonium bifluoride). Frosted glass is also referred to as Camphor glass.

FRUIT JAR
See Canning Jar.

FRUIT OR NUT DISH
A small flat or shallow circular container, with or without handle(s), and used for serving small fruits, nuts, candies, etc.

FRY, H. C.
An American glassmaker who founded the Rochester Tumbler Company in 1872 and the H. C. Fry Glass Company in 1901, both in Rochester, Pennsylvania. The glass that was produced in his later factory is sometimes referred to as Fry glass and included some art glass as well as tableware. Fry closed for good in 1934.

FULGURITES
Crude, brittle, slender glass creations in the shape of small tubes that are created when lightning strikes a sandy area with the right combination of minerals.

FULL LEAD CRYSTAL
Colorless glass containing a minimum of 30 percent lead content.

FURNACE
An enclosed structure for the production and application of heat. Furnaces today are usually heated by natural gas for clean burning. In glassmaking, furnaces are used for melting a batch of glass, maintaining pots of glass in a molten state, and reheating partially formed objects at the "glory hole."

FUSION
The process of liquefying or when the melting point is reached for a batch of glass. Temperatures can range from 2,000 to 3,000 degrees Fahrenheit, depending on the ingredients used.

GADGET
A special rod developed to replace the pontil to avoid leaving a mark on the foot. A spring clip at the end of the gadget grips the foot of a just-finished piece of glass while the worker trims the rim and applies the finishing touches on the glass.

GADROONING
A decorative band derived from a silver form made of molded, applied, or deep cut sections of reeding. Gadrooning is sometimes referred to as knurling.

GAFFER
A term of respect for an experienced master or head glassmaker dating back to the 16th century.

GALL
A layer of scum that forms at the surface of a batch of glass during the heating process (it is skimmed off).

GALLE, EMILE
A French glassmaker and pioneer in the 19th century art nouveau–styled glass. He is noted for art cameo and floral designs created in several color effects and styles.

GATHER
A blob of molten glass attached to the end of a blowpipe, pontil, or gathering iron.

GIBSON GLASS
Established in Milton, West Virginia, by Charles Gibson in 1983, Gibson is known for animals, figurines, paperweights, and other novelty items produced in a variety of colors and styles.

GILDING
An applied decorating technique with gold leaf, enamels, dust, or paints to finished glass objects.

GILLINDER & SONS
Founded by English immigrant William T. Gillinder, who once was superintendent of the New England Glass Co., Gillinder and his sons James and Frederick established their own cutting and art-glass business in 1867 in Philadelphia. The firm later became part of the U.S. Glass Co. in 1892 as Factory G.

GIRANDOLE
An elaborate branched candleholder that usually contains attached cut-glass prisms.

GLASS
A hard, brittle, artificial substance made by fusing silicates (sand) with an alkali (soda or potash) and sometimes with metallic oxides (lead oxide or lime).

GLASSBORO GLASSWORKS
An American factory established in Glassboro, New Jersey, by Jacob Stanger in 1781; the company produced windows, bottles, and tableware into the 20th century.

GLASSHOUSE
The building that contains the glass-melting furnaces and in which the actual handling and shaping of molten glass takes place.

GLASS PICTURE
A design that is ordinarily etched on flat sheets or flat pieces of glass.

GLORY HOLE
A small-size opening in the side of the furnace used for inserting cool glass objects to reheat them without melting or destroying the shape (sometimes named the reheating furnace).

GLOVE BOX
A rectangular glass object, with or without cover, used specifically on dressing tables or vanities for holding gloves.

GOBLET
A drinking vessel with a large bowl of

various sizes and shapes that rests on a stemmed foot.

GOLD
A metallic coloring agent that produces cranberry or a deep ruby red color. The metal itself is also used to decorate glass (see also Gilding).

GONE WITH THE WIND LAMP
A kerosene or electric table lamp containing a glass base with a round, globe-shape glass shade.

GRAAL
A technique developed by Orrefors of Sweden. Graal is created by cutting a pattern within the core of colored glass that is encased in clear glass and then blown into its final shape (much like the reverse of cameo glass since the cut-away portion forms the design instead of the background).

GRAPEFRUIT BOWL
A concave glass vessel, usually circular in shape, ordinarily with a wide foot, and used for serving half of a grapefruit.

GRAVY BOAT
An oblong bowl-like object with handle and spout used for pouring gravy (may or may not be accompanied by a matching platter or pedestal).

GREEN GLASS
The natural color of ordinary alkaline or lime-based glassware, usually produced by iron present in the sand. Additional iron and chromium are added to make a clear green. Uranium was once added, too, to produce a vibrant, glowing green color.

GREENSBURG GLASS CO.
Established in Greensburg, Pennsylvania, in 1889; the company produced pressed glass until becoming part of the National Glass Company in 1899.

GREENTOWN GLASS
A general name for pressed tableware and other glass products produced in and around the town of Greentown, Indiana, in the late 19th and early 20th centuries. Firms included the Indiana Tumbler & Goblet Co., the National Glass Co., McKee Brothers, and Jacob Rosenthal.

GRILL PLATE
A large individual or serving plate with divisions (similar to relish dishes only larger).

GROUND
The background or base glass object on which decorations are applied.

GUNDERSON GLASS WORKS
Robert Gunderson, along with Thomas Tripp and Isaac Babbitt, purchased the silverware and glass departments of Pairpoint in 1939 and continued production until Gunderson's death in 1952. Glass made by Gunderson is often referred to as Gunderson's Pairpoint.

HAIRPIN BOX
A small square, rectangular, or circular glass container, with or without cover, used specifically on a dressing table or vanity for holding hairpins.

HAIR RECEIVER
A circular glass object, usually with a cover that has a large hole in the middle, and used on tables, dressers, and vanities to hold hair that accumulates in a hairbrush.

HALF LEAD CRYSTAL
Colorless glass containing a minimum of 24 percent lead content (lower quality than full lead crystal).

HAMMONTON GLASSWORKS
An American factory established at Hammonton, New Jersey, by William Coffin and Jonathan Haines in 1817. The company produced windows, bottles, and

some tableware before going out of business.

HANDBLOWN GLASS
Glass formed and shaped with a blowpipe and other hand-manipulated tools without the use of molds.

HAND COOLER
A solid ovoid or small glass object originally developed in ancient Rome for ladies to cool their hands. Later, hand coolers were also used by ladies when being wooed or for darning. Modern hand coolers are made in the form of animals and eggs.

HAND-PRESSED GLASS
Glass that is made in hand-operated mechanical presses.

HANDEL, PHILIP J.
An American glassmaker who founded the Handel Company in Meriden, Connecticut, in 1885. He was noted for producing Art Nouveau acid cut back cameo vases and Art Nouveau lamps similar to, but less expensive than, Tiffany lamps. The firm closed in 1936.

HANDKERCHIEF BOX
A rectangular glass receptacle with cover used for storing handkerchiefs.

HANDKERCHIEF VASE
A style of vase whereby the sides of the object are pulled straight up and then randomly pleated to resemble a large ruffled handkerchief.

HAT OR HAT VASE
A whimsical glass object in the shape of an upside-down head covering or top hat. The space where one's head would usually rest is often used for flowers or holding tiny objects.

HAT PIN HOLDER
A tall glass object in the shape of a cylinder used on tables, dressers, and vanities for holding hat pins.

HAWKES, T. G. & CO.
An American company established at Corning, New York, in the late 19th century by Thomas Gibbon Hawkes. The company produced high-quality cut crystal tableware and blanks for others. In 1903, T. G. Hawkes and Frederick Carder merged to form the Steuben Glass Works.

HAZEL ATLAS GLASS CO.
An American factory founded in Washington, Pennsylvania, in 1902; they produced large amounts of machine-pressed glassware, especially during the Depression period. Factories were added throughout Ohio, Pennsylvania, and West Virginia until the company sold out in 1956.

HEISEY, A. H. GLASS CO.
An American company established at Newark, Ohio, in 1896 (though A. H. Heisey himself produced glass as early as the 1860s). Heisey was known early on for cut patterns and finely etched glass. The company produced some carnival glass, above-average pressed wares during the Depression era, and collectible glass animals. The factory closed for good in 1957.

HELIOS
A name given to a style of carnival glass by the Imperial Glass Company. Helios is characterized by a silver or gold iridescent sheen over green glass.

HIGBEE GLASS CO.
Established by John B. Higbee in 1900 in Bridgeville, Pennsylvania; Higbee once worked with John Bryce in 1879 before opening his own business. Higbee operated for only a short period of time, but his glass is easily identified with the famous raised bee trademark.

HIGHBALL GLASS
A tall narrow tumbler of at least 4-ounce capacity used for mixed drinks.

HOARE J. & CO.
Established in Corning, New York, in 1868 by John Hoare, Hoare formed many partnerships beginning in 1853 (Hoare & Burns, Gould & Hoare, and Hoare and Dailey, among others) before forming his own cut-glass department under the Corning Flint Glass Co.

HOBBS, BROCUNIER & CO.
Established in Wheeling, West Virginia, in 1863 by John Hobbs. Hobbs formed many partnerships beginning as early as 1820 (Hobbs and Barnes) before teaming up with Brocunier. One of their employees, William Leighton, is credited for developing a cheap lime glass formula as a substitute for lead glass. They became part of the United States Glass Company in 1891.

HOBNAIL
A pressed or cut pattern in glassware resembling small raised knobs referred to as "hobs" or "prunts." The name originated in England from the large heads of hobnail fasteners.

HOCKING GLASS CO.
An American factory established in Lancaster, Ohio, by I. J. Collins in 1905; they began as a hand operation but converted fully to automation during the Depression era. They were one of the largest manufacturers of machine-pressed tableware and merged with the Anchor Cap and Closure Corporation in 1937 to form Anchor-Hocking.

HOLLY AMBER
A type of art glass made only in 1903 by the Indiana Tumbler and Goblet Company; it is a pressed design characterized by creamy opalescent to brown amber shading (golden agate) with pressed holly leaves.

HONESDALE DECORATING CO.
An American factory founded by Christian Dorflinger and his sons at Honesdale, Pennsylvania, in 1901. They produced hand-cut, high-quality crystal wares with some gold decoration until the business closed in 1932.

HONEY DISH
A tiny flat or shallow dish used for serving honey.

HONEYCOMB PATTERN
A decorative pattern in the shape of interlocking hexagons that are usually molded onto a glass object. The pattern can be traced back to Roman times in the 4th century A.D. and has been a popular design on pressed wares since the 18th century.

HOPE GLASS WORKS
Established in Providence, Rhode Island, in 1872 by Martin L. Kern, the company was best known for cut glass. In 1891 Kern's son resumed the business; in 1899 it was sold to the Goey family, who continued to operate under the Hope name until 1951.

HOREHOUND
A Northwood iridized carnival-glass color named after horehound candy. The color is often compared to root beer.

HORSERADISH JAR
A small to medium-size covered glass receptacle used for serving horseradish.

HOT PLATE
An unusually thick, sturdy flat glass object used to sit under hot items to protect the surface beneath it.

HUMIDOR
A glass jar or case used for holding cigars

and/or tobacco in which the air is kept properly humidified.

HUNT GLASS CO.

Established in Corning, New York, in 1895 by Thomas Hunt, the company used blanks from the Corning Glass Works as well as pressed blanks from the Union Glass Co. They operated as a cut-glass operation until the early 1910s.

HURRICANE LAMP

A style of lamp that usually contains a glass base, a separate glass shade, and a glass chimney. Some are shaped much like candlesticks with wicks, whereas others are powered by electricity. Hurricane lamps debuted in the late 19th century.

HYDROFLUORIC ACID

An acid similar to hydrochloric acid but weaker that attacks silica. It is used to finish as well as etch glass.

ICE BLUE

A very light shade or tint of transparent blue-colored glass (the color of ice), usually applied as an iridescence on carnival glass.

ICE BUCKET OR TUB

A glass vessel shaped as a medium-size bucket or pail, with or without semicircular handle, and used for holding ice.

ICE CREAM PLATE

A small flat glass plate, usually round in shape, and used for serving a single scoop of ice cream.

ICE CREAM TRAY

A large shallow or flat glass container used for serving ice cream.

ICE GLASS

A type of art glass characterized by a rough surface that resembles cracked ice (see Crackle Glass, and Crackling).

ICE GREEN

A very light shade or tint of transparent green-colored glass (the color of ice) usually applied as an iridescence on carnival glass.

ICE LIP

A rim at the top of a pitcher that prevents ice from spilling out of the spout when tilted or poured.

IDEAL CUT GLASS CO.

Founded by Charles E. Rose in 1904 in Corning, New York; the company moved their cut-glass business to Syracuse, New York, in 1909 and operated until 1934.

IGC LIQUIDATING CORPORATION

A subsidiary of Lenox, Inc. of New Jersey, Lenox purchased the Imperial Glass Company in 1972 and continued to produce glass under the IGC name until it was sold to Arthur Lorch in 1981. Lorch sold out to Robert Strahl in 1982, and the company closed for good in 1985.

IMPERIAL GLASS CO.

An American manufacturer founded in Bellaire, Ohio, by Edward Muhleman in 1901; they were a major producer of carnival glass in the early 20th century and were responsible for many reproductions of it later. The company was sold in 1972 to Lenox, which continued producing glass under the IGC Liquidating Corporation name until 1982.

INCISING

The technique of cutting or engraving designs into the surface of glass.

INCRUSTATION

A sulphide design within crystal or clear glass paperweights.

INDIANA GLASS CO.

An American manufacturer founded in 1907; they were noted for many machine-pressed Depression patterns and more recent reproductions of them. The company continues to operate today as a subsidiary of the Lancaster Colony Corporation.

INDIANA TUMBLER & GOBLET CO.

An American manufacturer founded in 1894 in Greentown, Indiana. They are noted for unique though inexpensive experimental colored tableware, including caramel slag glass. The company became part of the National Glass Company in 1899. The factory closed permanently when it burned in 1903.

INKWELL

A small but heavy glass container used for holding ink (originally for quill pens).

INLAY

An object that is embedded into the surface of another.

INTAGLIO

An engraving or cutting made below the surface of glass so that the impression left from the design leaves an image in relief (Italian for engraving).

INTARSIA

The name given to a type of glass produced by Steuben in the 1920s. It is characterized by a core of colored glass blown between layers of clear glass, then decorated by etching into mosaic patterns.

IRIDESCENCE

A sparkling rainbow-colored finish applied to the exterior of glass objects that is produced by adding metallic salts.

IRIDIZED

Glass that has been coated with iridescence.

IRVING CUT GLASS CO., INC.

Established in Honesdale, Pennsylvania, in 1900 by William Hawken and five partners, they purchased blanks from H. C. Fry and were noted for cutting flowers and figures. Many of their products were shipped to Asia, South Africa, and Spain. The company closed in 1930.

IVORY

A cream- or off-white-colored opaque glass (the color of ivory).

IVRENE

A white-colored opaque glass with a light pearl-like iridescent coating; originally made by Steuben.

JACK-IN-THE-PULPIT

A style of vase made to resemble the American woodland flower. It usually consists of a circular base, thin stem, and large open ruffled bloom at the top.

JADEITE OR JADE-ITE

A pale lime-colored opaque green glass (the color of jade).

JAM JAR

A tiny covered glass receptacle used for serving jams and jellies. The cover usually has an opening for a spoon handle.

JARDINIERE

An ornamental glass stand or vase-like vessel used for holding plants or flowers.

JARVES, DEMING

An early pioneer instrumental in getting glassmaking started in America. He founded the New England Glass Company in 1818, the Boston & Sandwich Glass Company in 1825, and several others.

JEANNETTE GLASS CO.

An American company established in Jeannette, Pennsylvania, in 1902; they were noted for several color patterns during the Depression era and continue to make glassware today.

JEFFERSON GLASS CO.

A pressed-glass manufacturer established in Steubenville, Ohio, in 1901. The firm moved to Follansbee, West Virginia, in 1907 and closed in the 1930s.

JELLY DISH OR TRAY

A small flat or shallow dish used for serving jelly, jam, marmalade, and other preserves.

JENKINS, D. C. GLASS CO.

Once part of the Indiana Tumbler & Goblet Co. and the Kokomo Glass Co., David C. Jenkins built his own factory in Kokomo, Indiana, in 1905. His new company produced some pressed wares until the early 1930s.

JENNYWARE

The nickname for kitchenware glass made by the Jeannette Glass Company.

JERSEY GLASS CO.

An American company founded in Jersey City, New Jersey, by George Drummer in 1824; they produced cut- and pressed-glass tableware.

JEWEL BOX

A glass receptacle, usually rectangular in shape, with or without cover, and used for storing jewelry.

JEWEL CUT GLASS CO.

Established in Newark, New Jersey, in 1906 by C. H. Taylor; the company had previously begun as the C. H. Taylor Glass Co. and made cut-glass products.

JUG

A large, deep glass vessel, usually with a wide mouth, pouring spout, and handle, and used for storing liquids.

JUICE GLASS

A short narrow glass tumbler, with or without feet, with a capacity of 3–6 ounces,

and used for drinking fruit and vegetable juices.

KANAWA GLASS CO.

Founded in 1955 in Dunbar, West Virginia, Kanawa was noted for glass novelty items, pitchers, and vases. The company was purchased by the Raymond Dereume Glass Company in 1987.

KEMPLE, JOHN E. GLASS CO.

A pressed-glass manufacturer established in Kenova, West Virginia, and East Palestine, Ohio, in 1945. The firm reproduced many McKee patterns from original molds before closing in 1970.

KEW BLAS

A name given to a type of opaque art glass produced by the Union Glass Company in the 1890s. The primary color is brown with various shadings of brown and green.

KEYSTONE CUT GLASS CO.

Established in Hawley, Pennsylvania, in 1902; the company produced cut glass until 1918.

KEYSTONE TUMBLER WORKS

A short-lived pressed-glass manufacturer established in Rochester, Pennsylvania, in 1897. The firm joined the National Glass Company in 1899.

KICK

A small indentation in the bottom of a glass object.

KILN

An oven used for firing or refiring glass objects. Kilns are also used for fusing enamels onto glass objects.

KIMBLE GLASS CO.

Colonel Evan F. Kimble purchased Durand's factory in Vineland, New Jersey, in 1931; Kimble operated for a short period of time and was noted for the art-glass Cluthra style.

KING, SON, AND CO.
An American company founded in 1859 as the Cascade Glass Works near Pittsburgh, Pennsylvania. The firm was renamed Johann, King, and Company in 1864, and then the King Glass Company in 1879. They were another manufacturer of tableware that became part of the United States Glass Company in 1891 as Factory K.

KNIFE REST
A small thick barbell-shape glass object used to hold knife blades off the table when eating.

KNOP
An ornamental ball-shape swelling on the stem of stemmed glassware such as wineglasses.

KOSTA GLASSWORKS
Established in 1742 in Sweden, it is one of the oldest glassmakers still in operation today. The factory originally produced windows, then later added chandeliers and tableware. In 1946 it merged with the Boda Glassworks to form Kosta-Boda and is noted for decorative cut glass and tableware.

LABELLE GLASS COMPANY
An American company founded in Bridgeport, Ohio, in 1872. They operated as a maker of pressed and some limited engraved glassware until the factory burned in 1887. The rights to the firm were purchased by the Muhleman Glass Works in 1888.

LACE GLASS
A mid-16th-century Venetian-styled glass characterized by transparent threaded designs layered on the sides of various glass objects.

LACY PRESSED GLASS
A mid-19th-century American style of pressed glass characterized by an overall angular and round braiding pattern.

LADLE
A handled (long or short) spoon used for dipping jam, gravy, punch, or other foods and liquids from jars or bowls.

LALIQUE, RENE
A French glassmaker who got his start in glassmaking in the late 19th century by designing fancy perfume bottles for Coty. He is noted for multiple-faced or figured crystal and colored art-glass items, and his success continued well into the 20th century. The firm continues in operation today under the Lalique namesake.

LAMP
A glass vessel with a wick or bulb used to produce artificial light. Those with wicks usually burn an inflammable liquid such as oil or kerosene. Those with bulbs are lighted by electricity. The huge variety of lamps includes fairy lamps, hurricane lamps, table lamps, desk lamps, pole lamps, and many more.

LAMP SHADE
Glass coverings that shelter lights to reduce glare. At times, large glass bowls are converted to lamp shades by drilling holes in their center to attach them above the light.

LAMPWORK
The process of forming delicate glass objects out of thin rods or canes while working at a small flame (the flame is referred to as the *lamp*, hence the term *lampwork*). Along with sulphide and millefiore, lampwork is one of the three basic types of paperweight styles.

LANCASTER GLASS CO.
Lancaster was established in the city of

Lancaster, Ohio, in 1908; they sold out in 1924 to the Hocking Glass Co., which continued to use the Lancaster name through 1937.

LATTICINO
A 16th-century Venetian-styled glass characterized by white opaque glass threads applied to clear glass objects.

LAUREL CUT GLASS CO.
Founded in 1903 as the German Cut Glass Co. in Jermyn, Pennsylvania, this company changed its name to Laurel soon afterward. In 1906 it changed briefly to the Kohinur Cut Glass Co., but it switched back to Laurel in 1907. The company produced a limited amount of cut glass and merged with the Quaker City Cut Glass Co. after World War I. The two split soon afterward, and Laurel disbanded in 1920.

LAVA GLASS
A style of art glass invented by Louis Comfort Tiffany characterized by dark blue and gray opaque hues (the color of cooled lava) and sometimes coated with gold or silver decorations.

LAVENDER
A light pastel shade of purple-colored glass produced by the addition of manganese (see also Amethyst, and Purple).

LAYERED GLASS
Glass objects with overlapping levels or layers of glass.

LAZY SUSAN
A large revolving tray used for serving condiments, relishes, or other foods.

LEAD CRYSTAL
Crystal or colorless glass made with a high lead content (see Half and Full Lead Crystal).

LEHR
An annealing oven with a moving base that travels slowly through a controlled loss of heat until the objects can be taken out at the opposite end. The rate of speed is adjustable as needed.

LIBBEY GLASS CO.
An American company originally established as the New England Glass Company in 1818 and purchased by William L. Libbey in the 1870s. Libbey produced high-quality cut and pressed glass and continues to operate today as one of the nation's largest glass producers.

LIBERTY WORKS
An American company established in Egg Harbor, New Jersey, in 1903; they produced some cut- and pressed-glass tableware before going out of business in 1934.

LID
A covering for closing the mouth of a jar, box, mug, stein, tankard, tea caddy, or similar object. Lids are usually attached to the body of an object with a metal hinge (covers usually do not include hinges).

LILY PAD
A name given to a decoration applied to glass objects characterized by a superimposed layer of glass. Several styles of leaves (including lily pads), flowers, and stems were then designed on this layer.

LIME GLASS
A glass formula developed by William Leighton as a substitute for lead glass. Calcined limestone was substituted for lead, which made glass cheaper to produce. Lime glass also cools faster than lead glassware but is lighter and less resonant.

LIME ICE GREEN
A light shade or tint of transparent yellowish-green-colored glass (the color of ice), usually applied as an iridescence on carni-

val glass. Note that lime is slightly darker than ice green carnival glass.

LINER
A glass object made to fit snugly within another vessel to prevent contents such as food from coming in contact with the underlying vessel. The underlying vessel may be made of a metal such as silver or other materials including wood or even glass.

LITTLETON, HARVEY
A professor of ceramics at the University of Wisconsin in the 1960s. In March 1962 he held a workshop at the Toledo Museum of Art and proved that art glass could be blown by independent artists in small studios. He established a new graduate design program at Wisconsin and is credited with spawning the new studio art-glass movement in America.

LOCKE, JOSEPH
An English pioneer in the art-glass field who moved to America. He is noted for designing and creating several varieties of art glass, including Agata.

LOTZ OR LOETZ GLASS
Art nouveau glass produced by Johann Lotz of Austria in the late 19th and early 20th centuries.

LOVING CUP
A glass drinking vessel, with or without a foot, that usually contains two or three handles. Loving cups were often passed around at celebrations or even shared simultaneously by more than one person.

LOW RELIEF
An engraving process in which the background is cut away to a very low degree (see Relief Cutting).

LUNCHEON PLATE
A flat glass object, usually round in shape, about 6"–8" in diameter (an inch or two smaller than a dinner plate but larger than a salad plate), and used for serving lunch.

LUSTRED
An iridescent form or finish applied to glass by use of a brush to apply metallic salt solutions to glass that has already been cooled to room temperature. The glass is then placed in a lehr to produce the lustrous iridescent finish.

LUTZ GLASS
A thin clear glass striped with colored twists first created by Nicholas Lutz of the Boston & Sandwich Glass Company. It is sometimes referred to as Candy Stripe Glass.

LUZERNE CUT GLASS CO.
Established in the early 1900s in Pittson, Pennsylvania; the company made some cut-glass products before going out of business in the late 1920s.

MACBETH-EVANS GLASS CO.
An American company established in Indiana in 1899; they began as a hand operation and switched to machine-pressed patterns. They were acquired by Corning in 1936 and continue to operate today.

MALLORYTOWN GLASS WORKS
A Canadian company founded in 1825 in Mallorytown, Ontario; they were Canada's first glassmaker, producing blown vessels and containers. They closed in 1840.

MANGANESE
A metallic coloring agent used in glass to produce amethyst or purple hues. When combined with cobalt, it produces a dark amethyst that is nearly black (see also Black Amethyst, and Black Glass).

MANTEL LUSTRE
A decorative candleholder or vase for use above fireplaces. Mantel lustres usually contain attached cut-glass prisms as well.

MAPLE CITY GLASS CO.
Established in 1910 in Honesdale, Pennsylvania; the company produced a limited amount of cut glassware into the early 1920s.

MARBLED GLASS
Glass objects with single or multiple color swirls made to resemble marble.

MARIGOLD
The most common iridized form of carnival glass. Marigold consists of a flashed-on iridescent orange color.

MARMALADE DISH
See Jelly Dish.

MARMALADE JAR
See Jam Jar.

MARQUETRY
A decorating technique whereby hot glass pieces are applied to molten glass and then marvered onto the surface, creating an inlaid effect.

MARVER
A marble, metal, or stone plate or base on which blown glass is shaped. Marvers are also used to pick up surface embellishments such as mica or gold leaf.

MARY GREGORY
Clear and colored glassware decorated with white enamel designs of one or more boys and/or girls playing in Victorian scenes. Mary Gregory actually worked as a decorator for the Boston & Sandwich Glass Co. from 1870 to 1880 but did not decorate the glass of her namesake. The original Mary Gregory was produced in Bohemia in the late 19th century and has been made throughout Europe and America in the 20th and 21st centuries.

MASON JAR
See Canning Jar.

MATCH SAFE
A small container used to safely carry matches in one's pocket. Match safes date back to around the 1850s and were made of metals such as tin, silver, and brass. Later examples were produced in glass and porcelain.

MAYONNAISE DISH
A small flat or shallow indented dish used specifically for serving mayonnaise.

MCKEE BROTHERS
An American company founded in Pittsburgh, Pennsylvania, by Samuel and James McKee in 1834. The firm was moved to Jeannette, Pennsylvania, in 1889 and briefly joined the National Glass Company in 1899 (until 1904). McKee began as a hand operation and continued producing a variety of glass tableware until 1961, when the company was purchased by the Jeannette Glass Company.

MERCURY GLASS
Glass objects characterized by two outer layers of clear glass with an inner layer of mercury or silver nitrate between them. It is also sometimes referred to as silvered glass.

MERESE
An ornamental notch or knob between the stem and bowl of stemware.

MERIDEN CUT GLASS CO.
Established in 1895 in Meriden, Connecticut; this cut-glass outfit operated as a subsidiary of the Meriden Silver Plate Co., which in turn became part of the International Silver Co. They produced cut glass until 1923.

METAL
A term used by chemists for a batch of glass (see Best Metal).

MILK BOTTLE
A glass container with a narrow neck and

mouth designed to hold milk. Milk bottles usually do not contain handles but do have a threaded cap or foil seal at the top. Many are mold-embossed or enameled with the name of a dairy.

MILK GLASS

A semi-opaque opalescent glass colored originally by a compound of arsenic or calcined bones or tin. The result is a white color resembling milk. Modern milk glass usually contains aluminum and fluorine as additives.

MILLEFIORI

An 18th-century European-style paperweight made with several different colored glass rods together in a pattern and then covered with an extremely thick outer layer of glass. Multicolored canes are embedded in clear glass to create the "thousand flower" design. Millefiori techniques have been applied to other objects as well, such as vases, bowls, perfume bottles, and jewelry.

MILLERSBURG GLASS CO.

An American company established in Millersburg, Ohio, by John and Robert Fenton in 1908; they were a major producer of carnival glass but the business lasted only until 1911. After filing bankruptcy, Millersburg Glass continued to be produced under the Radium Glass Company name until 1913; it was then sold to the Jefferson Glass Company, which briefly produced lighting glassware until 1916 and then closed the plant. Note that Millersburg glass is often referred to as Rhodium Ware or Radium because of the minor traces of radiation measurable within the glass.

MINT CONDITION

A perfect, undamaged glass object with no scratches that appears brand new. "Mint in the box" refers to an unopened item in its original packaging.

MINT DISH

See Bonbon or Fruit Dish.

MITRE CUT ENGRAVING

Glass cut with a sharp groove on a V-edged wheel.

MODEL FLINT GLASS CO.

A short-lived pressed-glass manufacturer established in Findlay, Ohio, in 1888. The firm moved to Albany, Indiana, in 1891 and joined the National Glass Company in 1899. The factory closed permanently in 1903.

MOIL

Waste glass left on the blowpipe or pontil.

MOLASSES CAN

A small cylindrically shaped vessel, with or without cover, and used specifically for serving molasses. If lids are present, they may or may not contain an opening for a matching spoon.

MOLD

A wooden or iron form used to shape glass. Pattern or half molds are used before glass has totally expanded. Full or three-part molds are used to give identical or same-size shapes to glassware. The common British spelling of *mold* is *mould*.

MOLDED GLASS

Blown or melted glass that is given its final shape by the use of molds.

MONART GLASS

An art glass originating in Spain in the 1920s. It is characterized by opaque and clear marble swirls.

MONAX

A partially opaque or nearly transparent cream-colored or off-white glass first produced and named by the MacBeth Evans Glass Company.

MONROE, C. F. CO.

Established in Meriden, Connecticut, in 1880, they were noted for some art-glass designs, particularly Kelva, Nakara, and Wave Crest (all similar in style). They also made some cut glass and novelty items before ceasing operation in 1916.

MORGANTOWN GLASS WORKS

Established in Morgantown, West Virginia, in the 1880s, the company produced primarily pressed wares along with some colored glass. The business closed permanently in 1972.

MOSAIC

A surface of a glass object that is decorated by many small adjoining pieces of varicolored materials such as stone or glass to form a picture.

MOSER, LUDWIG

A famous Austrian glassmaker who opened an art-glass studio in 1857 in Karlsbad, Czechoslovakia; he is known for deeply carved and enameled wildlife scenes upon glass.

MOSS AGATE

An art-glass first created by Steuben characterized by red, brown, and other swirled or marble-like colors.

MOSSER GLASS COMPANY

An American company founded by Tom Mosser in Cambridge, Ohio, in 1964. The firm is noted for glass miniatures and novelty items and continues to operate today.

MOTHER-OF-PEARL

An art-glass technique produced by trapping air between layers of glass.

MT. VERNON GLASS CO.

An American art-glass company founded in the late 19th century noted for fancy glass vases and glass novelty items.

MT. WASHINGTON GLASS WORKS

An American art-glass manufacturer established in South Boston, Massachusetts, in 1837 by Deming Jarves; they were noted for high-quality and innovative art-glass designs such as Burmese Glass, Crown Milano, and cameo-engraved designs. The company sold out to the Pairpoint Manufacturing Company in 1894.

MUFFLE KILN

A low-temperature oven used for refiring glass to fix or fire on enameling.

MUG

A cylindrical drinking vessel with one handle; larger mugs with hinged metal lids are usually referred to as steins.

MURANO

A single island that is part of an archipelago of islands, linked by bridges, in the Venetian Lagoon. Glassmakers settled on Murano in the 10th century, and all Venetian glass has been produced here since 1292 (the year glassmaking was banned on mainland Venice, for fear of fire). Today, there are more than 100 small glassmaking firms on Murano.

MURRHINE OR MURRINA

A Venetian technique in which colored cane sections are embedded within hot glass before a piece is blown into its final shape. The result is a colorful mosaic design.

MUSTARD DISH OR JAR

A small flat or shallow dish, with or without cover, and used specifically for serving mustard. If lids are present, they may or may not contain an opening for a matching spoon.

NAILSEA GLASS HOUSE

An English glass factory established in Somerset, England, in 1788. They were noted for producing many unusual glass items such as rolling pins and walking canes. Nailsea glass is characterized by swirls and loopings (ordinarily white) in a crystal or colored base.

NAPKIN RING

A small circular glass band used for holding napkins.

NAPOLI

Glass objects that are completely covered with gold or gold enamels, both inside and out. Additional decorations may be applied to the gold covering.

NAPPY

An open shallow serving bowl without a rim that may contain one or two handles.

NASH

A wealthy American family of English heritage that included several glass designers and manufacturers. They are noted for expensive high-quality art glass similar to Tiffany designs and styles.

NATIONAL GLASS CO.

A short-lived pressed-glass manufacturer established in 1898. National was a brief conglomeration of merged companies in 1899–1900. The company broke up in 1905, and many of its members became independent firms once again.

NEAR CUT

Pressed-glass patterns similar to the designs of hand-decorated cut glass.

NECK

The part of a glass vessel such as a bottle, jug, or similar article between the body and mouth.

NEEDLE ETCHING

A process of etching glass by machine. Fine lines are cut by a machine through a wax coating upon glass and then hydrofluoric acid is applied to etch the pattern into the glass.

NEW BREMEN GLASS MANUFACTORY

An American firm established at New Bremen, Maryland, by Johann F. Amelung in 1784. They were one of the first glassmakers in America of useful tableware. Many of their products were signed and dated (rare for that time period).

NEW CARNIVAL

Reproduction iridescent glass made since 1962, sometimes with the original carnival glass molds.

NEW ENGLAND CRYSTAL COMPANY

Established in 1990 by Philip E. Hopfe in Lincoln, Rhode Island; the company is noted for hand-cut and copper wheel–engraved art forms as well as Pate de Verre styles.

NEW ENGLAND GLASS CO.

An American glass company established at Cambridge, Massachusetts, by Deming Jarves and associates in 1818. One of the first highly successful American glass companies, they produced pressed, cut, and a variety of art glass such as Agata, Amberina, Pomona, and Wild Rose Peachblow. They were purchased by Libbey in the 1870s.

NEW GENEVA GLASS WORKS

An American company established in Fayette County, Pennsylvania, by Albert Gallatin in 1797; they made some tableware and windows before closing.

NEW MARTINSVILLE GLASS CO.

An American company established in 1901 in New Martinsville, West Virginia; they began as an art-glass company and later produced pressed pattern glass, some novelty items, and Depression glass. In 1944, they sold out to the Viking Glass Company.

NICKEL PLATE GLASS CO.
A short-lived pressed-glass manufacturer established in Fostoria, Ohio, in 1888. The firm joined the U.S. Glass Company in 1891 as Factory N.

NIPT DIAMOND WAVES
A pattern applied to glass objects produced by compressing thick vertical threads into diamond-like shapes.

NORTHWOOD GLASS CO.
An American company established in Wheeling, West Virginia, in 1887 by Harry Northwood. They were noted for decorated glass with gold and opalescent edges as well as for producing carnival glass in some quantity before going out of business in 1925. The firm became part of the Dugan Glass Company in 1896, joined National Glass in 1899, and reverted back to Northwood around 1908.

NORTHWOOD, HARRY
Born in 1860 in Stourbridge, England, Northwood, Brocunier came to America in 1881 and served as a glass etcher for Hobbs. He founded his own company in 1887 and, after several moves, remained in business until his death in 1919.

NOTSJO GLASSWORKS
A Finnish glass firm founded in 1793 in Nuutajarvi, Finland. By the middle of the 19th century, it had become the largest glass-producing firm in Finland. It became part of the Wartsila Group in 1950 and continues to produce a variety of tableware as well as some art-glass products today.

NOVELTY
A glass object made in the form of a toy, animal, boat, hatchet, souvenir, flower, etc.

NOVELTY GLASS CO.
A pressed glass manufacturer established in La Grange, Ohio, in 1880. The firm

moved to Brilliant, Ohio, in 1882, and then joined the U.S. Glass Company in 1891 as Factory T. The company was moved to Fostoria, Ohio, in 1892, and then it burned a year later.

NUT DISH
A small flat or shallow dish used for serving nuts.

OBSIDIAN
A mineral that resembles dark glass that is formed by volcanic action. Black glass is sometimes referred to as obsidian glass. Obsidian is considered the first form of glass ever used by humans (in arrowheads, spears, knives, and other simple tools).

OFF-HAND GLASS
Glass objects such as whimseys, art pieces, or other novelty items created by glassmakers from leftover or scrap glass.

OGIVAL-VENETIAN DIAMOND
A pattern applied to glass objects produced by pressing or cutting. The shape is of large or wide diamonds and is sometimes referred to as Reticulated Diamond or Expanded Diamond.

OHIO FLINT GLASS CO.
A short-lived pressed-glass manufacturer established in Lancaster, Ohio, in the early 1890s. The firm became part of the National Glass Company in 1899.

OIL BOTTLE
A glass receptacle with top used for serving vinegar or other salad oils (see also Cruet).

OLD GOLD
A deep amber stain or amber applied to glass made to resemble gold.

OLIVE DISH
A small flat or shallow glass object, oblong or rectangular, that may or may not be di-

vided and is used specifically for serving olives.

OLIVE GREEN
A green color in glass similar to army olive drab. Olive green can be found in regular transparent glass as well as some flashed-on carnival glass items.

OLIVE JAR
A small to medium-size glass container with wide mouth and cover used for serving olives.

ONYX GLASS
A dark-colored glass with streaking of white or other colors made by mixing molten glass with various color mediums.

OPAL GLASS
An opalescent opaque-like white milk glass usually produced by the addition of tin or aluminum and fluorine (see also Milk Glass).

OPALESCENCE
A milky or cloudy coloring of glass. Opalescent coating is usually made by adding tin or zinc and phosphate. Opalescent glass was first made by Frederick Carder at Steuben in the early 20th century.

OPALINE GLASS
A semi-opaque art glass, pressed or blown, that was first developed by Baccarat in the early 19th century.

OPAQUE GLASS
Glass that is so dense in color that it does not transmit light (milk glass, for example).

OPEN HANDLES
See Tab Handles.

OPTIC MOLD
An open mold with a patterned interior in which a parison of glass is inserted and then inflated to decorate the surface.

ORANGE GLASS
Glass that is colored by the addition of selenium and cadmium sulfide. Orange flashed glass is referred to as marigold in carnival glass.

ORMOLU
A decorative object usually made of brass, bronze, or gold applied to glass objects (such as a knob on stemware).

ORREFORS GLASBRUCK
Established in 1898 in Smaland, Sweden, the company continues to operate today. They are best known most for contemporary art-glass forms, including engraving. The Graal line is of particular note. (See Graal.)

OVERLAY GLASS
The technique of placing one colored glass over another, with designs cut through the outermost layer only.

OVERSHOT GLASS
A type of glass with a very rough or jagged finish produced by rolling molten glass objects into crushed glass.

OWENS, MICHAEL J.
A glassblower who began his career at Libbey in 1888. In 1903 he invented the automatic bottle blowing machine, which produced bottles quickly and efficiently at a much lower cost. He went on to form Owens-Illinois, Incorporated.

OWENS-ILLINOIS, INC.
An American company established in Toledo, Ohio, in 1929 when the Owens Bottle Machine Company under Michael Owens merged with the Illinois Glass Company. In 1936 it acquired the Libbey Glass Company and continues producing

huge quantities of glass under the Libbey name today.

PADEN CITY GLASS CO.
An American company established in Paden City, West Virginia, in 1916; they were noted for many elegant Depression glass patterns and closed in 1951.

PAIRPOINT MANUFACTURING CO.
An American company established in New Bedford, Massachusetts, in 1865. They acquired the Mt. Washington Glass Company in 1894 and continued producing glass until 1958. A new Pairpoint opened in 1967 in Sagamore, Massachusetts, producing handmade glassware.

PANE
A large piece of flat sheet glass used for glazing windows.

PAPERWEIGHT
A small heavy glass object with an inner design used as a weight to hold down loose papers. Paperweights are often oval or rounded and are made of extremely thick glass. The three most popular styles are Millefiori, Lampwork, and Sulphides.

PARFAIT
A tall narrow glass with short stem and foot used for serving ice cream.

PARISON
A blob of molten glass that is gathered at the end of the blowpipe, pontil, or gathering iron (same as "gather").

PATE DE VERRE
Meaning "Paste of Glass," it is an ancient material made from powdered glass or glasslike substances that is formed into a pastelike material by heating and then hardened. The resulting form is carved, painted, or applied with other decorations.

PATERNOSTRI
An Italian or Venetian term for glass beads used commonly in prayer and in jewelry. Glass beads have been produced on the island of Murano since the 13th century.

PATTERN GLASS
Glass produced by mechanically pressing it into molds. The design is cut directly in the mold.

PATTERN-MOLDED GLASS
Glass that is first impressed into small molds and then removed and blown to a larger size (blown-molded).

PEACH OPALESCENT
Peach-colored glass with a white opalescent edge or background (usually found in iridized Carnival glass).

PEACHBLOW GLASS
An American art glass produced by several companies in the late 19th century. It is characterized by multicolored opaque shades such as cream, white, pink, orange, red, and others.

PEARL OR PEARLIZED GLASS
Custard glass with a delicate, pastel iridescence.

PEARL ORNAMENTS
A molded glass pattern consisting of diamonds, squares, and other diagonal bandings.

PEARLINE GLASS
A late-19th-century-style art glass with color variance of pale to deep dark opaque blues.

PEGGING
The technique of poking a tiny hole in a molten glass object to trap a small quantity of air or bubble. The hole is then covered with other molten glass that expands the

bubble into a tear shape or teardrop inside the object.

PEKING CAMEO
Cameo-engraved glass first made in China in the late 17th century in the city of Peking. It was made to resemble more expensive Chinese porcelain.

PELOTON GLASS
A style of art glass first made by Wilhelm Kralik in Bohemia in 1880. It is produced by rolling colored threads into colored glass directly after it is removed from the furnace.

PERFUME BOTTLE
A tiny glass receptacle with narrow neck and stopper used for holding perfume.

PERTHSHIRE PAPERWEIGHTS, LTD.
Established in 1970 by Stuart Drysdale in Crieff, Scotland; Perthshire is noted for high-quality paperweights. Many are produced in limited editions.

PHIAL
A small glass bottle used for ointments, medicines, and perfumes (same as *vial*).

PHOENIX GLASS
A term usually applied to cased milk glass, also known as mother-of-pearl, made by the Phoenix Glassworks Company in Pittsburgh, Pennsylvania, in the late 19th century.

PHOENIX GLASS CO.
Established in Monaca, Pennsylvania, in 1880; they later moved to Pittsburgh and were noted for cut-glass gas and electric lighting fixtures, general glass items, and some figured art glass. Phoenix became a division of Anchor-Hocking in 1970 and was later sold to the Newell Group in 1987.

PHOTOCHROMIC GLASS
A glass developed by the Corning Glass Works in Corning, New York, in 1964. When the glass is exposed to ultraviolet radiation such as sunlight, it darkens; when the radiation is removed, the glass clears.

PICKLE CASTOR
A glass jar held within a silver or silver-plated metal frame, usually with handle and matching spoon, and used for serving pickles. They were most popular during the Victorian period.

PICKLE DISH
A flat or shallow dish, usually oblong or rectangular, and used specifically for serving pickles (smaller than a celery dish).

PIE PLATE
A large, shallow round glass dish used for baking and serving pies.

PIEDOUCHE
A French term for a paperweight that is raised on a low, applied crystal foot.

PIGEON BLOOD
A color of glass characterized by brown highlighting over ruby red.

PILGRIM GLASS CO.
A contemporary art-glass company founded in 1949 by Alfred E. Knobler in Ceredo, West Virginia; Pilgrim is noted for paperweights and modern cameo cut glass.

PILLAR CUTTING
A decorative pattern of cut glass in the form of parallel vertical ribs in symmetrical pillar shapes (similar to flute cutting).

PILSENER GLASS
A tall narrow glass vessel with foot used primarily for drinking beer.

PIN TRAY
A tiny flat or shallow glass dish used for holding hairpins.

PINK GLASS
Glass that is colored by the addition of neodymium and selenium. Pink-colored glass was most popular during the Depression era.

PITCHER
A widemouthed glass vessel usually with spout and handle, with or without lip, and used for pouring or serving liquids.

PITKIN & BROOKS
Established as a cut-glass operation and distributor of crocks and glassware in Chicago in 1872, Edward Hand Pitkin and Jonathan William Brooks operated as a partnership until closing in 1920.

PITTSBURGH FLINT GLASS WORKS
The early name for Benjamin Bakewell's first glass company established in 1808 (see Bakewell, Pears & Company).

PITTSBURGH GLASS
High-quality pressed glass made in America by several companies in and around Pittsburgh, Pennsylvania, in the late 18th and 19th centuries.

PLATE
A flat glass object usually round in shape (occasionally square or oval) used for serving dinner, lunch, desserts, and other foods.

PLATED AMBERINA
A style of cased art glass developed by Joseph Locke, an employee of the New England Glass Company, in 1866. Glass objects were created with a creamy opalescent lining, and then cased with an outer layer of Amberina. The pieces were difficult to make and were produced in limited

quality. They are also far more valuable than regular amberina items. (See also Amberina.)

PLATED GLASS
Glass that is covered by more than one layer; usually clear glass that is dipped or completely covered with colored glass.

PLATINUM BAND
A metal silver-colored trim applied to rims or by banding around glass objects (made of genuine platinum).

PLATONITE
A heat-resistant, opaque white glass first produced and named by Hazel Atlas in the 1930s and 1940s.

PLATTER
A large flat glass object, usually round or oval in shape (larger than dinner plates), and used for serving large amounts of foods.

PLUNGER
The device that presses molten glass against a mold to create the interior or primary pattern of an object (the mold produces the pattern on the outside surface).

POKAL
A Bohemian-style goblet with stemmed foot and cover (cover may or may not contain a finial).

POLYCHROMIC GLASS
Glass characterized by two or more colors.

POMADE BOX
A small rectangular, circular, or oval glass receptacle with cover used for storing perfume, oils, or hair dressing. Pomade boxes were popular in the Victorian era and were part of dresser sets. Note that pomade ointment was originally made from apples.

POMONA GLASS
An art glass created by applying or dipping the object into acid to produce a mottled, frosted appearance. It was first developed by Joseph Locke at the New England Glass Company and patented in 1885.

PONTIL
A solid shorter iron used to remove expanded objects from the blowing iron, which allows the top to be finished. Before the 19th century, it left a mark but since then has usually been grounded flat. Pontil is also referred to as pontie, ponty, and puntee.

POT
A vessel made of fired clay in which a batch of glass ingredients is heated before being transferred to the furnace. Many varieties include open, closed, smaller for colored glass, and so on but most last only three to six weeks before breaking up. Modern pots hold 1,100 to 1,650 pounds of glass.

POT ARCH
A furnace in which a pot is fired before being transferred to the main furnace for melting.

POTASH
Potassium carbonate that is used as a substitute for soda as an alkali source in a glass mixture.

POWDER JAR
A small glass receptacle, usually with cover, used for holding various body powders. Powder jars are ordinarily part of dresser sets.

PRESERVE DISH
A small flat or shallow dish, with or without a foot, and used for serving jelly, jam, and other fruit preserves.

PRESSED GLASS
Hot molten glass mechanically forced into molds under pressure. An important American invention in the 1820s was the hand press.

PRESSING
The process begins with molten glass poured into a mold, which forms the outer surface of an object. A plunger lowered into the mass leaves a smooth center with a patterned exterior. Flat plates and dishes are formed in a base mold, and an upper section folds down to mold the top (like a waffle iron).

PRISM
A type of decorative oval or triangular dangling glass piece used in chandeliers, mantel lustres, and candelabras. In optics, a prism is a thick piece of crystal used to refract light.

PRISM CUTTING
Cut glass made with long horizontal grooves or lines that usually meet at a common point.

PROOF
A term often used in carnival glass to describe a trial impression from a plunger and mold combination. Often in a proof, certain areas contain incomplete patterns; if noticed by glassworkers in the factory, proofs were usually pressed back into the mold to complete the pattern.

PRUNTS
A German decoration or ornamentation characterized by small glass knobs or drops attached to drinking vessels; they later became another name for hobs on hobnail patterned glass.

PUCELLAS
A glassmaker's tool shaped like tongs used for gripping or holding glass objects while being worked.

PUFF BOX
A small square, rectangular, or circular glass container with cover used on dressing tables or vanities for holding powders.

PUMICE
Volcanic rock that is ground into powder and used for polishing glass objects.

PUNCH BOWL
A huge concave glass vessel, usually hemispherical in shape, and used for serving beverages.

PUNCH CUP
An open, somewhat bowl-shape or cylindrical vessel, usually with a single handle, and used for drinking punch as dipped from a punch bowl.

PUNCH LADLE
A long-handled utensil with a concave dipping cup at the end used for dipping out liquids from a punch bowl. Punch ladles are longer than all other ladles.

PUNCH STAND
A matching support base on which a punch bowl rests.

PURLED GLASS
Glass characterized by a ribbing applied around the base of the object.

PURPLE
A violet-colored glass produced by the addition of manganese (see also Amethyst, and Manganese). Note that purple is usually a bit darker than amethyst; this is particularly true in carnival glass.

PYREX
A type of glass created by Corning Glass in 1912. It contains oxide of boron, which makes the glass extremely heat resistant (sometimes referred to as borosilicate glass).

QUAKER CITY CUT GLASS CO.
Established in Philadelphia in 1902; they produced cut-glass products until 1927.

QUARTZ GLASS
An art glass consisting of a wide variety of colors and shades created by Steuben (designed to imitate the appearance of quartz).

QUATREFOIL
A form based on four leaves or four-petaled flowers originally applied to stained-glass windows in medieval Europe. It was later applied to glass objects.

QUEZEL ART GLASS & DECORATION CO.
An American company founded in Brooklyn, New York, in 1901; they were noted for producing opalescent art glass known as Quezal glass.

QUEZAL GLASS
An iridescent semiopaque imitation of Tiffany's Favrille art glass made by the Quezal Art Glass & Decoration Company in the early 20th century.

QUILLING
A wavy pattern applied to glass by repeated workings with pincers.

RADIUM
A brilliant transparent iridescence applied to carnival glass (most by Millersburg). The base color can usually be observed without holding radium iridized pieces to a light.

RADIUM GLASS CO.
Established by Samuel Fair, John W. Fenton, C. J. Fisher, and M. V. Leguillon, Radium assumed control of the Millersburg Glass Company after it filed for bankruptcy in 1911. Radium continued to produce glass until 1913, when it was sold to the Jefferson Glass Company.

RANGE SETS
Kitchenware glass sets developed during the Depression period. Items might include canisters, flour jars, sugar jars, shakers, and others.

RATAFIA GLASS
A small cordial-like stemmed glass used to serve the liquor ratafia. Ratafia is distilled with fruit like brandy and usually flavored with almonds.

RAVENSCROFT, GEORGE
The first commercially successful glass-maker in England, who developed a high-quality durable lead crystal formula in the 17th century (1632–83).

RAYED
A sunburst cut design usually applied to the bottom of glass objects.

READING ARTISTIC GLASS WORKS
This American company was established by French immigrant Lewis Kremp in Reading, Pennsylvania, in 1884, but closed soon afterward, in 1886. In their two years of operation, the factory produced several styles of high-quality art-glass products.

REAMER
A juice extractor with a ridge and pointed center rising in a shallow dish, usually circular in shape.

RED CARNIVAL GLASS
An iridized coating produced by a gold metallic coloring agent that in turn produces a brilliant cherry red finish. Red carnival glass is rare and very valuable.

REEDING
A decorating technique applied with very fine threads or tiny ropelike strings of glass. The strings are usually colored and applied in a variety of patterns. It is also sometimes referred to as ribbing.

REFRIGERATOR DISH
Stackable square or rectangular covered glass containers of various sizes used for storing foods in the refrigerator.

RELIEF CUTTING
A difficult and expensive method of cutting glass by designing the outline on the surface and then cutting away the background. The design is then raised in relief similar to that of cameo-engraving.

RELIQUARY
A glass vessel used for storing sacred religious relics.

RELISH DISH
A small to medium-size shallow glass serving tray with divisions, usually rectangular or oval in shape, that may contain one or two handles.

RENNINGER BLUE
A medium iridized blue color named by the Northwood Glass Company for some of their carnival glass products. The color is darker than sapphire but lighter than cobalt.

REPRODUCTION
A close imitation or exact copy of an original object made at a later time. Reproductions pose problems for collectors, particularly for originals that are rare and valuable.

RESONANCE
The sound that results when a glass object is struck; sometimes used as a test for crystal, though other types of glass resonate similar sounds.

REVERSE PAINTING
Designs that are painted on the back side of glass that appear in proper perspective when viewed from the front.

RIB MOLD

A pattern mold for bowls, bottles, tumblers, and so on that is marked with heavy vertical lines or ribbing.

RICHARDS & HARTLEY FLINT GLASS CO.

An American glass company founded by Joseph Richards and William T. Hartley in Pittsburgh, Pennsylvania, in 1869. They moved to Tarentum, Pennsylvania, in 1881 and manufactured pressed wares before becoming part of the U.S. Glass Co. in 1891.

RICHMOND, JAMES N.

A glassmaker of Cheshire, Massachusetts, Richmond built a glass house in 1850 that attracted many curiosity seekers. He is credited with being the first to make plate glass in America.

RIGAREE

A narrow vertical band decoration applied to glass in various colors.

RIM

The narrow area adjacent to the edge of a glass vessel. Rims are usually associated with bowls, vases, cups, plates, and so on. Rims are sometimes decorated with applied colors or enamels or may be ruffled, flared, scalloped, and the like.

RINGTREE

A glass object in the shape of a miniature tree with knobs that taper upward (the knobs are used to hold finger rings).

RIPLEY AND CO.

Established in 1866 in Pittsburgh, Pennsylvania, by Daniel Ripley and George Duncan; they produced pressed-glass items until they parted ways in 1874. Both continued on their own (Ripley & Co. and George Duncan & Sons) until becoming part of the U.S. Glass Company in 1891 as Factory F.

RIVERSIDE GLASS COMPANY

Established in Wellsburg, West Virginia, in 1879, the company produced pressed glass until they joined the National Glass Company in 1899.

ROASTER

A deep round, oblong, or angled dish; with or without cover; with or without handles; and used to bake or cook foods.

ROBINSON GLASS CO.

A pressed-glass manufacturer established in Zanesville, Ohio, in 1893. The firm joined the National Glass Company in 1899. The plant burned in 1906 and was not rebuilt.

ROCHESTER TUMBLER CO.

A pressed-glass manufacturer established in Rochester, Pennsylvania, in 1872. The firm joined the National Glass Company in 1899.

ROCK CRYSTAL

A somewhat translucent pale white form of natural quartz. Rock crystal is carved into decorative objects, and glassmakers from early times sought to imitate it in their creations.

ROD

A thin solid cylinder or small stick of glass. Many are used together to form a cane.

ROLLED EDGE

A curved lip or circular base on which glass objects may turn over or rotate.

ROPE EDGE

A twirled threadlike design usually applied around the edge of glass objects.

ROSE

A deep red cranberry-colored glass applied by staining or flashing (not as deep or as dark as ruby red).

ROSE BOWL

A small round concave glass vessel usually with three feet (tri-footed) with a small opening in the center for holding a single rose bloom or a few flowers.

ROUSSEAU, EUGENE

A French glassmaker and pioneer in the 19th-century art nouveau–styled glass. He is noted for floral and Asian designs created in several color effects and styles.

ROYAL FLEMISH GLASS

An art glass made by the Mt. Washington Glass Works characterized by a raised gilding decoration and light staining.

RUBIGOLD

A name given to a marigold-colored carnival glass by the Imperial Glass Company. Rubigold was advertised as a dark red iridescence with tints of other colors, but it is truly marigold only and not red carnival glass.

RUBINA GLASS

Glass that gradually changes in color from crystal at the bottom to a cranberry or rose color at the top (also spelled *rubena*).

RUBINA VERDE

Glass that gradually changes in color from a light yellow-green at the bottom to a cranberry or rose color at the top (also spelled *rubena*).

RUBY RED

A gold metallic coloring agent that produces the most powerful red color within glass. Since the mid-20th century, ruby red glass is produced by the chemical selenium instead of gold.

RUBY STAINED

Pressed clear or crystal glass that is decorated by fusing metal (gold) oxide onto the surface. Gold oxide produces the somewhat transparent light red color or stain. Ruby stained items were popular as souvenirs in the 1880s until the Depression. Many were etched or engraved with tourist attractions, names, dates, fairs, etc.

SABINO, MARIUS-ERNEST

A French art-glass maker noted for opalescent gold figurines produced in the 1920s–1930s and 1960s–1970s.

SACHET JAR

A small glass receptacle, with or without cover, used for holding perfumed powders for scenting clothes and linens.

ST. CLAIR

A small novelty glass operation founded in 1941 in Elwood, Indiana, by the St. Clair family. The company produces lamps, paperweights, and miniature novelty items.

ST. LOUIS

A famous French glassmaking town that was producing glass as far back as the 16th century (1586). In the 1840s it was noted most for paperweight production but most companies closed when the popularity of paperweights severely declined. The art form was revived in the 1950s and continues today.

SALAD PLATE

A flat glass object, usually round in shape, ordinarily about 6" to 7½" in diameter (slightly smaller than the average lunch plate) and used for serving salads.

SALTCELLAR

A small open bowl, with or without a foot, and used for sprinkling salt on food before the development of shakers (may or may not have a matching spoon). They are also known as salt dips.

SALTS BOTTLE

A small glass bottle with a silver or silver-plated top used for holding smelling salts.

They were most popular during the Victorian period.

SALVE BOX
A small jar with cover used on dressing tables and vanities for holding salves, ointments, or cold creams.

SALVER
A large platter or tray used for serving food or beverages. Most have a pedestal foot.

SAMOVAR
An urn-shape lamp usually containing a metal spigot and metal hardware (base, top, and handle). Samovars originated in Russia.

SAND
The most common form of silica used in making glass. The best sands are found along inland beds near streams with low iron content and low amounts of other impurities.

SANDBLASTING
An American-developed process where the design on a piece of glass is coated with a protective layer and the exposed surfaces that remain are sandblasted with a pressurized gun to create the design.

SANDWICH GLASS
An American pressed glass produced in the eastern United States in the 19th century. It was a substitute for more expensive hand-cut crystal glass.

SANDWICH SERVER
A large platter or serving tray with an open or closed center handle.

SAPPHIRE BLUE
The color of sapphire or sky blue, darker than ice blue but much lighter than cobalt blue.

SARDINE DISH
A small, oblong or oval, flat or shallow dish, used for serving sardines.

SATIN GLASS
An American art glass form characterized by a smooth lustrous appearance obtained by giving layers of colored glass an allover acid vapor bath.

SAUCE BOAT
A glass oblong bowl-shape vessel, usually with a handle on each end, used for serving sauces or gravy.

SAUCE DISH
A small, usually flat or shallow dish, with or without handles, possibly footed, and used for serving condiments or sauces.

SAUCER
A small flat or shallow plate usually with an indentation for a matching cup.

SAWTOOTH
See Serrated.

SCALLOPING
A decorative technique applied during the molding process that gives an object a wavy or ruffled rim. It is usually applied to the rims of bowls, plates, and vases.

SCENT BOTTLE
See Cologne Bottle or Perfume Bottle.

SCHNEIDER GLASS
Founded in 1913 in Epiney-sur-Seine, France, by brothers Ernest and Charles Schneider. Charles had previously worked for Daum and Galle. The firm is best known for art-glass items, but they also produced some tableware, lamps, and stained glass. Robert Schneider, Charles's son, assumed control of the company in 1948 and moved the operation to Loris, France, in 1962.

SCONCE
A glass candlestick bracket with one or more sockets for holding candles.

SCREEN PRINTING
A decorating technique that involves the passage of a printing medium through a stenciled specialized fabric.

SEEDS
Tiny air bubbles in glass indicating an underheated furnace or impurities caused by flecks of dirt or dust.

SELENIUM
A chemical element that produces red or ruby red coloring in glass. Selenium serves as a gold substitute in the modern era for achieving red glassware.

SENECA GLASS CO.
Established in 1891 in Fostoria, Ohio; the company later moved to Morgantown, West Virginia, where they continue to make pressed tablewares and novelty items today.

SERRATED
A form of notching along the rims of glass objects that resembles the edge of a saw blade. It was a popular finish on cut glass and is sometimes referred to as sawtooth.

SHAKER
A small glass upright container, usually cylindrical or angular in shape, with metal or plastic covers containing tiny holes, and used for sprinkling salt, pepper, sugar, and other spices on foods.

SHAM
Very thin, fragile glass tumblers.

SHAVING MUG
A cylindrical glass vessel, with or without handles, usually larger than a drinking mug, and used for repeated dipping and rinsing of shaving cream from a razor.

SHERBET
A small footed dish, with or without a small stem, and used for serving desserts such as pudding, ice cream, Jell-O, and so on.

SHERRY GLASS
A tall glass with foot and stem with a shallow angled or straight-edged bowl.

SHOT GLASS
A small whiskey tumbler with a capacity of at least 1 ounce but not more than 2, and a height of at least 1¾" but strictly less than 3".

SHOULDER
The bulged section just below the neck of a glass object (usually present in vases and bottles).

SICKNESS
Glass that is not properly tempered or annealed that ordinarily shows random cracks, flaking, and eventually breaks or disintegrates.

SIGNATURE
The mark of the maker or manufacturer usually applied near the bottom or the underside of glass objects.

SILICA
An essential ingredient in making glass. The most common form is sand, which is an impure silica. Sand is usually taken from the seashore or along inland beds near water. The Venetians historically used ground white pebbles from rivers. Powdered flints were once used, too, as silica (see also Flint Glass).

SILVERIA GLASS
The technique of rolling an extremely thin layer of silver over glass and then blowing it, which shatters the silver into glittery decorative flecks.

SILVERINA

A type of art glass created by Steuben in the early 20th century using particles of silver and mica applied to the glass object.

SINCLAIRE, H. P. & CO.

Established in Corning, New York, in 1904 by H. P. Sinclaire; Sinclaire used blanks from Dorflinger for cutting and engraving. The company closed permanently in 1929.

SKITTLE

A small fire-clay pot used for melting a specialized small batch of colored glass or enamel.

SLAG GLASS

A type of glass made with various scrap metals, including lead, that was first produced in England in the mid-19th century. Slag is characterized by colorful swirling or marbleized designs.

SMITH, L. E. CO.

Established by Lewis E. Smith in 1907 in Mt. Pleasant, Pennsylvania; Smith left in 1911, but the company continued producing many unique novelty items as well as colored glass during the Depression era. The firm is still in operation today.

SMITH BROTHERS

Harry A. and Alfred E. Smith worked in the art-glass decorating department of Mt. Washington in 1871. They opened their own shop in 1874 in New Bedford, Massachusetts, and produced cut, engraved, and other art-glass products.

SMOKE

A smoky or light to medium gray charcoal color. Smoke is most often found on iridized carnival glass.

SODA

Sodium carbonate, which is used as an alkali in a glass mixture. Soda serves as a flux to reduce the melting-point temperature of a batch of glass.

SOUTH JERSEY GLASS

Tableware made in America in the New Jersey area in the 18th century; it was fairly crude but bold, and the style spread to Europe.

SOUVENIR GLASS

Glass objects decorated with a variety of techniques (enameled, painted, transferred, embossed, etc.) depicting cities, states, countries, advertising, tourist attractions, and so on.

SOWERBY & CO.

Established in the city of Gateshead-on-Tyne in England in 1763 (originally called the New Stourbridge Glass Works) by John Sowerby, the name was officially changed by John's son, John George Sowerby. After John George's death, the name was changed again by his son-in-law to Sowerby's Ellison Glassworks, Ltd. Sowerby was a large producer of pressed glass, including carnival glass.

SPALL

A shallow rounded flake on a glass object that is usually applied near the rim of a piece.

SPANGLED GLASS

A late-19th-century American art glass made with flakes of mica in the clear glass inner layer and then overlaid by transparent colored glass. The majority of items produced in this style were glass baskets with fancy decorated handles and rims.

SPATTER GLASS

An opaque white or colored glass produced in both England and America in the late 19th century. The exterior is sometimes mottled with large spots of colored glass.

SPECIALTY GLASS CO.

A short-lived pressed-glass manufacturer established in East Liverpool, Ohio, in 1889. The firm closed in 1898.

SPITTOON

A fancy glass vessel or receptacle used for containing saliva (or spit, hence the name *spittoon*). Spittoons are sometimes referred to as cuspidors.

SPOON DISH

A flat or shallow glass object, rectangular or oval in shape, used for holding dessert spoons horizontally.

SPOONER OR SPOON HOLDER

A tall cylinder-shape glass vessel, with or without handles, and used for holding dessert spoons vertically.

SPOUT

A tubular protuberance through which the contents of a vessel are poured.

SPRAYED-ON IRIDESCENCE

Adding iridescence to glass by spraying it with particles of metallic salts.

SPUN GLASS

Glass threading that was originally spun by hand upon a revolving wheel. Glass fibers are automatically spun by machine today.

STAINED GLASS

An imitation colored glass created by painting clear glass with metallic stains or transparent paints.

STAR HOLLY

A milk-glass design created by the Imperial Glass Company in the early 1900s. It was made to duplicate pressed English Wedgewood glass and was characterized by intertwined holly leaves raised in relief with background color mattes of blue, green, or coral.

STAVE

A basketlike enclosure used in millefiori paperweights.

STEIN

A cylindrical or square drinking vessel with a single handle, ordinarily larger than a mug (originally they had a capacity of 1 pint), with or without a hinged lid (the lid as well as handles may be metal), used for serving beer.

STEM

The cylindrical support connecting the foot and bowl of glass vessels (these vessels include all types of stemware, such as goblets, wineglasses, comports, etc.).

STEMWARE

A general term for a drinking vessel that is raised on a slender pedestal or stemmed base (wine, goblet, claret, champagne, cordial, etc.).

STERLING CUT GLASS CO.

Established in 1904 in Cincinnati, Ohio, by Joseph Phillips and Joseph Landenwitsch; they were noted for cut-glass production. The company closed for good in 1950.

STEUBEN GLASS CO.

An American company founded in Corning, New York, by Frederick Carder in 1903. They were a leader in art-glass styles and production early on and were purchased by the Corning Glass Works in 1918. Corning continues to produce some of the finest-quality crystal in the world today with the Steuben name.

STEVENS & WILLIAMS

English glassmakers who produced art-glass products, including a cheaper method of making cameo glass. They operated at the Brierly Hill Glassworks in Stourbridge, England, from the 1830s to the 1920s.

STIEGEL GLASS

A style of 18th-century glass made in both Europe and America. The name originated with Baron Henry William Stiegel, who founded a glass factory in Manheim, Pennsylvania, in 1769. Stiegel glass consists primarily of some limited colors but was mostly made of crystal. Most pieces were practical tableware items, such as barware, bottles, and flasks, and may or may not contain enameled decorations.

STIPPLING

A decorating technique consisting of shallow dots or short lines produced by striking a diamond or steel point against a glass object. Image highlights are produced by the dots while the untouched finished glass leaves a shadowy background.

STOPPER

A matching piece that fits into and closes the mouth of a glass vessel. They are made in many shapes and styles (ball, faceted, triangular, cylindrical with possibly a finial, among others) and are ordinarily found on perfume or cologne bottles, decanters, cruets, and so on.

STOURBRIDGE FLINT GLASS WORKS

Established in Pittsburgh, Pennsylvania, in 1824 by John Robinson, the name was changed to J. & T. Robinson in 1830, and then to Robinson, Anderson & Co. in 1836. The firm produced some pressed wares and a little opalescent glass before closing in 1845.

STOURBRIDGE GLASS

Glassware made as far back as the 16th century in or near Stourbridge, Worcestershire, England. Many English factories later sprang up in this area, including Webb, Stevens & Williams, Stuart & Sons, and others.

STRAUS & SONS

Established by German immigrant Lazarus Straus in 1872 in New York City; they began as a retailer of china and glass products but began cutting glass in 1888. As the demand for cut glass declined, the company returned to the retail market.

STRAWBERRY DIAMOND CUTTING

One of the most popular patterns in cut glass. As a variation of raised diamond cutting, an uncut space is left between the diagonal grooves so that a flat area results instead of pointed diamonds. The flat areas are then cross-hatched to form a group of low relief diamonds that is sometimes confused with hobnail. Grooved fans were also a popular addition above the strawberry diamond region to produce the strawberry and diamond with fan cut design.

STRETCH GLASS

A type of iridescent or carnival-like glass made with an onion-skin surface effect. It was primarily made in America during the carnival glass era (early 1900s–1920s).

STRIPED GLASS

An American art glass from the late 19th century characterized by wavy bands of contrasting colors.

STUART & SONS, LTD.

Established in Stourbridge, England, in 1881 by Frederick Stuart, the firm produced a high volume of colored glass and chandeliers before World War II. After the war, the firm produced crystal only. It is still in operation today and is carried on by descendants of Frederick.

SUGAR

A small glass cuplike vessel that may or may not have handles and is used for serving sugar (often paired with a creamer for serving tea and coffee).

SUGAR AND LEMON TRAY
A two-tiered object used for serving lemons and sugar. Cut lemons are placed on the bottom level while sugar held in a bowl makes up the top level.

SUGAR SHAKER
A small glass upright container, usually cylindrical or angular in shape, with metal or plastic covers containing holes, and used for sprinkling sugar on various foods (larger in size than typical salt and pepper shakers).

SULPHIDE
A ceramic relief incrusted within a clear glass paperweight, usually a portrait of a historical figure. It is also spelled *sulfide*. Along with lampwork and millefiori, sulphide is one of the three basic types of paperweight styles.

SUNSET-GLOW GLASS
An early (18th century) European milk or opalescent white glass.

SUPERIMPOSED DECORATION
A glass decoration separate from the object that it is applied to.

SWEETMEAT DISH OR COMPOTE
A small flat or shallow tray or bowl-like glass object used for serving sweetmeat hors d'oeuvres.

SWIZZLE STICK
A thin glass rod with an enlarged end that is used to stir liquids (swizzle originally was a sweetened alcoholic beverage made with rum).

SYRUP PITCHER
A small widemouthed vessel with spout, handle, and hinged metal lid, used for pouring syrup.

TAB HANDLES
Small protrusions usually attached or connected to the rims of bowls and plates allowing one to grasp the object. Tab handles may be closed (solid glass) or open (holes within the handles). Bonbon dishes typically have a single tab handle.

TANK
A large holding vessel constructed in a furnace for melting a batch of glass. Tanks replaced pots in large glass factories in the later 19th century.

TANKARD
A large drinking vessel, somewhat straight edged, with a single handle that may or may not contain a hinged lid (as in steins, the lid and handle may be made of metal).

TARENTUM GLASS CO.
A pressed-glass manufacturer established in Tarentum, Pennsylvania, in 1894. The firm closed in 1918.

TAYLOR BROTHERS
Established in 1902 in Philadelphia by Albert Taylor and Lafayette Taylor, they operated as a cut-glass company until 1915.

TAZZA
An unusually wide dessert cup or serving plate with or without handles mounted on a stemmed foot.

TEA CADDY
A large widemouthed glass canister with cover used for storing tea bags or loose tea.

TEAL
A bluish-green-colored glass (a little darker with a stronger blue coloring than ultramarine).

TEAPOT
A vessel with handle, spout, and lid used to serve tea. Glass teapots are typically found in miniature children's tea sets.

TEAR OR TEARDROP

A bubble of air trapped in glass that is sometimes purposefully created for a decorative effect.

TEKTITES

Small, rounded bodies of glass that form as a result of the impact of fiery meteorites upon sand on both the Earth and moon. Tektites have been found in Eastern Europe, Indonesia, Vietnam, Australia, America, and other places. Yellowish lumps of tektites are occasionally found in the dunes of the Sahara Desert.

TEMPERED OPAL

A heat-resistant translucent milk glass that was developed during World War II by the Corning Glass Works. Tempered opal is the basis for colored Pyrex kitchenware products.

TEMPERING

A technique that increases the strength of glass by heating it slightly below the softening point and then suddenly cooling it with a blast of cold air.

TENDRILS

Slender, coiling stemlike glass trailings that resemble those by which a plant attaches itself to a support.

THATCHER BROTHERS

Established by George and Richard Thatcher in 1891 in New Bedford, Massachusetts; they produced cut-glass products until going out of business in 1907.

THOMPSON GLASS CO.

A short-lived pressed-glass manufacturer established in Uniontown, Pennsylvania, in 1889. The firm closed in 1898.

THREAD CIRCUIT OR THREADING

A decorative pattern applied with rope-like strings or twists of glass. The strings or threads are often colored and applied in concentric circles or other symmetrical patterns.

THUMBPRINT

A decorative style usually made by pressing in the form of oval-shape shallow depressions arranged in rows. Several variations of the basic thumbprint pattern exist, such as almond thumbprint and diamond thumbprint.

TIDBIT TRAY

A tiered dish with a pole connecting two or more levels. The pole usually runs through the center and the size of the levels gradually decrease as they go up.

TIFFANY, LOUIS COMFORT

The most celebrated and renowned leader of the art nouveau style of glass in America in the 19th century. He established a glass factory in Long Island, New York, in 1885 and was known for several famous worldwide designs, including Favrile, lamps, and a host of other items (1848–1933).

TIFFIN GLASS CO.

An American company established as the A. J. Beatty & Sons Company in 1888 in Tiffin, Ohio. It became part of the United States Glass Company in 1892 and began operating as a distinct subsidiary in 1916. Employees purchased the plant in 1963. After a few additional ownership changes (1966 Continental Can, 1969 Interpace), the company closed for good in 1980. Tiffin is noted for good-quality table, bar, stem, and decorative glasswares, including a line of black glassware in the 1920s referred to as Black Satin.

TOBACCO JAR

A large canisterlike glass container with cover used for storing tobacco.

TODDY JAR

A tall, widemouthed glass receptacle used for serving hot toddies (alcoholic beverages consisting of liquor, water, sugar, and spices).

TOILET WATER BOTTLE
A glass receptacle with narrow neck and stopper used on dressing tables and vanities for holding water (larger than a cologne bottle).

TOOTHBRUSH BOTTLE
A tall, narrow, and cylindrical-shape glass container with cap used to store a single toothbrush.

TOOTHPICK HOLDER
A small glass or ceramic receptacle of small capacity designed to hold toothpicks; usually cut or patterned to taper inward at the top.

TOOTHPOWDER JAR
A small glass receptacle with cover used for holding toothpowder.

TOPAZ
A mineral used as a coloring agent to produce a bright yellow color within glass.

TOY MUG
A miniature glass vessel in the shape of a mug with a handle and a capacity of 1 to 1½ ounces.

TOY WHISKEY TASTER
A small glass tumbler first made in America around 1840 for the tasting, sampling, or consuming of whiskey in tiny amounts.

TRAILING
The process of pulling out a thread of glass and applying it to the surface of a glass object in spiral or other string designs.

TRANSFERS
A complete design printed on a paper backing that is removed from the backing, applied to glassware, and then fired on in a special enameling lehr.

TRANSLUCENT
Glass that transmits or diffuses light so that objects lying beyond cannot be seen clearly through it.

TRANSPARENT
Glass that transmits light without appreciable scattering so that objects lying beyond are clearly visible.

TRAY
A flat glass object, usually oval or rectangular in shape, and used for holding or serving various items.

TRIVET
A glass plate, usually tri-footed, and used under a hot dish to protect the surface (such as a tabletop) beneath it.

TUMBLE UP
An inverted glass set for a dresser or nightstand that usually includes a water bottle and other items such as a tray and tumblers. A tumbler usually serves as the cover when placed upside down on the bottle.

TUMBLER
A drinking vessel ordinarily without foot, stem, or handle, and containing a pointed or convex base.

TUREEN
A round or oval covered serving bowl ordinarily used for serving soup or other foods. Some have an accompanying stand. Most were made in porcelain but occasional glass examples have been produced.

TUTHILL CUT GLASS CO.
Established in 1900 in Middletown, New York, by Charles G. Tuthill, James F. Tuthill, and Susan Tuthill, they were noted for cut glass and some intaglio engraving before shutting down for good in 1923.

TWISTS
See Air Twist.

ULTRAMARINE
A bluish-green aqua color produced by the mineral lazulite or from a mixture of kaolin, soda ash, sulfur, and charcoal.

UNDERCUTTING
A technique of decorating glass in relief by cutting away part of the glass between the body of the object and its decoration.

UNGER BROTHERS
Established in 1901 in Newark, New Jersey; they began as a silver manufacturer of household items and added cut-glass products shortly afterward. They later switched to cheaper pressed blanks before closing permanently in 1918.

UNION GLASS CO.
Established in 1851 as the Bay State Glass Company in East Cambridge, Massachusetts, under the direction of Amory Houghton, the firm moved a few short years later to Somerville, Massachusetts, where it was renamed the Union Glass Co. It operated as a cut-glass operation. Houghton later sold his interest to Julian de Cordova (whose initials are sometimes found on the liners of certain objects). The company closed in 1927. Houghton went on to form Corning (see also Corning).

UNITED STATES GLASS CO.
An American glass conglomerate that was established in 1891 when 18 separate companies from the Glass Belt (Ohio, Pennsylvania, West Virginia, and others) merged.

URANIUM GLASS
A brilliant yellowish-green glass produced by the addition of uranium oxide. Uranium glass is mildly radioactive (not harmful) and glows brightly under a black light. It was first made in the 1830s.

URN
An ornamental glass vase with or without pedestal (may or may not have handles); also a closed glass vessel with spigot used for serving liquids.

VAL ST. LAMBERT CRISTALLERIES
A Belgium factory established in 1825 by Messieurs Kemlin and Lelievre. They are still in operation today and are noted most for engraved, cut, and cased colorful art styles.

VALLERYSTAHL GLASS
A glass-producing region in Lorraine, France, established in the 18th century. In 1872 the Vallerystahl Glassworks and the Portieux Glassworks merged and produced a good deal of art glass. The factory is still in operation today.

VARIANT
A glass item that differs slightly from the original form or standard version of a particular item or pattern.

VASA MURRHINA
An American 19th-century art glass characterized by an inner layer of colored glass that has powdered metals or mica added for decoration.

VASE
A round or angled glass vessel, usually with a depth that is greater than its width, and used for holding flowers.

VASELINE GLASS
Glass made with a small amount of uranium that imparts a light greenish-yellow color (a greasy appearance like vaseline). Vaseline glass usually glows under black light.

VENETIAN GLASS
Clear and colored glassware produced in Venice and the surrounding area from the 13th century to the present (see also Murano).

VENINI & COMPANY

Founded in 1921 in Murano, Italy, by Paolo Venini, the company is noted for a revival of filigree techniques and innovative use of canes and murrhine. Venini is one of the most recognizable names in modern Venetian glassmaking and continues to operate today.

VERLYS GLASS

Verlys was established in 1932 as an artglass branch of the French Holoplane Company in France. The Heisey Glass Company of Newark, Ohio, obtained the rights and formulas for Verlys and produced similar, but somewhat cheaper, products from 1935 to 1951. French-made pieces have a molded signature, whereas the American-made pieces have a diamond-etched signature in script. The glass itself is usually crystal with satinized frosting and/or etching (similar in style to Lalique).

VERRE-DE-SOIE

An art glass first produced by Steuben characterized by a smooth translucent iridescent finish.

VESICA

A cut-glass technique whereby a pointed oval is cut into an object.

VICTORIAN GLASS

English-made glass from about the 1820s through the 1940s characterized by colors, opalescence, opaqueness, art glass, and unusual designs and shapes, named for Queen Victoria (1837–1901). The entire Victorian era or period encompasses colored art glass during this time.

VIKING GLASS CO.

Viking purchased New Martinsville in 1944 and continued using some of New Martinsville's original molds. In 1991 Viking was purchased by Kenneth Dalzell

(former president of Fostoria) to become Dalzell-Viking. The company closed in 1997.

WAFER DISH

A small flat or shallow dish, usually square or rectangular in shape, and used for serving crackers or wafers.

WAISTED

A vessel (usually a vase) that has a smaller diameter in the middle than at the top and bottom. The sides then form a continuous inward curve.

WATCH BOX

A small rectangular or circular glass vessel, with or without cover, and used for storing a single wrist watch.

WATER BOTTLE

A glass container with narrow neck and mouth, usually without handle, and used for drinking water or other liquids.

WATER SET

A tableware set consisting of a large pitcher and a set of matching tumblers or goblets (usually six).

WATERFORD

The first Waterford glass company was established in Waterford, Ireland, in 1783 by the Penrose family and then sold to the Gatchell family in 1799. The handmade crystal produced contained a bluish tint and heavy cuts. The factory closed in 1851. A new Waterford factory was built in 1951, and since then Waterford has become the world's largest manufacturer of handmade crystal. Today they operate as Waterford Wedgewood PLC.

WEAR MARKS

Tiny, barely visible scratches on the base, foot, or rim that indicate normal wear and tear through years of use. Glass with wear marks is usually not considered mint glassware, but it holds much more value than damaged glass.

WEATHERING
The harmful effects of age, moisture, and chemical action, which all lead to glass's decomposition.

WEBB, THOMAS & SONS
Established in 1837 in Stourbridge, England, by Thomas Webb; the company has been in continuous operation since then and is best known for several art-glass styles, such as cameo, Peach Blow, Alexandrite, Burmese, and others.

WEST VIRGINIA GLASS CO.
A pressed-glass manufacturer established in Martins Ferry, Ohio, in 1861. The firm joined the National Glass Company in 1899.

WESTMORELAND SPECIALTY CO.
An American company established in Grapeville, Pennsylvania, in 1889; they were noted most for English hobnail patterned glassware. The company closed in 1985.

WHEELING GLASS
Glass made in the city of Wheeling, Virginia, in the 19th century (before West Virginia became a state).

WHEELS
Cutting wheels developed from lapidary equipment. Large stone wheels are used for deep cuts, and smaller various-size copper wheels are used for finer engraving.

WHIMSEY
A small unique decorative glass object made to display a particular glassmaker's skill (sometimes called a frigger).

WHISKEY JUG
A large, deep glass vessel or decanter, with a small mouth, with cover or stopper, usually with a small handle, used for serving whiskey.

WHISKEY SAMPLE GLASS
Small whiskey tumblers and cordials with a capacity of up to 4 ounces for sampling whiskey or other distilled spirits. Sample glasses were produced in the late 19th century until Prohibition (1919). Most contained advertising of a distiller or brand of whiskey (also referred to as pre-prohibition advertising glasses).

WHISKEY TUMBLER
A small shot-glass-size drinking vessel usually without foot, stem, or handle, and containing a pointed or convex base used for drinking distilled spirits in small amounts.

WHITNEY GLASS
An early American 18th-century glass consisting of bottles and flasks.

WINEGLASS
A tall glass with foot and stem with a large, round, deep bowl. As a unit of measure for serving size, 4 ounces is the most prevalent.

WINE SET
A decanter with matching wineglasses (may or may not include a matching tray).

WISTAR, CASPAR
An early American glass designer and manufacturer who established a glass works in Allowaystown, New Jersey, in 1739. His unique, wide, bulbous-form glass objects were dubbed South Jersey Glass and are also characterized by a superimposed winding thickness on the bottom.

WITCH BALL
A spherical glass globe, usually 3 to 7 inches in diameter, and dating from early 18th-century England. They were used to

ward off evil, for fortune-telling, and for other superstitious means.

WRYTHING ORNAMENTATION
A decoration consisting of swirled ribbing or fluting.

YELLOW GLASS
Chromate of lead and silver act as the primary coloring agents in producing a deep yellow color within glass (see Canary Yellow and Topaz). Also note that antimony added to lead will provide an opaque form of yellow.

ZANESVILLE GLASS
An American art glass produced in Ohio in the mid-19th century.

ZWISCHENGOLDGLAS
An 18th-century Bohemian or German glass characterized by gilding and inlaid gold decoration within another straight-sided glass.

MANUFACTURERS' MARKS

Abraham & Straus, Inc.

Akro Agate Co.

C.G. Alford & Co.

C. G. Alford & Co.

Almy & Thomas

American Wholesale Corp.

Anchor-Hocking
Fire-King

Anchor-Hocking
Glass Corp.

M.J. Averback

Baccarat Glass Co.

Bartlett-Collins Co.

J. D. Bergen Co.

J. D. Bergen Co.

House of Birks,
Montreal, Canada

Blenko Glass Co.

George L. Borden & Co.

George Borgfeldt
& Co.

Boyd Art Glass, 1978–1983

Boyd Art Glass, 1983–1988

Boyd Art Glass, 1988–1993

Boyd Art Glass, 1993–1998

Boyd Art Glass, 1998–2003

Boyd Art Glass, 2003–present

Bradley & Hubbard

Buffalo Cut Glass Co.

Burley & Tyrrell Co.

Cambridge Glass Co.

T. B. Clark & Co.

Conlow-Dorworth Co.

Corona Cut Glass Co.

Crown Cut Glass Co.

Crystal Cut Glass Co.

Crystolyne Cut Glass Co.

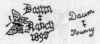

MADE
DeVilbiss
IN U.S.A.

Czechoslovakia,
20th Century

Daum Glass
Nancy, France

De Vilbiss Co.

SILVART

D

Deidrick Glass Co.

Diamond Cut
Glass Works

Dominion Glass Co. Montreal,
Canada

C. Dorflinger & Sons

George Drake
Cut Glass Co.

G.W. Drake & Co.

FLORAL CRYSTAL

Duffner & Kimberly

Duncan Dithridge

Durand Art
Glass Co.

937

O.F. Egginton
Co.

Empire Cut Glass Co.

Eska Mfg. Co.

Federal Glass Co.

Fenton Glass Co.,
1969–1970

Fenton Glass Co.,
1980s (with 8)

Fenton Glass Co.,
1985–

Fenton Paper Labels

Fostoria Paper Label
1920

Fostoria Paper Label
1924–1957

"Iris" Fostoria Glass
Co. Paper Label

Festoria Paper Label,
1924 to 1957

FRY

Fostoria Paper Label,
1957

H.C. Fry Glass Co.

Emile Gallé

GILLINDER

Gibson Glass

Gillinder & Sons

Gowans, Kent & Co., Ltd.,
Toronto, Canada

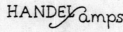

Gundy-Clapperton Co.,
Toronto, Canada

Handel & Co.

T. G. Hawkes
& Co.

Hazel Atlas Glass Co.

A. H. Heisey Glass Co.

L. Hinsberger Cut Glass

939

J. Hoare & Co.

Hobbs Glass Co.

Hobbs, Brocunier & Co.

Hocking Glass Co.

Honesdale
Decorating Co.

Hope Glass Works

Hunt Glass Co.

Imperial Glass Co., 1951–1972

Imperial Glass Co. as the IGC
Liquidating Corp., 1973–1981

Imperial Glass Co.
under Arthur Lorch,
1981–1982

Imperial Glass Co. 1904–1950

Indiana Glass Co.

Iorio Glass Shop

Irving Cut Glass Co.

PEERLESS

Jeannette Glass Co.

Jewel Cut Glass Co.

Kelly & Steinman

**MARS
STRAND**

Keystone Cut
Glass Co., Ltd.

Kings Co. Rich Cut
Glass Works

Edward J. Koch
& Co.

Kosta

Kosta Boda Limited
Edition Label, 1970s

Kosta Boda Label, 1980s

941

Krantz, Smith & Co., Inc.

Lackawanna Cut
Glass Co.

René Lalique

Lansburgh & Bro.

Lansburgh &
Brother, Inc.

Laurel Cut
Glass Co.

Apr. 16, 1901
(for use on pressed
[figured] blanks)

W. L. Libbey & Son

Joseph Locke

Loetz Glassworks

Lotus Cut Glass Co.

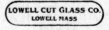

Lowell Cut Glass Co.

Wm. H. Lum

Luzerne Cut Glass Co.

Lyons Cut Glass Co.

MacBeth-Evans Glass
Co./Corning Glass Works

Majestic Cut Glass Co.

Maple City Glass Co.

Master Glass Co., 1970s

McKanna Cut Glass Co.

McKanna Cut Glass Co.

PRESCUT

McKee Glass Co.

McKee-Jeannette Glass Works

Meriden Cut Glass Co.

Millersburg Label

KELVA

"Kelva"
C.F. Monroe Co.

"Nakara"
C. F. Monroe Co.

"Wavecrest"
C.F. Monroe Co.

C.F. M.Cº

C. F. Monroe Co.

Moser Glass Works

Moses, Swan & McLawee Co.

Mosser Glass Co., 1980s

Mt. Washington Glass Works
Paper Label

"Crown Milano"
Mt. Washington
Glass Works

"Royal Flemish"
Mt. Washington
Glass Works

Mt. Washington Glass Works
Paper Label

Mt. Washington Glass Works
Paper Label

Richard Murr Co.

A. Douglas Nash
Corp.

National Association of Cut
Glass Manufacturers

Newark Cut Glass Co.

New England Glass Works
Paper Label

Northwood Glass Co.   *J. S. O'Connor Co.*

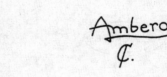

OHIO CUT GLASS COMPANY

NEW YORK SALESROOM, 66 West Broadway.
CHICAGO SALESROOM, Silversmiths' Building.
ST. LOUIS SALESROOM, Holland Building.

Ohio Cut Glass Co.

The Pairpoint Corp'n

Pairpoint Mfg. Co.

Pairpoint Mfg. Co.

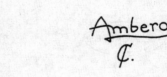

*Pairpoint Mfg. Co./Mt. Wash-
ington Glass Works*

P. X. Parsche & Son Co.

Phoenix Glass Co.

Pilgrim Glass

Pilkington Glass Co.

Pitkin & Brooks

DIAMONKUT

*Pope Cut
Glass Co., Inc.*

U.S.A. Pyrex Corning Glass Works

English Pyrex

Canadian Pyrex

French Pyrex

Pyrex Label

Quaker City Cut Glass Co.

Quezal Art Glass & Decorating Co.

Roden Brothers, Toronto, Canada

Sabino Art Glass Co., France

St. Louis, France

Seattle Cut Glass Co.

Seneca Glass Co.

947

Signet Glass Co.

H. P. Sinclaire & Co.

Smith Brothers
Decorating Co.

Standard Cut Glass Co.

Sterling Glass Co.

Steuben Glass Works

Steuben Glass Works

Various Frederick Carder Signatures, Steuben Glass Works

"Cire Perdue"
Steuben Glass Works

AURENE

Steuben Aurene

Stevens & Williams,
England

L. Straus & Sons

Taylor Brothers Co.

Thatcher Bros. & Co.

Tiffany Favrile

Tiffin Glass Co.

Tuthill Cut Glass Co.

Unger Brothers

Unger Brothers

"Kew Blas"
Union Glass Co.

United States Glass Co.

Val St. Lambert, Belgium

Van Heusen, Charles Co.

United States Glass Co.

E.J.S. Van Houten Co.

Venini, Murano, Italy

Viking Glass Co., 1970s

*Viking Glass Co.
Label, 1970s*

Waterford Glass Co.

*Thomas Webb & Sons
England*

Westmoreland Glass Co.

*Westmoreland Glass Co.
1949–1983*

*Westmoreland Glass Co.
1983–1985*

C.E. Wheelock & Co.

*L. G. Wright Glass Co.,
1970s–Present*

*Wright Rich
Cut Glass Co.*

BIBLIOGRAPHY

Angus-*Butterworth. British Table and Ornamental Glass.* New York: Arco Publishing, 1956.

Archer, Margaret, and Douglas Archer. *The Collector's Encyclopedia of Glass Candlesticks*. Paducah, KY: Collector Books, 1983.

Imperial Glass. Paducah, KY: Collector Books, 1978.

Arwas, Victor. *Art Nouveau to Art Deco*. New York: Rizzoli International Publications, 1977.

Tiffany. New York: Rizzoli International Publications, 1977.

Avila, George C. *The Pairpoint Glass Story.* New Bedford, MA: Reynolds-Dewart Printing, 1968.

Baldwin, Gary, and Lee Carno. *Moser*

Artistry in Glass 1857–1938. Marietta, OH: Antique Publications, 1988.

Barber, Edwin A. *American Glassware.* Philadelphia: Press of Patterson & White, 1900.

Barbour, Harriot Buxton. *Sandwich: The Town That Glass Built.* Boston: Houghton Mifflin 1948.

Barlow, Raymond E. and Joan E. Kaiser. *A Guide to Sandwich Glass.* Windham, NH: Barlow-Kaiser Publishing Co., 1987.

Barret, Richard Carter. *A Collectors Handbook of American Art Glass.* Manchester, VT: Forward's Color Productions, 1971.

A Collector's Handbook of Blown and Pressed American Glass. Manchester, VT: Forward's Color Productions, 1971.

Barret & Forward. *Popular American Ruby-Stained Pattern Glass.* New York, NY: Richard Carter Barret and Frank L. Forward, 1968.

Battersby, Martin. *Art Nouveau: The Colour Library of Art.* Middlesex, England: Hamlyn Publishing Group, 1969.

Batty, Bob H. *A Complete Guide to Pressed Glass.* Gretna, LA: Pelican Publishing, 1978.

Beard, Geoffrey. *International Modern Glass.* New York: Charles Scribner's Sons, 1976.

Belknap, E. McCamly. *Milk Glass.* New York: Crown Publishers, 1949.

Bennett, Harold, and Judy Bennett. *The Cambridge Glass Book.* DesMoines, IA: Wallace-Homestead Book Co., 1970.

Bing, S. *Artistic America, Tiffany Glass and Art Nouveau.* Cambridge, MA: Massachusetts Institute of Technology Press, 1970.

Bishop, Barbara, and Martha Hassell. *Your Obdt. Servt., Deming Jarves.* Sandwich, MA: Sandwich Historical Society, 1984.

Blount, Berniece, and Henry Blount. *French Cameo Glass.* Des Moines, IA: Published by the authors, 1968.

Blum, John, et al. *The National Experience: A History of the United States.* New York: Harcourt Brace Jovanovich, 1981.

Boggess, Bill, and Louise Boggess. *American Brilliant Cut Glass*. New York: Crown Publishers, 1977.

Bones, Frances. *The Book of Duncan Glass*. Des Moines, IA: Wallace-Homestead Book Co., 1973.

Bossaglia, Rossana. *Art Nouveau*. New York: Crescent Books, 1971.

Bount, Henry, and Berniece Bount. *French Cameo Glass*. Des Moines, IA: Wallace-Homestead Book Co., 1968.

Bredehoft, Neila, George Fogg, and Francis Maloney. *Early Duncan Glassware: Geo. Duncan & Sons 1874–1892*. Boston: Published by the authors, 1987.

Bridgeman, Harriet, and Elizabeth Drury. *The Encyclopedia of Victoriana*. New York: Macmillan, 1975.

Brown, Clark W. *A Supplement to Salt Dishes*. Des Moines, IA: Wallace-Homestead Book Co., 1970.

Burns, Carl O. *The Collector's Guide to Northwood's Carnival Glass*. Gas City, IN: L-W Book Sales, 1994.

⸻. *Imperial Carnival Glass*. Paducah, KY: Collector Books, 1996.

The Cambridge Glass Co. Cambridge, OH: National Cambridge Collection, 1978.

Carved and Decorated European Glass. Rutland, VT: Charles E. Tuttle Co., 1970.

Charleston, R. J. *English Glass*. London: George Allen and Unwin, 1984.

Chase, Mark E., and Michael J. Kelly. *Contemporary Fast-Food and Drinking Glass Collectibles*. Randor, PA: Wallace-Homestead Book Co., 1988.

Cloak, Evelyn Campbell. *Glass Paperweights of the Bergstrom Art Center*. New York: Crown Publishers, 1969.

Collector's Guide to Heisey's Glassware for Your Table. Gas City, IN: L-W Book Sales, 1993.

Conder, Lyle, ed. *Heisey's Collector's Guide to Glassware for Your Table*. Gas City, IN: L-W Book Sales, 1984.

The Complete Book of McKee. Kansas City, MO: The Tuga Press, 1974.

Contemporary Art Glass. New York: Crown Publishers, 1975.

Cosentino, Geraldine, and Regina Stewart. *Carnival Glass*. New York: Western Publishing Co., 1976.

Cousins, Mark. *20th Century Glass*. Secaucus, NJ: Chartwell Books, 1989.

Cudd, Viola N. *Heisey Glassware*. Brenham, TX: Herrmann Print Shop, 1969.

Curtis, Jean-Louis. *Baccarat*. London: Thames and Hudson, 1992.

Daniel, Dorothy. *Cut and Engraved Glass 1771–1905*. New York: M. Barrows & Co., 1950.

⸻. *Price Guide to American Cut Glass*. New York: M. Barrows & Co., 1967.

Davis, Derek C., and Keith Middlemas. *Colored Glass*. New York: Clarkson N. Potter, 1967.

⸻. *English Bottles and Decanters 1650–1900*. New York: World Publications, 1972.

Deboni, Franco. *I Vetri Venini*. Torino, Italy: Umberto Allemandi & Co., 1989.

Diamond, Freda. *The Story of Glass*. New York: Harcourt, Brace, and World, 1953.

Dibartolomeo, Robert E., ed. *American Glass Volume II: Pressed and Cut*. New York: Weathervane Books, 1978.

Dorflinger C. and Sons. *Cut Glass Catalog 1881–1921.* Hanover, PA: Everybody's Press, 1970.

Doros, Paul E. *The Tiffany Collection of the Chrysler Museum at Norfolk.* Norfolk, VA: Chrysler Museum, 1978.

Drepperd, Carl W. *ABC's of Old Glass.* New York: Doubleday, 1968.

Duncan, Alastair. *Tiffany at Auction.* New York: Rizzoli International Publications, 1981.

Duncan, Alastair, Martin Eidelberg, and Neil Harris. *Masterworks of Louis Comfort Tiffany.* New York: Harry N. Abrams, 1989.

Ebbott, Rex. *British Glass of the 17th and 18th Centuries.* London: Oxford University Press, 1972.

Editors of the Pyne Press. *Pennsylvania Glassware 1870–1904.* Princeton: Pyne Press, 1972.

Edmonson, Barbara. *Old Advertising Spirits.* Bend, OR: Maverick Publications, 1988.

Edwards, Bill. *Northwood – King of Carnival Glass.* Paducah, KY: Collector Books, 1978.

Ehrhardt, Alpha. *Cut Glass Price Guide.* Kansas City, MO: Heart of America Press, 1973.

Eige, Eason, and Rick Wilson. *Blenko Glass 1930–1953.* Marietta, OH: Antique Publications, 1987.

Elville, E. M. *English and Irish Cut Glass 1750–1950.* New York: Charles Scribner's Sons, 1951.

Ericson, Eric E. *A Guide to Colored Steuben.* 2 vols. Corning, NY: Lithographic Press, 1963–1965.

Evers, Jo. *The Standard Cut Glass Value Guide.* Paducah, KY: Collector Books, 1975.

Farrar, Estelle Sinclaire, and Jane Shadel Spillman. *The Complete Cut and Engraved Glass of Corning.* New York: Crown Publishers, 1978.

Fauster, Carl U. *Libbey Glass Since 1818.* Toledo, OH: Len Beach Press, 1979.

Feller, John Quentin. *Dorflinger: America's Finest Glass, 1852–1921.* Marietta, OH: Antique Publications, 1988.

Florence, Gene. *The Collector's Encyclopedia of Akro Agate.* Paducah, KY: Collector Books. 1975.

The Collector's Encyclopedia of Depression Glass. Paducah, KY: Collector Books, 1990–1998, volumes 1–14.

Collectible Glassware from the 40's, 50's, and 60's. Paducah, KY: Collector Books, 1992–1998.

Kitchen Glassware of the Depression Years. Paducah, KY: Collector Books, 1981–1998, volumes 1 to 6.

The Queen of Carnival Glass. Paducah, KY: Collector Books, 1976.

Rarities in Carnival Glass. Paducah, KY: Collector Books, 1978.

The Standard Encyclopedia of Carnival Glass. 14 vols. Paducah, KY: Collector Books, 1982–1998.

Forsythe, Ruth A. *Made in Czechoslovakia.* Marietta, OH: Antique Publications, 1993.

Frantz, Susanne K. *Contemporary Glass: A World Survey From the Corning Museum of Glass.* New York: Henry N. Abrams, 1989.

Freeman, Larry. *Iridescent Glass.* Watkins Glen, NY: Century House, 1964.

Garage Sale and Flea Market Annual. Paducah, KY: Collector Books, Annual Guide, 1991–1999.

Gardner, Paul F. *Frederick Carder: Portrait of a Glassmaker.* Corning, NY: Corning Museum of Glass. 1985.

Gardner, Paul F. *The Glass of Frederick Carder.* New York: Crown Publishers, 1971.

Garmon, Lee, and Dick Spencer. *Glass Animals of the Depression Era.* Paducah, KY: Collector Books, 1991.

Grimmer, Elsa H. *Wave Crest Ware.* Des Moines, IA: Wallace-Homestead Book Co., 1979.

Grist, Everett. *Covered Animal Dishes.* Paducah, KY: Collector Books, 1988.

Grover, Ray, and Lee Grover. *Art Glass Nouveau.* Rutland, VT: Charles E. Tuttle Co., 1967.

Carved and Decorated European Art Glass. Rutland, VT: Charles E. Tuttle Co., 1967.

English Cameo Glass. New York: Crown Publishers, 1980.

Hand, Sherman. *The Collector's Encyclopedia of Carnival Glass.* Paducah, KY: Collector Books, 1978.

Hardy, Roger, and Claudia Hardy. *The Complete Line of the Akro Agate Co.* Clarksburg, WV: Clarksburg Publishing, 1992.

Harrington, J. C. *Glassmaking at Jamestown: America's First Industry.* Richmond, VA: The Dietz Press, 1952.

Hartung, Marion. *Carnival Glass in Color.* Emporia, KS: Published by the author, 1967.

Hartung, Marion. *Northwood Pattern Glass in Color.* Emporia, KS: Published by the author, 1969.

Haslam, Malcolm. *Marks and Monograms of the Modern Movement, 1875–1930.* New York: Charles Scribner's Sons, 1977.

Hastin, Bud. *Avon Collectibles Price Guide.* Kansas City, MO: Published by the author, 1991.

Heacock, William. *The Encyclopedia of Victorian Colored Pattern Glass (Books 1–9).* Marietta, OH: Antique Publications, 1974–1988.

Fenton Glass: The First Twenty-five Years. Marietta, OH: O-Val Advertising Corp., 1978.

Fenton Glass: The Second Twenty-five Years. Marietta, OH: O-Val Advertising Corp., 1980.

Fenton Glass: The Third Twenty-five Years. Marietta, OH: O-Val Advertising Corp., 1989.

Heacock, William, and Fred Bickenhauser. *The Encyclopedia of Victorian Colored Pattern Glass (Book 5).* Marietta, OH: Antique Publications, 1974–1988.

Heirmans, Marc. *Murano Glass 1945–1970.* Antwerp: Gallery Novecento, 1989.

Hettes, Karel. "Venetian Trends in Bohemian Glassmaking in the 16th and 17th Centuries." *Journal of Glass Studies* V: 1963.

Hollister, Paul, and Dwight Lanmon. *Paperweights.* Corning, NY: Corning Museum of Glass, 1978.

Hollister, Paul Jr. *The Encyclopedia of Glass Paperweights.* New York: Clarkson N. Potter, 1969.

Hotchkiss, John F. *Art Glass Handbook.* New York: Hawthorn Books, 1972.

Carder's Steuben Glass Handbook and Price Guide. New York: Hawthorn Books, 1972.

Cut Glass Handbook and Price Guide. Des Moines, IA: Wallace-Homestead Book Co., 1970.

House, Caurtman G. *Relative Values of Early American Patterned Glass.* Medina, NY: Published by the author, 1944.

House of Collectibles. *The Official Price Guide to Carnival Glass.* New York: Random House, 1986.

The Official Price Guide to Depression Glass. New York: Random House, 1988.

The Official Price Guide to Glassware. New York: Random House, 1987–2000.

Huether, Anne. *Glass and Man.* New York: J. B. Lippincott Co., 1965.

Hughes, G. Bernard. *English Glass for the Collector 1660–1860.* New York: Macmillan, 1968.

Hunter, Frederick William. *Stiegel Glass.* New York: Dover Publications, 1950.

Husfloen, Kyle, ed. *American & European Decorative & Art Glass.* Dubuque, IA: Antique Trader Books, 1994.

Antiques & Collectibles. Dubuque, IA: Antique Trader Books, 1985–1998.

Huxford, Sharon, and Bob Huxford, eds. *Flea Market Trader.* Paducah, KY: Collector Books, Annual Edition 1993–1999.

Imperial Glass Corporation. *The Story of Handmade Glass.* Ballaire, OH: Imperial, 1941.

Innes, Lowell. *Pittsburgh Glass 1797–1891: A History and Guide for Collectors.* Boston: Houghton Mifflin 1976.

Jarves, Deming. *Reminiscences of Glassmaking.* Boston: Eastburn's Press, 1854.

Jefferson, Josephine. *Wheeling Glass.* Mount Vernon, OH: Guide Publishing Co., 1947.

Jenks, Bill, and Jerry Luna. *Early American Pattern Glass 1850–1910.* Radnor, PA: Wallace-Homestead Book Co., 1990.

Jokelson, Paul. *Sulphides: The Art of Cameo Incrustation.* New York: Thomas Nelson & Sons, 1968.

Kerr, Ann. *Fostoria.* Paducah, KY: Collector Books, 1994.

Ketchum, William C. Jr. *A Treasury of American Bottles.* New York: Ridge Press, 1975.

Klamkin, Marian. *The Collector's Guide to Carnival Glass.* New York: Hawthorn Books, 1976.

The Collector's Guide to Depression Glass. New York: Hawthorn Books, 1973.

Klein, Dan, and Ward Lloyd. *The History of Glass.* New York: Crescent Books, 1989.

Koch, Robert. *Louis C. Tiffany, A Rebel in Glass.* New York: Crown Publishers, 1964.

Kovel, Ralph, and Terry Kovel. *The Complete Antiques Price List.* New York: Crown Publishers, 1973–1999.

The Kovels' Antique and Collectible Price List. New York: Crown Publishers, 1990–1999.

Kovels' Bottles Price List. New York: Crown Publishers, 1992–1998.

Kovels' Depression Glass and American Dinnerware Price List. New York: Crown Publishers, 1992–1999.

Krantz, Susan. *Contemporary Glass*. New York: Harry N. Abrams, 1989.

Krause, Gail. *Duncan Glass*. New York: Exposition Press, 1976.

Lafferty, James R. *The Forties Revisited*. Canterbury: published by the author, 1968.

Lee, Ruth. *Boston & Sandwich Glass Co.* Boston: Lee Publications, 1968.

———. *Reflections on American Brilliant Cut Glass*. Atglen, PA: Schiffer Publishing, 1995.

———. *Early American Pressed Glass*. New York: Ferris Printing Co., 1946.

———. *Nineteenth-Century Art Glass*. New York: M. Barrows and Co., 1952.

———. *Sandwich Glass*. New York: Ferris Printing Co., 1947.

Leybourne, Douglas M. Jr. *The Collector's Guide to Old Fruit Jars*. North Muskegon, MI: Published by the author, 1993.

Lindsey, Bessie M. *American Historical Glass*. Rutland, VT: Charles E. Tuttle, 1967.

Mackay, James. *Glass Paperweights*. New York: Facts on File, 1973.

Madigan, Mary Jean. *Steuben Glass: An American Tradition in Crystal*. New York: Harry N. Abrams, 1982.

Manley, Cyril. *Decorative Victorian Glass*. New York: Von Nostrand Reinhold Co., 1981.

Mannoni, Edith. *Classic French Paperweights*. Santa Cruz, CA: Paperweight Press, 1984.

Mariacher, G. *Three Centuries of Venetian Glass*. Corning, NY: Corning Museum of Glass (translation), 1957.

Markowski, Carol, and Gene Markowski. *Tomart's Price Guide to Character and*

———. *Promotional Glasses*. Radnor, PA: Wallace-Homestead Book Co., 1990.

Marshall, Jo. *Glass Source Book*. London: Quarto Publishing Co., 1990.

McClinton, Katharine Morrison. *Lalique for Collectors*. New York: Charles Scribner's Sons, 1975.

McGee, Marie. *Millersburg Glass*. Marietta, OH: Glass Press, 1995.

McKean, Hugh F. *The "Lost" Treasures of Louis Comfort Tiffany*. New York: Doubleday & Co., 1980.

McKearin, George, and Helen McKearin. *American Glass*. New York: Crown Publishers, 1968.

———. *Nineteenth-Century Art Glass*. New York: Crown Publishers, 1966.

Measell, James. *New Martinsville Glass, 1900–1944*. Marietta, OH: Antique Publications, 1994.

Mebane, John. *Collecting Brides' Baskets and Other Glass Fancies*. Des Moines, IA: Wallace-Homestead Book Co., 1976.

Melvin, Jean S. *American Glass Paperweights and Their Makers*. New York: Thomas Nelson Publishers, 1970.

Miles, Dori, and Robert W. Miller, eds. *Wallace-Homestead Price Guide to Pattern Glass,* 11th ed. Radnor, PA: Wallace-Homestead Book Co., 1986.

Miller, Robert. *Mary Gregory and Her Glass*. DesMoines IA: Wallace-Homestead Book Co., 1972.

———. *Miller's International Antiques Price Guide*. London: Reed International Books, 1996.

Miller, Robert, ed. *Wallace-Homestead Price Guide to Antiques and Pattern Glass*. Iowa City IA: Wallace-Homestead Book Co., 1982.

Moore, Donald E. *The Complete Guide to Carnival Glass Rarities.* Alameda, CA: Published by the author, 1975.

Moore, N. Hudson. *Old Glass European and American.* New York: Tudor Publishing Co., 1924.

Mortimer, Tony L. *Lalique.* Secaucus, NJ: Chartwell Books, 1989.

National Cambridge Collector's, Inc. *Colors in Cambridge Glass.* Paducah, KY: Collector Books, 1997.

Neustadt, Egon. *The Lamps of Tiffany.* New York: Fairfield Press, 1970.

Newark, Tim. *Emile Galle.* London: Quintet Publishing, 1989.

Newbound, Betty, and Bill Newbound. *Collector's Encyclopedia of Milk Glass.* Paducah, KY: Collector Books, 1995.

Newman, Harold. *An Illustrated Dictionary of Glass.* London: Thames and Hudson, 1977.

Nye, Mark. *Cambridge Stemware.* Miami: Mark A. Nye, 1985.

Oliver, Elizabeth. *American Antique Glass.* New York: Golden Press, 1977.

Over, Naomi L. *Ruby Glass of the 20th Century.* Marietta, OH: Antique Publications, 1990.

Padgett, Leonard E. *Pairpoint Glass.* Des Moines, IA: Wallace-Homestead Book Co., 1979.

Papert, Emma. *The Illustrated Guide to American Glass.* New York: Hawthorn Books, 1972.

Paul, Tessa. *The Art of Louis Comfort Tiffany.* New York: Exeter Books, 1987.

Pears, Thomas C. III. *Bakewell, Pears & Co. Glass Catalogue.* Pittsburgh, PA: Davis & Warde, 1977.

Pearson, Michael, and Dorothy Pearson. *American Cut Glass for the Discriminating Collector.* New York: Vantage Press, 1965.

A Study of American Cut Glass Collections. Miami: Published by the authors, 1969.

Percy, Christopher Vane. *The Glass of Lalique.* New York: Charles Scribner's Sons, 1983.

Pesatova, Zuzana. *Bohemian Engraved Glass.* Prague: Knihtisk Publishing, 1968.

Peterson, Arthur G. *400 Trademarks on Glass.* Takoma Park, MD: Washington College Press, 1968.

Phillips, Phoebe, ed. *The Encyclopedia of Glass.* New York: Crown Publishers, 1981.

Pickvet, Mark. *The Definitive Guide to Shot Glasses.* Marietta, OH: Antique Publications, 1992.

The Encyclopedia of Shot Glasses. Marietta, OH: Antique Publications, 1998.

The Instant Expert Guide to Collecting Glassware. Brooklyn, NY: Alliance Publishers, 1996.

Official Price Guide to Glassware. New York, NY: House of Collectibles, 1995–1998.

Shot Glasses: An American Tradition. Marietta, OH: Antique Publications, 1989.

Pina, Leslie. *Fifties Glass.* Atglen, PA: Schiffer Publishing, 1993.

Fostoria, Serving the American 1887–1986. Atglen, PA: Schiffer Publishing, 1995.

Popular '50s and '60s Glass. Atglen, PA: Schiffer Publishing, 1995.

Polak, Ada. *Glass, Its Tradition and Its Makers.* New York: G. P. Putnam's Sons, 1975.

Pullin, Anne Geffken. *Signatures, Trademarks and Trade Names.* Radnor, PA: Wallace-Homestead Book Co., 1986.

Rainwater, Dorothy T. *Encyclopedia of American Silver Manufacturers.* New York: Crown Publishers, 1975.

Revi, Albert Christian. *American Art Nouveau Glass.* New York: Thomas Nelson and Sons, 1968.

American Cut and Engraved Glass. New York: Thomas Nelson and Sons, 1970.

American Pressed Glass and Figure Bottles. New York: Thomas Nelson and Sons, 1968.

Nineteenth-Century Glass. New York: Galahad Books, 1967.

Ring, Carolyn. *For Bitters Only.* Boston: Nimrod Press, 1980.

Rinker, Harry. *Warman's Americana and Collectibles.* Elkins Park, PA: Warman Publishing, 1986.

Rockwell, Robert F. *Frederick Carder and His Steuben Glass 1903–1933.* West Hyack, NY: Dexter Press, 1966.

Rogove, Susan Tobier, and Marcia Buan Steinhauer. *Pyrex By Corning.* Marietta, OH: Antique Publications, 1993.

Rose, James H. *The Story of American Pressed Glass of the Lacy Period 1825–1850.* Corning, NY: Corning Museum of Glass, 1954.

Ross, Richard, and Wilma Ross. *Imperial Glass.* New York: Wallace-Homestead Book Co., 1971.

Rossi, Sara. *A Collector's Guide to Paperweights.* Secaucus, NJ: Wellfleet Books, 1990.

Schmutzler, Robert. *Art Nouveau.* London: Thames & Hudson, 1978.

Schroeder, Bill. *Cut Glass.* Paducah, KY: Collector Books, 1977.

Schroeder's Antiques Price Guide. Paducah, KY: Collector Books, 1993.

Schroy, Ellen. *Warman's Glass.* Radnor, PA: Wallace-Homestead Book Co., 1992.

Schwartz, Marvin D., ed. *American Glass Volume I: Blown and Molded.* New York: Weathervane Books, 1978.

Scott, Virginia R. *The Collector's Guide to Imperial Candlewick.* Athens, GA: Published by the author. 1980.

Selman, Lawrence H. *The Art of the Paperweight.* Santa Cruz, CA: Paperweight Press, 1988.

Shuman III, John. *American Art Glass.* Paducah, KY: Collector Books, 1988.

Art Glass Sampler. Des Moines, IA: Wallace-Homestead Book Co., 1978.

Shuman III, John, and Susan Shuman. *Lion Pattern Glass.* Boston: Branden Press, 1977.

Sichel, Franz. *Glass Drinking Vessels.* San Francisco: Lawton & Alfred Kennedy Printing, 1969.

Spillman, Jane Schadel. *American and European Pressed Glass in the Corning Museum of Glass.* Corning, NY: Corning Museum of Glass, 1981.

Glass Tableware, Bowls & Vases. New York: Alfred A. Knopf, 1982.

Glass From World's Fairs 1851–1904. Corning, NY: Corning Museum of Glass, 1986.

Masterpieces of Glass: A World History From the Corning Museum of Glass. New York: Harry N. Abrams, 1980.

Spillman, Jane Schadel, and Susanne K. Frantz. *Masterpieces of American Glass.* Corning, NY: Corning Museum of Glass, 1990.

Stevens, Gerald. *Canadian Glass.* Toronto: Ryerson Press, 1967.

Early Canadian Glass. Toronto: Ryerson Press, 1967.

Stout, Sandra McPhee. *The Complete Book of McKee.* North Kansas City, MO: Trojan Press, 1972.

Depression Glass Price Guide. Radnor, PA: Wallace-Homestead Book Co., 1975.

Depression Glass III. Radnor, PA: Wallace-Homestead Book Co., 1976.

Swan, Martha Louise. *American Cut and Engraved Glass of the Brilliant Period in Historical Perspective.* Chicago, IL: Wallace-Homestead Book Co., 1986.

Tait, Hugh, ed. *Glass, 5,000 Years.* New York: Henry N. Abrams, 1991.

Toledo Museum of Art. *Libbey Glass: A Tradition of 150 Years.* Toledo, OH: Toledo Museum of Art, 1968.

Toulouse, Julian. *Fruit Jars: A Collector's Manual.* Camden, NJ: Thomas Nelson & Sons, 1969.

Traub, Jules S. *The Glass of Desire Christian.* Chicago: Art Glass Exchange, 1978.

Truitt, Robert. *Mary Gregory Glass.* Kensington, MD: Published by the author, 1992.

Truitt, Robert, and Deborah Truitt. *Collectible Bohemian Glass, 1880–1940.* Kensington, MD: B & D Glass, 1995.

U.S. Patent Records

Viking Glass Company. *Beauty Is Glass from Viking.* New Martinsville, WV: Viking Glass Co., 1967.

Wakefield, Hugh. *19th-Century British Glass.* New York: Thomas Yoseloff Publishing, 1961.

Warman, Edwin G. *American Cut Glass.* Uniontown, PA: E. G. Warman Publishing, 1954.

Warner, Ian. *Swankyswigs, A Pattern Guide and Check List.* Otisville, MI: Published by the author, 1982.

Warren, Phelps. *Irish Glass.* New York: Charles Scribner's Sons, 1970.

Watkins, Lura Woodside. *Cambridge Glass.* Boston: Marshall Jones Co., 1930.

Weatherman, Hazel Marie. *Colored Glassware of the Depression Era.* Springfield, MO: Weatherman Glass Books, 1974.

Colored Glassware of the Depression Era II. Springfield, MO: Weatherman Glass Books, 1974.

Fostoria: Its First Fifty Years. Springfield, MO: Weatherman Glass Books, 1979.

Weatherman, Hazel Marie, and Sue Weatherman. *The Decorated Tumbler.* Springfield, MO: Weatherman Glass Books, 1978.

Webber, Norman W. *Collecting Glass.* New York: Arco Publishing, 1972.

Weiner, Herbert, and Freda Lipkowitz. *Rarities in American Cut Glass.* Houston: Collectors House of Books Publishing Co., 1975.

Welker, John, and Elizabeth Welker. *Pressed Glass in America.* Ivyland, PA: Antique Acres, 1986.

Wheeling Glass 1829–1939: A Collection of the Oglebay Institute Glass Museum. Wheeling, WV: Oglebay Institute, 1994.

Whitehouse, David. *Glass of the Roman Empire.* Corning, NY: Corning Museum of Glass, 1988.

Whitmyer, Margaret, and Kenn Whitmyer. *Children's Dishes.* Paducah, KY: Collector Books, 1984.

Wilson, Kenneth M. *New England Glass and Glassmaking.* New York: Thomas Crowell Co., 1972.

Wilson, Jack D. *Phoenix & Consolidated Art Glass.* Marietta, OH: Antique Publications, 1989.

Winter, Henry. *The Dynasty of Louis Comfort Tiffany.* Boston: Henry Winter, 1971.

Yeske, Doris. *Depression Glass: A Collector's Guide.* Atglen, PA: Schiffer Publishing, 1998.

Zerwick, Chloe. *A Short History of Glass.* New York: Harry N. Abrams, 1990.

Numerous advertisements, trade catalogs, journals, newsletters, and other publications were used that are not listed above:

American Antiques

American Carnival Glass Association Newsletters

American Glass Review

American Pottery and Glassware Reporter

Antiques Journal

Antique Trader

Antiques Trade Gazette

M. Bazzett & Co.

A. C. Becken Co.

Butler Brothers

China, Glass, and Lamps

The Connoisseur

The Cosmopolitan

Crockery and Glass Journal

The Crockery Journal

The Daze

Enos' Manual of Old Pattern Glass

Glass Art Society Journal

Glass Line Newsletter

Good Housekeeping

Gordon & Morrison

Harper's

Heart of America Carnival Glass Association

Higgins & Seiter

International Carnival Glass Association Newsletters

The Jeweler's Circular Weekly

Journal of Glass Studies

Krantz & Smith Co.

Marshall Field & Co.

McClure's

Montgomery Wards

S. F. Myers Co.

N. A. & Co.

New Glass Review

Oskamp, Nolting Co.

Pattern Glass Previews

Pottery and Glassware Reporter

The Pottery, Glass & Brass Salesman

R. T. & Co.

Charles Broadway Rouse Wholesale Catalogs

Scribner's

Sears, Roebuck & Co.

William Volker & Co.

Woolworth & Co.

Woman's Day

Companies publishing catalogs, brochures, trade journals, and advertisements not included above:

Adams & Co.

Akro Agate Co.

Alford Cut Glass

Anchor-Hocking Glass Co.

Averbeck, M. J.

Baccarat Glass Co.

Bakewell, Pears & Co.

Bergen Cut Glass Co.

Blackmer Cut Glass

Blenko Glass Co.

Boston & Sandwich Glass Co.

Boyd Art Glass Co.

Bryce Brothers

Cambridge Glass Co. by National Cambridge Collectors, Incorporated

Central Glass Co.

T. B. Clark & Co.

Consolidated Lamp & Glass Co.

Correia Art Glass Co.

De Vilbiss Co.

Diamond Glass Co.

Diamond Glass-Ware Co.

Dominion Glass Co.

C. Dorflinger & Sons

Dugan Glass Co.

Duncan & Miller Glass Co.

Durand Art Glass Co.

O. F. Egginton Co.

Empire Cut Glass Co.

Federal Glass Co.

Fenton Art Glass Co.

Fostoria Glass Co.

H. C. Fry Glass Co.

Gibson Glass Co.

T. G. Hawkes & Co.

Hazel Atlas Glass Co.

A. H. Heisey & Co.

J. Hoare & Co.

Hobbs, Brocunier & Co.

Hocking Glass Co.

Carl Hosch Co.

Imperial Glass Co.

Indiana Glass Co.

Indiana Tumbler & Goblet Co.

Jeannette Glass Co.

Keystone Cut Glass Co.

King, Son & Co.

Lalique

Libbey Glass Co.

Loetz Glass

MacBeth-Evans Glass Co.

Maple City Glass Co.

McKee Brothers

Meriden Cut Glass Co.

C. F. Monroe Co.

Moser Glass Works

Mt. Washington Glass Works

New England Crystal Co.

New England Glass Co.

New Martinsville Glass Co.

Northwood Glass Co.

Orrefors Glasbruck

Paden City Glass Co.

Pairpoint Manufacturing Co.

Perthshire Paperweights Ltd.

Phoenix Glass Co.

Pilgrim Glass Co.

Pitkin & Brooks

Quaker City Cut Glass Co.

Quezal Art Glass & Decorating Co.

Sabino Art Glass Co.

H. P. Sinclaire Co.

L. E. Smith Co.

Steuben Glass Works

L. Straus & Sons

Taylor Brothers

Tiffany

Tipperary Crystal Co.

Tuthill Cut Glass Co.

Unger Brothers

U.S. Glass Co.

Waterford Crystal Ltd.

Thomas Webb & Sons

Westmoreland Glass Company or Westmoreland Specialty Company

L. G. Wright

Auction Houses, Catalogs, Brochures, and Advertisements:

Albrecht & Cooper Auction Services; Vassar, Michigan

Sanford Alderfer Auction Co.; Hatfield, Pennsylvania

Apple Tree Auction Center; Newark, Ohio

Arman Absentee Auctions; Woodstock, Connecticut

Artfact, Inc.; Computer Auction Records' Services

Auctioneers International; Salt Lake City

James Bakker; Cambridge, Massachusetts

Frank H. Boos Gallery, Bloomfield Hills, Michigan

Ron Bourgeault & Co.; Portsmouth, New Hampshire

Richard A. Bourne Co.; Hyannis, Massachusetts

Bullock's Auction House; Flint, Michigan

Burns Auction Service

Christie's and Christie's East; New York City

William Doyle Galleries; New York City

Du Mouchelles; Detroit

Dunnings; Elgin, Illinois

Early Auction Co.; Milford, Ohio

eBay Auction Service

Robert Eldred Co.; East Dennis, Massachusetts

Emerald Auctions; London

Fine Arts Co. of Philadelphia; Philadelphia

Garth's Auction, Inc.; Delaware, Ohio

Glass-Works Auctions; East Greenville, Pennsylvania

Grogon & Co.; Boston

Guerney's; New York City

Hanzel Galleries; Chicago

Justglass.com On-Line Auction Service

Leslie Hindman, Inc.; Chicago

Martin Auctioneers Inc., Intercourse, Pennsylvania

Milwaukee Auction Galleries; Milwaukee

M-Live On-Line Auction Services

Mordini, Tom and Sharon, Carnival Glass Auction Reports; Freeport, Illinois

Old Barn Auctions; Findlay, Ohio

Phillips Fine Art Auctions; New York City

PK Liquidators; Flint, Michigan

David Rago; Trenton, New Jersey

Roan Brothers Auction Gallery; Cogan Station, Pennsylvania

SGCA Auctions; Flint, Michigan

L.H. Selman Ltd.; Santa Cruz, California

Sotheby's; New York City

Western Glass Auctions, Tracy, California

Antiques Shows and Dealers:

AA Ann Arbor Antiques Mall; Ann Arbor, Michigan

W. D. Adams Antique Mall; Howell, Michigan

Americana Shop; Chicago

Antique Alley; Phoenix

Antique Gallery; Detroit

The Antique Gallery; Flint, Michigan

The Antique Warehouse; Saginaw, Michigan

Ark Antiques; New Haven, Connecticut

Artesian Wells Antique Mall; Irish Hills, Michigan

Bailey's Antiques; Homer, Michigan

Bankstreet Antiques Mall; Frankenmuth, Michigan

Bay City Antiques Center; Bay City, Michigan

Bell Tower Antique Mall; Covington, Kentucky

Burton Gallery Antiques; Plymouth, Michigan

Cherry Street Antique Mall; Flint, Michigan

Estes Antiques Mall; Blissfield, Michigan

Flat River Antique Mall; Lowell, Michigan

Flushing Antique Emporium; Flushing, Michigan

Gallery of Antiques; Detroit, Michigan

Gene Harris Antiques; Marshalltown, Iowa

Gilley's Antique Mall; Plainfield, Indiana

Glick's Antiques; Galena, Illinois

Grand Antique Mall; Apache Junction, Arizona

Hemswell Antiques Centre; Gainsborough, England

Hitching Post Antiques Mall; Tecumseh, Michigan

Indianapolis Antique Mall; Indianapolis

Main Antique Mall; Ardmore, Oklahoma

Memories on Lane Street Antiques; Blissfield, Michigan

Plymouth Antiques Mall; Plymouth, Michigan

Reminisce Antique Mall; Flint, Michigan

Showcase Antique Center; Sturbridge, Massachusetts

Water Tower Antiques Mall; Holly, Michigan

Williams Crossroads Antiques and Collectibles; Blissfield, Michigan

Wolf's Gallery; Cleveland

Special thanks to the numerous dealers and auction companies who allowed me to snap a few photographs and provided helpful advice on pricing and market trends.

INDEX

H

Hald, Edward, 90
Hamilton pattern, 223–224
Handel and Company, 406–408
Harp pattern, 781
Harrach, Count Arnost, 21
Hartmann & Dietrichs, 21
Hastings, Daniel, 141
Hawken, William, 331
Hawkes, T. G. Company,
322–326
Hawkes, Thomas Gibbons, 317,
322, 326, 330
Hawkes, Thomas J., 460
Hazel Atlas Glass Company
　Aurora, 572
　Chevron, 581
　Cloverleaf, 583–584
　Colonial Block, 584–585
　Florentine No. 2, 613–614
　Florentine No.1, 612–613
　Fruits, 617
　Moderntone, 641–643
　New Century, 648–649
　Newport Hairpin, 649–650,
　810–811
　Old Florentine, 612–613
　Ovide, 654–655
　Poppy No. 1, 612–613
　Poppy No. 2, 613–614
　Royal Lace, 681–682
　Sailboat and Windmills, 839
　Ships and Windmills, 839
　Sportsman Series, 839
　Starlight, 689
Hazel Ware, 737–739, 805–806
Heart With Thumbprint pattern,
224–226
Heavy Grape pattern, 515–516
Heavy Panelled Grape pattern,
260–261
Heisey, A.H. Glass Company,
408–410
Heisey and Company, A.H.,
782–784
Heisey animals, 782–784
Heisey Glass Company, The,
126–127
Hemingway insulator, 795
Heritage pattern, 618–619
Herringbone pattern, 219–220
Hex Optic pattern, 226–229,
619–620
Higbee Glass Company, 241–242,
262–263, 517
Hitchcock, W.B., 330
Hoare, J. and Company, 326–329
Hoare, John, 322, 326
Hobbs, 142
Hobbs, Brocunier and Company,
197–201, 410–411, 437–440

Hobnail pattern, 323, 517–519,
620–621, 784–789
Hobstar pattern, 518–519
Hobster and Feather pattern,
519–520
Hobster Band pattern, 520
Hocking Glass Company
　Banded Rib, 587
　Banded Rings, 673–674
　Block or Block Optic, 574–575
　Cameo, 576–578
　Circle, 582
　Colonial Knife and Fork,
　585–587
　Coronation, 587
　Diamond, 640–641
　Fire-King dinnerware, 608–609
　Fortune, 616–617
　Hobnail, 620–621
　Lace patterns, 629–630
　Mayfair Open Rose, 586,
　638–640
　Miss America, 640–641
　Old Cafe, 652
　Princess, 665–667
　Queen Mary, 668–669
　Ribbon, 672–673
　Rings, 673–674
　Roulette, 679–680
　Saxon, 587
　Spiral, 688–689
　Vitrock Flower Rim, 700
　Waffle, 700–701
　Waterford, 700–701
Holiday pattern, 789–790
Holly Amber art glass, 411–412
Holly pattern, 520–521
Holly Sprig pattern, 521–522
Homespun pattern, 790–791
Honesdale Decorating Company,
412–413
Honeycomb pattern, 226–229,
619–620
Honeycomb with Flower Rim pat-
tern, 288–289
Hope Glass Works, 329
Horizontal Ribbed pattern,
636–637
Horn of Plenty pattern, 229–231
Horseshoe pattern, 621–622
Hosch, Carl, 21
Hungarian glass, 56–58
Hunt, Thomas, 330
Hunt Glass Company, 330

I

Ice sculpture, 62–64
Ideal Glass Company, 330–331
Identification, vii, xi–xii
Illinois pattern, 231–233
Imperial Glass Company

Animals, 791–793
Art glass, 414–415
Beaded Block, 573–574
Candlewick, 726–733
Cane, 484
Chesterfield, 489–490
Colonial, 491–492
Columbia, 491
Crab Claw, 493–494
Diamond Lace, 494–495
Diamond Point Columns, 496
Diamond Quilted, 595–596
Fashion, 499–500
File, 502
Flat Diamond, 595–596
Floral and Optic, 503
Flute, 504–505
Four Seventy-Four, 506
Frosted Block, 506–507
Golden Honeycomb, 509
Grape, 509–511
Heavy Grape, 515–516
Hobstar, 518–519
Hobster Band, 520
Lace patterns, 629–631
Lustre and Clear, 524, 527
Lustre Rose, 528–529
Melon Rib, 529–530
Moon and Stars, 250–251
Octagon, 530–531
Omera, 531–532
Optic and Buttons, 532, 533
Pansy, 535
Poppy Show, 540–541
Prism & Daisy Band, 541–542
Ranger, 542
Robin, 543
Smooth Rays, 546
Star and File, 548–549
Star Medallion, 549–550
Stippled Rays, 550–551
Tree Bark, 553–554
Twins, 554
Twisted Optic, 696–697
Waffle Block, 556–558
Whirling Star, 558–559
Wide Panel, 559–560
Windmill, 560–562
Wishbone, 561
Imperial pattern, 355
Indian glass, 58–59
Indiana Custard pattern, 793–794
Indiana Glass Company
　Avocado, 572–573
　Christmas Candy, 748–749
　Daisy, 761–762
　Flower and Leaf Band, 793–794
　Horseshoe, 621–622
　Indiana Custard, 793–794
　Lorain Basket, 634
　No. 601 pattern, 572–573
　No. 610 pattern, 667–668